BLUEPRINT
For
BLACK POWER

A Moral, Political and
Economic Imperative for
the Twenty-First Century

AMOS N. WILSON

Copyright © 1998 Afrikan World InfoSystems

First Edition
FIFTH PRINTING January 2005

All rights reserved. No part of this publication may be reproduced or transmitted in any form or by any means, electronic or mechanical, including recording, photocopy, or any information storage and retrieval system, without prior permission in writing from the publisher, except by a reviewer who wishes to quote brief passages in connection with a review written for inclusion in a newspaper, magazine, or broadcast.

Executive Editor: SABABU N. PLATA
Assistant Editor: Adisa Makalani

Cover Illustrator: Joseph Gillians

ISBN: 1-879164-06-X (soft cover)
ISBN: 1-879164-07-8 (case bound)

Library of Congress Cataloging-in-Publication Data

Wilson, Amos N.
    Blueprint for Black power: a moral, political, and economic imperative for the twenty-first century / Amos N. Wilson. — 1st ed.
      p. cm.
    Includes bibliographical references and index.
    ISBN 1-879164-06-X (alk. paper). — ISBN 1-879164-07-8 (alk. paper)
    1. Black power—United States. 2. Afro-Americans—Social Conditions—1975- 3. Afro-Americans—Economic conditions. 4. Afro-Americans—Politics and government. 5. African diaspora.
6. Twenty-first century—Forecasts. I. Title.
E185.615.W54 1998
305.896 073—dc21   98-22964
                                                                                     CIP

AFRIKAN WORLD INFOSYSTEMS
743 Rogers Avenue, Suite 6
Brooklyn, New York 11226

E-Mail: AFRIKANWORLD @ AOL.COM
www.Afrikanworldinfo.com

Printed in Canada

BLUEPRINT
For
BLACK POWER

A Moral, Political and
Economic Imperative for
the Twenty-First Century

AMOS N. WILSON

New York 1998
Afrikan World InfoSystems

About the Author

Professor AMOS N. WILSON is a former social caseworker, supervising probation officer, psychological counselor, training administrator in New York City Department of Juvenile Justice, and Assistant Professor of Psychology at the City University of New York.

Born in Hattiesburg, Mississippi in 1941, Amos completed his undergraduate degree at the acclaimed Morehouse College in Atlanta, Georgia. He later migrated to New York where he attained his Ph. D. from Fordham University in New York City.

Familiarly referred to as Brother Amos, he availed himself for numerous appearances at educational, cultural and political organizations such as the First World Alliance, the Afrikan Poetry Theatre, Afrikan Echoes, House of Our Lord Church, the Patrice Lumumba Coalition, the Slave Theatre and CEMOTAP to name just a few. His travels took him throughout the United States, to Canada and the Caribbean. Dr. Wilson's activities transcended academia into the field of business, own ng and operating various enterprises in the greater New York area.

A prolific writer, Dr. Wilson has penned other pertinent works in the areas of education, child development and therapeutic psychology which we hope to share with our readers in the near future.

Dedication

*Those who will to transform destiny
must first will to transform history*

Acknowledgments

A work of this magnitude could not be accomplished without the blessings and contributions of noteworthy and trusted friends and associates from both near and afar. Our heartfelt appreciation to one and all. However, there are some whose mention must be specially noted.

Gratitude to Lorenzo Tyson, Ralph King, Franklin Joseph, Ivor Alleyne and Andre Gray for unequivocal and unwavering support, diverse participation, and economic undergirding in publishing this opus.

My indebtedness to Adisa Makalani for typing and editing this manuscript and being ever present in all times of need; Kwaku Oronde, whose revolutionary fervor fired this attempt; Joseph Gillians, graphic artist, able friend, and thinker.

Worthy of special adulation are Osei Tutu, Yero Bandele, Aramintha Grant, Linda Milner, Gerald Joshua, Andre Deputy, Kabari Jordan and Nzinga Nosakhene for commenting, critiquing and proofing the manuscript; staff members extraordinaire Dorothy Lewis and Akua S. Culbreth; volunteers Tara Edwards, Karen Campbell, Isha Tafara, Lolita Lopez, Leah Mullen, Melanie Scott; friends Djed Wade, Tabu Djata and Robert Dobson. Without you all, this task would still be in gestation.

Appreciation to Rosa Plata for her serene understanding and total support in the protracted nature of these endeavors. To Sankofa Plata, for the many moments missed in your flowering. Special thanks to Judith Jeffrey, for your years of companionship and warmth. One would be remiss to not laud Dr. Janice Montague whose Afrikan-centered diligence held ajar local academic doors. Special thanks to the Wilson extended family for the credence necessary to complete this work.

To the many others worthy of mention, you too occupy a revered space in our hearts. Thanks for the many concerns, proddings, reassurances, finances, trust, patience and graciousness, efforts however seemingly small but which served to weave the tapestry of this epic volume. May this Blueprint be of assistance to you in your life travails. We thank you for allowing us into your consciousness.

Other Books By Amos Wilson

The Developmental Psychology of the Black Child
The best-selling text on Black child development. The iconoclast in the field.
ISBN 0-933524-01-3
PB. Pages: 216

Awakening the Natural Genius of Black Children
A must-read for educators and parents concerned with helping Black children reach their full potential.
ISBN 1-879164-01-9
PB. Pages: 144

Black-on-Black Violence: The Psychodynamics of Black Self-Annihilation in Service of White Domination
A piecing insight into the nature and causes of Black-on-Black violence.
ISBN 1-897164-00-0
PB. Pages: 224

Understanding Black Adolescent Male Violence: Its Remediation and Prevention
Clairvoyant in its analysis, and unsurpassed in its prescriptions. The original from which much is borrowed.
ISBN 1-879164-03-5
PB. Pages: 100

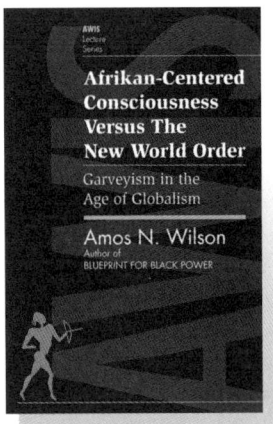

Afrikan-centered Consciousness Versus the New World Order: Garveyism in the Age of Globalism (with maps and charts)
A splendid introductory text on the continued survival of Afrikan Nationalism in the face of new imperialism.
ISBN 1-879164-09-4
PB. Pages: 141

The Falsification of Afrikan Consciousness: Eurocentric History, Psychiatry and the Politics of White Supremacy
A triple feature. Contains two of Wilson's most memorable lectures along with brilliant analysis.
ISBN 1-879164-02-7
PB. Pages: 160
Hard cover. 1-879164-11-6

Contents

Dedication   *v*
Acknowledgments   *v*
Foreword   1

Chapter 1

What Is Power   5
    The Typology of Power 7
    Force as Power 9
    Coercion as Power 12
    Influence as Power 15
    Competent and Legitimate Authority as Power 16
    Manipulation as Power 22
    Summary: White Domination – Black Subordination 23

Chapter 2

Bases of Power: Organization and Ethnic Resources   27
    Power and Property 29
    Organizations and Institutions as Power Sources 33
    Organized Networks and Power 36
    Sources of Organizational Power 41
    Factors Affecting Group Power 42
    Social Power of Unorganized Masses 42
       The Expression of Mass Power 42
    Ethnic Solidarity and Power 45
    Ethnic and Class Resources, Race Ideology and the
       Exploitability of Black Americans 46
    Organizing for Black Power 49
    The Black American Nation-within-a-Nation 51

Contents

Chapter 3
Social and Cultural Origins of Power   **56**
Culture and Power 56
The Family as a Power System 57
Black American Culture and Identity 59
Cultural, Social, and Personal Identity 60
The Need for a New Afrikan Self-Identity 63
Destruction of Black Family Power 64
Religious Institutions and Power 67
The Institutional Black Church 68
The Black Church and the Myth of Individualism 75
The Nation of Islam 80
The Spirit of War 83

Chapter 4
Consciousness and Power   **85**
Consciousness as Power 85
Social Control Theory: Consciousness as an Instrument
   of Social Control 89
Values as Instruments of Social Control 92
Group Consciousness 94
White Consciousness versus Black Consciousness 96
White Power – Black Consciousness 96
The Realization of Afrikan Consciousness 98

Chapter 5
Self-Concept and Power   **100**
The Self-Concept, Ethnocentrism and Social Power ... 102

Chapter 6
Power and Personality   **109**
Personality Differences as a Division of Labor 110
Personality as an Instrument of Social Power 111
The Other-Directed Afrikan American Personality 115
Other-Directedness and the Reconstruction of the
   Afrikan Personality 123
Sociogenetic Maladaptiveness 125
The Socioeconomic Functions of the Maladaptive
   Afrikan Personality 127
The Reconstruction of the Afrikan Personality 129

Contents

The Afrikan Centered Thematic Inventory 131

Chapter 7

Class, Race and Power in America   **136**
Social Classes and Class Conflicts 136
Social Class and Ethnicity in the United States 137
The White Elite Power Structure and the White
    American Nation-within-a-Nation 141
Preparing for Power 147

Chapter 8

The Power Processes of the Ruling Class   **152**
The Political, Economic and Ideological Processes
    of the Ruling Class 153
The Special Interest Process 155
Lobbyists and Committees 157
The Second Government-within the Government 162
Blacks and Government 164

Chapter 9

The Policy-Formation Process   **166**
The Functions of the Policy-Planning Groups 169
The Role and Function of Selected Influential
    Policy-Planning Groups 172
Think Tanks 175
Leading Think Tanks 179
Foundations 182
Foundations as Vehicles of Social Engineering 185
Education for Servitude: Corporate Philanthropy
    and the Shaping of Black Higher Education 189
Foundation and Think Tanks: The Selling of Newt Gingrich
    and the Republican Party 1994 193
Foundation Influence on the Afrikan Community 197
The Need for Afrikan-centered Information
    and Strategy Centers 200
On the Black Hand Side: Black Power Networks and
    Institutions of Higher Learning 204

Chapter 10

The Candidate-Selection Process   **209**

Contents

The Selling of the Candidate 209
Party Politics 212
The Need for a Black Political Party 216

Chapter 11
Ideology and the Legitimization of Dominance — 220
The Ideology Process 223
Media and the Ideology Process 227
Ideological Process of Afrikan-centered Opposition 230
The Lack of an Afrocentric Ideology Process 233
The Black Media: White Media in Black Face 234
The Black Bourgeoisie – Black Political Establishment
    Alliance against Afrikan Liberation 240

Chapter 12
The Economic Order and Power — 246
Economic Powerlessness means Political Powerlessness ... 246
The Afrikan American Community as Colony 248
Economic Segmentation 253
White American and Afrikan American Economies in
    Post-Industrial America 254
Echoes of Decline 255
American Decline – Black Decline 260
Industrial and Government Policy 262
Jobs Move Abroad 267
The Powerlessness of the Government to Resolve
    Human Problems 269
Reactionary Outcomes of Global Competition 273
Losing Ground 277
Taking Charge of Economic Destiny 286
A Contrarian Point of View 289
The Economic Future of the Afrikan American
    Community 292

Chapter 13
The Financial-Corporate Elite: *The New World Government* — 295
World Ascendancy of Private Capital 295
The Private Financial-Corporate Complex – U.S. Second
    Government 297
The Federal Reserve: Private Controller of the Public

Contents

Economy 299
Tyranny of the Free Market 300

Chapter 14

Race and Economics — 307

Social Relations and Economics 307
Ethnic-Cultural Identity and Economics 308
Global Economic Network of the Ethnic Chinese 311
Kuan-Xie: The Economic Power of Social Relationships 312
The Local Tribe 317
    The Koreans 317
The Ethnic Road to Riches 329
How They Do It 335
Afrikan Immigrants 339
Black American Racial Solidarity and Economic
    Development 343
Immigration and the Afrikan American Community 345
Costs and Benefits of Immigration 346
A Refrain: Wealth and Power 353
The Asian Brotherhood Collective 354
The White Brotherhood Collective 356
The Black Brotherhood Collective 360

Chapter 15

Afrika Agonistes — 366

Dangerous Economic Straits of Contemporary Afrika 366
Impoverishing of Afrika: *IMF/World Bank and U.S. Policy* 367
Benign Neglect of Afrika by the World Community 370
The Self-Inflicted Wounds of Afrikans at Home and
    Abroad 374
The Planned Suffering of Afrika 377
The Afrikan American Monoculture 385
Open Markets, Open Shelves, Most Favored Nations
    and the Manufacturing of Wealth 387
Reasons for Optimism 393

Chapter 16

Investing In and Trading With Afrikan Nations — 398

Pan–Afrikan Trade Alliances 403
Global Policy Is Local 404

Contents

The Possibilities of an Afrikan Investment Fund 406
The Power of Investment Funds 407
International Trade Centers.......................... 409

Chapter 17

Empowerment Through Wealth   **415**
   The Tradition of Trade and Self-Help among
     Afrikan Nations 415
   Tulsa, The Black Promised Land 421
   Black Phoenix Rises from Its Ashes 422
   All-Black Towns in America 423
   Early Afrikan American Investment in Afrika:
     The Case of Marcus Garvey 425
   Repression of Afrikan American Economic Power 431
   Black American Communities as Economic Brothels 439
   The Black Bourgeoisie's Repression of Black
     Entrepreneurialism 442

Chapter 18

Benevolent Fronts Assault Local and Global Afrikan Markets **445**
   The Community Development Corporation as
     Economic Front 445
   A Mall Comes to a Black Township 454
   Inner-City Shopping Malls 461

Chapter 19

The Paucity of Black Wealth   **469**
   Some Facts About Wealth Ownership 472
   Business Ownership and Investment: Keys to Black
     Wealth 476
   The Case of Reparations 486
   Collective Capitalism 487
   Afrikan American Collective Capitalism 488

Chapter 20

The Myth of the Market Economy and Black Power   **491**
   Self-Defeating Economic Ideology and Trade Strategy
     of the Afrikan American Community 495
   Lessons of History 497

Contents

Chapter 21
Nation-within-a-Nation — 503
The Afrikan American Community: Separate and
 Unequal 504
The Afrikan American Community as a de facto
 Third World Nation 507
The Advantages of an Afrikan American Nation 509
Economic Proposal to the Afrikan American Community .. 510

Chapter 22
Demographic Foundations of an Afrikan American Nation-within-a-Nation — 517
The Importance of a Sense of Nation 517
The Power of the Black Consumer 520
Demographic Distribution of Afrikan Americans in
 Contrast with Other non-White Ethnic Groups 521
The Economic Potential of Urban Black America 530
Suburbanization and Economics 536
Cooperative Economics in Los Angeles 542
Prince George's County 543
The Power of a Black National Vision 551

Chapter 23
The Black Church: Key to Black Economic Empowerment? — 555
The Black Church's Potential for Transforming
 the Black Nation 569
Church-sponsored National Chain Stores 577
Church Businesses as Community-owned Businesses 580
The Economics of the Nation of Islam 581
The Trade Relations of Other Ethnic Nations to the
 Afrikan American Nation 585

Chapter 24
The Black Consumer and the Economics of Afrocentrism — 588
Black Consumer Power 588
Alien Merchants and Black Consumers 591
The Civil Rights Movement – A Consumer Movement 596
The Black Civil Rights/Consumer Movement: Victorious
 Self-Defeat 598
Spending Habits of the Black Consumer 602

Contents

Native American Nations and Economic Empowerment ... 609
Black Tourism As Industry 613
Creating and Meeting Black Consumer Needs 621
The Politics of Black Consumer Tastes 625
The Economics of Afrocentrism 626
Afrikan American Entrepreneurs and Afrikan-centered
    Marketing 635
The Economics of Cultural and Subcultural Identity 643
Afrikan Peoples: The White Man's Golden Geese 650
Black Self-Employment 652

Chapter 25
The Relationship of White-owned Banks to the Black Community   657
Banks Rob Customers 657
Lending Bias Against Black-owned Businesses 660

Chapter 26
Black-owned Banks: *Creators of Wealth*   676
Creating Money 677
Historical Overview of Black-owned Banks 680
The Possibilities of Black Community Banking 685
The Combined Deposits and Assets of Black-owned Banks . 686
Black-owned Banks and Capital Levels 691
Black-led Institutional Investment in Black-owned Banks . 692
Pension Funds, Corporate America and Black Banks 695
Black Financial Self-Help 697
Interstate Banking 700

Chapter 27
Financing Black Economic Development   704
Development Bank 704
Credit Unions 708
Types of Credit Unions 711
Community Development Credit Unions 715
The Community Development Corporation 718
Venture Capital 719
Black-owned Venture Capital Funds in the Expansion
    of the Afrikan American Economy 723

Contents

Chapter 28

Rotating Credit Associations: *The Prime Importance of Saving*   **729**
    The Rotating Credit Association 731
    The "Susu Account" 738
    Micro-Loan Funds and Underwriter's Loans 740
    Small Business Incubators: Creating a Conducive
        Environment for Black Leadership 742
    Small Business Administration Loans 744
    The Afrikan American Development Corporation:
        National Underwriter of Black Economic Power 747
    Cases In Point 750

Chapter 29

The Investment Club   **755**
    Investment Trends in the Black Community 755
    The Investment Clubs 756
    Investment Companies 760
    Wealth and Knowledge: A Case in Point 761

Chapter 30

Franchises, Cooperatives, Corporations
    and Collective Capitalism   **766**
    Franchises 766
    Some Afrikan American Franchises 768
    Blacks and Burger King 771
    Co-operatives 776
    Co-ops as Large Businesses 778
    The Non-Profit Mode of Economic Development 781
    A CASE IN POINT Community Organizations and
        Institutions: *The Struggle for Economic Democracy*
        in South Afrika 785
    A Note on Concessionary Financing 791
    Investment Banking 797
    An Afrikan American Stock Market 817
    The Need for an Afrikan American Stock Market 820

Chapter 31

The Crisis of Leadership   **824**
    Leaders and Followers 824
    The Cry for New Leadership 827

The Assimilationist/Moralistic-oriented Leadership
    Establishment 830
The Dilemma of Assimilationist Leadership 833
Black Neo-Conservatism 837
Black Nationalist Leadership 848
Why Black Nationalism 849
Contemporary Black Nationalism: Absence of
    Organization, Creed and Plans 852
A Black Nationalist Party 856

BIBLIOGRAPHY   859
INDEX   865
EDITOR'S NOTE   890

Table of Illustrations

Title	Table	Page
America's Long History of 100 Percent Racial Quotas in Favor of Whites	2-1	34
Universally Practiced Race Discrimination as Cartel Power	2-2	35
National Political and Economic System	2-3	50
Complementary White-Black Social, Political and Personality Role Dispositions	6-1	118
Founding Fathers Classified by Known Economic Resources	8-1	156
The Policy-Formation Process	9-1	170
Black Proportions in Occupations	12-1	259
African-American Share of the Major Occupations in 1991 and Projected Occupation Growth Rates 1990-2005	12-2	259
Where Black Losses Were Most Disproportionate	12-3	280
The Master Plan	12-4	294
Damage Count	14-1	318
Where Markets are Developing (Sub-Saharan Africa)	16-1	401
Black Business Establishments and Business Persons in Tulsa, Tulsa City Directories, 1921	17-1	424
Wealth Ownership, 1988	19-1	471
Receipts and Numbers of Firm in 1987 by Industry	19-2	473
Black and White Share of Wealth per Capita in 1992	19-3	476
Top 75 Black Enterprise (B.E.) Industrial Service 100 Companies, June 1997	19-4	477
1994 Black Enterprise 100s	19-5	481
1997 B.E. 100s	19-6	481
B.E. Top 10 Employment Leaders	19-7	482

Contents

Title	Table	Page
The B.E. 100s: 25 Years of Growth	19-8	482
Afrikan Americans in Metropolitan Populations 1990	22-1	522-3
Black Population Percentage above Percent in Cities with 100,000 or More Inhabitants in 1990	22-2	525
Black Urban Demographics Money Income of Families	22-3	526
The Most Blacks	22-4	537
Black Concentrations	22-5	538
Changes in Black Suburbs	22-6	539
The Fastest-Growing Black Suburbs	22-7	540
Affluent Blacks	22-8	541
Demographics of Black Church Denominations	23-1	560
Black Buying Power by Place of Residence for U.S. and the States, 1994–1995	24-1	592
Black Share of Total Buying Power for U.S., and the States, 1994–1995	24-2	593
Federal Contributions to Selected City Budgets	24-3	595
10 Largest Metropolitan Cores: Percentage White	24-4	600
Ethnic Shifts in Cores of 10 Largest Metropolises	24-5	600
Corporate Return on the Black Consumer Dollar	24-6	605
Top 10 Cities for African-American Conventions	24-7	615
Sample Economic Plan	24-8	622
Proposed National Economic Plan	24-9	623
Market of the Future	24-10	635
Hiring Patterns	24-11	653
Narrow Market	24-12	654
Bank Loans to Black- and White-owned Firms	25-1	660
1993 Bank Summary	26-1	687
1997 Top 25 Financial Institutions (update)	26-2	687
1993 Savings & Loans Summary	26-3	688

Title	Table	Page
The Range of Risk Reduction Activities of a National Minority Development Corporation	28-1	750
The Power of Compounding	29-1	758
Black Enterprise 15 Largest Black-owned Investment Banks	30-1	803
B.E. 15 Largest Black-owned Investment Companies (updated)	30-2	804

Table of Boxes

Title	Box	Page
The Realm of Alert Consciousness	4-1	91
Financing Export Trade	15-1	381
Afrikan American Entrepreneurial Milestones	17-1	417
The Planned Permanent Economic Depression	17-2	440
Myths About Entrepreneurs	18-1	467
Jobs versus Ownership	19-1	484
The Black Church and Economic Development	23-1	564
Black Buying Power	24-1	589
The Power of Refusal	24-2	618
Economic Democracy	24-3	620
A Note of Caution Concerning Borrowing from Mainstream Institutions	25-1	667
Capital Accumulation	26-1	684
Corporations versus Proprietorships	30-1	793
Why Blacks Should Own Government Securities	30-2	801

Foreword

THE FORUMS, CONFERENCES, conventions, workshops, lectures, talks, teach-ins, seminars, informal conversations, everyday encounters, newspaper, magazine and journal articles, radio and programs to which the Afrikan American community is exposed with profusive and bewildering frequency, almost invariably involve discussions of some aspect of White American oppression and Black American victimization. Such discussions in their various incarnations have, no doubt, taken place since 1619 when the first Afrikans, enslaved, arrived on this continent. In seeking to develop various means for coping with their oppression, these colloquies, lectures, soliloquies, monologues, programs, essays and articles seek to answer the questions among others: Why do Whites oppress us? By what means are we oppressed by them? How may we end our oppression?

Many answers to the first of this triumvirate of questions have been proposed. They run the gamut from the sublime, i.e., that Whites are divinely ordained to be the oppressors of Blacks, to the ridiculous, e.g., that Whites are inherently more intelligent than Blacks and are thus naturally enabled to dominate them, whether as determined by God or by Chance. Of course there are many interesting proposed answers which fall in between the extremes of this continuum, including the White Man's icy origins in contrast to the sunny beginnings of the Black Man, as reflected in their contrasting frigid and temperate predispositions. Also included is the minority White Man's inordinate need to steadfastly guard his recessive gene pool, the pristine source of his racial purity and identity, against pollutive and miscegenous admixture with the majority Black Man's dominant gene pool.

Declarations proposed as answers to the first question implicitly answer the second. Color, its intensity, has been accepted as the measure of God's favor — from blessedness to cursedness, from brilliant giftedness to dimwittedness, from cold calculation to warm gullibility, from vulnerable recessiveness to threatening domination. Therefore the darker ones, the darkest race is destined to grasp at the shorter end of the stick, to remain unaccepted, unassimilated. "If you're white, you're all right": "If you're yellow, you're mellow": "If you're brown, stick around": "If you're black, stay back."

However, a brief review of history very quickly disabuses us of the idea that color, or the lack of it, is destiny. For the White Man's ascendance has been but a moment in the history of mankind. The 500-year rise of Europe, the 200-year rise of the United States, even the lifetimes of the Greek, Roman and Holy Roman empires are but flashpoints of time relative to Egypt's 10,000 years, the ancientness of Ethiopia, the thousand years of Ghana, and the thousands of years of a plethora of Afrikan kingdoms and empires — free, virile, ingenious, and independent. For Europe is Afrika's wayward, bastard child and therefore not her ordained master. So, Europe and her White children's supremacy today must be accounted for in far less than cosmological terms. For their supremacy, like the supremacy of any race, is but the ascendancy of the mundane. And their fall from grace will be but the result of the working of mundane forces.

Hence, our answers to the three questions will be starkly terrestrial — the White Man oppresses Afrikan peoples because he possesses the power to do so. The Black Man is oppressed because he has not developed the power to prevent his oppression. His oppression will end when the power of his oppressor is countered by his own power. More specifically to the point, no matter how we choose to explain White oppression or global supremacy, whether cosmologically or mundanely, the ultimate reason the White Man does what he does is because he possesses the power to do so. The reason why the Black Man is victimized by White power is because he has not developed the power to prevent his victimization. Therefore, if the Black Man is to prevent his victimization by the White Man, he must neutralize, balance or destroy the power differential which favors his domination by the White Man. The Black Man, the Afrikan race must study power — its sources, its acquisition, its increase, its preservation — and its application to the successful achievement of his liberation from White oppression and to enhance his autonomous quality of life.

It is to this end that these volumes are dedicated. It is our intent here not to be ingeniously original or purely academic, for we wish to solve practical problems which revolve around the development of Afrikan Power.

We hope these volumes will in some good ways contribute to the empowerment and liberation of Afrikan peoples.

AMOS WILSON
The Pan–Afrikan Research
& Development Foundation

Chapter I

What Is Power

THE DEFINITIONS OF POWER are various and conflicting. This is due mainly to the multifarious nature of power itself, rather than due to its unreality or ephemeral spirit. Few, if any of us, doubt the reality of power and the tangible effects its application engenders. Our confusion as to its exact definition more likely flows from the fact that power, depending on context and circumstance, assumes ubiquitous shapes and forms, varying degrees of transparency and visibility. Power is a chameleon: it takes on the texture of its environment.

It is not our purpose here to untangle the web of power definitions. It is not necessary for us to do so. However, a review of a number of definitions and of several forms of power will provide an intuitive understanding of its essential meaning, which is all that is necessary to our mission.

Power comes with being; with interactive existence; with being alive. It is the essence of life and the motive force of growth and development and of the adaptability of living things to environmental changes and demands. Power refers to the ability to do, the ability to be, the ability to prevail. Beingness and aliveness originate with power. To be powerless is to be will-less, impotent and lifeless; without effect or influence; to be nothing, of no account. Thus, we concur with Rollo May when he contends that:

> Power is essential for all living things. Man, in particular, cast on this barren crust of earth aeons ago with the hope and the requirement

that he survive, finds he must use his powers and confront opposing forces at every point in his struggle with the earth and with his fellows.[1]

The unimpeded intentionality of living systems, including especially human beings, is self-realization and self-actualization, the fulfillment of genetic potential or possibilities. This intentionality must be *empowered* to be realized. Thus, to paraphrase Friedrich Nietzsche, "Wherever we find the will to live, there we find the will to power." Power is essential to our existence and the most influential factor in determining our quality of life. As Wartenberg contends, "Power is one of the central phenomena of human social life."[2] And as Parenti argues, "All sorts of interpersonal [and we may add, intergroup] relationships can be seen as involving power, including between lovers or between parent and child." Power! There is no escaping its presence in some form. There is no escaping its use by others to influence in some form our person, our minds and behavior and our own use of it to influence the persons, minds and behavior of others.

We deny the ubiquity of power to our peril. It does not vanish from reality or lose its influence by our refusal to acknowledge its existence. Therefore, we are behooved to recognize its permanent reality and make the best of it, control it and use it to good purpose. Power in and of itself "can be both a detrimental and a beneficial aspect of social relationships" and can be made to play "the negative as well as the positive role...in the constitution of human social life" (Wartenberg). Power can be utilized to achieve personal, social, political and material ends if it is appropriately developed, organized and applied. The question of whether power is beneficial or harmful can only be answered in regard to the specific use to which it is put in a particular situation.

Many in our audience will find this discussion of power disturbing or dis-easing. Having been victimized by the abuse and misuse of power, often crushed by the powers-that-be, the reader who identifies himself as among the powerless or as a member of a relatively powerless group, e.g., an Afrikan American, will be the more perturbed by our discussion. The oppressed and downtrodden, having been traumatized by the abuse of power by their powerful oppressors, often come to perceive power itself as inherently evil, as by nature corrupting and therefore as something to be eschewed, denied and

---

[1]. Rollo May, *Power and Innocence* (New York: Norton, 1977).

[2]. Thomas E. Wartenberg, *The Forms of Power: From Domination to Transformation* (Philadelphia: Temple University Press, 1990), p. 9.

renounced. The pursuit of power is viewed as unworthy of virtuous persons, and the desire to possess it as sinful. Therefore, many among the powerless and poor feel compelled to find in their powerlessness and poverty the emblematic signs of their Godliness and redemptive salvation. How convenient a precept for rationalizing and maintaining the power of the *haves* over the *have-nots*! As the result of their ideological manipulation by the powerful and their own reactionary misperception of reality, the poor and powerless have been made to perceive the pursuit, possession and application of power in their own behalf as unbecoming to themselves. This is even more the case when through their naive acceptance of the self-serving deceptive propaganda perpetrated by the powers-that-be, their own reactionary self-negation, and their nursing of their internalized inferiority complexes, the poor huddled masses perceive the possession and exercise of power as the inherent and exclusive prerogative of the ruling classes or races.

There are many Blacks who have been convinced by racist propaganda that supreme power is divinely deeded to dominant Whites. They therefore suffer anxiety attacks and feel as if they are blasphemously rebelling against God, Himself, if they — even for a moment — seriously dare consider conspiring to wrest power from the hands of their oppressors. More unfortunate than this sorely mistaken theological perception is the self-abnegating perception by many Blacks that they are inherently incapable of mounting a successful campaign against oppressive White power and therefore must sulkingly seek the least onerous accommodation to it. This perception of and orientation toward power on the part of Afrikan peoples, is but a pre–scription for their unending subordination, exploitation, and ultimately, when it is convenient to the purposes of their oppressors, their genocidal demise. Therefore, if they are to survive and prosper in freedom then, like it or not, Afrikan peoples must come to terms with power. We must be ever conscious of the fact that "...the establishment, whatever rewards it gives us, will also, if necessary to maintain its control, kill us."[3]

The Typology of Power

In perhaps its most general sense, Rollo May defines power as "the ability to cause or prevent change." Power is fundamentally ambivalent in that it exists in both latent and manifest forms, is both stabilizing and destabilizing, both a causal factor in bringing about

---

3. Howard Zinn, *The Twentieth Century: A People's History* (New York: Harper & Row, 1984).

certain changes in social and environmental circumstances as well as in preventing them. Power may conceivably refer to the ability to achieve a desired goal, or to the ability to willfully resist or overcome certain social and environmental conditions imposed on oneself by others, or the ability to impose on others against their will or outside their awareness, certain social, environmental circumstances and behavioral demands.

Instances of defining power as the "ability to" or *"power to"* include the definition of power as "the ability to get what one wants" (Parenti); as "the capacity of some persons to produce intended and unforeseen effects on others" (Wrong); or as the ability a person or group has to "produce intended effects upon the world around them, to realize their purposes within it, whatever these purposes happen to be."

Power as the *"power over"* in contrast to power as the *"power to"* emphasizes the use of power by one person or group to *constrain* or *restrict* the possibilities or options of another person or group. "Power-over" refers to power that "is exercised over an agent [i.e., a person or group] when he is not able to act freely, that is, with a full set of possibilities available to him." Wartenberg explicates the concept of "power-over" more clearly in the following statements:

> An agent who acts in a context in which someone else has power over her is not able to do as she wishes, but faces a situation in which the structure of her action-environment is in the control of someone else. She is therefore not in the normal circumstances of human action and, as a result, her responsibility for her actions is modified.[4]

Instances of defining power as "power over" include the definition of power as "the possibility of imposing one's will upon the behavior of other persons" (Weber); "the ability to influence or control the actions of others, to get them to do what we want them to, and what they would otherwise not have done," and finally, as "the capacity to affect the conduct of individuals through the real or threatened use of rewards and punishments."[5]

The person or group which possesses and applies "power-over" another person or group is thereby enabled to structure and restrict the action range of the subordinate person or group and to limit the options available to him or it. "Power over" as defined above, characterizes the primary power relationship between Whites and Blacks. As such, it essentially defines the character of White supremacy relative to Black subordination.

---

4. Wartenberg, p. 86.

5. Thomas R. Dye, *Power and Society: An Introduction to the Social Sciences*, 3rd ed. (CA.: Brooks/Cole, 1983).

Power, whether as "power to" or "power over," manifests itself in a variety of forms or types. We shall briefly define certain types or forms of power and their relevance to White racist domination and exploitation of Blacks and to the necessity of Blacks to develop the power to end such domination and exploitation.

Force as Power

Power as force involves the exercise of biological and physical means to prevent another person or group from doing what he or it prefers to do or "to get something to happen to the [person or group] that [he or it] would prefer it did not" (Wartenberg). The force utilized may involve "the infliction of bodily pain or injury including the destruction of life itself, and the frustration of basic biological needs."[6] It may also involve the construction of human and physical obstacles to constrain or restrict the freedom and range of movement of another person or group.

Force may be utilized instrumentally rather than directly, to achieve certain ends. The instrumental use of force may involve its use to inhibit or destroy another person's or group's ability to develop and mobilize his or its human and material resources which might be used against the interests of the powers-that-be. The strategic and tactical purpose of instrumental force is to limit or eliminate the subordinate individual's or group's capacity to act in certain ways. Instrumental force may be used to establish in the mind of the subordinate person or group the powerholder's capability and willingness to use force as an instrument of punishment for non-compliant behavior on his or its part. It also may be used as a means of motivating the non-complying party to return to or to re-establish a pre-existing power relation.

Force, per se, rather than being utilized as the primary and exclusive means of exerting power over another may serve more to reinforce or "back up" other forms of power relations (to be discussed below). That is, "force, although a reality in many social situations, achieves its full scope by undergirding other types of power" (Wartenberg). In so-called advanced societies like the United States, force is more likely to be applied as the "final persuader or arbiter" when compliance is not attained by other means.

Force as Inefficient Power — In the context of the modern nation-state, the use of force as the primary regulator of social and power relations,

---

6. Dennis Wrong, *Power: Its Forms, Bases and Uses* (Chicago: Univ. of Chicago Press, 1988), p. 24.

as the primary means of achieving the results desired by power-holders is more often than not, inefficient, counter-productive and fraught with onerous complexities and unintended outcomes. It is also often socially, economically and materially costly to exert and maintain. Wrong perceptively notes, as follows:

> Force is more effective in preventing or restricting people from acting than in causing them to act in a given way... Force can achieve negative effects: the destruction, prevention or limitation of the possibility of action by others. But one cannot forcibly manipulate the limbs and bodies of others in order to achieve complex positive results: the fabrication or construction of something, the operation of a machine, the performance of a physical or mental skill.[7]

Wartenberg further notes:

> Force is uneconomic for a number of reasons. In the first place, it requires that the dominant agent make some physical effort in order to keep the subordinate agent from doing what she would otherwise do... As a result, maintaining the use of force requires a constant expenditure of energy by the dominant agent....
>
> *Force is also uneconomic because it inherently occasions resistance...* it is always perceived by those over whom it is used as a hostile presence, an alienating experience that restricts their ability to act. Because of this it engenders a dynamic of resistance in those over whom it is exercised.
>
> ...[Thus], force *by itself* is less effective as a means of power than is often assumed.[8] [Emphasis added]

The problematics of using unadorned force as the chief instrument of power utilized by a dominant group to achieve complex social-material ends with economic efficiency and the barest minimum of social disruption, motivates that group to develop and apply more subtle forms of power. These will be discussed below. However, at this juncture we should note that current forms of domination of Continental, Caribbean, North, Central and South American Afrikans, respectively, by Europeans, is secured by more subtle and efficient means of political control than by the use of oppressive physical force. Consequently, the "independence" of Afrikan countries and former Caribbean colonies and the social "assimilation" of Afrikan Americans into the mainstream of White America by no means represent the lessening of European and Euro-American domination of or a fundamental change in the nature of European and Afrikan power

---

7. Ibid., p. 27.
8. Wartenberg, p. 95.

relations in favor of the Afrikans, as persons so erroneously assume. Quite to the contrary, these historically apparent social/political changes instead represent the increased subtlety and efficiency of European domination of Afrikan peoples. It should be noted that the ability to use physical/militaristic force as the final arbiter of power relations still lies overwhelmingly in the hands of Europeans and EuroAmericans. It is this "force differential" that Afrikans across the Diaspora must in some way resolve, neutralize or frustrate if they are to gain true parity with Europeans and EuroAmericans and indeed gain their liberation from European domination.

Psychic Violence — The most powerful obstacle against the liberation of Afrikan peoples from White domination and exploitation is not the ability of Whites to use superior military or police firepower or their threat to use it against Afrikan insurgency, but is their ability to engage in unrelenting psychopolitical violence against the collective Afrikan psyche. It is the White monopoly on psychic violence and their devastatingly ingenious use of it against the minds of Afrikan peoples which represent the greatest threat to Afrikan survival. Wrong insightfully points out the nature of this form of violence:

> [T]here is a form of conduct, often described as psychic, psychological or moral force or violence, which does not fit readily under the rubrics of any of the other forms of power. If physical violence involves inflicting damages on the body of a person, how is one to classify the deliberate effort to affect adversely a person's emotions or his feelings and ideas about himself by verbally, or in other symbolic ways, insulting or degrading him? If...power includes the production of purely mental or emotional effects and is not confined to the eliciting of overt acts, then the psychic assault of, say, a nagging, browbeating spouse or parent, *the defamation of the character of a political foe or even of an entire group, constitute exercises of power.*
>
> ...*Damage to the psyche is surely as real as damage to the body... It is plainly not true that 'sticks and stones may break my bones but names can never hurt me'. Psychic violence, in which the intended effect of the perpetrator is to inflict mental or emotional harm, is continuous with physical violence....*[9] [Emphasis added]

The ultimate force in the world is the force of mind. When that force is defeated all is lost.

Dominant Whites have used words and symbols to violently and unrelentingly attack oppressed Blacks in a thousand and one nefarious ways, including the projection of dehumanizing stereotypes

---
9. Wrong p. 28.

and caricatures of them; the falsification of their history and culture; the miseducation of Blacks; and the engaging in chronic derisive media attacks on their morals, behavior, intelligence, ways of life, sexuality, physical features, motives and values.

The final end of the violent White-instigated psychic assaults against the collective psyche of Blacks is to induce in them states of false consciousness, self-alienation and self-hatred so as to irreparably impair their capacity to overthrow their White oppressors through the mobilization of their human and material resources.

False consciousness, self-alienation and self-hatred are conjoining states of mind which motivate oppressed Blacks to engage in continuing self-defeating, self-destructive assaults against their own interests and against themselves. Consequently, by these means Blacks are unwittingly manipulated into forming alliances with their oppressors and exploiters in disempowering themselves and in empowering those who dominate and exploit them all the more.

Coercion as Power

The instrumental use of force or the threatened use of force by the powerholder to attain the compliance of another is often referred to as coercion. Coercion is therefore a form of power. It is of the utmost importance to note as did Wrong that "a coercer may succeed without possessing either the capability or the intention of using force, *so long as the power subject believes he possesses both*" [Emphasis added]. That is, the coercive power of the powerholder may rest significantly less or not at all on his actual capacity to harm the subject, but may rest more or less completely on the subordinate subject's *belief* that the powerholder can do so. This perspective, commonly referred to as "bluffing," allows us to recognize the fact that in many instances powerholders exercise power over their subjects because of the subjects' misperceptions and misunderstandings, or false beliefs about the powerholders' ability to restrict their options or possibilities. Wartenberg refers to this situation as the *Oz Phenomenon*, "for it shows that agents are able to coerce other agents by acting upon their beliefs rather than by controlling their action-environment directly." He further contends

> ...that coercive power relations can be brought into existence by means of the subordinate agent's false understandings about the ability of the dominant agent to harm him. *This is an important source of power for a dominant agent so long as her ability to realize her threat is not questioned [and challenged]*.[10] [Emphasis added]

---

10. Wartenberg, p. 101.

While the ability of the dominant agent to coerce the subordinate subject may rest heavily on the subject's exaggerated misperception of the dominant agent's actual capacity to do him harm, equally and often of greater importance, the ability of the dominant agent to coerce the subject may rest on the subject's misperception and underestimation of *his own* capacity to successfully thwart the coercive or punitive actions of the dominant agent. The often anemic self-concept of subordinate persons and groups, their low self-esteem, their ignorance of their actual strengths, are more the causes of their subordination than is the actual strength of their oppressors.

The long history of White American domination of Black Americans — which has been enforced and reinforced by the use of physical force and violence, psychic violence and coercive power — has in effect convinced the majority of Blacks that Whites are invincible. Moreover, this history has undermined the self-confidence of most Blacks, narrowed their vision of their possibilities and power, restricted their aspirations to the narrow confines of racial accommodation and assimilation, to being the paternalistic recipients of White sympathy rather than expanding their aspirations to include the overcoming of White power and achieving full, unfettered self-liberation. The unending maintenance of this self-defeating state of mind in Blacks is the fundamental objective of White power and the keystone upon which the infrastructural facade of White power rests.

We are not arguing here that White power is purely delusional or does not contain truly lethal actualities. However, we are arguing that if Black Americans and Afrikans the world-over do not permit themselves to be "psyched out" by White racist propaganda; if they both recognize and actualize their potential to neutralize White power in either its imagined or actual forms, they can by these means neutralize it.

The Productivity of Coercion — We can recall from our prior discussion that the use of force is essentially socially negative, expensive and prone to provoke overt resistance to its application by those subjected to it. We also intimated that force is essentially restrictive and preventative in character, more effective in obstructing people's behavior than in causing them to behave in certain productive ways (from the powerholder's point of view). Coercion, in contrast to the use of raw force, permits the powerholder to benefit more readily from the subordinate subject's actions and reactions. According to Wartenberg, "Unlike force, coercive power actually functions by getting an agent to *do* something. The logic of the threat is precisely its positing an action that an agent is able to forestall by acting in an appropriate manner."

For Wartenberg, coercive power is productive in that (1) it *produces* action on the part of the subordinate subject, and (2) because the actions of the subordinate subject elicited by coercive threat may actually *produce* something of value or of benefit to the coercive powerholder. The scope of coercive power, particularly in its political and institutional forms, is, as argues Wrong, "at least in the short run, ...undoubtedly the most effective form of power in extensiveness, comprehensiveness and intensity...."

However, despite its efficiency and productivity relative to force, the exercise of coercive power like the exercise of force may be expensive, socially and politically costly, and provokes resistance from those subjected to its application. Because the subjects of coercive power are aware of its application against them and realize that freedom to act has been threatened or restricted, they resent such an imposition and may attempt to break or thwart the powerholder's coercive power over them. The use of coercive power as its chief means of control often means that the dominant group must maintain constant surveillance and must constantly keep itself fully informed as to the thoughts, attitudes and activities of its subjects. Consequently, to the costs of acquiring and maintaining the means of production (if they are an owning class) the cost of procuring, maintaining and deploying the means of force and violence must be added the costs of information-gathering and espionage operations (Wrong). The relative inefficiency, counter-productivity and costliness of exercising force and coercive power as the primary means for dominating other groups serve to motivate powerholding groups to develop other more effective but less obvious or intrusive ways of exercising coercive force and power so as to reduce, if not eliminate altogether, the reactive resentment and resistance of their subordinate subjects. This end is accomplished when powerholders discover and utilize ways and means of obscuring or hiding the use of coercion by inducing misperceptions and misunderstandings among their subjects about whether they are actually being coerced (Wartenberg) or are being subjected to a "power play." The other forms of power we shall discuss below have in good part been developed and are utilized to obscure the actual nature of the coercive power relationship between powerholders and their subjects. However, we should note at this juncture that the ability of powerholders to obscure their coercive and exploitative actions from their subjects will be critically successful to the degree that their subjects have not developed and utilized their own analytical/critical, perceptive, and creative capacities to see through and subvert the hidden coercive machinations and intentions of their oppressors.

Influence as Power

Influence occurs when a person acts in compliance with the wishes or directions or suggestions of another, based on his sheer positive regard for love and admiration of the other, or based on a desire to please or serve the other because of the other's personal significance to him. Influence is achieved when the subject's behavioral compliance is attained without the influential party having to possess or use force, coercion, material rewards or making appeals to authority. This is especially the case when the subject complies with the wishes, suggestions, or commands of the other while engaging in no relevant, independent or deliberate thinking, reasoning, or rational processes whatsoever; or when the subject complies out of a "conditioned habit of obedience" in regard to the other.

Wartenberg mentions two important types of influence with which we are familiar: *rational persuasion* and *personal persuasion*. (He also mentions a third, *expertise*, which we discuss as "competent authority," presently.) In the first instance the subject retains the use of his critical or rational faculties but is led to reassess his understanding or perception of a situation or of reality, or to accept as reasonable or correct the conclusions reached and recommendations suggested by the other as the result of the other's apparently logical argumentation or reasoning. In the second instance the subject's behavioral compliance, the argumentation or demands of the other occur essentially because he wishes to satisfy the desires of the other as he perceives them to exist. As Wartenberg posits, "The central feature of influence via personal persuasion is that the influenced agent does not make her choices on the basis of reasons that she can present in the form of rational argument, but rather on the basis of the desires of the influencing agent." Another form of persuasion might be referred to as *propagandistic persuasion*, wherein through various media and forms of indoctrination techniques the subject is influenced to accept certain opinions or beliefs which lead him to think that he is acting in his own interests when this really is not the case.

Influence as power involves the powerholder's ability to gain his subordinate subject's "voluntary" acceptance of and behavioral compliance with the powerholder's interpretations of reality, value judgements, prescriptive suggestions and commands, based on the powerholder's perceived status, resources, personal/social attributes, competence, expertise, or legitimate authority. When powerholders as a group possess a monopoly of the positions of influence due to historical and other social factors, they may use their influence as a means to secure and obscure their possession of other types of power, and at times render unnecessary the naked use of force and coercion.

Influence requires that the subject subordinates his judgement to that of the other, that he is guided by the judgement of the other. As such, influence is a more secure and "hidden" form of power in that the influenced subject complies with the demands of the powerholder either without questioning the role or motives of the powerholder or after being persuaded by the powerholder's apparently logical argumentation. Consequently, influence as a type of power, as a type of rational, personal, propagandistic persuasion, may serve to render the possession and exercise of other types of power unnecessary and more secure, or to obscure them altogether. Thus, influence may itself function as an exceedingly potent or subtle form of power.

To a very significant extent White domination of Blacks, which initially and until relatively recently was expressed in terms of physical force coercion, the threatened use of force along with its occasional use, now expresses itself as influence. By means of the various forms of influence we have discussed, Whites dominate Blacks without appearing to deliberately do so and without having to revert to the sheer use of force and coercion. Consequently, they convince or persuade many Blacks to behave in ways compatible with maintaining White power, and incompatible with generating Black Power, while Blacks self-deceptively think that such behavior on their part is purely "voluntary," reasonable, or obligatory. This situation devolves from Blacks having accepted Eurocentric frames of reference and perceptions of reality. Only by choosing to accept and live by an Afrocentric frame of reference will Blacks escape the dispowering White influence and, correspondingly, enhance their own power.

Competent and Legitimate Authority as Power

Competent authority involves the achievement and exercise of social power derived from knowledge and skill and where behavioral compliance is obtained from the subject in return for his receipt of some benefit or service awarded by the authority.

Wrong defines competent authority as "authority that rests solely on the subject's belief in the superior knowledge or skill of the exerciser rather than on formal position in a recognized hierarchy of authority."[11] He further contends that "competent authority is a power relation in which the subject obeys the directives of the authority out of belief in the authority's superior competence or expertise to decide which actions will best serve the subject's interests and goals."

---

11. Wrong, p. 53.

Competent authority or expertise may crucially be used as a mask for social privilege and power exercised by one group over another. It hides social privilege and power because it appears to merely exist to advance the public interest. Moreover, competent authority or expertise, particularly if it is held in high social esteem and is well organized, may use its claims to superior knowledge and skill, and to operating in the public interest, to legitimate the rule of the powers-that-be. The legitimacy of their rule under other circumstances may be questionable or denied. Hence, competent authority, if monopolized by one social group, may serve to facilitate that group's social power over a dependent, less competent, subordinate group. In such an instance, the latter group may be relatively unaware of the extent and the degree to which it is dominated by the former. Even if it is aware it remains relatively powerless to the degree to which it lacks or does not exercise expert knowledge.

European Americans monopolize the positions of competent authority in addition to monopolizing the means of certifying (legitimating) and delegating such authority. They, through racial discrimination against Blacks, monopolize the means of gaining access to competent authority. They make use of these monopolies not only to command the obedience of subordinate Afrikan Americans, but to justify the "legitimacy" of their preponderant power over them. Moreover, they utilize their monopoly and competent authority to both obscure from and legitimate their social power, its exploitative, oppressive nature and intent, upon Black Americans.

The legitimacy of competent and other forms of White authority to which Afrikan Americans "voluntarily" submit or "freely give their consent," are but special cases of the overall "legitimacy" of White power they have been conditioned, seduced and otherwise compelled to accept and believe as morally justified.

Legitimate authority refers to a power relation in which the powerholder possesses an acknowledged *right to command* and the subject an acknowledged *obligation to obey*. "The *source* rather than the *content* of any particular command endows it with legitimacy and induces willing compliance on the part of the person to whom it is addressed" (Wrong, 1988). Authority can be said to be legitimate to the extent that it conforms to established rules; to the extent to which the rates used to justify it are based on shared beliefs or norms and are based on the expressed consent of the subject, i.e., on the extent to which the subject consents to the particular relations of power which the exercise of such authority requires (Beetham, 1991).

The norms which constitute a legitimate authority relationship are generally shared within a larger group or community to which both the person exercising that authority and the person subject to it belongs. Interestingly, as Wrong notes, submission to legitimate authority is widely regarded as "voluntary" and based on "consent" rather than on coercion and yet at the same time is felt to be "mandatory" or "obligatory." We must keep in mind that legitimate authority and the power relations it entails are based on the acceptance by those who submit to it of certain beliefs, values, rules and modes of giving consent (e.g., voting). The functional superiority of legitimate authority as a form of power is delineated by Wrong thusly:

> Legitimate authority creates far greater reliability of anticipated reactions than the other forms of authority, just as internalized social norms ensure more reliable conformity than norms the observance of which is more dependent on situational sanctions or *ad hoc* negotiation over their meaning and applicability. Legitimate authority is more efficient than coercive or induced authority in that it minimizes the need for maintaining means of coercion in constant readiness, continual surveillance of the power subjects and regular supplies of economic or non-economic rewards. For these reasons, naked (that is, coercive) power always seeks to clothe itself in the garments of legitimacy. Or, as Franz Neumann puts it even more strongly: 'Those who wield political power are compelled to create emotional and rational responses in those whom they rule, inducing them to accept, implicitly or explicitly, the commands of the rulers.'[12]

To a significant degree Afrikan Americans accept and obey predominant White American power and its authorities (at least from a social-psychological standpoint) because they agree with the rules of their establishment and expression as defined by White Americans; share with White Americans the moral, legal, and other values and perspectives which justify them; and to some extent (limited and of recent origin) because they, i.e., Blacks, have been permitted by White Americans to participate in political and social processes by which White power is given legitimacy. To a limited degree, Afrikan Americans have been permitted access to certain positions of competent and legitimate authority. These factors contribute mightily to their acceptance of White American power (domination) and the White American monopoly of positions of authority as legitimate. These forms of giving consent to the social power status quo on the part of Blacks help to obscure as well as deny the fact that they are in fact a dominated and severely exploited group (regardless of class);

---

12. Wrong, p. 52.

and helps to obscure the fact that their uncritical acceptance of the "rules," moral beliefs, perspectives, and their customary-traditional participation in the "American" (White) political-economic process and system is tantamount to the legitimation of their own oppression and to the consensual ensurance of their own powerlessness.

Rules, beliefs and consent are manufactured by those in power to justify, legitimate and serve their interests. In its origins White American power was not legitimated (i.e., voluntarily or contractually consented to, morally justified or politically-socially ratified) by Afrikan Americans who at the time of its origination were held in captivity (slavery) and to this point in time have been largely excluded from significantly participating in American legitimation processes.

From the historical point of view of Native and Afrikan Americans, White power, in whatever form, is illegitimate. This is because such power rests essentially on the near physical and genocidal decimation of Native Americans, the theft of their properties, on the exploitation or the forced labor (enslavement) of Afrikans, and on the systematic exclusion by Whites of both Black and Native Americans from the influential exercise of practically all forms of "legitimate" power and authority in the United States. The rules and beliefs which provide the means for legitimating White power were in fact pre-established, pre-ordained and imposed on Blacks against their will by Whites from the beginning. The illegitimacy of White American power is founded on the illegitimacy of its original sins — genocide, theft of property, and enslavement. It is apropos to note here a very telling statement made by Beetham in regard to power and legitimacy:

> ...the occupancy of property, the development of a hierarchal division of labour, or the establishment of a command structure [authority structure] can occur, and historically frequently has occurred, *through acts of forcible appropriation, exclusion or subjection which take place in violation of existing rules or outside of them* [even those promulgated by the usurpers themselves]. *Such usurpations cannot be legitimate.* However, the resulting power relations typically become consolidated and perpetuated through the establishment of rules which underpin and give legal form to the original usurpation. From that time on, subsequent positions of power come to be derived from the rules, in the same way those whose rules originate through custom or agreement. Although the memory of the original usurpation may be kept alive, with the passage of time the issue of the rules' legitimacy becomes less a question of their origin than one of the ongoing character of the relationships they embody, and the nature of the requirements they impose.

Here lies the...reason *why power is not necessarily legitimate, even when it is legally valid,* ...that legality constitutes only one dimension of legitimacy; it is a necessary but not a sufficient condition for it.[13] [Emphasis added]

Our questioning of the legitimacy of White power, particularly White American power, does not amount to a call for the overthrow of the American government. However, it does amount to a call for Afrikan Americans to critically examine the origins and functions of the rules, morals, values, customary attitudes and behavior, common perspectives and folkways they have been convinced to accept as the result of White American physical and coercive impositions, ideological propaganda and conditioning procedures. Uncritical acceptance of Eurocentric rules, morals, customs and so on by Afrikan Americans hides from them the fact that despite the norms and values they share with White Americans and which serve to legitimate the American social-political-economic system, White Americans possess a preponderant and dangerous power advantage over them. The power advantages of Whites place them in positions to deny Blacks political and economic freedom and survival at will and enables them to engage in an almost unimpeded genocidal attack against Blacks whenever it may suit their power needs to do so.

The establishment, whatever rewards it gives us, will also, if necessary to maintain its control, kill us.[14]

Therefore, the very vulnerability of Afrikan Americans to the arbitrary and injurious application of physical force and coercive power, legitimate and competent authority, and other forms of power now possessed by White America should in and of itself motivate them to as rapidly and judiciously as possible neutralize such power. This is necessary to Black political-economic well-being, let alone Black biological survival.

The failure of Black Americans to gain access to and fill significant numbers of positions of power and influence in America is not the result of a large number of Black individuals who lack initiative, drive, etc., but is ultimately the result of the nature of the power relations which inhere between White and Black Americans. White Americans, in hypocritically projecting the American political-economic system and opportunity structure as egalitarian, i.e., as "color blind" and race neutral, justify their monopoly of positions of influence and power in terms of their superior individual characteris-

---

13. D. Beetham, *The Legitimation of Power* (New Jersey: Humanities Press, 1991), p.57.
14. Howard Zinn, *The Twentieth Century: A People's History* (N.Y: Harper & Row, 1984).

tics, training, experiences and much else. In other words, according to dominant Whites there is nothing wrong with or racially discriminatory about the White-dominated social system, only something wrong with individuals; the largest percentage of those who happen to have something wrong with them just "happen to be Black." Many Black Americans give consent to this line of reasoning. Notwithstanding, Beetham's observations in this regard are well worth noting:

> However, it is a notable feature of power relations that they are themselves capable of *generating* the evidence needed for their own legitimation. *Thus the evidence of superiority and inferiority which justifies the inequality of condition between dominant and subordinate is itself largely the product of that condition.* Those who are excluded from key positions, activities or resources are thereby denied the opportunity to acquire or demonstrate the capacities and characteristics appropriate to their occupation or exercise, so justifying their subordinate position. *This is true even where relatively open processes of selection are at work, once the selection is performed by an education system which is given the task of preparing children differentially for their respective future roles.* Evidence about the fitness or appropriateness of people to exercise power thus tends to be structured by the relations of power themselves, and therefore to have a self-fulfilling quality about it.
>
> * * * *
>
> If we look, finally, at consent, then we find that it is precisely the lack of some key resource or skill deriving from the rules of power themselves that leads the subordinate to voluntary acceptance of their dependency upon the powerful...[to their conformity to established rules and to giving their consent to the particular power relation].[15]

The conditioned consent to ideological acceptance and behavioral conformity of Black Americans to White American political and economic domination as legitimate, are designed to blind them to the fact that they can only gain access to and occupy a very significant number of positions of influence and power by creating, developing and applying ideological-action perspectives which go beyond, and stand outside, the existing relations of power, their supporting social customs, traditions, and arrangements. If Blacks are to empower themselves they must question White-originated and self-serving rules and ideological justifications for establishing and maintaining White domination as a legitimate expression of power consented to by Blacks themselves. These rules and ideological justifications must be

---
15. Beetham, pp. 60–61.

directly challenged or subverted by Blacks in order to enhance and exercise a Black power counter to White power. Even if the American political-economic system is now "colorblind" or race-neutral, which most assuredly it is not, this counter-factual situation occurred after almost three and a half centuries of White racial prejudice toward and oppression of Blacks. It was during this long period that Whites developed and accumulated the collective cultural, social, political, familial and individual capital that their domination of Blacks afforded. These accumulated advantages are used by Whites, even in a race-neutral egalitarian society, to provide themselves with further huge advantages compared to Blacks who have suffered three and a half centuries of accumulated disadvantages. A contemporary race-neutral society, in terms of its neutrality alone, would in no way resolve the problem of gross inequalities between Whites and Blacks. In fact, such a society would function only to maintain, if not in actuality enhance them. Blacks must develop means of overcoming White sociopolitical and socioeconomic advantages regardless of the racial status quo.

Manipulation as Power

Manipulation involves the attempt by the manipulator to elicit certain desired responses from his subject while concealing his efforts to do so. In this way the manipulator seeks to constrain, restrict, or prevent certain undesirable actions on the part of his subject and/or to subtly direct his subject to behave in certain desired ways outside his subject's knowledge and awareness.

Manipulation involves a more "efficient" exercise of power than force, coercion and influence because it is less likely to evoke resistance since the subject is unaware of the effort to influence him or may think that the manipulator is exercising his influence to achieve an end desired by both the manipulator and the subject himself, when in actuality the subject is being influenced toward an end which may be detrimental to himself and beneficial only to his manipulator. Thus, the manipulated subject may be led to perceive his own responses and behavior as expressions of his own free will and choice. Commonly, manipulation is achieved by skillfully presenting information, rewards and deprivations in ways which shape the consciousness and behavior of the subject and motivates him to freely "choose" to act in ways compatible with the concealed intentions of his manipulator.

Wrong notes two important general forms where manipulation may occur:

> First, the power holder may exercise concealed control over the power subject through symbolic communications designed to make veiled suggestions, to limit or determine selectively the power subjects' information supply, or to inculcate without appearing to do so certain positive or negative attitudes....
>
> But an equally widespread kind of manipulation occurs where A alters B's environment in such a way as to evoke a desired response from B without interacting directly with B at all.[16]

Wrong further notes that manipulation may involve the most dehumanized, and as far as we are concerned, perhaps the most dehumanizing exercise of power of all because, unlike the exercise of obstructive physical force, visible coercive and authoritarian power where the intent of his adversaries and the sources of assault and frustration are known to the subject, manipulation "is a form of power that cannot be openly resisted by the power subject since he is unaware of the powerholder's intent or even sometimes of his existence. There is no visible command for him to disobey, no identifiable adversary against whom to assert his freedom."

The manipulation of Afrikan American political and economic attitudes by the White ruling elite is designed to effectively secure, enhance and exercise power while not appearing to do so; while appearing to provide Blacks with power or options equal to that or those of Whites. The point of this type of manipulation is to win the acceptance by Blacks of the legitimacy of White power, its moral integrity, its legitimating ideology, and the acceptance by Blacks of their obligation to obey the directive of White power while believing their obedience to be expressive of their own free and moral will. Only by basing their behavioral orientation on their own Afrikan history, culture, values, interests, consciousness and identity can Blacks prevent their behavioral manipulation by self-serving Whites and act under the influence of their own self-generated enhanced power.

Summary: White Domination — Black Subordination

All of the forms of power we have discussed as well as those not discussed here when used by Whites to maintain their power over Blacks, add up to one overarching social power relation between Whites and Blacks — White domination, Black subordination.

Social domination occurs when the power of one person or group over another is exercised in a systematic manner at the expense of the dominated person or group. Wartenberg uses the term "domination" to refer to:

---

16. Wrong, p. 29.

...the power that one social agent has over another in situations in which that power is exercised by the dominating social agent repeatedly, systemically, and to the detriment of the dominated agent. The concept of *domination therefore refers to a specific manner of exercising power.* Such an exercise of power must be one that conditions the relationship between two agents in a longstanding manner. "Domination" refers not to a single exercise of power but to a *relationship* between two social agents that is constituted by the existence of a power differential between them.[17] [Emphasis added]

Our characterization of the White American-Black American power relationship as one of White domination of Blacks is based on the fact that in large part the White American power structure possesses and uses its ability to adversely affect the welfare of Blacks to further its own interests and to the detriment of those of Blacks.

The subordination of people of color is functional to the operation of American society as we know it and the color of one's skin is a primary determinant of people's position in the social [power] structure. Racism is a structural relationship based on the subordination of one racial group by another. Given this perspective, *the determining feature of race relations is not prejudice toward blacks, but rather the superior position of whites and the institutions — ideological as well as structural — which maintain it.*[18] [Emphasis added]

The power relationship between Blacks and Whites is an *interactive* one — one where White power, to a significant extent, arises out of certain types of social interactions between Whites and Blacks where Blacks unwittingly play a very important role in constituting and sustaining their powerlessness relative to Whites. White domination of Blacks in our current social context is primarily facilitated by the fact that Blacks think of themselves and of reality in terms created by the self-serving interests and perspectives imposed on them by Whites, and act on the basis of biased and false information provided them by Whites without realizing it. They therefore contribute to their powerlessness and domination by Whites simply by thinking about themselves and reality in a manner that allows them to be subjugated. Thus, White domination of Blacks is, to a significant degree, covered-over by ideology, beliefs which Blacks have been conditioned by Whites to unwittingly accept. To this degree their domination and powerlessness is self-imposed. Blacks obscure their unnecessary domination by Whites and contribute to that

---

17. Wartenberg, p. 117.
18. David T. Wellman, *Portrait of White Racism* (New York: Cambridge Univ. Press, 1977), pp. 35–36.

domination by their own gullibility and too-ready acceptance of Eurocentric ideology and their obsequious willingness to think and act only within the confines of White-generated ideas, social definitions, relations and ethics (not often honored by Whites themselves). Hence, the minds of Blacks are used to forge the links of their own mental chains.

When Afrikans in the Americas and the world-over choose to critically examine the "received" ideas and biased perceptions of "reality" imposed on them by Europeans and choose to know reality for what it is — to create themselves through gaining a thorough knowledge of self, knowledge of the world, and through studying and acquiring power — they will then have attained the keys to their own liberation.

Even a cursory review of the relations of the social domination of Blacks by Whites demonstrates its repeated, systematic and detrimental nature. All of the types and forms of power we have so far discussed, as well as others not discussed, have been and are currently used by hegemonic Whites to maintain a system of social domination immensely beneficial to them as it is devastatingly detrimental to Blacks.

The use of sheer, unadorned physical force as a means of dominating Blacks has been used by Whites from the 16th century to the present moment. It has assumed many forms, from war, captivity, lynching, beating, torture, mob violence, police brutality and repression, to martial law and the like. The threatened use of physical (police and military) force stands behind White power in all its deceptive metamorphoses. But more effective and deeply enduring than the use of physical force or the coercive threat to use it in maintaining the domination of White over Black, is the long-term use by Whites of harshly unrelenting psychic violence against the collective Black persona. For this violence more effectively neutralizes Black opposition to and possible overthrow of White domination than the preponderance of White military might. Psychic violence hobbles the most powerful of human weapons — the human mind and its productive creativity, ingenuity, innovativeness and vision. Moreover, it hobbles the human capacity to develop and press into service the social identity, social consciousness, unity and solidarity, and the cooperative social spirit which combined empower a race to overcome impossible odds posed by other hostile and apparently more powerful races of men.

Psychic violence makes the victimized individual or group vulnerable to the "soft", yet ultimately more treacherous and effective forms of social domination — social coercion, influence, manipulation, allegedly legitimate and competent authority, and ideological hypnosis. Nothing less than the healing of the wounds occasioned by White-instigated psychic assaults against the collective Afrikan mind, body and spirit can enable Afrikan peoples to regain their liberation. A deep and fundamental transformation of the subordinated Afrikan psyche via the steadfast acquisition of an Afrikan-centered consciousness and identity will provide the social-psychological, and if need be, military power tools for breaking through the imprisoning walls of White supremacy.

However, in this liberating Afrikan-centered consciousness and identity must be included an indomitable will to Afrikan Power! This will must be informed by a profound knowledge of the means of acquiring and of the exercising of power as well as a strategic and tactical knowledge of the enemy's power. To an examination of these factors we will now turn.

Chapter 2

BASES OF POWER
Organization and Ethnic Resources

> Overconcentration of power resources is dangerous... Underconcentration of power resources is equally as dangerous... Conflict is an inescapable social fact...Power struggles are not necessarily bad.
> — ALVIN TOFFLER, *Powershift*

FOR SOCIAL POWER TO BE EXERCISED effectively the powerholder must possess or control some important or valued material and/or social resource(s) which is the basis of his power. By strategically rewarding or depriving others of these resources, he may use them to influence behavior in ways compatible with his interests. Resources when used for such ends is referred to as power bases or resources. Power bases or resources may include physical safety, health and well-being, wealth and material possessions; jobs and means to a livelihood; knowledge and social skills; social recognition, status and prestige; love, affection, social acceptability; a satisfactory self-image and self-respect (Dye). Dye rightly cautions that power is not a "thing" exclusively possessed by an individual or group but essentially refers to the nature of a *relationship* between individuals, groups, and institutions within a social system in which some individuals or groups have applicable control over certain vital or important social and material resources needed or desired by others. Social power is based or rests on social desires and needs. Toffler (1990) asserts forthrightly that "because people have needs and desires, those who can fulfill them hold potential power. Social power is exercised by supplying or withholding the desired or needed items and experiences." A power relationship and the inequality between the parties in such a relationship presuppose that the weaker party either lacks appropriate power resources, or relatively fewer of them, or if he possesses them does not possess the will and/or the ability to employ them effectively in his interest.

We have no intentions to review the quite sizable number of possible power bases here. We shall constrain ourselves to brief, but pertinent, discussions of those power resources which are of important relevance to Afrikan Americans and the power relations between them and European Americans. These power resources include *property*, organization, race consciousness and ideology. We do not include state politics in our discussion at this juncture because in the context of contemporary Afrikan American social, political and economic culture and the more basic issues it must resolve, state politics is of secondary importance to the Black community. Black politics and activism without the Black ownership of and control over primary forms and bases of power such as property, wealth, organization, etc., is the recipe for Black political and non-political powerlessness. The rather obtuse pursuit of political office and the ballot box as primary sources of power by the Black community and its politicians without its concomitant ownership of and control over important resources, has actually hindered the development of real Black power in America. More ominously, there appears to be a paradoxical and positive correlation between the number of Blacks elected and appointed to high office and retrogressions in the civil and human rights extended to Black Americans during the past twenty years. Increases in homelessness, poverty, unemployment, criminality and violence in the Black community; disorganization of the traditional Black family, inadequacies in education, increases in health problems of all types, and a host of other social and political ills have all attended increases in the number of Black elected and appointed officials. That is, the more elected and appointed Black politicians, the more social-economic problems the Black community has suffered. While we are not implying a causal relationship between the increase of the number of Black appointed and elected officials and the increased misery indices of the Black community, we are implying or asserting that their increase obscures those things which are responsible for and do little to ameliorate or uproot the increasing prevalence of social and economic problems in the Black community. The community's concern with the election and appointment of Black political figures helps it to maintain false hopes that their attainment of office will significantly resolve its problems. The activities of Black politicians, given the current inadequacy of social organization and economic resources, harmfully distract the Black community's attention from recognizing and eradicating the true causes of its problems and the remediation of its powerlessness.

We shall presently look at ethnic groups whose economic, educational, social and political progress in America have been phenomenal and often surpasses that of Black Americans, yet, who have not acquired one elected or appointed official to high political office. We will see that it has been and is their effective acquisition and application of more fundamental power values or resources which are far more responsible for their progress and power than their political-electoral activism or lack of it.

In our ensuing discussion of the bases of power we will therefore put first things first, and Black American "politics as usual" is not one of these.

Property and Power

It seems apropos at this juncture to emphasize a statement made by Thomas Dye: *"Power is never equally distributed. There is no power where power is equal. For power to be exercised, the "power holder" must control base values."*[1] Inequality of power in social systems is correlated with inequality of the distribution of power resources within them. The distribution of power resources is rarely, if ever, randomly distributed among the individual and group constituents of a society. As we have already intimated, inequality of power between individuals and groups must devolve from their unequal share of important or relevant resources of power among which includes "property, wealth, organization, social prestige, social legitimacy, number of adherents, various kinds of knowledgeability and leadership skills, technological skills, control of jobs, control of information, ability to manipulate the symbolic environment, and ability to apply force and violence" (Parenti). It is the first two items on this list we shall now very briefly discuss.

---

1. Thomas R. Dye, p. 5.

Property, Wealth and Power — Property and wealth represent a class of power resources commonly referred to as economic resources. As Dye contends:

>...control of economic resources provides a continuous and important base of power in any society. Economic organizations decide the basic economic question or *who gets what.*[2]

Economic power is the power to decide what will be produced, how much it will cost, how many people will be employed, what their wages will be, what the price of goods and services will be, what profits will be made, how these profits will be distributed, and how fast the economy will grow (Dye, 1983).

In capitalistic America the foundation of economic power is private property whose ownership not only refers to real estate but also to the ownership of "the means of production," of accumulated capital (factories, machinery, etc.), wealth, surplus production or surplus material goods as belonging to private individuals or groups instead of to the people or nation as a whole. Racial and class domination fundamentally involves the unequal interaction between the owners of property and wealth and the propertyless and poor, the greater power residing in the hands of the first group.

The concept of property in advanced capitalist societies is complex. Property resources as owned by private individuals and private institutions rather than the society or government, i.e., private property, is one of the central defining characteristics of capitalist ideology and societies. The private ownership of property refers to far more than the ownership of concrete things like land, houses, factories, personal items, production tools, machinery and the like. Property also refers to rights and interest and claims in and to things, to certain privileges relative to things, people and activities (Bazelon, 1963). This includes property as a right of use or disposition. The private ownership of things, rights and claims as property combined with "the right and the freedom to negotiate binding legal contracts, permits private persons or businesses to obtain, control, employ and dispose of property resources as they see fit" (McConnell and Brue, 1990). In sum, Bazelon reminds us to think of property as being of two kinds — "thing property" and "rights-property". The latter may refer to "pieces of paper, like stock certificates and bonds, representing certain direct entitlements relating to certain things and productive activities such as the right in one person of the fruit of another's labor." Bazelon goes on to remind us "that money-and-credit are simply the most generalized and so most obvious form of property."

---

2. Dye, p. 82.

Ultimately, property is what the state — as adjudicated by its legislative bodies and courts — says it is, the things, rights, claims and privileges to which the state accords its enforcement and protection. The central function of the modern state is the protection and regulation of the private property system — to defend the owners of property and wealth from the propertyless and poor. With the ownership or claim to certain properties and rights goes the right to exercise certain privileges and powers from which those who do not own or hold claim to those properties and rights are excluded. The ownership of property demarcates the borderline between inclusion and exclusion. With the ownership of property comes the right to exercise more rights and privileges than comes with the lack of ownership. Consequently, the ownership of property is one of the most important bases of power. Beetham elaborates this point:

> Central to the social organization of power ... are the processes of exclusion, typically embodied in rules, which prohibit general access to key resources, and which determine who may acquire the use or possession of them, and by what means. These are usually called rules of property; and it is through the possession of, or the privileged access to property that some people acquire and maintain power over others who lack or are denied such access.[3]

Hence, power relations are inextricably reflective of property relations. The dominance and subordination of classes and races are constituted by the power deriving from the ownership of property, more so from control over key resources and the means of production. The propertyless classes and races by the fact of their propertylessness, are compelled to bow to the demands of the propertied as a condition for obtaining their daily bread. Therein is the basis for dominance and subordination.

The unequal distribution of power between Whites and Blacks in America in accordance with the greater ownership of property and capital, and therefore power by Whites, did not originate from the fabled "economic genius" of the former relative to the lack of it in the latter. White power, based on the White monopolistic ownership of property and accumulated capital, is the alchemical product of "blood and fire," i.e., of the genocidal murder by Whites of Native Americans, the outright theft of their lands and resources, the brutal enslavement and murder of Afrikans as well as the naked, direct exploitation of their uncompensated labor — all made possible by the unrestrained use of White-instigated physical violence, psychic terrorism and psycho-political economic manipulation. Afrikans were brought to the

---
3. Beetham, p. 48.

Americas as the private property of Europeans. The surplus production of their labor was expropriated and accumulated both during and after their enslavement. This, along with the theft of Indian lands are the fundamental sources of European American-African American property-power relations to this very moment. Moreover, White America's "long history of 100 percent racial quotas in favor of Whites" and its use of racial discrimination as "a standard form of cartel power" (Cross, 1987) has provided Whites (and some of their non-White immigrant group imitators) with the propertied means of bending the will and shaping the behavior of relatively propertyless, dependent Black Americans. Cross depicts this relationship in *Tables* 2–1 and 2–2.

In capitalistic America, since with property comes power, it stands to reason that if Afrikan Americans are to obtain substantial and sustainable power, they must obtain control of substantial property and with it substantial economic power. The rapid accumulation and applied organization of property and wealth by any means necessary must become top priority goals of the Afrikan American community if it is to maximally ensure its own future survival and well-being. The accumulation and organization of property and wealth as means of securing their survival, enhancing their well-being and power, are imperative for immigrant groups entering and establishing themselves in the United States. Adherence to these imperatives are in good part responsible for their remarkable economic progress compared to the relative economic stagnation of Afrikan Americans.

A review of *Tables* 2–1 & 2–2 indicates that contrary to the Horatio Alger myths and the myths of individualism, where the rugged individual gains fame and fortune through frugality, thriftiness, dogged determination and creativity; or through the convenience of marrying into wealth; or through the convenient receipt of a huge helping hand from some dolting wealthy benefactor, the principal means by which White men gain wealth and power is through aggressive, ruthless, race-based organization. The history of White American capitalism and wealth creation and the generation of near-tyrannical White political-economic power is replete with the organization and violent operation of White, race-based cartels, syndicates, "rings", private armies, gangs and thugs. The "captains" of American industry by all sorts of nefarious and violent means, literally organized or seized control of federal, state, and local governments in order to cede to themselves all types of special benefits, protections and keys to the public treasure. Government, business and the military — those entities which have permitted White America to dominate the national and world industrial complex from their inception until this very moment — are essentially exclusive organizations and the special preserves of the White male ruling elite and of White men in general.

The American economic system, as is its system of government, its military and paramilitary system, as well as its religious and media systems — the key power systems of any modern society — are systems organized by, of and for White men vs. Black men, White people vs. Black people. And these systems are not the creation of Adam Smith's mythical "invisible hands" guiding self-interested, self-serving individuals into the coincidental building of an equilibrated market economy, free market and democratic government. These systems were and are constructed and operated by highly conscious and deliberate men, men well aware of what they are about and what it is they want to achieve — the holy grail or power and the perks of power. These organizations and systems can only be neutralized or defeated by counterpoised organizations and systems and the oppositional consciousness which informs them.

Organizations and Institutions as Power Sources

Power, particularly its effective exercise to achieve certain ends, does not flow solely from the ownership and control of property as thing and property as right. Effective, working power — the essence of social power — requires the coordinated organization of power resources. It is not the mere possession of power resources and of the power which flows from their possession which enables some groups to dominate others, but it is more so the organization of power on the part of the dominant group, in contrast to the relative disorganization of the subordinate group (which may possess potentially more powerful human and/or material resources than the dominant group), which ensures their control over the subordinate group. We concur with Beetham when he asserts that *"the relative differences of power between people are largely the result of social arrangements. And the relations of power between them are typically the product of collective organization"* [Emphasis added]. To paraphrase Beetham, the manner in which a group's internal social relations, i.e., power relations, are organized has obvious consequences for the power of the group and of the society as a whole. For as Beetham further contends, "It is rare for subordinate groups to lack any means of power of their own, even if it takes the defensive form of a power of limitation or veto in face of the power of initiative exercised by the dominant. The subordinate are often more numerous, and their contribution within the social division of labour [and within the social division of consumption] makes them

AMERICA'S LONG HISTORY OF 100 PERCENT RACIAL QUOTAS IN FAVOR OF WHITES

For 300 Years the American Colonies, the States and the Federal Government Allotted Untold Billions of Dollars of Public Wealth Exclusively to Members of the White Race.

1675 — Massachusetts Bay Colony cedes plantation rights in six-square mile tracts to "worthy" individuals. The population of the Colony included Black slaves as well as free blacks. Neither were treated as "worthy" individuals eligible for land grants.

1683 — Maryland and Virginia establish fifty-acre land grants to settlers who pay their own way across the Atlantic. Blacks were given a free ride in slave ships and thus were not eligible for grants.

1785 — The federal Ordinance of 1785 authorizes the sale of 640-acre tracts to settlers for $1 per acre. As slaves, blacks were legally prohibited from owning property.

1800 — The federal government establishes liberal credit privileges in western territories for buyers of public land at a price of $1 acre an acre. Slaves not eligible and free blacks generally considered uncreditworthy.

1830 — The federal Preemption Act grants land settlers rights to purchase up to 160 acres each at $1.25 per acre. The vast majority of blacks are still slaves and ineligible to own property. No evidence of significant participation by free blacks.

1850 — The beginning of the massive federal land grant program for private railroad companies. Outright awards of 130 million acres frequently include property for twenty miles on either side of roadbeds. These lands later found to contain billion of dollars of petroleum and mineral reserves. Black businessmen never considered qualified to acquire, finance, or operate railroad franchises.

1862 — The Homestead Act grants settlers 160-acre tracts of federal lands without charge. Over 250 acres of public lands transferred almost exclusively to whites in the most important land program in American history. Negro claimants blocked by lynch mobs, intimidation and refusals of local authorities to protect their claims.

1889 — In the celebrated Oklahoma Land Rush, 150,000 white settlers scramble to claim the choicest. Savage lynchings, Ku Klux Klan terrorism and Jim Crow legislation kept Negroes out. Later the heirs and successors of white settlers were to discover billions of dollars of petroleum resources on these lands.

1920 — The Mineral Leasing Act authorizes the federal government to lease public land for the exploration of oil, gas, and other minerals. Affluent Negroes need not apply. Race discrimination in public awards was the established policy of the federal government in the 1920s.

1926 — The federal Air Commerce Act authorizes the granting of monopoly air routes to qualified aviators. The nation's airlines are born. Twenty thousand white pilots learned their trade in the rigidly segregated World War I Army Air Corps ensuring that the ownership of commercial aviation would be lily white.

1927 — The federal Radio Act authorizes the award of radio station broadcast franchises to private citizens. Under settled policy of the federal government, no grants were made to negroes. Radio broadcast licenses currently valued in the billions of dollars now held almost exclusively by whites.

1939 — The Federal Communication Commission issues the first licenses for television broadcast station. No grants made to Negroes until token awards of the late 1970s. In 1980, all television franchises, valued at $5 million to $10 billion held exclusively by whites

1941 — Government contracting becomes a major factor in the sales revenues, and profits of private enterprises. Race discrimination in government contract awards becomes the official policy of the United States government. During the years 1941 to 1980, approximately $3 trillion in contract awards were made almost exclusively to white-owned firms.

Sources: A thorough historical summary of American public land grants may be found in Peter Wolf, Land of America (New York: Pantheon Books, 1981). Mineral rights information is from Stephen L. McDonald, The Leasing of Federal Land for Fossil Fuel Production (Baltimore: John Hopkins University Press, 1979). The history of aviation is detailed in Carl Soberg, Conquest of the Skies (Boston: Little Brown & Co., 1979). Information on the history of radio and television franchising appears in Erwin G. Krasnow and L.B. Longley. The Politics of Broadcast Regulation (St. Martin's Press, 1973). Government procurement data are from the federal Office of Management and Budget.
[Cited in THE BLACK POWER IMPERATIVE, Theodore Cross, pp. 122–23.]

Table 2–1

> **UNIVERSALLY PRACTICED RACE DISCRIMINATION IS A STANDARD FORM OF CARTEL POWER**
>
> In allocating places and opportunities according to race rather than merit, whites in the United States have used the full armory of coercive weapons commonly employed by the traditional combination in restraint of trade.
>
> In common with a classic cartel, the collective racial prejudgment mounted against black people:
>
> - used collusion and gentlemen's agreements to keep targeted groups out of jobs and markets.
> - allocated employment, credit, and capital through the commands of law and private agreement among cartel members, rather than through free market forces of open competition.
> - employed public resources and subsidies to enrich cartel members and to aid—or prop up—favored groups or classes or citizens.
> - ostracized defectors and deputized vigilantes to punish those who broke the exclusionary rules of the cartel.
> - resorted to the use of terrorism and violence whenever it could not accomplish its goals by non violent means.
> - provided special franchises, loans, job privileges, government contracts, and exclusive bidding rights for cartel members.
> - used legislatures and government agencies to enact licensing laws and administrative rules that safeguarded the favored position of members of the cartel.
> - established customs, rules of etiquette, and gentlemen's agreements to prevent potential competitors from acquiring the training and skills necessary to equip them to perform the tasks or to take advantage of the opportunities that the cartel wished to reserve for its own members.
> - proclaimed its fervent and undying devotion to restrict employment and free trade while steadily pursuing the closed membership objectives of the cartel.
> - called for open competition and a fair fight, but not until it had succeeded in becoming the biggest kid on the block.
>
> Source: *The Black Power Imperative*, Theodore Cross, p. 132.

Table 2–2

indispensable, as a group, to the dominant." He goes on to argue that essentially, one of the purposes of the organization of power on the part of the dominant is to ensure the relative disorganization among the subordinate. Thus the subordinate, through effective social organization, may enable themselves to change the nature and outcomes of the power relations between the dominant and themselves, perhaps to the extent of revolutionizing those relations.

Even if we were to argue that the individual and that individual behavior are the foundation of social systems and the powers they manifest, we still must give due respect to power born of organization. The power man represents in the world, whether as individual or group, is a power operationally founded on physical, mental, and social organization and on the organized behavior which flows therefrom.

Hence, human social organization, not mere individual self-interested behavior, is central to the generation and application of power. The upcoming discussion of ethnically based economic development amply supports the assertion made by Adolf Berle that "No collective category, no class, no group, of any kind in and of itself wields power or can use it. Another factor must be present: that of organization." Berle goes on to correctly contend that "Power is invariably organized and transmitted through institutions." Social organization refers to the interactive uniting of a number of persons into a group, who through the structured use of their aggregate resources, act to achieve the group's purposes and goals. As alluded by Wrong (1988) "the more people who contribute their holdings [or personal, social and/or material resources] to a common pool the greater the aggregate resources to pursue a group's goals and enhance its power are likely to be." As Galbraith (1983) asserts, through organization a group and the individuals who constitute it or speak and act according to its mandates may thereby gain access to condign (punitive), compensatory (reward), and especially to conditioned (behavior and "mind-controlling") power. "Organized groups as collective actors controlling resources [provide themselves with] the capacity to exercise power over non-members: the general public, particular clienteles, the local community, and political leaders."[4]

Organized Networks and Power

To be organized is to be structured; to assume and operate according to a discernable pattern. Organizations systematically channel and distribute energy or force along definite pathways in order to achieve some definite outcome. Organization imposes order and direction on otherwise random, relatively diffuse, unfocused, or erratic phenomena in order to generate a focused concentrated form of power directed toward accomplishing particular goals.

---

4. J.K. Galbraith. *The Anatomy of Power* (Boston: Houghton Mifflin, 1983).

A social organization is composed of two or more persons or groups of persons, each of whom, operating under centralized human control or direction, plays a more or less specialized role; each behaving as a component part of the organized whole and whose active output is channeled and coordinated in some special way in order to perform work and achieve definite outcomes. Social organizations exert influence on their component membership in such ways as to achieve definite effects on both their internal and/or external environments.

Since a social organization wields influence, brings about changes, i.e., *does work*, it may be said to express *power*. The dynamic pattern of social relations or interactions between the members of a social organization, provides the means by which it does its work or expresses its power. This may be said to represent a *power network*. That is, organization itself may be conceived of as a power network or as composed of power networks.

Various organizations may coordinate their specialized activities in order to do the work or achieve the ends of a society or culture of which they are component parts. When performing their societal or cultural duties such organizations operate as instruments of societal and/or cultural power, as social tools of power. They thereby are the means by which a society and/or culture adapts to its world and seeks to adapt its world to its special needs or desires.

Since social organizations may be conceived of as social power networks, the societies they may be said to constitute may in turn be perceived as consisting "*of multiple overlapping and intersecting sociospatial networks of power.*"[5]

> Conceiving of societies as multiple overlapping and intersecting power networks gives us the best available entry into the issue of what is ultimately "primary" or "determining" in societies. *A general account of societies, their culture, and their history can be best given in terms of the interrelations of what I will call the four sources of social power: ideological, economic, military, and political* (IEMP) *relationships.* These are (1) *overlapping networks of social interaction*, not dimensions, levels, or factors of a single social totality. This follows from my first statement. (2) They are also *organizations, institutional means of attaining human goals*. Their primacy comes not from the strength of human desires for ideological, economic, military, or political satisfaction but from the particular *organizational means* each possesses to attain human goals, whatever these may be.[6]

---

5. Michael Mann, *The Sources of Social Power: A History of Power from the Beginning to A.D. 1760* (New York: Cambridge Press, 1986).

6. Ibid., p. 2.

The strength or power of organizations reflects their capacity to channelize and control people, to utilize their human and material resources, interests and/or those of the larger society of which they are members or parts. Social organizations as power networks are structured forms of social control and simultaneously are the means of attaining social control. The four sources of social power, as designated by Mann — the ideological, economic, military, and political — "offer alternative organizational means of social control." As the means of structurally transforming and enhancing human relations and capacities, social organizations of various types can often facilitate fundamental social changes and radical changes in the social power relations which hitherto characterized a particular society or social situation.

Social organization amplifies power. It is a collective source of power in that it involves a means by which persons may enhance their joint power over third parties or their environment by cooperating with each other. *Collective power,* i.e., the power of a group as a whole, may be maximized by its *distributive power*, that is, by its internal organization and division of function or labor, the specialization of function at appropriate levels and the coordination of functions through supervision and under central direction. Collective power is enhanced and stabilized in a social group to the degree that its control is institutionally based on commonly accepted values, rules, laws, and norms. Cultures and societies normally achieve their routine goals through institutionalizing much of their social behavior and activities, by founding and operating institutions designed to organize social attitudes and behavior toward the accomplishment of certain tasks. Weakly organized groups — groups which lack collective organization or whose collective organizations are inadequate — are vulnerable to being or in actuality organizationally out-maneuvered by more powerfully organized groups. The weaker group may be thereby forced to comply with the demands of the stronger due to the greater power and tactical advantages held by the latter group. Or the compliance of the weaker group is obtained by having been forcibly integrated into inferior or subordinate positions within the confines of the collective and distributive [social class or stratification] power organizations controlled by the stronger group.

The ability of a social group to defend its independence or to be liberated from domination is related to its *extensive power*, that is, "its ability to organize large numbers of people over far-flung territories in order to engage in minimally stable cooperation; its *intensive power*, its ability to organize tightly and command a high level of mobilization or commitment from the participants, whether the area and numbers covered are great or small"; its *authoritative power*, the degree to which participants willingly comply to the commands and recommendations of its legitimate institutions and authorities; and its *diffused power*, that is, to the degree to which participants spontaneously, consciously and unconsciously, individually and of their own free will, engage "in similar social practices that embody power relations but are not explicitly commanded... — [based on] an understanding that these practices are natural or moral or result from self-evident common interest" (Mann, 1968). It should be noted that it is diffused power — power generated spontaneously based on commonly held attitudes, values, and modes of behavior — which facilitates the *conspiring* of one group against another, without their conspiracy being deliberately planned and executed by any one person, group, or groups within them. At times cultures, societies and various types of social organizations may be conceived of as conspiracies, as the means whereby persons cooperate towards an end, whether good or evil, their effects on their own and other groups being more determined by the very compelling logic of their *shared beliefs* and *practices* than by the machinations of some apparent or secretive group within them consciously pursuing some particular goal.

Extensive, intensive, authoritative, and diffused power tend toward maximization in modern nation-states or cultural groups who are exceedingly conscious of their special status and are proactively and effectively organized, have established strong solidarities based on commonalities of ethnicity, language, custom, religion, values, a sense of superiority, a strong sense of mission, and the determination to dominate others or to liberate themselves from, or protect themselves against, domination by others. These powers, to the extent to which they are socially accepted and supported, effectively organized and coordinated, are realistically and relevantly based on a sound knowledge of the nature of its current social, political and economic universe by the group that exercises them. These powers coalesce to maximally enhance that group's social power by making maximum use of its collective human and material resources. Note that the emphasis in the prior statement is on group organization, attitudes, support and use of its collective resources. Collective identity, consciousness, intentionality and solidarity are the key determinants as to whether a group recognizes the resources it has in its possession and whether and how it will use those resources.

For as Wrong (ibid) cogently states, "Possession of means or resources that may be employed to wield power over others is not, however, any guarantee that they will in fact be so employed." To paraphrase Wrong's statement in regard to individuals, groups may possess power resources without using them at all or, more commonly, using them only to pursue non-political goals. Wrong very astutely points out the social factors whose operative presence is necessary for converting potential collective resources and power into kinetic resources and power: social organization and collective identity. He notes that:

> Social organization and collective identity are clearly matters of degree with respect to which groups or social categories vary widely. *But organization and identity (or solidarity) are themselves the fundamental collective resources underlying and making possible the mobilization of all others* [Emphasis added].
>
> The most obvious collective resources are those created by *the pooling of individual resources* for employment in the service of a common aim.
>
> The most important collective resources are unambiguously classifiable as non-reducible or global properties of groups: namely *solidarity and organization.* They constitute, in fact, the major defining attributes of a group itself in the sociological sense as distinct from a mere population or statistical category. Collective resources resulting from the aggregation of individual resources, as well as group size and job or skill monopoly which I have chosen to consider non-reducible collective resources, can only be mobilized for political uses, or even acquire existence *as* collective resources, because of the prior achievement of a degree of minimal solidarity and organization by a plurality of individuals....
>
> Both solidarity and social organization can be subdivided into a number of variable aspects which might also be regarded as distinct collective resources. Solidarity includes the degree of awareness of boundaries between group members and non-members (the familiar Sumnerian 'in-group-out-group' distinction), the intensity of mutual emotional identifications with one another based on a sense of similarity or 'consciousness of kind', rituals symbolizing belonging and collective identity, and so on. Social organization comprises the degree and complexity of division of labour, the presence of leadership or a power structure, rules governing interactions between members and between members and outsiders, and much else. These different aspects of solidarity and social organization amount, of course, to well-known variable characteristics of what sociologists call 'social structure'.[7]

The crucial importance of social solidarity to group survival and a group's effective use of power to secure its survival and for other

---

[7]. Wrong, pp. 134–39.

important purposes can hardly be overstated. Social solidarity not only facilitates the maximum use of already available group resources, but social solidarity in pursuit of common goals in conjunction with effective social organization and leadership is of critical importance to the *creation* of collective resources — the means by which social power is generated and exercised.

The crucial importance of ethnic identity or solidarity and social organization among Afrikan Americans and their relationship to that community's ability to exercise extensive and intensive, and authoritative and diffused power in order to successfully counter its domination by the White American community, underlies the White community's unceasing efforts to atomize the Black community into a mere aggregate of disunited individuals — individuals lacking or weak in social solidarity and organization.

Sources of Organizational Power

Horton and Hunt (1968) correctly point out that "The struggle for power often appears to be largely a contest between organizations ...the power of highly organized groups is only checked by the opposition of other groups." These authors further delineate a number of sources of organizational power and some factors which affect group power:

Wealth, numbers and specialized facilities. The obvious advantage of organization is that it brings together the efforts of a large number of people along with a great deal of wealth. When an organization represents millions...it has at least a potential claim to speak for a considerable fraction of the population. An organization can accumulate a large treasury from the dues and small contributions of many members. By joining together, even the poor and unknown may gain some of the attributes of power often attributed to the elite.

The specialized facilities of the organization also increase its influence. [Its individual members may make their] ...views known through the activities of the organizational lobbyist who is constantly in contact with those who make government decisions.

Coordinated membership response. The major source of organizational power lies in the ability to enable many people to take planned, concerted action to affect social decisions. [Organizations can exert power through]... (a) ...some form of coercion — either through force or through non-violent coercion; (b) ...the organization of blocs of voters [or activists] to influence government policy, non-violent coercion through economic pressure and occasional use of violence.

Factors Affecting Group Power

Size and organizational power. While large groups are not always effective, a large membership does give them a large power potential. ...Large organizations become highly active and overwhelmingly powerful when their vital interests are threatened.

Cohesiveness and action orientation. Solitary groups which can unite their members in a given program have a great advantage over loosely structured organizations which must seek agreement through an education and decision process and may seldom be able to count on a concerted response from their members.

Perceived role as a power factor. The members of an organization have an image of what kinds of activities are proper for the organization, and this image limits the areas in which it can exercise power....

The power of an organization is also limited by the role assigned to it by the community... Thus the public's perceived role of an organization or group limits its social power by determining the public support its actions will receive.

Organizational alliances. Some of the advantages of large size may be won if smaller groups join in united action. This alliance is simplified when the organizations involved are led by interlocking directorates... Thus an overlapping network of membership links the organizations together, making for easy cooperation and vesting control of many organizations in a very small group of persons....

An alliance between entirely separate groups may be forged when their interests converge.

Countervailing power. The opposite tendency of organized groups — to oppose each other rather than to cooperate — has been given the name of countervailing power [Galbraith, 1952]. This theory states that the exercise of great power to inspire the organization of opposing power usually keeps any one group from gaining complete control.[8]

SOCIAL POWER OF UNORGANIZED MASSES

The Expression of Mass Power

Horton and Hunt, in addition to discussing the factors affecting group power briefly list some of the means by which "the unorganized masses can exert a decisive power over social developments..."

---

8. Paul B. Horton & Chester L. Hunt. *Sociology* (N.Y.: McGraw-Hill, 1968), pp. 328–34.

The power of mass markets In a democratic society the masses exert influence through their choices of what goods to buy, what papers to read, what television programs to watch, and so on.... But in a competitive market the consumer's preferences are rarely disregarded for very long. [Therefore, the masses may exert influence and power through choosing to buy or not to buy certain goods and services in order to achieve certain social, political, or economic ends].

Mass veto power through noncooperation Some decisions can become effective only through mass cooperation. ...Wherever a decision cannot be effective without mass cooperation, the veto power of the masses must be considered. [The masses through noncooperation, e.g., passive resistance, may exert power to bring about change.]

Direct political power of the masses Who...holds the reins of power in our society? No single group, for power is of several kinds and is very diffused among many groups. The paradox of power in the twentieth century is that although our society is largely controlled by highly organized groups dominated by an elite leadership, this leadership may be blocked by the action of normally unorganized and apathetic masses of men whose basic attitudes towards life are often sharply different from those of the influentials who normally set the pace. Even this pace-setting function of the elite is restricted by the need to draw in the participation of the masses as consumers, workers, and participants... [The masses may use the elite's need for their support and participation as leverage for getting the elite to act in their interest].[9]

To Horton and Hunt's list we have added one of our own which follows.

Breaking the habit of obedience. The social order and social power relations of a society depend on "the habit of obedience" of a critical mass of its members. To be viable and stable, social systems — systems consisting of dynamically structured power relations between persons and groups — require conventionalized responses to authority, other social symbols and signals. If a critical mass of a society's members fail to emit the "appropriate" behavior or responses, the social system tends toward destabilization and may eventually bring about its breakdown.

Most often the institutional or social chain of command is not perceived by those subject to it as coercive and as an expression of dominance by a particular social class for which the command

---

9. Ibid., pp. 334–5.

structure is designed to undemocratically benefit. The chain of command or class structure is generally perceived by those who benefit from it least, or who are oppressed by it, as functionally necessary. In this instance, compliant behavior, even when such behavior perpetuates gross inequities, is seen as morally compelling, as "right and proper" in and of itself. As Parenti argues:

> *Obedience in such cases is not felt as a submission to the interests of the powerful but as proper, constructive behavior of a person who freely accepts responsibilities.* It is not uncommon for people to make *a virtue of the necessities they face; in that way are their life situations made more bearable for them.*
>
> Of interest to us is the function of such propensities for organizational control. *This attitude of obedience* disseminated among subordinates in any institutional structure or within the entire society *becomes a social norm, acting as both an externalized and internalized force for compliance upon the individual.*[10] [Emphasis added]

In an unjust social order, an order where one group abusively dominates another, "the habit of obedience" in the subordinate or abused groups functions to maintain that order. Subordinate groups thereby collude with the dominant group to perpetuate its own subordination and exploitation. This situation can only be changed by the destabilization and breakdown of the unjust social order, i.e., by radically reorganizing its structure of power relations. And this can only be bought about by subordinate groups' refusal to comply with the demands of the dominant group, the compliance with which (by the subordinate groups) are often responsible for or crucial to maintaining the onerous social order in the first place. The subordinate group must break its "habits of obedience" and engage in "civil disobedience." It was primarily through civil disobedience that Ghandi broke the social order of British colonialism in India and Martin Luther King, Jr. radically transformed the social order of the southern United States. Civil disobedience is one of the primary means by which the masses of the oppressed may successfully oppose the power of a dominant oligarchy. Breaking the habit of obedience on the part of the oppressed may not only include the refusal to cooperate with unjust laws, but may include boycotting and refusal to consume certain goods and services sold by the dominant group, disrupting the social and behavioral routines and machinery which maintain the operations of the dominant social order, and by devaluing the commercial and cultural output, products and values of the dominant

---

10. Michael Parenti, *Power and the Powerless* (New York: St. Martin's Press, 1978), pp. 123–4.

group. Sometimes social disruption is the only expression of social power left to the masses. Of course, such actions as just discussed may be adjunctively supported by petition and letter writing campaigns, political demonstrations, marches, protests and pickets.

Ethnic Solidarity and Power

Most often a group is formed based on the sharing among its members of a common history, set of values, fate, plight, or on their consciousness of a shared collective identity, e.g., socioeconomic class, political or social category, or ethnicity. These shared factors form the basis for the construction of a group solidarity and the use of solidarity to generate and exercise social power.

With regard to solidarity and its relation to group power, Galbraith makes the very important observation that an organization "wins submission to its purposes outside the organization only as it wins submission within. The strength and reliability of its external power depend on the depth and certainty of internal submission." He further notes that the power of an organization depends on association with, access to and application of other forms and sources of power. There is an interesting circularity here in that an organization is strong to the degree that it has effective access to certain important forms of power, and the most effective way of gaining access to certain forms of power is through organization.

The achievement of group solidarity and organization results from the mobilization of previously disunited individuals in order to create or activate power they may already have possessed but could not employ or wield due to the absence of will and a facilitating group ideology.

It may be cogently argued that it is the will of immigrant groups, such as the Koreans, combined with their ideology of racial or ethnic solidarity expressed via appropriate socioeconomic organization which permits them and other ethnic groups, though possessing fewer human and material resources and numbers, to achieve greater economic prominence and well-being, and ultimately, greater power, than Black Americans. In fact, a good deal of their economic power and their increasing political power will be gained through their economic exploitation of Afrikan Americans. Social organizational differences between Black Americans and these groups are the factors most responsible for the growing economic and political power differential between certain immigrant groups and Black Americans in spite of the fact that Blacks possess the greater potential for socioeconomic and political power.

Ethnic and Class Resources, Race Ideology and the Exploitability of Black Americans

In the sections to follow we will discuss how ethnicity and organization based on ethnicity are utilized as sources of power in order to develop ethnically-based economic power resources. That is, ethnic groups, such as the Asians, have utilized their immigrant status, the ethnic solidarity demanded by that status, and their ethnic resources to systematically develop economic enterprises and social power. The active combination of these factors by immigrant groups has been and is employed to fuel the growth and development of what Light and Bonacich (1988) refer to as *immigrant entrepreneurship* and more specifically, ethnic entrepreneurship. They define these factors in the following way:

> *Immigrant entrepreneurship* means self-employment within the immigrant group at a rate much in excess of the general rate. *Ethnic entrepreneurship* denotes ethnic minority specialization in self-employment without, however, imposing the requirement of foreign-born origin.[11]

Light and Bonacich argue that "the entrepreneurship of immigrant groups is explained by their resources." These resources are used by various ethnic groups to support the firms owned by their co-ethnics, to sustain their competitive position and "competitive edge" relative to other ethnic groups or outsiders. Light and Bonacich define these *ethnic resources* as those "social features of a group which co-ethnic business owners utilize in business or from which their business passively benefits." According to those authors, "ethnic resources include values, knowledge, skills, information, attitudes, leadership, solidarity, an orientation to sojourning, and institutions." The tendency of immigrant groups, particularly Asians at this time, to employ such resources will be documented in the chapters to follow. To the employment of ethnic resources to advance the economic interests and power of immigrant groups, Light and Bonacich add the employment of what they refer to as *class resources*. Class resources include material factors: private property and ownership of means of production or distribution, personal and familial wealth, and investments in human capital (education, training, etc.); and cultural resources: "bourgeois values, attitudes, knowledge, and skills transmitted intergenerationally in the course of primary socialization."

---

11. Ivan Light & Edna Bonacich, *Immigrant Entrepreneurs: Koreans in Los Angeles 1965-1982* (California: University of California Press, 1988), p. 18.

In the specific case of Koreans in Los Angeles, both ethnic resources and class resources supported the entrepreneurship of group members. That is, Koreans were highly educated in their country of origin, often well endowed with money upon arrival in the United States, and commonly middle or upper middle class in social origin. These were class resources. On the other hand, Koreans also passed business information among themselves; worked long hours; mobilized unpaid family labor; maintained expected patterns of nepotism and employer paternalism; praised a Calvinist deity; utilized alumni, family, and congregational solidarities; thought of themselves as sojourners; expressed satisfaction with poorly remunerated work and utilized rotating credit associations [Keh] in financing their businesses. All of these ethnic characteristics also contributed to Korean entrepreneurship simultaneous benefit from class resources and old-fashioned ethnic resources.[12]

Light and Bonacich's conclusions corroborate our initial contentions that the ownership of property, wealth, organization, race consciousness and ideology as potential and actual power resources can be combined to increase group well-being and power. The essence of economic organization and power does *not* revolve around the mere possession of money, property, human resources, population size, density and location, and ethnic identity. For Afrikan Americans have these in abundance relative to a number of the immigrant groups who have penetrated and currently dominate their community markets and who have rather successfully competed with them for educational resources, job and business opportunities in the larger society. An economic system is ultimately a *social system* — a system of coherent, cohesive, social values, attitudes, relations, arrangements and behaviors consensually shared by a distinguishable group, a group which possesses and expresses a group consciousness, self-consciousness, awareness and identity, all held together and motivated by a group-based, self-interested system of ideas or ideology. The group must take pride in its identity, ideologically rationalize and justify its right to act in terms of its interests as a group, to exclude outsiders, to place its survival and well-being above the interests of other groups (where those outside group interests may injure or threaten to destroy its viability). A group whose members share a strong sense of identity and purpose that are employed to define and motivate its organization, a shared sense of group solidarity and a shared sense that it can determine its destiny rather than have it determined by outsiders, possesses the preconditions and prerequisites for power. These factors

---

12. Ibid., pp. 19–20.

and orientations coalesce to form a group-based idea system, philosophy or ideology which in turn provides reasons and rationales for the construction of social institutions and social structures by whose means power can be generated, enlarged and effectively applied. We, like Berle, are "convinced that a philosophy or idea structure [in the instance of this discussion, an ideology based on group identity and interest] is a pre-condition of the formation of any organization — that is, it precedes the coming into existence of power in any form or at any level." The history of group economic relations in racist America demonstrates quite clearly that the "ideologies of ethnicity" — ideologies regarding group identity and interests, intergroup roles, relations and positions — have been and are key factors in struggles for group survival, advantage, defense, equity, achievement and supremacy. The absence of a strongly held, coherent, well-centered group ideology and related positive, proactive group identity and solidarity, even when that group may possess *potentially* powerful material and human resources, only exposes such a group to the almost invariably rampant, shameless, degrading exploitation and domination by other groups who may actually possess relatively fewer material and human resources, but which do not lack aggressive group ideologies upon which are based their identity, organization and solidarity.

To a very significant degree the absence of a coherent, strongly-held, ethnicity-based system of ideas in the Afrikan American community and in the Afrikan community world-wide has facilitated the pillaging and exploitation of the resources and power potentials of those communities by other groups organized on the basis of their own ethnicity and singularity of interests.

The power of Black consumers has been long recognized and is currently receiving attention (see "Waking up to a Major Market," *Newsweek*, 4/6/92). Immigrant groups and the White American business community have taken note and advantage of the fact that Black Americans represent an exploitable and rapidly expanding consumer market. This market now estimated to be worth $300 billion (near $400 billion by 1995) has yet to be significantly tapped by Afrikan American entrepreneurialism as a source of very influential communal economic wealth, power and well-being. In fact, Afrikan American business persons and groups have been largely excluded from or marginalized in their own ethnic markets by both new immigrant and domestic ethnic groups.

At first blush, two broad, interacting factors would seem to account for the domination and exploitation of the relatively large

Afrikan American consumer market by other ethnic groups — the absence of a strongly held, Afrikan-centered, economic ideology and of a well-organized, Black-owned and controlled market system on the part of the Afrikan American community.

Some argue that it is the attitudes and socioeconomic relations and "natural" organization of non-Black groups, their apparently inherent, innate, cultural penchant for hard work, to work long hours, for self-employment; their use of kinship and communal networks to raise capital; their taking of individual responsibility; their drive for high educational and occupational achievement, and much else, which are responsible for their ability to outperform Blacks economically and otherwise. In this instance, non-Afrikan American groups appear to be naturally endowed with entrepreneurial initiative and talent, and Afrikan Americans to be naturally bereft of such factors. Such contentions and appearances are not supported by historical nor psychological investigation and evidence. The economic subordination of Black Americans is not the result of some erstwhile natural anti-economic tendencies characteristic of their Afrikan genetic and cultural heritage. Black American economic subordination is the result of deliberate economic oppression by other groups, primarily the White American community, aided and abetted by immigrant groups, and secondarily, the result of the failure of Afrikan American leadership to forge a race-based ideological consensus and economic program. Such a consensus and program is necessary if Afrikan Americans are to utilize their formidable ethnic resources to achieve power and liberation. The Afrikan American community must organize itself to take power. Suggested forms for organizing the community to achieve Black Power are presented below.

Organizing for Black Power

Flow Chart of a proposed Afrikan American National Political and Economic System. The establishment of this or a similar "nation-within-a-nation" system of governance for the national Afrikan American community would allow for its coordinated and systematic political, economic, social development and empowerment. The proposed National Council would debate and propose specific political, economic, and social policies which apply to the community as a whole as well as to its relations to other national communities, foreign communities, Afrikan diasporan nations, and the Pan–Afrikan Economic System. The National Executive Offices would create and execute practical ways and means of carrying out the proposals of the National Council and monitor their success and effects on the national

National Political and Economic System

```
┌─────────────────────────────────────┐
│      President of The Council       │
└─────────────────────────────────────┘
                  │
┌─────────────────────────────────────┐
│   The National Council of Presidents of  │
│  Major Black Organizations and Institutions │
└─────────────────────────────────────┘
                  │
┌─────────────────────────────────────┐
│ The National Executive Officer of Economic │
│ Development, Education, External Relations, etc. │
└─────────────────────────────────────┘
                  │
┌─────────────────────────────────────┐
│  State/Regional Councils of Presidents of │
│  Major Black Organizations and Institutions │
└─────────────────────────────────────┘
                  │
┌─────────────────────────────────────┐
│      Local Councils of Major Black       │
│       Organizations and Institutions     │
└─────────────────────────────────────┘
                  │
┌─────────────────────────────────────┐
│    Community of Individuals, Groups,     │
│      Organizations, and Institutions     │
└─────────────────────────────────────┘
```

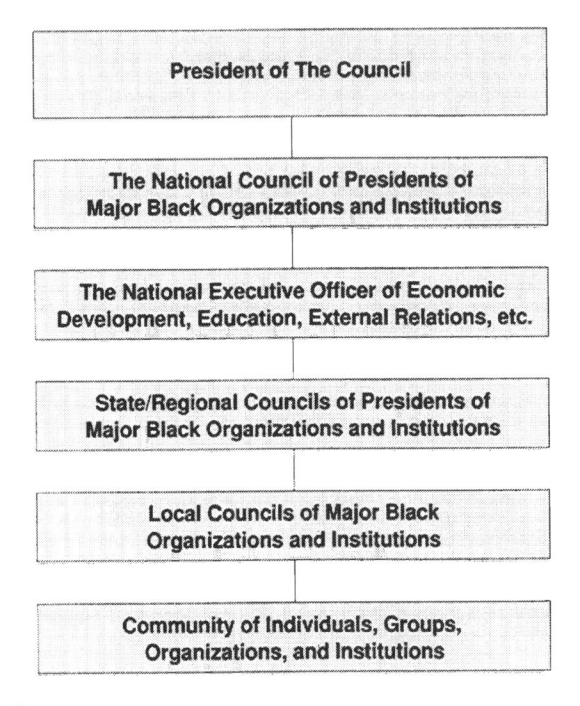

Table 2–3

community. The State/Regional Councils, Local Councils and local individuals, groups and institutions are finally responsible for translating national proposals and programs of the National Council into everyday social relations, activities and institutional development on the grassroots level. Proposals generated from the grassroots would also flow through local, state, and regional organizations into the National Council for consideration and policy decision-making.

Based on its present configuration, the full development of an Afrikan American economic system requires that it undergoes a number of phases. The first phase will involve the founding and establishing of a broad base of retail and service outlets by individuals, partners, corporate groups, institutions, professional and lay organizations. With the support of Afrikan American consumers these retail establishments, if numerous and prosperous across all regions and urban-suburban centers of the nation, can together initiate and sustain phase two — the institution of wholesale and distribution centers to service the already established retail and services markets.

The operative presence of large retail and service as well as wholesale and distribution markets, together provide the bases for the founding and expansion of a manufacturing and raw-materials sector as the third phase of economic development. The fourth phase involves the founding and expansion of the financial services sectors which will supply the financial needs of the consumer, retail and services, wholesale, distribution and manufacturing sectors of the community. Moreover, the financial services sectors will facilitate the purchasing of equity in mainstream corporations and businesses, real estate and other investment properties in the larger national economy. The fifth phase involves the entering into export-import trade relations across the Afrikan diaspora as part of a global Pan–Afrikan Economic System and with other nations selling both goods and services. This phase also involves enriching the Black nation by the increased selling of goods and services by Black workers, professionals and businesses in non-Black communities while returning and spending their earnings to aid in the community. This is equivalent to maintaining a favorable "trade balance" by the earning and building up of "foreign reserves" through exporting more goods and services outside the community than are imported.

The phases of economic development just outlined need not be linear or sequential but rather somewhat cross-sectional and roughly simultaneous. However, the economic development of the community should occur under the guidance of nationally coordinated plans directed by a national governing council and executed by national, regional and local organizations.

The Black American Nation-within-a-Nation

Well-organized, socially coherent and cohesive nation-states provide the best means for the accumulation and exercise of collective power resources. To the degree that a social group can approach nation-state status, even on an informal, non-declared level, it can create, accumulate, and maximally utilize its collective resources as media of its social power and will. The failure of the Afrikan American community to exercise considerable economic and political power despite its large population and broad national expanse as well as ample human and material resources, is directly linked to its failure to conceive of itself as a nation within a larger White American-dominated nation and to organize itself as such. Consequently, it is dominated and exploited by White America and is economically monopolized and exploited by Whites, Asians, Arabs and any other ethnic group that possess a modicum of social solidarity and organization.

The failure of the Afrikan American community to think of and organize itself as a nation in America means that it cannot maximize the use of its ample collective resources and create new ones as media by which it greatly enhances and exercises its power in its own best interests. This also means that the community cannot appropriately reconstruct and maximize the development and exercise of the four power sources or organizations of power mentioned earlier — the economic, ideological, military, and political institutions.

If Black America is to actualize and exert its tremendous potential for power, it must organize itself to do so. For it is subordinated, exploited and victimized by organized alien peoples and forces. As little more than an aggregate of individuals, isolated groups and loose reactionary confederacies of weak organizations, the community is literally prostrate before other well-organized groups. Furthermore, in the absence of a guiding national consensus regarding overall goals and a shared sense of national mission, a set of regulatory principles, an Afrikan-centered consciousness and identity, a socialization system and system of governing institutions, the Afrikan American community not only faces further subordination and exploitation, but possible fatal disintegration and annihilation. This possible fate it shares with the whole of the Afrikan world-wide community.

Chancellor Williams in Chapter 25 of his classic book, *The Destruction of Black Civilization*, lays out a detailed, race-based plan for the organization of the Afrikan American community and the benefits such organization can bestow on it. As a sort of preamble to this plan he discusses some of the things a "massive consolidation of unused [Black] power can do."

1. It can influence American foreign policy and actions in regard to crucial matters affecting Afrikan nations just as effectively as American Jews can influence this country's relations with Israel. This would be real Pan Afrikanism.

2. An overall race organization can deal with some important problems at home than any smaller, independent group can do nationwide. What the people need is a national defender to further expose [and victoriously end] the silent war that is quietly being carried on each day against a now helpless people, many of whom are not really aware of its extent.

3. It can carry on a nation-wide education program directly into the homes, reversing the "poor and deprived homes" negative outlook to a positive one... .

4. It can oversee the welfare of the race by maintaining a check on the extent Blacks are secretly used exclusively as guinea pigs in dangerous experiments by various medical projects.

5. Such a race movement would be superficial indeed if it proceeded without its principal foundation, which is the ownership of vast tracts of farm and timber land in various parts of the country. The current ideological cry of "We must have land!" is valid only if we answer the question, "for what purpose?" or "to what end?"

6. It can have, on behalf of the race it represents, a Central National Bank as the people's national depository and central financing agency; a national auditing and accounting service; a general insurance system covering especially those categories where Blacks are arbitrarily denied protection or are charged much higher rates than those now paid by whites; home improvement, building and small loans could all be handled by community credit unions, organized on a somewhat different basis than existing credit unions. For one thing, all community credit unions in various sections of a city would be united as one to reinforce each other's services when needed.

7. It can give hope and a new sense of direction to the thousands behind prison walls and, in time, practically empty the prisons of those convicted of crimes for which the whites go free. The important thing, however, is that the youths, men and women coming out of prisons would have something to come to: training, or retraining for much needed service in helping to build and advance themselves as they build and advance their race. They have never had such an opportunity.

8. The great change in outlook and the new inspiration that would come to Black children and youth are immeasurable. Just to know that their parents are engaged in, and actively a part of a great movement will give a new sense of worth and dignity. It will no longer be necessary to shout in unison, "I *am* — somebody!" We are great if we are an active part of a great movement.

Finally, and obviously, none of the above can be achieved on a nation-wide scale without a nation-wide movement of several million members, organized as a race, working *as a race* for its interests as full-fledged American citizens.

Williams proceeds to go much further than outlining what a nation-wide Afrikan American organization for Black Power can do. He presents a working *Master Plan*, i.e., a plan as a focus for discussion, revision and amendment by which such an organization could be structured, legitimated and functionally achieve its goals. In the preliminary stages of development Williams proposes that an Organizing Committee composed of representatives from exclusively Afrikan American national organizations, or smaller organizations, lodges, clubs, etc., be instituted for the purpose of studying, revising and amending *The Master Plan* and setting the course for future action. Further developments of a national organizing committee would involve ensuring that its membership includes representatives from various sections of the country. After outlining the work of the National Organizing Committee in eleven proposals, Williams very aptly proposes that *The Master Plan* with its revisions and amendments be considered tentative proposals "until approved by the people." Williams makes the following recommendations with regard to the overall structure of a nation-wide Black Power organization:

> The functioning organization would be under the overall administration of a National Council of Leaders, headed by a National chairman (following traditional patterns of Afrikan Council of Elders). Every state, city or community division, would also be organized under councils of leaders.
>
> The organizational structure of the Movement should be by major divisions for the major activities, each divided into departments for carrying on their respective programs....

The structural organization Chancellor Williams suggested includes the following divisions: economic planning and development; political action; public education; community services; youth activities; Afrikan affairs; intelligence and security; and the commission for spiritual assistance. The division of economic planning and development is further subdivided into seven departments. Williams provides additional ideological suggestions and guidelines for actualizing his master plan for Black Power. These include recommendations having to do with the achievement of organizational unity, financing, and administration.

Chancellor Williams recognized that the plan he set forth was "rather clearly *one way out.*" However, he also recognized that any overall plan finally adopted by the Black community, as a matter of integrity and efficiency must include many of its central recommendations, provisos and rationales. While the Chancellor Williams' plan is a grand one in terms of scope and vision as well as detail, and no doubt a bit daunting, it or some similar plan must be actualized if the Afrikan American community is to empower itself to the maximum extent possible. A number of prototypical organizations in some of the areas and divisions proposed by Williams already exist. Their invigoration, expansion and "Afrocentrization" would do much to move them toward a good fit with the Williams model. For example, local, state, regional, and national associations like the National Association of Black Social Workers, Black MBAs, Black psychologists, Black teachers, etc. could expand or reconstruct their present organizations to meet the demands of a Williams-like plan, or create special divisions within their organizations in order to achieve the goals of the divisions of the Williams' plan. Ultimately, a National Organizing Committee or National Council of Leaders composed of the leaders of such organizations could be created in order to administer and coordinate the activities of its various member organizations.

We must again emphasize that member organizations should be unequivocally Afrocentric in composition, structure and purpose. They should avoid like a plague the significant influence in or the leadership of their organization by persons tied to the Democratic or Republican parties, Marxist groups, proselytizing or overzealous religious groups, Eurocentric socialists, and assimilationists. The inclusion of such groups, because of their ambivalent loyalties and conflicting priorities and values, surely will be the death-knell of organizations committed to the advancement of Afrikan peoples.

The work and goals of a national system of divisions as proposed by Chancellor Williams, or of more specialized organizations of the types we just discussed, should be fortified and supported by an openminded, creative and productive Afrocentric policy-formation and planning network. This network, as we shall discuss later, would in basic outline and function parallel that of the White elite policy-formation process also to be described later. This network, like its White counterpart, must include independent, Black-funded foundations, institutes, study or seminar groups in order to develop and provide education and training regimes, research and analytical reports, political and economic development experts and personnel when needed within the Afrikan American and Pan-Afrikan communities.

Chapter 3

SOCIAL AND CULTURAL ORIGINS OF POWER

Culture and Power

SOCIAL POWER is *situated* in that it is embedded in a broader social network or a social field. Social power is generated by the *social alignment* or "relative positioning" of individuals within groups, and the alignment and position of groups vis-à-vis each other within large social organizations, societies, cultures, nations and various coalitions or alliances, in order to achieve mutually desired ends.

One of the most important contexts in which the alignment of individuals and groups is utilized to generate and exercise social power is that of culture. A culture is a type of "power system" which includes all of its members and the various groups and institutions which constitute it. A society or culture as a power system may be subdivided into a number of smaller and smaller power systems nested within, or organically related to, one another. The overall power of a culture or society operationally emerges from these smaller power systems which may include familial, kinship, communal, regional, and other types of social and institutional organizations.

Culture is man's adaptive dimension. "Man alone among the forms of animated nature is the creature that has moved into an adaptive zone which is an entirely learned one. This is the zone of *culture*, the man-made, the learned, part of the environment" (Ashley Montague).

If societies are to survive, they must minimally satisfy certain biological, psychological and social needs of their members. They must successfully counter those forces of nature and man which threaten their well-being and their very biological survival. Culture is the social-institutional instrument which is crucial for facilitating a people's adaptation to the complexities of their world. Therefore its functional structure, cohesiveness, resilience, flexibility, responsivity to reality, evolutionary growth and development, or the relative lack thereof, to a very significant extent, determine its longevity and quality of life. Culture is learned and is the result of historically and conceptually created designs and patterns for living with and relating to others and the cosmos.

The Family as a Power System

Culture is a social machine, a power grid or system. As a holistic system it is composed of a number of sub-systems, power systems in their own right. The family is one such fundamental cultural subsystem. It is a system of social relations, hierarchical in structure, where different members exercise different privileges, prerogatives and different levels of authority. The family is a primary organization, a fundamental generator or source of power where the human and non-human capital resources of its members are pooled and shared as means of achieving its vital goals. These goals include sexual reproduction, socialization of its children, securing a common habitation, providing protection and affectional relations among its members, maintaining and enhancing the social status of its members and providing for their economic well-being.

The family is a system where power is customarily and legally exercised; where its members are not only related by kinship ties, by blood and a shared history, but relate to each other in terms of membership rights, duties, behavioral expectations and authority. The character and personality of individual family members, especially its young, are developed, shaped and continuously influenced by the organization and exercise of power and authority inside and outside the family unit. Consequently, the family as a power system markedly influences its members', particularly its youngs' attitudes toward and relationships to power and authority both within and without the family. Thus there is an important continuity between the nature of power, its quantity, quality and organization within the family and the nature of social and power relations between the family and its physical and social environment including other families and institutions which together constitute a larger social system such as a clan, tribe, nation or culture. Hence, the effective nature of power generated and exercised by a culture is intimately and reciprocally related to and dependent on the effective nature of the power generated by its family and other subcultural units. Generally, the power generated by a culture derives from the structured coalescence of interdependent family kinship groups, clans and tribe for mutual defense against outsiders and other mutually beneficial outcomes. This coalescence of subcultural social units is usually organized and motivated by a mutually recognized leadership or governing establishment. This establishment usually fulfills its responsibilities through the creation, issuance and enforcement of policies. At this level of organization a culture may be defined as a political organization which exercises political power in its defense, economic and social interests as a whole, and in the interest of its subcultural group and individual members. As Dye contends, "true political (power) organizations begin with the *development* of power relationships *between* family and kinship groups." He goes on to state that

> ...the habitual association of human beings in communities or local groups generally leads to the introduction of some sort of political (power) organization. The basic power structures are voluntary alliances of families and clans who acknowledge the same leaders, *habitually work together in economic enterprises*, agree to certain ways of conduct for the maintenance of peace among themselves, and cooperate in the conduct of offensive and defensive warfare. Thus, power structures begin with the development of cooperation between families and kinship groups.
>   Warfare frequently leads to another purpose for power structures — ruling and exploiting people who have been conquered in war. *...Well-organized and militarily successful tribes learn to subjugate other peoples for purposes of political and economic exploitation*, retaining them as subjects. The power structure of the conquering tribes takes on another function — that of maintaining control over and exploiting conquered peoples.[1] [Emphasis added]

If we substitute the phrase "economically successful tribes" for the phrase "militarily successful tribes" in the latter italicized paragraph above, and think in terms of "economic and political warfare" instead of "military warfare," we would more closely approximate the contemporary political-economic relations between White Americans and immigrant Americans and Black Americans in the contemporary United States. That is, the rather superior organization of family-

---

1. Dye, p. 35.

kinship and communal groups and resources of the White Americans and various immigrant groups have facilitated their political and economic exploitation of the Afrikan American community. Besides the fact that the organizations are based on family-kinship, community and ethnic relationships, they are based more profoundly on cultural identity, values and attitudes. A culture generates effective power when it aligns its subcultural, social and individual units, especially its family and communal units, in such ways that they can most effectively create and exploit its human social and material resources to its own advantage relative to its environment and other groups or cultures.

Black American Culture and Identity

What is culture? Horton and Hunt provide a workable answer to this question. "From their life experiences, a group develops a set of rules and procedures for meeting their needs. The set of rules and procedures, together with a supporting set of ideas and values, is called a culture." Anthropologist Clyde Kluckhon has defined culture as all the "historically created designs for living, explicit and implicit, rational, irrational and non-rational which may exist at any given time as potential guides for the behavior of man."

As a set of designs for guiding the behavior of its members, i.e., a set of guidelines for directing and regulating the behavior of its members, a culture provides standards of proper cognitive, emotional, and behavioral conduct; a set of proverbial precepts as to what reality is, and an accompanying set of rationalizations or ostensible explanations for its nature and purpose. Thus, culture, though a product of the actual lived experience of a people — the primal source of much of their daily personal and social activities, their forms of labor and its products, their celebratory and ceremonial traditions, modes of dress, art and music, language and articulatory style, appetites and desires — is essentially ideological in nature based as it is on shared beliefs, customs, expectations, and values. Culture constructs definitions, meanings and purposes. These cultural constructs are used to proactively and reactively mold the mind, body, spirit and behavior of the constituent members of a culture. These active constructs become the cultural and social heritage of the members of a particular culture. Hence, culture does not exist outside and independent of its human subjects. Culture is represented symbolically and operationally in the minds and characteristically mental/behavioral orientations or styles of its members, and is incarnated in the customary ways they move and use their bodies. The culture is represented "in" the minds and bodies of its members, and expresses itself through the systematic ways they attend, experience, categorize, classify, order, judge, evaluate, explain and interact with their world. Mentally, culture involves the socially shared and customary ways of thinking, a way of encoding, perceiving, experiencing, ordering, processing, communicating and of behaviorally expressing information which distinguishes one cultural group from another. All these activities are dedicated to the end of adapting the culture to the consistent and changing demands of its physical and social environment and reciprocally adapting the environment to the demands of the culture.

Socially, culture patterns the ways its members perceive each other, relate to and interact with each other. It facilitates the ways they create, develop, organize, institutionalize and behaviorally apply their human potential in order to adapt to the conditions under which they live so as to satisfy their psychological, social and survival needs. To the degree that the shared beliefs and behavioral orientations of the members of a culture are consensually consistent, reasonably rational and realistic, are effectively and consistently socialized and reinforced, the culture is characterized by coherence, somewhat low levels of internal conflicts and contradictions, relatively smooth, automatic, coordinated operation, and thereby effectively functions in the interest of its members.

It is very important to keep in mind that a culture is to a significant extent a *historical* product, a *social* product. A culture is socially manufactured, the handiwork of both deliberate and coincidental human social collusions and interactions. A culture also manufactures social products. Some of the most important social products it generates include its own cultural identity, and the social and personal identities of its constituent group and individual members.

Cultural, Social, and Personal Identity

The cultural identity of an individual or group is the social product of a socialization process, a process in which new responses, values, perspectives and orientations are acquired and existing behavioral repertoires of the individual or group are modified to some extent, as the result of his or its subjection to direct or indirect social conditioning experiences. Cultural identity also results from the patterning of its modal thoughts, feeling, or actions after other cultures or groups who serve as models.

The reader may wonder why we include cultural identity as a group phenomenon, as the result of a socialization process, something ordinarily used to explain the development of personal and individual identity. Can a culture be socialized? We believe it can; especially when a distinct subcultural group is to a large extent embedded, completely dependent on, controlled, structured and conditioned by a totalitarian dominant culture. This is particularly the case when the members who constitute the subculture have been uprooted and isolated from and have lost knowledge of their own original culture and been forced to adapt to the new and strange one. Black American culture in large part is the "socialized" product of historical and power relations between White and Black Americans. Consequently, Black American cultural identity, while riddled with indigenous Afrikan cultural elements, residuals and fundaments, is still an amalgamated product of the American experience primarily conditioned by dominant Whites who do not have the best interests of Blacks in mind or at heart.

Dager quite aptly describes socialization as "the most efficient and effective means of social control." It is through the socialization process that the necessary ingredients for social order are instilled in the personality (or in the context of this discussion, the subordinate culture). The socialization of a subordinate culture involves the inculcation of its young with values and attitudes that serve to perpetuate the dominant social system.

A realistic and objective analysis of the social structure and dynamics of American society, particularly those pertaining to White-Black race relations will vividly reveal that Blacks are "doubly socialized", i.e., first by the environing and dominant White culture and secondly, reactively and proactively by partly indigenous Black culture. Consequently, Black culture and each of its members are introjected with and afflicted by the "double consciousness" so famously defined by W.E.B. DuBois. Hence, with little modification Dager's definition applies equally to individuals and the subordinate Black culture. "Socialization, broadly defined, is the process by which the infant [or subordinate culture] learns the ways a given social group [the dominant culture] and is molded into an effective participant." Dager adds that:

> Because of imperfections in this process, the infant [subordinate culture] is not completely "molded," but in the course of his [its] development he [it] acquires behavior, attitudes, values and other personality [cultural] traits that are at once unique to him [it] and at the same time characteristic of the group or groups [dominant culture] that serve as the socializing agent.

Dager contends that the socialization process is facilitated by the process called identification. He defines *identification* as the "process by which the infant [and in the present context of discussion, the subordinate Black culture] becomes or behaves like some other or others and/or like others expect [the final three words in this statement are particularly apropos to oppressed Blacks]. It involves psychological processes and includes motives, both conscious and unconscious.... During and following the [identification] process, the adult [dominant culture] normally in control of the resources, dispenses them according to the desirability of the behavior performed by the infant [subordinate culture]. The infant [subordinate culture] will identify [i.e., behave the way he is expected to behave, or to attempt to imitate usually in a considerably caricatured manner the attitudes and behavior of his role model] with the adult [dominant culture] because he [it] is dependent on him [the dominant culture]; in order to receive certain rewards and avoid punishments of various kinds the infant [subordinate culture] will be motivated to conform to expected behavior [or barring this, engage in various forms of deviant behavior in order to attain the same equivalent ends]."

Moreover, identification involves the process by which the individual or group is socialized to acquire those attitudes, values, interests, morals, ethics, tastes, skills, emotional and behavioral tendencies, and ways of thinking that the socializer deems appropriate to the person's gender, the person's or in the case of Whites and Blacks, the group's race and social role. In other words, identification refers to the process of fitting a person or group to its ascribed or prescribed social role. The social role for which the person or group is fitted is usually the one(s) the socializer perceives as important in supporting his or its own position and in achieving or satisfying his or its own goals and needs; or in terms of group relations, important to supporting, enhancing and empowering and helping the socializing group to achieve its economic, political, social and psychological objectives.

The socialized individual or group is considered to have achieved his or its identity when he or it behaves and thinks in ways befitting his or its social role(s) as designated by the socializer and accepts his or its role(s) "voluntarily", or as "natural", or as destined for himself or itself. Depending on the socialized individual's or group's own autonomous characteristics, the nature of the relationship he or it has with the socializer, the attitudes he or it has regarding the socializer, and the particular conditions under which his or its socialization takes place, the socialized individual or group may be inadvertently fitted to a social role identity whose behavioral, emotional and cognitive tendencies may be opposed to those of the socializer. This defiant social role identity if powerful or effective will threaten to or upset the social order or relations intended by the socializer. Under an oppressive socializing regime the social role identities achieved by the socialized person or group though opposed to his or its oppression may yet be self-defeating or self-destructive, and inadvertently self-subordinating. Some social role identities of individuals or groups while diametrically opposed to those intended by the socializer may still unwittingly operate to empower the socializer and strengthen and maintain the social order and relations they defy.

The Need for New Afrikan Self-Identity

Under certain social-economic circumstances cultural identity can become the instrument for the expression of the power of the predominant cultural system which molded it, and may also become the instrument used by the dominant culture and its members to further its survival and enhance its empowerment. Black cultural identity, even in its stratified and diffused state, even on the individual level, is a political economy or essentially an organization of lacks, deficiencies, interests, needs, desires, passions, tastes, ideals, motives, values, etc., the response to which on the part of Blacks helps to maintain or enhance the social power relations, prerogatives, and integrity of the White-dominated racial status quo.

In the context of White American supremacy, Afrikan Americans must ask ourselves: What is the political economy of oppressed Black culture and the various personal and social identities it produces? We must no longer through the abuse of reality, denial and distortion fail to recognize that our basic identities as an oppressed people are largely socially manufactured by the White-dominated American culture and its related social practices in which we as a people are immersed. These identities are therefore incarnations and instruments of their social power; and are socially designed and conditioned when activated, to unwittingly serve the political-economic interests of dominant White America to the detriment of subordinate Black culture. Afrikan American cultural identity and behavioral orientations as currently defined, are functionally defined to perpetuate self-negating, self-defeating, and under certain circumstances, self destructive behavior in Black Americans.

The salvation, empowerment and liberation of Afrikan peoples require an appropriate, thorough, pragmatic cultural analysis of the deculturation and reculturation of ourselves by dominant European peoples, of reactionary "Black culture," and their social products as represented by reactionary Black identities. We must analyze how these identities, whether considered prosocial or antisocial, function to maintain the oppressive power of Whites and the subordinate powerlessness of Blacks. Our salvation further requires that we perceive White supremacy as the major social, political, economic, and spiritual problem to be resolved by Afrikan peoples, and that we ask and answer definitively the questions: What kind of a culture must we construct in order to overthrow White supremacy? What kinds of social identities, relations, arrangements, alignments, institutions, values, etc., which when actualized, will allow us to attain and protect out liberty?; enhance our quality of life? What kinds of socialization practices must we institute in order to empower ourselves to become the kinds of people we must become if we are to secure our right to be free?

Certainly the answers lie in the direction of the reclamation of our Afrikan identity and the reconstitution of our Afrikan-centered consciousness supported by commensurate Afrikan-centered cultural, social, political and economic values, institutions and relations.

Destruction of Black Family Power

We have indicated that the family is a power system. It is an alignment of persons usually related by blood or adoption (formal or informal), a shared history, a shared sense of mutuality, identity, values and fate. The power generated by the family system can be utilized to enhance and maintain the family's own well-being and self-sufficiency as well as the well-being and autonomy of the community and culture of which it is a member.

Dominant groups, in seeking to achieve or maintain their power over subordinate groups, are for this reason compelled in some ways to constrain, restrict, reduce, destabilize, misdirect, or destroy the family systems, and with those, the communal and cultural systems of the groups they subordinate. The oppression, distortion and destabilization of the Afrikan American family by dominant White America began with the enslavement of Afrikans and continues to this day.

Slavery initiated and over the long term, motivated the disintegration of the social organization, traditional social sanctions, strictly regulated family life and rigidly enforced moral codes, which legitimated and supported the pre-slavery Afrikan family (Stampp). Although during and after Emancipation the Black family outwardly resembled that of the White family functionally, psychosocially and socioeconomically it was (and is) distinctly different. *The main difference is that it was and is a family under oppression.* Not permitted the full freedom, the full access to and use of the same or similar resources and supports available to the dominant White family, the Black family exercises less power than its White counterpart. The same may be said of Black culture, which is constituted by Black families. Stampp's description of the slave family still fundamentally fits that of the modern Black family:

> ...they were regulated by whatever laws the owners saw fit to enforce....
>
> Not only did the slave family lack the protection and the external pressure of state law, it also lacked the centripetal forces that gave the White family its cohesiveness. In the life of the slave, the family had nothing like the social significance that it had in the life of the white man. The slave woman was first a full-time worker for her owner, and only incidentally a wife, mother, and home-maker...*and children soon learned that their parents were neither the fount of wisdom nor the seat of authority*...Lacking autonomy, the slave family could not offer the child shelter or security from the frightening creatures in the outside world.
>
> *The family had no greater importance as an economic unit...* slaves labored most of the time for their masters in groups that had no relationship to the family. *The husband was not the director of an agricultural enterprise; he was not the head of the family, the holder of property, the provider, or the protector...* In an age of patriarchal families, the male slave's only crucial function within the family was that of siring offspring....
>
> The husband was at most his wife's assistant, her companion, her sex partner. He was often thought of as her possession ("Mary's Tom"), as was the cabin in which they lived. *It was common for a mother and her children to be considered a family without reference to the father.*
>
> Given these conditions — ...*the family's minor social and economic significance, and the father's limited role* — it is hardly surprising to find that slave families were highly unstable.[2] [Emphasis added]

We do not have to elaborate the fact that the economic role of the Black family and the role of the Black father have remained essentially the subordinate to and dependent on the socioeconomic needs of their dominant White equivalents. The stability, economic foundations and functions of the Black family, given its dependence on White largesse, have always been relatively fragile and tenuous, exuding an air of impermanence which, except for a few decades of relative stability, has rarely blown away. The place and role of the Black male

---

2. Kenneth M. Stampp, *The Peculiar Institution: Slavery in the Ante-Bellum South* (New York: Vintage Books, 1956), pp. 341–44.

in the family and in the society during slavery throughout American history to the present moment are still ambivalent, confusing and contradictory. Much in Stampp's description of the Black male during slavery applies today.

> The average bondsman, it would appear, lived more or less aimlessly in a bleak and narrow world. He lived in a world without schools, without books, without learned men; he knew less of the fine arts and of aesthetic values than he had known in Africa; and he found few ways to break the monotonous sameness of all his days. His world was the few square miles of earth surrounding his cabin... *His world was full of mysteries which he could not solve, full of forces which he could not control. And so he tended to be a fatalist and futilitarian, for nothing else could reconcile him to his life.*[3] [Emphasis added]

The conditions of life and resulting state of mind of the Black male under slavery were deliberately constructed and induced in order to secure and maintain his powerlessness, to expropriate the product of his labor, to capitalize on his human and material capital resources so as to make possible the accumulation of capital surplus and social power by his White exploiters. Even after Emancipation the Black man's cultural alienation (i.e., deprivation of Afrikan culture), reactionary dealings with his oppression, self-contempt, his pseudo-imitation of White cultural behavior, internalization of White racist attitudes in regard to himself and his fellows, served as stumbling blocks to his achievement of the type of collective values, behaviors, arrangements and unity which would ultimately empower him to successfully counter White racism and oppression. The disempowerment of the Afrikan male, the Afrikan family and culture virtually assures continuing Afrikan American powerlessness and economic exploitation by other ethnic groups. The groups that exploit the Afrikan American community most expertly are patriarchal and male-headed; groups whose family structure are relatively stable and well organized, are political-economic systems, and whose sense of ethnicity, of tribe (i.e., ethnocentrism) are strong and enduring. Generally, these groups are proud of their differences from "the mainstream" White culture, do not resent their residential separation from Whites, and are not seeking to commit "biological suicide" by miscegenation or intermarriage with Whites to such an extent that their racial stock disappears from the face of the Earth. While not the whole of the Afrikan American community exhibits these sentiments, probably not even the large majority, a relatively small but influential

---

3. Ibid., p. 361.

segment does. This segment is over-represented in Black community leadership positions and organizations which mediate between the White power structure and the Black community. Their social-political positions garner them ready access to mass media, to White liberal resources and support such that they repeatedly frustrate and often destroy positive Black ethnocentric sentiments and operational efforts. This assimilationist segment of the community is quite vocal in its condemnation of ethnocentric and self-help leaders and organizations in the Afrikan American community. Pathologically committed to the consumption of White-owned manufactured products and gaining the unadulterated approval of Whites as well as its self-effacing assimilation into White society, this influential group unwittingly enters into an alliance with the exploiters of the Afrikan American community in managing its continuing disempowerment.

The Black family — as long as and to the degree to which it is dependent on the dominant White power structure, to the degree to which it is not founded on Afrikan-centered consciousness, cultural traditions and values, social, economic arrangements or alignments, its organization and disorganization, stability and instability, power or powerlessness — will reactionarily reflect the political-economic interests of the White power structure in which it is operationally embedded. And these interests are, more often than not, detrimental to those of the Black family. The relative powerlessness of the Black family portends the relative powerlessness of Black culture, and vice-versa.

Religious Institutions and Power

Fundamentally, a people's culture is a mental-behavioral system used by them to rationalize and justify, organize and regulate, give meaning and purpose to their individual and group behavior, social relations, lives and existence. Culture is essentially a way of thinking, perceiving, evaluating, and interpreting the world; a way of relating to others and to the physical-metaphysical world, and involves an explicit and implicit set of rules of conduct which orders the overall social relations, arrangements and attitudes of a society. The power generated by such social relations, arrangements (alignments) and attitudes is utilized for maintaining and enhancing the well-being and integrity of the society; for procuring, processing and producing the material and non-material products characteristic of the society; and for substantiating its abilities to defend and advance its interests in cooperation with or in opposition to other societies or groups.

At center of a culture's guiding mental-behavioral system is its moral-religious-ethical system. That is, its attitudes concerning right and wrong feelings and conduct; its acknowledgment of a God, of divine, pre-eminent, cosmic or universal principles, and a related system of beliefs, faith and worship, ritual and practical piety; as well as a doctrine or system of morals, or moral philosophy and code of moral-behavioral precepts. A people's religious system (which we will use here as a short-hand phrase for moral-religious-ethical system as just defined) to a very significant degree serves as an organizing entity in their personal and social life. As a major factor in social organization, often as the linchpin of sociocultural organization, the religious system of a society serves as its fundamental power center, or at least as one of its most influential centers of power. Often the heads of religious institutions of a society may simultaneously serve as heads of its governmental regime or heavily influence its policies and operations.

The Institutional Black Church

The institutional Black Church and the Black preachers are cultural icons in the Afrikan American community. Black preachers have led the Afrikan American community from slavery to the present. Rarely has a secular leadership establishment gained long-term and broadly effective influence in the Afrikan American community superior to that of the ministerial establishment. Black preachers have been consistently and almost exclusively supported by the Black community. This type of support has provided many of them with the power of relative independence. The relative independence and the relatively open time schedule enjoyed by the ministerial profession have permitted them larger degrees of freedom and social latitude than is the case for would-be secular leaders who practice other professions or work at other jobs, usually in the employ of White establishments. However, the foundation of Black ministerial power, influence and leadership in the Afrikan American community is in largest part due to the custodial control of the key cultural institution, the institutional Black Church; the use of institutional Christian theology, ideology, doctrine, dogma, and ritual by Black preachers; their own "divinity" as God's representatives on Earth; and their ministering to the centrally important spiritual, supernatural needs of their congregations. As the Afrikan American community's preeminent leaders, as custodians and leaders of its central cultural establishment, the fabled Black Church, the nature, organization and functionality of Black cultural power must be attributed more to the quality of the leadership of Black preachers than to any other alternative leadership group. Therefore, the theological-ideological rationales which undergird the legitimacy, power and direction of the Black preacher establishment and its leadership of the Afrikan American community must be critically analyzed if we are to understand the relative potency and impotency of "Black American culture".

The Black Church has not only underdeveloped the power-potential of the Black community, but has actually squandered its potential, impaired it, and prostituted it in service to alien peoples and cultures, particularly White peoples and Eurocentric culture. This profligate wasting of the tremendous power potential of the Black community, its feeble and misdirected growth and development, are not due to malicious intent on the part of the Black preacher leadership establishment. Nor is it due to a lack of courage or dim-wittedness of this group. The fault lies in the nature of the imposed /borrowed theological-ideological rationale which undergirds the Black Church and which guides the perceptions, expectations, social relations and behavior of its leadership.

We must keep in mind that enslaved Afrikan were not Christians when they were brought to the New World. They were predominantly practitioners of their indigenous Afrikan religions and behaved in accord with indigenous Afrikan codes of ethics. Therefore, the Christian religion along with its ideological doctrines was taught to and imposed on enslaved Afrikan by their White masters. Obviously, the masters taught the slaves Christianity for their own conscious and unconscious self-serving reasons. The theology they passed on to their slaves was necessarily biased in order to serve and justify their dominance. Therefore, in essential ways the theology which undergirds the practice and outcome of White Christianity was distinctly different from that which undergirds Black Christianity, despite the apparent and superficial sameness of the two. In other words, Blacks do not relate to, pray to, and serve Jesus Christ in the same way, for the same reasons Whites do, even though it appears they do. Christianity as a central cultural institution, has not empowered the Black community in the same ways it has empowered the White community, or as it has the other alien Christian communities, or in ways other communities are empowered by their own religious institutions. As a matter of fact, Christianity as it is practiced in the Afrikan American community has probably done as much to disempower that community than to empower it. A brief review of the history of the development of Christianity among Afrikan slaves in America readily reveals why this is the case. A very schematic presentation of Stampp's review of the development of the Black Church during slavery will provide us with some idea of why that institution has retarded Black empowerment as much as it has advanced it.

- Many [masters] ...considered Christian indoctrinations an effective method of keeping slaves docile and contented.

- When the first Africans were imported in the seventeenth century, some purchasers opposed converting them to Christianity *lest baptism give them a claim to freedom*. After the colonial legislatures provided that conversion would not have this effect, the opposition diminished. *Thereafter most masters encouraged Christian proselytization among their bondsmen, and conversion proceeded rapidly.*

- ...*the master class could look upon organized religion as an ally.* Church leaders now argued "that the gospel, instead of becoming a means of creating trouble and strife, *was really the best instrument to preserve peace and good conduct among the negroes.*" This was a persuasive argument. "In point of fact," recalled one churchman, "*it was this conviction that ultimately opened the way for the gospel on the larger plantations.*"

- Through religious instruction the bondsmen learned that slavery had divine sanction, that insolence was as much an offense against God as against the temporal master.

- It [Christian doctrine] taught them [the slaves] "respect and obedience to their superiors," made them "more pleasant and profitable servants," and aided "the discipline of a plantation in a wonderful manner."

- The master class understood, of course, that only a carefully censored version of Christianity could have [the] desired effect. Inappropriate Biblical passages had to be deleted; sermons that might be proper for freemen were not necessarily proper for slaves. Church leaders addressed themselves to this problem and prepared special catechisms and sermons for bondsmen, and special instructions for these concerned with their religious indoctrination.... Religion, in short, should underwrite the status quo.[4]
[Emphasis added]

The ambivalent nature of the Christianity to which Afrikan slaves were converted and to which large segments, if not the large majority of the Afrikan American community and its preacher leadership are

---

4. Kenneth M. Stampp, *The Peculiar Institution*, pp.156–60.

committed to today, is readily discernable. We use the term "ambivalent," meaning "to act in two opposite directions simultaneously; to serve two opposing purposes at the same time," to bring attention to the fact that Christianity taught the slaves by their masters or by the dominant Whites, served to rationalize and justify the status quo of White mastery and Black slavery; White dominance and Black subordination; White command and Black obedience. This ambivalent function of Christianity as taught to Afrikan slaves remains embedded in the church theology of the contemporary Black Church. This theology and the ethics derived therefrom function to sustain White domination, domination by other groups, and Black subordination, by means of inducing Blacks to believe in and follow what appears to be divine, objective, "race-neutral," sayings, proverbs, ethical rules and moral preachments. However, any cursory examination of the mundane outcome of the belief in and practice of such preachments is startlingly different and almost completely opposite for Whites and Blacks.

For Whites, Christianity empowers; justifies their sense of moral superiority; justifies and dictates their dominance of non-Whites; provides material enrichment; provides material comforts, reduces material suffering; is self-affirming; produces tangible and desirable results in this world as well as the world to come; promotes the worship of a god whose image bears their likeness; provides a rationale for their racial self-centeredness, selfishness, and exclusivity by confining the practice of brotherly love and equality, self-sacrifice, and the like within the borders of the White race. For Blacks, Christianity disempowers; induces a sense of moral inferiority; preaches submission, subordination and obedience; is associated with material deprivation; sanctifies material discomfort and suffering; is self-negating, self-effacing; produces relatively few tangible and desirable results in this world while emphasizing "pie-in-the-sky" other-worldly rewards; promotes the worship of a god that wears a non-Afrikan face and bears the facial image of their White dominators and enemies (leading them to consciously worship White people, to think of them as more god-like than themselves, to perceive them as divinely ordained to rule over themselves, to associate whiteness of skin with all that is good and blackness of skin with all that is bad); provides a rationale for racial self-denial, selflessness, inclusiveness, etc. by expanding the practice of brotherly love and equality, self-sacrifice, and the like to all beyond the borders of the Afrikan race.

Christian theology and ethics, especially in the form of good/evil, good/bad percepts and behavior, constitute the principal form of White

White (and other groups) domination of Blacks. The acceptance by Afrikans of White valuations and definitions of good versus evil, good versus bad attitudes and behavior and the Afrikan acceptance of White valuations and definitions of good and evil, good and bad as objective, divinely inspired, universal and race-neutral, allows them to be duped and dominated by Whites simply through the media of ideas. The uncritical acceptance of such non-Afrikan religious precepts as universal, as applying with equal effect across all groups and individuals, without regard to sociohistorical context or situation; without asking, "Good for what?", "Good for whom?", "Evil for whom?" "Good from whose perspective?" "Evil from whose perspective?", can become the vehicle for dominance by the group whose good/bad, good/evil precepts are accepted and thus the vehicle for subordination by the group which accepts them.

Germane to this discussion of how one group can dominate another through the acceptance of the ideas of the dominant group by the subordinate group, is Wartenberg's analysis of Nietzsche's philosophy of domination based on the premise that one group can dominate another through ideas alone. Wartenberg argues that

> Nietzsche has demonstrated that it is possible for one group to dominate another group by means of ideas, by getting that group to think about themselves in a manner that allows them to be subjugated. Such a form of domination is able to succeed because the true nature of the ideas by which it occurs is concealed in a form of language that has the appearance of objectivity. His analysis of the use of the term "good" is intended to demonstrate that, despite the appearance of objectivity, such a term functions subjectively in that its use is only justified from a certain perspective. Since this perspectival aspect of judgment is concealed, however, the subordinate group views the judgments as valid independently of the perspective from which they are made. As a result, a group can come to think of itself [and behave] in terms created by the perspective of another group without realizing it. It is this particular mechanism that Nietzsche highlights as the origin of domination.[5]

Wartenberg goes on to contend that "All evaluative judgments are made from the perspective of the ability of an item to fulfill its function. In fact, judgments using the term "good" without qualification merely conceal the fact that the term "good" always means "good for the following end." The attribution of "good", "bad", or, "evil" to human attitudes, thoughts and behaviors, "fits *someone's* purposes, even though the judgment itself does not make reference to these

---
5. Wartenberg, p. 132.

purposes." These types of attributions lie at the heart of Black Church theology and ideology and at the center of the political ideology operationally accepted by the Afrikan American community, its Black Church and secular leadership. Both the theologies and ideologies imposed on them by the White American Church and political communities are designed to serve as the mental means by which Whites (and other non-Afrikan groups) manipulate and exploit Blacks. Black preachers as ardent advocates of racially biased theologies and political ideology become the unwitting allies and mercenary surrogates for the domination and exploitation of the Afrikan community by Whites and other outsiders whose theologies and ideologies they uncritically adopt.

For little do these ministerial leaders seem to know that the term "good" as used by Whites and other outsiders functions "as a means of affirming their own self-evaluation", "grows out of [their own] triumphant self-affirmation"; equates "good/noble/power/beautiful/happy/favored-of-the-gods" in reference to themselves; and posits the characteristics of their own group is "worthy of emulation" (Wartenberg, with all quotes except the first and last from Nietzsche). For Whites and other groups the term "bad" is used to characterize the traits and behavior of those unlike themselves and those who do not live up to their cultural ideals and expectations, which they themselves readily and shamelessly violate in the interest of their self-preservation and predominance. *For it is most interesting to note that if Afrikan Americans thought and behaved in ways judged as "good," in terms of ways which facilitate their economic and social enrichment, material well-being; their ability to exploit their own economic and cultural resources, such thought and behavior on the part of Blacks would be condemned by other ethnic groups as "bad," "reverse racism," "racist," "selfish," as "creating racial tensions," "race hatred," "unchristian," and a host of other derogatory terms, the use of which, in the final analysis, is designed to maintain the racial / economic /political status quo — that is, maintaining Blacks in positions of subordination.* Unfortunately, they would be joined in chorus by a host of influential Black preachers, Black Christians, their Black ideological sympathizers, and Black assimilationists, all unwittingly indoctrinated by imposed, borrowed, or inherited White self-serving Christian theology and political ideology "charading" as divinely inspired, universal precepts and expectations.

There is one central tendency of the Black Church and the Black preacher leadership establishment with which it has saddled the Afrikan American community, has doomed that community to one disempowering failure after another, and doomed it to unrelenting subordination and exploitation by outside groups. That is its predilection to *moralize* every problem which confronts the Black community — no matter how mundane. Every problem is perceived in moral terms and is perceived as solvable by moral means ("moral suasion") only. The problem of White domination is seen as a moral problem the solution to which involves persuading Whites to think and behave according to Christian moral precepts and ethical codes in addition to convincing Blacks to be more "Christ-like" in their attitudes and behavior. In reference to this "fatal flaw" in Black ministerial leadership, Harold Cruse reached the following conclusion (regarding the leadership of the Southern Christian Leadership Conference [SCLC], the apotheosis of Black Church ministerial leadership, at one time led by Martin Luther King, Jr.):

> After King's death, the SCLC vowed valiantly to carry out and expand the black church role that King had envisioned. This was an exemplary ambition for the SCLC, for it was beyond the scope of its collective social imagination, beyond the range of its *institutional* experience, to understand that as a *social organization* the black church could not give the kind of leadership that had been lacking since the 1920s unless *the black church changed itself*....The economic, social, political, cultural, and institutional problems of American blacks are beyond the reach of moral preachments — as King was, finally, forced into understanding.
>
> * * * *
>
> ...It was overwhelmingly white liberals, *not* the political ruling class, who flocked to the support of Martin Luther King on the question of the moral imperative. No one knows better than the political ruling class that *the political, economic, and cultural policies that monitor the internal affairs of American society are not inspired by moral considerations, but are based on the imperatives of power — especially economic power*. Placing segregation and race prejudice on the nation's up-front agenda for examination by means of moral suasion had its unquestionable value. However, after that, *practical solutions require not moral means, which are unavailable, but a pragmatic reorganization of the institutional bases of race relations by both Blacks and Whites*.[6] [Emphasis added]

The Black Church/community leadership along with Black assimilationist leadership and Black neo-conservative leadership (?), like that of King's, fail to fully comprehend and come to terms with the essentially amoral, secularized nature and functioning of the

---

6. Harold Cruse, *Plural But Equal: A Critical Study of Blacks and Minorities and America's Plural Society* (New York: William Morrow, 1987), pp. 232–33.

American/European-political-economic system. Cruse notes this when he argues that:

> The racial politics of a racist (or, better, an ethnocentrically imbued) capitalistic society such as the United States cannot tolerate for long the brand of moral imperative that King was preaching. The free-enterprise money markets know no morality other than the morality of the power to determine marketable exchange values.[7]

The Black Church and the Myth of Individualism

In addition to accepting, inculcating and misleading the Afrikan American community with its White racist tainted religious theology and ideology, the Black Church establishment along with its bourgeois class retainers addicts the community to an ever more socially poisonous political ideology — the myth of individualism. The wholesale adoption and communal promulgation by Black Church and non-church leadership of the mythologies of *laissez-faire* capitalism, unrestrained individualism, self-centered, self-serving, narcissistic, competitive self-promotion and careerism as the cultural foundations of the Afrikan American community have been and is greatly responsible for its disempowerment and social underdevelopment. EuroAmerican cultural, economic and political mythologies are designed to maintain White domination and facilitate the White political-economic exploitation of the Afrikan American community. This accords with the political ends of White American theological mythologies. The crude myth of individualism propagated in the Black America community includes the idiotic contention that a people, a nation, can achieve its *w*holistic social and economic goals as the result of the self-centered, self-interested, self-aggrandizing, competitive pursuit of material and non-material advantages by each individual in competition with all other individuals. These self-elevating advantages are to be energetically, single-mindedly pursued without regard for their injurious interpersonal and anti-social effects on others. The right to such pursuit is an article of faith and considered to be inalienable. The individual is perceived as independent of and opposed to his community. And sacrifice of individual pursuits to communal ends is perceived as an unlawful usurpation of basic human and civil rights, as an imposition on "individual liberty."

The building of the United States, its ability to support individual freedom and self-realization, its evolution as a world economic, military and cultural power center is *not* the result of the independent individual pursuit of advantages even though it may appear so, but

---

7. Ibid., p. 252.

is the result of socially organized efforts, White ethnocentrism, racism, social cooperation, mutual aid, socially shared values and attitudes, constraints and restrictions on individual expression and liberties, governmental grants, supports, subsidies, regulations, protections, institutional rules and practices as well as all types of binding social relations and arrangements. We cannot separate individual motivation and self-realization from its social nexus or matrix. For as Michael Mann contends:

> The pursuit of almost all our motivational drives, our needs and goals, involves human beings in external relations with nature and other human beings. Human goals require both intervention in nature — a material life in the widest sense — and social cooperation. It is difficult to imagine any of our pursuits or satisfactions occurring without these. Thus, the characteristics of nature and the characteristics of social relations become relevant to, and may indeed structure, [individual] motivations.[8]

Individual development, success and fulfillment are social products. They are made possible by and are the product of social relations and organizations. The nature, organization and goals of individual self-definition reflect *social* experience, organization, shared *social* ideals and values, *social*, institutional and opportunity structures, all of which facilitate or inhibit individuals, their formation, structure and general orientation. Individual success and accomplishment and failure only take on meaning if they occur within a definable social system.

White America, its propaganda regarding individualism notwithstanding, is a nation or community built on social interdependence and cooperation. This is clearly delineated by anthropologist David Maybury-Lewis who contends that:

> In the modern world we shroud our *interdependency* in an ideology of independence. We focus on individuals, going it alone in the economic sphere, rather than persons, interconnected in the social sphere.

Recall that in the case of White moral preachments to the Black community relative to expressions of "brotherly love", "self-sacrifice", etc., wherein among Whites such sentiments are to be expressed only within the limits of the race and not toward outsiders, their expression among Blacks instead are essentially directed toward outsiders, especially Whites. White political preachments about individual

---

8. Michael Mann, *The Sources of Social Power: A History of Power from the Beginning to A.D. 1760*, vol. 1. (New York: Cambridge University Press, 1986), p. 5.

freedom, "open markets" and "free trade," while denying such rights and privileges to Blacks and granting them to themselves, are truly designed to facilitate the exploitation of the Black community by the White corporate establishment. White-defined individualism as propagated and understood within the contextual reality of the Black community, a reality whose social transformation cries out for collective sentiments and action, instills in Blacks a hunger for personal aggrandizement and a competitiveness which tends to negate or impair their human capabilities for collective action and cooperative economics which together would empower the Black community to achieve liberation and prosperity. The strengthening of intra-group ties and obligations, collective identity and action in the Black community, is neither anti-individualistic nor does it deny the achievement of individual distinction and fulfillment within the community or in the larger world. In fact, these factors motivate Black individualism to a greater degree than is presently the case, where Blacks are stereotyped and permitted relatively little individual, non-stereotypical recognition and freedom. As stated by Ralston, "The highest meaning of the social group is to foster the development of individual potential, for the community's own well-being depends on it." A group must empower itself as a whole if it is to empower its individual members.

We agree with Michael Lewis when he argues that American culture is first and foremost a culture of inequality. It is a culture characterized by massive class and ethnic differences in wealth, power, privilege, prestige, and quality of life. The ideology of American individualism principally functions to justify and rationalize White America's culture of inequality. Lewis explains it in the following manner:

> The emergence of this individualistic moral sensibility is of considerable significance, for as we shall see it has become central to the existence of the American *culture of inequality* — an interpretation of unequal outcomes given the assumption of equal chances. It is a sensibility that virtually ignores the impact of social structure upon personal achievement and mobility. According to this sensibility, it is the individual alone who is socially significant, who determines what his or her contribution to the commonweal will be, and who is therefore responsible for the degree of personal success achieved. Society is seen as benign, offering up opportunities and waiting to be enriched by those who have the will and the capacity to make productive use of them. This sensibility therefore removes inequality of personal perquisites from the category of social conditions in need

of reform. If such inequality is seen as the product of traditional restrictions on opportunity it becomes a target for social reformers to whom it is the arbitrary and unjust outcome of a reactionary system. If, however, such inequality is simply an indication of differentials in the productive exertion of individuals, free to exercise their ambitions and talents to the fullest, then the presumption of social arbitrariness cannot be sustained and only the individual can be held accountable for the state of his or her well-being. If inequality exists it is nothing more than a reflection of different personal qualities.[9]

As Lewis further notes, "In reality such a system [as the racist modern American capitalist system] limits the success most of us can achieve, even as the individual-as-central sensibility [American individualism] encourages us to believe otherwise." Inspired by American individualism, White and Black Americans alike are encouraged and conditioned to believe "that opportunity is virtually unlimited and that the extent of one's success or failure depends solely upon the quality of one's efforts." Thus when we do not succeed, when we are impoverished and powerless, we are more likely to believe "that we lack the ability or character to succeed than [to believe] ...that we have been victimized by the requisites of American [race- and class-based] capitalism." Believing uncritically in American individualism, Afrikan Americans, reviewing their relative lack of success and powerlessness in White American dominated society, falsely conclude that "their problem is not an opportunity structure which [they] perceive as constraining, but is rather an insidious intimation of personal [and social/cultural/ethnic] inadequacy, a sense that lacking the success [wealth and power they] have aspired to [they] are thereby lacking in worth."[10] Thus is the ideological trap sprung. The uncritical internalization of American individualism by the Afrikan American community as a whole and Afrikan Americans as individuals in the face of obvious personal and communal powerlessness, motivates their placing themselves in social and psychological jeopardy. Their obvious problems, failures, and powerlessness in the face of their unqualified belief in American individualism (those problems, failures, and powerlessness having been mandated and socially engineered by European American power needs and aspirations), leads Afrikan Americans to self-defamation, self-abnegation, self-blame, self-alienation, self-hatred, loss of self-confidence, self-esteem and a lowering of aspirations. These prevalent feelings are typically correlated with the Afrikan American culture of poverty and

---

9. Michael Lewis, *The Culture of Inequality* (NY: New American Library, 1978), p. 8.
10. Ibid., p. 16.

powerlessness. These traits and tendencies generated and "bred" into Afrikan Americans by European American-Afrikan American power relations, are made to appear as intrinsic, inherent Afrikan traits and the true causes of their personal and communal powerlessness by Eurocentric social scientific propaganda.

If the Afrikan American community is to successfully counteract its socialization for subordination, powerlessness, and poverty by the dominant European American community, then it must oppose White power, rationalized by the ideology of Eurocentric individualism, with Black Power, rationalized by the ideology of Afrocentric communalism. The culture of inequality of necessity, in order to establish its preeminence as a culture in contrast with, other cultures or subcultures, generates and sustains the subordination, poverty and powerlessness of the other cultures and subcultures. Ironically, the ideology of American individualism with which the wealthy and powerful European American community indoctrinates the subordinate Afrikan American community is neither really accepted nor practiced by that dominant community, especially its ruling elite. Neither does this class actually accept or practice the ideology of individualistic, free market capitalism into which it so skillfully socializes its lower classes and the Afrikan American community. For the implicit acceptance and extreme practice of these ideologies are individually isolating, overly competitive and communally divisive and disunifying. Their overemphasis is therefore both communally and individually impoverishing and disempowering. That is the reason they are foisted on the Afrikan American community.

The abiding characteristics of the culture of wealth and power and of the ruling elite are these:

1. Class, community, and/or ethnic consciousness.
2. Wealth.
3. Control of social, political and other important institutions necessary for reaching group goals and of realizing group values.
4. Control of, or effective influence on, the government, its agencies, policies and operations necessary for achieving group interests.
5. The founding and funding of hierarchical and socially and institutionally appropriate organizations necessary to achieve group power and security.
6. The availability of high quality and skilled, imaginative and creative human resources.

7. A set of social relations, arrangements, and attitudes which facilitate intragroup social unity, identity, acceptance, cooperativeness and exclusiveness relative to out groups.
8. Control of community resources, socialization, educational and training institutions wherein group members and future group leaders are developed and oriented.
9. An ideology of group superiority or worthiness and the overwhelming desire to be free and independent — a drive for hegemony.
10. Control of superior coercive physical forces, important human intellectual, physical, and economic resources with a willingness to fully and effectively use them to achieve and defend group interests.

The individual who is a member of the culture of wealth and power with a bit of ambition and ability is markedly more likely to realize his aspirations than is an individual who is a member of the "culture of poverty and powerlessness" despite an abundance of ambition and ability. For the social, institutional, and economic advantages provided by the social matrix of the culture of wealth and power greatly enhances the probabilities of success for those who are positioned in and supported by that matrix. The contextual nature of middle and upper class individual and group success, the social matrix which makes such success possible, are conveniently ignored by Eurocentric social scientific propaganda. All success is attributed to drives, values and other characteristics supposedly inherently possessed and spontaneously expressed by fortunate individuals and/or groups. This is done to obscure from the powerless and social failures the fact that both individual and group power and success are fundamentally communal and organizational in nature, are founded on the possession of a group consciousness, an appropriate set of social relations and organization, and *group* control over some important basic human and material resources. If the Afrikan American community is to gain its liberation and independence, is to achieve wealth and power it must socialize its collective personality and character to internalize and express the modal collective personality and character of an Afrikan-centered culture of wealth and power.

The Nation of Islam

In stark contrast to the Black Church as a religion and cultural power center stands the Black Muslims or the Black Nation of Islam, especially when under the leadership of The Honorable Elijah Muhammad. Paradoxically, the "Nation" as a religious-cultural institution, and the psychosocial outcomes which flow from its unique theological-ideological infrastructure, resemble those of the White Church far more than those of the Black Church. Like White Christianity, Black Islam is *a religion and culture which serves a people*, not a religion which the people serve as is the case for the Black Church. The God of Black Islam has a special relationship with the Black Nation *exclusive* of other racial groups. He, in a rather special way, is *their* God, a God who has provided them with a special mission, a "manifest destiny." This special relationship with God, the special mission assigned to them by their God, the unorthodox and unique religio-historical, mytho-ideological system which undergirds that relationship and mission, imbues the true believers with feelings of specialness or superiority. They do not perceive themselves to be the footstools of other peoples by divine decree as is the case with many Black Christians. They are not to be sacrificial lambs in the interests of other peoples or in the name of some foreign notion of universal "brotherly love." Others outside "the nation," particularly Whites, are to be rejected as models of emulation; are not to be targeted for racial assimilation or integration. White power and domination are to be subdued, not to be worshiped.

The Nation of Islam is not a "copycat" imitation of orthodox (Arabized, Semitic) Islam and therefore does not rely on outside Islamic authorities or theologians to validate its authenticity (and by their agency subvert it to their interests) and does not seek the acceptance by outside co-religionists as its central goal or *raison d'etre*. Its theology, though in good part borrowed from orthodox sources, has been significantly "Afrikanized" and is therefore uniquely its own creation and is therefore instrumental in advancing the exclusive interests of the Nation and its Black members. More than a religious institution, the Nation of Islam is a full-fledged Black Culture, a nation-within-a-nation. For it includes all the major institutions which define a people as having a culture: a group identity and name; a religious institution unique to themselves; family and economic institutions; a military or paramilitary establishment; a distinct system of ethics, mores, folkways and values; distinct modes of dress; distinct culinary and dietary styles; a system of production and resource ownership and development. The Nation is patriarchal in leadership and organization, meaning that its males have developed ways and means of intra-group cooperation and organization which permit them to act on coherent, cohesive and collective terms. The Nation presents a "masculine" face to the world of outsiders and relates to them on "masculine" terms, terms of equality and power.

As a consequence of its self-definition and self-determination, Black Islam, like White Christianity, empowers its adherents; provides them with high self-esteem, self-confidence, a sense of high intellectual and moral superiority; motivates a drive toward and sense of self-control, control of environment, self-sufficiency and independence; justifies and provides the means for material enrichment, producing desirable and tangible results here on earth as against "pie-in-the-sky"; provides a rationale for "race first" self-centeredness, and emphasizes the fact that brotherly love, self-sacrifice, integration, assimilation, and the like, must occur first *within* the nation of Black people prior to their application to outsiders. This orientation strikingly contrasts with that of the Black Church. By means of this and other related orientations, cultural and moral ideals the Nation of Islam has had and currently has a major impact on the consciousness of the Afrikan American community and has garnered a grudging and often resentful, respect from some prominent leaders of the Black Church and the assimilationist Black leadership and their followers. The Nation has demonstrated entrepreneurial drive and provided a model for Afrikan American economic development.

We must hasten to notify our readers that we are not herein proselytizing for the Nation of Islam. We merely use it as an example of a Black-centered organization and of the cultural, psychosocial, socioeconomic and empowerment outcomes which can devolve from organizations whose founding ideology is Black- or Afrikan-centered in context compared to those whose ideology is White- or European-centered, or centered around outside ethnic group philosophies, ideologies, cultures and religions. We are fully aware of the influence of other Black- or Afrikan-centered organizations or movements such as that led by Marcus Garvey (the precursor of the Nation of Islam in a number of very important ways). The key ingredients which define the Nation of Islam's and its socioeconomic, sociocultural outcomes, influence and power potential, can be utilized by other Black organizations and the Black community as a whole to gain power, liberation, independence and respect, without converting to Islam as a religion. These include an Afrikan-centered identity and consciousness; Afrikan-centered ideological systems based on a thorough knowledge of and admiration for Afrikan-centered, "race first" educational and economic institutions and relations; an Afrikan-centered "do for self" orientation; Afrikan-centered Manhood-

Womanhood-Familyhood training and institution building; Afrikan-centered sense of high self-esteem, self-confidence, self-love, self-assertiveness, expressive-creative intelligence, values and behavior. Whatever the religious, political, or cultural foundation of a group of Afrikan people, however borrowed or synthesized their guiding ideologies and principles may be, to work for Afrikan peoples (if not, what would be the point of adopting them) they must be thoroughly and practically "Afrikanized", otherwise they will become the facilitators of the exploitation, manipulation, if not the domination of Afrikan peoples by outsiders and their enemies.

The Spirit of War

It is important to note that the Nation of Islam is organized, as its name implies, as a permanent nation-state. And like a nation-state, it exists within a more or less well-defined border or territory (at least psychosocially and institutionally) and is governed by a recognized leadership establishment which makes and enforces rules of conduct. State societies also develop an organized and trained military or paramilitary establishment for offensive and defensive purposes. It should also be noted that the Nation and the White Christian Church share in common an assertive, war-like, or martial tradition, a tradition of making war against their enemies or defending themselves against their enemies by force of arms. The tradition of Jihad permeates the Nation of Islam as much as the warrior and war-like European tribal traditions and Christian soldierly traditions permeate the White Christian Church and European Christendom as a whole. The Black Muslim God — just as his White counterpart — easily assumes the aspects of a God of War, or at least approves of war in the interest of his adherents.

In this light it is interesting to note that the study of war strategy and practice of war, the codification and expostulation of war, have held a long and honored place in the annals of the European and Asian groups who socioeconomically and politico-economically occupy and exploit the Afrikan American community and the Pan–Afrikan community worldwide. The Black Church, servant of White American interests that it is, and the Afrikan American community, shorn of its Afrikan cultural traditions, are bereft of a warrior tradition, mentality and outlook. Except when called into military service by their White masters, they not only ignore the study and practice of war and of military strategy but, in essence, eschew them. The military and warrior traditions, the marital arts and military strategic thinking indigenous to Afrikan history and culture was lost to the Afrikan

American community as the result of its deculturation during and after slavery. The patriarchal organization, identification and cooperation required and imbued by warfare has been lost to the Black community, along with the ability to utilize and apply military-like strategy and military-like organization to non-military arenas.

The Afrikan American community though by and large physically separated from the White American and other ethnic communities, especially in the large inner cities across America, is surrounded and economically penetrated by these same groups. It is like a fortress under siege whose walls have been breached at many places and whose foundations are in the process of being razed by its attackers. It stands nearly defenseless against its invaders and is in danger of being completely overrun, captured and forced to pay onerous tribute to its captors, to supply labor for their labor camps and to have most of its able-bodied men interned as prisoners of war. The Afrikan American community must recognize that if it cannot achieve its economic and social well-being by the "usual" ("legitimate") means, then it must achieve them by unusual means. For this community is not obligated to sacrifice its well-being, its children, to ransom its future to any other people in the name of God or Man.

To ensure its survival and well-being, its full empowerment and liberation, the Afrikan American community must not only capture its internal markets but capture a significant portion of America's national production facilities and markets, and vigorously engage in international trade. To accomplish these necessary goals the community must painstakingly examine the nature and functionality of its culture and cultural institutions. It must especially examine and revise its family and religious institutions, rebuild and build anew its economic and educational institutions. Of especially great importance, the Afrikan American community must train its boys very carefully, intelligently and intensely for manhood. Afrikan American manhood must be redefined in ways which positively redefine the relations of Afrikan men to women, their families and community. Above all, they must be taught the skills of manly intimacy, honor, cooperation, reliability, and loyalty to community. They must re-assume their role as warriors, defenders of family and community, as assertive and skillful traders, strategic thinkers and superb tacticians. The power of community is the power of its men and women. It cannot long survive half slave and half free.

Chapter 4

Consciousness and Power

Consciousness as Power

THE STATE OF BEING CONSCIOUS and states of consciousness are inextricably related but not synonymous. The state of being conscious refers to the attainment and maintenance of a level of physiological and psychological arousal or alertness which permits the conscious being to be aware of, to remember, to recall both past and contemporary, internal and external events; to wilfully and selectively attend to some stimuli rather than others; to deliberately choose and execute an action in response to environmental and personal goals. The state of being conscious essentially refers to a state of wakefulness or knowingness. The state of being conscious enables the conscious being to amazingly and deliberately behave in certain ways for whatever reasons. How the conscious being actually behaves, for what express reasons, and to what end, reflect its *state of consciousness*.

Consciousness refers to a state of mind which includes varying degrees of awareness and which, depending on its particular organization and condition, both facilitates and sets limits on the ability of the individual to engage in various types of mental and behavioral activities. For example, wakefulness is a state of consciousness which facilitates certain types and forms of self-determined mental and physical behavior not possible during sleep as a state of consciousness or vice versa. Each level of consciousness makes the achievement of some goals possible while inhibiting the achievement of others. It includes, consciousness as a *w*holistic mental or psychological state, simultaneously enables and disenables, allows and disallows the individual to achieve certain ends. In both cases it acts as a force which either expands and/or contracts behavioral possibilities. Hence, consciousness is a form of power. What type of power, how much power it exhibits, depends on its level, organizational and functional state.

Wakeful consciousness is an active, goal-oriented, all-inclusive psychophysiological state of being. It includes the operational influence of conscious and unconscious processes as well as the behavioral repertoire and possibilities which can influence the mental and physical behavior of the conscious individual. It encompasses and is largely characterized by the fairly consistent ways the individual tends to perceive, interpret, respond to, and behave toward stimuli based on past and current experience, prior conditioning, perceived knowledge, values, and intentions. These factors interact and coalesce to organize consciousness as an attitude, i.e., as a general and ongoing predisposition to behave in certain ways based on operationally available information, experience, abilities, skills, needs, values, and expectations; on a characteristic world-view and perception of the self.

To possess consciousness is to be possessed by consciousness. For consciousness "takes over" and represents itself in the body as feelings, emotions, tastes, values, intelligence, and behavior. When relatively stable or consistent, habitual dispositions and tendencies which dynamically structure and are reciprocally structured by consciousness, incline the individual or group to act or react in certain fairly predictable ways. Bourdieu (1991) refers to such a set of related tendencies as a *Habitus*. The related tendencies which characterize an individual's consciousness, conjoin to generate practices, perceptions and attitudes which may appear to the individual and others to be natural, cultural, or compulsive in nature. As interpreted by an editor of his work (Thompson, 1991), Bourdieu contends that:

> The body is the site of incorporated history. The practical schemes through which the body is organized are a product of history and, at the same time, the source of practices and perceptions which reproduce that history.

Thompson goes on to contend that Bourdieu's work implies that:

> Structured dispositions are also *durable*: they are ingrained in the body in such a way that they endure through the life history of the

individual, operating in a way that is pre-conscious [and unconscious] and hence not readily amenable to conscious reflection and modification....As a durably installed set of dispositions, the habitus tends to generate practices and perceptions, works and appreciations, which concur with the conditions of existence of which the habitus is itself the product.

The habitus also provides individuals with a sense of how to act and respond in the course of their daily lives. It 'orients' their actions and inclinations without strictly determining them. It gives them a 'feel for the game', a sense of what is appropriate in the circumstances and what is not, a 'practical sense' (*le sens pratique*). The practical sense is not so much a state of mind as a state of the body, a state of being. It is because the body has become a repository of ingrained dispositions that certain actions, certain ways of behaving and responding, seem altogether natural.

Thompson cautions that:

> ...when individuals act, they always do so in specific social contexts or settings. Hence, particular practices or perceptions should be seen, not as the product of the habitus as such, but as the product of *relation between* the habitus, on the one hand, and the specific social contexts or 'fields' within which individuals act, on the other.[1]

In addition to consciousness expressing or representing itself as the habitus, it actively incarnates itself in the organization of the body and the habitual ways the body expresses or deploys itself in the world. Bourdieu refers to this as the bodily 'hexis'. Consciousness as bodily hexis is to a very good extent personal, cultural and political history and mythology incarnate. That is, consciousness as shaped by political history and mythology, as personal experience and beliefs, is "*embodied*, turned into a permanent disposition, a durable way of standing, speaking, walking, and thereby of feeling and thinking."[2] Hence, to shape and organize consciousness is to a measurable extent to shape and organize the mind and body as well as their behavioral deployment and expression.

What we perceive as our ordinary, wakeful consciousness is a very active state of mind, or psychobiological state of being, which involves applying or using cognitive processes — i.e., selectively attending, encoding, thinking, reasoning, recalling, recollecting, evaluating, choosing, imagining, fantasying, daydreaming, processes to achieve

---

1. P. Bourdieu, *Language & Symbolic Power*, ed. John B. Thompson (Cambridge, MA.: Harvard University Press, 1991), pp. 12–14.

2. J.L. Austin, *How To Do Things With Words*, 2nd ed., J.O Urmsson & M. Sbisa, editors (Howard Univ. Press, 1975).

certain ends. In addition, it involves the application of various methods of information processing to what is known, or recalled, believed, anticipated, expected, desired or hoped for, relative to what is not, and using their outcomes to direct or regulate mental and physical behavior in order to achieve some intended result.

The states of consciousness which typify a given individual, his ranges of awareness and organizational character, are structured, defined, energized and purposively directed by sets of values, needs, desires, modes of cognition, self-perceptions, self-concepts, perceptions of others, knowledge, skills, beliefs, emotional tendencies, past experiences, interests, ignorances and expectations that the individual habitually uses to guide his behavior. States of consciousness, particularly wakeful consciousness, are generally organized under the influence of the individual's predominant intentionality or sense of purpose. Of course, this does not negate the fact that the individual's intentionality or sense of purpose is also reciprocally determined by the state and nature of his personal consciousness. That this is the case highlights the interesting fact that human beings are self-conscious and have the capacity to know or be aware of the fact that they are aware or conscious. This "self-reflective consciousness" enables the person to review aspects of his own experience and experiencing; to know that he knows or that he is ignorant. Therefore, through self-reflective knowledge or awareness, individual consciousness can motivate its own transformation, can, through positive and negative feedback based on both internal and external sources, regulate and modulate its own state of being.

The characteristic modes of cognition used by a person, his range, depth and efficiency, deeply influence the nature and operation of his consciousness. They are adjunctive instruments of consciousness. That is, to the degree to which the individual utilizes various modes of logic or reasoning (e.g., deductive, inductive, analogical), modes of thinking (e.g., conceptual, intuitive, analytical), as means of testing reality, comprehending and interacting with reality, for guiding his responses and behavior, determines, within limits, the degree to which his consciousness falls under his own control. They determine the degree to which he can utilize his consciousness as a relatively independent, versatile instrument to adaptively change himself, his behavior, the results of his behavior, and his reality for his benefit. Thus his consciousness and behavior exude power.

Hence, consciousness is a type of intelligence. It is creative, inventive and innovative and is therefore an adaptational instrument in both the reactive and proactive sense, which is used to deal with internal and external environmental demands. It can be used to influence the individual's self and his environment relative to his perceptions, needs, desires and expectations. Its formative past experiences determine the degree and extent to which it is able to generate and sustain the working relations of its internal and external universes in ways which enable the individual to realize his desires. That is, consciousness, the modes of intelligence it characteristically develops and utilizes, is influenced to a marked degree by the types of social relations to which the individual has been exposed during his most impressionable developmental periods.

Social Control Theory: Consciousness as an Instrument of Social Control

Consciousness is a psychophysiological control mechanism. It is an instrument of behavioral control. Through its states and levels, humans control their mental, physical and emotional behavior. However, consciousness can be socialized, meaning that its defining functional contents — methods of processing and expressing information, its guiding values and parameters — are deeply influenced and conditioned by the nature and consistency of our interactions with other human beings and the various social conditions under which we live. In other words, the consciousness that directs the individual's behavior is to a great degree under social control, and is used as a means of controlling his behavior by the culture, society and groups of which he is a member and under whose influence he operates. Consciousness is therefore the premier instrument of social control. Consequently, its contents, character, abilities and intentions are the objects of social concern and social engineering. To control consciousness is to control behavior or at least, to limit its possibilities.

The character and level of consciousness is related to the degree to which it is controlled by its host, by others and by non-human circumstances. Wakeful consciousness represents the highest levels of mental and physical integration. It is reflective of, or is characterized by the highest levels of self-awareness, i.e., awareness of our own mental activity, awareness of the fact that one is aware. Consciousness operates as a regulatory field for behavior and is intimately related to action (Coleman, 1969). To be self-aware, self-knowing, that is, to be aware of and in some degree in control of our own motives and feelings, is to be self-controlling, to possess the ability to exercise voluntary control over our own behavior. High levels of self-knowledge and self-awareness facilitate high levels of self-control, control over impulses; the ability to delay action and gratification; enables the undertaking of constructive critical analysis and adaptive readjustment of one's own behavior; facilitates the routine and creative use of symbols to actively guide thinking and communication as well as to systematically and rationally solve problems. Low levels of self-awareness and self-knowledge bring about the opposite effects. In sum, self-knowledge/self-consciousness = individual self-control, i.e., the relative gain of power over his own behavior by the individual himself. "Other-consciousness" (i.e., where the level and character of individual consciousness is determined by others through social conditioning, through the creation and manipulation of powerful unconscious drives and motives by others) = control by others, the relative loss of self-control and the exercise of an inordinate, possibly harmful amount of power over the individual by others.

Thus, consciousness is about power, whether as generated and exercised by oneself and/or by others. It is the medium by which the individual and others control his state of being and behavior. To the degree that others shape and direct the individual's consciousness, to that degree is his state of being and behavior under their control. To the degree that the individual shapes and directs his own consciousness, to that degree is his state of being and behavior under his control. In sum, consciousness is an instrument of social control and power. It is the means by which personal and social behavior is controlled. Hence, the society and culture, particularly those who represent and exercise societal and cultural authority, seek to shape and direct the consciousness of each of the society's and culture's members in ways which maintain their integrity and advance their (i.e., the society's, culture's and the authorities' — though often not the same) interests. It is through its shaping and directing of individual consciousness that the society achieves social control, i.e., power over individual and social behavior. The socially shaped and directed individual consciousness thereby becomes the society's instrument of social control. The individual empowers the society to control him when he cedes or surrenders the creation and direction of his consciousness to the virtual complete, unquestioned, unopposed control of others who represent the society to him. *It is very important to keep in mind that what we have said here as it applies to individual consciousness, also applies without qualification to group consciousness.* And it is group consciousness that is the central subject of our discussion herein. Helpful to the reader's understanding of our objectives and meanings would be to automatically translate references of individual consciousness to mean group consciousness as well.

> **Box 4–1 The Realm of Alert Consciousness:**
> **The Primary Source of Individual and Social Power**
>
> Consciousness refers to a level of physiological and psychological arousal which permits the individual to be conscious or aware of his internal and external environments and facilitates his ability to regulate his cognitive and behavioral capabilities toward achieving goals he finds desirable. Consciousness is a type of *active* intelligence. By that, it is an adaptational force which utilizes instinctual, habitual, innovative, inventive, and creative approaches in responding to various environmental demands and incentives. Because of its ability to bring about mental, social and physical change in both the individual's internal and external circumstances, consciousness may be perceived as the fundamental and essential form of human power. How much power it represents, the nature and outcomes of its influence on the individual's internal and external worlds, depend on its level of arousal, organizational and functional state.
>
> The organizational and functional state of consciousness which determine the impact it will have on its world depends on the interactive relations between three of its major componental factors: its factual-experiential contents, mental-behavioral instrumentalities, and directional-organizational orientations.

The Functional Elements of Consciousness: How Afrikan Consciousness is Disempowered and Empowered

Consciousness is characterized and determined by its contents, instrumentalities, and directional-organizational factors.

Factual-Experiential Contents: Perceived and factual knowledge/Beliefs/ Attitudes/Opinions/Temperament/Conditioned behavioral and Emotional tendencies/Unconscious motives and drives/Self-perception/World view/ Current perception of internal and external environments.

These broad classes or types of contents, stable personality traits and tendencies are the bases for determining the general character orientation of human behavior.

Mental-Behavioral Instrumentalities: Physical skills/Personal-social skills/ Intellectual-cognitive (e.g., reasoning, intuitive, critical-analytical, problem-solving skills, etc.) abilities/Academic skills/Occupational skills/Learning skills.

Major kinds of intellectual and behavioral skills are utilized to process or operate on the factual-experiential contents of consciousness and to behaviorally express the outcome of that process or operation.

Directional-Organizational Orientations: Needs/Desires/Values/Interests /Aspirations/Ideals/Sense of Purpose/Culture.

These factors are used to decide what problems need to be solved and what goals are to be pursued. They heavily influence which contents and what instrumental methods of processing those contents and modes of expression will be used by the individual to achieve particular ends or to solve particular problems.

The Disempowerment and Empowerment of Afrikan Consciousness

In resolving problems, creating new or innovative possibilities, and adapting to environmental demands, the conscious individual (1) applies one or more of the instrumentalities of his consciousness to process its contents under the guiding influence of one or more of his directional-organizational orientations or values and (2) uses the outcome of his mental-behavioral processes to direct and regulate his mental and physical behavior in order to achieve some intended result.

How is Afrikan consciousness disempowered by White power? White power seeks to disempower Afrikan consciousness by adversely falsifying, limiting, or manipulating its contents and/or impairing or constricting its instrumentalities and/or misdirecting its directional-organizational orientations under the guiding influence of self-serving European-centered values.

How is Afrikan consciousness empowered by Black power? Black power seeks to empower Afrikan consciousness by expanding the factual knowledge base of its contents and making its factual and other contents functionally relevant to resolving the problems of Afrikan peoples; maximally enhancing and expanding its instrumentalities; and by bringing both its contents and instrumentalities under guiding influence of Afrikan-centered directional-organizational orientations or values. ∎

Values as Instruments of Social Control

Values, as a key factor in the individual's orientation toward himself and his world, regulate and direct consciousness. Values are the standards by which we determine what is preferable, appropriate, important, good, desirable, or what ought to be. They help us to regulate and direct our behavior. They give meaning to behavior. Valu-ing involves the making of choices, choices which not only operationally influence behavioral activities, but significantly helps to shape the type of life the individual builds for himself and the kind of person he becomes. However, values, in tandem with the consciousness which they help to guide and direct, are instruments for controlling behavior. Moreover, values, like consciousness, are socialized, in that they are deeply influenced and created by the cultural, religious and life experiences undergone by the individual, as well as the social environment in which he currently operates. Therefore, the degree of self-control an individual or group exercises under the influence of values, is related to the degree to which his or its operative values are intrinsically (determined by his or its own interests) or extrinsically (determined by the interests of others) generated and activated.

To the degree that the values Blacks use to determine their own behavior are originated and controlled by Whites, is the degree Black behavior falls under White control, is the degree Whites retain and exercise social power over Blacks, is the degree Blacks are powerless relative to Whites. This allows Whites to socially control the behavior of Blacks while Blacks believe themselves in control. Black Power requires that Blacks originate their own values and that those values be exercised by them in their own interests.

Cultural values are means by which a cultural group achieves and retains self-control, control regulated and directed by its own values. Culture is a form of social control and as such, is a form of social power; a means by which a people gain power over themselves and their behavior in order to achieve certain desired ends. In this light, it is not difficult to infer that to achieve deep and practical social control or social power over Blacks, dominant Whites had to "deculturate" Blacks, i.e., strip them of their original Afrikan cultures, languages, consciousness, and values in order to instill in them a new subordinate culture and cultural values compatible with White economic and social interests.

Money follows values — we pay for what we value. Afrikans must value things European, things manufactured and marketed by Europeans, thereby enriching and empowering Europeans while impoverishing and disempowering themselves. The degree to which Afrikans value things Afrikan, things manufactured and marketed by Afrikans, they enrich and empower themselves. Thus, to the degree that the operational values which determine Afrikan behavior are truly Afrikan-centered, to that degree Afrikans become self-controlling, self-empowering, and will be liberated from European domination and exploitation.

The character and strength of consciousness is structured, defined, motivated, and directed by sets of values, needs, desires, interests, tastes, emotional tendencies it contains within itself. Therefore, the White Power establishment seeks to determine the character and strength of Black behavioral achievement by its skillful and self-serving manipulation of the values, emotions, needs, and such which influence, regulate and determine the direction and functionality of

Black consciousness. The ability of individual consciousness to have an impact on and to change its relations to its world and thereby change the social order is founded in good part on the adjunctive use his consciousness makes of its cognitive and intellectual faculties. Hence, the White Power establishment seeks to effectively impair or misdirect the development and functionality of those faculties in Blacks in order to misdirect and weaken the consciousness of Afrikan peoples and, consequently, impair their ability to revolutionize the racial status quo. All of the disempowering manipulations of Black consciousness by the White supremacy establishment are powerfully aided and abetted, even legitimated, by its pervasive promulgation of racial myths designed to not only to induce in Blacks a diffuse sense of racial inferiority, but to also induce in them the belief that the character and relative powerlessness of the states of consciousness which characterize them under White oppression — states of consciousness deliberately and purposely created and manipulated by dominant Whites — represent their inherent, innate, God-given consciousness. Thus, Blacks are induced to believe that what is, is what has to be.

Once this inducement takes hold and is identified with by Blacks, their consciousness becomes possessed by a set of White-fabricated predispositions, dispositions and tendencies which incline them to act and react in ways that bring them into an unconscious collusion with Whites in perpetuating their own domination and exploitation.

Group Consciousness

If the sets of values, modes of thinking, beliefs, and much more which define and direct an individual's consciousness are shared by or are compatible with other individuals who mutually consider themselves to be the members of a distinct group; who socially and behaviorally interact in order to achieve mutually desired ends; who initiate and regulate their individual behavioral interests in accordance with the interests of the group of which they are members; who identify many of their personal interests with interests of the group of which they are members; and who see membership in their group as vitally important to achieving both personal and group aims, then it may be inferred that they have generated and share in group consciousness. To the degree that such groups have been formed as the result of a shared or common social history, a shared or common ancestry and ethnicity; have been socialized according to the same or similar social practices as prescribed by the same or similar institutions; have been trained and motivated to act and interact in ways which maintain and advance the interests of the larger society, it can be inferred that they participate in sharing a cultural consciousness.

A group or culture that shares a common consciousness empowers both itself and its individual members. This common consciousness facilitates the achievement of many of the ends desired by both the group and its individual members which would be difficult or impossible for either to achieve if such a consciousness did not operationally exist. Thus both individual power and group power are markedly and mutually extended and enhanced by the operational presence of a group consciousness. To the degree that a group's consciousness is relatively narrow, inflexible or labile, conflicted or ambivalent, its social power is diminished and its ability to assert its will and realize its interests in the world is also commensurately diminished or dysfunctional.

Group consciousness is an adaptational tool, a means the group uses to adapt to environmental demands and adapting the environment to its demands. The presence of group consciousness motivates otherwise exclusively self-interested individuals to cooperatively coordinate and organize their activities as a group toward the achievement of goals they find mutually desirable. The stronger or more powerful the group consciousness the more likely the group is to achieve its aims. Group consciousness is necessary to the self-determination and autonomy of a group, and to maintaining its cohesiveness in the face of opposition from other groups. The strength of group consciousness — the degree to which the members of a group are loyal to its values, committed to its survival and enhancement, and the degree to which the members of a group can work together to defend the group against the negative intentions of others and achieve its aims — depends on:

- the degree to which its members are proudly aware of their membership in the group;
- are esteemed to be identified by others and themselves as members of the group; and
- are revered of the group, embrace it in high esteem, and are committed to enhancing its social status and power relative to other groups.

The power of a group is weakened or destroyed (i.e., its ability to achieve its aims, protect and enrich its and its members' viability) to the proportion its members (a) are ashamed of being members of it; (b) wish to deny their membership in it; (c) crave membership in a rival group; (d) do not hold themselves or their group in high esteem; (e) are alienated or psychologically separated from or resist identifying with the group, its history and culture, ethnic and/or social characteristics, because these seem incompatible with the standards of other groups whom they esteem more highly than their own and whose acceptance, recognition and approval are considered more important than those of their own group; (f) have failed to develop their personal potential, cognitive, social and occupational skills for the benefit of themselves *and* their group because their unwanted or embarrassing membership in it has destroyed their confidence in their ability or need to do so; and (g) if they have developed themselves (within severe limits) and their skills only as means of gaining employment by and/or the acceptance of a rival group.

White Consciousness versus Black Consciousness

As a form of intelligence, consciousness is the central instrument for human problem-solving activities, for guiding the types of interactions we have with ourselves, others, and the environment. It determines the effects we have on the world and, conversely, the effect the world has on us. It is therefore a power; a power because it can enable and facilitate the achievement of certain ends; because it can create, motivate and inform assertive and defensive behavior. Hence, because of its power to determine human social power relations, *the control of consciousness* is a primary objective of interpersonal and intergroup interactions. Because consciousness is instrumental to the achievement of certain ends, one individual or group often strives to shape and control the consciousness of the other as a means for helping to achieve its own goals. This almost invariably occurs where one person or group has inordinate power over another or where one group or person is inordinately dependent on another person or group. Such has been and still is the case with White and Black group relations. Consequently, the consciousness of Blacks, because it is shaped and utilized as an instrument of White Power, exhibits a required restrictiveness of range, shallowness of depth, an overriding level of emotional reactionariness; the underdevelopment and underutilization or misdirected use of a variety of modes of thinking, reasoning, logic and creativity; and a limited breadth and depth of intragroup identity, mutual, concern, love, loyalty, cohesiveness and solidarity.

White Power – Black Consciousness

The relative powerlessness and nature of Black consciousness as the reactionary product of White-Black power relations is operationally created through the sabotaging and manipulation of the fundaments of Black consciousness through their social and educational conditioning by Whites. Since the power of consciousness is related to its available fund and accuracy of knowledge, Whites have determined the strength and potential of Black consciousness by deliberately supplying it with operational non-knowledge or ignorance, inappropriate, inadequate, or otherwise faulty knowledge. The strength and behavioral character of Black consciousness depends on its accurate perception of and its willingness to directly confront and come to terms with reality. Consequently, in order to weaken and misdirect Black consciousness, Whites through obscuring and misdefining reality, by associating its discovery by Blacks with social rejection and with other forms of punitive and painful consequences, have induced in many Blacks a compelling need to also obscure and misdefine reality, to chronically seek to escape from it, and to accept the self-serving depiction of reality by Whites as valid.

The power of Whites as a group to dominate and exploit Blacks as a group is primarily due to their manipulative inculcation in Blacks of the belief in the mythology of individualism, the belief in the purely autonomous, detached, self-defined, self-centered individual who rejects all group identities and loyalties. More important, White power over Blacks rests on the ability of Whites to create and provoke in Blacks feelings of shame, inferiority, low self-esteem and all manner of negative feelings because they are members of a race negatively stigmatized by Whites to begin with. These efforts on the part of Whites have successfully induced in a critical number of Blacks the psychological attributes which characterize a weakened group or inadequate group consciousness. Black powerlessness flows from these deliberately created and sustained psychic assaults on Black consciousness perpetrated by the social machinations of the White supremacist establishment.

No amount of individual achievement or the gaining of personal acceptance by Whites on the part of Black individuals, will remove from them the stigma of their membership in a powerless race. It will not truly enhance their personal power or freedom. The fact that they have to deny an intrinsic part of their being and identity to achieve "success" and White approval means that a crucially important part of their full humanity has to be negated, that their authentic sense of power and efficacy, their need to be loved unconditionally remains ache-ingly unfulfilled. It connotes that they are isolated and defenseless because they must reject the ability of their group to protect and shelter them in times of social and personal upheavals; that their power is a counterfeited, delegated power, conditionally, tenuously and arbitrarily based on their willingness to ally themselves with Whites in their genocidal assault against the interests and lives of their Afrikan brethren whose fellowship they disdain. The racially isolated Afrikan individual will learn too late that he cannot aid and abet the destruction of his "former" race without ultimately aiding and abetting his own personal destruction.

Black Power will be achieved and become a most potent power in the world to the degree that disempowering ideologies, propaganda and social conditioning techniques employed by the White supremacist consciousness and the negative feelings and tendencies they actively invoke are compellingly refuted and neutralized by Blacks themselves. This can be fully achieved only by the reinstitution in Blacks of an Afrikan-centered identity and group consciousness. This can only be achieved when Blacks proudly accept who they in reality are, when they accept themselves as Afrikans and willingly act under the influence of that acceptance to enhance the power and prestige of Afrikan peoples everywhere.

The disempowerment of Afrikan consciousness occurred when it ceased to be Afrikan, to be Afrikan-centered; when it was set adrift from its Afrikan moorings based on a basic knowledge and practice of Afrikan history and culture. The disempowerment of Afrikan consciousness and of Afrikan peoples will continue as long as they deny their inherent Afrikaness, that they are *Afrikan* human beings, not just abstract, identity-less human beings; as long as they are utterly dependent on other peoples for self-definition, self-perception, for their bread of life; as long as they cannot make themselves believe that they have it within themselves, within their culture to do for themselves and to equal or subdue the power of any other people; as long as they believe the fantasy that they shall be accepted as equals by Whites, shall be integrated into some mythical raceless, classless society in the near future or believe that they are hopelessly left behind the leading races of humankind; as long as they do not take responsibility for the creation of their own consciousness.

The Realization of Afrikan Consciousness

Afrikan consciousness will realize its full power, second to none, when it dedicates itself exclusively to the advancement and satisfaction of Afrikan interests before all others; when it bases its organization on a realistic and truthful knowledge of Afrikan history and culture, a truthful knowledge of the history, culture, intentionalities, and powers of the enemies or would-be enemies of Afrikan peoples;

when it acquires a solid and courageous knowledge of reality, and self; when it becomes determined to achieve self-control, high self-esteem; when it achieves self-acceptance, and develops its ability to form more affirmative, affectionate, cooperative intragroup relations; when it produces to and for its own satisfaction; when it organizes itself to overcome and overthrow White supremacy and successfully defend Afrikan peoples against the deprecations of other ethnic groups.

A sense of purpose organizes consciousness and motivates it to develop the required abilities and relations to achieve desired goals. The more intense its sense of purpose, the more is consciousness compelled to develop the mental and social faculties required to achieve its purposive ends. If the central purposes which organize Afrikan consciousness are the lowly ones of futilely seeking to gain the acceptance and love of Afrikans by Whites and other ethnic groups; to be employed and cared for by others instead of being self-employing and caring for self; to continue to be dependent on others for their survival and sustenance, then Afrikan consciousness and its adjunctive abilities and attributes will be lowly and powerless. The royal road to Afrikan Power, to Black Power, to a powerful Black Consciousness runs through the reclamation by Afrikan peoples of their Afrikan identity and their irresistible will to be the determiners of their own ultimate destiny.

Chapter 5

SELF-CONCEPT AND POWER

A CULTURE, SOCIETY, OR GROUP are organized, dynamically structured, social arrangements where members relate to each other in fairly predictable ways over time and space. Generally, the members of a stable culture, society, or group may be seen as playing particular social roles or a set of roles which are more or less designed to achieve both individual and group goals. According to Horton and Hunt (ibid), "The orderliness of a society rests upon a network of roles according to which each person accepts certain duties toward others and claims certain rights from others. An orderly society can operate only as long as most people reliably fulfill most of their duties toward others and are able successfully to claim most of their rights from others."

We must keep in mind that not only individuals make up the network of roles upon which a society rests. Certain groups (e.g., ethnic groups) and social classes also act out and fulfill certain social roles in the network of group roles which characterize a society. The roles individuals and groups play in a society are generally ordered, that is, ranked and classified. Moreover, the social standing or prestige, the material and social benefits, and other social prerogatives the individual or group receives, are generally correlated with his or its position in the hierarchy of social ranks. Hence, a society generally includes a *social order,* "a system of people, relationships and customs operating smoothly to accomplish the work of a society" (Horton and Hunt). As Horton and Hunt contend, "Unless people know what they may expect from one another, not much will get done. No society, even the simplest, can function successfully unless the behavior of most people can be reliably predicted most of the time." However, on a more fundamental level, networks of social roles, of reciprocal rights and duties which define the social order of a society, must consistently be held in place and reinforced if the society itself is to remain functionally stable.

Social roles must be defined and maintained and the members of a society conditioned to fulfill and identify with them. Thus the maintenance of a social order, a social system or society, calls for an underlying system which maintains and regulates its order — a system of *social control*. Again Horton and Hunt provide us with a succinct definition — "Sociologists use the term *social control* to describe *all the means and processes whereby a group or a society secures its members' conformity to its expectations*...the means through which people are led to fill their roles as expected...." One among a number of important means by which a society, more specifically, the dominant group or class in a society, maintains the social order which is beneficial to its interests is through markedly influencing the ways individuals and groups who make up the social order perceive or define themselves. Such a socially conditioned perception or self-definition is generally referred to as the person's or group's *self-concept*. The self-concept is one of the major means by which a person or group guides or orders his or its behavior. Thus, to the degree that a person's or group's self-concept is influenced or shaped by another, that person or group behavior is socially influenced by the other. For better or worse, we must conclude that to the degree to which an individual or group is behaviorally directed according to his or its perception of his or itself, i.e., the degree to which his or its self-concept is conditioned and defined by another, the self-concept acts as an instrument of social control, or more precisely, an instrument of social power. Hence, the self-concept of a subordinate individual or group which has been conditioned and defined by a dominant individual or group provides the means by which the subordinate individual or group is controlled or at least, noticeably influenced by the dominant other. The self-concept of the subordinate party may be said to reflect in its character and behavior the power of the dominant party and, moreover, to serve in effect as the instrument of the other party's power.

In sum, people are largely controlled by being socialized or socially conditioned to perceive themselves in certain ways and thereby to behave in certain ways so as to fill their roles in maintaining a social order. The social order is most efficient and stable when individuals and groups "fill their roles in the expected way through habit and preference" as well as identify with their roles to the extent that they perceive them as defining who they *naturally* are. They and the role become one and the same (Horton and Hunt). If a social order is to function efficiently, "its members must acquire the kind of character which makes them *want* to act in the way they *have* to act as members of society. They have to *desire* to do what objectively is necessary for them to do."[1] When a dominant group conditions the self-concept of a subordinate group, it in effect shapes the character of the subordinate group, "which makes them *want* to act in the way they *have* to act" as members of a particular social order or system controlled by the dominant group. The subordinate group is thereby conditioned by the dominant group to desire, to feel and act in ways which necessarily help to maintain the power of the dominant group and the social order which oppresses and exploits them. Consequently, the subordinate group's self-concept at the same time that it is the instrument of the dominant group's power, is also the instrument of its own powerlessness.

Self-Concept, Ethnocentrism and Social Power

Since we contend that the self-concept is an instrument of social control and power, it is important that we briefly define its composition and development. We remind the reader of perhaps what he or she has already surmised; that our interest in the self-concept is premised on our contention that the self-concept which characterizes Afrikan peoples under the various regimes of White supremacy are the instruments of White Power and, conversely, of Black Powerlessness. This is because the self-concept of Blacks is markedly influenced by the social impositions and conditioning paradigms of Whites. Blacks, through having their perceptions of themselves conditioned by Whites, empower Whites and disempower themselves when they identify with and behave in accordance with their White-conditioned self-concepts. This implies, to anticipate our conclusion a bit here, that if Blacks are to liberate themselves from the detrimental social control and power of dominant Whites, then they must re-define their self-perceptions in ways which will empower themselves.

In our rather cursory analysis of the composition of the self-concept we shall follow the very clear exposition of that concept written by James Coleman. He defines the self-concept and its composition as follows:

---

1. Erich Fromm, *Escape From Freedom* (New York: Holt, Rinehart, Winston, 1941).

Self-Concept and Power ✧ 103

The individual's self-concept is his picture or image of himself — his view of himself as distinct from other persons and things. This self-image incorporates his perception of what he is really like (self-identity) and of his worth as a person (self-evaluation), as well as his aspirations for growth and accomplishment (self-ideal).[2]

Self-Identity — Coleman goes on to posit the body image as central to the individual's (and group's) self-concept. He contends that the individual's:

> ...early perception of [his] physical self is called the *body image* and appears to form the primitive core of his self-concept. Since others perceive and react to the individual — at least partially — in terms of his physical appearance, it is not surprising that the individual's body image may continue to be an important component of his identity and self-concept throughout his life.*[3]

We need not elaborate on Coleman's statements here in terms of their relevance to Afrikan people's self concept under the propagandistic influence of White supremacy's association of Black skin and body with all manner of negative attributes and connotations. The reader is well aware, we are sure, that the internalization of White racist attributes and connotations by Blacks, has done much to inculcate, in Afrikans, a self-concept and self-identity which impair the full development of their positive human potential and severely restrict their range of active possibilities. Coleman goes on to say:

> When we think of *me* or *my*, we may include possessions such as our home, the people we love, the groups we are loyal to, and the values we believe in. Of key importance here is the individual's position and role. The individual is treated in consistent ways by others in accordance with his position in the group; and role behavior considered appropriate to his status is demanded and reinforced by those around him. Thus his self-identity is confirmed by recurrent and relatively consistent social interactions.*

By the means just depicted in regard to individuals, the consistent ways Whites as a group relate to Blacks as a group serve to define the role behavior that Whites consider appropriate to their status of Blacks in American and global society.

Self-Evaluation — Inextricably related to self-identity is self-evaluation, whether an individual or group behaviorally perceives his

---

2. James Coleman, *Psychology and Effective Behavior* (Glenview, Illinois: Scott, Foresman & Co, 1969), p. 62.

3. *Ibid., p. 62.

or itself as good or bad, worthy or unworthy, adequate or inadequate, superior or inferior. In a way similar to his acquisition of self-identity, the individual's (and group) self-evaluation "is heavily dependent upon the way in which others view him" — on the ways he (and it) uses the standards of others "for measuring his [or its] adequacy and worth" (Coleman, ibid). Another term often synonymous with the term self-evaluation is *self-esteem*. To a good extent the individual or group's self-esteem determines what he or it thinks he or it are capable of achieving. A person or group's self-esteem therefore sets limits on his or its levels of aspiration. Thus the self-evaluation to which Blacks subscribe as conditioned into them by Whites, is the psychological means by which Whites seek to limit, fix, and shape the behavioral possibilities of Blacks. Also, by shaping the self-esteem of Blacks, Whites seek to shape and limit the behavior of Blacks as well as make Black behavioral outcomes compatible with the interests of White Power and the maintenance of Black Powerlessness.

Self-Ideal — Coleman defines the individual's self-ideal as his "image of the person he would like to be and thinks he should be..." Like self-identity and self-evaluation, the self-ideal is shaped by social conditioning and experience. It is related to the identification individuals or groups make with various models. Consequently, the self-ideal also sets limits on levels of aspiration. However, the "ideal" self may be markedly different from the "real" self; the ideal may be markedly less or more than what the person is really capable of achieving. In the first instance, the person may suffer disabling underachievement, inner conflict and self-devaluation. Under White supremacy Blacks are often inculcated with impossible self-ideals (e.g., being perceived and accepted as "white" by Whites) which subject them to disempowering inner conflicts and motivate them to behave in ways that perpetuate the power of Whites to define and control their reality and life in ways compatible with White interests which may ultimately prove detrimental to their own.

We can thus surmise that the self and the way the self is perceived and evaluated, the ideals the self aspires to realize, together form a self-system — a system which shapes and determines behavior; which evinces fairly consistent and characteristic ways of experiencing, knowing, striving, doing, thinking, remembering, and reacting that distinguishes a person or group from other persons or groups. These patterns of perception, information processing and behaving tend to be consistent with the person's or group's perceptions of himself or itself, with the assumptions he or it makes concerning him- or itself and the world he or it perceives him- or itself to inhabit. These patterns of thinking, feeling and behaving are subsumed under the concept of the self-concept which typifies the individual or group.

The key elements which are integrated into the self-concept of a group or individual may provide it or him with the power of self-determination, the power to act effectively in its own or his own best interests, or may be the means by which it or he is controlled and made instrumentally to act in the best interests of others and to the detriment of his or its own interests.

Ethnocentrism, Self-concept and Power — One key element in the make-up of the self-concept of an individual or group is his or its ethnicity or race. It is to the role that ethnicity and ethnocentrism play in the making of the self-concept, and in their relationships to the engendering or disengendering of social power that we will now examine. We have indicated that self-identity and self-evaluation are key elements in defining the character of the self-concept. We should recognize that these elements are in good part collective in that many of the perceptions of reality, assumptions, values, motives, behavioral tendencies and goals which underlie an individual's self-concept were inculcated in him by his primary and peer groups and by the society of which he is a member. Many of the perceptions he holds about himself he holds in common with other members of his group and society. Many values the individual ascribes to himself are quite typically ascribed to his group as a whole. For as Coleman (ibid) contends, *"As an individual's experience broadens, his self-identity comes to include things outside of himself with which he feels strong, personal involvement "*[Emphasis added]. One of the principal things with which the individual feels strong personal involvement and which helps to determine his self-concept is his ethnicity. Self-identity, self-evaluation and self-ideal combined as the self-concept, are primally related to and based on the individual's ethnic identity. (Even when and if the individual denies membership in a particular ethnic group, his identity is markedly influenced by the concept of ethnicity — his behavioral and attitudinal orientations are still to a significant degree determined by his "lack of an ethnic identity," by his ethnic "anti-identity". He defines himself by who he is not.) In other words, the ordinary self-concept of individuals and groups is to a measurably important degree *ethnocentric,* i.e., in good part determined by the view the individual or group has of his or its ethnicity.

According to Horton and Hunt (1968) "ethnocentrism is the tendency for each group to take for granted the superiority of its culture.... Ethnocentrism makes our culture into a yardstick with which to measure all other cultures, which are good or bad, high or low, right or queer in proportion as they resemble ours." While it is customary in America, especially among Blacks, to denounce ethnocentrism and to hold it responsible for the most heinous expressions of White racism and racial hatred, it is also important that we take note of the fact that "All known societies are ethnocentric"; [that] "Ethnocentrism is a universal human reaction, found in all societies, in all groups, and in practically all individuals; [and that] "Most, if not all, groups within a society are also ethnocentric" (Horton and Hunt, ibid). When a behavioral tendency may be said to exist spontaneously across all cultures, much the same way that all cultures speak a language, it implies that such a tendency plays a primal, fundamentally positive role in human social existence. *"Ethnocentrism gets us into many of our muddles; yet it is doubtful whether groups can survive without it"* (Horton and Hunt, ibid). Horton and Hunt go on to assert that "ethnocentric groups seem to survive better than tolerant groups." Why does this seem to be the case? For a number of reasons we shall explain.

Ethnicity provides a primary basis for social identity and group definition, organization, and solidarity. As pointed out earlier, ethnicity is a crucial aspect of the individual or group's self-identity, providing both with a sense of place and belongingness. The taking of pride in one's ethnic group is basis for holding oneself in high or positive self-esteem. The level of a group's social standing, success and power is crucially important to its individual members own positive self-esteem, sense of security, well-being and purpose; is of central importance to its members' wholesome existence and functioning; and is central to the promotion of group unity, loyalty and morale. An appropriately high level of group pride (or ethnocentrism) combined with effective group organization, generates group social power. This makes it more likely that the group will provide for the biological, material, social, and psychological needs of itself and each of its members. Ethnocentrism helps to increase a group's probability of surviving and of maintaining its autonomy, thereby providing its members some modicum of protection or freedom from the negative impositions and tyrannies of outsiders. Ethnocentrism provides the basis for a group or national consciousness, reinforces nationalism and patriotism, provides the emotional preparation for identifying with personal and group interests, and justifies and sanctifies individual sacrifices for maintaining group integrity and existence (Horton and Hunt, ibid). Ethnocentrism provides for group stability and solidarity by preventing and/or discouraging the acceptance of alien, perhaps damaging or lethal, elements into the group culture which may lead to its disintegration, subordination, or demise.

Ethnocentrism is an enabling factor in human groups and individuals. Its operational presence enables a group and its members to utilize vital and important means, cohesive group action to achieve ends that could not be achieved otherwise. Hence, ethnocentrism is a central force of power in almost any group. Consequently, "Almost every race, social class, regional or sectional group, occupational group, recreational group, or group of any kind encourages the ethnocentrism of its members" (Horton and Hunt, ibid). Ethnocentrism is akin to the concept of *esprit de corps*, the spiritual heart and soul of a group. Thus when a group's ethnic pride is negated, its ethnocentric self-esteem is lowered; its members are demoralized; its unity threatened by disintegration; its mental and physical agility and stamina fatigued; its power dissipated. This is the major reason why since the slavery period until the present moment dominant Whites have unrelentingly negated Afrikan ethnicity, culture and character in every possible way at every possible level of intensity. An attack on a group's ethnicity is an attack on its center of power. To control the definition and depiction of a group's ethnicity is to control a group's self-definition, its self-perception, and is thereby tantamount to the reactionary control of its behavior.

When the members of a group internalize the negative definition of their ethnicity and a host of negative associations regarding their ethnic identity and character, the organizational ability of the group is severely weakened and made dysfunctional — a condition of relative powerlessness. Since the self-concept helps to motivate and organize behavior; determines interests and tastes, levels of aspirations; determines what abilities will be sharply developed and others left to atrophy; helps to determine the type and quality of the individual's personal attitudes toward and relations with others in his group, with his group as a whole, the shaping of the self-concept is tantamount to shaping all these things. To shape the self-concept is to gain power over personality, or at least, to place limits on its range and capability.

Ethnicity is one central element which helps to shape the individual's or group's self-concept. Therefore, the characterization of an individual or group's ethnicity conveys the power to characterize his or its self-concept. Consequently, the self-concept of individual or group becomes an instrument of power of those who have effectively characterized that individual or group's basic sense of ethnicity to begin with. This mechanism is one of the most influential means by which dominant Whites have gained possession of the Afrikan self-concept and thereby exercise power over Blacks.

However, the White Power that has found its way into the central headquarters of the collective Afrikan self-concept is not often felt by Blacks to be an alien intrusion into their collective personality because as a part of the self-concept it is perceived to be a "natural" or innate aspect of the personality. Hence, to paraphrase Fromm, Afrikans who have internalized an ethnic self-concept depreciated by racist Whites are thereby made to *want* to act the way they *have* to act, to *desire* to do what is objectively necessary for them to do in order to unwittingly collude with racist Whites in perpetuating the system that dominates, exploits, and deprives them of power.

Thus, if Afrikans are to liberate themselves from European domination, empower themselves, enrich their quality of life, they must repudiate the power of Europeans to characterize their ethnicity and through it, gain power over them by characterizing their own perception of themselves. Afrikans must become the primary definers of their own ethnicity and determiners of their self-perception, character and behavior. This means that Afrikans must develop a robust, wholesome ethnocentrism. The ethnocentrism of the European and Asian nations which exercise global economic and military power is notoriously high. No nation of people can arise to power without pride of nation and race.

Ethnocentrism need not lead to racism. Pride of ethnicity empowers a group to best actualize its human potentials and possibilities, to protect its vital interests, enhance its quality of life and maintain its autonomy. This does not require that it abusively dominate and exploit other groups and attempt to justify those activities in terms of racial superiority. Racism has given ethnocentrism a bad name. But Afrikans must not reject positive ethnocentrism for that reason. For to reject positive Afrikan ethnocentrism is to reject Black Power.

Chapter 6

POWER AND PERSONALITY

WE HAVE PREVIOUSLY INTIMATED THAT the power generated and expressed by a particular group reflects in good part its social structure and organization. To a marked degree a group regulates its own and its members' actions which are expressions and instruments of its powers, under the influence and guidance of its collective norms and standards. We have indicated that organized groups tend to generate and express their power in terms of divisions of labor and function wherein social roles and responsibilities, positions of authority and execution are systematically and interactively delineated as means of achieving collective and individual goals. Generally, the social power of a group reflects the appropriateness and efficiency of its organization. However, we must be careful in our discussion of the power of which groups are capable of generating and expressing, not to make their organization the be-all and end-all of their power. For maximizing power a group's formal organization may be necessary without at the same time being sufficient. Because on a more fundamental level the power of a group is heavily dependent upon the abilities and characteristics, in short, the personalities of its individual members who constitute it and perform its organizational roles and functions. James Coleman (1969) very aptly describes the impact of the characteristics of group members on group effectiveness:

> A group's effectiveness depends heavily upon the individuals within it, since ultimately it is individuals who actually make and implement

group decisions. Members with serious personality weaknesses, immaturities, or lack of essential skills may disrupt or prevent group progress, just as mature, competent, and dedicated members help to ensure group effectiveness and success. Characteristics of members — especially in terms of the possession of essential competencies and commitment to group goals — are especially important when the group is under severe stress. A group's loss of dedicated and capable members, particularly those with outstanding leadership skill or other key abilities needed by the group, can be seriously disruptive to group performance and effectiveness.[1]

We may infer from Coleman's exposition that a group's power potential or actuality may be remarkably enhanced or gravely weakened by enhancing or impairing the abilities and characteristics of its individual members. Where the personal qualifications and qualities of its individual members are too scarce or inadequate; where they may suffer conflicting needs, (i.e., needs which pull them in opposing directions); where their emotional conflicts and tensions cause debilitating irritations among them leading to their inability to objectively consider their problems as well as distracting their attention from the tasks at hand, the group may fail to achieve its goals or may reach inadequate or unsatisfactory resolutions of its problems.

In sum, the personality characteristics of a group's membership or the overall general personality orientations of the members of a group heavily influence that group's ability to solve problems. *To a measurable degree the power of a group reflects the power of the personalities of its members.*

Personality Differences as a Division of Labor

In an interesting sense, the personalities which together compose the membership of a group, a society or a culture, provide for a somewhat natural division of labor or function within it. For within limits, individual differences, i.e., differences in personality, among the members of a group, society or culture, function together to enhance the group's survivability and serve to maintain its adaptability. Personality differences within a group provide a pool of alternative ideas and behaviors with respect to customary and routinized ideas and behaviors which, if appropriately utilized, increase the probability of the group's adapting effectively to changing conditions by making needed changes within its own structure and functioning. Personality differences within a group increase the probability that

---

1. Ibid., p. 282.

some person or persons within it may recognize and make other members of the group aware of changing or new conditions, propose new modes of behavior, and motivate other group members to make the necessary changes for effectively dealing with changed or new circumstances.

Since the personalities that compose a group are key sources of its power, are themselves sources of power, it behooves us in discussing the bases of social power, to examine personality as a unit and instrument of the social power of a group, society, or culture. We will begin by posting a working definition of personality and proceed to look at personality as an instrumentality of social power.

Personality as an Instrument of Social Power

We shall define personality, without claims of definitivity, as more or less enduring psychophysically organized ways of thinking, feeling, desiring, and behaving as they are assumed to be partly determined by an individual's fairly consistent or characteristic attitudes, values, perceptions, motives and other abilities — all of which may be said to uniquely describe him or her as a person.

It is important to note in this context that personality is generally perceived as organized, as a dynamic *organization* of traits, tendencies, abilities, intentions, and behavior. The behavior elicited from an individual in response to internal and/or external stimuli is organized, i.e., is an expression of his personality organization. Under normal circumstances human behavior is coordinated, not random, and is initiated and mediated by the organized functioning of an organized brain and body — a coordinated system of *organs,* themselves composed of cellular subunits and homeostatically regulated substances and activities. All of this is to say that the powers expressed by the individual as person and personality emanate in an organized psychological system known as his body. Hence, even at the individual level, at the level of the individual personality, organization, as defined by its many structurally and functionally related levels and complexities, is the base or source of power — of the ability of the individual to solve problems in the world. This implies that the "contents" of personality — its abilities, tendencies, interests, tastes — and the nature of their dynamic organization, largely determine the power of the person, and in the context of our current discussion, the contribution, for better or worse, he can make to his group, society, and/or culture. We reiterate an earlier statement to the effect that one major way of controlling the power of a group is to control the contents, abilities, tendencies, interests and tastes, and their collective organizational expression in its constituent members.

There is a general tendency amongst Eurocentric psychologists to overemphasize the uniqueness or utter differentness of individual personalities. This is perhaps to be expected in a culture whose guiding ideology is that of "rugged individualism" or which idealizes almost unbridled individual freedom, and one which is horrified by almost any form of collectivism, cooperativism, socialism or communalism. However, as we remarked earlier, one of the most remarkable things about individuals is their inveterate tendency to form groups. The gregariousness of humans as well as many other animals has fascinated behavioralists, philosophers and pundits across the ages. What is most remarkable about individuals who form distinct groups is their exceedingly high level of conformity and obedience to customary values, expectations, and legal standards. Even more remarkable is their sameness or similarity of interests and tastes — their apparent love of or need to eat much the same foods and drinks prepared in much the same ways; to be entertained by much the same amusement; to dress pretty much alike; speak the same language; express similar attitudes; like the same kinds of music; and behave pretty much within a rather narrow range of a very broad spectrum of behavioral possibilities.

Perhaps this is not as remarkable as it seems at first when we recognize the fact that an effectively functional group must maintain some necessary measure of conformity and unanimity if it is to achieve its goals in a planned and coordinated manner. In fact, "overlapping" personality tendencies and tastes which characterize the differing personalities of the individuals who constitute a group, provide that group with its necessary degree of conformity; their "non-overlapping" tendencies and tastes, however, provide it with its necessary degree of flexibility, both together being necessary for maximizing its adaptability to changing circumstances. Conformity and unanimity in service essential to coordinated group functioning and effectiveness, serve a basic need of the group for self-preservation and therefore must operationally develop in any organized group. Consequently, in spite of individual differences, organized groups tend to exert some initial and ongoing pressure on their members toward conformity in vital areas of group life. Groups seek to induce conformity in their members through role definitions, setting limits to permissible behavior, convincing them of the validity of group goals and values, conditioning them through the manipulation of a broad variety of rewards and punishments. Moreover, a large proportion of basic and acquired individual needs can best only be satisfied through group activity and institutions. The individual is attracted to the group in terms of his and its commonality of interests, values, and goals; the success and status of the group; its exclusivity; its ability to provide him security and anxiety reduction, and to relieve him of his loneliness and alienation among other things (Coleman, ibid).

More profoundly, the dynamically organized contents, abilities, tendencies, interests and tastes which uniquely characterize the individual, are derived in large part from social systems and culture through socialization, i.e., "the developmental and ongoing social interactions and experiences the individual has had with his social environment."[2] To paraphrase Parsons in reference to how a child develops an attachment to its mother and has its budding personality organized to some significant degree thereby — the organization of the emerging and ongoing personality and motivational system of the individual are functions, not simply of his own independently given needs, but of the way in which his sociocultural group responds to these needs which themselves have been organized. In reference to the infant and the shaping of personality, Parsons contends that "the infant in the first few weeks, if not days, of life comes to be integrated into a social system." And we may add that through the internalization of its symbols the social system is integrated into the personality of the individual. Parsons goes on to contend that the "internalization of the sociocultural environment [brought on by the social relations which the individual has experienced in the course of his life history] provides the basis, *not merely of one specialized component of the human personality, but of what in the human sense, is its central core"* [Emphasis added]. The social system in which the personality is bred, matured and embedded is characterized by an immense inequality of power relationships, especially in its early phases, and the relatively systematic and organized sanctions (i.e., rewards, punishments, incentives) it imposes on the individual, "eventually leads to the learning of a complementary pattern of responses [by the individual], which is also organized and generalized" (Parsons, ibid).

In sum, the predominant social system and those who define and control it, substantially help to shape the organized personalities of its individual members. This means that much of the contents, abilities, tendencies, interests and tastes which uniquely characterize its members, are derived from it and are integrated into their unique personalities. However, the uniqueness of their personalities is like the uniqueness of all the individual waves which make up the ocean — while paradoxically uniquely shaped, they are fundamentally made pretty much of the same stuff. The individual is essentially an

---

2. Talcott Parsons, *Social Structure and Personality* (New York: The Free Press, 1964).

"individuated *social* being."[3] Hence, in spite of its vaunted uniqueness, personality is socializable — that is, it is to an important degree organized by the system of social relations in which it is embedded and with which it reciprocally interacts. Since personality as an organization is a base or source of social power, since its unique organization of contents, abilities, tendencies, interests and tastes is to a measurably important degree determined by the predominant social system of which it is a subunit or member, the social power it generates and expresses is also largely determined by the social system of which it is an integral part. Consequently, the personalities which constitute a particular social system, in spite of their uniqueness, share numerous common orientations promoted by that system and are thereby instruments of that system — and are instrumental to its survival and maintenance. They, in effect, are the power instruments of its social power, of its ability to socially engineer its continued existence and functionality. Thus, personality inherently serves both the individual and society. It is most useful to the predominant social system when it conforms to the needs of the system while expressing its conformity in uniquely personal ways.

Ultimately, personality is a functional social unit of society. Major questions in its study involve asking what function does it serve? Who determines its functions? Who stands to benefit most from its functionality or dysfunctionality?

In the context of White-Black social power relations we may easily infer from the foregoing discussions that the social powerlessness of Blacks relative to Whites devolves in part from the ability of the predominant, White-controlled social system to impose certain patterns and limitations on the organized ability and behavioral tendencies which characterize the multitude of Afrikan American personalities. This imposition creates Black personalities, in spite of their individual uniqueness, whose character, tendencies and behavioral outcomes are compatible with maintaining the White-controlled system which dominates them. Consequently, those personalities become the variety of expressions of White systematic power and its instruments of social power against their own best interests. In a word, Black personalities created and formed by a White-controlled social system are inherently self-defeating. The energy yielded by the conglomerate of Black personalities empowers the dominant White-controlled social system as it disempowers the potential of a Black-controlled social system, or at least a social

---

3. H. Gerth & C.W. Mills, *Character and Social Structure: The Psychology of Social Institutions* (New York: Harcourt Brace Jovanovich, 1953).

system equally controlled by Blacks and Whites. However, Black empowerment and Black power whether epitomized by a relatively autonomous Black-controlled social system or by a social system equally controlled by Blacks and Whites, require that the personalities of Blacks be organized by a Black-controlled social system so that their contents, abilities, tendencies, interests, and tastes are compatible with the self-preserving, liberated interests of that system and the individual interests of its members.

The Other-Directed Afrikan American Personality

The ruling White male corporate elite utilizes a variety of processes to maintain the sociopolitical-socioeconomic system from which it benefits munificently and from which it derives its status and power. A major objective of these processes involves defining and controlling the political socialization of the members of the society to accept elite authority, and arouse in them a certain level of "diffuse support" for the reigning political system. Political socialization essentially involves the conservative process which facilitates the maintenance of the 'status quo' by inducing people to accept the system under which they exist, to accept the decisions of the powers-that-be without question.

It is important to note that as Barbagli and Dei (1977) demonstrate, "political socialization is already present at the preschool age (that is, between birth and five or six) and...its most important phase of development occurs between the ages of eleven and thirteen...." In both indirect and direct ways political socialization involves the transmission and inculcation of values which may influence and help to shape the individual and collective political personality of persons, ethnocultural groups and social classes. The nature of individual and group attitudes toward and responsivity to political authority differ widely, the differences most often reflecting their past socialization, current circumstances and future expectations. Dye characterizes such differences extensively in the following passage. We ask the reader to take the liberty of mentally substituting the word and concept of the "group" where Dye refers only to "individuals" because we believe in this instance, his description applies equally well to individuals or groups.

> Individuals react toward power and authority in characteristic ways. In many different situations and over a relatively prolonged period of time, their responses to power and authority are fairly predictable. Some individuals regularly seek power and authority while others avoid it. Some individuals are submissive to authority, while others

are habitually rebellious. Some individuals try to conform to the expectations of other people, while others are guided by internalized standards. Some individuals feel powerless, helpless and isolated; they believe they have little control over their own lives. Other individuals are self-assured and aggressive; they speak out at meetings, organize groups and take over leadership positions. Some individuals are habitually suspicious of others, unwilling to compromise; they prefer simple, final, and forceful solutions to complex problems. Some individuals are assertive, self-confident and strong-willed, while others are timid, submissive, and self-conscious. There are as many different ways of responding to power as there are types of personalities.[4]

Intergroup Interaction — The nature and character of a group's relative political predisposition, is in important part determined by the nature and character of its intergroup interactions, i.e., its interactions with other groups. In the case of a particular group, e.g., Afrikan Americans, the political disposition of the group is more likely to be reflective of intergroup interactions when those groups are in constant contact and differ measurably in power, influence and prestige, or when one group heavily dominates another, such as the domination of Blacks by Whites. Groups, in ways similar to individuals, develop social role-determined attitudes and behaviors and an awareness of self by their interaction with the environment. "*A role* is a pattern of expected behavior associated with a given position in society..." (Dye, ibid). The emergence or submergence of group consciousness and self-identity in significant part reflects certain types of intergroup relations or interactions just as the emergence or submergence of individual self-consciousness and self-identity reflects certain types of interpersonal interaction over time.

Through the process of fairly habitual and consistent interpersonal relations or interactions, the individual acquires or internalizes a number of influential values, attitudes, and judgments from others. This is called the *socialization process*. By *interacting* with others, people come to understand what is expected of them and to internalize these expectations as parts of their personalities. (The internalization of certain values and so forth, does not necessarily imply that the individual will act according to them. He may act against them. Yet the values have been internalized and act nonetheless as behavioral stimulants. Similarly, a group by interacting with another, may also come to understand what is expected of it and internalize these expectations as a part of its social and political predispositions.)

---

4. Dye, p. 113.

The domination of Blacks by Whites, the establishment and maintenance of White authority over Blacks, of White supremacy, requires that Whites as the more powerful members of the Black-White group dyad, maintain and reinforce a rather distinct pattern of intergroup relations or interactions with Blacks. White domination requires that Whites continuously seek to contain and control the character of the *life space*, i.e., the character of the environment and social experiences which significantly influence the collective and individual personality and behavior of Blacks. The determination of the character of the intergroup interaction between the two groups by Whites, as well as the White determination of the character of Black life space, have been instituted by Whites as a means of producing and reproducing in Blacks a distinctive pattern of Black intergroup (and intragroup) response traits and political predispositional traits generally consistent with and supportive of the continuance of White power and supremacy. By maintaining certain pivotal intergroup relations or interactions with Blacks over time, Whites, in the interest of maintaining White domination, hope to reproduce in Blacks certain relatively consistent and stable predispositions to respond in distinctive ways toward Whites and White authority.

The intergroup political predispositions or response traits Whites expect Blacks to internalize are generally the opposite of or complementary to those traits Whites expect to internalize themselves, particularly Whites who belong to the ruling elite. A brief list of White-Black intergroup complementary power relations, response traits and political dispositions which the White supremacist establishment strives to create and sustain, would resemble in general outline the list in *Table* 6–1.

The process of White supremacy is founded on a Black-White mythical polarity. White imperialism and racism is founded and maintained on the basis of racial distinctions and the cultural/behavioral differences attributed to them. The social meaning assigned to the racial polarity between Black and White permeates every aspect of Eurocentric culture. The social meanings dominant Whites project onto biological racial differences serve the function of rationalizing and naturalizing social differences, that is, making the social and material differences which typify the Eurocentric racial status quo appear to be reasonably justified and naturally what they should be. For as J.C. Smith contends:

> The need for turning the contingencies of history into the determinations of nature is obvious. *A political system can be seen as a social*

Complementary White-Black Social, Political and Personality Role Dispositions

WHITE	BLACK
Role Dispositions	
Ascendance (social assertiveness)	Descendance (social timidity)
Dominance (power-oriented)	Submissiveness (subservient to power)
Social Initiative (active)	Social Passivity (apathetic)
Independence (mastery)	Dependence (servile)
Sociometric Dispositions	
Rejecting of others (exclusiveness)	Accepting of others (inclusiveness)
Discriminate sociability	Indiscriminate sociability
Internally controlled sympathy	Externally uncontrolled sympathy
Expressive Dispositions	
Competitiveness	Noncompetitiveness
Stable social-emotional poise	Volatile social-emotional disposition
Conservatism	Liberalism
Proactive	Reactive
Intellectual Dispositions	
Higher IQ	Lower IQ
Abstract/Conceptual	Concrete/Specific
Analytical	Global
Precise	Diffuse
Obsessive/Compulsive	Distractible/Labile
Basic Dichotomies	
Mind	Body
Culture	Nature
Strength	Weakness
Good	Evil
Reason	Non-rationality
Authority	Obedience
Light	Darkness

Table 6–1

order made up of dominant and servient power relationships. For such a system to be effective, and economical, compliance with the exercise of power must be substantially voluntary. *For compliance to be voluntary, the hierarchical ordering of the power relationships and the exercise of power must be considered legitimate by the subjects of that power.* As Rousseau stated, "The strongest is never strong enough to be always the master, unless he transforms strength into right, and obedience into duty."

A social order is considered by its subjects to be legitimate when it is believed to reflect, comply with, or be in accordance with the natural order. This is how power relationships are legitimized. To this extent, all theories of political or legal obligation, or theories of the moral foundations of government, are directly or indirectly "natural" in the sense that they assume a particular view of nature.[5] [Emphasis added]

White supremacy, whatever form it takes, wherever it exists, must achieve three major goals if it is to socialize Blacks into accepting its "natural" rights of final authority and primary privilege. It must establish the human racial ideal as White in contrast to Black. It must proclaim that Blacks are innately destined to serve Whites, and that the fulfillment of their true nature requires their happy commitment to this service. Finally, it requires that Blacks be persuaded that they are incomplete without Whites and that their highest calling involves the sacrificing of themselves for the benefit of Whites.

White supremacy posits that Whites relative to Blacks are autonomous agents who are free to set and order their own goals and priorities, and are free to act in order to pursue their own ends. Blacks are by nature denied such autonomy and therefore are destined to act to achieve the goals set for them by Whites rather than to act to achieve their own self-determined goals. Blacks are therefore an extension of White agency. How are Blacks induced to "voluntarily" or "naturally" accept the role to which White supremacy has assigned them? This is accomplished by the creation and projection of racial myths against the background of ultimate reality; by associating Black with negative values and associating White with positive ones through myths of White superiority and Black inferiority. Blacks are required to internalize and integrate into their central identity the racial images and roles furnished them by Whites. White supremacy conditions Blacks to achieve this end through its ability to pattern and structure the external and experiential world of Blacks and through this process induce them to unconsciously incorporate into their collective psyche negative views of themselves. Under White supremacy Blacks are socialized or conditioned from conception to serve the will of dominant Whites. They are positively reinforced for conforming to the social roles assigned them. They are made to suffer if they do not conform. Thus is the collective Black personality transformed and shaped to meet the demands of White supremacy.

For Whites, the Black-White complementarity of political predispositions is functional in maintaining their power relations and

---

5. J.C. Smith, *The Neurotic Foundations of Social Order: Psychoanalytic Roots of Patriarchy* (New York: New York Univ. Press, 1990), p. 77.

in maintaining the "smooth," racially "harmonious" operation of the political-economic system. For Whites who wish to maintain their supremacy, a Black population whose general political predisposition would duplicate their own would mean racial conflict and disharmony and a racial struggle for power. The racially negative stereotyping of Blacks by Whites, reinforced by the multifarious forms of racial discrimination practices by Whites against Blacks, functions to reproduce in Blacks orientations and characteristics complementary to those of Whites. Even in the case where the political disposition of many Blacks overlap those of Whites, these dispositions are alienated and restricted in such ways as to motivate such Blacks to be supportive of the fundamental racial power status quo, or at least, not to struggle for the complete reconstruction of the American political-economic system and the neutralization of the White-Black power differential.

The subordination and increased vulnerability of Afrikan Americans to European American authority, Eurocentric ideology and propaganda; their addiction to the consumption of European American-manufactured psychosocial and material products, require that the Afrikan American political-economic personality be predisposed to be rather more easily directed by others or outsiders than by itself or from the inside. It must seek its basic satisfactions and identity in the external world rather than its internal world. In other words, in order for Blacks to more readily respond to the social, political and economic dictates of Whites, they must be more intensely "other-directed" in their personality dispositions than "tradition-directed" or "inner-directed" in contrast to the relatively more self-directed personality dispositions of Whites, particularly the White ruling elite. The terms *tradition-directed, inner-directed*, and *other-directed* were first defined by David Reisman in his book, *The Lonely Crowd*. Dye provides a relevant description of these orientations:

> Modern mass urban society — with its weakened family, community, religion, and social group ties — may increase the individual's sense of powerlessness. In the absence of meaningful social interaction, people search for synthetic ties to replace the ones lost in the process of modernization. They become *other directed* — that is, *decreasingly* reliant on their own consciences and *increasingly* dependent upon other people for their ideas and actions. The other-directed person is easily manipulated by the mass media, by demagogic leaders, and by mass political movements....
>
> The *tradition-directed* character is found in traditional societies, where obedience to the family and adherence to traditional ways of

life are dominant values. Things that are old and long-established are considered good. Traditional norms are the dominant guide for individual behavior. Traditional societies existed in the Western world through the Middle Ages and still exist in many rural areas of the non-Western world.

The *inner-directed* character is associated with the rise of Protestantism and capitalism. Parents implant general rules and norms in the child at an early age. Mature, inner-directed adults have internalized these values and norms and use them to guide their behavior throughout life, regardless of changing conditions or the values of others around them. The values of the inner-directed person in the Western world generally include respect for work and self-sufficiency, a desire for personal achievement and production, strong moral restraints on sexual behavior, devotion to family and children, the postponement and sacrifice of pleasure for future well-being, and emphasis on personal savings and the accumulation of wealth. But the important aspect of the inner-directed person is an internalized "gyroscope" for behavioral guidance. Inner-directed people are punished by feelings of guilt when they violate these inner-norms...For the other-directed person, social control lies *outside*, rather than inside the individual. As parental control weakens, and family and church influences wane, the individual seeks guides for behavior in the approval of peers — classmates, friends, groups, society at large. Other-directed persons have few internal restraints upon their behavior, and so are guided primarily by what is fashionable, what is popular, what others are doing. Instead of guilt, they experience anxiety when their behavior does not conform to group expectations. Their parents want them to be popular, and even the school curriculum emphasizes getting along with others — "life adjustment." The mass media, the advertising industry, and the clothing, music, entertainment, and recreation industries reinforce pressures on youth to be fashionable, "hip," "with it." Other-directed adults care more about what their friends and neighbors think than about what they want for themselves and their children. They are "organization men," seeking security in large corporate or governmental bureaucracies. Their values constantly shift as conditions change and social values fluctuate. They are more concerned with leisure and consumption than work and production, less "hung up" about sexual standards, more interested in the immediate "now" than in planning for the future, and oriented toward spending money rather than saving it.

Other-directed people are powerless in the face of group pressures and their own need for group approval. Conformity results from the need to belong and to be accepted by a group. Individual freedom, dignity and self-reliance are submerged in the necessity for conformity and social approval.[6]

Parsons and White provide us further insight regarding the other-directed person relative to consumption.

> Where the inner-directed person pioneered on the frontier of production, the other-directed is "moving to the frontiers of consumption" — not just consumption of goods, but of words, images, and personal relationships themselves, particularly those aspects that deal with "the minutiae of taste or speech or emotion which are momentarily 'best'." Approval is bestowed on those who embrace the momentarily right consumption preferences, the "fandoms and lingoes" of the peer group.
>
> Since the preferences are momentary and not seen as structured — as was production by the goals of attaining it — they are dominated by swings of fashion. "To escape the danger of a conviction for being different from the 'others' requires that one can be different — in look and talk and manner — from *oneself* as one was yesterday."
>
> Thus the only source of guidance that remains in other-direction is the approval by one's peers of shifting consumption preferences. Or, to put it in our terms, the only determinate reference point is the sanctioning by other agents of performances of an indeterminate nature. In the utilitarian conception, these sanctions become the "glad hand" that replaces the invisible hand; the consumption preferences of the group replace individual wants as "givens."[7]

By attempting to create and maintain the conditions conducive to making the general Afrikan American political-economic personality almost completely other-directed, dominant White America not only discourages Afrikan American striving for autonomy (which can only flow from inner-directedness) by manipulating their attentional focus on the single-minded pursuit of the immediate satisfaction of their needs and desires (many artificially conditioned and stimulated by Whites), on consumption, and on the futile striving for White acceptance; it seeks to limit the imagination, restrict the vision, narrow the range of interests, and lower the ceiling of aspirations of Black Americans compatible with its continuing supremacy.

Thus, we may conclude from the foregoing discussion that the relative powerlessness of the Afrikan American community in good part flows from it permitting its behavioral orientation and attentional focus to be reactionarily manipulated and its political

---

6. Dye, 3rd ed., pp. 130–32.

7. Talcott Parsons with Winston White, "The Link Between Character and Society" in *Social Structure and Personality* (New York: The Free Press, 1964), p. 188.

disposition to be conditionally other-directed by the White American community. Ultimately, the relative powerlessness of the Black community flows from its inability to find a sense of worth, purpose, direction, meaning and significance from within its own history, culture and reality; from its fear of striving for an Afrocentric reconstruction of all of its social-psychological dispositions; from its fear of engaging in a struggle to the death to gain true Afrikan-centered autonomy. But regardless of its trepidation, the Afrikan American community must struggle to achieve autonomy or face the very likely possibility of its genocidal demise.

The achievement of true Black Power by the Afrikan American community and the Pan–Afrikan community first and foremost requires that these communities reconstruct their modal socio-psychological pre-dispositions founded on an inner-directed Afrikan-centered self-knowledge, self-awareness and identity.

Other-Directedness and the Reconstruction of the Afrikan Personality

The other-directedness of the modal Afrikan political-economic personality is compatible with White American and European domination of Afrikans because it permits Afrikan consciousness and behavior to be manipulated by "others than themselves," primarily by White Americans and Europeans. The center of psychological gravity, the source of motivation of the other-directed Afrikan, lies outside himself and in the hands of others than himself. Who this type of Afrikan thinks he is, his self-perception, is the product of the history of his interactions with others than himself, i.e., with aliens. For he has no knowledge of himself prior to his coming into contact with his exploiters and dominators. For him, prior to his captivity and enslavement or his colonization by aliens, especially Europeans and White Americans, he was practically non-existent, unconscious, invisible, or at best, possessed of a savage consciousness and existence he would rather not recall. Consequently, his identity was and is one given him by others; one he infers from how others — aliens — interact with him; one he infers and abstracts from accounts and histories of himself written by his alien exploiters and dominators. Moreover, the world he inhabits is constructed by others, his captors, his past and his future delimited by those who despise him. He is the plaything of the other. Bereft of a knowledge of self, of his own history and culture, subjected to a distorted and twisted sense of his origins and reality, all these conditions perpetuated deliberately by his White handlers, he identifies with the alienated images, history and culture fashioned and imposed on him by alien Whites who are free to re-fashion them, and do when the occasion calls for it. His consciousness, constructed as it is by the other, essentially the reactionary product of his domination by the other, brought into existence by the other, he cannot conceive of a future existence independent of the other, a future wherein the other is no longer in some way supreme. For him, there is no world for him without White people in it, without White people defining it, or world where he is the dominant force and is self-creating and responsible for bringing his consciousness into being and visibility through his interactions with himself and his kind.

The other-directed Afrikan personality is one characterized by subjective feelings of personal and group inadequacy; resentful dependency and submissiveness; conservatism and conformity; intolerance and frustration; either low self-esteem or narcissistic high self-esteem; inadequate or inappropriate self-confidence; negative or socially unproductive relations with others; immaturity; limited imagination and a range of interests. It is a personality designed for powerlessness, gullibility, exploitation, and to futilely seek merger and identification with those who exploit it; fashioned to seek the approval and love of those who spitefully hate it above all else in life.

The other-directed Afrikan personality is a vacuous personality, an empty shell, a bottomless pit, an Afrikan container devoid of Afrikan content and therefore suffering a chronic sense of emptiness, an insatiable craving for satisfaction. The vacuum created in this personality comes from it being emptied of its Afrikan core by its European enslavers. The niggerized version of the original, introjected into this personality by its Eurocentric creators, is designed not to be satisfied — for it is designed to consume...consume things produced by others, consume others like itself, consume itself!

The other-directed Afrikan personality is a wounded personality, a personality produced by crippling blows to its Afrikan-originated ego, to its self-esteem, self-love and self-knowing. Being a wounded personality it is a vulnerable personality, a personality under severe stress and highly conflicted. But an empty shell, subject to insatiable cravings for fulfillment, a wounded personality and suffering from chronic stress and pain, it is a personality vulnerable to addictions — addictions to consumption, religion, sex, excitement, the search for ecstasy, painkillers and sedatives, stimulants, analgesics and hypnotics.

The other-directed Afrikan personality has the feeling of being always under pressure; always under threat; always under attack. It chronically strives to recover its balance, to protect its ego and self-system from further devaluation and disorganizing assaults from others, from aliens, other alienated Afrikans, Afrikans alienated from themselves just as he is alienated from himself. Thus the other-directed Afrikan, intimidated by the other, dependent on the other, is first and foremost a defense-oriented personality. His primary purpose in life is defending himself against further self-devaluation and emotional hurt. His obsessive-compulsive concern is with the alleviation or avoidance of anxiety. As a defensive personality, he is prone to deny and/or distort reality by a multitude of self-deceptive schemes in order to hold on to what he perceives as a tenuous, sane and relatively pain-free existence. However, the other-directed Afrikan personality is so single-mindedly caught-up in defending itself against the assault on its person by others, by aliens; against the disorganization of its ego brought on by its denial of and its attempt to escape from its germinal Afrikanicity, of its fundamental and uneradicable Afrikaness, it neglects the discovery and development of means for ridding itself of the true causes of its displeasures and *dis*eases. So caught up in dealing with the emotional effects rather than the realistic causes of its doldrums, it is unable to develop the means of identifying the true sources of its discontent and of developing and executing strategies and tactics for realistically meeting the demands of its problematic situation based on a creatively planned, dynamic, yet objectively appraised, conscious, rational, and constructive course of action.

Sociogenetic Maladaptiveness

We emphasize the reclamation of the Afrikan identity by Afrikan peoples and their construction of an Afrikan-centered consciousness because we recognize that it was and is the repression of these two factors that made the mental conquest and continuing domination of Afrikan peoples possible. This repression out of consciousness of their original identity and consciousness is essentially what is referred to as "alienation" or "self-alienation." When the repression of Afrikan identity and consciousness, the refusal to learn of Afrikan history and culture are motivated by shame, guilt, anxiety, fear, embarrassment of being identified as an Afrikan (most often induced by the politico-economic machinations of the dominant Whites); when the Afrikan person uses these attitudes and feelings to reject his Afrikan identity and heritage (the identity and heritage being an objective fact whether he accepts it or not), then we refer to that person as "self-hating" or self-alienated. The general attitude is one of "self-hatred." In being ignorant of (self-alienated) or in rejecting his objective historical/cultural identity (self-hatred) the person is compelled to assume a new identity, albeit a false one, or suffer identity confusion, ambivalence, or a lack of self-definition usually characterized by a chronic search for purpose and meaning.

The important thing to note at this juncture is that attitudes of self-alienation or of self-hatred and the behavioral tendencies that these attitudes generate, e.g., assuming a new identity, are themselves induced in the self-alienated or self-hating person or group by a powerfully dominating alien group. This powerful, or dominant, group deliberately induces these attitudes in the subject group by denying it the knowledge and practice of its history and culture; by denigrating and negatively distorting its history and culture; by punishing any attempt on its part to positively identify with its history and culture, as well as by rewarding it for assuming a new and false identity compatible with the interests of the dominant group. The false or alienated identity of the subject group, if compatible with the interests of the dominant party, supports and often strengthens the dominant-subordinate relationship, i.e., maintains or enhances the power of the dominant party and increases the benefits it receives from the relationship, while simultaneously maintaining or accelerating the relative powerlessness of the subordinate party. Ultimately, the subordinate party may become exhausted by the relationship. A subordinate group is other-directed to the degree to which it is ignorant of the processes by which its collective personality has been and is created, shaped or conditioned by the dominant group; the degree to which it is unaware of the fact that it is psychologically and behaviorally motivated and directed by the dominant group; believes itself to be self-directed when such is not the case; it has been unconsciously induced to behave in ways which maintain, if not enhance, its subordination by the dominant group. Thus, it perpetuates its own subordination, its own powerlessness and exploitation.

Working against their self-interests on the part of the dominated, works best when they are falsely assured that they are working for themselves and in their best interests. This deceptive orientation is achieved when the dominated identify completely with a character and general behavioral disposition created for them and introjected into them by their oppressors. Even if the artificial character and disposition of the dominated are seen by many of them as unattractive, deficient, maladaptive and inferior, the sources of social ridicule and social rejection, especially by their oppressors whose acceptance they crave beyond all else, they will tend to see such a character and disposition as inherently their own. They come to believe that their faulty character and disposition were thrust upon them by fate or divine curse. For the mechanism of how important segments of their faulty character and dispositions have been conditioned into them by their oppressors is hidden from them as have been the knowledge of how these orientations empower their oppressors as they disempower themselves.

The Socioeconomic Functions of the Maladaptive Afrikan Personality

The pervasive political-economic condition of Afrikan Americans is that they are under European American domination, that they are first and foremost a dominated, dependent people. Afrikan American dependency *benefits* European Americans, who dominate them and condition their dependency. Both Afrikan Americans and European Americans are to a significant degree defined and identified by the power relations of domination. One cannot be fully characterized without reference to the other. Yet their characterization requires that they be defined in opposition, as complementary, mirror images of one another. Their power differentials, relations and social, political, economic roles require an opposition in character and complementarity in disposition if the relations of White domination are to operate with maximum efficiency.

> [W]e cannot give an undistorted account of 'a person' without giving an account of his relation with others. Even an account of one person cannot afford to forget that each person is always *acting* upon others and *acted upon* by others. The others are there also. No one acts or experiences in a vacuum. The person whom we describe, and over whom we theorize, *is not the only agent in the 'world'*. How he perceives and acts towards the others, how they perceive and act toward him, how he perceives them as perceiving him, how they perceive him as perceiving them, are all aspects of the 'situation'. They are all pertinent to understanding one person's participation in it.
>
> * * * *
>
> All 'identities' require an other: some other in and through a relationship with whom self-identity is actualized. The other by his or her actions may impose on self an unwanted identity.[8]

Basically all the important behavioral and characterological orientations which inhabit Afrikan Americans may be depicted by others and themselves as flaws — maladaptive or maladjustive, self-

---

8. R.D. Laing, *Self and Others* (Baltimore, Maryland: Penguin Books, 1971), pp. 81–82.

defeating and self-destructive, perhaps neurotic and psychotic flaws. All the important social problems which may be defined as socially dis-empowering and socially dysfunctional for the Afrikan American community are to a very measurable degree conditioned by their domination by European Americans, including many of which on first sight appear to be "self-inflicted."

To more fully and productively understand the Afrikan American character and disposition, particularly those factors which are self-defeating and dis-empowering, it is important to begin with and keep in mind the political-economic context in which the collective Afrikan character is conditioned and shaped as well as acted out. It is also important to continue to ask the questions: Who benefits from the typical orientations and behavioral tendencies of the subordinated Afrikan personality? How and in what ways? Any adequately logical and evidentiary attempt to answer these questions will reveal the following concatenation of facts and outcomes:

• Afrikan Americans are dominated by and dependent on European Americans.

• European American domination generates basic social problems for Afrikan Americans (also for European Americans but in an importantly different way).

• White domination therefore generates and maintains the social problems (e.g., academic underachievement, criminality, poverty, mental maladaptiveness, etc.) of Afrikan Americans.

• Domination (and exploitation) of Afrikan Americans benefits European Americans materially, socially and psychologically.

• In sum, European Americans benefit from the social problems generated and maintained by their domination of Afrikan Americans and are therefore motivated to continue to maintain those social problems.

Since European Americans benefit from the social problems their domination of Afrikan people generates, they have an investment in perpetuating the symptoms resulting from these problems and in interacting with Afrikan Americans in such ways as to reinforce those symptoms and/or create new ones.

Moreover, the social problems presented by Afrikan Americans (*recall*: problems generated by European domination of Afrikan Americans) are utilized by European Americans as evidence which justifies and supports their domination of Afrikan Americans.

Following the logic of William Ryan, European American domination creates social problems and maladaptive behavioral tendencies in Afrikan Americans. The European social research establishment "discovers" and identifies these problems and maladaptive tendencies. It then studies how Afrikan Americans are affected (infected?) by these problems and tendencies and how they differ from European Americans and other supposedly unaffected groups — and concludes that the *differences* between Afrikan Americans and the other groups are the causes of their social problems and maladaptive behavioral tendencies, not the power relations of domination and exploitation to which they are subjected. Finally, the alleged differences which characterize Afrikan Americans and the social and personal deficiencies these differences generate are used by the dominant European Americans to further justify, rationalize and sustain their domination and the power relations which make such domination possible.

The Reconstruction of the Afrikan Personality

Of course, the means by which the other-directed Afrikan can resolve his problematic situation cannot be supplied him by the other, the alien. For it is the other, the alien, who profits most from his problematics, who is invested in his dilemma, who above all *is* his problem. As the other-directed Afrikan's problems began with his loss of his Afrikan-centered self, his Afrikan consciousness and identity, they can only be resolved through their re-discovery, reclamation and integration into his self, consciousness and identity. There can be no substitutes. This means that the true empowerment and liberation of Afrikan peoples can only be achieved in the process of the Afrikan-centered reconstruction of the Afrikan personality by means of the re-education of Afrikan adults, adolescents and children in accord with Afrikan-centered curricular regimen.

Kwame Agyei Akoto impressively defines the essence and ideology of what is meant by Afrikan-centered education:

> Afrikan centered education is rooted in the unique history and evolved culture of Afrikan people. It is defined in its singular commitment to the elucidation of that history, that culture, and the confirmation, invigoration and perpetuation of the Afrikan collective identity that emanates from that history and culture. Afrikan centered education is concerned with the origins, current status and future of the Afrikan world. Afrikan centered education is committed to correcting the historical distortions born of three millennia of foreign invasion, destruction, enslavement, physical and mental

colonialism, cultural disruption, and dependency. Afrikan centered education is committed to rooting or anchoring the spiritual and intellectual energies of Afrikan people in the spiritual, moral and philosophical traditions of Afrika. Afrikan centered education, whether in the several nations of the diaspora or on the motherland, is concerned to fully develop the sense of Afrikan nationality within a broader Pan Afrikan world. Afrikan centered education is concerned to sever irrevocably the pathological and slavish linkage of Afrikans to the European or Asian ethos. Afrikan centered education is concerned to enable the Afrikan person with nationbuilding, nation management, and nation maintenance abilities. Afrikan centered education is concerned to motivate teacher, student, parent and community to advance the Afrikan nation/world by any means necessary.

Historical and Ideological Currents

The future of the Afrikan world must begin with a confirmed sense of Afrikan nationality defined within the universe of Afrikan spiritual, moral and philosophical traditions and committed to the material and spiritual development and independence of the Afrikan world. Only an unambiguously Afrikan centered education can possibly accomplish this goal.

Afrikan centered education is to be distinguished from the current educational philosophies being employed in independent Afrikan nations and national enclaves in the Americas, Asia, the Pacific, and Europe. Afrikan centered education rejects the implicit and explicit superiority of European and Asian intellectual, political, and spiritual traditions that characterize the systems of former colonies, dependencies, and slave populations of the Afrikan world. It rejects the false historical notion that Asian (Arabic) and European civilizations rescued Afrika from barbarism and godlessness. Afrikan centered education seeks to restore the traditions of Afrika to prominence, to revitalize those traditions and imbue them with the liberating and progressive dynamics of nationbuilding.[9]

Akoto's Afrikan Centered Thematic Inventory provides "the major recurrent themes in Nationalist/Pan-Afrikan theories of liberation... [and] the philosophical foundation of the Afrikan centered curriculum." It is presented in abridged form below. Following the inventory is a representation of Akoto's "Curricular Domains", which "provide the basis for the organization of the subject matter within [a prototypical Afrikan-centered] ...curriculum."

---

9. Kwame A. Akoto, *Nationbuilding: Theory and Practice in Afrikan Centered Education*. Washington, D.C.: Afrikan World Institute, 1992), pp. 46–7.

The Afrikan Centered Thematic Inventory

I. *Spirituality and the Psycho-Affective*

SPIRITUAL AWARENESS

Aim:
> To transmit the knowledge of Afrikan spiritual tradition, and develop an appreciation for tradition and the ability to apply the major principles to self, family and community

MORAL CONSCIOUSNESS

Aim:
> To foster an understanding and willingness to be guided by those principles that characterize the righteous and just person

FAMILY AS BASIC SPIRITUAL AND MORAL UNIT

Aim:
> To develop an understanding and appreciation for the dynamics affecting the Afrikan family; to recognize its centrality to the Afrikan nationality, and work to revitalize it

SELF-KNOWLEDGE/PRACTICE

Aim:
> To facilitate the achievement of total knowledge of self as a unique extension of the collective, defined by the collective and committed to it

ANCESTRAL VENERATION

Aim:
> To facilitate the acquisition and valuing of the wisdom of the ancestors; and to foster a commitment to restore their works and make those works even better than before

II. *Cultural and Ideological*

THE PRIMACY OF AFRIKAN CIVILIZATION AND THE
AFRIKAN ORIGIN OF THE HUMAN SPECIES

Aim:
> To develop and inform a complete and more comprehensive historical consciousness, from antiquity to the contemporary, that will be the basis for Afrikan unity and development

AFRIKAN HERITAGE AND CULTURAL UNITY

Aim:
> To develop an appreciation of the need to foster cultural, and political unity among all Afrikan people, and to commit oneself to that task

AFRIKAN CENTERED HISTORICAL PERSPECTIVE
(Afrikan Perspective on all Knowledge and Intellectual Endeavor)

Aim:
> To develop a commitment to reconstruct Afrikan culture through the reclamation of Afrikan history and the critical/creative analysis of all knowledge and experience from an Afrikan centered perspective

IDEOLOGICAL CLARITY AND COMMITMENT

Aim:
> To foster an identification with and a desire to participate in the ongoing dialogue aimed at creating a coherent and dynamic Afrikan/nationalist ideology for the liberation and independence of Afrikan people

BEAUTY AND AESTHETICS

Aim:
> To foster the development of a sense of the beautiful and righteousness that is Afrikan centered

WHITE SUPREMACY AND RACISM

Aim:
> To develop an awareness and sensitivity to the dynamics of white supremacy. To facilitate the development of personal and collective strategies to counteract the effects of racism/white supremacy

III. *Socio-Political and Economic*

PAN AFRIKAN POLITICAL AND ECONOMIC UNITY,
COOPERATION AND DEVELOPMENT

Aim:
> To instill commitment to developing Pan Afrikan cultural, political and economic unity and cooperation

AFRIKAN AMERICAN NATIONALITY

Aim:
> To foster the commitment to the development of an organized, unified, productive and dynamic nationality of Afrikans in America

NATIONAL AND COMMUNITY LEADERSHIP

Aim:
> To develop an awareness of the necessary qualities of leadership and to inculcate those necessary values and skills of leadership that are essential to the liberation and development of Afrikan people

COEQUALITY OF MEN AND WOMEN: EQUAL RESPONSIBILITY
AND PARTICIPATION

Aim:
To develop a sensitivity and commitment to eliminate any behaviors typical of sexism and sexual exploitation

DEMOCRATIC PLURALITY OF RACIAL/ETHNIC NATIONALITIES
IN THE AMERICAN POLITICAL ECONOMY

Aim:
To foster a profound awareness of the psychic and constitutional entrenchment of the white racial/ethnic supremacy in the U.S. and to advance the Afrikan nationality within the "nation of nations" that the American political economy in fact is

HUMAN AND CIVIL RIGHTS

Aim:
To foster an awareness of one of the higher goals of social activism, the creation of a world order that is culturally pluralistic and truly democratic, equalitarian, and just

IMPEDIMENTS

Aim:
To inculcate a clear understanding of the historical impediments to Afrikan liberation and development, and further to provide a clear criteria for identifying and handling those less obvious impediments to the advancement of the race

INSTITUTIONAL GOALS

Aim:
To foster a clear understanding of our mission to build the institutional infrastructure of an independent nationality, and to foster a conscious commitment to advance the Afrikan nation and race toward independence and freedom, and the human race toward greater humanity

Curricular Domains

The five curricular domains provide the basis for the organization of the subject content within the curriculum. Each curricular domain consists of one or more curriculum fields. The curriculum fields provide the actual structural basis for the organization and presentation of subject matter within the curriculum. The purpose of listing the several fields under the curricular domains is to establish their relationships with the assumptions and aims of the ACTI [Afrikan Centered Thematic Inventory]. The curriculum fields are listed below under the curricular domains, and include the subject areas that would comprise the respective fields.

I. Cultural/Ideological
   A. Culture and Ideology
   B. Creativity

II. Spiritual/Psycho-Affective
   A. Self Knowledge
   B. Ethics and Morality

III. Socio-Political and Economic
   A. Political Economy
   B. Cognition and Inquiry
   C. Technology
   D. Mathematics
   E. Sciences
   F. Computer Sciences

IV. Technology
   A. Mathematics
   B. Science
   C. Computer Science
   D. Functional Skills

V. Nationbuilding (Practical Applications)
   A. Career Development Apprenticeships
   B. Research Theory and Practicums
   C. Community Development Projects
   D. Organizational Experience

Each curricular domain includes several specific subjects that are integrated to reduce the compartmentalization that is typical of subject centered curriculums.[10]

We endorse Akoto's proposals and regard them as excellent working models for the education of Afrikan peoples into the reclamation of their god-given identity and source of liberating power. In his ground-breaking work, *The Afrikan Personality in America: An Afrikan-centered Framework*, Kobi Kazembi Kambon (a.k.a. Joseph Baldwin) describes in detail the structure and basic traits of the prototypical Afrikan personality. The acquisition of this personal-orientation would permit Afrikan peoples to rid themselves forever of the eurocentrically-created, other-directed Afrikan personality — the personal and collective source of Afrikan powerlessness — and to empower and liberate themselves through the reclamation of their Afrikan heritage, identity and destiny. Our Afrikanicity is our power.

---

10. Ibid., 129–47.

Summary: The reclamation of their Afrikan identity and the construction of an Afrocentric consciousness by Afrikan peoples is crucial to the empowerment of the Afrikan individual and the Pan–Afrikan community. Such a reclamation of identity and transformation of consciousness would permit Afrikans to shed their "other-directed" personality and behavioral dispositions, to greatly diminish their reactionary orientation to the world, particularly their reactionary relationship to European Americans and other ethnic groups. This would greatly reduce the power of these groups to adversely shape the attitudes, interests, motives and behavior, and consciousness of Afrikan peoples and thereby markedly reduce their ability to exploit, manipulate and dominate them as well. The Afrikan-centered personality is primarily pro-active in orientation. It is a self-defined, self-directed personality that is both "inner-directed" and "tradition-directed" as well as responsive to immediate and future reality. *It is an autonomous construction, not one created and motivated by aliens.* Its potentials and resources are developed and utilized primarily for its own perpetuation and enhancement, and for the benefit of humankind.

Chapter 7

CLASS, RACE AND POWER IN AMERICA

Social Classes and Class Conflicts

ALL COMPLEX SOCIETIES ARE CHARACTERIZED by the uneven distribution of wealth and income, prestige, privilege, authority, and power. They also exhibit unequal levels of consumption, differences in styles of life, attitudinal-behavioral orientations, and sets of values among the individuals and groups who constitute them. These uneven distributions and differences among individuals and groups that constitute a complex society provide the bases for ranking them according to class as well as on other measures of relative degrees of inferiority and superiority. As noted by Dye:

> ...*the most important bases of stratification in a modern industrial society are the different roles that individuals play in the economic system.* Individuals are ranked according to how they make their living and how much control they exercise over the livelihood of others.[1]

Social class simply refers to all individuals who occupy a broadly similar category and ranking in the stratification of a social system. Social class may be defined functionally, i.e., in terms of its division of labor, such a division deemed necessary for maintaining the

---

1. Thomas R. Dye, *Power and Society*, 3rd ed. (Monterey, CA: Brooks/Cole, 1983) p. 58.

structural and functional well-being of the society. Certain occupational and social positions may be perceived as more important to a society's survival than others, requiring the acquisition and possession of special skills, special abilities, training and resources, motivation and other personality characteristics not equally shared by others. Individuals occupying such positions may incarnate the prestige and power associated with these higher-ranked social positions and the conferred advantages and privileges such positions may offer. Social class may also be defined as the outcome of ongoing social competition and conflict between individuals and groups over *scarce* resources including property, income, wealth, power and prestige, the outcome of competition and conflict between those who may already possess or control such resources and those who do not; between those who want to take possession of such resources or who wish to see them more equitably shared and distributed, or who want opportunities to gain access to them remain equally open to all seekers. Class conflict may not inevitably result from the mere inequality of distribution of material and social resources, power, and prestige among various individuals and groups in society. For all members may, to a significant degree, share and accept an ideology which "explains and justifies the distribution of power and reward in society ...[such acceptance thereby helping] to reduce tensions between the classes [or groups], perhaps maintaining class harmony of a sort" (Dye). Class conflict may ensue, however, when higher-ranked classes are perceived by the "have-nots" as having gained and as maintaining their positions by immoral means, at the expense of the other classes; as seeking greedily to expand their possession and control of social resources and products; as seeking to monopolize social and material resources while depriving the others of their rightful and necessary share of them; as seeking to protect their position in society and to confer their advantages on their descendants exclusively; as self-servingly restricting occupational opportunity and social mobility by using various forms of political, economic and physical oppression.

Social Class and Ethnicity in the United States

The United States of America is a nation-state. As such, it contains within its well-defined borders a fairly large and concentrated multiracial population whose conduct, institutions and economy are regulated by a recognized central government. It is a pluralistic society where wealth, income, property, authority, prestige, privilege, and power are markedly and unevenly distributed according to race or ethnicity, and social class standing. Indeed, the uneven distribution of goods and services, resources and privileges, power and prestige among individuals and groups, (a form of distribution legislated, administered, and maintained by the central government through the use of positive and negative sanctions, justified and explained by a generally accepted cultural and social mythology-ideology) provide the bases for classifying and ranking these individuals and groups according to levels of class and degrees of superiority and inferiority.

American society's superordinate race and classes are peopled by Whites of mostly western European descent. Its most subordinate race and classes are peopled by Blacks of mostly western Afrikan descent. Decisive governmental and social political power are centered in the White race, especially in a relatively small, virtually all-White male, generally hereditary, elite. In this White-dominated nation-state the Afrikan American population, though internally stratified along class lines, is essentially incorporated as a tributary, servant/consumer-orientated, social caste. White elitist domination is dependent on a fully-developed system of power relationships synonymous with the organized state and on White elitist-controlled governmental and economic power employed to legislate and enforce order among the various subordinate peoples and classes. The predominance of White power, or more accurately, of White corporate elite class power, is maintained by the backing of the centralized authority of the U.S. federal government, whose authority itself is backed by the military, paramilitary, and coercive power it has at its disposal. This use of governmental power is legitimated by a generally accepted sociocultural mythologized ideology designed to justify the class-racial status quo.

The upper, White corporate class which generally possesses and controls the largest amounts and most highly valued productive properties and boasts the highest income, power and prestige, is essentially motivated by and organized to realize its desire to consolidate its superordinate position in both the national and international communities. Dye, in his comments regarding C. Wright Mills' *The Power Elite*, aptly describes the characteristics of the ruling White elite:

> The *unity* of the top elite rests on several factors. First of all, these people are recruited from the same upper social classes; they have similar education, wealth, and up-bringing. Moreover, they continue to associate with each other, which reinforces their common feelings. They belong to the same clubs, attend the same parties, meet at the

same resorts, and serve on the same civic, cultural, and philanthropic committees. Members of the elite incorporate into their own viewpoints the viewpoints, expectations, and values of those "who count." Factions exist and individual ambitions clash, but their community of interest is far greater than any divisions that exist. Perhaps what accounts for their consensus more than anything else is their experience in command positions in giant institutions.[2]

He goes on to note that:

Power in the *executive branch* [of the U.S. government], which most analysts now see as more important than Congress in policy formulation, is also exercised by individuals from the [White] upper and upper-middle classes.[3]

Throughout the history of America the white corporate elite has utilized the government and the social system for its own self-aggrandizement, self-enrichment, and political-economic hegemony. This trend has reached tremendous proportions in the last two decades, especially during the Reagan-Bush administrations. The economic and political power gaps between White and Black America, between rich and poor America have widened alarmingly. In January 1991 the Census Bureau reported that the typical White household was 10 times wealthier than the typical Black household. During the last decade and a half the richest *one* percent of American families achieved the largest gains in prosperity. Three-fourths of the increase in pre-tax income went to the wealthiest 660,000 families out of a total of 66 million families. While Black inner-cities experienced actual declines in income and phenomenal increases in unemployment, "the average pre-tax income of families [almost exclusively White] in the top percent swelled to $560,000 from $315,000, for a 77 percent gain in a dozen years...in constant dollars" (*New York Times*, 3/5/92). By the end of the 1980s business executives were earning 120 times as much as the average worker, up from 35 times as much as in the mid-1970s. Aiding and abetting the accelerated enrichment of the rich and impoverishment of the poor was the fact that the top one percent paid slightly less than 27 percent of their income in taxes in 1989, compared with more than 35 percent in 1977. On April 21, 1992 the *New York Times*, citing Federal Reserve and Internal Revenue Service data, reported the following:

By 1989, *the top 1 percent* (834,000 households with about $5.7 trillion of net worth) *was worth more than the bottom 90 percent of*

---

2. Ibid., p. 77.
3. Ibid., p. 75.

Americans (84 million households, with about $4.8 trillion in net worth).

The *New York Times* (10/5/93) reported that the most affluent one-fifth of all families had incomes averaging 8.4 times the poverty level in 1992, compared to six times that level in 1967. This occurred at the same time that the least affluent one-fifth of all families saw their income decline from 97 percent of the poverty level in 1967 to 91 percent in 1992. The poverty rate for Blacks was 33.3 percent in 1992, nearly three times the 11.6 percent rate of Whites. The *Wall Street Journal* (10/5/93) reported that the richest 20 percent of households accounted for 46.9 percent of the nation's income, while the poorest 20 percent accounted for just 3.8 percent of income.

A more telling comparison concerns the fact that total income earned by 400 full-time workers paid the minimum wage of $4.50 an hour for 50 weeks a year, which equals $3.6 million, does not equal the salary of the average chief executive at a large corporation — $3.8 million.

The hugely increasing wealth of the wealthiest families in America is not merely the result of salary and earnings increases, increases in the value of money and capital market instruments, property-holding and reduced federal taxes, but is also the result of federal entitlement spending, i.e., federal benefit payments to individuals. As reported by the *Atlantic* (April, 1992), "...only *one of every eight* federal benefit dollars actually reaches Americans in poverty." It further reported that "the most affluent Americans actually collect more from the welfare state than do the poorest Americans." Moreover, the magazine reports:

> the aggregate amounts received by the non-needy in 1991 were staggering. One half (at least $400 billion) of all entitlements went to households with incomes over $30,000. One quarter (at least $200 billion) went to households with incomes over $50,000.

If we were to add to the enormous entitlements the wealthiest classes receive from government (some of which were merely alluded to above) including inflated monies earned by the military-industrial complex and various types of government procurements, consulting services, and subsidies of all shapes, forms and fashions forged by these classes, it would be glaringly obvious that the elite classes are *looting* the nation's treasury, pillaging its resources, and "mugging" its working and poorer classes. And yet the paradox is that these poorer classes (including Black Americans) seem to approve of their exploitation by the reigning elite when judged by the fact of their repeated voting into office national, state and local regimes those who serve as the instruments for facilitating their wholesale robbery by the elite classes. More succinctly, the paradox is that Black America while complaining of oppression and exploitation by White America has not consolidated its own considerable resources and reorganized its community so as to revolutionize its power relationship with White America and end its subordination to that community. Even though the scope of this volume will not allow adequate answers, we must at least tentatively ask: *By what means does the ruling White elite, and by extension the White race, maintain its political-economic dominance and power over America in general, and Black America in particular?* This question suggests the counter question *central* to this book: By what *means* and *methods* of organization can Black America markedly attenuate or neutralize the power of White America — White domination — and its economic exploitation by this and other ethnic groups?

The White Elite Power Structure and the White American Nation-within-a-Nation

White political and economic domination of America is founded on the fact that Whites are an exclusive nation on American soil. They are organized as a state-within-a-state, having firmly established their own political system and central government, their own economic system, cultural and social institutions and hierarchical social class structure. Additionally, this nation of Whites maintains a standing military establishment of enormous war-making and defensive prowess, a preponderant national guard establishment and police force. Through these armed services it seeks to maintain both internal and external order in the interests of its national and international hegemony. The White nation-within-a-nation is practically always misidentified as synonymous with the United States as a whole by both its White and non-White "citizens" and by the peoples and governments of other nations. Even a cursory review of the history and current social dynamics of American race relations leads one very rapidly to the same conclusion as expressed by Andrew Hacker, a foremost scholar in the field.

> America is inherently a "white" country: in character, in structure, in culture. Needless to say, black Americans create lives of their own. Yet, as a people, they face boundaries and constrictions set by the white majority. America's version of *apartheid*, while lacking overt legal sanction comes closest to the system even now being reformed in the land of its invention.[4]

---

4. Andrew Hacker, *Two Nations: Black and White, Separate, Hostile, Unequal* (New York: Macmillan, 1992), p. 4.

Hacker goes on to assert, "Rather than as a cauldron [melting pot], many commentators today prefer to see America as a mosaic or even a lumpy stew. At best, the pot still contains plenty of unmelted pieces." As a nation-within-a-nation, White America strictly and stringently controls entry and naturalization of outsiders within its bounds. This is especially the case in regard to Black Americans. Membership and naturalized citizenship within the White nation are carefully scrutinized, given long consideration (especially for non-Europeans) and is grudgingly and tentatively tendered. For Blacks, special laws, court rulings, judicial reviews, special commissions, periodic reviews and legislative abrogations of, or amendments to prior civil rights laws, affirmative action laws, rules and regulations, customary racial discrimination and the like, all point to the fact that — despite the entry of some conspicuous Blacks who are given permits as "honorary Whites" — a would-be-nation of over 35 million Blacks are forbidden citizenship in the White nation; or even if granted tentative citizenship, Blacks assimilated into the White nation are always subject to identity checks, must be prepared to present their "passports", "pass books", certificates of authority and work permits on request in order to establish and prove their loyalty — and are subject to immediate revocation of citizenship and deportation without due process for minor infractions of social codes. Again, Hacker makes an astute observation in this regard:

> the question is not "Who *is* white?" It might be more appropriate to ask "Who *may* be considered white?" ...In a sense, those who have already received the "white" designation can be seen as belonging to a club, from whose sanctum they ponder whether they want or need new members, as well as the proper pace of new admissions.[5]

Hacker proceeds to say that White America as nation-within-a-nation, reserves the exclusive right to validate or invalidate as needs be the "whiteness" or "non-whiteness" of those seeking admission into its domains. While this nation may allow any number of ethnic or racial groups a valid claim to being "white," "African Americans were never given that indulgence. The reason is not that their coloration was too dark to allow for absorption into the "white" classification... The point is that white America has always had the power to expand its domain. However, in the past and even now, it has shown a particular reluctance to absorb people of African descent." After noting that "a very considerable number of black Americans have achieved impressive careers, winning many of the rewards bestowed

---

5. Ibid., p. 9.

by white America," Hacker attests to the existence and exclusivity of the White nation when he argues that, "Still, there is no way that even the most talented of these men and women will be considered eligible for the honorific of 'white.' They are and will remain accomplished blacks, regarded as role models for their race. *But White Americans, who both grant and impose racial memberships, show little inclination toward giving full nationality to the descendants of African slaves.*"[6] [Emphasis added]

Thus we see that the White American nation has effectively marginalized Black America and closed its borders to their absorption into its society and culture. Black representation and effective participation in its political affairs are minuscule and paternalistically indulged. Black American ownership and control of its wealth-producing resources are small to the point of invisibility. Blacks are essentially excluded from full participation in its economic system. They are granted what is tantamount to a "work permit" or "working papers" in order to earn a living working at jobs reserved for outsiders and "resident aliens." The wonder is that the vast majority of Black Americans still consider themselves citizens of the same nation as Whites despite their placement on and containment in physical and psychological reservations and "native bantustans."

America essentially consists of three large political-economic, ethnic constituencies — the White American nation-within-a-nation, a set of rather articulated non-White ethnic tribes, and the rather diffuse tribe of Afrikan Americans. We have already indicated the basic characteristics of the White American nation. In fact, when the United States is described in terms of a nation-state it is essentially the White American nation that is being described.

An articulated tribe may be best represented by any one of a number of immigrant groups, e.g., the Korean Americans. In this instance, we have a group organized around cohesive families or kinship groups, land or communities, and confederations, with formal power organizations extending beyond family ties. The articulate nature of these groups devolves from their high levels of group and cultural identity, group and class consciousness, racial-ethnic exclusiveness; their relatively high level of intragroup cooperativeness and self-sufficiency, economic assertiveness and monopolistic business practices; their concentrated populations with an informal leadership establishment generally composed of highly respected or regarded individuals whose authority rests on their power to persuade, influence and organize their followers. Authority and leadership

---
6. Ibid., p. 15.

status is generally attained by personal achievements and abilities, and often as the result of leading important cultural institutions such as economic enterprises and/or religious establishments. The articulate tribal arrangement may yield relatively high levels of economic subsistence or surplus. In the United States, any group which achieves substantial economic surplus combined with cohesive economic-political organization and distinctive group consciousness and identity, can and does exert power and influence beyond their actual numbers in the general national population. An economically enriched, articulate tribe can use its leverage to significantly influence the actions and attitudes of the dominant White American nation and perhaps make deep inroads into its social, economic and political infrastructure. Ultimately, some of these tribal groups may be truly assimilated into the White American nation.

The Afrikan American community at this juncture in history is essentially a diffuse tribal grouping. This implies that it exhibits a number of inadequate, relatively weak, poorly focused and organized power organizations which extend beyond family ties and community groups. Its sense of self-identity, self-awareness and Afrikan-centered consciousness is unstable, tenuous and basically reactionary — meaning that its self-definition is arrived at more by default than by considered intent, more by its marginalization from and domination by the White nation than by a proactive, proud form of self-expression or self-actualization. It therefore operates around relatively low levels of group and cultural identity, group and class consciousness. Its racial-ethnic boundaries are extremely porous and over-inclusive. Its relatively low-level of intragroup cooperativeness, mutual support and self-sufficiency — its economic dependency, relatively low level of entrepreneurial drive and accomplishment and lack of control of any economic niches; its concentrated populations poorly served by a generally assimilationist, preacher-led informal leadership establishment — dissipates, squanders, underdevelops and stunts its enormous economic-political potential. This rather amorphous, reluctant tribal arrangement and the weak, ambivalent consciousness it generates and which in turn generates it, yields relatively low levels of economic surplus and political power for its own benefit. Its economic earnings and surpluses, which if conserved for its own uses would be quite large on a world-class scale, due to its diffuse organization are rapidly withdrawn from it primarily by the exploitative White nation which dominates it, and secondarily, by other more articulate tribal-ethnic groups, such as the South Koreans. The amorphous tribal nature of the Afrikan American community vitiates its capacity to develop and conserve an economic surplus and thereby destroys its ability to achieve a cohesive, economically and politically well organized community with a clear pro-active community consciousness and identity. Consequently, it has failed thus far to realize and exert its full power and influence to gain its complete liberation, independence, prosperity and self-respect.

The most effective organization for the generation and delivery of Black Power in the United States and the world would be a nation-state organization to counter that of the White American nation-state as well as the articulated tribal organizations of other immigrant-ethnic groups. Next to the nation-state stands the articulated tribal state as an effective power vehicle for Afrikan Americans. Why, given their concentrated population, their exclusion from the White American nation, their human resource and economic capacity, have Afrikan Americans not used either of these vehicles as the medium of Black Power? The scope of this volume will not allow us to pursue the answer to this question in any of the detail it deserves. However, we may summarily answer that it is primarily due to the machinations of the White American nation-state, led by its ruling White male ruling elite establishment, and the absence of political-economic sophistication within its own ranks which have thus far frustrated the ascension of the Afrikan American community. White racial and ruling class dominance requires a diffused tribal identity and organization of the Black American community as opposed to a cohesive tribal identity and organization of its own. For as Wellman contends:

> ...the social hierarchy based on race is a critical component in the organization of modern American society. The subordination of people of color is functional to the operation of American society as we know it and the color of one's skin is a primary determinant of people's position in the social structure. Racism is a structural relationship based on the subordination of one group by another. Given this perspective, the determining feature of race relations is not prejudiced toward blacks, but rather the superior position of whites and the institutions— ideological as well as structural—which maintain it.[7]

White American political and economic supremacy primarily requires a White race and White ruling class consciousness. White racism generates and unites Whites as a whole around a sense of race awareness and White consciousness. White race awareness reflects the feeling that, though the members of the race do not all share the

---

[7]. David Wellman, pp. 35–36.

same class and political interests, they perceive themselves as one in their struggles against opposing or subordinate races or groups. Dye defines class consciousness thusly:

> *Class consciousness is the belief that all members of one's social class have similar economic and political interests that are adverse to the interests of other classes and ought to be promoted through common action.*[8]

White class consciousness is embedded within white race awareness. The level, scope and integrity of class consciousness varies from one extreme to the other — i.e., while the members of the lower classes in a society may possess class awareness, the sense that they belong to the lower or low-income classes as opposed to the middle and upper classes — they as a class "do not always share political interests, feel collective class action is necessary, or see themselves as locked in a struggle against opposing classes" (Dye). In sum, the lower classes tend to lack a relatively strong sense of class consciousness. However, it is important to keep in mind that whether in reference to the White lower classes or in reference to Blacks, the weakness of class and race consciousness, respectively, are to a great extent the deliberate result of an ongoing, aggressive, ideological campaign against such consciousness led by a highly class- and race-conscious White male elite. At the top of this elite are White businessmen.

> *Businessmen collectively constitute the most class conscious group in American society.* As a class they are more organized, more easily mobilized, have more facilities for communication, are more like-minded, and are more accustomed to stand together in defense of their privileges than any other group.[9] [Emphasis added]

It is this group, allied with other White elite and not-so-elite interest groups, whose ownership and control of the most influential political, economic and sociocultural institutions, which defines reality and promulgates the values that form the bases of moral judgments, attitudinal and behavioral orientations for the White lower classes and Black Americans of all classes. It was Marx and Engels who asserted that "The ideas of the ruling class are, in every age, the ruling ideas." The ideology projected by the White ruling elite, as we should expect, is one contrived to justify and rationalize the class-race status quo and, moreover, designed to limit the range and acceptability of alternate ideologies and ways of thinking so that alternatives to

---

8. Dye, 1983, p. 71.
9. Schattschneider in Parenti, 1984.

established arrangements appear risky and irresponsible (thereby undercutting dissent). "People who are unhappy about the status quo are persuaded that any other system would be worse" (Katznelson and Kesselman, 1975).

The ability of the ruling White classes to maintain and successfully exploit the class-race status quo, requires that the material and social conditions which generate and undergird that status quo function so as to foster their own race and class loyalties and cohesions while simultaneously permitting them to structure the material conditions and socialization experiences of Blacks and the poor in ways which destabilize and destroy their race and class consciousness, loyalties, and cohesions.

> Once again we see that power is used not only to pursue interests but to define interests, or the range of interest choice, and therefore the range of class consciousness....
>
> The absence of competing images, symbols, and organization from working-class [and Afrikan American national] sources, especially evident in the United States, leaves the capitalist culture unchallenged and prevents the emergence of a competing class [and race] consciousness, thus further sustaining the impression that class [and race] interests are harmonious and the needs of most people are being satisfied, or that the deprivations suffered by many stem from innocent causes and individual deficiencies. Even when new demands arise, they are expressed in a context that accepts as a "realistic" given the exploitative, asymmetrical nature of the ongoing exchange relations between classes [and races].[10]

Preparing for Power

Educational Establishments. Sociologists Horton and Hunt (1968) note that each class in society is a subculture, each exhibits a characteristic set of attitudes, beliefs, values, behavioral norms, lifestyles and interests. Ethnocentrism and the relative cohesion of ruling White classes are not coincidental. The "virtues" of these classes are consciously and institutionally cultivated. The similarity and relative exclusivity of the educational and socialization experiences of key members of the ruling elite are two of the major means by which they are prepared to exercise power and authority in the interests of their class. Generally, it is in the early childhood, primary and secondary educational establishments, as well as in the undergraduate, graduate and post-graduate institutions attended almost exclusively or predominantly by members of the ruling elite, where

---

10. Michael Parenti, *Power and the Powerless*, p. 110.

they learn the roles, behaviors and social abilities which prepare them to wield social power. As Domhoff observes:

> From infancy through young adulthood, members of the upper class receive a distinctive education. This education begins early in life in preschools that frequently are attached to a neighborhood church of high social status.[11]

This distinctive education continues through private elementary schools, boarding schools and a handful of heavily endowed private schools and universities, e.g., Harvard, Yale, Princeton, and the like. Education at these institutions is not necessarily superior to that of lesser prestigious or public institutions, and is often inferior to the latter relative to the development of technical abilities. However, as Cookson and Persell (1985) contend, acceptance into these schools is tantamount to acceptance into an exclusive private club where shared attitudes, beliefs, lives and a sense of "character" and collective identity are forged through training and social encounters. As Domhoff (ibid) argues, "This separate educational system [or set of related educational experiences] is important evidence for the distinctiveness of the mentality and lifestyle that exists within the upper class for schools play a large role in transmitting the class structure to their students." Upper-class schooling provides the members of that class with *rationales and justifications for socioeconomic inequality* and aids them in the acquisition of styles of behavior and social relations that legitimate unequal relationships, prerogatives and privileges. In addition, they provide the educated upper-class members with "legitimate" authority to exercise the power they already possess and to acquire new powers when necessary.

Cookson and Persell cogently sum up the social purpose and historical foundation of upper-class private prep schools thusly:

> The preservation of privilege requires the exercise of power, and those who exercise it cannot be too squeamish about the injuries that any ensuing conflict imposes on the losers. The people who founded American boarding schools during the time of the robber barons were far from innocent or naive about how the world worked, and deliberately chose heads who were adept at portraying the world in moral terms. *The founders of the schools recognized that unless their sons and grandsons were willing to take up the struggle for the preservation of their class interests, privilege would slip from the hands of the elite and eventually power would pass to either a competing elite or to a rising underclass.*

---

11. G. William Domhoff, *Who Rules America Now? A View for the '80s*, p. 24.

Thus the idea of taking boys, in particular, away from their mothers and placing them in barracks where their personal identities were stripped away begins to make sense. *These boys were meant to become soldiers for their class and to become "combat ready."* They had to be made tough, loyal to each other, and ready to take command without self-doubt.[12] [Emphasis added]

With little modification the above statements also apply to White upper-class private colleges, universities, special institutes and think tanks.

Social Clubs. Upper-class private social clubs provide arenas for orienting the lives of upper-class adults in line with their class interests. These organizations provide points of social-cultural interaction, serve as means of establishing a place in the social hierarchy and, as argued by Brinton, take "the place of those extensions of the family, such as the clan and the brotherhood, which have disappeared from advanced societies."[13] Many families and individual members of the upper class belong to two or more social clubs in several cities nationwide. Many of the memberships are overlapping. Some of the colleges and other male-dominated or exclusively male clubs engage in secret private initiatory ceremonies and rituals reminiscent of tribal rites of passage conceived to create a sense of class-ideological cohesion and solidarity. Hence the emphasis on tradition, appropriate etiquette, modes of expression and social interactive styles advocated and supported by these clubs and the informal gatherings among the elite at their favorite resorts and "watering holes." These social institutions and activities create within their upper class members "an attitude of prideful exclusiveness that contributes greatly to an in-group feeling and a sense of fraternity" (Domhoff, 1983).

The educational and social organizational patterns which maintain the class and ethnocentrism of the ruling elite are supplemented by the marriage practices of this group. The continuity and cohesion of upper class families are maintained by a fairly high rate of within-class marriage.

Consumerism and Individualism as the Industrial Instruments of White Elite Power — Following the trend of Parenti's thought, the

---

12. Peter W. Cookson, Jr. and Caroline H. Persell, *Preparing For Power: America's Elite Boarding Schools* (New York: Basic Books, 1985), pp. 24–25.

13. In E. Baltzell's *Philadelphia Gentlemen: The Making of a National Upper Class* (Glencoe, New York: The Free Press, 1958), p. 373.

White ruling elite, or as Parenti refers to them, the White "owning class," i.e., "those who possess income-producing corporate property rather than income-consuming personal-use property,"[14] creates and maintains the political-economic weakness and disarray of Black America and the lower classes by using a broad variety of methods. Two of the major means by which these ends are accomplished include the infusing of Blacks and the lower classes with a psychology of consumerism and by indoctrinating them with the ideology of individualism. Under the hypnotic influence of consumerism propagated by the White elite-controlled major media and socialization institutions, over-consumption provides meaning and definition for life for the lower orders. As Parenti notes, their "feeling of accomplishment and personal worth seldom found in work are sought in commodity accumulation." He goes on to define "*consumerism*" as the "tendency to treat consumption and accumulation of goods and services as a central purpose of life." Consumption as an end in itself, as a means of symbolizing social status, absorbs the life energies of those committed to personal acquisition and thereby serves to dissipate and retard, in the case of lower-class whites, class consciousness, and in the case of Blacks, both class and race consciousness. Parenti recognizes that "under capitalism, the acquisitive impulse...is constantly instigated and developed into a life imperative that cannot easily be put to rest." The "consumerist's" life becomes focused and bounded by his obsessive devotion to social-economic success and psychophysical passions and satisfactions. Caught up in or carried away by the unrelenting struggle for survival or insatiable status-striving drives, communal and social goals receive little consideration and low priority. Collective betterment through collective cooperation and action is blightly ignored or resentfully rejected as time-wasting, pointless, personally unrewarding nuisances.

The ideological individualism with which Black and lower class America is indoctrinated by the White ruling elite, an ideology which it does not apply to itself, is designed to atomize those collective groups into aggregations of individuals each of whom is almost exclusively concerned with his or her private or personal interests and life in opposition to the collective, social interests and life of the group as a whole. The ideological pablum of individualism fed to Black America produces in that community the concept of the individual as one who "exists as something abstracted from a social matrix, apart from the web of tasks, obligations, affections, and collective relationships which give people their identities, their social meaning, and

---

14. M. Parenti, *Power and the Powerless*, p. 101.

their experience of humanity and of themselves."[15] This privately defined, socially abstract, deracialized, de-ethnicized individualism is perfectly designed to induce a false and self-defeating, alienated state of consciousness in the members of the Afrikan American community in order to sap its vitality and potential. Furthermore, it functions to induce and motivate in Afrikan Americans the behaviors, attitudes and social relations which perpetuate their own subordination which at the same time, and by the same means, support and empower the racist status quo — thereby making the Afrikan-centered collective overthrow of White power an impossibility.

---

15. Ibid., p. 106.

Chapter 8

THE POWER PROCESSES
OF THE RULING CLASS

THE RULING WHITE MALE ELITE'S STRUGGLE for national hegemony includes its struggle to maintain Afrikan American subordination and is waged on three broad levels — the *police-paramilitary, political-economic*, and *ideological* (to paraphrase Trumphour, 1989). The *police-paramilitary* level entails the use of police and/or other forms of coercive physical or armed force, violence or constraints by the ruling class to overcome or neutralize the actual or possible opposition or resistance and to achieve the overt compliance of the subordinate classes to its edicts. Physical force is used by the ruling class in order to realize or defend certain interests considered vital or necessary to maintaining or expanding its privileges and prerogatives, especially when other forms of gaining compliance of the opposition are considered inadequate or have proved ineffective or too costly. In the modern nation-state the use of physical force by the ruling class to impose its will on the subordinate classes is usually justified or rationalized in accordance with certain ethical-moral values, certain legislative, legalistic, and judicial codes that it subscribes to or enacted itself. The deployment of the physical force is usually administered by bureaucracies under orders from the ruling class.

The use of force of violence by the ruling class usually occurs when its use of power by nonviolent means, e.g., political, economic and ideological persuasion and manipulation, has failed or broken down. Violence is generally utilized as the final persuader of the recalcitrant subordinate classes. Obviously, the control over the means of physical force and violence by the ruling class enables it to "obstruct, constrain, hurt, harm or destroy those who lack them, [the subordinate classes] and to compel them to action or inaction through the threat [and/or actual exercise] of such inflictions" (Beetham, ibid). Beetham aptly notes that "To possess superior physical power or resources is not only to be able to compel others; it is also to be able to offer protection against physical coercion or destitution, and hence to establish relations of dependency." This type of dependency may become the basis of a continuous, unequally beneficial power relationship between the classes or groups.

Within the United States the use of physical force and violence as an expression of ruling class power is generally only occasionally or episodically applied, mainly during social upheavals or disorders. Their use is primarily implied as a basis for reinforcing the more complex and effective relations of power, such as power exercised at the political-economic and ideological levels. It is for this reason we shall spend the remainder of this chapter very broadly discussing these levels rather than the police-paramilitary level, even though we are ever mindful of its existence and prime importance.

The exercise of power by the White male elite at the *political-economic* level entails the domination and manipulation of the governmental and economic systems by that group to control the behavior and attitudes, limit the interests, shape the experiences and thereby the consciousness of others. The exercise of power at the *ideological* level refers to the control over and manipulation of the symbolic environment, i.e., the creation, definition and presentation of language, image and symbols by the elite in order to determine or influence the character, range and behavioral expression of consciousness of others. Thus, the ruling elite needs to control or heavily influence the media, educational curricula and institutions, and all important information sources and services if its manipulation of the symbolic environment is to be effective.

The Political, Economic and Ideological Processes of the Ruling Class

Our main interest here is to very sketchily outline the means by which the White male ruling elite dominates America, especially Black America, through its influential impact on governmental decision-making and policy-making processes. In the interest of brevity and expediency, our discussion of these matters will principally consist of a fore-shortened review of G. William Domhoff's book *The Powers That Be: Processes of Ruling Class Domination in America.* We will briefly follow his outline. Unfortunately, the limited scope of these chapters will not allow us to present many of Domhoff's and our own examples which would illustrate and substantiate our admittedly inadequate summations of the processes discussed herein. We suggest that those who wish to examine the relevant examples and substantiations read Domhoff's publications regarding these matters as well as William Greider's *Who Will Tell The People: The Betrayal of American Democracy*, a recent best-seller, and the works of Parenti, Chomsky, Zinn, Schattschneider, Mills, and others.

Domhoff describes four general processes by which the ruling class in the United States dominates the government and subordinates other social classes (and Black America) to its interests. He argues that "the ruling class, working with the aid of highly trained and carefully selected employees, are able to dominate the United States at all levels" by means of the following four processes:

1. *The special-interest process*, which comprises the various means utilized by wealthy individuals, specific corporations, and specific sectors of the economy in influencing government to satisfy their narrow, short-run needs;
2. *The policy-formation process*, which is the means by which general policies of interest to the ruling class as a whole are developed and implemented;
3. *The candidate-selection process*, which has to do with the ways members of the ruling class ensure that they have "access" to the politicians who are elected to office;
4. *The ideology process*, which involves the formation, dissemination and enforcement of the assumptions, beliefs and attitudes that permit the continued existence of policies and politicians favorable to the wealth, income, status and privileges of members of the ruling class.[1]

Domhoff defines the *power elite* as "the leadership group or operating arm of the ruling class. It is made up of active, working members of the ruling class and high-level employees in institutions controlled by members of the ruling class. It is the members of this power elite or leadership group who dominate within each of the four processes." Domhoff listed the following indicators as evidence of the power of a ruling class in America:

---

1. G.W. Domhoff, *The Powers That Be: Processes of Ruling-Class Domination in America*, New York: Vintage-Random House, 1979), p. 10.

1. A disproportionate amount of wealth and income as compared to other social classes and groups within the state;
2. A higher standing than other social classes within the state on a variety of well-being statistics ranging from infant mortality rates to educational attainments;
3. Control over the major social and economic institutions of the state;
4. Domination over the governmental processes of the country.[2]

The Special Interest Process

The process of national governance is of pre-eminent interest to the ruling White elite and moneyed classes inasmuch as the functional-structural form and dynamic-directional outcomes of governmental actions have marked impacts on their wealth, power and influence. This has been true since the founding of the White American nation as represented by the construction of its constitution in ways that contain the spread of democracy in the United States and work to the advantage of propertied and commercial class interests. This essentially elitist document drawn up by the predominantly "rich and wellborn" was and still is designed primarily to make property and its protection the central objective of government. As noted by a number of historians and political scientists, and to use the words of Parenti, "The Constitution was framed by financially successful planters, merchants, and creditors, many linked by kinship and marriage and by years of service in Congress, the military, or diplomatic service."

Parenti goes on to indicate that this segment of the White male elite, as social myth would have it, was not possessed by a nonpartisan, exclusively high-minded "dream of nation-building," but rather by a newly acquired nationalism that "was a practical response to material conditions affecting them in a most immediate way. Their like-minded commitment to federalism was born of a common class interest that transcended state boundaries." The best that can be said of the high-mindedness of this Constitution-constructing, White male elite who "possessed more time, money, information, and organization..." (characteristics that would continue to mark the ruling elite to the present day) than any of the other classes (Afrikan slaves not counted) was that they perhaps devised ways they could "serve both their nation and estates."

The conditions of governance necessarily influence the shape and maintenance of the social order which in turn influences the form,

---

2. Ibid., p. 12.

Table 8–1   Founding Fathers Classified by Known Economic Interests

Public Security Interests

Major	Minor	Real Estate and Land Speculation	Lending and Investments	Mercantile Manufacturing and Shipping Interests	Plantations and Slaveholdings
Baldwin	Bassett	Blount	Bassett	Broom	Butler
Blair	Blount	Dayton	Broom	Clymer	Davie
Clymer	Brearley	Few	Butler	Ellsworth	Jenifer
Dayton	Broom	FitzSimons	Carroll	FitzSimons	A. Martin
Ellsworth	Butler	Franklin	Clymer	Gerry	L. Martin
FitzSimons	Carroll	Gerry	Davie	King	Mason
Gerry	Few	Gilman	Dickinson	Langdon	Mercer
Gilman	Hamilton	Gorham	Ellsworth	McHenry	C.C. Pinckney
Gorham	L. Martin	Hamilton	Few	Mifflin	C. Pinckney
Jenifer	Mason	Mason	FitzSimons	G. Morris	Randolph
Johnson	Mercer	R. Morris	Franklin	R. Morris	Read
King	Mifflin	Washington	Gilman		Rutledge
Langdon	Read	Williamson	Ingersoll		Spaight
Lansing	Spaight	Wilson	Johnson		Washington
Livingston	Wilson		King		Wythe
McClurg	Wythe		Langdon		
R. Morris			McHenry		
C.C. Pinckney			Mason		
C. Pinckney			C.C. Pinckney		
Randolph			C. Pinckney		
Sherman			Randolph		
Strong			Read		
Washington			Washington		
Williamson			Williamson		

Adapted from Thomas R. Dye, *Power and Society*, 5th ed. (Pacific Grove, CA: Brooks/Cole, 1990), p. 188.

range, needs, and functionality of the commercial economy. They help to organize social, national and international business and trade relations and therefore affect the ability of the various social classes, particularly the ruling elite, to defend and advance their group interests, and political-economic agendas. The primary interests of the ruling elite include the practically exclusive control over access to or possession of key material and social resources, physical force, social activities and skills, and positions of authority which permit it to acquire and maintain power over the subordinate classes who are denied significant access to them. It is of great importance to the ruling elite that the government allows it to "legitimately" achieve these ends. These concerns and the process of managing them to its advantage, help to define the ruling elite as a special interest group. They also provide the motivation for its recruitment of personnel, organization of groups, and to continually subject the government to its special-interest process by means of which it can increase its private wealth and power at public expense and the expense of democracy. Domhoff describes the special interest process of the ruling class as follows:

> Ruling-class domination of government can be seen most directly in the workings of lobbyists, backroom super-lawyers, trade associations and advisory committees to governmental departments and agencies. It takes place in a network of people and organizations that is knit together by varying combinations of information, gifts, bribes, insider dealing, friendship and, not least, promises of lucrative private jobs in the future for compliant government officials... This is the level of what I call the special-interest process; it consists of the several means by which individuals, families, corporations and business sectors within the ruling class obtain tax breaks, favors, subsidies and procedural rulings that are beneficial to their short-run interests.[3]

Lobbyists and Committees

One of the major means by which the ruling White male elite influences governmental operations and policies in ways favorable to its interests is through the employment and heavy use of lobbyists. Lobbyists are persons and organizations hired by various interest groups to influence legislative and governmental policies by (1) gaining access to pertinent officeholders; (2) attempting to shape officeholders' perceptions of issues by providing them with information that favors the interest group's concerns; (3) providing the

---
3. Ibid., p. 25.

officeholders with arguments supportive of the lobbyist's own views; (4) helping legislators to perform tasks normally done by congressional staffs; (5) drafting legislation, writing speeches and handling favorable publicity in the press for legislators and officeholders, and (6) the barely concealed bribing of officeholders. Parenti sums up the techniques used by modern lobbyists in the following way:

> Supposedly the techniques of the "modern" lobbyist consist of disseminating data and giving informative testimony before legislative committees rather than the obsolete tactics of secret deals and bribes. In fact, the development of new lobbying techniques have not brought an end to the older, cruder ones. Along with the slick brochures, expert testimony and technical reports, corporate lobbyists still have the succulent campaign contributions, the secret slush funds, the "volunteer" campaign workers, the fat lecture fees, the stock awards and insider stock market tips, the easy-term loans, the high-paying corporate directorship upon retirement from office, the lavish parties and prostitutes, the prepaid vacation jaunts, the luxury hotels and private jets, the free housing and meals, and the many other hustling enticements of money. "Many a financial undertaking on Capitol Hill," writes Washington columnist Jack Anderson, "has been consummated in cold cash — that is, with envelopes or briefcases stuffed with greenbacks, a curious medium for honorable transactions."[4]

While lobbying may be used to represent and protect the legitimate interests of a group of citizens or segment of the society, lobbying as utilized by the corporate elite is often in effect tantamount to the purchase or leasing of the government. It provides the media by which vast sums of money are moved through the governmental system in order to influence, if not determine its outcomes. The $4.1 million spent by Gulf Oil; $75 million a year spent by the American Petroleum Institute, only hint at the tremendous sums spent by corporate America in order to not only present and fight for their legitimate claims but more often to subvert the legislative and administrative process, if not destroy much legislative, governmental and administrative integrity. When all is said and done one can conclude that the United States has the best government that money can buy.

The extent to which big business has come to virtually dominate the government may be illustrated by an observation regarding the Reagan-Bush administration made by William Greider.

---

4. Michael Parenti, *Democracy for the Few*, 5th ed., p. 201.

In Ronald Reagan's White House, it was the office of vice-president that was designated as the chief fixer for aggrieved business interests. Industries that were unhappy with any federal regulations, existing or prospective, were instructed to alert George Bush and his lieutenants. *The power of the White House would be employed to intimidate and squelch any regulatory agencies that seemed upsetting to American business.*[5] [Emphasis added]

Greider provides a succinct indication of the extent to which the monied interests have come to seek marked influence in the policy-making process through the enlargement of lobbying organizations.

In 1970, only a handful of the Fortune 500 companies had public affairs offices in Washington. Ten years later, more than 80 percent did. In the same period, not coincidentally, business political-action committees displaced labor as the largest source of campaign money. In 1974, labor unions accounted for half of the PAC money; by 1980, they accounted for less than one fourth.[6]

Business Week magazine, October 21, 1988, in an article titled "Knights of the Business Roundtable" described some of the activities of organized big business in arriving at consensus decision-making and influencing governmental processes. It noted that a few dozen of the country's top corporate chiefs met at an exclusive club in New York to discuss public policy. This business group composed of executives of companies the likes of IBM, Xerox, American Express, Exxon, DuPont and Pepsico, who refer to themselves collectively as the Business Roundtable, cultivates contacts at the highest levels in Washington. The Business Roundtable, notes *Business Week,* was "founded in 1972 on notions that business and government share mutual interests and that government actions can have great impact on the bottom line. Membership in the Roundtable is limited to chief executives of almost 200 of the nation's largest industrial, financial, and service companies." *Business Week* further noted that the policy committee of the Roundtable "forges the broad positions and goals of Big Business. These positions, in turn, are conveyed directly to politicians [e.g., the vice-president and through him, the president] and policy makers: no big support staff, no phalanx of hired lobbyists — just one-on-one." Representatives of the Roundtable meet frequently with the important Senate and Congressional committee chairmen, such as the chairman of the Senate Finance Committee, and dine with influential House and Senate aides to express its opposition to

---

5. William Greider, *Who Will Tell the People,* (N.Y.: Simon & Schuster, 1974), p. 141.
6. Ibid., p. 48.

pending bills, regulations, and things relevant to its business interests. *Business Week* notes, for example, that "The Roundtable helped to weaken some of the toughest provisions, such as the Gephardt protectionist amendment. It also threw its weight against the provision forcing companies to give workers 60 days notice before closing a plant or major layoffs..." According to *Business Week,* the Roundtable was formed during the Nixon administration at the suggestion of then Secretary of Treasury John Connally and Federal Reserve Board Chairman Arthur Burns, "who saw the need for a group of first-tier titans to counter the influence of organized labor."

The Business Roundtable along with similar business organizations, industry trade groups, corporate Washington offices, corporate political action committees, corporate lawyers, broad-based business-oriented organizations such as the Chamber of Commerce and the National Association of Manufacturers, have not only managed to significantly influence government tax policy, thwart governmental regulatory agencies, provide self-serving advice to the bureaucracy and lobby congressional committees, but have managed to obtain lucrative welfare benefits for the rich. Parenti indicates the history and nature of welfare for the rich in the following way:

> After the war, the Eisenhower administration sought to undo the "creeping socialism" of the New Deal by handing over to private corporations vast offshore oil reserves, government-owned synthetic rubber factories, public lands, public power, and atomic installations, some $50 billion worth of resources and enterprises. Nor were things much different by the 1980s when the Reagan administration sold or leased — at fees of 1 to 10 percent of true market value — billions of dollars worth of coal and oil reserves, grazing and timber lands, and mineral reserves. In any given year, the federal government hands out more than $100 billion to big business in price supports, loan guarantees, payments in kind, research and development, export subsidies, subsidized insurance rates, promotion and marketing services, irrigation and reclamation programs, and new plants and equipment. In recent times, the government has provided billions to bail such giant companies as Chrysler and Lockheed — while small independent businesses are left to sink or swim on their own. In 1984, when one of the nation's largest banks, Continental Illinois, was on the brink of failure, it received $7.5 *billion* in federal aid.
>
> Probably the most outrageous case of compensation involves corporations such as DuPont, Ford, and ITT, which owned factories in Germany during World War II that produced tanks, bombers, synthetic fuels, and other such things for the Nazi war effort. After the war, rather than being prosecuted for aiding and abetting the enemy, ITT collected $27 million from the United States government

for war damages inflicted on its German plants by Allied bombings. General Motors collected more than $33 million in compensation for damages to its enemy war plants.[7]

Through the shrewd construction and manipulation of tax laws, policies and tax breaks the ruling business elite and the wealthy classes use tax revenues and public spending as a major means of soaking the poor and less-well-off to redistribute wealth in their favor. By influencing the writing and rewriting of tax codes the largest businesses, banks and corporations may pay little or no taxes, or even achieve a negative tax rate, meaning that through various accounting procedures they may receive cash rebates from the public treasury. Moreover, entitlement programs and special taxation allowances which benefit the wealthy and corporations encourage "deficit spending" by the government, i.e., the tendency of the government to spend more than it collects in revenues. These deficit expenditures often mean that greater and greater amounts of public monies are spent in support of the rich and large companies in the form of subsidy guarantees and procurements for private firms owned by the wealthy. Furthermore, it means that the government must borrow from financial institutions, wealthy individuals and other creditors at home and abroad to finance its debt, thereby helping to increase and maintain capital accumulation among the rich by mortgaging the future earnings of the masses to enhance and protect the earnings of the wealthy:

> By buying up government bonds and securities, wealthy creditors can put their surplus capital into the federal deficit and watch it grow risk-free at public expense....In almost every enterprise, government has provided business with opportunities for private gain at public expense...provides financial aid and military protection to support the global expansion of multinational corporations...there prevails a welfarism for the wealthy of such stupendous magnitude as to make us marvel at the big businessman's audacity in preaching the virtues of self-reliance whenever lesser forms of public assistance threaten to reach hands other than his own.[8]

The social myth is that the welfarism of the rich, special tax breaks and exemptions in favor of the wealthy and the large companies or corporations, provides them with extra investment capital which is invested in production facilities at home thereby increasing employment, income and "trickle down" wealth to the masses. This

---
7. Ibid., p. 82.
8. Ibid., p. 103.

"supply side" mythology is only another facet of a mass propaganda campaign perpetuated by the rich in order to rob the poor of their money, lives and freedoms while making them think otherwise. The social mythology of "trickle down" economic betterment for the masses is but a con game, a sting operation, a swindle of mass proportions pulled off by the ruling elite. Beetham speaks to the "con" when he makes the following assertion:

> Once some necessary social resource [e.g., capital, expertise, authority] or activity [e.g., domination and control of vital governmental agencies, offices] comes to be controlled by a particular group, *it follows that the interests of society at large can only be met through satisfying the interests of that group, and on terms acceptable to them.* Those who have historically controlled the means of production or subsistence, of violence and administration, have been in a position to ensure that general needs for welfare, employment or security could only be met through the power relations that simultaneous secured their own privileges.[9] [Emphasis added]

However, the irony is that the investment policies of the ruling elite have of late proved detrimental to the general needs for welfare, employment and security for the working and lower classes in general, and the diffused Black American tribe in particular. For the wealth which is being stolen from these groups is being in ever larger portions increasingly invested abroad, thus precipitating a flight of capital, industry and jobs from the United States. Consequently, the diffused Black American tribe along with the working and lower classes (the middle and lower-middle classes as well) have been duped into financing their own underemployment, joblessness and impoverishment by a pretentiously paternalistic ruling White male elite. These groups have sacrificed their labor and capital so that the White male elite-controlled government can use public monies and resources to subsidize and finance multinational corporate foreign investment. And if needs be, these same groups will be called on by that same elite-controlled government to sacrifice their very lives as members of a military force to defend the private capital invested by the said elite in those foreign countries — capital disinvested from the lower order in the first place — against the depredations of alleged enemies.

The Second Government-within the Government

The tasks of corporate and other special interest lobbyists are simplified by the fragmentation of congressional and senatorial power

---
9. Beetham, *The Legitimation of Power*, p. 61.

among over 300 subcommittees, each having its own staff and legislative, policy-making jurisdiction. These subcommittees along with the twenty or so standing or permanent committees essentially determine the destiny and scope of bills and laws. In a sense the fragmented subcommittee system has produced cadres of "special interest legislators", i.e., members of legislative subcommittees specially concerned with particular businesses or industry interests such as energy, agriculture, etc. Thus these committees offer almost each special-interest group its own special-interest congressional subcommittee, which, if represented on the subcommittee by one or more legislators, can shape or subvert legislation in their behalf. The monopolization by congressional subcommittees of decisions in specific areas that potentially benefit specific groups, permits them under the influence of strong lobbies, PACs and other well-organized, moneyed interest-groups to serve up a broad smorgasbord of "protections, grants, subsidies, leases, franchises, in-kind support, direct services, noncompetitive contracts, loan guarantees, loss compensations, and other forms of public largesse" in favor of the more influential of these groups (Parenti, 1988).

The legislative committees and subcommittees and the legislative process itself are often equaled in importance and effect by the rulings of a vast network of non-elected agencies of government — the bureaucratic agencies. In the absence of specific guidelines from Congress (many times deliberately non-specific), bureaucracies may issue rulings as or more significant than major pieces of legislation. Bureaucracies and agencies may raise or lower all types of rates; influence the administration, enforcement or non-enforcement of laws; influence the interpretation and writing of laws and policies; and under pressure from various influential groups, ignore, fail to implement, or outright subvert the intent of the law. Bureaucratic enforcement of the law is often sabotaged by influential interest groups, often with the help of legislators, representatives from the Presidential offices and top policymakers. The promise of a lucrative position with a large or private firm after administrators leave governmental service is often used to influence their judgment while in office. The vulnerability of many ambitious public administrators to such influence from corporate and elite class interest organizations, implies that a large number of agencies, bureaucracies and their decisions service the interests of those organizations and that class, contrary to the interests of such groups as the Afrikan American community.

It is widely known that any number of administrative bodies under the direct command of the president as well as ostensibly independent regulatory commissions which make quasi-judicial rulings, fall under the influence of special interest groups, e.g., the corporate elite, and often become protectors of the "rights" of the industries they are supposed to regulate, in contradiction to the rights or interests of the people. At the cost of billions of public dollars yearly, these agencies often grant monopoly privileges to big companies and elite corporate entities. These agencies may favor corporate and elite interest groups with generous subsidies, contracts, research and development services, and infrastructural improvements and new construction when necessary. When private, elite interests in effect achieve the subversion of public agencies, public authority falls into private hands and is used to achieve private ends. Since the private and public good often do not coincide, elite and corporate propaganda and ideology notwithstanding, the public good is often left unattended or damaged by the public's own agencies of governance. The damage done may be prolonged, extensive and hidden from public view because of the secrecy and unaccountability which surrounds governmental activities. Secrecy in public bureaucracies strongly favors the machinations of private business and ruling class interests.

Blacks and Government

There is a very significant difference between involvement in the process of legitimating a government and involvement in the process of governance. Afrikan Americans help to legitimate the White American national governmental structure, i.e., its presidency and congressional houses, through ratification by voting and even electing some of their own to governmental office in the process. They garner a handful of token appointments to high federal office where they become peripherally or marginally involved in various of its governmental processes. However, the Afrikan American community through its representatives, has very little, if any, direct one-on-one or face-to-face influence on the day-to-day decision-making process of government or on the decisions of civil authority which directly influence its quality of life. In the absence of direct access to and influence on relevant government centers of power, of independent moneyed lobbies, PACs, and the like, the absence of an organized, independent political party or organization permanently installed in Washington, and of an influential, wealthy, nationalistic upper or leading class, the Afrikan American community is unable to effectively and more fully secure its special interests. It is unable to penetrate and favorably influence public authority through the exercise of its own power. The Afrikan American community has far less influence on American governance processes than have many foreign nations though it resides on American soil and participates in the election of its government.

Our brief review has indicated that, in reality, America is not a democracy — not even a pluralistic democracy — as far as Afrikan Americans are concerned. It is obvious that public policies favor the White American nation as a whole, and large-investor, ruling White male-elite interests in particular. This favoritism is bought at a very substantial cost to the Afrikan American community, the lower classes and other out-groups in general. Under present circumstances the government serves those who can best serve themselves (Parenti). And those who can best serve themselves are those groups who possess a strong group consciousness and identity; who know their interests well and pursue them with energetic single-mindedness; who are well-organized, exclusive and cohesive; who possess the requisite economic concentration of wealth and clout; who possess the political savvy and expertise, information processing and dissemination know-how, as well as the courage and will to exercise power without being squeamish. We have seen, as Parenti avers, that power in America, "In reality...is distributed among heavily entrenched, well-organized, well-financed politico-economic conglomerates that can [produce and] reproduce the social conditions needed for continued elite hegemony." To wield power in America the Afrikan American community, or an economically powerful, nationalistic class which represents its interests, must establish itself as one of those "heavily entrenched, well-organized, well-financed, politico-economic conglomerates."

The power and influence of the Afrikan American community must be fortified by a variety of internal, social, economic, institutional and governmental arrangements. It must use its internally fortified power to penetrate and influence the institutional and governmental arrangements of the White American nation. The Afrikan American community, in ways paralleling the White male elite and the White American nation in general, must control the socialization and indoctrination of its constituents and the recruitment and training of its business, governmental and nongovernmental leadership. This leadership must deeply apprise itself and the community of the real workings of the U.S. government and the means of influencing it to its own benefit.

Chapter 9

THE POLICY-FORMATION PROCESS

WE MAY REFER TO POLICY rather informally and imprecisely, yet pragmatically, as "the rules of the game", as "the rules of power" used to organize, direct and regulate the activities, the production and consumption of the resources, internal and external social relations and institutions of a society in order to defend and advance what it perceives as its overall interests. The policy-process involves the means whereby a society attempts to reach certain self-defined goals or to satisfy certain social needs, and arrives at the rules by which it will govern its behavior in doing so. This process involves conflicting and collusive interactions between various groups of society who project different perceptions of its goals and needs and who wish to legitimate and exercise different rules by which the society's goals are to be attained and its needs satisfied. Which group will get its views and rules, or a significant number of them, to prevail and be accepted as the legitimate views and rules adopted by the society as a whole, will depend on the social power and effectiveness of that group compared to other groups. Once rules are adopted and sanctioned by a society, once they are accepted as morally justified, they can themselves be used to justify and legitimate certain social relations, privileges and prerogatives of individuals and groups relative to other individuals and groups. In the context of our subject, the acquisition and exercise of social power, the social relations with which we are primarily concerned, are power relations between groups, between

White people and Black people, between dominance and subordination.

Hence, the policy-formation process involves, above all, the process of promulgating, establishing and enforcing, among other rules, those governing the acquisition and exercise of power, the "rules of power" (Beetham, 1991). For, as Beetham argues, "when power is acquired and exercised according to justifiable rules, and with evidence of consent, we call it rightful or legitimate." Furthermore, as Beetham propounds, "to be justified power has to be derived from a valid source of authority (this is particularly true of political power); the rules must provide those who come to hold power to have the qualities appropriate to its exercise; and the structure of power must be seen to serve a recognizably general interest, rather than simply the interests of the powerful." These goals essentially define the outcomes the ruling elite attempts to achieve by means of the policy-formation process. The policy-formation process is essentially the process of rule creation. As Becker cogently contends, rule creation is an enterprising act.[1] Behind every rule is an entrepreneur or interest group who, for one reason or another, sought to have the rule created and by whose efforts legislation came into being in an effort to defend or advance his or its interests.

Predominant social power can only be acquired and maintained by a particular group to the extent to which other groups can be systematically excluded from gaining equal or greater power by denying them access to sufficient social and material resources by means of which they may acquire and exercise effective power. Both access and denial of access to these means are usually determined by rules, especially the "rules of access" and the "rules of exclusion" (Beetham, ibid). It is through their influence on and manipulation of the policy-formation process that dominant or advantaged groups establish the rules (or policies) which provide them with privileged access to property and resources, the possession and use of which permit them to acquire and maintain power over subordinate or advantaged groups. The policy-formation process is a reciprocal operation. More specifically, it is a circular process.

We must be mindful of the fact that advantaged or powerful groups derive their ability to establish the "rules of the game" from their having achieved by some preliminary means (not necessarily "legitimate") the important resources which enable them to impose their self-serving rules on others in the first place. After having initially set the rules, their ability to negate old rules and to generate

---

[1]. Howard Becker, *Outsiders: Studies in the Sociology of Deviance* (New York: The Free Press of Glencoe, 1963).

new ones permits them to gain access to more power resources, which in turn enables them to acquire and exercise more power or to retain enough power to protect their interests as long as the social system which makes their power possible retains its basic organizational and functional structure.

Our argument here is that while the federal government may appear to be independent and autonomous, a government of the people and for the people, it is very heavily influenced, if not dominated, by a White male business elite network to the advantage of its members and class, and to a lesser extent to the "trickle-down" benefit of the constituents of the White American nation, in general contrast to the marginalized Black American community. The essence of class rule involves the ability of a class, in this instance the White male business elite class, to influence the structure of government, obtain access to decision-making agencies and positions within government, and the ability to help shape the general political, social, economic and foreign policies of the government. Governmental policy is not made by the President or the executive branch alone after approval by Congress. As indicated by Anker et al., the image that government decision-making is primarily carried out by the President and his staff working late at night, developing guidelines he will present to a hostile Congress, has little to do with reality. They contend that

> every important political policy is the result of careful research, multiple authorship, collective judgment, and in most cases, a long period of incubation. *And usually, the policy-making process will begin outside of government in groups that are established and financed by major business interests.*
>
> *Such groups constitute a corporate policy-making superstructure,* which is based ultimately on the intercorporate and interpersonal links...which have grown and evolved since the founding of the National Civic Federation, [i.e., the first major corporate policy-planning organization] at the beginning of this century.[2] [Emphasis added]

The policy-planning groups which compose the corporate policy-making network and regulate the overflow and outcome of the policy formation process are not solely concerned with narrow economic interests. The purview of these policy-planning groups are nearly all-encompassing, dealing with the issues which extend far beyond corporate business and trade matters. Funded by leading corporations and major foundations, these tax exempt research and discussion

---

2. L. Anker, P. Seybold & M. Schwartz, "The Ties That Bind Business and Government," in *The Structure of Power in America* (New York: Holmes & Meier, 1987), p. 106.

organizations recruit their members from a *Who's Who* of prominent individuals from leading American businesses and corporations, government leaders and administrators, outstanding academic experts and researchers.

The position papers, reports and related policy proposals produced by the various organizations who are members of the network are often translated into public policy. Their programmatic proposals or recommendations are often translated into guidelines for governmental and American policy in a host of important areas. Domhoff describes the nature and function of the policy-planning network:

> It is within the policy process that the various sectors of the business community transcend their interest-group consciousness and develop an overall class consciousness.
>
> The staid and dignified policy formation process...appears as disinterested and fair-minded as the special-interest process seems self-seeking and biased...only the "national interest" is of concern. "Non-partisan" and "objective" are the passwords.
>
> *The policy formation process begins in corporate board rooms and executive suites.* It ends in the innermost private offices of the government in Washington... In between the beginning and the end there are *a handful of foundations that provide the experts with money for research*, as well as *blue-ribbon presidential commissions which legitimate the policies* to the general public *and present them formally to the President. Research institutes and think tanks also are found in the inner circles of the network* and *influential newspapers and magazines* are important in bringing the views of the policy groups to the attention of governmental personnel. *However, the central units in the policy network* are such official-sounding organizations as the Council on Foreign Relations, the Committee for Economic Development, the Business Council and the American Assembly, which *are best categorized as the policy-planning and consensus-seeking organizations of the power elite.* **They are also the training grounds in which new leaders for government service are informally selected** [Emphasis added].[3] [See page 170]

The Functions of the Policy-Planning Groups

Domhoff lists several important functions of policy-planning groups including the following (abbreviated):

> 1. They provide a setting wherein members of the power elite can familiarize themselves with general issues in a relaxed and off-the-record setting.

---

3. G.W. Domhoff, *The Powers That Be*, p. 61–62.

The Policy-Formation Process

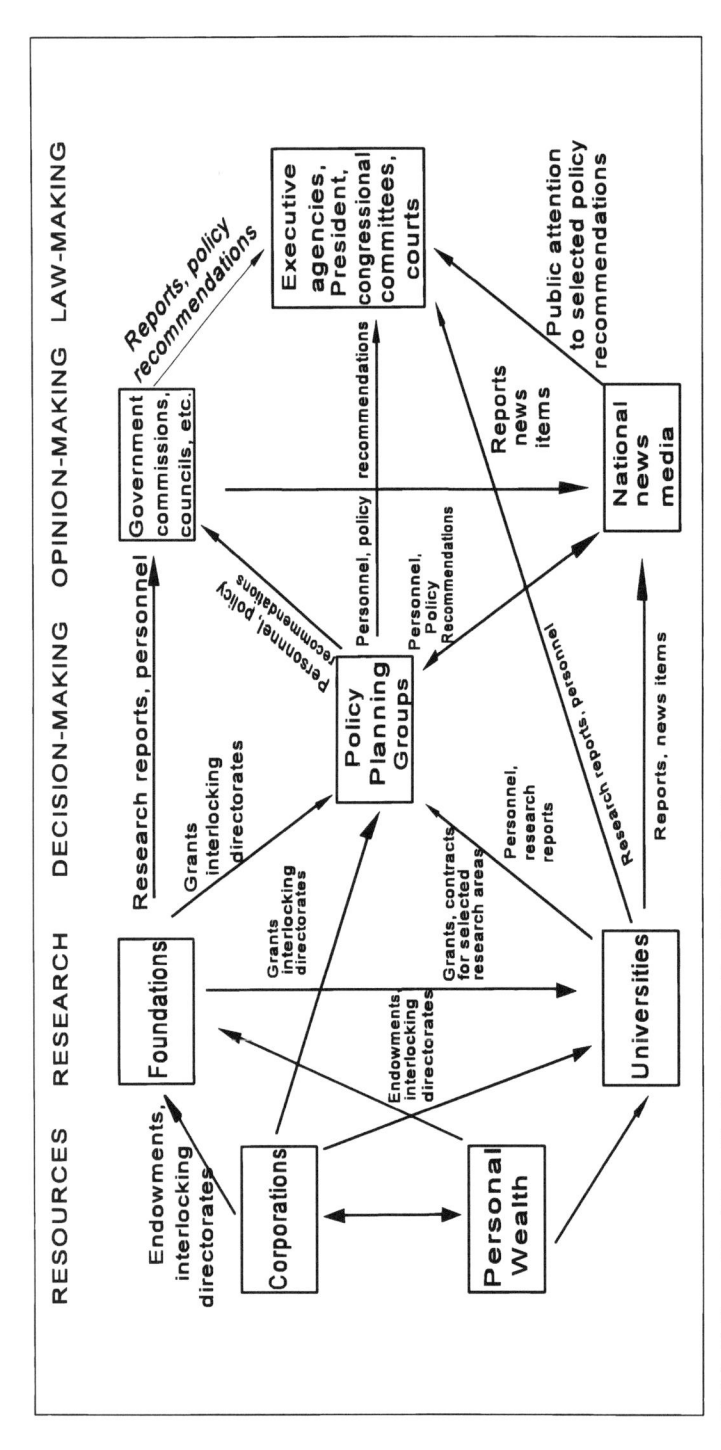

Table 9–1 Cited from *The Powers That Be*, G.W. Domhoff, p. 63.

–170–

2. They provide a setting where conflicts within the power elite can be discussed and compromised.

3. They provide a setting wherein members of the power elite can hear the findings of various academic experts. In some cases, study groups within the policy-planning organizations can be characterized as ongoing seminars or briefing sessions for the corporate rich, with experts doing most of the talking.

4. They provide a framework for commissioned studies by experts on important issues, thereby assuring leaders within the power elite that they have the latest and best information on the subject at hand.

5. They provide an informal training ground for new leadership within the power elite. It is in these organizations that big businesspeople can determine which of their peers are best suited for service in the government.

6. They provide an informal recruiting ground for determining which academic experts may be suitable for government service, either as faceless staff aides to the numerous lawyers and businesspeople who take Washington positions or as executive-branch appointees in their own right.

In addition to their functions within the power elite, the policy-planning groups perform at least two major functions for the power elite vis-à-vis the rest of society.

1. These groups legitimate their members as "serious" and "expert" persons capable of government service and selfless pursuit of the "national interest." This is by virtue of the fact that group members are portrayed as giving of their own time to take part in highly selective organizations which are nonpartisan in nature.

2. Through such avenues as books, journals, policy statements, press releases and speakers, these groups influence the "climate of opinion" both in Washington and the country at large.[4]

Advisory Committees — We shall specifically and briefly describe the roles of the "independent" research and policy organizations and "think tanks" presently. However, we should also note another important means by which the corporate elite seeks to shape and direct governmental policy — the advisory committees. Hundreds of these committees help to oversee the functions of government agencies. In 1972, as the result of a Senate investigation, it was revealed that there were between 1,000 and 1,500 of these unknown-to-the-public advisory committees working with and for the federal government during any given year. Many of these committees may consist of scientists, technicians, and academicians who evaluate

---

4. Ibid., p. 120–21.

government programs and select recipients of research grants and contracts, or many may consist primarily of people from the industry affected by a particular agency (Domhoff, ibid). In contrast to and in support of the strategic formulations of the policy-planning organizations, the advisory committees, a routine part of the governmental policy formation process, help to refine and implement policies which have been adopted by the government. These committees, like their policy-planning counterparts, essentially consist of business representatives, politicians and experts, with the business segment usually over-represented. Advisory groups usually take one of three forms; blue ribbon, formal and ad hoc (Anker, Seybold & Schwartz, 1987). The blue ribbon advisory committee is designed to assess or evaluate newly introduced proposals. Formal advisory committees oversee operations once policies have been fully formulated. Finally, ad hoc committees are relatively short-term groups which function to advise government on important and critical decisions concerning ongoing programs. Anker and her colleagues note that an ad hoc group may engage in meetings that are not reported, "nor is its existence mentioned with any regularity by the press. Such a committee can arise, function, and die without any public notice." Advisory committees may heavily influence the character and direction of government policies by shaping the information flow into any number of governmental agencies and of the executive departments, and by helping to instigate and ensure a smooth and highly renumerative flow of funds from government to the coffers of business and industry interests of their members. The operation of certain advisory committees and their significant impact on policy change and implementation sometimes may exclude the input of relevant public bureaucracies, the cabinet and elected representatives, thereby leaving it up to the well-represented corporate elite to elaborate and determine official governmental policy.

The Role and Function of Selected Influential Policy-Planning Groups[5]

The Council on Foreign Relations. Founded in 1920–21 by East Coast bankers, lawyers and academicians, this organization, comprised primarily of financial executives and lawyers and secondarily of journalists and academic experts, plays an "unofficial but influential role in shaping U.S. policies and recruiting elites for leadership posts during both Democratic and Republican administrations."[6] Members

---

5. See G.W. Domhoff's *The Powers That Be*, pp. 64–81.
6. M. Parenti, *Democracy for the Few*, 5th ed., p. 198.

of this and other similar upper-class organizations go on to serve in the highest offices of the nation, i.e., as U.S. presidents, vice-presidents, secretaries of state and defense, and have at times virtually monopolized the membership of the National Security Council, the nation's highest official policy-making body. The Council on Foreign Relations was very influential in the creation of the International Monetary Fund and the World Bank. It publishes the influential periodical, *Foreign Affairs*. Major foundations such as the Ford, Rockefeller, and Carnegie with which it has numerous director and executive interlocks, fund many of its special projects.

The Council, which intensely concerns itself with the role the U.S. plays in international affairs, is preeminent in helping to shape U.S. foreign policy. Its New York clubhouse hosts government officials and national leaders from all over the globe, of the highest rank and influence, as luncheon and dinner speakers as well as auditors. The Council's discussion groups and policy groups, generally consisting of about twenty-five business executives, government officials, scholars and military officers, engage in detailed discussions of various topics and issues having to do with foreign affairs. These groups attempt and define issues and alternatives which their general exploration or problems in international affairs imply or suggest. The discussion and policy groups play the most important roles in the Council's program. The Council's study defines and shapes many U.S. foreign policy initiatives. According to Domhoff (1979), "Study groups revolve around the work of a council research fellow (financed by Ford, Rockefeller and Carnegie foundations) or a staff member. This group leader and other experts present monthly papers which are discussed and criticized by the rest of the group. The goal of such study groups is a detailed statement of the problem by the scholar leading the discussions."

But the work of the Council's discussion and study groups is not merely academic, because many of its members are directly involved in making foreign policy in Washington. Many of its members are called on by the national government to assume important posts and to undertake important official responsibilities. It is not unusual for a sizable segment of the overwhelming majority of major appointments to the State department and presidential advisory groups to be a member of the Council.

The Committee for Economic Development. Founded in the early 1940s, it was created by its corporate founders to help plan the post-WWII world, particularly to help avoid a possible postwar depression.

It also was designed to present economic plans for the postwar era acceptable to the corporate community and which would block the presentation and influence of economic ideas and plans proffered by other sectors of the society. All of this was to be done under the cover of non-partisan "national interest." In its early years the Committee for Economic Development (CED) consisted of 200 corporate leaders, later including a small number of university presidents. The CED is advised by leading economists, public administrations and academic experts. Its policy statements on a broad range of domestic and international issues are developed by study groups aided by academic specialists. The statements are published and disseminated widely in business, government and media circles. They have had considerable influence in that they are often translated into official policy. CED's staff is relatively small, consisting of about twenty-four persons and a highly competent research advisory board. Working through subcommittees, CED's two hundred trustees meet to discuss policy problems with experts and after lengthy deliberations publish their policy recommendations. CED also commissions numerous research papers from academic experts and publishes them as background papers.

In 1988 about 1,300 companies contributed $3.3 million to CED. Private foundations contributed some $370,000. These contributions and others like them support CED's annual revenues and expenses of about $4 million. Like the Council on Foreign Relations, many of the members of CED come to serve in government posts in both Republican and Democratic administrations.

The Business Council. The Business Council was founded in 1933 as an official advisory agency to the Department of Commerce. Since the end of WWII the group no longer functions as the official advisory body to the Department of Commerce. But it continues to meet as a policy-planning forum for inner circle business leaders. Its 154 members listed in *Who's Who in America*, in combination held 730 directorships in 435 banks and corporations, 49 foundation trusteeships, and 125 trusteeships with 84 universities (Parenti). This organization whose members are drawn from the ranks of the nation's top financiers, bankers and industrialists, e.g., Chase Manhattan Bank, Morgan Guaranty, GE, GM, meets about six times a year with high government officials. During these usually three-day, strictly confidential meetings held at luxury hotels, paid for by private contributions, the Council conducts panels, holds informal talks, and presents its views on a broad range of public issues. Its views are influential in Washington and significantly influence governmental and bureaucratic policy. Moreover, the relaxed and friendly atmosphere of the Council's meetings with high governmental officials, the alternation of discussion sessions with banquet-style dinners, golf tournaments, tennis matches and other social events, serve to create and maintain feelings of camaraderie, class identity and consciousness between corporate elite and government officials.

Think Tanks

The work of influential policy-planning organizations such as the Council on Foreign Relations and the Business Council is reinforced by a coterie of specialized research information and expert advisory groups and institutes. Indeed it is within these think tanks (further supported by university-based research) that the deepest and most critical thinking takes place within the policy-planning network. The most important institutes and research centers, centers connected with universities, receive much of their funding from foundations. A number of the larger and less specialized independent think tanks often undertake contract research for businesses or government agencies.

Via think tanks, foundations, university centers, the corporate elite finances "a counterrevolution of ideas that would overwhelm the voices of vigilant citizens" (Greider, 1992). They also counter the reign of true democracy in America and the ideas and policies which could make it a reality. Since the 1970s and '80s, a period of increasingly conservative ideas and presidential administrations, think tanks such as the American Enterprise Institute (AEI) and the Hoover Institute moved from intellectual marginality to become primary sources of Washington and national opinion. The intellectual output of these and similar centers are utilized to inform and shape the thoughts and behavior of the media and politicians. By 1983, the AEI budget had increased nearly eighteen-fold from 1965, i.e., from $600,000 to $10,600,000. This explicitly conservative think tank has over 600 corporate contributors, including Citicorp ($100,000); Chase Manhattan Bank ($171,000); AT&T ($125,000); Chevron ($95,000) General Motors ($100,000); Exxon ($130,000); General Electric ($65,000); Proctor & Gamble ($165,000) (Greider, 1992), as well as the support of corporations like IBM, Morgan Guaranty Trust, Ford, Firestone and Goodyear. Located in Washington, D.C., the AEI produces policy prescriptions and intellectual parameters for important political debates and issues. It has argued copiously against the minimum wage, producing some nine or more scholarly reports on the matter

(Greider, 1992). These arguments were obviously favored by their corporate funding sources. Centers like AEI often seek to hide their political biases behind a veneer of disinterested scholarship.

The Hoover Institution at Stanford University is another well-funded (over $8 million, in addition to regular corporate sponsors including right-wing millionaires like Joseph Coors, the beer magnate) think tank which concerns itself with a range of public policy issues. The Heritage Foundation aggressively intellectualizes the class objectives of its generally right-wing corporate investors. It is the source of many ultraconservative legislative ideas and critiques of social programs. This think tank has also received funding from Coors ($100,000) to aid its conduct of research and educational activities on major public policy issues.

Since the early 1970s a host of additional right-wing think tanks and institutes have been resuscitated or created. The Institute for Contemporary Studies (under the aegis of Ed Meese, one-time Reagan Attorney General), the Georgetown Center for Strategic and International Studies, the Center for the Study of American Business, were among a number of centers designed to promote "free enterprise" (Schwartz, 1987). The latter organization, founded by conservative economist Murray Weidenbaum who later became Chairman of Reagan's Council of Economic Advisors, engaged in strong intellectual attacks against governmental regulation. It did much to promote deregulation.

It must be kept in mind that these conservative think tanks have their moderate and liberal rivals. To AEI, Hoover and Heritage may be opposed the Brookings Institute, the Committee for Economic Development (CED) and the Council on Foreign Relations (CFR). The Brookings Institution, formed in 1927, conducts some study groups for government officials as well as general study groups. More importantly, it is "a kind of postgraduate school for specialists in a wide range of policy areas. Employing a very large number of social scientists, it functions as a source of new ideas and consultants for policy groups and government leaders" (Domhoff, 1979). Its board of directors greatly overlap with the CED and CFR. The Brookings Institute, once the preeminent home of liberal intellectuals, has reportedly steadily shifted rightward in ideology and personnel of late, apparently under pressure from its newly financed conservative rivals (Greider, 1992).

We would be remiss if we did not include the Cato Institute in our present discussion. This organization, founded in 1977 as the research and policy think tank of California's Libertarian party, is one of the most influential corporate bodies in Republican politics and in Washington today. Founded in San Francisco, it moved to Washington in 1981. Neither wholly traditionalist, neoconservative or liberal, Cato has advocated replacing social security with a system of individual retirement accounts, the privatization of the federal deposit and the savings and loan insurance programs, a phased withdrawal of the U.S. from NATO, and the decriminalization of drug use. Cato, though no longer an exclusive libertarian think tank, shares with other libertarian research operations the belief that governmental functions — federal, state, and local — should be turned back to the private sector.

Once considered fringe thinkers, Cato's intellectuals exert tremendous influence throughout the capital. For 15 years a fountain of ideas, books, policy statements, op-ed pieces and media broadcasts, Cato is now perceived as having significantly influenced the retrogressive politics which characterized the new Republican congress of 1994. It is currently engaged in developing a handbook which seeks to show congress what the future government should be like. It is also in the process of advocating the abolishment of the federal domestic departments and giving their powers back to the states (*Wall Street Journal*, 12/14/94).

Cato works closely with Newt Gingrich, the Speaker of the House, on term-limitation issues. Two of its staff members went on leave work with Dick Armey, the House Majority Leader, on the Joint Economic Committee. Armey supports Cato's free-market ideas about the economy. Representatives Tom DeLay, the House majority whip, and Henry Hyde, head of the House Judiciary Committee, have a close relationship with Cato.

K. Tucker Anderson, a New York investment banker and Cato board member, is one of Gingrich's chief financial bankers. Another of the chief financial backers for Cato is Charles Koch, heir of the Koch family interests in Kansas oil, gas, and petrochemicals. Cato has also won broad financial backing among conservatives as a result of attacking the Bush administration's moderate Republican stance. The Koch family which now contributes about twenty percent of Cato's $5 million annual budget, has been joined by new donors including Coca-Cola, Citibank, Shell Oil, Philip Morris and Toyota. The money is so plentiful that Cato just recently moved into a new $13 million headquarters. With this kind of financial and political clout Cato was able to garner the most newspaper citations per dollar spent of all but two of 21 Washington-based think tanks (WSJ, ibid). Its ideas are frequently presented in the editorial pages of the *Wall Street Journal*.

Cato demonstrates most clearly how the corporate elite develops and funds propaganda agencies and how such agencies become intricately intertwined with the government and influence its policy directives.

Our discussion of think tanks would assume book-length proportions if we merely very briefly described the dozens of such organizations not mentioned above. Important organizations like the RAND Corporation, the Urban Institute, the National Bureau of Economic Research, Resources for the Future, and centers for international studies at MIT, Harvard and Georgetown, are certainly worthy of further study. The most important thing to note here is the fact that regardless of the scope or political leanings of any number of influential think tanks, they tend to be supported by the same corporations and all represent efforts by the ruling elite to shape governmental and public opinion across broad areas including foreign policy, economics, social values and cultural orientations. The corporate elite spends millions of dollars in financing the organizations which further its interests; by providing legal help, free advertising space in newspapers and magazines and a variety of free services for organizations in the policy-planning network; and by serving as the directors and trustees of these organizations. By these means the corporate elite seeks to determine the general direction of such organizations as well as to select the personnel who will manage their operations (Domhoff).

Efforts by the ruling elite to shape opinion in vital social areas are extensive. The work of the Joint Council on Economic Education illustrates these efforts skillfully. Receiving much of its initial funding from the Ford Foundation at its founding in 1949, and receiving the bulk of its current funding from corporations and corporate foundations, this organization seeks ostensibly to enhance general "economic literacy." It seeks to determine the parameters of the field of economic education through its promulgation of a variety of programs designed to influence the teaching of economics. The extensive efforts of the Joint Council on Economic Education to influence the nature of economic education in America may be gleaned from the following statements by Domhoff:

> At the most obvious level, it publishes books, pamphlets, movies, and teaching aids and provides school systems with curriculum guides and the literature and films of affiliated corporations. Equally important, it seeks to change the views of teachers through council-sponsored classes and workshops. These efforts began in the late 1940s and early 1950s with in-service mini-courses and summer workshops. The program expanded to the point where, in 1974, for example, 17,000 teachers participated in the in-service workshops

and 2,500 took part in 84 summer workshops. Graduates of the early workshops provided the joint council with the basis for local and regional councils designed to give support to economic education in the schools.

However, the real backbone of the joint council's strategy is its program in the 122 council-affiliated Centers for Economic Education at colleges and universities in 48 states. By the late 1970s, over three-fourths of the teacher-training programs in the country required social studies teachers to take an economics course, and the percentage of elementary teachers taking economics courses for teachers had risen from 13 percent to over one-third.

The program of the joint council, then, begins in corporate board rooms and foundation offices, flows through affiliated councils and university centers, and ends up in teacher-training programs and public school curricula. In that regard, it is an ideal example of the several steps and organizations that are usually involved in attempts to shape public opinion on any domestic issue. However, the level of economic illiteracy, according to polls taken for the corporations, remained as high in the 1970s as it was in the 1940s.[7]

Referring to the role an organization such as the Joint Council plays as a part of a corporate-sponsored elite and financed ideology network, Domhoff contends that their most important role may involve the network's ability "to help ensure that an alternative view does not consolidate to replace the resigned acquiescence and lack of interest in policy issues that are found by pollsters and survey researchers to permeate the political and economic consciousness of Americans at the lower levels of the socioeconomic ladder."

Leading Think Tanks

There are over a thousand think tanks in the United States. Some fade in and out of favor depending on political and social circumstance. Some endure and increase in influence across the years having somehow mastered an adaptational fluidity which allows them to respond positively to political and social change. The list which ensues was adapted from the more detailed one developed by James D. Smith. Our intention here is to merely acquaint the uninitiated reader with the names and the general orientations of some of the more prominent and influential think tanks of the last fifteen years.

American Enterprise Institute for Public Policy Research. Founded as a business research group in 1943 and one of Washington's most influential policy-research centers, this politically conservative

---

7. Domhoff, *Who Rules America Now?* pp. 103–4.

institute's research program is organized in three broad areas: economic policy, foreign and defense policy, and social and political studies. In addition to its bi-monthly publication *The American Enterprise*, AEI publishes forty to fifty books each year and disseminates hundreds of articles and op-ed essays.

Brookings Institution. Founded in 1916, the Brookings Institution is Washington's oldest policy research center. With an annual budget of over $17 million and an endowment of roughly $100 million, the institution's program focuses on economic studies, foreign policy and government studies, and educational policies among other matters of national and international importance.

Carnegie Endowment for International Peace. Founded in 1910 with a $10 million gift from Andrew Carnegie, this institution uses its approximately $85 million endowment to support its interest in international relations. It has published its influential quarterly journal *Foreign Policy* since 1970.

Cato Institute. Founded in 1977, this institution has gained outstanding prominence via its intimate relations with the Reagan-Bush administration and with the Republican party's ascendance in 1984. Concerned with what it perceives as traditional American principles of individual liberty, limited government, and peace, the Cato Institute publishes roughly ten books and fifteen to twenty policy analyses annually, along with its *Cato Journal* three times per year. In addition to a series of Cato Policy Reports, the institution publishes hundreds of op-ed articles and radio commentaries. The Cato Institute uses a broad network of some fifty to sixty adjunct scholars who work at other research institutes and universities to do much of its research and publishing.

Center for Strategic and International Studies. This institution with some 50 senior researchers among its 147-member staff and network of adjunct scholars, senior associates, and councilors describes its mission as "providing a strategic perspective to decision makers that is integrative in nature, international in scope, anticipatory in its timing, and bipartisan in approach." The center publishes *The Washington Quarterly* and generally co-publishes with commercial and university presses books designed to deal with such matters as arms control and technology, international business, energy and environmental issues, international communications, and political-military issues. It supports specialists who focus on regions such as Afrika, Latin America and the Middle East.

Committee for Economic Development. This institution which defines its mission as based on "the belief that the private sector should involve itself as early as possible in the development of ideas that will shape public policy," was founded by businessmen in 1942. The committee primarily concerns itself with the federal deficit, the job market, reformation of the educational system, of trade policy, the health care system and tax policy. It also concerns itself with economic development at the state level.

The Economic Policy Institute. Founded in 1986, this politically liberal institute is designed to counter what it perceives as a major shift to the right in the national policy debate. It seeks to encourage more active government intervention in the economic and social life of the nation. Backed by a coalition of unions such as the American Federation of State, County and Municipal Employees, the United Steel Workers of America, the United Mine Workers of America, the institute concerns itself with living standards, the labor market, unions, trade policy and economic competitiveness.

Heritage Foundation. As the flagship of the "New Right", this intellectually conservative establishment founded in 1973 by a group of conservative legislative aides, seeks to cultivate a new generation of conservative leaders who will become directly involved in the Washington policy process. The Foundation's research program focuses on foreign policy, defense studies, hemispheric development, Asian studies, domestic and economic studies. It produces over 200 publications including its journal *Policy Review*, with a paid circulation of over 15,000, and the *Annual Guide to Public Policy Experts*, which lists nearly 1,500 conservative experts in various important fields. It has been noticeably successful in disseminating its programmatic publications and policy proposals via the mass media.

Hoover Institution on War, Revolution, and Peace. Established in 1919 with a gift from Herbert Hoover as the Hoover War Library and now supported by a budget of some $17 million drawn from Stanford University allocations with which it is loosely affiliated, this institution has very measurable influence in the areas of international and domestic policies, and national security affairs. With the support of an endowment of over $125 million, foundation and corporate support, the institution avidly defends the preeminent role of the market in the allocation of goods and services, wealth and welfare.

Joint Center for Political and Economic Studies. The center was founded in 1970 by a group of Black intellectuals, politicians and professionals with the financial backing from the Ford Foundation and under the auspices of Howard University and the Metropolitan Applied Research Center, directed by Kenneth Clark. Its current objectives include its research, publication and educational efforts "to improve the socioeconomic status of Black Americans; to increase their influence in the political and public arenas; and to facilitate the building of coalitions across racial lines." The center sponsors training and technical assistance programs for Black elected officials and publishes a magazine *Focus*, aimed at Black political leaders. Its central concerns presently involve research on public policy and the incorporation of economic issues into its program of political and social research. The center is concerned very much with urban poverty, educational achievement, minority businesses, Afrikan affairs and human rights. It publishes about half a dozen books each year and has produced well-regarded radio and television programs.

Manhattan Institute of Policy Research. Originally known as the International Center for Economic Policy Studies in 1978, it was renamed the Manhattan Institute for Policy Research in 1981. This politically conservative institution has supported along with a provocative program of lectures and conferences, controversial authors such as George Gilder (*Wealth and Poverty*) and Charles Murray, who completed *Losing Ground* under its aegis and later authored the very controversial, *The Bell Curve*. This organization is also host to such Black conservatives as Thomas Sowell and Walter Williams. Supported by corporations which supply about one-third of its annual income of more than $2 million, this organization, through its Center for New York Policy Studies, is highly influential in the Giuliani administration of New York City. It also sponsors another center in Washington which enrolls and utilizes highly conservative Black and Hispanic scholars to vigorously attack what it perceives as liberal, pro-Black, pro-minority governmental policies and programs, as well as the Afrocentric movement and Black nationalism.

Foundations

We must note the important role foundations play in the policy-planning network and in shaping the political consciousness of the American populace. As observed by Horowitz and Kolodney in *The Poverty Establishment,* "the foundations sustain the complex nerve centers and guidance mechanisms for a whole system of institutional power." They go on to point out the central purpose for their existence.

> Obviously, nominally philanthropic institutions like Rockefeller and Ford fail to coincide with the popular conception of a charitable institution or an altruistic mission to uplift the poor. *They were after all designed first for the purpose of preserving wealth, not undermining it.* This is why the largest area of foundation support has been

research and higher education: the development of techniques and the training of the social elite.

"The problem of our age," Andrew Carnegie said in *The Gospel of Wealth*, is not the redistribution but "the proper *administration* of wealth, that the ties of brotherhood may still bind together the rich and poor in harmonious relationship." For the foundations, this effort takes many forms, from charting national policies designed to make the world safe for Standard Oil to engineering a proper course of moderation for America's black minority.[8]

The most influential foundations are an inextricable part of the two-faced, carrot-and-stick, good cop-bad cop, olive branch-arrow approach of American domestic and foreign policy. They are the velvet glove which clothes the iron fist of the U.S. military and police establishment as well as other more crude coercive technologies. As Horowitz and Kolodney aptly note, they are "private and non-governmental, they could leave the task of repression to their friends in other agencies while they pursued a benevolent, enlightened course without apparent hypocrisy." The foundations while presenting a benign, humanitarian facade, function to preserve a total social-political-economic system rife with inequities and injustices, national and international in scope; to resist and repress the massive redistribution of income and power by rationalizing and helping through an array of non-belligerent, non-military and apparently non-repressive means to maintain the wealth, power and prestige which define their way of life. Again to cite Horowitz and Kolodney:

> The foundations, however, are only the beginning, the base of the network of organizations through which the nerve centers of wealth impress their will on Washington. This network, the ganglia of foundation intelligence, is composed of a panoply of "independent" research and policy organizations, jointly financed and staffed by the foundations and the corporate community, which as a group set the terms and define the horizon of choice for the long range policies of the U.S. government.[9]

We intimated earlier the observation by Horowitz and Kolodney that "the foundations sustain the complex nerve centers and guidance mechanisms for a whole system of institutional power." In 1974, they reported that "The income of the 596 largest tax-exempt foundations is more than twice the net earnings of the nation's 50 largest

---

8. David Horowitz with David Kolodney, *The Poverty Establishment*, ed. Pamela Roby (New Jersey: Prentice-Hall, 1974), p. 50.

9. Ibid., p. 58.

commercial banks."[10] The wealthiest and most influential of the foundations form a network of interlocking directorates among themselves as well as between themselves and the policy-planning organizations and think tanks whose work they finance. Moreover, these foundations sustain substantial upper-class and corporate representation on their boards of trustees and directors. The influence of the foundations on public policy and opinion via their influence on the policy-planning process is considerable. Domhoff notes the types of foundations which seek to significantly influence and shape public opinion and policy thusly:

> Among the many thousands of foundations that exist in the United States, only a few hundred have the money and interest to involve themselves in funding programs that have a bearing on public policy. They are of three basic types:
>
> 1. There are 26 general-purpose foundations with an endowment of $100 million or more that were created by wealthy families. Most of them are controlled by a cross-section of leaders from the upper class and corporate community, but there remain several ultraconservative foundations in the general purpose category that are tightly controlled by the original donors.
>
> 2. There are dozens of corporate foundations that are funded by a major corporation and directed by the officers of that corporation. Their number and importance has increased greatly since the 1960s, especially in donations to education, medical research, and the arts.
>
> 3. Many cities have community foundations that are designed to aid charities, voluntary associations and special projects in their home cities. They receive funds from a variety of sources, including other foundations, wealthy families, and corporations, and they are directed by boards that include both corporate executives and community leaders.[11]

The foundations are unequivocally extensions of the corporate community and are instrumental to the achievement of corporate and White male elite-class intentions and goals. A number of foundations have become involved with specific public policy areas. For example, Domhoff observes that the Carnegie Corporation and its affiliates take special interest in the area of higher education. He notes:

> Their study groups, commissions, and fellowship programs have been central to the history of college and university development through-

---

10. Ibid., p. 43.
11. G.W.Domhoff, *Who Rules America Now?* p. 92.

out the twentieth century. For example, the Carnegie Commission on Higher Education of the late 1960s and early 1970s spent $6 million and produced 80 books with policy implications for all aspects of higher education.[12]

Foundations as Vehicles of Social Engineering

Foundations in a number of instances can become the vehicle for the restructuring of important social institutions. The newly restructured or created institutions may themselves become vehicles for the "transmission and ultimate institutionalization of ruling class interests into the cultural sphere" (Seybold, 1987). Thus the ruling elite in effect, through its foundations, mounts a "cultural war" against alternative and competitive ideologies by attempting to shape and delimit intellectual discourse in academia and in the larger society. Foundations using their funding mechanisms may seek to not only change the types of questions academia and the general populace may ask and the issues they may perceive as important, but also the methods by which these questions and issues are confronted.

We must note that method and technique are not value-free or politically neutral. Marcuse speaks to this issue when he asserts that

> the very concept of technical reason is perhaps ideological. Not only the application of technology but technology itself is domination (of nature and men) — methodical, scientific, calculated, calculating control. Specific purposes and interests of domination are not foisted upon technology "subsequently" and from the outside; they enter the very construction of the technical apparatus. Technology is always a historical-social project: in it is projected what a society and its ruling interests intend to do with men and things.

The story of how the Ford Foundation transformed the focus and methodology of political science is a case in point in demonstrating the impact large foundations can have on academic and public discourse and opinion. Peter Seybold outlines the process beginning with the following observation:

> Before World War II, the field of political science had focused either on the formal operation of government institutions or on the moral and ethical issues of government policy. By 1960, its attention was riveted on voting patterns. The lone scholar sitting in the library, examining the details of a state constitution or philosophizing on the morality of legislature actions, was replaced by a team of survey researchers who sought to understand the electoral choices of

---

12. Ibid., p. 94.

American voters through the use of random samples and questionnaire surveys.

This transformation became known as the behavioral revolution. In a little more than ten years the whole foundation of political science was altered as behavioralists came to dominate the major journals and departments in the field. Traditional scholarship was brushed aside — labeled as too philosophical and abstract and therefore unable to meet the task of scientifically understanding modern political behavior. The victory was so complete that, in 1961, the *American Political Science Review* published what amounted to an official declaration of victory by Robert Dahl, a leading behavioralist, entitled "The Behavioral Approach to Political Science: Epitaph for a Movement to a Successful Protest."

A crucial factor that determined the intellectual complexion of post-World War II political analysis was the institutional leverage exercised by the foundation as a representative of the interests of the corporate elite. The rise to prominence of the political behavior approach did not signal the victory of a particular perspective in the marketplace of ideas; rather, it demonstrated the very significant influence that institutional support by major foundations can have on the production of ideas in our society.[13]

> The behavioral revolution referred to above was not primarily the result of spontaneous internal changes in the attitudes of political scientists, the development of academic schools of thought, or of changes in political science research technique. The revolution was deliberately engineered by external forces. These forces sought to determine the primary or "principal determinant of what questions are considered important by the discipline and what methods are used to research these questions." Seybold goes on to demonstrate that the behavioralist revolution in the American political science establishment "was largely the product of the Ford Foundation's efforts to restructure political science to meet the needs of the economic elite."

> From this perspective, the triumph of the behavioralists in political science was not principally the result of the mood of social scientists nor was it the result of the development by behavioralists of a more accurate portrait of how the system operates. Rather, it was a consequence of the operation of social forces in the larger political economy as mediated by the Ford Foundation.*

The Ford Foundation as a major institutional representative of the ruling elite whose major concern is to preserve the stability of the

---

13. Peter Seybold, "The Ford Foundation and the Transformation of Political Science," in *The Structure of Power in America*, ed. Michael Schwartz, pp. 185–86; *Ibid., p. 186.

American class-race status quo and institutional social order, sought to define the agenda for social research. "The role of the Ford Foundation in this process was to identify actual and potential threats to the status quo and address them with a program of political research which could aid the struggle to maintain political stability" (Seybold, 1987). By what means did the Ford Foundation accomplish the "behavioralist revolution"? There were a number of well-thought-out approaches designed to achieve its goals.

1. Concerned with what it referred to as the "practical problems of democracy" and with the scientific study of people, i.e., values, motivation and maladjustments as well as the application of social science knowledge and technique to every aspect of democratic life, the Ford Foundation institutionalized the Behavioral Science Division. It engaged in institution building in a number of related areas as well.

2. Between 1951 and 1957, the Behavioral Sciences Division invested over $23 million in individual scholars, graduate departments, research institutes, and professional associations who shared its special commitments.

Statistics regarding the foundation's Foreign Area Fellowship Program illustrates its influential impact on political science research.

> Statistics will demonstrate just how successful this program has been in strengthening American higher education. Of the 984 former fellows, 550 hold faculty positions in 181 colleges and universities in 38 states....
>
> Some twenty-nine universities employed five or more fellows, and ten universities have employed ten or more. In addition to academic and teaching careers, eighty-two former fellows are now in government service, thirty-eight are now in philanthropic or non-profit organizations, and forty-five are in business or professions. Many former fellows have added to our knowledge of the non-Western world through the publication of results of research. Altogether they have published some 373 books and over 3,000 articles and short monographs; moreover, they have edited or contributed to another 516 volumes. (Beckman, 1964, p. 18)[14]

3. In order to further transform the research orientation and social functionality of political science into an empirical discipline, the

---

14. Ibid., pp. 190-91.

foundation not only provided support for individual scholars, established and supported research institutions; it also engaged in the reorientation of professional journals, the utilization of intermediary organizations, and the training of upcoming scholars in the methodology of behavioralism.

4. The foundation encouraged and supported the creation of a number of programs designed to develop behavioral political theory in places such as the University of Chicago, Columbia University, and the University of Michigan. Furthermore, it issued a variety of grants to research institutes, e.g., the Bureau of Applied Social Research at Columbia University, the National Opinion Research Center at the University of Chicago, the Russell Sage Foundation, the Center for Advanced Study in the Behavioral Sciences in Palo Alto, and the Social Science Research Council.

> The grant to Russell Sage was especially significant since it helped create two different sorts of institutional niches for behaviorally oriented researchers. It financed the appointment of postdoctoral scholars to residencies in operating agencies or professional schools, many of which had not been previously exposed to empirical political science. It also provided funds for the appointment of empirical political scientists to faculty positions, thus facilitating the addition of these scholars to the staffs of many universities.[15]

5. A large part of the literature of the behavioral political science revolution resulted from research committees funded by the foundation. For example, the Committee on Political Behavior distributed $340,000 in research support for individual researchers concerned with American governmental processes at the federal, state, and municipal levels. Some 15 landmark books in political science were published under the aegis of this committee between 1952 and 1959.

6. The foundation also funded the Committee on Comparative Politics. This committee was designed to generate up-dated information and practical knowledge about underdeveloped and emerging nations whose policies and/or systems of government are uncongenial or incompatible with United States interests. The body of information generated by the committee was also to be used for propagandistic purposes as well, i.e., to demonstrate the superiority of American capitalism, economic developmental approaches and public policies. Moreover, the committee generated a number of "area specialists" who

---

15. Ibid., p. 193.

could provide valuable information regarding previously under-researched regions and countries to government officials and corporate leaders.

The schematically brief history presented here of a representative institution of the moneyed interests, e.g., the Ford Foundation, gives some indication of how these interests can and do subtly but powerfully influence the agenda and orientation, not only of the social sciences, but of any number of important academic, research and applied fields, including the natural sciences. This history also indicates that intellectual discourse, the generation and application of knowledge, can be and is shaped in ways favorable to ruling elite interests and in ways unobserved by the public or certain target populations such as the Afrikan American community.

Education for Servitude: Corporate Philanthropy and the Shaping of Black Higher Education[16]

The Prospect of Black Education for Social Equality. The history of Black higher education essentially involves the origin and evolution of the Black private college system, beginning from the Reconstruction era to World War II. This is the case because up to 1938 and for quite some time thereafter, when the United States Supreme Court ordered the states to provide "substantially equal facilities" for Black and White state and land-grant colleges, the vast majority of Black college students were enrolled in private institutions of higher learning. And these institutions were controlled by or identified with Black church organizations, White missionary and industrial philanthropy. As late as 1930 Black church organizations controlled colleges which enrolled 14 percent of Black students. Missionary and industrial philanthropy controlled colleges which enrolled 61 percent of those students. The Black state and land-grant colleges enrolled most of the remaining 25 percent. The mission societies made their most important contributions to Black higher education from the 1860s to 1915. By then the mission societies had established over thirty colleges attended by the majority of Black and professional students. Many of these institutions were and remain the leading Black centers of higher learning.

The Triumph of Black Industrial Education. Missionary philanthropy was soon replaced by industrial or corporate philanthropy as the dominant force shaping the quality, character and mission of

---

16. The following sketch of the role of industrial philanthropy in Black higher education is abstracted from James D. Anderson's article titled "Philanthropic Control over Private Black Higher Education" in *Philanthropy and Cultural Imperialism* (J.D. Anderson, editor).

Black higher education. By the turn of the century, mission philanthropy, the organizations such as the American Baptist Home Mission Society, the American Missionary Association, the Methodist Episcopal Freedman's Aid Society, Presbyterian Board of Missions for the Freedmen, and other Northern missionary societies were virtually bankrupt and their campaign to develop Black higher education sputtered out before getting in sight of their goal, the extension of equal education, civil and political rights to Afrikan Americans. The colleges they had supported were left without sufficient endowments to insure their survival. From the eve of the First World War onward, industrial philanthropy gained ascendence as the major force in Black higher education after having struggled with missionary philanthropy for that position since 1867 when the Peabody Educational Fund was established. Beginning about 1918 Black colleges became increasingly dependent on industrial philanthropy to fund "faculty salaries, retirement benefits, scientific equipment, laboratories, substantial endowments, libraries, and other material resources...necessary for colleges to be recognized as accredited institutions" (Anderson, ibid).

Crucial to the economic viability and educational development of Black private colleges were the philanthropic organizations financed primarily by northern industrial capitalists such as the Southern Education Board (founded in 1901) and the General Education Board (established by John D. Rockefeller in 1902). The former board was absorbed into the latter in 1914 under the title of the General Education Board. The General Education Board, which served as a clearing house for industrial philanthropy and which markedly influenced the character of southern education through its disbursements of grants to the region's educational institutions and state departments of education, became the premier philanthropic trust among a number of powerful northern industrial funds. By 1909 Rockefeller had supplemented his initial grant of $1 million by others amounting to $53 million. As Anderson (ibid) notes, "By 1921 Rockefeller had *personally* donated $29 million to the board. Moreover, the board became an interlocking directorate of northern industrial philanthropy as its members directed disbursements of old and new foundations." The General Education Board either directly controlled such funds as the Peabody and Slater Funds or gained the cooperation of funds such as the Phelps-Stokes, Julius Rosenwald, Carnegie Corporation and the Laura Spelman Rockefeller Funds, all established between 1902 and 1917. Anderson quotes historian Louis Harlan as saying that the General Education Board exercised "virtual monopolistic control of educational philanthropy for the South and the

Negro." Anderson himself further asserts that "The role of industrial philanthropy in shaping black education, then, is largely a story of the General Education Board and its trustees, agents, and cooperating foundations."

The ascendance of industrial or corporate philanthropy in determining the character of Black education represented no mere change in the funding of Black education from missionary to industrial philanthropic hands, but more importantly, it represented a seismic change in the perception of the role Blacks were to play in Southern society and the nation as a whole. Missionary leaders tended to be politically liberal, basically equalitarian in their views of civil rights and race relations. They generally saw Black higher education institutions as primarily designed to prepare "a college-bred black leadership to uplift the black masses from the legacy of slavery" and to lead the ex-slaves "into the mainstream national culture, largely free to do and become what they chose, limited by their own intrinsic worth and efforts" (Anderson, ibid). Toward this end, the missionary philanthropists offered their Black students the New England college curriculum, a regimen including the study of Greek and Latin, of Western civilization and its great events, and literary and philosophical works of such writers such as Shakespeare, Locke, Descartes, as the keys to Black social progress. This educational orientation and ideology which supported it were for the most part diametrically opposed to those of industrial philanthropy.

Black Education in the Service of White Domination. Equal rights for southern Blacks was of little or no concern to northern businessmen. They had virtually no interest in transforming the region's racial caste system. In fact, they sought to stabilize southern society by organizing its industrial market, restoring its agricultural prosperity, and achieving racial cooperation on southern White terms by educationally preparing Blacks to work efficiently within that system. "Negro industrial training" was recognized by industrial philanthropists as the most appropriate form of education for Blacks, who were expected to help maintain the racial order and political stability, and help advance the material prosperity of the South by keeping to their assigned "place" and playing their designated roles in the social and economic system of that region. We must add here that the "place" and role of Blacks in the South as perceived by the northern industrial philanthropists was not significantly different from their perception of the place and role of Blacks in the North and America in general.

The industrial model of Black education "was designed to develop habits of industry, instill an appreciation for the dignity of labor, and to primarily train a cadre of conservative black teachers or 'guides' who were expected to help adjust Afro-Americans to a subordinate role in the southern political economy." Any review of the perceptions of the primary purposes of Black education held by the White corporate elite today would quickly reveal that they do not differ fundamentally from those of their counterparts during the early to mid-1900s.

Higher Education for the Few. In general, the northern industrial funds, including the Rockefeller-financed General Education Board, the Peabody, Slater, Jeanes, Phelp-Stokes, and Rosenwald, avoided giving support to Black higher education (in contrast to industrial education) during the late 19th and early 20th centuries. This is not to say that industrial philanthropists were totally and exclusively committed to the idea of Black industrial education. While they had no intention of making Black higher education broadly accessible to a college-age population of over 250,000 Black youths in the first two decades of the 1900s, these philanthropists did support the idea of developing a very small number — i.e., two high-quality universities and three high-bred colleges — of Black institutions of higher learning designed primarily to produce educated leaders whose role it was to inculcate White American values into the Black masses. At its highest levels Black education was to be an education for "service", education designed to supplementarily improve and support southern and American industrial efficiency. Black intellectuals were still expected to uncomplainingly accept the South's and America's racial hierarchy. From 1902 to 1960, the General Education Board expended slightly less than $41,500,000 on Black higher education. However, Black higher education was and still remains dreadfully underfunded.

The Legacy of The Corporate Funding of Black Education. Black colleges remain dependent on industrial philanthropy and the wealthiest among them is not endowed sufficiently to garner a major portion of their annual income from investments. Anderson notes that in 1958 "the combined endowment of UNCF [United Negro College Fund] colleges was less than the endowment of Northwestern University." The combined endowment of the 41-member colleges pales in significance compared to the $6 billion endowment of Harvard University which is now in the second year of a 5-year drive to raise $2 billion to eliminate deficits and to shore up its economic well-being. The whole of the 41 UNCF colleges must satisfy themselves with raising a few million dollars to be shared among themselves. They are still held hostage to the self-serving, political-economic ideology and to the miserly philanthropic largesse of industrial funds like the Ford, Sloan and Taconic Foundations, the Duke and Mellon Charitable Trusts among other foundations which replaced the General Education Board after it was phased out in the 1950s. The industrial foundations are still a powerful force in Black higher education as Black colleges must still beseech them for gifts to aid them in their day-to-day struggles to survive. As a result Black colleges must retain conservative curricula, restrict themselves to preparing their students to serve White corporate interests, to work for White-owned and controlled companies and institutions, and to assist White supremacy in its domination and exploitation of Afrikan peoples. The education of Blacks in predominantly White colleges and universities is fundamentally no different. Education in these institutions also falls heavily under the mercenary influence of corporate philanthropy as we have already discussed. It is obviously not the intention of White industrial philanthropy and the White powers-that-be in education that Black higher education play a major role in liberating Afrikan peoples and nations from White politico-economic domination and in empowering those same peoples and nations to challenge the industrial-military-technological hegemony of White peoples and nations.

Foundations and Think Tanks: The Selling of Newt Gingrich and the Republican Party 1994

In November 1994 the nation and the Afrikan American community were astonished by a near-revolutionary change in the political composition of their national legislative chambers. Both houses of government came under the solid control of the Republican party. In the House the Democrats were routed after 40 years of predominance. The ascendance of the Republican party in the House and Senate was accentuated by its stunning takeover of numerous statehouses, state legislatures, and local governments.

To many pundits and ordinary citizens, especially in the Black community, the triumph of the Republican party ominously signaled a drastic turn to the political right of a very large segment, if not the large majority, of the White American population. In the aftermath of a campaign based on race politics and the rejection of liberal values, many in the Black and progressive communities were pervaded by a lingering sense of foreboding and menace. The expectation that national and state governments shall grow increasingly mean-spirited and repressive is palpable. This expectation will grow should a Republican be elected president of the United States.

For many in the Afrikan American and progressive communities the menace of Republican party rule is incarnated in the person of Newt Gingrich of Georgia, Speaker of the House. Within a decade Gingrich has risen to become the chief spokesman for the Republican party and the personification of its race-based, anti-Black, market-oriented politics. His and the Republican party's ascendance is perceived by many in the Black community to represent the electoral expression of the heartfelt, spontaneous racial sentiments and economic fears of the majority of the White American community. While this perception may be based on fact, the Republican sweep was a good bit more complex than the mere expression of political discontent. The Republican victory was to a significant degree deliberately orchestrated by well-funded political operatives. The ascendance of Newt Gingrich and the Republican party is a tribute to the White elite's masterful manipulation of the candidate-selection, psychopolitical, and communication processes. The triumph of Newt Gingrich and Republican party is one with the triumph of conservative White elite corporations, foundations and think tanks. Their triumph is also one with the White elite corporate ownership and control of the electronic and print media.

The Selling of Newt Gingrich and Right Wing Politics. The far-ranging political thrust of the *New York Times* (12/18/94) detailed report of Newt Gingrich's victory in 1994 was perfectly encapsulated by its title: *Gingrich: Man in Spotlight and Organization in Shadow.* The lengthy report begins as follows:

> Back in 1987 when most people thought Democratic control of the House would last forever, Newt Gingrich had a vision: Raise millions of dollars and spend it to nurture a dynamic new generation of Republican politicians — a farm team that could some day march from the state-houses to Congress.
>
> He had a vehicle as well: a political action committee called Gopac that is the centerpiece of what has become known as "Newt Inc.," an interlocking set of entities that in recent years has grown to include a think tank and college course beamed around the country.

While the *Times* readily admits that the Republican's sweep of the Congress had a number of causes, including "the failings of President Clinton and Democrats," it attributes a good proportion of their success, along with many important Republicans, "to the spade work done by Gopac and the energy of Mr. Gingrich, its general chairman..."

Founded in 1978 by former Delaware Governor Pierre (Pete) duPont, scion of the famous duPont family, and 12 other Republican governors, Gopac not only raised the money to fund Gingrich's political ambitions but helped to construct Gingrich's and the Republican party's ideology and campaign strategies. The *Times* goes on to intimate that:

> Gopac was already trying to build its "farm team" of local candidates when Mr. Gingrich took the helm in 1986.
> Gopac gave Mr. Gingrich new stature in his fund-raising efforts. As its head, he could "speak to Republicans of means in a direct manner," said Terry Kohler, a businessman and former gubernatorial candidate in Wisconsin. He and his wife have given the group $715,457 since 1985.
> Gopac, Mr. Kohler said, appealed to Republicans like him who long dreamed of reclaiming the House of Representatives. "We've won the Presidency time and again, but let's face it — the House initiates all spending and all taxing bills," he said. "That's where the power is, that's where the money is, and Gopac was the only one with a plan."

Most of Gopac's and Gingrich's planning, development and operational strategies occurred largely out of public view. Gopac has thus far refused to release the roster of its charter members. However, it is known to be primarily supported by corporate executives, investment bankers, health executives and others whose bottom lines are affected by Federal legislation. This coterie of Gopac supporters were able to raise $7.8 million (from Jan. 1, 1991 to Nov. 28, 1994) to help pay for Gingrich's media exposure and to train the "farm team" of Republican candidates it developed over seven years. Gopac credits 33 of the 73 freshman Republicans in the House with being members of its "farm team". Representative Bill Paxon, New York Republican, who is chairman of the National Republican Congressional Committee, is reported to have said that "Up to 80 percent of our new members were recipients over the years of Gopac activities-tapes, seminars, meetings" (NYT, 12/18/94). Training videos developed by Gingrich and Gopac were distributed free of charge to prospective candidates for congress. According to the *Times*:

> Over time, the training videos became much more professional. They offered case studies of successful campaigns — how they got rolling, how they exploited opponents' weaknesses, how they harvested money from political action committees in Washington.
> The manual even recommended a language for the candidates, and it echoed Mr. Gingrich's favorite themes: "greed," "decay," "liberal," "devour," "waste," "corruption."

"Part of our objective, and this was Newt's approach, was to get people to think on a larger scale than they had before," said Mr. Morgan [Gopac's former training director]. "We would say, 'People who support Dukakis believe X, we believe Y, and here's what it means to your life.' "

Focusing on big-picture issues helped Mr. Gingrich "nationalize" the 1994 elections and turn voters' attention away from the Democrats' long-perceived strength of boasting about local pork barrel projects. Mr. Gingrich thus reversed Speaker Thomas P. (Tip) O'Neill Jr.'s famed axiom that "all politics is local."

"Gopac was important because it provided an ideological framework for a lot of the candidates," said Paul Weyrich, the conservative thinker who founded National Empowerment Television. "The party was never good at this, in fact shied away from it."

Gopac is one of the several political organizations, wealthy individuals and families which aided and abetted Gingrich and the Republican's capture of the congress. Two of the major political organizations who greatly helped the Republican cause include the Progress and Freedom Foundation and the Friends of Newt Gingrich Campaign Committee. The Progress and Freedom Foundation, a think tank supervised by some of the intellectual advisors closest to Gingrich, was projected to have raised $2.3 million for Gingrich's efforts between March 31, 1994 to April 1, 1995 (NYT, 12/20/94). The Friends of Newt Gingrich Campaign Committee raised $6.3 million between January 1, 1987 and November 28, 1994. The Foundation, whose current projects include the development of plans to reorganize the Food and Drug Administration, "underwrites Mr. Gingrich's weekly call-in program on National Empowerment Television, the conservative cable network" (NYT, 12/18/94). The Foundation also contributes heavily to Gingrich's other communications projects. The *New York Times* reports that:

> The Foundation raises money for a college course taught by Mr. Gingrich called "Renewing American Civilization," which is beamed by satellite to more than 130 classrooms across the country. Although it is avowedly nonpartisan, one of Mr. Gingrich's associates wrote in a fund-raising letter last year that the course hoped to "train, by April 1996, 200,000 citizens into a model of replacing the welfare state and reforming our government."
>
> Each entity — Gopac, the foundation and the college course — has raised its money from an overlapping pool of businessmen, investment bankers and other longtime supporters of Mr. Gingrich. And that has stirred a dispute now that Mr. Gingrich has moved from the back bench.

A number of corporations who helped to foot the $400,000 bill for producing Gingrich's course and broadcasting it across the nation were warmly endorsed by Gingrich on the air. The Progress and Freedom Foundation paid about $125,000 in 1993 to underwrite an hour-long television call-in program hosted by Gingrich and to underwrite Gingrich's college course broadcast on National Empowerment Television. Gingrich's "Renewing American Civilization" course reached tens of thousands of students every week. This 20-hour course carried on National Empowerment Television every Wednesday and which is available on videotape, speaks to the central premise "that an America in decay must take radical steps to restore individual opportunity and prepare for a new age based on information, not industry. The overall goal, he says, is to transform the welfare state into what he calls an opportunity society" (NYT, 12/20/94). In addition to studying ways to accelerate the licensing and testing of new medical technologies, matters of intense material interest to its backers in the health industry, the Progress and Freedom Foundation plans to study how the Government regulates the telecommunications industry, a matter of intense interest to the corporate and ruling elite in general.

Jeffrey Eisenbach, head of the Foundation, was previously the chairman of Gopac. Gopac handled much of the arrangements for Gingrich's satellite broadcasts and registration for his course. Corporate sponsors of the course were reported to have been told that "if they contributed $50,000 or more, they would have the chance to "work directly" with the project's leaders in developing the course" (NYT, 12/18/94). Owen Roberts, who was ambassador to Togo under President Ronald Reagan and who gave Gopac $324,513 between 1985 and 1993, sat in with the students during one session of Gingrich's television broadcasts. No doubt the Corporate Sponsors who bought the right to "work directly" with Gopac's leaders, who include Gingrich as their head, have also bought the right to "work directly" with those leaders as they assume government policy-making positions and as they call in the political debts owed them by those elected to congress, and perhaps, ultimately, to the presidency of the United States.

Foundation Influence on the Afrikan American Community

With regard to the Afrikan American community one can confidently argue that a number of its leading social-political institutions, e.g., the NAACP and the National Urban League, have to measurable degrees compromised the interests of the community in response to their being heavily financed by White wealth in general and White institutional wealth in particular. Foundations, such as Ford and Rockefeller, have loomed large in the lives of these and similar Black "civil rights" organizations and in the life of the Black community in general. For example, in an effort to cool down racial tensions in Cleveland, Ohio in 1961, the Ford Foundation granted CORE $175,000 for voter registration efforts which were instrumental in the election of Black mayor Carl Stokes (since deceased), a Democrat and supporter of the Vietnam War (Horowitz and Kolodney, 1974). Stokes was also considered to be politically "moderate" and friendly toward business.

The Ford Foundation also influenced the generation of information regarding the Afrikan American community through its funding of research organizations, such as that led by Black social psychologist Kenneth Clark's Metropolitan Applied Research Center, to the tune of a half million dollars. Also in an effort to calm racial tensions in Cleveland in 1961, this organization is reported to have "sponsored a secret meeting of civil rights leaders (nine major groups were represented) ...in order to execute a joint campaign in that regard" (Horowitz and Kolodney, ibid).

Even apparently Black militant and liberation politics and movements were not spared the influence of the White corporate elite, who were ostensibly an enemy of Black Power advocates. According to Horowitz and Kolodney, "In 1967, a Black Power conference was held in Newark, financed by 50 White corporations." They provide a very apt example of how White elite foundations sought and seek to shape and direct the social-political character and orientation of the Afrikan American community:

> [A]t the end of the month [July, 1967], the most massive rebellion to date took place in the Motor City of Detroit, leaving 45 blacks dead and millions of dollars worth of property damage in its wake. On August 1, the day after troops left the city, 22 American leaders called on the nation to revise its priorities and bring more resources to bear on domestic problems, and announced the formation of an Urban Coalition to do just that. The Urban Coalition, headed by John Gardner, former secretary of Health, Education and Welfare and former president of the Carnegie Foundation, included moderate Negro leaders Roy Wilkins of the NAACP and Whitney Young of the National Urban League, as well as labor leaders, big city mayors and businessmen like David Rockefeller and Gerald Phillipe, chairman of the board of General Electric and trustee of the National Industrial Conference Board, a foundation-financed policy organization. The funds for the Urban Coalition were to be provided by the Rockefeller Brothers Fund Inc., the Carnegie Foundation and the Ford Founda-

tion. Regional coalitions between labor, Negroes, businessmen and politicians were to be formed (the New York coalition was headed by Christian Herter Jr., vice president of Standard Oil of New York) and they were to work in close cooperation with the National Alliance of Businessmen headed by Henry Ford II. Not surprisingly, the coalition placed primary emphasis not on massive income redistribution and federal reconstruction and rebuilding programs, but on the vigorous involvement of the private sector in the crises in the cities by commitment of investment, job training, hiring and "and all other things that are necessary to the full employment of the free enterprise system, and also to its survival."

This basic strategy of salvation was echoed in the Report of the Special Advisory Commission on Civil Disorders (the Kerner Commission) which had been empowered by the President at the same time, July 27, 1967, in the wake of the Detroit insurrection) to look into the causes of riots and prescribe remedial action.[17]

The efforts of the White male elite establishment to redefine reality and define important and possibly revolutionary political-ideological concepts are illustrated by Horowitz and Kolodney's following example of how that elite sought to redefine the concept of "Black Power" and publicize its redefinition:

> While vigorously repressing — i.e., killing, jailing, framing, ostracizing — Black Power advocates for whom Black Power meant confrontation with the system and agitation for revolutionary change, the rich white establishment and its press began to promote recognition of the reasonable connotations which the term "Black Power" had in the mouths of "responsible militants." As the Wall Street Journal reported in July 1968, "Black Power" is being "newly defined in a way that may not be quite so frightening to the white man" — and particularly to Wall Street Journal readers. "What now seems to be happening in the tortuous history of race relations in America," commented the Journal, "is that the black man is coming of age." While maintaining that "extremist blacks, and their radical ideas must be purged," the Journal noted that "White America is the majority, and the new black leadership, while adopting more and more of a 'do-it-ourselves' stance, still does not want a complete break with the rest of America."
>
> Black Power as self-help within the system, then, was the Journal's preferred interpretation, and it was pleased to find that the black organizations, which are heavily subsidized by Journal readers on the one hand and savagely repressed by the forces of law and order on the other, are coming around to this point of view: "What is really

---

17. David Horowitz with David Kolodney, *The Poverty Establishment*, p. 53.

being said now, in different ways by different leaders, is that the black man is beginning to feel strong enough to rely more on himself and less on the white man. This new emphasis on self-help is, in a sense, a return to the turn-of-the-century philosophy of Booker T. Washington."[18]

Thus, it is plain to see that in the single-minded pursuit of its class interests the ruling White male-corporate elite seeks to bias the policy-formation process of the government in its favor, often to the detriment of other groups and classes. This class views the government and the resources of the country and world as its very own special preserve to dispose of as it sees fit. Therefore it uses its immense material and human resources to create and redefine reality; to shape and deceive the consciousness of those it seeks to shamelessly exploit.

The Need for Afrikan-centered Information and Strategy Centers

Our review of the White male elite-dominated policy-formation network, the power and influence it generates and exerts, obviously implies that if detrimental effects on the Afrikan American community are to be neutralized, they must be countered by an effective Afrikan American-controlled network. This network must provide "the powers that be" in the Afrikan American community with the relevant information, intelligence, strategies and tactics for advancing the community's interests, and for liberating Afrikan peoples from their oppressors. We fully endorse Theodore Cross' proposition regarding the need to "organize a Black-controlled intelligence agency and strategy center":

> IN THE COLLECTIVE OPINION of millions of blacks in America, their numerical minority position keeps Negroes from claiming power and position in this country. This conclusion wholly ignores the potential of minority power in a democracy. The fact is that black powerlessness is due in large measure to the inability of Negro people to develop a winning scenario for taking up positions of economic and political power. This is not a failure of numbers; it is often a failure of *intelligence* operations. In a nation that allocates resources according to power as well as ability, blacks simply lack the information and plans necessary to set in place a strategy for becoming both strong and equal.
>
> Intelligence power uniquely belongs to those who can read maps. In modern times powerful people possess and read the mapped-out

---

18. Ibid., p. 54.

channels of the federal bureaucracy. They find, and skillfully interpret, the intricate charts of Wall Street finance, the complex folkways of large corporations, and the obscure roads of entry into credentializing institutions. They scout out the thickets of legislative and administrative bodies. Powerful people and groups tend to be the people who know the ropes because they have charted the maze of business, government, education, and banking.

Like other activities associated with power, expert training in map reading and other intelligence activities has been reserved for members of the white race. In recent years, many of the critical charts that describe the engines of power in the United States have been unlocked and made available for distant inspection by blacks. But few blacks have learned to use the charts and scrutinize the maps; few have discovered how to move comfortably through the maze of political and economic information that is indispensable to those who would locate, harness, or blunt institutional power.

In order to come to power and finally reach equality in the United States, blacks, too, must become expert map readers. To this end they must organize and *control* a competent and well-funded intelligence-gathering agency. Staffed by expert chart readers and intelligence operators, the intelligence unit is necessary to provide black leaders and strategists with all the charts and other strategic information that they need to "scope out" their problems, detect the presence of barriers, find ways of entering closed places, set agendas, plan political strategies, and act rationally to attain agreed-on objectives.

What kinds of information will this new black intelligence agency search out, analyze, and publish? Answers are needed to some basic questions:

- What are the principal underlying causes of black inequality?
- What, in order of importance, are the current forces that pose the greatest obstacles to the progress of blacks?
- To what extent, if any, is racial inequality self-repairing if openly competitive and bias-free markets can be established?
- Are simple and well-enforced laws against racial bias in commercial and employment selections sufficient, in due course, to cause blacks to catch up to whites?
- What is the effect on blacks of minimum wage laws and similar protective legislation?
- How can standardized tests be prevented from perpetuating the economic and educational advantages of whites?
- To what extent does affirmative action and similar racially oriented policies reinforce race prejudice and otherwise hurt blacks?
- What states, cities and congressional districts offer the best opportunities for building black political strength?

- What are the reasons for the disintegration of the black family?
- How is black progress to be measured?[19]

These and more profound questions must be asked and answered. However, centers founded to deal with those important questions and issues and to provide in-depth and pragmatic analyses as well as to plot strategies and tactics for Black empowerment, must be totally funded by the Afrikan American community. Efforts of nominally Black-controlled think tanks like the Joint Center for Political and Economic Studies, though necessary, are insufficient and limited by their funding sources. For example, this center, which was founded in 1970 by a group of Black intellectuals, politicians and professionals, opened under the auspices of Howard University and Kenneth Clark's Metropolitan Applied Research Center (this center is designed to undertake research dealing with issues that most affect Afrikan Americans). Its objectives include in addition to research and the dissemination of relevant information, the improvement of the "socioeconomic status of Black Americans; to increase their influence in the political and public policy arenas; and to facilitate the building of coalitions across racial lines." Moreover, the Center provides training and technical assistance for Black elected officials, and issues reports on political and management techniques for Black officials and political leaders. It publishes a magazine, *Focus*, which mainly speaks to Black politicians. The Center publishes about a half-dozen books per year and produces radio and television programs. While the Center's objectives may be laudable and its active interests relevant to issues of concern in the Black community, we may expect its objectives and interests will be confined within the limits defined by the White corporate and foundation elite which funds it and, therefore, within limits set by the demands of White supremacy. Its staff of approximately 50 persons is supported by a budget of approximately $3.5 million originated through the financial backing of the Ford Foundation. And we can rest assured that it continues to receive similar backing from Ford or some other White elite funding sources. This being the case, it is easy to see that certain perspectives, questions, answers, strategies and tactical approaches are practically precluded from discussion and study by its various committees. The questions it asks, answers it suggests, and tactics it executes will not likely challenge the "free enterprise" system — of which the Ford Foundation along with other White elite foundations are products, and the White supremacist ideology they advocate. It does not seek to change the fundamental social structure and relations responsible for

---

19. Theodore Cross, *The Black Power Imperative,* pp. 673–75.

creating and maintaining the general oppressive conditions which characterize much of the Afrikan American community in the past as well as the present. The best that White-funded Black organizations can achieve is a repetitive and tired call for government support, private (White) investment, job training, affirmative action and other "solutions" which affirm and strengthen the very system that is the major source of suffering in the Black community to begin with. Thus, creative, courageous, imaginative, novel and innovative ideas, solutions and possibilities escape this dependent intellectual Black elite. Consequently, they can only maintain and exacerbate "the crisis of the Negro intellectual", the crisis of leadership in the Black community, and the crisis in the Black community.

The need for the Afrikan American community to establish self-supporting institutions should be evident if the community is to generate and exercise genuine Black Power. This need should also underscore the community's further necessity to increase its wealth by capturing its internal markets and extending its reach into the larger national and international market systems if it is to financially support its vital institutions and defend their integrity.

To return to the need to establish Black-controlled information agencies and strategy centers, Cross suggests a number of important characteristics which define such agencies and centers as well as their objectives. These include the following characteristics and purposes:

- [Be] sufficiently sophisticated to detect and expose where appropriate, tax policies and administrative rulings that do harm to the economic prospects of most Blacks.
- Must be staffed by expert economists, sociologists, political strategists, and investigators sufficiently worldly and knowledgeable to challenge and refute the prescriptions issued by "think tanks" that ponder the problems of minorities and then unwittingly recommend public policies that perpetuate the power advantage of Whites.
- An important purpose of a Black intelligence agency is to shape the black political agenda and plan its tactics. The ... agency would lay out the possible scenarios for winning and losing in particular political campaigns.
- Must discover the "open windows" where Black political power can move in and share control of institutions and cities...devise political penalties and rewards to convert opponents of Black-backed legislation.
- [Must] ...set straight the public record when Black politicians act irresponsibly or dishonestly and then blame their failure on racism.

- Must free themselves from the important constraint that much of what they now know, or are likely to know, is controlled by government and private media power, which at best, wants to help Blacks but is endemically opposed to empowering them. Just as Blacks must break the White monopoly of the means of production, they must also dismantle the White monopoly on information, the raw material for thinking and planning.
- The strategic purpose of the Black intelligence agency is to define what Blacks should do and how they might do it. With the aid of superb intelligence operations, American Blacks must develop a concrete and definite plan for achieving the five or ten things they *must* have to obtain parity in American society...Blacks...must prepare themselves to be first-class spies and sleuths. The Black nation in the United States, like any other nation, will be no stronger than its information and intelligence.[20]

Utilizing another suggestion by Cross in another context, the "organization of a nation-wide system of Black caucuses within all major corporations," federal and state government agencies, legislatures, educational institutions, financial organizations, hospitals, industrial firms, etc., can provide extremely valuable information. Such information carefully processed by the relevant Black-controlled establishments can be immensely empowering in a world where information and knowledge are the major bases of power.

On the Black Hand Side: Black Power Networks and Institutions of Higher Learning

We have sketched an outline of how the White male-dominated ruling class in America seeks to bend the public policy-formation process to its will. We have looked briefly at the policy-planning and policy-formation network of corporate interests, research and educational institutions, policy-planning groups, opinion-shaping apparati, and the governmental law-making regulation and executive institutions it utilizes to actualize its class interests. It is tempting to perceive the foregoing discussion as primarily a description of how the predominant class in a class society seeks to work its wiles on the subordinate classes without regard for their racial composition. Therefore, there are those who think that a "class analysis" instead of a "race analysis" would be appropriate here. They may argue that racism is only instrumental to ruling-class interests. This proposition implies that the common enemy of both the Black and White masses

---

20. Ibid., 675–77.

is their domination by the ruling class, whose processes of ruling we have described so far.

The ruling elite of America is practically lily White, almost exclusively led by White males. Black Americans are excluded from this club and are in no way influentially a part of its special-interest processes or its policy planning/policy formation processes or network. Even if Black Americans were significantly a part of these power systems, they would be Black only in skin-color, i.e., "honorary Whites," assimilated Blacks working in the interest of continuing White domination and supremacy. This is the standing price of their admission to the club of the ruling corporate elite. As to the masses, including Blacks and Whites of all classes, we agree with W.E.B. DuBois (1968) who described them as not split along horizontal lines, i.e., an integrated division of Blacks and Whites along middle-class, working-class, lower-class lines, but as split along "a vertical fissure, a complete separation of classes by race, cutting across economic layers." He goes on to argue:

> Even if on one side of this color line, the dark masses were overwhelmingly workers, with but an embryonic capitalist class, nevertheless *the split between white and black workers was greater than that between white workers and capitalists*; and this split depended not simply on economic exploitation but on a racial folk-lore grounded on centuries of instinct, habit and thought and implemented by the conditioned reflex of visible color.[21]

The verticality of the split between Blacks and Whites from the ruling elite (if there were an equivalent Black class) down through to the very lowest of classes implies that in reality we are dealing with an exclusively White nation-state which excludes Blacks at all of its class levels. This connotes that despite the exploitation of the subordinate classes of both ethnic groups by the ruling White elite, the White lower classes are joined in racial solidarity with the White elite against the realization of the true and full citizenship of Blacks in the United States. Even the nominal citizenship of Blacks in this White nation means a sacrifice of "Black Power" since full membership in that nation would require Blacks to no longer see themselves as Black; that they shed their identity and consciousness of themselves as a people with cultural and other interests separate from those of Whites. This means that "Black Power" can only be realized and exercised in the interest of Afrikan people at home and abroad if it is consciously based on an Afrikan-centered identity and conscious-

---

21. W.E.B. DuBois, *Dusk of Dawn: An Essay Toward an Autobiography of a Race Concept* (New York: Schocken, 1968), p. 205.

ness and is motivated and guided by a conscious intent of Afrikan peoples to gain power equal to or in excess of that held by European peoples.

If Black Power is our goal, we must develop and use an intimate and expert knowledge of the nature and organization of White Power and of the White American nation. We should study its class interest structures, its policy formation and execution networks, and its governmental structures and operations in terms of how they may be counterbalanced by equivalent Afrikan American-based political-economic structures, policy formation/execution networks, governing structures and operations. This implies the development of a Black nation-within-a-nation which would fund, organize and operate its own power networks in order to penetrate, favorably influence or counter those of the White elite.

The need for the full economic development of the Afrikan American community, the need for its material enrichment and heavy penetration of the now White American economic system, should be by now quite clear. For it is clear that given the current design and functional operation of the White American nation, its governmental operations and outcomes can only be influenced in favor of Black Americans through the solid, appropriately structured social and political organization, and the purposeful creation and use of wealth by the Black community.

Black institutions chartered by the White elite, funded and influenced in their composition and direction by that elite, for those very reasons cannot operate freely and fully in the interest of the Afrikan American community and in the interest of the world-wide Afrikan community. There is a severe need for the Afrikan American and Pan–Afrikan communities to develop Afrikan-funded special interest and policy-formation institutions as well as several world-class universities and research institutions. We must recognize that the major function of education involves securing the survival of a people, advancing their interests, enhancing their quality of life. Educational establishments are as much a part of the defense establishment of a people as is their army. A people bereft of educational institutions dedicated and designed to defend their interests and to *solve their problems*, are essentially a defenseless people, a people vulnerable to the exploitation of other peoples as well as vulnerable to annihilation. We cannot advance or appropriately defend our interests and lives as an Afrikan people if we place the fate of our community in the hands of the educational establishments of our oppressors and enemies, and in the hands of those Afrikans educated in them. Afrikan peoples and Afrikan leaders should be the recipients of an Afrikan-centered education. No Afrikan should be granted leadership in the Afrikan community who has not been certified through education or experience as Afrikan-centered in consciousness, identity and orientation. In the absence of such institutions today, it is incumbent on the so-called predominantly Black colleges and universities and the Black and Afrikan Studies programs in these and the predominately White institutions to develop teaching, training and research departments in all areas vital to Afrikan communal interests. Intense education and research must not only occur in the areas of history, culture, political science and victimology (toting all the ailments of Black suffering followed by White establishment-dictated or defined recommendations). Every department in predominantly Black colleges and universities should require all their students to attend courses taught from an Afrikan-centered perspective and designed to achieve Afrikan-centered ends. This includes business, economics, the social and physical sciences. For example, Black students should not only be taught "business administration" courses which only prepare them for work and servitude in White-owned businesses. They should also be taught the development and administration of Black-owned businesses; how to develop and execute business and economic strategies in the interest of the Black community's control of its own markets; to run specific types of businesses; to finance businesses from within the Black community; to solve business and economic problems facing the Black community; to penetrate the White business world as entrepreneurs; to gain control of White markets and businesses; to engage in import-export businesses; to compete as international businesspersons heading multinational Black-owned corporations and the like. In the physical sciences Black students should be instructed in the politics of science, the sociology of science (i.e., what social, political, economic, cultural formations are conducive to the creation and continuing development of science and technology; what are the scientific and technological issues and needs in Afrikan communities; how trained Afrikan scientists and technicians can profitably work in the interest of Afrikan peoples, etc.).

Black universities and think tanks must increase their Afrikan-centered research, their consultancy relations with the Black community, and fully engage themselves with Black community development on all levels and in all areas. For all Afrikan American-controlled institutions must come to the realization that their primary reason for being is the protection and betterment of Afrikan peoples.

They must recognize their place and the role they must play in a vast network of institutions, groups and individuals designed to achieve these ends. For if Afrikan peoples cannot be protected and their quality of life optimized by Black Power, then what is the point?

Chapter 10

THE CANDIDATE-SELECTION PROCESS

The Selling of the Candidate

A BRIEF REVIEW OF OUR PRIOR DISCUSSION of the special interest and policy-formation processes and a re-examination of the schematic diagram depicting the policy-formation process should impress us with the fact that electoral politics, particularly as represented by the every-four-years voting ritual in the U.S., has relatively little to do with the actual process of day-to-day governance, policy-making and execution, or with the actual exercise of power by the mass electorate imposing its will on the U.S. government. We have seen that democracy in America has essentially been betrayed by the domination of governmental processes by a relatively small class of powerholders. This is also true of the candidate-selection/election processes. The existence of an exclusive two-party electoral system; the decline in party organization; the fundamental similarities between the two parties; the need for candidates to be backed by rich contributors, large and costly individualized staffs, to engage in very expensive media campaigns, to place individual ambition, image-building and winning above dealing with substantive issues, means that the "will of the people" as expressed through their voting patterns rarely expresses itself in actual governmental policy, decision-making and practical governance.

The need for a candidate to obtain strong financial backing before mounting a credible primary campaign, let alone before making a final run for political office, often means that he has been compromised, if not bought, before he presents himself to the people for election. The power to influence the process of governance begins before the election and those groups who generally lack the monetary and other relevant resources to influence the pre-election candidate selection process are already out of the running for achieving significant influence in the governance process. This, despite their heavy voting in favor of one candidate as against another. This is aptly implied by Parenti's observation that, "Supposedly one of the great gifts of our democracy is the right to vote for the candidate of one's choice. But...the "choice" is often narrow and/or restructured by a variety of undemocratic features." Parenti in the same vein notes the following:

> The ostensible purpose of electoral competition among political parties is to hold rulers accountable. According to Western democratic theory, popular elections counteract the oligarchic tendency by institutionalizing the power of numbers. An election, like an opinion poll, is supposedly a measure of mass sentiment, but also a mandatory decision, an exercise of sovereign power by the many. The democratic goal is not only that the many shall have their say but that their say shall have an empowering effect, that it shall be both the public *opinion* and the popular *will*. The right to free speech and dissent, even assuming such a right could be exercised without risk to the dissenter, is not democracy's sum total but merely one of the necessary conditions for holding those in office accountable to their constituency. One can imagine a situation — as exists in our better universities and prisons — in which the constituents might be free to complain of conditions, petition the authorities, read critical newspapers and books, and even write them, while exercising little or no power over decision makers. "Democracy," as it is practiced by institutional oligarchs, consists of allowing others the opportunity to *say* what they want while the oligarchs, commanding all institutional resources, continue to *do* what they want.[1]

It has been noted by a number of political scientists that the candidate-selection process had become increasingly individualistic. Name recognition and personal image are important assets in any politician's run for high office. However, the candidate's personal ability to buy the kinds of services with which to achieve recognition, to publicize his or her positions and abilities, is often very limited.

---

1. M. Parenti, *Power and the Powerless* (N.Y.: St. Martin's Press, 1987), p. 203.

Herbert Alexander concluded from his study of how political campaigns are financed that: "Because of its ability to buy the kinds of services that produce name recognition and exposition of positions, money wields its greatest influence on campaigns — particularly presidential races — during the prenomination period."[2] Consequently, candidates become vulnerable to the influence of "fat cats," effective fund-raisers, and the contributions of political action committees, many of which are connected directly or indirectly with the corporate oligarchy. The ability of the power elite to provide crucial financial support for both parties on the national level generally far outweighs that of the unions and other sources of funding more closely related to the masses of the population. Domhoff argues that through relatively simple and direct means and large campaign contributions, members of the ruling class can in good measure dominate the candidate-selection process as prospective officeholders seek to distinguish themselves from their competitors and to project an image which will compel the electorate to vote for them. He goes on to argue:

> In the guise of fat cats and money raisers, the same men who direct corporations and take part in policy groups play a central role in the careers of most politicians who advance beyond the local level or state legislatures in states of any size and consequence: "Recruitment of elective elites remains closely associated, especially for the more important offices in the larger states, with the candidates' wealth or access to large campaign contributions. Moreover, the role of the wealthy donor and the fund raiser seems to be especially crucial in the nomination phase of the process. This was the conclusion of one of the earliest systematic studies of campaign finance:[3]

The legitimacy of the electoral system is put into serious question in light of the central role played by heavy campaign contributions and services provided by the ruling elite and those under its ideological influence. The legitimacy of this system is especially questionable when one looks at the products of the candidate-selection process. This system generally produces a legislative and governmental system top-heavy with lawyers and other professional "go-betweens."

> [T]he major results of the candidate-selection process are, first, a large number of well-to-do-politicians who are eager and willing to "go along to get along," precisely the kind of politicians who are necessary if the special-interest process is to operate the way it does, and

---

2. Herbert E. Alexander, *Financing Politics* (Congressional Quarterly Press, 1976), p. 44, cited in Domhoff, *The Powers That Be*, p. 144.

3. G.W. Domhoff, *The Powers That Be*, pp. 143–44.

second, a great many politicians with few strong policy positions of their own, who are thus open to the suggestions put forth to them by the corporate executives and academic experts who have been legitimated as "serious" statesmen and leaders within the institutions of the policy-planning process. In other words, the evidence shows that the candidate-selection process naturally produces the kinds of elected officials whom we know must be in office because of the ways in which the special-interest and policy-planning processes operate. We can begin to see why the three processes mesh together so well even though they are relatively independent.[4]

Party Politics

Another outcome of the American candidate-selection process dominated by "big money" and ruling elite influence, is a two-party system which downplays, discourages or ignores substantive policy issues and discussions, neglects the political education of its constituencies, does not satisfy voter preferences, and which produces two major parties whose ideological orientations are many times barely distinguishable and whose political views and goals overlap at many important points. The blurry difference between the two parties has led one labor leader to wryly observe that "We don't have a 2-party system in this country. We have the Demopublicans." It is one party of the corporate class with two wings — the Democrats and Republicans. Domhoff (ibid) argues that "the major effect of the two-party system in the United States is that it discourages policy discussion, political education and any attempt to satisfy majority preference, rather than encouraging them. It helps to create the confusion and disinterest for which pluralists constantly scold the general public." Parenti asserts that though there are enough discernable differences between the parties to prohibit their being accurately described as identical twins, the differences are not wide enough to prohibit their identification as fraternal twins. He contends that:

> On most fundamental economic class issues, the similarities between the parties loom so large as frequently to obscure the differences. Both the Democratic and Republican parties are committed to the preservation of the private corporate economy; huge military budgets; the use of subsidies, deficit spending and tax allowances to bolster business profits; the funneling of public resources through private conduits, including whole new industries developed at public expense; the use of repression against opponents of the existing class structure; the defense of the multinational corporate empire; and interven-

---
4. Ibid., p. 162.

tion against social revolutionary elements abroad. In short, Republicans and Democrats are dedicated to strikingly similar definitions of the public interest, at great cost to the life chances of underprivileged people at home and abroad.[5]

Greider (1992) argues that "The Democratic party, as a political organization, is no longer quite real itself...It exists as historical artifact, an organization fiction... It acts neither as a faithful mediator between citizens and the government nor as the forum for policy debate and resolution nor even as a structure around which political power can accumulate." Like the Republican party, the Democratic party essentially regards the vast majority of its rank and file members or grassroots supporters as an impediment to governing. They are sensitive to the public mood and constantly measure its pulse by means of opinion polls, surveys and the like. This partisan interest in public opinion polls and focus groups is not designed to enhance their responsivity to the electorate and to produce responsive government, but to manipulate the public mood in order to win office. The people and their welfare are not the end of the electoral process but merely the means for winning. For both parties electioneering is more of a social device for selling to the public, for shaping its opinion than for standing to account for past behavior and receiving instructions from the public regarding governance and policy decisions. The Republican party is currently notorious for "the strategy that requires the party to agitate latent emotional resentment and turn them into marketable political traits. The new raw materials for this are drawn from enduring social aggravations — wounds of race, class and religion, even sex" (Greider).This strategy which centers around projecting the idea that the White populace is threatened by overwhelming alien forces, particularly Black criminals and Blacks demanding welfare and special entitlements, is not a strategy for governance. Again, as Greider notes, "The party's method deliberately coaxes emotional responses from people — teases their anxieties over values they hold important in their own lives — but then walks away from the anger and proceeds to govern on its real agenda, defending the upper-class interest of wealth and corporate power." He concludes that "The Republican party is not a party of conservative ideology. It is a party of conservative clients. Wherever possible, the ideology will be invoked as justification for taking care of the client's needs. When the two are in conflict, the conservative principles are discarded and the clients are served."

---

5. M. Parenti, *Democracy for the Few*, 5th ed., pp. 174–75.

However, the contemporary Democratic party does not differ significantly from its Republican counterpart with respect to servicing the interests of the ruling White male corporate and wealthy elite. The contemporary leadership of this party, the Democratic Leadership Council (DLC), is determined to jettison the party's image of being beholden to left-of-center interest groups, racial minorities, labor unions, women's rights groups, and the like, and return it to the "mainstream." The boundaries of the mainstream, as Greider argues, is "defined by the DLC's donors from corporate America — ARCO, American Petroleum, Dow Chemical, Prudential-Bache, Georgia Pacific, Martin Marietta...." One of the major objectives of the Democratic party leadership is to distance the party from its association, in the collective psyche of the White suburban America, with predominantly inner-city Black America. This distancing process is symbolized by the Democratic party leadership's distancing treatment of Jesse Jackson, the major spokesman for Blacks and other minorities and for the progressive wing in the party. To the broad White electorate the party's relationship with Jackson, its visible treatment of him, is synonymous with or emblematic of its relationship with Afrikan Americans and its attitudes toward and treatment of progressive, anti-elitist, anti-capitalist groups in general. The distancing process undertaken by the Democratic party leadership in effect compelled it to reject the claims and influence of some of its most loyal constituent groups. Greider thus explains the objectives of the DLC at a 1990 conference in New Orleans as follows:

> The DLC's main objective, however, was an attack on the Democratic party's core constituencies — labor, schoolteachers, women's rights groups, peace and disarmament activists, the racial minorities and supporters of affirmative action. Its stated goal was to restore the party's appeal to disaffected white males, especially in the South, but the DLC discussions did not focus on the economic decline afflicting those citizens. Instead, it promoted the notion that Democrats must distance themselves from the demands of women or blacks or other aggrieved groups within the party. The Reverend Jesse Jackson and his provocative economic agenda aimed at workers, white and black, was a favorite target of the Democratic Leadership Council and, on Capitol Hill, the DLC was sometimes waggishly referred to as "the white boys' caucus."
>
> Thus, in addition to all its other organizational weaknesses, the Democratic party is divided by nasty ideological combat between the party's Washington elites and its rank-and-file constituencies — the people at the grassroots who are most active in Democratic politics. The establishment's quarrel was with the party's own voters. The

people they belittled as "activists" and "interest groups" were the very people who cared most intensely about public issues and who formed the faithful core of the party's electorate, win or lose.

The Democratic establishment did not wish to initiate a dialogue with these citizens, only to make them go away or at least keep their mouths shut. The party elite had no intention of sharing its own policy deliberations with Democrats at large or trying to re-engage people in governing politics by building the organizational connections that have been lost. The elites wished only to form a governing consensus around the supposed "mainstream" — their mainstream, the one they have already formulated in Washington.[6]

Thus, as Greider surmises, "In the contemporary Democratic party, the 'regulars' at the grassroots are regarded as an impediment to governing." And the major impediment to governing is the troubling presence of Black America. This is not only the case for the Democratic party but for the Republican party as well. This is the case for the White American nation-within-a-nation, period.

Blacks: The Primary Impediment to Governing — At the center of American politics and governance stands the alien presence of Black America. This presence is White America's number one domestic issue and problem. This presence in its own peculiar way very significantly defines the shape and character of the collective White American psyche and body politic. This group, the Afrikan American community, intrudes disturbingly into White consciousness as insistently and persistently as White America seeks to exclude it from its midst and to deny and distort its reality through projective and self-deceptive stereotyping processes. Thomas and Mary Edsall cut right to the heart of the matter in their introductory remarks to an article titled "Race" published in the *Atlantic Monthly* (May, 1991):

> RACE IS NO LONGER A STRAIGHTFORWARD, morally unambiguous force in American politics; instead, considerations of race are now deeply imbedded in the strategy and tactics of politics, in competing concepts of the function and responsibility of government, and in each voter's conceptual structure of moral and partisan identity. Race helps define liberal and conservative ideologies, shapes the presidential coalitions of the Democratic and Republican parties, provides a harsh new dimension to concern over taxes and crime, drives a wedge through alliances of the working classes and the poor, and gives both momentum and vitality to the drive to establish a national majority inclined by income and demography to support policies benefitting the affluent

---

6. W. Greider, *Who Will Tell The People: The Betrayal of American Democracy*, p. 263.

and the upper-middle class. In terms of policy, race has played a critical role in the creation of a political system that has tolerated, if not supported, the growth of the disparity between rich and poor over the past fifteen years. Race-coded images and language changed the course of the 1980, 1984 and 1988 presidential elections and the 1990 elections for the governorships of California and Alabama, the U.S. Senate in North Carolina and the post of Texas secretary of agriculture. The political role of race is subtle and complex, requiring listening to those whose views are deeply repellent to some and deeply resonant for others. The debate over racial policy has been skewed and distorted by a profound failure to listen.

The Edsalls give further evidence of the antipathy many in the White American nation have for Afrikan Americans in reporting the results of an analysis of the attitudes of White "Reagan democrats," i.e., White, nominally Democrats who supported Ronald Reagan and Republican party politics during the past decade.

The views of working-class defectors from the Democratic Party were examined in a 1985 study of suburban Detroit by Stanley Greenberg, the president of the Analysis Group, a Democratic polling firm. The study found that

> these white Democratic defectors express a profound distaste for blacks, a sentiment that pervades almost everything they think about government and politics. Blacks constitute the explanation for their [white defectors'] vulnerability and for almost everything that has gone wrong in their lives; not being black is what constitutes being middle class; not living with blacks is what makes a neighborhood a decent place to live... These sentiments have important implications for Democrats, as virtually all progressive symbols and themes have been redefined in racial and pejorative terms....
>
> The special status of blacks is perceived by almost all of these individuals as a serious obstacle to their personal advancement. Indeed, discrimination against whites has become a well-assimilated and ready explanation for their status, vulnerability and failures.

The Need for a Black Political Party

The foregoing discussion should strongly indicate that Black America is in no important way an assimilated part of White America. The latter community is a nation unto itself, an exclusively White American nation-within-a-nation. The former is a diffused, essentially reactionarily and loosely organized, overly inclusive community lacking the self-knowledge, self-acceptance and types of social attitudes, relations and institutions which can actualize, organize and apply its relatively abundant power potential. The Afrikan American community is excluded from the decision-making and governance processes of the White nation which dominates and exploits it. It is excluded from the policy-planning and formation networks which guide or influence governmental policy. It has no effective, Afrikan American-funded lobbying and political action organizations which can influence governmental and electoral processes in its favor. Not only is the Afrikan American community and its representatives excluded from the power centers of White America; it has now been excluded for all practical purposes from the National Democratic Party. This party and its Republican counterpart go to great lengths to dissociate themselves from being perceived as advocates for Black community interests and concerns. The firm establishment of this dissociation in the minds of the predominant White electorate is seen as the key to gaining presidential office and many other national and state offices by both parties. Thus, Afrikan Americans are indeed excluded from significant influence in governance and in the two parties which share the governance process between them.

The "exclusion problem" alluded to above can be solved in many ways, a variety of which will be discussed herein. In the context of this chapter, one of the possible solutions points to the full development of an independent Afrikan American political party. While we harbor no illusions about the ability of such an organization to win national office, that would not be its primary purpose, we believe that it could, both as a single party and in coalition with other similar parties, very significantly influence presidential, statewide, and local candidate selection and election processes, and more importantly, favorably impact the decision-making and governance processes on the international, national, state and local levels. More determining than running for office and winning elections, an independent Black political party would be able to do the following things:

1. Articulate and debate major issues relevant to Afrikan Americans.
2. Formulate coherent and distinct programs designed to realize the important interests of Afrikan Americans.
3. Implement national, state and local programs whether in and out of office.
4. Fund the cost of gathering information and developing policies.

5. Raise and organize money in order to engage in the process of developing leading ideas and goals that will form the Afrikan American community's internal and public policy agendas and strategies for actualizing its interests.
6. Undertake the responsibility of overseeing federal, state and local law writing and enforcement in the community.
7. Serve as a civic agency which assists Afrikan American communities with their concrete needs.
8. Act as faithful mediator between the Afrikan American community and the U.S. government and foreign governments as well as the governments of the Afrika and Afrikan-Caribbean nations.
9. Serve as a forum for policy debate and resolution and as a structure around which political and economic power can accumulate.
10. Serve as a "communiversity," a university for the people — an educational institution where the people discover how the world really works. Serve as a place where people learn mutual trust, loyalty, purpose and collective activity, to draw together in relationships which lead to real, potent political and economic power.
11. Serve as the means for training and developing leaders, experts and community organizers. Foster research and development projects and provide a nationally coordinated network of political and economic administrative centers in order to carry out local, regional, national and international programs and policies according to a democratically sanctioned strategy.
12. Serve as a primary source for the development of concentrated cooperative and private business enterprises, trade associations, for the development of financial resources for Afrikan American personal, communal, and business success and prosperity. Provide the means for supporting the social, industrial, technical and business training of Afrikan Americans.
13. Maintain an independent, highly informative, ethnically committed media center.
14. Promote Pan-Afrikan cultural unity and development through the study of Afrikan history and culture and through serving as a conduit for cultural and economic exchange between Afrikan peoples across the Diaspora.

The scope of this volume will not allow us to detail the process of developing, organizing and administering an independent Black political party. However, we think a basic caveat is in place here. Such a party should *not* permit dual party membership. That is, Afrikan Americans who are members of other political parties, including and especially those belonging to the Democratic and Republican parties, should not be admitted membership into a Black independent party — under no circumstances. No Black politicians affiliated with any other party should be allowed entré at any level of the organization. They should be dealt with as members of rival parties. Persons and groups representing Marxist, communists, or Eurocentrist ideological leanings should be discouraged from seeking membership. The party should be secularly led, i.e., not led by preachers and other religious leaders. While their membership is welcomed, the party should not become the battleground for religious, sectarian interests or moralistic, moralizing institutions. The party's orientation should be clearly Black nationalistic in character and intention — definitely not assimilationist and integrationist in the traditional sense. While open and willing to enter into advantageous coalitions with other parties and groups, the Afrikan-centered nature and purpose of the party should be clearly and universally recognized.

Chapter 11

IDEOLOGY AND THE LEGITIMIZATION OF DOMINANCE

IN OUR SECOND CHAPTER WE DISCUSSED a number of sources or bases of power, e.g., economic resources, authority, class membership, family, culture, organization, and the like. However, a source of power more fundamental than these, in fact the ultimate base of power for the other power sources, is that of the power of ideas. The power of mind, of thought, imagination and vision; the power of symbols and the word; the power of ideation and the translation of ideation into action, are manifested in a multitude of personal, social, cultural and physical forms. For ideas are actualized and incarnated in patterns of social attitudes, relations and organization; in social and physical products; in abilities and inabilities, superordinations and subordinations. Knowledge is idea, the product of ideation reciprocally interacting with reality. Therefore, if knowledge is power, ideas have power. Ideas can be coercive and compelling. Beliefs, symbols, doctrines, and idea systems can enable or empower men through their capacity to induce them into states of consciousness conducive to the achievement of certain personal and social goals which would not be achievable by other means. "Indeed," as Thomas Dye asserts, "whole societies are shaped by systems of ideas that we frequently refer to as ideologies." He goes on to define an ideology as "an integrated system of ideas that provides society and its members with rationalizations for a way of life, guides for evaluating "rightness" and "wrongness," and emotional impulses to action."

The relationship between socioeconomic power and social ideology is an intimate one. For ideology legitimates power systems, hierarchal structures and social relations through its provision of rationales and justifications for the exercise of power and the necessity of certain social relations. If ideology successfully justifies the distribution and exercise of power within social relations, then it represents itself as a potent source of control over the consciousness and behavior of the participants.

> Ideologies control people's behavior in several ways: (1) Ideologies affect perception. Ideas influence what people "see" in the world around them. Ideologies frequently describe the character of human beings in society; they help us become aware of certain aspects of society but often impair our ability to see other aspects. Ideologies may distort and oversimplify in their effort to provide a unified and coherent account of society. (2) Ideologies rationalize and justify a way of life and hence provide legitimacy for the structure of society. An ideology may satisfy the status quo, or it may provide a rationale for change, or even for revolution. (3) Ideologies provide normative standards to determine "rightness" and "wrongness" in the affairs of society. Ideologies generally have a strong moral component. Occasionally, they even function as "religions" — complete with prophets (Marx), scriptures (the Communist Manifesto), saints (Lenin, Stalin, Mao), and visions of utopia (a communist society). (4) Ideologies provide motivation for social and political action. They give their followers a motive to act to improve world conditions. Ideologies can "convert" individuals to a particular social or political movement and arouse them to action.[1]

In the context of this chapter we will speak of ideology in terms of its use by the ruling class or dominant group(s) to justify the existing social order. In this sense we follow Jeffrey Reiman (1990) in asserting that "when ideas, however unintentionally, distort reality in a way that justifies the prevailing distribution of power and wealth, hides society's injustices, and thus secures uncritical allegiance to the existing social order, we have what Marx called *ideology*." So to the naive but acute observer of the American political and economic system it is amazingly baffling that in the face of gross and rapidly increasing inequities in wealth and power, social status and influence, social health and welfare, the vast majority of the population who bare the burden of those inequities do not utilize their vaunted

---

1. Thomas R. Dye, *Power and Society*, 3rd ed., pp. 201-2.

freedom of speech and assembly to engage in fundamentally questioning the political-economic-legal institutions of the system and organize to transform them so that they produce more equitable and salutary outcomes. The fact that this system has not been transformed toward such outcomes implies that despite its gross inequities and inadequacies a critical mass of the populace must accept the ideology used to rationalize and justify its existence. Obviously, those most interested and active in inculcating and sustaining such an ideology would be those who are the chief beneficiaries of the socioeconomic status and those who believe they stand to gain in the future from its continuance and/or who fear losing what they have, though it may be less than they need if the system were to be reconstituted. It should be apparent that in such a system the rich and powerful have an especially strong interest on promulgating and elaborating the prevailing ideology which legitimates their socioeconomic status. The rich and powerful, in this context, of all the groups which compose American society, have the greatest need for ideology and to see that the other groups are well-indoctrinated with it.

> A simple and persuasive argument can be made for the claim that the rich and powerful in America have an interest in conveying an ideological message to the rest of the nation. The have-nots and have-littles far outnumber the have-plenties. This means, to put it rather crudely, the have-nots and the have-littles could have more if they decided to take it from the have-plenties. This, in turn, means that the have-plenties need the cooperation of the have-nots and the have-littles. Because the have-plenties are such a small minority that they could never force this cooperation on the have-nots and have-littles, this cooperation must be voluntary. For the cooperation to be voluntary, the have-nots and the have-littles must believe that it would not be right or reasonable to take away what the have-plenties have. In other words, they must believe that for all its problems the present social, political and economic order, with its disparities of wealth and power and privilege, is about the best that human beings can do. More specifically, the have-nots and have-littles must believe that they are not being exploited by the have-plenties. Now this seems to me to add up to an extremely plausible argument that ours is a social system that requires for its continued operation a set of beliefs necessary to secure the allegiance of the less well-off majority. These beliefs must be in some considerable degree false, because the distribution of wealth and power in the United States is so evidently arbitrary and unjust. Ergo, the need for ideology.[2]

---

2. J. Reiman, *The Rich Get Richer and the Poor Get Prison: Ideology, Class, and Criminal Justice*, 3rd ed. (New York: Macmillan, 1990).

The Ideology Process

In addition to the special interest, policy formation, and candidate-selection processes, the ideological process is crucially used by the powers-that-be to maintain and enhance their power over the masses. Domhoff discusses the ideology process thusly:

> The ideology process consists of the numerous methods through which members of the power elite attempt to shape the beliefs, attitudes and opinions of the underlying population. It is within this process that the power elite tries to create, disseminate and reinforce a set of attitudes and values that assure Americans that the United States, is for all its alleged defects, the best of all possible worlds. The ideology process is an adjunct to the other three processes, for they would not be able to function smoothly without at least the resigned acquiescence of a great majority of the population. Free and open discussion are claimed to be the hallmarks of the process, but past experience shows that its leaders will utilize deceit and violence in order to combat individuals or organizations which espouse attitudes and opinions that threaten the power and privileges of the ruling class.
>
> The ideology process is necessary because public opinion does not naturally and automatically agree with the opinions of the power elite....Without the ideology process, a vague and amorphous public opinion — which often must be cajoled into accepting power-elite policies — might turn into a hardened class consciousness that opposed the ruling-class viewpoint at every turn.
>
> In order to prevent the development of attitudes and opinions contrary to the interests of the ruling class, leaders within the ideology process attempt to build upon and reinforce the underlying principles of the American system. Academically speaking, these underlying principles are called laissez-faire liberalism, and they have enjoyed a near-monopoly of American political thought since at least the beginnings of the republic. The principles emphasize individualism, free enterprise, competition, equality of opportunity and a minimum of reliance upon government in carrying out the affairs of society.[3]

The principal ideological goals of the ruling White male elite in America and of the White American nation taken as a whole relative to its domination of the Afrikan American community, are to legitimate and justify their superordinate position and power; generate the evidence which substantiates their claims to power and legitimacy; have their rule and domination appear inevitable and "natural," i.e.,

---

3. Domhoff, *The Powers That Be*, 1979, pp. 169.

not the result of deliberate, perhaps malicious intentions on their part; gain the "freely given" consent of Afrikan Americans to subordination to White Power; and to continuously reproduce the conditions of Afrikan American community dependency and relative powerlessness. The "manufacturing of consent" of the Afrikan American community to its own subordination — i.e., the ideological indoctrination of the Afrikan American community in such ways as to neutralize its capacity to realize its potential power, to liberate itself from EuroAmerican domination — is achieved not solely through the White ruling elite's ownership and control over all the major ideological vehicles in the society, e.g., the electronic media, print media, educational and socialization institutions and processes.

The receptivity of the Afrikan American community to White American ideological propaganda is chiefly the result of having been socially and mentally conditioned by the systematic control of its concrete living conditions by the White American nation. The sustenance, control and organization of Afrikan American life by EuroAmericans permit them to significantly shape the perceptions, experiences, capacities, expectations and interests of Afrikan Americans so that justification for the rules of White power appear credible. EuroAmerican control of the Afrikan American historical and contemporary social and experiential context is such that it is extremely difficult for many Afrikan Americans to mentally position themselves outside that context so as to compare EuroAmerican propaganda and rules of power with alternative ideologies (specifically Afrikan ideologies) and rules of power and challenge their apparent plausibility and credibility. Thus, as Beetham explains:

> [T]he justifications advanced for a given system of power are vindicated by effects generated by the power system itself, but which are not understood as its effects, because they appear autonomous or independent of it. As Marx himself understood well, though not all later Marxists have followed him, or worked out the implications for other dimensions such as gender, it is the appearance of the socially constructed as *natural* that lies at the heart of all ideology. What is socially constructed is not itself imaginary or illusory, and its evidence gives credibility to the justifications advanced for a given system of power. Yet the fact that it is constructed indirectly by that same system of power is obscured by the complexity of the processes involved; and by the fact that these processes, such as those of socialisation, are not necessarily managed by the powerful, but often by the subordinate themselves.[4]

---

4. David Beetham, *The Legitimation of Power*, p. 107.

The most effective means of disseminating and reproducing ideas in society, and in the Afrikan American community in particular, is to have that community perceive their dissemination and reproduction as the work of disinterested, unbiased, non-manipulative, liberal yet authoritative, White American individuals, groups, or institutions, or as flowing from sources independent of the marked influence of the powerful. Thus, White America strongly pushes and projects the powerful mythology of independent, liberal American media, universities, and other information processing establishments. That is, America loudly congratulates itself for what it calls its "free press" and mass media which permit the free exchange of ideas. Most Black Americans utilize White media and these factors as their primary, if not sole, source of information. Most are not mindful of the fact that the American press and mass media are privately owned, profit-making, White elite-controlled corporations. The press is one among other institutions, "and one of the most important in maintaining the hegemony of the corporate class and the capitalist system itself," advances Parenti.

> If the press cannot mold our every opinion, it can frame the perpetual reality around which our opinions take shape. Here may lie the most important effect of the news media; they set the issue agenda for the rest of us, choosing what to emphasize and what to ignore or suppress, in effect, organizing our political world for us. *The media may not always be able to tell us what to think, but they are strikingly successful in telling us what to think about....*
>
> It is enough that they create opinion, visibility, giving legitimacy to certain views and illegitimacy to others. The media do the same to substantive issues that they do to candidates, raising some from oblivion and conferring legitimacy upon them, while consigning others to limbo. This power to determine the issue agenda, the information flow, and the parameters of political debate so that it extends from ultra-right to no further than moderate center, is if not total, still totally awesome.[5]

The central aim of the ruling elite's ideology process is to define the "domain of discourse." That is, the corporate elite seeks to define the limits of "acceptable ideas" and to define what is worth talking about, worth learning, teaching, promoting, and writing about. Of course, the limits of the "acceptable," the "responsible," are set at those points which support and justify the interests of the elite itself. To a great extent the elite ideology process essentially involves the reinforcement of long-held, orthodox "American" values, perspectives,

---

5. Michael Parenti, *Inventing Reality: The Politics of the Mass Media,* 1986.

practices and ideals (which the system of power relations has already indirectly shaped to begin with). These factors are the ideological bases of elite power. It is a well-known fact that propaganda works best "when used to reinforce an already existing notion or to establish a logical or emotional connection between a new idea and a social norm" (Hirsch, 1975). It is important to note that many of these pre-existing notions are the products of elite propaganda and conditioning processes harking back to earlier historical eras; to socialization experiences in the early childhood, adolescent and young adulthood years in the family, educational institutions, peer groups; and to media exposures during these impressionable years as well. The ideas, attitudes and response tendencies implanted by these early experiences are often mistakenly identified by their hosts as self-generated; these previous "selective exposures and experiences" become the infrastructure which helps to maintain a later accrued "selective attention," "tunnel vision" orientation. This orientation serves to resist new ideas and practices not compatible with the old or pre-existing set of ideas and practices. This may be the case even when such pre-existing ideas or practices are not producing desired or satisfactory outcomes. Thus, through its monopoly of the media and the means of disseminating and "validating" information and interpreting reality, the ruling elite not only reinforces and channels those orthodox values which support its supremacy but also utilizes its monopolies to simultaneously prevent "groups with a different ideology from presenting their interpretation of events" As Hirsch further contends:

> In order to preserve ideological hegemony, it is only necessary for the ruling group to reinforce dominant values and at the same time *prevent the dissemination of opinion that effectively challenges the basic assumptions of the society.* Public knowledge of inequality and injustice isn't so damaging as long as these perceptions are not drawn together into a coherent, opposing ideology.[6]

David Sallach[7] very aptly observes that the ruling elite achieves its ends when it prevents groups with opposing ideologies from attaining a value consensus through its attempt to create confusion, fragmentation and demonstrate inconsistency in their belief systems or, as Domhoff argues, when it ensures that opposing opinions and

---

6. Glenn K. Hirsch, "Only You Can Prevent Ideological Hegemony: The Advertising Council and Its Place in the American Power Structure," *The Insurgent Socialist*, Spring 1975, p. 79, cited in G.W. Domhoff, *The Powers That Be*, pp. 192–93.

7. David Sallach, "Class Domination and Ideological Hegemony," *The Sociological Quarterly*, Winter 1974, p. 42, cited in G.W. Domhoff, *The Powers That Be*, p. 192.

values are only partially developed, remain isolated, and are made suspect. Thus, as Domhoff summarizes, the elite ideology process and network "is not the be-all and end-all of ruling-class domination. ...It does not function to eliminate conflict [thereby maintaining the illusion of "the free flow of ideas," "freedom of speech"] but to keep conflict from leading to an alternative ideology that provides the basis for an anticorporate, anticapitalist [anti-White supremacy] social movement."

Domhoff concludes his review of the processes of ruling class domination in America, which parallels and conditions the processes of White supremacy in America and the world, with the very important reminder that "the struggle for power is a continuous one." The contradictions and tensions inherent in ruling class domination and in White global supremacy make such domination vulnerable to a successful challenge from insurgent mass class and ethnic-based movements. An appropriately innovative, united, well-organized, political-economic counterattack by such movements can take successful advantage of the economic or political conflicts and vulnerabilities now present in the White supremacist establishment, or of its inevitable future contradictions and conflicts.

Media and the Ideology Process

Social institutions are the primary means by which a society defines itself, its views of and relationship to its world. This is the case whether we refer to a society's religious, family, education, scientific, economic, health care, political, or other social institutions. Social institutions structure and give meaning to a society's social thoughts, practices and interactions. They regulate and socialize its members and provide the instrumental means by which the society instructs and polices itself, propagates and reinforces its dominant values, maintains and advances its dominant interests, generates social power, and structures its internal and external power relations.

Institutions in an oppressive society function to maintain its structural status quo. As Michael Parenti contends, "Most American institutions, be they hospitals, museums, universities, businesses, banks, scientific laboratories, or mass media, are...owned...by a relatively small number of corporate rich. When trying to understand the context and purposes of the media, this pattern of ownership takes on special significance." In the context of ethnically pluralistic America, the latter part of the next to the last sentence of Parenti's statement can be usefully transliterated to "...owned...by the White American community." However, it remains true that within that community the major institutions, and in the context of our present focus, the mass media, are owned by a relatively small number of the corporate rich. Parenti proceeds to ask and answer the following question:

> Who specifically owns the mass media in the Unites States? Ten business and financial corporations control the three major television and radio networks (NBC, CBS, ABC), 34 subsidiary television stations, 201 cable TV systems, 62 radio stations, 20 record companies, 59 magazines including *Time* and *Newsweek*, 58 newspapers including the *New York Times*, the *Washington Post*, the *Wall Street Journal*, and the *Los Angeles Times*, 41 book publishers, and various motion pictures companies like Columbia Pictures and Twentieth-Century Fox. Three-quarters of the major stockholders of ABC, CBS, and NBC are banks, such as Chase Manhattan, Morgan Guaranty Trust, Citibank, and Bank of America.
>
> The overall pattern is one of increasing concentration of ownership and earnings. According to a 1982 *Los Angeles Times* survey, independent daily newspapers are being gobbled up by the chains at the rate of fifty or sixty a year. Ten newspaper chains earn over half of all newspaper revenues in this country. Five media conglomerates share 95 percent of the records and tapes market, with Warners and CBS alone controlling 65 percent of the market. Eight Hollywood studios account for 89 percent of U.S. feature film rentals. Three television networks earn over two-thirds of total U.S. television revenues. Seven paperback publishers dominate the mass market for books.
>
> Of the existing "independent" television and radio stations, 80 percent are network affiliates. Practically the only shows these "independents" produce are the local evening newscasts, the rest of their time being devoted to network programs. Most of the remaining stations are affiliated with the Public Broadcasting System (PBS), which receives almost all its money from the federal government and from corporate donors and their foundations, with a smaller share from listener subscription.[8]

We must keep in mind that when Parenti presented these data in 1986, the ownership and control of the mass media was still diffuse compared to its narrow monopolistic ownership today. Not only has traditional electronic and print media been far more consolidated under far fewer owners since then, but the communications revolution currently underway in the forms of "information superhighways" and giant national and international "interactive" media networks are the

---

8. Michael Parenti, *Inventing Reality: The Politics of the Mass Media*, 1986.

sources of furiously combative conflicts over their ownership and control by less than a handful of media and information processing conglomerates. The mass media and information/communications systems are the major tools for generating, maintaining and converting individual and public opinions into social power — power used to oppress and exploit.

The White corporate elite media/information establishment uses its control of the mass media to create and reinforce "the ideology that transforms [its] interests into a "general interest," justifying existing class relations as the only natural and workable ones, the preferred and optimal, although not perfect, societal arrangement."[9] The corporate elite-owned and -controlled media function to create a climate of opinion, to shape social perception by framing the reality and information which basically shapes the formation and expression of opinions. They do this mainly through setting the issues agenda, that is, by controlling the "domain of discourse," e.g., determining what is worthy of public exposure and discussion. They choose what issues and information are to be emphasized, to be ignored or suppressed. Consequently, they create visibility and legitimacy for certain persons, groups and opinions and thereby impose limits on public knowledge, interest, discourse, understanding, behavioral orientation and capability.

These contentions can be solidly substantiated by an analysis not only of the ownership and control of the mass media but even more relevant, of their general programmatic content.

> Conservatives, and religious New Rightists make over 17,000 weekly television and radio broadcasts across the country, with much of the air time donated by sympathetic station owners. Hundreds of radio and TV stations are owned outright by conservative organizations. Over 1,000 radio and TV outlets beam a fundamentalist evangelical message around the nation [also Afrika, Central and South America, the Caribbean, and the Pacific].
>
> The right is not seeking changes of a kind that burden or threaten the interest of the dominant corporate class. If anything, it advocates a view of the world that wealthy media owners look upon with genuine sympathy, unlike the view offered by left protesters. The centrist media is, in a word, more receptive to the right than to the left because its owners and corporate heads share the right's basic feeling about free enterprise, capitalism, communism, labor unions, popular protest, and U.S. global supremacy, even if not always seeing eye-to-eye with it on specific policies and certain cultural issues. In

---

9. Ibid.

addition, the right has the money to buy media exposure and the left usually does not.[10]

Again, an updated version of what Parenti noted in 1986 will convincingly demonstrate the preponderance and pervasiveness of a general center-to-right political media establishment arrayed against Black America and progressive non-Black Americans. A review of the most popular TV and radio talk programs saliently reveals that they owe their popularity to barefaced and barely disguised anti-Black, anti-liberal sociopolitical orientations and content. In a major urban market like New York City, "hate radio", unadorned, crude expressions of hatred of Blacks are a 24-hour, seven-days-a-week fare. The radio stations and hosts who broadcast such attitudes receive markedly higher ratings and are listened to by enormously larger audiences, numbering in the millions, compared to their milder or even more liberal counterparts. Rush Limbaugh, nationally syndicated TV and radio personality who transparently disguises his Reaganite conservative views, anti-Black, anti-liberal attitudes as "entertainment" and political satire, speaks daily to an audience approaching 20 million, 70% of whom are middle to lower class Whites. His first book sold over 3 million and his second, published in the Fall of 1993, had a first printing of 3 million, the largest in U.S. history.[11] Limbaugh's blustery, vacuous rantings laced with clichéd conservative "ideolo-guese", earn him not only his large national audience as well as audiences with conservative U.S. presidents and high administrative officials, but an estimated $4 million from radio annually. Sales from his first book grossed over $8 million and his 12-page monthly newsletter supported by some 370,000 subscribers, grosses $11 million.

These earnings pushed Limbaugh's income in the area of $20 million for 1993. Anti-Black propaganda, conservative, ideological publications not only help to maintain the White supremacist status quo but, to put the icing on the cake, are the sources of fabulous wealth, fame and prestige.

Ideological Processes of Afrikan-centered Opposition

The foregoing discussion only hints at the social-political construction and power of the White-owned and -controlled media/establishment system, a system founded on political and economic oppression and exploitation of the masses in general and of Afrikan peoples in

---
10. Ibid.
11. "Voice of America?"*Time*, November 1, 1993.

particular. In the aftermath of that discussion we need not belabor the need for an aggressive Black-owned and -controlled countercultural media information network. However, to counter the propagandistic White media/establishment the Black media information network must be supported and financed by Black-owned businesses which in turn must be primarily supported by Black consumers. The Black press today is not a free or powerful press because it lacks these necessary supporting pillars. The more "successful" and wealthy the Black media become, meaning the more they are financed by White-owned corporate advertising, the less free and weaker they become. Fear of incurring the disapproval of their White advertisers effectively prevents them from providing their audiences with truthful, critically astute and informative analyses of the nature of White domination. Forget their providing a detailed political-scientific, political-economic, social-scientific, historical/cultural education to their audiences: an education which would revolutionize their consciousness and prescribe the practical means for overthrowing their oppressors and exploiters. This media *fears* becoming the focal establishment for politically, socially and economically organizing a truly nationalistic Black American community.

If an Afrikan-centered liberation movement is to be successful it must rescue the collective Afrikan mind and soul from the clutches of Eurocentric and non-Afrocentric ideology. Such a movement must organize itself for a struggle to the death against the continuing internalization of self-defeating, self-destructive ideas by Afrikan peoples. It must unite these peoples around the ideology of Afrocentrism and inculcate within their breasts a life-saving, life-giving, liberating, Afrikan-centered consciousness and identity. It must incite the peoples to new self-knowledge, to the discovery and development of creative, operative strategies, social relations and arrangements; new values and visions with which they will break asunder — forever — the shackles of White supremacy. These ends can only be attained if the Afrocentric movement goes on the ideological offensive with an overpowering vengeance.

The "powers that be," i.e., the ruling White male elite, has already sensed the tremendous power potential of ideological Afrocentrism and is loudly sounding the alarms. For no one knows better than this establishment the power ideology can generate when it imbues a critical mass of people with a rationale for action and revolution. A review of the most important White mass market publications such as *Time*, *Newsweek*, magazines; newspapers, e.g., *The New York Times*; books, e.g., *The Disuniting of America*; radio and television programs; academic struggles over curricula of inclusion, Afrocentric curricula and the like, would quickly convince us that the ruling establishment and its cohorts are mounting a comprehensive campaign against the Afrocentric movement. That this coordinated offensive makes use of every possible weapon in the Eurocentric propaganda armamentarium indicates just how dependent the White power elite is on the indoctrination of the Afrikan masses by Eurocentric ideology, and more important, its indoctrination by self-alienating, self-defeating, self-destructive, self-subordinating ideologies, attitudes, social relations and behavioral orientations. Any Afrocentric ideology which successfully induces Afrikan peoples to shed Eurocentric ideologies, attitudes, relations and orientations will at one and the same time induce them to shed themselves of their subordination to White supremacy. In addition, this revolutionary ideology would empower Afrikan peoples to overthrow their European masters and non-European exploiters and to enjoy the bounty of their own labor, lands, resources and humanity. To these ends the White male ruling elite and the White nations are opposed. For them, Afrikan liberation, independence and prosperity is a zero-sum solution, i.e., and real Afrikan gains add up to European losses.

It is in this light that the ruling White elite and the Eurocentric ideological establishment it controls have seen fit to subject the Afrocentric movement and its ideological arm to an "intellectual cointelpro." The militant police-erected cointelpro of the 1960s and 70s decimated Afrikan-centered armed resistance groups and radical ideological encampments in the Afrikan American community through outright police murders and executions; malicious espionage, propaganda campaigns, and prosecution; personal character assassination and intimidation. Ideological warfare was also mounted by the ruling elite against the nascent ideology of Black Power and the Black Power Movement. In some interesting ways the Afrocentric movement represents the resurrection of Black Power and is its transcendent.

In its current struggle to defeat the Afrocentric movement the ruling establishment has resorted to its old strategic tactics and invented new ones. The process of discrediting Afrocentric ideology; discrediting its rationales, undergirding thought and scholarship; assassinating the characters of its proponents; intimidating, isolating and dis-employing them, is in full-throttle. A relatively new wrinkle in the ruling elite's strategy involves the invention and employment in vastly increased numbers of a species of Afrikans referred to as *"neo-conservatives."* These "academic Uncle Toms and Thomasinas" who occupy chairs in prestigious White elite institutions are the war dogs of the establishment whose purpose is to accomplish two of the central ends of elite propaganda discussed above — to prevent among Afrikan American peoples the dissemination of an Afrocentric ideology that effectively challenges the basic assumptions which justify and undergird White supremacy, and to thwart the coalescence of an Afrikan-centered consciousness and identity among Afrikan peoples through the generation of ideological confusion, fragmentation and contradiction. The appointment by the White ruling elite of neoconservative Blacks to chairs in their most prestigious universities, underwriting their publications, permitting them editorial space in their most influential publications and the providing them with valuable electronic media interviews, only hints at the fact that the ruling White establishment means to use all and every means at its disposal to maintain ideological supremacy over the Afrikan world — the key to its supremacy.

Black "neo-cons" write White propaganda in Black face. Their primary goal is to try and defeat the "conscientization" of Afrikan peoples. More dangerous than their writings, which are generally repudiated by the Afrikan community when and if they are read or discussed, is the possibility that these academicians as heads of Afrikan studies and related departments will use their positions to indoctrinate future Afrikan American teachers, professors and intellectuals in addition to students pursuing other vocations with ideologies compatible with White supremacy. If the graduate students of these academicians go on to become heads of Afrikan Studies departments across the country as well as influential journalists, columnists, community leaders and the like, the Afrocentric movement will be markedly hampered, if not completely thwarted in its great leap forward. To a measurable degree the pressure to remove outstanding Afrocentric chairs in Afrikan studies is already moving apace. A number of these chairs have been replaced by academic "Toms" and many Afrikan Studies departments have been restricted in their scope and squeezed dry of life as a result.

The Lack of an Afrocentric Ideology Network

More important than the ideological warfare between Afrocentric and *neo-con* academics in the battle to win the minds of the Afrikan masses is the absence of an effective Afrocentric ideology network which influences the popular as well as the academic mind. Such a network would include not only academic publications but more crucially, the mass media, i.e., popular books, magazines, newspapers, radio and television programs, community education and training seminars, and rallies. While there has been a manifold increase in the paper and electronic media in the Afrikan American community, and a corresponding emphasis in these media on Afrikan culture and Black identity, Black programming and Black-centered writing and perspectives, this must not be construed to mean that Black-controlled media are fully supportive of Afrocentrism. One can safely describe the popular Black-controlled and -oriented media, dependent as it is on White ruling-elite licensing and largesse, as essentially integrationist, assimilationist, and accommodationist in orientation. As a media they are tied to and promote Americanism as much as the White media, even when they permit a harmless amount of Black radical political dialogue.

The Black Media: White Media in Black Face

The most popular Black media productions, e.g., *Ebony, Emerge, Black Enterprise, Essence, Upscale*, and other similar magazines; the Black radio stations and television programs which feature Black-oriented formats, have in large measure been victimized by their very success. For such success, dependent on White elite financing and underwritten by White elite advertising revenues, has made "successful Black media" extremely sensitive to Afrocentric ideology and even circumspect about "radical chic" Black-oriented ideology, i.e., ideology emphasizing Black identity and culture that is a bit critical of Eurocentrism, a bit left-of-center in its social and economic value orientations, but still within acceptable White liberal conversational domains. On the whole, the Black media are essentially a parochial establishment lacking vision and courage, craving White media acceptance and recognition. Specializing in racial ego massage, commiseration, complaints and victimization, they are of relatively low-educational value and provide little worthwhile leadership for the Afrikan American community. They are dark imitations of their white counterparts which set their reactionary agendas, news stories, editorials and features. Even though Afrocentrism is phenomenally increasing in the Afrikan American community and popular culture viz., rap music, the popularity of Afrocentic T-shirt art, Afrocentric personal dress and adornments, the demand for Afrocentric and Afrocentric-oriented multicultural education in the Afrikan American community, etc., one would be very hard-pressed to find any popular Afrikan American magazines, such as *Ebony*, or radio or television series which have produced in-depth, thoroughly descriptive explanations of the ideology and goals of Afrocentrism. Nor would one readily find a clear indication of an Afrocentric scholar, spokesperson, columnist or editor consistently or unrestrictedly published in their pages or hosting their programs. For, essentially, the current Black media establishment is still one with what it was when it received its most severe criticism by sociologist E. Franklin Frazier in his much-acclaimed book *Black Bourgeoisie* published in 1962.

> The Negro press is not only one of the most successful business enterprises owned and controlled by Negroes; it is the chief medium of communication which creates and perpetuates the world of *make-believe* for the black bourgeoisie. Although the Negro press declares itself to be the spokesman for the Negro group as a whole, it represents essentially the interests and outlook of the black bourgeoisie. Its demand for equality for the Negro in American life is concerned primarily with opportunities which will benefit the black bourgeoisie economically and enhance the social status of the Negro. The Negro press reveals the inferiority complex of the black bourgeoisie and provides a documentation of the attempts of this class to seek compensations for its hurt self-esteem and exclusion from American life. Its exaggerations concerning the economic well-being and cultural achievements of Negroes, its emphasis upon Negro "society" all tend to create a world of make-believe into which the black bourgeoisie can escape from its inferiority and inconsequence in American society.[12] [Emphasis added]

He then argued that "In reporting any recognition which the Negro may receive, the Negro press is not concerned with principles or values except where status, in a narrow sense, is concerned...the Negro press is not concerned with broader social and economic values." The contemporary Afrikan American press, except for its marked increase in size and composition, which now includes a much larger electronic, i.e., radio and television sector, maintains the essential character and purpose attributed to it by E. Franklin Frazier. The Afrikan American media establishment still "represents essentially the interests and outlook of the black bourgeoisie." In a number of ways it is even more bourgeois in outlook and interest than in the past. Until the decade of the '60s and '70s the major Black media, particularly some newspapers and magazines like *Ebony*, still expressed the character of the original Black press, that of organs of "Negro protest." Many publications following the traditions of the first Black papers in America, *Freedom's Journal*, *North Star* (later renamed *Frederick Douglass' Paper*), *New York Age*, and the *Chicago Defender*, were staunch defenders of the rights of Black Americans,

---

12. E. Franklin Frazier, *The Black Bourgeoisie: The Rise of a Middle Class in the United States* (New York: Collier-Macmillan, 1962), p. 146.

exposed and fulminated against racial oppression and discrimination. The editorials of *Ebony* magazine regarding the civil rights struggles of the late '50s and '60s were outstanding. Their emphasis on the historical and contemporary achievements of Afrikan Americans served to enhance Black self-esteem and encourage continuing struggle against American apartheid.

The central ideological thrust of the Black print media was primarily assimilationist and integrationist in character. They struggled mightily against what was then called the "second-class" status of Black Americans and for full equality for Blacks in American society. The ideological thrust and the struggle for social equality manifested by the Black press were in accord with Black bourgeois interests and outlook as well as those of the Black masses, and were generally supported by the White liberal press and White liberal establishment. At the end of the Civil Rights era when most of the important Black bourgeois goals were nominally achieved — school and housing desegregation, affirmative action (which accelerated the movement of Black bourgeois professionals into previously exclusively White employment areas), expanded equal opportunity programs in many social and employment areas for Blacks, tokenism, national Black suffrage, and so forth — the Black bourgeois press and expanding electronic media establishment while still serving as the watchdogs for Black bourgeois interests and speaking for Black community interests, increasingly follows the party line of the liberal White American media establishment. The Afrikan American media establishment in essential ways more closely fits Frazier's characterization of it today than in the late '50s and early '60s when his media critiques were first published.

The Black print media as exemplified by *Ebony, Essence, Emerge, EM* and other similar national publications fit Frazier's characterizations "to a *T*." These publications along with their electronic media brethren are boringly innocuous, inoffensive and bland. Apparently frightened of provoking the disapproval of their national and multinational advertisers and of raising the ire of the White ruling establishment on whose favor they depend for survival, these media assiduously concern themselves with reporting the activities of Black celebrities, of the Black bourgeoisie, and with selling the products of White-owned manufacturers to Black customers. The Black media literally "deliver" the Black market to White merchants, their *raison d'etre*. The Black print media, especially the popular magazines which increasingly project the fashionable lives of Blacks "who have made it" in White society, are little more than fashion and consumer magazines. Their stock-in-trade is now fundamentally the same as White mass publications — celebrity features, male-female relations, career choices and opportunities, exercise and fitness features, self-help and pop psychology features. Controversial issues are superficially treated when dealt with at rare instances and are carefully and inoffensively "balanced." They are careful not to take any editorial position which can be interpreted as Black nationalist or Afrocentric in orientation. The deeper issues and controversies involving Afrocentrism and Black nationalism, involving deep ethnic confrontations between the Black and non-Black communities are virtually ignored or dealt with so gingerly and benignly as to be devoid of any real substance while not revealing where the Black media themselves stand relative to such issues. Afrocentric and Black nationalist interpretations of events and ethnic reality are essentially excluded from the national Black print media and local and regional electronic media. The views of Black nationalist scholars and intellectuals as well as activists are rarely featured in the Black media except when they are the objects of White media attack or have aroused broad White social disapproval, or are engaged in some controversial struggle with the White powers-that-be. Some nationalists and activists are not interviewed or presented even under these circumstances if their mere mention or presence may be interpreted by powerful Whites as representing Black media approval or support for their ideological orientation or social-political activism.

The Black media establishment is highly reactionary. Its agenda is generally set by the White media and ruling/corporate elite establishment. Once a Black person has evoked the full notice and approval or disapproval of the White media and ruling establishment, the Black media establishment compellingly presents him or her to their Black public. The Black media interaction with these noted or notorious persons or groups as defined by the White press or establishment, usually lasts as long as White media focus is maintained on them. Consequently, the White press markedly still determines the visibility or invisibility, the esteem or lack thereof, of Black persons, groups and ideas in the Black media establishment. Rarely does the Black media raise a Black person, group or ideology to prominence based on the intrinsic nature of their relevance to the Black community and to Afrikan liberation without having received some signal from the White media.

Thus, the Black media in its reactionary fashion seconds the motions of the White media in excluding unpopular, anti-White supremacy, anti-Eurocentric, anti-capitalist, and other radical ideological approaches that may provide possibly promising, pragmatic solutions to problems faced by the Black community. They thereby help to deny the Black community innovative and creative alternatives to the failed, yet socially accepted, approaches advocated by the general media (including the Black and White media). In this sense the Black media enters into complicity with the White media against Afrikan liberation from White supremacy.

When expert opinion is sought by the Black media regarding problems facing the Black community, e.g., Black-on-Black violence, drug abuse, economic deprivation, etc., this establishment with its penchant for recognizing as expert only those Blacks so designated by the White media and educational establishments (or celebrities such as movie directors, actors, comedians and other erstwhile Black entertainment or media personalities) will publish the sayings or writings of these "experts" regardless of the fact that they generally express opinions of no real substance or relevance, or more often than not, express regressive and outdated approaches to problems. Typically, the Black media will treat the expositions of Black academics attached to prestigious White elite universities as holy writ without apparently considering the fact that such experts have eschewed any ideological perspectives and pragmatic solutions to problems in the Black community which would meet with the disapproval of their White colleagues and the White institutions for which they work. Their espousal of unorthodox ideologies and approaches would no doubt have precluded their employment by the White establishment institutions in the first place. Obviously, their solutions to problems confronting the Black community will fit within the range of acceptable White elite opinions. Their Black faces and positions in White institutions serve essentially to sanction White elite ideas and values which are antithetical to Black liberation and independence, to give these ideas authority and present them in ways which deceive the Black public into assuming that they operate in its interest when the opposite is true. Moreover, the ready access these White institution-supported Black experts have to the Black and White media, allows them to not only reinforce the ruling ideas of the dominant White elite but to literally block a fair hearing of unorthodox, though often more realistic ideas of independent Black experts, activists and everyday citizens. Frazier succinctly summarizes the scope of the Black press thusly:

> The lack of interest of the black bourgeoisie and its mouthpiece, the Negro press, in the broader issues facing the modern world is due to the fact that the Negro has developed no economic or social philoso-

phy except the opportunistic philosophy that the black intelligentsia has evolved to justify its anomalous and insecure position. Of course, plain ignorance of the nature of the modern world and the revolution which is in progress accounts also for the outlook of the Negro press...They are generally careful, however, never to offend the black bourgeoisie nor to challenge white opinion on fundamental economic and political issues. In fact, except in regard to race relations, the columnists generally echo the conservative opinions and platitudes of the white world on crucial issues... By echoing the opinions of the white community the intellectual leaders of the black bourgeoisie hope to secure the approval and recognition of the white propertied classes with whom they seek identification.[13]

The Black broadcast media is a major culprit in mesmerizing the Afrikan American community, particularly its youth, with stupefying, mind-numbing, retrograde music and DJ claptrap — music created and recorded by the lowest elements of its street culture and sold and distributed by White-owned, Japanese-owned record companies who have shown nothing but the nastiest contempt for the peoples whose music is the principal source of their fabulous wealth and power. In general, Black electronic media feed the mind-destroying, self-defeating addiction Blacks have for music, whether rap, jazz, hip-hop, or gospel. Black celebrity-driven electronic and print media saturate their audiences with Black bourgeois political nostrums and palliatives, hokey clichés and hopelessly wrongheaded prescriptions for Black social and economic advancement and liberation. Black reactionary media push the same corporate conglomerates as do the white media; and like the white media, virtually ignore, suppress, or invalidate more radical, alternative points of view, social, political, economic prescriptions and programs for Afrikan empowerment and liberation. Unlike the white media, however, the Black media does not see as one of their most important roles that of "creating visibility and thereby legitimacy" by raising from relative obscurity those persons, groups and organizations, those publications which speak directly and practically to the liberation of Afrikan peoples from the mental and physical bondage to white supremacy.

Relative to publication of books which target the Black American community, one need only look at the Black literary review sections of magazines like *Black Enterprise, Ebony, Emerge, Essence*, and literary quarterlies or supplements like the *Quarterly Review of Black Books* and the *City Sun* Literary Supplement to note that 99% of the books reviewed are by Black authors published by White-owned

---

13. Ibid., pp. 159–60.

presses. Thus, not only is the white-owned book industry pedaled by the Black press, but the rather innocuous books — books edited according to the needs and standards of white supremacy, books specializing in victimology, self-pity, self-aggrandizing autobiographies and inflated biographies of people who were or are famous because they achieved the condescending approval or reactionary disapproval of whites, books advocating solutions to Black problems which have long ago been demonstrated to be complete failures, harmful even — are routinely recommended to a gullible Black public. Books by both Black and white authors that have gained critical acclaim or propagandistic visibility in the white press, that have made the *New York Times Best-sellers List* are routinely reviewed, their authors lionized and interviewed regardless of their content or genuine social importance or relevance to the Afrikan American community and its critical struggle to survive. Authors and books which address this struggle and prescribe for its success, particularly if they run counter to the social and political status quo, are contrary to "acceptable" [*read:* white liberal] opinion and Black bourgeois interests, are ignored and actively suppressed by an obsequious Black media or a Black media which is gutless and lacking in vision. The publishing companies more likely to publish such books are the Black-owned publishing houses.

The Black Bourgeoisie – Black Political Establishment Alliance against Afrikan Liberation

Since Afrocentrism and the Afrocentric movement encompass Black nationalism, advocate an economic and social philosophy contrary to that of the ruling White establishment, are avowedly committed to the overthrow of White supremacy and to the development of Pan–Afrikanist solidarity and independence, all such orientations which are viewed with alarm by the White powers-that-be, it is obvious that the Black media as currently constituted will be of little direct value for achieving true Afrikan liberation. In fact, they may retard its progress in this regard. Consequently, the Afrocentric movement and the movement to develop authentic Afrikan Power at home and abroad must continue to develop alternative means of its own to reach the Afrikan masses. The ideological struggle for Afrikan Power will therefore involve ideological struggle against not only the White media establishment but also the Black media establishment. The latter establishment must be subverted by various means into serving the power interests of the Afrikan community or its political and ideological voice and clout must be muted by a more vigorous, relevant and practical Afrikan-centered media-ideological process. Whatever pressure the Black liberation movement can bring to bear against the Black media establishment in order to reach the masses of Afrikan Americans must be applied.

The sociopolitical role played by the Black media establishment must become the object of scholarly and utilitarian analysis and critique. A thoroughgoing critique of the Black press has been too long delayed since Frazier's critique. The relationship of the Black media establishment with the Black political establishment should be the focus of intense critical analysis from the nationalist and Afrocentric perspective. For as Frazier so pointedly noted, the orientation of the Black political establishment is at one with that of the Black bourgeois media establishment and with the Black bourgeoisie as a whole. He observed that:

> SINCE THE BLACK bourgeoisie is composed chiefly of white-collar workers and since its small business enterprises are insignificant in the American economy, the black bourgeoisie wields no political power as a class in American society. Nor does the black bourgeoisie exercise any significant power within the Negro community as an employer of labor...In the political life of the American society the Negro political leaders, who have always had a middle-class outlook, follow an opportunistic policy. They attempt to accommodate the demands of Negroes for better economic and social conditions to their personal interests which are tied up with the political machines, which in turn are geared to the interests of the white propertied classes.[14]

The Black media-political establishment alliance can best be seen in its almost uncritical and very adulatory support for Black politicians. The Black media lionizes Black incumbents without critical examinations of their records and supports Black candidates for political office essentially on the basis of their Blackness (generally as long as they are not Republicans). The Black press makes little or no demands on Black politicians while it constantly parades them before the Black community as role models, regardless of their success or lack of it in advancing the interests of the community. The achievements of Black politicians, no matter how dubious, are often presented by the Black press as vicarious achievements of the Black community as a whole. Black incumbents are given ready access to Black media outlets to massage the Black community, to maintain their public persona, and to rationalize their very frequent failures to

---
14. Ibid., p. 77.

provide the Black community with responsive and effective political leadership. Thus, they keep their opposition out of the media limelight and the community is cajoled into re-electing a political establishment whose accomplishments are meager when not plainly regressive.

> Except in the case of a crisis such as that created by the Depression when the Negro masses changed their political affiliation, the Negro politician may even mobilize the masses to vote against their economic interests. In his role as leader, the Negro politician attempts to accommodate the demands of the Negro masses to his personal interests which are tied up with the political machines. He may secure the appointment of a few middle-class Negroes to positions in the municipal government. But when it comes to the fundamental interests of the Negro masses as regards employment, housing, and health, his position is determined by the political machine which represents the propertied classes of the white community.[15]

The Black media establishment's gung-ho, indiscriminate support of Black politicians and the White male elite-dominated American political system is most clearly exposed during elections when it beats the drums to get Black voters to the polls to elect Black officials. This establishment strives strenuously to convince the Black electorate that every conceivable problem which confronts it can be resolved through voting heavily for Black and friendly White politicians. The Black media is ever quick to remind the Black electorate of the historical struggles necessary to achieve their right to vote. It indicts the community for its electoral apathy and seeks to evoke guilt feelings in those who do not participate in the electoral process — making such ritualistic participation emblematic of democracy and first-class citizenship. This is of special interest when it is realized that very few, if any, of the major political, economic and social goals achieved by Black America, including the Voting Rights Act, were accomplished through Black voting prowess. The ballot box has been a relatively impotent weapon in the achievement of major victories by the Black community. Suddenly vigorous protest and direct-action legal suits and extralegal processes such as boycotts, sit-ins, and the like, which were used so effectively by the community to achieve its sociopolitical ends and to fight injustice and oppression, have fallen far behind the election of Black politicians to achieve the same ends. The mystery of the Black media establishment's complicity with this type of political fraud — the electing of politicians to a bankrupt

---

15. Ibid., p. 95.

political system dominated by the ruling corporate elite whose values and aims are inimical to the cause of Black liberation; the election of Black politicians who are but pawns of the White Democratic Party machine and who seek to have the Black community identify its communal interest with the politicians' personal interests; the election of politicians who in no way are interested in developing a program for the economic emancipation and empowerment of the Black community, and who are not committed to the final overthrow of White supremacy, becomes clear when we recognize their bourgeois interests.

The realization that the Black owners of the major Black media outlets have been financed by White funding sources, are supported by White advertisers, have gained access to their media properties through special dispensations, provisos, set-asides and affirmative action programs promulgated by the two political parties, especially the Democratic Party; the realization that the holding of political office or high appointive positions in government and the private sector on the part of a large and influential segment of the Black bourgeoisie, that their social standing in the Black community was achieved and is maintained by their ties to the Democratic Party and the American electoral system — make it obvious as to why this Black social class seeks to convince the larger Black community that voting is the end-all and be-all of Black liberation. Consequently, the Black community is spared a true, realistic and thorough education as to how the American political system really works by the Black media establishment. It is not informed as to how the system is subverted by the White corporate elite; as to how the process of governance is almost unrelated to the electoral process and electing of politicians; as to how an economically powerless people are almost invariably a politically powerless people as well. The Black community is misled by electoral mumbo-jumbo and antiquated, ethereal political theory into placing all its hopes for survival, security and liberation in the hands of politicians who are as powerless as the community they represent. Because of their personal and career ties to the White American political system, electoral processes and political parties, Black politicians, along with their Black media supporters are almost instinctively opposed to an independent, nationalistic political and economic movement. This is particularly the case when those movements rival their own leadership and influence in the Black community, and when they cannot control or squash them at the behest of their White political and party bosses. Thus, if the Afrikan American community is to achieve truly substantial power in America it must rid itself of the leadership and influence of the Black political-media alliance as it exists today. The stranglehold on Black opinion by bourgeois publications such as *Ebony, Essence, Jet, Emerge, Black Enterprise, EM, Upscale, Class* magazines and the like by electronic media outlets like *BET, Ebony-Jet Showcase, Tony Brown's Journal*, must be successfully challenged by the nationalist and Afrocentric movements.

To a good extent the popularity of Afrocentrism and Black nationalism at this time in the Black community attests to the effectiveness of the Black nationalist Afrocentric ideological thrust. The effectiveness of the ideological tactics of the Afrocentric movement is also attested to by the over-reaction and vigorous ideological counterattacks and preemptive strikes of the White media, White academic and political establishments. However, the ideological struggle by the Afrocentric movement is far from won. It is currently at near-deadlock with its White establishment opponents and their fifth column Black "neo-con" lackeys. This means that the Afrocentric campaign must increase in its intensity and scope. Such an increase involves:

- Exposure of Afrocentric ideas through a broad range of publications regarding all important subject matter areas, e.g., political science, history, culture, anthropology, the social sciences, mathematics and science, literature, economics and economic development, military strategy and tactics, propaganda and ideological warfare, espionage, etc.
- Taking advantage of every opportunity offered by the media to spread Afrocentric ideology.
- Developing and widely distributing Afrocentric books, booklets, pamphlets, articles, records, tapes, CDs, newsletters, journals, clothing items and symbolic adornments.
- Sponsorship of Afrocentric community seminars, festivals, cultural events, training sessions; develop mental projects.
- Establishment of Afrocentric rehab centers, recreational programs, educational programs and schools. Seeing to it that the chairs of Black studies programs are filled by Afrocentric scholars. Push for the establishment of all-male training programs and schools and Afrocentric curricula throughout the early childhood, primary, secondary and higher education institutions.
- Challenges to neo-con and bourgeois ideological publications and public utterances.

- Development of a prosperous Afrocentric economic business and financial network. Spearheading capture of the internal markets of the Black community as well as penetrating those of aliens and Whites. Development of a full-fledged import-export business network across the Afrikan Diaspora as well as with other trading partners.
- Establishment of independent political party.
- Establishment of a nation-within-a-nation.

All of this implies that the Black nationalist press must challenge the Black bourgeois media relative to their duplicity, cowardliness and lack of imagination. It must accelerate its organization and clout and seek to overthrow what little influence the bourgeois Black media has in the Black community as well as counter that of the more dominant White media.

Chapter 12

The Economic Order and Power

Economic Powerlessness means Political Powerlessness

THE IDEA THAT THE AFRIKAN AMERICAN community can exercise effective power, political or otherwise, without simultaneously exercising economic power, is a fantasy. The election of Blacks to high office, even to the highest office, and their plenteous appointments to various courts, powerful directorates, boards, commissions, heads of multinational corporations, powerful regulatory agencies and the like, will do relatively little to enhance the power of the Afrikan American community or release it from its subordinate relationship to the White American community. Neither will it measurably increase the probability of its future survival. For while hundreds of Afrikan Americans may be fortunate enough to attain positions of influence and affluence in America, millions of average Afrikan Americans are marginalized and impoverished simultaneously.

Ultimately, the power of office reflects the power of the constituency it represents and which supports it. As long as the Afrikan American community is relatively weak so will be its representatives, no matter how high their offices. And this community will remain relatively weak as long as it remains in relative economic disorder, and will not amass and effectively utilize significant wealth. The greater power and influence of Jewish Americans, the growing power and influence of Korean Americans in Los Angeles and New York City, and other ethnic minorities in America despite their relatively small populations and national voting numbers compared to the much larger population and voting populations of the Afrikan American community, clearly indicate that power and influence are borne of effective social organization and the effective use of organized wealth compared to that of ineffective social organization, unorganized wealth and sheer population size.

In prior chapters we discussed various forms of power, e.g., coercive power, physical force, authority, as well as various bases of power. Control over important economic resources and the ability to make economic decisions which significantly impact on the lives of others permit those who own or control these resources to wield a considerable amount of power. Thomas Dye cogently describes the relationship between power and economic resources in the United States:

> A great deal of power in America is centered in large economic organizations — corporations, banks, utilities, investment firms, and government agencies charged with the responsibility of overseeing the economy...*Control of economic resources provides a continuous and important base of power in any society.* Economic organizations decide the basic economic question of *who gets what.* Deciding "who gets what" entails deciding what will be produced, how it will be produced, how much will be produced and how much it will cost, how many people will be employed, who will be employed and what their wages will be, how the goods and services that are produced will be distributed, what technology will be developed, what profits will be made and how they will get distributed, how much money will be available for loans and what interest rates will be charged, how fast the earnings will grow, and so forth.[16]

Dye goes on to define the economic system as consisting *"of the institutions and processes by which a society produces and distributes scarce resources."* He adds that where resources are "scarce some scheme must be created to decide who gets what." At this time, the Afrikan American community has not appropriately addressed and resolved the problem of economic scarcity which prevails within it. This problem distorts all of its social and personal relations, social institutions and general well-being, as well as weakens its power relations with other ethnic communities. If the Afrikan American community is to maximize its political-economic power then it must maximize its wealth through the organization of an economic system by which it can acquire, produce and distribute economic resources in

---

16. Thomas R. Dye, *Power and Society*, 3rd ed., pp. 81–82.

such ways as to provide for its own needs and can use them in pursuit of its own political interests in the nation and the world.

The maximization of the economic power of the Afrikan American community in particular, and the worldwide Pan–Afrikan community in general, requires that we realistically appraise the economic structures of those communities and the nature of their economic relations with European and other ethnic national and international communities. Given the relatively poor economic conditions which inhere across the Afrikan diaspora and the correlated powerlessness which they generate, the full economic empowerment of Afrikan communities everywhere requires that their internal structural dynamics and external relations be radically transformed.

The limited scope of our volume explicitly prohibits us from dealing with the issues raised in the prior paragraph with the great descriptive and prescriptive detail such an undertaking necessitates. However, we strive to provide broad conceptual frameworks which render us a sound working approach to economically and politically empower the Afrikan American community. We reason that by conceptually looking at the Afrikan American community as a colony, a "nation-within-a-nation," along with viewing Afrikan nations and large Afrikan populations in predominantly non-Afrikan nations as neocolonial nation-states and "nations-within-nations" respectively, we can both more simply and productively describe their current poor economic circumstances and powerlessness as well as prescribe for their remediation.

The Afrikan American Community as Colony

The virtual exclusion of the Afrikan American community from full participation in the White-dominated, political-economic system and its practically total physical, residential and social separation from the White American community; the generally tenuous, if not hostile, relations between these two communities, in effect serve to define them as *de facto* nations sharing the same continental space. The Kerner Commission Report attests to this in its poignantly famous quotation:

> [The United States is] moving toward two societies, one black, one white — separate and unequal. ...[To continue present policies is] to make permanent the division of our country into two societies; one, largely Negro and poor, located in the central cities; the other, predominantly white and affluent, located in the suburbs.[17]

---

17. U.S. National Advisory Commission on Civil Disorders, *The Kerner Report* (New York: Pantheon Books, 1958).

On the basis of the division and separateness of the Black and White American communities as well as the gross political and economic inequalities which inhere between them, we believe that the relationship of the White to the Black community can be more accurately and productively described as that between an imperial nation and its economically dependent colony. Our perspective which conceptually views the Afrikan American community as a "less-developed country" or as a "colony", essentially follows the argumentation of economist William K. Tabb that:

> The black ghetto is best viewed from the perspective of development economics. In its relations with the dominant white society, the black ghetto stands as a unit apart, an internal colony exploited in a systematic fashion. There are limits to such a parallel, but it is helpful as an organizational construct. Through it, current policy alternatives may be viewed in a more meaningful perspective than heretofore....
>
> The economic relations of the ghetto to white America closely parallel those between third-world nations and the industrially advanced countries.[18]

Tabb goes on to specify two key relationships that must exist to support the analogy of the Afrikan American community as colony: (1) economical control and exploitation, and (2) political dependence and subjugation. That this is the case can easily be established through a rather cursory study of the history of White American political repression and economic exploitation of Black American communities from slavery to the present. Moreover, a description of the economic characteristics of the typical Afrikan American ghetto readily fits that of a typical less-developed, neo-colonized country. Such a description includes the following traits (Tabb, 1970; Offiong, 1982):

    a. Relatively low per-capita income; high birth rate; a small, weak middle class; low rates of increase in labor productivity, capital formation, domestic savings; and a small monetized market.

    b. An economy heavily dependent on external markets where demands for its human and material resources are relatively static or declining.

    c. A relatively high desire to consume the products enjoyed by wealthier populations which works to increase the quantity and value of imported goods and services over and above the quantity and value of goods and services (human and non-human capital) exported. Its major export is unskilled labor.

---

    18. William K Tabb, *The Political Economy of the Black Ghetto* (New York: W.W. Norton, 1970), pp. 20–21.

d. Much of the small modern sector of the economy is owned by outsiders. Local entrepreneurship is limited as is managerial know-how.

e. Local markets are relatively limited; businesses lack capital; savings rates are low and what is saved is usually not invested locally. The incidence of credit default is high.

f. Unemployment is prevalent. Welfare payments, i.e., governmental transfers, are needed to help pay for the community's requirements. Important jobs in the local public economy (e.g., teachers, firemen, policemen) are held by outsiders.

g. The economic and social infrastructure are relatively disarticulated, i.e., fragmented, disorganized and disunited.

h. The cultural and intellectual elite are "penetrated," i.e., the community's most influential leaders, opinion shapers and molders ideologically identify with the ruling elite of the dominant cultural/economic group and are dependent on a continued relation with them.

i. An education establishment structured by the political, social and economic dynamics of the dominant group so as to perpetuate the miseducation, poor or inadequate education and training of the community populace thereby perpetuating its underdevelopment, non-competitiveness, and dependency.

In light of the foregoing list, we must take care and not adopt the same fallacious tendency so prevalent among Eurocentric economists and social scientists, i.e., to treat the Afrikan American community as a self-contained unit whose political, social or economic system can be analyzed out of the context of its domination by the larger White American community. Otherwise, the characteristics of "underdevelopment" listed above will be erroneously identified as reflections of the inherent characteristics of Afrikan Americans themselves; as the absence of certain crucial values, attitudes, beliefs, levels of aspiration and motivation or other personal and communal inadequacies. An equally fallacious approach prevalent among Eurocentric economists is to reduce the problem of the underdevelopment of the Afrikan American community (and the worldwide Afrikan community as well) to the prevalence of an aggregation of factors such as those listed above, as if they are the causes rather than the effects of White imperial domination and exploitation. The way the Afrikan economic system(?) has been and is structured is directly related to the history and current nature of the social-economic relations between the White and Black American communities and to the ways in which the Afrikan American community has been and is affected by national and international industrial and economic policies of the White-run

U.S. government. The essence of the Afrikan American economy is its subjugation to White American economic imperialism.

We think that Theotonio dos Santos' description of the dependency of some Third World nations on White American imperialism aptly describes Black American communal dependency on White American imperialism. He defines such dependency as:

> a situation in which a certain group of countries have their economy conditioned by the development and expansion of another economy, to which the former is subject. The relation...assumes the form of dependence when some countries (the dominant) can expand and give impulse to their own development, while other countries (the dependent) can only develop as a reflection of this expansion...The dominant countries have a technological, commercial, capital resource, and social-political predominance over the dependent countries... This permits them to impose conditions of exploitation and extract part of the domestically produced surplus.

This definition which describes the economic situation of dependent nations, especially Afrikan nations relative to European imperialism, applies with equal force to large Afrikan populations in non-Afrikan nations, particularly to the Afrikan American community in the United States.

The economic underdevelopment of the Afrikan American community cannot be veridically traced to alleged innate or enculturated lacks and deficiencies in its constituents or to pre-existing defects in its fiscal and financial infrastructure. Just as with the historical and contemporary underdevelopment in Afrika, the conditioned dependency of the Afrikan American community can be traced precisely to the trans-Atlantic slave trade, to external and internal colonialism and neocolonialism as rationalized by White economic and social racism.

Like any colonial economy, the Afrikan American economic community has never operated in an open and free economic market. It has never engaged in unrestrained free trade inside or outside of its economic borders or has never been permitted to engage freely or fully in competitive national or international labor, commodity, and capital or financial marketplaces.

Theodore Cross (1987) accurately describes the deleterious effects of internal, race-based American colonialism on Black economic development when he contends that "racial prejudgment as power" is a form of coercive power "working in the marketplace for labor, goods, and capital."

It is self-evident that people operate as either buyers or sellers in the market. Racial prejudgment occurs on the buying side of the market whenever the user of labor, capital, goods, or services rules out, or refuses to use, the work, money, goods, or services offered by members of a specific racial group. On the selling side, the racial mode of decisionmaking operates whenever someone who offers work, capital, goods, or services on the market declines to consider offers from buyers, borrowers, or even employers who come from a particular racial group. Both of these processes of making economic judgements may be called *primary* forms of race discrimination. The important point to notice is that whenever the racial prejudgment occurs, coercive power is at work because the judgement tends to limit or block the freedom of the outcast person [group] to enter certain jobs or places where economic benefits may be obtained.

A secondary form of racial prejudgment occurs whenever members of a racial majority reject or ostracize members of *their own group* who agree to trade with a castigated racial group. This *secondary* form of racial prejudgment is a particularly potent form of economic power because it reinforces and makes certain that no one will depart from the original racially biased economic decision....

The dimensions of racial prejudgments as a form of economic power thus begin to emerge. In its several forms, race discrimination takes on the characteristics of an economic boycott or blacklist.[19]

Cross goes on to note that "the white majority used the forces of terrorism and intimidation to regiment the activities of negroes and define the acceptable limits of their economic, social, and political aspirations. [They also] enlisted the powers of federal, state, and local governments to physically segregate Negro people and to enforce the limited zones of economic activity and entry that had been assigned to them." He further notes that through the enlistment of federal, state, and local government power, dominant Whites, "acting as a unified political body, embarked on one of the most ambitious programs of social engineering undertaken in the history of the nation... [to legislate] *inferior* opportunities and status for blacks [and to legislate] *superior* opportunities and status for them." Moreover, Black America was and is decapitalized by White America's use of skin color as a basis for the restrictive regulation and control of the distribution of capital and capital instruments and the restriction of credit and other forms of financial leverage indispensable to capital formation and to the accumulation of wealth in the United States.

---

19. Theodore Cross, *The Black Power Imperative: Racial Inequality and the Politics of Nonviolence* (New York: Faulkner Books, 1987), pp. 102–4.

Economic Segmentation

The history of White racism has been such as to segment the American marketplace between a White imperial economy and a Black dependent economy, a segmentation which in effect segregates Blacks from the more freely competitive and lucrative economy enjoyed by Whites. Thus, the labor and capital economy of the Afrikan American community cannot be adequately and correctly explained by orthodox labor and classical economic theory which assume that the marketplace is perfectly competitive. This means, as Sullivan (1989) contends, that "Inner-city residents do not compete as equals in the existing labor market. Their access has been blocked by the organization of the labor market itself, as well as by institutional arrangements in the education and welfare systems which perpetuate the isolation of inner-city residents from sufficient access to decent jobs." Hence the organization and function of the Afrikan American economy can better be described according to dual economy or segmented market theory. A dual or segmented labor market is defined by Piore as consisting of:

> a *primary* market offering relatively high-paying, stable employment, with good working conditions, chances of advancement and equitable administration of work rules; and a *secondary* market, to which the urban poor are confined, decidedly less attractive in all of these respects and in direct competition with welfare and crime for the attachment of the potential labor force.[20]

In a broader, more general sense, the primary and secondary labor markets are adjunctive segments of parallel dual economies consisting of "(1) a center economy with a high degree of corporate and bureaucratic organization, great diversification, technically progressive means of production and distribution, and national and international accounts; and (2) a peripheral economy [which] contains firms which are small, dominated by one individual, use outdated techniques of production, and operate in small restricted markets" (Butler, 1991). The segmented labor market warehouses an inflated pool of marginal and surplus labor which provides relatively low-wage, low-cost services to the benefit of the center economy. The segmented labor and economic market functions to produce a largely non-competitive Black labor and entrepreneurial community for the economic and political benefit of White labor and capital.

---

20. Michael J. Piore, "Public and Private Responsibility in On-the-Job Training of Disadvantaged Workers," *Department of Economics Working Paper*, Number 23 (Cambridge, Mass.: The M.I.T. Press, June 1968), pp. 2–3.

White American and Afrikan American Economies in post-Industrial America

The bifurcation or segmentation of the American marketplace between a predominantly White center business and primary labor economy and a predominantly Black peripheral business and secondary labor economy, preserves "a continuous drain of income and resources that keeps the Afrikan American relatively poor" and as a whole, economically and politically weak (Fusfeld and Bates, 1984). The remarkable and continuous drain of savings, physical capital, human resources and incomes, leaves the Afrikan American community bereft of the most important resources needed for its development and communal well-being, and of the resources it needs to support its social institutions and enhance its political clout. As intimated by Fusfeld and Bates (1984), a very substantial portion of the savings of the Afrikan American community goes into White-owned financial institutions, e.g., banks and savings and loan societies. These institutions' investment policies and "redlining practices" siphon funds out of the Black community and into business loans, mortgages, and other investments elsewhere, with little or no earnings returning to support that community's economy and development. The withdrawal of capital by non-Afrikan American owners of inner-city housing probably represents the largest flow of wealth out of the community.

The drain of income from the Afrikan American community derives mainly from the purchase of goods and services produced and sold by outsiders; from spending in stores and business establishments owned and staffed by outsiders; from servicing enormous external debt and credit accounts. The drain of human resources means the hemorrhagic loss of many of the community's most intelligent, capable, and imaginative young people "into the progressive sectors [center economy] where rewards are greater and opportunities are wider...leaving the economy of the ghetto — whose chief resource is labor — without many of its best products" (Fusfeld and Bates, 1984).

The outflow of physical capital, i.e., industrial and manufacturing concerns, the historically primary sources for Black upward mobility and viable income, has dealt the most devastating blow to the economic well-being of Black communities in the inner-cities of America. The communal organization and well-being of the inner-cities were conditioned by being located in proximity to concentrated blue-collar manufacturing and distribution centers (Fusfeld and Bates, 1984; Casarda, 1985). The effects of industrial decentralization or de-industrialization, increasingly evident since the mid to late 1940s, are therefore concentrated in the inner-cities where the character of the local center economy has shifted from an industrial to a post-industrial system of production; from industrial production to human, administrative, financial, information processing and analytic services. Fusfeld and Bates describe the processes of industrial centralization and decentralization thusly:

> Manufacturing production employment has largely moved out of the central city. Wholesale and retail employment has declined substantially while central city jobs in services, government, and nonproduction manufacturing have increased. Growth in business service employment has been rapid and sustained, along with substantial growth in finance, insurance, and real estate. In contrast to the central city, the suburban periphery has experienced strong growth in retail, wholesale and manufacturing industries.... Decentralizing manufacturing employment, the leader of the shift from the central city to suburbia, [from the northeastern and midwestern cities to sunbelt and west coast cities], was motivated by both technological and economic changes, such as changes in production methods, developments in transportation, and changes in the relative attractiveness of suburban and central-city tax and service programs [as well as conducive federal industrial and tax policies].
>
> Decades of deindustrialization have coincided with important changes in the nature of business enterprise, especially in the large corporation, that brought increasing use of white-collar as opposed to blue-collar workers...A fundamental shift in the nature of the corporation.[21]

These and other shifts in the national economy have, according to Sullivan (1989), "resulted both in the degradation of employment conditions for much of the population and the disruption and impoverishment of inner-city neighborhoods." Changes in both the center and inner-city economies over the past decades have been such that a condition of permanent depression may be said to prevail in urban poverty areas where high unemployment and retarded business performance remain stubbornly persistent.

Echoes of Decline

The permanent economic depression which characterizes the Afrikan American community is in good part an outcome of American social history, particularly of historical White-Black race relations.

---

21. Daniel R. Fusfeld and Timothy Bates, *The Political Economy of the Urban Ghetto* (Chicago: Southern Illinois Univ. Press, 1984), p. 84.

These relations have been and are such that the largest number of Afrikan Americans have been excluded from full and equal participation in the American social-economic-political system. They are deliberately excluded by White racism from equal employment, equal access to capital resources, equal opportunities to develop their economic resources, and equal opportunity to reside and work in areas where economic growth and development is advancing instead of stagnating or rapidly declining. All of these and other race-based factors and practices are very much responsible for the economic conditions which inhere in the inner-cities.

However, since World War II other factors in addition to White American racism (although related to it) have been having an increasingly greater overall negative and more ominous impact on the economic conditions and prospects of the Afrikan American community. Two of these factors include the relative economic decline of the United States in the global economy and the dramatically rapid structural changes occurring both within the U.S. and global economies. Paul Blumberg discusses these trends:

> The transformation of the American economy from a position of apparent invincibility to one of growing weakness has occurred so quickly and dramatically that economic irony is piled on irony in a continuing and almost unbelievable economic melodrama....
>
> For decades, the United States enjoyed the highest per capita income of any industrialized nation; many people in fact come to consider it part of the natural order of things. How disconcerting then, that in 1975 the Organization for Economic Cooperation and Development (OECD), composed of the 24 leading non-Communist industrial countries in Europe, North America, and Asia, announced that in national income per capita Switzerland had for the first time bumped the U.S. into second place. In 1976, the U.S. fell to third place behind Sweden. In the 1978 OECD yearbook, the United States with per capita GNP of $7,910, dropped to fourth place behind Sweden with $9,030; Switzerland with $8,870; and Canada with $8,410.[22]

It is not our purpose here to discuss the reasons for relative de-industrialization and the global competitive difficulties of the U.S. as have been noted and detailed in numerous contemporary articles and books. That the drastic changes in the nature and character of the American and global economy have deep and serious implications for the continuing economic well-being of Black America is attested to by the inclusion of the following description of the contemporary U.S.

---

22. Paul Blumberg, *Inequality in an Age of Decline*, 1980, pp. 108–9.

economy by the National Urban League in its annual report, *The State of Black America 1993*:

U.S. Competitiveness: Lapses, Lags, and Losses

The United States no longer enjoys the distinction of being the world's undisputed economic superpower. Led by Japan and Germany, other industrialized nations have made remarkable advances that have altered radically the global economic order. The erosion of American preeminence appears in several key indicators of economic performance.

- The U.S. productivity growth rate has slowed dramatically, falling behind that of major international competitors. From 3.1 percent in the 1960s, U.S. productivity growth dropped to 1.1 percent in the 1980s. Japan's productivity growth in the last decade was more than triple the U.S. rate.
- The real gross domestic product (GDP) in the United States rose by just 2.6 percent per year in the 1980s, compared to 2.8 percent in the 1970s and a robust 3.8 percent in the 1960s.
- U.S. trade deficits over the last decade totaled $1 trillion. In 1980, the United States was the world's largest creditor nation, to the tune of about $400 billion. By 1990, we were the largest debtor nation by an even larger amount, much of it borrowed from Japan.
- The United States now trails other industrialized countries — including Japan, Germany, Canada, and the United Kingdom — in national saving rate. The saving rate in Japan more than doubles the U.S. rate. Likewise, the U.S. investment rate is less than half that Japan and lags well behind that of other competitor nations.
- The federal budget deficit has skyrocketed to $300 billion, while the national debt has soared to $4 trillion. The debt averages to about $50,000 for every American family.

There are still other, equally revealing correlates of economic weakness that fuel concerns about U.S. economic competitiveness.

- Real wage growth has dipped sharply, down by 12 percent since 1969. Manufacturing workers have been especially hard-hit. Meanwhile, wages in competitor nations have been on the rise.
- Family incomes in the United States have stagnated, but income inequality has widened. Families in the upper fifth of the income distribution have progressed; those in the lower fifth have lost ground. There now is more income inequality in the United States than in any other industrial nation.
- Unemployment in the 1980s rose over average levels in the 1960s and 1970s, and it remains over 7 percent at this writing. Simi-

larly, the poverty population expanded during the last two decades. In 1991, 35.7 million persons, 14.2 percent of the U.S. population, were poor. The 1991 poverty rate was well above the recent low of 11.4 percent in 1978.[23]

The report goes on to comment: "In combination, these conditions and trends bespeak a reduction in the American standard of living and have even more ominous implications for the future.... Afrikan Americans have suffered disproportionately and face the bleakest prospects." One of the major structural changes in the U.S. economy has been its increasingly steady shift from the production of manufactured goods to the production of services. The report notes that this shift which includes the continuing long-term contraction of the industrial sector of the U.S. economy, "is arguably the most profound economic change to occur in the United States since the Industrial Revolution." Blumberg along with many others have noted that the loss of their hold on the industrial infrastructure, i.e., the almost precipitous decline of manufacturing, in the inner-cities of America is primarily responsible for their assumption of the "contours of underdevelopment". From his analysis of the effects of American de-industrialization on inner-city communities in his book, *The Truly Disadvantaged*, William Julius Wilson concludes that the chief factor behind the rapid deterioration of Afrikan American inner-city communities across the nation has been the loss by Blacks of manufacturing jobs, a primary source of Black employment and livable wages. The continuing loss of manufacturing jobs and of the relatively high wages and job security they provided has contributed mightily to the growth of an increasingly large "Black underclass." It has resulted in the destabilization and destruction of working-class and poor Black families, the creation of female-headed families, and in assorted social problems prevalent in the inner-city today.

The still heavy dependence of Afrikan Americans on the manufacturing sector of the economy and on the service sectors which are likely to decline in the near future, means that there is a "bad fit" between the current distribution of the Afrikan American work force and the reconfiguring industrial and service base" (*State of Black America 1993*). A review of *Tables* 12-1 & 12-2 clearly indicates why the fit between the economic prospects of the Afrikan American community and projected growth rates for the major occupational categories between 1990–2005 is not very good.

---

23. The following data and information was adopted from Billy J. Tidwell, "Afrikan Americans and the 21st Century Labor Market: Improving the Fit" in *The State of Black America 1993* (New York: National Urban League), pp. 37–38.

Black Proportions in Occupations
(Proportion of Total Work Force: 10.1%)

Janitors	21.0	Designers	2.9
Correction Officers	23.3	Lawyers	2.6
Short Order Cooks	23.3	Architects	2.1
Security Guards	23.5	Cabinetmakers	2.1
Vehicle Washers	25.4	Bartenders	2.0
Laundry & Dry Cleaning	26.1	Dentists	1.5
Hotel Maids & Housemen	27.2	Commercial Pilots	1.5
Postal Clerks	27.7	Speech Therapists	1.3
Domestic Servants	29.3	Dental Hygienists	1.1
Nursing Aides	31.2	Geologists	0.7

Source: Bureau of Labor Statistics

Table 12-1

African-American Share of the Major Occupations in 1991 and Projected Occupation Growth Rates 1990–2005

Occupation	African American Percent in 1991	Occ. Growth Rate 1990–2005
Total	10.1	20.1
Exec., admin, & managerial	5.7	27.4
Prof. specialty	6.7	32.3
Technicians and related support	9.3	36.9
Sales	6.6	24.1
Admin. support, including clerical	11.4	13.1
Service	17.2	29.2
Precision prod., craft, & repair	7.8	12.6
Opers., fabricators, & laborers	15.0	4.2
Agri., forestry, fishing, etc.	6.4	4.5

Sources: Bureau of Labor Statistics. *Employment and Earnings, January 1992*. Table 22. pp. 185-190; Bulletin 2402, May 1992, Table 1, p. 63 (*State of Black America 1993*, p. 49).

Table 12-2

As can be readily surmised from this review, "Afrikan Americans are greatly under-represented in the fastest growing occupations and over-represented in those having the slowest projected growth."[24] This pessimistic assessment is not helped by the fact that educational status and human capital characteristics of the Afrikan American

---

24. Ibid.

community as a whole, are generally very unfavorable relative to its ability to gain its fair share of high-growth, high-paying jobs and its ability to engage in highly compensatory entrepreneurial activities. In light of these and other facts the National Urban League, in part, concluded:

> In short, the shifting occupational structure does not bode well for the economic future of African Americans. Both their current placement in the labor market and their relative position on the hierarchy of educational attainment are major constraints. Relieving these constraints, i.e., "improving the fit," is essential to the overall economic well-being of the African-American community in the years ahead. But the challenge may be even more complicated than that.[25]

The economic outlook of Black America, particularly its "underclass" is such that one writer concludes:

> Black Americans have outlived their usefulness. Their raison d'etre to this society has ceased to be a compelling issue. Once an economic asset, they are considered an economic drag. The wood is all hewn, the water all drawn, the cotton all picked, and the rails reach from coast to coast. The ditches are all dug, the dishes are put away, and only a few shoes remain to be shined.[26]

American Decline – Black Decline

While many analysts may attribute America's relative economic decline to foreign competition, other analysts have given greater priority to other factors. Of course, the overwhelming balance of payment problem, unprecedented trade deficits, the growing non-competitiveness of much of American industry, must in part be held accountable for many of the economic problems plaguing the United States. However, as much, if not more, of these problems can also be attributed to White America's external and internal policies having to do with power and race relations.

Both the attempt by White America to maintain its economic and military dominance in the world and racial domination in the nation has worked to negatively skew and to weaken its overall economy and jeopardize the living standards of large segments of its native population, including the Afrikan American community. On the global level, White America's attempt to maintain, expand and protect its worldwide political-economic empire is based on its development and maintenance of a *permanent* war economy. While there is evidence that military spending associated with war might temporarily invigorate an economy

---

25. Billy J. Tidwell, "African Americans and the 21st Century Labor Market: Improving the Fit," in *The State of Black America 1993*, National Urban League, p. 51.

26. Samuel F. Yette, *The Choice: The Issue of Black Survival in America*, p. 18.

as did war production during World War II, a permanent war economy, i.e., permanent war production, as has essentially been the case with the U.S. economy since World War II, may ultimately debilitate or distort it. Citing the work of Melman (1965; 1974), Bergman (1980) asserts that for the past several decades "the United States had diverted gargantuan amounts of money, manpower, and resources into military production, the inevitable by-products of which have been the neglect, depletion, deterioration, and exhaustion of vast areas of the civilian economy, its industrial base, and the underlying infrastructure." Economic dislocations occur in a war economy which tends over time to retard its ability to produce products of ordinary economic use, value, products useful for enhancing standards of living through the production of new and innovative consumer goods and services, and useful for further production, e.g., machine tools used to make the other products (Melman, 1974). This can and does occur despite "spinoffs" from defense production to civilian production (e.g., commercial aircraft, computers). The military priorities of the U.S. have been such that a vast proportion of its enormous wealth has been siphoned off by relatively nonproductive military and geopolitical investments, thereby forcing it to lose vital opportunities to build and rebuild the American civilian and commercial economy and to expand and upgrade the American economic infrastructure. Capital, manpower, and research funds largely dedicated to military and geopolitical priorities essentially exposed the underfunded and inadequately organized economic structure to damaging, often fatal, foreign competition. This sentiment is supported by Paul Kennedy's two major works related to the subject, *The Rise and Fall of the Great Powers* (1987) and *Preparing for the 21st Century: Winners and Losers* (1993). Kennedy in an article in the *New York Review* (1993) contends that:

> Yet while [its] military power boosts the United States' place in world affairs, that may not necessarily be a blessing for the nation as a whole. The high defense burden has caused some economic damage, and given an advantage to commercial rivals like Japan and Germany...While some strategic thinkers debate whether forces should be withdrawn from Europe and concentrated against "out-of-area" threats in the developing world, others wonder about the utility of military force in general, since the threats to America may now come not from nuclear weapons, but from environmental hazards, drugs and loss of economic competitiveness...Three hundred billion dollars a year bought military security for the United States, but it also diverted resources — capital, the armed forces' personnel, materials, skilled labor, engineers, and scientists — from nonmilitary production. In 1988, for example, over 65 percent of federal R&D [Research and Development] money was allocated to defense, compared with 0.5 percent to environmental protection and 0.2 percent to industrial

development. Moreover, while engaging Moscow in an expensive arms race, America has had to compete for world market shares against allies like Japan and Germany which have allocated smaller percentages of their national resources to the military, thus freeing capital, personnel, and research and development for commercial manufacture, which has undermined parts of the American industrial base.

While the issue as to whether high defense spending enhances or slows down the commercial, if not the overall, economy is not resolved, it seems quite clear that such spending otherwise changes the structure of the economy. Such changes and possible distortions which hobble the economy with an unhealthy mixture of strengths and weaknesses, occupational dislocations, indebtedness, financial frailties, deficits in trade and current accounts, low productivity in important sectors, and markedly uneven distribution of its wealth, inevitably trail immense social problems in their wake. And among those social problems is the economic destabilization and social ruination of predominantly Afrikan American inner-city communities.

Industrial and Government Policy

American industry has also contributed to the breakdown and restructuring of the civilian economy through its own competitive relations with its foreign counterparts. The rapid diffusion of technology and managerial know-how across international borders has been and is presently aided and abetted by their sale and transfer to the industrial and service sectors of other nations (European and Asian) by the American industrial sector itself. Blumberg comments on this situation thusly:

> It is not the natural process of technological diffusion alone that has eroded America's [technological] lead, however. By their massive sale of advanced technology abroad, via licensing agreements, patent sales, and other forms of technology transfer, American corporations are exporting America's future and undermining its industrial base. The United Electrical, Radio and Machine Workers of America (UE) reported that of some 11,600 foreign technical aid agreements concluded by Japanese firms from the end of World War II to 1970, approximately 6,000 were with American companies. Developing these patents in the U.S. originally cost over $120 billion, but Japanese industry bought the patent rights for these technological developments for only 2.7 billion, or at what the AFL-CIO calls "fire-sale prices."[27]

---

27. Paul Blumberg, *Inequality in an Age of Decline*, pp. 146–47.

While such transfers were beneficial to international economic development and to some American multinational corporations, their contribution to devastating foreign competition and to injurious domestic dislocations and restructuring which are undermining the economic viability of the Afrikan American community and of the worldwide Afrikan community cannot be denied. While the sale or transfer of notoriously aged or virtually obsolete technology and know-how to Afrikan enterprises move at a snail's pace, American corporations sell or transfer the latest generation of advanced technology to Western Europe and East Asian countries. This has permitted sophisticated foreign corporations to develop and innovate these factors and "eventually outflank the U.S. in international trade" (Blumberg, 1980). After reviewing this process he further concludes:

> Finally, as America loses its comparative advantage in many areas of manufacturing, some U.S. companies are gradually shifting their corporate efforts from manufacturing domestically to developing and marketing technology abroad...Instead of directing their energies toward producing competitively in the U.S., some firms now find it easier and more profitable simply to transfer manufacturing operations — and the advanced technology underlying it — abroad.[28]

It is also important to note that not all foreign competition is "foreign." A measurable proportion of the foreign competition which is creating problems for the American economy has been and is created by the investment and industrial policies of the U.S. government and American corporations themselves. In order to gain access to foreign markets and to better position themselves to reduce costs so as to compete more effectively with foreign corporations, many U.S. multinationals corporations have been investing increasing billions dollars in manufacturing facilities abroad. Moreover, such investments often involve the downsizing or closing of domestic factories, or removing them offshore to Europe, Asia, Mexico, and other non-Afrikan Third World countries. The investment facilities created in foreign countries by American corporations form a major portion of what is referred to as direct foreign investment. While such investment may earn foreign exchange for the investing corporation and nation, it may also markedly damage the domestic economy for the reasons that it:

A. Alters the distribution of income in favor of capital and to the disadvantage of labor;

---

28. Ibid., p. 149.

B. Causes a loss of domestic employment and of government tax revenue, especially where tax laws provide incentives for overseas investment (as in the U.S.);
C. Speeds the diffusion of economic power and technological know-how abroad;
D. Increases the domestic market concentration of large firms.[29]

For the past two decades foreign investments by U.S. corporations have been immense. By 1976, U.S. direct foreign investment amounted to $137 billion (Blumberg, 1980). Between 1975 and 1991, U.S. direct investment amounted to $450 billion, the largest bulk of which went to Western European countries, with some $26 billion (in 1990) going to emerging countries with the skilled work forces (*Fortune*, 12/14/92).

In 1991 U.S. manufacturers invested largely in the industrialized countries of Europe and Canada (WSJ, 10/20/92). As reported in the *Journal*, a study conducted by the firm of Ernst and Young notes that "less than one-third of the 659 major investments abroad by U.S. manufacturers in 1991 went to countries with low labor rates." Contradicting the popular notion that U.S. manufacturers would automatically elect to invest in countries where labor is cheapest, if given the opportunity, these countries use their foreign investments chiefly to gain access to markets. Apparently, "looking to build market share in industrialized countries by accessing customers, technology and skills"(WSJ) as well as in responding to financial incentives and low corporate tax rates offered by these countries, U.S. companies placed more than half of their investments abroad in Europe. The most popular single recipient of U.S. investment, however, was Canada where 84 of the 659 major investments were made. The *Journal* reported that "Mexico and the now-disbanded Soviet Union were the only countries with low hourly wages that were among the top 10 choices where U.S. manufacturers chose to invest [in 1991]."

Edward Greenberg aptly cautions us about drawing erroneous conclusions from the apparent character of U.S. foreign direct investment.

> Now it may be argued that the heavy investment in Western economies disproves the contention that American corporations are involved or interested in the exploitation of Third World natural resources. It is important to point out, therefore, that much of the investment in Western Europe, Canada, and Japan is in firms that are themselves heavily involved in the Third World. Moreover, the 40 percent of direct investment in the less developed parts of the world

---

[29]. Blumberg, 1980; Gilpin, 1975.

is important. Forty percent is not an insignificant figure. It is a major portion of all overseas United States economic activities by corporations, and accounts for a very high percentage of its profits.[30]

Moreover, the trend for foreign direct investments by U.S. and foreign corporations is moving increasingly in favor of the developing nations (this is also the case regarding portfolio investments). Robert Ross and Kent Trachte in their study of global capitalism also noted this trend.

> U.S. foreign investment in manufacturing in the Third World has grown both absolutely and relatively to investment in traditional sectors. This supports the proposition that spatial mobility has emerged as a new and critical form of competition for U.S. manufacturing capital.
>
> The available data show recent increases in the flow of manufacturing investment to the periphery for the other major core industrial powers. As of 1971, 42 percent of the stock of British direct investment in the periphery was in manufacturing industries; by 1979, that figure had increased to 57 percent. In 1980, 68 percent of the outflow of German direct investment to the periphery was in manufacturing. The surge of Japanese foreign investment to the periphery during the 1970's was also concentrated in such manufacturing industries as textiles, iron and steel and electronics.
>
> Overall, according to the United Nations Centre on Transnational Corporations, in the 1970s, particularly the latter years, foreign investment in manufacturing accounted for an increasing share of direct investment from developed to developing countries.
>
> In contrast to the era of monopoly capitalism, manufacturing capital from other regions is now flowing to the Third World in substantial amounts. In fact, investment in manufacturing in the periphery now exceeds investment in raw material extraction.[31]

Ross and Trachte go on to indicate how standard foreign direct investment figures may inadvertently obscure the true magnitude of this type of economic activity.

> While the data on foreign direct investment in manufacturing are impressive, they do not capture comprehensively the relocation of manufacturing production to the periphery by core capital. Subcontracting is one means of capital relocation not included in direct investment data. For example, in the apparel industry, firms

---

[30]. Edward Greenberg, *Serving the Few: Corporate Capitalism and the Bias of Government Policy* (New York: John Wiley, 1974), p. 61.

[31]. Robert Ross and Kent Trachte, *Global Capitalism: The Leviathan* (Albany: State University of New York Press, 1990).

frequently subcontract the sewing of garments to independent "jobbers" located in a low-wage country. The "jobbers" are not formal subsidiaries of the apparel firm, and the firms may make no direct equity investment in plant and equipment in the low-wage site. Yet, in a very real sense the payment to a "jobber" is the functional equivalent of a direct foreign investment. For it is the foreign apparel firm that provides the capital to finance the sewing machines needed to sew the garment.

Joint ventures are another means of redeploying production whose impact is not fully reflected in direct foreign investment data. General Motor's joint venture with a Korean automobile manufacturer illustrates the point. By acquiring a share of the Korean firm and agreeing upon a joint project to produce a new subcompact car for the U.S. market, GM began the process of shifting production from plants in the United States that currently make subcompacts to plants in Korea. Yet, because the Korean firm has existing plants, the amount of capital flow recorded is less than would have occurred if GM had to build new plants in Korea.

Global finance capital has also played a role in the movement of manufacturing production to the periphery that is not reflected in direct investment data. The available research suggests that a significant portion of the enormous loans that have been extended to Third World countries in the past fifteen years have financed private and state-owned manufacturing facilities in the periphery.

The means global capital has available for shifting manufacturing production to sites in peripheral countries are many and varied. Direct investment is the most visible but it understates the magnitude of the employment that has transpired in recent decades.[32]

In regard to the developing countries *Fortune* magazine (12/14/92) noted as follows:

> FDI [Foreign Direct Investment] in developing countries is unevenly distributed. The economies of East Asia take the tiger's share. Between 1986 and 1990 the developing countries altogether received, on average, $26 billion of the FDI a year. Of that, East and South-East Asia's share was $14 billion, Latin America's $9 billion *and Africa's $3 billion.* [Emphasis added]

As can be readily inferred from these figures, the overwhelming bulk of FDI involves investments from the industrial U.S. to industrialized countries elsewhere. These countries are ethnically, predominantly Caucasian or Asian. Afrika receives very, very little, reflecting a lack of U.S. government and industrial sector interest in that

---
32. Ibid.

continent. In fact, direct foreign investments in sub-Saharan Afrika amounted to only 0.46 of the total U.S. FDI *abroad in 1990*.[33] We can easily see that the nature of the American investment and trade relations follows the "color line" in rapidly decreasing proportion from White to in-between to Black. Consequently, the trend of ethnic power and economic relations which inhere domestically is also reflected by U.S. foreign trade and investment patterns abroad.

Jobs Move Abroad

The magnitude of U.S. foreign direct investment which involves the founding, development and expansion of industries abroad; the entering into joint ventures of various types with foreign corporations; the moving of manufacturing facilities abroad and the like by American transnational corporations, ultimately leads to change in the quantity and character of both the domestic industrial sector and labor force. U.S. foreign direct investment along with that of other industrialized Western and some Asian nations have led to "the emergence of a truly global labor force, talented and capable of accomplishing just about anything, anywhere."[34] *Fortune* magazine goes on to indicate that "A fundamental shift is underway in how and where the world's work gets done — with potentially ominous consequences for wealthy industrialized nations." And we may add, actually ominous consequences for the Afrikan American community. The global redistribution of industry brought on by current investment trends and other national and global economic structural dynamics, has led to the de-industrialization of much of inner-city America; the post-industrial age; the stagnation of the growth of the American manufacturing workforce which has not expanded much beyond its 1946 level despite a five-fold increase in its productivity; and has at least, since the 1960s, disenabled the richest economy in the world to provide significant, full-employment at livable wages to lift the 30–40 percent of the Afrikan American population above the government's anaemic poverty and near-poverty thresholds.

Not only are industrial facilities moving abroad; so are jobs. As employment of Afrikan Americans stagnate and decline, American direct foreign investment appears to be creating jobs abroad, not only in so-called developing and Third World nations where wages and other monetary and political costs are low, but in high-wage countries like Canada and in Europe. *Fortune* magazine (ibid) reports that after a measurable decline in the early eighties, "The number of foreign

---

33. "Retreat from Africa," *Foreign Affairs* (1992/93) Vol. 72, No. 1, p. 95.
34. *Fortune*, 12/14/1992.

workers employed by U.S. companies...rose by half a million between 1986 and 1990 to 6.7 million."

The rearrangement of the global workforce as well as the global redistribution of industry have led some experts to predict that "It is a fallacy to think that industry will increase employment overall in the Western world...; Western European and American employment will just shrink and shrink in an orderly way. Like farming at the turn of the century" (*Fortune,* ibid). While discussing the movement of jobs and industrial facilities abroad we must be careful not to be left with the impression that such jobs are mainly going to low-wage, unsophisticated workers and managers. Quite to the contrary, *Fortune* magazine reports that "increasingly sophisticated work is indeed being parceled out to faraway nations, where labor forces are exceedingly capable." It indicates that a vice president in a firm specializing in global manufacturing notes that "new factories abroad, even in low wage countries, tend to be more labor efficient than their counterparts in the company's home country."

It is very important to note that the globalization of the service industries and jobs are increasingly being moved abroad in a manner which parallels movement of blue-collar jobs abroad. This includes managerial, designer and engineering jobs as well as research and development work. In many instances responsibility for design, manufacture, marketing and profits are being transferred wholesale.

This trend in industrial and job movement abroad as outlined will most likely be intensified if efforts to eliminate trade barriers between Canada, Mexico and the United States are successful. The North American Free Trade Agreement (NAFTA) to which these efforts refer, may further erode well over a 100,000 or more jobs, especially blue-collar jobs, which describes the larger proportion of jobs in the Afrikan American community. In addition, the wages paid to remaining blue-collar workers may stagnate and their rate of growth decline relative to prior decades. The AFL-CIO has predicted a loss of 500,000 jobs as the result of NAFTA. While the actual loss or gain of jobs is difficult to quantify, an indication of the flow of jobs to Mexico may be garnered from the fact that employment in factories constructed by U.S. companies there already has climbed from 120,000 in 1980 to 500,000 in 1991.

We must keep in mind that the exact outcome of NAFTA is highly uncertain. Certainly it will eliminate a significant number of jobs. It will also create more jobs, perhaps many more, as U.S. companies process increased exports to Mexico. One thing is certain, however: the America industrial profile will be markedly changed. It could be that the shift in the American economic landscape in the long run may be a shift for the better. It may generate new ideas, new products, new markets and expanding employment, none of which we can perceive at the moment. But we cannot ignore the fact that at this historical moment and perhaps for a few historical moments more, fundamental changes have and are occurring. Old paradigms, old and reliable assumptions and approaches no longer apply. As noted by the *Wall Street Journal* (10/28/92):

> By 1973, Bretton Woods [where] statesmen designated "the dollar", pegged at $35 an ounce [of gold], as the centerpiece of international exchange... [and set] the seal on America as the world's ruling financial power] was dead, scuttled in large measure by an America no longer willing, and increasingly less able, to bear its burden. Today America is $4 trillion in debt. It passed the hat to wage the Persian Gulf War. It remains the global leader, but one in the midst of historical transition: away from unquestioned supremacy....
>
> Since Bretton Woods, the global economy has shifted like a tectonic plate. First the global upheaval reshaped American corporations and American lives. Now, inevitably, it is shaping American politics as well.
>
> The economic shift is starkly visible. "Creative destruction," in the Orwellian term coined by the economist Joseph Schumpeter, mowed down three million jobs in the 1980s. The world's seven largest banks are now Japanese.

The U.S. economy is being shaped profoundly by a global economy over which it is having less direct control and against which it can do less and less to protect its own workforce and maintain its vaunted high standard of living. The steady stream of remarkably large layoffs, cutbacks and terminations by big corporations such as IBM, Westinghouse, Boeing, "underlines the continuing turmoil in America's corporate economy"(NYT, 1/28/93). The fast-changing economy and its markets, which are compelling more and more companies to shrink or downsize, to remain small and flexible, to engage in new types of relations and corporate partnership arrangements with co- and sub-contractors, can no longer provide long-term job security with ample lifetime benefits and guarantees for an increasingly large segment of the workforce.

The Powerlessness of Government to Resolve Human Problems

Our foregoing analysis speaks to the fact that in order for the U.S. and global capitalist nations to maintain world-wide military and economic dominance, the U.S., as the principal capitalistic military/economic power, must sustain a constant mobilization to ensure national and international security. We have documented the tremendous monetary costs ($300 billion+) and injurious distortion of the domestic economy this global posture generates (over 65% of research and development geared to military weaponry). These massive monetary and commercial/economic distortions effectively determine domestic priorities in ways chiefs of state are powerless to change. Since national military and economic security are top priorities regardless of who is head of state, regardless of the political composition and orientation of the legislative and judicial branches, and regardless of who heads state and local governments, domestic priorities which speak to the basic social needs of citizens are reduced in importance. Gerald and Patricia Mische succinctly define the matter when they contend that "Fuller human development and the realization of such higher human values as justice, peace, unity, truth, etc., are restricted and subverted by dominance of security priorities."[35] The Misches list a number of issues which concern people and need the priority attention of government. They include:

–Hunger	–Care of the Aged
–Housing	–Racial Justice
–Health Care	–Women's Rights
–Education	–Religious Freedom
–Employment	–Penal Reform
–Environment	–Urban Planning
–War Prevention	–Population
–Crime Prevention	–Democratic Participation
–Prevention of Alienation and Addiction	

We agree with the Misches when they suggest that "Most political leaders would insist that they personally embrace the above agenda." They, however, are compelled to acknowledge that "first priority is given to policies which enhance a nation's ability to survive...global competition. The above priorities are consequently relegated to the back burners of national agendas." In this political context, the Misches argue, "even the best intentioned of national leaders [are powerless] to move person-centered, social justice priorities up from the bottom of their country's agenda."

---

35. Gerald and Patricia Mische, *Toward A Human World Order: Beyond the National Security Straitjacket* (New York: Paulist Press, 1977).

A review of the above priorities accurately expresses the social concerns of the Afrikan American community. If these priorities are made subservient to national security and international economic competition concerns, then the issues most vital to the survival and enhancement of the Afrikan American community will receive inadequate or no resolution.

Demands of Global Capitalism. On Monday, July 25, 1994, the *New York Times* reported that the foreign investment trends we discussed earlier are accelerating. In fact, the *Times* reported that "American companies are once again rapidly expanding their operations — demonstrating that no matter what the incentives for keeping business in the United States, the urge to spread factories offices, stores and jobs overseas is irresistible."

The *Times* reported that "American companies employ 5.4 million abroad, 80 percent of them in manufacturing." The bulk of the $716.2 billion American companies invested in 1993 was concentrated in manufacturing in Europe, Canada and Japan. The companies also invested substantially in the booming economies of East Asia, especially China, Singapore, and Hong Kong. This was also the case with countries in the Western Hemisphere, especially Canada, Mexico, Argentina and Bermuda [an offshore enclave for American banking and insurance companies]. While manufacturing represents some 40 percent of American foreign investment, the percentage of investment outlays for retail, finance and service facilities rose twice as rapidly as those for manufacturing.

Change in the Power Relations between Global Capital and Labor. While opening a factory abroad implies or actually means that one in the U.S. may be closed, an equally important ramification of this process is the change in power relations between big capitalists or the financial-corporate elite and labor, and in regard to our central concern here, the change in power relations between this elite and the state. That a favorable change in power relations between itself and labor and the state is as important to the financial-corporate elite as is the movement of manufacturing, finance, retail, research and service facilities abroad as means of enhancing profits, is implied in a statement reportedly made by Thomas Skelly, a senior vice president in the Gillette Company (NYT, ibid). When questioned as to why Gillette's new Sensor XL razor blade cartridge, to be sold in the United States starting this year, would not lead to the expansion of its Boston plant where production was started two years ago — thereby creating additional jobs in the U.S. — rather than adding the extra capacity to its Berlin plant, Skelly answered, "We are also concerned about having one place where a product is made. There could be an explosion, or *labor problems*" [emphasis added]. Gillette has put 62 factories in 28 countries and employs 2,300 people in the manufacture of razors and blades in the U.S. and 7,700 abroad. The emphasis we placed on Skelly's reference to labor problems speaks to the fact that by placing manufacturing and other productive facilities abroad, global capitalists are able to neutralize or negate U.S. labor's power to successfully execute its wage and benefit demands on industry by using the labor strike as its most effective tool. Global capitalists are increasingly able to counter labor's attempts in this direction by making up for production losses due to strikes in the U.S. by increased production elsewhere, and through the importation of the relevant products into the U.S. market by other means. More often, they may threaten to close down their American operations in the face of union and labor demands and thereby unemploy their American workers rather than accede to their demands. Consequently, the power of global capitalism has been massively increased relative to that of labor due to the fact that global capital can balance its foreign labor forces against its domestic workforces. The relative weakness of labor can be gauged by the steep decline in union membership in America and the "give backs" unions and workers have been forced to make under the threat of global capital to close factory facilities and lay off or cut domestic workforces.

The relative weakness of labor power in America, the wholesale transfer of jobs abroad and the relatively low wages paid to workers abroad, translate into little employment and benefits protection, joblessness, low wages, and general economic stagnation for the American workforce in general, and the Afrikan American workforce and community in particular.

Change in the Power Relations between Global Capital and the State. The ability of global capital to export jobs and displace manufacturing, financial, service, and research facilities not only permits it to oversee federal, state and local governments by threatening to ship productive facilities abroad and to disinvest in the domestic economy, but also increasingly enables global capital to get the state to generate laws and policies favorable to it and unfavorable to labor and the welfare of the citizenry in general. In the name of maintaining a "favorable investment climate", i.e., a climate which benefits capital at the expense of labor and other social groups, and in the name of maintaining America's competitive edge in international trade, global capital uses its capacity to increase unemployment by withholding domestic investment; by transferring jobs abroad; by refusing to fund national, state and local debt and thus force the state to reduce its social costs — welfare, unemployment benefits, etc.; to reduce expenditures for job training, education, health and other human services if it deems such costs and expenditures to be against its economic interests. Such reductions fall heaviest on the already overburdened Afrikan American community. And they occur at precisely the times the community needs to not only maintain prior levels of human services but when these levels need to be increased.

The state is now less able to protect the human and civil rights, to meet the human and economic, educational and social needs of the Afrikan American community than it was prior to the 1970s, before the significant globalization of labor and productive facilities empowered global capitalists to neutralize the just demands of domestic labor and the people. At this juncture, even if a progressive Afrikan American were elected president of the U.S., he or she would ascend to office at the point where it would be least able to positively impact on Black social problems. In addition to White racism, its old nemesis, the Afrikan American community is now faced with a new nemesis in the form of the negative fallout from the globalization of labor, which will have an impact on the community equal to or greater than that of racism. This dilemma — the dilemma of having to deal with the detrimental impacts of both racism and globalism simultaneously — defines the critical vulnerability of the contemporary Afrikan American and Pan–Afrikan communities. It is to this dilemma that this volume speaks. We believe that our proposals for enhancing Black Power point to its only viable resolution.

Reactionary Outcomes of Global Competition

The reactions of American companies to global economic assaults are bewildering and often frantically revolutionary. Besides reducing their workforces and forcing the remaining workers to take on more jobs and work overtime (while earning fewer benefits) in order to increase productivity and cut costs, many firms are now increasingly resorting to the use of contract labor and job temps. The *Wall Street Journal* (3/11/93) describes this trend thusly:

> This is the 1990s workplace. After spending years at one company, more American office and factory employees are getting transplanted overnight to a temporary or subcontracting netherworld. They do the same work at the same desk for less pay and with no health insur-

ance or pension benefits. Others are farmed out to an employment agency, which puts them on its payroll to save the mother company, paperwork and cost.

The *Journal* goes on to note that "Temporary-help employment grew 10 times faster than overall employment between 1982 and 1990. In 1992, temporary jobs accounted for about two-thirds of new private-sector jobs." Temporary, contract and part-time workers now compose some 25 percent of the workforce. This phenomenon has led to the coining of names to designate this growing pool of temporary and part-time help, contract and leased employees — "contingent workers", "disposable workers", "flexible workers", "assignment workers", or "throwaway workers". While such changes in workforce permanence, job security guarantees and designations reflect current recessionary conditions, labor market specialists expect that many of the shifts are permanent.

The *Journal* (3/16/93) recently chronicled in detail an approach to industrial organization it refers to as *"re-engineering"*. Re-engineering involves the reconfiguration, redesign and reconstruction of the workplace, the workforce, and its procedural organization in ways meant to maximize its efficiency and productivity while simultaneously reducing the number of its personnel. Consequently, it may markedly accelerate productivity growth while creating job losses. Some analysts estimate that the re-engineering may wipe out as many as 25 million jobs in a private sector economy which employs approximately 90 million people. The *Journal* quotes John C. Skerritt, managing partner in the financial services group at Anderson Consulting, concerning possible jobs outcomes of re-engineering: "We can see many, many ways that jobs will be destroyed, but we can't see where they will be created... This may be the biggest social issue of the next 20 years." It further quotes John Scully, then chief executive of Apple Computer Inc., who commented that the "reorganization of work could prove as massive and wrenching as the Industrial Revolution." Some experts have ventured to estimate that job losses due to re-engineering may amount to between a million and 2.5 million jobs each year for the foreseeable future. These job losses may include millions of service workers such as clerical workers, supervisors, middle managers and support workers. Interestingly, the *Journal* (3/16/93) reports that layoffs due to re-engineering may hit hardest at the level of middle management, whose ranks now constitute 18 to 22 percent of workers let go. "By that count, middle managers are three times as likely to be put out of work by re-engineering" (WSJ, ibid). At this juncture it is apropos to note that compared to an overall employment rate which rose by 21 percent between 1989 and 1991, un-employment rates for executives, administrators and managers jumped by 28 percent. The growth rate of managerial occupations is projected to slip to fourth place between now and the year 2005 from its first place position during the 15 years between 1975–90 (*State of Black America 1993*). Consequently, the Urban League in its 1993 report suggests that "credentials that formerly served management-oriented Afrikan Americans well may no longer assure their economic success."

Thus the restructuring of the overall American economy and the re-engineering of many of its corporate workplaces translate into job losses by both factory workers and professionals. However, not all the job losses suffered by professionals are due to re-engineering and recession or to foreign competition, but also due to the fact that American firms are hiring highly skilled workers abroad for lower pay to perform jobs once reserved for American professionals (WSJ, 3/17/93). Highly skilled workers from Asia, the former Soviet bloc and Europe are also being employed by American companies to temporarily replace American professionals in America itself. For example, the *Journal* reports that companies, namely:

> Texas Instruments Inc., Chase Manhattan Corp., International Business Machines Corp. and scores of other companies have contracted with Indians, Israelis and other foreigners to write computer programs. The importing of foreign professionals, their hiring abroad by branches of multinational corporations and American "runaway" companies, the movement of business units abroad, along with hundreds of high-paying managerial and research jobs, and the availability of an abundance of low-paid professionals in Malaysia, Hungary, China, India and elsewhere calls into question the idea, popular in the Clinton administration, that US workers can raise their own wages or job prospects by acquiring more skills.

The *Journal* further notes that "The number of applications [by American companies] to bring in foreign professionals has nearly doubled to more than 100,000 annually over the past five years." Many foreign professionals also come to the U.S. to get training as well as to work alongside Americans during "peak" times, some remaining in the country and others returning to their native lands to find full-time employment in national corporations as well as transplanted U.S.-owned production facilities abroad.

Social Conflict. The scenario outlined above not only speaks to the ensuing drastic economic and industrial changes in America but also to the possibility of increasingly dangerous political and social upheavals or, at least, increasing social-political instability and conflict in the U.S. as well. Richard Freeman, a Harvard labor economist, suggests that the current changes in the American industrial sector threatens to bring "a further division in society between those who have long-term jobs and those who lose their jobs.... We will see a further increase in the income-inequality problem." Blumberg (1980) speaks directly to this issue when he contends that "the United States has entered a period in which growth is no longer an alternative to redistribution. As the size of the pie remains relatively constant, a larger slice for one group necessarily means a smaller slice for everyone else." As economic growth atrophies, the only way one class can increase its living standards is at the expense of others. What we shall likely see is not the withering away of the strike but what used to be called the "intensification of the class [and if we may interpolate here, ethnic] struggle." Blumberg cogently argues that the cleavages which already exist in America may deepen as the economy slows, stagnates or shrinks and scarcity of opportunity increases. Racial conflicts, he predicts, are "almost inevitable, for Blacks and other minorities aspire to mobility at a time of growing scarcity." The technology of "taking care of number one" may become the predominant theme in American political and economic life. After completing a learned and detailed review of national and global economic trends, David Swinton, then Dean of the School of Business at Jackson State University, concluded that:

> To be sure, some African Americans have advanced. However, the central tendency of the group as a whole has been stagnation or retrogression in absolute status and increased disparities in relative status.
>
> The latest data in 1991 and 1992 on income, poverty, and labor market status reveal a continuation of the disadvantaged status of blacks....However, for African Americans, the entire period has been characterized by conditions that would be considered depression level if they were experienced by all Americans.[36]

Swinton correctly concludes that "history teaches us that recovery by itself will not resolve the underlying problem of racial inequality. The swings in the black economic status attributable to the stages of the business cycle are only a few percentage points. General [government] policies will not result in secular improvements for the black

---

36. David H. Swinton, "The Economic Status of African Americans during the Reagan-Bush Era: Withered Opportunities, Limited Outcomes, and Uncertain Outlook," in *State of Black America 1993*, pp. 135.

population." The Afrikan American community must drastically revise its social and economic practices and organization if it is to ensure its economic survival, to greatly expand its economic and political power and achieve its final goal of liberation from oppression. However, for these things to occur the Afrikan American community must not only vastly increase its economic power but also must implement the economic empowerment of the Pan–Afrikan community as well. Its economic and political alliance with the Afrikan motherland is crucial in this respect. The Afrikan American and continental Afrikan communities must mutually empower each other if either is to survive happily in the future. An economically strong Afrikan continent is necessary for an economically strong Black America, and both for an economically strong Pan–Afrikan worldwide community.

Losing Ground

Economic recessions, unemployment and the concomitant social and economic problems they generate may be caused by any number of factors including the traditional slowdowns in consumption, saturations or contractions of markets, failed governmental policies, competitive conflicts, to name a few. There are some analysts who contend that sometimes recessions are more or less deliberately engineered by a segment of the corporate elite as a means of increasing surplus labor, especially in an economy nearing full-employment which strengthens the bargaining power of organized labor. Therefore by creating a sizable unemployed or underemployed workforce big capital is positioned "to discipline" labor by threatening increased layoffs if wage demands, work rules and other benefits to workers are not held in abeyance or reduced; if workers do not make certain concessions or provide some "givebacks" compatible with corporate-elite economic interests. Some analysts also argue that recessions often allow for the restructuring by big capital of its production facilities, of the market, and possibly the economy itself. An obsolete or less efficient, less profitable economic and production system is replaced by a presumably more upgraded, efficient, profitable and productive one. This may mean many who were employed under the old economic regime may not be re-employed due to their new obsolescence, i.e., their inability to fit into the new system, or because the new, more efficient, productive system requires fewer workers, and due to the possibility that the new system, even though no longer in recession, may restrict employment opportunity rather than expand it, at least for some of the segments of the workforce.

While we will not enter this interesting argumentative arena on one side or the other, we will contend that recessions, whether "accidents of economic nature," the deliberate creations of fiendish big capital, or the un-intended result of inept governmental policy-making, sometimes do provide marvelous opportunities for covertly settling some old scores on the part of the powers-that-be. And the scores to be settled may not be exclusively against organized labor. They may also include old political and/or ethnocentric scores against certain unpopular political regimes or certain unpopular political or ethnic groups.

Dis-Affirmative Action. The 1990-91 recession had all the earmarks of providing an economic cover for the execution of a political and racist vendetta against the Afrikan American workforce and community by the White corporate establishment and White American community. While we are not contending that the recent recession was deliberately fomented for that reason — it was not — it did provide a convenient opportunity for a racist, resentful White American community, smarting from being slapped with affirmative action requirements, "racial quotas", and other "equal opportunity employment programs", to strike back at the Black American community which it believed was the source of its irritations. Forced against its traditional racist will by governmental edicts and political pressure from the Black activist community to hire increasing numbers of Black Americans at all levels of its industrial and professional establishment, the White corporate establishment and the conservative White American community submitted to affirmative action with a vengeance. They would not only increase the hiring of Blacks, the original "minority" group and the one with the most valid claims for preferential hiring and treatment (due to its unique history in America shared by no other ethnic or immigrant group, save Native Americans) but they would simultaneously increase the hiring of all excluded "minority groups and women." This was affirmative action with a vengeance — the introduction of "diversity in the workplace." Consequently, Blacks would have to share the prize of equal employment opportunity and the affirmative action programs which facilitate it — the prizes they rightfully earned after hundreds of years of slavery, of fighting, bleeding and dying in every American war, of racial oppression and exploitation — with White women, Asians, Hispanics, ethnic Jews and ethnic White Americans. Equal opportunity employment, the long-fought-for holy grail of the Black American community, when finally placed within its grasp would be filled with poisonous hemlock which it would be forced to drink as a salute to its own economic un-health — a toast to multi-ethnic equality.

In an extensive analysis of the effects of the 1990–91 recession on the employment of Blacks, Whites, Asians and Hispanics, the *Wall Street Journal* (9/14/93) graphically detailed the egregiously serious erosion of the Black American workforce in the corporate American workplace. In a two-page spread titled *"Losing Ground — In Latest Recession Only Blacks Suffered Net Employment Loss,"* it analyzed the reports of 35,242 companies filed with the Equal Employment Opportunity Commission (EEOC) covering more than 40 million workers. Its analysis revealed the following facts:

- Blacks were the only racial group to suffer a net job loss during the 1990–91 economic downturn...Whites, Hispanics and Asians, meanwhile, gained thousands of jobs....
- [T]he nation's largest corporations shed black employees at the most disproportionate rate. At Dial Corp., for instance, blacks lost 43.6% of the jobs cut, even though they represented 26.3% of Dial's work force going into the recession. At W.R. Grace & Co. and ITT Corp., blacks lost jobs at more than twice the rate of their companies' overall work-force reductions. [See accompanying chart [Table 12–3] for Black work-force reductions at selected companies.]

In an analysis of the 35,242 companies that filed EEOC reports for more than 40 million workers in both 1990 and 1991, the *Journal* found:

- Blacks lost a net 59,479 jobs at these businesses during the recession, which officially began in July 1990 and ended in March 1991. Overall, blacks' share of jobs at the companies dropped for the first time in nine years, wiping out three years of gains. Black employment at the companies fell in 36 states and in six of nine major industry groups.
- By contrast, Asians and Hispanics, who in recent years have become more vocal about getting their share of jobs, both made gains. Asians gained a net 55,104 jobs during the recession and Hispanics a net 60,040 jobs. Whites, who outnumber blacks nearly eight to one at these companies, gained 71,144 jobs.
- Black workers were especially hard hit in blue-collar jobs, losing nearly one-third of the net 180,210 such slots lost. They were the only group to lose service-worker positions, dropping 16,630 such jobs while businesses added 53,548 new ones. They were the only group to lose sales jobs.
- Blacks did show some progress in several highly prized white-collar job categories. They gained a disproportionately high number

WHERE BLACK LOSSES WERE MOST DISPROPORTIONATE

Major federal contractors where jobs fell by at least 500 in 1990-91, ranked job-loss index. The higher the index, the more blacks' share of job losses exceeded their share of the 1990 work force.

COMPANY	BLACKS' % of 1990 Work Force	BLACKS' % of Total Decline	BLACKS' Job-Loss Index
BankAmerica	7.90	28.11	3.56
Sears*	15.85	54.32	3.43
Pet	13.71	34.53	2.52
W.R. Grace	13.09	32.16	2.46
Coca-Cola Enterprise	17.89	42.06	2.35
ITT	11.81	27.40	2.32
American Cyanamid	11.17	25.19	2.26
Safeway	8.62	15.66	1.82
Campbell Soup	16.40	29.62	1.81
J.P. Morgan	16.59	27.66	1.67
Dial	26.29	43.56	1.66
Deere	4.23	6.90	1.63
Digital Equipment	6.84	11.04	1.61
Schering-Plough	17.80	28.55	1.60
Fluor	11.67	18.64	1.60
General Electric	7.86	12.55	1.60
McDonald's	23.19	36.52	1.57
USX	12.55	19.72	1.57
TRW	8.94	13.88	1.55
Emerson Electric	6.88	10.51	1.53

*Based on company's original report to EEOC

Table 12-3

of managerial, professional and technical jobs. But they held such a small percentage of these jobs before the recession began that their actual gains were meager. Companies added a net 2,719 black managers during the recession, bringing the 1991 number to 248,915, which is just 5.2% of the total for all races.

• The better-educated Asians managed to gain jobs even in states that cut tens of thousands of workers. Overall, Asians gained jobs in midsize and big business in 39 states, while blacks lost ground in 36 states.

- Blacks were hit particularly hard in Florida losing jobs at EEOC corporations at a rate more than five times that of the overall work-force reductions. They were the only racial group to lose jobs there as well as in Illinois, where 43.4% of jobs lost were held by blacks; in 1990 they represented 13.4% of all workers in the state. Their work force was devastated in New York, where they lost more than 21,000 of the 91,746 jobs cut in business. And they also got slammed in California, losing more than 11,000 of the 72,230 jobs eliminated while Asians were gaining more than 9,000 positions.

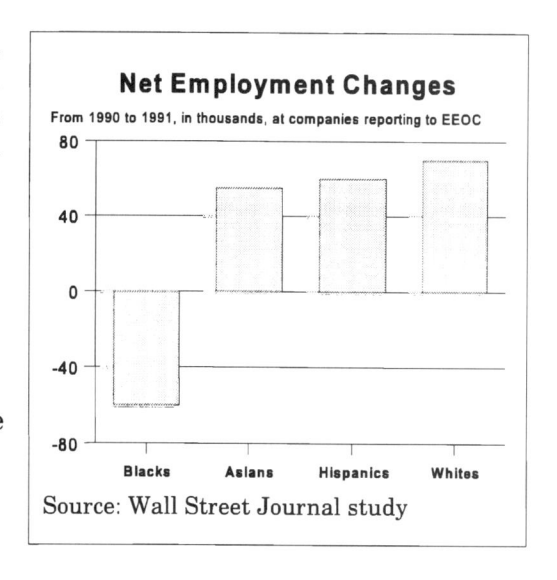

Net Employment Changes
From 1990 to 1991, in thousands, at companies reporting to EEOC

Blacks	Asians	Hispanics	Whites
~-60	~50	~55	~65

Source: Wall Street Journal study

- Only in three Southern states — Alabama, Arkansas, and Louisiana — did blacks add a substantial number of jobs.

Many and diverse explanations for these startling statistics were offered by the spokespersons representing the companies involved. A number offered the obviously lame set of excuses that the markedly increased gains by Whites, Hispanics and Asians in contrast to the marked decline of Blacks was the result of an unexplained "sudden demographic shift", "a statistical fluke", "the unintentional fallout of corporate cutbacks and reorganizations". That we are asked to believe that the capture of a total of 185,288 jobs by Whites, Hispanics and Asians at the same time that Blacks lost 59,479 jobs is just "a statistical fluke"!; that we are asked to take it on faith that this in no way indicates the operation of racial bias — besides mocking the limits of our credulity — adds insult to injury. Even the *Journal* itself, not exactly the paragon of the White liberal establishment or a friend of labor regardless of its color or creed, could not accept the facile explanations offered by corporate spokespersons. That this was the case is indicated by its following excerpt:

> The losses can be partially explained by blacks' relatively low seniority in companies and their heavy concentration in the types of

jobs eliminated. Corporations' continuing decisions to abandon inner-city offices, factories or franchise outlets didn't help blacks either.

But the demographic change suggests something more fundamental has occurred, a pronounced shift in the way affirmative action operates. Several companies with poor records of retaining blacks say they were mostly concerned with their aggregate minority employment rates and never calculated whether blacks bore a disproportionate share of cutbacks. Thus, they could claim to the government continued progress by minorities as a whole even as blacks were suffering reversals — in some cases dramatic ones.

Black workers had their biggest setbacks at retailers. About half of their losses were in retailing, where blacks lost jobs at a 50% higher rate than the overall work force.

It is interesting to note that about half the job losses sustained by Blacks were in retailing. This implies that Black job losses to Whites, Hispanics and Asians were not primarily due to the imputed paucity of high-tech job skills or high educational qualifications — at least in this area. This implication is sustained by the following revelation by the *Journal*:

> Blacks who held jobs involving public contact had an especially rough time during the recession, EEOC records show.
>
> Those lost 5,823 sales jobs overall in 1991 for instance, even though companies added a net total of more than 63,000 white, Asian and Hispanic sales workers. "There's a continuing problem that white companies will not buy from a black salesperson," says John Work, a career consultant and author of "Race, Economics and Corporate America."
>
> At least one recent study suggests that racism still plays a role in some personnel decisions. In 1990, the Urban Institute sent out teams of black and white job applicants with equal credentials. The men applied for the same entry-level jobs in Chicago and Washington, D.C., within hours of each other. They were the same age and physical size, had identical education and work experience, and shared similar personalities. Yet in almost 20% of the 476 audits, whites advanced farther in the hiring process, researchers found.
>
> "The simple answer is prejudice," says Margery Turner, a senior researcher at the Urban Institute involved in the study. "Clearly, blacks still suffer from unfavorable treatment."

Some Black job losses may be attributed to relatively low seniority — the old, "last hired, first fired" syndrome. Whether this explains a really significant proportion of Black job losses is belied by the experience of Black workers like those at USX, where seniority in their favor was disallowed or neutralized by the institution of new work rules or qualifying criteria under reorganization:

> But at USX, the new rules that allowed blacks' advancement in the 1970s ended up accelerating their job losses in the 1980s, when the company had massive layoffs. That's because of USX's plantwide labor pool, which allowed blue-collar workers who were laid off to bump people out of jobs in other departments, if they met qualifications and had seniority.
>
> Blacks who could overcome the seniority hurdles often stumbled when faced with the company's new testing requirements, says Billy Hawkins, chairman of a union grievance committee at USX's plant in Gary, Ind. Suddenly, blacks with 25 years' seniority were being rejected for jobs because they couldn't read rulers — even though rulers weren't even used on the jobs. USX says the stiffer tests are all job related and needed since the steel industry is more technology-driven than before.
>
> Blacks could no longer get training to qualify for skilled jobs either, as USX eliminated its crafting programs in the mid-1980s because of the availability of unemployed craftsmen. As a result, parts of the plant that were traditionally black have started turning white, Mr. Hawkins says.
>
> "It's really ironic," adds Frank Webster, another union representative. "Blacks were caught by the very thing that was supposed to protect them. We're seeing the best results of discrimination. We're right back to square one."

While corporate "downsizing" or "right-sizing" may account for a measurable proportion of Black job losses, a proportion that is disproportionate for Blacks to begin with, it has been reported by a number of Black workers that a disproportionate number of their white counterparts were hired back to take jobs in newly reorganized companies compared to themselves. In fact, the Black workers indicated that they were rarely rehired. It is also of interest to consider the possibility, based on suggestive data only, that White women, many of whose entry length of employment is not much longer than Black males or perhaps a bit shorter, have suffered a disproportionately smaller percentage of layoffs. This is certainly the case at some specific corporations.

The explanation that "demographic shifts" are in good part responsible for Black job losses, in some particular instances, may be valid as the following citation from the *Journal* seems to corroborate:

> Geography plays a major role in black-employment patterns. At Bank America, blacks did poorly during the recession because of attrition

combined with the fact that the company expanded in states that have low black populations, such as Arizona and New Mexico, says spokesman Russ Karrow. Blacks accounted for 28.1% of the lost jobs, even thought they made up just 7.9% of the company's work force before the recession.

However, it should be noted that a large part of the "demographic shifts" referred to by the *Journal* are demographic shifts not of the Black population but of the corporations themselves — shifts to parts of the country where Blacks are sparsely located. And it cannot be said that such shifts were purely arbitrary or without racial motives. For any current study of demographic shifts will reveal that the movement of some 10 million Whites from America's inner-cites have not only been to nearly exclusive white suburbs and edge cites but in rapidly increasing numbers to once underpopulated states like Oregon, Nevada, Wyoming, Colorado, Arizona, New Mexico, the Dakotas — places known to harbor relatively very few Blacks. The corporations have led as well as followed the "White exodus" into the wilderness of the country, leaving severely shrunken or closed operations in the inner-cities. Neither the *Journal* nor the company spokespersons they interviewed apparently bothered to discuss the "demographic shifts" of Asians and Hispanics from their native lands to America where they are apparently handily competing with Black Americans for jobs. Neither did the *Journal* bother to discuss in its analysis the deliberate recruiting of Asians by American corporations where they just "happen" to be appropriately located and qualified to be recruited under the aegis of equal employment opportunity.

When all is said and done, the following quote by the *Journal* sums it up:

> Critics consider many companies' explanations about black job losses hollow excuses, designed to hide unspoken bias. Charges Westley Poriotis, who heads Wesley, Brown & Bartle, one of the nation's oldest minority search firms: "There's a deep sourness in corporate America that had to hire minority professionals. *Downsizing has been their first opportunity to strike back.*"
>
> Civil-rights advocates argue that under the guise of fairness for all, employers can hide differential treatment of blacks. "Affirmative action has gotten so diluted that companies can trade one minority against the other," says Aileen Hernandez, who was an EEOC commissioner under President Johnson [Emphasis added].

Paradoxically, it seems that Blacks are fast becoming the ignored minority in the rush of companies to increase the hiring of minorities and diversity in the workforce.

Many companies may not even realize how their black employment shifted during the recession. Personnel executives often focus primarily on minorities' overall progress, in part because that is what the federal government focuses on when it evaluates affirmative-action efforts.

Even at companies with aggressive diversity programs, such as Dial, black workers can lose ground. Dial says its attorneys carefully reviewed layoff plans for diverse impact before any downsizing took place. But company officials say they assessed the effect on overall minority and female employment rather than on blacks, Hispanics or Asians separately.

It is interesting to note, as did New York City's the *City Sun* (9/22–28/1993), that:

Despite the fact that the Democrats invented the EEOC and the concept of affirmative action, and that Blacks overwhelmingly vote Democrat in both local and national elections, Secretary of Labor Robert B. Reich [nor any national representatives of the Democratic party] has no response to...the *Wall Street Journal* report.

This was generally true for both the mainstream print and electronic media. Despite the racist over- and under-tones that thread themselves throughout the *Wall Street Journal's* analysis of Black job losses during the 1990–91 recession, Afrikan Americans must take a good, hard, objective look at the facts it presents and its implications regarding their perilous current and future economic status.

General Accounting Office finds greater Black Job Loss. In a study of job losses during the 1990–91 recession released on September 16, 1994, the General Accounting Office found that Blacks and Hispanics had a greater chance of losing their jobs during that period than other groups (*Wall Street*, 9/19/94). Blacks and Hispanics had at least a 15 percent greater chance of losing their jobs than Whites. They had a 43 percent greater chance of job loss than Asians. When they lost jobs Blacks remained unemployed slightly longer than members of other groups and suffered the highest losses in weekly income. Even when Blacks found new jobs their average weekly earnings fell 10.1 percent compared with a 5.3 percent decline for Hispanics and a 9.5 percent wage loss for Whites.

Moreover, compared to White workers, Blacks suffered a greater long-term loss of health benefits as a result of losing their jobs. Commenting on the GAO study, the *Wall Street Journal* reports that "while more than 50 percent of blacks had such benefits before they were displaced, only 38% had them once they found new jobs. By contrast, 56% of white workers had health benefits before they lost their jobs, and 60% had them upon gaining new jobs."

Layoffs were more concentrated among young, less-educated workers and in clerical and machine-operator jobs. The average age of displaced Black and Hispanic workers was 36 and 35, respectively. The average age for White and Asian displaced workers was 38 and 40, respectively. While 82 percent of displaced Whites and 77 percent of displaced Asians had high school educations or less, 90 percent of displaced Blacks and Hispanics had a high school diploma or less.

The discrepancy in job losses between Blacks, Whites, Hispanics and Asians can only be partially explained by differences in age, educational levels, and job choices. "Blacks and Hispanics had a greater chance of losing their jobs — even when age, education, gender and occupation were taken into account, the General Accounting Office concluded in [its] report" (WSJ, ibid). The GAO report acknowledged that racial discrimination may account for some portion of the difference even though it claimed that there is no way to measure its extent.

Taking Charge of Economic Destiny

It is clear from this analysis and any number of similar ones, that the Afrikan American community must become much more self-centered and active in seeing to it that Blacks are hired in rapidly increasing numbers at all levels in corporate America. In light of our tenure in America, our social and military sacrifices to its growth, development, security and greatness; in light of the fact that America — against the will of our ancestors — is our native land in the sense that we are born here and can claim no other country and therefore are mystically and historically attached to it regardless of our traumatically ostracized relationship with it, we should justifiably and loudly demand that we be first in line to receive its benefits. We have not been reparated for our contributions to America, whether extorted from or voluntarily shared by us. We have *never* been the enemy of America in its wars, whether of imperial conquest or in self-defense. And yet we are told that those peoples who not only have not paid the price we have paid to become first-class citizens of America — but many of whom at one time were its enemies — are as immigrants allowed to enjoy rights not only equal to our own but are to boast superior privileges. We should *not* let cries of "reverse racism" or our own rhetoric regarding racial equality and our sincere commitment to it prevent us from demanding our rightful and proportionate returns on our heavy investment in this nation. We, its foundation, must be determined not to be treated as if we are mere immigrants.

The structural changes going on in the American global economy require that the Afrikan American community not only assess its vulnerability to economic poor health but must proactively deal with this problem, aggressively. It must adeptly deal with the fact that its constituents tend to be heavily concentrated in the most expendable jobs. As intimated by the *Wall Street Journal* (ibid) "more than half of all Black workers held positions in the four job categories where companies made net employment cuts: office and clerical, skilled, semi-skilled and laborers, according to EEOC records." If this situation is to be rectified before half or more of the Black workforce is to be dismissed and the Afrikan American community be economically and socially devastated as a result, then it must rapidly and on a large scale, upgrade the educational levels, skills, training and experience of its workers and future workers. Moreover, it must take charge of its own economic destiny, put its economic and cultural house in order, and act to actualize its enormous economic and political potential.

Capitalism as a System of Social Relations. As our guide through this economic space we have chosen the noted economist Robert L. Heilbroner, Norman Thomas Professor of Economics at the New School for Social Research. Heilbroner seems to corroborate our earlier contention that an economic system is not one wherein capital or money-as-capital is merely possessed individually by the members of a community; that an economic system is more fundamentally a social system, a system of organized social relations within a community of persons. He argues persuasively that "*capital is therefore not a material thing but a process*....It is, moreover, a social process, not a physical one." Heilbroner goes on to argue that "money in itself is not capital: it is money-in-use that is capital."[37] "[C]apital...[is] a web of social activities that permit the continuous metamorphosis of M-C-M' [the 'process of a continuous transformation of capital-as-commodities, followed by a re-transformation of capital as commodities into more capital-as-more-money'] to take place." He elaborates further:

> At the center of this process is a social relationship between the *owners* of money and goods, the monetary embodiments of capital, and the *users* of these embodiments, who need them to carry on the activity of production on which their own livelihoods depend. The

---

[37]. Robert L. Heilbroner, *The Nature and Logic of Capitalism* (New York: W.W. Norton, 1985), pp. 36–37.

legal crux of this relationship lies in the right of exclusion: a central, although often ignored, meaning of "property" is that its owners can legally refuse to allow their possessions to be used by others.[38]

Heilbroner contends that it is the right of the owners of money or capital goods as private property to withhold them from use as their owners see fit. "It is this right that enables the capitalist to dominate the sphere of trade and production in which his authority extends." Cutting to the chase, he outrightly contends that "The idea of capital as a social relationship leads directly to the core of that relationship: *domination*." Readily admitting that power wielded by capital differs in subtle but substantial ways from "owners" of other aspects of social authority or coercive power, under social conditions that make the withholding of capital an act of critical social consequence, capital can exert its organizing and disciplining influence on the state, individuals and groups in its commercial, social and political interests. More directly to the point, Heilbroner delineates the source of the dominative power of capital (and coincidently, the dominative power of Whites over Blacks):

> ...the domination of capital hinges on the appearance of a class of workers who are dependent for their livelihood on access to the tools and land that can be legally denied to them by their owners.
> The relationship of domination has two poles. One of them — the social dependency of propertyless men and women without which capital could not exert its organizing influence — ...[and] ...the other,... — the restless and insatiable drive to accumulate capital.[39]

Heilbroner further contends that while the possession of substantial capital may or may not confer on its owners good repute, authority, or prestige, it does confer on them "the ability to direct and mobilize the activities of society." It also confers on the owners of the goods that constitute wealth "an attribute that goes beyond prestige and preeminence. This is power." He rightly concludes that "*Wealth is therefore a social category inseparable from power.*" And he again points to the unadorned social-economic bases for this power:

> Per contra, wealth can only come into existence when the right of access of all members of society to an independent livelihood no longer prevails, so that control over this access becomes of life-giving importance. The corollary is that wealth cannot exist unless there also exists a condition of scarcity — not insufficiency of resources themselves, but insufficiency of means of access to resources. As

---
38. Ibid., p. 38.
39. Ibid., p. 41–42.

Adam Smith put it, "Wherever there is a great property, there is great inequality. For one very rich man, there must be at least five hundred poor, and the affluence of the rich supposes the indigence of the many."[40]

"Domination in human society," Heilbroner cogently points out, "entails a structured inequality of life conditions that has no parallel in the animal world." Moreover, he forthrightly reminds us that the insatiable drive to amass wealth, which is probably the most obvious characteristic of capitalism and of the capitalist, "is inextricable from power, and incomprehensible except as a form of power." He says elsewhere that "the process of accumulating capital is pursued in part because it is the manner in which the dominant class expresses and renews its social control." He pointedly asserts that *"Capitalism is the regime of capital*, the form of rulership we find when power takes the remarkable aspect of the domination, by those who control access to the means of production, of the great majority who must gain "employment."[41]

It should be an obvious and compelling conclusion that if Afrikan Americans and Afrikans across the diaspora are to achieve their liberation from White domination whose ruling instrument is the regime of capital, they must either overthrow or subvert White capitalism; bring it crashing like Humty Dumty, hard to the earth, or masterfully wrest it from the hands of their White masters and victoriously fight fire with fire. But before we blare the clarion call of final battle we must honestly assess our current position, resources and potentialities and those of our adversaries, for it is from such assessments a winning set of strategies and tactics must be derived.

A Contrarian Point of View

Not all economists agree with the contention that the reconfiguration of the U.S. workforce is primarily due to foreign competition, increased imports, and foreign direct investment trends. Paul Krugman, professor of economics at Stanford University, is one of the most prominent of these.[42] In a recent article in the prestigious journal *Foreign Policy* (Summer, 1994) titled "Europe Jobless, America Penniless," Krugman makes the following argument:

> Most people who worry about growing earnings disparities in the United States and rising unemployment in Europe blame those

---
40. Ibid., p. 46.
41. Ibid., pp. 47–52.
42. Paul Krugman, *Peddling Prosperity: Economic Sense and Nonsense in the Age of Diminished Expectations* (New York: Norton, 1994).

trends on international trade. The pressure of global competition, in particular from newly industrializing countries with their much lower wage rates, is widely believed to be the fundamental cause of the decline in wages and jobs for the less-skilled.

That is an understandable view. In principle, it is entirely possible that increased trade with countries teeming with cheap labor could drive down the real wages of less-skilled workers in the West. It is also true that trade in general, and the manufactured exports of the Third World in particular, have increased rapidly since the 1970s. From that perspective, the hypothesis that international trade is at the heart of the story is highly persuasive.

Unfortunately, it is not true. A number of careful studies have come to the conclusion that international trade explains at best only a small fraction of the rise in earnings inequality in the United States or the employment problems in Europe. The basic point in all these studies is that if international trade reduces an economy's demand for unskilled labor, it does so by changing the industrial mix. That is, if the United States responds to growing world economic integration by producing more skill-intensive goods like aircraft and fewer goods, like garments, that employ primarily unskilled workers, the effect will be to raise the demand for skilled workers while reducing it for unskilled — and hence to bid up the wages of the former and drive down the wages of the latter. In fact, however, very little of the decline in the relative demand for unskilled labor in Western countries has been due to changes in the mix of goods produced. Instead, employment has shifted noticeably toward skilled employment *within* each industry — including those "nontraded" industries, accounting for about two-thirds of U.S. employment, that are largely insulated from international competition.

The pervasiveness of the shift toward highly skilled labor suggests that the explanation for growing inequality lies not in international trade, which affects labor demand by changing the mix of industries, but in technological changes that have reduced the demand for the worst-paid workers in all industries.

At the time of the publication of this volume the U.S. economy is undergoing a fairly strong economic recovery. Unemployment is declining rather steadily. For many, particularly in the Afrikan American community, this appears to be good news. But appearances can be deceiving. Krugman spoke of the appearance of the current recovery thusly:

> As this article was being written, the Bureau of Labor Statistics announced a sharp fall in the U.S. unemployment rate. Most economists expect that rate to decline even further, eventually

approaching the 5.5 per cent level generally regarded as "full employment." It is also probable, though by no means certain, that within a year or two recovery will begin in Europe and Japan. As growth accelerates and the number of jobless falls, much of the current despondency over the state of the world economy will surely dissipate. Stories about the "jobless recovery" will fade from the press, to be replaced by upbeat tales of business success.

The optimism that is likely then to dominate economic commentary will, however, be misguided — even more misguided than the doom-and-gloom pessimism that prevails today. The fact is that all of the industrially advanced countries are in deep economic trouble. The irregular rhythm of recessions and recoveries sometimes exaggerates their problems, while at other times it masks them; but to anyone who looks behind the business cycle the disturbing long-term trends are unmistakable. In Europe, in the United States, and increasingly in Japan, it is becoming obvious that something has gone wrong with the promise of economic growth.

The failure of that promise may be summarized by two words: jobs and wages. For a generation after World War II, the economies of the West offered both — that is, there were jobs for the great bulk of those who wanted them, and those jobs paid wages whose purchasing power rose steadily for just about everyone. Since the early 1970s, however, the economies of North America and Western Europe have not delivered that kind of broad prosperity. In the United States, the problem is essentially one of wages: Most people who seek jobs still get them, but an increasing fraction of our workers receive wages that both they and the rest of us regard as poverty-level. In Europe, wages at the bottom have declined less, but in their place long-term unemployment has consistently risen. On both sides of the Atlantic, there is now a growing sense that many people are in effect economically disenfranchised, shut out of the prosperity that one might expect in what are still wealthy societies.

Ironically, the rise of poverty and unemployment in the Western world over the last 20 years has taken place in a time of spectacular technological progress. That progress has not quite resulted in the productivity growth that one might have expected, yet the economies of the advanced countries are by any measure substantially richer and more productive than they were in 1970. The economic troubles of the West therefore present a paradox of growing misery in the face of growing wealth.

Krugman sees economic forces as splitting American (and European) society in two. The society will be composed of "those who have good jobs and whose standard of living continue to rise and those who are faced either with falling incomes or the prospect of a more or less permanent life on the dole." Interestingly, Krugman does not see the upgrading of the skills and education of workers as resolving this socially disturbing trend, at least not immediately. While acknowledging that the trend toward growing economic inequalities is likely to reverse itself, he suggests that this reversal may take more than a decade. He notes that "The Industrial Revolution created high inequalities in its first half-century, but eventually produced a middle-class society of unprecedented affluence. The Information Revolution will probably do the same. Unfortunately, the crisis of jobs and wages is here now and will not go away anytime soon." Krugman suggests that retraining and raising the quality of basic education "will not have an impact on labor markets for at least a decade."

The Economic Future of the Afrikan American Community

Whether the reader accepts our earlier general analysis of the changing character of the American workforce, American employment trends and income inequalities, or Krugman's analysis, the outcome for the Afrikan American community is generally the same — high levels of unemployment and underemployment. Even with "full employment" the unemployment rate for the Black community will average around 13 percent. This point is corroborated by an analysis of this matter by economist Andrew F. Brimmer, former member of the Federal Reserve Board, now president of Brimmer & Co. Inc. His analysis as reported by *Black Enterprise* (6/94) in an article titled "No Real Recovery for Black Jobs or Incomes," includes the following information:

> The economy is picking up steam. However, economist Andrew F. Brimmer, president of Brimmer & Co. Inc., says that while "the progress of black Americans will improve slightly," the black population and labor force will grow faster than their share of employment and income. As a result, he predicts, "the jobs and income deficits which blacks suffer will widen further."
>
> This year, the black civilian labor force should grow to 14.4 million, or to 11.1% of the total workforce, vs. 14.1 million, or 11% of the total in 1993. African-American employment, meanwhile, is likely to hit 12.6 million, or 10.32% of total employment, vs. 12.2 million, or 10.2%, last year.
>
> This means that there will be nearly 1 million more black workers in 1994 than there are jobs for them. As the nation's gross domestic product (GDP) picks up, black unemployment will be slightly lower than last year, but it will stand at 2.27 times that of whites. Black joblessness is projected to average 1.83 million in 1994, or 23.2% of all

those unemployed vs. 1.89 million or 21.7% last year. That translates into a black unemployment rate of 12.7% this year vs. 13.4% in 1993.

By contrast, total unemployment in the U.S. may dip to 6.1% for all workers vs. 6.7% last year, and to 5.2% for whites vs. 5.9% in 1993.

On the bright side, if black employment grows, so does black money income. Of course, the parity share of money income would be larger if blacks were employed in numbers equal to their share of the civilian labor force. In 1994, total U.S. money income is projected to be 4.17 trillion, and the black share may rise to $319.8 billion or 7.7% of total U.S. income vs. $300.6 billion or 7.6% last year. If blacks received a parity share of income, their share would rise by $142.6 billion more this year.

The average unemployment rate for Afrikan American teenagers and young adults is likely to be many times higher than the average rate for Blacks as a whole. Many members of the Black community who will be employed will be part-time employees or will be employed at minimum wages. Many will belong to the class of the "working poor". This implies that the Afrikan American community must fully and vigorously exercise the few options it has available to it. These options include: a more effective push for Affirmative Action and struggle against racial discrimination in the workplace; a massive increase in the quality of Afrikan American human resources, i.e., increases in the level of job skills, training and education; political agitation for the passage of Earned Income Tax Credit or "negative income tax" legislation, i.e., the provision of income supports that gradually taper off as income rises; and the increase of Black wealth and employment through the economic expansion of the Black community mainly through the ownership of business enterprises and equity investments in income-earning resources. We shall discuss the latter option throughout the rest of this volume.

THE MASTER PLAN

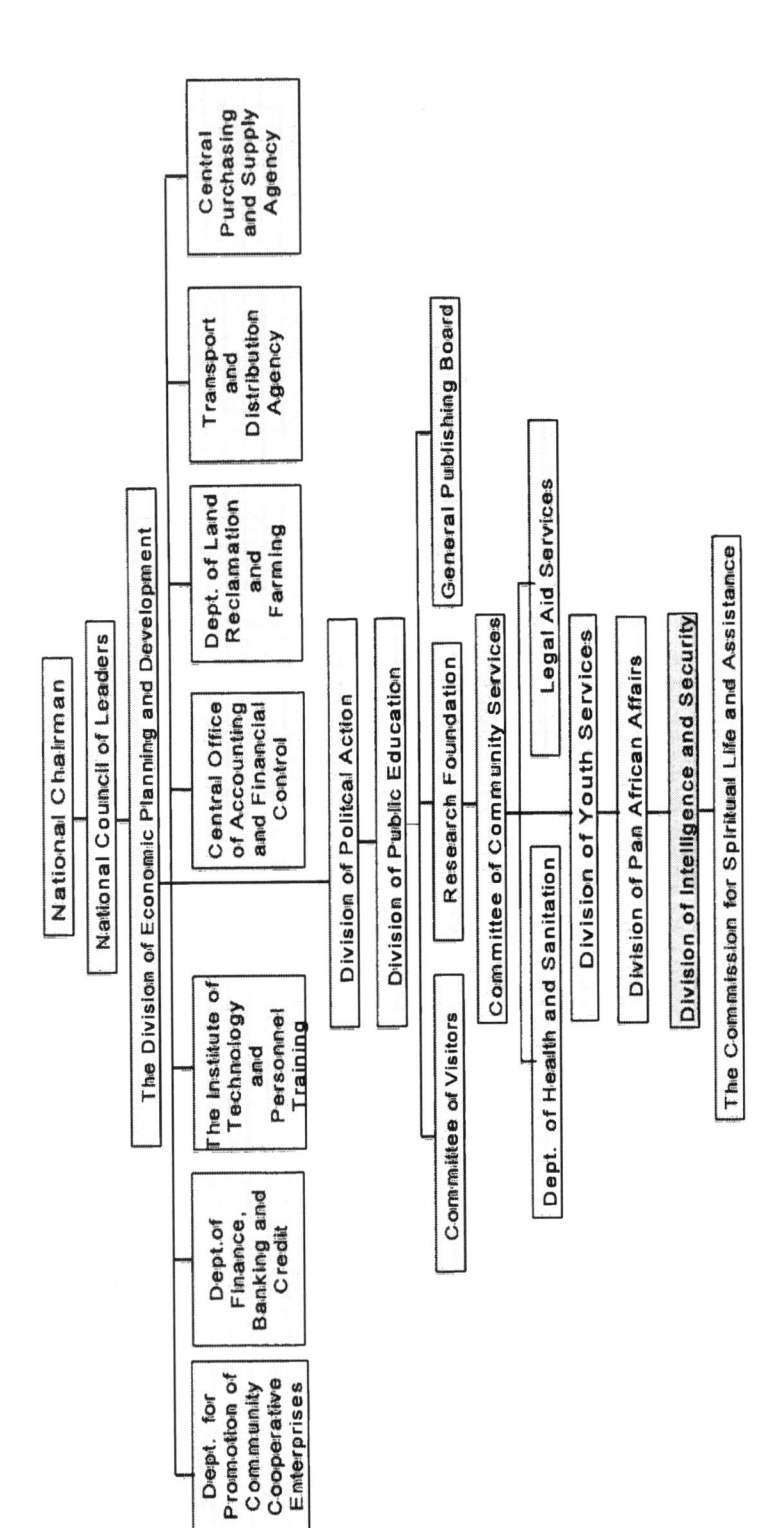

- National Chairman
  - National Council of Leaders
    - The Division of Economic Planning and Development
      - Dept. for Promotion of Community Cooperative Enterprises
      - Dept. of Finance, Banking and Credit
      - The Institute of Technology and Personnel Training
      - Central Office of Accounting and Financial Control
      - Dept. of Land Reclamation and Farming
      - Transport and Distribution Agency
      - Central Purchasing and Supply Agency
    - Division of Political Action
    - Division of Public Education
      - Research Foundation
      - General Publishing Board
    - Committee of Visitors
    - Committee of Community Services
      - Legal Aid Services
    - Dept. of Health and Sanitation
    - Division of Youth Services
    - Division of Pan African Affairs
    - Division of Intelligence and Security
    - The Commission for Spiritual Life and Assistance

Table 12–4

Pg 294

Chapter 13

THE FINANCIAL-CORPORATE ELITE
The New World Government

World Ascendancy of Private Capital

OWNERSHIP IS SOVEREIGNTY. The owners of the means of production in effect dominate those people who depend on them for survival and for maintaining and enhancing their quality of life. In capitalist societies national and multinational corporate hegemons and their satellites markedly influence the quality, rhythms, order and direction of people's lives, their self-perception, the nature of their social interactions, their values, tastes and desires more directly than do their governmental, cultural and religious institutions. In the face of the organized national and transnational corporate elite — the owners of the means of production — the citizens of supposedly independent nations lose control over their lives. The masses rapidly lose their power to determine their collective fate directly and indirectly through their elected delegates and heads of state to the owners of vital financial and business capital, to large local, regional, national and multinational corporations, and to powerful governmental, quasi-, and non-governmental agencies who represent the interests of the owners of the means of production instead of the people. Therefore the organized business ownership community, the owners and managers of financial capital, the owners and managers of corporations are self-selected governors who, going beyond certain limits, may surreptitiously usurp the power of representative governments thereby undermining the power of the people to elect governments which serve their interests before all others — including those of the financial-corporate elite.

When national governments' ability to control the national economy and budget is superseded by international trade agreements such as GATT, NAFTA; by indebtedness to or dependency on international financiers, large foreign national banks, the World Bank, the International Monetary Fund, various foreign aid arrangements and the like — all extensions of or related to the machinations of private financial capital — then their national sovereignty or self-determination is essentially an institutional fiction. This is the case with virtually all of the continental Afrikan and Afrikan diasporan nations today and an increasing number of nations of all stripes — White, Asian and Semitic. For example, on June 20, 1994, the *New York Times* reported that "through its structural adjustment programs, I.M.F. and the [World] Bank now effectively oversee and supervise the economies of some 30 countries in sub-Saharan Africa." Indebted nations are indebted to the owners and managers of public and private financial capital and to the nations and international agencies who represent them and enforce their contracts. Consequently, these private international financiers, financial institutions, multinational corporations and multinational governmental agencies, in conjunction with the hegemonic nations whose domestic and international policies they effectively influence, dictate the economic, social and political fate of weaker nations against the wills and best interests of their peoples. Increasingly, private financial capital is able to achieve these ends under its own power.

Felix Rohaytn, investment banker and former Chairman of the Municipal Assistance Corporation for the City of New York, the famous "Big MAC" which took control of the city's budget during its financial crisis under the Beame administration, noted this trend:

> For the last fifty years, the Bretton Woods institutions, the World Bank and the IMF, have been directly involved in financial economic development in the emerging economies. This role will, more and more, be taken over by the global capital markets. The cold-blooded selection process by which world capital is invested will determine the economic progress of many developing countries.[1]

Today, the international supremacy of financial capital and the global corporate elite is almost complete. Together they are colluding

---

1. Felix Rohaytn, "World Capital: The Needs and the Risk" in *The New York Review of Books*, August 14, 1994.

to form a new world order — a world government to which all nations will give prostrated obeisance.

This fledgling financial-corporate world government will not be democratically representative of those it shall govern, though it intends to rule all nations and peoples. It is intended to be a world government dominated primarily by the United States (White America), the European Economic Community, and secondarily by Japan, China, and one or two other Southeastern Asian nations. The head of the world government is expected to be the White American financial-corporate elite disguised as the democratically elected government of the United States. Its power to rule will be ideologically justified and legitimated in terms of the natural ascendance of private property, private enterprise, privatization, "the free market", and U.S. military supremacy.

The Private Financial-Corporate Complex – U.S. Second Government

The fact that a private financial-corporate complex and its governing elite are the second government of the United States, is evident to all who care to analyze the fundamental social structure of American economic and political power. That is, the elected U.S. government may, for all practical purposes, be perceived as an extension of this private government. Its primary function under such circumstances is to legitimate and execute private rule by making it appear to be public policy. Thus is the fascist, corporate state produced, wearing a benign public persona.

By the private "financial-corporate complex" we mean that combination of the largest, wealthiest and most influential financiers and privately owned financial institutions, syndicates and corporate bodies which seek by various methods to influence and direct governmental policy in favor of its own self-serving interests and often against the best interests of the public. One of the more important means by which this complex influences governmental policy in its favor is through the appointment of some of its most politicized members to head powerful government departments, offices and agencies. Parenti notes this in his contention that:

> the top state and federal offices and party leadership positions, to this day, have remained largely in the hands of White, Protestant, middle-aged, upper-income males of conventional political opinion, drawn from the top ranks of corporate management, from the prominent law and banking firms of Wall Street and less frequently from the elite universities, foundations and the scientific establishment....

Not every member of the ruling class is born rich but most are. Not all wealthy persons are engaged in ruling, some preferring to concentrate on making money or on living a life of ease. "The ruling class contains what could be called the politicized members of the upper class," writes Alan Wolfe....

The policies they pursue in office frequently are connected directly to the corporate interests they represent in their private lives. Thus the decision-makers involved in the U.S. armed intervention against the worker-student uprising in the Dominican Republic in 1965 consisted of Abe Fortas, A.A. Berle, Jr., Ellsworth Bunker, Averell Harriman and a half-dozen others who were stockholders, directors or counsels for large sugar companies that depended on Dominican sugar and molasses for their operations. "Even without these direct economic interests, it would be difficult for these gentlemen in their 'neutral' decision-making roles to escape the assumptions, inclinations and priorities inculcated by their economic and social milieu."[2]

In the fifth edition of his book, Parenti further discusses what we refer to as the financial-corporate complex. He writes:

Less than 1 percent of all corporations control two-thirds of the corporation assets of the entire economy. Forty-nine of the biggest banks hold a controlling interest in the 500 largest corporations. Thus, ITT, Sears, American Express, IBM, BankAmerica, and Citicorp can all claim J.P. Morgan, Inc., as one of their top investors. J.P. Morgan is the nation's largest stockholder, with more than $15 billion invested in the stock market. In the United States, as in most other industrial countries, finance capital dominates other forms of capital formation, including manufacturing.

The trend is toward greater concentrations of corporate wealth as giant companies are bought up by supergiants. ...Instead of enlarging the economic pie, corporate and financial elites cut bigger slices for themselves. This is why, despite repeated recessions and sluggish economic growth, profits doubled in the early 1980s.[3]

It is certain that the quality of life of the average American citizen is more dependent on the functionality of the corporate sector than on the governmental sector. For it is the corporations and companies which hire and fire, promote and demote, who determine the economic standing and fate of millions of individuals and families. American corporations and companies can, through control of wages, salaries, working conditions, layoffs, job cuts and much else, more directly affect the social order and the quality of life of American citizens than

---

2. M. Parenti, *Democracy for the Few*, 2nd ed., 1977, pp. 217–20.

3. M. Parenti, *Democracy for the Few*, 5th ed., 1988, pp. 11–12.

can the American government. It has been decided by constitutional fiat and political tradition that the private financial-corporate sector can exercise these vital powers with relatively little interference from the public sector. The cry for "less government", "deregulation", an "unrestricted market economy" or a "free market economy"; for "letting the market determine outcomes", by the private financial-corporate sector, is not a call for full individual freedom of choice and democracy as it may appear to be on the surface. It cloaks a call for governance by financial-corporate authoritarian rule in place of public democratic rule. For where public government does not reign or protect, private government will establish its tyrannies. And the private citizen will not be the freer.

The Federal Reserve: Private Controller of the Public Economy

The tyranny of the private financial-corporate complex over the quality of American life can be no better illustrated than by observing the immense influence exercised over the national economy by private financial-corporate capital in the form of the Federal Reserve System. The Federal Reserve is self-described as: "An efficient monetary mechanism [which functions] to foster a flow of money and credit that will facilitate orderly economic growth, a stable dollar, and long-run balance in our international payments."[4] Heilbroner and Thurow describe the Federal Reserve thusly:

> For many years the banks themselves decided what reserve ratio constituted a safe proportion of currency to hold against their demand deposits. Today, however, most large banks are members of the Federal Reserve, a central banking system established in 1913 to strengthen the banking activities of the nation. Under the Federal Reserve System, the nation is divided into twelve districts, each with a Federal Reserve Bank owned by the member banks of its district. In turn, the twelve Reserve Banks are themselves coordinated by a seven-member Federal Reserve Board in Washington. Since the President, with the advice and consent of the Senate, appoints members of the board for fourteen-year terms, they constitute a body that has been purposely established as an independent monetary authority.[5]

The Federal Reserve is essentially a central bank and like all central banks it seeks "to exert control over the direction and extent

---
4. Board of Governors of the Federal Reserve System, *The Federal Reserve System* (Board of Governors: Washington, D.C., 1963), p. 1.

5. Heilbroner and Thurow, *Economics Explained*, 1987.

of changes in the money supply" (Heilbroner and Thurow, ibid). Like all central banks, it seeks to supply the national economy with the "right" amount of money through inflating or deflating the money supply by manipulating bank reserves, interest rates, and the buying and selling of U.S. government bonds on the open market. Despite the fact that it may, independent of government interference, have a major impact on the national economy and for better or worse, on the lives of American citizens, the Federal Reserve is not a public governmental agency. It is not democratically controlled by the people to whose lives it is of crucial importance. For it is an "independent" private organization owned by its member banks and like any other privately owned and operated institutions, its employees are not civil servants. Referring to this privately owned system which controls the nation's issue of money and commands its financial resources, Wright Patman, former Chairman of the House Banking and Currency Committee, is reported to have said:

> In the United States today, we have in effect two governments. We have an independent, uncontrolled and un-coordinated government in the Federal Reserve System, operating the money powers which are reserved to Congress by the Constitution.[6]

Tyranny of the Free Market

Thus, we can surmise from our foregoing discussion that relative to the most vital areas of life, the making of a living through stable employment and the maintenance of a viable national economy, the social and economic fate of Americans, rests in private hands and reflects, predominantly, the policies of a private government — the government of the White male financial-corporate elite. This barely visible government not only rules in the shadow of the public government but more perniciously, rules in the name of "the free market", of "free trade", two phrases most American citizens think are synonymous with individual freedom, freedom of choice, and democracy. However, free market and free trade economies may operationally represent political, social and economic tyranny as well as provide the foundations for class and racial domination.

The "free market" or the "open market" is ultimately owned by those who buy and sell within it. The "market" consists of *human* beings engaged in the varied activities of buying and selling properties, commodities, futures, and the swapping of options. The market is human activity and is therefore biased by human attitudes and

---
6. Gary Allen, "The Bankers: Conspiratorial Origins of the Federal Reserve," *American Opinion* (March 1978), p. 1.

values. The nature and effects of markets on the lives of ordinary citizens are determined by the marketing activities of their biggest and most influential buyers and sellers, brokers and dealers. And when those buyers and sellers, brokers and dealers who dominate the markets belong primarily to one class or two races, "free markets" are not free, and "open markets" are closed. The oligopolistic character of the contemporary "free market" clearly corroborates John Kenneth Galbraith's[7] contention that the primary objective of the modern giant corporation is to avoid the unpredictability, instability, and riskiness of a marketplace "free for all". The corporate elite's drive to maintain marketplace predictability, stability; to avoid or minimize marketplace risk, has led to the situation where, as described by Greenberg:

> [G]iant corporations have amassed sufficient power to allow them, in general, to tame and transcend dealings in the marketplace. Instead of the market system envisioned by Adam Smith, a system characterized by vigorous competition between many small firms, a new system has emerged on the American scene, one the economists term *oligopoly*. Oligopoly leads to private control of prices and profits, and thus wide discretion in the decision making power of corporate executives. Oligopolistic power means that a few firms are able to control the marketplace, to deny entry to new firms, to control sources of raw materials, and to generate their own internal sources of capital for investment and expansion.[8]

If one or two racial groups and one class of capitalist dominate capital and other important markets through their or its monopolistic or oligopolistic ownership and control of the means of production, then the establishment and expansion of such markets represent the establishment and expansion of race and class tyrannies over non-market or peripheral market participants. Consequently, the ideological call for free markets and free trade may be in reality a call for racist and for nationalistic economic and military hegemony. Under such circumstances the free market may provide the rationale and means by which one race or class economically and politically dominates and exploits other races and classes. We argue that such is the case relative to the domination of the global economy and of the lesser developed nations by the American-European communities (in collusion with some members of the Asian community). Via privately owned and controlled national and international financial-corporate agencies, a relatively small group of ethnically homogeneous men and

---

7. John Kenneth Galbraith, *The New Industrial State* (N.Y.: Houghton Mifflin, 1968).

8. Edward Greenberg, *Serving The Few: Corporate Capitalism and the Bias of Government Policy* (New York: John Wiley, 1974), p. 41.

nations seek to privately dominate and exploit the economic and human resources of the universe for their own national, ethnic, social and individual benefit at the expense of the vast majority of the world's peoples.

Ideological evidence for our concern here is provided by an article published by Benjamin C. Schwarz, foreign policy analyst at the RAND Corporation, published in the May 1994 issue of *Salmagundi* and adapted for the op-ed section of the *New York Times*, May 23, 1994. In the op-ed column titled "Is Capitalism Doomed?" Schwarz makes the following assertions and proposals:

> Today's global economy depends upon American power,...
>
> In fact, international capitalism has enjoyed only two golden ages: the periods following the Napoleonic wars and the two World Wars. The key to both these episodes of peace and prosperity has been the same — the ability and will of a single state to become a hegemonic power, taking over the security problems of weaker states so they need not pursue autarkic policies nor form trading blocs to improve their international positions. This suspension of power politics through hegemony has been the fundamental aim of American foreign policy since 1945.
>
> Even though the cold war has ended, America's security leadership — for instance, its dominance of NATO and the alliance with Japan — is still necessary to hold in check the rivalries that would otherwise disrupt the stability that a global economy requires. Thus, the U.S. must continue, as the Pentagon's 1992 draft Defense Planning Guidance argues, to dominate the international system by "discouraging the advanced industrialized nations from challenging our leadership or even aspiring to a larger global or regional role." Assuming this awesome responsibility, the Pentagon asserts, insures "a market-oriented zone of peace and prosperity that encompasses more than two-thirds of the world's economy."
>
> Imposing a protectorate over two-thirds of the world economy means not only that the United States must dominate wealthy and technologically sophisticated friendly states, but that it must also deal with such nuisances as Saddam Hussein, Kim Il Sung and Slobodan Milosevic so that potential great powers need not acquire the means to deal with those problems themselves. This, in turn, dictates that America must spend more on national security than the rest of the world combined....
>
> The indispensable foundation for integration among the advanced industrialized nations was — and remains — American hegemony. To hold that U.S. hegemony is no longer needed because the political,

economic and military cooperation among the great powers now insures stability and peace is to put the cart before the horse.

Most everyone applauds the highest stage of capitalism — today's complex web of global trade, production and finance — as the dawn of a brave, new world. But, a genuinely interdependent economy is extraordinarily fragile. Today the emergent high technology industries, for instance, are the most powerful engines of world economic growth, but they require a level of specialization and a breadth of markets that is possible only in an integrated world economy. It is difficult to see, therefore, how capitalism can survive the decline of the Pax Americana.

So there we have it in blunt, plain English: White American, Western European, Japanese, and perhaps Southeastern Asian economic prosperity and capitalisms depend on the existence of "a market-oriented zone...that encompasses more than two-thirds of the world's economy" protected by the military and economic hegemony of the United States. There can be little doubt that Afrikan peoples, both inside and outside the United States, are expected to largely compose the one-third of the world's economy not included in "zone of peace and prosperity."

In support of his argument Schwarz refers to the February 18, 1992 draft of the Pentagon's Defense Planning Guidance for the Fiscal Years 1994–1999. This draft which outlined "ways to thwart challenges to the primacy of America" and which proposes to maintain "a one-superpower world" is in part described by the *New York Times*:

> WASHINGTON, March 7 — In a broad new policy statement that is in its final drafting stage, the Defense Department asserts that America's political and military mission in the post-war era will be to insure that no rival superpower is allowed to emerge in Western Europe, Asia or the territory of the former Soviet Union.
>
> A 46-page document that has been circulating at the highest levels of the Pentagon for weeks, and which Defense Secretary Dick Cheney expects to release later this month, states that part of the American mission will be "convincing potential competitors that they need not aspire to a greater role or pursue a more aggressive posture to protect their legitimate interests."
>
> **Policy of Deterrence**
>
> The classified document makes the case for a world dominated by one superpower whose position can be perpetuated by constructive behavior and sufficient military might to deter any nation or group of nations from challenging American primacy.

To perpetuate this role, the United States "must sufficiently account for the interests of the advanced industrial nations to discourage them from challenging our leadership or seeking to overturn the established political and economic order," the document states.

With its focus on this concept of benevolent domination by one power, the Pentagon document articulates the clearest rejection to date of collective internationalism, the strategy that emerged from World War II when the five victorious powers sought to form a United Nations that could mediate disputes and police outbreaks of violence...

WASHINGTON, March 7 — *Following are excerpts from the Pentagon's Feb. 18 draft of the Defense Planning Guidance for the Fiscal Years 1994-1999:*

This Defense Planning Guidance addresses the fundamentally new situation which has been created by the collapse of the Soviet Union, the disintegration of the internal as well as the external empire, and the discrediting of Communism as an ideology with global pretensions and influence. The new international environment has also been shaped by the victory of the United States and its coalition allies over Iraqi aggression — the first post-cold-war conflict and a defining event in U.S. global leadership. In addition to these two victories, there has been a less visible one, the integration of Germany and Japan into a U.S.-led system of collective security and the creation of a democratic "zone of peace."

DEFENSE STRATEGY OBJECTIVES

Our first objective is to prevent the re-emergence of a new rival, either on the territory of the former Soviet Union or elsewhere, that poses a threat on the order of that posed formerly by the Soviet Union. This is a dominant consideration underlying the new regional defense strategy and requires that we endeavor to prevent any hostile power from dominating a region whose resources would under consolidated control, be sufficient to generate global power. These regions include Western Europe, East Asia, the territory of the former Soviet Union, and Southwest Asia.

There are three additional aspects to this objective: First, the U.S. must show the leadership necessary to establish and protect a new order that holds the promise of convincing potential competitors that they need not aspire to a greater role or pursue a more aggressive posture to protect their legitimate interests. Second, in the non-defense areas, we must account sufficiently for the interests of the advanced industrial nations to discourage them from challenging our leadership or seeking to overturn the established political and economic order. Finally, we must maintain the mechanisms for deterring potential competitors from even aspiring to a larger regional or global role. An effective reconstitution capability is important here, since it implies that a potential rival could not hope to quickly or easily gain a predominant military position in the world.

The second objective is to address sources of regional conflict and instability in such a way as to promote increasing respect for international law, limit international violence, and encourage the spread of democratic forms of government and open economic systems. These objectives are especially important in deterring conflicts or threats in regions of security importance to the United States because of their proximity (such as Latin America), or where we have treaty obligations or security commitments to other nations. While the U.S. cannot become the world's "policeman," by assuming responsibility for righting every wrong, we will retain the pre-eminent responsibility for addressing selectively those wrongs which threaten not only our interests, but those of our allies or friends, or which could seriously unsettle international relations. Various types of U.S. interests may be involved in such instances: access to vital raw materials, primarily Persian Gulf oil; proliferation of weapons of mass destruction and ballistic missiles, threats to U.S. citizens from terrorism or regional or local conflict, and threats to U.S. society from narcotics trafficking.

REGIONAL THREATS AND RISK

With the demise of global military threat to U.S. interests, regional military threats, including possible conflicts arising in and from the territory of the former Soviet Union, will be of primary concern to the U.S. in the future. These threats are likely to arise in regions critical to the security of the U.S. and its allies, including Europe, East Asia, the Middle East and Southwest Asia, and the territory of the former Soviet Union. We also have important interests at stake in Latin America, Oceania, and Sub-Saharan Africa. In both cases, the U.S. will be concerned with preventing the domination of key regions by a hostile power.[9]

Pax Americana and Pan-Afrikan Prosperity. The Pax Americana on which world capitalism and "free enterprise" presumably depends, according to the Pentagon draft, obviously requires United States (the White American financial-corporate elite) global politico-economic and military hegemony. As the draft recognizes, such hegemony can only be challenged by national, regional or collective blocs of peoples determined to maintain their relative autonomy and ability to be the prime beneficiaries of their own human and material resources. If

---

9. "U.S. Strategy Plan calls for Insuring No Rivals Develop," *New York Times*, March 8, 1992,

Afrikan nations and peoples are to be salvaged from the impoverished third of the world's economy under the aegis of United States economic and military hegemony, then it is vitally necessary for the Afrikan American nation to be deeply and inextricably intertwined in the American industrial-military complex. This means that the Afrikan American community must deeply penetrate and co-own the "mainstream" American financial-corporate sector and through its influence on American foreign policy, move to direct that policy in ways favorable to the security and prosperity of all Afrikan nations and peoples. It also means that Afrikan nations and peoples, including the Afrikan American community, must with urgent care, develop a global cooperative/corporate system in order to counterbalance White American-European and Asian systems which are now taking exploitative advantage of the currently weak and disorganized state of these same nations and peoples. The power of national and transnational corporations must be counterbalanced by organized national and transnational consumer unions which will refuse to support those corporations and corporate complexes which operate against their sociocultural and politicoeconomic interests. In their counteractions against hegemonic financial-corporate capital, organized consumers must be joined by national and international organized labor, which refuses to accept wage slavery and peonage as conditions for being employed by piggish transnational corporations. Only strategically passive and active resistance on the part of the organized masses the world-over can overcome the tyranny of the international financial-corporate elite if it is their will to do so.

Chapter 14

RACE AND ECONOMICS

Social Relations and Economics

AN ECONOMIC SYSTEM, like any other social system, is fundamentally founded on dynamically organized and systematic social relations of exchange within a community of persons and between communities of persons. An economic system does not come to existence because of the mere presence within a group or between groups of individuals or classes of individuals who possess or control commodities, items of use-value, money, and various services which other members or classes of persons may desire to possess or utilize. While such conditions are necessary for the evolvement of an economic system, they are not in themselves sufficient to bring it into functional existence. In order for an economic system to evolve within a group, members of that group must choose to enter into ongoing, organized social relations of exchange with each other based on a complementarity or mutuality of interests, purposes, values, tastes, means of production, and a functional level of trust and fidelity. The conditions sufficient to the development of an economic system are generally and best achieved within a group which shares a common ethnic, group, or national identity (especially if based on a shared gene pool), a shared history, set of experiences, customs, traditions, language, values, mythology, and culture. Societies and cultures pattern or organize the ways their members perceive, relate to, and interact with each other. They also pattern the ways their members develop, organize, coordinate and apply their human potential in order to adapt to the conditions under which they commonly live, satisfy their common psychological, social and survival needs, and in order to achieve other important social, spiritual and ideological goals.

It is of utmost importance to keep in mind that an economic system is fundamentally a social system, a system of social relations. An economic system cannot exist prior to or apart from a system of social relations. The products, goods and services which characterize a social system, their allocation, distribution, use, ownership, symbolic value and associations with social status power and privilege, are socially determined and ultimately derive from the nature of social relations which define that system. When the members of a society accept the social relations which characterize its economic system, they become subject to the power differentials and arrangements those relations create and sustain. These socially created and sustained power differentials and arrangements tend over time (and due to concerted propaganda and other efforts put forth by those who benefit most from the system) to appear to the members of that society to be autonomous and "natural." When this occurs, habituation, force of habit, social inertia, among other factors, may prevent certain potentially powerful groups in that society from changing the nature of the social relations which sustain its particular economic system and the system of social power derived therefrom, even when that group is being victimized by those social relations and the economic and social power systems they sustain. White capitalism (mistakenly referred to as mere "capitalism") is a system of social relations and social power which exploits and victimizes Blacks. Blacks will only transform their situation if they transform the nature of the social relations and consequently, the nature of property and power relations which characterize White capitalism. White capitalism (for Blacks are not capitalists of any significance) is the instrument of White supremacy and domination of Blacks. It is important that we understand the social relations that define White capitalism and are the sources of its power.

Ethnic-Cultural Identity and Economics

Identity is the social and personal outcome or product of an historical or experiential process during which new or habitual responses are acquired and existing repertoires of behavior are modified as a result of subjection to direct and indirect social conditioning or learning paradigms or schemes. Generally, the operational conditioning and learning experiences which interactively combine to produce identity are provided by the primary group or culture.

Identity is achieved when as a result of having undergone an identification process, the individual or group comes to perceive himself or itself as possessing a unique personality or character; of being a person or group in his or its own right; as being able to answer to his own satisfaction, the question: Who am I? Who are we? What am I? What kind of people are we? What do I do with my life? What do we do with our existence?

Identity, like personality, to the extent it is a cultural product, is the incarnation of cultural ideology, ecology and practice; is culture made flesh, experienced and perceived as emotional, cognitive and behavioral manifestations; is an instrument used for the expression of cultural power and is an instrument of personal, group and cultural survival, accomplishment and continuity. A group identity exists when each member of a group, or a significant majority of them, perceives his or her membership in the group and his or her sharing of its defining characteristics, its defining values, attitudes and behavioral tendencies as the most important or the primary defining characteristics of himself or herself as an individual. Group identity is evident when the success and well-being of the group and its other members are the highest priorities of each group member and are perceived by each member to be one with or crucial to his or her own sense of success and well-being. Group identity is evident when each member of the group holds the group and its other members in the highest regard relative to other groups and their members and perceives the advancement and defense of his or her group's interests as synonymous with or more important than his own. Group identity is evident when each member of a group organizes and directs his or her behavior in ways intended to maximally or primarily benefit his or her group, one or more of its other members, as well as him- or herself.

Group identity as an adaptational instrument, provides the means by which the members of a group while under the influence of a shared sense of belonging and unanimity rationalize, regulate, and systematize their emotional, cognitive, attitudinal and behavioral relationships with each other so as to achieve individual and group goals with maximum efficiency. The character and depth of group identity determines the nature and intensity of the sympathetic and emphatic interactions which provide the all-important emotional-behavioral foundation of a group's capacity to act in unison to maintain its cohesion and single-mindedness. The presence of group identity eases the ability of a group to recruit into loyal service to it those who identify themselves as members of it.

The value of group identity to both individual and group survival and success is obvious when one observes the distress, vulnerability, loneliness or aloneness, perhaps victimization or subordination, relative powerlessness, emptiness, intrapsychic and intragroup conflict or ambivalence of those individuals or groups who possess too little or no group identity.

Identity as a personal or collective phenomenon is as much, if not more, a political-economic entity as it is a purely social or psychological entity. As a political economy, identity is an organization of interests, tastes, desires, passions, ideals, motives, values, knowledges, abilities, skills, etc., the pursuit, satisfaction, exercise and realization of which helps to maintain the social power relations, social prerogatives and the integrity of social, political, economic systems which characterize a particular culture and its status quo. Thus, in both the commercial and noncommercial sense an ethnocultural group trades on its identity. This is the case because the individual's personality is formed by and reflects the political, social and economic character of the culture and society into which he is born and nurtured. Societies and cultures socialize individuals to adapt to, contribute to, and to operate in their unique socioeconomic system.

Related to identity is social consciousness — the awareness of one's identity or relatedness to another, to the group; the awareness of a mutuality of interests and self-acknowledged engagement in behavior intended to maintain, enhance and advance the interests of the group with which one identifies, and of its individual members. Group consciousness, like group identity, comes easiest for a group which shares a common ethnocultural background. Group or ethnic identity and consciousness together provide a social field which best facilitates various types of coherent, cohesive social organizations — be they cultural, social, religious, political, economic, or military — which are the bases of group power, the instruments of group's survival, influence, wealth, prestige and hegemony.

Ethnicity, religion and identity have been the enduring, almost irreducible factors which motivate and sustain a group's social and economic development and the power which it derives therefrom. Even a very cursory review of the history of the economic success and power of various ethnic groups in America and in the world would corroborate this contention. Joel Kotkin in his book *Tribes: How Race, Religion and Identity Determine Success in the New Global Economy*, recognizes this fact when he substantiates the thesis that "ethnicity [is the] defining factor in the evolution of the global economy." In his review of the economic history and future of "global tribes," e.g., Jews, the British, Japanese, Chinese, and the Indians, Kotkin concludes that "Global tribes combine a strong sense of common origin and shared values, quintessential tribal characteristics... [and] do not surrender their sense of a peculiar ethnic identity...but utilize their historically conditioned values and beliefs to cope successfully with change." Kotkin posits, along with writers like Brezinski and Moynihan among others, that the end of the twentieth-century, far from demonstrating "the triumph of a rational and universal order", a multicultural brotherhood of man, is demonstrating instead "an increased interest in the power of race, ethnicity and religion..." Furthermore, he predicts that "it is likely that [globally dispersed ethnic groups] and their worldwide business and cultural networks — will increasingly shape the economic destiny of mankind." He argues that although global tribes, such as the British (and Western European Whites) and the Japanese, possess a different history, they all share the following three critical characteristics:

1. A strong ethnic identity and sense of mutual dependence that helps the group to adjust to changes in the global economic and political order without losing its essential unity.
2. A global network based on mutual trust that allows the tribe to function collectively beyond the confines of national or regional borders.
3. A passion for technical and other knowledge from all possible sources, combined with an essential open-mindedness that fosters rapid cultural and scientific development critical for success in the late twentieth-century world economy.

Global Economic Network of the Ethnic Chinese

Kotkin illustrates his case by reviewing the economic history and economic global network of the five groups mentioned earlier. Besides reviewing the economic history of the most outstanding global tribe today, the Japanese, who he describes as "The first Asian group to form a truly global ethnic economic network...second in size and scope only to Anglo-Americans," Kotkin also reviews the lesser known but growing global economic network of the Chinese. He depicts the Chinese thusly:

The fifty-five million overseas Chinese are the fastest-growing economic force in the world, controlling an empire that includes the booming regions of coastal China, the high-tech centers of California's Silicon Valley and the most vibrant sections of Manhattan. The three major financial centers of the Chinese — Singapore, Taiwan and Hong Kong — possess combined foreign reserves twice as large as those of Japan, Germany or the United States.[1]

Kotkin's assessment of the growing global economic prowess of the Chinese is corroborated by an investigative article published in the *Harvard Business Review* (March–April, 1993) by John Kao titled "The Worldwide Web of Chinese Business." Therein Kao goes on to demonstrate that:

> In fact, Chinese businesses — many of which are located outside the People's Republic itself — make up the world's fourth economic power. The very definition of "China" is up for grabs. What we think of as Chinese now encompasses an array of political and economic systems that are bound together by a shared tradition, not geography. For many generations, emigrant Chinese entrepreneurs have been operating comfortably in a network of family and clan, laying foundations for stronger links among businesses across national borders. And Chinese-owned businesses in East Asia, the United States, Canada, and even farther afield are increasingly becoming part of what I call the *Chinese commonwealth*.

Kuan-Xie: The Economic Power of Social Relationships

> [P]ower,... exists in *relationships* — it has a primary location in the ongoing, habitual ways in which human beings relate to one another.
>
> [P]ower exists primarily in social relationships and not in isolated exercises.
>
> — THOMAS E. WARTENBERG.[2]

The ability of the ethnic Chinese to finance their own phenomenal economic growth, development, and prosperity is based on the nature of their social relationships. So is their increasing economic and social power, whether in the Chinatowns and cities of the U.S. and Canada,

---

1. Joel Kotkin, *Tribes: How Race, and Identity Determine Success in the New Global Economy* (New York: Random House, 1993), front cover flap.

2. T.E.Wartenberg, *The Forms of Power: From Domination to Transformation.* (Philadelphia: Temple University, 1990).

in booming Southwestern Asia, or in the global political economy. Chinese economic power is generated by the structure of a broad social network which defines their culture and community.

If one is to understand and function effectively in China, he then must understand two important concepts — *Kuan-Xie* and *Ho-Tai*. *Kuan-Xie* means "relationships" or "connections"; *Ho-Tai* means "backstage". As noted by Chin-Ning Chu, President, Asian Consultants Inc., together *Kuan-Xie* and *Ho-Tai*

> refer to an individual's personal influence and powerful connections. In China, simple merit has never been enough to advance one's cause. A highly placed Chinese official once lamented to me, "In China, it does not matter how many laws and how much righteousness are on your side, without *Kuan-Xie*, you have nothing. Even if you are outside the law and there is no righteousness to your position, if you have the right *Kuan-Xie* and *Ho-Tai*, you can do no wrong."
>
> Anywhere in the world, influential contacts can be a great asset. But one needs to magnify their importance many times to understand the significance of *Kuan-Xie* in China....
>
> The importance of influential contacts is characteristic of all Asian societies. If you have an introduction or reference from the right person, you will receive a warm welcome. If you knock on the door cold, there is a distance created that is difficult to overcome. Western companies could save immeasurable work by arranging to have their representatives introduced by the right people. This is true elsewhere in the world, but it is not as necessary a prerequisite to doing business as it is in Asia. Use *Kuan-Xie* there and your way will be made smooth.[3]

Chin-Ning Chu goes on to emphasize the important roles identity and family ties play in Chinese society and culture.

▪ Regional Identity

The Chinese recognize a strong bond to village and province. There is an instant rapport when you discover someone is from the same province or village, and this relationship plays an important role in the game of *Kuan-Xie* and *Ho-Tai*.

In large cities like Los Angeles and New York, Chinese from the same province or city will settle close together. Although some Chinese, as I mentioned, stay apart in order to avoid being the target of gossip, others enjoy the game. They socialize together and support each other, and have fun fighting within their own local association and with other associations and groups.

---

3. Chin-Ning Chu, *The Asian Mind Game,* pp. 199–200.

■ **Family Ties Are All-Important**
Strong family ties are the pillars of Chinese civilization. It is these ties that have allowed the people to survive China's seemingly unceasing internal wars, and it is these ties that make the Chinese civilization indestructible.

Often among Overseas Chinese, those who share the same surname form associations. The Chinese believe that those who share the same surname are from the same ancient family.[4]

The nature of social relationships and connections between Chinese Americans are fundamentally important to the way they organize and utilize their monetary resources in order to finance their extraordinary economic success in cities like Los Angeles and New York. Chinese social relationships along with their attitudes toward money and its use directly affect the nature of credit and finance and how they are used to achieve personal, familial and business goals in the Chinese-American community.

In a recent article about the growing prosperity of the Asian commercial community in one area of New York City, i.e., Flushing, Queens, a region whose economic growth will be discussed, the *New York Times* (10/2/94) reported:

> Actually, running a bank in Chinatown is a good-news/bad-news situation. The typically cavalier attitude that many Americans take toward debt — leverage is synonymous with growth opportunity, credit cards are a means to buy something now that you could not otherwise afford — is anathema in Chinese culture.
>
> "Chinese people do not feel comfortable borrowing, they consider debt a big weight on their shoulders," said Ms. Min of Chemical Bank. Moreover, added Mr. Ho of Shanghai Bank, there are many alternative sources of funds in Chinatown. "Often, Chinese business owners can get money from wealthy individuals coming from abroad, or from relatives," he said. "And they are usually quite willing to pool their money and open, say, a new restaurant as partners."
>
> * * * *
>
> But while loan business may be sparse, savings deposits are ample. And since Chinese people are unlikely to take chances with money, what loan business there is, is generally lucrative. Asian culture is such that family members, friends, even acquaintances, will often chip in to help someone in financial trouble, rather than let them renege on their debts. And Chinese people are more likely to assume debt to expand a business that has already been successful, making the loan a better risk for both the borrower and the bank.

---

4. Ibid., pp. 200–1.

"Nonperforming loans are almost non-existent here," said Mr. Aleffi of Chemical Bank. "The credit character of the Asian market is exceptionally strong."

For all these reasons, banks clearly pursue Asian business. Most Flushing branches, whether American- or Asian-owned, have automatic teller machines that offer transactions in Mandarin as well as English.

* * * *

Citibank has a special Asian Banking Center where Korean, Mandarin and Cantonese are spoken. And most of the banks are open on weekends to accommodate local people who may work in Manhattan but prefer to do their banking in a Chinese-speaking bank.

Local institutions that ignore the demand for Chinese-oriented services do so at their peril. Look at the history of the Sheraton, a now thriving hotel that has become not only the place for visiting Asians, but also the place for local events.

When it opened in February 1992 it marketed itself as an airport hotel with proximity to La Guardia, to Shea Stadium, to the National Tennis Center in Flushing Meadow-Corona Park and to transportation to Manhattan rather than its location in the heart of a bustling Chinatown. Floundering is a euphemism for how it fared.

So the hotel changed its approach. It subscribed to Chinese cable television stations for its rooms, provided Chinese newspapers and put together tour packages aimed at Asian travelers. And it sent an Asian salesperson to Beijing, to Shanghai, to Taipei, all over Asia, to call on government offices and persuade them to send delegations to New York. "That opened the flood-gates," Ms. Petrus said.

Today the hotel's occupancy is about 50 percent Asian. It is finally also getting spillover La Guardia traffic too. It reaped a bonanza from the U.S. Open tennis tournament in Flushing Meadow last month. And it has become a popular spot for local weddings and banquets.

"We advertise in Spanish, Chinese and Korean newspapers," Ms. Petrus said. "We've learned that marketing to the ethnic community really works."

The primary importance of ethnic identity and consciousness and the types of socioeconomic relationships they engender are well illustrated by the economic success stories of the ethnic Chinese and other ethnic groups in America. They provide a very valuable economic orientation for the Afrikan American community. A radical change for the better in the economic fortunes of the Afrikan community requires a commensurate radical change in the nature of the character of the social relationships and connections its members share with each other. For an economic system and the political power it generates are finally founded on the system of social relationships which inhere in a community of persons. And that foundational system is but itself the concrete behavioral manifestation of the group identity and consciousness shared by that community of persons.

Thus, it should be apparent that ethnicity plays the central role in a group's economic empowerment. Over the centuries the preeminence of such groups as the Babylonians, Egyptians, Phoenicians, Greeks and Romans, Incas, Mayans, and Aztecs, the ancient Chinese, Ghanian and Islamic empires have demonstrated the economic and political outcomes of a strong sense of ethnic-cultural identity. The current economic power of the Europeans, the Anglo-Americans and other global tribes illustrate the point in the present century.

Moreover, the trend toward ethnic nationalism is not decelerating in this age of the "global village". This is attested by a recent article published in the *Wall Street Journal* (6/20/94) titled "Global Paradox: Growth of Trade Binds Nations, But It Can Also Spur Separatism." In this lengthy article which begins thusly: "It's a paradox of global proportions: the closer that trade and technology bind nations together, the bolder the moves to break nations apart," the writer notes the following:

Errant Predictions

Who would have expected all this? Following World War II, many predicted that a global economy and global communications would lead to a world-wide community. Nationalism, they said, would decline as ever more people saw us all as passengers on lifeboat Earth.

But the growth of the global economy and of more powerful transnational institutions is producing the opposite effect. Instead of fading away, nationalism is flourishing, and not just in the war-ravaged Balkans. Now even tiny groups of people can contemplate breaking away from the central state and plugging into the world economy on their own. Regions nursing ancient grievances are claiming independence, or at least autonomy, confident they aren't committing economic suicide. At the same time, the big corporations and institutions shaping the world economy seem so remote that many people turn to local ethnic groups and obscure languages for their identity, furthering the world's political fragmentation.

"This is a world we didn't expect to happen and we haven't planned for," says Paul Goble, a specialist in ethnic movements at the Carnegie Endowment for International Peace. Over time, he believes, the world may fracture into 500 states from the current 200. Others put the ultimate number lower but talk of a new kind of state —

something akin to a corporate holding company — with the central government little more than a shell and power residing in the regions.

Regional Identities

But the global economy doesn't just make the world safer for many breakaway movements; it also reinforces their desire to assert regional identities. International bureaucracies don't create a sense of belonging, and many people fear ceding control to them....

This contemporary trend compels us to take notice that ethnicity and ethnic nationalism are alive and well. For better or worse, their reality must be acknowledged and utilized in our best interests.

THE LOCAL TRIBE

Economic networks based on ethnicity are not only discernible on a global scale. In fact, local economic networks are the acorns from which global oaks grow. For our purpose herein, local networks may prove the more instructive and pertinent since our interest is primarily in the economic development of the Afrikan community in the United States. We are all familiar with the economic and political success stories of various immigrant groups in America who utilized their ethnic identity and consciousness to catapult themselves into national and international fame and fortune. We shall briefly review the visible, economic success of recent emigrant groups such as the Indians, Afghans, and Koreans. Because of their ambivalent relations with the Afrikan American community and the wealth they have managed to extract from it, we will review the conscious efforts of Korean Americans to transform their new-found economic success into political power based on their ethnic identity and consciousness.

The Koreans

A recent *Wall Street Journal* report noted that "Korean immigrants have built a thriving community of nearly 400,000 in Southern California, the largest concentration of Koreans outside Korea." It further noted that in its population of small-business owners "an estimated 1 in 10 Korean American adults owns a business, compared with one in 15 Whites and one in 67 Blacks." A very large percentage of Korean businesses in southern California are supported by Blacks, as they are in many American cities across the country. The riotous reaction of a number of Afrikan Americans in Los Angeles' predominantly Black South Central District, with a population of 500,000, to the not-guilty verdict for four police officers accused of beating

Number of Korean-American businesses damaged in the Los Angeles riots following the Rodney King verdict	
Auto Repair Shops	82
Dry Cleaners	95
Electronic Stores	72
Furniture Stores	20
Jewelry Stores	64
Liquor Stores	220
Markets	314
Swap meets*	385
Restaurants	106
Clothing stores	288
Video Stores	43
Other	546
Total	2,240

*Swap meets are collections of small retailers who share space inside a large building. This figure reflects the number of small retailers affected.
SOURCE: Survey of Businesses by a Committee of Local Korean Language Media. Adapted from the *Wall Street Journal*, 1992.

Table 14-1 **Damage Count**

motorist, Rodney King, revealed the amazing degree to which the Koreans had come to dominate the economic life of that community. The *Journal* reported that *"An estimated 20% of the area's Korean American businesses, or about 2,000 companies, had been damaged or destroyed."* If this figure is somewhat accurate, a simple mathematical calculation would allow us to estimate that the Koreans must own some 10,000 businesses in the area. A "damage count" by the *Wall Street Journal* of the number of Korean-American businesses damaged in the Los Angeles "riots" following the first Rodney King verdict, will provide some idea of the depth and breath of Korean-owned businesses located in South Central, Los Angeles.

Let us look for a moment at one of the businesses the Koreans monopolize in predominantly Black South Central, Los Angeles. The *New York Times* (11/29/92) reported that "There is perhaps no other inner-city business that has been as lucrative as liquor." This is a business which the Koreans monopolize in South Central. The *Times* goes on to report that "In fact, liquor stores have done so well in urban centers that before the spring riots, *South Central, with a population of 500,000, had nearly three times as many outlets — 728 — as Rhode Island, which has 1.3 million people and 280 liquor stores.*" As an aside the *Times* reported in the same article that for the liquor industry as a whole, the thousands of liquor stores located in inner-cities across the country are the endpoints of a multi-billion dollar pipeline. Malt liquor and fortified wines sold predominantly in urban centers accounted for $2 billion in sales in 1991 — the bulk of which, i.e., three-quarters, came from malt liquor.

The story of the success of Korean-owned businesses is by now a familiar one. However, the transformation of that success into political power is just beginning to unfurl. The basic foundations of Korean economic success and political transformation are the Korean-centered organizations such as the Korean American Small Business Service Center of New York, the Korean-American Grocers Association of New York, the Korean Produce Association, and the umbrella organization, the Korean Association of Greater New York (KAGNY). Such associations are duplicated across the country. Via the Korean Produce Association, which began some 20 years ago with only 30 members and which now numbers over a thousand, Korean-Americans have come to dominate the retail end of the produce industry in New York. This ethnocentric organization which functions "to help the new merchants with the various problems associated with owning a retail business in New York City" (*Manhattan Spirit*, 4/7/93), along with other Korean businessmen, is seeking to establish the New York Korean-American Cooperative. As reported in the *Times* (3/22/93) the idea of the cooperative "is to escape buying from wholesalers [non-Koreans] by banding together to buy as a group, and thereby attract lower prices directly from manufacturers." The Korean-American Grocer's Association which began in Brooklyn, New York City, in 1985 with 20 businesses as members, now has 2,500 members.

The KAGNY is widely recognized as the leader of Korean American business organizations. Its current president, Dr. Jae T. Kim, sees its special mission as creating and maintaining the unity of the Korean community; as the chief social and political organization designed to meet the needs of the Korean community; and to mediate relations between Korean New Yorkers and other ethnic minorities in the city. The KAGNY currently sponsors "cultural unity concerts, conflict and mediation training, a college to teach English to immigrants, guidance for the socially disadvantaged, voter registration, and minority scholarship opportunities."[5]

---

5. *Manhattan Spirit*, April 7, 1993.

In the interest of ethnic unity, identity and consciousness, the Korean Produce Association of New York City sponsors the Annual Korean Harvest and Folklore Festival started in 1982, which has been attended by as many as 80,000 persons. It features professional entertainers brought over from Korea, traditional activities such as Korean wrestling, circle dancing as well as professionally prepared Korean traditional foods.

Buying the Black Community on the Cheap. Of special interest here is the Korean community's organized public and political relations efforts directed toward the Afrikan American community at large and the predominantly Afrikan American city administration then headed by Mayor David N. Dinkins. An indication of the clout wielded by the Korean community in New York City is provided by the fact that the Korean-American Grocers Association had the Reverend Al Sharpton, an immensely influential local and national Black leader and politician, give the invocation at one of its annual awards meetings in February, 1993.

Pinning the Tail on the Donkey: Korean Public Relations Efforts in the Black Community. Responding to its troubled relations with the Afrikan American community the Korean community has, through its various associations, targeted the former community for a public relations blitz. Korean associations have sponsored spots of Black radio stations honoring heroes like Thurgood Marshall. The Korean Produce Association ran a scholarship program for minority students in conjunction with the *Amsterdam News* [the leading Black weekly newspaper in New York City].[6]

In the March 20, 1993 edition of that publication, Dr. Jae T. Kim, president of the KAGNY is pictured with the vice-president of the association, Kwi-Sook Koh-Taylor, and three Black American and one Latino American high school students. These students were given scholarships by the KAGNY to study as Kyung Hee University in Seoul, Korea. It was further reported that "A total of 100 scholarships were given for studies on the undergraduate and graduate levels. Under the arrangement, the students are to be sent in groups of 20 over a five-year period."[7] In addition to this transparent tokenism, the embarrassingly cheap buying of favor from the Afrikan American community, the Korean Produce Association engages in "charitable works" in the Afrikan American community by donating "produce to help feed homeless New Yorkers, and those in senior centers"

---

6. *New York Times*, March 22, 1993.

7. *New York Amsterdam News*, March 30, 1993.

(*Manhattan Spirit*, 4/7/93). Moreover, according to the *New York Times* (3/22/93), "For years, in relative anonymity, Korean grocers have given turkeys to the needy, and Korean dry cleaners have distributed unclaimed clothes. By contrast, the 10 minority students winning $1,000 scholarships in the grocers' "Share the Dream" essay contest co-sponsored by Coca-Cola, will be honored at Harlem's Apollo Theater." In an effort to maintain their monopolies and to soothe the ruffled feathers of the exploited Afrikan American community, Korean business owners are employing more non-Koreans (mostly Mexicans) and are giving seminars where Koreans are taught to smile more frequently, a relative rarity in their culture and a much sought after amenity demanded by their Black customers.

In the face of mounting tensions between themselves and the Black communities in whose economic infrastructure they play a very significant and sometimes near dominant role, the Korean merchant community has undertaken a number of other diplomatic and public relations initiatives designed to mollify their Afrikan American clientele. To ease and pacify the resentments of a community which perceives them as often discourteous, hostile, or only mildly courteous, as merchants who care only to commercially exploit the community, who contribute little or nothing to its betterment or create little or no job opportunities for its constituents while exporting its capital, members of the Korean community in New York City in conjunction with sympathetic Blacks launched the Black-Korean Mediation Project in September, 1993.[8] The project is designed to strengthen Black and Korean communication and cooperation by bringing together volunteers from both communities to serve as mediators who will co-mediate interracial and intercultural disputes. The mediating teams consisting of one Black and one Korean, undergo a three-month training program, and after being certified by the State, work in mediation centers located throughout the city.

In Chicago, a Black woman has been employed by the Korean business community to monitor and critically evaluate Korean-Black market relations and consult with Korean merchants with respect to improving their customer relations with the Black community, as well as improving their rather poor business image. The consultant also functions as a liaison between the Korean merchants and Black community by acting to forestall or quietly resolve disputes between the two.

In a major diplomatic initiative, the South Korean federal government extended an invitation and welcome to an Afrikan American Congressional delegation which visited the country in

---

8. *City Sun*, "New Community Effort Aids Interracial Communication," 9/22-26/93.

August 1993. Consisting of six members of the Congressional Black Caucus — Edolphus Towns and Major Owens of Brooklyn, Donald Payne of New Jersey, Lucien Blackwell of Pennsylvania, Eva Clayton of North Carolina, and Corrine Brown of Florida — the delegation in a week-long trip interacted with Korean government leaders, church officials and corporate executives.[9] The cross-cultural junket was co-sponsored by the Korean-American Friendship Society, a diverse group of leading Korean citizens who founded the organization in 1990 to concern itself with easing tensions stemming from Black-Korean trade issues, and the New York-based Cross-Cultural Pastor's Association for Peace, led by the Rev. Henry H. Hyong, a Korean clergyman who pastors an Afrikan American congregation. The Korean-American Friendship Society, based in Seoul, South Korea, also sponsors festivals and holiday celebrations for American servicemen and women as a way of improving ties with the U.S.

The delegation met with members of the Korean National Assembly, President Kim Young Sam and members of his administration, including the ministers of foreign affairs, of commerce and industry, as well as visited several large Korean corporations such as Hyundai, Pohang Iron and Steel Corporation, and Korea United Technologies. The delegation was given the "royal treatment" — including police escorts — throughout their visit and made a brief visit to the International Exposition in Taejon City where they toured the Korean and American pavilions. During this trip, ostensibly designed to "launch" a systematic, ongoing effort aimed at improving communications between Korean-Americans and Afrikan Americans (*New York Amsterdam News*, 9/4/93) and at initiating trade exchange, the Black Congressional Caucus delegation participated in a two-hour seminar titled "How To Promote Harmony Between Korean-Americans and African-Americans." Members of the delegation reportedly explored the development of retail chain outlets for Korean electronic and other products to be jointly owned by Korean-Americans and Afrikan Americans.

"*Killing Me With Your Love.*" The breadth and depth of Korean public relations initiatives toward the Afrikan American community are impressive. The reason for these initiatives is obvious — to ease and camouflage the continuing and growing Korean commercial exploitation of the Black community; to maintain their dominance of its economic markets along with other non-Black merchants; and to

---

9. *New York Amsterdam News*: "Black lawmakers visit Korea in cultural, trade exchange," 9/4/93; "U.S. Congress persons to take cross-cultural trip to S. Korea," 8/17/93).

export its wealth and thereby impoverish it, while pretending that such is not the case, by deceiving its constituents with cunning public relations techniques. Manipulating the conditioned needs of many Blacks to be treated kindly by non-Blacks, to be respected, socially acknowledged and accepted by non-Blacks — needs conditioned into them by the long history and nature of White oppression; needs apparently far greater than their need to own and control their own marketplaces, control their own economic destiny, and to pass on an economic legacy to their children — the Koreans are frenetic ally selling Blacks "the sizzle instead of the steak." Their public relations campaigns and, worse still, their transparent lobbying and buying of Black-elected officials, the blatant attempt to use those representatives to advance Korean interests at the expense of Afrikan American interests by making vague promises to enter into joint ventures with Afrikan American business persons, are insultingly designed to beguile the Afrikan American community into stupidly aiding and abetting its own economic exploitation and retardation.

The Afrikan American community must resist and overthrow its conditioned addictive need to be "loved" by other ethnic groups who can only "love" it to the extent that they can exploit its commercial and economic potential. Even if their "love" was genuine, the community is in no way obliged to impoverish itself, neglect and abuse its children, literally sacrifice its physical and psychosocial body politic by giving away its wealth in a Faustian bargain with the devil to gain that love. The Afrikan American community's dedicated use of its wealth to maintain the employment, health and welfare of its members and its children, to socially and economically improve itself through the preservation and use of its resources as allocated through its own social, cultural and economic institutions, should have absolutely little to do with permitting Korean and other communities free and full access to its marketplaces, only to economically exploit it while smilingly pretending to "love" it.

The Koreans' "Political Economy." Above and beyond their public relations campaigns Korean associations are, according to the *New York Times* (3/22/93), organizing to use "the strength of their numbers [and their wealth] to try to increase their political influence..." in New York City. The *Times* further reported that "on the political level, the Korean immigrants are banding together to push their concerns by voting as a bloc in this year's [1993] Mayoral race." The *Times* further intimated that Mayor Dinkins [since deposed] as well as his challengers "are already campaigning among Korean Americans." Besides the above-mentioned efforts to elicit municipal help to set up a huge new food cooperative, the *Times* reported that Korean business owners also have on their political agenda the squashing of "a city plan for zoning changes that would allow bigger food stores into the city, as well as lobbying the City Council to crack down on illegal food vendors." Promising to deliver at least 6,000 votes to the mayoral candidate whose stand on vending seems best, "Myong Y. Juch, president of the Korean American Grocers Association of New York, and his organization is seeking to force the city to crack down on illegal vendors and more tightly regulate legal ones." This demand presents a special irony since a very large number of the vendors the association wishes to run out of business or to severely restrict are those of Afrikan origin having to vend in the streets for a living as a result of Korean and other ethnic groups' monopoly of the stores in communities where their customers are almost one hundred percent Black! This is the final payback for the tremendous financial support the Black community has given the Korean community over the years, a community which has chosen not to reside among its customers, nor has given generously to support its social institutions — a community which was the beneficiary of the great human and monetary sacrifices made by Afrikan Americans to protect their liberty during and after the Korean War.

Such are the benefits and fruits of economic organization and clout.

In a city which contains more than two million Blacks, Mr. Juch, president of the Korean American Grocers Association, counts some 300,000 Koreans in the metropolitan region, some 10,000 Korean-owned businesses of which 3,500 are groceries, delis or supermarkets. The total sales of this estimated 15 percent of such businesses in the city approaches $1.5 billion. This figure was enough to provoke giants of the food industry, from Anheuser-Busch to General Mills, to stream to the association's second annual food and trade show in February, 1993 (NYT, 3/22/93).

It is pertinent to note that on April 13, 1993, just weeks after the *New York Times* (3/22/93) reported the KAGNY's demand that the New York City administration crack down on illegal street vendors, it reported that the Dinkins administration announced it would "step up its efforts against the 10,000 unlicensed street vendors who have flooded New York City sidewalks with everything from tube socks to fake Rolex watches" (4/13/93). Apparently responding to the Koreans' new-found, wealth-based political clout, the Mayor announced that he would assign 36 additional police officers to an already 46-member peddler enforcement unit and would deploy along with 12 additional vans and trucks, 31 more city inspectors as well as other personnel. That the political purpose of their pronouncement and its political targets were immediately recognized by the *New York Times* (4/13/93) can be inferred from the following paragraph in its report:

> The Mayor's get tough policy comes at the beginning of his election campaign in which the votes of small shop owners [read: Korean shop owners] and politically potent organizations that represent them [read: the Korean American Association of Greater New York and other Korean business associations] are regarded as far more compelling than the power of illegal sidewalk vendors who are breaking the law and who have virtually no political constituency.

We have gone on at length about the growing economic and political clout of Korean Americans in New York City in order to demonstrate how a group's conscious, judicious use of its ethnicity and identity can facilitate its achievement of power and influence in this society, even if it composes a very small percentage of the human and voting population. The Korean saga in America can provide a workable model for the far larger Afrikan American population in its struggle to achieve its full measure of power and freedom in America.

A Sweeping Thank You Note: ON MONDAY, OCTOBER 17, 1994, *over 400 uniformed police officers, some in riot gear and others on mounted horses, some deployed as undercover officers and others as public relations personnel, combined to demonstrate a massive show of force and callously swept all street vendors from 125th Street, in Harlem. Operating at the behest of New York City Mayor Rudy Giuliani and a few local elected officials, the police proceeded to arrest some 26 vendors and place the street under military occupation. The police state which effectively established its presence all along 125th Street and adjoining avenues was posted 24 hours a day, seven days a week. It was in its third week as this note is being written [and 15 months hence]. Thus far, no solution which would allow the return of the vendors, or some portion of them, to 125th Street has been reached.*

Thus, the circle has closed. Blacks who provide approximately 95% of the customers along 125th Street, one of New York City's major commercial streets, support a host of storeowners, shopkeepers, professional services and other businesses, 95% of whom are non-Black. Until about two to two-and-a-half decades ago, would-be Black entrepreneurs were not allowed to rent storefronts in the most lucrative blocks of this street by White and non-Black landlords.

Several decades ago Adam Clayton Powell, Jr. led an historic boycott of the storeowners along 125th Street in order to pressure them into hiring Blacks as salespersons and as other types of employees in their businesses. Currently on this street, whose real estate is primarily owned by Whites and other non-Blacks, rents for storefronts on a per-square-foot basis are extraordinarily high even when compared to storefronts in downtown Manhattan. This situation effectively bars many would-be Black storeowners from entering into business selling goods and services to an overwhelmingly Black clientele. Black street vendors filled the breech between the practical absence of Black-owned storefront businesses and a cornucopia of Black consumers, many of whom desired to support those vendors and their families by shopping with them.

In a city where the unemployment of Blacks is among the highest in the country; where several *hundred thousands* of jobs have been lost over the last decade; where tens of thousands of city employees are being cut from their jobs and crucial public service organizations such as schools, hospitals, youth services, colleges and universities, are being disinvested and defunded; and in a region of the country which has not fully recovered from the last recession, Black street vendors represent an attempt of the Black community to capitalize on its own wealth in order meet the basic and vital needs of its constituents. According to Danny Perez, outgoing chairman of the Economic Development Committee of Community Board 10 in Central Harlem, on 125th Street alone, local Black consumers and hoards of shoppers from around the metropolitan area as well as tourists — for the colorful street vending market attracted many tourists and visitors — spent an estimated $300 million annually with the vendors.

With 20-20 hindsight it is now apparent, judging by the near empty street, that the Black street vendors were the life-blood of 125th Street. Their presence there served as a magnet drawing customers not only to themselves but also to the in-store merchants who complained that they were taking away their business from them. Be that as it may, the case of the Street vendors on 125th Street demonstrates the absence of any intention by non-Black merchants and businesspeople — who do not live in the community, who do not contribute materially, socially or financially to its economic and social welfare, do little to stem its high unemployment, and who are generally racially hostile toward its inhabitants — to share any of the wealth they earn in the Black community with its constituents. This case also highlights the misguided sentiments of Black community and national leadership establishments which ignore the imperatives of communal self-preservation and which under the influence of false economic ideologies and deceptive religious dogmas, deliver the wealth of the community into the hands of alien merchants who are snatching the bread from the mouths of hungry Black children.

The 125th Street vendor's case symbolizes the condition of Black entrepreneurs all around the globe — Black entrepreneurs as outsiders in their own markets, as alien merchants in markets dominated by Black consumers; non-Blacks in the stores taking the lion's share of Black consumer dollars and Black vendors on the street picking up the change. This is the case in virtually all Black communities and in communities where Blacks own a significant portion of the buying power in North America and in Black nations in Central and South America, the Caribbean Basin, Afrika and the Pacific Islands. It should be obvious that if the worldwide Afrikan community is to achieve economic self-sufficiency and self-respect, if it is to wield sufficient political and economic power to protect its vital interests and to enhance its quality of life, then its current economic posture relative to other ethnic groups in its midst and with whom it does business must be radically reversed! It is obvious that other ethnic communities, even when they earn a living in the Black community and moreover, wax rich and fat from doing business with it, feel that they owe it nothing, not even common courtesies or respect. They feel that every penny the community spends should be spent with them exclusively and that not even a fraction of a cent the community spends should be spent with its own native merchants. This situation and attitude in a world of incredibly rapidly shrinking employment opportunities, fiercely competitive markets, and of protectionistic trading blocs, bodes very badly for the future well-being of Afrikan peoples throughout the diaspora.

The Afrikan community despite its long tradition of sharing with all strangers who enter its gates must face up to the fact that it does not owe non-Afrikans a living at the expense of its own economic viability. The Black community simply cannot support itself and everybody else at the same time. Other ethnically related nations and economically interdependent groups have recognized that same fact relative to themselves. While globalization is occurring at a breathtaking pace, so is regionalization — the joining of nations, often ethnically and culturally related, to form regional trade blocs and associations for advancing and protecting the economic self-interests of their members. The globe is now currently organized around three regional centers — Western Europe, North America, and East Asia. Central and South America are in the process of organizing. There is the probability that the nations which form that region will become full members of the North American Free Trade Agreement, or NAFTA. Note that intra-regional trade and finance are increasing at the moment in spite of the overall globalization of trade and finance. This means that in a global universe, intragroup, intraregional, intracommunal economic organization is of the greatest importance. For example, in assessing the new world order Klaus Schwab & Claude Smadja noted the following:

> As the world economy continues both to globalize and to organize itself around the three regional centers, we are witnessing another revolutionary development that may actually help to contain interregional tensions: a desynchronizing of economic cycles in the three regions. East Asia, for example, has been booming despite the accelerating decline in the Japanese economy from 1991 to the beginning of 1994, while Europe and the United States have been stuck in one of the most severe recessions in contemporary history. And although the U.S. economy would receive an additional boost from a recovery in Europe, it has been able to climb out of the recession while Europe is still struggling to do so.
> The process of regionalization and the desynchronization of regions in the world economy are, in fact, linked. Six years ago, Japan exported one-third more to the United States than it did to the rest of East Asia. Today the situation is reversed. East Asia's intraregional trade now constitutes about 43% of the region's total, compared with 33% in 1980. Meanwhile, East Asia's intraregional investment and financial flows represent the fastest growing share of the region's exchanges: from 1986 to 1992, almost 70% of all investment in East Asia came from within the region, while 10.3% came from Europe and 10.9% came from the United States.
> These developments are creating a pattern in East Asia that is increasingly similar to the one that already exists in Western Europe (where intraregional trade accounts for almost 70% of the total) and that will come about in North America with the implementation of NAFTA. Under these conditions, each region is becoming less and less vulnerable to fluctuations that may occur within the others. In other words, desynchronization means that if the United States sneezes, the rest of the world will no longer automatically get the flu.[10]

In light of the sweeping changes in national, regional and international economies, Afrikan communities, nations and regions can no longer permit their economies and to be owned and exclusively

---

10. "Power and Policy: The New Economic Order," *Harvard Business Review* (10/12/94) pp. 40–50.

exploited and their resources to be disemboweled by outsiders whose only interest in them is to suck them dry of their lifeblood.

The Ethnic Road to Riches

Social power theorist Robert Dahl has advanced a rather comprehensive list of political power resources or bases. Most germane to our discussion here is his listing of "solidarity" as one important source of power and influence. He defines the term thusly — *"solidarity: the capacity of a member of one segment of society to evoke support from others who identify him as like themselves because of similarities in occupation, social standing, religion, ethnic origin, or racial stock"* [Emphasis added]. Wrong (1988) argues that "the most obvious collective resources are those created *by the pooling of individual resources* for employment in the service of a common aim." The following examples of ethnic economic solidarity amply corroborate Dahl's and Wrong's viewpoints.

The Growth of Asian American Enterprises — In August 1991, based on new census data, the U.S. Small Business Administration reported that Asian American business growth between 1982 and 1987 was six times the national rate. This rate of growth demonstrated that Asian American businesses make up the fastest growing sector in the U.S. As reported by SBA Administrator, Patricia Saiki:

> Their numbers and receipts are growing fast; they are creating more jobs and contributing to the economic well-being of their communities and country....We expect this expansion to continue as the businesses owned by these groups [Asian Americans and Pacific Islanders] mature and branch more strongly into manufacturing, finance and construction.[11]

According to the U.S. Bureau of the Census data, the number of Asian American-owned businesses increased by 989.3 percent between 1982 and 1987. The rate for all U.S. businesses during the same period was 14 percent. Comparatively, the rate of growth for Latino-owned businesses for the period was 80.5 percent; women owned businesses, 57 percent; Afrikan American-owned businesses, 38 percent.

The number of Asian American-owned businesses increased from 187,691 in 1982 to 355,331 in 1987. More specifically, among the Asian American groups the number of Vietnamese American businesses grew from 4,980 in 1982 to 25,671 in 1987, a growth rate

---

11. *Big Red News*, 8/1991.

of 414.55 percent. Korean American businesses increased from 30,919 to 69,304; Asian Indian American businesses grew 119.9 percent, from 23,770 to 52,226.

Korean Entrepreneurial Success — The success of the Koreans is aptly notorious. A small Korean population, relative to the much larger Black and other ethnic group populations in metropolitan New York City, owns more than 85 percent of the 1,600 greengrocer establishments (NYT, 1/12/92). The more than 100,000 Koreans who have emigrated to the New York City area since the 1970s also own numerous novelty shops, beauty salons, liquor stores and drycleaning establishments. The *Times* also reported that "since the 1970s *65 percent of Korean families own at least one business* "[Emphasis added]. This group is the most highly self-employed of all ethnic groups. As early as 1980 Koreans in Los Angeles County, as reported by the U.S. Census Bureau, were engaged nearly three times more frequently in entrepreneurship than were non-Koreans. At that time about 62 percent of Koreans in Los Angeles County were either self-employed or were employees of Korean-owned firms (Light and Bonacich, 1988). The *New York Daily News* (1/22/89) describes the nature of the current Korean community as follows:

> The Korean population in the United States has grown to an estimated 750,000 from 70,000 in the 1970 Census. While there is a thriving Korean section in Flushing, Queens, the largest concentration is in Southern California, home for about 300,000 Korean immigrants. The nerve center of the community is the vast Koreatown west of downtown Los Angeles, focus of 150 associations, 500 Christian Churches, 15 Buddhist Temples, 32 newspapers and a 24-hour radio station. The jumble of Korean signs, restaurants, coffee houses, hotels and offices shout immigrant success. Already, Korean grocers control 18 percent of the beer, wine and liquor licenses in Southern California and 5 percent of the total grocery market including supermarkets. Census and other data indicate that Korean entrepreneurship is a national phenomenon instead of merely local New York City or Los Angeles events.

The Korean entrepreneurial record in the New York City green grocer business is quite typical of Korean entrepreneurial activities in other business areas. There are over 1,400 Korean green grocers in New York City. They now own and operate about 90% of its retail fruit and vegetable businesses (*New York Daily News*, 1/22/92).

Banks and the Asian Immigrant Community — The area of New York City called Flushing, Queens, like other areas in other cities, has been flooded by thousands of Asians, mostly Chinese and Koreans, over the past decade. Virtually a new "Chinatown" in New York City, this area which contained few Asians 10 years ago now supports a population of over 140,000 Chinese and Korean immigrants. It is home to "200 stores in a three-block area and 800 restaurants in the neighborhood...[with] a new 175-room Sheraton Hotel [soon to] open." (NYT, 8/7/91). More remarkable is that seven banks crowd into just two blocks of this area, with an eighth being currently constructed. This Asian neighborhood altogether contains *at least 35* [banks] — American, Chinese, Korean, British, Indian, Pakistani, and Columbian. The *Times* went on to report that in the first two weeks of opening, the Chinese Trust branch bank "took in $6 million from 400 depositors." Referring to the ethnic basis of his branch's success, the local manager of the China Trust branch is reported to have stated that "Chinese people have a lot of savings... *They will come to us because we are Chinese.* Chinese people are traditionally shy. They won't talk to strangers" [Emphasis added].

A New Chinatown Grows in Brooklyn — Flushing, Queens, hosts the *second* Chinatown in New York City. The original and most famous Chinatown is located in Manhattan. Now, New York City — Brooklyn, to be specific — is host to a new and third Chinatown. This thriving ethnic enclave was described by the *Wall Street Journal* as follows:

> A new Chinatown is blossoming in Brooklyn, N.Y., as small businesses started by immigrants rescue a neighborhood once marked by abandoned buildings and rising crime....
>
> For nearly a century this was Brooklyn's Scandinavian community; then it became infested with drug dealers. But in less than a decade, Chinese immigrants, many of them illegals, have pushed the dealers out, creating jobs, businesses and a local real-estate boom. The 13-block stretch has become New York City's third largest Chinatown — following the Manhattan original and another near La Guardia Airport in Queens.
>
> The arrival of the Chinese in this neighborhood typifies New York's settlement by immigration. Illegal Chinese immigrants first came looking for cheap housing in commuting distance of Manhattan sweatshops. Chinese-American investors gradually bought property and advertised rentals in Chinese-language newspapers. More illegal immigrants arrived, often looking for Chinese-speaking landlords. Sweatshops followed the work force, as did stores. Eighth Avenue's once-empty storefronts began to fill with Chinese-American appliance stores, bakeries, hairdressers, restaurants, even herbal pharmacies.

The transition hasn't been trouble-free: Along with sweatshops, the Chinese have brought gangs and tensions with oldtimers. But today, bright Chinese-lettered signs dominate the avenue, replacing graffiti. Cantonese rock music blares. A dozen minibus services, many improperly registered, shuttle fares to Manhattan's Chinatown at $1.50 a ride. Last year, Taiwan-controlled China Trust Bank and Chinese-American-owned Abacus Federal Savings Bank opened branches in a neighborhood that hadn't had one for years.

According to 1990 U.S. Census Bureau data, in the Northeast the Afrikan American population is approximately 14 times larger than that of the Chinese. In 1989, the estimated total per capita income of Asians in the tri-state area including New York, New Jersey and Connecticut was roughly $17–20 billion compared to $62–70 billion for Blacks. The bulk of the population for both Black and Chinese reside in the New York City metropolitan area. Yet the Chinese have been able to establish solid and economically viable communities there while Blacks have not established a single one. The difference undoubtedly has to do, in great part, with differences in ethnic identity and consciousness as well as ethnic-based values and solidarity. The heavy proactive presence of these orientations in the Chinese and their relatively reactionary presence in Blacks go far in explaining the economic growth and development of the Chinese community compared with the relative economic stagnation of the Black community, even though the Black community is far older and contains far more social and economic resources on the whole than its Chinese counterpart.

As in our prior story about the Chinatown in Flushing, Queens, ethnic identity, consciousness, and the exclusive use of ethnic resources are essential to Sunset Park Chinatown's prosperity. The *Journal* noted the extremes to which the ethnic Chinese were willing to go in order to establish a stable social and economic community for themselves. It reported that *"Chinese community leaders acknowledge that the Chinese prefer to patronize one another, which is helping to drive some non-Chinese shopkeepers out of business. Chinese landlords also sometimes evict Hispanic tenants illegally to put in Chinese"* [Emphasis added]. The *Journal* goes on to report that the neighborhood has become more prosperous. This is primarily the result of well-known Chinese frugality and ethnic chauvinism. This virtually assures Chinese merchants and financial institutions that they will be, for all practical purposes, the *sole* beneficiaries of Chinese consumer spending and wealth. The following quote from the *Journal* attests to this assertion: "Poor-looking [Chinese] people will walk in off the street and deposit $50,000 in cash," says Carolyn Chen, who runs the Local China Trust Bank branch. You can't tell anything by looking at them."

Other Immigrant Success Stories — In a front page article titled "An Ethnic Road to Riches" the *New York Times* reported the illustrative story of Parmjit Singh, a Punjabi who left his job as a mechanic on a Greek-owned ship in 1981 and settled in New York City. There he met a fellow Punjabi who owned a gas station and who taught him to run one as well. By 1990, "Mr. Singh, with an Indian partner, owned 13 gas stations in the New York area." Mr. Singh and his partner "has competitors, however — chiefly, other Punjabi Sikhs who began buying and working in gas stations in the city at the same time he did, some of whom now own as many as 40." Moreover, about 40 percent of the city's filling stations are run or owned by South Asians.

Afghan Refugees — One of the smallest groups of refugees in the New York City area, the Afghans, numbering less than 4,000 — almost all war refugees — own more than 200 fast-food chicken restaurants (NYT, 1/2/92). Lacking higher education, trade skills, and having little knowledge of English, Afghans have become specialists in the fast-food chicken business. "To circumvent language and discrimination barriers, *even the carpenters and chicken suppliers they use are Afghans*" [ibid, (Emphasis added)]. One Afghan owns as many as 40 enfranchised fried chicken restaurants — all named Kennedy's Fried Chicken. The owner when asked how he and other fellow Afghans so recently arrived in New York City have succeeded in the fast-food business, replied that he and other established immigrants undertake to lead new arrivals by the hands through the business and to teach the intricacies of running a business. "It's like a formula," he was reported to have said. "We tell them how to go to the building department, how to save money by cutting and installing their own bulletproof glass." He went on to say, "You have to have some connection with somebody to succeed... We all know each other. When the new ones come to the store, they sit. They watch. They learn and then they work."

Thriving Where Others Won't Go — The Dominicans of New York City are well known for the many grocery stores they own in the ghetto neighborhoods (along with numerous other types of businesses). However, their success has not only been marked by their ownership of small grocery stores but by their increasingly rapid ownership of supermarkets as well. These stores are located in areas — Black and Latino ghettoes — abandoned by national supermarket chains such as A&P. According to a *New York Times* (1/7/92) report, about half of the 167 stores the C-Town supermarket group owns in the New York City area are owned by Dominicans. In addition, at the time of the publication of this report the owners of some 32 Bravo supermarkets were almost entirely Dominicans. Moreover, the *Times* reported that "The Dominican grocery store owners who succeed, as well as Mr. Diaz [who owns a supermarket in Harlem], have followed a quick but steep route to six-figure incomes, often planting their stores in tough neighborhoods where major chains have pulled out or seldom ventured. This intrepid entrepreneurialism has permitted "the region's Dominicans [to] sell more than a billion dollars worth of groceries a year."

Where Hispanic Merchants Thrive — Creating, maintaining and serving ethnocultural identity and tastes provide the fundamental bases for the economic growth and development of any particular ethnocultural community. The growth of Hispanic businesses in Westchester County, New York, illustrates this case. The main city in Westchester, New Rochelle, exhibited all the signs of urban decay and decline — boarded-up, abandoned storefronts and lifeless streets — attendant on White flight when the Hispanics began to move there in sizable numbers in the 1970s and 80s. Between 1980 and 1990 the Hispanic population doubled to 86,000, creating ethnic Hispanic enclaves whose ethnocultural tastes and needs were soon to be satisfied by an obliging coterie of Hispanic merchants. From 1977 to 1987, the number of Hispanic businesses in Westchester blossomed from 229 to almost 1,700, an average of about 140 new, successful businesses per year.[12] In the county, "Cuban, Peruvian and Mexican restaurants abound as well as several groceries that sell chili peppers, green tomatoes and tender cactuses, and a cluster of travel agencies, social clubs and bodegas that cater to Spanish speakers" (NYT, ibid).

The phenomenal growth of Hispanic businesses has not only helped bolster the economy of New Rochelle, but has helped bolster the county economy as a whole. Where Hispanic populations have grown significantly in other cities in the county, e.g., White Plains, Port Chester and Yonkers, patterns of Hispanic entrepreneurial growth similar to that of New Rochelle have also occurred. David and Carlos Aliaga started the Village Taxi company in Port Chester in

---

12. "Where Hispanic Merchants Thrive," *New York Times*, 7/12/94.

1990 in order to meet the transportation needs of the growing Hispanic population there. Since that time their fleet of cabs has grown from seven to more than 30 in 1994.

Like other ethnic groups that have succeeded in the county, the Italians, Jews and Koreans, Hispanic merchants primarily rely on relatives to get their businesses off the ground and the free labor from their wives, children, siblings, parents, and other relatives to carry them until they achieve independent profitability. But above all, the Hispanic merchants and business persons of Westchester county, like their ethnic cohorts and counterparts in ethnic communities across America, ultimately depend on the loyal support of their ethnic group to provide them with the crucial foundation for entrepreneurial success.

How They Do It

The examples of ethnic enterprise could be multiplied extensively. However, the ones cited here serve to substantiate the fact that ethnicity can be and is used as a base for creating and developing one of the most important sources of social power — economic resources. Needless to say, the ethnically owned and operated businesses referred to above require relatively substantial sums of money to establish in the first place. Since recently arrived immigrants are generally rarely rich or considered credit-worthy by banks and other financial establishments, the question arises as to how these entrepreneurs "cultivate cash" to invest in their fledgling businesses. In this instance, the ethnic card is again played. We will use the Korean approach to cultivating cash as an example of how entrepreneurial immigrant ethnic groups develop monetary investment resources from within. While recognizing that other such groups may utilize differing methods, we also must recognize that these methods generally involve the use of ethnic resources.

The Family as Financier — The *New York Daily News* (1/22/89) depicted a typical means of cultivating cash through family financing in the Korean community using Choi and his family, who live in the Bronx, New York City, as a case in point. Choi wished to purchase a second green grocer business from its retiring Hungarian owner. The selling price of the business was $28,000 and Choi was to assume the $1,500 monthly rent. He first sought family support "over a traditional family meal in his mother-in-law's apartment."

> Present were Choi's mother-in-law and father-in-law, a brother and sister-in-law, his little girl and very important, his wife. All live in the same building...

He figured he needed about $60,000 to buy and start the... store. The financing was no problem because, like many other Korean merchants in the city, his family also is his bank. The members pool their money to start a business they hope will profit them all.

They bankrolled him once before, for $50,000, ...

Choi doesn't like borrowing from real banks.

"That's dangerous, loan at the bank. If a business falters, the bank, unlike one's family, would insist on prompt repayment no matter what, Choi says."

The next key step was to call a carpenter, not just any carpenter, but a Korean carpenter, because they work hardest and fastest, Choi and other Korean merchants say...

[The Korean carpenter's] bill for the...store would be $20,000 — "All cash job — everything cash. Cash is more cheap and fast," Choi says, laughing. "Korean deal cash."

There's a reason. "Pay a check, maybe he charge $1,200" he says of a hypothetical businessman. But cash, maybe he come down (to) $1,000.

The *Daily News* report further elaborates how the Koreans "do it."

Koreans now own about 90% of the fruit and vegetables stores in the city and buy about 40% of the wholesale produce supply daily at Hunts Point [a major wholesale supply depot].

That robust growth, say local Korean business leaders, has been accomplished with *money raised almost exclusively within the Korean community*, usually from personal savings or loans from relatives, *friends and fraternal or business associations*... [Emphasis added].

It typically costs from $30,000 to $150,000 to start a fruit and vegetable business...some Korean immigrants start by going to work for an established store owner for two or three years, working the requisite long hours.

In return, the owner promises to help the worker finance a store of his own when the time comes....

Still another funding source is the money-pooling *Keh*, a kind of very informal, nonchartered loan club.

Though not illegal, the Kehs operate outside U.S. banking laws. For Korean and other immigrants who've found it hard to get banks to take a risk on them, the Kehs have become an important alternative.

A typical Korean *Keh* consists of 10 to 12 people. Each kicks in the same amount of cash each month to a kitty. Then, on a rotating basis, the entire kitty is loaned to the members, one at a time. Each member, including the borrower, keeps up the monthly payments until every member has gotten a loan at least once. By the time the cycle is complete, each member has borrowed and paid back the whole loan.

As can be surmised, the Korean *"Kye"* or *"Keh"* (pronounced KAY), a holdover "from the old country", is a kind of privately ethnic group-based banking club where a loan can be had without the usual applications or promissory notes required by the more formal institutions. They are relatively efficient means of raising investment capital in a hostile, or unfriendly financial environment controlled by outsiders. However, the Korean facility for raising money and reliability in paying back loans has gained increasing respect from establishment bankers, who are discovering a lucrative new loan market in the Korean community. The Kehs have been so influential until, as reported by the *New York Times,* "a Korean-American bank, Hammi Bank, has devised a legal *imitation* of them. The would-be borrower agrees to deposit, for example, $100,000 over 24 months. After three or four months, he becomes eligible to borrow the full $100,000 at 2.5 points above the prime rate." (That is about half what he would pay a Kye had he chosen to borrow from one at the interest rate of 24 percent or higher.)

In addition to familial and intragroup sources of financing entrepreneurial enterprises Koreans utilize other means as well, e.g., the smuggling out of South Korea of relatively large sums of money, $20,000-$60,000+, by some rather "well-heeled immigrants in defiance of currency laws, which may then be "laundered" by investing it in small business enterprises" (Light and Bonacich, 1988). According to Light and Bonacich, "A Korean social scientist...reported that intricate international networks existed among Los Angeles Koreans by means of which these already here could, with the contrivance of friends and relatives still in Korea, sneak additional capital sums out of South Korea, possibly by way of Europe or Southeast Asia." Moreover, in Los Angeles Koreans have founded their own thrift institutions and borrowed money from California branches of Korean banks. The Koreans also use non-ethnic financial sources such as the Small Business Administration. However, the bulk of their capitalization comes from intragroup, intrafamilial sources.

Insider's Edge and Special Niches — Various enterprising immigrant groups work at developing *specialized niches* in local economies. By these means they may come to virtually monopolize certain businesses or professions and slowly change the original commercial, political, and cultural makeup of the economic field and the city. These ethnically based, quasi-monopolies upon reaching "critical mass" in a particular economic niche, tend to become self-generating, creating "a snowball effect, gathering in labor from that ethnic group and expanding exponentially" (NYT, 12/2/92 [Emphasis added].

In sum, as noted by the *Times*, "The common thread linking all immigrant work niches is the insider's edge on the profession. "Recruiting through the *ethnic network is the most efficient way the employer gets labor.*" [Emphasis added].

The *Times* further elaborates the ethnic-based success of the Koreans when it noted that:

> The snowballing success of Korean grocers is due in part to an *extensive and well-organized support group*. New arrivals can rely on a 500-page Korean business directory, as well as *dozens of business groups*, including the Korean Green Grocer Association. When black residents of Flatbush, Brooklyn organized a boycott of the Korean grocers in 1990, for instance, *fellow Korean grocers put up money to help the stores remain in business* [Emphasis added].

The Koreans' use of extensive ethnic, social kinship and business association networks is duplicated to significant degrees by other immigrant groups. In a multi-ethnic nation such as the United States, ethnic divisions are reflected in ethnic differences in social status, economic well-being, wealth, and political power. These differences do not always accord with ethnic differences in population size, aggregate earned or expendable income, language, and any other number of demographic characteristics thought at first to be important in this regard. In explaining ethnic differences in economic achievement, ethnic and cultural consciousness and identity cannot be overlooked. Ethnic social structures and relations (both internal and external), ethnic self-perception, and other-perception must also be taken into consideration. Ethnic solidarity is of supreme importance. Where an ethnic group possesses and expresses these factors to a relatively high and positive degree along with the will, organization, and creative wherewithal to fully enter into the contested terrain of the marketplace, it greatly enhances the probability that it will win significant social, economic and political benefits for its members. We have seen that this is indeed the case for the immigrant groups we have just discussed. Nominally disadvantaged ethnic groups, if they posses strong, or at least, functional, cultural and affective ties, can utilize their ethnocultural organization and solidarity to subvert or transform the nature of the economy or market for their own benefit.

Organized ethnic groups tend to act in ways that maximize the benefits and advantages that flow to the group. They also tend to act in ways which better benefit the specific interests of individual ethnic members as well as the general interests of the ethnic group. Individual leverage and power is increased in a variety of interactions with ethnic outsiders if that individual is a member of an ethnic group which possesses and exercises system-wide power. As long as the Afrikan American community perceives itself as a mere conglomeration of individuals each pursuing his own individual needs, wants and actions without regard for their negative outcome relative to the status, well-being and power for his group, without concern for broadening his ethnic affiliations and networks and strengthening his ethnic inter-connectedness, it shall suffer unnecessarily low status, poverty, social problems and powerlessness.

Afrikan Immigrants

Economics is embedded in culture. A culture is in good part an economic system, a system which produces and allocates economic resources according to the social relations, structure, values and beliefs which characterize it. Ultimately, it is culture, not racial genetics, which determines economic inputs, outputs and distribution. The entrepreneurial success stories of Afrikan emigrants — stories which rival those of other emigrant groups — corroborate our contention.

The Nigerians — The saga of Nigerian Chris Chidueme, and the entrepreneurial success of Nigerian and Senegalese immigrants in Washington, D.C. and New York City, respectively, underline the roles that Afrikan culture, consciousness, and identity play in economic achievement. The story of Chris Chidueme is told by the *Washington Post* (October, 1994):

> Chris Chidueme, the 40-year-old founder of Bamboo End Restaurant at Georgia Avenue and Kennedy Street, started in 1989 with an $8,000 loan from a local bank. Having managed a McDonald's while earning a business degree from American University, Chidueme thought he could make it with a West African bistro. But with no credit history of his own, he needed someone to co-sign the loan. A friend from Nigeria, from Chidueme's hometown, was happy to comply. The restaurant was a hit, and Chidueme branched into grocery stores, a logical move, he says, because more Nigerians eat at home than in restaurants. He owns two stores now, and is moving into the wholesale business. With annual revenues around $1 million,

Chidueme paid over $200,000 in state and local taxes last year, and another $600,000 in employee salaries. He expects to become a U.S. citizen next year.

Chidueme's path is being followed by quite a number of other fellow Nigerians in Washington, D.C. They provide mutual financial and social support for each other's entrepreneurial undertakings through their traditional revolving credit associations or community savings clubs. Continuing support for their business expansion and economic development is provided for by various culturally and ethnically based business associations, some of which may include native-born Afrikan Americans.

Community savings groups, called *isusus* in Nigeria and Ghana, *tontine* among Senegalese and Guineans, are a cheap source of credit for African entrepreneurs. Five or 10 members of a tontine circle agree to contribute $100 each for five or 10 weeks, each member taking home the pot until everyone has received his share. Tontine pays for a livery cab license or bolts of Ghanaian cloth to fashion into clothing to peddle on the road. Bigger circles finance restaurants, grocery stores and beauty salons....

There are dozens of these African savings clubs in Washington, after New York probably the most popular destination for African emigrants. The many students, taxi drivers and embassy employees here form social organizations — first by nationality, then by ethnic affiliation, finally by village or clan. One linking dozens of Washington-area Ibo from Nigeria is called the Onye Aghalanwaneya Mbaise.

"It means, Let Nobody Leave His Brother Behind Association," explains Bina Avery, a member of Nigeria's Izon group who works with the People's Involvement Corporation, a nonprofit community development association on Georgia Avenue. *Avery counts nearly a hundred businesses opened by African-born entrepreneurs along the strip over the past five years, making Georgia Avenue one of the few commercial strips in the city where Korean businessmen are actually a minority....*

"They're here and they're thriving," agrees Donna Younger, president of the Upper Georgia Avenue Business and Professional Association, of the African entrepreneurs. "They bring fashion and cuisine from the homeland, things you can't find anywhere else in Washington." Twelve of the 46 members of her organization are African-born.

...[U]p and down Georgia Avenue, from the Howard University campus to the District's border with Silver Spring, there are African or Caribbean businesses on almost every block, the greatest number founded by Nigerians.

Working south from the Masjid Madrassa, a mosque on the 5900 block of Georgia Avenue, you'll pass the Kendejah West African restaurant, then, around at the corner of Missouri Avenue, the Soukous Club. Amina's Tailoring, run by an immigrant from Sierra Leone, is on the 5600 block.

Working north, you'll pass Homeland Travel, then Pro Bono Tropical Food ("a division of Pro Bono Enterprises," says a sign on the door) and Ghigis Afrikan Fashion & Textile Gallery, all owned and run by Ibos from Nigeria.

"We consider ourselves African-American too and our clientele is 90 percent African-American," says Ghigi, a former student of Niang's at Howard. [Sulayman Niang is a professor of African Studies at Howard University]. "We're Ibos, first. They call us the Jews of Africa."

The prospects for repeating these immigrant success stories are promising. This spring, in what was called the country's first "diversity lottery," the State Department assigned more than a third of the 55,000 immigrant visas it offers each year to applicants from Africa, the most visas offered to any region of the world after Europe. While the lottery sharply cut back the number of would-be citizens from Asia, Latin America and the Caribbean, the invitation to 20,000 African strivers has the potential to work wonders for urban economies.[13] [Emphasis added]

The Senegalese — The Senegalese in New York City are blazing an entrepreneurial trail as dazzling as the one blazed by the Nigerians in Washington, D.C. Typical of Afrikan emigrants, the Senegalese have settled in the Afrikan American community where they find a ready market for their goods and services. The Senegalese, like the Nigerians and many other Afrikan peoples, have centuries-old traditions of trading. Unlike Afrikan Americans, these traditions were not mortally impaired by racial and cultural oppression. These traditions and their cultural adjuncts, e.g., ethnic identity and solidarity, permit them to prosper in the relatively freer economic markets of the United States and to ably exploit the relatively noncompetitive and receptive markets within the Black inner-cities of the country. The *Washington Post* continues:

> The first wave of Senegalese, for example, came to the United States as peddlers, appearing on New York City's streets in the mid-1980s with briefcases filled with counterfeit designer watches, or canvas sacks filled with knock-off handbags. They had a reputation for sleeping eight to a room in fleabag hotels off Broadway and for being

---

13. *The Washington Post*, October 1994.

first on the corner with $3 made-in-Taiwan umbrellas seconds after the first raindrops fell.

The peddlers who spent the workweek hawking goods to office workers in midtown Manhattan spent the weekends on the road. Like the peddlers of the 1800s, they went deep into the provinces, to what many Americans would consider hostile territory — the ghettos of Detroit, Cleveland, St. Louis and New Orleans. They sold African imports to the African Americans: cloth from Ghana, carvings from Zaire, even gold from the Gold Coast. The peddlers' network spawned the first African stores, which spawned further immigration....

The critical mass of lumpen emigrants is being joined quickly by university-educated elites, who are setting themselves up as real estate agents, wholesalers, shopkeepers and accountants serving fellow emigrants. With time, prosperous enclaves have sprouted amid the devastation of some of this country's worst ghettos.

It is important to note that as is the case with Korean Americans and other entrepreneurially successful emigrant groups, the Senegalese skillfully combine both class and ethnic resources in order to maximize their possibilities of business success. That is, general ethnic identity and solidarity are used to garner the financial and material wherewithal to establish and support various enterprises. The services, wealth and human capital possessed by the middle and upper class or educated and highly skilled members of their community are recruited in order to help finance, service, manage and ensure the economic prospects of the ethnic group as a whole.

The Senegalese in Harlem — *Forbes* (9/26/94) introduces us to Harlem's "Little Senegal" thusly:

> Near the mosque, [Masjid Malcolm Shabazz — Malcolm X's old mosque on Lenox Avenue] along 116th Street, lies the heart of Harlem's Little Senegal. The Horizon 96 insurance agency, run by Makhtar Ndoye, offers all-American products, although French and Wolof are spoken. A framed text of the Koran hangs on a wall behind his desk. An ex-cab driver, Ndoye worked his way through New York University, and became a citizen in 1990. "New York has become the promised land for Senegalese," he smiles.

Ndoye is typical of many of the current wave of Afrikan and Korean emigrants in that they tend to be highly over-educated for the first jobs they find or the new businesses they found. However, their ascent of professional and business ladders also tends to be relatively rapid. Within a very short time Ndoye was joined in his entrepreneurial pioneering efforts by Senegalese fellow travelers. The *Washington Post* (ibid) reported the events this way:

> Last summer, there was one African-owned business on Harlem's 116th Street, Makhtar Ndoye's Horizon 96 insurance agency. Since 1993, Ndoye has been joined by nearly a dozen entrepreneurs: four hair-braiding boutiques; two restaurants, two groceries, a halal (kosher for Muslims) butcher, a travel agency and an African crafts store. "New York," Ndoye smiles, "is the promised land for Senegalese."
>
> This neighborhood, New York City's Little Senegal, boasts between 10,000 and 15,000 residents, many of whom arrived only since 1990.

As discussed earlier, the Senegalese finance their business enterprises through utilizing their traditional financial network, the *tontine*. Like so many other immigrant groups, the entrepreneurial success of the Senegalese is founded on a highly developed sense of ethnic identity and solidarity, a will to succeed, and on an informal or traditional system for raising finance capital.

Black American Racial Solidarity and Economic Development

In our discussion of the racial solidarity of immigrant groups and the economic growth and opportunities it engenders for them, we do not wish to leave the impression that Black Americans are not capable of or have not experienced racial solidarity and its associated economic outcomes. Racial solidarity and self-help have a lengthy history in the Black American community and were particularly intense in the years following Reconstruction. It is no coincidence that this period was also characterized by a heavy emphasis on economic development and activity as major means of solving the economic and social problems confronting the recently emancipated Black community. August Meier (1966) informs us that "Negro conventions of the late 1870's also placed their strongest emphasis on racial solidarity, self-help, and economic advancement." He goes on to intimate that "The delegates, many of them the most distinguished leaders in the Negro community, were more concerned with self-help and economic development than with the decline of political and civil rights." Meier takes note of John Wesley Cromwell's advice to the Black American community, as editor of the *People's Advocate,* that in the name of "racial patriotism", Blacks should "award their work to colored men even where whites would perform it more cheaply, in order to build up colored tradesmen to the point where they could compete with whites."

During the 1880s and 1890s the emphasis on race pride and unity grew immensely in popularity. This emphasis on race pride was accompanied by an increased emphasis on race history. The increased interest in and writing of race history was primarily designed to refute the myth of Black racial inferiority as perpetuated by racist Whites as well as to stimulate racial solidarity. Hence, these motives coalesced to form a general movement which might be referred to as cultural nationalism. For prominent Black writers and orators frequently used the term *nation* or *nationality* when referring to the Black community of that time. Meier (ibid) noted that "In the years between the compromise of 1877 [which involved the withdrawal of Federal protection of the rights and privileges of Blacks in the South] and the Compromise of 1895 [Booker Washington's capitulation to White domination in the New South] emphasis upon race loyalty, race pride and racial solidarity, upon a sort of cultural pluralism — all evidence of ethnoculturalism or "nationalism" — visibly increased. The idea of nationalism was frequently expressed, for example, in connection with the appeal to economic racial solidarity.

The high tide of Black American entrepreneuralism and the operational establishment of corporate cities, industries, small businesses and shops, professional services, schools and universities as well as a high level of inventions by Black inventors, reflected the emphasis on Black pride dating from the failure of Reconstruction to the advent of Marcus Garvey in the 1920s. Evidence of this phenomenon was still fairly strong in many areas up until the late 1950s and early 1960s. A perusal of our review of Black entrepreneurial history in the following chapter will substantiate our claims relative to the late 1800s and early 1900s.

Thus, it is evident that conscious race solidarity, a certain level of ethnocentrism and nation-ness are as necessary to the entrepreneuralism, economic growth and development of Afrikan Americans and Afrikans the world-over as they are to non-Afrikan immigrants, White Americans and other ethnic groups elsewhere. If Afrikan American entrepreneuralism, economic growth and development are to occur again and reach the levels necessary not only for economic prosperity but for liberation from white domination, then Afrikan American race solidarity and nationalism must also be revived. For the first is not possible without the second. This means that racial solidarity must be adopted by all classes of Afrikan Americans, especially and including the relatively wealthy and Black bourgeoisie class. For to a very significant extent the failure of the Black elite, the Black wealthy and influentials to support the concept and activities denoting racial solidarity, self-help, and group economy, along with the rest of Black America, spells doom for the liberation hopes of Afrikan peoples both at home and abroad.

Immigration and the Afrikan American Community

In addition to the generally negative influence on the economic prospects of the Afrikan American community currently brought on by radical structural changes in both the national and global economy on those same prospects, the contemporary influence of waves of immigrants to the U.S. has been far from benign. This is as true today as in the past; particularly since the periods between 1970–80 and 1980–90 which saw an influx of some 6.25 and 8.7 million immigrants, respectively. *Business Week* (7/13/92) reports that "In the 1980s alone a stunning 8.7 million people poured into the U.S. matching the great immigration decade from 1900–10." It goes on to intimate that the newcomers compete for jobs with Americans, "particularly with the less skilled" [which includes the largest segment of Black workers]. Furthermore, it reports that:

> the U.S. is reaping a bonanza of highly educated foreigners. In the 1980s alone, an unprecedented 1.5 million college-educated immigrants joined the U.S. work force. More and more, America's high-tech industries, from semiconductors to biotechnology, are depending on immigrant scientists, engineers, and entrepreneurs to remain competitive. And its immigrants' links to their old countries are boosting U.S. exports to such fast-growing regions as Asia and Latin America.

A cursory look at some salient aspects of the influx of immigrants during the 1980s will allow us to make some important inferences regarding the impact of immigration on the prospects for Black American empowerment and economic well-being.

- In 1965, Congress overhauled the immigration laws that made it easier to bring relatives into the country. Prior to that, it was difficult for anyone who was not European or Canadian to settle here.
- As a result of the overhaul of the immigration laws a surge of immigrants flooded into the country from Asia and Latin America, especially from countries like South Korea and the Philippines that had close economic and military ties to the U.S. And once a group got a foothold in the U.S., it would continue to expand by bringing over more family members.

- Over the last 10 years, the U.S. granted permanent-resident status to about 1 million refugees, mostly from Vietnam, Cambodia and Laos. Over the last three years, the fastest-growing group of settlers have been from refugees from Eastern Europe and the former Soviet Union.
- Throughout the 1970s and 1980s, a total of some 5 million illegal immigrants from Mexico and other countries settled in this country.
- In the 1980s the proportion of illegal immigrants coming from Latin America and Asia rose from 31% to 84%, including illegal aliens granted amnesty under the 1986 law.
- The number of skilled immigrants has been increasing in tandem with the overall increase in numbers over the last 10 years. The level of education of recent immigrants has measurably increased.
- About one-quarter of the immigrant workers are college graduates, slightly higher than the native-born Americans. Some groups, such as Indians, Filipinos, Chinese, Koreans, are on average much better educated than today's Americans.
- U.S. industry has been eager to take advantage of the influx of immigrants. About 40% of the 200 researchers in the Communication Sciences Research wing at AT&T Bell Laboratories were born outside the U.S. The next generation of scientists and engineers at U.S. high-tech companies will be dominated by immigrants. About 51% of computer-science doctorates in 1991 went to foreign-born students.
- The 1990 changes in the immigration law, by increasing the number of visas for skilled immigrants, will increase the number of foreign graduates who remain in the U.S.
- Immigrant entrepreneurs have also made big contributions to the U.S. export boom. Businesses run by immigrants from Asia, for example, have ready-made connections overseas. They bring a global perspective and international contacts to American businesses as well as the "spirit of competing globally."
- According to an analysis of 1989 Census Bureau survey, 46% of the Asian-born immigrants have four or more years of college, compared with 34% of native-born Asian-American.[14]
- Twenty-two percent of Black immigrants have four or more years of college compared with 13% of native-born Blacks. Among Black men, the gap rises to 30% vs. 13%.*
- Between 1980-90 Asians provided 35.2%. of immigrants; Mexico, 23.7%; Caribbean, 13.1%; Central and South America, 11.1%; Canada, 1.8%; Europe 12.0%; Rest of the World [including Afrikans], 3.1%.*

Costs and Benefits of Immigration

It may be relatively easy to argue that overall, immigrants overwhelmingly of non-Afrikan descent (only a relatively small

---

14. *Cited from the *Wall Street Journal*, 3/5/93.

percentage of immigrants are of Afrikan descent: largely Afro-Caribbean, with only a rather insignificant percentage from mainland Afrika) are an economic and social benefit to the country. Certainly we cannot gainsay the fact that they have invigorated cities and suburbs, turned around some decaying neighborhoods in the inner-cities, helped to reverse the shrinking populations of at least 10 of the nation's largest cities. Moreover, immigrants provide a workforce to fill low-paid jobs and on the whole may pay more taxes than they consume. It has been estimated that some 11 million immigrants earn at least $240 billion a year and pay more than $90 billion in taxes. However, all of these favorable facts cannot belie the fact that they place added stress on scarce resources, especially educational services. Many cities are experiencing enormous difficulties in educating an exceptionally large influx of immigrant youngsters. This has added to the problems of preexistent overcrowding, general inadequacy and under-funding in many school systems as well as the need to expand services to meet the special needs of immigrant school children. For example, some school systems must deal with a school population which speaks well over 100 different languages. A similar situation exists with regard to health services.

Even the contention that immigrant families pay more in taxes annually than they receive in public services is questionable. Donald Huddle, Professor Emeritus of economics at Rice University, in a letter to the editor of the *New York Times* (1/26/94) argues that the above contention is "clearly wrong." He further asserted that based on his and the research of other experts:

> ...each permanent Mexican immigrant in California had a public service deficit of more than $1,000 annually in 1982.
>
> My own recent national study found that the national after-tax deficit of post-1970 immigrants, both legal and illegal, exceeds $2,000 per immigrant — a total cost of more than $42 billion. Comparatively, the native born had a surplus on public services after taxation.
>
> This is not surprising. Data from the 1990 Census show that the poverty rate of post-1970 immigrants is 42 percent higher than that of the native born... High welfare usage, combined with low earnings (meaning low taxes), means that immigrants must run a public-service deficit that is financed by the native born with low welfare and higher earnings (meaning higher taxes).
>
> [...The] belief that immigrants do not displace Americans in the labor market has been repudiated by a number of careful studies in recent years. A consensus is developing...that for each six or seven immigrants, one unskilled or blue-collar job is lost to Americans. As Richard Bean of the University of Texas recently showed, slow growth

areas are particularly prone to labor displacement. As in California during the 1990's, many native born, according to Randy Filer in a National Bureau of Economic Research study, end up fleeing the region to avoid job losses and falling wage levels.

We cannot deny that there is a struggle between Afrikan Americans and newcomers over jobs and access to scarce public and private resources. Many Afrikan Americans, 73% according to a *Business Week*/Harris Poll,[15] believe that the success of immigrants has in good part come at the expense of the Black community. They also believe that both White-owned and immigrant-owned businesses would rather hire immigrants than Afrikan Americans, especially Afrikan-American males. Furthermore, immigrants do most damage to the job prospects of native-born high school dropouts, already hard-pressed to find meaningful employment. John Sullivan, who researches immigration, summarizes some of the economic and social costs of the high influx of immigrants to Afrikan Americans thusly:

> Congress is considering a number of bills designed to combat illegal immigration, which is praiseworthy, but the need to address legal immigration is being ignored. Especially ignored is the crippling effect legal immigration has on inner-city African Americans.
>
> A study of General Accounting Office illustrates this effect. The GAO found that in Los Angeles, three-fourths of the unionized African American janitors who cleaned high-rise office buildings were displaced by Mexican immigrants in only a five-year period. This displacement occurred even though total janitorial employment rose because the Mexicans were willing to work for lower wages. These Mexicans were not illegal immigrants stealing jobs but were legally admitted to this country.
>
> In Miami, Cuban immigration is keeping African Americans out of jobs where Spanish proficiency is required. In Houston and San Diego, this same barrier exists. Even in shops in neighborhoods that are virtually all African American, African Americans are seldom employed.
>
> The reason is not necessarily racism on the part of the store owners. The explanation is more likely found in the family unification policy at the heart of American immigration.
>
> Since 1965, the primary goal of immigration has been family unity. Immediate relatives of American citizens — spouse, children, parents, even cousins — can join their family without numerical limit. The result of "this migration" has been disastrous to the job hopes of inner-city African Americans.

---

15. *Business Week*, July 13, 1992.

Take the example of a Korean convenience store owner. Typically, the Korean immigrates to the United States and, through the virtues of working long hours and living frugally, manages to save money. His savings, coupled with a loan at 30 percent interest from the local Korean businessman's association, allow him to open a convenience store. Now that he is a store owner, he brings over his wife and brother to work in the store. Korean is spoken here; the employees may speak little or no English. Anyone hoping to work in the shop will have to speak Korean, which disqualifies area African Americans.

My intention is not to single out Koreans; with some variations, this story applies to Vietnamese, Pakistanis, or any of dozens of immigrant groups. Ethnic networking shuts out African Americans so thoroughly that a study of immigration in New York City concluded, "There are tens of thousands of jobs in New York for which the native born are not candidates."

...Blue-collar, entry-level jobs served as the first step up the ladder into the mainstream economy for groups like the Irish, Italians and Jews. Continued widespread immigration in fact deny too many inner-city African Americans the same opportunity to step onto the bottom rungs of the ladder and begin the ascent from poverty.[16]

Many Afrikan Americans have come to perceive entrepreneurial immigrants as aggressively exploiting their communities, this while hiring few community persons, entering into few business partnerships and other mutually beneficial arrangements with native residents, refusing to reside in the communities where they do business, and demonstrating the same anti-Black attitudes and prejudices as do native-born White Americans. It is clear that the immigrant and non-Black owners of the business and service organizations which thrive in Afrikan American communities or serve predominantly Afrikan American clients, do not reside in those communities, provide little financial support to community in the form of taxes and other types of contributions, and as a result, help to intensify the hypersegregation, economic and social isolation of Afrikan Americans. The denuding of inner-city communities of their resources and wealth and the further isolating of their residents serve to concentrate poverty, joblessness, welfare dependency, single-parenthood, teenage pregnancy, drug abuse, disease and sickness, poor education, crime — a complex interlocking set of social and economic disorders in those same communities. Without malice toward non-community, immigrant and native-born non-resident owners of inner-city businesses and services, we must acknowledge that the tremendous outflow of monetary, human, material and non-

---

16. *The City Sun*, 8/25–31/1993.

material resources from the Afrikan American inner-city communities at the hands of these agents, in addition to the institutional racist practices of the nation as a whole, cannot but grievously harm these communities. The continuation of these private and public practices will not only maintain and hasten the further decline of the already too-low level of Afrikan American political and economic power, but will also accentuate and accelerate the precipitous increase in the social disorganization of inner-city communities. These practices help to increase their social problems, such as violent crime, homicide, family decomposition, joblessness, drug addiction, and the like.

It can be clearly demonstrated that throughout the history of the United States, immigrant groups, first white ethnics followed by non-white ethnics, have benefitted from racist governmental and private social practices and restrictions against Black Americans. Cross (1987) contends that "Immigrant American groups were major participants in erecting the racial codes that excluded qualified blacks from jobs...White ethnics in large numbers not only used the political system to economic advantage, but also were prime actors in politically disenfranchising blacks and in unconstitutionally manipulating state power to prevent Blacks from voting and influencing the political process." The same discriminatory governmental and social practices, which, as in the past, vitiated "the strong Afro-American services businesses which had been developing since the 1700s [and which] were replaced with other ethnic businesses", are still operating against Black economic interests today (Butler, 1991). The economic progress of Afrikan Americans has historically correlated with the ebb and flow of immigrants. For example, Fusfeld and Bates (1984) point out that "only with the cessation of immigration and the start of World War I did economic opportunity open the way to ending the coerced labor of the rural South." Butler (1991) elaborates this point:

> Given the development of legal segregation in the South and racial distinctions in the North, the pattern of racial interactions was set for decades to come. While Japanese, Italians, Jews, and other ethnics developed business activities and were free to place their enterprises in the major growth areas in the city (and, of course, in their own neighborhoods) and take advantage of the free enterprise system, Afro-Americans found themselves limited by law and unable to pursue this simple tenet of free enterprise.

Light and Bonacich (1988) in their study of immigrant entrepreneurs, particularly of Koreans in Los Angeles, conclude that "The United States plays an important role in driving immigrants to its doors...Immigration policy does not exist in a vacuum — as much as politicians would like to keep it there. It is intimately tied to foreign policy, including economic aid, trade, cultural influence, military assistance, and political interferences. U.S. foreign policy in South Korea (as in many other countries) has a direct and indirect impact on the immigration of peoples to this country." Light and Bonacich go on to contend that in particular, "...Korean enterprise has various links to segments of the American capitalist class. Korean small business served as a cheap labor sector from which both monetary and non-monetary benefits could be drawn. Korean immigrant enterprise helped U.S. big businesses to earn greater profits. And these small firms helped to undermine the local class struggle. As such, the U.S. capitalist class had an interest in encouraging immigrant entrepreneurship." Furthermore, they contend "that government policy may have provided special encouragement to immigrant entrepreneurship above and beyond the general national fostering of small business enterprises."

The impact of immigration on its power and socioeconomic prospects, must be realistically and objectively faced-up to by the Afrikan American community. This customarily liberal, sharing community must confront the fact that in its relative poverty and powerlessness it cannot continue to permit its vital resources to be commandeered by aliens. It must aggressively accumulate external earnings, retain as much of its internal resources as possible, and invest in itself first, if it is to survive and prosper throughout the coming centuries. Moreover, the Afrikan American community must enhance its political power to the degree that it can effectively influence U.S. internal and external policies in its own interests and the interests of Afrikan peoples worldwide.

Internal Migration within the United States: The Flight from Diversity. It is tempting to imagine the influx of immigrants into the United States as producing an ethnically and culturally mixed population which values and profits from its cultural diversity. However, an analysis of recent U.S. census data indicates that this is not the case. Actually, the opposite trend seems to be occurring. In reporting on a demographic study of census data, *Forbes* magazine (8/94) revealed the following results.

> According to University of Michigan demographer William H. Frey, the 1990 census shows clearly that international immigration and internal migration are resulting in a spontaneous phenomenon of racial self-sorting in the U.S. Only in a few big cities, like New York and Los Angeles, are all racial groups present in force.

Individuals of every race, of course, can be found anywhere. But Frey thinks the U.S. may be on its way to becoming a collection of several unique different societies, at least in terms of their racial makeup. This is in sharp contrast to 1900, when the U.S. was white, with a black majority that was still virtually confined to the South....

Racial self-sorting is being exacerbated by minority immigration unleashed by the 1965 immigration reform. Only 15% of the 6 million legal immigrants to the U.S. in the 1980s came from Europe or Canada; 45% came from Asia; 38% from Latin America.

These new Americans tend to stick together. Three-quarters of all immigrants go to six states: California, Texas, Illinois, Florida, New York, New Jersey.

Forbes goes on to report Frey as saying, "And now, for the first time, we're also seeing native-born Americans leaving whole regions." Current ethnic migratory trends point to Blacks leaving California and midwestern "rust belt" states for the South. Native-born Whites from the Bay Area of Southern California, Texas, New York City and other areas are migrating or gravitating toward the north and east. Much of the U.S. interior remains more than 95% White (*Forbes*, 8/94). The general migratory trend of Blacks is now toward the South, a reversal of earlier trends for this group. U.S.-resident Cubans continue to converge on Miami and Asians on California from various points in the nation. Even in states and regions where all ethnic groups tend to gravitate, such as Florida, they tend to converge on racially distinct regions or areas. *Forbes* goes on to intimate the following:

Of course, immigrants have formed enclaves before. "What's new, says demographer Frey, "is the scale. The immigrant flow is relatively larger and has lasted longer. What's also new is that with today's easy mobility, it's easier for native-born Americans who don't like living among the newer groups to flee into their own enclaves. *We seem to be seeing the beginning of a flight from diversity*" [Emphasis added].

The trends we have discussed along with other similar and related data included in this volume and elsewhere, clearly point to the fact that while it is trendy to speak of the "global village", of multi-culturalism", "diversity", and the like, ethnocentrism, ethnic conflicts, and ethnic sub-partitioning of the nation and world seem to be accelerating rather than diminishing. This implies that the assimilationistic ideology which guides the thinking of the Afrikan American leadership establishment and forms the emotional and cognitive platform for its political and socioeconomic plans and activities, is not grounded in reality. Therefore, the programmatic approaches and activities sponsored by this establishment and which it imposes on the Afrikan American community are not only unrealistic and counterproductive, but are actually undermining and destroying the ability of the community to survive, let alone prosper.

A Refrain: Wealth and Power

The economic stories of Korean Americans, Jewish Americans, White Americans, and other ethnic Americans overwhelmingly demonstrate the substantial positive correlation between ethnic self-centered identity and the accumulation of wealth and political and various other forms of power. Under the regime of American capitalism these forms of power are ultimately founded on the ownership and control of property, resources, means of production, and of vital and influential institutions. This brings us directly to the point of the political-economic powerlessness of America's largest minority group — Afrikans in America.

Black economist David Swinton, in a lengthy series of annual reports regarding the economic status of African Americans for the National Urban League's *The State of Black America 1993*, has noted time and time again that the "persisting relative inequality in the current economic status of black Americans reflects the persistence of limited economic power." He further noted that "in many respects, the absolute and relative labor market position of African Americans worsened [over the 12 years of the Reagan-Bush era, i.e., 1980-1992]; ...the central tendency of the group as a whole has been stagnation or retrogression in absolute status and increased disparities in relative status." Swinton concludes that "it is unlikely that economic parity could ever be obtained in our capitalistic economic system without significant attenuation of the racial gaps in ownership." After making the very pertinent observation that "Economic power flows from ownership of human and nonhuman capital," Swinton further contends that the "*empowerment of the African-American community to obtain and maintain economic parity through its own efforts will be impossible without the elimination of the large and glaring disparities in wealth ownership.*"[17] [Emphasis added]

Swinton goes on to argue that both the absolute and relative economic status of an individual or group is to the largest extent, determined by business and resource ownership. He provides the following reasons in support of this contention:

---

17. *State of Black America 1993*, p. 137.

1. Ownership provides income either in the form of the earnings from assets or in the form of the services provided by the asset...Thus, the individual or group that owns more will also have higher income and consumption, all else equal.
2. Ownership of wealth is important because owners organize and control production either directly or indirectly in a capitalistic system. They determine the quantity, location, and nature of investment; how much, what type, and whose resources to employ; and they determine how much, what type, and whose goods and services to purchase. Thus, ownership enables an individual or group to have greater influence on the development, employment, and renumeration of their human and nonhuman resources.[18]

Swinton's references to capitalism, to the capitalist system, and to the fact that ownership of resources is closely bound up with power in that system, underlies the central thrust of our contention in this section: *If the Afrikan American community is to exercise effective power and influence in American society and in the world, then it must concomitantly exercise ownership and control of some of America's and the world's important economic resources.*

The Asian Brotherhood Collective

The global balance of economic power is undergoing a phenomenal shift as the economies of East Asia threaten to catch up with and overrun those of Japan and the West. In the economies of Hong Kong, Taiwan and China, business classes are dominated by *ethnic Chinese* who do business according to a distinctively *Chinese model*. In just one generation they are creating their own wealth at a speed and scale unmatched in recent history. The East Asian governments, which include China, Hong Kong, Indonesia, Malaysia, Singapore, Taiwan and Thailand, enriched by years of export surpluses, high savings rates (China's savings rates alone amounts to 40% of GNP and Taiwan's savings rate is currently 27% of GDP, down from 40% in the mid-80s) and prudent management of their wealth, have amassed some $250 billion in foreign reserves. This is in addition to the $600 billion in cash reserves held by the region's corporations. It is generally expected by many economic analysts that with savings increasing some $550 billion annually, East Asia's purchasing power will surpass that of Japan's within 10 years.

The region is fast becoming the world's largest source of liquid capital and of investable wealth. In 1993, Hong Kong alone held $235 billion in investable capital by its government and corporations, and

---
18. Ibid., p. 137.

in foreign reserves. Taiwan held $215 billion dollars, Malaysia 46, Singapore 76, Thailand 45, and Indonesia 36. In 1990, China held $38 billion, and though figures are not available for 1993 it is certain that the current growth of investable capital it holds has grown very significantly. All of this adds up to the fact that East Asia is very rapidly becoming able to finance its phenomenal economic growth and meet most of its development needs from its own internal resources. The region no longer depends on Western capital markets to the critical degree it did in the past.

What is relevant to our discussion here is the role ethnicity plays in the remarkable economic growth of East Asia (a role played in the growth and development of peoples, nations, empires, and regions throughout history). We have already indicated that the business classes of Southeast Asia are dominated by the ethnic Chinese. Through what is referred to as *guanxi* [connections] the ethnic Chinese are funding the emergence of a thriving China. Ethnic Chinese-based *guanxi* revolve around a number of brokers whose deal-making depends on extensive personal ties between wealthy private citizens and regional leaders. This extraordinarily powerful, informal network and its financial structures have yet to be fully comprehended or penetrated by outsiders. As noted by *Business Week*, the network serves a critically important function:

> [I]nterpersonal networks are critical for moving information and capital quickly.
>
> To get into the loop, insiders spend years cultivating politicians and building trust. When they learn of an opportunity, they give friends first crack. Financing for a $100 million property deal can be arranged in days, with personal trust taking precedence over due diligence.[19]

Business Week goes on to indicate that while one is not excluded from these networks because he is not Chinese, he must understand how the deals are done and must bring something to the table. The networks are seen by many analysts as transitional institutions which will be replaced by more sophisticated financial systems, systems that operate according to the clarity and transparency of law. This will facilitate the movement of Asia's wealth out beyond the rather narrow financial networks (networks which if they become corrupt oligarchies may impoverish once-rich nations, e.g., the Philippines, once the region's richest nation is now one of its poorest) into a much more broadly based and coherent financial/economic system. Those nations

---

19. "Asia's Wealth," *Business Week's* cover story, 11/29/93.

best able to accomplish this are expected to achieve a high level of success, not inevitable for all Asian nations.

> Asia's winners will be those countries that harness the billions generated by shopkeepers, small manufacturers, and white-collar workers, making them the driving force of development.

The same axiom may be said to apply in the case of the Afrikan American community and in all the communities of the Afrikan diaspora. However, the lesson that the fascinating story of East Asia teaches us is that it is fundamentally an *Asian* story, a story in which *Asians*, ethnic Chinese to be more exact, are among its principal characters. Ethnicity plays a major role in the Asian economic drama. It has and does play the major role in the economic drama of all nations and peoples. More accurately, it may be said that ethnicity and culture, culture which stresses cooperation, altruism, work, education, merit, thriftiness, concern for the future, solidarity, creativity, innovativeness, ethical behavior, are key elements for markedly improving a nation's or community's economic fortunes. Isn't it curious that ethnic Afrikan Americans are taught and motivated to realize the very opposite values? — that they should downgrade or deny their ethnicity, not develop an Afrikan-centered culture, should assimilate themselves out of existence, practice no level of ethnic exclusion, allow all other groups to monopolize their markets; that to support their own businesses and community first is to engage in "reverse racism"; that undiscriminating, unbridled consumption — particularly of non-Afrikan manufactured, wholesaled and retailed products and services — means freedom and equality; that they cannot finance their own growth and betterment without outside or government aid! Can there be little wonder why this community whose gross earned income ranks it among the richest nations in the world is functionally impoverished?

The White Brotherhood Collective

The archetypal White brotherhood collective, like the brotherhood collectives which characterize other ethnic groups, has taken and takes many different forms such as bands of warriors, priesthoods, monastic orders, guilds, consortiums, and the like (Smith, 1990). These collectives, based on commonalities of ethnicity, cultural values and goals, take advantage of the group-mind their association breeds to "create a wide variety of rule-governed social practices such as language, games, trading, and markets, and mythic structures such as law, politics, and religion" (Smith, 1990). Generally, all the members of the brotherhood are considered to be equal to each other and strive to achieve homogeneity. They are disturbed and disrupted by difference and therefore are motivated to deny it and to exclude or marginalize those members within the group whose biological and/or cultural differences may be too obvious. For these reasons such groups tend toward racism and sexism.

Black men, particularly if they insist on not denying their Afrikan descent, will rarely, if ever, be accepted as the same as White men by the White brotherhood collective. Their achievement of equal status within this brethren is highly unlikely or impossible. The White brotherhood collective as such, functions primarily as the central instrument of White power — a power in good part based on its subordination and exploitation of Afrikan and other non-White peoples, as well as the lower classes of White peoples. Therefore Blacks cannot simultaneously be at one with and at the same time separate subjects of White power.

As J.C. Smith contends, "monopoly is the essence of power." The exercise of power by the White American ruling elite requires that it retains a monopoly of three kinds of power — physical or military power, economic power, and ideological power. "Physical power entails the capacity to use brute force on other persons [or peoples]. Economic power entails the capacity to grant or withhold economic benefits, whether in terms of money, property, or resources. Ideological power consists of the capacity to affect other people's actions by persuasion" (Smith, ibid). It is the monopolistic possession by the ruling White brotherhood collective of a combination of physical, economic, and ideological power which enables it to dominate the other white classes and the Afrikan American community. That this view of power monopolies allows the White brotherhood collective to dominate American society is in essence the same as that advanced by C.W. Wright Mills in his seminal and controversial analysis of power in America, in his popular book *The Power Elite*. Power in America, according to Mills, is possessed and controlled by a single, interlocking structure of power — *a power elite* whose power is concentrated at the top of three domains: "the corporation chieftains, the political directorate [governmental organizations], and the warlords [military organizations]. Other important institutions are subordinate to and generally supportive of those three major institutions of power.

The brotherhood in which we are most interested at the moment is the corporate brotherhood of the White male collective — "the brotherhoods of producers, merchants, and bankers [who] organize and control economic power" (Smith, ibid). These brotherhoods together represent the apex of the White pyramidal structure, since economic power is the primary means of directly and indirectly controlling military and ideological power. The insatiable drive to accumulate wealth, which characterizes capitalism and the White male corporate brotherhood, is synonymous with the drive to dominate, to exercise power primarily through the withholding or granting of capital. Thus the "free market" capitalism, the central source of power of the White Brotherhood collective, cannot be truly free and access to it not be really freely available to all other groups — especially to a brotherhood collective of Afrikan males, members of a subject people. The market system as created and monopolized by the White Brotherhood Collective is an economic instrument by which the White male corporate elite disciplines and orders American society; by which it maintains its quintessential class and race-based social order. The market system is the White Brotherhood Collective's instrument of power and social control, its primary instrument for maintaining the racial and social inequalities that are essential to its very existence and functionality. Capitalism is a social and political regime wherein those who own and control property — e.g., the means of production (land, capital, equipment and other resources) enter into unequal contracts with the propertyless (i.e., workers, laborers), with classes of people who are unable to secure a living unless they can gain access to privately owned resources or wealth, and who in exchange for wage payments, must surrender all claims to the products of their labor to the owners of capital.

> *What is of essence under capitalism is that gains from whatever origin normally accrue to the owners of capital, not to workers, managers, or government officials.*[20]

The American market economy, dominated as it is by the White Brotherhood Collective, is not a "free market," for access to it is withheld or granted by this brotherhood based on any criteria it chooses — one exclusionary criterion includes being of Afrikan descent. Consequently, the White man's "free market" imprisons the Black man — when it does not enslave him. It is a system that by its very logic, structural dynamics, rules, and the ideology which justifies it, operates to maintain the supreme power of the White Brotherhood Collective which monopolizes it. The power of the White Brotherhood Collective is coterminous with the power of the market forces themselves, power which rests on conventionalized responses to its movements by the propertyless, their programmed acceptance of its

---

20. Robert Heilbroner, *Behind the Veil of Economics: Essays in the Worldly Philosophy* (New York: W.W. Norton, 1988).

legitimacy and ready obedience to its demands. This aspect of the capitalist market system leads Heilbroner to conclude:

> that economists take for granted that the dispositions of the market will not be resisted by other means of material allocation, such as force. If men and women are unable to enter into successful market relations — whether as workers or consumers — it is assumed they will acquiesce in social defeat even though the enforcing agency is only the impersonal authority of the exchange mechanism itself. The assumption is amply borne out in reality: Only on the rarest and most desperate occasions do unsatisfied individuals attempt to disobey the market system by violating its dispensations. In the vast majority of cases, its provisioning arrangements are accepted without question; and the law, which silently stands behind the market, remains uninvoked — but not on that account unneeded.

The capacity of the market to secure acquiescence in a provisioning process in which the surplus automatically accrues to the property of only one class obviously makes the market mechanism an executive instrument for a particular social order, precisely as the dispositions of command or reciprocity make these systems the instruments for the reproduction of their respective social orders. Put as simply as possible, this is to say no more than that capitalism, like tribal societies, imperial kingdoms, feudalisms, or socialist states, are at bottom regimes of power and privilege, built on the granite of family ties, community norms, and above all, on a deeply inculcated "habit of subordination."

The White Brotherhood Collective's uncontested monopoly of capital and the dominating power it undergirds rests largely on a would-be Black Brotherhood Collective's "habit of subordination", on its atomized individuality, and its vitiating ambivalence in regard to its collective identity and unwillingness to use its identity as a basis for acquiring capital and property, and deriving from them the power to challenge that held by its White counterpart. Every ethnic or immigrant group that has gained a significant foothold in the American market system and has gained substantial economic and political benefits for itself and its members has done so by making full, practical use of its ethnocultural resources. The problems which face all immigrant and subordinate groups in America who are concerned with achieving power and prosperity, or just good, decent wages, have been how to gain and maintain control over their ethnic resources, over access to their markets, and how to harness the power potential contained in their ethnicity to activate and direct it for achieving their social, economic and political goals. While these groups have made and are making use of their ethnicity to found brotherhood collectives as means of advancing their economic and political interests, Black Americans are discouraged from utilizing the same mechanism, most often by their well-meaning "friends", and by an uninformed, assimilationist, bourgeois leadership establishment.

The Black Brotherhood Collective

It is interesting and important to reiterate the fact that the primary financiers funding the phenomenal growth and development of Southeastern Asia are the ethnic Chinese. They are also the leading entrepreneurs and power brokers setting the pace and defining the form of the rapidly maturing world-class economy. What is equally interesting and important is the fact that the leading Asian financiers and powerbrokers are Asian *males*. They are in essence an Asian Brotherhood Collective, an informal and formal fraternal group of males who combine their resources and talents, utilize common languages and symbol systems, social-bonding rituals and values, in order to empower themselves to achieve mutually beneficial ends. In this they follow a long and grand tradition, one beginning perhaps with the hunting band and apparently founded in the primal genetic urge of humans to socially bond together to form enduring social institutions (i.e., definite, consistent ways of relating to and interacting with each other) within gender and ethnic boundaries. As J.C. Smith contends, "The proliferation of male fraternal organizations throughout the world and throughout history reflects a male complex which drives the male to band together into close-knit groups. Whether these are sacred priesthoods, monastic orders, military orders, secret societies, fraternal orders, or merely private men's clubs, they are a product of behavior which reflects a psychological basis." For better or worse, dominant corporate structures whether economic and/or political, or religious regimes, have generally been founded, developed and controlled by brotherhood collectives — males often belonging to the same ethnocultural or racial group. This is still true today. Men band together against other men and in games of war, sports or business, struggle against each other for supremacy or in defense of their independence and liberty. The struggle for economic supremacy or self-defense between ethnic bands of males may in good part be seen as a more benign form of warfare operating essentially according to rules of the game, the strategies and tactics which are in essence the same as or similar to those of war — with essentially the same or similar outcomes. To the victor goes the spoils and the power; to the vanquished, the bitter fruits of defeat. In economic warfare as in military warfare, the losers may face not only political subordination and tyranny, humiliation and social degradation, but poverty and starvation, and perhaps genocidal elimination.

Perhaps not coincidentally, in the same *Business Week* publication (11/29/93) which so excitedly reported on how ethnic male Chinese-led "financial power is creating new markets, industries, and cities ...[which] will change the world," a special report titled "Inside The Black Business Network – A far-flung web of entrepreneurs and executives is driving African American economic growth," was also included. This network is predominantly composed of Afrikan American males — 40 of them, and 4 females. Included in this "brotherhood collective" of, for all practical purposes, Black males are the likes of Ron Brown, commerce secretary [since deceased]; Earl Graves, owner, *Black Enterprise;* Percy Sutton, owner, InnerCity Broadcasting; General Colin Powell, former chairman, Joint Chiefs of Staff; Robert Johnson, CEO, Black Entertainment Television; John Johnson, owner, Johnson Publications (*Ebony*); Bill Cosby; Quincy Jones; Michael Jackson; Julius Erving; Earvin "Magic" Johnson; Spike Lee; Michael Jordan; J. Bruce Llewelyn, owner, Queen City Broadcasting, Philadelphia Coca-Cola Bottling; A. Barry Rand, Executive VP, Operations, Xerox; John Jacobs, former President, National Urban League, among other Blacks prominent in business, politics, religion and entertainment. *Business Week* describes the network:

> Welcome to *The Network* — an informal, but powerful, system of contacts and relationships that is helping drive economic growth in the African American business community. At its core it is a cadre of entrepreneurs and a smattering of high-ranking corporate executives who together make up the black business elite. But it envelops countless of the African American businesspeople and heavy hitters in politics, social activism, and religion. With much the same energy that characterized the civil rights struggle, this network is focused squarely on economic development. The eyes still on the prize these days is a slice of wealth and influence in what remains *a business world dominated by white males* [Emphasis added].

After frankly noting "that ethnic groups have been networking in this country for years to claim a share of the nation's wealth and power," e.g., the Polish in Chicago, Irish in Boston, Jews and Italians in New York, Cubans in Miami, and the Koreans in Los Angeles, the report points out that the Black network is distinguished by its national scope and reach which "is far deeper than that of other ethnic networks." An example of how members of this group mutually interact follows:

Leg up. A prime example is Bruce LLewellyn, arguably the most prosperous black entrepreneur in mainstream business. In building his three main companies — Philadelphia Coca-Cola Bottling, Queen City Broadcasting, and Garden State Television — he used all the benefits the network has to offer.

LLewellyn proved himself during the 1970s, when he built up Bronx-based Fedco Foods Corp. from $18 million in sales to the largest minority retailer in the U.S. Annual sales neared $100 million when he sold it in 1982. After that, he turned to soft-drink bottling and got a leg up with Coke when his cousin, General Colin L. Powell, put in a good word with Charles W. Duncan Jr., who was president of Coca-Cola Co. before becoming Deputy Defense Secretary and Powell's boss of the late 1970s. It didn't hurt that Operation PUSH was targeting Coke at the time, charging that it has done little to open its lucrative bottling franchises to minorities.

When he ventured into broadcasting in 1985, LLewellyn was similarly resourceful. First, he tapped a roster of investors that reads like a Who's Who in the African American community. He has drawn on Ed Lewis from *Essence* and Bill Cosby. Betty Shabazz, Malcolm X's widow, invests with LLewellyn, as do wealthy sports figures O.J. Simpson and Julius Erving.

Part of the allure was that during the 1970s, a handful of white and black members of Congress had persuaded the Federal Communications Commission to bestow rich tax advantages on those who sold broadcast properties to minorities. Since the program, there have been more than 300 such sales. The properties that make up Queen City and Garden State Cable are among them.

For the black network, the linkage of politics, activism, and business is key. While Caucasian ethnic groups have been able to gain wealth and fold seemlessly into the white power base, that's not always possible for blacks. Prejudice remains a barrier. "There's a multistage process through which you emerge into the mainstream," says Northwestern University economist Marcus Alexis. "Blacks have to look at how others have moved along and understand where we are in relationship to where we have to go. This is just the beginning."[21]

This "beginning" is a rather auspicious one. The fact that this so-called Black Business Network or as we choose to call it for heuristic purposes, the Black Brotherhood Collective, is ethnically based, provides it with what could be a solid, workable foundation for future growth and empowerment. However, despite its ethnicity, there are some serious doubts as to its deeply rooted connections with the Afrikan American community in particular, and the worldwide

---

21. *Business Week*, 11/29/93.

Afrikan community in general, and its full commitment to enhancing the lives and power of Afrikan peoples across the diaspora. There is certainly among the network members many who sincerely entertain such concerns and commitment and whose careers have demonstrated the same. But the fact that, as *Business Week* reports, "Most of the elite belong to the same civic organizations, from the NAACP to the Urban League," and are for the most part racial assimilationists, puts in question whether they possess or will develop the know-how and the persistence of will to advance the interests of the Afrikan American community and of the international Afrikan community — or any other interests than their own insular concerns. While "some worry the network risks leaving large portions of the African American community behind," and Northwestern University economist Marcus Alexis expresses the sentiment that "our greatest challenge is finding a way to make opportunities for the people in the inner cities," there are others who not only do not express such a concern or sentiment but are hostile to its implications. *Business Week* (ibid) notes such hostility, or at best, ambivalence, in the following:

> Others, such as consultant Andrew F. Brimmer, the first black governor of the Federal Reserve Board, believes holding blacks to such a standard is unfair. "I do not see why black businesses should have any more responsibility that anyone else to improve life for blacks," Brimmer says.
>
> Most networks fall somewhere in between. While many give copiously to groups such as the Urban League and United Negro College Fund, the prevailing ethic is that a rising tide lifts all boats. And that leads to another concern: *For all of its enthusiasm, some worry that the black businesses community is continually co-opted by white-owned businesses with deeper pockets.*

An Afrikan nationalist cabal, this group is not. A number of its members and a significant number of Black businesses and professional persons who refuse membership in this group resonate to the sentiments expressed by non-member, "and superlawyer Vernon E. Jordan [who] takes great pains to underscore his independence, bristles at the notion of lumping black business people in a separate group." "I don't have a role in that network," Jordan says, noting that he's a lawyer, not a businessperson. "You have to transcend race in this process." Jordan puts his finger on the irritating and paralyzing dilemma the Network and would-be "successful" Black business persons and professionals face. Their assimilationist orientations, and client status relative to their White patrons and sponsors, and their need to be fully accepted in White society in order to acquire wealth, "freedom" and respectability, to achieve their acceptance into the White corporate elite as "honorary" White men, require their self-negation, self-alienation, the transcendence of their race, (note that Whites and other ethnics do not have to meet such stringent requirements) and rely on their not reminding Whites of their ethnic difference. Their "success," like the success of their White counterparts with whom they urgently desire to merge to the point of invisibility, requires the "unsuccess" of the Afrikan American community as a whole. This means, however, that their success depends on their not being perceived as Afrikans, their not being perceived as Afrikans representing the interests of Afrikan peoples in addition to their own. Their position as "honorary" Whites is tense, tenuous and revocable, weak, schizophrenic, ineffectual, powerless and cowardly. They correctly intuit that their success can do little to enrich or empower the Afrikan American community. Their worry is whether they, for "thirty pieces of silver", have allied themselves with forces bent on its total disempowerment and possible genocidal demise, and whether they will suffer the same fate as the community from whom they have so valiantly sought to dissociate themselves.

If the Network would regain its common sense and apprise itself of the history of how the world works, how financial empires and great ethnic and national economies have and are truly built and protected, it would realize that its attempts to gain entry into the White corporate elite by cutting itself off from its cultural and ethnic base is foredoomed to ignominious failure. The Network suffers from a massive and inexcusable lack of understanding of the workings of the White American brotherhood collective as well as of its economic underpinnings.

The Network, or as we shall refer to it, the Black Brotherhood Collective, is unlikely to empower the Afrikan American community for the very reason that its assimilationist yearnings motivate it to disassociate itself from its power bases — its Afrikan ethnicity, Afrikan-centered identity and consciousness. This establishment renders itself powerless by its futile attempts to merge with the White Brotherhood Collective and thereby regain the manhood it has lost, and fears it cannot re-gain by dint of its own will to power. In trying to "transcend race" it becomes neither Black nor White and therefore cannot be accepted into full membership by either Black or White brotherhoods. It can only exist in limbo, in an in-between, identity-less, pointless world.

The White Brotherhood Collective or any fully functional brotherhood collective captures and yields power not because it "transcends race," but because it single-mindedly pursues its self-centered interests; not because it wishes to disassociate itself from its ethnocultural group but, to the contrary, because of it. For members of the White Brotherhood Collective, the group-mind it generates through exclusive association

> functions [first] as an object of the ego ideal into which the self can be merged, and second, *it functions as an instrument of power. Individuals seek both to merge the self into the group and to merge the group into the self.* As a person becomes a part of the group, the group becomes a part of him. Group and individual merge so that the power of the group is felt and enjoyed by its individual members. Outside of the group the individual is naked and alone. The self is minuscule. Within the group each self takes on the power of the group and shares the sense of omnipotence.[22] [Emphasis added]

If a Black Brotherhood Collective is to successfully counter this group it, too, must in no uncertain terms proclaim its Afrikanicity and act in terms of its group identity. Each of its members, too, must merge the self into the group and merge the group into the self. It must gain the loyal followship of its community by being the community's primary patron, protector and nurturer. It must become the primary arbiter of Afrikan community values, beliefs, ideologies, modes of consciousness, tastes and desires as it acts to facilitate the ownership and control of its internal markets by the community itself; to facilitate increases in the community's savings rate so that it can accumulate large amounts of capital and property under the control of its own financial institutions; to facilitate the development of large, cooperatively owned financial and commercial institutions and networks whose resources can be utilized to penetrate the White-dominated market system successfully and influentially as well as help to finance the growth and development of Afrikan nations and peoples across the diaspora; to facilitate the political organization of the community such that it can not only influence American domestic governmental policies for its own benefit but also for the benefit of Afrikan peoples everywhere. These goals are achievable not by playing by all of the mythological and mythical rules of the market system as hypocritically broadcast by the White Brotherhood Collective, but by mastering the techniques by which the resources and power potential of both the national and international Afrikan community are enhanced and are owned and controlled by Afrikans, and are transformed into instruments of Black Power.

---

22. J.C. Smith, p. 326.

Chapter 15

AFRIKA AGONISTES

Dangerous Economic Straits of Contemporary Afrika

Just as domestic and global economic structural changes are threatening the economic future of the Afrikan American community so are they threatening the future viability of the Afrikan continent. The benign neglect which defines the economic policy of the national community toward the Black American community also defines the economic policy of the White American/European community toward the international Afrikan community. The scope of this volume will allow for only the sketchiest description of the economic position of continental Afrika vis-à-vis the United States, Europe and Asia. However, this too brief description should provide us with enough information to accurately surmise that if the Afrikan American and continental Afrikan communities do not revolutionarily restructure and reprioritize their social-political relations, identity and consciousness, values and goals, economic organizations and cultural wills to power, they shall quite likely perish or be trampled time and again under the boots of domination of one ascending ethnocultural group after the another.

The consequences of EuroAmerican policy prescriptions and practices with regard to Afrika have left her as exploited, impoverished and disempowered today as she was after having been subjected to wave after wave of colonial land-grabbing during the great "scramble for Afrika" in the 1880s.[1]

Impoverishing of Afrika:
IMF/World Bank and U.S. Policy

The following citation taken from a very lengthy three-part series published in the *New York Times* on the contemporary economic and social world of Afrika titled, "Survival Test: Can Africa Rebound" (6/19, 6/20, 6/21/94) provides a very sketchy description of Afrika's overall economic situation.

> It is hard to exaggerate the depth of Africa's economic crisis.
> Consider this fact: Excluding South Africa, the 1991 gross national product of all countries south of the Sahara — a swath of the globe that is home to almost 600 million people — was about the same as the gross national product of Belgium, with a population of 10 million.
> Eighteen of the world's 20 poorest countries are African, and 30 of the poorest 40. Caught in a downward cycle that began with the oil price explosion of the 1970's and then accelerated with the plunge of the commodities markets, they are getting poorer still. Per capita G.N.P. declined by 2 percent a year throughout the 1980's.
> Their debt, tripled since 1980, now amounts to over $180 billion. The debt burden — caused by borrowing to keep budgets afloat and to pay for imports — is so gigantic (amounting to 110 percent of G.N.P. in 1991) that virtually no one thinks the sum can ever be repaid. Just servicing it costs the countries $10 billion every year — four times more than they all spend on health and education.
> Africa's share of world trade has fallen below 4 percent and is now closer to 2 percent. That is so marginal it is almost as if the continent has curled up and disappeared from the map of international shipping lanes and airline routes that rope together Europe, North America and the booming Far East. Direct foreign investment in Africa is so paltry it is not even measured in the latest World Bank study.

Some one and a half to two decades ago many Afrikan countries were ideologically committed to some form of socialism and sought to follow a socialist path to economic independence and prosperity. Today these countries along with the rest of the Afrikan countries are committing themselves to some variant of capitalism and as one official observer put it, "all the talk is about floating currency, private enterprise, and getting hold of capital" (NYT, 6/30/94). The *Times* describes this situation thusly:

---

1. Michael Brown and Paul Tiffen, *Short Changed: Africa and World Trade* (London. Boulder, Colorado: Pluto Press, 1992).

The I.M.F. and the World Bank are the purveyors of the new orthodoxy. They come in to bail out a country that is bankrupt. They do so by drawing up a "structural adjustment program," a tight package of economic prescriptions designed to bring about free market enterprise and minimize governmental interference.

Because the package is tied to millions of dollars in aid from Western donor countries, it is an offer that can't be refused. And so the I.M.F. and the bank end up calling the shots on a broad range of issues — even political matters like calling multiparty elections — that effect the lives of millions.

Through its structural adjustment programs, the I.M.F. and the bank now effectively oversee and supervise the economies of some 30 countries in sub-Saharan Africa.

The imposition of structural adjustment programs on Afrikan nations has generally proved not only counterproductive, but disastrous. Two students of Afrikan economics, Michael Brown and Paul Tiffen outline the typical International Monetary Fund (IMF) World Bank adjustment demands in the following way:

- *Currency devaluation* to improve the balance of payments by raising the cost of imported goods and making exports more competitive.
- *Domestic demand management* to cut back government budgets, especially for social expenditure and for subsides.
- *Freeing of prices* to remove the distortion resulting from subsidies on food, fertiliser and other essentials from import taxes on luxury items, and to provide an incentive for exports where prices are set in the world market.
- *High interest rates and credit squeeze* to reduce inflationary pressures.
- *Import liberalisation* to open local industry to competition from more industrially developed countries and encourage an expansion of foreign trade exchanges.
- *Privitisation of state and para-statal enterprises* to reduce government protection of inefficient economic activities.

Each of these economic instruments has problems, some more than others:

- *Currency devaluation* increases prices for imported food and hits those who depend on it, mainly the urban poor, while increased prices of imported equipment raise production costs. Devaluation can lead to inflation, but reduces imports of food in competition with local farm production. Devaluation increases commodity

exports, unless other producing countries do the same, as they are also under pressure from the World Bank to do.
- *Domestic demand management* reduces public funds available for development, for the local financial component of joint development projects and infrastructure improvements. Incentives through tax concessions for exports are not affected. The impact of *freeing prices* may be nullified if all countries follow suit and world prices are generally falling.
- *High interest rates and a credit squeeze* tend to result in bankruptcies, especially of small local businesses, and may push up costs all round.
- *Import liberalization* increases dependence on foreign suppliers.
- *Privitisation of state and para-statal enterprises* may not distinguish between fledgling, but strategically important enterprises which add value to raw materials, and the merely inefficient. Local businesses, especially those in export markets, become prone to foreign takeover.[2]

Despite the fact that the stated intent of the IMF/World Bank structural adjustment programs is to resuscitate Afrika, many analysts and observers generally agree with the conclusion reached by Kevin Watkins, senior policy advisor for Oxfam, the British relief agency. He contends that instead of generating economic recovery in Afrika the programs have imposed unbearably costly social burdens on the poor of the continent (NYT, 6/20/94). This outcome may be in large part due to the World Bank as well as the IMF and other money center banks and agencies' imperial approaches to Afrikan development. Such approaches demean Afrikan peoples' ability to make crucial choices regarding solutions to their problems since foreign agencies do not see them as the people perceive them. The approaches of international agencies often involve talking to and interacting with all the wrong people, e.g., corrupt politicians, self-serving bourgeois cadres. Consequently, agencies such as the World Bank and the IMF make more wrongheaded choices than right ones and their putative beneficiaries are left to foot the bill. World Bank/IMF mistakes are paid for by the very people who can least afford them. The error-strewn, economically counterproductive record of the World Bank is clear as the following citation from *Business Week* (7/11/94) indicates:

> **MONEY HOLES.** It is difficult to see how the World Bank can carry its loans at face value when its commercial bank partners in co-financing have had to write down their portfolios. The World Bank's policy is especially puzzling in view of its own analyses, which show that only

2. Ibid.

a fraction of the programs financed with the loans are deemed to be successful.

Two recent World Bank reports show that projects it has financed are failing at a rate that would quickly lead to bankruptcy if the institution were a private commercial bank. The February, 1992, report, *Evaluation Results for 1990*, assessed 359 projects in all economic sectors at completion of World Bank funding, representing investments of some $43 billion. The report found that 36% of the projects had failed by the time their funding was completed, and only half of the remaining 64% would survive over time. In other words, the report projected a success rate of only 32%.

The following year, project performance was even worse. *Evaluation Results for 1991*, released in March, 1993, evaluated 278 projects involving World Bank investments of more than $32.8 billion. It concluded that 37% of the projects had failed by the time funding was completed. The report estimated that only 42% of the remaining 63% would survive over time. Thus only 26% of the projects were deemed to be successful.

The March, 1993, report noted that the 1991 results were part of an "overall downward trend in project performance" that had been observed over the previous two years. The report also pointed out that lending to the World Bank's best customers in Asia is declining while lending to Africa, the poorest performer overall, is increasing.

Benign Neglect of Afrika by World Community

The benign neglect and misguided policy of the international community toward Afrika can be fairly typified by current U.S. relations with the continent. The February 1993 edition of the journal *Foreign Affairs* titled *America and the World 1993*, features an article by Marguerite Michaels titled "Retreat from Afrika" which foresees very little hope for the economic future of Afrika and describes how little Afrika's future is of important concern to the so-called developed nations, especially the United States and the European nations. Her depiction of declining American interest in Afrika is quite to the point:

> The United States has been retreating from Job's continent since the implosion of the Soviet Union left America to pursue its own interest in Africa — and found it did not have any.
> In the last six months the State Department's bureau of African Affairs has lost 70 posts, a nine-percent cut. Consulates in Kenya, Cameroon and Nigeria are to be closed, and perhaps also the U.S. embassy in the Comoros Islands — bodies and budgets are needed in eastern Europe and the Commonwealth of Independent States. Over the last three years the Africa desk for the U.S. Agency for Interna-

tional Development has lost 30 to 40 staffers out of 130 for the same reason. USAID has already phased out missions in five countries, and this fiscal year it will phase out three more. The National Security Council's bureau of African Affairs has gone through six directors in the last four years.

With the end of the Cold War, the U.S. strategic interest in Africa is minimal. But now the old pretext for intervention — the global containment of communism — may be replaced with a new one — global humanitarianism. Somalia is a case in point, and it fits the pattern of US policy toward the continent even during the Cold War: *neglect, benign or otherwise, or hyperintervention* [Emphasis added].

Michaels, voicing the conclusions of many other experts, further contends that "Afrika is simply not commanding the kind of attention in the new world order to keep it from dissolving into new world disorder." Moreover, she rightly adduces that since "Global Economy" is the foreign policy king, there has been no foreign policy rationale for dealing with sub-Saharan Afrika, especially since the continent began its free fall in the 1980s. She goes on to point out some of the more salient characteristics of U.S. economic relations to Afrika:

1. Africa was never a magnet for U.S. exports or investment.

2. In 1983, for example, Africa received 2.2 percent of total U.S. exports and it sent 4.1 percent of total U.S. imports. Only five years later, however, American exports to Africa were a mere 1.2 percent, and the U.S. imports were halved.

3. Direct U.S. investment in sub-Saharan Africa — 0.46 percent of the U.S. total abroad in 1990 — has also fallen as the rate of return on investment in the continent slides [moving down from 30.7 percent in the 1960s to just 2.5 percent in the 1980s].

Between 1970 and 1985 Afrika's already very inadequate share of the world's non-oil primary products market fell from 7 percent to 4 percent. This statistic, in combination with others just as dire — the fact that Afrika's economic growth rate at 1.5% is the world's lowest — indicates the devastation of the continent's prior fragile standard of living. Since the 1980s, Afrika's national growth has relatively and absolutely slipped backward and its population has outgrown its economies. In 1965, sub-Saharan Afrika's percentage share of world trade in manufactures was 0.4%. In 1986, it was 0.2%. This is in stark contrast to the percentage shares of the newly industrialized economies of East-Asia (excluding Japan) whose growth increased that same period from 1.55% in 1965 to 8.5% in 1986. The nature of this difference may be illustrated by the case of Ghana and South Korea, countries which in the 1960s both had exactly the same per capita income and GNP (US $230). With far fewer natural resources to begin with, South Korea is now ten to twelve times more prosperous than Ghana.

In its study of Afrika the *New York Times* (ibid) concludes that "In more general terms, if the most optimistic growth forecasts prove accurate, it will take 40 years for Afrikan countries to regain the per capital income level they reached in the mid-1970s."

The countries south of the Sahara, the traditional division between black Africa and the Arab world, have turned in a decade and more of devastatingly bad economic performance. The economic failure is undercutting a drive for political liberalization, raising ethnic rivalries to a dangerous level and forcing countries to impose politically inflammatory austerity programs, often under the dictates of Western financial institutions.

But most of all it is spreading misery. In living standards, Africa is falling further behind the rest of the world. It is now the only continent where most people are getting still poorer and where health and education are deteriorating.

As political changes similar to those that shook Eastern Europe and the Soviet Union four or five years ago now reverberate in Africa, Africans seem more concerned about the social and welfare problems caused by the economic decline. Their views emerged during scores of interviews in the course of a six-week trip through nine countries in East, West and Southern Africa...

Overall, sub-Saharan's population of 600 million people could reach 1.6 billion by the year 2030.

The danger in such growth is that economies have to move full steam ahead just to avoid standing still. And in Africa they hardly moved at all; in the 1980's per capita income declined by almost 2 percent a year leaving everyone except for a tiny elite significantly poorer by the end of the decade.

According to a World Bank report in 1992, some 200 million Africans south of the Sahara — more than one out of three — now live in "absolute poverty," meaning they are unable to meet their most basic needs. Some studies predict that half of the population will be in poverty by the end of the century.

In the terms of health and food production, the 1980's were catastrophic. Because of war, drought and degradation of the soil through desert encroachment — combined with the damage wrought by policies that worked against making agriculture profitable — overall food production dropped to a level 20 percent below that of in 1970.

The downward trend continued into 1993. Per capita cereal production fell in 18 of the poorest African countries last year, by more than five percent in nine of them....

"The overall status of children is getting worse in sub-Saharan Africa," said Djibril Diallo, deputy director of public affairs for the United Nations Children's Fund. "We have 10,000 children dying every day from preventable causes. And another 10,000 crippled for life. So every 24 hours, 20,000 children are being wasted. What future is there for the continent?...

In terms of education, Unicef calls the 1980's a "lost decade." Expenditure per student declined by about one third, primary school enrollment fell from 79 percent to 67 percent and an estimated one third of all college graduates left the continent, according to the figures from the United Nations Development Program and the African Development Bank.

Ghana is facing a crisis because an insufficient number of secondary school students passed exams to qualify for college.

The lack of American interest and investment in sub-Saharan Afrika is echoed by other members of the international community. Paul Kennedy in *New York Review of Books* (2/11/93) observes that "Following the repeated debt re-scheduling, Western bankers — never enthusiastic to begin with — virtually abandoned private loans to Afrika" [How similar to the behavior of White American banks toward the Afrikan American community]. He goes to say that, "As a result, Afrika's economy is in far worse condition now than at independence, apart from a few countries like Botswana and Mauritius" [Cameroon, Congo, Gabon, Kenya]. Brown and Tiffen (1992) in their study of foreign investment in Afrika, reached the following conclusion — "Not only is foreign investment being withdrawn from Africa, it is bypassing sub-Saharan Africa completely."

This relative lack or paucity of investment in Afrika by the international community at large should not be taken to mean that Afrika is only a recipient of international charity and adds nothing to the bottom lines of the trade balances of special and powerful members of that community. Quite to the contrary, as Paul Kennedy points out:

> although much international aid goes to the developing world, in fact far more money flows out of impoverished countries of Afrika, Asia, and Latin America and *into* the richer economies of Europe, North America, and Japan — to the tune of $43 billion each year. This outward flow of interest repayments, repatriated profits, capital flight, royalties, fees for patents and information services, makes it

difficult for poorer countries to get to their feet; and even if they were able to increase their industrial output, the result might be a large rise in "the costs of technological dependence... .

In sum, as we move into the next century the developed economies appear to have all the trump cards in their hands — capital, technology, control of communications, surplus foodstuffs, powerful multinational companies — and, if anything, their advantages are growing because technology is eroding the value of labor and materials, the chief assets of developing countries. Although nominally independent since decolonization, these countries are probably more dependent upon Europe and the United States than they were a century ago.

The Self-Inflicted Wounds of Afrikans at Home and Aboard

Comparative studies of the Afrikan American and Continental Afrikan communities reveal the many political and economic ills they have in common. Both exhibit a poor to near-catastrophic prognosis for the future, with the next decade of the crisis being absolutely critical. A good deal of the blame for Afrika's and Black America's economic and political maladies may be placed on a shared history of slavery, colonialism, neocolonialism, and racism. However, a sufficient amount of the blame — and possibly the determining portion of the blame in our contemporary world — can be placed on Afrikans themselves, both at home and abroad. A good number of the wounds from which both suffer are self-inflicted. There is no question that many if not most Afrikan leaders have squandered the admittedly few but crucial opportunities for positive change they have had and presently have. There is little excuse for the mismanagement of their economies and their debts by many Afrikan governments, as difficult and heavy as they may be. While overstating his case in attempting to demonstrate "How Africa Ruined Itself" (*Wall Street Journal*, 12/9/92), we agree with the general tenor of George Ayitley's argument with regard to Afrika's management of its economic and social affairs. A Ghanaian, and associate professor of economics at American University, in Washington, D.C., he contends that:

> According to Africa's elites, ...the causes of Africa's problems are forever external: Western colonization and imperialism, the effects of the slave trade, exploitation by multinational corporations, the injustice of the international economic system, inadequate flows of foreign aid and now "marginalization."
>
> But a new and angry generation of Africans reject the claptrap and lay greater emphasis on *internal factors*: misguided leadership,

systemic corruption, economic mismanagement, senseless civil wars, tyranny, flagrant violations of human rights and military vandalism.

The lack of vision and creativity on the part of too many Afrikan leaders, as well as their refusal to exercise self-control and common sense to vigorously and steadfastly reform their economies, and their self aggrandizing, self-defeating behavior, have led some experts — including some Afrikan Americans themselves — to "argue that disengagement by developed countries might have the positive effect of compelling Africans to begin a *self-driven* recovery as well as ending the misuse of aid monies" (Kennedy, ibid). A similar argument could be made regarding the quality and direction of Afrikan American leadership. For racial self-alienation and self-hatred deeply afflict both groups of leaders. These twin afflictions deny both sets of leaders and their followers the use of their greatest power instruments — a race-centered consciousness and identity, a sense of racial solidarity, and a commitment to race first-ness. No race of people have triumphed without these vital motivational, mental and behavioral orientations, for they are the keystones in the construction of liberated and prosperous peoples.

The U.S., Western Europe and the Problem of Afrikan Debt. The problems of Afrika are manifold. Its lamentations are monotonously familiar — familiar to the point of indifference. It only manages to break through the jaded or otherwise preoccupied consciousness of the world community when one or another of its many nations collapses thunderously into chaos and famine. For a moment it becomes the object of humanitarian concerns and of mercenary ministrations, after which it is left to its fate.

Afrika is no longer of great strategic importance to the West since the fall of the Soviet Union and the termination of the Cold War. The world's agenda has changed since then and Afrika, and the actualization of its human and material potential are not on it. Its shrinking per capita income, the underdevelopment of its markets for Western goods, its seemingly endemic political instability and poorly educated and underskilled workforce, make it unattractive to Western investors. Its economic significance continues to decline as Western demands for its raw materials are reduced as the result of the development of new technologies and of increased competition from other major producers of raw materials like Russia. As indicated earlier, direct private investment in Afrika has declined since 1985, as it has tripled in Latin America and increased five-fold in East Asia. Afrika stubbornly remains burdened by increasingly unpayable debts, even as it has been the recipient of dramatically increased foreign aid. According to the *Financial Times* (9/1/93), "In 1962, the outstanding debts of sub-Saharan African countries were less than $3 billion, with a debt service ratio of less than 2 per-cent... By 1990, debt exceeded $146 billion, equivalent of 110 per-cent of GDP [Gross Domestic Product]; service payments would take up to three times its annual export earnings."

The United States and its European allies have contributed in no small way to the debt crisis which is paralyzing the economic potential of Afrika. While the U.S. and other G-7 nations freely forgive many other nations their indebtedness or offer them some measurable debt relief, they have granted Afrika little or no such forgiveness or relief. According to Lamond Goodwin, an Afrikan American and senior director at American Express Bank, the United States

> forgave 7% of all of Poland's bilateral debt to the United States and organized G-7 nations to forgive fifty percent of what Poland owed them. We forgave $7 billion of Egypt's official debt and led an effort, again, to get the other countries to cancel 50% of all Egyptian bilateral debt. In the Enterprise for the Americas Initiative, we forgave or set in place a mechanism that enables Latin American countries, forgiveness of up to 80% of their bilateral debt restructuring and, again, trade liberalization as well as a $1.5 billion multilateral investment fund for Latin American countries.

Goodwin charges that one of the major reasons Poland received such favored treatment in contrast to Afrika is political. "We gave more attention and support to Poland because of political constituencies for Poland in the United States which are very strong, very well organized, starting with the chairman of the Ways and Means Committee in the Congress and then moving on to...where the Polish American community is highly organized." As Goodwin further notes, Afrika lags in financial support from the U.S. essentially because it lacks the organized support of a strong political Afrikan American constituency.

Afrika's present growth rates are so relatively low and its debt so high until even its most successful countries would take approximately 20 years to be ranked among the world's lower middle-income nations. It would take even longer for many of them to return to their per capita incomes of the 1970s. Consequently, Afrika is being left far behind in its economic, political and technological development as its institutional capacities to resolve its problems become increasingly inadequate. Many of its schools and universities are bereft of adequate facilities, teachers and teaching materials. Its civil services have been weakened, corroded and corrupted by tyrannous or inept government administrations, and its infrastructure has fallen into disrepair or is grossly underdeveloped. Its poor management of its human and material resources has meant economic and social repression even in nations such as Nigeria which in 1965 had a GNP higher than that of Indonesia. Today Indonesia's GNP is three times higher and growing even more rapidly.

Such economic woes translate into tangible social and physical woes for Afrika's peoples. Four million or more of Afrika's children die before age five; a third are severely malnourished; one in eight is severely disabled; one in three receives no elementary school education (*Financial Times*, 9/1/93). Afrika's skilled urban class, on which the hope of the nations depends, is being ravaged by the AIDS virus. With more than 1.2 million already killed by AIDS, it is estimated that Afrika contains half of the world's 15 million victims, a number which is expected to increase to 14 million by the year 2000. The list of woes seems excruciatingly endless.

The Planned Suffering of Afrika

It is to some significant degree justifiable and it is certainly easy to blame the sufferings of Afrikan nations and peoples on the ineptness, kleptomania, and the lack of genuine concern for the general welfare of the people, on Afrika's heads of state, its ruling elites, and its self-serving bureaucracies. But the significance and validity of these charges are vastly inflated when we stop to consider the fact that all the socially dysfunctional orientations which now characterize much of collective Afrikan political behavior occur within the context of, and in reaction to, European colonialism and neocolonialism as well as Western imperialism. The regrettable conditions of Afrika can in no way be extracted from the even more regrettable and more reprehensible impositions and outcomes of European and American hegemonic capitalism. For the collective orientations of Afrikan nations and peoples today are inextricably intertwined with and reflective of the perverse intricacies of global White supremacy.

We cannot elaborate on this matter here. That is and has been the subject of other books. But suffice it to say that we agree with David Keen, a research officer at Oxford University and author of *The Benefits of Famine*, who said that "Probably nothing will change either, until the world acknowledges that famine and violence are typically manipulated in a rational (if immoral) manner by those who expect to benefit from them" (*New York Times*, 8/15/94). The famines, poverty, "tribal warfare", governmental tyrannies and kleptocracies, economic stagnation and distortion too prevalent in Afrika today are the legacies of 18th and 19th century European colonialism and the ill-effects of the 20th century American and European world capitalism.

The Eurocentric Distortion of Afrikan Economies. It is of signal importance to recognize that it was not and is not Afrikan peoples and nations who were or are dependent on hegemonic economies of the West, but it was and is those economies which were and are dependent on the distorted economies of Afrika and of Afrikan diasporan nations and communities. We must not forget that it was from the profits of crops such as tobacco, cotton, cocoa, tea, coffee, and sugar that both the Europeans and White Americans generated the capital necessary for the industrial expansion of 19th and 20th century Western Europe and North America. It was and is the cheap raw materials, the cheap food, the low-wage labor, the consumer markets for Western industrial goods, the foreign indebtedness, and militarized instability of Afrikan nations and peoples which are the foundations of American and European political and economic ascendance. Anne Buchanan cogently states our case in the following way:

> Although most of the former colonies are now politically independent the pattern continues very much the same because they have inherited warped economic structures and because the elites to whom power was handed over on independence have every reason to continue the system of the former colonisers and thus share in the profits which still drain out of the poor nations to the rich ones.
>
> Thus we see that there are not really two different groups of nations — one 'developed' and the other, because of some internal deficiency on their part, 'underdeveloped'. Rather, the two sets of nations are part of the same system, two sides of a single coin. The development of the Centre has been achieved only by the *mal*-development of the Periphery, by the transfer of wealth from one to the other...
>
> Today, Third World elites and giant transnational corporations (also called 'multinationals') take the place of the colonisers, owning or controlling vast tracts of land on which the highly profitable export crops are grown. [And the land from which the highly profitable export mineral wealth is extracted]... And so the inequalities continue to grow, the result, as Dumont and Cohen stress, of "the removal of control over production from those who work the land into the hand of those who merely speculate on and profit from it" (1980: 27). These

inequalities today divide the world into those who eat and those who hunger.[3]

The distortion of Afrikan economies is marked by several primary indicators: inadequate infrastructure, insufficiency of food, malnutrition, indebtedness, and vulnerability to Western economic "whitemail". Space limitations do not allow a detailed exposition of each of these indicators. We can only generalize by pointing out that the primal need of the colonial and imperial powers to export the minerals and crops of Afrika to their markets led to the construction of railways, roads, communications, and port facilities designed specifically for that purpose, not for the internal economic, social and political development of Afrikan nations themselves.

The agricultural techniques and cultural traditions of Afrika were designed to meet its food and nutritional needs. However, the demands of colonial and contemporary Western agribusiness with their emphasis on the maximal use of arable land to produce cash crops, exportable meat and poultry and fodder to satiate the Western hunger for proteins, rather than for feeding the indigenous population, have reduced Afrika's ability to feed its people and to meet their nutritional needs. It is bitterly ironic that "while Third World nations could still export 12 million tons of grain in the 1930s, by the late 1970s they had to *import* nearly 80 million tons" (Buchanan, 1982). The indebtedness for which Afrikan nations are so infamous has more to do with the fact that these nations have to pay out more money than they collect in order to pay for the imports, goods and services they must purchase from the West as the result of their having their own economies stunted and distorted by the West to begin with. They have been forced by the West to deal their raw materials, practically their only sources of income, at too low-a-price to pay in full for their imports. As Buchanan (1982) points out, this unequal trade relationship has been good for the industrialized nations of the West because "prices paid for imported raw materials and certain manufactured goods relying on cheap labor have been kept low while export prices for their own capital-intensive manufactures have been kept high." In reference to the worsening economic plight of Afrikan nations Buchanan (1982) further notes the following:

> And the relation between the price they get for their export crops and the price they pay for imported goods has steadily worsened as is shown, for example, by the often quoted banana/tractor ratio: in 1960 3 tons of bananas were enough to buy a tractor, by 1970 it took 11

---

3. Anne Buchanan, *Food, Poverty and Power* (Nottingham, England: Bertrand Russell House, 1982).

tons for 1 tractor. Similarly we can take other leading crop and mineral exports and relate them to oil purchases or to interest repayments on debts and get a similarly depressing picture as does *South* each month with fourteen different exports for the 1975-81 period...The poor nations can do little about this situation because they rely so heavily on one or two key exports which the developed nations can stop buying temporarily to force prices down. They would get more money if they processed the goods themselves (e.g. if they exported instant coffee rather than coffee beans) but are again blocked in this development because of the high tariffs which the developed world places on such processed exports. The profit is in the processing and the developed nations keep a tight hold on this lucrative stage of the game.

The situation is aggravated when the Third World elites use scarce foreign exchange to pay for ostentatious western-style urban projects and luxuries: Gerard Chaliand gives data from French West Africa in the 1960s, for example, which show that the value of imports of alcohol and perfumes was as large as the total value of imports of fertilisers, tractors, agricultural equipment and machine tools combined.

Food as Weapon. The dependency of a lot of Afrikan nations on Western food distribution means that the West may use food as the ultimate weapon to maintain its domination of Afrika. This situation prompted the CIA to publish a study entitled "Potential Implications of Trends in World Population, Food Production, and Climate," in 1974 (cited by Buchanan) in which it intimates that "The world's increasing dependence on American surpluses portends an increase in US power and influence, especially vis-à-vis the food deficit poor countries... In bad years, when US could not meet the demand for food of most would-be importers, Washington would acquire virtual life and death power over the fate of multitudes of the needy. Without indulging in blackmail in any sense, the US would gain extraordinary political and economic influence."

The United States and its European allies have rigged the rules of trade and commerce such that they win all the bets. These rules are designed to exclude, by the manipulation of tariffs and quotas, the manufactured goods of Afrika, and consequently, help to maintain its dependence on primary products for the large majority of its exports. In sum, the European-engineered "monocultures" of Afrika make them highly vulnerable to the not unplanned steady decline of commodity prices. That is, the economic dependency of many Afrikan countries on the selling of one or just a few commodities to the industrialized nations, makes them vulnerable to the prices those nations decide to pay for such commodities. And those prices are often engineered in favor of these buyer nations and not by market forces as we are often told. Therefore, the much-ballyhooed balance of payment deficits of Afrikan nations are often engineered by the West which, while raising the prices of its exports to Afrika, simultaneously lowers the prices it pays for Afrikan exports.

The Charade of Western Aid. After engineering and exploiting the poverty and indebtedness of Afrikan nations the West attempts to convince itself and others that it possesses charitable feelings toward those same nations by recompensing their losses with "foreign aid." These "grants" which amount to hardly two percent of the West's Gross National Product and inflated in their importance and size, are made to appear to be generous and voluntarily given "from the heart." Western aid is propagandistically made to appear to be designed to support the development and growth of the social and economic infrastructure of recipient Afrikan nations. But, as Buchanan points out:

> contrary to the impression given by the 'donors', most aid is not, in fact, 'given' at all. About half of world aid is actually loans and three-quarters of world aid is 'tied' which means the recipient has to spend it on goods provided by the donor country, often at prices much higher than the goods could be bought elsewhere... In other words the 'aid' is actually a subsidy for the donor's manufacturers. Even direct food aid is "in essence little better than a dumping of the surpluses produced by the protectionist policies of Europe and North America" (Harrison 1980: 213-4). It also creates a future market for the donor country's agricultural products.

Box 15-1 Financing Export Trade

Loans or "tied aid" is a variant of a well-worn technique for financing a nation's or firm's export trade. Similar methods were practiced in foreign markets by England and Germany around the turn of the century. The basic approach involves the stimulation of big export trade by lending foreign governments the money with which to pay for the goods. This arrangement permitted the lender to gain both the return on the loan and the profit from the exports. Perhaps a less exploitative but similar approach to stimulating and increasing export trade might be used by the Afrikan American community and its individual corporations relative to diasporan Afrikan nations, communities, and firms. The extension of credit lines, underwritten trade contracts, swapping and bartering agreements, etc. of various types to overseas Afrikan firms, may be initiated by Afrikan American companies in order to promote the export activities of these companies.

An Afrikan American International Corporation may be capitalized by the Black business community to investigate opportunities for investments in projects in a number of major areas throughout the Pan-Afrikan world. Its interest may follow several lines of activity, from finance, to agriculture, to mining. Such a corporation may found wholly or partly owned subsidiaries in various diasporan Afrikan countries and communities. ■

Alternatives. Lappé and Collins have noted that "Hungry people cannot eat that which is exported. Nor are they likely to eat from export earnings or benefit from the so-called development achieved through these export earnings. People will escape from hunger only when policies are pursued that allow then to grow food and eat the food they grow."[4] Afrikan peoples will escape from their other material hungers — the hunger for economic and technological growth and development, for stable governments and societies, and for an enriched quality of life — when they can enter into trade relations which are mutually beneficial to themselves and their trading partners; when they trade and technologically cooperate within their own nations and regions, with other Afrikan peoples and nations overseas and with non-Afrikan nations in ways which permit them to produce for themselves and to cultivate interdependent self-reliance.

The Continuing Reign of Colonialism. The degree to which many Afrikan regimes and countries can be held fully responsible for their adverse political and economic conditions is quite unclear when we recognize the fact that these nations, though nominally independent, continue to be under the control of their former European colonial metropoles. The economies of many Afrikan countries, whether bankrupted or not, have yet to be owned by the indigenous Afrikans themselves. The former colonial powers have hardly ceded political and economic self-determination to their formerly wholly-owned and -operated Afrikan fiefdoms. A prime example of the Eurocentric neocolonial control of Afrikan economies is provided by France's control of its former (?) Afrikan colonies.

Paris still is in the position to open and close the economies of the 11 Afrikan countries whose currency is the Afrikan franc, to international investment and trade. As noted by the *New York Times*

---

4. Lappé and Collins, *Food First: Beyond the Myth of Scarcity* (Boston: Houghton Mifflin, 1977).

(9/10/94), France still perceives its former colonies as its own private reserve:

> In international business circles, France's advantages in its former African colonies earned this region the reputation of being Paris's chasse gardée, or private game reserve.
> The exchange rate for the African franc, fixed at a value of 50 to 1 against the French currency from 1948 until its value was cut in half this year, gave Paris another strong commercial advantage over other exporters to this region.
> Since the devaluation, however, Paris has grown anxious as West Africans have begun scrambling in search of the best deal, rather than automatically looking to France. "The days when all roads ran through the former metropolis are over," wrote the French daily *Liberation*.

France is not ready to "throw in the towel" relative to its extraordinary influence on the political and economic fate of its former colonies. It is still primarily concerned about protecting its privileged access to Afrikan markets as well as protecting and expanding the markets it already has established there. As the *Times* notes, "while France has urged the countries [its former colonies] to open their economies, many people...say that it has shown little willingness to make room for other influences in an area where its hold remains powerful after more than three decades of independence." The *Times* goes on to reveal that "in countries like Ivory Coast, Senegal and Gabon, boulevards are named for every French president since de Gaulle and French troops train their Afrikan counterparts and serve as the ultimate republican guard." French experts from Paris continue to supervise important government services, from the police to the postal service.

French companies, corporations, retail and service firms enjoy decisive advantages over their non-French counterparts, including indigenously owned Afrikan firms. French-owned corporations are almost always first in line whenever major national and international contracts are being awarded. The French are known to deliberately encumber the efforts of non-French companies to do business in her former colonies. The *Times* (9/10/94) gives some examples of how this is accomplished:

> Hoping to protect long-cozy markets, the French have been scrambling. In an effort to head off African pharmacies seeking medicines from lower-cost suppliers in Europe and Asia, for example, the French Government recently began encouraging the export of generic medicines to the continent for the first time.

Businessmen and diplomats in Ivory Coast and elsewhere tell of mysterious port delays holding up the arrival of new Canadian telecommunications gear and discreet political intervention from Paris urging that a major cocoa trading concern here not be sold into American hands.

No recent case has drawn more attention than that of an independent American oil company, United Meridian, which in March discovered enough oil and natural gas offshore here to meet this country's fuel needs, and perhaps eventually allow it to become a small exporter.

French Challenge

A French group led by the civil engineering company Bouygues had rights to an adjacent field, and nurtured hopes of building a pipeline to the coast, where it would install turbines to generate electricity from the natural gas offshore. Bouygues which already controls the national electricity and water companies, and is believed to be interested in Ivory Coast's telephone business as well has long enjoyed close ties to the Ivorian political elite and diplomatic support from Paris.

"We felt we could negotiate with them and sell them gas from our well, which was ready to produce," said Steve Thornton, director of United Meridian's Ivory Coast operations. "Their response was, 'Thank you, but you have no right to exploit gas in the Ivory Coast.'"

Several people with knowledge of the dispute said that what ensued was a fullcourt press by the French company, supported by France's diplomatic machine, aimed at shoving the American company out of the picture....

In the end, United Meridian won out over its French rival, but not before what many said was rare support from the State Department and Energy Department in Washington. Also not before Bouygues was itself awarded a contract to go ahead with its gas turbines, which will be fueled from the American-developed field.

As can be easily inferred from the foregoing, native Afrikans have yet to play the major role in the control, operation, growth and development of their economies. This not only applies to the so-call Francophone or French-speaking Afrikan countries but to the Afrikan countries who were the former colonies of other European countries as well. A good portion of the problem of poverty in Afrika may be attributed to the fact that that continent is still being robbed blind of its resources and sustenance by neo-colonial and imperialistic Europeans. As long as non-Afrikans dominate and shamelessly exploit the economies of Afrika the vast majority of her peoples will always suffer poverty and social retardation.

The domination of Afrikan economies by Europeans and other non-Afrikans raises a number of questions: What is an *Afrikan* national economy? What do we mean when we refer to *Afrikan* economies as "weak", "lesser developed", "indebted", etc.? How can *Afrikan* economies, laboring under and restricted by non-Afrikan "structural adjustment programs", hemmed in and hampered by high tariffs and other trade barriers, and low or non-existent international investment, be accurately defined as Afrikan? Is there a true *Afrikan* economy in the World?

It is the duty of Afrikans across the diaspora to work in concert to wrest their control over their local and national economies from greedy European hands. This call to battle sounds loudest for the Afrikan American nation in the United States.

The Afrikan American Monoculture

Labor: Black America's 'Cash Crop. "The Afrikan American nation stands at the nexus of a potential network of mutually beneficial trade and cultural relations between Afrikan diasporan nations, and these nations and non-Afrikan nations such as the United States. For Black America's financial and trade relations with Afrika and other Afrikan nations and communities are crucial to the economic liberation of all Afrikan peoples from unrestricted exploitation by industrialized nations whether White or non-White. Increased Afrikan American political power is necessary for it to effectively safeguard and advance the interests of Blacks at home and abroad. For if American and European trade, economic and political policies which now impoverish and disempower Afrika and Afrikan peoples everywhere are to be reversed, then it is the Afrikan American community which is best positioned to lead such a reversal. The Afrikan American community is the chief bulwark against a total American-European usurpation of the freedom and vitality of Afrikan peoples the world over.

However, the Afrikan American community cannot successfully undertake such an awesome responsibility unless it realistically recognizes its own sociopolitical and politicoeconomic plight. This community must resolve its own dependent relationship with White America. It must, with extraordinary haste, learn to "do for self." It must resolve it own economic "monocultural" relationship with White America. Like many diasporan Afrikan nations and communities, Black America exports only one "cash crop" or commodity. That commodity is *labor*. And like many "dependent" Afrikan nations and communities, its sole export commodity is devalued by White America. More ominously, not only is its labor commodity being steadily discounted by White America, it is increasingly no longer being bought at any price. Hence, the creeping "Third World" conditions of joblessness, poverty, unhealthiness, criminality, extreme class stratification, social disorganization, and internal conflicts are spreading across the urban centers of Black America at a rapidly accelerating pace.

While White American claims that its devaluation of Black American labor is "market driven" in that such labor is relatively unskilled, out-dated, untrained, unreliable, inferior, and the like, it has demonstrated its bad faith and hypocrisy by the fact that it has by all means, refused to invest in the upgrading of Black labor by institutionally providing the means by which it may be upgraded. In fact, White America has disinvested the upgrading of Black labor by its almost wholesale withdrawal of funds used for the education, training, re-skilling and employment of Black labor. In the meanwhile it keeps raising its prices for the goods and services it exports to the Black community.

The "foreign aid" White America grants to Black America in the form of governmental transfer payments, e.g., welfare and social services, economic development programs, food stamps, etc., and similar to White American foreign aid to Afrika, is essentially designed to subsidize White-owned firms and professionals in that the largest bulk of these funds which are used to finance such initiatives are ultimately spent with these parties. Little, if any, of the money is spent with or remains in the hands of its reputed Black recipients. Consequently, the basic economic and social formation of the recipient Black community is not fundamentally changed and matters are often made worse. And the continuing dependency of that community assured.

Alternative. The alternative to this problematic situation is for the Afrikan American community, as must be the case for the Afrikan community of nations, to engage in increased internal production and trade, and in lateral trade with partners across the Afrikan diaspora as well as friendly non-Afrikan nations and communities.

Afrikan nations trade far more with European nations, America and non-Afrikan nations than they do among themselves. This trade orientation we refer to as "vertical trade relations". Trade between Afrikan nations and communities we refer to as "horizontal, or lateral, trade relations". The major trade imbalance relative to Afrikan nations on the continent and across the diaspora is not so much the one that inheres between these countries and the industrialized countries of Europe, America and Asia, but the imbalance between vertical trade and horizontal trade. That is, because the volume and value of trade between Afrikan nations and regions is relatively low compared to their trade with Europe and the U.S., they are far less able to resist trade pressures and the manipulation of prices for their commodities by these industrial giants. A parallel situation defines Afrikan American-White American trade relations. The virtual absence of horizontal trade within the Afrikan American nation also leaves it less able to resist economic and political manipulation by White America.

Open Markets, Open Shelves, Most Favored Nations and the Manufacturing of Wealth

Markets and Economic Growth. It is not enough to produce. There must exist a market where what is produced can be bartered, swapped, traded or sold. The major incentive for the manufacturing of products and the reaping of profit from their sale is the existence of an active market wherein those manufactured products can be sold at a profit. However, the mere existence of relevant markets wherein certain manufactured products may be sold in no way guarantees that they will be sold therein, even if the demand for them is high. The sheer ability to manufacture a product and the actual existence of a market wherein that product can be sold in no way assures that the product will be sold there, even if it could be physically transported to the market and be offered for sale. This may be the case because those in control of the market where the manufacturer would want to sell his product may, for any number of reasons, close that market to him. In sum, just as not all markets are free, not all markets are open. It is not enough to manufacture a product for sale. In order to sell it, it must be accessible to a market of buyers. If extant markets where a manufactured product can be sold remain closed to its entry by those who control them, then the manufacturing of that product will cease since it cannot be sold. If the same applies to a broad range of products then the broad range of manufacturers who produce them will go out of business and cease to exist, or will not come into existence in the first place. And if these manufacturers or potential manufacturers whose products have little or no access to profitable market outlets happen to reside in certain countries or locales, those countries or locales will exhibit relatively low levels of product diversity, export of manufactured goods, income from the sale of manufactured products, technology and technological organization and advancement, income per capita (unless the sales of raw or primary commodities brings very high income relative to population size), employment and wages, and of their general quality of life.

Such international market conditions and their correlated low levels of manufacturing and exportation of manufactured products, and low levels of technological development and advancement, along with a bevy of attendant socioeconomic problems, are characteristic of Afrikan nations and peoples across the Afrikan diaspora including the Afrikan American nation. Despite the European and American cultural and political advocacy of "free markets" or "open markets", of "letting the market determine the distribution of goods and services" in theory — *in practice they operate in terms of protected trade, protected markets, and managed trade*, that is, their trade relations with other nations are managed with the objective of maintaining their economic domination and preponderance and protecting important segments of their internal economies and markets (both internal and eternal) from the threat of foreign competition.

Race-based Trade Relations. The trade relations and economic foreign policies of Western Europe and America are often based on White supremacist and White racist motives, attitudes, biases, stereotypes and intentions. They are meant to create and maintain a self-serving internal and international division of labor based on skin color — with the darker and black-skinned nations and communities functioning as low-wage laborers, producers of raw and primary commodities and materials, and functioning as poverty-stricken servants to and dependents on the relatively more prosperous White, Yellow, and Brown nations and communities of the world.

This race-based, color-based national and international division of labor is structured and maintained by trade policies which embargo Afrikan-manufactured products for any number of reasons, including placing high taxes or tariffs on their entry and sale within American and European markets, the placing of economically disadvantageous restrictive quotas on the quantity of these products admitted into those markets. Western European and American economic foreign policy includes the restriction of foreign aid, technological aid, loans and other international developmental programs in ways which provide little or no finance to Afrikan nations to aid them in the creation and development of significantly productive manufacturing and technological institutions. Moreover, Western European nations and America in creating and maintaining the heavy indebtedness of Afrikan nations, leave them with little or no money to invest in the development of their manufacturing and technological sectors as well as to invest in their general economic growth and development. Furthermore, the European-American manipulation of Afrikan tastes, appetites for Euro-American manufactured and exported products in order to increase their consumption by Afrikans through mass media advertising and cultural imperialism, through the European-American control and ownership of Afrikan commercial markets, structure the spending habits of Afrikans in ways that undermine their ability to save and their ability to accumulate wealth in the quantities and ways which will permit them to finance their own economic development, produce for their own consumption, and to create or manufacture a broad variety of products for sale in the international market.

Lack of Access to Internal Markets. An even more insidious phenomenon occurs within the internal commercial markets of Afrika themselves. That is, not only are Afrikan-manufactured products denied access to external markets, they are denied access to their own internal markets. This situation is due to the fact that there exists few Afrikan-owned manufacturing facilities of sufficient size, productivity, efficiency and marketing clout which can penetrate Afrika's own national and continental markets. If and when such manufacturing and marketing facilities exist in Afrika they are or will be far more likely than not, to be owned and operated by Europeans or other non-Afrikans. Or they are branches and affiliates of giant multinational corporations. The existence of these non-Afrikan-owned facilities militate effectively against the development of an indigenously owned manufacturing and marketing establishment which can effectively compete against non-indigenously-owned industries and marketing prowess in Afrika's internal markets whose main customers are Afrikans themselves. Moreover, the vast majority of wholesale and retail outlets, i.e., the stores, shops, etc., which serve the Afrikan market are not owned by indigenous Afrikans. So, even when products are manufactured in Afrika itself and by Afrikans themselves they still may not be stocked on the shelves of the retail shops which constitute Afrikan market places. Hence struggling, near-impoverished, Afrikan vendors are forced out on the street by their non-Afrikan shopkeeping rivals to sell in the open-air and side-street markets where they must hawk their goods to customers who have already spent the bulk of their income with non-Afrikan merchants.

Non-Discriminatory Trade Accords. There have been international agreements such as the various rounds of the General Agreement on Tariffs and Trade (GATT) which have supposedly reduced or eliminated the numerous trade barriers erected by developed nations against imports from developing countries. In this instance, international trade between these nations and countries would operate on the principle of non-discrimination. Each trading partner under this agreement would receive the same benefits awarded to all or any of the other trading partners. In some instances, the U.S. and the European community have, in order to aid the development of some lesser developed countries (LDCs), instituted a General System of Preferences (GSP) thereby permitting more favorable or liberal, or duty-free, special quota access to U.S. and European markets of products from LDCs and Afrikan Caribbean and Pacific (ACP) countries. While these are important concessions in theory, as Tiffen and Brown (1992) note:

> In practice the effect of any concessions to developing countries' exports has been limited, particularly because tariffs have remained high for products which compete with the developed countries' own production and because of their high residual tariffs and internal taxes on imports of manufactures — coffee (12 per cent), tobacco (67 per cent) and tropical fruit (13 per cent). In addition, reach has been indiscriminate. A 1987 study found that Hong Kong, South Korea and Taiwan together received 44 per cent of the total gains from the current GSP system and Brazil was the third biggest recipient, although none of these is a typical LDC and the Asian trio could arguably be termed developed countries. ACP concessions have worked better, allowing duty-free entry for most products, although it is notable that several products on which tariffs remain directly affect prospects for diversifying African exports — namely, roasted coffee, margarine, canned fruits and meat.

Tiffen and Brown further explain why the apparently generous agreements between the developed nations and the LDCs, specifically Afrikan nations, achieved through GATT and other international or bilateral negotiations, do not often work in practice:

> The World Bank distinguishes between internal and external blockages or obstacles to economic development. It is generally insisted that internal blockages are at the heart of Africa's crisis. In fact, external factors influencing Africa's economic development are at least as important and indeed constitute almost insuperable obstacles. It has been exceedingly difficult for Africa to break out of the primary commodity straitjacket inherited from its colonial past and to end its reliance on TNCs [transnational corporations] — both processors and traders — whose objectives may not, and cannot be expected to prioritise Africa's economic and social development. The protective barriers against imported manufactures and against the

more processed stages of primary products defy most efforts to develop viable and independent industry. Of all developing regions, sub-Saharan Africa has fared the worst, because despite some duty-free access, African products with development potential, notably textiles, processed coffee and canned fruits, are still prohibitively taxed on entry to markets in developed countries. Finally, the most serious of all, there is a growing crisis for Africa, as direct foreign investment bypasses Africa and the collapse in primary commodity prices and export earnings makes the already crippling foreign debt ever harder to service.

The Parallel Case of White American-Black American National Trade Relations and Accords. If we perceive the economic relations between White and Black America as that between relatively autonomous nations, we will readily perceive that their trade and commercial relations parallel those of Western European-American trade and commercial relations with Afrikan nations we have just described. Like its continental Afrikan counterparts, the Afrikan American nation manufactures relatively few products which are exported into the general American market and which can provide really significant levels of employment within the Black community as well as provide for the economic prosperity for its inhabitants. As a matter of fact, as in the case of Afrika in general, there does not exist in the Afrikan American nation enough non-Black-owned manufacturing facilities to employ even at low wages a truly significant number of its inhabitants. Also, as is the case of Afrika, non-Afrikan Americans own and control both the external and internal markets where Afrikan Americans buy and attempt to sell. (We must recognize that if Afrikans and Afrikan Americans were permitted to be in charge of the wholesaling, distribution, retailing and general marketing of products in their home markets, even if the products they moved were produced by European and American manufacturers, they would be significantly more economically advanced and prosperous than they presently are. This end of the market must be captured by Afrikan peoples across the diaspora as the necessary preparatory stage of their competitive entry into the manufacturing industry in general.)

Consequently, even when Afrikan American manufacturing and marketing entrepreneurs establish and develop the relevant manufacturing and marketing facilities, their products and services are denied unencumbered access to both the external general American markets and to the internal specific Afrikan American market. Obviously, such a market structure discourages the founding, growth and success of a full-blown Afrikan American-owned manufacturing and marketing establishment which contributes significantly to the employment and economic prosperity of Black Americans in general. The closed markets of America — of both non-Black and Black America — to Afrikan American products, goods and services virtually assures an impoverished manufacturing, marketing, technically backward or retarded Afrikan American economic establishment and population.

This situation, like the one concerning continental Afrikans, is race- and color-based. The refusal of White-owned financial institutions to provide funding for the development of Black-owned manufacturing and marketing facilities — even when the monies they would release are composed of the banking and financial deposits of and the earned income from Black consumers — transparently represents a racist scheme on the part of White Americans to keep Black Americans out of competition with themselves. It represents a White racist scheme to maximize the economic exploitation of the Afrikan American nation. The degree of White American economic greed is so prevalent and intense, its greed for power and supremacy so obsessive and compelling, until it will not let Black entrepreneurs pick up the crumbs dropped in either the general American or Afrikan American market places. Afrikan American-manufactured or originated goods and services are generally denied access even to the shelves of wholesale and retail outlets, of the shops and stores which service the Black community exclusively. The shops and stores of Black America are owned by the White-, Yellow-, and Brown-skinned peoples of America. Only the streets and sidewalks and the open-air are left to the Black-skinned entrepreneurs.

This situation continues even in the face of Government initiatives such as the Community Reinvestment Act, Enterprise Zones, Set-Asides, Affirmation Action, Quotas, the Small Business Administration, and a plethora of other economic development programs supposedly designed to prime the pump of an overflowing stream of Black capitalist production and prosperity. As in the case of Afrika, economic and social matters have grown worse for Black America as these governmental and private initiatives have been undertaken. The key reason for this situation is because truly significant Afrikan American and Afrikan economic autonomy and power is compatible with continuing White economic domination and exploitation of Afrikan peoples and with national and international White supremacy. Consequently, even when White America appears to be consciously supporting the full economic development and power of Black America; when it appears to be seriously inclined to bring Black

America into full socioeconomic equality with itself, its compulsive need to still dominate, exploit, and control Black America — a need which possesses its collective consciousness — will undercut and vitiate its good intentions. This means that the political, social and economic liberation of Blacks from White liberation cannot depend on the apparent goodwill and intentions of Whites. Afrikan peoples must cleverly utilize and manipulate whatever resources they can wrangle from Whites — for many of those resources originate from the soils, labor, consumption, and exploitation of Afrikan peoples themselves — to their advantage. They must learn to beat Whites at their own game. More important, Afrikan peoples must recognize that they possess within themselves all the means by which they can achieve socioeconomic liberation and prosperity. They must specifically identify and cultivate these means. They must radically change the way they perceive and relate to themselves and others and be willing to courageously endure the necessary sacrifices they must make and the abuse to which they will be subjected, if they are to empower themselves to be free and wholesome peoples. We hope this volume will significantly contribute to these ends.

Reasons for Optimism

Despite this apparent doom and gloom, Afrika's destiny is far from hopeless. Generalizations about this huge continent are just that — generalizations. Examples of economic growth, political stability, social and technological development are present and increasing in some Afrikan nations. It must be kept in mind that Afrika is the world's second largest continent consisting of 53 countries which encompass a broad array and assortment of social systems, human and material resources, and cultures. A number of these nations are not only characterized by political and financial stability but also present great promise and opportunity for intrepid investors. As several Afrikan nations expand into new business, mining and manufacturing areas, they are experiencing unprecedented economic growth. There are a number of stock markets open to foreign investors in such countries as Botswana, Ivory Coast, Ghana, Kenya, Mauritius, Morocco, Nigeria, Tunisia, and Zimbabwe. In fact, Botswana, along with Mauritius and South Afrika were given high ratings for creditworthiness by *Institutional Investor* magazine in March, 1993. Listed as Afrika's poorest country by the World Bank in 1967, Botswana's economy grew at a phenomenal 13.8% a year between 1971 and 1987. One of the best managed countries in Afrika, it has a balance-of-trade surplus and budget surplus and "is one of the few developing nations that has never restructured or defaulted on its debt" (WSJ, 9/24/93). Mauritius, an island off southwestern Afrika, has an economy which has been growing at about 6.6% a year since 1985. Once primarily a sugar producing country, Mauritius is increasingly expanding its economy to include textile manufacturing and tourism. Zambia, Morocco, Tunisia, Zimbabwe and Ghana are also receiving increasingly favorable notice from investors.

According to *Fortune* magazine (6/27/94), "Ghana's infant stock market has already doubled in price since opening to foreigners in 1993." *Fortune* further notes that Miles Morland, CEO of Blakeney Management in London, asserted that Ghana is "a well-governed country with a very promising future". Morland estimated that Ghana's $5.3 billion GDP will rise 5% in 1994. Morgan Stanley Africa Investment fund sells on the New York Stock Exchange for a discount of 12%. A manager at Morgan Stanley contends that "countries like Zimbabwe, Botswana, and Ghana are doing all the right things to get their economies on track."

The Responsibility of the Afrikan American Community for Afrika's Economic Development. The ignoring of Afrika by the Western nations provides windows of opportunity open to native Afrikans to drastically reduce the massive outflow or flight of capital, which has been estimated to exceed 80 percent of the Gross Domestic Product, and to reinvest it in their own countries. Afrikan peoples and nations across the diaspora must apprise themselves of a full, ongoing knowledge of the social, economic and cultural history of Afrikan nations as well as their contemporary status and reorganize their sociocultural and economic structures so as to initiate and fuel continental Afrika's growth and development. The Afrikan American community, especially, should vastly overhaul and reconstruct its educational orientation toward a knowledge of the Motherland. It must realize that its own economic salvation is coterminous with or tied to that of Afrika's. It must invest money and human resources in Afrika's development and perceive its economic prosperity as its special responsibility and mission.

The Afrikan American community must no longer be afraid to be constructively critical of tyrannous, repressive, corrupt and inept governments in Afrika and across the diaspora. Such regimes are a threat to the vitality and survivability of the whole Pan-Afrikan community. The Afrikan American community must become vigilantly and jealously interested in U.S. and European policies toward Afrika and seek to influence those policies in both its own and Afrika's favor.

While being constructively critical of erring Afrikan governments and actively opposed to those which are repressive, the Afrikan American community must cooperate with Afrikan nations and peoples by providing and attracting markedly increased investments in their economies; by providing and brokering finance for the development of small business enterprises and manufacturing establishments which can greatly reduce unemployment; by supporting privatization programs, where appropriate, and by fostering the full development of capital markets, e.g., markets where economic growth may be aided and accelerated through the purchase fixed-interest and equity securities by U.S. investors, particularly Afrikan American investors themselves.

Afrikan Americans as well as continental Afrikan business-school graduates and economics professionals should be trained in the knowledge and expertise regarding the various financial sectors of Afrika; regulatory reform, the liberalizing of interest rates, institution-building and reform, the development of appropriate technologies, the restructuring of banks and financial institutions and the construction and operation of appropriate systems for the prudential regulation of banking, financial and economic systems which will help the Pan–Afrikan community to realize and abundantly enjoy the wealth with which it has been so naturally blessed.

The rapid expansion of the Afrikan diasporan nations and communities and Afrikan American investment in them must be very substantial if the Afrikan American community is to attain and sustain economic prosperity. The economic growth and development of Afrika and the disaporan communities are crucial to future economic and social well-being of the Afrikan American community. Since this is the case, it is of paramount importance that the community actively assist in the economic expansion of the Pan-Afrikan world community, first, through private and institutional investments in its member nations and communities, second, through influencing United States public and private economic and trade relations policies in favor of Pan–Afrikan economic growth and stability, and third, through prevailing on international agencies of the United Nations, The World Bank, and the IMF to initiate and execute truly viable and productive projects across the Afrikan diaspora.

Our proposal parallels that of Felix Rohaytn (ibid) with regard to the importance of the rapid growth in the developing world to the U.S. economy in particular, and the Western economies in general. In this context Rohaytn makes the following argument.

Without rapid growth in the developing world the West itself will be in great difficulty. The need for such growth has been little noticed, but it becomes clear when one considers how much demand for US exports depends on countries outside Europe, and other than Canada and Japan. During the past three years, exports to the other countries that make up the G-7 — Japan, Germany, Canada, the UK, France, and Italy — have grown at an annual rate of only 0.6 percent. By contrast, shipments of US goods to the rest of the world have risen at a rate of 7.6 percent. Although Europe and Japan are likely to recover eventually, the differences in the rate of growth are likely to continue.

The economist Henry S. Rowen recently published an article in the *Wall Street Journal* estimating growth rates between 1990 and 2020 in what he called "Rich Countries" — the G-7 and countries like Switzerland with comparable income levels — and the "Non-Rich Countries," including, for example, India, China, Indonesia, and Russia. Rowen estimated that the output of the rich countries would grow from $13 to $24 trillion during the period for an average annual growth rate of less than 2 percent per year. The output of the "non-rich" countries is expected to grow from $9 trillion to $34 trillion over the same period; that is, at about 4.5 percent per year.

These estimated growth rates are hardly exact but when considered along with other relevant data, such as the sources of demand for US exports, they clearly show that strong growth in the poorer parts of the world will be needed to sustain enough growth in the West to maintain adequate levels of employment and to enable Western governments to deal with their pressing social problems. It is also obvious that if added output of over $25 trillion is to be produced in the "non-rich" part of the world, huge amounts of capital will be required.

In order to help create a favorable investment climate in Afrikan diasporan nations and communities, the Afrikan American community must create its own stable and productive investment infrastructure. Moreover, it must appropriately organize its political economy and political system so that it may influentially interact with diasporan nations and communities. The major political objective of these national initiatives, on the part of the Afrikan American community, is the political stability of diasporan communities without which social and economic health both at home and abroad is impossible. The economic objective of these initiatives include the creation and expansion of productive capital markets, i.e., stock and bond markets, domestic banks that can lend and invest in their local economies, trading companies, alliances, joint ventures, subcontractors, and the elimination or significant reduction of barriers to, as well as the construction of channels for, the confident investment of Afrikan American money and Afrikan American brokered investments in enterprises and basic infrastructured facilities in Afrika and other Afrikan diasporan communities. If these ends are to be achieved it will be necessary that the Afrikan American community so develop its economic and political clout within the U.S. and develop such political, cultural and economic ties with the other diasporan communities that it can measurably help them to achieve three major goals necessary to its and their economic prosperity: growing economies, stable currencies, responsive and responsible social and political institutions. All of these ends are to be pursued in the hope that increasing Afrikan American investment — as well as domestic investment — will lead to increasing diasporan trade with the Afrikan American community and increasing employment both within that community and other Afrikan communities across the globe.

We do not deceive ourselves about the Afrikan American community's economic and political capacity to finance and undertake the projects we have just cited. The cost of such undertakings are enormous and cannot be borne by the Afrikan American community alone. However, we do think that the Afrikan American community has the ability to achieve high levels of sociopolitical organization and economic growth, and along with them, high levels of Black Power within the U.S. We believe that it can exercise such power in the U.S. and thereby in the world; that it will be able, in partnership with the rest of the diasporan communities, to move the international community to invest in Afrikan peoples so as to help them become prosperous and influential members of the world community of nations.

Chapter 16

INVESTING IN AND TRADING WITH AFRIKAN NATIONS

WHILE FEW AFRIKAN AMERICAN INDIVIDUAL and business investors may be prepared to engage in direct foreign investments in Afrika (the founding and owning of businesses, entering into joint ventures, partnerships, etc.), there is increasing opportunity for them to engage in portfolio investments there (the buying of stocks and other equities). As *Table* 16-1 indicates, stock markets have been developed and are developing in a growing number of sub-Saharan countries. In fact, the *New York Times* on April 3, 1994, reported:

> Africa, particularly that part of the continent south of the Sahara, has become a new hot target for international investing. In the last two months, brokerage firms in New York have floated three new funds — and raised more than $350 million — to invest in southern [not just *South*] Africa. And according to Fund Decoder, an industry newsletter, four more funds are in the works, including two that plan to invest across the continent....
>
> Investment experts also point to a variety of factors, from the end of the cold war to signs of improving commodity prices that may ultimately make Africa the greatest emerging market of them all.

The *Times* went on to point out that "The allure of Africa is its potential for economic growth that will far surpass that of industrial nations. A few African countries, including Botswana, Ghana and Kenya, have sustained growth rates of 5 percent a year in their gross national products...[according] to a portfolio manager for Morgan Stanley Asset Management in New York. That's almost twice last year's growth in the United States." The *Times* further reported on 4/3/94:

> Other African markets [i.e., other than the relatively large South Afrikan market] have shown even more spectacular increases, at least in local currencies. Last year, for example, stocks rose 41 percent in Nigeria, 67 percent in Mauritius, 116 percent in Ghana, 117 percent in Kenya and 161 percent in Zimbabwe.
> Nevertheless the stocks remain inexpensive by most measures.

The *Times* aptly warns that "Africa's markets are far riskier than those of the big developed countries, in part because they are so small."

While these assertions seem quite optimistic, especially given the political instability, weak currencies, small and fledgling stock markets — all indicative of high-risk investment environments — they point to a growing recognition of the ample manufacturing capabilities and markedly undervalued natural resources of a number of Afrikan nations. Moreover, while the current investment fad threatens to raise more money than there are stocks in Afrika thereby portending a possible market bust or collapse in the short run, long-term portfolio and direct investments may prove mutually profitable for both investors and the recipient nations. This could especially be the case if solid political and economic reforms take root in nations across the continent. Investors who are willing to take reasonable risks may take advantage of the fact that Afrikan stocks are inexpensive, and because Afrika is starting at a lower base, the investor enters the market at levels which allow sizeable room for growth. Investors can spread or hedge their risks by investing in a mutual fund that invests in emerging Afrikan markets. Perhaps such funds could be funded and operated by Afrikan American funds and/or joint ventures and alliances founded and operated by Afrikan Americans and continental Afrikans. A brief perusal of *Table* 16–1 indicates the population sizes and sizes of the Gross National Product (the total market value of all final goods and services produced in the economy in one year) of Afrikan nations where capital markets have been developed or are in the process of developing. In light of the great favorable differences in exchange rates between the United States and these countries, as well as the relative advantages in monetary and human capital possessed by the Afrikan American nation, its citizens and entrepreneurs could mutually benefit themselves and their continental brethren economically and otherwise by considering Afrika and Black nations and populations across the diaspora as natural locations for capital investments and business alliances. They should also be considered as possible places to resettle and contribute to their economic, social and political-cultural development.

Early American and European Investment Relations. The kind of nation-to-nation investment and trade relations we suggest relative to the Afrikan American nation and other Afrikan nations have a long history relative to other ethnically related nations. From the colonial era to the first World War, the United States was a debtor nation in international accounts, owing more than it was owed.[1] This situation was mainly due to the outstanding level of nonresident investment from abroad by European entrepreneurs, i.e., merchant houses and corporations in crucial sectors of the developing American economy. These investments included both direct (investor ownership and control of invested enterprise) and portfolio investments (where the investor lends to or purchases part ownership, i.e., buys equity in an enterprise but relinquishes control of it to its managers). European investors made major investments in American land, mining and manufacturing as well as in insurance, trading, banking and finance, transportation, i.e., railroads, government securities and other commercial activities.

Historian Mark Thomas describes the scope and influence of European foreign investments in the economic growth and development of the United States as follows:

> it was foreign capital that gave Americans the opportunity to forge a strong, dynamic economy. This was recognized as early as 1791 when Alexander Hamilton, one of the greatest economic minds produced by this country, observed that
>
>> Instead of being viewed as a rival [foreign capital] ought to be considered as a most valuable luxury, conducing to put in motion a greater quantity of productive labor and a greater proportion of useful enterprises, than could exist without it.
>
> A decade earlier, Robert Morris, financier supreme to the new Republic, had said much the same thing: "Money lent by the City of Amsterdam to clear the forests of America would be beneficial to both." This was not mere Federalist rhetoric. Hamilton and Morris

---

1. Mira Wilkins, *The History of Foreign Investment in the United States to 1914* (Cambridge, Mass.: Harvard University Press, 1989).

Where Markets Are Developing (Sub-Saharan Africa)

Country	Status	Population (million)	GNP (billion)
Cameroon	Establishing stock market		
Malawi	"	9.1	1.9
Tanzania	"	26.0	2.6
Uganda	"	17.5	2.9
Zambia	"	8.6	2.6
Botswana	Established stock market		
Ghana	"	1.4	3.8
Ivory Coast	"	12.8	8.7
Kenya	"	25.8	8.5
Mauritius	"	1.1	3.0
Namibia	"	1.5	2.5
Nigeria	"	101.9	32.5
South Africa	"	39.8	106.0
Swaziland	"	.86	930(mill)
Zimbabwe	"	10.4	5.9

Sub-Saharan Afrikan countries with stock markets and those establishing stock markets. Figures from 1992. Source: The *New York Times*, 4/3/94 – "Investors Who Discovered Africa."

Table 16-1

were describing the reality of colonial economic growth. It has been estimated that the accumulated debt of the colonies to Britain alone amounted to $40 million (about $1 billion at today's prices) by the time of the Revolution. Much of that was short-term credit, rather than long-term investment. Nevertheless, it was vital to the smooth working of the colonial economy. The plantations of the Chesapeake, the factory houses of Norfolk and Charleston, the trading concerns of New York and Boston, the iron works of rural Pennsylvania and the shipyards of Newport were all dependent on British finance. Immediately after the Revolution, John Lord Sheffield declared that "the greater part of the colony commerce was carried on by means of British capital" with more than four-fifths of European imports being "at all times made upon credit." Foreign money oiled the wheels of colonial commerce as well as colonial prosperity.

THAT COMMANDING POSITION

Independence saw no weaning of the American economy from the mother country as far as investment was concerned. ...Canal builders and railroad barons, symbols and architects of American expansion, went directly to London for capital. Foreign investors were absolutely crucial to the success of the canal boom of the 1830s, from the Erie Canal on down. Even the railroads glorified by that most American of board games, Monopoly, were owned in large part by the British, Dutch, and French in the 1850s. Indeed, so much of the stock of the Philadelphia and Reading was in British hands in 1857, that when the board of directors searched for a new president, they went to London to find him. Foreign capital was no less crucial to the opening up of the transcontinental system. When Jay Cooke, a father of the American capital market, wanted money to expand his Northern Pacific Railroad in the early 1870s to connect the east and west coasts, he turned to Europe, going from one banking house to another to raise the $50 million he needed. ...The Illinois Central, the Baltimore and Ohio, the New York and Erie, the New York Central — the list of pioneer American railroads dependent on European finance is impressive. No wonder that it has been argued that foreign capital "meant the difference between slow, self-generated development and the very rapid development" that did in fact occur.

Railroads were the most visible beneficiaries of foreign capital, but Europeans invested in every conceivable aspect of the American economy where profits could be made: oil in Wyoming, textiles in Massachusetts and Georgia, land and agriculture in Colorado and Kansas, fruit and oil in California, mining in Virginia, California, and Nevada. Money flowed from the London Stock Exchange, and from the bourses of Paris, Amsterdam, Berlin, and Vienna. Firms as crucial to the American Industrial Revolution as Western Union, AT&T, Eastman Kodak, Carnegie Steel, and General Electric, all borrowed from overseas in large volume. Borrowing from abroad was very much part of the American way of doing business in the nineteenth century.[2]

Thus, the basic economic development of the United States was not solely or primarily financed by indigenous means. European financial establishments, investors and trade alliances crucially abetted the development of the European-American nation — the United States. These financial alliances were further abetted by waves of European immigrants who additionally contributed in various ways to its ultimate economic and political supremacy. We must not forget that the economic-political developmental relationship between the United States and Europe, especially Western Europe, has been reciprocal and synergistically beneficial, empowering the White reign of supremacy in international relations. Similar invest-

---

2. Mark Thomas, "Who's Afraid of the Big Bad Trade Deficit?" in *Second Thoughts: Myths and Morals of U.S. Economic History,* Donald N. McCloskey, ed., (New York: Oxford University Press, 1993), pp. 90–91.

ment relations between the Afrikan American nation and Afrikan nations and communities across the diaspora are crucial to the mutual development of all concerned.

Pan-Afrikan Trade Alliances

The mutual economic development and political empowerment of Black America and Afrika require the functional development of Afrikan American-Continental Afrikan business and financial alliances as well as social-cultural relations. According to Peter Drucker, renowned management consultant, business writer, and business scholar, "All economics is international." Drucker goes on to say:

> *An additional lesson of the world economy is that investment abroad creates jobs at home.* In both the 1960s and the 1980s, expanded U.S. business investments overseas spurred rapid domestic job creation. The same correlation held for Japan and Sweden, both of which invested heavily in overseas plants to produce goods for their home markets.[3] [Emphasis added]

Drucker further notes that, "The services trade of all developed countries are growing fast, and it may equal or overtake their merchandise trade within ten years. Knowledge is the basis of most service exports and imports." One of the major bases for facilitating this trend is the formation of business alliances such as joint ventures, partnerships, sub-contracts, knowledge agreements and outsourcing arrangements. An international business alliance need not involve any investment at all or the required investment may be secondary. For example, an Afrikan American company may assume responsibility for the design and marketing for "afrocentric sneakers" or other products and enter into an alliance with a continental or diasporan firm to manufacture those sneakers or other products (the designing, financing, construction, and management development of the relevant manufacturing facilities could be handled by Afrikan American firms if need be). Such an alliance would consequently create jobs and opportunity in both the Afrikan American community and the allied continental or diasporan country or communities. Afrikan or diasporan companies could produce through joint ventures, American and Afrikan American-designed goods in Afrikan and diasporan countries for the markets in those countries. It is so common as to be almost unremarkable to find many products sold by

---

3. Peter Drucker, "What Kind of Trade Policy?" *Foreign Affairs*, Jan/Feb., 1994, Vol. 73, No. 1.

giant retail chains such as K-Mart, Walmart and Woolworth are manufactured in foreign countries such as China and Taiwan. The populations of immigrant communities in the United States from such nations are small compared to that of the Afrikan American community. Yet it is very unusual to find manufactured products made in Afrika or Afrikan diasporan nations sold by America's retail chains or discount stores, or as a matter of fact any stores in America, in spite of the very significant support given these establishments by Black American consumers. For example, one can go into a Woolworth store and buy a "steam/dry iron", an aluminum polished soleplate, lightweight smoothing iron which sells for $12.99 (at least in New York City) made in China. There is no apparent reason why an Afrikan American-Continental Afrikan business alliance cannot manufacture a similar product, among others, just as well or better designed, as inexpensive or less expensive, marketed by the F.W. Woolworth and other major retailers. There is no reason why such a product could not be sold worldwide.

Formal and informal alliances must become the dominant vehicles of the integration of the Pan–Afrikan economy. These alliances must pool knowledge, finance, and markets. Alliances between Black universities, their research staffs, labs and departments, between university research labs and departments and businesses, both within the Afrikan American community and across the Afrikan diaspora, must be operationally consummated. Alliances between banks, producers, mutual funds and other institutions are also possible.

All of these things must take place within the context of an Afrikan American nation-within-a-nation which makes itself effectively responsible for the nature and direction of U.S. foreign policy and trade relations relative to Afrika, and Black nations and peoples across the Afrikan Diaspora.

Global Policy Is Local

Michael Clough, Senior Fellow at the Council on Foreign Relations, correctly points out "that the wall separating foreign affairs from domestic influences has come crumbling down... The idea of a separation between domestic and foreign affairs has become untenable."[4] In a review of *Afrikan World* magazine's interview with Lamond Godwin (a senior director at American Express Bank) cited earlier, he asserts that Poland receives more attention and support from the U.S. government, in good part due to the activism of "very strong, very

---

4. Michael Clough, "Grass-roots Policymaking," *Foreign Affairs*, Jan./Feb. 1994, Vol. 73, No. 1.

well-organized" political constituencies for Poland in the U.S. His assertion corroborates Clough's general argument that "global policy is local." Clough goes on to reveal that many state and local institutions are establishing direct links with their counterparts around the world for various economic, technical and cultural reasons; that regions in the U.S. are developing their own economic interests and orientations, trade offices and other institutions necessary to pursue them on a global scale. He further notes that the economic, social and political incentives for individuals and groups to emphasize their ethnic identities are increasing as the U.S. becomes more ethnically diverse. Clough's central contention is best summarized thusly:

> In the 1980s, for example, African Americans, motivated in part by the model of Jewish-American support for Israel, largely succeeded in laying claim to U.S. policy toward Africa, especially toward South Africa. More recently, Mexican-American groups have begun to play a critical part in the NAFTA debate and in the formulation of U.S. policy toward Mexico generally. Similarly, a growing Chinese-American community has played an increasingly significant role in the policy toward China, and the American cousins of embattled East European nationalities have begun to mobilize as well.
>
> This trend is reinforced by the economic advantages that can accrue to ethnic groups who serve as a bridgehead for potentially prosperous countries such as China and Mexico. More and more foreign countries are beginning to see their ethnic brethren in the United States as natural allies in campaigns to develop more favorable bilateral relationships....
>
> Concentration of ethnic groups in particular geographic areas heightens the impact of the regionalization of foreign affairs.
>
> ...ethnic organizations may not only attempt to influence U.S. foreign policy but also to develop their own global policies.

The levels of immigration into the U.S. in the last twenty-four years approach those at the turn of the century. And the ethnic composition of this tidal wave of immigrants is far more diverse. The drive for current immigrant groups to divest themselves of their original language, culture, national identities and linkages to become "americanized", i.e., "real Americans", is not as intense as it was previously. As implied by multiculturalism, cultural orientations seem to have been reversed — ethnic immigrants now appear to be intensely resistant to losing their cultural identity and dissolving in the "American melting pot." This means that American society is becoming increasingly globalized, that is, the interconnections between local ethnic communities and their countries of origin will be maintained, and that developments abroad will measurably influence political, social and economic activities locally, and vice-versa. Thus, thinking and acting in global terms are becoming more common. The reciprocal relationship and influence between local ethnic communities and their ethnic cohorts abroad imply that planning for change in the local ethnic community may involve planning for coordinated change in ethnic communities abroad — planned changes in the nature and quality of their social, political and economic relationships.

While Afrikan Americans do not constitute an immigrant group in the classic sense of that term, they are interconnected by descent, culture, history, and ethnicity with Afrikan peoples across the diaspora. They share similar sociopolitical, socioeconomic problems and issues as well as a common fate with Afrikan peoples all over the globe. This fact requires that the interconnections between Afrikan peoples – wherever they exist – must be operationally strengthened. Where such interconnections do not exist, they must be created. For the globalization of the Afrikan community is essential to the salvation and the liberation of all local Afrikan communities.

If the Afrikan American community can markedly increase its internal trading, finance and service activities within and between its local and regional communities and markets, and within the general American market; if the Afrikan American community can become the central trading, finance and service hub for the vast Afrikan diasporan community and build its trade alliances with this community, it can thereby stem its increasing unemployment resulting from the de-industrialization of America and create increased employment opportunities for its members both at home and aboard.

The Possibilities of an Afrikan Investment Fund

While Afrikan stock markets are in their infancy (except for South Africa), are small, labile and may be considered high risk, their existence and growth may provide effective investment vehicles by means of which the Afrikan American community can contribute significantly to the economic advancement of the Continent. Of course, returns from investing in Afrikan markets are expected to economically expand and enrich the Afrikan American community reciprocally. Investment risks may be shared and spread across the investing Afrikan American community if large sums are invested by means of mutual investment funds and according to an investment plan in Afrika. Such a fund would permit individual Afrikan American institutions to not only contribute to the growth and development of the Motherland but will also permit them to gain equity ownership of Her wealth and production as well as to establish binding ties with Her which will permit them to socially share Her history and culture.

An "Afrikan Diasporan" Management Corporation may be created to raise several hundreds of millions, or perhaps more than $1 billion for a fund to invest in large, long-term infrastructure projects in Afrika. Such a fund would possibly make investments in projects for developing agricultural sectors, products and plantations, projects for developing energy, transportation, electrical power and petrochemicals, housing, retail, export, and health-care industries. Investing and trading in Afrika by Afrikan American corporations have already firmly started and their experience and know-how may possibly be used to aid the development of various investment funds. One such corporation is the African Development Public Investment Corporation of Hollywood, California, Dick Griffey, CEO. Founded in 1985, ADPI specializes in Afrikan commodities, air trading service, and oil trading. ADPI achieved sales of nearly $60 million in 1993. Fund investors may in some instances include various indigenous government agencies. With the exception of South Afrika, sub-Saharan Afrikan markets do not provide enough publicly traded stocks to invest large amounts of money. However, large sums may be readily invested in plants and equipment, ports and other major projects.

The Power of Investment Funds

If large and savvy enough, international mutual funds can possibly come to wield very significant clout in their invested nations. Mutual funds may in some ways take over the financing role of big banks and quasi-governmental institutions such as the International Monetary Fund.[5]

The roles of the World Bank and IMF are being undermined to such a degree by private capital that a columnist in the *Wall Street Journal* calls for their role redefinition. He contends:

> The World Bank and International Monetary Fund, once the chief doctors of the world's ailing economies, are battling to stay relevant.
>
> Times have changed since the two institutions held sway in countries desperate for a loan or project funding. Now, the surge in private financial activity in many emerging economies offers nations a different — and often more efficient — funding option.

---

5. "Some Mutual Funds Wield Growing Clout in Developing Nations," *Wall Street Journal*, June 14, 1994.

Last year, foreign direct investment in developing countries swelled to more than $56 billion — greater than the $51 billion in official development assistance, and far greater than disembursements by the bank and fund. Despite recent turmoil in emerging-market debt, the private flows are likely to grow in the 1990s, threatening to reduce the IMF and the World Bank to high-priced extras on the global financial stage. For one thing, Wall Street is likely to dominate the widely anticipated $300 billion in privatizations, mostly in developing countries.

These forces weren't evident 50 years ago, when representatives of 44 countries, meeting in Bretton Woods, N.H., created the World Bank and IMF to oversee postwar reconstruction and manage the world's monetary system. However, what the institutions need to do today isn't to retire, as some critics say. They need to redefine themselves.

Speaking at a State Department seminar last week, Deryck Maughan, chairman and chief executive of Salomon Brothers Inc., noted that private capital ruthlessly seeks economies where profits can be generated and shuns those where prospects are shakey. That means capital is concentrated on the reforming economies of East Asia and Latin America. "You'll get very little help from private capital" in the former Soviet Union and Africa, he said.

World Bank President Lewis Preston makes a similar distinction. He points to ballooning private capital flows but notes, "The problem is, it's only going to about 20 countries — the successful adjusters in Latin America and East Asia." The World Bank, he acknowledges, "shouldn't be lending these countries money."

This means that in the future the bank should leave the traditional financial work in countries such as Thailand and Mexico to the private financial engineers already flocking there. It should concentrate on places that private capital won't touch.[6]

According to the *Wall Street Journal*, in "the emerging economies of Eastern Europe, Latin America, Asia and Afrika, mutual funds are now one of the biggest suppliers of badly needed capital." Such investment clout allows funds to influence government policies in ways that maximize returns as well as general economic policies. The active presence of influential funds may motivate indigenous investment managers to raise their standards of policy making. The funds may facilitate easier access to powerful government officials. The *Journal* further comments that "the funds' ability — and propensity — to withdraw their money at any time gives them a

---

6. "It's Time to Redefine World Bank and IMF," *Wall Street Journal*, 7/25/94.

negotiating clout that perhaps is greater than that of the banks or the IMF, which allow countries time to solve their financial problems." Perhaps, viable funds financed by the Afrikan American community can help to empower Afrikan nations to neutralize the negative or maladaptive policies of the IMF, World Bank, and private financial-corporate cartels.

International Trade Centers

The ability of the Afrikan American community, more specifically of Afrikan American firms, to trade across the Afrikan diaspora, could be maximally facilitated by the active involvement of international trade centers. Such centers could be located in major metropolitan areas across the country. The functions proposed for these centers are based on those suggested by the Harlem Third World Trade Institute and the Harlem Urban Development Corporation of the State of New York. Both of these institutions along with Congressman Charles Rangel (Democrat of New York) are advocates for the construction of The International Trade Center to be located in Harlem. [These projects and organizations have come under the axe of the Pataki administration.]

Decentralized trade centers would be designed to achieve purposes similar to those of the Harlem Third World Trade Institute and those of the proposed International Trade Center. That is, the main purpose of the trade centers would be to stimulate and promote international trade between the Afrikan American community and the nations of the world, especially the developing nations, e.g., the Afrikan diasporan nations. Additionally, the trade centers would provide one-stop complexes which would handle all aspects of trade negotiations and transactions. A look at some of the program services and projects of the Harlem Third World Trade Institute gives some idea of the scope of service that could be provided by well-managed trade centers.

The concept for the proposed International Trade Center is a very intriguing one, as the prospectus published by its proponents indicates.

- **Purposes**

The purpose of the complex is to provide a multi-use, 24-hour activity center that will function as a business center for United States international trade. In addition to strengthening trade ties between the United States and developing nations, it is hoped that the center will be a catalyst for the social and economic revitalization of Harlem.

> **Program Services & Projects of
> The Harlem Third World Institute**
>
> - "How To" Export/Import Sessions
> - Trade Conferences & Seminars
> - Marketing Research
> - Referrals' Network (Public/Private)
> - Brokerage Services
> - Business Enterprises Development Program
> - Trade Leads Opportunities/Joint Ventures
> - Creative Financing/Countertrade Arrangements
> - Language Laboratory (Classes/Translation)
> - Trade Winds (International Trade Newsletter)
> - International Trade Intern Program (Academe)
> - Diplomatic Minority Service Directory
> - Job Skills Data Bank (Overseas Work)
> - Foreign Visitors' Program
> - Arts and Crafts Merchandise Mart

- **Services**

The complex and its facilities are expected to encourage technological development in health and agriculture, foster trade education through conferences and seminars, and promote tourism through its tourist information office.

- **Participants**

Developing nations and businesses, international financing institutions, United States agencies involved in international trade, major United States corporations, and major international airlines will participate in this ambitious project.

CONCEPT

In general, the ITC complex is designed to achieve the following goals.

- the establishment of New York State as the center for trade for developing nations
- the acceleration of development in Harlem and the expansion of jobs and business opportunities in the Harlem community
- the development of a one-stop trade center to facilitate export/import business between developing nations and the U.S.
- the collection and dissemination of trade information from U.S. firms and developing nations, and

- the provision of service for U.S. companies, particularly small and medium-sized companies, which are unable to send representatives to foreign countries.

Obviously, the basic concept and operation of local trade centers need not be as elaborate as the ones just depicted. Fundamentally, an upstart trade center may be little more than a computer facility with a conference room attached. The computer facility would maintain a complete and up-to-date data bank containing businesses, entrepreneurs, agencies and the like located in Afrikan diasporan countries who are seeking various services, business contacts and deals, joint ventures, etc.; Afrikan American businesses, professionals, persons and services interested in international trade, financial and consulting services; governmental agencies and bureaus, private financial services, transportation services, etc.; all the information which can facilitate the making and closing of trade deals and agreements.

Full use should be made of local universities, particularly Black Studies departments, in constructing and administering the trade center. A partnership with the local community college, university, or Black Studies department — and perhaps with helpful business firms and corporations — can help build a program of services like the ones cited earlier. Such a program, more fully described, could make the following offers (adapted from a brochure published by the Harlem Third World Trade Institute):

SERVICES

- **Brokerage**

Sellers and buyers are bought together and are taken through the steps of a trade deal: letters of credit, document filing, insurance, and freight forwarding.

- **Referrals**

If the needs of a business person cannot be met by the [trade center], referrals are made to government agencies that can best help that individual. The network includes, the International Trade Administration, the U.S. Department of Commerce, the Exim Bank, and the Overseas Private Investment Corporation.

- **Language Laboratory**

Designed to assist minority and small entrepreneurs in understanding the most widely used languages in international markets, notably: French, Spanish, Chinese, and Arabic. By providing these language tools, the [trade center] assists participants in international trade overcome some of the sociocultural barriers of working in and training with foreign countries.

- **Translation**
In dealing in international trade, many minority and small businesses enter into negotiations with countries where the official language is other than English. Contracts, joint venture proposals, letters, and telexes have to be translated.

- **Conferences/Seminars**
The [trade center] regularly conducts workshops and seminars. These meetings have panel presentations on marketing strategies, export opportunities, local export/import incentives, legislation on international trade, and United States and foreign governments' trade regulations.

PROGRAMS

The emphasis of the programs of the [trade centers] is on providing fledgling entrepreneurs with practical information necessary for the completion of international trade.

- **Export/Import Development**
Designed to assist individuals, businesses, and foreign governments in the arrangement and negotiation of transactions in international trade. Components include export/import financing through private lending institutions and government agencies; joint venture investments in overseas markets; and trade missions to and from developing nations.

- **"How To" Sessions**
An ongoing service for entrepreneurs who want to explore export potential. The different types of export firms are covered: Export/Import Companies, Export Trading Companies, Trade Consultants, Manufacturer's Representatives, Agents/Distributors, etc.

- **Educational Program**
The provision of information to minority and small businesses on the advantages, complexities, and possible pitfalls of international trade. The program draws on the knowledge and insights of professionals in business, government and academia. The center in collaboration with [the local university and city college, may conduct] an internship program which provides undergraduate and graduate level students with practical experience in international trade.

- INTERNATIONAL NETWORK
  Africa and the Caribbean [are] the areas of the Third World in which much of the center's programs and activities [will be] focused. By and through letters of introduction to firms across the world, other nations have indicated an interest in opening trade doors to the U.S.

through the [trade centers]. The [centers should also sponsor] a program to establish ongoing relationships with countries in Asia, Latin America and the South Pacific Islands.

- **Arts and Crafts Merchandise Mart**

The central objective of the project is to assist Third World countries in their economic development by providing a vehicle to market handcrafted merchandise in the U.S. and Canada.

The [center] realizes that craft export sale is a potential major foreign exchange earner and that the handicraft industry is a primary source of sustained employment for rural households within the Third World.

- **Job Skills Data Bank Service**

A program which offers employment opportunities in developing nations to the many United States-based minority professionals and technicians: In conjunction with other public and private agencies, provides training facilities and partial funding of specific manpower planning and development projects in research, labor recruitment, counseling and consulting, socioeconomic development, agriculture, and human services.

Each individual firm and organization which undertakes a project abroad under the auspices of the [trade center] is expected to place an emphasis on training the host country's manpower through skills transferral. Only through such efforts can the work of the Skills Data Bank participant be considered a service to the host country and a fulfillment of its objectives.

- **FOREIGN VISITORS**

In its bid to foster mutual trade relationships between public and private concerns in the Third World and small minority businesses in the United States of America, the [trade center should] regularly play host to heads of state and government, and dignitaries and entrepreneurs from Third World countries visiting the U.S.

Current Status of the International Trade Center. On November 14, 1994 the New York Times reported that the construction of the International Trade Center was to receive final approval when the state's Urban Development Corporation was expected to approve a revised plan for the 22-story complex at 125th Street and Malcolm X Boulevard the following Thursday, November 17, 1994. The U.D.C.'s approval, according to the Times, "would clear the way for the next phases of development: the selection of a hotel and the signing of tenants for the office space."

The revised plan for the trade center calls for 22 stories instead of the original 30. However, the 100-room hotel and the conference center for up to 750 people and a first-class office building, remain as holding retail space. Meeting rooms, a ballroom and exhibition halls will be housed in an adjacent building to be built above an existing parking garage. Trade center officials hope to draw their tenants mainly from companies and trade delegations from Afrikan and Caribbean nations as well as local corporations and organizations. Construction which is expected to start in early 1996 is to be completed two years later. [Though these projects have suffered under the budget cuts of the Republican administration of Governor Pataki, the need and concepts are still worthy of mention here.]

Institutions are social organizations whose central purpose is to further public welfare. They include a relatively stable set of social attitudes and relations which endow groups and their members with legitimacy and power, status and resources of various kinds. The power of a society is coterminous with the power of its institutions. The weakness or powerlessness of the Afrikan American community reflects the scarcity, ineptitude, dysfunctionality, and inappropriateness of its institutions. Appropriate, efficient institutions in the Afrikan American community, such as the trade centers just discussed, would contribute heroically to the empowerment and liberation of that body politic. They must be established with urgent care if the community is to secure its survival.

Chapter 17

EMPOWERMENT THROUGH WEALTH

The Tradition of Trade and Self-Help Among Afrikan Americans

THE CONTEMPORARY AFRIKAN AMERICAN community is heir to perhaps the longest tradition of commerce and entrepreneurialism of any group on earth. It is often not recalled that the most ancient Afrikan civilizations such as those of Ethiopia and the Nile Valley were founded on economic systems of trade and commerce. The fabled kingdoms and empires of both Eastern and Western Afrika were based on commercial enterprise, on monopolies and control over important economic material resources, centers of trade and major trade routes.

Basil Davidson notes in his book, *A History of West Africa*, that the specialness of that region rested "in the interplay of...three factors...metal working, production for trade, and markets of exchange." He writes extensively about the influence of these activities on many of the peoples of the Western Sudan and in the larger world including the so-called Middle East and Europe. He demonstrates that these trade activities and their reverberations along the long-distance trade routes across the Sahara fueled a "socio-economic motor of effective change" which facilitated "the notable political organization of Ghana" and the Western Sudan, the fatherland of the bulk of Afrikan descendants in the "New World." Davidson records the following basis for early trade in ancient West Afrika:

Old West Africa possessed two kinds of wealth that were greatly desired by the peoples of the far north and east, whether in Africa or Europe or Asia. These were gold and ivory.

...So the basis of trade between the Western Sudan and the Berbers of the Sahara lay in the exchange of salt for gold. But this was only the basis of trade. The total system was much wider. For the Saharan Berbers sold the goods they bought from the Western Sudan to the traders of North Africa, and the traders of North Africa sold them again to Europeans and Asians. European and Asian goods came down into West Africa by the same methods. Needless to say, there were other items of trade besides gold and salt.[1]

This trade led to the founding of cities which began as small trading settlements and evolved to become centers of government, centers for the employment of a variety of craftsmen who worked in "leather, wood, ivory and metals" (Davidson). Whether we study the particular empires or kingdoms of Ghana, Mali, Songhai, Kanem-Bornu, the Hausa States, Benin, Dahomey, the Asante Empire, etc., we note that they were centered around and based on trade, production, distribution and commercial activities of various types. Describing sixteenth-century West Africa, Davidson notes that:

> There was much development. Craftsmen worked in a wider range of skills. Farmers cultivated new crops for food, trade, and manufacture. Traders extended their business: scarcely any fragment of Western Africa, from the waters of the far Atlantic to the hills of Cameroon, now lay beyond the reach of their middleman skills and trading trails. Outstanding men ruled and judged, made war or pursued the arts of peace, wrote books and spoke poetry, composed music or carved in wood and ivory and clay.*
>
> West Africa exported a wide range of goods to the outside world. These included gold, ivory, cotton stuffs, animal hides and leather, kola, peppercorn, and mutton.*
>
> There also took place a...stratification of society, caused by the changing and expanding methods by which people worked and produced wealth. Craftsmen formed themselves into different groups, according to their skills: metalworkers, boat-builders, fishermen, farmers, diviners, priests, singers of songs and many others.*[2]

These observations by Davidson, drawn from his large corpus of work on the history and culture of Afrika, in conjunction with the voluminous histories of ancient and pre-slave Afrika by other

---

1. Basil Davidson, *A History of West Africa: to the Nineteenth Century* (New York: Doubleday Anchor Books, 1966), p. 33.

2. *Ibid., pp. 107, 153 & 175, respectively.

renowned Afrikan and Afrikan American historians, provide copious evidence that Afrikans who were forcibly imported into the Americas were the heirs to long traditions of trade and commerce, craftsmanship and entrepreneurialism. That the business and social organizational skills, the inventive and entrepreneurial genius to which they were heirs did not wither and die under the trauma of slavery, is evidenced by the following examples of Afrikan commercial activity in pre-revolutionary and ante-bellum America.

Race and Entrepreneurship — In his praiseworthy publication, *Entrepreneurship and Self-Help Among Black Americans,* John Sibley Butler points out that the lengthy business experience and traditions of commercial enterprise of Afrikans in America, i.e., Afrikan Americans, have been virtually ignored in the sociology of entrepreneurship and have not been included in building theories of group entrepreneurship. He cogently argues that "the literature on the sociology of enterprise leads to the assumption that Afro-Americans did not develop a strong business tradition — but this is far from being correct. The historical business tradition developed by this group, when measured by theories which guide the sociology of entrepreneurship was quite strong." Butler, utilizing his research and the outstanding research by students of Afrikan American business history such as DuBois, Minton, Pierce and Harris, provides very substantial evidence to support the contention that, in general, Afrikan Americans exhibited the same type of entrepreneurial spirit as other groups who migrated to this country. The list of Afrikan American entrepreneurial milestones and experience extracted from Butler's work only hints at the length, breadth and depth of the Afrikan American entrepreneurship.

Box 17–1	Afrikan American Entrepreneurial Milestones

- Anthony Johnson was probably the first person of African descent to become an entrepreneur in the New World. Having arrived in America before the pilgrims, he accumulated property in Jamestown, Virginia.

- The first wholesaler, merchant and settler of Chicago, Jean Baptiste Du Sable, was also a businessman and capitalist. As America began to take shape as one of the leading capitalist countries, Afro-Americans tried to carve out a business place for themselves.

- Afro-Americans developed enterprises in almost every area of the business community *prior* to the Civil War, including merchandising, real estate, manufacturing, construction trades, transportation, and extractive industries. This underscores the fact that Afro-Americans are woven historically into the economic fabric of America and *cannot be looked upon in totality, as a recently arrived ethnic group.*

• The reality of slavery was that slaves, despite acquired skills, could not become entrepreneurs in the true sense of the word... Nevertheless, the fact that *some degree of Afro-American entrepreneurship has been documented as existing during slavery* is testimony to the fact that this form of capitalism is able to exist under the most extreme conditions.

• In the late 1700s and the 1800s African American entrepreneurs were simultaneously involved in almost every major industry during this time period. This was especially true in the North where they excelled in all of the important occupations and formed an impressive and cohesive business class.

• "The Negro in the South was not only proficient as a carpenter, blacksmith, shoemaker, baker, tailor, and cook, but as a result of almost two and a half centuries of slavery up to the outbreak of the Civil War, the knowledge of these skills was concentrated almost exclusively in the hands of the Negroes, free and slaves" (Kinzer and Sagarin).

• Despite hardships presented by governmental restrictions and White racist social attitudes and practices, *wherever there were free Afro-Americans, a business tradition was developed.*

• In 1838, a pamphlet, perhaps the first of its kind, was published. Entitled "*A Register of Trades of Colored People in the City of Philadelphia and Districts,*" it listed 656 persons engaged in fifty-seven different occupations. ...The register also listed businesses which were independently run by women of African descent.

• During the 1700s and 1800s African Americans dominated and controlled a number of business niches and figured significantly in other business areas. Many of the businesses were lucrative and many business persons made a fortune.

• A significantly large number or class of free Black artisans, grocers, barbers, caterers, hotel owners, coal dealers, tailors, blacksmiths, craftsmen, and professionals existed prior to the Civil War. In a number of places those Blacks played a leading or dominant role in certain trades and their numbers increased after the war.

• A number of Atlanta's most important contractors and real estate dealers were Black during the 1800s and well past 1900.

• In Charleston, S.C. the butcher's trade and barbering were at one time dominated by Blacks. Black entrepreneurs were the backbone of the shoemaking trade, and until after World War I among the city's most prominent contractors.

• Before the Civil War, African American entrepreneur Thomy Lafon of New Orleans, achieved considerable notoriety as a merchant, moneylender and real estate dealer. When he died in the 1880s he left an estate worth a half-million dollars.

- In the late 1800s entrepreneur Wiley Jones not only generated a reputed fortune of some $200,000 through farming, horsetrading, liquor selling, and transportation, but also through his ownership of a streetcar line in Pine Bluff, Arkansas.

- When R.R. Church died in 1912 in Memphis, he had reportedly accumulated a fortune of over a million dollars gained through speculation and investment in Memphis real estate as well as investments in White-owned corporations.

- According to historian August Meier (from whose work the six prior citations were drawn) "There was a real burgeoning of Negro enterprise after 1890 and especially after 1900, though it was based more on the Negro market than were earlier enterprises. According to the National Negro Business League, the number of business enterprises had risen from 20,000 in 1900 to 40,000 in 1914. In that period banks had risen from 4 to 51; undertakers from 450 to 1000; drug stores from 250 to 695; retail merchants from 10,000 to 25,000. Perhaps the most celebrated of these newer enterprises was that of the millionaire, Madame C.J. Walker, a St. Louis laundress who invented the first successful hair-straightening process."

- In addition to development of business enterprise during this early period, Afro-Americans displayed an active role in the area of inventions... They participated in significant numbers in the development of the nation during its early years.

- There are records which show that, as early as 1789, Afro-Americans found it difficult to borrow money in order to establish business enterprises. Nevertheless, through hard work and thrift, many were able to do so.

- In order to generate capital, Blacks organized mutual aid societies for mutual assistance. These mutual-aid societies were combinations of secular fund raising and religious institutions. Many of these societies also provided some form of insurance for their members.

- In addition to mutual-aid societies, and because of the success of many Afro-Americans, there was *trade in money lending.*

- Before the Civil War in the North and South *the clients of Afro-American business persons were interracial.* However, whenever they became very successful, Euro-Americans tried to disrupt their businesses. There were *laws passed by some states which made it very difficult to make their enterprises successful.*

- At the turn of the century, commentators and scholars were as excited about Durham, North Carolina, as they are today about the Cuban-American experience in Miami [or the Korean-American experience in New York City and Los Angeles].

- W.E.B. DuBois noted after visiting Durham that "there is in this city a group of five thousand or more colored people, whose social and economic development is perhaps more striking than that of any similar group in the nation."

- Sociologist E. Franklin Frazier, in complimenting the business acumen of Black Durham businessmen noted that "As we read the lives of the men in Durham who have established the enterprises there, we find stories paralleling the most amazing accounts of the building of American fortunes. We find them beginning their careers without much formal education and practicing the virtues of the old middle class... These men have mastered the technique of modern business and acquired the spirit of modern enterprise."

- Durham began as a financial district as early as 1907... In many publications throughout America, it was called the "Wall Street of Negro America." The strength of one of its larger firms, The Mechanics and Farmers Bank, is demonstrated by the fact that it helped most, if not all, the Afro-American businesses in Durham to survive the Great Depression, a feat which the great majority of American small businesses were unable to match.

- One observer wrote that "a common feature of the Negro business interests of Durham is the fact that *not one* of their group organizations failed during the period of depression."

- Just as the Japanese were able to develop economic success in California at the turn of the century, Afro-Americans were able to do the same... Although other cities throughout the country were not as strong as Durham, Afro-Americans in other cities also developed a strong middle class which was grounded in entrepreneurship and the professions. In cities throughout the country, entrepreneurship flourished in part because of the structure of racial discrimination.

- Stories of successful businesses run by free Afro-Americans in both the North and South since the 1700s had been passed down through the decades. Drawing ideas from the experiences of Afro-American business persons Booker T. Washington sought to organize Black businesses nationally.

- In 1900, Booker Washington spearheaded the development of the National Negro Business League to encourage enterprise. The League was founded on certain fundamental assumptions which were designed to: (1) generate high character; (2) develop racial respect; (3) develop economic stability; and (4) lay the economic groundwork for future generations.

- It was the economic experience of African Americans, the economic opportunities available to them as they organized to take advantage of them, and the organizational efforts of Booker Washington in this regard, that inspired and attracted Marcus Garvey, the consummate advocate of Black self-help, to the U.S.[3]   ▪

---

3. The above list was adapted and quoted from John Sibley Butler, *Entrepreneurship and Self-Help Among Black Americans: A Reconsideration of Race and Economics* (Albany, New York: State University of New York Press, 1991).

Tulsa, The Black Promised Land

The Durham model was duplicated across Black America. There existed quite a number of Black towns across the country and a large number of Black "main streets" in many American towns and cities where Black-owned businesses and Black professionals prospered.

One rather famous Black "main street" was Greenwood Avenue, north of Archer, better known as "Deep Greenwood", in Tulsa, Oklahoma. In fact, "Deep Greenwood" comprised the heart of Black Tulsa's business community. It was regularly referred to by many as the "Negro Wall Street" (Ellsworth, 1992). Ellsworth describes Tulsa's Black business district and neighborhood during the first decades of the 1900s:

> By the year...1921, the black population had grown to almost 11,000 and the community counted two black schools, Dunbar and Booker T. Washington, one black hospital, and two black newspapers, the Tulsa *Star* and the Oklahoma *Sun*. Black Tulsa at this time had some thirteen churches and three fraternal lodges — Masonic, Knights of Pythias, and I.O.O.F. — plus two black theaters and a black public library.
>
> A focal point of the community was the intersection of Greenwood and Archer. This geographical location — a single corner — has had something of a symbolic life of its own in Tulsa for most of the twentieth century, as it has been a key spot of delineation between the city's black and white worlds. The corner has even been mentioned in song. Beginning about 1941, Bob Willis and his Texas Playboys, a white "western swing" group which drew their music heavily from black sources, sang:

> Would I like to go to Tulsa?
> You bet your boots I would,
> Let me off at Archer,
> I'll walk down to Greenwood
>
> Take me back to Tulsa...

> And in the 1970s, a nationally known black musical group from Tulsa, the Gap Band, drew its name from Greenwood, Archer, and Pine streets.
>
> ...Two- and three-story brick buildings lined the avenue, housing a variety of commercial establishments, including a dry goods store, two theaters, groceries, confectionaries, restaurants, and billiard halls. A number of black Tulsa's eleven rooming houses and four hotels were located here. "Deep Greenwood" was also a favorite place for the offices of Tulsa's unusually large number of black lawyers, doctors, and other professionals. The district would especially come

alive on Thursday nights and Sunday afternoons and evenings — the traditional "days off" for black domestic workers living in white neighborhoods."

...Along Detroit Avenue and certain other streets were the neat, sturdy homes of some of those black Tulsans who owned businesses lining Greenwood Avenue, augmented by the houses of the city's black professional class. Within this elite group, some were rumored to have assets in excess of $100,000.[4]

Black Tulsa's prosperity was interrupted in May 1921 when an exceedingly destructive race riot eventuated in the almost total burning down of its business district and surrounding neighborhoods by raging White mobs, inflammatory police and national guard tactics.

Table 17–1 provides some idea of the broad variety of businesses and professions owned and practiced by Blacks in Tulsa.

Black Phoenix Rises from Its Ashes

The greater testimony to the heroic character of Black Tulsans is not only brilliantly illuminated by their pre-riot entrepreneurial accomplishments, but more so by their post-riot rebuilding of their enterprises. Ellsworth succinctly pays tribute to their courage and ingenuity when he writes that "In the aftermath of the Tulsa race riot, black Oklahomans employed their own resources, and in doing so they endured."

Ellsworth describes the rebuilding of "Deep Greenwood" in the following way:

> The rebuilding of black Tulsa after the riot, particularly that of "Deep Greenwood," is a story of almost as great importance as the riot itself. Perhaps more than anything else, this rebuilding was a testament to the courage and stamina of Tulsa's black pioneers in their struggle for freedom.
>
> Many of the buildings along the first block of Greenwood Avenue running north from Archer Street were rebuilt by the end of 1922. Although the burned-out shells of the pre-riot structures were for the most part torn down, many of the new buildings assumed the form of their predecessors. The 1922 Williams building, for example, bears a great resemblance to its pre-1921 predecessor. Many of these later buildings were constructed, as the original ones had been, with red bricks from a local brickyard located two blocks north of the avenue.

---

4. Scott Ellsworth, *Death in a Promised Land: The Tulsa Race Riot of 1921* (Baton Rouge, LA.: Louisiana State University Press, 1992), pp. 14–16.

"A little over a decade" after the riot, Henry Whitlow has written, "everything was more prosperous than before. Most of these businesses even survived the Depression." Furthermore, Whitlow tells us that a local Negro Business Directory was published, a Greenwood Chamber of Commerce organized, the National Negro Business League hosted here, and a black entrepreneur by the name of Simon Berry established a black-owned bus system. "Tulsa's Negro owned and operated business district became known nationally."[5]

All-Black Towns in America

In tandem with the idea of the development of predominantly Black owned and controlled business districts in towns and cities across the country, ideas about establishing all-Black communities, even of all-Black states within the United States and all-Black nations outside the U.S. — especially in the Caribbean and in Afrika — were also extremely popular in the Afrikan American community of the 19th century. More than two dozen all-Black towns were founded in the late 1800s. Among the better known all-Black towns across the country were Kowaliga (Alabama), Mound Bayou (Mississippi), and Boley (Oklahoma).

Kowaliga, Alabama, was established about 1897 by William Benson. A graduate of Howard University, Benson founded an "industrial settlement" populated primarily by farmers, landowners and skilled craftsmen who would be able to minister to their own and the needs of the entire community. His Dixie Industrial Company purchased large tracts of land which it sold on easy terms to members of the community, constructed a 15-mile railroad, and operated a timber company, sawmill and retail stores. The town's Kowaliga School was designed to produce skilled farmers and mechanics as well as good husbands and housewives rather than servants.

Mound Bayou was founded in 1887 by Isaiah T. Montgomery, former slave and staunch defender against the disenfranchisement of Black Mississippians. Charles Banks, a graduate of all-Black Rust University at Holly Springs, Miss., as Mound Bayou's leading merchant founded a bank, a cottonseed oil mill, and a loan and investment company after he moved there in 1903. Besides Banks' enterprises the town boasted a sawmill, a farmers' Co-Operative Mercantile Company, real estate ventures, a newspaper, a Normal and Industrial Institute, and an electric power company.

Boley was also among the earliest of some 25 all-Black towns founded (1898) in America. In 1914 Boley boasted of a $150,000 high

---
5. Ibid., p. 108.

**Black Business Establishments and Business
Persons in Tulsa as Listed in Tulsa City Directories, 1921.**

Establishments	21	Professionals	21	Service Workers	21	Skilled Crafts Persons	21	Semi-Skilled Workers	21
Bath Parlors	2	Dentists	2	Barbers	12	Bakers	5	Expressmen and Messengers	2
Billiard Halls	9	Druggists and Medicine Manufacturers	4	Cleaners, Hatters, Dryers, and Pressers	5	Blacksmiths	2	Housemovers	
Cigars and Tobacco	4	Jewelers	1	Hairdressers	3	Contractors, Carpenters, Builders, House and Sign Painters	5	Newsdealers	
Clothing, Dry Goods, Racket, Second-hand, Music, Furniture, Paints and Oils, Shoes	1	Lawyers	3	Launderers		Dressmakers	2		
Confectionary, Soft Drinks	2	Nurses		Shoe Shiners	6	Milliners			
Feed and Grain	4	Photographers	2	Total	26	Plumbers			
Furnished Rooms, Boarding and Rooming Houses	1	Physicians and Surgeons	15			Printers	1*		
Garages, Auto Repair and Filling Stations	11	Real Estate, Loans, and Insurance Agents	6			Printers	1		
Grocers, Meat Markets	2	Private Detectives				Shoemakers and Shoe Repairers	4		
Hotels	41	Total	33			Tailors	10		
Restaurants	5					Upholsterers	1		
Theaters	30					Total	24		
Undertaker's Parlors	2								
Total	108								

Adapted from: Scott Ellsworth, *Death in a Promised Land*, pp. 115–17.

Table 17-1

– 424 –

school, cement sidewalks, attractive residences, a Masonic temple, electric power plant and waterworks, and eighty-two business concerns, including a bank, three cotton gins, and a telephone system.

The story of Tulsa is the story of Black American entrepreneurial triumph and tragedy. A story now almost forgotten in America — the nation which epitomizes entrepreneurialism — it is a story almost uncelebrated in Black folklore. And Black America is economically the poorer and politically the weaker for such preterition.

The entrepreneurial spirit of Black Tulsa, Durham, Atlanta, Philadelphia, Chicago, Kansas City and many other pre-Great Depression Black main streets across the nation, must be rediscovered and revived if the Afrikan American community is to realize its economic and political power.

Early Afrikan American Investment in Afrika: The Case of Marcus Garvey

Many in the Afrikan American community perceive and wish to relate to continental Afrika in ways similar to the ways the European community perceived and related to America during its early history. Just as the Europeans saw America as a locale for emigratory resettlement, as a trading and commercial partner, and as providing opportunities for mutually profitable capital investments, many Afrikan Americans perceive Afrika as a place for the realization of similar possibilities relative to themselves. This perception on the part of Afrikan Americans has a somewhat lengthy history. It achieved its most dramatic expression in The Honorable Marcus Garvey's attempts to re-settle Afrikan Americans in Liberia and initiate economic trade relations between the continental Afrikan nations and the Afrikan American community.

In 1920, Marcus Garvey as head of the Universal Negro Improvement Association (UNIA) set in motion a plan to "colonize" Liberia and to establish trade relations with that Afrikan nation then founded as a locale for the re-settlement of Black Americans in Afrika under the aegis of the United States government.

As intimated by historian August Meier, among American Blacks "Interest in colonization in tropical lands abroad had had a long antebellum history and enjoyed its greatest vogue in periods when the outlook seemed the most discouraging, particularly during the decade preceding the Civil War, when the emigration conventions represented a full-blown nationalist movement."[6] Meier goes on to relate

---

6. August Meier, *Negro Thought in America: 1880-1915* (Ann Arbor, Michigan: Univ. of Michigan Press, 1966).

that "By the time of the Civil War, almost every Negro leader of consequence ... either favored or was at least open to the idea of colonization in Africa or one of the Caribbean lands." Afrika consciousness was the hallmark of the Black immigration and nationalist movements during this period.

In this context, historian Richard B. Moore has noted the numerous books written by Afrikan, Afrikan American, Afrikan Caribbean, and European authors about ancient and contemporary Afrikan history during the period of the mid-1800s to the first three decades of the 1900s. These publications, in addition to pamphlets, newspapers and other types of literature along with the numerous lectures and conventions pertaining to emigration, trade and cultural relations between Black America and Afrika, point to the general "Afrika consciousness" then prevalent among Afrikan Americans. Moore provides a brief list of the many book titles published at that time, including the two cited below:

> Though written in 1886, the challenging book, *Liberia: The Americo-African Republic* by T. McCants Stewart urged AfroAmericans to "put their own ships on the sea... We must have our own vessels carrying our Afrikan workers, our civilization, and our wares back to the 'Fatherland,' and bringing back its riches." This exhortation concluded with the confident vision of a great "Americo-African Republic," extending 'into the Soudan, throughout the Niger and into the Congo; and under a mighty African ruler, there will arise a stable and powerful Government of Africans, for Africans, and by Africans, which shall be an inestimable blessing to all mankind."
>
> Likewise far-visioned were the writings of Alexander Crummell: *The Future of Africa* and *Africa and America*. The last contained his classic essay on *The Relations and Duties of Free Colored Men in America to Africa*, originally published in 1861. This dedicated thinker affirmed "a natural call upon the children of Africa in foreign lands, to come and participate in the opening treasures of the land of their fathers."

Moore goes on to further substantiate his contention of a general Africa consciousness prevalent in the Afrikan American community of the 1800s.

early ties to Africa

Consciousness of their ancestral homeland has thus been historically evident from the first arrivals when some of these Africans, brought as slaves into the Americas, killed themselves believing that they would thereby return to Africa. Awareness of their heritage of culture and dignity continued during the colonial period and the early days of this republic. The name *African* was then preferred and used instead of the slave-masters' degrading epithet "negro." Witness thus The Free African Society, founded in Philadelphia in 1817 by Richard Allen and Absalom Jones. This was the forerunner of the African Protestant Episcopal Church of St. Thomas and also of the African Methodist Episcopal Church. Note also the African Lodge of Prince Hall Masons in Boston; the African Methodist Episcopal Zion Church, African Society for Mutual Aid, African Grove Playhouse in New York; and many so named throughout the country.

As early as 1788 an organized body of Afroamericans in Newport, R. I., which included Paul Cuffee who was soon to make history in this respect, wrote to the Free African Society of Philadelphia proposing a plan for emigration to Africa. In 1811 Paul Cuffee sailed in his own ship to Sierra Leone to investigate the feasibility of founding a settlement there. In 1815 at his own expense amounting to some $4,000, Captain Paul Cuffee, consummating twenty years of thought and effort, sailed forth again to Sierra Leone, this time commanding the good ship *Traveler* with 38 Afroamerican emigrants abroad, which included several whom he had boldly rescued from slavery along the Atlantic seaboard.

Paul Cuffee's achievement gave impetus to the founding of the American Colonization Society in 1817. But this body was dominated by slaveholders with the object of getting rid of free Afroamericans whose very presence and example encouraged the slaves to seek freedom. Hence the American Colonization Society was powerfully opposed by free-spirited Afroamericans and their Abolitionist allies.

Nevertheless, several Afroamerican leaders took advantage of the operation of the American Colonization Society to foster self-government in Africa through the founding of Liberia... [Afrikan American] Joseph Jenkins Roberts was elected first president of Liberia in 1848. By this time the population of Liberia included some 3,000 persons of African descent who had emigrated from the United States of America and the Caribbean.

The distinguished Afroamerican scholar, Rev. Alexander Crummell, after graduating from Cambridge University in 1853, spent 20 years teaching and laboring in Africa. Commissioned by a convention of Afroamericans held in Chatham, Canada West, in 1858, Martin R. Delaney led an expedition into what is now Nigeria and published his *Official Report on the Niger Valley Exploring Party* in 1861. This mission had even signed a treaty with African rulers at Abeokuta which authorized a projected settlement, but this project lapsed after the outbreak of the Civil War in the U.S.A. The other commissioner of this expedition, Professor Robert Campbell, published his report in *A Pilgrimage to My Motherland*.

After the Civil War and Reconstruction, interest was revived in African settlement as a great exodus from the south, due to the wholesale massacre of some 40,000 Afroamericans by such terrorist organizations as the Ku Klux Klan. This reign of terror reached monstrous proportions after the withdrawal of federal troops from the south. A new movement for immigration to Africa was fostered jointly by Afroamerican Baptists and Methodists; Bishop H.M. Turner played a leading part in this endeavor. Organizations were established in several states, notably the Liberian Exodus and Joint Stock Company in North Carolina and the Freedmen's Emigration Aid Society in South Carolina. This last acquired the ship *Azor* for $7,000 and this ship actually carried 274 emigrants to Africa on one of its trips, despite the efforts of prejudiced European Americans to impose outrageous costs and to hinder its operation. The *Azor* was soon stolen and sold in Liverpool; the attempt to recover it failed when the U.S. Circuit Court refused even to entertain the suit brought to this end.

About 1881 a descendant of Paul Cuffee, Captain Harry Dean, sailed to Africa commanding his ship the *Pedro Gorino* with the object "to rehabilitate Africa and found an Ethiopian Empire as the world has never seen." Another expedition took 197 emigrants from Savannah, Georgia to Liberia. "Chief Sam" of Kansas launched a movement to sail ships and build a state in Afrika but this movement failed to achieve its goals.

The idea of Blacks moving to areas where they would possess an independent state, a place where they could escape the psychosocial, political and economic ill-effects of endemic White American racism, and enjoy life as a free people, was not merely confined to overseas locations such as the Caribbean and Afrika. As previously corroborated, many sought to found independent, all-Black towns and states in America. Many such towns were established and an attempt to create an all-Black state in Oklahoma Territory in the 1890s was vigorously pursued by a number of Black leaders and organizations.

It must also be underscored the motive for the desire of many Blacks to migrate or emigrate to all-Black towns, states, or nations was not merely to escape adverse political and social conditions. In many instances economic motives predominated. Nationalistic sentiments, the desire to found economically and culturally great nations, were inextricably intertwined with other social and economic drives. There existed in the 1870s a South Carolina Liberian Joint Stock Company. This is the legacy to which the Honorable Marcus Garvey and the U.N.I.A. were progenies.

The U.N.I.A. and Afrikan American-continental Afrikan Trade Relations. Amy Jaques Garvey, Garvey's widow, in her book *Garvey & Garveyism* writes the following about Garvey's attempts to colonize and trade with Liberia:

> In May 1920, the Executive Council of the U.N.I.A. decided to send a delegation to Liberia to negotiate with the government regarding colonization over there. It was difficult to get passports in a hurry, which was necessary since they wanted a reply for the August convention; so only Elie Garcia was able to go, as he had a Haitian passport. He was given the rank of commissioner and empowered to negotiate all business.
>
> In a letter dated June 8, 1920, addressed to Hon. C. King, President of Liberia, Mr. Garcia stated the purposes of his mission, and specifically stated that,
>
>> it is the intention of the U.N.I.A. to establish trade routes through a line of steamships, etc., to encourage emigration to build up the country, to transfer its Headquarters to Liberia, to bring with it medical and scientific units, etc. Therefore the Organization asks for written assurance that every facility will be given it to procure lands for business, agriculture and industrial purposes. In return the Organization with its vast membership will lend financial and moral support to the Government to help her out of her present economic plight.
>
> After many interviews, inspection of sites, and collection of statistics, the Government and people signified their happiness in having the U.N.I.A. operate in Liberia.[7]

Garvey made good on his stated intentions and objectives. The U.N.I.A. sent a delegation of six persons to Liberia after receiving a favorable reply from Liberia's secretary of state to the letter just cited. This delegation included an agricultural officer, surveyor, pharmacist, and a builder. They carried machinery and supplies with them and were recipients of subsequent shipments. They were later joined by many other U.N.I.A. members. In December 1923, another delegation was sent to Liberia to make arrangements for a full-scale, colonization program and to work out further details of trade, commerce and resettlement. Also at this time Garvey went full steam ahead in laying the concrete foundations for actualizing the U.N.I.A.'s Afrikan-Afrikan American trade program. Amy Jacques Garvey writes:

> From December 1923, when the delegates reported by letters the Liberian government's approval of the colonization plans, Garvey

---

7. Amy J. Garvey, *Garvey & Garveyism* (New York: Macmillan, 1970).

went ahead with the formation of another steamship line, called The Black Cross Navigation and Trading Company, and the purchase of one large ship to ply between Liberia and America, in keeping with the recommendations from Liberia. Later on they were to get a smaller coastal ship to trade on the West Coast of Africa, as there was a great need for this. The ship would act as a feeder for the larger vessel. This new company bought the S.S. *General Goethals*, paid $60,000 down and spent an additional $20,000 fitting it up for passengers and freight. All stocks were held by the U.N.I.A., which borrowed moneys from the members on terms of five to ten years for repayment. The ship was rechristened the *Booker T. Washington*.

These activities were followed by interactions between the U.N.I.A. and Liberia:

In June 1924 the U.N.I.A. sent out a team of experts to prepare camps for the colonists. They were: O'Meally, commissioner; William Strange, mining and civil engineer; Roberts, electrical engineer; Walcott, shipwright and builder; Hurley, carpenter and builder; Nicholas, mechanical engineer, and Rupert Christian, Secretary. With these men went thousands of dollars of material for ready use on landing. Additional shipments on a later ship were contracted to be sent for, when there were storage facilities.

Unfortunately, due to the skullduggery of White businessmen whose interest in Liberia's minerals and rubber was stimulated by the U.N.I.A.'s economic explorations, the Firestone Rubber Company (who received a 99-year lease on a million acres of Liberian land), and machinations of the U.S., British, and French governments, the U.N.I.A. project was summarily aborted.

Black Nationalism and Afrikan American-Afrikan Trade Relations. Garvey's initiatives remain central to the programmatic intentions of contemporary Black nationalists. However, such initiatives are not mere partisan concerns. Their acceptance, elaboration, and realization are crucial to Afrikan American and Pan-Afrikan liberation, survival, prosperity, and power as they have always been. The need for Afrikan-based trade, economic and cultural cooperation cannot be overstated.

For liberating, enriching and empowering trade, economic and cultural relations to take place within the context of the world-wide Afrikan community, the Pan–Afrikan economic intentions of pre-World War I Afrikan American leadership and of Marcus Garvey must be rediscovered, revitalized, and refurbished by the contemporary Afrikan leadership and community. The success of continental Afrikan-Afrikan American trade relations depends to a significant degree on the "colonization" of Afrika by segments of the Afrikan American community and vice versa with regard to continental Afrikans. That is, the Afrikan American community must initiate a deliberate diaspora of regular immigrants, business and professional persons, business, professional and service establishments across all the important trade areas of Afrika so as to permit the rapid development of trade alliances and relations between Afrikan Americans at home and those abroad. It is expected that the Afrikan Americans located in Afrika would have thoroughly integrated their business activities with those of native-born Afrikans thereby facilitating true continental Afrikan-Afrikan American trade rather than Afrikan American enclave-Afrikan American trade which exclude native Afrikans. Integrated continental Afrikan-Afrikan American business communities on both sides of the Atlantic would help immensely to overcome cultural and linguistic barriers as well as barriers of distrust to consummating and operationalizing trade and economic relations. This type of arrangement is not unprecedented in history. By these and other means, the Afrikan American community and the community of Afrikan nations can mutually accelerate and motivate each other's economies in ways similar to the mutual growth and development of the economies of Western Europe and the United States.

Repression of Afrikan American Economic Power

One of the most important and potent sources of social power is access to and control over economic resources. The relative powerlessness of Afrikan Americans is directly related to their relative lack of control over important economic resources. However, as demonstrated in the prior section, this lack is neither due to the absence of an entrepreneurial tradition nor an absence of "economic virtues" so celebrated in White Americans and economically successful immigrant groups, including the fabled Koreans and Cubans. The relative feebleness of Afrikan American enterprise has been deliberately induced and maintained by a number of concrete socioeconomic, sociopolitical actions taken against their economic growth, development and power by three major groups — White Americans, immigrants, and Blacks themselves — particularly the Black leadership establishment.

The study of early Afrikan American entrepreneurial history reveals that when Black business persons were permitted relatively free access to full American markets, i.e., allowed to develop clientele from all racial groups, many of their businesses prospered. Moreover, Afrikan Americans gained a number of economic niches and monopolized a number of trade and service areas in the American market place. They demonstrated the characteristics celebrated later in economically aggressive immigrant groups. However, unlike the immigrant groups who followed Blacks into American business, Black business progress was deliberately retarded, completely destroyed or marginalized by the federal and state governments and White racist social attitudes and practices. Black business activity was not *laissez-faire*, i.e., free to pursue its own ends unhindered by racial barriers, attitudes, practices and governmental interference as were other ethnic groups. In this regard, Butler aptly notes the following:

> It is significant to point out the system of segregation which was implemented as a program in the South applied exclusively to Afro-Americans. For Chinese Americans, Mexican Americans, Jewish Americans, or Native Americans, the system did not apply. Thus, in the South and as late as the 1960s, Mexican Americans did not have to drink, eat, and sleep at segregated fountains or in segregated hotels. This is also true for other ethnic groups such as Italians and Jews who moved into the Southern states.
>
> Although there were competitive conflicts between ethnic non-black ethnic groups, there were never explicit legalistic codes and practices developed by state governments to control their every movement. *This governmental control took away the opportunity for Afro-American business to compete in a truly open market. This is one of the fundamental differences between Afro-American business and ethnic American business.* For example, while the Japanese in California were able to develop a White clientele, Afro-Americans were forced to find clients from within their own communities. Such a governmental policy negatively impacted the program which Washington [Booker] designed for business development in the South.
>
> This reality was also taking place in the North. As ethnic groups began to migrate to America, and as Afro-Americans from the South began to go North, the relationship between Afro-American business, and White clients began to change. Most importantly, the strong Afro-American service businesses which had been developing since the 1700s were being replaced with other ethnic businesses [Emphasis added].

Thus, as Butler demonstrates, Afrikan American business and economic development and the economic power these factors afforded were forced to take what he terms an *economic detour*, due to governmental "Jim Crow" laws in the South and *de facto* segregation and informal racism in the North. This early American anti-Black business pattern was to continue formally and informally to this very day. Butler contends, "While Japanese, Italians, Jews, and other ethnics developed business activities and were free to place enterprises in the major growth area of the city (and, of course, in their own neighborhoods) and take full advantage of the free enterprise system, Afro-Americans found themselves limited by law and unable to pursue this simple tenet of free enterprise." This near-total governmental interference in the common and business lives of Afrikan Americans and in support of White racist market practices, e.g., excluding Black vendors from competing on equal terms for business contracts or gaining access to doing business and providing services with and for federal, state, and local governments and their various agencies, still continues. For example, as recently as December 23, 1991, the *New York Times* reported that thousands of minority companies were forced to close as government contracts with them began to evaporate. The *Times* further reported that "wave of suspensions and cancellations began with the United States Supreme Court's ruling in January 1989, invalidating a city law in Richmond [Virginia] that set aside 30 percent of public works contracts for minority companies. In a vote of 6 to 3, the Justices held that the law violated the right of White contractors to equal protection of the law." The *Times* further reported that "After being nurtured for a decade by state and local governments that set aside a portion of their contracts for minority businesses, thousands of such companies have closed or are floundering in the aftermath of court rulings that the racial preferences are unconstitutional." This, after centuries of exclusive 100 percent government set-asides for White American businessmen. The *Times* went on to quote Ralph C. Thomas, 3rd, executive director of the National Association of Minority contractors, who asserted that, "Thousands of minority businesses went under or were neutralized, and thousands of strong businesses became weak. Most of the minority community's business comes from government programs, and when these programs are struck down they no longer have a place to sell their goods and services."

The economic development and concomitant economic power of Afrikan Americans have not only been concretely repressed by White social and governmental power, but the entrepreneurial history and character of Afrikan Americans themselves have been subjected to slanderous, degrading attack. Harold Cruse sums up this approach thusly:

While force and persuasion told blacks they should not attempt to participate as equals in such economic activities, at the same time they were accused of being shiftless, lacking in thrift, lacking in industriousness, being lazy, eschewing the virtues of hard work and individual initiative, being of innate criminality, being unfit candidates for acceptance into the society of *men* endowed with the capacity to participate as free individuals in the America of democracy and free enterprise.[8]

The internalization of these racist lies by Afrikan Americans and the deliberate, though most often covert, restriction, undermining and destruction of Black business and economic progress, in no small way has contributed to the lowering of Black business self-esteem and self-confidence, the loss of confidence in Black business acumen and professionalism, the fear of taking business risks by Blacks, and their relative lack of faith that their business enterprises will be supported by their Black customers — let alone their White customers. (A contemporary *Black Enterprise* magazine survey of self-employed Afrikan Americans reported that 70 percent of them consider lack of community support their most formidable problem.)

Immigration and Black Economic Stagnation. As noted in a prior chapter, immigration in important instances also operated against the job and business opportunities of Afrikan Americans. In collusion with and sometimes stimulated by regressive White racist governmental and social practices, immigrants often dislodged and replaced Afrikan American workers and business persons from the economic niches they held in the U.S. occupational and market structures. The immigrants more often than not internalized and expressed the same racist attitudes toward Blacks as did (and still do) native racist Whites.

Graham and Beck (*City Sun*, 6/3/92) provide an important analysis of the significantly negative impact immigration has had on Black economic prospects for the past several decades as well as today. They note that "This country has a long and sad history of allowing the massive importation of low-skilled foreign workers to displace African Americans..." They intimate that Booker Washington in his famous 1895 Atlanta Exposition address, implored White industrialists to turn to the under-employed, freed slaves and their descendants to fill the factories then opening up by rapid industrialization, instead of importing millions of workers from Europe. He was not heeded, however. Graham and Beck further observed that

---

8. Harold Cruse, *Plural but Equal*, 1987, p. 163.

in 1965, *when the Civil Rights Act provided for major political advancement, Congress revised the immigration law, once again allowing millions of foreign workers to pour into our inner cities.* The effect on lower-skill urban Blacks has been devastating.

More than 25 million immigrants and their descendants since 1970 have flooded the unskilled-labor markets, causing poor wages to decline to still lower levels, according to labor economists such as Vernon Briggs of Cornell University [Emphasis added].

When this continuing flood of unskilled (and skilled labor) combines with so-called "ethnic networking" (negating laws against racial discrimination and favoritism) the impact of immigration on Black life-chances and economic empowerment is doubled. Through networking, according to Graham and Beck, "Recent immigrants achieve positions of authority within a business and begin to recruit relatives, friends and acquaintances from their country of origin. Wages and working conditions often stagnate or decline in the firm. *Often the language of the workplace changes from English. Blacks, effectively, are barred from employment* "[Emphasis added]. Additionally, they point out that *"Affirmative action and other remedies, which originally were intended to redress two centuries of exploitation of and discrimination against Blacks, now must be shared with recently arrived, foreign-born populations "* [Emphasis added].

This series of events is all the more interesting and galling for conscious Afrikan Americans in view of the fact that these groups received citizenship and civil rights almost immediately on their arrival, when Blacks themselves did not enjoy these same privileges and had to struggle mightily — often bloodily — and over centuries to attain them. The recent arrivals were and are permitted the same, if not freer, access to governmental, financial and social resources, when they had or have virtually no service-to-country to their credit as do African Americans (Butler). Essentially, all that Afrikan Americans have struggled to gain after having their labor production expropriated through slavery and criminally low wages and after their joining and fighting in all of America's wars — from the Revolutionary War onwards — has been their exclusion from full participation in the American market economy. The loyalty of Afrikan Americans to this country for centuries has apparently not earned them enough credits to step to the head of the line in front of immigrants who not only recently "got off the boat," but many of whom at one point in time may have been active enemies of the U.S.

> Any type of foreigner, Oriental or "what not," can usually attract to his business a surviving degree of patronage of the native American.

No matter that he may be fresh from foreign shores with no contribution to the national welfare to his credit; no matter that he sends every dollar of his America-earned profit back to his foreign home and uses it to help finance organizations dedicated to the destruction of the government that furnishes him his new golden opportunity; yet he can find a welcome place on the economic broadway of America. But the Negro, despite centuries of unrequited toil to help build and maintain the highway, must turn to a detour that leads to he knows not where.[9] [Emphasis added]

Blacks As Immigrants. It is popular today to compare Afrikan American economic efforts or the lack thereof to immigrants, especially Asian immigrants. The comparisons are insidious and specious. The difference in favor of non-Blacks in terms of economic progress is attributed to their "willingness to work long hours"; to work at two or three low-wage jobs, save their money and invest it in business"; the use of common ethnic contacts to obtain credit, advice and patronage" (*Wall Street Journal*, 5/28/92); to "do business with their own"; "hire their own"; "strong economic solidarity"; "a strong desire for education"; "large numbers of intact families," etc. What is forgotten when these comparisons are made is the fact that Afrikan Americans exhibited those characteristics well into the 1900s. We have quoted extensively from Butler's work (and he from other works) which clearly establishes that Blacks have some five to ten decades earlier basically exhibited nearly all of the economic characteristics, orientations, capital funding techniques now attributed almost exclusively to later Asian immigrants.

Afrikan Americans are *not* immigrants! They are native born. Native-born groups of any race do not exhibit the same entrepreneurial drive characteristics of new immigrant groups. When the currently celebrated new immigrants become third, fourth, ...generation "Americans", new immigrants from their own ethnic stock will quite likely surpass them in entrepreneurial drive. Even Thomas Sowell, Black neoconservative economist who indulges in misleading Black American-new immigrant comparisons, in his book *Ethnic America,* arrives at the following conclusions regarding the entrepreneurial spirit of different ethnic groups across generations:

> In the United States, Canada, Great Britain, and Israel, the same striking pattern emerges: *immigrants begin economically below the levels of existing members of their own ethnic group already in the country, but eventually rise not only to equal but surpass them.* In the United States, native-born Americans of Cuban, Japanese, Mexican,

---

9. M.S. Stuart, *An Economic Detour.*

Negro or Filipino ancestry are overtaken by immigrants of the *same* respective ancestry. Cuban immigrants reached the income level of native-born Cubans after eighteen years and surpassed them thereafter. Mexican immigrants take fifteen years to overtake native-born Mexican Americans. Japanese immigrants take eighteen years to overtake native-born Japanese Americans. Immigrants from the Philippines overtake native-born Filipino Americans in thirteen years, and black West Indian immigrants overtake native-born black Americans in eleven years.[10] [Emphasis added]

These findings support that the rapid economic progress of new immigrant groups relative to native-born Afrikan American groups has little or nothing to do with the inherent ethnic character of the non-Black groups since similar differences in economic progress occur within those same groups between "native-borns" and "new arrivals."

Native-born Afrikan Americans, a group which has inhabited American soil for nearly four centuries, are not to be insidiously equated with immigrants within or outside the race. As Harold Cruse contends, "White liberal propaganda of the seventies [eighties, nineties] ...relegate[s] blacks to being just another *immigrant* group." He justifiably castigates Black leadership for not possessing the command to pronounce to those who defame Black American economic enterprise and who lump Afrikan Americans in with other "minorities and women" as well as newly arriving immigrant groups, that *"American blacks were not to be classified as an immigrant group, and should not allow themselves to be classified as such; that American black history involved a specific relationship to the constitutional* [and racist] *history of the United States not shared by other ethnic immigrants."*

The comparing of Black Americans with immigrants; the attempts to perceive and treat them in the same way as one perceives and treats immigrants; and to demand that Afrikan Americans behave like immigrants, new arrivals "just off the boat", manifests stereotypical attitudes and negative intentions held by non-Afrikan Americans, especially White Americans, in regard to Afrikan Americans. These insidious comparisons, perceptions and demands substantiate Hacker's thesis:

> Black Americans are Americans, *yet they still subsist as aliens in the only land they know.* Other groups may remain outside the mainstream — some religious sects, for example — but they do so voluntarily. *In contrast, blacks must endure a segregation that is far from freely chosen.* **So America may be seen as two separate nations**. Of

---

10. Thomas Sowell, *Ethnic America: A History* (N.Y.: Basic Books, 1981), p. 283.

course, there are places where the races mingle. Yet in most significant respects, the separation is pervasive and penetrating. *As a social and human division it surpasses all others — even gender — in intensity and subordination.*[11] [Emphasis added]

To compare Afrikan Americans to immigrants is to compare apples and oranges. No immigrant group, no matter how low its status may have been during its early history in America, was ever enslaved for well over two hundred years. The relations of Black Americans to White Americans are essentially reproduced in Black Americans' relationships to other ethnic Americans, including newly arrived immigrants such as Korean Americans. Black Americans are segregated, racially isolated and ghettoized relative to other non-White ethnics (except for Puerto Ricans) in ways similar to their separation from Whites. As with Whites, their segregation serves one primary purpose — to facilitate their economic exploitation. Fusfeld and Bates in their perceptive book succinctly sum it up this way:

> The urban ghetto is a depressed and underdeveloped enclave within a prosperous and progressive economy. It produces little that can be sold outside the ghetto other than low-wage labor. *Underdevelopment is preserved by a continuous drain of income and resources that keeps the ghetto poor.* The pool of low-wage labor is preserved by barriers that make exit difficult, while other social and economic forces provide recruits from outside the ghetto. These flows of income, resources, and people interact with conditions of poverty and underdevelopment in a system of circular causation that maintains the ghetto as a characteristic feature of the national economy.
>
> * * * *
>
> One of the most striking characteristics of the urban poverty area is a continual drain of resources out of the area and into other sectors of the economy. The drain includes savings, physical capital, human resources, and income. As a result, urban poverty areas are left without the most important resources needed for development and improvement, and the economic infrastructure of supporting institutions is seriously deficient.
>
> ...Programs that enable some individuals to escape the ghetto serve to preserve ghettoization for many more. *The best and brightest are drawn out of the ghetto to serve themselves and contribute to the further advancement of the progressive sector of society outside the ghetto.*
>
> The drain of capital is equally striking. A substantial portion of the savings of the urban ghetto goes into financial institutions whose

---

11. Andrew Hacker, *Two Nations: Black and White, Separate, Hostile, Unequal*, p. 3.

investment policies draw funds out of the area and into business loans, mortgages, and other investments elsewhere.¹² [Emphasis added]

Black American Communities as Economic Brothels

In sum, both the Black urban ghettoes and the Black *suburban* ghettoes (for these no more control the wealth, resources and businesses of their communities than do the inner-city communities) are essentially "economic brothels" where the White American community in alliance with immigrant communities exploitatively achieve a good deal of economic satisfaction at the expense of the Afrikan American community. The intense consumer-orientedness and entrepreneurial non-competitiveness of the Afrikan American community make it a perfect target for economic and labor exploitation and resource drainage. As intimated by Fusfeld and Bates (ibid), "the entire economy outside of the ghetto benefits from the income, capital, and manpower resources that are drawn out, just as it benefits from a pool of low-wage labor that provides relatively low-cost services to those outside."

If we were to conceptually consider the collective Afrikan American community as a Third World nation, one encapsulated within a first world nation, the source of its economic, political and social problems would be readily apparent — it suffers a negative balance of payment. The Black American community is a *de facto* alien nation located on American soil. Like a typical Third World country, it imports or buys more than it exports or sells. It is therefore not self-sustaining. Its local economy is not locally owned or controlled. Unable to invest in its own infrastructure and productive facilities, i.e., produce for its own needs, it suffers chronically-massive external debt. Consequently, it cannot provide enough monies to fund its cultural and social institutions; to maintain and enhance its political-economic organization; to materially support, reinforce and reward its positive social values, ethical attitudes and behavior; to support its families, maintain and enhance the dignity, self-esteem and social standing of its residents. It is therefore constantly on the edge of self-destructive social disorganization, bankruptcy, social indiscipline, criminality and violence. We concur with the assessment of Fusfeld and Bates that "Economic growth is particularly difficult for the ghetto economy. Its weak infrastructure, lack of local initiative and entrepreneurship, and the shortage of capital make it difficult to generate a growth process. They create instead a self-generating poverty cycle.... Any program or programs that seek to improve the

---

12. Fusfeld & Bates, *The Political Economy of the Urban Ghetto*, pp. 136–37.

Box 17-2   The Planned Permanent Economic Depression

Many of the social and political problems prevalent in the national Afrikan American community stem from the fact that for the past several decades it has suffered economic depression. In a sense, the Great Depression has virtually never left a very large segment of the community. The Black community has always been the major source of surplus labor in America. That is, it is always the "first fired" when White business employers decide that they need to cut their workforce for whatever reasons, and the "last hired" after other ethnic groups, especially White workers, are hired, rehired, trained or retrained during labor shortages, i.e., during periods of high labor demand or economic recoveries or booms.

On the basis of the traditional economic and hiring trends just described, many in the Afrikan American community may reach the conclusion that economic upturns or conditions which approach full-employment would be in their best interests since as increasing economic growth soaks up unemployed Whites and other preferred ethnic groups, they will be increasingly hired in turn. There is one major problem with this wished-for scenario, however. Both business and government do not see full-employment or even really low unemployment as necessarily a good thing. For business employers, full-employment means that the workers would take advantage of the scarcity of labor and force them or "black-mail" them into paying higher wages, by that increasing business costs and perhaps reducing profits. For the government the concern is that full-employment or very low unemployment in pushing up wages will also increase inflation thereby decreasing the value of real income or reducing the purchasing power of the dollar. Consequently, both business and government have a vested interest in maintaining a certain level of average unemployment. The debate between economists and government bureaucracies and quasi-governmental agencies such as the Federal Reserve, concerns what level of unemployment should be maintained in order to hold down wages and inflation rates. The current "economic recovery" has occasioned the debate as to whether unemployment should be allowed to remain at eight million or seven million unemployed before "a shortage of workers begins to push up the inflation rate".[13] According to the *Times*, "About 8.5 million people are now jobless, for a 6.5 percent unemployment rate..."

When government and business policy requires a standing unemployment rate of between 5.5 to 6.5 percent, then it in effect requires that the standing unemployment rate in the Afrikan American community remains between 14 to 17 percent — deep recessionary or depression rates given that the Black unemployment rate is consistently approximately 2½ times the average rate of the nation as a whole. This amounts to a virtual governmental and corporate conspiracy to maintain the Afrikan American community in planned permanent recession

---
13. "Growth of jobs may be casualty in inflation fight," *The New York Times*, 4/24/94.

or depression. The White American corporate establishment and other ethnic American groups as owners of businesses and as employers, therefore collude with a White American-controlled government to maintain a mutually beneficiary employment rate for themselves by creating, maintaining and containing the highest unemployment rate in the Afrikan American community.

This collusive policy all but assures excruciating levels of social problems in that community as well.

This being the case, the Afrikan American nation is faced with a major decision: it must increase its ownership of businesses and productive investments; its savings; its equity in productive corporations of all sizes; its quality of human capital (highly trained, highly skilled personnel); and its ability to favorably influence governmental economic policy to the greatest possible degree, or sink into irreversible economic and social degradation. ◘

economy of urban poverty areas *must reverse the drain of skilled manpower, capital and income if a cumulative process of growth is to be established"* [Emphasis added].

The reversal of Black ghetto deterioration, economic decline and collapse requires that it must, in no uncertain terms, capture and control its economic infrastructure, i.e., eject foreign and immigrant owners and controllers of its internal economy from its midst. It must retard its capital flow outward, retard the outflow of its human resources and circulate those resources within its borders as many times as possible before they flow out. In addition, the Afrikan American community must at least balance its trade imbalance with the larger society, i.e., see that at least as much money flows into the community as flows out. Better yet, the community should establish a trade surplus by earning more from trade with the larger community *and the world community* by selling goods and services to those outside communities and returning, spending, saving and investing that outside earned income within its own confines. This requires a deep and abiding sense of ethnic solidarity, organization based on ethnicity and ethnic identification, a healthy degree of ethnic selfishness and self-centeredness, ethnic pride, high self-esteem and self-confidence, ethnically based economic aggressiveness and acumen, all justified and rationalized by an appropriate ethnic ideology.

The latter characteristics are neither new to the Afrikan American collective personality, nor must they be borrowed from immigrants. For as we have already seen, they have been long present in the Afrikan cultural character, arguably, longer than in the character of any other people. They therefore only need to be resuscitated and expressed. They have only been heavily repressed, not extinguished.

The Black Bourgeoisie's Repression of Black Entrepreneurialism

We have indicated some of the reasons for the repression of the Afrikan American entrepreneurial spirit — immigration, restrictive governmental laws, trade restrictions, and White racist social practices. However, there is an additional set of reasons which, in the end, is almost as repressive as the others — a regressive Black bourgeois leadership establishment held mentally captive — to an anti-Afrikan assimilationist ideology. This leadership is typified by the NAACP, the Urban League, the late Dr. King, Jesse Jackson, a coterie of Black preachers, politicians, intellectuals and professionals who not only neither advocate nor aggressively promulgate an economic program for the Afrikan American community, but actively fight against such a program. They seem to perceive the problems facing the Black community as essentially problems having to do with Civil Rights, Human Rights, and moral "turpitude," i.e., the failure of America to live up to its highly publicized moral, constitutional, political, and civic values. Thus the program these leaders have imposed on the Afrikan American community is the one political scientists have aptly captioned, *noneconomic liberalism*. The emphasis on noneconomic liberalism as the guiding philosophy of "responsible" Black bourgeois leadership, *involves the projecting of "strong reformist impulses in the realms of civil liberties, race relations, and foreign affairs but not in the basic distribution of wealth and power"* [Emphasis added].[14] Harold Cruse, who best explicates and critically analyzes the philosophy of noneconomic liberalism, sums up its self-defeating irrelevancy thusly:

> In any event, the civil rights of "racial adjustment" was destined from the outset to be noneconomic. In a society where the making of money, the eager search after profits, the entrepreneurial activity, the superexploitation of labor and natural resources, the ownership of land, the perfection of technology, the expansion of industry, and where the apotheosization of every financial scheme imaginable for individual enrichment (even organized crime) was worshipped as the highest virtues, transcending religion itself, the American Negro was being advised by white liberals [and their Black counterparts] to waive any program of economic advancement as a matter of priorities. *When it is realized that not a single European* [Asian] *immigrant, not even the most unfavored, was ever told that the land of opportunity held such restraints on his or her citizenship ambitions, then the real*

---

14. Arnold Rose, as quoted by Harold Cruse.

economic relationship between native-born blacks and immigrant whites [Asians, Arabs, etc.] is better understood.[15] [Emphasis added]

The assimilationist, integrationist Black bourgeois leadership which essentially reduces all the racial, economic subordination and exploitation of Afrikan Americans to race discrimination in employment, public and private accommodations, vehemently opposed the self-help economic ideologies of Booker T. Washington, Marcus Garvey and those who preceded and followed them, popularly known as "Black Nationalists." The Black bourgeois' antipathy for Black Nationalism — for those who support Black self-help, Black economic self-control, aggressive Black entrepreneurship, Black identity, consciousness and power — is legendary. This leadership evinces a fundamental and self-defeating ambivalence. It promotes Black identity and solidarity in support of its programs aimed at submerging and obliterating that very identity and solidarity while in the process of achieving complete racial assimilation into the White mainstream [and bloodstream]. To paraphrase Oliver Cox, for Black assimilationists "...social [racial] solidarity is not a virtue in itself." Consequently, an ideology of Afrikan American solidarity expressed as Black economic self-determination and Black power is an anathema to them; this, despite the obvious relationship between White economic self-sufficiency, political power and well-being as well as immigrant entrepreneurialism and immigrant well-being. The Black bourgeois social-political leadership, stupefied by its indiscriminate internalization of the White American ideology of individualism, and according to Cruse, "whose status [is] predicated on the very existence of the segregated urban ghettoes, ...reject[s] the legitimacy of the ghetto's existence." Cruse further argues that "The general logic of this political leadership would be to eschew and disdain all *social* policy aimed at internal economic, social, and cultural improvements in the ghettoes, on *the assumption that such improvements amounted to the perpetuation of segregation.*" Even though the contemporary, "Kente cloth" Black bourgeois political-professional establishment may now faddishly, blatantly and self-servingly give lip service to such improvements, their inability or unwillingness to initiate, administer, and fund tangible, workable programs toward these ends, and their reactionary opposition to and underhanded sabotaging of such efforts when they have been proposed or led by Black nationalist or grassroots organizations, betray their true character and motives. Unless and until the Black community rids itself of its dominant assimilationist leadership establishment and institutes a new, race-

---

15. Cruse, pp. 76–77.

conscious, race-first leadership which will facilitate its acquisition of economic self-control and considerable ownership of America itself, it will continue to suffer relative powerlessness, and perhaps in the near future, biological annihilation.

Chapter 18

BENEVOLENT FRONTS ASSAULT LOCAL AND GLOBAL AFRIKAN MARKETS

The Community Development Corporation as Economic Front

THE MOVEMENT TO EXPAND LARGE supermarket chains and develop commercial projects in lower-income urban areas is not only receiving its greatest impetus from local community organizations but also from national organizations as well. One such national organization is the Local Initiative Support Corporation, known as LISC, headquartered in New York City. Founded in 1979, LISC is mainly identified with low-income housing development for which it raised $648 million through 1991 in donations from foundations and investments by corporations (NYT, 11/8/92). The *Times* reports that in September, 1992 LISC "began a national equity fund to funnel corporate and individual investments to local nonprofit community development corporations engaged in retail ventures." LISC hoped to raise $10 million to $13 million within six months for its equity fund, called Retail Initiative Inc., to be used as a "financial cushion" for supermarkets and private developers. Retail Initiative Inc. offers investors an annualized rate of return of 10 to 13 percent over a 10-year holding period. That is, the Retail Initiative Corporation expects to generate an annual pretax return of at least 10% for investors. Investors will be given stakes in the stores constructed by the Initiative. It principally provides the equity to get commercial projects started by developing the site and leasing spaces to chain stores and independent retailers. The LISC equity fund provides community groups with initial financing and low-interest loans to cover up to 30 percent of the development costs. Additional costs are generally covered by conventional loans at market rates.

In this context it is of interest to note that in September, 1994 LISC announced that it intended to use private money to build supermarkets in low-income communities across the country (*New York Times*, 9/22/94). Beginning in East Harlem, New York City, on famous 125th Street, LISC plans to start retail projects in Philadelphia, Washington, Chicago, Los Angeles, Phoenix, Miami, Kansas City, San Diego, Houston, Boston, Seattle and San Francisco. Moreover, LISC expects its corporate fund to provide start-up money for two supermarkets in the South Bronx and in Newark. LISC, a community development group started by the Ford Foundation, has collected $24 million from 10 major corporations including Prudential, G.E. Capital, Bank of America, Home Savings of America, and the venerable J.P. Morgan, to help finance a proposed 53,000 square-foot Pathmark supermarket in East Harlem and similar stores, e.g., Safeway supermarkets, in other inner-city areas. The supermarket in East Harlem, which is scheduled to open in 1997, expects to employ about 250 people. The program is expected to permanently employ some 2,000 people across the country in its first two years of operation. According to the *New York Times* (ibid) $4 million of the $24 million fund will go to the East Harlem project and the project itself is expected to be administered by the development arm of the Abyssinian Baptist Church and the Community Association of East Harlem Triangle. These organizations will build the store and lease it to Pathmark supermarkets.

In addition to the expected 10 percent annual return on their investment over a 10 year period, the corporate investors will reap handsome public relations benefits from demonstrating their apparent interest and willingness to invest in the economic development of inner-cities, areas they have been roundly criticized for withdrawing from and ignoring in the past.

The LISC Initiative: A Trojan Horse. The Local Initiative Support Corporation's projects are very impressive on first hearing. It certainly is heartwarming to learn that inner-city residents will gain access to goods and services commensurate with those accessed by suburban residents. The reduction in the cost of living commercial projects like that proposed by LISC will make possible for Afrikan American families is welcome indeed. So are the increased jobs such projects will produce, along with the measurably positive collateral economic and social benefits they will bestow on their local communities and urban areas. No doubt the foundations and corporations whose donations and investments will make such projects a reality will feel justifiably proud of their socioeconomic handiwork.

But be that as it may, the Afrikan American community must not renege on its self-interested obligation to look this gift horse in the mouth. In fact, the LISC initiative may be better described as a Trojan horse. Even though basically funded by nonprofit foundations like the Ford Foundation and administered by non-profit community development organizations, LISC is not merely a philanthropic entity or initiative or charitable trust. LISC, like any number of other similar organizations, functions, in its role as a commercial developer at least, as a nonprofit shil or front for profit-making undertakings whose returns on investment will exclusively benefit America's largest White-owned capitalist juggernauts.

The humanistic intentions of the proposed LISC commercial initiatives to economically rehabilitative inner-city communities is belied by the fact that it is perfectly clear to any astute observer that these initiatives are little more than financial stalking horses for bringing White monopoly capitalists back into the same communities to plunder them again after having plundered and abandoned them earlier. In this instance we can easily discern the imperialistic role played by major White "philanthropic" organizations such as the Ford and Rockefeller foundations — that of clearing the grounds for the establishment of new White corporate construction. The natives on whose territory these new White-owned establishments will be pre-emptively constructed will profit little. Having been displaced by "progress," they will only see their monies sucked out of their pockets into the overstuffed pockets of White and alien financiers, merchants and shopkeepers.

Why Not Black-owned Shopping Centers? In their flashy press releases LISC and its local cohorts leave unexplained how the Afrikan American community may come to own and operate the collateral businesses associated with the anchoring supermarkets and in the neighborhoods surrounding the proposed inner-city shopping malls or centers. Neither are we told how or if Black institutional and individual investors will be prime or major beneficiaries of the dividends to be earned from these projects. Why are no Black-owned banks, investment houses, insurance companies, individuals, families, and other institutions not mentioned as major investors in LISC's projects? Moreover, why must the anchor supermarket in the LISC projects be a White-owned corporation?

There are Black-owned supermarket corporations and other Black-owned food service and distribution companies, such as Restoration Supermarket Corporation, Community Foods, Inc., Calhoun Food Supermarket, TLC Beatrice International Holdings, and the Anderson-Dubose Company, who might welcome the opportunity to expand their operations by leasing spaces, anchoring major inner-city shopping centers, malls, and commercial streets. J. Bruce Llewellyn, CEO of the Philadelphia Coca-Cola Bottling Co. Inc. ($290 million in sales) and of the Garden State Cable TV ($96 million in sales), was once the owner of a supermarket chain in the inner-city neighborhoods of New York City. There are any number of experienced Afrikan American supermarket owners, managers and executives who could form a core group for organizing a national chain of Black-owned supermarkets and other retail outlets. The "charitable" thing for White-owned foundations and capitalists to do would be to lend their monetary and human resources to the development of truly Black-owned and controlled business and financial establishments so that the Black community may captain its own economic ship. Since this is a highly unlikely proposition, the Black community must find and develop ways of harnessing its own monetary and human resources to achieve the same goal. (See our discussion of Leon Sullivan's "10-36" plan for financing the largest Black-owned shopping center in the U.S. and of Wheat Street Baptist Church's sponsorship of shopping centers in Atlanta.) National and local consortiums of Black for-profit and non-profit organizations can be used to establish the same or similar retail systems as can be established by White and alien interests. Black electoral pressure can be utilized to remove political barriers to the development of Black-owned commercial undertakings. Black consumer pressure can be brought to bear on White-owned retail and financial establishments (who depend on Black consumer savings, and investment dollars for their financial well-being) to get them to invest in the development of Black-owned commercial enterprises in non-controlling ways. Black-owned local and national underwriting establishments and investment companies such as the ones we discuss in this volume, can provide the means by which the Afrikan American community can instrumentally invest in the development of commercial projects of its own design constructed by its own companies so that it may substantially profit from them. Such undertakings can best be initiated and successfully completed under the aegis of a nationally organized body of Afrikan American agencies depicted in the **Master Plan** discussed in Chapter 2.

> The lesson is clear, but not simple. Development does not start with single projects, financed from abroad through aid, commercial loans, or joint ventures. This strategy creates only modern islands in a sea of backwardness — cathedrals in the desert. Development starts within the society when switches are put in the right position and traffic lights are turned from yellow to green.
>
> –WILHELM HANKEL, "The Role of Finance in the Market Economy" *Sais Review*, Summer-Fall 1994, Vol. XIV, No.2, pp. 47-59.

> One common fallacy about aid programs is that they benefit the African people. They do not. As can be expected, each foreign group advances its own agenda. It is naive to believe that aid agencies pursue the interests of the African people. Far too long, outsiders have arrogantly assumed that role, and for far too long, average Africans (in contrast to the ruling elite) have been excluded from defending their own interests.
>
> –GEORGE B.N. AYITTEY, "Aid for Black Elephants: How Foreign Assistance Has Failed Africa," *Perpetuating Poverty: The World Bank, The I.M.F, and the Developing World*, eds. Doug Bandow & Ian Vasquez (The Cato Institute: Washington, D.C., 1994), pp. 125-46.

It is Afrikan Americans who must ultimately solve their own social and economic problems. When outside governmental agencies, corporations, foundations, and non-profit organizations plan and execute developmental programs for the Afrikan American community, they do so in their own alien interest and for their own benefit, not in the interest and for the benefit of the Afrikan American people.

White-planned, financed and executed commercial development projects can only lead to the development of White-owned, commercial establishments located in the midst of commercially exploited Black communities. The primary beneficiaries of these inner-city commercial projects will not be the Black consumers whose monies they will insatiably devour, but will be the White entrepreneurs and investors who actually own and control the business establishments which constitute those commercial contrivances in the first place. Given their very financial and ownership structures, such projects cannot enhance the overall economic development and wealth of the Black neighborhoods which surround them. In fact, they primarily represent the most efficient means the White community can devise to vampiristically suck the last coin from the pockets of an already exploited and impoverished population, thereby exploiting and impoverishing it all the more. The presence of White commercial elephants in inner-city communities cannot help but trample to near death the smaller grassroots economic and entrepreneurial establishments.

White-planned and financed projects do more harm than good. Projects planned and developed by outsiders deny Afrikan Americans a say in decisions purportedly made in their behalf. Furthermore, they deny Afrikan Americans the right to be the first to benefit from their own economic activities and consumption habits. They impair the ability of Afrikan American community to provide its own solutions to its own problems; to set its own pace and direction of development according to its own cultural agenda.

No One Should Confuse the Retail Initiative with Philanthropy. Statements by Paul Grogan, president of LISC, substantiate our contention that LISC's inner-city commercial projects are essentially mercenary, i.e., purely profit-making ventures, not primarily acts of charity. In an article published by the *New York Times* (10/2/94) titled "Inner Cities Beckon Savvy Retailers," Grogan spoke directly to the point:

> Late last month, a group of corporate investors unveiled an unprecedented fund to re-establish major supermarkets in more than a dozen poor urban areas.
>
> *But no one should confuse this effort, the Retail Initiative, with philanthropy. That's not why the likes of Bank America, Bankers Trust and GE Capital have signed up. The fund, as much as $90 million when leveraged, is a hard-headed investment tool for breaking into a surprisingly lucrative market — the inner city.*
>
> You read it right. First, any pioneering supermarket would encounter little competition in these areas. Years ago, when the neighborhoods lost blocks and blocks of housing, supermarkets boarded up their windows and moved out. Since then, nonprofit, community-based developers have rebuilt many of these areas. But the often-activist residents of these comeback communities still have few places to buy a loaf of bread or quart of milk — let alone the fixings for a salad.

And supermarkets can do very well against the inner-city competition that does exist — delicatessens and corner stores. With their high volumes, supermarkets have buying power and can survive on razor-thin profit margins. Not so the small stores, which charge up to 40 percent more than supermarkets, often for inferior goods, and do not stock some items at all [Emphasis added].

Obviously, Grogan has little or no concern for the possible bankruptcy of local merchants and shopkeepers which may occur as the result of the entry of giant supermarkets and chain stores into their markets. Neither does he show any appreciation of or respect for the economic needs and goals of inner-city inhabitants, especially those of the Afrikan American community. The social movement of Black Americans toward greater economic self-sufficiency and self-determination; the need of the Black community to gain greater control of its internal markets in order to advance and enhance its economic prospects as well as to empower itself politically, will be vitiated by Grogan's brazen belief that "what's good for multinational corporations is good for Black America." He gives little or no thought to the primary economic problem in the Black American community — how may Black consumer and business dollars be retained longer and made to circulate more frequently within the Black community before leaving it, thereby benefitting a larger number of its inhabitants and enhancing its general welfare. Instead, the community is greedily looked at as a plump chicken ready for easy plucking by corporate butchers. Grogan goes on to contend, as noted earlier, that

> despite the inner cities' lower incomes, their high population density gives them potent buying power — as the few supermarkets that do operate in such neighborhoods prove. A Pathmark supermarket in Newark, for example, routinely outperforms many other Pathmark stores. Also ranking high in industry profitability are a Safeway in Washington, a Winn-Dixie in Miami and a Dominick's in Chicago.
>
> The inner city offers supermarkets low rents, too. And while these neighborhoods do present some business problems — higher security costs, for example — the comeback communities are by definition areas where residents are dedicated to improving where they live. This attitude sets in motion positive forces that can help overcome many inner-city problems. And, such involved residents are likely to give supermarkets that come to their areas something businesses spend much money to court: customer loyalty.
>
> What is the bottom line? That there are markets for the asking for urban retailing pioneers. Not only supermarkets, but banks, pharmacies, fast-food restaurants, even health maintenance organizations.

While a bit overstated, Grogan's contentions do speak to the economic potential represented by a significant number of inner-city communities across the country. What they do not speak to is how that potential can be realized by the inhabitants of those communities for their own benefit and not the exclusive benefit of corporate monopolies whose only concern is their bottom line and not the economic and social well-being of the communities they so selfishly exploit.

Low-Income: High Profits. Paul Grogan's assertion that inner cities beckon savvy retailers is corroborated by real estate consultant Steven Greenberg, whose Long Island, N.Y. firm locates profitable low-income neighborhoods for the children's apparel chain Young World. Greenberg also reveals that "Low-income neighborhoods that are densely populated can be a gold mine for sharp retailers" (*Crains New York Business*, 11/7/94). Greenberg further adds that residents of such neighborhoods "like apparel. They're very fashion-conscious. If good retailers can focus in, they will do quite well."

Greenberg's proposition is substantiated by the retailing experience of Jimmy Khezrie, 33, owner of 15 stores, primarily located in low-income neighborhoods. Khezrie, who recently opened his Jimmy Jazz and Hyperactive shops on Brooklyn's Flatbush Avenue, a predominantly Black shopping area, also asserts that "If stores service the ethnic customer the right way and give the right services, they will be very successful" (*Crains*, ibid). Within six years of opening his first Jimmy Jazz store in 1988, Khezrie's retail units have generated more than $30 million annually by selling fashion labels to residents of New York City's low-income neighborhoods. *Crain's* reveals that:

> Overall, Mr. Khezrie is in a hot segment of the retail market. According to a recent national survey by Dun & Bradstreet Information Services and G.A. Wright Inc., employment at men's and boys' clothing stores similar in size to Jimmy Jazz grew 48% between 1985 and 1993. Jobs at similar women's stores rose only 16%, while positions at general family clothing stores grew 21%. Employment at children's clothing stores vaulted by nearly 500%, however.

Crain's goes on to report:

> *Mr. Khezrie's customers, mostly African-American and Hispanic boys and men between the ages of 13 and 30, have a taste for style but are neglected by major retailers.* "If they want better quality," he says, "the only way to find it is to go to midtown Manhattan."

Quality at Jimmy Jazz is not cheap. A long-sleeve Champion sweatshirt sells for $36.99, a Calvin Klein T-shirt for $19.99 and a nylon Fila jacket for $109.99. Mr. Khezrie made a profit of 14 cents on every dollar that was spent in his stores last year....

Woolrich plaid flannel shirts, nylon Fila jackets, Guess jeans and Calvin Klein T-shirts are some of the basics that customers can always find stocked in Mr. Khezrie's stores. *Baseball caps, socks, belts and shoes — which account for 50% of sales —* are also available to give the customer the entire "hook-up," or outfit.

Some of the more "fashion-forward" items, such as Karl Kani jeans or Fila jackets, are limited to six to 12 styles at a time, to give what Mr. Khezrie calls a "freshness" to the store. "It's the No. 1 reason for my success," he adds.

Another is business acumen. While rents for retail space in low-income neighborhoods can be as high as some areas of midtown Manhattan, Mr. Khezrie has managed to pinpoint strips where foot traffic is constant. "He's picked very good locations within the shopping districts," says Harold Weidman of Brooklyn-based Storefinders Inc....

He feels good about the future, too. Mr. Khezrie plans to open six new stores in 1995 in the New York metropolitan area and is negotiating with two shopping malls to lease space [Emphasis added].

There is no good reason why Khezrie, a Syrian immigrant, and other alien merchants like him should be virtually the exclusive retailers in the Black community when Black retailers can provide the same services while keeping their businesses as well as their earnings "in the family." Khezrie's success, as well as that of other alien merchants located in Black neighborhoods, discredits the common myth in the Afrikan American community that it is not possible to achieve a high level of business success by servicing Black consumers almost exclusively. This myth has done more to discourage Black entrepreneurialism than the reputed unavailability of finance capital to would-be Black entrepreneurs. If Black entrepreneurs and prospective Black investors, both individual and institutional, are confident that Black consumers have the wealth and the will to support Black-owned businesses, then they will be more forthcoming in making the increase and predominance of such businesses a reality in the Afrikan American community.

Shopping Malls in the "New" South Afrika. A remarkable instance of how White supremacists the worldover use the same or similar techniques to oppress and exploit Afrikan peoples is the one where White South Afrikan entrepreneurs, in a manner similar to White

American entrepreneurs, after having suddenly discovered that shopping malls in Black townships are good business decided to found them there by using the wealth and other advantages they gained from their prior exploitation of Blacks to begin with. As in the case of the proposed Harlem mall discussed above, White South Afrikan entrepreneurs after years of benign and malignant neglect of Black commercial needs have now decided to atone for their past sins by returning to Black townships in order to more thoroughly exploit them in the name of the "new" South Afrika. In typical white supremacist fashion, they make elaborate claims of helping Afrikan peoples while greedily helping themselves to their god-given and hard-earned resources. While claiming that they are meeting the commercial needs and advancing the economic development of Afrikan peoples, these White-owned corporate leviathans are in reality only concerned with attempting to satisfy their own insatiable appetites and advancing their own exclusive economic agendas. The *New York Times* (10/26/94) describes the South Afrikan situation in this way:

A Mall Comes to a Black Township

Soweto, South Africa, Oct. 23 — Late last year, a group of white executives from Sanlam Properties, a leading South African development company, piled into a mini-van and rode into terra incognita, the sprawling black metropolis of Soweto.

As Jacobus A. Swanepoel, Sanlam's regional manager, recounts that journey, it is tempting to imagine a carload of cartoon capitalists with dollar signs ringing in their eyes — ka-Chung, ka-Chung. Soweto, impoverished alien, oppressed, battle-torn Soweto, suddenly seemed a land of untapped opportunity.

The first result of that trip materialized here on Sept. 29; the biggest and most modern shopping center any black township has ever seen, complete with a family steakhouse, a triplex cinema, automated teller machines, an appliance store, clothiers, and the ne plus ultra of suburban life in South Africa, a gun shop.

At the mall's heart is a vast airconditioned Shoprite supermarket that has brought some Soweto shoppers close to joyous tears. After years of commuting to stores on the periphery of the black enclave, or paying the inflated prices of tiny township convenience shops, they have discovered in the wide aisles and sale prices of Shoprite an equality nearly as satisfying as the one conferred by last April's elections.

Soweto, which once appeared to white business as a ghetto teeming with squatters and bristling with political upheaval all at once acquired a more alluring identity; a city of more than three million consumers without a grocery store, appliance dealer or clothing outlet of national stature.

Furthermore, the *New York Times* observes:

> Until now, most white businesses have shunned black townships. Whites were prohibited by apartheid law from owning township property. Then, after the repeal of that barrier in June 1991, the townships seemed too turbulent to be worth the risk.
>
> Instead, Sanlam and other developers built huge indoor malls on the outskirts of Soweto, forcing township residents to come to them.
>
> A mini-van taxi ride from Soweto to one of these malls cost the price of half a gallon of milk or two loaves of bread, and it ate up most of a morning, but as Alfred Hlatchwayo observed over his basket of groceries in the new Shoprite, "it was that or do without."
>
> Now that the April elections have restored political peace, developers have turned to the townships with a more open mind. Following the lead of gasoline station and fast-food chains, which moved in earlier with franchise outlets, banks, developers and retailers are now scouting hungrily.
>
> "If you look at the strategic plans of most of the larger firms, you see that they have their eye on the townships," said Johan Jacobs, marketing director of the South African Chamber of Commerce and Business.
>
> Soweto's shopping mall was developed with capital from Sanlam, which historically catered to white Afrikaners, but the mall's success suggests that foreign investment could follow into the neglected townships.
>
> Mr. Swanepoel said Soweto had grown ripe for business at a time when most white suburbs are already saturated with retail stores.

Sanlam Properties is a subsidiary of South Afrika's second largest insurance company, the Sanlam Group, the country's largest developers of shopping centers. Here, as in the Afrikan American case where after having abandoned or ignored the Black communities when it suited their economic and political purposes to do so, giant White capitalistic enterprises return to or enter those communities to exploit them all the more. The return or entry of these gluttonous entrepreneurs is obviously self-serving in that they demonstrate little concern for the true economic well-being and self-determination of the Black community. Their entry into Black township markets merely reflects their search for new markets after having saturated their traditional (White) markets. It also reflects their unrelenting intention to economically and politically dominate Afrikan peoples all over the globe with impunity.

For White supremacists, the more things change the more they remain the same. In fact, they change things in order to maintain their sameness. Despite social changes from colonialism to neo-colonialism, from social segregation to neo-racial desegregation (nominally referred to as "from colonialism to independence, from segregation to integration"), the motive of white supremacy remains the same — the unending domination and exploitation of Black peoples by White peoples and to profit therefrom. Just as Whites in America and Whites in South Afrika profited from apartheid, the legal racial segregation of Blacks, they now profit from so-called racial equality, the legal desegregation of Blacks. The amount and rate of profits that Whites gain under desegregation are even greater than under segregation. In either case, Blacks were and continue to be relatively poor and dependent as well as politically powerless.

To add insult to injury, as in the LISC case discussed above where White-owned chainstores plan to open shopping malls in some 14 inner-city neighborhoods, Sanlam Properties plans to open other shopping malls in several Black townships. According to the *New York Times*, Sanlam has "two other township projects near announcement, including a mammoth "hyper mall" in another part of Soweto, and another half dozen on the drawing board." In like manner to the East Harlem project discussed above, Sanlam and other White entrepreneurs make full use of Black organizations to run political interference in establishing White-owned and controlled commercial projects. Thus, they put a Black face on White power. The *Times* points out that Sanlam "entered Soweto on political tiptoes. It assembled a committee of 40 local organizations to review its plans." In perpetrating the charade that it is truly interested in advancing Black economic development and in order to ease its entry into the Black township markets, Sanlam makes use of a familiar White American entrepreneurial tactic — that of promising more than it is actually going to deliver. Sanlam claims it has created a trust fund to train local entrepreneurs. It also intimates that it plans to sell 49 percent of the project as shares to local investors. (Note that it did not offer to sell 49 percent of Sanlam to Black investors.) Sanlam has permitted three small Black-owned businesses to occupy spaces in its new 68-store mall. The clincher in Sanlam's package for the Black township is a promise of 600 permanent jobs for local residents. As reported by the *Times*, Afrikan South Afrikan businessman Max Legodi's attitude toward this approach by Sanlam seems quite to the point.

> Mr. Legodi of the Soweto chamber of commerce applauded Sanlam for its diplomacy, but said black businesses resented the fact that the

Shoprite supermarket chain, which has no connection with the American supermarket chain of the same name, had not enlisted black partners in the store that is the centerpiece of the project.

"We feel that appointing a few black faces in Shoprite doesn't give you a passport to come in and exploit the emerging black market," he said.

The promise of jobs in return for the right to greedily exploit the Black community is business as usual for White entrepreneurs and the White politicoeconomic establishment whose true intention is to maintain Blacks as servants, wage earners, and general subordinates, not owners and managers, in their own neighborhoods and nations. Some prominent Afrikan South Afrikan businesspeople and organizations, much to their credit — in contrast to their Black American counterparts — have seen through the deceptive games being played by white entrepreneurs and the White supremacist establishment. The *Times* reports that

> the new interest of white retailers has generated a bitter outcry from some black businessmen in the townships. They complain that after decades of weathering the strains of an apartheid ghetto, black entrepreneurs are being bulled aside by the economic power of white outsiders who have discovered gold in black townships.
>
> "I feel like a man on a bicycle who's been overtaken by a jet," said Paul Gama, chairman of the black-controlled Blackchain Ltd., which owns three modest and struggling grocery stores in black townships.
>
> Max M. Legodi, head of the Greater Soweto Chamber of Commerce and Industries, which speaks for hundreds of small retailers in the township, was sympathetic. "All these years we had no access to capital, no access to credit," he said. "We were not able to gain expertise in business management. We did not have relationships with suppliers to buy in bulk. We could not do business in white areas."
>
> These men argue that white entrepreneurs moving into the "emerging markets" of black townships should be obliged — by political pressure, if not by law — to take local partners, as do many foreign companies that come to South Africa.

Gama describes the typical pattern of White entrepreneurial strangulation and impairment of Black entrepreneurial growth and development opportunistically followed by White entrepreneurial oppression and exploitation of Black peoples. Typically, with the legal approval of the government and the support of traditional White racist social practices, White entrepreneurs and financial institutions deny equal quality goods and services as well as credit and capital to the Black community during long periods of White racist political and economic oppression of Blacks, sometimes lasting for centuries, followed by continued denial of finance, credit, training, and economic opportunity to Blacks during periods of so-called Black political liberation and independence. The tremendous financial and human resources White entrepreneurs and capitalists have accumulated during the former period are used to enter into overwhelmingly unequal competition with Black entrepreneurs during the latter period. Any attempt on the part of Blacks to even the "entrepreneurial playing field" by asking and demanding that compensatory considerations, preferences and advantages be awarded them for past racist practices in favor of Whites, is loudly hooted down by conservative Whites and ignorant, self-serving Blacks as "reverse racism". This is an interesting response in light of the obvious fact that "reverse racism" would be a just solution to "forward racism" which permitted Whites to gain almost irreversible advantages over Blacks.

Afrikan South Afrikan Paul Gama underlines this point when he, according to the *Times,* explains that

> his Blackchain stores had remained in business, without laying off workers, despite political violence that scared away customers and drove the company repeatedly to the brink of bankruptcy. He fumed at the thought of white companies now reaping the dividends of the struggle.
>
> "White businesses know the devastation of apartheid won't leave them any competition," he said. "It is a walkover for them."

Justice as well as the current and future economic well-being of the Black community require that Black peoples *own and control* their community and national markets, and not act as mere workers and consumers in them. Blacks, like any other ethnic group and nation, should be the first to profit and benefit from their markets and resources. To do otherwise would be tantamount to willfully giving away the commonwealth of the group to others and consequently impoverishing themselves as well as denying their future generations the right to inherit the god-given traditional and accumulated wealth of their ancestors.

That Afrikan South Afrikans are at least conscious of this issue is demonstrated by the *Times* when it reported the following:

> Whether businesses should be required to team up with black capitalists when tapping black markets is now a topic of heated negotiation in business groups and within the Government. Major business groups generally favor such joint ventures, although they are opposed to enforcing them by law.

We can only wish that such a heated discussion was underway in the Afrikan American community. At this time this community seems hell-bent on the self-destructive path of robbing itself and its future generations of the material basis for "life, liberty, and the pursuit of happiness."

Justice requires Afrikan Ownership and Control of Markets. Afrikan South Afrikans and Afrikan Americans have endured all manner of indignities, sufferings, deprivations, losses and impairments under the reign of White supremacy in its various historical and contemporary forms. The negative effects and aftereffects of White domination shall last for generations among all Black peoples, its primary subjects. The central function of White-commandeered apartheid was to forcibly and exploitatively extract the material, human and productive wealth of Black peoples and redistribute them to their White overlords. The wealth, power and influence Whites expropriated through their coercive domination and exploitation of Black land, labor and productivity have continued to *exponentially* expand and perpetuate themselves by compounding the interest on their original and concurrent principal. White domination of Blacks, even if confined to the past, allowed Whites to accumulate astronomical wealth. Moreover, it has allowed Whites to capitalize that wealth by developing socioeconomic technologies and sociopolitical advantages which will facilitate their continuing economic and political domination of Blacks in the present and into the future even under governmental regimes which do not legally or politically sanction racial discrimination of any kind, whether of the forward or reverse variety.

Consequently, while prior forms of White domination and exploitation of Blacks may have ceased and desisted, the economic injustices and inequalities they imposed continue unabated. The legal prohibition of further injustices does not necessarily mean that the injurious effects of past injustices no longer persist and do not require rectification. Justice requires not only the ceasing and desisting of injustice but also requires either punishment or reparation for injuries and damages inflicted for prior wrongdoing. The essence of injustice is the redistribution of gains earned through the perpetration of injustice. If restitution is not made and reparations not instituted to compensate for prior injustices, those injustices are in effect rewarded. And the benefits such rewards conferred on the perpetrators of injustice will continue to "draw interest", to be reinvested, and to be passed on to their children, who will use their inherited advantages to continue to exploit the children of the victims of the injustices of their ancestors. Consequently, injustice and inequality will be maintained across the generations as will their deleterious social, economic and political outcomes.

Therefore it is not enough that Blacks forgive Whites their past sins; that they merely "forget the past"; that they "forgive and forget". It is not enough that Whites cease and desist their prior injustices and racially discriminatory practices while they retain all the advantages those prior injustices and practices afford them. For even under a color-blind political and economic regime they will use their previously accumulated and unredistributed wealth and power to continue to invest to their advantage and to the disadvantage of Blacks.

Blacks must remain very aware of the fact that when they let Whites purchase or gain control of their resources by means of the wealth and the other advantages they acquired through the perpetration of prior racial injustices, they will continue to be victimized by White-instigated racial inequalities and exploitation even though such ends may not be consciously intended by Whites. Whites will plea that they are only taking advantage of market opportunities equally available to all without regard to race. It is imperative that if Blacks are to acquire true equality and power relative to Whites, then, they must demand and get reparations from Whites or that Whites, through committed long-term affirmative action, compensate them for their losses due to their prior oppression by Whites. If this cannot be accomplished then it is necessary that Blacks, by any means necessary, prevent Whites from further investing in their territories where Blacks themselves are not included as equal or predominant partners and where Blacks are not the primary beneficiaries of such White investment. Moreover, Blacks should raise whatever resources they have at their disposal to gain ownership and control over their own resources and the resources of others so as to provide for and empower themselves to achieve self-sufficiency and self-determination.

Crime, family instability, social disorganization, poverty and disease in the Black community are all related to the absence of Black *ownership* of important and vital resources. The mere convenience provided by White-owned retail facilities placed in Black community is by no means a substitute for Black ownership of those facilities and the ancillary goods and services they require. Social problems in the Black community will not be prevented because shopping will be more convenient for Black consumers. Those problems will be solved through the Black ownership and equitable distribution of the Black commonwealth and through the Black community's empowering itself relative to other communities to protect and advance its interests. This cannot happen if other communities own and control all that is vital to the Black community, no matter how convenient or inexpensive to Black consumers. Ultimately, the convenience provided by such arrangements will become much too inconvenient and the cheap prices they afford will become much too much to pay.

Inner-City Shopping Malls

One of the many harmful myths about inner-city communities is that their generally low average income makes them unprofitable locales for retail and other investments. Even though this myth is belied by the heavy retail investment in these communities by immigrant merchants such as Koreans, Indians, Arabs, Hispanics, etc., it has inhibited investments in these areas by prominent White retailers, and more important, by would-be Black retailers. In fact, many mainstream retailers, e.g., major supermarkets, have steadily withdrawn from the inner-cities over the past two decades. During this time major supermarket chains and other major retailers have generally severely restricted their business activities or refused to do business in low-income inner-city neighborhoods.

Supermarket chains such as A&P, when they have not withdrawn from inner-city markets have refused to invest further in them, generally claiming that the poverty of their residents and the high cost of security make investing and doing business in them risky undertakings. This has led to a two-tier marketing system where large supermarket and other retail chains serve the predominantly White suburbs and wealthy White inner-city enclaves, and ignore predominantly Black suburbs and inner-city neighborhoods. This system in effect has devalued the dollars of Black consumers. That is, Black consumer dollars buy less than do White consumer dollars. This is the consequence of the fact that the absence of convenient large discount outlets in the inner-cities force Black consumers to shop in over-priced, understocked, and out-dated small stores.

Discount stores, outlet malls and warehouse clubs, places where relatively inexpensive goods may be purchased, have largely bypassed inner-city communities. According to the *Wall Street Journal* (7/2/92) "the gap between prices paid by the rich and poor appears to be widening at the same time the income gap is growing." In 1991, the New York City Department of Consumer Affairs "found that grocery shoppers in poor neighborhoods paid 8.8% more or $350 more a year for a family of four — than shoppers in middle-class areas." In a spot check of five grocery items in 1991, staff members of the Chicago City

Council found that the poor paid 18% more than their middle-class counterparts. A 1968 Federal Trade Commission study demonstrated that furniture and appliances cost an average of 52% more in the inner-city of Washington, D.C. than its surrounding suburbs. We have no reason to believe that this difference has diminished significantly since that time. It is of interest to note that studies made by industry trade groups have found that since 1970 Boston has lost about two-thirds of its supermarkets, Chicago about half and Los Angeles more than one-third. A trade group in New York City, the Community Resource Center, reported that inner-city consumers spend as much as $400 to $1,000 per year traveling to supermarkets by taxi or mass transportation.

Relative to large ticket items and long-term purchases, the *Wall Street Journal* (7/2/92) noted that "Finance charges for the poor...have soared in recent years because of the de-regulation of consumer interest rates in many states. Today, it isn't uncommon for the poor to pay annual rates of 40% or 45%..." It is usual for the poorest 10% of Americans to devote 70% to 75% of their budgets to food, housing, utilities and medical care, compared to 55% for the average American. Obviously, the poor are confiscatorily "taxed" because of their low-income and status in American society. Poor consumers who make purchases via catalog payments may pay annual interest rate charges several percentage points more than the average bank rate banks charge their more affluent counterparts or credit card purchases.

However, this trend may be reversed as major retailers discover that while incomes in many (but by no means all) inner-city neighborhoods are lower than in other neighborhoods, their population densities increase their buying power. That is, while the Black residents of certain inner-city neighborhoods may have lower average incomes than other ethnic neighborhoods, the fact that there may be many more Black residents per square mile in some Black neighborhoods compared to their more affluent, but more scarcely populated White counterparts, the combined income or buying power of those Black neighborhoods may compare quite favorably with their White cohorts.

The Fulton Mall: Example of a Successful Inner-City Shopping Center. At first sight the Fulton Mall, located in an overwhelmingly Afrikan-American/Afrikan-Caribbean neighborhood in Brooklyn, N.Y., looks a little down at the heels. Its open, often unkempt storefronts facing a crumbling cobblestone street over-running with traffic and sidewalks over-running with street peddlers and teen-age roustabouts, belies its social significance and economic profitability. Despite its extravagance of beeper outlets, gold, jewelry and "going-out-of-business" electronics stores, its merchandise stores with their merchandise heaped on tables and counters, their racks filled with gaudy T-shirts, this 200-store marketplace hosts a 100,000 people who spend more than a million dollars daily. According to the *New York Times* (8/18/94) "The great profitability of the mall is belied by its appearance....[It] remains a highly successful shopping street. Jill Kelly, acting executive director, said Fulton Mall ranks *sixth* in sales among the nation's commercial streets." The *Times* goes on to indicate that according to David Milder, a development consultant, "sales at Fulton Mall average $200 a square foot, compared with $234 at a giant regional mall." The 44,000 square-foot Pathmark supermarket located in the mall since 1978 has annual sales of $25 million. Fulton Mall refutes the myth that because most of an area's customers may be Black, it must for that reason be a failed shopping area.

The Fulton Mall as a public-private shopping-center venture has been emulated by a number of similar ventures in cities such as Newark, Chicago, and Kansas City, Missouri. For example, the not-for-profit New Community Corporation located in Newark, developed a three-acre shopping center through a limited partnership arrangement with Pathmark Foods, a major discount supermarket chain. According to the *New York Times* (11/8/92):

> Pathmark invested about $400,000 of the nearly $3 million in construction financing and owns one-third of the store against New Community's two-thirds. New Community also owns a Dunkin' Donut franchise, a print shop, two restaurants and a health spa, all in the shopping center, which opened in 1990. Both Pathmark and New Community say all the ventures are profitable, although neither will disclose the profit margin.

The development of inner-city shopping malls like the Fulton Mall and the New Community are the result of community groups and developers who, in addition to focusing on building and renovating housing for low-income people, have decided that commercial development of inner-cities should also receive high priority attention as well. These groups believe that urban neighborhoods provide good opportunities for commercial development should commercial developers take certain calculated and well-managed risks. The groups help to assure positive outcomes for commercial developers and investors by raising start-up development funds, acquiring property, and removing political and other cost barriers to the development and profitability of commercial undertakings in their local communities. Noting the role giant supermarkets play in anchoring urban shopping malls, the *Times* (11/8/92) describes how a public-private partnership generally operates to found and develop the typical urban shopping center:

> Depending on the location, size, design and available local subsidies, the deals will vary. Typically, a for-profit entity will form a partnership with the non-profit, community-based developer. Sometimes the supermarket chain will buy its store and in other deals it will lease from the community group....
>
> Even successful groups acknowledge that the cost of developing and operating such centers is substantially higher than in suburban sites. Land acquisition often proves the primary obstacle.
>
> Appropriate sites in ready-to-build condition are hard to find in cities. For each square foot of store space, most food-store chains want about four square feet of parking. Urban developers sometimes spend 5 to 10 years assembling the parcels of commercially zoned land.
>
> Higher real estate taxes and higher maintenance and security costs have also impeded commercial development in city neighborhoods. Studies have found that while urban shoppers spend as much as suburban shoppers they typically make more trips to the market, which increases operation and maintenance costs....
>
> Along with low-interest financing, the community-based developers bring another important, if less tangible, contribution to a commercial project: neighborhood support for the shopping center.
>
> "With community involvement, our stores are more quickly assimilated into the community," said Harvey Guttman, a senior vice president for retail and development with Pathmark. The project also faces fewer challenges from local politicians when it comes to zoning changes or Government subsidies.

As not-for-profit corporations, community groups can generally lower construction costs with government grants or low-interest loans.

The Role of Finance in the Afrikan American Market Economy. The establishment and control of an Afrikan American market economy is imperative for the enrichment and empowerment of the Afrikan American community. The main reason the Black community is commercially and politically exploited by aliens is that it lacks a financial system which provides for its self-sustained and self-financed development. (*Note:* The following discussion closely follows the outline of the article by Wilhelm Hankel, cited above. While Hankel's discussion concerns itself with the role of finance in Third

World countries we think it applies equally well to the role of finance in the Afrikan American community — a Third World country in the United States.)

As we emphasize in this volume, the Afrikan American community does not suffer from an absence or inadequacy of financial resources which can be utilized to maximize its wealth, economic and political power. What the community lacks is a domestically based financial sector which functions to collect its monetary and savings resources and transform them into working capital used to finance the development of Black-owned and controlled commercial, economic, and cultural establishments. Increased employment and economic opportunity, enhanced wealth, cannot occur within the Afrikan American community without the building of its own banking and finance sector. An efficient Afrikan American market economy cannot be created unless the community understands the role and functions of an interdependent banking and finance system. The major reason alien and White communities are able to fund their own internal economic development as well as take advantage of economic opportunities which exist outside of their communities, is because they have developed traditional or formal systems of finance which collect and transform their monetary and socioeconomic resources into investable capital. At this time the Afrikan American community does not possess a formal or informal banking system capable of constructing and sustaining a domestic money market system based on credit and refinancing institutions.

The paucity of Black-owned banks where the savings and receipts of Black consumers and businesspeople are deposited, means that the Black community lacks a systemic mechanism for transforming those deposits and receipts into expanded credit and other investments which economically benefit the community. This means that the community must develop an adequate network of banks, investment banks, insurance companies, pension funds, and other financial systems which intermediate between Black savers and borrowers to expand the money supply available for economic development. As Hankel (ibid) contends, "the credit economy splits economic actors into classes of savers and investors. They can be identical in terms of person or function, but must not be identical if the credit economy is to function. It is up to the banking sector [its equivalent, e.g., the "susu" system or the Korean "Kye" system, and other traditional systems of collecting savings from one group and lending them to others] as intermediary to bring them together."

Banking systems markedly increase capital formation through their unparalleled capacity to accumulate in a select number of places a sizable amount of monetary resources. A functioning banking and financial sector promotes the growth of the entrepreneurial sector by its capacity to increase the supply of capital and credit. Through the centralization of its monetary reserves in the hands of its financial and cultural institutions which will in turn utilize these reserves to expand the money supply, the Black community can exert a powerful force behind the process of nation building and the necessary building of the Pan-Afrikan economic system. A growing network of Black-owned and controlled financial institutions which are capable of disbursing increasing quantities of money and credit contracts between Black savers and investors and the Black-owned and controlled entrepreneurial sector as well as among individual consumers to finance the growing exchange of goods and services, will permit the Black community itself to generate the market forces necessary to achieve its economic growth and development. This will permit it to replace alien merchants and financiers who now dominate and exploit its moribund economy. This translates into increasingly effective Black political and economic power as well as increasing community self-determination and individual freedom.

Since the capital market, e.g., the system of banks, financial institutions and other financial arrangements decide by means of credit allotment interest charges who gets capital for which project and under what terms, Black ownership and control of this market would permit the Black community to allot credit in its own economic interest. A Black-owned and controlled capital market would be maximally responsive to the direction and intensity of Black consumer demand and needs. This will permit the Black consumer to more effectively influence the profits and prices, and to measurably influence the flow of funds and use of capital in the Black community. A Black-controlled financial system would permit the Black community to be the primary regulator of its own investment priorities, projects, and preferred instruments.

The failure of the Black community to establish its own domestic formal and informal banking and financial systems and schemes for financing its own economic growth has the following consequences:

- The large consumer buying (some $400 billion) and productive capacities (some $1 trillion$^+$) of the community cannot be collected and converted by the community into investment and consumer credit and made available to its entrepreneurial enterprises and consumers for fueling economic growth the community's quality of life.

- The discrepancy between the demand for funds for needed investments and consumption in the Afrikan American community and the inadequate supply of intracommunal funds compels Black entrepreneurs and consumers to borrow or import larger amounts of capital than would be otherwise required from outside resources. Consequently, credit that could be produced within the community, must be provided by outsiders. This leads to the chronic over-indebtedness of Black consumers, leading to the continuing flight of community capital into the coffers of outside business and financial establishments as well as the chronic underfunding of Black-owned and controlled enterprises, leading to Black economic under-development with its attendant social problems.

- To quote Hankel (ibid), "The recourse to foreign banking and credit markets instead of domestic resources and facilities, however weak, only worsens the illness instead of curing it."

The development of an efficient financial sector in the Black community through the expansion of Black-owned banks, credit unions, co-operatives, underwriting institutions, informal credit associations and the like, would facilitate the rapid increase in Black-controlled capital formation, real income, and employment. By these means the Black community can avoid its onerous indebtedness to and control by outside financial and social-political institutions. The development in the Black community of financial institutions which can effectively counter those of the White community can be realistically achieved only if the Black community perceives, organizes and behaves itself as an Afrikan nation-within-a-nation and that nation fully commits itself to its liberation from White domination through its the active reclamation of its Afrikan identity and consciousness.

Box 18-1   **Myths about Entrepreneurs**

A large number of myths characterize our perception of the typical new entrepreneur and of the typical start-up enterprise. For example, many people believe that only a relative few adults try to start new businesses; that most entrepreneurs are rugged individualists; are great risk takers; recent immigrants; untraditional; young adults; and are now mostly women. A generally accepted myth about business and entrepreneurship is that a good business climate is required for entrepreneurial activity and that entrepreneurship is a cultural trait. Studies by Paul Reynolds of Marquette University in Wisconsin and Sammis White of the University of Wisconsin, among others, appear to have put the lie to these myths. While studying the business start-up process by doing phone surveys with random samples of the adult population, Reynolds and White asked a series of questions of those who said they were trying to start a business. The pattern of answers were the same in both Wisconsin and national U.S. samples. Contrary to the myths cited above Reynolds and White discovered following facts:

- More U.S. adults are trying to start new businesses than are training children or getting married. One person in 25 is actively involved in trying to start a new business. More than 7 million people a year are trying to start more than 3 million new businesses.
- Only about one-third of nascent entrepreneurs — those actively trying to start a business — go it alone. About two-thirds of new entrepreneurs include two or more persons. The average size of a start-up team is 2.2 people.
- More than two-thirds of those trying to get a business started have full-time or part-time jobs or are running another business. Most only devote full-time efforts to the new venture after it is truly up and going. Fewer than 10% of those starting a new business are unemployed at the time. Thus it appears that new entrepreneurs are not necessarily great risk takers.
- Recent immigrants, current popular media images notwithstanding, are not the major force in new ventures. About 50% of those trying to start businesses have resided in their county for more than 15 years. About 80% of new entrepreneurs have resided in their county for more than 5 years.

Almost all entrepreneurs trying to start a new business are high school graduates (college or graduate work does not increase participation). Most earn household incomes above the poverty level and are in their middle years — between 30 and 50 years old. Thus it appears that most entrepreneurs are not your typical social maverick.

- About twice as many men are likely to start businesses as are women. Women comprise about one-third of those starting new businesses. Though their role in starting new enterprises has increased very substantially in the past several decades, they are still a minority.
- Personal judgments about a specific location rather than feelings or knowledge about the goodness or badness of the general business climate, seem more important in determining whether or not an entrepreneur would start a new venture. In fact, those who had started a new business in the Wisconsin sample were the most negative about state's entrepreneurial climate. Those trying to start a new venture were neutral.
- Educational attainment, length of residence, age, and household income appear to be the primary factors leading to business start-ups. Cultural traits or background seems to play a lesser role than is generally thought. Once the factors cited above are considered, there is little difference among ethnic groups (Native Americans, Asian Americans, Afrikan Americans, and Hispanics). This finding may be an artifact of the small population samples used in the study of this variable.[1] ■

---

1. Adapted from Paul Reynolds, "What WE Don't Know May Hurt Us," *Inc.* Sept., 1994, pp. 25–26.

Chapter 19

THE PAUCITY OF BLACK WEALTH

IN THIS CHAPTER WE SHALL FOLLOW the central contention argued by David Swinton in a series of articles published since 1988 in the National Urban League's annual *The State of Black America*. He asserts that "only when Blacks own enough to be equal participants in the nation's economy will they be able to ensure their own prosperity and equality" (1993). Swinton recognizes the fact that the general economic well-being of Black America depends on the overall performance and structure of the American economy. However, more to his credit is his insistence on the idea that *"the economic status of blacks depends on the level and character of black participation in American economic life"*[Emphasis added].[1] Also, while recognizing that there has been a substantial increase over the past two decades in the proportion of Afrikan Americans who can be classified as solidly middle and upper-middle class according a number of income and social measures, trends indicate that an increasingly larger proportion of the community is experiencing economic stagnation, decline, and deterioration. It is also important to keep in mind that approximately one half of Black children belong to poor families. With reference to the character and level of Black participation in American economic life Swinton has consistently argued that:

> The low relative economic status of blacks and the high share of economic burdens borne by blacks have their economic origins in

---

1. *The State of Black America 1988*, p. 138.

blacks' limited ownership of human and nonhuman capital. These limitations have two impacts. They limit the extent of ownership and control of business enterprises. This limitation forces blacks to be dependent on white-owned or -controlled businesses for jobs, income, and goods and services. This makes them vulnerable to the possibility of discrimination. The limited human capital of blacks may make them less attractive to potential employers, which would limit the quantity and quality of opportunities that business owners are willing to provide for them. These three factors — limited ability for self-employment, limited attractiveness to employers, and racial discrimination — combine to produce the high level of racial disparities.[2]

While economic analyses of Black America have fittingly emphasized the adverse effects on its economic well-being of its poverty of human capital, (e.g., education, high skills) and racial discrimination, unless there are significant reductions in racial disparities in wealth and business ownership there will be little really significant improvement in the economy and power of the community. Reductions in racial disparities in wealth, business ownership and human capital, argues Swinton, "are necessary to eliminate the income disparities that arise from returns on ownership of productive wealth and self-employment."

In sum, economic well-being depends on the amount of assets (rent, interests, profits) or wealth one owns, in addition to earned income (e.g., wages). Wealth refers to the difference between assets and liabilities (debts). It "reflects savings and investments that can be drawn on in times of need...those resources that can be passed on from one generation to the next."[3] As we implied in our introductory statements, wealth is a major source of power in the U.S. and in the world. Disparities in wealth between Afrikan Americans and White Americans and other ethnic Americans are the primary reasons Blacks have been unable to overcome racial inequality and relative political powerlessness.

> General policies to promote national economic recovery...will not resolve the underlying problem of racial inequality. During a recovery, all boats may rise, but the black boat will remain a small canoe next to the white yacht. The swings in the black economic status attributable to the stages of the business cycle are only a few percentage points. General policies will not result in secular improvements for the black population.[4]

---

2. Ibid., p. 150.

3. W.P. O'Hare, *Wealth and Economic Status: A Perspective on Racial Inequality* (Washington D.C.: Joint Center for Political Studies, 1983).

4. *The State of Black America 1993*, pp. 198–99.

Wealth Ownership, 1988 (in millions of 1991$)

	Mean Wealth Holdings		Percent Owning Each Type of Wealth		Per Capita Wealth Holdings			Aggregate Wealth Holdings		
	Black	White	Black	White	Black	White	B/W	Black	White	Gap
Total Net Worth	27,230	116,661	100.00%	100.00%	$9,359	44,980	20.81%	279,870	9,235,958	1,065,224
Interest Earning at Financial Institutions	5,008	21,748	44.48	76.58	766	6,421	11.93%	22,904	1,318,506	169,118
Regular Checking	822	1,243	30.11	50.92	85	244	35.04%	2,555	50,070	47,367
Stocks & Mutual Funds	4,220	32,582	6.97	23.92	101	3,005	3.36%	3,023	617,100	86,849
Equity in Business	29,053	76,604	3.66	13.57	366	4,008	9.13%	10,938	822,943	108,913
Equity in Motor Vehicle	4,568	7,378	64.67	89.15	1,015	2,536	40.02%	30,353	520,812	45,497
Equity in Home	42,334	73,871	43.46	66.72	6,323	19,003	33.27%	189,094	3,902,024	379,184
Equity in Rental Property	46,926	95,965	4.55	9.61	734	3,556	20.63%	21,938	730,078	84,388
Other Real Estate	18,895	44,294	4.37	11.35	283	1,938	14.62%	8,476	397,991	49,486
U.S. Savings Bonds	1,165	3,589	11.01	18.47	51	212	23.95%	1,309	52,424	63,260
IRA or Keoghs	6,394	19,010	6.87	26.43	174	1,786	9.73%	4,518	397,777	53,412

Aggregate gaps = white per capita - black per capita * 1988 black population (29, 904,000)
Inequality Index (B/W) = black per capita/white per capita
Source: U.S. Department of Commerce, Bureau of the Census, *Household Wealth and Asset Ownership: 1988*, December 1990, Table 3.

Table 19–1

Some Facts About Black Wealth Ownership

- Afrikan Americans have a mean net worth of only $27,230 compared to $116,661 for Whites. On a per capita basis, blacks have a net worth of $9,359 versus $44,980 for whites.

- 76.58 percent of white households had assets which earned interest at financial institutions, but only 44.48 percent of blacks had this type of wealth.

- Moreover, those blacks who had interest-earning assets at financial institutions had mean holdings worth $5,008 compared to $21,748 for white households.

- Blacks have only $766 per capita in interest-earning assets at financial institutions compared to $6,421 for whites.

- Afrikan Americans had only one-third as much equity in housing as did white Americans. Greatest inequality existed for ownership of stocks and mutual funds, equity in business, and IRAs and Keoghs.

- The greatest equality in ownership of assets between blacks and whites involved the ownership of consumption-oriented assets such as motor vehicles, housing and regular checking accounts.

- In 1987, blacks owned 424,000 businesses compared to 17,526,000 business in the nation as a whole.

- There were only about 14 firms per 1,000 black persons compared to 73 firms per 1,000 persons for the country as a whole.

- Blacks were 12.1 percent of the population in 1987 but owned only 2.4 percent of the businesses. Black-owned businesses together generated receipts of only $22.8 billion compared to receipts of $11,893 billion for all businesses.

- Black businesses accounted for only 0.19 percent of total receipts. Black businesses had total receipts of $775 for each black person compared to $49,310 per person for the economy as a whole.

- In the selected services sector black-owned businesses generated only $7.1 billion out of a total of $996 billion. This amounted to only seven-tenths of 1 percent of total receipts.

Table 19–2 provides the latest data on Black business ownership.

Receipts (in billions of 1991$) **and Number of Firms** (1,000s) **in 1987 by Industry**

	Black Receipts	Total Receipts	B/T**	Black Firms	Total Firms	B/T***	Receipts per Firm Black	Receipts per Firm Total	B/T	Receipt Gap	Firm Gap
Total	$22.8	$11,893	0.016	424	17526	19.8%	53,774	678,592	7.92	$1,427	1,713
Construction	2.6	616	3.7%	37	560	53.9%	70,270	1,100,000	6.34	72.9	32
Manufacture	1.2	3,185	0.3%	8	642	10.2%	150,000	4,961,059	3.02	387.7	70
Trans. and Public Util.	1.8	909	1.7%	37	735	41.2%	48,649	1,236,735	3.93	108.4	53
Wholesale Trade	1.5	1,466	0.9%	6	641	7.0%	250,000	2,287,051	10.93	177.2	73
Retail Trade	6.7	1,802	3.2%	66	2,658	20.4%	101,515	677,953	14.97	212.6	258
Finance, Ins., & Real Estate	0.9	1,814	0.4%	27	1,426	15.5%	33,333	1,272,090	2.62	220.9	147
Selected Services	7.1	996	6.0%	210	7,095	24.2%	33,810	140,381	24.08	114.6	656
Other Industries*	0.9	1,105	0.7%	34	3,769	7.5%	26,471	293,181	9.02	134.4	425

Note: 1987 dollars were converted to 1991 dollars using CPI-U-XI
*: Includes Agriculture, Mining, and Industries not elsewhere classified.
**: (Black Receipts/Black Population) divided by (Total Receipts/Total Population).
***: (Black Firms/Black Population) divided by (Total Firms/Total Population).
Black population in 1987: 29,417,000; total population in 1987: 241,187,000.

Source: U.S. Dept. of Commerce, Bureau of the Census, *Survey of Minority-Owned Businesses: Black, 1987*, and *The Statistical Abstract of the United States*, 1990, Table 859, 521.

Table 19-2

According to Swinton, "The B/T inequality index suggests that Black businesses generated only about 1.6 percent as much revenue as would be required to have ownership parity as measured by receipts." A similar ratio was developed for the number of Black-owned businesses relative to the Black American population. For example, in construction, the 37,000 Black-owned firms comprise 53.9 percent of the firms required for parity. The B/T numbers clearly indicate the high degree of inequality in the number of firms across the whole of the industrial/services spectrum. Moreover, there is evidence that during the 12 Reagan and Bush years progress towards parity in business ownership was retarded and that the Afrikan American business sector may have generated a relatively smaller share of total business receipts despite an overall rise in the per capita receipts during that period.

Although the growth rate of Black-owned firms (37%) in 1987 was substantially higher than the average of all American firms (26.2%), these firms comprise only about 3.1% of the total U.S. business enterprises and account for only 1% of sales/receipts of all U.S. firms. Only 17% of Afrikan American firms have paid employees. This may be in great part due to the fact that not only do Black-owned firms tend to be relatively small, but that 94% of Afrikan American firms are organized as sole proprietorships, the remaining 6% consisting of 3% partnerships and 3% sole corporations. Approximately 63% of Afrikan American firms are concentrated in the services and retail trade industries.

Lenneal Henderson, Professor of Government and Public Administration at the University of Baltimore, like David Swinton, has been emphatic in emphasizing the intimate relationship between Afrikan American enterprise ownership and Afrikan American political-economic empowerment. His concept of empowerment is presented in his article titled "Empowerment through Enterprise: African American Business Development" published in *The State of Black America 1993:*

> Empowerment is a complex and comprehensive concept consisting of at least five interrelated components.
>
> (1) The formation of strategic goals and objectives by individuals and institutions that focus on creation, expansion, distribution, and utilization of human, financial, technological and information resources, particularly for a given group or organization;
> (2) The mobilization of those resources through strategic interaction with individuals/institutions within and beyond the current range

or field of interaction to achieve even higher levels of resource attainment;
(3) As resource mobilization generates higher levels of resource attainment, entrepreneurs build skills, capacities, and networks that position them for even greater resource development and diversification. This is the economic concept of "multiplier effect" applied to psychological, socioeconomic, and institutional outcomes as well as financial consequences;
(4) As resource development and diversification occurs, entrepreneurs are able to transact, contract, and interact across more and more community, financial, institutional, and other boundaries both within and beyond their own locations, further extending their networks, skills, and resource base; and;
(5) The enabling and building of the individual, organizational, and institutional network, of which the empowered organization is part. In other words, when one force is empowered, most forces connected with it are actually or potentially empowered as well.[5]

Henderson goes on to contend that in light of the overwhelmingly negative balance of trade between the Black and White American communities, "the concept of empowerment for African American entrepreneurs includes a two-dimensional imperative: (a) conception, development, and enrichment of economically and socially productive and enterprising *organizations* and (b) mutually enriching and collectively productive relationships between Afrikan American *enterprise organizations* and African-American *individuals, households*, and *communities.*"

Empowerment begins at home. A major dilemma faced by Afrikan American business persons is the fact that in the virtual absence of a deep and abiding sense of race solidarity, they cannot rely on the full, loyal patronage of their ethnic community. They, unlike many other ethnic business persons, cannot assume that they will be more or less automatically supported by a substantial portion of their community based on common ethnic-cultural bonds. In fact, Black business persons must, much more often than necessary, engage in a losing battle with other ethnic business persons for the business support of their own people. Even though Afrikan American business persons earn the highest percentage of sales and receipts in areas where the demographic concentration of the Afrikan American population is the highest, there is still a "glaring disparity between the proportion of African Americans in the states' population and the revenues

---

5. *State of Black America 1993*, pp. 91–92.

generated by African American-owned firms."[6] For example, Henderson points out that in the District of Columbia where 69% of the population is Afrikan American, "it is clear that the African American community is not sufficiently strong to elevate those businesses even to the level of 50 percent of all sales and receipts generated [there]." Paltry indeed, Black-owned firms generated only 6.3 percent of the total sales and receipts in Washington, D.C.

Business Ownership and Investment: Keys to Black Wealth

In contrast to some other indices of Black American social and economic progress since the 1960s, such as increases in the number of high-ranking Black professionals in private industry and government, there has been little progress made toward equalizing the economic status of Blacks and Whites. Alarmingly, according to Census Bureau data collected in 1992, economic inequality between the two groups is continuing to widen. In 1992, the median Black family income of $21,761 was just 55.3% of the median White family income of $39,320. This disparity in significant part reflects compara-

Black and White Share of Wealth Per Capita in 1992

	Net Worth	Interest Earning	Stocks Mutual funds	Home Equity	Rental Property
BLACK	$10,651	872	115	416	7,196
WHITE	$51,191	7,308	3,420	4,561	21,627

*In thousands of 1992 dollars
Source: National Urban League, *State of Black America*, January 1994.

Black's share of American wealth per capita
is far less than that of Whites.
Adapted from *Black Enterprise* magazine, July 1994.

Table 19-3

tively higher levels of unemployment and lower average earnings, when employed, of Blacks. Inequality of wealth ownership between Blacks and Whites also accounts significantly for this difference.

6. Ibid.

Paucity of Black Wealth ❖ 477

Top 75 of B.E. Industrial/Service 100 Companies, and
selected others, abstracted from *Black Enterprise*, June 1997

RANK 1997	RANK 1994	COMPANY	TYPE OF BUSINESS	SALES*
1	1	TLC Beatrice International Holdings Inc.	International food processor and distributor	2,230.000
2	2	Johnson Publishing Co. Inc.	Publishing; broadcasting; TV production; cosmetics; hair care	325.712
3	3	Philadelphia Coca-Cola Bottling Co. Inc.	Soft drinks bottling	325.000
4	14	Pulsar Data Systems Inc.	Computer systems integration & network design	166.000
5	4	H.J. Russell & Co.	Construction development & management; communications	163.756
6	16	Uniworld Group Inc.	Advertising, public relations, event marketing; TV programming	157.865
7	30	Granite Broadcasting Corp.	Network TV affiliates	154.845
8	—	Convenience Corporation of America Inc.	Convenience stores	137.395
9	17	Burrell Communications Group Inc.	Advertising, PR, consumer promotions; direct response marketing	134.700
10	18	Black Entertainment Television Holdings Inc.	Cable television network; magazine publishing	132.700
11	12	The Bing Group	Steel processing; metal stamping distribution	129.500
12	11	Envirotest Systems Corp.	Vehicle emissions testing	124.472
13	6	The Anderson-Dubose Co.	Apparel manufacturer	122.200
14	21	Stop Shop and Save Food Markets	Supermarkets	108.000
15	38	Sylvest Management Systems Corp.	Computer systems & engineering	107.500
16	—	Midwest Stamping Inc.	Automotive metal stamping & assemblies	106.800
17	20	Mays Chemical Co. Inc.	Industrial chemical distributors	105.300
18	13	Barden Companies Inc.	Radio broadcasting, real estate, development, casino gambling	93.207
19	19	Essence Communications Inc.	Magazine publishing; TV production; direct-mail catalog	92.784
20	9	Soft Sheen Products Inc.	Hair care products manufacturer	91.400

RANK 1997	RANK 1994	COMPANY	TYPE OF BUSINESS	SALES*
21	23	Wesley Industries Inc.	Industrial coatings & grey iron foundry products	87.500
22	?	Thomas Madison Inc.	Automotive metal stamping, steel sales & processing	79.000
23	54	Digital Systems Research Inc.	Defense systems; engineering; computer systems integration	77.000
24	---	Fuci Metals USA Inc.	Ferrous & non-ferrous metals, seller and trader	75.000
25	--	Spiral Inc. / Powerline	Sanitation products	72.400
26	—	Sayers Computer Source	Value-added reseller of computers & related products	70.000
27	93	La-Van Hawkins Urban City Foods, LLC	Burger King fast foods	67.320
28	--	Karl Kani Infinity Inc.	Men's & boys' wear, footwear, sports apparel, licensing	65.000
29	?	The Bartech Group	Contract employment; staffing services	64.800
30	—	Reliant Industries Inc	Manufacturer of fasteners for auto industry	62.000
31	22	African Development Public Investment Co..	African commodities & oil trading	61.000
32	27	Surface Protection Industries Inc.	Paint & specialty coatings manufacturer	57.000
33	26	Pepsi Cola of Washington, D.C., LP.	Soft-drink distributor	55.643
34	60	The O-J Group	Transportation service	54.900
35	43	Beauchamp Distributing Co.	Beverage distributor-wholesaler	54.466
36	45	Advantage Enterprises Inc.	Project integrator for health care & construction	54.325
37	25	The Chisholm-Mingo Group Inc.	Advertising, public relations & promotions	54.292
38	?	Exemplar Manufacturing Co.	Auto parts manufacturing & assembly	51.578
39	34	Pro-Line Corp.	Hair care products manufacturer & distributor	50.386
40	15	Drew Pearson Marketing	Sports licensing & sportswear manufacturing	50.000
40	--	Health Resources Inc.	Medical ancillary networks	50.000
42	--	Community Pride Food Stores	Supermarkets	47.000

RANK 1997	RANK 1994	COMPANY	TYPE OF BUSINESS	SALES*
43	37	Grimes Oil Co. Inc.	Petroleum products distributor	43.500
44	28	Community Foods Inc. T/A Super Pride Markets	Supermarkets Restaurant & food service	43.000
44	29	Luster Products Co.	Hair care products	43.000
44	68	Regal Plastics Co. Inc.	Project integrator for health care & construction	43.000
44	24	Trumark Inc.	Beauty products manufacturer	43.000
48	—	Fair Oaks Farms Inc.	Meat processing	42.674
49	51	Edge Systems Inc.	Information technology	41.500
50	41	Metters Industries Inc.	Information technology, technical services, software development	40.277
51	—	Intellisys Technology Corp.	Computer systems integration, network engineering & mgt.	39.885
52	36	Calhoun Enterprises	Supermarkets	38.841
53	49	R.OW. Sciences Inc.	Biomedical & health information systems & research	38.308
54	39	Gourmet Companies Inc.	Food services, golf course management	37.000
54	50	Rush Communications & Affiliated Companies	Music publishing, TV, film, radio production, music & fashion	37.000
56	47	Am-Pro Protective Agency Inc.	Security guard services	36.796
57	44	Thompson Hospitality, L.P.	Restaurants, food services, lodging	36.000
58	70	V and J Foods Inc.	Burger King franchisee	36.000
59	31	Capsonic Group Inc.	Designs & manufactures composite metal/plastic components	35.000
60	42	Integrated Packaging Corp.	Manufacturers of corrugated paper products	34.800
61	33	Maxima Corp	Systems engineering & computer facilities management	34.500
62	81	Terry Manufacturing Co. Inc.	Apparel manufacturing	34.000
62	53	Yancy Minerals Inc.	Industrial metals, minerals & coal distributors	34.000
64	?	Perfection Industrial Distributors	Medical & industrial supply distributor	33.800
65	?	Telecommunications Systems Inc. (TCS)	Advanced technology systems engineering, integration & manuf.	32.700

RANK 1997	RANK 1994	COMPANY	TYPE OF BUSINESS	SALES*
66	90	Solo Construction Corp.	General engineering construction	32.621
67	46	Dudley Products Inc.	Beauty products manufacturer & cosmetology training	32.500
68	—	Innolog	Logistics systems engineering & information technology	32.000
68	—	Management Technology Inc.	Information systems technology	32.000
70	86	Ozanne Construction Co. Inc.	General construction & construction management	31.800
71	88	Resource One Computer Systems Inc.	Computer hardware & software	31.000
72	63	Restoration Supermarket Corp.	Supermarket & drugstore retail sales	30.500
73	?	C.H. James & Son (Holdings) Inc.	Wholesale food distribution/ produce processing	30.100
73	72	Earl G. Graves Ltd.	Magazine publishing	30.100
75	—	Sentel Corp.	Engineering & aviation services for the U.S. government	30.000
77	67	The Navcom Systems Group	Engineering and aviation	28.522
78	?	Integrated Systems Analysts Inc.	Systems engineering & computer systems services	28.400
81	—	Social & Scientific Systems Inc.	Technical and information support services	28.066
82	57	Cimarron Express Inc.	Truckload transportation services	28.000
83	52	Inner City Broadcasting Corp.	Radio, TV, cable TV, franchise	27.389
88	69	Lundy Enterprises Inc.	Pizza Hut restaurants	25.000
88	?	Washington Cable Supply Inc.	Electrical & telecommunications equipment distributor	25.000
90	?	American Urban Radio Net.	Radio broadcasting	22.700
95	—	Dynamic Concepts Inc.	Telecommunications services, operations & maintenance support	22.211
98	—	GB Tech Inc.	Information systems support, systems engineering & integration	21.062
99	—	Advanced Technological Solutions Inc.	Computer and electronic services	21.000
100	—	Red River Shipping Corp.	Ocean transportation	20.509

*In millions of dollars, to nearest thousand. As of Dec. 31, 1996. Prepared by B.E. Research Reviewed by Mitchell & Titus, L.L.P.

Table 19–4

1994 B.E. 100s

	1992	1993	DIFFERENCE	PERCENT CHANGE
Total Sales*	$9,028.449	$10,280.801	$1,252.352	13.9%
Total Staff	38,020	45,628	7,608	20.0

1994 B.E. INDUSTRIAL/SERVICE 100

	1992	1993	DIFFERENCE	PERCENT CHANGE
Total Sales*	$5,691.557	$6,156.821	$465.264	8.2%
Total Staff	31,668	38,649	6,981	22.0

1994 B.E. AUTO DEALER 100

	1992	1993	DIFFERENCE	PERCENT CHANGE
Total Sales*	$3,336.892	$4,123.980	$787.088	23.6%
Total Staff	6,352	6,979	627	9.9

*In millions of dollars, to the nearest thousand.
Prepared by B.E. Research. Reviewed by Mitchell/Titus & Co.

Table 19–5

1997 B.E. 100s

	1995	1996	DIFFERENCE	PERCENT CHANGE
Total Sales*	$13,092.832	$14,107.600	$1,014.768	7.75%
Total Staff	51,057	55,242	4,185	8.20

1997 B.E. INDUSTRIAL/SERVICE 100

	1995	1996	DIFFERENCE	PERCENT CHANGE
Total Sales*	$7,399.179	$8,182.356	$783,177	10.58%
Total Staff	42,386	46,034	3,648	8.61

1997 B.E. AUTO DEALER 100

	1995	1996	DIFFERENCE	PERCENT CHANGE
Total Sales*	$5,693,653	$5,925.244	$231,591	4.07%
Total Staff	8,671	9,208	537	6.19

*In millions of dollars, to the nearest thousand.
Prepared by B.E. Research. Reviewed by Mitchell/Titus & Co.

Table 19–6

TOP TEN EMPLOYMENT LEADERS

COMPANY	LOCATION	Employees	1996 Sales*
TLC Beatrice International Holding Inc.	New York, NY	4,700	$2,230.000
Envirotest Systems Corp.	Sunnyvale, CA	4,000	124.472
Johnson Publishing Co. Inc.	Chicago, IL	2,702	325.712
The Bartech Group	Livonia. MI	1,614	64.800
Barden Companies Inc.	Detroit, MI	1,450	93.207
H.J. Russell & Co.	Atlanta, GA	1,416	163.756
La-Van Hawkins Urban City Foods L.L.C.	Baltimore, MD	1,390	67.320
V & J Foods Inc.	Milwaukee, WI	1,385	36.000
Thompson Hospitality, L.P.	Reston, VA	1,350	36.500
Am-Pro Protective Agency Inc.	Columbia, SC	1,181	36.796

In millions of dollars, to the nearest thousand. **In thousands of dollars, as of December 31, 1996. Prepared by B.E. Research. Reviewed by Mitchell & Titus, LLP.

Table 19–7

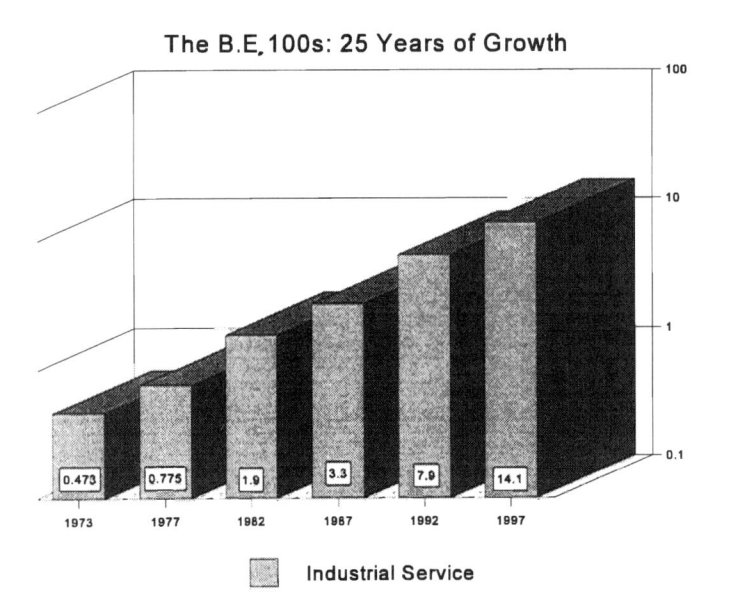

The B.E. 100s: 25 Years of Growth

Year	Industrial Service
1973	0.473
1977	0.775
1982	1.9
1987	3.3
1992	7.9
1997	14.1

Table 19–8

David Swinton, now a member of the Black Enterprise Board of Economists and president of Benedict College in Columbia, S.C., best speaks to this issue when he explains the reason for Black-White disparities in income:

> The reason: There has never been a significant effort to equalize racial disparities in ownership. In a free enterprise economy, economic forces flow from ownership of human and other resources. Lack of ownership means lack of income-earning resources and organized enterprises to create jobs. And any group not owning business and financial capital becomes dependent on others.
>
> In 1987, the last year for full data, there were significant black-white ownership gaps (see chart). Blacks owned fewer than 15 businesses per 1,000 persons compared with more than 72 businesses per 1,000 persons for whites. Moreover, black-owned businesses generated only $775 in revenues per employee, compared with $56,120 for white businesses. Consequently, black per capita net worth was only $10,651, and 80% of these holdings were in home and motor vehicle equity. Whites had a net worth of $51,191 per capita, and less than half of that was in the same types of equity.[7]

Swinton goes on to contend that if Blacks are to achieve business ownership parity with Whites they would have to own approximately 2.1 million enterprises. That is, they must own some 1.7 million more businesses than the 424,000 they now own. Swinton elaborates:

> The aggregate of ownership gaps is also tremendous. In 1987, blacks owned 424,000 businesses. But to achieve parity, they would have had to own another 1.7 million enterprises. These businesses had revenues of $22.8 billion (of which $6.2 billion was generated by the 200 largest black businesses as represented by the BLACK ENTERPRISE 100S) but another $1.624 trillion would be needed for parity. And the total household wealth gap exceeded $1.2 trillion in 1988. In addition, the human capital wealth gap was over $650 billion.
>
> How did the gaps appear? They are a legacy of slavery, segregation and discrimination. And this legacy is self-perpetuating without the reparations needed to equalize the opportunities for ownership.
>
> Society can close these ownership gaps within a 25-year time period, without straining the economy. But if we do not, the current chasms of racial economic inequality will be with us forever.

For Swinton, poverty in the Black community is more a matter of net worth than income.

---

7. *Black Enterprise*, July 1994.

Box 19-1 — Jobs versus Ownership

Slavery, colonialism, neocolonialism, and politico-economic subordination, condition dependent people to expect to be provided employment, sustenance, and supervision by those on whom they depend. Their conditions of dependency, especially if long, intense, and pervasive, understandably impair and delimit their initiative, self-direction, self-determination and self-fulfillment. For under oppression these tendencies in the dependent are restricted or punished by their oppressors. Under such oppression the dependent often utilize apathy, narrowness of vision and range as survival mechanisms. Enterprise is the special prerogative and preserve of their masters or of outsiders. The spirit of enterprise in the dependent, their self-confidence — the essential aspects of entrepreneurship — are systematically militated against them by their masters, who greedily seek to reap all the fruits and profits from any and all productive materials, undertakings and labor. Therefore, the dependent are only of value to their masters as laborers, servants and consumers — not as entrepreneurial competitors. Consequently, they subsist primarily through jobs supplied by their masters. They are thus conditioned to work for others who own and manage the enterprises which employ them.

Thus, the dependent become inveterate job seekers. Their moribund spirit of enterprise motivates them to secure their survival through constantly beseeching their masters to provide them with jobs, opportunity, job creation, job training, affirmative action, quotas. Success and security for the dependent are one with the fantasy of rising to the highest ranks in the workshops owned by their masters or by people other than themselves. They have lost faith in their ability to create their own employment opportunities, to own their own workshops and master their own enterprises. Perhaps they have lost even the desire to do these things. The thought, too often, seems never to occur to them.

This reflects the power of the slave plantation — a power that extends over generations. Life and its sustenance require working on and maintaining the plantation; succeeding on the plantation. Even after Emancipation the plantation mentality remains fixed, so stubbornly rooted in the consciousness under the intractably influential "desire to return to the plantation" that like the "desire to return to the womb" it negates or neutralizes apparent opportunities to "do for self"; to be one's own boss; to independently create abundance through the creative use of one's own human and material resources.

These passages speak to contemporary conditions of job-orientated Afrikans in America and across the Afrikan diaspora: poverty-stricken, powerless, though possessors of overwhelming human resources and occupants of lands blessed with abundant material possibilities. Afrikans are job seekers in their own communities, territories, economic markets, and lands — properties whose ownership and economic exploitation they have ceded to aliens. For them, jobs are more important than ownership.

The High Cost of Jobs. We are, of course, mindful of the fact that Afrikan Americans are job orientated mainly as the result of having been conditioned to servitude and dependence by those who monopolize the ownership of the economy. However, the fact that Black Americans own less than 3 percent of the economy should not blind them to the economic and political advantages of business ownership versus jobholding. This is especially applicable to the case where such jobholding occurs even within Afrikan American community markets consisting of businesses which are fully or significantly supported by Black consumer dollars. More specifically, we are referring here to the case, too prevalent in Afrikan American and Afrikan diasporan communities, where virtually all businesses are owned or managed by aliens. These businesses are predominantly, if not exclusively, supported by Blacks, and yet local Blacks seek and may find little employment in them (where it is far more likely that the family members, fellow ethnics or members of ethnic groups other than local Blacks are employed). Even if local Blacks were the sole employees of these non-Black-owned businesses, especially retail businesses, the cost of employing them and of maintaining these establishments in business is borne by the local Black community. And the cost to the community is relatively high and regressive in its tendency to further impoverish an already poor community. When a local Black community maintains a non-Black-owned firm in business by spending with it, the community in effect is paying that business to employ the local residents it hires. When the business owner is a non-resident, i.e., removes all monies he earns from the community and spends it elsewhere; when virtually all of the business expenses are paid to absentee landlords for rent; to non-Black-owned wholesalers — who also may have relatively few or no Black employees; to other non-Black firms and professionals as well as to other persons who provide a variety of services, the local community pays more for the employment of its local residents by the alien-owned business firms than that business and the goods and services it apparently provides is worth to it. For instance, suppose a non-Black-owned business earns $100,000 per year from sales to its local Black customers and from that amount it pays two local Black employees a combined total of $20,000 per year. (For simplicity, we are ignoring other operating expenses and costs paid to non-Black vendors). In effect, the community is paying the alien merchant $100,000 to hire and pay two local employees $20,000. Thus, the community spends $100,000 to retain $20,000. The alien merchant walks away with $80,000 to spend in his own community and to support its institutions, traditions, values, and quality of life.

Obviously, if the community spent the same $100,000 with a resident, community-owned business which employs the same two local employees, the $100,000 spent with community merchant would be retained in it, spent in it, and used to support its community-based institutions, traditions, values, and quality of life. Hence, the monopolistic ownership of businesses located in Black community markets cannot be blightly justified in terms of their mere provision of goods and services, that of their "revitalization" of the community and paying of taxes, and more to the point, in terms their provision of customarily minimum wage jobs to a relative handful of local residents. This is no substitute, or at best is a poor substitute for a Black, residentially owned community or cooperatively owned business which employs from community residents, buys its goods and services from community and Black-owned vendors to whatever extent is possible or reasonable, and spends or invests its earnings or profits in support of other community-owned businesses and institutions.

Ownership of significant equity in businesses where it spends its monies for the goods and services they provide, should be Black community economic policy applied to both community-based and non-community-based firms. Significant equity should be pursued in large national and multinational corporations which Black communities support through consumer spending nationally and internationally.

Those businesses which resist significant Black equity ownership should *not* be supported by Black consumers. Local alien-owned businesses which do not leave the bulk of their earnings in the community, which do not support its local institutions and vendors, should not be supported by Black consumers. All empowered nations "tax" foreign-owned firms and see to it that those firms in some way truly contribute to the enrichment and well-being of the host nation in return for exercising the privilege of doing business there. The Black American nation and Afrikan peoples and nations should do no less. The Black community should not shop where it does not own. ▪

The Case for Reparations

Swinton makes a good case for reparations. The slave experience and White racism has been extremely costly to Blacks. It will continue to be costly in a myriad of ways for Blacks and the nation until White America reparates and repents its exploitative racist past and present. A decision by White America to immediately cease and desist its racist practices against Black America and engage in a range of affirmative action initiatives will not suffice to repay Blacks the damages which have been done to them. Only reparations can economically redeem the injustices of slavery and White supremacy.

Therefore, Black Americans must vociferously demand reparations and seek their payment by all means. Black Americans must not, however, let its self-sustained efforts to achieve maximum economic wealth and power under current or future circumstances be arrested by awaiting the day when reparations will be paid, if ever, no matter how justified their recompense appears to be. The Black American community must maximally invest in itself, in its economic and political expansion and power. For, to the degree to which Black economic and political power expands and increases, to that degree it will be enabled to attain reparations from White America. Moreover, an appropriate, well-developed and efficient Black political and economic establishment would provide the best means by which reparations to the Black community could be absorbed, invested, and distributed. Even if reparations are not forthcoming, the functional existence of a highly efficient Afrikan American/Pan Afrikan political economy could achieve White-Black socioeconomic parity by other means.

Collective Capitalism

Collective capitalism refers to a set of institutional relationships wherein the principle of planned coordination is extended across corporate enterprises, firms, within firms, and to business-government relations. According to Lazonick (1991) "The distinguishing features of collective capitalism are (1) *the organizational integration of a number of distinct firms (i.e., units of financial control) in pursuit of a common investment strategy,* (2) the long-term integration into the enterprise of personnel below the managerial level, and (3) *the cooperation of the state in shaping the social environment to reduce the uncertainty facing private-sector investments*" [Emphasis added]. The enterprise group is a fundamental institution of collective capitalism. In this instance, one or more dominant enterprises or social institutions take the lead as "core" companies in the planned coordination of a group of subcontractors (for the core companies) as a means of creating new businesses, strengthening already existent enterprises, and gaining increased market share or predominance in a certain market. The satellite firms which are in principle independent, tend to view themselves as members of an integrated organizational structure. This permits them to vertically integrate their production and distribution, not only through coordinated planning and activity but to organize cooperative investment strategies across enterprises. Consequently, the shareholding of individual enterprises is distributed across industrial and financial companies. Mature companies and institutions through investing financial and human capital in "satellite" companies and by committing themselves to maintaining long-term exclusive contractual relationships with them, can thus facilitate the protection of home market of these firms and thereby free them to develop and employ their productive resources to the point where they attain competitive advantage in open national and international competition. Hofheinz and Calder provide a cogent example of the operation of such an enterprise group in Japan:

> The industrial groups, led by their main banks and trading companies, pool risk and allocate credit from mature sectors into rapidly growing sectors largely without government intervention. Sometime in the late 1960s, for example, the Mitsui group, after months of behind-the-scenes discussion, proposed at one of its regular Thursday meetings that the company enter the field of aluminum refining. Mitsui Aluminum shares were subscribed to by all the major firms in the group. Mitsui Bank joined the trust bank and the insurance affiliates of the group to supply the financing, and the trading company, Mitsui Bussan, proceeded to buy bauxite and take contracts to sell the product. In this way a multimillion-dollar company was conceived, financed, and launched entirely in-house.[8]

State and institutional systems play a key role in collective capitalism by helping to protect the home market, promoting cooperative research and development among business competitors by helping to create and shape an economic and social environment conducive to economic development; and helping to formulate investment strategies, and building organizational structures to execute them.

Afrikan American Collective Capitalism

Obviously, the collective capitalism which typifies Japanese economic culture and organization cannot be directly applied to the economic circumstances of the Afrikan American community. However, indirect and analogous applications of Japanese-style collective capitalism are possible. For example, the institutional Black church and other large, predominantly Black institutions and organizations — such as colleges and universities, the Urban League, NAACP, National Association of Black Social Workers, along with the many organizations and trade groups we discussed earlier — can function as quasi-governmental, quasi-large business enterprise agencies. These institutions and organizations, much like a federal governmental system, can use their influence to help shape the attitudes, values and behavior of very large segments of the Afrikan American public in ways conducive to attaining its increased and loyal commitment to supporting community economic development. As major purchasers of goods and services they, by contractually committing themselves to the joint procuring of such goods and

---

8. Roy Hofheinz, Jr. & Kent E. Calder, *The Eastasia Edge*, p. 128.

services from Black-owned firms, can encourage the creation or enhance the development of such firms. Moreover, by providing these firms with an assured market they may help to stabilize and protect them until they are able to compete in the general market. For example, if large Black-owned businesses, predominantly Black educational institutions, large Black organizations and Black-owned publishing houses and magazine companies pledged all or a large part of their printing contracts to a Black-owned printing establishment, that firm could then confidently invest in state-of-the-art printing equipment and trained blue- and white-collar personnel, which would permit it to efficiently print high-quality, cost-effective materials and allow it to competitively win government and business contracts in the general market. Such an establishment or set of establishments would not directly create jobs in the community in meeting their own staffing needs only, but indirectly, by farming out to and integrating its productive activities with subcontracting firms and professionals. Black-owned business firms may regionally and nationally organize their purchasing activities in printing and other areas in such ways as to greatly increase demand from already established Black-owned suppliers. Or, Black-owned firms within and across various industries may form an enterprise group and in conjunction with Black-owned financial institutions and Black private investors collaborate in the founding and funding of firms which would supply their needs as well as compete in the general marketplace. Such enterprise groups can help to provide or train expert personnel for these firms in order to fully professionalize them and may, through interlocking boards of directors and interactive CEOs, assume supervisory or executive input over trainees so as to shepherd their efficient growth and development. The group may also use its influence to garner extra business for its newly founded or invested firms. Black-owned enterprise groups may buy cooperatively from pre-existing Black-owned suppliers, or themselves found cooperative production or shared warehouse-wholesale facilities. Revolving credit associations among Black-owned enterprises may be founded to provide financial and investment capital for their members. It is interesting in this context to note that the Congress of National Black Churches (CNCB), an organization consisting of seven historic Black denominations, has proposed to establish a large cooperative publishing company. Furthermore, it has already established a joint insurance company.

In sum, we think that through an adaptationally creative use of the concept of collective capitalism, cooperative economics and the organizational development of enterprise groups, the Black community, its social and economic institutions, can create an economic and social environment conducive to remarkable business enterprise growth, development, and jobs creation. We believe that the Afrikan American community can, as a whole, create economic opportunity and stability for itself by perpetuating the heavy ideological commitment of the institutional Black Church and other influential Black organizations, corporations, business associations and educational institutions, as well as their long-term economic commitment to the purchasing of goods and services from Black-owned firms in conjunction with founding, investing in, and supplying them with highly trained and motivated personnel. It can prepare its business organizations to compete effectively in national and international markets. Small Black-owned businesses by cooperatively buying their sales merchandise and other supplies from wholesalers and manufacturers, by founding cooperative wholesale establishments themselves, could bring costs down and offer their customers prices which would be reasonably competitive with those of alien merchants. The institutional Black Church, Black media and Black educational establishments are crucial to such a process in that their ideological preachments and educational indoctrinal regimes, if effectively appropriate, can motivate the whole of the Afrikan American community, and perhaps other communities, to commit themselves to giving their full, enthusiastic financial support to such collective capitalist or cooperative approaches which we have just described. Furthermore, in light of the fact that Black college enrollment quadrupled to a million between 1965 and 1980, and the experience of Blacks in business over the past three decades, Black entrepreneurs should draw from this sizable talent pool in order to staff and found increasingly competitive and growing business enterprises. Such enterprises need not be set up in Black ghetto communities exclusively, but in all the *downtown* retail and office areas, suburban edge cities and shopping malls of America and the world. The Afrikan-Caribbean, Central and South American, and continental Afrikan nations should be perceived as providing copious entrepreneurial opportunities for venturesome Afrikan American businesspersons and professionals. It must be kept in mind that Afrikan peoples compose one of the largest population and geographical groups in the world. There is no reason why Afrikan peoples cannot and should not found and develop global entrepreneurial establishments to meet their extensive material and social needs. Imagination, vision, creativity and an indomitable will to power is needed to fashion for ourselves a wholesome and secure existence here on earth.

Chapter 20

THE MYTH OF THE MARKET ECONOMY AND BLACK POWER

THE HISTORY OF NATIONS both great and small, whether as imperial powers or colonial fiefdoms, is in great part the history of their economic ideas, organizations and stratagems. This is also true for those nations-within-nations, that is, ethnoculturally distinct peoples who may together with their ethnocultural counterparts, constitute one larger nation. The United States of America is a prime example of a nation of nations. These are customarily referred to as "ethnic groups". However, if examined closely it becomes apparent that the differences in their political and economic achievements and powers reflect differences in economic ideology, organization and strategy. Each ethnic group or nation, in economically and socially interacting with other groups or nations over time, may be said to have a history of economic ideas which have guided their economic behavior and which have led to discernibly different economic — and political — consequences. As this is true of the White Anglo-Saxon Protestant nation, of the Chinese, Japanese, Italian, Korean, Cuban, ... nations, it is also true of the Afrikan American nation.

Afrikan American Economic Ideology — The history of economic ideas and beliefs, organization, stratagems and tactics of the Afrikan American nation has changed over time in response to external changes in the economic history of the larger White American nation in which it is embedded. But they have also changed in response to internal dynamics within the Black American nation itself. Generally, the economic ideology of the Afrikan American community is more implicit than explicit. It is often overlooked that the Civil Rights Movement was and is not only a political movement but also an economic movement, a movement based on an economic set of ideas, stratagems and tactics. This is the case for Black nationalist movements as well. As is readily apparent, both these movements actively advocate radical changes in both the social and economic orders of the White American-dominated United States, along with changes in its power relations. These movements, therefore, have been resisted, and to some degree, accommodated for those very reasons.

While it would be interesting to pursue a history of Black American economic ideology with all of its ramifications, space and time does not allow us the privilege. However, suffice it to say that to a very significant extent the current economic and political situation in which the Afrikan American community finds itself today and will find itself tomorrow is closely correlated with the economic ideology and organization it has manifested in the past, manifests currently, and will manifest in the future.

We argue here that the economic ideology promulgated by the Afrikan American community, or by its most influential leadership establishments, is such that it has inadvertently foredoomed itself to economic penury and political powerlessness as well as economic and political subordination — not only to the much larger and economically better organized White majority but to other minimally organized ethnic minorities as well. We argue that it has been brought to this pass and shall remain there, or continue to decline rapidly, along with other Afrikan peoples and nations because its economic ideology is antiquated, of the 19th century, and based on the myth of the market economy. In good part, its economic vulnerability is directly the result of its naive commitment to *laissez-faire* or free market economics in the absence of such orientations and commitments (despite their vociferous lip-service) on the part of any of the other ethnocultural groups in America. The belief in the myth of the market economy and practice of the concept of free markets by the Afrikan American community along with its concomitant belief in and practice of the myth of individualism, have laid it open to economic penetration and domination by White and non-White communities. The subsequent exploitation of the Black community by non-Black commercial interests has left it economically and politically prostrate.

In the present context, *laissez-faire* economics involves the belief that there should be no legislated or cultural or ethnic barriers to the movement of capital, capital investment and business activities in those areas which their owners, regardless of race, color, creed or nationality, deem it most profitable to employ them. It is the belief that all barriers to entry into productive, profit-making activities and product markets should be without restriction and when this occurs the self-interested pursuit of these activities and markets will produce the broadest possible mutual benefits for all concerned. Related to the concept of *laissez-faire* economics is that of the market economy or the free market. William Lazonick's intriguing book very much shapes the discussion which follows. He distinguishes a market from an organization in this way:

> What is it that distinguishes a market from an organization? The defining social characteristic of a market is the impersonal relation between buyer and seller. Both sides pursue their self-interests independently of one another, both in specifying their goals and in engaging in activities to achieve those goals. The impersonality of the market is manifested by the willingness of sellers of goods and services to enter into exchange with the highest bidders. As long as a buyer has the purchasing power to pay the highest price, his or her identity is of no concern to the seller.[1]

Lazonick goes on to state that in the absence of impersonal exchange, "*Market exchange* does not exist, that is, if particular buyers have *privileged access* to the goods and services of particular sellers, or vice versa. By definition, the existence of market exchange requires that buyers have *equal access* to the resources of sellers." Lazonick proceeds to define the concept of the perfectly competitive market (a market from which Blacks have been and are excluded, even in its imperfect form):

> In a *perfectly competitive* market, as idealized by neoclassical economists there is no organization among or between buyers and sellers. In the pursuit of their own self-interests, buyers compete among themselves for access to marketed goods and services, while sellers compete among themselves for access to the currency of buyers. But whether markets are characterized by perfect competition or bilateral monopoly, the necessary and sufficient condition for the existence of a market is the impersonal relation between buyer and seller.[2]

---

[1] W. Lazonick, *Business Organization and the Myth of the Market Economy*, p. 59.
[2] Ibid., p. 60.

Finally Lazonick concludes, based on the concept of the market economy, that:

> The political message is that the exercise of social power plays no role in the operation of the capitalist economy because control over the allocation of resources is so widely dispersed among households. In a market economy, individuals are free from inherent personal commitment and dependence on the will of others. They are, as Milton and Rose Friedman have put it, "free to choose."
>
> The economic message is that the invisible hand of the market will ensure that resources are allocated to their most productive uses, with the net satisfaction, or utility, *that individuals derive from producing and consuming marketable commodities serving as the ultimate measure of productivity. If we let impersonal market forces direct the allocation of resources and the distribution of income, so the story goes, individual freedom and economic well-being will go hand in hand.*[3]

The Anglo-American Economic Worldview — The economic ideology and strategy of a trade community or nation are related to its worldview. According to James Fallows, Washington editor of *The Atlantic Monthly*, the Anglo-American countries of Britain and the U.S. project a worldview that is market oriented (*The Atlantic Monthly* – 11/93, 12/93 & 1/94). This worldview is crucially different from that of some other countries, particularly Japan's. The Anglo-American worldview, first practiced by Great Britain and later by the U.S., emphasizes: (1) the unpredictability and unplannability of economics; (2) assumes that the ultimate measure of a society is its level of consumption; (3) emphasizes how the game is played, not who wins or loses; (4) focuses on how individuals fare as consumers and how the whole world fares as a trading system; (5) emphasizes the idea that everyone can prosper at once; and (6) that if a country disagrees with Anglo-American economic axioms, it doesn't just disagree, it is a "cheater". Fallows demonstrates how these views contrast with those of Germany and Japan. He contends that:

> In the German view, economics is not a matter of right or wrong, or cheating or playing fair. It is merely a matter of strong or weak. *The gods of trade will help those who help themselves. No code of honor will defend the weak,* as today's Latin Americans and Afrikans can attest. *If a nation decides to help itself — by protecting its own industries, by discriminating against products — then that is a decision, not a sin.*[4] [Emphasis added]

---

3. Ibid., p. 63.

4. Fallows in *The Atlantic Monthly*, p. 73.

Fallows, citing Lazonick and others, goes on to demonstrate that both England and the U.S. violated their worldviews and ideological preachments during long, crucial periods in their historical struggles to achieve international economic supremacy and hegemonic power.[5]

> When England was building its technological lead over the rest of the World, Lazonick said, its leaders did not care just about the process of competition. They were determined to control the result, so that they would have the strongest manufacturers on earth.
>
> British economists began talking about getting prices right only after they succeeded in promoting their own industries by getting prices wrong. Prices were wrong in that cheap competition from the colonies was forbidden. They were wrong in that the Crown subsidized and encouraged investment in factories and a fleet. They were right in that they made British industry strong.
>
> By the time Adam Smith came on the scene, Lazonick said, the British could start lecturing other countries about the folly of tariffs and protection. Why should France (America, Prussia, China...) punish its consumers by denying them access to cheap, well-made English cloth? Yet the British theorists did not ask themselves why their products were so advanced, why "the world market...in the late eighteenth century was so *uniquely under British control.*" The answer would involve nothing like *laissez-faire.*
>
> The full answer would instead include the might of the British navy, which by driving out the French and Spanish had made it easier for British ships to dominate trade routes. It would involve political measures that prevented the Portuguese and Irish from developing textile industries that could compete with England's. It would include the Navigation Acts, which ensured a British monopoly in a number of the industries the country wanted most to develop. The answer involved land enclosure and a host of other measures that allowed British manufacturers to concentrate more capital than they could otherwise have obtained.
>
> Lazonick summed up this process in a passage that exactly describes the predicament of the United States at the end of the Twentieth century. The nineteenth-century British advocated laissez-faire because, given the advanced economic development that their industries had already achieved, they thought that their firms could withstand open competition from foreigners. [They wanted] to convince other nations that they would be better off if they opened up their markets to British goods....[They] *accepted as a natural fact of life* Britain's dominant position as the "workshop of the world" [emphasis added]. They did not bother to ask how Britain had attained that position....

---

5. Ibid., p. 76.

But the ultimate critique of nineteenth-century laissez-faire ideology is *not* that it ignored the role of national power in Britain's past and present. Rather, the ultimate critique is that *laissez-faire* failed to comprehend Britain's economic future — a future in which, confronted by far more powerful systems of national capitalism, the British economy would enter into a long-run relative decline from which it has yet to recover.

America's economic history follows the same pattern. While American industry was developing, the country had no time for laissez-faire. After it had grown strong, the United States began preaching laissez-faire to the rest of the world — and began to kid itself about its own history, believing its slogans about laissez-faire as the secret of its success.

The "traditional" American support for worldwide free trade is quite a recent phenomenon. It started only at the end of the Second World War. This period dominates the memory of most Americans now alive but does not cover the years of America's most rapid industrial expansion.

Citing economic historians Thomas McCraw[6] and Alice Amsden,[7] Fallows concludes that the opportunistic American pattern of providing "the greatest possible protection for its own industries" and markets while hitching a "free ride" by getting the greatest possible access to the markets of Great Britain and other nations which remained committed to free trade and liberal trade strategies, is not the exception to, but is, the rule. As Fallows asserts, "the great industrial successes of the past two centuries — America after its Revolution, Germany under Bismarck, Japan after the Second World War — all violated the rules of laissez-faire. Despite the obvious differences among these countries, "the underlying economic strategy was very much the same." He further notes that "Every country that has caught up with others has had to do so by rigging its rules: extracting extra money from its people and steering the money into industrialists' hands."

Self-Defeating Economic Ideology and Trade Strategy of the Afrikan American Community

We have cited the example of Anglo-American economic worldview because it is similar in many important respects to that of the current Afrikan American community. However, the actual economic or trade strategies utilized by England, U.S., and by other nations

---

6. Editor of *America Versus Japan* (Boston: Harvard Business School Press, 1986).

7. *Asia's Next Giant*

during their economic ascendance and political empowerment, strategies which violated their worldview, have not been practiced to any marked extent by the Afrikan American community relative to other ethnic American communities. Yet, these other communities — Whites, Koreans, Cubans, etc. — have historically practiced and continue to practice such strategies relative to the Afrikan American community. They have gained economic and social ascendance at the expense of Afrikan American economic stagnation and social decline. As with the U.S., England, and Japan, ascending nations and communities take advantage of the "free trade" open-market orientation of other nations and communities, while protecting their own markets, to gain a "free ride" to economic prosperity. Paradoxically, slow growing or economically stagnant nations and communities often, because of their ideological *laissez-faire* economic and free trade orientations, finance their competitor's economic ascendance and their own economic decline.

Along with the deliberate repression of its economic development by the White American nation, in its economic openness to other non-Black communities the Afrikan American community has permitted these communities to, while protecting their own internal markets, economically monopolize the Afrikan American markets with little or no direct cost to themselves and with little or no real or significant benefit to the Afrikan American community itself. The "free market" attitude of the Afrikan American community enables these communities to build social and economic walls around their domestic markets, to protect and retain the income gained from their business earnings received from the Black community without fear of Afrikan American economic retaliation. Consequently, immigrant communities which have integrated with the Black community only to the degree to which they can economically exploit it, are in the position of gaining unprecedented opportunities to capitalize on the internal markets of community and its consumers without having to pay their share of the cost for resolving its socioeconomic troubles and advancing its social and political interests.

Lessons of History

According to Lazonick and other economic historians, the gaining of competitive economic advantages of some nations over others and the gaining of wealth by one nation at the expense of another in the twentieth-century, has become increasingly dependent not on the vagaries of the "free market" or "free trade" alone, but on the planned coordination that takes place within and between business organizations, their privileged access to finance, labor and technology, as well as the social organization of the society or nation in which they are embedded. The historical evolution and exercise of national power which allowed newcomer nations (as once was the U.S. and as are currently the collective capitalist nations of Asia) to achieve economic ascendance, depended on the strategic organization and development of their national political economies and ability impetus to provide critical protection of and support for their fledgling industries and businesses. This permitted them to block outsiders from wholesale entry into and exploitation of their internal markets and resources. These ascendant nations adopted strategies which depended on organizational coordination supported by educational institutions, communications networks, financial systems, research and development organizations which generate productive human and material resources. By making the bulk of their resources exclusively available to their enterprises, they enabled them to challenge or overcome their competitors. These nations at some critical point in their evolutionary history sought to protect and preserve their home markets for their own firms and protect them during their early developmental stages from more mature foreign competition. They sought to provide them with an appropriately trained and motivated managerial and labor force as well as privileged, if not exclusive, access to productive human and financial resources. Privileged access to productive human resources refers to the situation where well-trained, experienced, skilled and/or highly educated workers "commit their goods and services to the use of particular business organizations irrespective of currently available market opportunities to reap returns," with the hope of reaping even larger returns in the future for having so committed themselves (Lazonick, 1991). An appropriately motivated managerial and labor force includes one in which members interact in accord with collectively specified national goals and activities, in contrast to one where each individual pursues his or her own self-serving goals and activities with little regard for collective interests or good. A sense of national, cultural or ethnic pride, identity and consciousness together provides the basis for collectivizing the interests and activities of key institutions, organizations, groups and individuals, i.e., for making their interests and activities compatible with the achievement of national wealth, power, and self-determination. Privileged access to financial resources involves motivating the members of a nation or community to save and enhance their monetary and financial resources in an organized and coordinated manner that they will be made available for the exclusive use of national or community enterprises and to fund or finance national or community economic development to the relative exclusion of other nations or communities. One way of enhancing national or communal savings and investments may be the reduced consumption of and refusal to purchase the goods and services provided by outside nations and communities, subsequently investing and utilizing the savings accumulated in the development of one's own national or communal enterprises and to buy from them their increasing output of goods and services. Lazonick illustrates the process thusly:

> Individuals grant an enterprise privileged access to their resources when they expect that their personal goals will be better attained by long-term attachment to the particular enterprise rather than by reallocating their resources from one business to another via the market. For example, an individual might give privileged access to his or her resources to an enterprise in which he or she can exercise some control over work conditions and can interact with people with whom he or she has a common philosophical outlook, familial ties, or other personal bonds....
>
> As the creators of capitalist enterprises, entrepreneurs give their firms privileged access to their human and financial resources. They expect that over the long run the way in which the firm develops and utilizes its productive capabilities will make them better off than if these resources had been supplied to the highest bidder on the market. Ownership and control of their enterprises assure entrepreneurs that they will be able to appropriate returns if and when the firm achieves the necessary extent of the market to generate profits.
>
> At the initial stages of an enterprise, an entrepreneur may also secure privileged access to financial resources from relatives, friends, and associates who expect that the business vision, managerial capability, and personal commitment of the entrepreneur will result in the generation of internal economies that will eventually yield returns to their financial stake that more than offset foregone market returns. Even some career-oriented individuals who do not hold shares in the enterprise might be willing to give the entrepreneur privileged access to their human resources because they expect that over the long run their personal goals will be better served by the growth of the particular entrepreneurial organization than by other employment opportunities currently available on the market.

* * * *

To attain and sustain competitive advantage, however, the enterprise must not only develop and utilize productive resources, but also *appropriate* a share of the value gains. The business organization can then use its share of the value gains to give itself privileged access to financial resources that can be reinvested in the further development of the productive capabilities at its disposal. Alternatively, the organization can pass on the value gains to consumers in order to increase market share, which in turn increases the utilization of existing productive capabilities, thereby increasing the internal economies of scale.[8]

A review of alien or immigrant entrepreneurs indicates that economic mechanisms such as we have just described were utilized effectively to gain and sustain their economic monopoly of Afrikan American community markets. Hence, in its efforts to gain control over its own internal markets and to compete successfully in larger national and international markets, the Afrikan American community must utilize similar mechanisms on its own behalf. It must therefore:

1. Perceive itself as a nation among nations in America and organize itself and act according to its own national plans.

2. Develop its human resources appropriate to its achieving national goals and to their broadest and most superior extent. It must commit as much as practically possible those resources to the exclusive and creative use of its developing enterprises and collective economy.

3. Reduce its consumption as much as practically possible of the goods and services produced and sold by other communities while increasing its consumption of those goods and services produced by its own members and organizations.

4. Increase its savings by reducing consumption of extra-communal goods and services and by engaging in prudent, productive, investment strategies; depositing and investing monies in community-owned financial institutions by utilizing traditional modes of savings and investment such as "susu" and cooperative savings arrangements. It must in turn use those savings to invest in and finance its economic growth and development and to increase its individual and communal wealth.

5. Protect its fledgling economy and enterprises from alien competition though not in ways which reinforce economic inefficiency in its own businesses and service institutions but in ways which allow them to accumulate the necessary resources and highly efficient organization to compete in the open market. The community should note as does Lake (ibid) "that protection is not necessarily a sign of

---

8. Lazonick, pp. 76–77 and p. 82.

domestic political failure....Both protection and free trade are legitimate and effective instruments to be used in national advantage. We should not allow an economic ideology...to blind us to this historical and deeply political reality."

6. Pursue protection and export expansion. The community and its relevant institutions must discover and develop routinized ways of exporting and importing goods and services throughout the Afrikan Diaspora, Latin America, Asia, and North Afrika. "Local export" in the U.S. involves manufacturing, wholesaling, distributing, and retailing in the general American market; selling professional services and job skills in the general market and returning the income gained from these "outside" activities to the community to be saved and expended there with community-owned enterprises and institutions.

7. Found international corporations which include Afrikans from various countries and which operate in two or more Afrikan diaspora nations. Investments in these nations should be rapidly increased along with the establishing of numerous enterprises therein. Portfolio investment, i.e., the purchasing of shares in Afrikan corporations and other enterprises, should become a well-known, well-practiced tradition. Enhance institutional investments in important non-Afrikan multinational corporations, in start-up and growing corporations likely to have important impact on Afrikan lives and nations. These investments should be significantly large enough to influence their trade and economic policies in favorable ways.

8. Continue to found small, well-niched companies. For these companies are the engines of economic growth and employment in America. Continue to apply strong political and consumer pressure to gain set-asides and other preferences for Black-owned enterprises. Have no fear of demanding such preferences as forms of reparations for Afrikan peoples who endured the concentration camps of America.

9. Become the most educated and best-trained group in America and the world. Demand equal and preferential employment at all levels of American industry — in the name of *Afrikan* ancestry, not as a "person of color" or as a "minority." Be self-centered. As the development and utilization of *human* resources are the sources of the value of all other resources, are the foundational sources of all other human powers, heavy investments in the productive capabilities of its members are of the utmost importance to the Afrikan community.

10. Become actively aware of the fact that competitive advantage and economic growth and expansion are now being driven by the

planned coordination of individuals and groups or teams who participate in divisions of labor *within* business organizations and charted coordination of economic activities *across* business organizations. While Afrikan-owned firms may compete against each other, they must not let such competition constrain cooperation among themselves for developing their national industries, gaining competitive advantages as industries, and achieving the common interests of the community.

11. Develop and practice cooperative economics wherever and whenever appropriate. Afrikan entrepreneurs must become keen students and practitioners of corporate organizations and economies. They must master the art of forming "virtual corporations", i.e., developing operationally efficient joint ventures and strategic alliances; temporary networks of companies which rapidly organize among themselves to take advantage of fast-changing opportunities; form communicational and informational networks which facilitate their working together to begin and finish a mutually beneficial project, each contributing company bringing its "core competence" to their joint efforts; build in mutual interdependence, trust, and a sense of "co-destiny" in their relations; and demonstrate a willingness to cross the traditional boundaries and borders of legally distinct but interrelated companies.

12. Be willing to challenge convention and tradition, assume risks, and reconstruct, reconceptualize customary and accepted rules or routines. Develop "horizontal corporations" if they lead to the generation of productive internal and external economies. That is, reduce hierarchical structures by utilizing coordinated teams of equal status organized around processes for achieving specifiable and specific performance and product goals.

13. Invest heavily in the development of the community's productive capabilities, individual and organizational members, as prerequisites to stable and remunerative employment.

14. Community members must thoroughly prepare themselves to work for and succeed in both for-profit and non-profit organizations, in powerfully entrenched governmental and private agencies in the nation and world. They must also invest in their own enterprises and financial institutions as well as those of others as a way of best positioning themselves to gather intelligence, earn a high standard living, and maximally exercising power in the interest of the community.

Chapter 21

NATION-WITHIN-A-NATION

...the dark ghetto's invisible walls have been erected by the white society, by those who have power, both to confine those who have *no* power and to perpetuate their powerlessness. The dark ghettos are social, political, educational and above all — economic colonies. Their inhabitants are subject peoples, victims of the greed, cruelty, insensitivity, guilt and fear of their masters.

— KENNETH B. CLARK

But black segregation is not comparable to the limited and transient segregation experienced by other racial and ethnic groups, now or in the past. No group, in the history of the United States has ever sustained the high level of residential segregation that has been imposed on blacks in large American cities for the past fifty years. *This extreme racial isolation did not just happen; it was manufactured by whites through a series of self-conscious actions and purposeful institutional arrangements that continue today.* Not only is the depth of black segregation unprecedented and utterly unique compared with any other groups, but it shows little sign of change with the passage of time or improvements in socioeconomic status [Emphasis added].

— DOUGLASS MASSEY & NANCY DENTON

[The United States is] moving toward two societies, one black, one white — separate and equal. ...[To continue present policies is] to make permanent the division of our country into two societies; one, largely Negro and poor, located in the central cities; the other, predominantly white and affluent, located in the suburbs.

— THE KERNER REPORT

The Afrikan American Community: Separate and Unequal

The Afrikan American community is a *de facto* nation-within-a-nation. Except for its mainly second-tier alien employment status, its cultural entertainment contributions to the American market economy, its role as a mass consumer market for White American-manufactured products and services, its full-spectrum participation in and integration into American society is negligible. The hypersegregation of Afrikan Americans in the urban centers as well as the Black suburbs of the United States after over 200 years of its official existence, glaringly bears witness to White America's inability and lack of desire to assimilate the Afrikan American community into American society. We have already provided a rationale as to why the Afrikan American community can reasonably be described as an internal American colony. Its national colonial status has been attested to by a long list of social scientists and observers such as De Tocqueville, Gunnar Myrdal, W.E.B. DuBois, Kenneth Clark, Harold Cruse, The Kerner Commission, Andrew Hacker, Studs Terkel, among others.

The failure of the Afrikan American community along with its cadre of activists, leadership establishment and intelligentsia to recognize the community as constituting a nation-within-a-nation and to operate as such, is the primary, overarching reason for the relative powerlessness of Afrikans in America and Afrikans in the world. An agglomeration of individuals and small, unstable groups can never wield the power of an organized, cooperative, coordinated, consciously and subconsciously self-identified people. The relative powerlessness of the Afrikan American community is not primarily due to an absence or paucity of human resources, or even monetary and other material resources. It is due rather to its lack of efficient organization, coordinated development and application under the influence and guidance of a deep and abiding sense of peoplehood and nationhood, of national purpose and destiny. As an aggregation of individuals who can only momentarily act as a people in reaction to their common victimization, the Afrikan American community is "a house divided against itself." As such it cannot withstand even relatively weakly organized economic, social and political assaults by other non-white ethnic groups who easily overrun its territories and domains, let alone the far more powerfully organized and coordinated assaults of its arch enemy, the White American nation.

The Afrikan American community's nakedness before its enemies is due to its failure of vision and will to clothe itself and shield its loins with the armor of nationhood; its failure to protect its fleshy parts with the sword and shield of hard-cast Afrikan-centered consciousness and racial solidarity. It has for too long dangerously denied the reality of its exclusion from full participation in the predominant White American nation-within-a-nation as well as the nation as a whole. The Afrikan American community along with other non-White ethnic tribes and clans helps to constitute an ever-more multicultural, racially diverse United States — a society whose states are united but whose peoples are not.

But being largely excluded from full participation in American society is not the primary source of the relative weakness and vulnerability of the Afrikan American community. Its principal source of powerlessness is its obtuse refusal to conceptually and socially utilize the perception of itself as a nation-within-a-nation, and thus utilize its ostracism to its advantage, as its major instrument of power.

The failure to view the Afrikan American community as a nation-within-a-nation or in short, as a nation, by Afrikan American scholars, thinkers, social analysts, intellectuals (i.e., opinion shapers such as newspapers columnists, print and electronic media establishments and personalities, community activists and institutional leaders) and social commentators means that many of the problems which confront the community have not been appropriately and usefully analyzed or resolved. This means that a number of useful and powerful approaches to resolving those problems have been ignored or overlooked. The principal conceptual instruments that Afrikan American thinkers and problem-solvers utilize in dealing with the problems confronting the Afrikan American community have been those handed down to them by the liberal intellectual establishment which represents the interest of the White American nation. These instruments primarily include individualistic and familial analyses, and secondarily, institutional, communal and (sub)cultural analyses. Consequently, the use of these instruments and their analytical outcomes almost invariably leads to the victim-blaming conclusions; that the sources of all social problems in the Afrikan American community are either due to an aggregation of individual inabilities, capabilities, lacks, impairments, deficiencies, errant motives and drives; family weaknesses, values, pathologies, disruptions; institutional insufficiencies and dysfunctions; or to aberrant communal and subcultural mores, folkways and worldviews.

While other analysts may with sound reasons point the finger of blame at the racist, structural dynamics and hegemony of the White American nation, they all but ignore the structural dynamics of the

Afrikan American community and its organizational vulnerability to racism. This is principally the result of their stimulus-bound and reactionary belief that the Afrikan American community is hopelessly dependent on the White American community, is incapable of self-determination and therefore must await the favorable transformation of White racist attitudes, behaviors, and social structural dynamics before it can be rescued from its problems. Therefore, an inordinate amount of individual time and energy as well as organizational skill is utilized by this group of thinkers and activists not to productively, socially, economically, and politically transform the Afrikan American community, but to vainly importune, cajole or pressure the White community to change its ways. Meanwhile, the Black community is left to fester and decay, its potential to build a nation wasting away.

Individualistic, familial, institutional, and subcultural approaches to White racism in America and social problems in the Black community, can only yield problem-solving outcomes commensurate with their narrow analytical ranges. While social structural approaches to these issues are much broader in their analytical range, their analyses of the overall national dynamics which interact to the detriment of the Afrikan American community instructive, their relative lack of concern with changing the structural nature of the community leads to additional problems while not solving the original ones. Massey and Denton are certainly correct when they contend:

> The effect of segregation on black well-being is structural, not individual. *Residential segregation lies beyond the ability of any individual to change; it constrains black life chances irrespective of personal traits, individual motivations, or private achievements.* For the past twenty years this fundamental fact has been swept under the rug by policymakers, scholars, and theorists of the urban underclass. Segregation is the missing link in prior attempts to understand the plight of the urban poor.[1][Emphasis added]

It is pertinent to note that over 11 million Afrikan Americans live in areas that are more than 75 percent Black. In other words, between 35.5 percent and 45 percent of Blacks live in such areas.

While the ability of the White community to *dis*organize and constrain the lifestyles of the Afrikan American community lies beyond the ability of any individual, family, individual community, institution, or subculture to change them, they do not lie beyond the ability of the Afrikan American community as a nation, a nation joined in a worldwide alliance of Afrikan nations, to change. It is this

---
1. D. Massey & N. Denton, *American Apartheid,* pp.2–3.

fundamental fact that has been swept under the rug by policymakers, scholars, and theorists. The concept of nation is the missing link in prior attempts to understand the plight of the Afrikan American community as a whole, not just its urban poor.

The Afrikan American Community as a de facto Third World Nation

The destinies of individuals, families, subgroups and subcultures in the Afrikan American community are not only constrained by the structural characteristics of the White American-dominated society but are also more immediately constrained by their own self-determinable structural characteristics. That is to say, even as a subordinate community, the Afrikan American community has several degrees of freedom at its disposal within which it could transform its socioeconomic structure and thereby markedly increase the economic and social well-being of its constituents as well as increase its socioeconomic power as a whole. However, such benefits can only occur through the formulation and enactment of nationwide, nationally administered and coordinated initiatives. Furthermore, such initiatives can only be realized by an Afrikan American community whose individual constituents self-consciously perceive themselves as members of an Afrikan nation in America, and who behave in accord with that perception.

The power of the concept of nation as an analytical instrument used to arrive at a practical understanding of problems faced by the Afrikan American community, can be demonstrated by applying it in the analysis of a broad range of social problems. For example, the basic cause of institutional under-performance and/or dysfunctionality [e.g., inadequate educational, recreational, social(ization) institutions]; lack of employment opportunities; family instability and disruption; inadequate housing; antisocial, criminal behavior; individual distress and dysfunctionality; can, in significant part, be traced back to the general state of the Afrikan American community considered as a nation. For this litany of problems which afflicts the national Black community may in large measure be said to reflect the disorganization of the Black American economy. More specifically, if the Afrikan American community were perceived as a nation it would become immediately apparent that its fundamental problem, like many other Afrikan nations which present similar problems, is its national debt. Like other Afrikan nations, it suffers a net outflow of monetary and human resources; it is unable to retain for any reasonable length of time, hard currency reserves within its borders;

its economic infrastructure is dominated by alien business establishments which siphon its wealth; it is by far, more indebted to outside communities than to its own internal establishments and as a result, suffers a chronic liquidity crisis. It suffers from infrastructural problems (poor highways, streets, industrial facilities, housing, police protection, etc.) which hamper its economic growth potential and attractiveness to investors. It suffers an overwhelming trade deficit with other communities, meaning it buys far more from other communities than it sells to those communities, that it retains for itself far less of what it earns from other communities than what other communities earn from it and retain for themselves.

Any cursory review of economic history reveals that nations which suffer the problems we have just listed, i.e., whose flow of monetary and human resources is grossly imbalanced, ultimately suffer social and economic dysfunctionality and disorganization as a result thereof, breakdowns in social civility, law and order, increases in criminality, family disruptions, drug addiction, disease and death, and a host of other politicoeconomic sociopsychological problems. Moreover, these nations are likely to be exploited, if not colonized, by stronger nations.

Simply stated, many of the problems exhibited by the Afrikan American community reflect more its inadequate economic organization and management as a "nation," than its outright poverty or impoverishment of human resources, than its accumulation of alleged individual or familial deficits and deficiencies. Just as the White American nation has to realize that its national debt, national deficit and trade imbalances relative to such nations as Japan threaten its power and viability as a nation, threaten the economic well-being and lowers the standards of living of its citizens, generate social/political conflicts between its multicultural/multiracial groups, the Afrikan American nation must recognize that its debts, deficits and imbalances threaten its continuing viability nationally, and the viability of Afrikan nations internationally. Just as the White American nation is now engaged in a major review and revision of its foreign and domestic policies, its trade relations and industrial policies as a means of maintaining and enhancing its power vis-à-vis other nations in the world community, the Black American "nation" also must review and revise its domestic and foreign trade and industrial policies in order to maintain and enhance its power, influence, and quality of life vis-à-vis other national and international ethnocultural groups in both the national and world communities.

Similar to the relationship between the White American nation and Japan, whereas the U.S. permits Japanese businesses to enter and operate in its relatively "open market" but U.S. business access to the Japanese market economy is relatively restricted or frustrated by Japanese political-cultural barriers, the Afrikan American economic market is completely accessible, i.e., "open" and "free" to all other ethnic groups, while Afrikan American businesses are frozen out not only of the markets of these groups but are frozen out of its own ethnic markets by other groups thus creating the crippling trade deficits or imbalances from which the community suffers. Moreover, the establishment of alien businesses in the Afrikan American community has led to relatively little employment of Afrikan Americans in those establishments. Alien businesspersons along with their families do not reside in the Afrikan American community from which their derive their income. Massive sums of money are therefore "repatriated," i.e., taken out of the Black community daily without circulating within the community once before flowing out to economically benefit other communities. Also, since alien business persons and their families have not assimilated into the Afrikan American community, they make little monetary or cultural/social contribution to the development, functioning, and maintenance of its vital social institutions including its cultural, economic, educational, recreational, family, health care and other institutions.

The lack of an appropriate domestic and foreign policy means that the Black nation has no efficient social or economic instrument by which it can enforce economic parity and equilibrium between itself and its "trading partners." It is instrumentally unable to retain badly needed currency and credits within its own domain and thereby provide for the economic and social welfare of its constituents. The economic parity and currency retention goals of the Afrikan community cannot be achieved in isolation by its individual or subgroup constituents. Similarly, parity between Japan and the United States cannot be achieved by the self-interested activities of isolated individual persons, corporations and social groups, but only through strategic planning and tactics by national bodies and their representatives.

The Advantages of an Afrikan American Nation

The advantages the Afrikan American community may gain by perceiving itself and acting as a nation are many. They include the following:

- The creation and continuity of an Afrikan-centered and socioeconomically unified community.

- The development of a nationally unified and well-coordinated, Afrikan American-controlled market, economic and financial infrastructure.
- The increased employment of Afrikan Americans within the community; increased business ownership both within and outside of the community; the use of Afrikan American business and consumer clout to increase employment and business opportunities in both the larger national and international markets.
- The ability of the Afrikan American community to speak with one voice to other communities and nations.
- The political empowerment of the community resulting from its economic empowerment and the use of its increased power to influence U.S. foreign and economic policy in favor of the economic and technological development of the Afrikan nations around the world.
- The enabling of the Afrikan American community to expand its domestic markets and open them to trade with Afrikan nations; and to use its political clout to open the larger U.S. markets to the importation and sales of Afrikan-manufactured goods and other goods and services within the country.
- The enabling of the Afrikan American community to enter into trade relations with Afrikan and other nations; to market its products and services abroad and most importantly, to lead in the development of a global Pan–Afrikan economic system to rival those of Europeans, Asians, Hispanics and others.
- The enhancement of the ability of the Pan–Afrikan world to defend its economic and political interests and to protect its population from the military depredations of other nations.
- The enhancement of national and international Afrikan self-esteem and self-respect and the marked reduction of antisocial behavior, criminality and other social and physical problems in Afrikan communities both at home and abroad.
- The development of financial and social institutions which enhance the overall viability of the Afrikan worldwide community.

Economic Proposal to the Afrikan American Community

The reader who is familiar with the history of Afrikan American economic theory will easily recognize that the ideas presented above are but extensions and elaborations of Black nationalist economic ideology and the economic ideologies of such thinkers like Booker T. Washington and the Tuskegee school, Marcus Garvey and the Pan–Afrikanist movement, the Honorable Elijah Muhammad and the

Nation of Islam, and the historian Chancellor Williams. Some may not so easily recognize that they also follow the economic thought of W.E.B DuBois. In his book *Dusk of Dawn: An Essay Toward An Autobiography of a Race Concept*, particularly in Chapter 7 titled *The Colored World Within*, DuBois speaks about the development of an Afrikan American economic system directly. He begins the chapter thus:

> Not only do white men but also colored men forget the facts of the Negro's double environment. The Negro American has for his environment not only the white surrounding world, but also, and touching him usually much more nearly and compellingly, is the environment furnished by his own colored group. There are exceptions, of course, but this is the rule.[2]

DuBois accepted the reality of the exclusion of Blacks from what we would now refer to as "the American Mainstream." He acknowledged that "In the first place we have already got a partially segregated Negro economy in the United States. There can be no question about this." After further acknowledging "that the inner economy of the Negro serves but a small proportion of his total needs," he asserts *"...but it is growing and expanding in various ways; and what I propose is to so plan and guide it as to take advantage of certain obvious facts"* [Emphasis added]. Anticipating our own emphasis on the correlation between economic and political power, DuBois went on to express the following contention:

> It is of course impossible that a segregated economy for Negroes in the United States should be complete. It is quite possible that it could never cover more than a smaller part of the economic activities of Negroes. Nevertheless, *it is also possible that this smaller part could be so important and wield so much power that its influence upon the total economy of Negroes and the total industrial organization of the United States would be decisive for the great ends toward which the Negro moves.*[3] [Emphasis added]

In an extremely prescient statement, DuBois establishes the economic problematics which confront the Afrikan American community (and the Pan–Afrikan community) today.

> the American economic class structure — that system of domination of industry and the state through income and monopoly — is breaking

---

2. W.E.B. DuBois, *Dusk of Dawn: An Essay Toward An Autobiography of a Race Concept*, p. 173.

3. Ibid., p. 198.

down; not simply in America but in the world. We have reached the end of an economic era, which seemed but a few years ago omnipotent and eternal. We have lived to see the collapse of capitalism.... In Europe and in the United States as well as in Russia the whole organization and direction of industry is changing. We are not called upon to be dogmatic as to just what the end of this change will be and what form the new organization will take. What we are sure of is the present fundamental change.

There faces the American Negro therefore an intricate and subtle problem of combining into one object two difficult sets of facts: *his present racial segregation which despite anything he can do will persist for many decades; and his attempt by carefully planned and intelligent action to fit himself into the new economic organization which the world faces.*[4] [Emphasis added]

Thus DuBois, recognizing that the racial segregation of Afrikan Americans would persist, logically proposed that we "proceed to use it as a method of progress... [That] instead of letting this segregation remain largely a matter of chance and unplanned development, and allowing its objects and results to rest in the hands of the white majority or in the accidents of the situation, it would make segregation a matter of careful thought and intelligent planning on the part of Negroes."

Recognizing in the late 1930s and the early 1940s that, as in the 1980s and 1990s, "most of the well-to-do with fair education do not realize the imminence of profound economic change in the modern world...," rejecting communist dogma and dealing with the "difficulties and pitfalls" of Black redemption through membership in labor unions and the labor movement as well as arguing against the idea that Blacks should simply "join themselves to capital and become capitalists..." as ways of dissolving the color line, DuBois set forth an alternative proposal

...that is a racial attempt to use the power of the Negro as a consumer not only for his economic uplift but in addition to that, for his economic education. What I propose is that into the interstices of this collapse of the industrial machine, the Negro shall search intelligently and carefully and farsightedly plan for his entrance into the new economic world, not as a continuing slave but as an intelligent free man with power in his hands.

I see this chance for planning in the role which the Negro plays as a consumer. In the future reorganization of industry the consumer as against the producer is going to become the key man. Industry is

---

4. Ibid., pp. 198–99.

going to be guided according to his wants and needs and not exclusively with regard to the profit of the producers and transporters. Now as a consumer the Negro approaches economic equality much more nearly than he ever has as producer. Organizing then and conserving and using intelligently the power which twelve million people have through what they buy, it is possible for the American Negro to help in the rebuilding of the economic state.

The American Negro must remember that he is primarily a consumer; that as he becomes a producer, it must be at the demand and under the control of organized consumers and according to their wants;...Today we work for others at wages pressed down to the limit of subsistence. Tomorrow we may work for ourselves, exchanging services, producing an increasing proportion of the goods which we consume and being rewarded by a living wage and by work under civilized conditions. This will call for self-control.

...To a degree, but not completely, this is a program of segregation. ...We are now segregated largely without reason. Let us put reason and power beneath this segregation.[5] [Emphasis added]

Thus, as we may infer from the foregoing proposal, DuBois clearly perceived that the capture and control of its internal markets in conjunction with utilizing its potential as a major consumer group in its own interest, could enable the Afrikan American community to wield considerable power and influence in the United States. We shall return to DuBois' emphasis on the enormous potential power represented by Afrikan American consumerism, shortly.

We believe that our proposals for Afrikan American economic development are a bit more comprehensive than those of DuBois in that we not only propose that the Afrikan American community gain control of its internal markets but combine this control with the judicious use of its consumer power to markedly influence the American government and society. We further propose that these powerful instruments be used as means by which the Afrikan American community can deeply penetrate the larger White American economic market. Thus the community by using the wealth, know-how, expertise, leverage developed by its ownership of its communal resources and the leverage represented by its consumer dollars, could massively invest in and by this means, come to own very significant portions or segments of the overall American economy, e.g., its major corporations, utilities, real estate, banks and financial institutions, factories and manufacturing facilities, service industries and quasi-governmental authorities. By coming to own substantial portions of

---

5. Ibid., pp. 208–9 & 214–15.

America's "means of production" Afrikans in America may come to own very substantial portions of American power as exercised domestically and abroad. Such an advance would have the effect of expanding the economic and employment opportunities for an increasing number of the members of the community; for motivating them to pursue further education, training and skills development; and enhancing the physical and psychosocial well-being of the community as a whole.

While these economic steps are indeed necessary, they will not be sufficient to meet the economic needs of the community in light of the radical restructuring of the American and global economies. Given the trends of this restructuring, there still may not exist enough economic and employment opportunity in America to provide for the reasonably full occupational needs of the community. For in a global economy, we are compelled to compete in a global market and workplace. We must think and act globally. Therefore, the Afrikan American community must engage fully and competitively in international trade, in the export of products and services as well as in their import, in the ownership of services and production facilities abroad — and above all — function as a central part of a global Pan-Afrikan economic system. Consequently, the Afrikan American community by capturing control of its internal markets, by conjoining them into a national Afrikan American marketing system or network, by deliberately and self-interestedly applying its consumer power, by owning a significant proportion of the general American economy, can, under the umbrella of a national organization, engage in productive and enriching trade relations across the Afrikan diaspora and lead the development of a global Pan-Afrikan economic system. This would permit Afrikan power to be effective not only on the domestic stage but in the global theatre.

The proposals we make here are not mere wishful thinking. We no longer have the option of ignoring them. Their actualization is a necessity.

There are those who in reading our proposals and musing over their social, political, and economic implications may feel anxious and near-apoplectic disquiet about the possible menacing opposition their attempted actualization might provoke from an alarmed White American nation who may misperceive its power and prerogative as being threatened by such a movement. And for that reason they may be tempted to reject what otherwise may appear to them to be not only a sensible, but a necessary approach to the salvation of our national community and its constituent peoples. That DuBois was aware such opposition would occur and yet we must pursue this course is clear in his discussion of this possible fact in *Dusk of Dawn:*

> There are unpleasant eventualities which we must face even if we succeed. For instance, if the Negro in America is successful in welding a mass or large proportion of his people into groups working for their own betterment and uplift, they will certainly, like the Jews, be suspected of sinister designs and inner plotting; and their very success in cultural advance be held against them and used for further and perhaps fatal segregation. There is, of course, always the possibility that the plan of a minority group may be opposed to the best interests of a neighboring or enveloping or larger group; or even if it is not, the larger and more powerful group may think certain policies of a minority are inimical to the national interests. The possibility of this happening must be taken into account.[6]

DuBois was aware, as are we, that his proposal, as is ours, was and is not fundamentally "anti-American" or opposed "to the real interests of the nation." The United States as a nation cannot but benefit from the full participation of the Afrikan American community in its domestic economy and in the global economy. The enrichment of the community cannot but help enrich America as a whole, as it would help enrich the world. A fully-employed Black America; a physically and socially healthier Black America; a Black America unplagued by poverty, disease, drug addiction, miseducation, violence and criminality, disrupted families; a Black America characterized by high self-esteem, self-love and acceptance, self-confidence, self-control, self-knowledge, and high productivity — cannot but be a blessing and a boon to American society and to the greatness of America as a nation among great nations. Black America — *un*oppressed — is America's greatest secret weapon in its struggle for economic survival and supremacy.

The proposals we make here are very familiar because they are very American in their essence. The only thing radical about them is their application to and by Black Americans. These proposals follow the pluralistic traditions of a United States where ethnic groups and regional groups have in pursuing their economic and political interests come to enhance their general well-being and to exercise power and influence in the country, and by so doing, contributed to the well-being of the nation and its exercise of power and influence in the world at large. It is our sincere hope that anti-Black racism will not blind a significant portion of the Afrikan and White American

---

6. Ibid., pp. 215–16.

population to the overall beneficiary effects which may flow from the broad expansion of Afrikan American economic and political power. If White America vigorously and mistakenly opposes the economic and political maturation of the Afrikan American community in its pursuit of the "American way" of success, then the hypocrisy of White America will be plain for all to see and the American nation will ultimately suffer the consequences of its false pretensions.

We will now outline specific proposals for Afrikan American economic empowerment. However, this first requires that we examine the demographic distribution of the Afrikan American population and how its dispersal across the country may be utilized as the basis for the development of a national economy as administered by local, regional and national organizations along the lines suggested in Chapter 22.

Chapter 22

DEMOGRAPHIC FOUNDATIONS OF AN AFRIKAN AMERICAN NATION-WITHIN-A-NATION

The Importance of a Sense of Nation

UNDER ORDINARY CIRCUMSTANCES IT IS EASY to think of the United States of America as "united," i.e., as a unitary, monolithic nation; and economically speaking, to think of it as a capitalistic system, as one huge market. Yet, a little more analytical thinking will make it immediately apparent that the United States consists of a number of geographical and socioeconomic regions. It consists of many cities with distinct characters and facilities. Many of these cities are business centers, manufacturing, transportation, financial, administrative centers together forming a mosaic network of trading, transactional, and power centers. The regions in which these cities are located also differ in terms of the products and services they predominantly export as well as import. For example, some regions primarily produce certain kinds agricultural products, others manufacture certain types of products, others provide certain financial and business services, transportation services, overseas trade, and so on. It is the interaction of these different regions and cities under the aegis of the concept of nationhood; of a centralized government; of a sense of cultural-linguistic commonality; a unified economic/marketing system, which permits the United States to function as a nation and to define, develop and express itself as a national and international power. The politico-economic, sociocultural martial power and dominance of White Americans are derived from the systematic transactions/ interactions between socioeconomic regions/cities on every level — cultural, social, economical, political, and communicational.

These White American trading/transactional/power/political centers/regions are interconnected by an infrastructural maze of rivers, roads, bridges, rails, airline routes, all types of ground transportation systems; intricate, multilevel, overlapping, redundant mail, package, and electronic communications networks which facilitate the flow of enormous amounts of information, data, goods and services, and which permit a full variety of transactions to take place rapidly. These networks form the nervous system of the nation. This unified infrastructure is the basis for the transfer of goods and services; is the basis for physically and psychosocially unifying the nation; for the development and marketing of resources, and is the basis for national economic power and competitiveness on the whole. However, the sense of nation is central. This sense of nation is not founded in the terrain, nor the infrastructure of other networks or systems. It is only founded in the minds of the members of a self-identified populace. It is from this sense of belonging to a social group, of belonging to a social and immaterial entity which transcends their individual egos, that a national people embarks on the development of physical infrastructures reflecting their social relationships in spite of their demographic distribution according to regions, cities, villages, settlements and the like.

A momentary pause for thought allows us to realize that similar regional and municipal population distributions occur among Black Americans as among White Americans. The same transportation-communications infrastructure which systematically serves the White American nation and which is a major source of its economic and political prowess is also available to the Afrikan American nation. The highways and byways of America provide a distribution/ communication network for a potential Black commercial and market system. It also contains the potential to form a power grid for the marked increase and projection of Black Power. However, this infrastructure will essentially remain in its relatively barren state as long as the sense of nationhood is absent in the collective Afrikan American mind. With a sense of nation, infrastructural America would become the nervous system of a massive Afrikan American national and Pan-

Afrikan international social, political, and economic system. Various Black American inner-cities could serve as power centers and other more or less specialized centers in an inner city-suburban network interconnected not only by distributory ground, water and air transportation systems, but also by electronic highways utilizing all of the electronic media such as computer, interactive television, cellular telephone networks and systems.

Though widely spread across the United States and yet concentrated in many of its most productive areas, the hypersegregated, almost-homogenized nature of Black population densities could be turned to an advantage if they are first turned into major wholesale and retail marketing sites. This can happen if sizeable Black urban, suburban and rural communities would capture control of their internal wholesale and retail outlets, and capture the highest percentage of the Black consumer dollar. However, this would only be a first step. The second step would involve the penetration of downtown and shopping mall retail centers by Black-owned businesses. In urban and suburban centers where Black populations are economically and numerically significant, the general wholesale/retail market, not only the ghetto markets, should be general Black business territory. Franchise units of national and multinational corporations serving predominantly Afrikan American locales should come under Afrikan American ownership, management and/or influence (e.g., where they can be influenced to stock on their shelves items manufactured or wholesaled by Afrikan American-owned firms or serviced by Afrikan American professional service companies). As we shall later discuss, Afrikan Americans may penetrate White markets through the ownership of popular franchises and independent business units in those markets.

The ownership and control of numerous wholesale and retail outlets across the country by Afrikan Americans, would lay the basis for a distribution and marketing system for the selling of products produced by Black-owned manufacturing units located both within and outside the United States. The presence of manufacturing, wholesale, retail and service outlets across the country and the world, especially the Afrikan diaspora, would provide a platform for the formation and growth of a markedly significant Afrikan American–Pan Afrikan financial-service industry. Moreover, as we shall also later discuss, the instituting of these factors should be followed or accompanied by the acquiring of equity ownership in large American and multinational corporations on the part of Black community. The ownership of such corporations (through takeovers, the buying of corporate "spinoffs," etc.) can be used to open those corporate markets to Black-produced goods and services. We will now take a cursory, but instructive, look at some relevant Afrikan American demographic facts which together could serve as a platform for bringing our proposal into reality.

The Power of the Black Consumer

It is often said that the Afrikan American community represents an earned consumer income of more than $250–300 billion. This community of between some 35–40 million persons is larger than many nations and richer as well. If considered a nation it would be one of the richest in terms of earned income. It represents a very large consumer market coveted and sought after by many business and marketing firms. One only has to look at Black market magazines such as *Ebony, Emerge, Essence, Black Enterprise*, bulging with ads, whose per page cost may range from $10,000 to $50,000+, to realize the value the Afrikan American market represents to many business establishments. Magazines such as *Ebony* feature ad fold-outs in their monthlies which may cost $180,000 or far more to be included. A simple 1 by 2.5 inch black-and-white advertising space in Ebony magazine costs a minimum of $1,750. Another indication of the value the Black consumer market represents for a large number of firms is the news item published by the *Wall Street Journal*, June 14, 1993, in a column titled "Business and Race." A selected section of the column reported the following information:

> *Big Firms in Ethnic Research.* Consumer-Products' companies swelling interest in minority shoppers has drawn big research firms into the ethnic-survey business, with African-American media firms as interested partners.
>
> A new survey of black consumer attitudes by **Yankelovich Partners** and **Burrell Communications Group** [an Afrikan American advertising firm], Chicago, is selling briskly at $20,000 a copy... Simmons Market Research Bureau, New York, and Essence Communications, New York, plan to query 10,000 African-Americans on a continuing basis. A Simmons executive *says a pilot study of 1,000 people planned for next month is being funded by six large companies in packaged goods, services and other businesses.* [Emphasis added].

Special publications of some 150 pages containing marketing information regarding Black Americans now sell to business firms for approximately $2,000 each.

We must not allow the size of the Afrikan American consumer market to obscure the fact this market represents the *earned* income of the Black community. That is, it represents but a small fractional return ("take home pay") on the much larger wealth produced by that community for its White American employers and overseers. The overall wealth produced by Blacks may approach or exceed a trillion dollars. Unmistakably, Afrikan Americans can enrich themselves many-fold by the capture of a significant percentage of the productive wealth generated by they themselves. *Table* 22-3 lists the money income of Black families-percent distribution by income level from 1970 to 1990.

Demographic Distribution of Afrikan Americans in contrast with other non-White Ethnic Groups

Officially Afrikan Americans number 35 million persons or 12 percent of the total U.S. population (compared to 22.4 million Hispanics; 7.3 million Asians; 2.0 million Native Americans). American Afrikans are still America's largest minority with American Hispanics closing fast on them at 9 percent of the total U.S. population. Due to the traditional undercounting of the Afrikan American population by the U.S. Census Bureau, a more accurate approximation of the Black American population would probably number between 35-40 million persons. Afrikan Americans combined with America's other racial and ethnic minorities comprise the majority population in more than 2,000 counties, cities, towns and other locales, according to the Census Bureau (with Blacks comprising approximately 40-50% of this total subgroup). On the whole, "Minorities comprise the majority in six of the eight American cities with more than a million people: New York, Los Angeles, Chicago, Houston, Detroit and Dallas. Minorities have the biggest population share in Detroit — 80 percent."[1]

A perusal of *Table* 22-2 will reveal that Afrikan Americans in 1990 comprised from 45% to 80% of the total population in 16 cities with 100,000 or more inhabitants. This list includes the cities of Atlanta, Baltimore, Birmingham, Cleveland, Detroit, Durham, Flint, Gary, Indianapolis, Jackson (Miss), Macon (GA), Memphis, Newark, Newport News (VA), Richmond, Savannah, Shreveport (LA), and Washington, D.C. Afrikan Americans comprise from 25% to 44% of the population of 44 cities with 100,000 or more inhabitants, and from 10% to 24% of the population of 57 cities with 100,000 or more

---
1. *City Sun*, June 16-22, 1993.

Afrikan Americans in Metropolitan Populations 1990

Metropolitan Area	Black percent of Metropolitan Population
New York-Northern New Jersey-Long Island, NY-NJ-CT CMSA	18.2
Chicago-Gary-Lake County, IL-IN-WI CMSA	19.2
Philadelphia-Wilmington-Trenton, PA-NJ-DE-MD CMSA	18.7
Detroit-Ann Arbor, MI CMSA	20.9
Washington, DC-MD-VA MSA	26.6
Dallas-Forth Worth, TX CMSA	14.3
Houston-Galveston-Brazonia, TX CMSA	17.9
Miami-Fort Lauderdale, FL CMSA	18.5
Atlanta, GA MSA	26.0
Cleveland-Akron-Lorain, OH CMSA	16.0
St. Louis, MO-IL MSA	17.3
Baltimore, MD MSA	25.9
Cincinnati-Hamilton, OH-KY-IN CMSA	11.7
Milwaukee-Racine, WI CMSA	13.3
Kansas City, MO-KS MSA	12.8
Norfolk-Virginia Beach-Newport News, VA MSA	28.5
Columbus, OH MSA	12.0
Indianapolis, IN MSA	13.8
New Orleans, LA MSA	34.7
Buffalo-Niagra Falls, NY CMSA	10.3
Charlotte-Gastonia-Rock Hill, NC-SC MSA	19.9
Orlando, FL MSA	12.4
Nashville, TN MSA	15.5
Memphis, TN-AR-MS MSA	40.6

Metropolitan Area	Black percent of Metropolitan Population
Oklahoma City, OK MSA	10.5
Louisville, KY-IN MSA	13.1
Dayton-Springfield, OH MSA	13.3
Greensboro–Winston Salem– High Point, NC MSA	19.3
Birmingham, AL MSA	27.1
Jacksonville, FL MSA	20.0
Richmond-Petersburg, VA MSA	29.2
West Palm Beach-Boca Raton-Delray Beach, FL MSA	12.5
Raleigh-Durham, NC MSA	24.9
Greenville-Spartanburg, SC MSA	17.4
Toledo, OH MSA	11.4
New Haven-Meriden, CT MSA	12.1
Baton Rouge, LA MSA	29.5
Little Rock-North Little Rock, AR MSA	19.9
Charleston, SC MSA	30.2
Youngstown-Warren, OH MSA	11.1

Metropolitan areas are shown in rank order of total population of consolidated metropolitan statistical areas (CSMA) and metropolitan statistical areas (MSA).
Source: U.S. Bureau of the Census, press release CB91-229

Table 22–1

inhabitants. In other words, there are some 60 American cities of 100,000 or more inhabitants where Blacks comprise from 25% to 80% of the total population, and some 117 cities where they comprise from 10% to 80% of population over 100,000. There are a total of 194 cities of 100,000 or more inhabitants in America. Of 75 of America's largest metropolitan areas (e.g., NY – Northern NJ– Long Island, NY-NJ-CT; Chicago – Gary–Lake County, IL-IN-WI; Greensboro – Winston Salem –High Point, NC; etc.) 40 are comprised of 10% to 40% of Afrikan Americans (see *Table 22-1*).

Black Population Percentage above 10 percent in Cities with 100,000 or More Inhabitants in 1990

CITY	1990	CITY	1990
Akron, OH	24.5%	Flint, MI	47.9%
Albany, NY	20.6	Fort Lauderdale, FL	28.1
Alexandria, VA	21.9	Fort Wayne, IN	16.7
Arlington, VA	10.5	Fort Worth, TX	22.0
Atlanta, GA	*67.1*	*Gary, IN*	*80.6*
Aurora, CO	11.4	Grand Rapids, MI	18.5
Austin, TX	12.4	Greensboro, NC	33.9
Baltimore, MD	*59.2*	Hampton, VA	38.9
Baton Rouge, LA	43.9	Hartford, CT	38.9
Beaumont, TX	41.3	Houston, TX	28.1
Berkeley, CA	18.8	Huntsville, AL	24.4
Birmingham, AL	*63.3*	Indianapolis, IN	22.6
Boston, MA	25.6	*Inglewood, CA*	*51.9*
Bridgeport, CT	26.6	*Jackson, MS*	*55.7*
Buffalo, NY	30.7	Jacksonville, FL	25.2
Charlotte, NC	31.8	Jersey City, NJ	29.7
Chattanooga, TN	33.7	Kansas City, KS	29.3
Chesapeake, VA	27.4	Kansas City, MO	29.6
Chicago, IL	39.1	Knoxville, TN	15.8
Cincinnati, OH	37.9	Lansing, MI	18.6
Cleveland, OH	46.6	Las Vegas, NV	11.4
Columbus, GA	38.1	Lexington-Fayette, KY	13.4
Columbus, OH	22.6	Little Rock, AR	34.0
Dallas, TX	29.5	Long Beach, CA	13.7
Dayton, OH	40.4	Los Angeles, CA	14.0
Denver, CO	12.8	Louisville, KY	29.7
Detroit, MI	*75.7*	*Macon, GA*	*52.2*
Durham, NC	45.7	*Memphis, TN*	*54.8*
Elizabeth, NJ	19.8	Miami, FL	27.4
Erie, PA	12.0	Milwaukee, WI	30.5

CITY	1990	CITY	1990
Minneapolis, MN	13.0	Rochester, NY	31.5
Mobile, AL	38.9	Rockford, IL	15.0
Montgomery, AL	42.3	Sacramento, CA	15.3
Moreno Valley, CA	13.8	St. Louis, MO	47.5
Nashville-Davidson, TN	24.3	St. Petersburg, FL	19.6
Newark, NJ	*58.5*	San Bernardino, CA	16.0
New Haven, CT	36.1	San Francisco, CA	10.9
New Orleans, LA	*61.9*	*Savannah, GA*	*51.3*
Newport News, VA	33.6	Seattle, WA	10.1
New York, NY	28.7	Shreveport, LA	44.8
Bronx Borough	37.3	South Bend, IN	20.9
Brooklyn Borough	37.9	Springfield, IL	13.0
Manhattan Borough	22.0	Springfield, MA	19.2
Queens Borough	21.7	Stamford, CT	17.8
Norfolk, VA	39.1	Syracuse, NY	20.3
Oakland, CA	43.9	Tacoma, WA	11.4
Oklahoma City, OK	16.0	Tallahassee, FL	29.1
Omaha, NE	13.1	Tampa, FL	25.0
Orlando, FL	26.9	Toledo, OH	19.7
Pasadena, CA	19.0	Topeka, KS	10.5
Paterson, NJ	36.0	Tulsa, OK	13.6
Paoria, IL	20.9	Valeijo, CA	21.1
Philadelphia, PA	39.9	Virginia Beach, VA	13.9
Pittsburgh, PA	25.8	Waco, TX	23.1
Pomona, CA	14.4	*Washington, DC*	*85.8*
Portsmouth, VA	47.3	Waterbury, CT	13.0
Providence, RI	14.8	Wichita, KS	11.3
Raleigh, NC	27.6	Winston-Salem, NC	39.3
Richmond, VA	*55.2*	Yonkers, NY	14.1

Source: Abstracted from <u>Statistical Abstract of the United States 1992: The National Data Book</u>, 112 ed.: U.S. Department of Commerce, Economics and Statistics Administration, Bureau of the Census pp. 35-37.

Table 22-2

Black Urban Demographics
Money Income of Families

No. 702. Money Income of Families — Percent Distribution by Income Level in Constant (1990) dollars, by Race and Hispanic Origin of Householder: 1970 to 1990.

[Families as of March of following year. Beginning with 1980, based on householder concept and restricted to primary families. For definition of race, family, and householder, see text, section 1. Based on Current Population Survey; see text, sections 1 and 14 and Appendix III. For definition of median, see Guide to Tabular Presentation. See also Historical Statistics, *Colonial Times* to 1970, series G 1-8, G 16-23, G 190-192, and G 197-199]

Race and Hispanic Origin of Householder and Year	Number of families (1,000)	Under $10,000	$10,000-$14,999	$15,000-$24,999	$25,000-$34,999	$35,000-$49,999	$50,000-$74,999	$75,000 and over	Median income (dol.)
BLACK									
1970	4,928	20.9	13.6	23.9	17.6	13.9	8.3	1.6	21,151
1975	5,586	21.8	14.5	21.9	16.3	15.8	8.0	1.8	21,327
1980	6,317	24.3	14.1	20.9	15.7	14.1	8.7	2.2	20,103
1985	6,921	25.8	12.4	21.2	14.2	14.2	9.3	3.0	20,390
1987[2]	7,202	25.7	11.7	20.1	13.8	14.3	9.9	4.5	21,177
1988	7,409	25.2	12.8	19.0	13.3	13.9	11.3	4.4	21,355
1989	7,470	24.6	12.6	19.4	13.8	14.1	11.0	4.5	21,301
1990	7,471	25.6	11.3	19.5	14.0	15.0	9.8	4.7	21,423

[2] Beginning 1987, based on revised processing procedures; data not directly comparable with prior years. See text, section 14, and source.
Source of table 702: U.S. Bureau of the Census, *Current Population Reports*, series P-60, No. 174; and published data.

Table 22-3

Table 22–1 also specifies by population size the names of metropolitan areas which include 100,000 or more Afrikan American inhabitants. Table 22–2 provides the share and growth of Black population by state (1990). The Afrikan American population grew by 13% in the 1980s. An analysis of Black population growth during the 1980s by *American Demographics* revealed the following:

> The black population lost ground in the District of Columbia and West Virginia. It remained stable in Arkansas, and grew everywhere else. Because blacks are more widely distributed than other minorities in the U.S., many states had faster-than-average growth of the black population, but few saw tremendous growth. New Hampshire led with a growth rate of 80 percent, followed by Minnesota with 18 percent....
>
> More than 25 percent of the population of the deep South states of Mississippi, Louisiana, South Carolina, Georgia, and Alabama is black, but only Georgia had a higher-than-average black growth rate in the 1980s.

Demographic analysis illustrates the fact that as a percentage of the population Blacks are the largest minority except in the West. As can be inferred from the data, by far the largest bulk of the Black population is concentrated along the northeastern, and southwestern seaboards inward. Blacks in the west are also concentrated along the coastline inward of southern California (see NYT, "Minorities on the Move"). It is interesting as well as instructive to compare the geographical population concentration of Blacks with those of Hispanics and Asian/Pacific Islanders. As perhaps would be expected, Hispanics (predominantly Mexican) are mainly concentrated in the Western (California) and Southwestern (New Mexico, Texas, Arizona, Colorado) United States. Other relatively high concentrations of Hispanics — predominantly Puerto Ricans, Dominicans, Central and South Americans) are located in the Northeast and Florida (predominantly Cuban). Asian Americans (predominantly Chinese and Japanese) are mainly concentrated on the Pacific west coast and the northeastern Atlantic coast (predominantly Chinese and Korean).

Trade Relations between Ethnic American Enclaves and their Countries of Origin. It is noteworthy to observe that compared to the Afrikan American community, the Hispanic, and more so, the Asian communities, have and are developing internally integrated commercial/business markets as well as satellite markets in the communities of other ethnic groups. These markets are providing platforms for the entry into and penetration of the larger American economic system by the business segments of these non-Black ethnic communities. Moreover, it is interesting to note the geographical, "trade route" relationship of a number of immigrant residential/commercial/ business communities to their countries and regions of origin (e.g., the "Atlantic seaboard Hispanics" to the Spanish Caribbean basin and the east coasts of Central and South America; the "Pacific seaboard and southwestern Hispanics" to Mexico, Central America and western South America). These are rough correlations, obviously.

We are already familiar with rapidly consolidating and growing economic regional trade systems of southeastern Asia and Japan. These regions and the many nations which constitute them not only engage in internal and mutually beneficiary trade relations among themselves, but trade relations with the United States and other nations. More important in the context of our discussion is the fact these regional countries carry out significant trade and financial relations with their overseas compatriots or ethnic enclaves in America. Such intragroup-international trade adds to the economic stability and growth of the various ethnic American enclaves. These home country-ethnic enclave relations may also enhance the political power and influence of various ethnic American communities *vis-à-vis* the United States government, depending on the nature of U.S. foreign and trade policy initiatives relative to their countries of origin.

As discussed previously, Kotkin argues that ethnicity is "a defining factor in the evolution of the global economy, i.e., that "global tribes," peoples who though globally dispersed share "a strong ethnic identity and sense of mutual dependence, ...seem particularly well adapted to succeed within today's progressively more integrated world-wide economic system."[2] If this is the case, then the location in the United States of cohesive Latino and Asian economic systems provide the bases for the continuing growth and development of their national economic and political power. For example, the entry of Mexico into the North American Free Trade Association (NAFTA) could theoretically, at least, enhance the economic growth and development of the Mexican-American community, and its political power as well. It is important to note that South American nations have themselves established and are establishing a mixture of bilateral and multilateral trade compacts. These trade compacts generally involve the mutual reduction of tariffs and other barriers among member nations. Trade compacts have allowed a rapid expansion in regional trade among Latin American nations. These

---

2. Joel Kotkin, *Tribes: How Race, Religion and Identity Determine Success in the Global Economy* (New York: Random House, 1993).

nations at present have formed four fledgling regional trade groups: the Mercosul Treaty (Brazil, Uruguay, Argentina and Paraguay — formed March 1990); Chile-Argentina Friendship Treaty, formed in 1984; the Colombia-Venezuela Customs Union, instituted January, 1992; and the Andean Pact (Colombia, Peru, Bolivia, Ecuador, and Venezuela). The economic implications of these compacts are interesting. For example, export trade between the members of the Andean Pact approached a growth rate of 250% between 1986 and 1992, and their export trade with the rest of the world increased 50% during that same time period. The political-economic implications for these regional networks and their relations with and impact on Hispanic Americans in general and their ethnic-American enclaves specifically, are interesting indeed.

Even more interesting in this regard are the political-economic implications of an historic conference which was attended by the members of the various Latin American regional trade pacts in Cartagena, Colombia, in June 1994 (NYT, 6/17/1994). The leaders of Spain and Portugal were among Latin American heads of state who gathered in Cartagena for a meeting devoted to trade and the integration of the separate trade pacts which currently divide the South American continent. According to the *New York Times*, Latin America's 19 largest nations agreed to fuse the regions' several free trade pacts into one Latin American free trade zone by the end of the decade. Speaking with reference to the restructuring of the global economy, Chile's President, Eduardo Frei Ruiz-Tagle, was reported to have said that "If we look at the world economy today, Latin America confronts three blocs — Europe, NAFTA and the Pacific Rim — Our union is fundamental." It is also of interest to note that during the conference Columbian officials announced their intention to sign a free trade accord in Barbados with the eight-nation Caribbean Community within the following two weeks.

Similar implications hold for potential trade and economic relations between a cohesive, well-developed and dynamic Afrikan-American economic system and Caribbean Common Market communities such as CARICOM, and Afrikan regional economic communities including the Economic Community of West Afrikan States (ECOWAS); the Preferential Trade Area of East and Southern Afrika (PTA); The South Afrikan Customs Union (SACU); the South Afrikan Development Coordination Conference (SADCC); the Maghreb Permanent Consultative (Committee-MAGHREB); and the Central Afrikan Customs and Economic Union (UDEAC).

The Economic Potential of a United Black America

The foregoing discussion of the demographics of the Afrikan American national community draws the picture of a Black nation-within-a-nation containing some 117 large urban populations across the United States along with hundreds of sizeable smaller urban, suburban communities and towns. If organized under the guiding influence of a deliberate Afrikan American nation-centered consciousness, a cohesive Afrikan American community-controlled internal consumer and producer market unified by a network of communications and transportation systems, the Afrikan American community could come to wield formidable economic and political influence at home and abroad. However, the realization of such a national economic community fundamentally requires the organization and economic revitalization of Black urban communities across the U.S.A. ...and there's the rub.

We hear so much of "urban blight," the social disorganization and deterioration of Black central cities, Black political and economic apathy, until the realization of an Afrikan American economic community as outlined above appears to be a fruitless fantasy doomed to remain merely a figment of the Black Nationalist fevered imagination. However, a closer analysis of the Afrikan American community will reveal a rising tide in the community for economic self-sufficiency and unification. The call for such a community has a long and honored history in Black America. The economic legacy of Booker T. Washington, The Honorable Marcus Garvey, The Honorable Elijah Muhammad, Malcolm X, among others; the economic legacy of the pioneering Black Church and the Nation of Islam; the development of significant Black urban economic markets like Atlanta, Durham and Tulsa; the economic achievements by the individuals and corporations who make up the BE 100 and numerous other smaller Black enterprises and sole proprietorships, give illuminating testimony to the ability of Afrikan American individuals, institutions and communities to plot their own economic courses.

The L.A. Story. There are a number of Black urban centers currently undergoing portentous self-revitalization and self-development. A leading example of such activities which should stimulate many imitators is represented by Black Los Angeles, more specifically, riot-torn, economically depressed, criminalized, socially and racially oppressed South Central, L.A.[3]

---

[3]. South-Central, L.A., located in Los Angeles county, California, radiates for approximately three miles from the junction of Slauson and Vermont avenues of its total population of 523,156, 55 percent is Black (down from 65% as the result of losing 48,000 residents from 1980 to 1990); 45 percent is Hispanic (up from 17 percent to a rapid influx

Even before last year's spasm of violence, South Central Los Angeles was close to an economic wasteland, with a few stores, banks or well-paying jobs for its predominantly Black and Hispanic residents. Per capita annual income at $7,600 for the core of South Central in 1990, was 52.6 percent lower than for Los Angeles county as a whole. There is one supermarket for every 40,646 residents in South Central's core as against one for every 23,224 residents in the county. ...While most of California boomed, South-Central suffered from a flight of well-paid manufacturing jobs, an exodus of middle-class Blacks and a reluctance among large businesses to operate there.

The rapidly growing Hispanic population which has led to the taking of the majority of Black South Central's low-wage jobs, and the influx of Korean immigrants who have become the area's predominant merchants, employing very few people from the neighborhood in their family-run stores, have stoked Black resentment and racial tensions between Blacks and Koreans. Ethnic group antipathies have prevented the functional development (for Blacks and Hispanics at least) of a coherent political-economic power base or general consensus necessary for rebuilding the area. The *Times* (5/6/93) further reports:

> The looting, arson and violence, which destroyed thousands of businesses and caused as much as $1 billion in damage, exposed the fragile nature of the local economy... The un-employment rate in the core of the South-Central area in 1990 was 7.1 percent...as against 5.8 percent for all of Los Angeles county. Among Black teen-agers, the rate in South-Central was 43.8 percent, and among Blacks aged 25 to 54, the rate was 9.1 percent... Many economists think the census data substantially understates the unemployment rate in South-Central.

Self-Help In South Central. In the immediate aftermath of the Los Angeles uprising, promises and pledges of money and aid to rebuild the riot-torn sections of the city were profuse. In fact, a special loan fund was set up under the auspices of Rebuild Los Angeles (RLA), the official riot-recovery organization, to finance reconstruction and economic expansion. Among the major post-riot loan funds marked for Los Angeles's "neglected areas" were: U.S. Small Business Administration, $334 million; Bank of America, $25 million; Southern California Business Corporation, $10 million; RLA Community Lending Corporation, $6.3 million; Community Financial Resource Center, $4.1 million; and first A.M.E. Church (Disney/Arco Fund),

---

of 46,000 residents between 1980 to 1990). The *New York Times* (5/6/92) provides a general description of South-Central as it was just one week prior to the Social upheaval following the Rodney King verdict of 1992.

$1.3 million (*Wall Street Journal*, 4/28/94). National political leaders pledged more than $1.2 billion of aid. Now, more than two years after the Los Angeles uprising the vast proportion of those pledges have yet to materialize and of the monies available only a very small portion has been lent. Almost all of the $380-million loan fund noted above is earmarked to rebuild what was destroyed. (Obviously, the outcome of such a strategy would be to reinstitute the pre-riot racial and economic status quo, e.g., the reestablishment of the Korean monopoly of the Black community's commercial markets.) Only about $22 million is dedicated to spurring the growth of small businesses among the 55,000 located in target areas. Even little of this money has been forthcoming.

Where loan-fund money does exist, it is very difficult for both existing and would-be businesses to access. It turns out that $600 million of the $1.2 billion pledged by the Federal government is not intended to be a direct loan at all since it essentially involves an offer by the Federal Home Loan Bank to make money available to its member banks at about 1.5% below prime. This means that these member banks would make the final loan decisions based on rather strict lending criteria. These criteria, essentially no different from those applied by banks under ordinary circumstances, continue, as they always have, to generally work against minority small-businesses that operate in economically depressed areas. The *Journal* reported that "So far, the $6.3 million RLA loan fund has received 70 applications, turned down 45 and funded seven for a total of $1.4 million. The remaining 18 applications are pending." It is clear by now that the central strategy for responding to local unrest and to remedy local socioeconomic problems has failed. This generally is the case with "top down" solutions and other approaches to problems prevalent in Black American community.

Interestingly, the adversities described above as well as the contradictory outcome of the second trial of four White police officers accused of beating Rodney King, have provided the catalyst for a budding revolution in Afrikan-centered consciousness and economic thinking. Instead of despair, the mood of many in South Central appears to be one of courageous determination on the part of all classes to transform the community socially and economically through their own initiative. On May 4, 1993, the *New York Times* reported that one significant sociopsychological outcome of the "Rodney King trials" was the rethinking of their general relations to the larger society in general by well-to-do Blacks in Los Angeles and around the country. The *Times* reported their views as follows:

...they had lowered their expectations about race relations over the last years. They told of efforts to stand up to indignities and said they were rethinking their spending habits, putting money and economic clout behind other Blacks and Black-owned businesses....

The people who embraced integration in their climb into the middle class are now talking with bitterness and resignation about separation and solidarity. Last year's despair, they said, has turned to defiance...While others talk of healing, those interviewed talked of doing for themselves and supporting one another in the way they said Jews and Asians had done.

Many have turned inward in the last year, transferring money to Black-owned banks, seeking out Black businesses to repair their automobiles or buy wall-to-wall carpeting. They have been creating **consortiums** and **cooperatives** to serve the inner city and generally viewing the country as a more hostile place than they did before the Simi Valley jury verdict.

...Since the riots, some Black businesses are reporting banner years, with Black customers seeking out the companies to show their support. [Emphasis added]

Beautifully illustrating the relationship between Afrikan-centered consciousness, Afrikan-centered identity and the enhancement of economic and social well-being of Afrikan peoples is the following event as reported by the *Times* (5/6/93):

...three financial institutions in Los Angeles posted gains in deposits despite the recession, which slowed growth at some other banks. *At Founders National Bank in South-Central, deposits rose to $75 million from $60 million. The accounts held by Black churches tripled to 50 after the riots....*

Deposits at the Black-owned Broadway Federal Savings and Loan rose to $3 million from $2 million, while those at Family Savings Bank rose to $113 million from $109 million [Emphasis added].

It is of note in this context that the Founders National Bank established just three years ago, in 1991, has loaned out about $19 million to some 300 businesses in the region.

We discussed in Chapter 14 Light and Bonacich's (1988) concept of *ethnic resources* and *class resources*. They contend that the combination and coordination of these resources are primarily responsible for supporting the entrepreneurship of various immigrant groups and for providing resources which "support the competitive position of individual firms owned by coethnics." Light and Bonacich intimate that "Ethnic resources include values, knowledge, skills, information, attitudes, leadership, solidarity, an orientation to sojourning, and institutions." These resources not only include the willingness to work long hours; to save a large percentage of income; work for relatively modest reward; generously reciprocate business skills and information; hire exclusively from within the family and ethnic group; engage in maintaining ethnic control of markets and occupations, but also involve the utilization of ethnic-based financial and credit resources and associations for advancing the group's economic, social and political interests. Recall that class resources are defined by Light and Bonacich as including credit ratings, the ownership of private property in the means of production or distribution, personal wealth, ...human capital [i.e., educational credentials, occupational skills, social skills, "connections,"] on the material side and "on the cultural side, ...bourgeois values, attitudes, knowledge, and skills transmitted intergenerationally in the course of primary socialization. Class resources are relatively class specific rather than common to the entire...group regardless of class level." Light and Bonacich credit the combination of ethnic and class resources with the phenomenal entrepreneurial success of Koreans across the country.

An article titled " 'Buying Black' Approach Paying in Los Angeles," published in the *New York Times* (5/23/93) clearly illustrates the powerful potential represented by the combination of class and ethnic resources in the Black urban communities. The *Times* reported that:

> Frustrated by stalled government and corporate efforts to revitalize poor areas of Los Angeles in last year's rioting, the city's Black community has undertaken its own approach to economic development: it is investing in itself.
> In the year since civil unrest laid waste to huge tracts of commercial property in South-Central Los Angeles, Black community leaders have launched numerous programs to persuade Blacks to spend their money in Black-owned businesses...
> Over the past year, Black Churches, celebrities and consumers, including *many from the more affluent neighborhoods* of Baldwin Hills and Inglewood, have transferred *millions of dollars* from large traditional banks to small Black-owned ones that serve the South-Central area. Those banks say that as a result *they have hired more employees* to handle the growing numbers of new accounts and that *the increased cash reserves will allow them to make more money locally.*
> Throughout the city, businesses are posting signs in their windows that indicate they are owned by Blacks, and many Black consumers ...seek these out. Local groups are publishing directories of Black

businesses for consumers and merchants and *running networking seminars for professionals* [Emphasis added].

Of great importance to the advancement of Afrikan American entrepreneurship and economic development are institutional and organizational resources. Institutions such as the Black Church can provide a broad array of material and cultural resources for the advancement of the community's interests on all economic and social fronts. Religious institutions and secular organizations are the cultural repositories for large monetary and human capital resources in the Black American community. As we discuss in greater detail later, the appropriate and energetic mobilization of institutional resources and influence can generate revolutionary changes in the socioeconomic/politicoeconomic status of the Afrikan American and the worldwide Afrikan community. An illuminating example of the tremendous impact that the mobilizing of institutional and organizational resources can have on the reorganization of the economic structure of the community is provided by the following information reported in the same *New York Times* article cited above:

> *Transferring Assets*
> Mr. Boyd, who served as pastor of Bethel A.M.E. in Los Angeles, helped organize the effort to persuade Black churches to transfer their accounts to Black banks, after seeing a Bank of America study that showed *Blacks in Los Angeles County controlled about $9.5 billion in liquid assets but deposited only 3.5 percent of that in Black banks. Within the first 45 days of arranging the effort, more than $8.5 million flowed into Black banks, a trend that Mr. Boyd said is continuing.*
>
> Another group active in encouraging Blacks to patronize Black businesses is Recycling Black Dollars Inc., which provides establishments with banners that indicate they are Black owned... The banners were first used during the riots to discourage looters, but now the signs have become a source of pride in the community.
>
> The group plans to mail Black consumers 50,000 consumer discount cards at the enterprize participating in the program [Emphasis added].

Obviously, the initiatives depicted here are just commencing and have yet to catch their stride. However, they reveal the enormous potential the Afrikan American community has available to it for socioeconomic self-transformation and some of the means by which this end can be achieved. Transformations similar to those occurring in Los Angeles, if they sequentially or simultaneously occur across all

Afrikan American communities in the country, especially under the aegis of unified national Afrikan-centered organizations, would not only drastically change the economic-political circumstances of the Afrikan American community for the better, but also the fortunes of the worldwide Afrikan community as well.

Suburbanization and Economics

One of the major demographic phenomena which occurred during the 1980s involved the relatively large migration of Blacks to the suburbs of America. A record 6 percent increase in population from 1980 has led to the fact that by 1990, 32 percent of all Afrikan Americans in metropolitan areas lived in suburban neighborhoods. *American Demographics* reports the following:

> In 1990, there were 40 U.S. metropolitan areas with at least 50,000 black suburbanites, defined as blacks living outside of the central city. The largest suburban black population by far is found in Washington, D.C.; if considered by themselves, Washington's 619,239 black suburbanites would form a metro area larger than Toledo, Ohio. The second-largest market is Atlanta, where 462,832 suburban-blacks cluster in such neighborhoods as Brook Glen, Panola Mill, and Wyndham Park. The third-largest market is Los Angeles, with 400,936 suburban blacks....
>
> The ten metros with the largest suburban black populations are all major population centers, and they follow national patterns of black population distribution. Just over half (53 percent) of all blacks in the U.S. live in the South, for example, and five southern metros are in the top ten for suburban blacks: Washington, Baltimore, Atlanta, Houston, and Miami. The list also includes Los Angeles, along with four northern industrial metros: Philadelphia, Newark, Chicago, and St. Louis.[4]

Table 22–4 lists 40 Black suburbs ranked by population size of at least 50,000 Blacks, or more. *Table* 22–7 lists 40 of the fastest-growing Black suburbs (50,000+). *American Demographics* further reports that "In metropolitan areas with populations of 1 million or more, Black families who live in the suburbs have an average income of more than $32,000.... That is 55 percent higher than the average income of Black families living in the central cities of those metropolitan areas." As noted in *Table* 22–4, the average population for the 40 areas is 135,981. These 40 areas represent a combined spending power of well over 100 billion dollars. *Table* 22–8 ranks the counties in terms of the percentage of households with incomes of $50,000 or more (in 1989

---

4. "Black Suburbs," *American Demographics*, Sept. 1992, pp. 32–33.

The Most Blacks

Washington, D.C., is the nation's capital for black suburbs.

(metropolitan areas ranked by the number of black residents living in suburban areas)

metropolitan area	black residents in suburban areas	metropolitan area	black residents in suburban areas
Washington, DC	619,239	Columbia, SC	95,069
Atlanta, GA	462,832	Orlando, FL	89,005
Los Angeles-Long Beach, CA	400,936	West Palm Beach-Boca Raton-Delray Beach, FL	71,460
Miami-Hialeah, FL	291,352	Greenville, NC.	71,005
Philadelphia, PA-NU	240,483	Charlotte-Gastonia-Rock Hill, NC-SC	70,984
Newark, NJ	240,084	Pittsburgh, PA	68,538
Chicago, IL	213,970	Baton Rouge Parish, LA	60,163
St. Louis, MO-IL	182,538	Norfolk-Virginia Beach-Newport News, VA	59,927
Baltimore, MD	169,333	Tampa-St. Petersburg-Clearwater, FL	59,783
Houston, TX	145,581	Raleigh-Durham, NC	58,791
New York, NY	138,243	Fayetteville, NC	58,517
Riverside-San Bernardino, CA	133,690	Jackson, MS	58,279
Detroit, MI	132,740	Birmingham, Al	57,897
Ft. Lauderdale-Hollywood-Pompano Beach, FL	120,462	Bergen-Passaic, NJ	55,379
Oakland, CA	120,347	Mobile, AL	54,105
Cleveland, OH	120,214	San Diego, CA	53,460
New Orleans Parish, LA	120,128	Middlesex-Somerset-Hunterdon, NJ	53,398
Charleston, SC	119,788	Memphis, TN	52,363
Richmond-Petersburg, VA	112,530	Cincinnati, OH	52,341
Augusta, GA	98,489	**AVERAGE FOR AREAS**	**135,981**
Dallas, TX	95,803		

Note: List contains only metropolitan areas with at least 50,000 blacks living in suburban neighborhoods.

Source: 1990 census

Table 22-4

Black Concentrations

Northern metros may contain more black suburbanites, but southern metros are far more concentrated.

(metropolitan areas are ranked by the percent of suburban residents who are black)

metropolitan area	percent of suburban residents who were black	metropolitan area	percent of suburban residents who were black
Fayetteville, NC	29.4%	St Louis, MO-IL	9.9%
Jackson, MS	29.3	Orlando, FL	9.8
Charleston, SC	28.1	Birmingham, AL	9.5
Augusta, GA	28.0	Houston, TX	9.1
Columbia, SC	26.8	Cleveland, OH	9.1
Miami-Hialeah, Fl	22.5	Richmond-Petersburg, VA	9.0
Norfolk-Virginia Beach-Newport News, VA	21.3	Los Angeles-Long Beach, CA	8.7
Washington, DC	19.9	Oakland, CA	7.8
Baton Rouge Parish, LA	19.5	Philadelphia, PA-NJ	7.6
Atlanta, GA	19.3	Dallas, TX	7.2
Mobile, AL	19.3	Chicago, IL	6.8
Newark, NJ	16.7	Riverside-San Bernardino, CA	6.2
New Orleans Parish, LA	16.7	Middlesex-Somerset-Hunterdon, NJ	5.7
Raleigh-Durham, NC	16.7	Bergen-Passaic, NJ	4.9
Memphis, TN	15.3	Cincinnati, OH	4.8
Ft. Lauderdale-Hollywood-Pompano Beach, FL	13.2	Detroit, MI	4.2
Greenville, NC	13.2	San Diego, CA	4.2
New York, NY	11.8	Pittsburgh, PA	4.1
Charlotte-Gastonia-Rock Hill, NC-SC	11.1	Tampa-St. Petersburg-Clearwater, FL	4.1
Baltimore, MD	10.5		
West Palm Beach-Boca Raton-Delray Beach, FL	10.4	**AVERAGE FOR 40 AREAS**	**13.3%**

Note: List only contains metropolitan areas with at least 50,000 blacks living in suburban neighborhoods.

Source: 1990 census

Table 22–5

Changes in Black Suburbs

In most metros, black suburbs are growing fast. But Mobile and Birmingham actually lost suburban blacks during the 1980s.

(metropolitan areas ranked by change in the number of black suburban residents between 1980 and 1990)

metropolitan area	change in number of black suburban residents	metropolitan area	change in number of black suburban residents
Atlanta, GA	224,857	Middlesex-Somerset-Hunterdon, NJ	21,538
Washington, DC	5,395	New Orleans Parish, LA	21,519
Miami-Hialeah, FL	101,065	West Palm Beach-Boca Raton-Delray Beach, FL	20,737
Riverside-San Bernardino, CA	85,793	Charleston, SC	18,628
Chicago, IL	83,944	Columbia, SC	17,866
Houston, TX	75,665	Augusta, GA	17,166
Ft. Lauderdale-Hollywood-Pompano Beach, FL	53,090	Greenville, NC	12,341
Dallas, TX	52,252	Norfolk-Virginia Beach-Newport News, VA	11,626
Baltimore, MD	50,782	Bergen-Passaic, NJ	10,256
Philadelphia, PA-NJ	47,805	Cincinnati, OH	9,152
Los Angeles-Long Beach, CA	45,499	Fayetteville, NC6,	784
Newark, NJ	42,774	Memphis, TN	5,700
St. Louis, MO-IL	42,338	Raleigh-Durham, NC-SC	4,815
Oakland, CA	37,144	Pittsburgh, PA	4,312
Orlando, FL	36,839	Jackson, MS	4,179
Detroit, MI	29,576	Charlotte-Gastonia Rock Hill, NC-SC	2,974
Richmond-Petersburg, VA	28511	Baton Rouge Parish, LA	2,670
San Diego, CA	26,984	Mobile, AL	-161
Cleveland, OH	25,915	Birmingham, AL	-7,878
New York, NY	24,901	AVERAGE FOR 40 AREAS	38,448
Tampa-St. Petersburg-Clearwater, FL	23,422		

Note: List contains many metropolitan areas with at least 50,000 black living in suburban neighborhoods

Source: Census Bureau

Table 22-6

The Fastest-Growing Black Suburbs

Riverside-San Bernardino is the twelfth largest black suburb, but it grew fastest during the 1980s.

(metropolitan areas ranked by growth of black suburban population, 1980-90)

metropolitan area	growth of black suburban populations	metropolitan area	growth of black suburban populations
Riverside-San Bernardino, CA	179.1%	Norfolk-Virginia Beach-Newport News, VA	24.1%
Dallas, TX	120.0	Columbia, SC	23.1
Houston, TX	108.2	Bergen-Passaic, NJ	22.7
San Diego, CA	101.9	New Orleans Parish, LA	21.8
Atlanta, GA	94.5	Newark, NJ	21.7
Ft. Lauderdale-Hollywood-Pompano Beach, FL	78.8	Cincinnati, OH	21.2
Orlando, FL	70.6	New York, NY	21.1
Middlesex-Somerset-Hunterdon, NJ	67.6	Augusta, GA	21.1
Chicago, IL	64.6	Greenville, NC	21.0
Tampa-St. Petersburg-Clearwater, FL	64.4	Charleston, SC	18.4
Washington, DC	53.3	Fayetteville, NC	13.1
Miami-Hialeah, FL	53.1	Los Angeles-Long Beach, CA	12.8
Oakland, CA	44.6	Memphis, TN	12.2
Baltimore, MD	42.8	Raleigh-Durham, NC	8.9
West Palm Beach-Boca Raton-Delray Beach, FL	40.9	Jackson, MS	7.7
Richmond-Petersburg, VA	33.0	Pittsburgh, PA	6.7
St. Louis, MO-IL	30.2	Baton Rouge Parish, LA	4.6
Detroit, MI	28.7	Charlotte-Gastonia-Rock Hill, NC-SC	4.4
Cleveland, OH	27.5	Mobile, AL	–0.3
Philadelphia, PA-NJ	24.8	Birmingham, AL	–12.0
		AVERAGE FOR 40 AREAS	**40.1%**

Note: List contains only metropolitan areas with at least 50,000 blacks living in suburban neighborhoods.
Source: Census Bureau

Table 22-7

Affluent Blacks

Blacks who live in wealthy counties are likely to be wealthy themselves.

(counties or county equivalents ranked by percent of black households
with 1989 incomes of $50,000 or more, and total black households in 1990)

rank	county (metropolitan area)	all black households	percent affluent
1	Somerset, NJ (Middlesex-Somerset-Hunterdon)	4,447	50.0%
2	Nassau, NY (Nassau-Suffolk)	30,375	44.1
3	Howard, MD (Baltimore)	7,810	43.6
4	Norfolk, MA (Boston-Lawrence-Salem-Lowell-Brockton)	3,484	43.3
5	Morris, NJ (Newark)	4,122	42.4
6	DuPage, IL (Chicago)	5,208	40.8
7	Bergen, NJ (Bergen-Passaic)	13,202	38.5
8	Suffolk, NY (Nassau-Suffolk)	21,483	38.4
9	Fairfax, VA* (Washington)	20,246	38.2
10	Prince George's, MD (Washington)	126,282	37.0
11	Loudoun, VA (Washington)	2,137	36.3
12	Rockland, NY (New York)	7,204	36.0
13	Ventura, CA (Oxnard-Ventura)	4,761	35.7
14	Prince William, VA** (Washington)	8,871	35.6
15	Montgomery, MD (Washington)	33,228	35.5
16	Middlesex, NJ (Middlesex-Somerset-Hunterdon)	16,423	34.9
17	Oakland, MI (Detroit)	27,200	34.8
18	Orange, CA (Anaheim-Santa Ana)	14,000	34.5
19	Burlington, NJ (Philadelphia)	16,792	34.3
20	Santa Clara, CA (San Jose)	19,020	34.1

U.S. average = 13.2%

* Includes the independent cities of Fairfax and Falls Church.
** Includes the independent cities of Manassas and Manassas Park.
Note: Includes only counties with black populations of 5,000 or more.

Source: 1990 census

Table 22–8

dollars). A very rough estimate of the combined average spending power for the approximately 2,200 households in Somerset, N.J., which earn $50,000 or more, equals $110,000,000+. The more than 46,000 households in Prince George's County earning $50,000 or more possess a combined average spending power of well over $2 billion, or $2,325,000,000+ yearly, which equals approximately 23 times that of

Somerset county. These rough figures (underestimates) give us some idea of the monetary wealth each of these communities represents separately and as a combined whole. If even a good fraction (say, 25%) of the yearly income of these Black suburban areas could be spent with Afrikan American business establishments and in investing in other wealth-producing projects helpful to the Afrikan American community, their impact on the economic construction and shape of the community should be tremendous.

This type of information is especially stimulating when it is recognized, as noted by *American Demographics* (9/92), that "Suburban Blacks live in counties that still show a high degree of segregation at the neighborhood level." Although discrimination is a large factor in segregating Black suburbs, living in segregated or predominantly Black suburbs is very frequently a matter of choice for affluent Blacks. It is also important to note that many affluent Black suburbs are relatively contiguous with or near-majority Black inner-city neighborhoods. This proximity of relatively homogeneous and large Black neighborhoods with their combined numbers, human and material capital, if appropriately organized and coordinated would make for the economic revitalization and political empowerment of Black America.

Even the cursory analysis just presented points to a major problematic situation for Afrikan-centered urban planning and economic development specialists. That is, a major goal of Black inner-city economic and social development would involve finding ways that relatively affluent Black suburbs can connect infrastructurally, culturally and economically with Black inner-cities to their mutual benefit. For these two entities, i.e., the Black suburbs and Black inner-cities, together possess the class and ethnic resources which combined, as we discussed earlier, are the primary ingredients for ethnic economic achievement and success.

Cooperative Economics in Los Angeles

The Brotherhood Crusade and The Black Brotherhood United Fund, Inc. (BBUF) of predominantly Afrikan-American South Central Los Angeles, provide a remarkable example of cooperative economics. Responding to a situation now prevalent in large inner-city communities where the commercial market is dominated by Korean or other ethnic merchants and where Black entrepreneurs are virtually excluded from their own community markets, the Brotherhood Crusade and BBUF decided to make a place for businesses owned by the Afrikan American community to serve the community.

However, rather than use the standard capitalist tools whose utility and success in the Afrikan American community have a checkered and not too successful history for establishing enterprises, BBUF utilized a direct and unusual approach. The Brotherhoods solicited and obtained help directly from the community itself. First, the Brotherhoods decided that they would construct the Mom and Pop convenience store (which also displays on its facade the title, *Our Community Convenience Store*). The $500,000 fund for building the store came from contributions made by the community's residents and business leaders. According to Danny Bakewell, founder and president of the Brotherhood Crusade which oversaw the construction of the store in the heart of South Central Los Angeles, "No bank, no savings and loan venture capitalists would support our vision." The Brotherhood Crusade plans to open five more stores. A model for redevelopment of the Afrikan American community, half of the current store's profit will go to open new stores and the other half will be used to fund community projects.

The Brotherhood Crusade's approach to Afrikan American economic development is a fitting one indeed, given the economic character of the Black American community. It avoids the use of community accumulation approaches developed in and utilized by the White American community, approaches reflective of and compatible with its history, economic character and organization. In most instances these approaches are poorly designed to advance Black economic development because they do not reflect or speak to the history and economic character of the Black community. There is some question as to whether the exceedingly individualistic, oligopolistic capitalism inherent in "standard" White-American business-approaches and the values they imply should be adopted by the Afrikan-descended community given its rather diffused and relatively low-level capital base, and the historic cultural values Afrikans place on cooperatism and communalism. The approach just described seems to best fit the economic organization of the community as well as to best realize the Afrikan values of cooperatism and communalism as alternatives to the European values of individual competitiveness, private property, and monopoly capitalism.

Prince George's County

Prince George's County, Maryland, a suburb of Washington, D.C., represents in concrete form both the problem and promise of Black suburban America. This county of 729,268 persons (1990) is 50.7% Afrikan American. Thirty-seven percent of its 126,282 households

(46,724 households) earn an income of $50,000 or more; 39.8 percent of its households earn between $25,000– 49,999; 14.1 percent of its households (17,806 households) earn between $15,000–$24,999; and 9.1 percent of its households earn $14,999 and under. A household refers to a group of people living together in a house or apartment. A special article in the Sunday *New York Times* (6/14/92) titled the "New Black Suburbs" focused on Prince George's County where, "as an increasing number of Black Americans head for the suburban dream, some are bypassing another dream — the dream of an integrated society." These Black Americans are moving to *Black* upper- and middle-class neighborhoods, usually pockets in counties that have a White majority. The growth of many Black suburban areas have paralleled the increasing growth in Afrikan-centered consciousness across all Black social classes. The *Times* further notes that:

> The growing popularity of these neighborhoods over the past decade has coincided with the increasing enrollment at Black colleges and booming interest in African and African-American history, art, music and literature. These trends seem to represent a retreat from the days of the early post-civil-rights era, when status in the Black community was often tied to one's entree into the once-forbidden worlds of White America.

The school system in Prince George's County is now 66 percent Black. It has built magnet school programs featuring specialized classes which have received national recognition. A number of its Black parents are pushing for an Afrocentric approach to the education of their children over the objections of many White parents. Under the leadership of the NAACP the number of Blacks in the police department has increased from 8 percent in 1978 to a current 37 percent. Relative to its economic character, the *Times* notes that:

> Prince George's now has more than 8,000 black-owned businesses. Financing for the smaller businesses — beauty parlors and home-based companies — often comes from a black-owned bank and a black-controlled savings and loan in Washington. Some of the county's larger black-owned companies — high-tech firms and a million-dollar-a-year trash hauling business — have received financing for expansion by established banks in the county.

The earned income statistics of Prince George's Afrikan American population are revealing. For example, its 46,724 households which earn $50,000 or more annually, together earn between $2–4 billion (we must keep in mind that this class includes high earning doctors, lawyers, business persons, high government officials, university professors and the like, many of whom earn many times $50,000 annually). The 50,260 households that earn between $25,000 – 50,000 per annum earn between 1 to 1.5 billion dollars combined. Thus, these two classes which combined comprise 76.2% of the Prince George's Afrikan American household population, earn a total of between $3.5 to 6.5 billion. The earned income across all classes of Afrikan American households in Prince George's County amounts to between $4–7.3 billion. At its largest extreme Prince George's Black population earns (and basically spends) nearly 40 percent of the total receipts earned by Black businesses in the U.S.A. — $19+ billion. One could imagine the contribution Blacks in this county could make to the economic well-being and development of the Washington, D.C. metropolitan area and to Black America in general if they consistently spent a significant fraction of that income with Black businesses and developed more businesses themselves. Perhaps the rising ethnic consciousness in this county will lead to just such results.

The situational possibilities just described become even more striking when we recognize that Prince George's County is the largest of *five* affluent Afrikan American suburbs in the Washington, D.C. metropolitan area. In addition to Prince George's County there are Fairfax (VA), Loudoun (VA), Prince William (VA), and Montgomery (MD) counties. *Table* 22–8[5] lists these counties among twenty affluent Black counties across the country. The total number of Black households across all five counties equals 190,764. Of that number, 74,503 are households which earn $50,000 or more per year. In fact, these households combined earned between $4–7 billion. They amount to 36.94 percent of the total 190,764 households across all five counties. This percentage of affluent households is practically the same as that (37 percent) in Prince George's County alone. Assuming similar percentages across the five counties in regard to the various class income levels (for example, that 39.8 percent of households earn between $25,000 – $50,000), we estimate that some 75,924 households in this category all told earn between $2–4 billion annually. That implies that the top two income classes in the five most affluent Black suburbs surrounding Washington, D.C. earn a combined total of between $6–11 billion per annum. As a whole, i.e., across all classes, we estimate that suburban Blacks in the most affluent counties in the Washington metropolitan area earn a combined income between $6.5 to 12 billion.

One can surmise from these figures the remarkable impact a significant redistribution of Black suburban spending and investment income directed at Black businesses would have on their own and

[5] *American Demographics,* December 1992, p. 39.

their surrounding metropolitan areas. We can see that the amount of income earned (and spent) by Black D.C. suburbs approaches some 60 percent of all the receipts earned by all Black businesses across the country. If the total income earned by Blacks in D.C. suburbs were combined with the total income earned by Blacks in D.C. proper, it would not be difficult to infer that if that grand total were redirected (even only 10 to 25% of the total) toward Black economic development, the economic situation of the Afrikan American community would be visibly and significantly improved.

If we could extrapolate our inferences concerning the Washington, D.C. Black suburbs and inner-cities across Black metropolitan areas across the country, it would become immediately apparent that the transforming effect of redirected urban-suburban spending and investment orientations toward Black business would be phenomenal. *Table* 22-8[6] permits us to calculate that in the twenty most affluent Black counties across the country, that some 148,453 households earn $50,000 or more annually. This implies that these households earn a combined income of between $7·25 – 13·33 billion annually. Across all classes we estimate that Blacks in the 20 most affluent Black countries in the U.S.A. earn between $12·25 and 23 billion per annum. As can be surmised from *Table* 22-4,[7] between 5 to 6 million Blacks reside in 40 suburban areas containing 50,000 or more Black persons across the country. About 20 of these suburbs contain 100,000 or more Black residents — areas whose population densities are as large as middle-size American cities. One cannot but be awed by the thought of what a sense of unity, Afrikan-centered consciousness and identity combined with Afrikan-centered urban-suburban planning and development could do to change the economic and social character of these 40 areas. Not only these 40 areas, but the economic and social character of Black America as a whole as well as that of the Pan-Afrikan world in general.

Class Resources

Number of Black-owned Commercial Banks   36

Trade Associations
National Association Trade Associations of Urban Bankers
1010 Wayne Avenue, Suite 1210

---

6. Ibid., December 1992, p. 39.

7. Ibid., September 1992, p. 32.

Silver Spring, MD 20910-5600

National Bankers Association
1802 "T" Street, N.W.
Washington, D.C. 20009
202/588-5432

Number of Savings and Loan Associations   18

Trade Association
American League of Financial Institutions
1707 New York Avenue, N.W.
Washington, D.C. 20006
202/628-5624

Number of Black-owned Insurance Companies   23

Trade Association
National Insurance Association
P.O. Box 53230
Chicago, Illinois 60653-0203
312/924-3308

Number of Investment Banks   13+

Number of Black-owned Companies (1987)   424,165
Total Receipts $19.8 billion

*Number of Black-owned Auto Dealers   379
 Total Sales of 1993 B.E. 100   3,336.892

Trade Association
National Association of Minority Automobile Dealers
23300 Greenfield Road, Suite 227
Oak Park, Michigan 48237
313/967-1900 or 313/863-3655

Number of Black-owned Cable Companies & TV Stations   29
Number of Black-owned Radio Stations (Where both AM-FM
  are the same station counted as one)   148

Number of Black-formatted Radio Stations (includes above
  Black-owned Radio Stations)   289

548 ✦ Blueprint For Black Power

Number of Black-owned Networks　　　　　　　　　　　　3

Trade Associations
National Association of Black-owned Producers
1730 M Street, N.W. Suite 708
Washington D.C. 20036

Number of Black-owned Newspapers　　　　　　　　　191+

Trade Associations
National Newspaper Publisher Association
948 National Press Building
Washington, D.C. 20045
202/662-7324

Amalgamated Publishers Inc.
45 West 45th Street
New York, New York 10036
212/869-5220

Source: Blackbook　　A national newspaper advertising rep company representing 140 of the country's leading and oldest African American newspapers — reach 5.0 million weekly in 67 markets

Number of National Magazines and Journals　　　　　　45+

Number of National Fraternities and Sororities　　　　　13

Coordinating Agency
(For eight historically Black international fraternities and sororities)
National Pan-Hellenic Council Inc.
Suite 30, IMU
Bloomington, Indiana 47405
812/855-8820

Number of Black National Associations　　　　　　　146+
Number of Black Professional/Political Organizations　　34+
(some overlap with previous associations)

Number of Black Chambers of Commerce　　　　　　　58+

Trade Association
National Black Chambers of Commerce

117 Broadway at Jack London
Waterfront
Oakland, California 94607-3715
510/444-5741
Regional

Number of Purchasing Councils   13

Trade Associations
National Business League
1629 K Street, N.W. Suite 605
Washington, D.C. 20006
202/446-5483

National Minority Business Council Inc.
235 E. 42nd Street
New York, New York 10017
212/573-2385

National Minority Supplier Development Council
15 W. 39th Street, 9th floor
New York, New York 10018
212/944-2430

Number of Predominantly Black Colleges and Universities   92+

Associations
Office for the Advancement of Public
Black Colleges
1 Dupont Circle, Suite 710
Washington, D.C. 20036
202/778-0818

United Negro College Fund, Inc.
500 E. 62nd Street
New York, New York 10021
212/326-1190

Number of Black Churches	65,000+
Number of Black Church Denominations and Organizations	28+
Number of Black Bar Associations	80
Number of Black elected officials (1991)	7,445

Associations

Congressional Black Caucus
H2-344 House Annex #2
Washington, D.C. 20515
202/226-7790

National Black Caucus of Local
Elected Officials
1301 Pennsylvania Avenue, 6th floor
Washington, D.C. 20004
202/626-3120

National Conference of Black Mayors Inc.
1430 West Peachtree Street, N.W. Suite 700
Atlanta, Georgia 30309
404/892-0127

National Black Caucus of State Legislators Inc.
602 Hall of The States Building
444 North Capitol Street, N.W. Suite 206
Washington, D.C. 20001
202/624-5457

World Conference of Mayors Inc.
Tuskegee Office:
101 Fonville Street
Tuskegee, Alabama 36083
205/727-0065
Network composed of Mayors from cities in Africa,
the Near and Far East, the Caribbean and the U.S.A.

Number of Blacks on Major Corporate Boards	70
Number of Major Corporate Boards on which Blacks serve	189
Number of Top black Executives on Wall Street	25
Number of Leading Black Corporate Managers in Major White-owned Corporations	40

Sources[8]

8. *Blackbook* 1992; *Blackbook* 1993, publisher *Dollars and Sense Magazines*, National Publications Sales Agency Inc. National Plaza, 1610 East 79th Street, Chicago, Illinois 60649, (312/375-6800).
Dollars and Sense, November 1992; *Dollars and Sense,* January 1993.
Black Enterprise, "The B.E. 100s" June 1993; "40 Most Powerful Black Executives," February 1993; "25 Hottest Blacks on Wall Street," October 1992; 1130 5th Avenue, New York, New York.
The State of Black America 1993, National Black Urban League, Inc. New York, New York.
The Black Resource Guide, 10th ed. Washington, D.C.: Black Resource Guide, Inc.

The Power of a Black National Vision

We began this section by discussing the importance of physical infrastructure, i.e., roads, rails, rivers, communications, etc., to a nation's economy and power. However, of more importance to the economy and power of a nation are its human capital and resources, its intellectual and social capital, and the character of the consciousness of its people. For the physical infrastructure and other essentials of a powerful economic, social, and political system as well as the overall prosperity and general well-being of a nation are primarily the result of the propitiously dynamic combinations of these human factors. Above all, the forces which co-ordinate and amplify the effects of those factors are the shared identity and consciousness of a people.

Our cursory review has revealed clearly that Afrikan American people have all the physical and human resource makings of a powerful nation-within-a-nation. While compared to the European-American nation-within-a-nation Afrikan American resources may appear relatively meager, we must remind ourselves that these resources are many times larger than many nations — including many White nations — and their potential for growth is enormous.[9] The important thing to keep in mind is that these resources, which on a national and even more so on an international scale are considerable, have been developed by a people who are yet, basically, "unconscious" of their fundamental Afrikan identity and who possess relatively little consciousness of themselves as a positively unique people; as a nation; as a nation with world-class possibilities.

The acorn is not yet the mighty oak; the willowy sapling not yet the towering redwood giant. But they are their beginnings, their absolutely essential fundaments. So too are the fragile ethnic and class resources, the economic and human resources of the Afrikan American community, the foundations of a powerful people. Nurtured in the rich soil of an Afrikan-centered consciousness, Afrikan-centered sense of nation, guided by a high-spirited, creative Afrikan-centered intelligence, the economic seedlings which have just recently taken root can grow rapidly to become one of the mightiest trees in a forest of mighty trees.

Contrary to the disingenuous and dissembling ideology of individualism, the White American nation-within-a-nation has never operated on the basis of the mere unregulated pursuit by unsocialized uncultured individuals, families and clans, states or regions (wiz: the

---

9. If perceived as a nation in terms of income, the Afrikan American community would rank as the ninth or tenth richest nation on earth. How about if perceived as a nation in terms both of earned income and wealth production?

slaveholding South) of their own self-centered interests on the basis of all against all, each pursuing its own interests without regard for the effect their pursuits have on others or on the nation as a community. For the sense of belonging to a social/economic entity greater than themselves and at crucial times acting under the influence of that sense (the sense of nation); the willingness of individuals and groups to subordinate their personal and collective interests to the higher ones represented by the nation — is what has made America great, what has enabled it to provide a broad opportunity structure for both individual and group success.

The Afrikan American community retains its relatively powerless position not only because it is dispossessed of monetary and human resources but also because it is dispossessed of a vision, a perception of itself not imposed on it by those who would exploit and dominate it — namely, White America and other alien groups. As long as the Afrikan American community perceives itself and perceives the world in terms of concepts imposed on it by an exploitative, dominant White America (the same can be said of the worldwide Afrikan community vis-à-vis the worldwide European community) it will remain politically and economically weak, it will suffer unnecessary physical, ecological, social and psychological ills. For Pierre Bourdieu is most assuredly correct when he contends that:

> The categories according to which a group envisages itself, and according to which it represents itself and its specific reality, contribute to the reality of this group.[10]

The Afrikan American community, given its current disposition, is in need of new categories of self representation, of a new representation of the world. If it is to change for the better; to realize its potential; to achieve liberation, then it must change the perception of reality it has received from its exploiters. It must name the unnamed. By changing its self-perception from that of perceiving itself as a sheer conglomeration or aggregation of self-centered individuals — united only by their common misery, victimization, and skin color to that of a nation united by an Afrikan-centered consciousness and identity — the Afrikan American community can change for the better the organization and nature of the social world which now contributes to its unseemly reality.

To its current representation as an aggregation of second-class, dependent persons we counterpose another vision, another project or

---

10. Pierre Bourdieu, *Language and Symbolic Power* (Cambridge: Howard University Press, 1991), p. 133.

program which apprehends the representation of the Afrikan American community as that of a nation-within-a-nation. By representing itself as a nation-within-a-nation the Afrikan American community contributes practically to the reality of becoming such; it contributes practically to making itself a nation-within-a-nation conceivable and credible. This form of self-representation will markedly help in creating the collective consciousness and the collective will which will reflectively contribute to the productive reality of a nation-within-a-nation.

At center of the Afrikan American community's struggle for dignity and power is its struggle for self-definition and self-representation. Indeed, as Bourdieu so presciently noted:

> ...every group is the site of a struggle to impose a legitimate principle of group construction, and every distribution of properties, whether it concerns sex or age, education or wealth, may serve as a basis for specifically political divisions or struggles... Indeed, any attempt to institute a new division must reckon with the resistance of those who, occupying a dominant position in the space thus divided, have an interest in perpetuating a doxic [conventional, accepted, orthodox] relation to the social world which leads to the acceptance of established divisions as natural or to their symbolic denial through the affirmation of a higher unity (national, familial, etc). In other words, dominant individuals favour the consensus, a fundamental agreement concerning the meaning or sense of the social world (thus converted into the doxic, natural world) which is based on agreement concerning the principles of di-vision.
>
> ...*Dominated individuals* make common cause with discourse and consciousness, indeed with science, since they cannot constitute themselves as a separate group, mobilize themselves or mobilize their potential power unless they question the categories of perception of the social order which, being the product of that order, inclined them to recognize that order and thus submit to it.[11]

The Afrikan American community must recognize the economic and political practicality of representing or perceiving itself as a nation. By doing so it comes to realize the formidable economic, political and social resources it already has in its hands as well as the remarkable potential it has yet to develop. For in its misperception of itself and consequently its unconsciousness of its true possibilities, it remains unaware of the lethal damage it does to its own body politic. For example, the Afrikan American community only spends approximately 5 cents out of every dollar it earns with its own businesses and professional establishments. This is attested by the fact that the gross

---
11. Ibid., pp. 130–31.

business receipts of the Black business community amount to $19⁺ billion. This is approximately one-twentieth of the $290–300 billion consumer market that the Afrikan American community represents. It is immediately apparent that if the community increased its spending with Black business establishments by 5¢–10¢ per dollar earned, Black business receipts would increase by approximately $15 billion to total approximately $35 billion; if increased to 15 cents, total receipts would equal $60 billion; 20 cents – $75 billion; 25 cents – $90 billion; 30 cents – $105 billion, and so on (the actual business receipts would in each case actually be significantly larger due to the "multiplier effect" where the increase in income enables the enterprises to make more money through additional investment and thereby to enhance their wealth and holdings). In other words, if the average Afrikan American consumer were to spend 25 cents out of every dollar with Afrikan American firms, those establishments would increase their combined receipts from approximately $20 billion to $75 billion or more. This is equivalent to requesting the Afrikan American who earns some $25,000 per year to spend $6,200.50 out of that amount with Black firms. A perhaps more practical spending of 10 cents per dollar, which would increase Black business receipts to a minimum of $35 billion, would amount to the spending of $2,500.00 out of $25,000.00 or approximately $48.00 per week spent and deposited with Black businesses compared with $433.00 per week spent with non-Black businesses. Thus we see that even modest increases in Black spending with Black businesses could greatly increase the earnings, expansion, number of employees, political power and economic leverage of Black-owned businesses and the Black community in general. A heavier investment by the Afrikan American community in Black business, in general commerce, and international trade could multiply these factors a thousand-fold. However, to achieve these ends requires a more race-conscious consumer orientation of the part of the Afrikan American community. It requires that the community "tax" itself by spending and investing ever-increasing percentages of its gross earnings with Black businesses. These businesses would in turn be enabled to contribute a significant amount of their earned income to increased employment, to community institutions and to the economic and social betterment of the Afrikan American/Pan–Afrikan community in general.

Chapter 23

THE BLACK CHURCH: KEY TO BLACK ECONOMIC EMPOWERMENT?

IN HIS BOOK *THE NEGRO CHURCH IN AMERICA*, E. Franklin Frazier refers to the Black Church as "a nation-within-a-nation." The reference is apt, at least as a potential reality. The *w*holistic concept of the "Black Church" includes the incorporated "mainstream" or "established" denominations of the Christian church as well as a large host of independent, unincorporated, and "storefront" churches.

A number of these denominations are national and international in organization and scope, i.e., they are operationally structured around systems possessing national/international hierarchical administrative and communications structures. Churches are the major *growth industry* in the Afrikan American community. They provide its most influential, best trained, experienced and independent leadership cadre. Both before and after the Civil War the Black Church was the primary social institution which structured and organized life in the Afrikan American community. As indicated by its contemporary role in the Civil Rights Movement, Black political and social life, it remains the major social institution in the Afrikan American community.

While the Black Church has long functioned as the central religious, social and political institution in the Afrikan American community, it has also long functioned as *the* economic institution as well. Frazier noted this when he expressed:

> As DuBois pointed out more than fifty years ago, *'a study of economic co-operation among Negroes must begin with the Church group'*. It was in order to establish their own churches that Negroes began to pool their meagre economic resources and buy buildings and the land on which they stood.[1]

C. Eric Lincoln, distinguished student of Black religion, also writes that "most economic studies of the black community tend to ignore the contributions of their religious background to black economic mobility and development."[2] Along with DuBois and Frazier, Lincoln intimates that survival economics, the economics of upward mobility from poverty, of liberation and independence in the Black community, are inextricably intertwined with the economic ideology and activities of the Black Church. He further contends that the Black Church formalized and legitimated the traditions of mutual aid and self-help which emerged from the attempts of slaves to survive the traumas of enslavement and to humanize their servile conditions.

The early history of economic development in the Black community involves the productive interaction between Black churches, mutual aid societies and fraternal lodges, all of which concerned themselves with the material as well as moral well-being of the community. Regarding the economic thrust of these institutions, Lincoln observes:

> Mutual aid or beneficial societies and churches were among the first social institutions created by black people. They often existed in a symbiotic relationship. Sometimes mutual aid societies led to the formation of black churches, and at other times these societies were organized under the rubric of the churches. Freedmen often played a leading role in establishing both institutions. For example, in April 1794 Richard Allen and Absalom Jones founded one of the earliest mutual aid-benefit societies called the Free African Society. Out of that society in 1794 Allen organized the Mother Bethel A.M.E. Church of Philadelphia. A few weeks earlier Jones had become the pastor of the St. Thomas African Episcopal Church, the first church to be spawned by the Society. These societies themselves were often quasi-churches, attempting to meet both religious and social needs....
>
> Mutual aid-benefit societies spread rapidly in northern urban areas where there were a large number of free blacks. By 1830 in

---

1. E.F. Frazier, *The Negro Church in America* (New York: Schocken Books), p. 34.

2. C. Eric Lincoln, *The Black Church in the African American Experience* (Durham: Duke University Press, 1990).

Philadelphia, for example, there were more than a hundred of these societies with an average membership of seventy-five. In terms of functions and purpose, these societies were the forerunners of both the NAACP and the National Urban League....

Black churches, mutual aid societies, and the fraternal lodges contributed to the formation of the black self-help tradition and to the establishment of an economic ethos of uplift for the race that emphasized the following virtues and moral values: industry, thrift, discipline, sobriety, and long-term sublimation rather than immediate gratification. Of these three institutions, black churches led in spreading this ethic of economic rationality among the newly freed masses during the Reconstruction period, partly because they were the most inclusive community institutions and their membership often included members from both mutual aid societies and lodges. For example, the A.M.E. Church *Review*, the leading African American magazine in the post-Civil War era, published many articles which stressed "the importance of economic and moral development, self-help, and racial solidarity." Before he became a bishop, Benjamin Tucker Tanner, editor of the A.M.E. *Christian Recorder* from 1868 to 1884, urged black people to imitate the economic advancement of Jews in Europe. He also called for collective support for an African American press on a racial basis.

From their pulpits many black preachers preached the moral messages of saving for a rainy day, learning to read and write, getting an education, finding a job and working hard, supporting the family, and raising the children respectably and industriously.

The Black Church, the mutual aid societies and fraternal lodges functioned economically to help "ease somewhat the onerousness of abject deprivation" experienced by many Afrikan Americans in the aftermath of the Civil War, during Reconstruction, and the height of American apartheid during the first three decades of the twentieth century. However, the scope of these institutions was to extend far beyond the provision of emergency aid and subsistence support for their members during difficult times.

Black churches and their allied institutions like the mutual aid societies, the quasi-religious fraternal lodges, and the benevolent and burial associations, which often met in the churches, helped to create the first major black financial institutions: the black-owned banks and the black life insurance companies....

Toward the end of the nineteenth and at the beginning of the twentieth century the first black insurance companies began to appear, developing from the financial resources of both the mutual aid and burial societies and the fraternal orders. In examining the origins of one of the largest black life insurance companies, North Carolina Mutual, Meier and Rudwick see the following pattern: "In the life of John Merrick, the man chiefly responsible for North Carolina Mutual, one of the two largest black life insurance companies, one observes the evolution of Negro insurance from the quasi-religious fraternity society through the chartered mutual-aid organization to the legal reserve company." Merrick founded North Carolina Mutual in 1898, while Alonzo Herndon established the rival Atlanta Life Insurance Company in 1905. The Afro-American Industrial Insurance Society of Jacksonville, founded in 1901, began as a mutual benefit society in the Baptist church pastored by Rev. J. Milton Waldron.[3]

A deeper sense of the role played by Black churches and their pastors in the economic development of the early Afrikan American community may be garnered from the following facts (adapted from C. Eric Lincoln, ibid):

• Prince Hall, a Methodist minister, established the African Masonic Lodge of Boston in 1775.

• The fraternal lodges and churches helped to capitalize black banks like the True Reformer's Bank in Richmond, and the Capital Savings Bank of Washington, D.C., both founded in 1888.

• The True Reformer's Bank, the Galilean Fisherman's Bank, and the St. Luke's Bank were all either founded by ministers or closely connected with the churches.

• The 16th Street Baptist Church in Birmingham, Alabama, has records of the Penny Saver Bank which was established by that church for its members in the late 19th century. The bank's first president was the pastor.

• The first building and loan association in Philadelphia was founded in 1886 and in twenty years there were ten such associations.

• The economic role of Black Churches rapidly expanded under the leadership of Booker T. Washington, who often functioned as an unofficial preacher. The National Negro Business League, founded by Washington, and the first national organization specifically concerned with advancing the business interests of the Black community, mediated the dialogue and economic relations between the Black Church and business communities.

---

3. Ibid.

Today, as we shall document presently, an increasing number of Black churches have revived or are in the process of reviving their involvement with the business and economic development of their communities. As noted by Horace Baldwin, the Black Church is the Black community's cornerstone:

> For over two hundred years the black church has played various roles in the black community including: a temporary refuge from the oppressions of slavery, a needed sanctuary on the "freedom trail", a place of emotional release from racial discrimination, and vehicle of social change....
>
> Education has historically been a major focus of the black church. During the slave era, Sunday schools were often the first vehicles used to introduce Black people to the educational process...
>
> More than half of the historically black four-year colleges were founded by black religious bodies and many can be traced to the black church. For example, Morehouse College..., Spelman College..., Tuskegee Institute [now university]....
>
> * * * *
>
> Historically, the black church has been a major source of black leaders... Black preachers have been the inspiration of many in the black community and were the source of leadership during the civil rights era. Such leaders as the reverends Martin Luther King, Jr., Jesse Jackson, Ralph Abernathy, Joseph Lowery, Fred Shuttleworth, Wyatt T. Walker, Andrew Young, Adam Clayton Powell, Jr., C.T. Vivian, Walter Faunteroy, and Benjamin Hooks led marches, organized demonstrations and were routinely at the forefront of efforts to free black people from the injustices of a racial society.
>
> ...In today's environment, black preachers must also be successful fund raisers and motivators if the black church is to meet the economic challenges of society....
>
> Finally, the black church must become more prudent with their investments of economic resources. The black church manages financial resources which must in turn be invested back into the Black community... By leveraging real estate, establishing credit unions, and other initiatives the black church can be the catalyst of positive changes.[4] [Emphasis added]

The Black Church is central to the economic development of the Afrikan American community for a number of reasons:

- It is the largest socioeconomic institution in the Black community by far.

---

4. *City News* 1992 Special Supplement, "Salute: The Black Church."

- It is the largest repository of Black monetary wealth. Conservatively, the annual income of the institutional Black Church is between $2–3 billion.
- Seventy-eight percent of Afrikan Americans are church affiliated compared to 72 percent nationwide. The church weekly attendance rate was 43 percent in 1986.[5]
- It contains in its national and international congregations the largest pool of professional, semi-professional, working class, and other human resources in the Afrikan American and Pan-Afrikan communities.
- It is the politically most influential institution in the Afrikan American community.
- It is nationally and internationally organized; it is the most independent of Black institutions, being supported mainly by the Black community itself.

Demographics of Black Church Denominations

Selected Major Black Denominations	
Denomination	*Demographics*
African Methodist Episcopal Church	3.5 million members 8,000+ congregations worldwide [2,000 in Afrika]
African Methodist Episcopal Zion Church	1.5 million members 2,500+ churches [missions abroad]
Church Of God In Christ, Inc.	3.7 million members in 38 countries
National Baptist Convention of America Inc.	3.5 million members [mission fields in Caribbean & West Afrika]
National Baptist Convention U.S.A. Inc.	7.0 million+ members
Progressive National Baptist Convention Inc.	1.5 million members 1,600 affiliated churches
Christian Methodist Episcopal Church	863,000 members [churches in the Caribbean and West Afrika]

Table 23–1

---

5. Emerging Trends Vol. 9, No. 5 (May 1987); *State of Black America 1994*, National Urban League; C. Eric Lincoln and H. Mamiya (eds.), *The Black Church in the African American Experience*. Durham: Duke University Press, 1990.

The socioeconomic size of the institutional Black Church may be gauged by a random survey of Black churches in the New York metropolitan area conducted by the National Baptist Convention's New York Entertainment Committee in 1993. The committee discovered that 600 churches in the New York City area deposited $152 million annually in 21 banks. This implies that these 600 churches alone deposit an average of over $3 million in New York City banks every Monday.[6] If this *one* area of *one* denomination generates this amount of deposit weekly or annually, then it is not difficult to approximate the relatively remarkable amount of money generated by the institutional Black Church as a whole.

An example of the pool of professional and business talent available to many Black churches is provided by the 9,500-member First African Methodist Episcopal Church of Los Angeles. Mark Whitlock is executive director of the church's Renaissance Program, which funds community services, business and economic development programs through private and public funding sources. The church's membership base includes some 300 attorneys, 200 certified public accountants and 700 business owners (*Black Enterprise*, 12/93).

A perusal of *Table* 23-1 which comprises a very selected list of the major church denominations in Black America, dramatically outlines the immense scope of the Black Church and the revolutionary potential it possesses for transforming the Afrikan American community and America as a whole. Based on the minimal figures in *Table* 23-1 one could reasonably estimate that the totality of Black church members amounts to approximately 20 million+. The total number of congregations number between 60,000–75,000. According to analyst Emmett D. Carson "90% of all black giving is channeled through the Church." As noted by *Black Enterprise* (12/93) the level of Black giving through the church makes "it the one enduring institution in low-income black communities with the ability to secure major credit." It has been reported that "the Black Baptist church... collects in excess of $14 million per week".[7] This figure suggests that the Black Baptists *alone* collect and raise well over $1 billion per year. Given this amount one could imagine the size of the combined collection and fund-raising revenues of the totality of Black churches

---

[6.] W. Franklyn Richardson, "Mission to Mandate: Self-Development through the Black Church," *The State of Black America 1994*.

[7.] *Daily Challenge*, June 18–20, 1993.

throughout the country. Based on the fact that Black Baptists comprise approximately one-half of Black church membership, we estimate that on the whole the Black Church collects approximately $30 million weekly. This implies that the Black Church as a whole collects between $2–3 billion annually.

The Black Church is famed for its fund-raising capabilities. For example, it is not unusual for a relatively small congregation to raise millions of dollars to build its sanctuary and other institutions. The *New York Times* (6/14/92) provides an example:

> The Ebenezer African Methodist Episcopal Church has revitalized itself by moving its congregation to Prince George's [county, Maryland]. Membership at the 136-year-old church had dwindled to fewer than 100 members. Since the relocation from Washington, [D.C.] in 1983, membership has grown to nearly 7,000 and donations have provided $10 million for the construction of a new church building.

An inferential review of *Box* 23-1 which presents a small sample of primarily New York City Black churches in terms of their funding of some of their economic and social programs, provides a remarkable glimpse at the actual and potential monetary power of the national and international Black Church.

As noted earlier, the Black Church has pioneered the economic development of the Afrikan American community. In our following discussion we shall note how some Black churches, utilizing their own public and private sources, have helped to economically and socially transform their communities. As an illustration of what can be accomplished by the present-day Black congregation, we will quote at length C. Eric Lincoln's citation of the accomplishments of the Zion Baptist Church and its legendary pastor, the Reverend Leon Sullivan.

> since the civil rights period of the late 1960s there has been a very important development among black churches regarding economic issues in the black community, namely, the Opportunities Industrialization Centers under the leadership of Rev. Leon Sullivan of Philadelphia.
>
> The Opportunities Industrialization Centers grew out of the experience of the civil rights struggles in Philadelphia and developed under the leadership of Leon Sullivan, pastor of the Zion Baptist Church. Educated at the Union Theological Seminary in New York and having served under the tutelage of Adam Clayton Powell, Jr., at the Abyssinian Baptist Church, Sullivan organized the Selective

Patronage Campaign in the late 1950s, which was supported by four hundred black ministers in Philadelphia. The campaign successfully boycotted the Tasty Baking Company, Sun Oil, Gulf Oil, Atlantic Richfield, and Pepsi Cola. This success led to requests from potential white employers for black employees with skills in technical fields which many African Americans did not possess at that time. Sullivan then recognized the need for a community-based employment training facility, which was founded in 1964 as the Opportunities Industrialization Centers of America. Another economic development project which helped to prepare the way for OIC was Sullivan's "10-36" plan initiated in 1962 in his church. The plan called for church members to contribute $10 for 36 months to support the Philadelphia Community Investment Cooperative. This group of 227 original subscribers grew to over 5,000 with about 400 black churches participating, and $200 of every $360 subscription was invested in the for-profit Progress Investments Associates while the remaining $160 was donated to Zion Non-Profit Charitable Trust. The Progress Investments Associates built Progress Plaza Shopping Center, the first and largest black-owned and operated shopping complex in the United States. It also constructed an apartment building, a garment manufacturing plant and a chain of convenience stores. Zion Non-Profit Charitable Trust used foundation and government grants to sponsor programs like housing for the disadvantaged, remedial education, and other human services activities. Through these projects Sullivan was resurrecting the historical role of black clergy and churches being involved in the stimulation of economic development.

Following its organization in 1964, the Opportunities Industrialization Centers of America quickly became a nationwide phenomenon, operating in seventy cities within five years and handling federal government contracts worth $18 million. President Johnson's War on Poverty programs and Sullivan's old mentor, Rep. Adam Clayton Powell, Jr., aided in the development of an OIC-federal connection....

By emphasizing a community based vocational training and job placement operation, the OIC experience has been a relatively successful one. At its height in 1980 OIC was operating in more than 160 cities and close to 700,000 people had been trained and placed in jobs.

More contemporary examples of the involvement of Black churches with economic development in the Afrikan American community follow.

Box 23-1   The Black Church and Economic Development

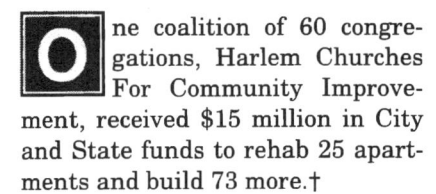

One coalition of 60 congregations, Harlem Churches For Community Improvement, received $15 million in City and State funds to rehab 25 apartments and build 73 more.†

Thessalonia Baptist, in the South Bronx, is constructing a $2 million community and youth center without asking anyone outside the church for a nickel.†

Concord Baptist [Church] reported a $1.7 million collection-plate income [in 1991] and Bethany Baptist [Church] in Bedford-Stuyvesant said its plate yielded $2 million.†

Berean Missionary Baptist [Church] in Crown Heights [Brooklyn]... has built 255 single-family apartments and with a $6 million federal grant, plans to build 77 more for seniors.†

The East Brooklyn Congregations [a coalition led by the Rev. Johnny Ray Youngblood of St. Paul Community Baptist in East New York, Brooklyn] has built 2,230 homes under the Nehemiah [housing program]. [Rev. Youngblood and his congregation has] gotten a go-ahead to build an alternative high school for 500 students.†[8]

The Allen African .Methodist Episcopal Church, pastored by the Rev. Floyd Flake, also a Democratic member of Congress, employs 742 workers and houses eight subsidiary corporations. Its annual budget is more than $17 million. In 1983, the Allen Christian School was constructed at a cost of $3.8 million. This active congregation of more than 6,000 persons has worked with city agencies to rehabilitate local stores and homes, and to build a 300-unit senior citizens complex at a cost of $11 million. Among the most outstanding enterprises of Allen's "empire" is the Charter Bus Company.

Moreover, Allen has started its own construction and rehabilitation company to repair homes. It has also expanded into the construction of new housing and into commercial real estate. Additionally, Allen has purchased a block on a commercial strip containing 10 stores in Jamaica, Queens, where its companies renovated the stores and leased them to businesses. The Allen Christian School serves 480 students, from kindergarten to eighth grade. The Allen Home Care Agency provides meals and home care services to more than 225 elderly and handicapped individuals daily. It also manages the South Jamaica Multi-Service Center which provides clinical services and nutritional programs to the community.[9] In December 1993, *Black Enterprise* magazine reported that the initial financing of these projects "began with the money from the collection plate." The magazine went on to point out that

---

8. † "Black Churches: Faith and Hope in Hard Times," *Daily News* (three-part series: 4/19, 4/20 and 4/21/93.

9. 1991 Educational Calendar, Carver Federal Savings, NYC.

...as its holdings grew, Allen Church was able to secure several hefty loans to keep up the momentum for these projects. Today, Allen Church continues to set aside one-third of the $3 million it collects annually from its 6,500 members for development projects. The church is currently negotiating to buy a Burger King and a Ben & Jerry's ice cream franchise. Also in the works is a $9-million new home for the church itself. "If our churches ever learn the power they have we can turn the urban communities of America around and have control of them," says Flake, who is also a U.S. congressman.

The Abyssinian Baptist Church, formerly pastored by Adam Clayton Powell, Jr., and currently pastored by the Rev. Calvin Butts, through its Abyssinian Development Corporation worked with Aadyus Corporation, a minority developer and contractor to renovate six abandoned buildings into a 38-unit condominium complex of two and three-bedroom apartments for about 18 new homeowners in Central Harlem.[10]

Concord Baptist Church, Brooklyn, N.Y., is over 145 years old and has a congregation of 10,000. While running many social service programs such as a senior housing program and center, a nursing home, an elementary school, full-service family center and its own charity, Concord Christ Fund, endowed with $1 million raised by the congregation, it has developed a credit union with over $2.1 million in deposits.[11]

REBUILDING BLIGHTED AREAS IN NEW YORK*

[I]n the Bedford-Stuyvesant section of Brooklyn, Bridge Street African Methodist Episcopal Church is transforming one of the most blighted areas in the city. The church owns and operates the Bridge Street Preparatory School, a credit union, apartment buildings and a soon-to-be-built 86-unit, $7.2-million senior citizens housing complex.

Bridge Street has also joined forces with 10 other local churches to revitalize the 40-block area surrounding the church. The massive project is spearheaded by the Consortium for Community Development, a nonprofit corporation. With financial assistance from several city, state and federal housing agencies, hundreds of vacant apartments and storefronts have been purchased and are currently being renovated. Several multimillion-dollar grants are enabling Bridge Street to renovate 40 housing units and erect 22 duplexes with the Enterprise Foundation and the New York Housing Partnership. Of the more than $1.3 million in tithes and offerings the church collected last year, over $600,000 was spent on renovation and construction projects.

---

10. "Abyssinian Housing Project Ready for Tenancy," *Amsterdam News*, 7/3/93.
11. *Daily News*, 4/19/92.

L.A. CHURCH PROVIDES LIFELINE*

Shortly after the 1992 riots in Los Angeles, the mammoth 9,500-member First African Methodist Episcopal (FAME) Church of Los Angeles swung into action. As an economic lifeline for the devastated community, the church created the FAME Renaissance Program to fund community services, business and economic development programs through private and public funding sources. FAME Corp. is a nonprofit organization established by the church.

Shortly after the Renaissance Program was formed, church officials competed for and received a $1-million grant from the Walt Disney Co., leading to the creation of the Micro Loan Program, which supplies low-interest rate loans of $2,000 to $20,000 to minority entrepreneurs in the area. So far, the program has approved about 34 loans totaling more than $500,000. Among the beneficiaries are day-care centers, transportation companies, restaurants, a medical billings business, cosmetics companies and a manufacturing firm. "We deal with people who won't qualify for a bank loan," explains Mark Whitlock, executive director of the Renaissance Program. "We don't mind if you have a couple of bad nicks on your credit. We don't mind if you're a brand new business that has never received a business loan before."

But FAME does mind delinquent repayment. It requires applicants to present their business plans to a panel of experienced entrepreneurs and bankers. Loan recipients whose businesses have been in operation less than two years must also go through the church's 10-week entrepreneurial training program.

Once completed, the church's moral and technical support network kicks in. "Our membership base has some 300 attorneys, 200 CPAs and 700 business owners," explains FAME's Whitlock. "For every loan we make the recipient also gets a mentor to help support that business." Finally, there's that crucial bottomline edge: "We suggest to the congregation that they do business with the company owner we just made a loan to."

The Micro Loan Program recently received a $500,000 grant from Atlantic Richfield Corp. Ultimately, the church hopes to raise $10 million from corporations to fund as many as one thousand businesses.

ATLANTA CHURCH SPREADS THE WEALTH*

While a number of African-American churches have just begun to launch the economic redevelopment projects for their communities, Atlanta's Wheat Street Baptist Church began changing the face of its historically black neighborhood in the early '60s. Today, it boasts more than $33 million in real estate holdings, making it one of the wealthiest African-American churches in the nation.

The church's nonprofit corporation, the Wheat Street Charitable Foundation, owns and manages two housing developments, several single-family dwellings and an office building. The foundation also owns Wheat Street Plaza North and South, two shopping centers located in the heart of the Martin Luther King, Jr. historic district. They were built in 1969 on land purchased with church monies and bank loans, and are currently getting a $120,000 face-lift thanks to an interest-free loan from the City of Atlanta.

RURAL CHURCHES BUILD BUSINESSES*

Not all African-American churches involved in economic redevelopment are located in major cities. A growing number of rural churches are launching businesses providing job opportunities for their members, many of whom are poor people with few skills.

When the nondenominational Mendenhall Bible Church was formed in the early 1970s in Mendenhall, Miss., church leaders knew that if they didn't provide jobs for their members, nobody would. So, they created Mendenhall Ministries, a nonprofit corporation, and built a business complex that today includes a health clinic, law office, elementary school, thrift store and recreation center. The projects were funded by private and public grants and a few bank loans.

In building its school, Genesis I, Mendenhall Ministries bought a long-abandoned school building for $20,000 — it took church members one week to solicit this money from residents and corporations. But the building was in such poor condition they soon realized that renovation would easily run into tens of thousands of dollars. That's when the church network stepped in.

"A church group from Aurora, Ill., brought 162 people down here to completely remodel and refurbish the building," recalls Rev. Dolphus Weary, associate pastor and president of Mendenhall Ministries. "They also brought about $75,000 worth of materials to do the job." Flooding the community with skilled and unskilled volunteers, the Aurora group spent one week reinforcing the two-story building's foundation, making it possible for the rest of the Mendenhall community to finish the restoration in about four months.

Mendenhall Bible Church, with only 125 members, is now trying to lure a manufacturing plant to the community to provide even more jobs for its people. It stands as proof that a church doesn't have to be large or rich to bring about tangible, positive change.[12]

---

12. * "The New Agenda of the Black Church: Economic Development for Black America" *Black Enterprise*, December 1993.

Serving the Needy

The city signs hundreds of contracts every year with black churches that provide social and human services. Here is a random sample:

- The Richard Allen Center on life, sponsored by St. Luke's AME, in Harlem: $15.65 million for foster care.
- DeWitt Reformed Church, lower East Side: $975,839 for Head Start.
- Church on the Hill Family Day Care Center, sponsored by church on the Hill AME Zion Church, Harlem: $1.25 million for day care.
- Sharon Baptist Church, Morrisania, the Bronx: $587,658 for Head Start.
- Allen AME Church, Jamaica, Queens; $133,845 to transport senior citizens.
- Allen AME Church; $246,271 for seniors meals.
- Allen Home Care Agency, Allen AME: $1.37 million for home-care services.
- Cornerstone Baptist Church, Bedford-Stuyvesant, Brooklyn: $861,114 for day care.
- Bridge Street, AME Church Bedford-Stuyvesant; Brooklyn; $87,216 meals for seniors.
- Concord Baptist Church, Bedford-Stuyvesant; $1.52 million for home care of seniors.
- Concord Family Services, Concord Baptist; $1.27 million, foster care and senior programs.
- Abyssinian Development Corp., sponsored by Abyssinian Baptist, Harlem; $619,924 for Head Start.
- North Presbyterian Church, Washington Heights, Manhattan; $534,662 for Head Start.
- Glorious Trinity Baptist Church, Crown Heights, Brooklyn; $75,197 for youth activities.
- Discipline Outreach Ministries Inc., sponsored by the Discipline Chapel, in Sunset Park, Brooklyn; $387,000 for youth programs.
- God's Deliverance Temple, Jamaica; $8,500 for youth programs.
- Canaan Baptist Church of Christ, Harlem; $44,205 for senior and youth programs.
- Miracle Makers Inc., sponsored by the Free Will Church of God in Christ, Bedford-Stuyvesant; $674,569 for day care.

The City of New York enters into hundreds of contracts with Black churches yearly. A sample of 23 Black churches and church alliances handed over $61,000,000 of government grants in 1990-91.*

The tax rolls list 5,268 houses of worship in the City of New York, with Brooklyn [a predominantly black area], "The Borough of Churches," leading with 2,206. This does not include hundreds of unincorporated storefronts.*

The effort [to become involved in economic development] at Greater Christ Temple Church in Meridian, Miss., dates back to 1977, when Bishop Luke Edwards gathered his 200-member congregation to discuss salvaging his parishioners pride and their decaying community.

The bishop's task was formidable. Back then, 96% of the Greater Christ Temple Church congregation was on welfare. "I showed the congregation that they have the buying power to deliver themselves, if they spend their money right."

Bishop Edwards combined church members' food stamps and purchased food items from a wholesale grocer. The church then began running a grocery store out of its auditorium. After *four* months, the members had earned enough to purchase a supermarket.

Today, the church owns a 4,000-acre farm, seven tractors, hundreds of cattle, two meat processing plants, a bakery, three restaurants, and an auto repair shop. It has expanded its ministry to Alabama. And none of its members are on welfare because they have been given jobs by the church.

Greater Christ Temple uses the profits from its businesses to invest in other ventures. It owns several dormitories, where most church members live. Young people who have problems at home or have been in trouble with the law also live there. The church operates office buildings, a computer room, a nursery, a cafeteria, a clinic, a library, a machine shop and a school. In short, it has created its own community.

Wall Street Journal, 1/1/93 — "More Black Churches Go Into Business."

Most members of Hartford Memorial Baptist Church on Detroit's northwest side aren't on welfare. In fact, many are doctors, lawyers, accountants and teachers. Hartford's pastor, the Rev. Charles Adams, was confronted by a challenge different from the one that faced Bishop Edwards. A decade ago, his sprawling church was surrounded by bottle-strewn dirt lots, abandoned buildings, drug houses and plots of wildly growing grass.

The 7,200 members of Hartford Memorial are largely responsible for that change. The church opened a social service center in 1977, and it provides food, clothing, medical help and emotional counseling to the underprivileged. It also started a school to train former criminals and drug addicts to be auto mechanics.

Next, Mr. Adams raised $1 million from his congregation to buy lots that he describes as "sitting foul and unused." The church leased them to Kentucky Fried Chicken and McDonald's restaurants, which quickly built large franchises and hired workers from the community.

Once those businesses opened, other companies began investing in the area. The neighborhood is now home to among other businesses, a Pizza hut, Bally's Hamburger restaurant, record shop and numerous convenience stores. Hartford also owns several small auto repair shops in the neighborhood. "The church awakened the financial community to the value of the property," says Mr. Adams.

Hartford Memorial works with a coalition of area hospitals and colleges to invest further in the community. With their help, it plans to open a "car care mall."

The Black Church's Potential for Transforming the Black Nation

Allen A.M.E. Church of Queens, N.Y., Greater Christ Church of Meridian, Miss., and Hartford Memorial Baptist Church of Detroit, Michigan, are three outstanding examples among a number of others that demonstrate what committed congregations can do for the economic uplift and viability of their communities. If we expanded these types of churches to include anywhere from one-quarter to three-quarters of the Black Church congregational population, it is easy and realistic to imagine how Black America could become socially and economically transformed as well as politically powerful.

This wished-for transformation could begin almost immediately if the Black congregations of America would in concert, *transfer* their full bank accounts or sizable portions thereof from White financial institutions to Black ones. This would make hundreds of millions of dollars available for better caring for and economically empowering the Black community. The judicious and creative use of funds provided by the institutional Black church along with other Black institutions (e.g., colleges) and organizations, corporations and businesses, as well as personal and family accounts, placed in Black owned, controlled or influenced financial institutions could provide billions of dollars for the takeover by the Black community of its own wholesale and retail markets. These funds could provide the base for the founding of new businesses, financial institutions, takeovers of small and large corporations in the general American corporate system, and provide the base for penetrating the general American economy and thereby provide greater economic opportunities for members of the community as a whole. More important, vis-à-vis their moral missions, the generation and very extensive control of Black-generated capital by Black institutions such as the Black Church and its use to improve the economic and social well-being of the community would do much to markedly reduce the economic and social causes of antisocial, immoral and criminal behavior which overwhelm the community today. Black families could be stabilized, the Black population better educated, housed and fed; the quality of life generally improved; the community held in higher regard by other communities, and more importantly, by itself.

While these things may be accomplished by individual congregations and small associations of churches acting within their immediate communities and larger areas within their metropoles, imagine how much more could be accomplished under the aegis of metropolitan-wide associations, regional, national and international associations. The Black Church "as nation" could construct a nationwide economic wholesale-retail network which could in turn form a distribution and market network which would then become the foundation of a Black owned and controlled manufacturing and import-export system. Moreover, because of their already extant national organizations, Black churches can provide the national administrative network necessary for coordinating the economic/political activities and development of the national Black economic community. For example, if Black churches working under the direction of a national coordinating council could more or less simultaneously support the entering into business of individuals, groups and organizations; support pre-existing businesses; open new businesses and urban-suburban shopping malls; aid in the purchase and support of franchises; influence White-owned franchises and businesses to open their shelves to the retailing of Black-manufactured products and open themselves to be consulted and served by

Black-owned service organizations; invest in White-owned financial and corporate institutions (sufficient to achieve positions of influence on their boards and executive staffs), the Afrikan American community would become a force to be reckoned with in America and the world.

The basis for a national council of Black churches may already exist in the Congress of the National Black Churches, Inc. (CNBC). As reported in *The State of Black America 1994*, published by the Urban League, "There are 65,000 churches connected with the Congress of National Black Churches alone. The Congress is composed of eight historically black denominations representing 250,000 church employees and in excess of 19 million worshipers."

How can such an ambitious plan be financed? We have already given some important suggestions and examples. We have already suggested the selective depositing of church monies and funds in Black financial institutions and White financial institutions whose policies can be practically and usefully influenced in favor of the Afrikan American community's achievement of certain politico-economic goals. A similar strategy can be undertaken relative to church-based investment policies. The Black Church not only has a large under- or mis-utilized cache of monetary resources or liquid assets in the absolute sense, i.e., in terms of hundreds of millions of dollars in White-owned institutions which "redline," or refuse to lend money and other kinds of aid to the community, but also has a large amount of under-utilized leverage relative to its assets, i.e., credit, or borrowing power based on its combined accounts.

Imaginative methods for funding and strengthening Black financial institutions and their ability to finance the economic development of the community can be executed once individual churches and church organizations commit themselves to these ends. An example of a mutually profitable relationship between a Black church and Black-owned financial institution is provided by the following report in the *City News* of Newark, New Jersey ("Salute to the Black Church," 1992):

> City National Bank of New Jersey, as New Jersey's only African American owned and managed commercial bank, understands the importance of the church to the African American community. City National has been a supporter of, and has been supported by, the Black churches. The churches have supported City National by maintaining significant account relationships. City National's support has come in the form of loans to finance church construction and expansion, banking services to the churches and their members, and

an annual breakfast where area members may inform the bank of the financial needs of their respective churches and congregations.

City National Bank of Newark, New Jersey, ranks 20th on the *Black Enterprise* magazine's 25 largest Black-owned banks list of June 1993, up from 21st place in 1992. Under chief executive Louis Prezeau and a staff of 35, the bank oversaw assets of $62 million and deposits of $58 million in 1992. It loaned $19 million that year. While this is very significant for a bank founded in 1973, its growth would be astounding if Black churches, organizations and individuals would increase their financial commitments to this important institution. Another illustrative example of Black church, Black bank and White bank relations which favor community development follows:

> Newark, [N.J.] St. James African Methodist Episcopal Church's call for financial support to build a prep school was heard March 26 by two of the state's landmark banks. First Fidelity Bank, the state's largest financial institution, presented the church with $67,500 that it will in turn invest in the stock of the state's only minority owned one, City National Bank.
> The church's St. James Preparatory School project, slated to break ground in the spring of 1993, will financially benefit from this arrangement as stock from City National Bank yields dividends. The school project will be the recipient of those dividends. City National Bank benefits from First Fidelity's indirect major capital infusion and still maintains its minority owned status.

Presumably, City National Bank will help the church to finance the school through a loan or other means. This implies that churches can enter into any number of creative and innovative relations with both Black and "mainstream" financial institutions in ways beneficial to the community as a whole. Churches and church associations with sizable accounts and deposits in mainstream banks can use their leverage in these institutions to influence them to enter into various supportive and enriching relations with Black-owned financial institutions.

Churches and church associations through their pledges and financial commitments may aid in the founding and development of new banks, financial instruments and arrangements which can help to revitalize the community. Any number of other approaches can be developed which can have a more visible, palpable, and immediate impact on transforming the ecology, opportunity structure, social welfare and behavior, and consciousness of the community. They may include the following approaches.

Endowment and Investment Programs. Despite their relatively large collections and famous ability to raise money for various causes to which they may commit themselves, Black churches as a whole possess very little in the way of invested wealth. Other than offertory collections, pledges, fund-raising drives such as dinners, sales, fashion shows, musicals, the churches have few other significant sources of income with which to sponsor their programs and missions. In a survey of sources of church income, Lincoln (ibid) found that only 2.2 percent of Black churches had endowment income and only about 15.6 percent had financial holdings such as portfolio investments, commercial businesses, income-producing property, or service enterprises. The investments of most churches were in money market certificates or high interest bank accounts. According to Lincoln, "only a handful of them have developed a stock portfolio."

An *endowment* refers to money or other property used for the permanent upkeep or benefit of an institution or organization. Institutional endowments are generally used for making and managing investments in various assets such as stocks, bonds, real estate, venture capital, leveraged buy-outs, mineral and other natural resources. The earnings from such investments are used to help finance and maintain the institution and its missions or interests. For example, Princeton University's endowment fund of $3.5 billion is managed by the Princeton University Investment Company. The Harvard Management Company is responsible for managing Harvard's $6 billion endowment. Institutions generally choose seasoned and highly regarded investment professionals and firms to help manage their assets. This is usually done under the supervision of the board of trustees or an advisory committee which may include some members of the board and investment consultants. Returns on institutional investment can be quite impressive. According to the *Wall Street Journal* (June 1994) Harvard's returns from its alternative asset investments (i.e., investments in relatively high-risk ventures such as real estate, and oil and gas) was 20%, "contributing strongly to the school's overall return of 16.9%."

Power of the Bond Market. Many wealthy individuals and non-profit institutions are substantially invested in the bond market (see below for definitions of this market). This group of investors — not including foreign institutions, pension funds, insurance companies, mutual funds, commercial banks and other institutions such as savings banks, credit unions, brokerage and investment firms — owns 13% or $1,355.3 billion (i.e., one trillion, three hundred and fifty-five billion[+])

of the $10.29 trillion United States long-term debt [debt held longer than a year] (NYT, 6/12/94). The influence of these and the other bondholding investors in the Bond Market on the U.S. economy is remarkable. As a matter of fact, the *New York Times* (6/12/94) reports that the bond market is "the pre-eminent force in the economy today. More than any other group, the bond market's members determine how many Americans will have jobs, whether the job holders will earn enough to afford a house or a car, or whether a factory might have to lay-off workers." The *Times* goes on to contend that "the American economy is governed by the bond market — a loose confederation of wealthy Americans, bankers, financiers, money managers, rich foreigners, executives of life insurance companies, presidents of universities and non-profit foundations, pensioners and people who once kept their money in passbook savings accounts (or under the bed) and now buy shares in mutual funds." The *Times* accuses the bond market, i.e., its members, of favoring and helping to bring about the current weak American economy.

Be that as it may, it should be apparent from the foregoing discussion that Black America has the potential for playing a much more powerful role in the American economy and political system through institutional investments in America's capital markets. The institutional Black Church through increasing its endowments and prudent asset management may provide one of the major means by which these ends are accomplished. The endowing of Black universities, the strengthening and growth of Black-owned insurance companies, banks, mutual funds and other financial institutions and management firms, may contribute heavily to these efforts.

Black churches and non-profit institutions may move forward in these areas by encouraging their members and supporters to found and contribute to endowment funds under their auspices. Some church members may choose to purchase endowment insurance, i.e., a policy providing for the payment to the church of an agreed sum of money at the end of an agreed time period, or upon at the death of the member. C. Eric Lincoln (ibid) notes that "taking into account the value of their property and holdings [as well as the potential for vastly increasing the value of such property and holdings through judicious acquisitions and asset management], the amount of charitable donations given, and the value of volunteer labor, the total institutional area of religion in the black community represents untold billions of dollars." However, if the institutional Black Church is to realize its and the Black community's economic potential, if it is to maximize its ability to realize its spiritual mission and to meet the material needs of the community which so desperately depends on its leadership and stewardship, it must remedy what Lincoln refers to as "one of the major weaknesses of the historic Black denominations... [the lack of the training and teaching of their denominational leaders, pastors, and laity about all aspects of economic stewardship, from careful record keeping, financial accountability, and investments to the economic development of their communities." Training and consciousness-raising in these areas must take place in the schools as well as in the local churches and community educational institutions. Financial consultants can be of invaluable service in this regard. While investment decisions and activities may take place at the congregational level there is no reason they may not occur at associational, regional, and denominational levels. They may occur at the national and international/interdenominational level as well. A vehicle of the latter type may involve an organization such as the Congress of National Black Churches. This congress, made up primarily of representatives from each of the seven historic Black denominations, held its first organizing meeting in 1978. Two of its stated objectives include undertaking social and economic institution-building in the Afrikan American community. We agree with Lincoln when he contends that aside from its central spiritual mission, "The final and most crucial challenge facing the Black church is to decide what kind of economic system would best serve the needs of everyone, with justice, equity, and fairness in the twenty-first century."

Community Development Credit Union. Many Black churches have credit unions for the benefit of their individual members. As noted above, some of their unions may well exceed $2 million. In the interest of community development, church associations or coalitions may combine their unions to found and develop a community development credit union, a member-owned and controlled nonprofit financial institution which can provide credit and financial services directly to individuals, home buyers and improvers, workers, and small business people. Churches may also join other organizations and institutions in establishing metropolitan, and regional *development banks* — organizations designed to help finance the economic and social development of Afrikan American communities in their areas. These institutions can directly transfer resources to fund projects and programs; provide technical assistance and institutional support; to mobilize external resources for investment purposes; support and administer Afrikan American economic integration through providing assistance, consultive management development and training; project co-ordination and financing.

Rotating Credit Associations. As defined by Ardener,[13] a rotating credit association is "an association formed upon a core of participants who agree to make regular contributions to a fund which is given, in whole or in part, to each contributor in rotation." In other words, as indicated by Light and Bonacich (1991), "A rotating credit association consists of a group who pool their funds on a regular basis then passes the pool around the group until all members have received it." We will later detail the operation of these associations. We have already alluded to them in our discussion of how Koreans finance their businesses chapter 14. The pooling of monetary resources between churches and other organizations as members of institutional rotating credit associations, would allow them to lend each other large sums of money on a regular basis which can be used to fund their individual economic and social projects and other commitments.

Business Establishments. Allen A.M.E. Church, Greater Christ Church and Hartford Memorial Baptist, all whose works were cited previously, provide excellent examples of how individual churches and the institutional church can transform for the better the economic circumstances of the Afrikan American community by directly founding business establishments. It takes but little imagination to recognize the economic impact, should we say "miracle(?)", which would be afforded if a good fraction of the 60,000 - 75,000 Black Church congregations across the United States founded, supported, and financed businesses of all types and sizes. This would especially be the case if the churches in the form of metropolitan and regional associations founded mini-malls, markets, malls, refurbished and revitalized deteriorated shopping streets, and placed small shops and other businesses in locations throughout the cities and region including downtowns and regular mainstream shopping malls.

Through national organizations and linkups, chains of stores and franchises could be established. In certain locales both large department and discount department stores could be established and administered by professional, impartial managements. Department stores, whether of the upscale or super discount (e.g., 99¢ stores) variety, could be established by a consortium or association of churches wherein each member church or combination thereof, would sponsor or fund a special department or departments. However, under such arrangements it is of key importance that store design, hiring practices, management, and the like be the responsibility of a

---

13. Shirley Ardener, "The Comparative Study of Rotating Credit Associations," *Journal of the Royal Anthropological Institute 94*, pt. 2 (1964): 201-29).

professional management team with the churches acting as investors and having seats on the board of directors. An alternate plan would be one where a duly constituted body of business persons, such as a corporation, may approach area churches to invest in a proposed business establishment or where the churches found their own for-profit corporation to run their businesses.

Church-sponsored National Chain Stores

While it may be tempting to invest in highly visible, "showy" projects, projects which are large, costly and risky, in order to maximize political, social and psychological influence, the small, manageable shop multiplied many-fold may be of more lasting and practical value, particularly in the beginning. Small specialty shops, well-appointed and well-managed can generate much goodwill and great earnings without the risks involved in exceedingly large undertakings, whose possible collapse or failure would backfire by impairing the business self-confidence and self-esteem of the community at large.

A prime example of the earnings possibilities and social/political impact a series or chain of small shops can have is provided by the Body Shop cosmetics chain owned primarily by Anita Roddick of England. The *New York Times* (5/27/93) reports that:

> ...in 17 years, she...turned a little cosmetics store in England into the Body Shop, a worldwide chain with about 900 stores, nearly $266 million in sales and $34 million in profit for the fiscal year that ended Feb. 28, making her one of the richest woman in England.

These specialty shops are not necessarily large or spacious, even though the space is well-designed, decorated, and efficient. The ingredients which constitute the sales products are mostly gathered and made from natural sources around the world. It is especially relevant that, as reported by the *Times*, "The stores are encouraged to participate in company-backed political programs, like a recent one in the United States to register voters." Furthermore, the *Times* reports that "There is no product advertising, nor do the stores have images of perfect women that might make the customer feel inadequate and driven to seek perfection through cosmetics." Anita Roddick has opened 130 stores in the United States — her fastest growing market — in five years, with 50 more planned for in 1993. She accepts offers to speak before progressive political and social organizations. She demonstrates a special sensitivity to minority-group interests and concerns as illustrated by the following example.

When she talks about the indigenous people in the United States, she doesn't mean the mall heads who linger in her stores, dipping fingers in the Body Shop's pots of strawberry lip gloss,...

By indigenous people, she means the Indians in New Mexico who are growing blue corn for the company. She means the Black residents of Harlem, where she recently opened a store, and she says she plans to return some profits to the community, a move that brought her company an award last week from the National Association for the Advancement of Colored People.

The Body Shop not only demonstrates the large monetary dividends which can be derived from the establishment of a chain of well-run, relatively small specialty shops. It demonstrates also that such a chain can dare be socially and politically responsible and community orientated. Moreover, it demonstrates through its exclusive use of products that do not use animals to test products; its purchase of raw materials from indigenous producers; its return of portions of profits to communities which support it; and its engagement in positive social causes and movements, that business practices can be utilized to further ethical, moral and pro-social ends. Herein lies its value as an example to church-owned or -supported businesses. Business development can be utilized for moral and social development, not only by reducing crime and other anti-social behavior through increased employment and business opportunities or through ameliorative ecological/psychological changes — but also as a means of propagating and demonstrating ethical, moral, and positive social concerns and principles.

The Effectiveness of Cause-oriented Campaigns. One may wonder if cause-oriented businesses and advertising campaigns such as the one we have just described with regard to Body Shop International and we are recommending for Black Church-based or privately owned businesses are effective tools for promoting sales and causes. A church-based or private business may overtly communicate to its customers that portions of its profits are used to support certain charitable and political organizations; for combating homelessness, crime, hunger, child abuse; for supporting educational institutions and programs; for dealing with teenage pregnancy; for providing youths with practical training in entrepreneurship or with jobs, and the like. Black consumers may be given pamphlets in their shopping bags informing them in colorful and illustrated terms of how their purchases of products manufactured, distributed, wholesaled and retailed by Black-owned companies help to create jobs and increase employment of Black adolescents and adults. The customer may thereby be prompted to see his or her purchase of items for personal consumption as, in part, a charitable and prosocial activity. These approaches are known as cause-related marketing or point-of-purchase politics. As intimated above, the institutional or individual Black church corporation may finance and further its social and religious missions by these means. This is also true for socially concerned private businesses. Cause-related marketing can provide a powerful means by which Black-owned business establishments may capture the attention and loyal support of Black and other ethnic consumers from their non-Black competitors. Cause-oriented marketing, if tied to competitive prices and good service, carries the very positive possibility of making the consumer feel good about making certain purchases, and more importantly, good about themselves and the retailer.

While the reader may readily concede the points we have just made, he or she, especially if he or she is a business person, may wonder or question if such a marketing technique is effective or really works — i.e., are consumers really moved by such appeals? It appears that the answer is yes, if the landmark study by the Roper Starch Worldwide market research company proves correct. As reported in the *New York Times* (12/6/93 – "The Media Business"), Roper conducted a national survey of 1,981 people for Cone Communications, a marketing and public relations agency based in Boston, in order to measure public attitudes in regard to cause-oriented marketing approaches. The results of the survey indicated that:

- [W]hile past experience, price and quality of products and services remained the far more important reasons consumers purchased items, the relative strength of corporate social responsibility was a surprisingly strong factor they considered when buying brands. "It's now in the second tier of important purchase influences" ... [according to Carol L. Cone, CEO of Cone Communications].

- If price and quality were equal, 66 percent of the people surveyed indicated that they were somewhat or very likely to switch brands "based on a good cause," while 62 percent said they were somewhat or very likely to switch retail stores.

- Seventy-one percent of those surveyed agreed somewhat or strongly that point-of-purchase politics "is a good way to help solve social problems," and 64 percent agreed somewhat or strongly that "it should be a standard part of a company's activities."

- Twenty percent said they bought something in the last year "because it was associated with a cause or issue." That figure doubled among social influentials — trend-setting socially active consumers.

In addition to Body Shop International, cause-oriented marketing is used by Ben & Jerry's Homemade and Members Only. Avon Products, sponsors of a program called the Breast Cancer Awareness Crusade, and Ryka Inc., a footwear company which has developed a foundation to combat violence against women, both utilize the services of Cone Communications which specializes in cause-related campaigns for its clients. Edward B. Keller, an executive vice president at Roper Starch, the New York City company which performed the survey for Cone Communications, suggested that the survey explored aspects of what he called "standing for something your customers stand for, to let them feel buying your product is an expression of their commitment,..."

The establishment of church-funded or -supported businesses, unlike many privately owned businesses, may be consciously instituted primarily to maximize service instead of profits, to provide economic opportunity, employment, and in particular, to provide training arenas to prepare Afrikan American youth with practical business and social skills and experience to aid in their character development, their diversion from antisocial involvements, etc., which would not otherwise exist. The perception of church-supported businesses as primary social institutions rather than exploitative institutions, would permit these establishments to more easily gain the acceptance and loyalty as well as monetary support of the community at large.

Church Businesses as Community-owned Businesses

Church-owned businesses are community-owned businesses. They are, therefore, primary communal and co-operative establishments. Their more socialized basis of ownership and control represents a significant departure from mainstream capitalist establishments and is in keeping with the moral precepts of the historical church and with ancient Afrikan cultural traditions of communal property versus private property.

While some may feel a bit uneasy about our suggestions regarding the direct involvement of the institutional church with economic development, the managing and founding of business establishments, *it should be kept in mind that in communities where business ownership and involvement is relatively high, where employment is relatively high and stable*, (e.g., the Korean community) the rates of violent crime and other visible and threatening anti-social behavior are also relatively low. The quality of life in these communities is much more desirable than in those where the opposite conditions inhere. Thus the institutional Black Church through its economic development activities can accelerate and enhance its "good works" in the everyday life of the nation. It also must be kept in mind that the theology, doctrine and practices of the church cannot in any real way, be separated from the economic character of the community in which it wields significant influence. A review of Tawney's *Protestantism and the Rise of Capitalism* and Weber's *The Protestant Ethic and the Spirit of Capitalism* demonstrates quite clearly the relationship between church doctrines and economic development. The generally ambivalent attitude, rather nonchalant attitude, and doctrinal insufficiency of the institutional Black Church are to a significant degree responsible for the poor economic quality of life which characterizes the Black community today. Interestingly, a review of Black churches which have established fully functional social and economic development programs show they tend to undergo marked increases in size and attendance as a result. Their programs apparently markedly enhance their ability to attract and retain younger members, especially males of all ages, and well-informed, educated, skilled, socially sensitive congregants. These churches have seen their missions expand and have been able to better reinforce and fund their primary mission — the salvation of souls and the care of the less fortunate.

The Economics of the Nation of Islam

The judicious involvement of institutional religious organizations in Black economic development cannot but vastly enhance their religious, social and political influence far beyond their numbers and denominational doctrines. The Nation of Islam while under the leadership of the Honorable Elijah Muhammad and now under that of the Honorable Louis Farrakhan is a remarkable case in point. Muhammad's was a nation indeed. As noted by *Emerge* magazine:

> Elijah preached mythology but rooted himself in solid ground. His motto was do for self. And he did just that. He ruled over 76 temples nationwide and 50,000 to 100,000 people. His nation owned 15,000 acres of farmland, a newspaper with a circulation of 500,000, several aircraft, a fish import business, restaurants, bakeries and supermarkets. A fire-eater with a whispery voice, Muhammad redeemed the disenfranchised in the ghetto, infusing them with pride....

The "nation" functioned as a nation with a national capital, Chicago; a head of state, Elijah Muhammad; a national, hierarchical administration; a binding religion and a political ideology; a set of distinct family, educational, economic, commercial, religious, martial, informational, and social institutions. Through these unified and allied institutions the nation forged a presence in the Black community, the United States and the world, one phenomenal given its rather small membership (compare 100,000 Black Muslims with 10 million Black Baptists, for example). By forging a unifying religious and ethnic identity and acting on these bases, the nation was able to generate enough wealth to fund the building of its temples, the education of its children, the establishment of businesses and industries of various types. It demonstrated in concrete and mortar, in its transformation of antisocial, derelicted and criminal persons, the effectiveness of its doctrines. This permitted it to ultimately win the admiration and support of many Black non-Muslims and permitted its best-known spokespersons, Malcolm X and Louis Farrakhan, to gain great popular acclaim in the Afrikan American community and to wield, conservatively speaking, enormous influence in that community as well. Its economic growth and success are as responsible for this outcome no less so than its unadulterated, forthright Black Nationalism.

The economic success story of the Nation of Islam (the Nation) is all the more remarkable in light of the general economic and intellectual level of its membership. The Honorable Elijah Muhammad himself completed only the third-grade. The economic and educational growth of the Nation of Islam, its growth as a religious body, and its political and social influence in the Black community and the United States hardly overstates the power that can be generated and exercised by a community that has a deep and abiding sense of nation and which comports itself as one.

Many in observing what they perceived as the "forced charity" or dues imposed on the members of the Nation and have complained that this is the foundation of its economic prowess and image, overlook a number of factors. These dues supported a number of independent institutions such as the schools which permitted the Nation to educate its youth as it saw fit. Little do these observers, i.e., regular taxpayers, see the *taxes* that they pay as "forced charity" — often used to support failing schools and other dysfunctional anti-Black, anti-life institutions and practices.

Tastes, Money and Power. Tastes and the accumulation and distribution of money, wealth and power are closely related. For example, the taste of Europeans for sugar transformed the economic destinies of both Europeans and Afrikans, helping to transform the former peoples into wealthy imperialists, landholders, industrialists and slave holders, the latter into poverty-stricken colonials, laborers, slaves and producers of cheap raw materials. As owners of the means of production and as the chief manipulators and producers of Afrikan tastes, appetites and needs which can only be satisfied by the consumption of European/White producers, White imperialists have induced Blacks to seek to satisfy their (created and natural) tastes in ways which only enrich Whites themselves. Hence the social role of Blacks almost exclusively as consumers.

Under the dominant influence of the White owners of the means of production Blacks are discouraged from seeking to create and produce for their own tastes and desires, that is, are not encouraged to own the means of producing to satisfy their self-created desires or those created in them by others. Thus, their very patterns of consumption lead to the enriching of their exploiters and oppressors and to their financing their own oppression. Through their consumption they forge the chains which bind them in powerless dependency on dominant Whites whose power they helped to enhance through their nondiscriminating (except against their own enterprises) political and consumer behavior to begin with. Thus, a vicious cycle is established and maintained.

The genius of the Honorable Elijah Muhammad lay in his ability to change or redirect the desires and tastes of the members of his nation, to in many instances, create tastes and desires in them as well. By demonizing many of the pernicious, yet overwhelmingly popular products of White society and many of its lifestyles, values and edibles, such as wines, liquors, cigarettes, drugs, "junk" foods, excessive eating, expensive and promiscuous clothing, and other consumer items and social activities, the Honorable Elijah Muhammad weaned his followers from unhealthy and economically self-defeating consumer addictions. He changed their appetites and tastes for items, the purchase of which not only enriched Whites and other exploitative ethnic groups but impoverished and often harmed the health of his followers themselves. He was able to induce his followers to save more of their earnings by neutralizing many of the tastes and desires produced in them by and for White-owned manufacturing, wholesale-retail and advertising establishments. These individuals and families saved between $2,000 to $5,000 per person, or between

$2,000 to $10,000 per family by not spending on "junk" foods, excessive food, beers, wines and liquors, egregious entertainments, and the like. Moreover, he induced his followers to produce and retail for the satisfaction of their own self-generated tastes and natural needs. Thus, these "national savings" like all national savings, could be used for investment purposes — to invest in schools and other social institutions; to invest in businesses, property and other economic development projects. Monies once spent outside the Nation, because tastes were created by outsiders, produced for and satisfied by outsiders (through White-owned manufacturing wholesale-retail-advertising establishments), were now spent inside the Nation thereby enriching and empowering it. Thus the Nation like all nations who can reasonably produce for internal demands and markets, can engage in successful import substitution; institute adequate savings rates and economic growth; adequately balance its internal deficits, i.e., not let its expenditures markedly outrun its revenues; reduce or eliminate external debts, i.e., monies owed to other peoples, foreign financial and business establishments, etc.; maintain internal stability and organization; achieve a significant degree of increasing prosperity and wealth, power and influence, as well as measurably enhance its standing in the world. We are not contending here that the Nation of Islam has attained all these ends — few nations do. But we are contending that a number of these ends were reasonably approached given its relative youth and the difficult circumstances under which it operated. We also contend that it had established the ideological and structural framework which, given more fortuitous circumstances, would have made it a virtual nation-within-a-nation exerting formidable economic and political power in America and the world.

The Nation of Islam provides an exemplary vantage point from which the Afrikan American community can critically analyze its national or community-wide economic, social and political options. More importantly, the Nation provides some intellectual and conceptual tools, a vocabulary which may be very helpful in creating workable solutions to the problems that confront the *de facto* Black nation in the United States. This vocabulary would permit the Black community to move away from unhelpful, outmoded and even harmful individualistic, familialistic, particularistic modes of analysis of and approaches to its problems.

For example, if the Afrikan American community perceived itself as a nation and not merely as aggregate of individuals who "happen to be Black," it could plan and successfully execute its own jobs development program without abjectly begging and importuning the increasingly hard-hearted U.S. government and intransigent White business establishment to do so. If it were to measure its own economic growth and output, its own trade relations as is done by sovereign nations, it could possibly execute programs to increase employment and economic opportunities for its constituents as well as enhance its wealth and power. When a nation measures the growth of its economy, say it finds it to be 1.5% or 3% a year, it is in part measuring the amount of jobs and economic opportunities it is producing for its citizens. Depending on its size and other demographic and economic factors, a nation growing at such rates may be producing thousands, hundreds of thousands, maybe millions of jobs per annum. The number of created jobs may be sufficient for the nation to employ all or a reasonable number of new workers entering its labor market and perhaps to employ large percentages of those who were un- or under-employed. If the growth of the economy is insufficient, certain policies such as the stimulation and/or redirection of private consumption may be instigated, thereby fueling economic expansion and with it the expansion of employment opportunity.

Trade Relations of Other Ethnic Nations to the Afrikan American Nation

To look at other ethnic groups in America as "nations-within-a-nation" is instructive. Virtually every ethnic economic enclave, whether White, Asian or Hispanic, maintains a nation-state, i.e., a foreign trade relationship with the Afrikan American community. None of these groups have permitted Black businesses and services to penetrate their markets to any significant degree. With the exception of some Hispanic subcultural groups, none are even residentially integrated with the Black community. Generally, they are socially and psychologically distant from the Black community and perceive it and its individual members in ways similar to the negative, stereotypic and racist ways manifested by racist Whites. Yet these same hostile ethnic groups have deeply penetrated Afrikan American consumer markets and exploit them with a single-minded, competitive passion.

By penetrating the Afrikan American market; earning large sums of "hard currency" there, "repatriating" these earnings, i.e., returning the money earned there to their own communities; by refusing to buy items sold or produced by Black-owned businesses; by spending and buying as much as possible within their own communities, other ethnic group enhance their savings rates and their accumulation of capital relative to the Black American community. Their non-reciprocal trade and business relations with the Black community generate huge trade deficits and imbalances in that community. Their trade relations impoverish the Black community and place it at a severe competitive trade disadvantage, i.e., leaving it with little that it can produce and sell competitively in its own or in the markets of other groups and by that not permitting it to accumulate capital.

The accumulation of capital achieved by other groups through their producing for and selling in the Afrikan American consumer market and by their refusal to buy from or trade with Black merchants and businesspeople, is utilized in good part by these groups to invest in their own community institutions and economies as well as to further fund their ability to more deeply penetrate and economically exploit the Black consumer and general American markets. Thus a self-perpetuating cycle is created, working to the economic disadvantage of the Afrikan American business community, devastating to its general wealth and well-being, while simultaneously enriching its alien exploiters.

The penetration of the economy and markets of the Black community by alien businesses leads not only to the exploitation of that community by taking approximately 95% of its income back to their own communities, but by hiring relatively few Blacks to work in their establishments and by not paying even those few a living wage, they help to maintain its impoverished conditions. This permits alien communities to increase the employment of their own members at the expense of the host Black community, i.e., permits them to create jobs for their members and to generally expand their job market and economy relative to those of the Afrikan American community.

The economic success of immigrant groups, such as the Koreans, cannot only be attributed to their entrepreneurial zeal and acumen. Often overlooked is the important fact that their immigrant economic strength in great part derives from their "consumer movement," the conscious refusal to buy from others more than from themselves, or what they can sell to themselves.

Essentially, the consumers in non-Black communities have instigated and maintained an economic boycott against Black businesses and the Black community while, at the same time, inducing that community to buy from them to the point of near profligacy. The situation is even more dire when the Black consumer inadvertently and foolishly allies him/herself with non-Black consumers in boycotting Black businesses as well. As one commentator put it: "The Black consumer has run the longest, most successful boycott in history — the boycott against their own Black businesses."

A careful examination of the economic character and configuration of the Afrikan American community in terms of its "national economic growth rate," indicates, as noted above, that stimulating Afrikan American consumers to reduce debts owed to non-Afrikan American businesses, to reduce the spending with such businesses thereby increasing their savings and using those savings to invest in already existing Black-owned businesses and to invest in new ones; to increase their spending with Black-owned businesses and to invest in income and wealth-producing instruments both inside and outside the community, would markedly increase the wealth of the community as well as the number of jobs available to its members. For instance, whereas now Afrikan Americans spend approximately 5¢ of every dollar to support about four hundred thousand business proprietors and their employees, by increasing their spending to 30¢ out of each dollar they will be able to support millions more Black business owners and workers (due to multiplier effects). Their investment in mainstream corporations will have the effect of generating new job opportunities for Black workers. Increased export-import trade across the Afrikan diaspora and in the general world market, stimulated by increased Black consumer spending with Black firms and selected non-Black firms, could markedly change the dismal economic figures which describe the Afrikan American community today.

However, as can be inferred from our discussion, the achievement of these desirable goals require Black consumer awareness and selectivity which has only been sporadically demonstrated to exist up to the present time. We believe it is possible that such Black consumer behavior can be realized provided an appropriate knowledge base and rationale for such behavior be supplied and amplified repeatedly and effectively by the Afrikan American intellectual, business, religious and general leadership establishments. We will now attempt to provide a modicum of a rationale and motivational stimulus package for activating Black consumer behavior in the interest of Black economic development and betterment in America.

Chapter 24

THE BLACK CONSUMER AND THE ECONOMICS OF AFROCENTRISM

Black Consumer Power

WE LIVE IN A CONSUMER SOCIETY. Consumer confidence, tastes, and spending greatly influence the character and rates of expansion or contraction of the nation's economy and with these the increase or decrease in job opportunities and standards of living. The same principle applies in the more particular case of the Black consumer relative to the character and power of the Black American economy. Again we refer to W.E.B. DuBois' prescient insights in this regard as outlined in his book, *The Dusk of Dawn*. Risking the dulling effects of redundancy, we think it important at this juncture to repeat portions of earlier quotations from DuBois. After carefully considering a number of possible solutions to the economic plight of the Black community, DuBois clearly proposed that the most hopeful solution "is a racial attempt to use the power of the Negro as a consumer not only for his economic uplift but in addition to that, for his economic education." Recall that DuBois advised that the Afrikan American must "intelligently and carefully and farsightedly plan for his entrance into the new economic world..." He further indicated that he saw "this chance of planning in the role which the Negro plays as consumer." He went on to say that "In the future reorganization of industry the consumer, as against the producer, is going to become the key man... Now as a consumer the Negro approaches economic equality much more nearly than he ever has as producer. Organizing then and conserving and using intelligently the power which twelve million people [the size of the Black American population in 1930] have through what they buy, it is possible for the American Negro to help in the rebuilding of the economic state." Furthermore, DuBois contended that "His [the Black consumer] social institutions,... are almost entirely the institutions of consumers and it is precisely along the development of these institutions that he can move in general accordance with economic development of his time and of the large White group, and also in this way evolve unified organization for his own economic salvation."

A rather cursory review of the character and structure of the Afrikan American consumer market fully substantiates DuBois' contention.

Box 24–1   Black Buying Power: 1990–1995

Black buying power is on the rise. The Selig Center for Economic Growth of the University of Georgia "projects that the nation's black buying power will rise from $298 billion in 1990 to $399 billion in 1995, up by 33.9 percent in five years — a compound annual rate of growth of 6 percent."[1] The Selig Center study demonstrates the growing importance of Black consumers, whose spending can make the difference between business success and failure. In many areas of the country Blacks control a very substantial share of the overall buying power in many locales. For example, by 1995, it is projected that Blacks will control 16.2 percent of the Atlanta metropolitan area's overall buying power.

Currently, Atlanta Blacks control $11 billion in buying power. They are expected to control $12 billion in 1995. Moreover, in the state of Georgia, for example, in 1995 Blacks are expected to control 20.3% of the buying power of Macon's metropolitan area; 19.4% of Savannah's; 21.3% of Columbus'; and 27.3% of Albany's buying power. The percentage of Black buying power will rank even higher in other Georgia counties and smaller metropolitan areas. For example, Blacks are expected to control 29.5% of the buying power in Baker, 28.9% in Burke, 33.7% in Clay, 29.6% in DeKalb, 45.1% in Hancock, 30.5% in Dougherty counties, by 1995. These and lesser, but very significant percentages not only hold true across Georgia, but hold true across several states and a multitude of metropolitan areas in the country.

---

1. Jeffrey Humphreys, "Black Buying Power by Place of Residence: 1990–1995," Vol. 54, No. 4, *Georgia Business and Economic Conditions*, July – August 1994.

Black buying power is defined as "the total personal income of black residents that is available, after taxes, for spending on goods and services — the disposable personal income of the black residents of a specified geographic area" (Humphreys, ibid). According the Selig Center, the District of Columbia, Mississippi, South Carolina, Maryland, Louisiana, Georgia, Alabama, North Carolina, Virginia and Delaware are the ten states with the largest shares of Black buying power. The states with the fastest rate of growth of Black buying power include Idaho, Hawaii, Nevada, Utah, Wisconsin, Florida, Colorado, Georgia, Texas and Oregon. It goes on to list the ten states with the largest Black markets (in billion dollars) include New York (43), California (32), Texas (25), Illinois (22), Florida (20), Georgia (20), Maryland (20), Michigan (17), New Jersey (17), and North Carolina (17), respectively. The New York, New Jersey, and Connecticut tri-state area with its compact Black population boasts a combined Black buying-power of some $64 billion. *Table* 24-1 underlines the ten largest Black markets in the United States. *Table* 24-2 underlines the ten states where the Black share of total buying power is largest. It is interesting to note that Black buying power is expected to grow faster than inflation. While the Consumer Price Index (the principal or most important measure of inflation — a measure of the prices the average consumer pays for a fixed amount of goods and services currently, compared to a prior base period) is expected to increase 16.4 percent between 1990-95, the percentage gain in Black buying power is expected to increase 33.9 percent.

In sum, the Selig Center report indicates that the Afrikan American market is a very large and growing one. It represents a market which is economically powerful and important. It contains geographically diverse sub-markets of great vitality and is one which yet provides numerous opportunities for the entry of new Afrikan American-owned businesses and the expansion of existing ones. For aggressive and savvy companies the Afrikan American market represents a strong potential area for new and existing products and services. We have seen that the Afrikan American share of the overall buying power of many states, counties and cities are crucial to their commercial and economic wellbeing. This means that if appropriately organized and directed, Black buying power could serve as a very effective political and economic instrument for advancing the community's interests. The overall political and economic weight of the community could be markedly increased if Black buying power were combined with the power of the Black vote. However, the maximization of Black Power would occur with the capture and control of the community's own internal markets through active internal, as well as external, trade and investment combined with the judicious use of electoral, sociopolitical organizational and consumer acumen. Recall that the total receipts of all Black-owned businesses combined, amounts to about $22 billion. Obviously, this is only a tiny fraction (a little more than 5%) of the $400 billion to be spent by Blacks in 1995. The capture of one quarter of the Black consumer dollars by Black-owned businesses would amount to over $100 billion. This amount of capital, if appropriately and productively invested by the Black business establishment, would permit it to capture greater portions of the Black consumer dollar and more importantly, to capture greater portions of "mainstream" consumer dollars and capital formations. These achievements will provide the economic platform for launching the Afrikan American community into the mainstream of international trade and commerce and thereby permit it to provide substantially greater employment and economic opportunities for its constituents as well as other Americans, and Afrikans across the diaspora.

However, these goals can only be achieved if the Afrikan American community becomes acutely self-aware and self-knowing. In addition, it must muster the courage to reacquire its Afrikan-centered consciousness and identity and a positive ethnocentrism. These orientations must be combined with its irresistible determination to be liberated from White domination and its utter dependence on White American-European economic power and largesse for its survival and well-being. It must seek unrelentingly to realize the existence of a powerful Pan-Afrikan politicoeconomic system which can liberate Afrikan peoples the world-over from poverty, dependence, and low esteem. ◼

Alien Merchants and Black Consumers

The importance of the Afrikan American consumer, the power that he and she collectively represents, is difficult to exaggerate. Hundreds of millions of dollars per year are spent by non-Black business establishments in their pursuit of the Black consumer. Relative to the Afrikan American economic system and the future development of Black Power which must be based on it, the behavior of the Black consumer is vitally crucial. As indicated earlier, the Afrikan American economic system, i.e., Afrikan American business and service establishments, have literally been boycotted by not only the non-Black consumer but also by the Black consumer. The Black entrepreneur has been practically excluded from both Black and non-Black marketplaces. This starvation of Black business has permitted other ethnic groups to economically thrive, or at least, survive in the Black consumer market, to monopolize and use it to perniciously exploit the Black community as a whole while at the same time disrespecting it, demonstrating racial hatred toward it, and not supporting it politically, socially, institutionally or in any other socially positive manner. Even as these alien merchants have invaded the community and earned their living or fortunes there they, in large part, have disdained to employ its residents; to pay a living wage to the few they

Black Buying Power by Place of Residence for U.S. and the States, 1994–1995
(Millions of dollars)

Area	1994	1995	Area	1994	1995
United States	375,429	398,741	Missouri	6,870	7,295
Alabama	9,652	10,197	Montana	19	19
Alaska	372	391	Nebraska	703	746
Arizona	1,410	1,488	Nevada	1,201	1,283
Arkansas	3,167	3,360	New Hampshire	117	121
California	32,210	33,678	*New Jersey*	16,731	17,794
Colorado	2,066	2,186	New Mexico	352	366
Connecticut	4,092	4,337	*New York*	42,830	45,837
Delaware	1,471	1,555	*N. Carolina*	16,527	17,510
D.C.	6,245	6,469	N. Dakota	45	48
Florida	19,893	21,535	Ohio	14,283	15,162
Georgia	20,075	21,436	Oklahoma	2,350	2,472
Hawaii	444	479	Oregon	541	575
Idaho	62	68	Pennsylvania	14,491	15,406
Illinois	21,551	22,876	Rhode Island	448	472
Indiana	5,425	5,778	S. Carolina	9,957	10,555
Iowa	556	602	S. Dakota	37	37
Kansas	1,774	1,880	Tennessee	8,732	9,234
Kentucky	2,960	3,146	*Texas*	24,603	26,273
Louisiana	11,369	12,007	Utah	141	150
Maine	72	76	Vermont	27	28
Maryland	19,559	20,802	Virginia	14,706	15,528
Mass.	4,330	4,596	Washington	2,165	2,245
Michigan	17,018	18,163	W. Virginia	579	604
Minnesota	1,166	1,241	Wisconsin	2,626	2,828
Mississippi	7,365	7,761	Wyoming	44	46

Source: The Selig Center for Economic Growth, Terry College of Business, The University of Georgia.

Table 24–1

Black Share of Total Buying Power for U.S., and the States, 1994–1995
(percent)

Area	1994	1995	Area	1994	1995
United States	7.5	7.6	Missouri	7.2	7.2
Alabama	14.2	14.3	Montana	0.1	0.1
Alaska	2.9	2.9	Nebraska	2.4	2.4
Arizona	2.1	2.1	Nevada	4.1	4.1
Arkansas	8.5	8.5	New Hampshire	0.5	0.5
California	5.2	5.3	New Jersey	8.6	8.7
Colorado	2.9	2.9	New Mexico	1.4	1.4
Connecticut	5.0	5.0	New York	10.6	10.7
Delaware	10.9	11.1	N. Carolina	13.6	13.7
D.C.	42.5	42.5	N. Dakota	0.4	0.4
Florida	7.3	7.4	Ohio	7.1	7.2
Georgia	16.0	16.1	Oklahoma	4.6	4.5
Hawaii	1.8	1.9	Oregon	1.0	1.0
Idaho	0.3	0.3	Pennsylvania	6.1	6.2
Illinois	9.0	9.0	Rhode Island	2.3	2.3
Indiana	5.3	5.4	S. Carolina	17.2	17.3
Iowa	1.2	1.2	S. Dakota	0.3	0.3
Kansas	3.8	3.8	Tennessee	9.7	9.8
Kentucky	4.9	4.9	Texas	7.5	7.5
Louisiana	16.7	16.8	Utah	0.5	0.5
Maine	0.3	0.3	Vermont	0.3	0.3
Maryland	18.4	18.6	Virginia	11.5	11.6
Mass.	3.2	3.3	Washington	2.0	2.0
Michigan	9.4	9.5	W. Virginia	2.1	2.1
Minnesota	1.3	1.3	Wisconsin	2.9	2.9
Mississippi	19.2	19.2	Wyoming	0.5	0.5

Source: The Selig Center for Economic Growth, Terry College of Business, The University of Georgia.

Table 24–2

reluctantly employ; and have seldom, if ever, entered into partnership or any other type of mutually beneficial economic arrangements with local Black business persons. This, in addition to the refusal of these merchants and their families to reside in the community or to contribute significantly to its fundamental well-being, is tantamount to wholesale exploitation. Moreover, their presence drains the community of valuable monetary and human resources thereby impoverishing it and diminishing its quality of life.

Despite their economic importance to a large number of alien merchants and the communities they represent, the Black consumer is very frequently rudely treated, insulted, gouged, and poorly served. Many are treated like criminals, are subjected to obvious, heavy surveillance, and sometimes refused entry into various establishments. These and many other forms of "economic racism" not only mean the chronic insulting and underserving of the Black consumer but more importantly, mean that the Black consumer pays more and gets less than other consumer groups. It is not uncommon for Black consumers to pay 2½ times more for certain items than middle-class White consumers.[2] The New York City Department of Consumer Affairs found that in 1991, "grocery shoppers in poor neighborhoods paid 8.8% more — or $350 more a year for a family of four — than shoppers in middle-class areas" (WSJ, 7/2/92). Chicago City Council staffers in spot checking five grocery items that same year found that poor Blacks paid 18% more than their middle-class counterparts. As we shall later detail, the financial institutions owned by alien communities and which are the repositories of billions of Black consumer dollars and financial accounts of various types — of union funds, city, state and federal employee retirement, pension and other funds to which Black employees contribute substantially — "redline" predominantly Black residential areas, refusing their inhabitants, business persons and landlords loans and mortgages.

Overall, while the Black consumer, worker, institutions have overgenerously spent or deposited their income (and have also invested it indirectly in White corporations and financial establishments through union and other employee funds) with non-Black merchants, businesses and financial institutions of all types, these establishments and the communities they represent have repaid the Black community's generosity by contributing little or nothing to it in return for what they have received from it. More often than not, they have responded by developing even more effective schemes for further exploiting the community. Moreover, as taxpayers, alien merchants

---

[2]. See *The Wall Street Journal*, July 2, 1992.

and the communities they represent, particularly the white suburban community, have chosen to disinvest Black urban communities by withdrawing private, state, federal and local government support for vital services to the inner-cities.

Table 24-3 depicts the devastating withdrawal of federal contributions from local urban budgets. The mostly suburban White population has been making war against the inner-cities over the last twenty years. This, while under the guise of "multiculturalism" or "diversity" its merchants have developed ingenious ways to further exploit the Black consumer, and through him and her, the whole Black community. In the end, this type of exploitation cannot but cause the economic collapse and social disintegration of very large segments of the Afrikan American community.

		1977	1985
1.	New York	19	9
2.	Los Angeles	18	2
3.	Chicago	27	15
4.	Philadelphia	20	8
5.	Detroit	23	12
6.	Baltimore	20	6
7.	Pittsburgh	24	13
8.	Boston	13	7
9.	Cleveland	33	19
10.	Minneapolis	21	9

Federal Contributions to Selected City Budgets (Percent)

Source: U.S. Bureau of the Census, *City Government Finances*, 1977-78 and 1984-85; and Preston Niblack and Peter Stan, "Financing Public Services in L.A.," in James Sternberg et al., *Urban America; Policy Choices for Los Angeles and the Nation*, Santa Monica, Calif.: Rand Corp., 1992 p. 267.[3]

Table 24-3

But the rapacious White American and immigrant merchant communities cannot be held fully responsible for those calamitous circumstances. The Black consumer, spending monies with alien merchants; Black depositors and investors placing their wealth in outside institutions, unconscious of the self-defeating disempowering outcomes of such behavior, unconscious of the tremendous potential power they are literally "tossing to the winds", must share a great

---

3. Mike Davis, "Who Killed L.A.? The War Against the Cities," *Crossroads*, No. 32, June 1993.

part of the responsibility for the economic and social degradation of the Afrikan American community.

The Civil Rights Movement — A Consumer Movement

The Afrikan American economic community can be revitalized, its economic and employment opportunities significantly expanded and secured, its overall well-being as well as that of the Pan –Afrikan community enhanced, only through the massive mobilization of Black consumers in support of those ends. And this is not impossible to achieve since Black mobilization and its power to transform the political and economic landscape not only of the Afrikan American community but of the nation as a whole has been demonstrated many times before. The last major demonstration of Black consumer power was during the civil rights movements of the late nineteen fifties, the sixties and early seventies.

It must be kept in mind that the civil rights movement was as much a Black consumer movement as it was a rights movement. Much of its thrust involved the struggle for equality in consumption privileges on the part of Blacks — the right and privilege of Black consumers to spend their earnings in the same ways and places as Whites. The landmark Montgomery Bus Boycott was essentially a Black consumer movement. Sit-ins at lunch counters and other White-owned businesses and institutions were also Black consumer demonstrations. In these and many other instances, Black consumers withdrew their economic support from offending White institutions, and through sit-ins, marches, demonstrations and other tactics blockaded consumers of other ethnic groups from supporting these entities as well. Its conscious and judicious use of its consumer power and capacity to influence the consumer behavior of other ethnic groups and individuals, permitted it to revolutionarily transform the American legal, social and economic landscape, especially in the South. In terms of increased economic opportunity, increased jobs and wages, affirmative action on any number of levels and arenas, the civil rights movement, strongly supported by consciously directed Black consumer behavior, was by all accounts significantly effective. In this context, it should be recalled that Black consumer power and the alliances forged with other consumer groups was of the greatest importance in transforming the South Afrikan political and economic landscape. Relative to both the expansion of employment opportunities and the increase of Black business and service participation in the American economy, Black consumer power as represented by Operation Breadbasket and Operation PUSH (People United To Save

Humanity) led by Reverend Jesse Jackson, also demonstrated its ability to effectively change Black economic circumstances for the better. The consumer strategy of Operation Breadbasket involved the boycotting of businesses that did not employ Afrikan Americans. This Black consumer movement resulted in the hiring of thousands of Afrikan American workers, the stocking of stores with products manufactured by Afrikan Americans, the hiring of Afrikan American contractors and service establishments, and the depositing of monies in Black-owned banks. Operation Breadbasket signed agreements with more than 10 major corporations, including Anheuser Busch, Coca Cola, Avon, and Burger King, within its first year of operation.[4] Utilizing Black consumer strategies identical to those of Operation Breadbasket, Operation PUSH was organized to press for Black business development. PUSH's efforts also led to increased economic opportunity for the community in terms of very significant increases in the quantity and quality of jobs held by Blacks and the number of Blacks who came to own business franchises, in addition to increased use of services offered by Black-owned firms by White-owned corporations. The following account of their negotiations with Coca-Cola company provides an instance of the work of the Reverend Jesse Jackson and Operation PUSH.

> In July 1981 the Rev. Jesse L. Jackson, founder of People United to Save Humanity, or Operation PUSH, had initiated a boycott after a stalemate in negotiations directed at increasing the company's support of African American enterprise.
>
> On August 10, in an announcement from its Atlanta headquarters, the Coca-Cola Co. promised to pump $30 million into Black-owned businesses and place an African American on its board of directors.
>
> Black involvement would be increased in eight areas of Coca-Cola's business system. In the year to follow, Coke would appoint 32 Black-owned distributorships and would commit itself to their success.
>
> Coca-Cola proposed to double its advertising in Black-owned newspapers and magazines. That would amount to $2 million.
>
> The company said that it had set a "goal" of eventually increasing the Black presence on its management force to 12.5 percent. In addition, it would place Blacks in 100 of its blue-collar openings in such areas as wholesale distribution in the year to come.
>
> Coca-Cola pledged, too, to increase its deposits and loans with Black-owned banks, to raise its annual contributions to Black

---

4. The African American Clergy And Economic Development 1991 Educational Calendar, Carver Federal Savings Bank, New York, N.Y.

organizations to $250,000 and to give a Black-owned advertising agency responsibility for a company brand with a budget of $8 million.

The boycott was over. PUSH had achieved one of the first of a number of major breakthroughs on the economic front toward an increase in African American input into areas of business that for decades had affected them directly as consumers.

The gains at Coca-Cola...served as a result of activity consistent with the objectives and efforts of PUSH toward mustering a certain ability on the part of African Americans behind the rights they had been granted, both in the past and more recently, to procure the means of survival.[5]

The Black Civil Rights/Consumer Movement: Victorious Self-Defeat

The civil rights movement, particularly in its manifestation as a consumer movement, undoubtedly expanded job and economic opportunities for Afrikan Americans, actually contributing to the remarkable expansion of Black middle and professional classes, as well as markedly reduced discrimination against Black consumers. However, such advances brought mixed results — some positive, others negative. While the expansion in economic and employment opportunities were commendable, and legal and social removal of legal and social restrictions on the freedom of Blacks are to be applauded, the interests of overall Black business and economic development were not well served. They in a number of important respects, may actually have been harmed. A case can be made in this instance when we recognize the fact that the economic emphasis of the civil rights movement was on jobs as supplied by White businesses instead of on community-based economic expansion; on income rather than wealth; spending rather than saving. The freedom to spend money with White businesses and establishments became almost synonymous with political freedom or "1st class" citizenship in the minds of many Afrikan Americans. Free and unrestricted consumption of White-produced consumables became identical to or indicative of freedom, per se. In actuality, while this freedom of consumption was not to be denied, it effectively led to the redistribution of Black consumer spending away from Black businesses toward White business establishments with the result that many Black businesses lost a large portion, if not their complete Black clientele. Many relatively prosperous Black business districts went into irredeemable

---

5. *The City Sun* (8/4–10/93).

or serious decline and Black business development underwent serious retardation and contraction as it was deserted or left unsupported by Black consumers. In many ways the civil rights movement proved to be a boon to White-owned businesses by providing them with a large, new clientele, a new market, and a very sizable pool of money unavailable to them before.

Curiously, attempts by some Blacks to improve the inner-cities and to expand the community of Black-owned businesses supported by a loyal core of Black consumers, was viewed by some other Blacks as forms of self-segregation, as indicative of separatism, anti-integrationist, anti- the struggle for racial equality. It must be noted that the enormously increased spending by Black consumers with White-owned businesses, as well as businesses owned by other ethnic groups; the broadly expanded opportunities for Black consumers to enter into markets previously closed to them; the remarkable opportunities for non-Black-owned business establishments to penetrate previously restricted consumer markets in the Black community, to very significantly increase their customer/client bases, and with them their gross and net incomes, were not paralleled by White and other ethnic group consumer spending in the opposite direction, i.e., spending with the Black community.

The increased business opportunities for non-Black firms to milk increased sales and earnings from Black consumers, were not matched by increased opportunities for Black firms to garner growing sales and earnings from non-Black consumers and, as for that matter, from Black consumers. In fact, through protests, court and legislative actions, the civil rights movement had to force an exceedingly reluctant and bitterly resentful White business establishment — through the development of "minority set-asides" — to spend a very miserly proportion of their vast wealth with Black and minority-owned businesses and service establishments. And even these forced concessions were rescinded by conservative court decisions shortly after their initiation.

As indicated above, the non-Black consumer has never demonstrated much of an inclination to spend with Black businesses. White consumers in fact distance themselves from the possibility of spending with Black firms to any really significant extent by literally leaving the central cities. White-owned business establishments obliged White consumers by the construction of suburban and rural shopping malls and the wholesale movement of business and production facilities out of the inner-cities into the suburban and rural areas as well. Consequently, both actual and potential Black business establishments and Black workers were abandoned by both White business establishments and White consumers. That is, assuming that these entities would have supported Black businesses and workers had they remained. *Tables* 24-4 and 24-5 show the degree to which White residents have abandoned the inner-cities since 1970. As noted there, some 8,000,000+ Whites have left the cities since that time and their demographic majorities have since become demographic minorities in many major cities.

10 Largest Metropolitan Cores: Percentage White			
		1970	1990
1.	New York	75.2	38.4
2.	Los Angeles	78.3	37.2
3.	Chicago	64.6	36.3
4.	D.C. Area	75.1	33.0
5.	San Francisco Bay Area	75.1	42.9
6.	Philadelphia	65.6	51.3
7.	Detroit	55.5	20.3
8.	Boston	81.7	58.0
9.	Dallas	75.8	49.8
10.	Houston	73.4	39.9

Source: U.S. Bureau of Census Population, 1970 and 1990. D.C. Area includes Baltimore; San Francisco Bay Area includes San Francisco, Oakland, and San Jose; Dallas includes Fort Worth.

Table 24-4

Ethnic Shifts in Cores of 10 Largest Metropolises
– 8,000,000 whites
+ 4,800,000 Latinos
+ 1,500,000 Asians
+ 800,000 Blacks
– 900,000 total population

Source: U.S. Bureau of the Census Population, 1970 and 1990.

Table 24-5

This problematic situation has not been systematically addressed by a Black leadership establishment that appears to be still futilely pursuing obsolete civil rights goals while using equally obsolete and counterproductive civil rights stratagems.

While an organized movement of Black consumers is still central to any new initiatives by the Afrikan American community and Black consumer-based stratagems must be utilized in their achievement, the goals the community must now strive to reach differ radically from those sought by the leaders of the civil rights movement. The main thrusts of movements like Operations PUSH and Breadbasket which utilized organized Black consumer movements to achieve assimilationist goals; for wringing token job concessions, half-hearted, minimally successful, affirmative action commitments and miserly set-asides from corporate America; to acquire a few franchises and distributorships to be distributed among a few already well-heeled Blacks — have essentially left the Black urban community bereft of a self-sufficient, self-perpetuating economic system.

In disdainfully rejecting the Garvey movement (UNIA) and the Nation of Islam as "Black Nationalists" or "separatist movements", the civil rights leadership missed an important opportunity to learn of and to utilize a Black consumer movement whose goals were much more practically relevant, politically and sociopsychologically beneficial to the community and much more national and international in scope than the anaemic ones it pursued. For the Garvey movement and the Nation of Islam initiatives were Black-consumer-based movements whose main thrust was the establishment of a new Afrikan-centered national and international economic and political order. These movements sought to organize and direct Black consumer spending in such ways as to increase and enlarge Black business ownership; to enlarge Black economic and job opportunities; enhance Black economic, social and political self-sufficiency and power; establish a free and independent Pan–Afrikan political and economic system; and by these means, to liberate Afrikan peoples from White domination.

These goals are still valid today and their achievement even more urgent. One of the means by which they are to be achieved must include the organization and redirection of Afrikan American and Pan-Afrikan modes of consumption. However, this can only be achieved through a realistic analysis of Black consumer spending attitudes and habits, their transformation and utilization to support the establishment of Afrikan American owned and controlled firms which can successfully compete for Afrikan American and non-Afrikan American national and international dollars. We will address the first of these requirements momentarily. We will begin by taking a very preliminary look at how and in what proportions the Black consumer spends his and her money. We shall then take a cursory look at what the Black community receives in return for the hundreds of billions of dollars it spends with non-Black establishments and the hundreds of billions of surplus value it produces for these establishments in terms of its surplus labor and talents.

Spending Habits of the Black Consumer

Data adapted from *American Demographics* (January, 1993) provides an interesting look at the spending habits of the average Black household. It provides insight not only into the tastes and the preferences of Blacks in comparison with those of Whites, demonstrating significant differences in many areas, but also quantifies in terms of tens and hundreds of millions of dollars, how much Blacks spend with mostly White-owned and non-Black-owned businesses. Even though a much smaller percentage of the population, and on the whole earning and spending less than White households in some areas, Black households spend nearly as much or more than their White counterparts. For example, Blacks spend over 75% more than Whites on boys' clothing. Interestingly, the money spent by Black households on boys' clothing alone amounts to well above $1 billion. This is even more noteworthy when it is recognized that Black households spend 1% less than Whites on girls' clothing. Further review, which also compares the average expenditure for products and services in 1988 for Black and White households,[6] indicates that Blacks spend over $12 billion for clothing and clothing services. Spending for these items and services, alone, accounts for substantially more than half of the total amount of receipts taken in by all of the more than 400,000 Black-owned business in the United States. The amount Blacks spend for food, $29 billion, overshadows the total receipts of Black-owned businesses by almost 50 percent. The following excerpts show some buying trends of Afrikan American consumers.

Food – In relative terms, African Americans spend more from their budget on food at home than Whites, a reversal from 1970. For instance, one food item heavily consumed by African Americans is soft drinks. Afrikan Americans spend more than $6 billion annually on this category alone.... African Americans are estimated to spend more than $500 million per year on McDonald's fast food.

Alcoholic Beverages – African Americans consume 32 percent of all malt liquor products and 20 percent of the scotch whiskey market.

Housing – Over $72 billion or 33 percent of Black American income goes toward housing, which includes shelter, utilities, and household

---

6. Margaret Anmbry, *Consumer Power: How Americans Spend* (Chicago: Probus. Publishing Co., 1992).

operations. Shelter — which includes owned and rented dwellings as well as other lodgings, such as hotels and motels — accounted for the bulk of housing expenses: $439 million. African Americans spent 2.1 times the amount of money on rented dwellings as white and other Americans, up from 1.33 in 1970. On an absolute basis, in 1991, African Americans spent more on rented dwellings than whites ($2,093 vs. $1,525 per household) per year.

Apparel and Services – In absolute dollars, African Americans spend more than whites on apparel and services each year. This is the only other category besides rented dwellings where this occurs. In relative terms, African Americans spend 1.6 times that of whites and others on apparel and services. African American males between the ages of 13 and 24, who are less than 3 percent of the total U.S. population, account for 10 percent of the $12 billion athletic shoe market, purchasing more than 1 out of 5 pairs of shoes made by Nike; they also account for 55 percent of the $275 million starter jacket market.

Transportation – African Americans spend more than $30 billion per year to acquire and maintain an automobile. They are also twice as likely as whites to own an Audi, a BMW, or a Mercedes. In the years since 1970, expenditures on private automobiles have grown from 9.5 percent to 13.9 percent of the [Afrikan American household] budget (a 4.6 percent increase).

Entertainment – According to *Black Enterprise*, African Americans spend over $4 billion on consumer electronics. One- fifth [20 percent] of all portable televisions are purchased by African Americans. African American consumers, who make up only 12 percent of the population, are estimated to buy 50 percent of the movie tickets.

Personal Care Products and Services – In relative terms, African Americans spend more on personal care products and services: one-third more than whites. African-American consumers reportedly buy 36 percent of all hair care conditioners and 25 to 35 percent of all detergent and toothpaste. African-American females, who equal approximately 6 percent of the total U.S. population, purchase 15 percent of the $4 billion cosmetics industry, or $600 million, and spend 26 percent more on perfume than any other group of females.[7]

Target Market News (9/93), the publication of a Chicago-based marketing information firm which specializes in gathering data on the spending habits of black consumers, analyzed the information it gathered from in-person interviews and diaries taken from more than 2,800 Afrikan American households. In findings similar to those

---

7. Adapted from *The State of Black America 1994*, p. 54–57.

published by *American Demographics* and cited from *State of Black America 1994* (above), *Target Market News* found that in general Black households spend three times more than non-Black households on small appliances, twice as much on laundry, dry-cleaning and perishable foods. They spend 50 percent more on footwear. The findings further indicated that:

• Compared to Whites, non-Black Hispanics, Asians and Indians who spend an average of $241 for footwear a year, Blacks spend an average of $363. For the 11,128 Black American commercial units as a whole, that equals an average of $4 billion per year.
• Black households on average spend a total 4 percent more on clothing, approximately $1,803, compared to the general population average of $1,726 annually. For the 11,128 Black commercial units combined, that averages about $20 billion annually.
• Black households spend an average of $72.49 on coin-operated laundry and dry cleaning, compared to the general average of $35.81. This annual amount approaches $1 billion for Black households combined.
• Compared to $307 for the general population, Black American households spend an average $632 per annum on meat, fish, poultry, and eggs. For Black households combined that averages about $7 billion per year.

In reviewing the statistics it becomes obvious that in almost no category do Black-owned businesses capture a really significant percentage of the Black consumer dollar. It should also be obvious that the capture by Black-owned businesses of even three or four of the product and services categories listed there, e.g., alcoholic beverages, tobacco and smoking supplies, television and radios, sound equipment, household furnishing and equipment, would add $12 billion or more to the total receipts of Black-owned businesses.

Little or No Return on the Black Dollar. Since Blacks own relatively few wholesale and retail and even fewer manufacturing establishments related to the categories listed above and in *Table* 24–4, it is immediately apparent that Black consumers spend enormous sums of money with non-Black establishments which, if consciously spent with the same or similar Black-owned establishments would revolutionize not only the Black business community but the entire Black community. A very pertinent question among many arises in this context. In light of the very huge sums of money the Black consumer spends with White-owned and other non-Black-owned business

COMPANY	1991 Sales ($billion)	Net Income ($mil)	MINORITY Employees (%)	Distrib-utors	Vendors ($mil)	Managers & Officers	Board Members	NON-PROFIT CONTRIBUTIONS Black ($ thou.)	Minority	Contribution
Anheuser-Busch	10.9	939.8	22.2 (B)	16	100.0	11% mgrs. 8.3% officers	16 2 Blk.	—	25.00	—
Brown & Williamson Tobacco Corp.	3.5	NA	24.0 (B)	0	40.0	8% mgrs.	—	—	1.20	—
Cola-Cola	11.6	1,600.0	19.9 (B)	0	122.0	8.4% mgrs. 5.5% officers	14 1 Blk	—	—	—
Coors (subsidiary Adolph Coors)	1.5	59.13 Op.Inc.	28.6 (B) Memphis	2	17.7	1.2% mgrs. .03% officers	—	561,240.00	—	*6% of sales attributed to Blacks $91.88 million
General Mills	7.15	472.7	14.0 (B)	0	4.4	7% mgrs	16 1 Blk	—	(Ed) 0.25 (org) 1.60	—
McDonald's	6.70	859.6	22.0 (Blk)	0	—	17% mgrs. 6% officers	17 1 Blk	—	—	—
Pepsico	19.60	1,080.0	—	0	243.0	—	11: 0 Blk	—	—	—
Phillip Morris	56.50	3,900.0	16.0 (Blk)	0	300.0	9% mgrs. & officers	19 1 Blk	—	—	—
Quaker Oats	3.50	205.8	12.0 (Blk)	0	10.3	5.4% mgrs. & officers	14 1 Blk	537,431.00	—	*12% of sales attributed to Blacks $420 million.
R.J. Reynolds	8.54	2,720.0	17.5 (Blk)	0	9.6	8.6% mgrs. 1.5% officers	—	974,290.00	—	—
Sara Lee Corp.	12.38	535.0	22.2 (Blk)	0	29.3	7% mgrs. 3.3% officers	17 2 Blk	—	—	—
Scheiefelint Somerset	NA	NA	15.0 (Blk)	0	—	105 mgrs.	—	—	—	—
Joseph E. Seagrams & Sons	6.30	727.0	9.6 (Blk)	0	18.3	12.5% mgrs. 2.2% officers	19 0 Blk	866,000.00	—	*20% of sales attributed to Blacks $1.26 billion.

Table 24-6 Corporate Return on the Black Consumer Dollar   – 605 –

establishments, what does it receive from such establishments in terms of employment opportunity, trade, and philanthropic returns to the community?

While we cannot answer this question in detail, we can provide some indications by reviewing Table 24-6. This table, adapted from *Dollars and Sense* magazine, November 1992, provides a review of the economic and social relations between thirteen White-owned corporate beverage, food and tobacco establishments and the Black American community in 1991. *Dollars and Sense* magazine in its 12th annual report on the beverage, food and tobacco industries, summarily reports the following:

> As a whole, they [the 13 companies who participated in the report] reportedly employ 721,784 people in the United States, with approximately 10 percent, 72,975, being Black. Within these same companies, however, *minorities occupy less than 1.5 percent of executive and management level positions. Those executives identified as being African-American (as opposed to "minority") amount to a mere 0.3 percent of the total workforce. Out of their 143 board members, only nine are black.*
>
> They spent nearly one billion dollars with minority vendors last year, with coca-cola leading the way in purchasing from black vendors, and spending over $130 million; Philip Morris and Pepsico purchased $300 million and $243 million, respectively, of goods and services from minority and black vendors. Seven companies were responsible for channeling over $30 million into non-profit organizations with *Anheuser-Busch contributing to black and minority organizations $25 million of that total.* Four companies — R.J. Reynolds, Joseph Seagrams & Sons, Inc., Coors Brewing Co. and Quaker Oats — clearly identified their gift recipients as being black but, perhaps due to this strained economy, collectively donated a reported combined sum of three million dollars.

This citation points to a crucial issue: What do Black consumers get in return for their exceedingly generous, consistently loyal support of White and other non-Black-owned businesses? Certainly, whether measured in terms of employment, rank and file and managerial positions, distributorships, franchises, wholesale-retail ownerships, stock ownership, or philanthropy, the returns Black consumers get for supporting non-Black businesses and communities, for enriching them while impoverishing their own, is arithmetically insignificant. Those non-Black merchants who greedily pursue the Black consumer do not hesitate to show their contempt for him in an ever-expanding number of subtle and not-so-subtle ways. Not only do the corporations which make billions from their trade with the Black consumers flee the inner-cities (often leading the rush); they join the rest of White America in damning those cities by withdrawing public support for their institutions, shrinking their tax bases, and by using their hegemonic political influence and enormous wealth to deflate the economic and social prospects of the consumers and cities they have jilted. Even when the major corporations remain in the central cities the Black populations there are forced to make various and sundry tax concessions, abatements, discounts and the like in order to maintain access to the ever-shrinking, insecure job opportunities they ostensibly provide.

A review of the contributions the Fortune 500 corporations make to Black non-profit organizations and institutions, community economic and social development programs[8] provide sobering evidence as to their rather sparse reciprocity with regard to their Black consumers who contribute mightily to their bottom lines. As seen earlier, Black consumers spend over $12 billion on apparel and apparel services; $29 billion on food; over $3 billion on beverages (alcoholic and non-alcoholic); well over $30 billion on vehicle purchases and related expenses; approximately $3 billion on personal-care products and services; over $3 billion on electronic products; more than $70 billion on housing, household supplies, services, furnishings, and equipment (not including the over $7 billion in mortgage interest); and more than $6 billion on health care. Yet a review of the combined annual philanthropic contributions to Black non-profit organizations by any of the Fortune 500 companies which do business in these and other industries very, very rarely exceed $500,000. More typically, they remain in the area between $100,000 to $200,000.

A prominent example of the meanness of corporate giving to Black non-profit organizations is provided by the annual United Negro College Fund TV Marathon. This annual song, dance and panhandling fest sponsored by Anheuser-Busch and hosted by singer Lou Rawls, is ostensibly designed to raise funds for its 41-member colleges. However, this marathon never manages to raise $1 million per member. Individual members of industries such as the automobile industry — with whom Blacks spend some $30 billion — may with great flourish, present a check before a national Black audience of from $5,000 to $10,000. The parade of multinationals, recipients of billions of dollars from their Black consumers, giving from their petty

---

8. According to *Fortune 500: The Directory of Corporate Philanthropy*, 8th edition, 1989–90, published by the Public Management Institute of San Francisco.

cash boxes, is endless. It is interesting that the executives who head these corporations, who demand tens of millions in salary and perks to support their individual lifestyles, feel that a $5,000 check to 41 Black colleges is sufficient to prevent the terrible wasting of Black minds. Thus, large White-owned corporations while appearing to support, actually help to underfund Black education and maintain its relatively non-competitive status compared to White education. While we cannot cite records with regard to its corporate philanthropy toward Black non-profit organizations in 1992, it is interesting to note that the Coca-Cola companies generated sales of more than $13 billion in that year. Its chairman, Roberto Goizueta, earned some $86 million in pay and bonus income in 1991 (NYT, 4/16/92). Giozueta's salary was $3.14 million. The restricted stock grant of one million shares of Coca-Cola stocks valued at $83 million, received by Goizueta, could have been doubled under Coke's rules. Moreover, Coke produced $50 million of additional wealth for its shareholders in 1991. The Coca-Cola company foundation rather atypically granted some $352,500+ ($300,000 to Atlanta University; $2,500 to the Bethune Museum Archives; $50,000 to Grambling State University for the Presidential Merit Scholarship Fund) to Black institutions in 1988 out of foundation grants amounting to $10,000,000. This can be considered very generous compared to other corporations that have generated similar amounts in sales and who have been similarly as generous in paying their principal officers and executives.

The real problem here is not the presence or the lack of generosity of White-owned corporations, but the fact that the Black consumer community asks little or nothing for the money it spends with these establishments. It gets what it demands. In fact, it appears that the more miserly the corporation the more the community spends with it.

What could the Black consumer demand from corporations with which they spend billions of dollars? Obviously, as was the case with Operations PUSH and Breadbasket, the answer involves increases in Black employment on all levels; in the numbers of Black distributorships, wholesale, retail and manufacturing outlets; increased Black ownership of corporate shares; increased grants to Black institutions; increased support given to the economic development of the Black American community. Of course, this requires that Black consumers be fully informed about the return they are, or not, receiving for the dollars they spend with the various corporations and industries. Furthermore, this requires that these consumers be motivated and organized to judiciously spend or not to spend their monies in such ways as to apply the needed pressures in the marketplace to achieve their goals. The application of such pressure must be exercised under the aegis of an effective leadership establishment. One of the major functions of all-Black-owned or Black-oriented media should be to repeatedly and as effectively as possible, provide the Afrikan American community and consumer with vital information and statistics regarding how the corporations and industries they support with their consumer dollars are aiding and abetting or are impairing their general well-being. If the Afrikan American community is to thrive, its consumers must be socially responsible in their spending with business establishments and must also demand social responsibility from those establishments with whom they spend.

In many ways the Afrikan American community is already basically organized to make its influence felt in corporate America. We have already alluded to the nationally organized institutional Black Church with its 60–70 thousand congregations. The NAACP alone has some 2,000 branches throughout all 50 states. Numerous other Black organizations are similarly organized and distributed across the country as well. These churches and organizations with their congregations and branches are quite capable of monitoring the racial sensitivity and inclusivity of major corporations and of spearheading Black consumer campaigns when appropriate to do so. [We must note here that an alternative to trying to persuade sometimes otherwise unresponsive Black consumers to withdraw their monetary support for certain cooperate products should the need arise, would be to persuade certain retail outlets, by various means, not to stock those products to begin with.]

Another important demand that can and should be made by the Black consumer community is that corporations increase their training of Black employees at all occupational levels. Moreover, from the point of view of politically and economically empowering the Afrikan American community Black consumers must encourage the corporations to enter an increased number of joint partnerships and joint ventures with individual, corporate, and organizational members of the community. However, the demands and relationships we speak of here are likely to be productively realized if they are made in the name and with the backing of the Black American community as the Afrikan American nation.

Native American Nations and Economic Empowerment

In this context it is interesting to note the growing beneficial relations between corporations and American Indian nations and tribal confederations. For example, *Fortune* magazine (4/19/93) describes the joint establishment of "an 80-acre industrial park, a gleaming shopping center, a new hospital, and a nursing home, topped off with the requisite Federal Express pickups station — in Mississippi; a power plant with more than $3 million a year in sales to Pacific Power & Light" in central Oregon; the operation of "an apparel company that has manufactured clothing for Nike" and which along with other tribally-owned businesses "produce revenues of around $80 million a year and employ 1,200", also in Oregon; the operation of nine enterprises by the White Mountain Apaches of northern Arizona which "generate over $45 million in revenue, including a ski resort, timber operations, and a plant that produces insulation and other materials for McDonnell Douglas's Apache helicopter." It is interesting to read of the business acumen of Philip Martin, 67, chief of the Mississippi community (some 5,500 members) of Choctaw Indians. Through extraordinary persistence, over fifteen years, the Choctaws in 1979 attracted their first manufacturing business partnership for assembling wire harnesses for GM's Packard Electric Division. *Fortune* further noted that:

> Today Martin presides over a portfolio of businesses with more than $60 million in sales, including plants that make wire harnesses and circuitboards for Ford and Chrysler, a factory built for American Greeting Cards, and a printing company. All these businesses except the joint venture are 100% owned by the tribe, and all but the printing plant operate on tribal land. Says Martin: *"our only resource is our people.* It took tenacity to convince businesses to come here at first. Now companies are approaching us" [Emphasis added].

Native American peoples form a number of official nations in the United States. Their nation-state status permits them certain formal possibilities not possessed by Afrikan Americans. However, above and beyond their formal or official status as nations, it has been their *acting as nations,* their movement based on their sense of a shared destiny, their sense of peoplehood, of nation, their openly avowed membership in a distinct ethnic community and their willingness to act in terms of these factors that are the keys to their increasing economic success.

The story of Patricia McGee, a member of the Yavapai Tribe of Arizona, is also a fascinating one.

> Also thriving is the 132-member Yavapai tribe in Prescott, Arizona, a bustling vacation town 95 miles north of Phoenix. The Yavapais are under the firm hand of President Patricia McGee, a sixtysomething dynamo. In 1984 she managed to secure a $1.2 million government

grant to build a resort hotel. Then she persuaded the town to issue $8.5 million in municipal bonds for the project. Still short of capital, McGee turned to non-Indian developer William Grace of Phoenix. "We didn't have the expertise to do commercial real estate development," she says, "so we found Bill."

Grace, who operates about two dozen shopping centers in the West, kicked in an additional $3 million and completed the 160-room Sheraton in 1988. Today the hotel is filled with conventioneers and weekenders fleeing the heat of Phoenix. The hotel's new casino, the first in the state, is jammed. McGee also leased part of the tribe's 1,400 acres to Grace, who built a shopping mall anchored by a Wal-Mart. The mall, done in high Santa Fe style, is almost full of tenants and packing in shoppers.

Visionary Indian leaders like McGee find that economic development and a healthy private sector reinforce rather than undermine traditional tribal values. Economic freedom fosters pride and independence and brings in precious dollars for language programs, schools, and museums.[9]

Further Signs of Economic Development. Although approximately one-third of the nation's two million Indians still live in poverty and suffer from a number of social problems such as high unemployment, suicide, alcoholism, domestic violence, street gangs and the like, these problems, as we have seen, are not hampering their advance toward economic empowerment. The new prosperity some Indian nations are deriving from their ownership of gambling casinos is the stuff of contemporary legend. For example, the Shakopee Mdewekantan tribe's Mystic Lake casino in Prior Lake, Minnesota, netted enough earnings in 1993 to pay each of its 200 members more than $400,000. Its 1994 earnings are expected to exceed $500,000 each.[10] The 81 casinos owned by American Indians across the nation earned combined gross revenues of approximately $567.7 million in 1992. From these revenues they obtained a net profit of approximately $141.9 million. At this time about 90 tribes have opened casinos, and dozens more are expected to open in the near future. Gambling profits for all reservations exceeded $1 billion in 1993. These profits are now providing a pool of start-up capital to diversify tribal economies and move the reservations toward self-sufficiency. They also are providing financing for new schools, housing, roads and hospitals.

But as our foregoing discussion indicates, the economic activities of the Indian Nations include far more than the owning and operating

---

9. "The Fortune 500," *Fortune* magazine, April 19, 1993.

10. "Economies Come to Life on Indian Reservations," *New York Times*, 7/3/94.

of gambling casinos. The *New York Times* (7/3/94) sums the matter up in the following way.

> And while nothing compares to gambling, Indians are beginning to find signs of prosperity in other areas as well — high-technology mining ventures, the tradition of herding bison, the surging growth of tribal colleges.
> The leaders in Indian Country today — from the bleached desert rock of the Navajo, to the windswept High Plains of the Sioux, to the Rocky Mountain foothills of the Southern Utes, to the Pacific fishing waters of the Quinalt — say they see more cause for optimism now than at any other time in generations, perhaps even since whites arrived.

The *Times* goes on to indicate what it perceives as a substantial number of new signs of hope for the economic expansion of the Indian nations.

> A burst of entrepreneurship on reservations in recent years has created jobs in manufacturing and retail businesses.
> A new trade group, the Indian Business Association, now represents 5,000 Indian companies. Indian tourism has been booming, from the elegant Inn of the Mountain Gods resort at the Mescalero Apache reservation to guided nature and hunting tours on the Lower Brule lands in South Dakota.
> Tribally run colleges, which have grown from a single two-year school in 1968 to some 26 colleges today, some with four-year degrees and graduate programs, are producing health workers, tribal government specialists and teachers in places like Rosebud in South Dakota, where most Sioux have grown up never seeing an Indian teacher.
> In a first for any tribe, the Southern Utes in Colorado have recently bought a gas-drilling company, a far more lucrative and autonomous venture than simply leasing the land to non-Indian businesses, which has always been the arrangement on Indian lands. And the Navajos of the Southwest, stewards of the largest reservation, 26,000 square miles, the size of West Virginia, have organized an oil company that plans to start drilling in two years.
> "There has emerged a consensus in Indian Country that if we're going to see economic growth, we're going to have to do it ourselves," said Wilma Mankiller, the principal chief of the Cherokee Nation. "Tribes have come to the realization that Federal resources are going to continue to decline, no matter who is in the White House."

The *Times* (7/3/94) notes another number of current economic initiatives undertaken by some native American tribes.

- The Choctaw in Mississippi assemble wire devices for automobiles. The Turtle Mountain Chippewa in North Dakota build house trailers. The Cherokee in Oklahoma produce parts for military contractors.

- Before gambling, perhaps the most lucrative business in Indian lands was artwork. Fueled largely by the popularity of Southwestern design, Indian art has become a $500 million-a-year industry, from the $15,000 black pots designed by Margaret Tafoya, a Santa Fe artist, to the $8 bracelets made by people living in adobe huts.

- In recent years, Indians have made inroads in publishing and broadcasting. There are now more than a dozen Indian-run radio stations, and a successful newspaper, Indian Country Today.

- Two years ago, using revenue from gambling, the Utes purchased some gas fields, and started their own drilling company, Red Willow. It was the first time any tribe had tried such a venture with natural gas.

The accomplishments of American Indians in the economic and social spheres just noted and the positive future economic prospects they express are not merely founded in their sense of nation and ethnicity. This is not to say that these elements are not fundamental. However, more specifically, Native American economic progress is also founded on their ownership of economic resources, e.g., real estate, minerals, equity in corporations. More important still, is their ownership of ethnic pride, their expectation to succeed, and their irresistible drive to liberate themselves from dependency and political powerlessness. Much of the ownership of Indian land and resources is communal. This form of ownership has not prevented the enrichment of the nations as well as their individual members. In fact, communal ownership seems to have facilitated the accumulation of wealth by the tribes.

The growing economic accomplishments of the Indian nations provide many lessons for the Afrikan American community. They teach us the possibilities inherent in the co-operative ownership of productive properties and resources, as well as the possibilities inherent in acting in concert based on ethnic identity and consciousness and on collective intent.

Black Tourism as Industry

The joint ventures, partnerships and outright ownerships and operations like those instituted by Native American tribes can also be achieved by the Afrikan American community, even more abundantly. Black-owned or controlled corporate groups, Black church organizations, and Black commonwealth corporations, i.e., community-owned corporate bodies (to be fully defined in the next chapter), with the support of organized Black consumers, together can economically empower the whole of the Afrikan American community.

In light of Patricia McGee's success in the tourist industry as previously described, it is interesting to note the possibility of Afrikan American community success in the tourist and convention industries.

The Black American community has a very long history of conventioneering. From the convention movement beginning prior to the Civil War to the present, Black organizations in rapidly increasing numbers meet in hotels and convention halls across the country. Today, the Black tourism, travel, and convention business is worth between $2–3 billion dollars yearly. It is not unusual for a Black convention to spend well over $10–15 million at an annual convention. In September 1993, The National Baptist Convention USA spent an estimated $40 million at its annual convention in downtown New York City. Approximately 50,000 persons were in attendance. The delegates booked some 30,000 hotel rooms (*New York Amsterdam News*, 8/21/93). It is somewhat of a tragicomedy to observe that Black organizations such as the National Urban League and the NAACP, the Black Congressional Caucus, the National Association of Black Social Workers, etc., spend collectively well over a billion dollars with White-owned hotels, convention halls and caterers, while discussing the poverty and degradation of the Black American community. And yet these organizations, jointly or separately, have not apparently seen fit to invest in, enter into partnership with established hotel chains such as those entered into by Patricia McGee. Neither have they together or separately decided to buy or build hotels or convention centers and catering facilities in their most popular convention cities. These cities generally have large Black majority populations such as Atlanta, Washington, D.C., New Orleans, or very large, centralized Black minority populations such as New York City, Philadelphia, Los Angeles. *Table* 24–7 lists the 27 most popular cities selected by Black professionals and conventioneers for their annual meetings. Virtually all of them are Black majority or heavily Black minority-based cities. This implies that if convention centers were built in these cities they not only would provide facilities for national convocations, but for local and regional ones as well. Such facilities can also function as community centers, recreational, cultural and entertainment centers for their local communities.

Despite the $2–3 billion dollars generated by Black conventioneers, travelers and tourists annually, Washington, D.C.'s Howard Inn, Miami's 265-suite Sheraton Suites and Atlanta's Barclay Hotel are the largest hotels owned and managed by Afrikan Americans. *Dollars and Sense* (1/93) reports that:

> ...of the 40,700 hotel properties in the United States, there are fewer than 35 black general managers....There are two executives of convention and visitor bureaus, approximately 10 auditorium managers, eight sports arena/stadium managers and eight convention center executives.

A phenomenon which has been observed by an increasing number of Black travelers, conventioneers and tourists is the fact that there appears to be fewer and fewer Black employees, e.g., doormen, bellboys, waiters, maintenance crews, in the rank and file of the hospitality industry than in the past, even when such hospitality facilities were closed to Black consumers. Thus it appears that Black ownership, partnership, and investment in the hospitality industry has not nearly kept pace, if not actually lost pace, with the burgeoning increase of Black consumer spending with the industry.

What cities do African-American meeting professionals select for their many meetings? *Dollars & Sense* **magazine undertook a nationwide random survey that resulted in the following list of the top 10 cities for African-American conventions:**

		And, what are the top second tier cities?	These cities are gaining ground in the convention game:
1.	Atlanta		
2.	Chicago		1. Charlotte
3.	Washington, D.C.	1. Dallas/Ft. Worth	2. Denver
4.	New Orleans	2. Houston	3. Detroit
5.	Philadelphia	3. Oakland	4. Indianapolis
6.	St. Louis	4. Baltimore	5. Kansas City
7.	Los Angeles	5. Cleveland	6. Minneapolis
8.	San Francisco	6. Memphis	7. Orlando
9.	San Diego	7. Nashville	8. San Antonio
10.	New York	8. Richmond	9. Seattle

— *Bernetta J. Hayes*

Source: *Dollars and Sense*, January 1993.

Table 24–7

Black Tourism and Trade in Miami. Miami, Florida, is a popular tourist and convention center for Afrikan Americans. It has been reported by a Black economic development group, Tools for Change, that over one million Blacks visit Miami and spend over $1 billion there annually (*N.Y. Amsterdam News*, 7/3/93). Moreover, Afrikan-Caribbean visitors to the Dade County area, where Miami is located, number well over 500,000 yearly. Furthermore, 20 percent of the international commerce which moves through the ports of Dade County is accounted for by the approximately $4 billion trade between that county and the Caribbean. According to economic projections, Miami is poised for record growth in international business in the near future.

Yet the Afrikan American natives of Dade County by all measures are literally shut-out of the tourist industry and from its general economy. Despite the hefty contributions of Black Americans and Caribbeans to the economy of Miami and Florida as a whole, Blacks in Dade County have been left far behind in the field of entrepreneurship by relatively recent immigrants to the area, especially Cubans. It was a Cuban leadership which successfully persuaded Dade County and Miami Beach mayors and officials to refuse requests by Blacks and other progressives to issue a proclamation recognizing the visit of Nelson Mandela, South Afrikan anti-apartheid leader, to South Florida. This was done in reprisal for Mandela's expressed gratitude for the support Cuban troops had given Angola against South Afrikan nationalist apartheid forces. Blacks in Dade County reacted to this rebuff by staging a boycott against the tourist industry beginning on July 17, 1990. The boycott ended on May 13, 1993. The boycott was primarily organized and led by H.T. Smith, a Miami-based criminal and civil attorney. Mr. Smith and Ms. Marilyn Holyfields, a member of Holland and Knight, the largest law firm in Florida, were the boycott's sole spokespersons. Black lawyers and professionals along with the working people of Miami pledged to continue the boycott for as long as it took to succeed. All the participants initially committed themselves to work for 10 years (*The Final Call*, 9/14/94). The National Bar Association, the organization of which Attorney Smith is president, was the first organization to cancel a convention scheduled for Miami. This cancellation was followed by the cancellation of 28 national conventions that had been booked. These convention cancellations amounted to approximately $50 million in loss revenues indirectly (*The Final Call*, ibid).

A positive side-effect of the Miami boycott was the economic benefit to Black-owned facilities and businesses. The number of people who began patronizing Black-owned businesses increased astronomically.

After a boycott which repeatedly precipitated the canceling of some 28 conventions and $50 million losses in revenues during the three years it was in effect, and after 18 months of negotiations, Blacks in Dade County consummated an agreement with the powers-that-be to pursue the following goals:

> Among the goals of the agreement are: an African-American-owned convention quality hotel; stepped up purchasing from African-American-owned businesses; scholarships, internships and workstudy opportunities for African-Americans in educational and training programs for visitor industry jobs; support for African-American financial institutions; loan and equity funds for African-American businesses; and recruitment of African-Americans for jobs in Dade's visitor industry and other business sectors.[11]

Overall, the agreement included 20 short-term plans to assist the Afrikan American community to achieve certain specified economic goals over a period of three years. According to the *Final Call* (ibid) "Those plans include creating 2,500 jobs in hospitality management, tourism in-roads programs, placing 20 blacks on the hotel's board of directors and 120 full scholarships in hospitality and management. The *Final Call* went on to report the following:

> **Miami**—In a historic move, The Miami Beach City Commission recently approved the Sheraton Suites project, a hotel that will be developed and owned by the HCF Group, a corporation led by four Black Miami businessmen.
>
> The project is designed to become the country's first hotel complex developed and owned by blacks and involves building a 265-room Sheraton Hotel in South Beach, Miami, and renovating two adjacent hotels. Its estimated $37 million cost includes $10 million in city financial incentives.
>
> Although the hotel now serves as a monument to the progress Blacks can make in Miami, what is equally compelling is the catalyst that prompted Miami's most influential business leaders and elected city officials to make overtures to open up such lucrative contracts to Blacks.
>
> H.T. Smith, a Miami-based criminal and civil attorney, said Beach commissioner approval of the hotel was one stop made by the city government and business leaders to fulfill promises made as part of a settlement that ended a powerful and effective Black boycott against tourism in South Florida's Dade County and Miami.

---

11. *New York Amsterdam News*, ibid.

Finally, some 1,050 days after he had been there and gone, the political establishment of the Metro-Dade area issued a proclamation welcoming Nelson Mandela. The Miami boycott dramatically illustrates what the power of an organized and fully committed movement of Afrikan Americans can achieve, especially when it includes and is supported by all the class and social units of the community. An organized Black consumer movement across the country is quite capable of achieving goals like and far beyond those achieved in Miami.

Box 24-2 — **The Power of Refusal**

Social Power is more effect than cause. It is generated by social relationships — the habitual ways in which human beings relate to and align themselves with one another. Power is based on the manner in which persons and groups interact with one another.

The powerful rule with the consent of the subordinate, consent created by ideological sleight-of-hand. Ultimately, the legitimacy and exercise of power by the powerful require the cooperation and active support of the subordinate, both behavioral orientations also skillfully manipulated by the powerful to begin with. If certain types of social relationships among the subordinate themselves and between the subordinate and the powerful are required to generate the power exercised by the powerful, then the self-determined changes of relationships among the subordinate and between the subordinate and powerful will lead to commensurate changes in the quantity and quality of power exercised by the powerful. If the cooperation and consent of the subordinate with and to the demands of the powerful are required to generate the power expropriated and exercised by the powerful, then a refusal of cooperation and consent on the part of the subordinate will lead to the disempowerment of the powerful. Successful non-cooperation, open disobedience, militant opposition, passive resistance, the withdrawal or refusal of consent and cooperation on the part of the subordinate not only lead to a reduction, neutralization or destruction of the power exercised by the powerful but more importantly, generate increased power which can be exercised by the subordinate themselves to achieve their own self-defined goals.

For example, an economic boycott organized by the subordinate, that is, where members of the subordinate participate in refusing to have certain commercial dealings with the powerful, substantially demonstrates how the subordinate may empower themselves and simultaneously disempower the powerful and change the relations and structure of social power. The following list of recent boycotts illustrates how unified actions on the part of the subordinate may effectively bring about social changes in power relations between themselves and the powerful. ◼

Avoidance maneuvers

Recent travel boycotts have cost states and cities millions, according to convention and visitors bureaus. A sampling:

Alaska
November – December 1992
- **Issue:** Animal rights. State planned to kill 300 gray wolves to promote growth of caribou, moose herds.
- **Economic cost:** Probably not much. Alaska hit record high 1.1 million visitors in '93.
- **Resolution:** Wolf kill delayed one year.

Arizona
January 1987 – November 1992
- **Issue:** Martin Luther King holiday. First the governor eliminated the holiday, then the voters agreed.
- **Economic cost:** $100–250 million in Phoenix, says city's Convention & Visitors Bureau.
- **Resolution:** Voters approved a King holiday in November '92.

Colorado
November 1992 – December 1993
- **Issue:** Gay and lesbian rights. Voters approved barring any law that protects homosexuals from discrimination.
- **Economic cost:** $38 million in Denver, says city's CVB.
- **Resolution:** Federal court ruled law unconstitutional.

Florida (Miami Beach)
July 1990 – May 1993
- **Issue:** Cuban-American politicians in Miami snubbed Nelson Mandela. Black conventions and meetings boycotted Miami/Miami Beach to show black economic muscle.
- **Economic cost:** $17-18 million, says Miami CVB.
- **Resolution:** Jobs, training, scholarships for blacks in hospitality industry; $10 million toward building a black-owned hotel on Miami Beach.

Louisiana (New Orleans)
June 1991 – December 1992
- **Issue:** Abortion rights. Legislature approved strict anti-abortion law.
- **Economic cost:** $116 million in New Orleans, says CVB.
- **Resolution:** Federal court ruled law unconstitutional.

Ohio (Cincinnati)
November 1992 – August 1993
- **Issue:** Gay and lesbian rights. Voters changed the city's human rights ordinance to eliminate protection based on sexual orientation.
- **Economic cost:** $19.2 million, says Cincinnati CVB.
- **Resolution:** Federal judge ruled it unconstitutional. Ruling is being appealed.

Source: USA TODAY Research
Adapted from USA TODAY, October 11, 1994.

By Elys A. McLean, USA TODAY

Box 24-3 — Economic Democracy

True economic development and empowerment of the Afrikan American community does not begin with the mere employment of its constituents by other ethnic communities which own and monopolize all the vital and important means of production and wealth creation. They begin and end with the *economic organization* of the whole of the Afrikan American community under its own auspices, direction and financial control to create opportunity for its constituents through its self-determined commercial and trade organizations and activities. Whatever the goals the community sets for itself, even when they may require the cooperation and financial support of other groups, it must achieve through its own cooperative efforts and financial genius. The ultimate goals of the community in addition to the acquisition of more jobs, small business loans and purchasing agreements, must include the establishment of genuine *Economic democracy* in America and the world. Economic democracy refers to the pluralistic ownership of the economy, its productive resources and facilities as well its wealth. By pluralistic we mean where ethnic groups *own* meaningful properties in the economy or where the economy is perceived and utilized as a public trust for the benefit of all the people instead of as the property of a particular race, social class, or a small group of races, ethnic groups, or classes. A more complete economic agreement of the Afrikan American community with White and other ethnic communities is one which involves not only their making available to Afrikan American businesses loans, equity funds and the like, but funds which would permit Afrikan American businesses and the community to own substantial equity in established and developing mainstream businesses.

Economic democracy is facilitated by the national Afrikan American community's development of the leverage and ability to form partnerships to buy substantial equities in ongoing mainstream business concerns; to purchase such businesses outright, and to invest in worldwide mining, manufacturing and financial ventures. Economic democracy involves the coming together of community institutions, organizations, individuals and investment groups to form large mutual fund establishments in order to purchase influential equity in major mainstream, national and multinational corporations. Economic pluralism involves the ideology that Black consumers will not continue to support industries and producers where Blacks are not substantially represented as investors and owners of equity. Black consumers with their leaders should no longer demand only jobs and a few franchises for their support of large corporations, but should demand significant equity in them — equity owned by Black not-for-profit organizations or by for-profit commonwealth mutual funds which the Black community owns through its investments in them. Afrikan American community commonwealth funds should therefore not only invest in the economic infrastructure and development of the community but also invest in corporate entities which profit significantly from the community both here and across the Diaspora.

Creating and Meeting Black Consumer Needs

We have just discussed how crucial Black consumers are to the economic expansion and power of the Afrikan American community. We emphasized the fact that if Black consumers were to spend only a fraction of their dollars with Black businesses, the economic system which now characterizes the community would be radically transformed and Black economic and political power decisively enhanced. It was noted that Black consumers spend approximately five cents out of each dollar with Black businesses. The reasons for this situation are many — the chief among them being the monopolistic domination of the Afrikan American market by the White American business establishments based on a long history of White racist repression of Black economic development and self-sufficiency. In a hierarchical fashion the White American monopolistic control of the Afrikan American market has been supplemented, and in numerous instances, supplanted, by other ethnic groups such as Cubans, Koreans, Arabs, Indians, and so on. As we have already pointed out, these groups have joined the White business and economic establishment in virtually excluding by various discriminatory and repressive maneuvers Black-owned businesses from the marketplace, even within the Black community itself. Obviously, the structuring of the American business/economic system along the race-based monopolistic lines we have just described, literally "compels" the Black consumer to spend the very large bulk of his dollars with non-Black businesses even if he were of a mind not to do so. The overwhelming effect of White-owned media advertising, the advantageous pricing and discount and stocking policies of White businesses; the imitation of White consumer patterns and tastes by many Blacks; the identification of shopping in non-Black business establishments by Blacks with "first class citizenship", among other comparative advantages held by White and non-Black businesses, converge to push the Black consumer away from what few Black businesses there are. The presence of ethnic monopolies as well as the relative paucity of investment capital discourage the entry of Black-owned businesses into the Black consumer market. The racist sociopsychological conditioning produces a "feel-good" worthy experience and a sense of heightened self-esteem when he shops in White-owned or non-Black-owned establishments; which makes him feel that somehow "the White man's ice is colder", "his sugar sweeter"; which stokes his need to curry the social acceptance of non-Black merchants by being acknowledged by them (a consequence of self-hatred), and the "crabs in a barrel" syndrome (fearing the success of other Blacks), etc., — has viciously militated

(1) *Weekly Income Level	(1) Number of Black Persons	(2) Proposed Minimum Weekly Spending	(3) Yearly Total Individual Weekly (52) Spending	(4) Total Yearly Spending Level	(5) Weekly Proposed Banking	(6) Total Yearly Banking For Capital Base
0 – $192	132,494	$20.00	$1,040.00	$137,793,760	$5.00	$34,448,400
$193 – $288	47,273	$39.00	$2,028.00	$95,869,644	$12.00	$29,498,352
$289 – $481	24,803	$66.00	$3,432.00	$85,123,896	$16.00	$20,636,096
$482 – $673	2,544	$89.00	$4,628.00	$11,773,632	$26.00	$3,439,488
$674 – $962	3,604	$98.00	$5,096.00	$18,365,984	$36.00	$6,746,688
$963 – $1,442	1,696	$129.00	$6,708.00	$11,376,768	$51.00	$4,497,792
	212,414			$360,303,684		$99,266,856

1. Total number of Black persons in the work force expected to participate in order that this economic plan is a total success.
2. Amount as a minimum that each income producing person should spend with Black owned business
3. The total weekly sum of the spending taken place in item #2 per individual.
4. The total yearly sum of the spending taken place in item #1 as shown in item #3.
5. The amount each person should have to build wealth and promote Black financial institutions.
6. Total funds available for financing the industrial growth.

* Statistical Abstract of the United States 1993, 113th Edition. (Bureau of the Census)

Note: This key also applies to Table 24–9 which additionally reflects both minimum and maximum ends of spending and saving levels of a proposed National Economic Plan.

Table 24–8 **Sample Economic Plan**

(1) 1991 Weekly Income Level	(1) Number of Black Households (million)	(2) Proposed Minimum Weekly Spending	(3) Total Yearly Spending Level	(4) Total Household Yearly Spending	(5) Weekly Proposed Saving	(6) Annual Total Available Saving for Capital Base
0 – $104	1.396	$10.00	$520	$725,920,000	$4.00	$290,368,000
$105 – $208	1.995	$11.00 – $21.00	$572 $1,092	$1,141,140,000 $2,178,540,000	$5.00 – $8.00	$518,700,000 $829,920,000
$209 – $312	1.259	$22.00 – $31.00	$1,144 $1,612	$1,440,296,000 $2,029,508,000	$9.00 – $12.00	$589,212,000 $785,616,000
$313 – $520	1.995	$32.00 – $52.00	$1,664 $2,704	$3,319,680,000 $5,394,480,000	$13.00 – $20.00	$1,348,620,000 $2,074,800,000
$521 – $729	1.529	$53.00 – $73.00	$2,756 $3,796	$4,213,924,000 $5,804,084,000	$21.00 – $30.00	$1,669,668,000 $2,385,240,000
$730 – $1,041	1.485	$74.00 – $104.00	$3,848 $5,408	$5,714,280,000 $8,030,880,000	$31.00 – $42.00	$2,393,820,000 $3,243,240,000
$1,042 – $1,562	.930	$105.00 – $156.00	$5,460 $8,112	$5,077,800,000 $7,544,160,000	$43.00 – $60.00	$2,079,480,000 $2,901,600,000
$1,563+	.410	$175.00	$9,100	$3,731,000,000	$75.00	$3,731,000,000
Total	10.999		$25,064 $32,344	$25,364,040,000 $35,438,572,000		$12,620,868,000 $16,241,784,000

Table 24-9 **Proposed National Economic Plan**

– 623 –

against Black entrepreneurialism. The merchants of other ethnic groups can take for granted the commercial support of their own particular group, the unreserved support of Black consumers, and a significant proportion of other ethnic consumers. Black merchants cannot take such privileges for granted, especially the commercial support from non-Blacks; they cannot take for granted the commercial support of their own ethnic group. Thus, even when Black entrepreneurs sell the same goods and services at or below competitive prices, civil rights, religious and liberal American political propaganda have succeeded in making many Black consumers feel that to support a business because it is Black-owned is a form of self-segregation, "reverse discrimination", is anti-American, racist, sinful, or morally unacceptable. Many Black consumers may feel guilty for consciously discriminating in favor of Black-owned businesses — despite the fact that all other ethnic group consumers engage in these practices vis-à-vis their own group-owned businesses relative to those owned by Blacks. The Black consumer represents a complex of motives and orientations for the Black merchant, which adds to the other daunting problems he or she must resolve in creating and maintaining his or her business establishment.

The Black consumer represents a complex riddle for the Black merchant and service establishment. Black business and service establishments must aggressively compete against other non-Black business and service establishments even when they offer goods and services loyal and better than their non-Black counterparts. However, this is not to say that the Black consumer is unreachable by Black businesses and the Black consumer is unalterably loyal or attached to non-Black, particularly to White-owned business establishments as our forgoing discussion might imply.

The Black consumer is not a White consumer "who happens to be Black." Black consumers exhibit different spending patterns, spending more or less on a variety of products and services than White consumers. Black consumer tastes differ from those of Whites on a number of dimensions. They react differently to advertising campaigns. For example, according to the *Wall Street Journal* (4/9/93) almost 60% of the nation's 31 million Black consumers feel that most commercials and print ads are designed only for White people (based on a study by Yankelovich Partners Inc. and the Burrell communications group). Based on the aforementioned study, the *Journal* reports that "African-Americans have more money to spend, are far more avid shoppers, and far less brand-loyal and more receptive to advertising than most marketers realize." Black consumers generally pay more attention to advertising than Whites and are particularly more responsive to commercials in which they are portrayed. A much larger percentage of Black than White consumers enjoy clothes shopping; are avid bargain hunters; are more likely to gather information about purchases by talking to salespersons, manufacturers and paying attention to advertising (*Wall Street Journal*, 4/19/93).

The Politics of Black Consumer Tastes

Black consumer tastes and habits are not monolithic or unchanging in that they reflect reactions to current fashions, trends, fads and the like. It is pertinent in this context to note that these tastes and habits also reflect current states of political consciousness and stages of political-social development. The fact that many Blacks have been deeply influenced by the Black Nationalist, Black Pride and Afrocentric movements is reflected in the very large number of them who consistently wear apparel projecting Afrikan-centered images. It is quite common to see Afrikan Americans sporting caps and T-shirts depicting other Afrikan American and continental Afrikan heroes/heroines, proverbs, geographical images, historical events. More striking is the wearing of Afrikan-style clothes of all types made from Afrikan fabrics. Dashikis, various styles of head-dress, Kente cloth garments of all types, Afrikan-style ornaments, Afrikan colors, etc., are very popular with a large segment of the Afrikan American population. The broad extent of Black consumer demand for things Afrikan and Afrikan American as well as things sold by Afrikan American merchants is demonstrated by the vast increase in the number of vendors, shopkeepers and wholesalers across the country in the past two decades who distribute and sell Afrikan-style merchandise. Huge Afrikan festivals featuring large numbers of vendors selling Afrikan-style items and merchandise, Afrikan-centered books and cultural icons, foods, art & crafts, music, etc., are now commonplace in many parts of the country.

The growing Afrikan-centeredness of Black consumers has been and is the result of, in large part, the Afrocentric movement which, taking advantage of American race politics, using all of the classic methods of propaganda and attitude change, has had a remarkable impact on the Afrikan American community and the nation as a whole. This applies to the spending habits and tastes of Black consumers as well. Black consumers — responding to Black nationalist appeals, Afrocentricism, to the obvious failure of the politics of assimilation, the virulent racism of White America, the crushing economic and social crises of urban Black America today, as well as to the possibility for developing really significant economic-political power in the world — are becoming increasingly more politically sensitive about their spending and consumption habits.

The Economics of Afrocentrism

The profitability of Afrocentrism is graphically demonstrated by Southern-born, Afrikan-American Carole Riley's success with her two McDonald's franchises. Carole Riley re-opened her two franchises in Harlem after completely refurbishing them with Afrocentric thematic designs. According to *Black Enterprise* (5/93):

> Last fall, Riley resurrected what was once a graffiti-plagued, cramped McDonald's restaurant and turned it into what Harlem patrons call "a joy" and McDonald's Corp. regional managers consider a financial success. Riley and her associate, graphics designer Kelly Givens, created a store adorned with Kente cloth and African-American art.
>
> McDonald's invested $1 million to overhaul the restaurant to Riley's unique specifications. "We wanted the community to know it was their McDonald's," Riley, 36, explains. Since reopening in September, Riley's 125th Street outlet has sales 40% higher than the same period last year.
>
> Riley, a graduate of Atlanta's Spelman College who holds an MBA from Atlanta University, also owns a second McDonald's franchise in Harlem, which she reopened on Lenox Ave. last May.
>
> That store also enjoys the Riley touch, with sales increases through the summer months of more than 35%, compared with the previous year. Riley's outlets employ more than 120 people.

Even Riley's McDonald's staff is outfitted in Kente hats, ties and vests. It is interesting to note that in the same edition of *Black Enterprise*, a full-page ad for Pepsico, Inc. presents a picture containing Larry Drake, a KFC vice president responsible for much of its business in the Midwest (KFC is a subsidiary of Pepsico), and four members of a staff, in one of KFC's outlets outfitted in Kente cloth uniforms. The ad reads in part:

> Larry and his KFC team members are not only actively involved in their communities, they recently re-designed their restaurants, uniforms and menus to represent the interest of Chicago consumers. They added collard greens, red beans & rice, and sweet potato pie to their menu and swapped KFC's traditional uniforms for vests, ties, and hats made of kente cloth. "KFC wants to be involved in our neighborhoods," Larry Drake says. "We serve on community boards, hire from the local market, support minority business development

and franchise ownership, and try to respond to the demands of our loyal customers. In Chicago, and all across America — KFC Is Cooking."

Many non-Black merchants are taking note of the enormous potential of the Black consumer market and the changing tastes and sensitivities of Black consumers. For example, cosmetics companies are all seeking to grab a significant percentage of the $600 million to $1 billion Black consumer market for cosmetics; such companies as Revlon, Esteé Lauder (which through its subsidiary, Prescriptive Inc., features the All Skins line of cosmetics), Maybelline, the IVAX corporation (an international conglomerate which purchased for $67 million the Black-owned, Chicago-based Johnson Products, whose products, e.g., Ultra Sheen, Classy Curl, dominated the Black consumer personal and hair care market), Proctor & Gamble (who spun out 72 new Cover Girl makeup shades for darker complexions), and Avon Products (long popular with Black consumers and which produces the Tones of Beauty line). In this context the following news story is of special interest.

Study Dispels Myths of Hair-Care Products

African American consumers were surprised to find that many of the hair-care products they have been using were not manufactured by African American companies, according to an extensive brand-awareness study conducted by Viewpoint Inc., a Chicago-based market-research firm.

The two-phased study included the use of focus groups and 500 telephone interviews with African American hair-care consumers in the 10 largest markets of the United States. The margin of error for the study is 4 percent.

The study further showed that Black consumers had assumed that brands such as African Pride, TCB, Dark & Lovely, Let's Jam, Right on Curl and Bone Straight were manufactured by African American companies.

Additionally, 79 percent of the African American consumers said it was important to them that they purchase hair products manufactured by African Americans.

Seventy-seven percent of these consumers said that if they knew which brands were African American, they would show a preference in purchasing these brands in the future.[12]

Obviously, there is gold not only in Afrikan soil, but also in Afrikan styles and tastes. Moreover, entrepreneurs have made the

---

12. *The City Sun* 8/4–12/93.

startling discovery that there is gold in the words "African", "Africa", and the Black nationalist colors — red, black, and green — a precious legacy left by The Honorable Marcus Mosiah Garvey to the whole of the Afrikan Diaspora as the symbolic colors for Afrikan peoples everywhere. While some White-owned companies are satisfied just to sell cosmetics in the Afrikan American market using Afrikan- or Black American-style logos, e.g., "African Pride", "Dark & Lovely", one of these companies has gone so far as to try and claim as protected trademarks the word "African" and related variations of this word as well as the Afrikan nationalist colors.

Many in the Afrikan American community were outraged to learn that "A White-owned hair product company masquerading as a Black company via red, black and green labels and logo and the name African Pride, [which] markets products for the Afrocentric trade in oils, braid sprays, etc, [was] suing a Black-owned company for the use of the trade mark "African" in their logo (*New York Amsterdam News*, 9/18/93 – "Stealing our Name and our Game!"). This company was unhappy with a Black company's use of the logo — "Mother Africa" — in conjunction with the colors red, black and green imprinted on its products. It was also unhappy with another Black-owned company's marketing of a new line called "African Royale". The same White-owned company sought to prevent a third Black-owned company from using the words "African Natural" on its products.

Kuba Cloth — Afrika from time immemorial has influenced the tastes and values of non-Afrikans in innumerable ways. In these times of anti-Afrikan, anti-Black sentiment, particularly in the United States, it is forgotten that Afrika, its raw materials, arts and crafts, food products, cultural arts and sciences were central to the trade and commerce of the ancient and modern worlds. The ability of things Afrikan, of Afrikan commodities, tastes, and styles to heavily impact the non-Afrikan world market is still very potent. However, in order for this to occur Afrikans must unashamedly claim their ethnocultural identity and consciousness, creatively cultivate and evolve their spiritual and material resources. When this happens, those products become the objects of interest and fascination for non-Afrikans as well as Afrikans and thereby become a part of trade relations both inside and outside the culture, leading to its material and spiritual enrichment.

Kuba cloth, a hand-embroidered grass cloth from Zaire sold by retailer African Home of Brooklyn, New York, illustrates our point. According to the *New York Times* (12/9/93), in 1989 Dent and Kim

Bressant-Kibwe, owners of African Home, opened their store specializing in objects and textiles made by Afrikan tribal artisans. They feature Kente cloth, imported fabric like damask, which they give an Afrikan touch through tie-dying or batik. Ochre and red-striped pillows are made from handwoven silk and Kente cloth-strips of fabric handstitched by Ghanaian men. They also feature other sophisticated stripes, spirals, geometrics and animal patterns freehand designed by Afrikan artisans, as well as baskets, fabric screens and other artistic creations. The *Times* reports that one year after they opened, the store grossed only $5,000. In 1992, it grossed $100,000. While sixty percent of its customers are Afrikan American, the remaining forty percent include people from other ethnic groups.

International Trade and Local Taste — The economic ascendance of Homeland Fashions of New York City richly illustrates the fact that trade follows the path of taste. The stimulation of taste lays the foundation for initiating and sustaining the entrepreneurial means for satisfying it. Changes in consumer tastes presage changes in economic production and trade as well as possible changes in trade relations and organization and in the redistribution of wealth. The European taste for sugar, molasses and rum, and for clothes made of cotton rewrote the economic history and map of the world. European wealth, power and monopolistic trade relations in contrast with Afrikan poverty, powerlessness and dependent trade relations are to a significant degree founded on the ability of Europeans to discover and/or socially engineer Afrikan consumer tastes and their ability to engineer the trade relations by which those tastes are satisfied. This discovery and production of desire are the pillars of local, national and international trade. And trade, needless to say, whether local, national or international, is a major source of wealth and power.

Our central contention in this section is that the discovery and/or social engineering of Afrikan tastes by Afrikan themselves can lay the economic foundations for the construction of Afrikan wealth and power, if Afrikans also engineer the trade relations by which those tastes are satiated. This is the fundamental challenge for Afrikan consumers and entrepreneurs across the Afrikan diaspora. For upon the rock of profitable Afrikan trade relations with other Afrikans will be built Afrikan trade relations with all peoples.

Homeland Fashions, founded by Mohamed Diop of Senegal, Afrika, has blazed an entrepreneurial and trade relations trail by his brilliantly successful efforts to satisfy the tastes of Afrikan Americans — tastes stimulated by the Afrikan nationalist movement — for things

Afrikan, for consumables from the Motherland. As noted by *Forbes* magazine (September 26, 1994):

> Homeland Fashions, based in New York, is cashing in on the demand from black Americans and fellow African emigrants for Afrocentric items. Homeland imports textiles from Senegal and Ghana to make over 300 Afrocentric items — from $200 evening suits to $8 *kente* baseball caps. He mails catalogs for both the wholesale and retail markets to individuals and small shops. From sales of $4 million in 1992, Diop expects to bring in $6 million this year, perhaps more if the Black Entertainment Television's new home shopping show takes off.

Diop employs several hundred of his fellow emigrants as workers at piecemeal. Diop's Homeland Fashions story is part of the larger story of Senegalese and American, especially Senegalese and Afrikan American cultural and trade relations. The Afrikan-centered consciousness and tastes of Afrikan Americans have become the bases for the reorganization and accelerated development of Senegalese tourist and international trade. *Forbes* goes on to note:

> In 1677 Senegal's Gorée Island was developed by French merchants as a place to warehouse goods bound for the New World or to swap for slaves. In the 1970s Gorée was developed by Senegal for tourism. Black Americans came and bought souvenirs.
>
> Soon Senegalese artisans and business people learned to manufacture for export their cowrie-shell bracelets and goatskin drums instead of waiting for tourists to come and buy them. An ebony carving selling for $5 in Dakar might fetch $20 in the U.S.; a boubou dress that cost $25 is marked up to $100 across the Atlantic. Like Soviet students who paid $100 for faded blue jeans, a lot of African-Americans pay a premium for authentic African wares, especially if an authentic African is the vendor.
>
> Then some of these people began developing their own distribution networks....
>
> As the trading networks grew, so did the product lines. Mohamed Diop created *kente* cloth fashions, hired emigrant tailors to make clothes and began moving his merchandise through African-American festivals.

The trade in Afrikan goods is such that one warehouse on Manhattan's West Side serves as an informal wholesale bazaar to "more than a 1,000 Afrikan businessmen," according to Mohammad DiBassy who handles large shipments of goods sent over from various Afrikan nations on container ships.

Diop and other such Senegalese vendors form a significant source of export trade and hard currency for the people and economy of Senegal. The significance of their trade is such that La Banque de L'Habitat du Senegal, a Senegalese-based bank located in New York, revealed that it transferred to Afrika about $4 million by September 1994, up from just $900,000 in the whole of 1993.

A major source of sales for Afrikan vendors, particularly the Senegalese, is Afrikan-centered cultural events sponsored and attended predominantly by Afrikan Americans all across the country.

> From April to September Senegalese travel the U.S. in cars and minivans, toting bags to dozens of black-oriented craft shows, jazz festivals or African Pride events. In Philadelphia a FORBES reporter counted five vanloads of vendors from Senegal and neighboring Mali at the River Blues festival. Detroit's annual African World Festival attracts on average 1 million patrons, and over 100 Senegalese vendors.
>
> By going on the road these sharp-trading peddlers increase the already attractive margins they're earning in New York. For example, a handmade *kora*, a stringed instrument played like a harp, that costs $10 in the market in Dakar and goes for $50 in New York, is marked up to $80 at the Detroit festival. And, besides individual sales, the peddlers unload hundreds of dollars worth of souvenirs to wholesalers who run their own boutiques across the Midwest. Most of their customers are African-Americans and Senegalese who are settling in other cities.
>
> "It's big business," says James Wyatt of the Museum of African American History, which sponsors the Detroit festival. "I've heard of peddlers clearing $15,000 in a single week-end." And much of the money is tax free, since much of the business is done in cash.

We should note that many street vendors and most of the vendors at Afrikan-centered festivals and craft shows who sell Afrikan wares are native-born Afrikan Americans as are many importers of Afrikan goods. Moreover, we should note the huge potential for international trade the Afrikan American market represents for Afrikans on the continent and Afrikan Americans in the United States. Afrikan Americans and Afrikans abroad can vastly and mutually enrich each other through the Afrikan-centered international trade of not only Afrikan arts, crafts and other cultural paraphernalia but also in continental Afrikan/Afrikan American-originated manufactures, goods and services from the simple to the complex, from low-tech to high-tech.

J.C. Penney's Afrikan Boutiques — The Black consumer market has now been especially targeted by White-owned corporations such as Mattel, Pillsbury, Quaker Oats, Toys "R" Us, K-Mart, and J.C. Penney. For example, *Newsweek* (4/6/92) reported J.C. Penney's targeting of Black consumers based on the increased Afrocentric consciousness of the Afrikan American community:

> Dallas-based J.C. Penney Co. has tested 20 "Authentic African" boutiques in its home-town and other cities such as Jersey City, N.J., and Cleveland where Blacks represent 20% or more of the population. The tiny shops, which are located inside J.C. Penney stores, featured clothing, handbags, hats, and other accessories that are imported from West Afrika.
>
> One problem: The stores have sold out of nearly all their initial $250,000 in merchandise. But Penney plans to restock for an August rollout in 50 to 150 stores. "Our customers really want this," says Bruce M. Ackerman, Penney's operations manager for merchandising. "It's brought in a lot of shoppers who wouldn't normally go into our store."

However, after successfully launching its pioneering "Authentic African" boutiques, J.C. Penney closed them in late 1992 because, as it reportedly intimated, "we had difficulty getting merchandise to meet our quality standards and experienced quite a few delays" (WSJ, 10/26/93 – "Stores Have Different Ideas on African Style"). These difficulties occurred at the time Penney was attempting to expand its Afrikan boutiques to 350 stores from 22. Authentic Afrikan cloth and garments made for the U.S. market are getting harder to come by because that the market is being flooded by mass-produced *Afrikan-style* prints manufactured by large Asian mills. These difficulties have by no means pushed Penney's off the field. This Dallas-based chain launched its "Global Effects" line in October, 1993 in 107 of its 1,266 outlets, featuring hundreds of products, from bath supplies to hats with bold fabrics and bright colors to wide-legged jeans to bedspreads with Afrikan mud-cloth designs, targeted for Afrikan Americans and Hispanics (*New York Daily News*, 9/9/93 – "An Ethnic Penney's Pitch"). This retail giant with national sales of $18 billion in 1992, also plans to sell these products through a Penney catalog aimed at these populations as well. For example, some of the products to be sold to Afrikan Americans "will include authentic African artwork; children's clothes sporting ethnic versions of Looney Tunes characters with Bugs Bunny in baggy pants and the Tasmanian Devil in Dreadlocks; darker shades of pantyhose and brightly colored full body suits" (*Daily News*, 9/9/93).

Afrikan tastes and styles have moved into the "upscale market" as evidenced by Montgomery Ward's announcement (WSJ, 10/26/93) that it plans to launch 30 in-store boutiques offering Afrikan styles and furnishings. The boutiques, referred to as "Homeland Authentics" were to open in about 8% of its stores in the Fall, 1993. According to a spokesman for the retailer, the boutiques will capitalize on the popularity of Afrikan-print cloth used in U.S.-style clothing and will capitalize on their experience which "found this niche to be profitable and it makes more of an impact when it's centrally displayed."

E Style and McCalls Patterns — A study by Essence Communications Inc. in conjunction with Simmons Market Research Bureau found that Black consumers spend some $180 million on books a year. Approximately $38 million of this total involves purchases made through book clubs. The study further revealed that Blacks spend about $5.2 billion on new cars and trucks and $3.3 billion on travel. The clothes buying habits of Blacks are such that Spiegel Inc. launched an "E Style" catalog targeting the readers of Johnson Publishing Company's *Ebony* magazine.

The merchandiser for E Style is Lori Scott of the Bronx, N.Y. whose father was a tailor. An Afrikan American, Lori Scott intimated that when she was growing up she could tell that the clothing companies were not designing clothes with Black women in mind. Her father often altered the clothes she bought. E Style was mailed to more than one million households in September, 1993. The slick four-color book features stylish Black women modeling "fashion-forward designs, bolder accessories, brighter colors and authentic ethnic fabrics and ensembles" (*New York Newsday*, 10/14/93 – "An Ethnic Appeal"). Spiegel interviewed and measured more than 1,300 Afrikan American women in developing the catalog. Many of the women suggested proportional changes such as longer sleeves.

In August 1993 *Essence* magazine introduced into major department stores Essence Pantyhose. Bucking the trend where mainstream designers and manufacturers produced one color of pantyhose or stockings for Black women, usually "coffee colored" versions of legwear originally designed for White women, Essence Pantyhose features narrower knitted ankles, fuller hips and a choice of color tones.

Not to be outdone in cashing in on the large market for clothes suited to the tastes of Afrikan American women as well as their increasing appetite to dress in Afrikan apparel, the McCall Pattern Co. recently introduced a group of patterns it calls "the only authentic African designs available to home sewers" (*New York Newsday*,

10/14/93 – "African Designs To Sew"). The patterns were created by Nigerian designer Emeaba Emeaba. Two weeks after their introduction the pattern reached McCall's top-10 best-seller list. Among the patterns are "Nne Uku," a dress that distinguishes an Afrikan man's first wife; "Ad'eze," a maternity-style outfit; a "Ball Boy," a lounging robe.

Afrikan Dolls — It is intriguingly interesting to find that 54 years after famed social psychologist Kenneth B. Clark discovered Black children's greater preference for White dolls over Black dolls, interpreted by him to indicate their low self-esteem and perhaps, self-hatred, Blacks dolls are the rage for White merchandisers and Black families. Apparently, this too speaks of the change in Afrikan American tastes stimulated by American racial and political history since that time. The influence of Black nationalism and Afrocentrism on the consciousness of the Afrikan American community is perhaps most responsible for this trend. As with all else, the White American capitalist system has proceeded to transform that consciousness into a "cash cow."

Although the contemporary marketing of Black dolls and toys was first pioneered by Black-owned companies like the Olmec Corp. of New York City, and people like Yla Eason, its creator who started the company when she could not find a Black superhero doll for her son, White-owned companies have now taken the field (*Business Week*, 4/6/92 – "Waking up to a Major Market"). In being preempted by established White firms, Eason entered her $2 million company, which markets more than 60 Black and Hispanic dolls, into a distribution partnership with Hasbro Inc. As reported by *Business Week*, both Mattel Inc. and Tyco Industries Inc. have fielded Black dolls. Tyco just recently introduced its female doll called Kenya and her little sister Baby Kiana (*New York Daily News*, 10/22/93 – "Tyco's Kenya, Kiana build Self-Esteem"). Mattel has introduced three slim fashion dolls, Shani, Asha, and Michelle plus Shani's new boyfriend Jamal. They come in three complexions — light, medium and dark and are outfitted in very colorful ethnic clothes.

Tyco reports that sales of Kenya, retailing for $29, have been phenomenal. She was completely sold out before Christmas of 1992. Besides their Afrikan American features and various skin tones, Kenya and Baby Kiana feature long thick curly hair that can be straightened with a "magic lotion", a moisturizing solution, or braided into cornrows with attached colored beads.

Toys and Games Industry — America spends some $17 billion on toys. According to Census Bureau figures, toys and games alone account for between $4.5–4.6 billion in American manufacturing output annually. Obviously, toys and games production and sales constitute a large industry and market. Afrikan American and other minority children form an increasingly significant segment of this market. As outlined in *Table* 24–10, 28% of the nation's 57 million children under the age of 14 are Black or Hispanic. By the year 2010, 35% of the nation's children will be Black or Hispanic. By the year 2020 or shortly thereafter, Black, Hispanic, and other minority group children will constitute a majority of the children in the United States.

Black Americans spent approximately $750 million on toys, dolls and games in 1992.

Market of the future

Breakdown of kids age 14 and under:

	Now	2010
Number of kids	56,824,000	60,463,000
Black	14.8%	16.0%
Hispanic	13.3%	18.8%
White	67.3%	57.8%
American Indian, Eskimo, Aleut	1.0%	1.0%
Asian, Pacific Islander	3.5%	6.4%

Note: Figures may not add up to 100% due to rounding.
Source: Census Bureau

Table 24–10

Afrikan American Entrepreneurs and Afrikan-centered Marketing

Afrikan American Entrepreneurs also play with Toys — It is encouraging to see the Afrikan American entrepreneurs we have cited here as well as the many others we could not cite, aggressively penetrate the toys and games industry. What is even more encouraging is to see that this penetration is being facilitated by Afrocentric-based toys and games — toys and games based on Afrikan ethnicity, culture and experience. This entrepreneurial approach is not only of crucial social importance but is economically productive as well. The social and economic productivity of this approach is illustrated by the examples cited earlier as well as the entrepreneurial success story of Jacob R. Miles as reported in the *Wall Street Journal* (12/2/93).

> Mr. Miles, a former toy industry executive, refocused his Cultural Exchange Corp. early last year to design and market a line of playthings largely aimed at minority groups. The company recently made its first shipments to retailers Toys "R" Us Inc. and Dayton Hudson Corp. Sales, which will exceed $1 million for 1993, are poised to reach more than $10 million for 1994, the first full year of production, Mr. Miles predicts.... After spending 21 years in the toy industry, Mr. Miles believed he had viable ideas for toys aimed at minorities. When he lost his job as a manufacturing executive for Hasbro Inc. (after the toy maker shut the St. Louis Park, Minn., operations of its tonka division in late 1991), he invested his severance pay and retirement money in Cultural Exchange.
>
> Mr. Miles and his wife Rosalind N. Bell, a marketing manager who helps Grand Metropolitan PLC's Pillsbury unit target minority consumers, founded their company in 1990 as a sideline. At that time, they spent most of their workday operating a Minneapolis art and crafts gallery, which subsequently closed in 1992.
>
> Early last year, Mr. Miles decided to develop toys, books, puzzles, greeting cards and other products. He says the toy industry has largely failed to specially tailor such items for minorities.
>
> *Began With 'Hollywood Hounds'*
> Mr. Miles began by creating three prototypes for stuffed animals, called Hollywood Hounds, "the pets of America's culturally diverse families." For example, a dog named Spike, with the same flat-top hairstyle now favored by many black youths, wears a shirt with African colors and design. The entrepreneur also fashioned a story line, linking the characters and emphasizing values such as home and love.

From three prototypes Miles broadened his line to 18 products and expects to have 60 on the market by the end of 1994.

However, it must be kept in mind that the entrepreneurial activity of Afrikan American business persons need not be necessarily restricted to the manufacture and sales of Afrocentric products only, though these activities are of the utmost importance. Afrikan-centered production and sales may serve as powerful platforms for thrusting Afrikan American entrepreneurs into the general national and international marketplaces — producing for and selling to cross-cultural markets.

Bill Becoat of Bect Enterprises, Inc., whose entrepreneurial adventure was presented in *Black Enterprise* magazine (11/93), provides such an example. Becoat developed a two-wheel-drive bicycle beginning in 1986. After numerous rejections while trying to perfect the manufacture and licensing of his very innovative machine, Becoat raised more than $200,000 in working capital from friends. With some $2 million from other sources in start-up capital, Becoat reached a license agreement with MacGregor Sports Products Inc. to sell the Taiwan-made bike through discount stores for $150 to $350. Becoat has joined with Afrikan American attorney and "bicycle engineer" Eugene Spices to develop a top-of-the-line two-wheel-drive bicycle "Deuce" which he expects to enter into a future Tour de France, the world's most prestigious two-wheeler race. The Deuce is expected to retail for $450 to $3,000 each.

Lonnie Johnson of Atlanta, was the inventor of the Super Soaker, a colorful, large capacity (a prominent feature being their oversized cylindrical and bulbous water containers), and powerful, long-distance, pump-and-nozzle water pistol, extremely popular in the summer of 1993. Through the Larami Corporation, the Super Soaker sold 27 million units — some models retailing for more than $50. The Super Soaker was the most popular water gun in American retail history.

Just-Us-Books — In 1976, Afrikan American husband and wife team, Wade and Cheryl Hudson, faced a dilemma very common to Black households during that period — they were unable to find Afrikan American images to decorate their child's, a daughter, nursery. Not to be outdone, Cheryl, then an art editor at Houghton Mifflin, a major mainstream publishing house, using letters featuring the faces of Afrikan American children, drew her child's name with what she called "Afro-Bets" (*New York Daily News*, 12/21/93). This auspicious beginning led Cheryl to join with her husband, Wade, then a magazine writer, playwright and public relations specialist, to begin publishing the well-received children's book series, Afro-Bets, around 1988. Their publishing house, Just-Us-Books, celebrated its fifth anniversary in 1993.

Since its founding Just-Us-Books has published 18 children's books, all of which focus on the Afrikan American experience — utilizing Afrikan American characters complete with full-features such as cornrows and the various hues which characterize the race.

In their books which focus on career choices, real-life Afrikan Americans who are outstanding in their various professions and advocations are prominently featured.

The Hudson's roster of books, to which they add four new ones each year, is dedicated to building the self-esteem of Black children. They are utilized in schoolrooms across the country. Furthermore, they can be found across the country in Toys "R" Us, Hallmark, and Kmart. There is a special irony in the Hudson's success story in that before starting Just-Us-Books with $7,000 from their savings account, they tried unsuccessfully to sell their ideas for Afrikan American children's books to mainstream publishers. In 1994, they expect to net well over $2 million and to achieve exponential growth in earnings as they expand to meet the rapidly increasing demand for books that focus on the Afrikan American experience.

Bill Becoat, Lonnie Johnson, the Hudsons, and such others vividly demonstrate that creative and persistent Afrikan Americans can utilize both cultural and cross-cultural bases to achieve entrepreneurial success in and across cultural markets.

Afrocentric Weddings mean Business — The sociopolitical influence of Afrocentric movements on the economic behavior of Black Americans is most graphically demonstrated by the increasing use of Afrikan traditions in wedding ceremonies and by the creation of companies which cater to them. In spite of loud laments about the disappearance of the Black family, it is estimated that Afrikan American couples are spending some $3.2 billion annually on their weddings. The wedding industry as a whole is estimated to generate $32 billion yearly. Wedding couples may accent their ceremonial dress with touches of Kente cloth here and there. Or they may dress in full Afrikan-style regalia complemented by drummers to announce the bride, dancers to entertain, and the throwing of kernels of corn as a wish for fertility (WSJ, 8/24/93 - "Firms Cater to Afrikan-style Weddings"). A variety of Afrikan and slave traditions may be utilized to celebrate and consummate the wedding — including ancient rites performed by Yoruba priestesses, the exchanging of wedding bands engraved with medu-neter [hieroglyphics], the cutting and eating of Caribbean black cakes (a kind of fruitcake), and "jumping the broom". This latter activity requires that the avowed couple leap over a broom lying on the ground as symbolic of their leaping into matrimony. The broom has traditionally been used as a symbol of the home in parts of Afrika, and during the enslavement period in America jumping the broom legitimated the marriage of a couple in the eyes of the slave community in lieu of the fact that initially slaves were generally not allowed to legally marry by the slaveholding White community.

In the typical American commercial tradition a social trend both stimulates an industry and/or is reciprocally stimulated by it. Contrary to the tendency we have been discussing where fledgling Afrocentric trends are rapidly catered to by White-owned businesses after their having watched pioneering Black-owned businesses create and establish the market and preempting them soon thereafter, the Afrikan-centered wedding tradition is so far engendering a rapidly growing Black-owned and controlled business sector. A popular guide to the broom jumping ceremony is Danita Green's 1992 primer, *Broom Jumping: A Celebration of Love*. Danita Green also publishes the newsletter, *Broom Lady,* to advertise Afrikan-centered bridal services. *Brides Today* magazine, a bimonthly which began publishing in 1991, already has more than 125,000 subscribers. *Kuumba Kollectives*, a greeting card company, sells custom-designed wedding invitations, programs and thank-you cards featuring various Afrikan motifs, including Kente cloth borders, Afrikan silhouettes and hieroglyphic symbols (WSJ, ibid). Other popular guides to Afrikan-centered weddings and services are being published in increasing numbers, and catering services such as wedding coordinator Metsa Mitchell's Always and Forever Wedding Chapel in Detroit, which offer a variety of the Afrocentric goods and services, are a growing phenomenon.

There is evidence that an increasing number of Black entrepreneurs are beginning to respond to Black consumer changes in taste, and to meet the culturally sensitized Black consumer more than halfway. It is often not remembered that business and success in business are to a significant extent culturally determined. Those businesses that create or detect and respond to enculturated needs and desires are more likely to succeed than are businesses which do not.

Colors 4 Afrikan Peoples — Carl Jones and Thomas Walker, then owners of Cross Colours, provide a very current example of how business success can be garnered by an enterprising Black entrepreneur sensitive to changing Afrikan American cultural tastes and who can use those tastes to penetrate both the Black and non-Black markets. Cross Colours received the Company of The Year Award in *Black Enterprise* magazine's BE 100 (June 1993). The *New York Times* (5/15/93) defines their success thusly:

> LOS ANGELES, May 14 — Three years ago, the apparel designer Carl Jones took a $200,000 bankroll from cashing out of a successful surf

sportswear maker and financed Cross Colours, which makes a line of hip-hop clothing that mainstream merchants are clamoring for.

Mr. Jones, an apparel designer who grew up in Watts, wanted to make clothes infused with black urban attitude and African accents that would appeal to resurgent black pride. "It was just a thing in the air, an idea," he said, in an interview today from his Commerce, Calif., factory.

The designs by Mr. Jones and his artist partner, Thomas J. Walker, so captivated buyers at the company's first trade fair that Cross Colours was swamped with $5 million in orders. Retailers that signed up ranged from Miller's Outpost, a large California sportswear chain, to the Washington specialty store, Up Against the Wall. From sales of $15 million in its first year, Cross Colours sales rocketed to $89 million in 1992....

Black Enterprise magazine began its lengthy tribute to Cross Colours in this way:

This *isn't* supposed to happen to a start-up. In 1990, Cross Colours co-owners Carl Jones and Thomas J. Walker set out to harness the hip-hop craze with a line of street-inspired fashions for young men. Targeting blacks, they lured the masses without a shrug. On a roll, the company segued from clothing to cups and saucers, wooing high-end stores with its African-themed housewares. Next came lines for women and kids, even a special collection endorsed by Earvin "Magic" Johnson. Spinning cash out of chaos, they saw sales explode from $15 million in 1991 to **$89** million in 1992.

Sounds whack? Well, to borrow a Cross Colours catchphrase, "Judge 4 Yo Self." Barely three years in the business, this Los Angeles-based company has cut a mean swath in the **$66** billion apparel industry, and is poised to become the nation's only black-owned fashion conglomerate. Playing off the vibrant themes of hip-hop music, its products — which range from **$20** T-shirts to **$800** leather jackets and **$15** ceramic mugs — have been snapped up by more than **3,000** retail outlets, including department and specialty stores such as Macy's, Bullock's, Oaktree and Merry-Go-Round.

"It's an unbelievable story, all that they've done in such a short time," says Derek Tucker, president of the St. Louis-based Oaktree stores. "I've never seen anything like it in my 18 years in the business."

The hype started with affordable T-shirts and base-ball caps, each accompanied by messages like "Stop D Violence" and "Educate 2 Elevate." Hip teenagers latched onto the stuff, which soon showed up on the backs of rappers and sitcom stars. In no time, the MTV generation had cozied up to the urban ethnic look, which Cross

Colours swiftly parlayed into women's fashions and tabletop items. Today, it seems, Cross Colours is stitching itself firmly into the fabric of pop — not just hip-hop — culture.

"We didn't intend to come across as a militant company," says Carl Jones, CEO and founder of Threads 4 Life Corp. d/b/a Cross Colours (commonly called Cross Colours). "We simply wanted to be known for making clothes for African-Americans. That's what our style is about, our colors, our fit." As for the other 220 million potential customers? "We figured, if they dig it, they do; if they don't, they don't."

Dig it they did. Though 1992 was a lackluster year for the rag trade, Cross Colours "was definitely one of the stars," says Robert Parola, sportswear editor for the fashion industry's *Daily News Record*. Make that a shooting star. Shipments in men/boys sportswear (Cross Colours' primary market) were up only 4% in 1992; Cross Colours pulled off an increase of 493%. Having debuted on the **BLACK ENTERPRISE INDUSTRIAL/SERVICE** 100 last year at No. 80, with $15 million in revenues, the company has this year rocketed to 10th place, posting sales of $89 million. For these accomplishments, **BE** recognizes Cross Colours as its Company of the Year.

The Cross Colours case indicates, as has historically been the case, that business is indeed a cultural affair and, to some significant degree, is based on the consumer's personal and cultural identity. This last factor, i.e., cultural identity, along with cultural solidarity and the related cultural tastes they generate, has been the bases for immigrant entrepreneurial success in America. Simply stated, the ability of immigrant cultural groups to produce for and sell in their own almost exclusive cultural marketplace, serves as the launching pad from whence they take off to penetrate the marketplaces of other groups. As Afrikan Americans achieve a more coherent and cohesive cultural identity and consciousness, a greater sense of racial self-esteem, they prepare the ground for the construction of an aggressive, creative Afrikan American and Pan–Afrikan economic community.

Addendum and Caveat — Cross Colours' success story is a fascinating one because it points to the brilliant possibilities of daring Black entrepreneurship. It is a model for success in a very trendy industry. While Cross Colours' dazzling achievement strongly encourages would-be entrepreneurs to take a headlong plunge into choppy commercial seas, while it encourages us to "Just do it", its subsequent fade away warns us not to be over hasty in our pursuit of the golden ring.

It seems that the source of Cross Colours' initial brilliant success was also the source of later problems which forced the company into reorganization, reducing its staff of more than 200 employees down to about 60 (NYT, 3/3/94). While, according to Carl Jones, CEO of Cross Colours parent company — Threads 4 Life — the famous logo is "alive and kicking", the firm will no longer make its own clothing. Production is now farmed out to manufacturers through joint ventures and licensing agreements. The company now has licensing agreements with one manufacturer to produce footwear and with another to manufacture a children's line. It also plans a comeback in 1995 through its marketing of sophisticated apparel for fashion conscious customers between the ages of 15 to 40.

As intimated earlier, Cross Colours' unexpected popularity overwhelmed their capacity to meet demands from distributors and retailers for their products. Consequently, shipments were often late and incomplete. Financial problems grew rapidly larger when the retail chain Merry-Go-Round, which has more than 1,400 stores and which accounted for about 60 percent of Cross Colours' revenues of $89 million last year, filed for chapter 11 bankruptcy protection. Moreover, the struggles of Carl Jones and his management team with the day-to-day production activities diverted required attention from the creative side of their business thereby hobbling the company's ability to appropriately respond to the fast-shifting trendiness of the industry and its consumers. This led to its failure to introduce new styles in a timely fashion.

Carl Jones' meaner and leaner company still expects to be a trendsetter in the industry with its soon-to-be introduced new designs. Jones expects the company to earn revenues between $30-40 million. Cross Colours' experience reminds us of the fact that controlled growth may in the long run be more productive than runaway growth and success, and that losing focus on one's strengths increases the possibility of failure. Making business commitments which are very difficult or impossible to manage should be resisted despite their monetary allure.

One Man's Failure, Another Man's Success — We often learn from our own and other people's mistakes. Trial and error are important to learning. Karl Kani is one person who seems to have learned good lessons from the mistakes of others. Kani, who has developed his own celebrated fashion line and is now CEO and president of his own new company Karl Kani Infinity, was once a major designer with Cross Colours. *Black Enterprise* (7/94) reports that "the 26-year-old designer broke with Cross Colours after the company announced plans to abandon its manufacturing operations for licensing." Kani also implied that his leaving Cross Colours was in part precipitated by that company's mismanagement, financial problems and shipping delays, factors we alluded to earlier. But it also appears that Kani's departure was more importantly motivated by his desire to test his mettle, to stand on his own as a major designer.

Kani acknowledges that he learned a lot of positive lessons while at Cross Colours — lessons having to do with getting to know the marketplace intimately, how to set trends, developing business contracts, developing a fully efficient and productive staff, and controlling growth. Kani was apparently an "A" student while at Cross Colours because *Black Enterprise* credits the Kani line with accounting for 65 percent of that company's $97M in sales in 1993.

Kani who claims to own 100% of his company projects that he will generate first year sales of $40 million [in fact, sales were $43 million]. His company jumped from obscurity to No.38 on the **B.E. INDUSTRIAL/SERVICE** 100 list of June 1995, and to 28 in 1997 with sales of $65M. Based in Los Angeles, Kani also has showrooms in New York. Born in Flatbush, Brooklyn, Kani maintains his roots with bi-monthly visits. Infinity employs 28 people and has embarked on a diversified product line.

So, "all's well that ends well." Carl Jones and Karl Kani, though no longer together, continue in their separate ways to be models for success within the context of the Afrikan American community. They both demonstrate the economic power of culture-conscious entrepreneurship.

The Economics of Cultural and Subcultural Identity

Cultural identity and its subcultural varieties are not merely social statements or forms of personal and group self-definition. They also define and determine economic behavior. People are much more likely to positively respond to and consume items which reinforce their personal and cultural self-image, their aspirations, their personal and social concerns, social-political consciousness, than otherwise. Entrepreneurs who market their products with these factors in mind are more likely to succeed in the cultural marketplace. Two new Black-owned business establishments illustrate this point quite clearly. Both happen to use the term "Homeboy" as either a company name or a brand name. The term itself has currency in the Afrikan American urban community, particularly in the "hip-hop" Black teenage-youth adult community, the market for which they are primarily designed to be sold. The fact that the products use a readily recognizable subcultural lingo provides them with immediate name recognition and cultural identity. Moreover, the products are designed to suit the food-tastes and food-values of the target teenage-young adult, hip-hop marketplace by re-affirming the identity of its constituents. But they also speak to and support their social concerns such as their concern about drugs, AIDS, and education. Hopefully, the types of orientation represented by the two concerns, which shall be described presently, will become the hallmark of Black-owned business establishments. Under the banner headline: *Homeboys Inc. Chips in to Help Inner-City Teenagers: Philadelphia Firm's Social Message on Packaging Win It Grocery Shelf Space* (WSJ, 5/21/93), the firm, co-owned by James Ridgley and Samir Muhammad, and the marketing approach it uses are described in part like this:

> For Homeboys Inc., fledgling Philadelphia company, success is marketing potato chips with a *social* message.
>
> Each bag of chips carries a message urging inner-city youths to stay away from drugs, stay in school and avoid premarital sex. But another message for entrepreneurs might be that trying to do good can sometimes help a business grow.
>
> Jerry Ridgley, who started Homeboys in 1991 after overcoming a drug problem, says he was inspired by the "need to save others from the plague of cocaine addiction." With 15 years of experience in the potato-chip business, the 39-year-old Mr. Ridgley teamed up with partner Samir Muhammad, 45, to "fight back against drugs" from the snack-food counter.
>
> After just one year on the market, sales last year reached $4 million, Mr. Ridgley says, and the company is profitable. Homeboys' chips now are sold from Boston to Texas in mom-and-pop stores and super-markets such as SuperFresh and Acme. Mr. Ridgley hopes the company will be a model for other African-American entrepreneurs....
>
> But good intentions aren't enough, experts warn. At Homeboys, the company's social goals are backed by street-smart marketing. A one-ounce bag of chips retails for 25 cents, affordable for most teenagers. And to appeal to urban youths, Homeboys uses slang from the streets to create the names and flavors for its chips.
>
> The first product was Chumpies, which is a commonly used term in Philadelphia for, "the best of the best," Mr. Ridgley says. Another is Homegirls, defined as girls from the neighborhood. A new flavor comes from "bumpin," which he says means something hot and good. So the "Bumpin Barbecue" flavor was created.
>
> **Favorite Among Vendors**
> Bartley Swartz, sales representative for Swartz & Sons, Baltimore distributor, attributes the chips' success not just to their social messages, but also to "their unique flavor and their 25-cent price." His

company distributes about 1,200 cases of Chumpies and Homegirls a week to inner-city stores in the Baltimore area and Washington. (One case holds 36 bags.) Even though the profit for merchants averages just six cents a bag, the chips are a favorite among vendors, Mr. Swartz says. "We receive calls from as far as Harrisburg, Pa., about them," he says.

On the back of the bags are the messages that have become a major draw. An antidrug message says drug peddlers are no heroes and urges: "Let's make it plain Homeboys! Tell those drug dealers to "STEP OFF," and "GET A LIFE"....

"Our community is so under siege with drugs and crime, we just wanted to be a part of the solution, not the problem."

Chumpies became the new chip on the block in late 1991 after Homeboys was started with a $100,000 investment, half of it from private investors. Sales grew from 1,000 cases a week in the first month to over 21,000 cases a week by the sixth month, Mr. Ridgley says. Homeboys now has over 100 distributorships in Philadelphia alone, he says.

The Neighborhood's Ills

Homeboys employs 17 people and has hired several young men from the neighborhoods of west Philadelphia. "We all have had either a family member or friend fall victim to the ills of our neighborhood," says Faruq Abdul-Ghaffar, director of sales. "I saw the opportunity to be a part of something positive and at the same time make money."

Mr. Abdul-Ghaffar, a former school teacher, takes the company's message to schools and recreational facilities. Mr. Muhammad, the company's vice president, says that "in some respects we are substitutes for parental guidance because we relay traditional, family values to the children."

Mr. Muhammad says the company also wants to set an example for other African-Americans to have the courage to start their own business: "For too long, African-Americans have been discouraged from being entrepreneurs. Once we begin to own, we will begin to promote positive images of our people."

Homeboys, meantime, plans to expand its product line to candy and freezer pops, as well as to offer healthier, sugar-free products such as whole grain cereals and health-food bars. A call-in number is also in the works. "Finally, the kids will be able to call and speak to Eric, Rafael and Kareem," says Mr. Ridgley. "Once the name is successful, you can sell just about anything" [Emphasis added].

Homeboy Soda — Bob Crowder, the producer of Homeboy soda, demonstrates a marketing orientation similar to that used by James Ridgley and Samir Muhammad. He also exhibits similar social interests. He clearly illustrates how a for-profit business can place top priority on social responsibility and can use the profits it earns from the community to further the community's socio-economic interests. The following partial depiction of Crowder's socially responsible enterprise published in the *New York Daily News* (5/20/93) notes the role of his Resource Enterprise Collective Fund plays in meeting the company's social goals.

> HOMEBOY SODA MAY sound like one of those bogus products spoofed on "In Living Color" — and, in fact, that's just about how it got its start — but the soft drink is real, and the businessman who created it says the hip-hop soft drink is designed to appeal to more than just inner-city youth.
>
> Bob Crowder, 44, a Brooklyn-based food and beverage broker with more than 20 years in the business, launched Homeboy last summer with his own money....
>
> The idea came to him in the Poconos, which is not exactly homeboy country. While at his vacation home, he caught a comedy skit on TV in which a woman joked about her boyfriend's giving her a bottle of "Homeboy Champagne."
>
> Crowder had seen Nike and Budweiser commercials that make reference to "homeboy," which when originally used among black young people meant someone from one's neighborhood....
>
> If there was any doubt that the term "homeboy" was becoming ubiquitous in the mainstream culture, it was eradicated by Bill Clinton's declaration on the eve of his election victory that he was "just a homeboy from Arkansas."
>
> "I realized that the term is no longer limited to a particular ethnic community or group," Crowder says.
>
> Crowder's Resource Enterprise Collective has begun producing the soft drink at the Brooklyn Bottling Co. plant in East New York and in other regions of the country. Homeboy is now sold in 28 states, and Crowder said a deal is in the works to start bottling in Europe.
>
> Homeboy comes in six fruit-blend flavors: cherry/berry, orange/mango, passion punch, raspberry/lime, blue-berry/grape wiz, and vanilla, peaches & cream.
>
> The notion that the soft drink will have its greatest appeal in the black community is something Crowder discounts....
>
> Still, Crowder's Resource Enterprise Collective is promoted as "an African-American-owned beverage company." A poster in the window of a local deli notes that the company has created a fund "to support charitable programs in our communities."
>
> For every case of Homeboy sold, 25 cents — or roughly 3% of the profit — goes into the Resource Enterprise Collective Fund, which will funnel money to charities selected by local distributors.

"There is a giveback to the community, a rebate, if you will. This is not a promotional gimmick. It's been done from case one," says Crowder, whom one wag called "the black Ben and Jerry."

Roughly $40,000 is in the charity fund, according to Crowder. Donations totaling $20,000 have gone to, among others, the United Negro College Fund, Hale House and a Brooklyn charity that distributes Thanksgiving baskets. "That isn't bad for less than a year," Crowder observes.

Crowder has started a snack line that includes chips, pretzels, candy, nuts and meat snacks — all sold under the Homeboy label. Four major snack-food distributors are handling the line, and Crowder reports brisk sales.

The black entrepreneurs has signed licensing agreements for the manufacture of Homeboy watches, Walkmen and boom boxes. He says he's negotiating with Kmart to produce Homeboy health and beauty-aids, T-shirts and jewelry.

What about making Homeboy brew?

You're never going to see a Homeboy beer or malt liquor," Crowder vows. "It's just not something I want to do, because it's not wholesome. I've been approached by a major, major brewery that heard about the soda and wanted to handle a Homeboy beer nationally. They offered me millions of dollars, but I had to tell them no. No one's going to make it because I have the trademark."

Food From The 'Hood: Greens into Gold — The hip-hop generation is more than a soda pop, junk food outlet for hip adult entrepreneurs. This generation has some entrepreneurial objectives of its own. One set of hip-hop entrepreneurs includes 39 predominantly Black and Latino students from Crenshaw High School. These teens sport all the emblems of hip-hop-dombaggy, low-riding jeans, expensive sneakers, earrings, lengthy T-shirts, and caps perched jauntily on their heads. They hail from South Central Los Angeles. These teenagers, while as fun-loving as any, are about serious business. In fact, they are taking care of business as the owners of Food From The 'Hood, a produce and salad dressing company located in South Central L.A. The *New York Times* (6/14/94 – "Students turn Greens into Gold") tells their story in the following way:

"We're hip-hop entrepreneurs," said Carlos Lopez, 15, one of the 39 students from Crenshaw High School who after the riots two years ago, turned an overgrown corner behind the school's football field into a garden and formed Food From The 'Hood to sell the vegetables and herbs they grew.

Last month, the company introduced Straight Out 'the Garden, a creamy Italian dressing. In the promotional material that the students wrote, the dressing is said to have a "kickin' taste," and "bumpin'" packaging. The dressing is already in 2,000 stores, primarily in Southern California, and it will be available nationwide within the next three months. More than 50,000 bottles of Straight Out 'the Garden have been sold, and the profits will go into a college scholarship fund for the 39 owners.

"What makes us hip is that we want to make a difference," Mr. Lopez said.

What makes them hop? Believe it or not, the students get very excited about gardening organically in raised beds on their quarter acre, selling produce at local farmers' markets, writing business plans and creating marketing campaigns. And they get even more excited talking about "line extensions" and "shelf presence."

"The uprising destroyed morale and a lot of property, and we just wanted to beautify a little corner and help people," said Jaynell Grayson, a 16-year-old partner in the business. "Real soon, we realized that the best way to give back to our community was to get a higher education. We figured that we sell lettuce, why not sell dressing?"

Food From The 'Hood is not just a serendipitous collection of teens each stepping on the other's toes. They are well supervised and organized by biology teacher, Tammy Bird, who oversees the garden, and former public relations executive, Melinda McMullen, who also does volunteer consulting for the group. Food From The 'Hood is well-connected and ensconced in a solid network of business relations and support services. The teenage management team receives free advice from Luther, Smith & Smith, a minority-owned investment banking firm. Sweet Adelaide Enterprises, a business owned by women, processes and bottles their dressing. And Bromar Southern California helps Sweet Adelaide with distribution.

The hip-hop owners of Food From The 'Hood did not come unprepared to accomplish their mission. They were taught basic business skills financed by a grant of $49,000 from the State of California's riot recovery fund. The Rebuild L.A. fund contributed $50,000 which was used to build the company's office and develop its salad dressing. Norris Bernstein, founder of Bernstein's Salad Dressing Company of Los Angeles, volunteered to help finalize the formula, price the product, and develop a marketing plan.

However, Food From The 'Hood does not want to be just another minority shil or minority-owned showcase business which serves as a contrived tribute to White liberal philanthropy and capitalism. The company has refused further donations and insists that future supporters invest in the enterprise under certain well-regulated conditions. Co-owner Mark Sarria provides an explanation for this prudent business and social policy when he exclaimed that "Taking something for free disempowers. Taking investment empowers because it means we're responsible for the payback."

Food From The 'Hood is an excellent illustration of the kind of productive activity the Afrikan American community can provide for its restless youth population if it decides to "take care of business". The founding of this company also provides a good case in point of how crisis and adversity can be transformed into productive opportunities by persons and communities who possess the appropriate consciousness, self-confidence, creativity, and persistence, and who are motivated to "do for self."

Sylvia's Restaurant — Bob Crowder's success story illustrates the additional point that like Chinese food and Black music, an identifiably culturally based product can "crossover" and penetrate cultural markets other than its own. The fact that a product is definitely designed to meet the demands of a particular cultural market does not necessarily hamper its appeal in other cultural markets. In fact, its appeal may be enhanced for the very reason of its identity with a particular cultural group or taste. The success story of Sylvia's Restaurant located on Harlem's Malcolm X Boulevard (previously named Lenox Avenue) between 126th and 127th Streets, illustrates this point quite elegantly. Sylvia's Restaurant is an eatery, owned and managed by Sylvia Woods and her husband, Herbert Woods, their family, and 62 employees. This restaurant, famed for its "soul food" cuisine (Sylvia is commonly referred to as "the queen of soul food") is a Harlem and New York City landmark. This establishment that began as an eight-stool café, now seats 250 in four separate dining areas. The restaurant celebrated its 30th anniversary in 1993 and serves a full spectrum of customers of all races, cultures and classes. It is a favorite of the "rich and famous", of powerful and aspiring politicians, and international business persons, including Japanese businessmen and other Orientals. Yet its principal clientele, the average and above-average Harlemite community, feels fully at home in its "down home" environment. Despite its service to people like Jesse Jackson, Muhammad Ali, Spike Lee, Marla Gibbs, former Mayor Dinkins, and other glitteraté, Sylvia's is still a community-based business, which demonstrates that things typically Black or Afrikan American can have consumer appeal in both the national and international market places.

More to the point, however, is the entry of Sylvia's Restaurant into the international marketplace through the manufacture and distribution of its food products. Beginning with its bottled barbecue sauce, Sylvia's Restaurant decided to roll out an entire line of Afrikan ethnic foods for the retail market. Through its Sylvia's Food Products, Inc., whose president is Sylvia and Herbert Woods' son, Van D. Woods, the restaurant's products have been received enthusiastically by many people of different ethnic backgrounds. Founded in 1992, Sylvia's Food Products, Inc. entered the mass market through supermarkets and community stores in the New York City region, the South East region (South Carolina — Sylvia's native state — North Carolina, Georgia), and the Mid Eastern region (Washington, D.C., Maryland and Virginia). Besides being sold by large foodstore chains such as Path Mark, Grand Union, Winn Dixie, Sylvia's products are sold by upscale, trendy specialty shops such as Zabar's Gourmet, Bloomingdale's, and Balducci's Gourmet.

We could easily extend our review of Black-owned companies that are making use of their cultural heritage and image to advance and enhance their business interests as well as the interests of the Afrikan American community as a whole. However, this very brief review serves to illustrate the immense power contained in Afrikanicity — the sense of Afrikan identity and consciousness, the sense of Afrikan-pride and self-esteem — for the generation of Black wealth, prosperity and political-economic power. However, the examples provided here as well as the sizable number of other examples we could have used must be multiplied many-fold if such wealth, prosperity and power are to be realized and achieve world-class status and influence. This requires a planful, deliberate approach by the Afrikan American and the Pan–Afrikan communities and their leadership. Most crucially, it requires that preexisting and newly founded businesses in the Afrikan American and worldwide community be adequately financed, managed and supported.

Afrikan Peoples: The White Man's Golden Geese

It has been the same since the beginning. In the Americas it began with slavery. It has continued unabated, in multitudinous shapes and guises, to the present moment — Afrikan peoples proving to be one of the White man's most fabulous sources of wealth; his golden geese who lay his golden eggs. Some may say that these people are golden sheep — sheep sheared of their golden fleeces by White rustlers.

No matter how it is metaphorically or allegorically described, it always amounts to the same thing — Black people producing and consuming to enrich others while impoverishing themselves. Whether we speak of slavery, peonage, menial labor, "glass ceilings," sports, music or cosmetics — wherever they generate millions or billions of dollars; whether through forced or wage labor, through creative, culturally based, productive activity or reactionarily conditioned consumerism — Blacks have allowed the fruits of their labor to be eaten by others while they hungrily scavenge among the leftovers. Since Emancipation this White-instigated feat has been accomplished through the activation of one basic Eurocentric "free market" rule: *prevent Blacks from having access to the marketplaces of others and prevent them from having access to their own marketplaces.*

The cosmetics industry provides a perfect case in point. Though some 12 to 15 percent of the U.S. population, Afrikan Americans reportedly consume more than 35 percent of its gross cosmetics production. Whether this figure is accurate or not, it is certain that Black business establishments control only a fraction of the $3 billion Black health and beauty aids market, and this fraction is shrinking. The same White-owned manufacturers, wholesale and retail stores which refuse to hire and promote Blacks, are rapaciously taking over previously Black-owned cosmetics companies. They instead are manufacturing counterfeit cosmetic beauty aids for the Afrikan American market, and habitually engage in all types of restraint of trade practices against Black-owned cosmetics manufacturers, distributors, dealers and retailers.

According to a report published by the *Final Call* (8/11/93 – "Kente Cloth and Red, Black, and Green mean Big Bucks for White Businesses"), Charles Johnson, president of Ashaway Inc., a Dallas-based lotion and creme manufacturer, complains that 15 major non-Black distributors deliver Black-oriented products made by White-owned companies to retailers but won't deliver products made by Black-owned companies. The *Final Call* goes on to report that Black business persons commonly complain that when these distributors reluctantly condescend to deliver Black-made products to retailers, they gouge Black consumers and make unconscionably large per unit profits by pricing these products some 40 to 60 percent higher than necessary. Major retailers such as giant supermarkets and drugstore chains collude with distributors in this process. The collusion between White-owned retailers and distributors operates to prevent many Black manufacturers from delivering their products directly from their plants to store shelves (when and if shelf space is even made available to them) with a single price markup. If this trade block were removed the price of the Black-manufactured cosmetics products would be markedly reduced and made competitive with their White-manufactured counterparts, more broadly distributed and easily retailed by Black-owned outlets in the Black community. Black manufacturers would then retain more income from sales, and as a consequence of these factors, could create new jobs in the industry.

Whether these ends will be accomplished depends first and foremost on the discernment and selectivity of Black consumers. Their achievement also depends on organized efforts in this direction by Blacks in the industry, by the efforts of concerned civil rights and community organizations, and most importantly, by the activities of a conscious Afrikan American community determined that it will benefit first and foremost from its own labor, wealth, productivity, creativity and industry, and from the commercial and business activities that other communities carry out with and within its business establishments and marketplaces.

The Afrikan American community can no longer afford to let other ethnic communities own, control and broker its labor, culture, and cultural products. The making and selling of its own cultural symbols and products in community and world markets by non-Afrikan manufacturers and merchants represent a gross insult to a poverty-stricken, under-employed Afrikan community which cannot afford to endure for one second more its exploitation by aliens. A people's cultural symbols and products are the very manifestations of its collective soul and spirit. They are the sources of its material wealth and social power. They permit these to be counterfeited, bartered, brokered and commercialized by aliens at peril to their very spiritual, moral and material existence.

In sum, a society's social, cultural production and consumption, and its ownership or control over these are the sources of its wealth and the determinants of its overall well-being, power and influence. These activities determine the deployment and employment of its constituents, their occupations and preoccupations. This is all the more pertinent for Afrikan American and Pan–Afrikan world communities which are being abandoned and economically isolated by the national and international economies of other ethnic communities which employ or disemploy Afrikan peoples only to the extent they can egregiously exploit them.

Black Self-Employment

We have already presented startlingly ominous statistics detailing the massive number of layoffs of Black workers by White-owned

Hiring Patterns

Sixty percent of black-owned firms have work forces that are at least 75% minority. A comparison with other firms:

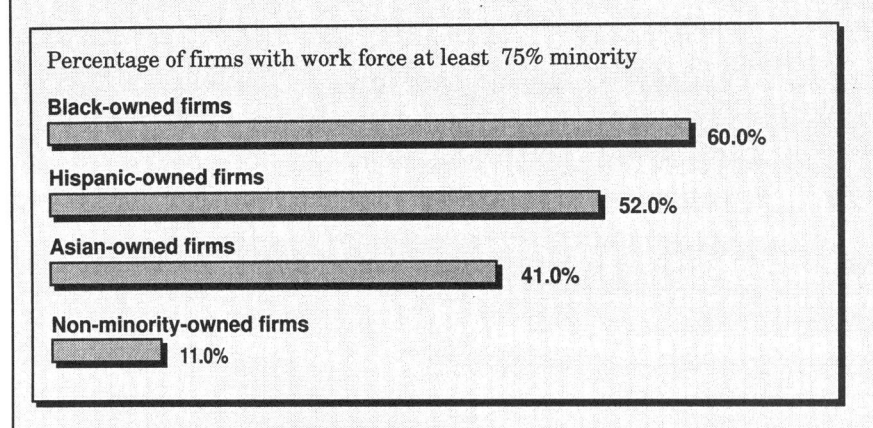

Percentage of firms with work force at least 75% minority

Firm type	Percentage
Black-owned firms	60.0%
Hispanic-owned firms	52.0%
Asian-owned firms	41.0%
Non-minority-owned firms	11.0%

Among black-owned businesses, financial-services firms have the greatest proportion of minority workers.

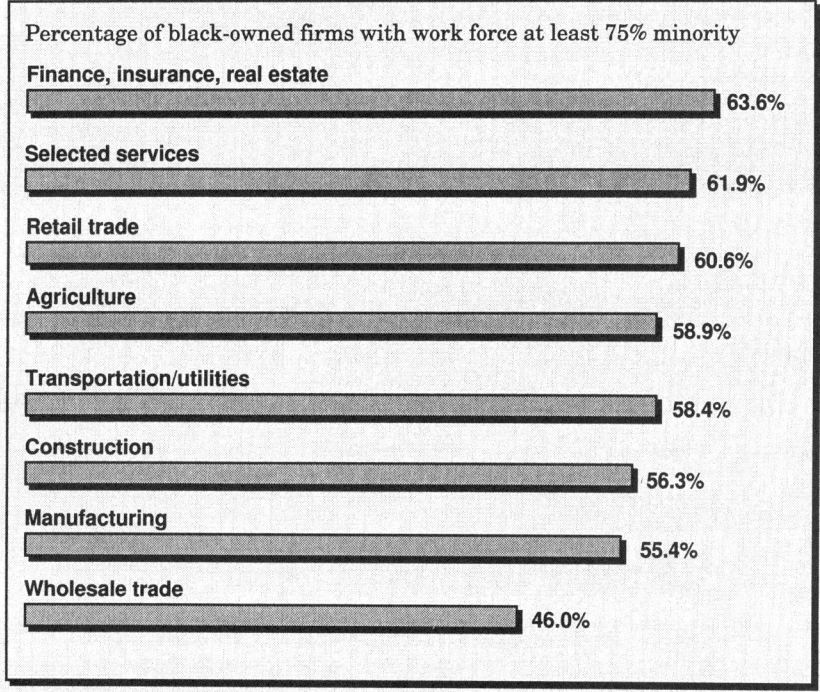

Percentage of black-owned firms with work force at least 75% minority

Industry	Percentage
Finance, insurance, real estate	63.6%
Selected services	61.9%
Retail trade	60.6%
Agriculture	58.9%
Transportation/utilities	58.4%
Construction	56.3%
Manufacturing	55.4%
Wholesale trade	46.0%

Source: Bureau of the Census, 1982

Table 24-11

Narrow Market

Almost half of black-owned businesses have a customer base that is at least 75% minority.

Percentage of firms with customer base at least 75% minority

- **Black-owned firms**: 45.3%
- **Hispanic-owned firms**: 28.5%
- **Asian-owned firms**: 26.1%
- **Non-minority-owned firms**: 11.9%

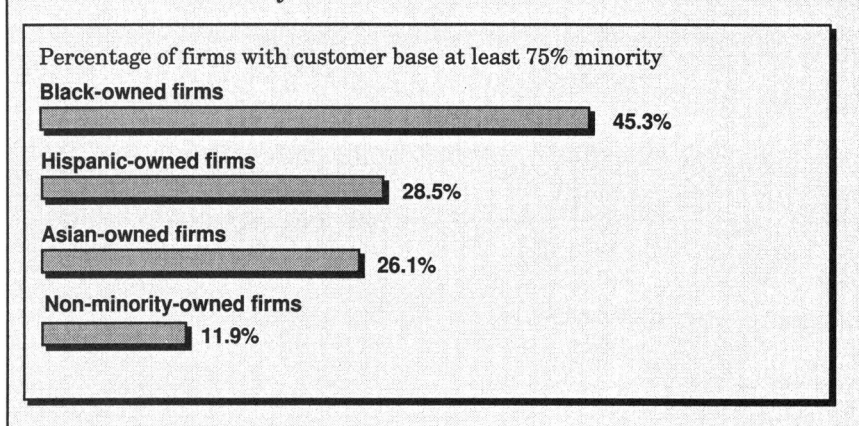

Among black-owned businesses, financial-services firms lead those reporting a customer base that is at least 75% minority

Percentage of black-owned firms with customer base at least 75% minority

- **Finance, insurance, real estate**: 56.6%
- **Retail trade**: 54.8%
- **Wholesale trade**: 46.2%
- **Selected Services**: 45.9%
- **Manufacturing**: 37.4%
- **Construction**: 30.6%
- **Agriculture**: 27.2
- **Transportation/utilities**: 24.2

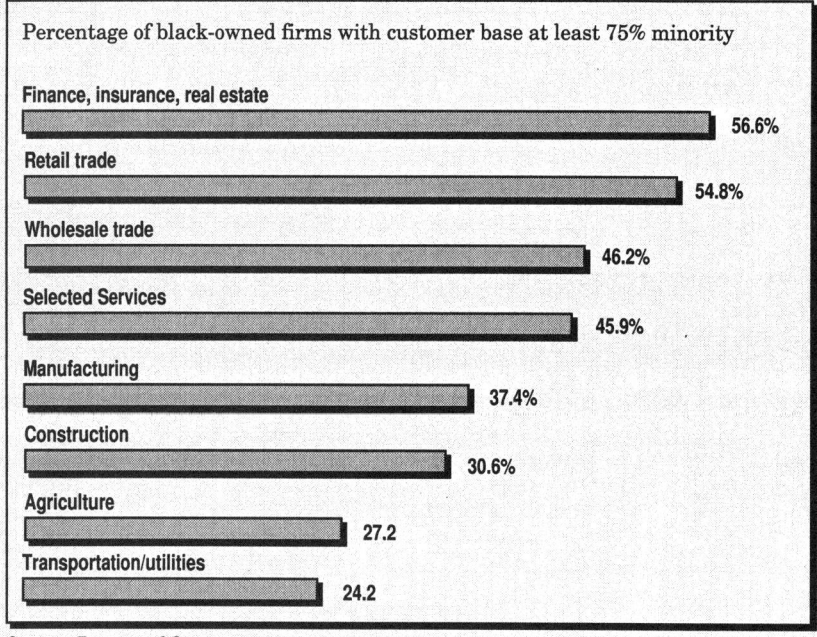

Source: Bureau of Census, 1982

Table 24-12

companies. This trend is expected to continue in spite of the current economic recovery and the ratification and institution of NAFTA and other international accords. This being the case, re-employment of and the creation of new jobs for Black workers must, in ever more increasing numbers, come from Black-owned companies. At this juncture at least 40% of Black-owned firms employ all Black employees. Some 60% of Black-owned firms employ a staff consisting of at least 75% Black and minority workers. This compares with non-minority-owned firms whose workforce consists of an average 11.0% Black and minority employees (WSJ, 4/3/92 – "A Delicate Balance"). For example, it can be observed in *Table* 24–11 which graphically illustrates the hiring patterns of Black-owned firms and those firms owned by other ethnic groups, that well over 60% of the Black-owned financial service firms employ 75% minority employees. This pattern is closely followed by other Black-owned firms across various categories.

Despite the overwhelming tendency for Black-owned firms to employ more Black and minority workers than their much larger White-owned counterparts, they are compelled to operate in much narrower markets. As can be surmised from *Table* 24–12 which depicts the customer base for Black and other ethnic group-owned businesses, nearly half of Black-owned businesses, overall, depend on a 75% minority customer base. In the finance and retail areas, more than half these businesses depend on this type of customer base. The wholesale trade and selected services are not far removed from this situation as well.

We must not construe these figures to mean that Black-owned businesses have captured the majority of Black and minority customers. Not by a long shot. They indicate that these businesses are more or less totally dependent on a very small percentage of Black and minority customers. This means that if they are to expand and increase their employment of Black workers they must capture a rapidly expanding number of Black customers and an increasingly larger share of the Black consumer dollar. Furthermore, if they are to compete in the national and international marketplaces they must strategically hire more Black workers and workers from other ethnic groups, redesign their establishments and redefine their tactics and techniques in order to overcome the market resistance of other communities. However, for Afrikan Americans and Afrikans across the diaspora, business begins at home. It begins with the capturing and servicing of their home markets and securing the loyalty of their own compatriots. It begins with actualizing the potentials of their own cultures, developing, controlling and owning their own cultural products. With their home base secured, then they may venture forth to capture new territories and bring home wondrous trophies of economic war.

Chapter 25

THE RELATIONSHIP OF WHITE-OWNED BANKS TO THE BLACK COMMUNITY

Banks Rob Customers

THE ESSENCE OF DOMINATION IS that the dominant benefits at the expense of the dominated. Domination is an uneven exchange. Unlike an honest or fair trade relationship, it does not involve equally beneficial reciprocity — an exchange of things of equal value. The dominated are forced to finance their own domination as their resources and productivity are expropriated by the dominant. This is obvious when domination is as directly tyrannous as in slavery, peonage, governmental-oligarchical repression, and colonial-neocolonial domination. However, it is complexly subtle to the point of invisibility when oppression and domination are convincingly *renamed* freedom and democracy as is the case with the current oppression and domination of Black people by White people in the United States of the Americas. Under such a deceptive regime the dominated are made to feel free-*est* when they are most exploited. They "voluntarily" chose their shackles. They "freely" spend their monies in ways that "just happen" to enrich those who dominate them. They gleefully purchase the chains which bind them all the more fixedly in servitude to those from whom they purchase their shackles since they have been convinced that such servitude is their natural state.

The habitual tendency of Blacks to "voluntarily" enrich "those who despise them, abuse and spitefully use them" can no better be revealed than by observing the banking behavior of Afrikan Americans relative to White-owned banks. The relationship of Black consumers to White-owned banks best illustrates the uneven, nay exploitative exchange which is the essence of domination: one gives all, the other takes all and gives back nothing in return. Yet, under White domination the indiscriminate spending or depositing of all their monies with White-owned establishments to receive little or nothing in return is perceived by most Blacks as the highest expression of freedom and "first class" citizenship. This, though their "generosity" ultimately impoverishes them, and eventuates into a billowing tide of criminality and social decimation in their midst.

Numerous studies throughout 1991 and 1992 repeatedly demonstrated that White-owned lending institutions where Black Americans have on deposit billions of dollars, reject Black mortgage applicants more than twice as often as White and Asian applicants.[1] These studies also demonstrate that the bias in lending is primarily a function of race, not income. For example, a survey of New York and national lenders released in October 21, 1991 by the Association of Community Organizations for Reform Now (ACORN), found general *redlining* — i.e., the refusal by lending institutions to extend credit to residents and businesses who live or are located in specific areas — regardless of qualification. For instance, in 1990, Chemical Bank, one of the largest banks in America, rejected 70% of upper-income applicants living in minority communities while at the same time it rejected only 40.5% of lower-income applicants living in White communities. It has been reported that while one Chemical Bank branch located in Central Harlem, a predominantly Black section of New York City, held over $100 million dollars in deposits, it loaned only $100,000 to Harlem residents and businesses. The ACORN survey showed that across the nation 33.9% of Black applicants for conventional and government-backed mortgage loans are rejected by lenders, compared to 15% of Whites, 12.9% of Asians, and 24.9% of Hispanic applicants. A more up-to-date study regarding racial bias in mortgage lending was released by the Nader group, Essential Information, Inc., on August 12, 1993. Demonstrating essentially the

---

1. See WSJ, 10/1/92, 10/28/92, 2/19/93; N.Y. *Amsterdam News*, 8/15/92; NYT, 12/11/91, 7/19/92, 2/9/92; New York *Daily News*, 10/22/91, 10/25/91, 1/22/92.

same racial biases as reported in previous studies, the *New York Times* (8/13/93) reported its major findings as follows:

> WASHINGTON, Aug. 12 — a computer study that matches loans and neighborhoods provides "strong evidence" that many of the nation's major mortgage lenders fail to serve minority areas, Ralph Nader's public interest group said today.
>
> A computerized nationwide study by the Nader group, Essential Information, Inc., suggests that 49 mortgage lenders in 16 big cities engaged in racial redlining, a practice in which banks and other lenders avoid making loans in low-income and minority communities.
>
> The group found evidence of 62 incidents of race-biased lending in violation of Federal fair-lending laws. In these instances, the report said, lenders in effect drew a red line around areas with a minority population of 75 percent or more, and chose not to make loans there.
>
> **Study Covers One Year**
>
> The one-year study analyzed Federal Reserve Board data of 1.25 million mortgage loan applications from 1990 and 1991, and used color-coded maps to highlight redlining hot spots around the country. The computer analyzed matched mortgage loan data with census tracts to create a visual depiction of lending patterns.
>
> Other local studies found similar, but more limited patterns of discrimination. Mr. Nader cited, for example, an October 1992 study by the Federal Reserve Bank of Boston on mortgage-lending discrimination, and a 1992 investigation by the Justice Department of Decatur Federal Savings and Loan of Atlanta that found that the institution had illegally excluded Atlanta's black neighborhoods in granting loans.
>
> Under the Federal Law known as the Home Mortgage Disclosure Act, lenders are required to provide information on all mortgage applications, including the incomes of applicants, their race and ethnic background and the amount they sought to borrow.
>
> The report comes just two months after the Comptroller of the Currency vowed to use undercover agents to test whether mortgage lenders are illegally discriminating among borrowers.
>
> Mortgage companies are responsible for two-thirds of the 62 lending patterns cited in the study. The study concludes that in New York City, five lenders practiced redlining: Prudential Home Mortgage Company, Apple Bank for Savings, Chemical Bank, Manhattan Savings Bank and Chase Home Mortgage Corporation.
>
> But many of the lenders said that the report which analyzed two- and three-year-old data, is misleading. They said they had already taken significant steps to insure that no communities were neglected, through outreach programs and other initiatives.

Lending Bias against Black-owned Businesses

We may surely infer from the findings cited in *Table* 25-1 with regard to racial bias and *redlining* in mortgage lending that such bias and lending practices also occur in regard to business lending as well.

Black and White

According to one study, black-owned firms are turned down for bank loans more often than white-owned firms. Moreover, the loans they receive, particularly in poor, inner-city neighborhoods, are smaller.

WHITE-OWNED FIRMS:

Percentage of White applicants that receive bank loans	32%
Average loan	$51,630
Average loan for borrowers in low-income, urban areas	$62,098

BLACK-OWNED FIRMS:

Percentage of applicants that receive bank loans	25%
Average loan	$20,604
Average loan for borrowers in low-income, urban areas	$28,324

Source: 1988 study of 10,139 small businesses in 28 U.S. cities by Timothy Bates, director of the urban policy analysis at the New School for Social Research in New York.

Table 25-1

Based on a study of 10,139 small businesses in 28 cities, *Table* 25-1 provides direct evidence for racial bias in business lending. It demonstrates that not only did Black-owned firms obtain fewer loans from White-owned banks than did White-owned firms, but the size of the loans received by White-owned firms was 2½ times larger than those received by Black-owned firms. In a poll of 500 Black entrepreneurs in 1992-1993, commissioned by the *Wall Street Journal*, 92% reported that they had been turned down by banks while trying to finance their firms (WSJ, 2/19/93). Moreover, they indicated, without qualification, that their problems were tightly linked to their racial background. Racial bias in lending occurs even when the success of a Black-owned company is clearly demonstrable in terms of years in business, healthy profit margins and growth rates, high cash flow, very adequate collateral and high caliber management. The following excerpt from a lengthy WSJ article (2/19/93) which speaks of the experience of George Fountain, co-owner of District Scientific & Medical Supply Inc., Gaithersburg, Maryland, and a petroleum dealer, is a case in point:

> The company is profitable now — as it has been for seven of its nine years with current annual sales roughly $1.1 million. But banks

routinely reject Mr. Fountain's requests for inventory financing. *Banks won't even accept signed government contracts as collateral*, he complains.

Indeed, a list of blue-ribbon customers is no guarantee that a bank will approve a loan request. "We sell to Fortune 500 companies," says Mr. Winters, the petroleum dealer. "The chances of them folding are minimal." He says that he "got shut out" at Portland's four major banks in his initial search for start-up funds, *while those same banks were financing "mom and pop companies" with non-minority owners.* Mr. Winters projects sales of $2 million for the year ending June 30 [Emphasis added].

Even when Black-owned businesses are successful in obtaining loans, about two-thirds of them feel that they are charged higher interest rates than their White counterparts (WSJ, 2/19/93). Another example also taken from the aforementioned article suffices to illustrate how secure, well-collateralized Black entrepreneurs with excellent track records very frequently have a rough time getting money to expand than less-secure, less-collateralized White entrepreneurs.

ARTHUR B. SCOTT figured that he had proved himself. He founded Kass Management Services Inc. in Oakland, Calif., in 1975. Seventeen years later, he says, the restaurant-management, catering and janitorial-services concern is profitable and has $4.5 million in annual sales.

But now, Mr. Scott says, he feels as if he has to prove himself all over again. Last year, the black entrepreneur's bank terminated Kass's credit line after the company graduated from a federal program that awards contracts to minority-owned firms. The departure cost Kass half of its business.

Mr. Scott tried to arrange new financing with another bank, but he was rejected. It didn't matter that he wanted to borrow only $250,000 — a fraction of his old $1.8 million credit line. "It's like starting over at day one," Mr. Scott says of his recent fund-raising effort. Despite his achievements, he says, "I feel like nothing has changed."

That same sense haunts many successful black entrepreneurs. They struggle for years, starting firms from scratch and slowly turning them into respectable money-makers. But success often doesn't make it any easier to raise money. Financing hurdles, they say, never go away for the black entrepreneur.

This type of example can be multiplied many-fold. In light of the racial bias against lending to well-established Black-owned businesses, it can be well-imagined that start-up Black entrepreneurs will have an extremely small chance of obtaining finance, if any, from White-owned banks. The rejection rates of Black-owned businesses and would-be businesses have been so long-standing and consistently frequent that many Blacks have given up shopping for capital and many more dare not even make the first attempts. In this way Blacks have literally been conditioned by the White-controlled financial establishment to avoid entrepreneurial undertakings or to undertake only small, marginal, undercapitalized, high-risk, often illegal, business ventures. The White-owned financial establishment through racially biased lending practices, through *redlining* and other detrimental lending practices have virtually declared war on the economic development and prosperity of the Afrikan American community. Evidence for this contention is provided by the easily substantiated fact that even when required by U.S. law to lend in all areas from which they accept deposits, White-owned banks generally have steadfastly and stubbornly refused to do so or have done so in a begrudging miserly manner, degrading to both themselves and their borrowers.

To add insult to injury, after accepting deposits from inner-city consumers and businesses and disinvesting in their communities, mainstream banks gradually reduced their services to them and gradually began disappearing from the scene altogether. As reported by the *New York Times* (9/6/93), the number of banks in low-income areas declined 10 percent between 1977 and 1989. Nearly one-third of the savings and loan institutions withdrew as did almost one-half the mortgage companies.

On the face of it, many people would perhaps be tempted to feel that the withdrawal of mainstream financial services and institutions is justifiable in terms of high loan default rates and the unprofitable prospects which characterize inner-city communities, especially Black areas. However, such a feeling is quite likely to be based on three stereotypical racial myths: that low-income borrowers are inherently "credit risky"; that the defaults on mortgages of low-income homeowners are significantly higher than those of low-income borrowers; and that doing business in inner-city areas is not profitable or capable of profitable expansion. Our earlier discussion of the low default rates and the profitability of the Shorebank Corporation belies those mythical beliefs.

Moreover, Maude Hurd, national President of the Association of Community Organizations for Reform Now, intimates that "available data from private mortgage insurance companies suggest that *low-income homeowners are far less likely to default on mortgages than high-income borrowers"* [Emphasis added]. Maude Hurd also notes the irony that "after a decade of record losses on speculative investments in commercial real estate, we have yet to see a bank or savings and loan institution go belly up because of too much lending to poor people" (NYT, 8/27/93).

Our discussion of the Shorebank demonstrated that lending in the community by mainstream bankers is both good social policy as well as good business. The experience of Antoci's American Savings, a large California thrift, in aggressively pursuing business in minority areas by opening branches there, speaks directly to the point. As reported by the *City Sun* (9/22–28/93) in a review of a hearing on the Community Reinvestment Act of 1977 held by Eugene A. Ludwig, Comptroller of the Currency, the thrift's unusual venture was unusually successful.

> The program began in Hispanic areas 4½ years ago and in Black areas about 3½ years ago. Antoci said fewer than 2 percent of mortgages made to minorities are 30 days or more delinquent compared to high levels to better-off customers — including a six percent delinquency rate for America's affluent customers.
>
> American is planning to open a dual branch in South-Central Los Angeles with tiny Founders Bank, the only Black-owned bank in California.
>
> Customers seeking business loans or checking or savings account will go the Founders side of the building; for home loans they'll go to the American counter.

American Savings Bank has become a leader in inner-city lending since it decided to enter this market in 1989. It opened branches in such places as Oakland and South Central Los Angeles, California. Its neighborhood branches are staffed with Afrikan American "urban lending specialists." These specialists are required to lend within low-income limits. As an incentive for motivating active lending in this area, American permits these specialists to earn commission rates 50% higher than what other loan officers get.

Between 1989 and 1992, American had granted $145 million of mortgages to California Blacks. In 1993, American made three times as many home-purchase loans as Bank America, which has 11 times its assets and immensely more marketing power.

Corroborating the comments of Maude Hurd, cited above, American Saving Bank has discovered that, contrary to a common myth, Blacks do not have a higher delinquency rate than do Whites. In fact, according to the *Wall Street Journal* (8/9/94), America's lending approach to inner-city neighborhoods "has been solidly lending approach to inner-city neighborhoods "has been solidly profitable, with an average five-year return on assets exceeding 1% and a delinquency rate in low-income areas that is one-fourth that of affluent towns such as Santa Monica."

The Clinton administration has demonstrated an intense interest in rectifying the most egregious practice of racist lending in the nation. This is a refreshing change given the benign neglect of this problem during the Reagan administration.

Ignored in the '80s

Proponents say it's about time. The legislation was passed in 1977 in response to concerns that banks were "redlining" around economically depressed areas excluding poor neighborhoods from credit. But the act was relatively ignored in the deregulatory environment of the 1980s.

Then in 1989, as part of the thrift-industry bailout, mortgage lenders were required to publicly report home loans according to borrowers' income, race and location. At last, community groups had the ammunition they needed: statistical evidence that black and Hispanic mortgage applicants, regardless of income, are more likely to be turned down than white applicants are.

At about the same time, new banking provisions put more teeth into the long-ignored act. The provisions called for periodic reviews and grading of banks' lending activities. Good CRA ratings became one of the key criteria for obtaining regulatory approval for banks' merger and acquisition plans.

Community groups knew a good weapon when they saw one: Using the CRA legislation, the groups could win loan commitments by threatening to challenge proposed mergers and acquisitions.

But while the act has been used to obtain inner-city lending commitments from banks, much of the money has been targeted for housing, with little toward small businesses. That's largely because banks aren't required to provide data on their small-business-lending practices, as they are with housing loans.

"That information is critical in accessing what is and what isn't happening to minority-business lending," says Mr. Taylor of the National Community Reinvestment Coalition.

Adds Allen Fishbein, director of the Washington, D.C., Center for Community Change, "We're shooting in the dark, and that's not going to change without quantitative data."

Failed Amendment

An effort to insert an amendment to the 1992 banking bill calling for banks to report their small-business-lending record was unsuccessful. Bankers denied they redline and argued that the provision would have added intolerable paperwork.[2]

Using the Community Reinvestment Act. Despite the difficulties just described, we still recommend that organized groups within the Afrikan American community take advantage of the Community Reinvestment Act to discover a bank's lending practices toward its residential and business clients and to bring pressure on banks to substantially increase their lending commitments to inner-city businesses and entrepreneurs. Moreover, these institutions should provide or fund support services to fledgling businesses by providing training, timely information and expert advice. Additionally, the Afrikan American community should back banking laws and regulations which would permit the establishment of Black-controlled, bank-financed, community-development corporations, especially through pre-existing and new Black-owned banks, in lieu of direct loans by mainstream banks as required by current CRA regulations. Laws and regulations which permit bank consortiums, presided over by Black-owned banks and financial institutions to provide small-business loans ranging in amounts from $50,000 to $300,000 or more, should be vigorously pursued by the community. Those White-owned banks participating in such a consortium may receive credits in favor of their community reinvestment ratings for so doing. However, the bases for making loans to Black-owned businesses by community-development banks, corporations, programs and consortium must be realistically pegged to the economic history and reality of the Black community, according to criteria developed by that community. For there are already large numbers of "commercial loan set-asides" or funds held by White-owned banks which are scarcely known to exist by the Black business community. Even if known and applied for, the qualifying criteria for obtaining loans are the same as those regularly used by the banks. Consequently, the loan rates to Black businesses from these special funds or set-asides are little better than those which use the banks' own general funds.

When all is said and done, the most effective measure for securing financial capital for Black-owned businesses and Black American residents is the wholesale depositing, to whatever degree possible, of monies in Black-owned banks and financial institutions controlled by Blacks themselves, even those coming from White government agencies. Secondarily, where no such banks exist or are too inconveniently located, the concentration of Black consumer and institutional

---

2. *Wall Street Journal,* 2/19/1993.

deposits in two or three White-owned banks and the willingness of Black clients to withdraw those deposits wholesale in defense of their economic interests should permit them to influence policies of those banks. Where the Black community has very substantial deposits and holdings in White-owned banks they should demand that aggressive, committed members of the community sit on bank boards and lending committees. Watchdog committees as ways of seeing to it that the community receives full return on its deposits and dealings with White-owned banking and financial institutions, should be installed and maintained on active duty to surveil banking practices and disseminate information regarding such practices throughout the community.

Where communities have established truly active organizations for monitoring banking activities and applying pressure when necessary, home mortgage lending to Blacks has, in general, markedly increased (*The City Sun*, 9/1–7/93). For example, in 1992, because of organizational surveillance BankAmerica Corporation of San Francisco increased its home loans to minority and low-income customers nearly 50 percent. It pledged to make $12 billion available for community development lending over the next 10 years. In 1992, Chemical Bank of New York City increased its mortgage lending to minority borrowers by 150 percent above a year earlier. It pledged $750 million in community reinvestment loans as well. Chase Manhattan Corporation of New York City and NationsBank Corporation of Charlotte increased their home loans to minorities significantly in the 1992–1993 period. However, it must be kept in mind that these increases were based on exceedingly small or low percentages to begin with. Great discrepancies based on race and residential areas remain. The overall quantity of lending to minorities, especially Blacks, remains small. Consequently, pressure on banks by community groups must be initiated where necessary, continued wherever it is already maximized, and increased wherever it is insufficient. The 1989 Home Mortgage Disclosure Act requires banks to release mortgage lending data by race, age, and income of the applicant — the type of information an activist community group needs to rationalize and organize its activities to improve the living conditions of its area.

CRA and Beyond. The Community Reinvestment Act generally requires banks to lend in the communities they serve. Once each bank has designated its service area, it is required to approve loans without bias and to seek new customers from all races and incomes. The purpose of the CRA includes guaranteeing that Blacks have access to

Box 25-1 A Note of Caution Concerning Borrowing from Mainstream Institutions

As our discussion in this chapter indicates, it is not uncommon for various mainstream banks and financial institutions under pressure of the Community Reinvestment Act to announce new loan commitments to minority communities. For example, in February 1992 the Fleet Financial Group Inc. announced plans to initiate a three-year, $8.5 billion loan commitment to low and moderate-income borrowers and minority-owned businesses (WSJ, 2/9/94). The NCNB and C&S/Sovran Corporations announced similar programs in 1991. These banks, which later merged, made a $10 billion loan commitment for community development over 10 years (WSJ, 2/9/94). These commitments primarily involve making mortgages available for low-income inner-city residents and the liberalization of lending criteria for minority- and women-owned businesses.

While we rightfully expect that as "American citizens," as Afrikan American consumers and business persons we should have equal access to consumer and business loans from mainstream [White-owned] banks and financial institutions as do other ethnic groups, we must be very prudent in our use of these non-community-owned resource markets. If we perceive the Afrikan American community as a nation-within-a-nation it will become apparent that borrowing money from the financial institutions of the "White Nation" or from the institutions of other "non-black nations" will indebt the Afrikan American nation to those other nations. In other words, the more the Afrikan American nation borrows from the other nations, the higher and more burdensome its "foreign debt," the more it will become a "debtor nation."

It must be kept in mind that when a big mainstream bank promises to make, say $10 billion available for loans to the Afrikan American community, it is not being charitable. That $10 billion loan will have to be repaid, and with interest! That money returns to that bank and its community. The borrowing of that $10 billion by the Afrikan American community represents a $10 billion addition to the "national debt" of the community — plus interest. If the economy of the community is not growing or expanding at a rapid enough pace, it will become impoverished by such debt in the long run. (*This is one of the major reasons the Afrikan American community should demand reparations — not loans, no matter how generous.*)

If its debts to outside nations and their institutions rise beyond certain critical levels the Black community will be forced to expend the greater part, perhaps virtually all of its income servicing the debts it owes to other communities and buying their imported products. All of its real estate, productive human and non-human resources will be owned and controlled by outsiders. All of its social institutions will be dependent on outside support and stripped of their positive cultural value and functionality. The Afrikan American nation would then be a dependent, underdeveloped nation with all the problems associated with nations of such status.

Thus, while it is obvious that we must borrow from outsiders, such borrowing should be kept to the barest minimum and that which we borrow should be invested as much as possible in wealth-producing projects. It is imperative that when feasible, monies needed for community growth and development should be attained from institutions which are community owned and controlled. This will maximize the circulation of wealth and money for longer periods of time within the community, thereby enriching and empowering it. The chart below schematizes the circular flow of output in the community consonant with our discussion. ∎

Maximization of Black Resources

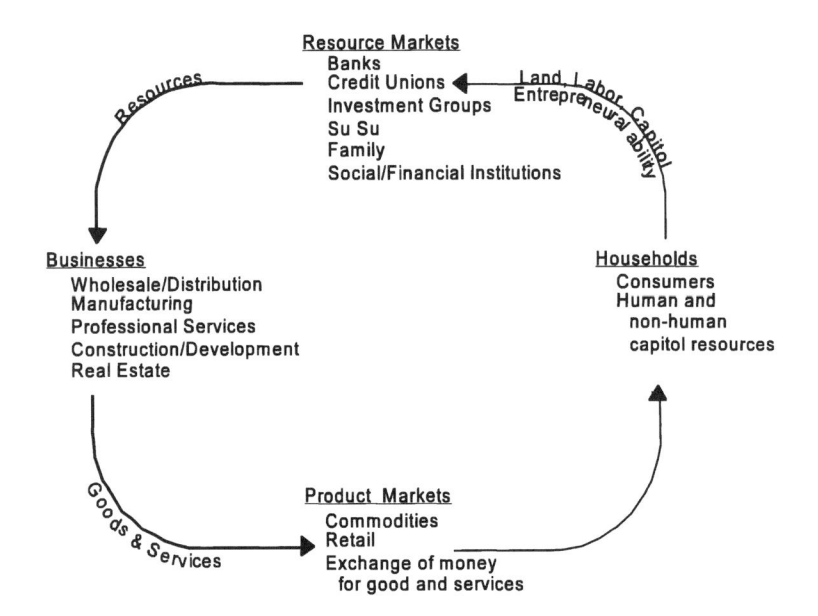

Resource Markets
Banks
Credit Unions
Investment Groups
Su Su
Family
Social/Financial Institutions

Resources → **Businesses**
Wholesale/Distribution
Manufacturing
Professional Services
Construction/Development
Real Estate

Land, Labor, Entrepreneurial ability, Capital ← **Households**
Consumers
Human and non-human capitol resources

Goods & Services → **Product Markets**
Commodities
Retail
Exchange of money for good and services

loans and banking services equal to that of Whites. Fair housing laws include among their major objectives that of ending race bias in lending by banks that provide mortgages. In this context the *New York Times* (8/25/94) quotes Paul Hancock, chief of the housing and civil enforcement section of the Justice Department, as saying that "Anyone who makes credit available on the basis of race is in violation of the Fair Housing Act. That includes lenders that say they do not do business in black neighborhoods." Under CRA some banks have been sometimes restricted from closing branches in poor areas as a remedy for credit discrimination.

A New Departure. However, in August, 1994, the Justice Department in a ground-breaking settlement forced a lending institution to open at least one new branch in an area it had not previously served (NYT, 8/25/94). Prior to this event, many banks managed to circumvent CRA and fair housing requirements by simply choosing to locate in and serve affluent White suburbs while avoiding poor and minority areas.

Chevy Chase Federal Savings of Chevy Chase, Maryland, the bank which was the object of the Justice Department's settlement, "had never opened a branch in an identifiably Black neighborhood in the Washington metropolitan area. Four of the bank's 74 branches were in black areas — two of them obtained by acquisition, one in an area that shifted to Black majority from white, and one in Annapolis, MD." (NYT, 8/23/94). Chevy Chase was found guilty by the Justice Department of refusing to market itself in minority neighborhoods.

The Justice Department construed such laws as the Fair Housing Act and the Equal Credit Opportunity Act as requiring banks to market themselves aggressively to minority customers by doing such things as opening branches in specific communities. Between 1976 and 1992 Chevy Chase made 97 percent of its loan in predominantly White areas.

Under the settlement Chevy Chase, with $5 billion in assets, whose suburban Maryland headquarters is about two miles from the District of Columbia line, agreed to: (1) make $140 million in concessionary loans available to people who might have suffered from the bank's redlining; (2) set up new branches and mortgage offices in the excluded communities, including Anacostia, an overwhelmingly Black neighborhood in the District; (3) spend $11 million to set up special loan programs to provide mortgages at either one percentage point below the prevailing market rate or at one-half point below the market rate along with a grant equal to two percent of the loan to be applied to the down payment and a waiver of $400 in fees in the excluded neighborhoods; (4) modify its commission scale in a way which makes it more rewarding to its staff to make smaller loans; (5) place at least 960 column-inches of advertising (for 5 years) in publications aimed at minority readers (NYT, 8/23, 8/25, 8/26/94).

The Justice Department's investigation was triggered by a series of articles which appeared in the *Washington Post* in mid-1993 about racial disparities in the number of mortgage loans. Chevy Chase and its subsidiary B.F. Saul Mortgage Company were among the banks revealed to have engaged in biased lending.

We included the Chevy Chase scenario in order to demonstrate the broadness of spread of the Community Reinvestment, Fair Housing, and Equal Credit Opportunity acts and how they may be used to curb race bias in bank lending, credit and services. The Chevy Chase case indicates that investigative knowledge of the lending practices of banks can be used under various government laws to help satisfy the need of the Black community for credit, financial support and other banking services. While maximum use of such knowledge and laws should be undertaken by relevant community organizations, we believe that the forced location of White-owned banking outlets in Black neighborhoods may, in the long run, be self-defeating. We think that the long-term and economic interests of the Black community would be better served by the establishment of Black-owned banking outlets in Black neighborhoods. A creative use of the laws to achieve this end would mutually benefit the Black and White banking communities, with the main beneficiary being the Black community.

Bank and Supplier-assisted Buyouts. Federal and state mandates such as the CRA and set-asides, combined with corporate support, community activism and excellent Black corporate talent, experience and organization can produce remarkable economic outcomes for the Afrikan American community. Prior and current efforts by the Black community to stimulate corporate support for minority suppliers and motivate mainstream financial institutions to provide financing for Black-owned franchisees, suppliers, manufacturers, professional services, and other vendors are beginning to show some signs of promise. In addition to reactively responding to the pressure of federal and state mandates, pressures by civil rights and community organizations by more actively searching for minority suppliers and vendors and by establishing large-scale minority supplier programs, large corporations are increasingly beginning to recognize that doing business with minority-owned companies provide them greater access to promising groups of minority consumers.

The Afrikan American community by "keeping its eyes on the prize", by maintaining its vigilance and activism in the areas of corporate finance and corporate-supplier relations, can greatly advance its economic developmental agenda. What can be accomplished is recorded throughout this volume. However, we shall very briefly review two cases which illustrate the good things that can happen in the community when big corporations and financial institutions respond to the call of Black entrepreneurs, not only without prejudice but with enthusiasm.

Ford Motors and Active Transportation. In 1980 Ford Motor Company began its search for minority suppliers and before long it found one in its own front yard, so to speak. He was Ford's own employee, Charlie Johnson, who along with his former college roommate Wade Houston had formed a small trucking company, the Johnson-Houston Corporation, which had won a small contract to haul parts to Ford Motor Company's plant in Louisville, Kentucky (WSJ, 11/10/94). In November 1994, as president and chief executive officer of Active Transportation Company, Louisville, a renamed metamorphosis of Johnson-Houston, Inc., Charlie Johnson signed a contract to complete the acquisition of the much larger Jupiter Transportation System, a trucking company with $240 million in annual revenues.

In a move that will make Active Transportation the biggest Black-owned trucking company and one of the largest Black-owned businesses, Charlie Johnson acquired Jupiter Transportation System of Kenosha, Wisconsin, a trucking unit of Jupiter Industries, Chicago, for $45 million in debt and equity. The support of Ford Motors was crucial to the success of the deal. Ford, followed by Jupiter's former customers, e.g., truck manufacturer Navistar International Corporation, Freightliner Inc. and Paccar Inc., guaranteed business and extended existing hauling contracts with the newly expanded Active Transportation.

When in 1981 Charlie Johnson's original company, Johnson-Houston, was asked to become Ford Motor's first minority contractor to ship cars from its assembly lines to dealers, Johnson chose Jupiter Transportation, a Chicago hauler, as its more experienced partner. Jupiter, which had lost its contract with now-defunct American Motors, brought to the joint venture it formed with Johnson-Houston, now re-named Active Transportation, its wealth of experience, computerized operations, balance sheet and expertise. Active's contracts with Ford rose over the next eight years. By 1993, Active employed more than 300 persons and earned more than $15 million in revenues. Active decided to bid for full ownership of Jupiter after one of its owners died and the company put up for sale.

In light of Ford's and other former Jupiter customers' long-term commitment to Active as Active's experienced and competent administrative staff, Active's bid was enthusiastically supported by a financial group, including First Chicago Corporation's subsidiary American National Bank & Trust Co., Heller Financial Inc., and Northwestern Mutual Life Insurance Company, a Milwaukee insurer. American National, which had had a prior relationship with both Jupiter and Active, provided the senior debt financing by helping to put together a $100-million financing package. Heller and North Western provided the actual funds which included $55 million in working capital.

Harriet Michel, president of National Minority Supplier Development Council, a New York organization that specializes in helping to create business contacts between corporations and minority-owned businesses, contends that Active's acquisition of Jupiter is "a vivid example of how relationships between big U.S. corporations and their minority suppliers are creating bigger and more viable minority businesses" (WSJ, 11/10/94). We contend that past, current and future mainstream corporate-minority business relationships of the type represented by Active's acquisition are and will be the outcome of organized political and consumer movements as well as institutional activism within the Afrikan American community relative to mainstream corporations. The most fundamental relationship is not that between corporations and minority suppliers but the relationship between the Black community, the corporations and the American power structure as a whole. It is this active relationship that is motivating large corporations to establish large-scale minority supplier programs. In this context the *Wall Street Journal* (11/10/94) notes that:

> Auto makers have been among the first to establish formal large-scale minority supplier programs. But others are active too. In telecommunications, for instance, AT & T Corp. and other telephone companies also have been aggressively working with minority suppliers. In health care and medical services, large pharmaceutical companies are actively seeking out and financing minority distributors and service providers.

The kind of contractual relations which Active Transportation, Ford Motor and the financial combine we have just discussed represents, vividly illustrates the possibilities that the construction of Black-owned industrial institutions located in the inner-cities of America can provide employment opportunities for its residents. They also represent the integration of Black-owned businesses into the economic mainstream of America and of the global business community. The strengthening and expansion of such relations under the influence of an organized Black community consumer movement can markedly change for the better the economic prospects and power of Black America as a whole.

Advanced Technological Solutions Inc.: Keeping the Business in the Family. Former IBM employee and current chief executive officer of Advanced Technology Solutions, Wesley D. Ratcliff of Brooklyn, N.Y., also provides a living example of how personal ingenuity, courage, know-how and organizational competence can beat the odds against the development of a viable inner-city industrial establishment. The *New York Times* (7/17/94) begins the fascinating story of Wesley Ratcliff's and employee-owned Advanced Technology Solutions (A.T.S.) on this note:

> As chief executive of a sprawling computer plant in the unlikely setting of Bedford-Stuyvesant, Wesley D. Ratcliff has received a wealth of mail from civic boosters in the South, the Middle West and elsewhere, suggesting that he move his company out of Brooklyn.
> "Those letters are in the trash," he said with a sweep of the hand. "You could say I owe my soul to this place.
> Indeed Mr. Ratcliff and his 260 employees at Advanced Technological Solutions Inc. has invested heavily in Brooklyn. A year after raising $6.5 million to purchase the 16-year-old Bedford-Stuyvesant plant from I.B.M., which was about to shut it down, they have taken charge of what experts say is the nation's largest company that is minority-owned and employee-owned.
> Although long-term success is by no means assured, the A.T.S. workers have salvaged one of the last major manufacturing operations in New York City. In doing so, experts say, they have beaten long odds against new business development in a poor inner-city neighborhood.
> "They are doing something almost unique and very important," said Corey Rosen, executive director of the National Center for Employee Ownership, a California advisory group that tracks the success of 9,500 employee-owned companies that have been formed since the mid-1970's. One of the largest and newest is United Airlines.
> "What is special about A.T.S. is that it provides a model of black entrepreneurship," he said. Unlike many black-owned companies,

which owe their success to an individual, "here you have a large group that is spreading the entrepreneurial culture," he added.

Wesley Ratcliff as CEO of A.T.S., is a graduate of predominantly black Prairie View University of Texas. He has an M.S. degree in math from the University of Houston. An ex-NASA engineer, he joined I.B.M. as a manager in 1976 and became manager of its Brooklyn plant in 1990. He is committed to providing quality jobs to Bedford-Stuyvesant residents in Brooklyn. The plant prospered during the 1980s, reaching peak employment of 400 workers in 1986. But as I.B.M. itself suffered well-publicized reversals in its economic fortunes the Brooklyn plant declined to the point that in 1990 it employed less than 200 workers. In 1993, I.B.M. decided to close it down. With 17 years experience as a manager with I.B.M., Ratcliff and 15 other managers at the Brooklyn plant decided that they had what it took to keep the plant open and operating. They offered I.B.M. a deal — they would buy the facility. Pooling their personal resources, Ratcliff and his partners came up with a $300,000 offer to I.B.M. This initial offer was supported by a $2.8 million low-interest loan by the New York State Job Development Authority. The late Thomas Watson, Jr., former chairman of I.B.M., offered to buy $1 million in nonvoting stock should Ratcliff and his employee group prove successful in its buyout. Ratcliff closed the deal when he was able to obtain bank financing from Chase Manhattan Bank to meet I.B.M.'s sale price of $6.5 million.

After the buyout was completed, workers at A.T.S. were offered the option of taking a 20 percent pay cut and receiving stock in the new company as supplements to their wages. One hundred and eighty former I.B.M. workers chose to remain. The *Times* concludes A.T.S.'s story as follows:

> The company which opened its doors under employee ownership on Oct. 1, has so far benefitted from a continued relationship with I.B.M., which has relied on it even more heavily for computer repair than it did before the buyout. A.T.S. said it was repairing 600 to 1,000 I.B.M. terminals a day, double the amount before the buyout.
>
> Such continued reliance on a single corporate patron could make A.T.S. vulnerable. "It is very important that A.T.S. diversify," said Mr. Rosen. "If I.B.M. were to withdraw suddenly, it could threaten their survival."
>
> Still, Mr. Ratcliff said, A.T.S. has made quick strides toward diversification. Chief among them is a $25 million contract it won in November to produce cable television circuit boards for Philips Broadband Networks Inc., the Syracuse subsidiary of a Dutch electronics company.

To meet the demands, A.T.S. has added 60 workers — for a total of 260. Sixty percent of the workers live in Brooklyn.

Mr. Ratcliff, who said he was seeking other new contracts for manufacturing and computer repair, said he hoped to increase employment to 600 within the next three years.

In the meantime, he said, he sometimes finds himself working as hard to sell the merits of Bedford-Stuyvesant as he does the products and services of A.T.S.

"Brooklyn does have negative connotations to a lot of people," he said. "But the first thing I do with customers is have them visit this plant. Once I can get them here, the job becomes easy."

The story of A.T.S. and the model it presents for inner-city industrial survival and prosperity should inspire the Afrikan American community to have greater faith in its ability to transform its economic situation for the better through unified, planful, creative, Afrikan-centered consciousness, organization and activism. We must keep in mind that while the example we gave of White corporate finance-Black business relations were exciting and exemplary of the positive path such relations should follow, they are very far from typical and frequent. They are not yet representative of a significant trend in White-Black economic relations. Even if they were to gain greater significance, as we expect them to do, these relations must not slow our drive to develop the far larger and more important Afrikan American/Pan–Afrikan Economic System. Ultimately, Black-White business partnerships, joint ventures and alliances must be adjunctively integrated into the Pan–Afrikan Economic System, instead of being merely integrated into the Pan-European economic system.

Chapter 26

BLACK-OWNED BANKS
Creators of Wealth

ONE OF THE MAJOR MEANS BY WHICH businesses are financed is through loans made by banks. Officially, i.e., as defined by Federal Law, a bank is "an institution that both takes in public deposits *and* makes commercial loans."[1] Banks, like many other financial intermediaries such as savings and loans associations and insurance companies, take deposits or funds from one group and lend these funds to another group.[2] A bank as a financial intermediary may accept deposits and funds from a number of sources including the usual savings and checking deposits from households, individuals or groups, firms and other organizations and then lend them to other households, individuals or groups, firms and businesses for any number of purposes. As summarized in *Table* 26-1, there are a number of types and categories of banks. These include commercial banks, which make up the largest class of financial establishments, which in general hold about 30 percent of all the assets held by financial institutions; savings and loans associations and mutual savings banks next in rank, holding about 17 percent of all financial assets. Other important institutions include credit unions, life-

---

[1]. Bradley R. Schiller, *The Economy Today*, 5th ed. (New York: McGraw-Hill, 1991).

[2]. Paul A. Samuelson and William D. Nordham *Economics*, 14th ed. (New York: McGraw-Hill, 1992).

insurance companies, pension funds and money market mutual funds (Samuelson & Nordhaus, 1992).

One of the primary functions of banks is to handle what are called *transactions accounts*. These accounts utilize deposits which can serve to make direct payments to a third party in market or business transactions without having to take a trip to the bank to withdraw funds. Transaction accounts include currency and checking accounts.

A bank in making a loan, in effect creates a transaction deposit which can be drawn on by the loan recipient. In making a loan a bank virtually creates money, i.e., makes money available where it did not previously exist.

Creating Money

Checking accounts are the most important and dominant form of money in the U.S. economy. Variously referred to as transactions accounts, demand or checkable deposits, checking accounts as represented by written checks, or checkbook money, are used in about 90 percent of all transactions involving the transfer of money. Checks are the means by which the ownership of deposits in banks and other financial institutions are transferred to others. They are therefore generally accepted as a medium of exchange. Transactions accounts demands or checkable deposits against which checks are written, are money. Thus, when a bank creates a transaction or checking account, or demand or checkable deposit it, in effect, creates money. This is particularly the case when a bank makes a loan by creating a demand (checkable) account in the name of the borrower. Schiller (1991) explains it this way:

> The making of a loan by a bank...is the heart of money-creation. Money effectively appears out of thin air when a bank makes a loan. To understand how this works, you have to keep reminding yourself that money is more than the coins and currency we carry around. Transactions deposits are money too. Hence, **the creation of transactions deposits via new loans is the same as creating money.**

When a bank makes a loan it in effect takes the borrower's IOU or promise to repay the loan, which in and of itself is not money, and provides the borrower with something that is money — a demand or checking account. The borrower now has more money (a demand or checking account) than he did before, yet no one else has any less. Consequently, since a demand account is in effect money, money has been created and the money supply enlarged or expanded.

What Is a Bank?

The essential functions of a bank are to:

- Accept deposits
- Offer drafts (check-writing privileges)
- make loans

In the United States, roughly 40,000 "depository institutions" fulfill these functions. These "banks" are typically classified into four general categories, even though most "banks" (and many other financial institutions) now offer similar services.

Type of Bank	Characteristics
Commercial Banks	Provide a full range of banking services ("time") and checking accounts and loans for all purposes. Hold nearly all demand deposits and nearly, half of total savings deposits. There are nearly 15,000 commercial banks in the United States
Savings and Loan associations	Begun in 1831 as a mechanism for pooling the savings of a neighborhood in order to provide funds for home purchases, which is still the basic function of such banks. The nearly 3,000 S&Ls channel virtually all of their savings deposits into home mortgages.
Mutual Savings banks	Originally intended to serve very small savers (e.g., the Boston Five Cents Savings Bank). Can use their deposits for a wider variety of purposes, including investment in bonds and "blue chip stocks. Almost all of the 575 mutual savings are located in only five states (New York, Massachusetts, Connecticut, Pennsylvania, and New Jersey).
Credit unions	A cooperative society formed by individuals bound together by some common tie, such as a common employer or labor union. Typically credit-union members hold members' savings accounts and enjoy access to the pooled savings of all members. Most credit-union loans are for consumer purchases. Although there are close to 22,000 credit unions in the United States, they hold less than 5 percent of the total savings deposits.

Adapted from Schiller, 1991.

Banks are able to *create money* because they are permitted by law to operate as part of a *fractional reserve system*. This system allows banks to lend at levels several times their actual store of cash. A bank is legally required to keep a cash reserve against its checkable and noncheckable deposits equal only to a relatively small percentage of those deposits (3% up to $41.5 million and 12% over $41.5 million of checkable deposits; 3% of noncheckable deposits, i.e., nonpersonal savings and time deposits, as of January 1989). A bank is allowed to lend all monies it possesses in excess of its required reserves. Excess reserves (which include the bank's own money) are equal to a bank's actual reserves minus its required reserves. For example, if a bank is holding $100,000 in demand deposits plus $10,000 of its own money, it is credited with $110,000 in actual reserves or cash. If it is required to hold 12% of the $100,000 in demand deposits in reserve, it will be credited with holding $98,000 in excess reserves [i.e., $110,000 (actual reserves) - $12,000 (required reserves) = $98,000 (excess reserves)]. The excess or extra reserves can be loaned by the bank to its customers and business clients. The ability of a bank to make loans depends on the existence and size of its excess reserves. Since required reserves are fractional, i.e., the size or quantity of a bank's checkable deposits may be 10 to 20 times as large as the cash it is required to hold in reserve or actually keep on hand, its ability to create money is greatly enhanced since it can lend its extra reserves and earn interest income by so doing. (Recall that money is created because the borrower has more money when he gets a loan, but no one else has less money as a result.) Fractional reserve is only possible because under normal circumstances as much cash will actually be brought into a bank as will be withdrawn. This reserve can retain only a small fraction of the money actually deposited by a bank's clients because, in practice, there is little likelihood that all its depositors will come to it at the same time to demand the full withdrawal of their money from their accounts.

As noted by McConnell and Brue, "It is through the extension of credit by commercial banks that the bulk of the money used in our economy is created."[3] Thus those social, political and economic forces which limit the ability of commercial banks or other financial institutions to create demand deposits — that is, to create "bank money" by lending — limit the economic and entrepreneurial possibilities of those who may depend on those institutions for expanding their money supply. It may be inferred from this that the few banks and financial institutions in the Afrikan American community, the paucity

---

3. *Economics,* 11th edition (New York: McGraw-Hill, 1990).

of monetary reserves held by those few establishments, the severely restricted access to credit from the "mainstream" banks, and the absence of traditional or cultural modes of saving or creating credit, among other factors, conspire to restrict the creation of money and the supply of money in the community to such a degree that it is made and kept needlessly impoverished and powerless.

Thus, through loans banks generate funds for business and economic development, among other things. Consequently, a paucity of banks, of bank reserves, other restrictions, regulations, and constraints on banks are directly related to the business and economic development of the communities they serve. So are various banking practices undertaken by the banks themselves.

It should be kept in mind that banks and other financial institutions essentially transfer funds from lenders to borrowers. In doing this, they create financial instruments like checking and savings accounts. In other words, it is through banks and other financial institutions that a community of lenders, i.e., depositors, makes money available to its individual or organizational members and other borrowers to pursue personal, social and economic ends — including the establishment, maintenance and expansion of business enterprises and activities. Many businesses are established, maintained and expanded through the use of "other people's money."

According to Mayer, banking has two distinct functions: "First, in symbiosis ... with the government, the banks provide and administer the money supply of the country. Second, they make loans to selected borrowers...." In regard to the latter statement, Mayer goes on to quote what he refers to as "the deliberately indiscreet phrase once used by John Bunting [former chairman of First Pennsylvania Bank of Trust]": *"We determine who will succeed and who will fail"*[4] [Emphasis added]. To the extent that banks can determine who will succeed and who will fail vis-à-vis ethnic economic communities, the banks and banking system have assuredly determined that the Afrikan American community will fail.

Historical Overview of Black-owned Banks

In Black America that failure was built-in from the beginning and has continued up to the present, even in banks apparently designed specifically to serve Blacks. Angela Wimes in an article "Blacks In Banking: A Historical Overview" published in *Dollars & Sense* magazine (January, 1993) describes the fate of the first bank designed

---

4. Martin Mayer, *The Bankers* (New York: Ballantine Books, 1974), pp. 23–24.

to aid in the economic development of the newly emancipated Afrikan American community.

The first major bank created for — although not by — emancipated blacks in 1866 was the Freedman's Savings and Trust Co. Badly mismanaged funds and lack of commitment to its black investors precipitated the bank's closing nine years later and the loss of approximately $3 million by over 61,000 African-Americans, thus stunting the economic growth for black people in America for a number of years.

It should be noted that the mismanagement of funds and lack of commitment referred to here was not the sole responsibility of the Freedman's Savings and Trust Company's Black managers and employees. A number of its principal managers were White, including White ministers, who share a very significant share of the blame for the banks ultimate downfall. The duplicitous role of the Federal government in this matter also cannot be overlooked. Interestingly, the great abolitionist and Black leader Frederick Douglass was called on to head the bank to try and avert its imminent demise. Referring to his impossible mission, Douglass alluded to his attempts to resuscitate the moribund institution as like being "married to a corpse." C. Eric Lincoln (1990) discusses the psychological aftereffects of Freedman's Savings and Trust Company's collapse.

Chartered by Congress in 1865, the Freedman's Saving Trust Company was the major bank which held most of the savings of many newly emancipated African Americans, the bounties which black soldiers received upon joining the Union army, and the deposits of numerous philanthropic organizations, benevolent associations, and churches. Its collapse resulted from both the national recession of 1873 and the incompetency of bank officials. Yet the collapse of the Freedman's bank and the loss of hard earned savings created a major distrust among African Americans toward banks, which for some took more than a decade to overcome and then only at banks organized by institutions they trusted. That distrust has not been fully dissipated in some sectors even to this day, and its effects lingers on in conventions which remain suspicious of black enterprise. According to Blassingame, for many other African Americans this distrust toward banks and other financial institutions never completely disappeared, but it helped to intensify a focus upon spending one's earnings for immediate pleasures.

However, those banks founded for and by Black Americans themselves were on the whole much more successful. Ivan Light

(1972) provides a very brief sketch of the history of Black-owned banks.[5]

BANKS AND BANK FAILURES

The earliest Negro-owned banks appeared in the South between 1888 and 1900. Fraternal orders created the financial institutions to serve as repositories for their funds. The banks thus established bore the name of the parent fraternal, for example, Knights of Honor Savings Bank. In the North on the other hand, the first bank did not appear until 1908. The banks of the North were fewer in number than those of the South and were usually nonfraternal in origin. Two Chicago banks, the Binga State Bank and the Douglass National Bank, achieved exceptional size in the world of Negro banking. The combined resources of these two nonfraternal banks amounted to 36 percent of those of all twenty-one Negro banks in existence in 1929.

Between 1884 and 1935, Negroes organized no fewer than 134 banking institutions in the United States. This sum does not include the numerous credit unions, industrial loan associations, and building and loan associations which blacks also organized in this period. Unfortunately, many of the 134 banks thus hopefully established later failed, a few in default of obligations. By 1929, only twenty-one Negro-owned banks still survived, and the Depression reduced this number to twelve in 1936. Eleven of these remained active in 1945. Thus, of the 134 banks founded, 92 percent were closed, liquidated, or suspended within a half-century. Since these bank closings took place before federal deposit insurance, the depositors lost their money.

Discouraging though this record was, Negro banks in this period were actually more successful than Oriental banks in California, among which the mortality rate was 100 percent. Japanese and Chinese opened ten state-chartered banks in California between 1900 and 1910. Of this number, six closed before the decade was out, victims of the California Banking Act of 1910. One bank survived until 1912, and three others limped along until the mid-1920s....
[Emphasis added].

PROBLEMS OF ADMINISTRATION

The Negro-owned banks experienced a chronic inability to recruit highly trained and qualified officials. This difficulty reflected the very low educational level of the entire Negro population and, of course, the inferior educational institutions which perpetuated the prevailing inequality of training and skill. However, the problem was exacer-

---

5. For an early detailed account of pioneering Black banks and bankers see Abram L. Harris' classic, *The Negro As Capitalist* (College Park, Md.: McGrath Publishing Co., 1936).

bated by the marked propensity of the best trained Negroes to enter the professions. Banking tended to recruit the uneducated or the less competent graduates of inferior educational institutions.... Consequently, "abject ignorance of elementary banking principles" among officials of Negro-owned banks was closer to the norm than the exception. Indeed, even today, the outstanding problem facing Negro banks is the *"severe shortage of management talent."* Lack of training and incompetence on the part of the Negro bankers was especially unfortunate in view of the small size and restricted investment opportunities of the Negro-owned banks. Other things being equal, these small banks had a heavier burden to bear than the larger white banks in simply engineering their survival. Only the best trained Negro bankers had a fighting chance of averting the destruction which stalked their minuscule institutions at every turn. There was less room for blunderers in Negro banking than in banking in general, but the Negro banks had more than their share of incompetents....

The allied problems of mismanagement and official venality that repetitiously plagued Negro-owned banks also afflicted the banks operated by Chinese and Japanese in California....

PROBLEMS OF INVESTMENT

In addition to the administrative problems of incompetence, mismanagement, and official venality, Negro banks also suffered from purely economic difficulties. Indeed, A.L. Harris regarded the administrative problems as epiphenomenal; in his view, insoluble economic contradictions would have condemned the banks to failure even had they been managed with exceptional skill instead of exceptional ineptitude. The unavoidable weakness of all Negro banking, according to Harris, was the eternal need to find profitable employment for capital and the chronic inability of the banks to do so because of the inability of black communities to support that capital.

Because of the contradiction between the banks' need for profitable investments and the lack of investment opportunity in the ghettos, Negro-owned banks were driven to make systematically unsound investments in ghetto real estate, faltering fraternal orders, unmarketable securities of fly-by-night enterprises, and unsecured loans to individuals. These investments temporarily propped up the tottering banks at the same time that they virtually guaranteed ultimate failure. In this manner the basic structural weaknesses produced a suicidal investment policy....

To be sure, had Negro-owned business been greatly stronger than it was, banks would have experienced less of a chronic problem in locating investment opportunities. That the banks did experience such a difficulty is evidence that black banking was developed entirely out of proportion to black business. But the experience of the

Negro banks also suggests that *formal banking could not antedate business development*. An important justification of Negro banking was the development of Negro business. However, in practice the Negro banks' record of failure indicates that banks could not create a business structure to support themselves. On the other hand, of course, business could not emerge so long as credit was unavailable.[6]
[Emphasis added]

It is encouraging to note that of the Black-owned banks which survived the Great Depression, five are still operating today. These include Consolidated Bank and Trust Co. of Richmond, Virginia (1903); Citizens Savings Bank and Trust Co. of Nashville, Tennessee (1904); Mechanics and Farmers Bank of Durham, North Carolina (1908); First State Bank of Danville, Virginia (1919); and Citizens Trust Bank of Atlanta, Georgia (1921). It should also be kept in mind that the failure of many Black-owned banks were paralleled by the failure of many White-owned banks at the same time and much later. In fact, more White-owned banks failed in the 1980s than the number created between 1888 and 1934 (Wimes, 1993). Overall then, the history of Black-owned banking is a tribute to the business acumen and steadfastness of Black business persons and the Black community. It not only demonstrates the entrepreneurial drive and spirit long present in the Black American community, but the ability of Black-owned enterprises to survive against overwhelming odds.

Box 26-1   Capital Accumulation

Banks, financial institutions and the functional roles these establishments play in the creation and distribution of wealth and power may be looked at from many practical perspectives. To state the obvious, the accumulation of relatively large amounts of money and the use of accumulated money to generate more money is the fundamental means of creating wealth — and the social power which flows from its possession and/or control. In the process of accumulating large amounts of money for investment purposes banks, along with other financial institutions, play a key role.

Banks may be perceived as institutions whose major role is to attract, collect, or accumulate large sums of money from various and scattered sources — sources each of which may possess relatively little money of themselves — at central locations. After collecting or accumulating relatively large sums of monetary capital, banks, by applying certain rules or acting on certain biases, make that capital available

---
6. Ivan Light, *Ethnic Enterprises in America: Business and Welfare Among Chinese, Japanese, and Blacks* Berkeley: Univ. of California Press, 1972), pp. 45–56.

to certain individuals or institutionalized groups through loans, credits and investments to be used for their mutual benefit. In other words, banks use other people's money — people who have been induced by various means to deposit their monies in the banks in the first place — to help make certain other people (and the owners of the banks as well) wealthy by supplying them with and permitting them to use, invest for their own benefit, the monies the banks have collected from their depositors.

Thus, the key to achieving wealth is to discover and execute some means of accumulating and controlling other people's money and using that accumulated money to increase one's own money supply. Banks, insurance firms, investment companies, the selling of corporate shares, taxation, outright robbery, sales of desirable commodities and so on, are among the means an individual or group use to gain access to other people's money. They then use their control over the monies or commodities accumulated from others for their own economic and social benefit. The power an individual or group gains through the use of various tactics for accumulating wealth from others may, ironically, be used against the very people who are the sources of his or its wealth.

In this context, it is readily apparent that by "voluntarily" placing or depositing their monies in White-owned banks, insurance companies, retail establishments, etc., multiple millions of Blacks concentrate or accumulate their monies under the control of the White elite in ways that immensely help that elite to further enrich itself and increase its power. This increased wealth and power is then used to dominate and disempower Blacks themselves. Hence, if Afrikan Americans are to gain access to and control wealth and are to make the most effective use of the social power derived therefrom, they must accumulate the monies in central institutions which are controlled and owned by themselves. These institutions must judiciously provide primary access to the accumulated wealth of Afrikan Americans to other Afrikan Americans, to the people who are the sources of their wealth to begin with, and to other Afrikan American institutions who will use the community's collective wealth to enrich and empower the community itself. ▣

The Possibilities of Black Community Banking

The history of Black-owned banking and financial institutions provides a richly mixed depiction of social and monetary success and failure. The brief sketch of that history, its unflattering description of Black American financial talent and the structural weaknesses which threatened the growth potential of Black-owned banks (as quoted earlier), while starkly realistic, need not be discouraging. The history of Black-owned banking is most instructive for those who possess a positive vision of the possibilities of Black financial wherewithal.

After all, the Afrikan American community is not a poor nation starved of financial resources and influence. The correct organization and mobilization of these resources can make that community a power to be reckoned with. Neither is the community starved of financial talent and genius, which is increasing daily through various types of formal educational and vocational experience. Black financial talent is no longer confined to parochial, backwater commercial banks, S&L associations, credit unions and the like. It is found leading well-run Black-owned banks and financial institutions, White-owned financial establishments, and sitting on a multitude of national and multinational corporate boards. A Black man currently serves as Secretary of Commerce in the cabinet of President Bill Clinton. A number of Blacks serve as CEOs and executives of a number of corporations and others are engaged in "high finance". While Black financial talent is not yet as abundant as it needs to be, it is not as dangerously scarce as it was in the past. It now needs, above all, unified community support, an Afrikan-centered sense of direction and commitment, and most importantly, the full support of the Afrikan American consumer and investing community.

Certainly the problems of investment discussed by Light are still vexing us today. For Black-owned financial institutions there still exists the problem of profitably employing their capital in the Afrikan American community. The relative paucity and anemic condition of Black-owned businesses and the paucity and relatively low value of Black-owned real estate and other financially productive services, properties, instruments and investments place certain restraints on the growth of financial capital. However, we believe that this problem can be surmounted in a number of ways. Obviously, the development of Black-owned businesses, the acquisition of productive properties, services, instruments and investments must achieve a certain critical mass prior to or simultaneous with the development of strong, rapidly expanding, Black-owned banks and financial institutions.

The Combined Deposits and Assets of Black-owned Banks

We will now briefly review the organization and character of contemporary Black-owned banks. The viability of these banks, that is, the value of their assets and deposits, their number and size, ability to meet the financial needs of the Afrikan American community, and related matters are of special interest since these factors circumscribe their role in advancing the economic development and political empowerment of the community.

A review of *Tables* 26–1 and 26–3 adapted from *Black Enterprise* magazine, June 1993 (The BE 100s), summarizes the financials of Black-owned Banks and Savings and Loans indicating that there were 36 and 18, respectively, of these institutions extant in 1993.

1993 BANK SUMMARY

BLACK-OWNED BANKS	1991	1992	PERCENT CHANGE
Number of Banks	38	36	5.3%
Number of Employees	1686	1,637	–2.9%
Assets*	$ 2,010.853	$ 2,107.865	4.8%
Capital*	$ 147.568	$ 158.952	7.7%
Deposits*	$ 1,778.716	$ 879.617	5.7%
Loans*	$ 827.976	$ 902.854	9.0%

*In millions of dollars to the nearest thousand.
Prepared by B.E. Research. Reviewed by Michael/Titus & Co.

Table 26–1

1997 TOP 25 FINANCIAL INSTITUTIONS SUMMARY (update)

BLACK-OWNED BANKS	1995	1996	PERCENT CHANGE
Number of Employees	1827	1,941	6.24%
Assets*	$3,275.252	$3,296.405	0.65%
Capital*	$271,651	$271.329	–0.12%
Deposits*	$2,811.518	$2,794.481	–0.61%
Loans*	$1,575.760	$2,103.249	33.48%

*In millions of dollars to the nearest thousand.
Prepared by B.E. Research. Reviewed by Michael/Titus & Co.

Table 26–2

According to the *Minority Bank Monitor* (Sept. 30, 1992), a newsletter published by Creative Investment Research of Washington, D.C., the combined net income of all 18 Black-owned Savings Associations in 1992 amounted to $4.1 million. Their total assets in 1992 amounted to approximately $1.2 billion and their total loans to $945 million. Their total deposits equaled $1.03 billion. The total deposits in Black America's 36 commercial banks amounted to $1.9 billion in 1992. At the same time, these banks held assets of $2 billion

1993 SAVINGS & LOANS SUMMARY				
BLACK SAVINGS & LOAN ASSOCIATIONS	1991	1992	PERCENT CHANGE
Number of Saving & Loan Associations	18	18	0%
Number of Employees	501	487	-2.8%
Assets*	$1,157.291	$1,226.104	5.9%
Equity Capital*	$ 62.815	$ 68.896	9.7%
Savings Capital / Deposits*	$1,012.038	$1,025.930	1.4%
Loans*	$ 921.038	$ 945.268	2.6%

*In millions of dollars to the nearest thousand.
Prepared by B.E. Research. Reviewed by Michael/Titus & Co.

Table 26–3

and made $903 million in loans. On the whole, profits at Black-owned banks rose from $7.4 million in 1991 to $14.7 million in 1992. Thus, we can surmise that as of 1992, the total assets held by Black-owned banks rose from $7.4 million in 1991 to $14.7 million in 1992. Thus, we can surmise that as of 1992, the total assets held by Black-owned banks equaled $3.2 billion, with deposits equaling $2.93 billion. The combined assets of the 25 largest Black-owned commercial banks equaled $2.8 billion in 1992. The 25 largest Black-owned banks loaned a combined $1.5 billion in 1992. The three largest Black-owned banks include New York City's Carver Federal Savings with assets of $320.9 million; Washington, D.C.'s Independence Federal Savings Bank, $239 million; and the nation's largest Black-owned commercial bank, Chicago's Seaway National Bank, $202 million.

We can infer from the foregoing statistics regarding Black-owned banks that the economic and social health of the Afrikan American community is puny indeed. At this point in their development Black-owned and financial institutions (including the 23 Black-owned insurance companies with combined assets of $720 million) certainly are not in the position to any very significant extent to "determine who will succeed and who will fail" in the community. While they provide needed services and are the seeds for the future growth in financial power of the Afrikan American community, their small numbers and inadequate levels of assets and deposits along with other legal and fiscal restrictions do not allow them to play a major role in the economic expansion of the community at the present time. This circumstance is the result of a number of remediable factors, only one or two of which we will discuss presently.

Reasons for Inadequate Assets and Deposits. The most obvious factor contributing to the rather low reserves of Black-owned banks, which places a severe restraint on their ability to lend money and fund the economic growth of the Afrikan American community, is the failure of the largest percentage of Afrikan Americans to deposit their monies in them. When one takes note of the fact that of the between $290–$400 billion Black consumer market Black banks have managed to snag only $2.9 billion in deposits and attain only $3.2 billion in assets, it is obvious that the average Black consumer, aided and abetted by Black institutions such as the institutional Black Church, is virtually ignoring the existence of their financial establishments. We very roughly estimate that on the whole Black-owned banks hold considerably less than 3 percent, i.e., less than 3 cents out of every Black bank deposit dollar, of Black money on deposit. [In fact, Afrikan Americans save an average of 2 percent of their earnings on the whole. The general population saves on average 4 percent. Asian Americans save about 20 percent of their earnings.] This estimate is based on our prior intimation that Black-owned banks in Los Angeles County held only 3.5 percent of the $9.5 billion in liquid assets held by Blacks in the banks of that locale. While this percentage may or may not be typical of the percentage of Black deposits held by Black-owned banks in general, we believe this to approximate the case in light of the fact that there are so few Black-owned banks relative to White-owned banks. Where Black banks do exist their often disadvantageous locations and small or non-existent number of branches make it difficult for them to garner Black consumer and institutional deposits, all other things being equal. However, the primary reason for the underfunding of Black-owned banks appears to be due to the negligence and the lack of knowledge of their importance to the economic well-being of the community by Black individual and institutional depositors. While we must acknowledge as did Alvin Boutte, Chairman and CEO of Chicago's Independence Bank, that "blacks have the same banking habits as everyone else; most people bank where they live or where they work," we must also recognize the truth in Walter Grady's and Jacoby Dicken's (president/CEO and Chairman of Chicago's Seaway Bank, respectively) statement to the effect that "The Polish go to Polish banks; Asians go to Asian banks; and Blacks go everywhere else."

In regard to ethnic banks, it is worthy of notice that in the Los Angeles area there exists some 30 Asian American banks. These establishments, some of which serve rather specific Asian groups (e.g., the Cathay Bank, whose principal clients are from the Canton region of China, and the General Bank, which primarily serves Taiwanese Americans) have been roundly criticized under the Community Reinvestment Act for failing to lend to Blacks and Hispanics.

If Black depositors increased their deposits with Black-owned banks by even 5 or 10 percent of their total deposits, these banks as well as the community would benefit phenomenally. That is, if Black depositors placed 10–25 cents of each dollar on deposit with Black-owned banks, the deposits held by these banks would increase four-fold to approximately $27 billion. Thus, even if Black-owned banks were utilized primarily as secondary depository institutions by Black consumers and institutions, their financial reserves and resources would expand rapidly and very significantly. Their ability to fuel the Afrikan American community's economic growth and development and its politicoeconomic power would be greatly enhanced. Additional deposits by Black consumers would not only encourage the increase in size of existing banks but also boost the financial services they can offer the Black community.

The Black community suffers a scarcity of Black-owned banks. This is another obvious reason for the paucity of low monetary reserves held by Black-owned banks. A total of 36 banking institutions serving a population of between 35–40 million Black Americans spread throughout the expanse of the United States, quite understandably could garner but a fraction of their deposits or banking business. An increase in the size and numbers of Black-owned banks and the financial services they offer would motivate competition by White-owned banks who now take Black consumers for granted and will force them to offer more services to the community on more generous terms. Thus the presence of a significant number of competitive Black-owned banks and financial establishments in the marketplace can in effect lead to the greater satisfaction of Black consumer and community financial needs. As Black-owned financial institutions increase in numbers, size and influence, their ability to participate in the "mainstream" financial and commercial marketplace will be vastly enhanced. This can be achieved through their increased ability to invest in larger White-owned institutions, corporations and other financially productive establishments; to gain significant equity and ownership of "mainstream" business establishments, valuable real estate, and services, as well as access to highly lucrative financial activities now virtually closed to Black financial institutions and business persons. All of these and other developments will permit the Black American community to enhance its social and economic power decisively. In the global context, a robust

Black-owned banking and financial establishment would do much to empower the Afrikan American community to influence U.S. foreign trade policies in favor of the economic and political empowerment of all Black nations and communities across the Afrikan diaspora. Moreover, Afrikan American financial power, if appropriately concentrated, distributed and creatively utilized, will enable that community to act as a financial engine motivating the economic development of other Afrikan economies, similar to the ways the White American economy serves as an engine motivating European, Asian and worldwide economic activity. A powerful Afrikan American financial establishment would provide empowerment and economic opportunities to the constituents of the Black American community as the result of its ability to generate domestic economic trade and employment activities; to sell financial resources and services to the Pan–Afrikan community; to engage in investment and export-import opportunities throughout the Diaspora and the world in general.

We will now discuss a number of options available to the Afrikan American community for strengthening its institutions and economic clout.

Black-owned Banks and Capital Levels

The Afrikan American community's general concern with community development through gaining access to federal funds earmarked for this purpose, should not divert its attention from the expanded role Black-owned banks can play in its economic development if they can be made to enlarge their capital reserves by any number of means in addition to acquiring more deposits from their Black consumers. Relative to the use of federal development funds, it is worth considering that instead of utilizing the $850 million fund proposed by the Clinton administration to create new community development banks, a sizable proportion of this fund could be divided among existing Black and minority-owned financial institutions.

This suggestion is made in light of the possibility that government grants to, and its creation of, community development banks could create competitive problems for community-based Black-owned banks. Exclusive grants to community development banks, loan funds and credit unions financially empower them to directly compete for the same target population served by Black-owned banks. Inadvertently perhaps, the pressure being placed on mainstream banks the Community Reinvestment Act to increase loans, credits and investments in inner-cities may also generate similar competitive problems for Black-owned banks. Overall, such competition may be for the better even for Black-owned banks, especially if it motivates them to improve their services, customer relations, pursue business more aggressively and develop more productive methods of seeking and doing business with large corporations, and to more aggressively exploit the potential in affordable housing loans.

However, while competition which encourages these activities has to be supported by the community, its support should not be such that it destroys the very financial institutions it wishes to strengthen. The track record of a significant number of Black-owned banks in supporting economic development is quite encouraging. A more adequately capitalized Black-owned banking establishment could provide superior financial services for the community at very competitive prices. According to Lucy J. Rueben, associate professor of finance at Florida A&M University, and her colleague, John A. Cole, the presence of minority-owned banks cuts financing costs to minority businesses and homeowners (WSJ, 12/16/92). They further contend that according to their research in more than two dozen cities where minority-owned banks exist, the after-tax borrowing costs for minority businesses are about 20% less on average than cities where they do not exist.

Black-led Institutional Investment in Black-owned Banks

Black individual and Black institutional depositors at mainstream banks and financial institutions can play a crucial role in very significantly increasing the capital levels of Black-owned banks. They can do this by using their organized and institutional influence to motivate mainstream corporate and financial institutions as well as their pension and union funds to utilize Black-owned banks for deposits, equity investments and involvement in various lines of credit. In light of the fact that well over 90 percent of Black-owned individual and institutional deposits and other financial instruments are held by White-owned banks and financial institutions, the demand by these clients that these establishments support the growth of Black banks is only just, not a begging for handouts. Capital infusions from major banks, pension funds and financial institutions would allow Black banks to substantially increase their lending to Black-owned businesses. For example, according to Wayne-Kent A. Bradshaw, president of Family Savings Bank, a minority-owned thrift in Los Angeles, $1 million worth of Family Savings stock sold to Keystone Holdings, a company that owns a major thrift American Savings Bank, supported an additional $20 million in loans by his institution (WSJ, 12/16/92). *Black Enterprise* magazine (6/94) elaborates the Family Savings Bank (FSB) saga. Noting that FSB moved to the rank of the fifth largest Black-owned bank, the magazine describes its remarkable recovery from near bankruptcy.

Family Savings Bank in Los Angeles returned to the fifth position on the list, and its win-win scenario for Family keeps getting better. Family posted assets of $181 million, up from $140.1 million a year ago. Deposits increased to $169 million from $114.8 million, and loans rose to $136 million from $115.2 million.

A year ago, Family Savings (FSB) was in danger of being shut down for failing to meet the minimum capital requirements set by the Office of Thrift Supervision. Located deep in South Central L.A., FSB is 93% owned by OFC Inc., a Washington, D.C.-based firm controlled by Opportunity Funding Corp. OFC solicits private capital for minority and community businesses.

Shortly before the L.A. riots wrecked the region last year, Keystone Holdings funneled $1 million through its subsidiary American Savings Bank to FSB. At the time, American had $17 billion in assets and its investment in FSB was lauded throughout the industry as a model use of the CRA.

Keystone is owned and operated by the billionaire Bass brothers of Texas, who also structured the investment to qualify as the first use of the qualified stock issuance provision of the Financial Institution Reform, Recovery and Enforcement Act of 1989. The provision allows an S&L holding company to acquire up to 15% in equity interests in an undercapitalized thrift without usurping control of that thrift. The cash infusion booted Family's assets up to $140 million and allowed the bank to acquire Enterprise S&L Association from RTC for about $20,000.

As the Family Savings Bank story indicates, equity investments in Black-owned banks by major White-owned banks and financial institutions need not devolve into the increasing ownership of these banks by White-owned institutions. White institutional equity investment in Black banks may actually increase Black institutional equity in these same banks. How this may be accomplished is illustrated in the following report published by the *Wall Street Journal* (12/16/92):

In April, City National Bank of New Jersey, a minority-owned bank in Newark with assets of about $65 million, received a $367,000 equity infusion from First Fidelity Bancorp., with assets of about $33 billion. *Much of the stock was given by First Fidelity to local charities and non-profit organizations, says Louis Prezeau, City National's president* [Emphasis added].

In other words, even though First Fidelity bought $367,000 equity in City National Bank, it did not retain its share of ownership this equity purchase allowed but gave it to community organizations, which now own shares of City National Bank as the result of Fidelity's generosity.

First Fidelity Bancorp's infusion to City National is a major part of a fascinating story of that bank's struggle to survive and prosper against great odds.[7] In the early years after its founding by Charles L. Whigham, a Newark businessman and community leader, City National grew rapidly and prospered. However, in 1989, due to past-due loans totaling some $3.55 million, or 23.5% of the bank's loan portfolio, the bank was faced with near insolvency. Its president, Louis Prezeau, a banker with 15 years of experience, has been with City National since 1990. Not one to avoid challenges, Prezeau rallied the community behind City National's survival. He was able to convince Newark's Mayor Sharpe James, to keep some of the city's accounts at the bank. With this vote of confidence, Prezeau weeded out bad loans and installed new, more efficient lending and accounting controls.

With the infusion from First Fidelity Bancorp, a $300,000 grant from the Ameliors Foundation, and $137,000 from private investors, Prezeau infused $50,000 of his own money. With these infusions, strong community support and audacious business acumen, Prezeau has been able to reduce the bank's nonperforming loans to just 2.2% of City National's $20-million portfolio, down from nearly 6% in 1989. In 1992, the bank earned a net income of more than $360,000. City National now expects to declare its first dividend since 1987, to open at least two more branches, and add services like automated teller machines and a City National Visa card. Within the first five months of 1993 the bank completed 10 minority business deals, with a number of others scheduled. City National's total assets increased some $11,289,800 from $50,622,000 in 1989, to $61,911,000 in 1992. From making some $15,027,000 in loans in 1989, City National made $20,156,000 in 1992. With increased support from its customer base, churches, small businesses, senior citizens and its regular depositors, increasingly aggressive customer services and banking activities, we expect that City National will prove to be a major asset to its local and national communities.

Thus, appropriate approaches to major financial institutions by organized Afrikan American groups can be utilized to increase the wealth and power of both their own financial institutions and

---

7. *Crain's New York Business*, 9/27/93.

communities. Besides, already existing federal banking laws and regulations can be of significant instrumental value to Black organizations in motivating major financial institutions to make very helpful equity infusions in Black-owned financial establishments of the type made by Fidelity Bank. For example, under the Federal Community Reinvestment Act of 1977, banks are required to increase their lending to underserved, resource-poor neighborhoods with large Black or minority populations. Seeking to lend to up-start and existing businesses by major banks in order to meet the legal requirements of the Act has been fraught with difficulty and only erratically enforced. Under a federal law passed in October, 1992, major banks can gain credit toward meeting their community reinvestment obligations by investing in minority-owned banks (WSJ, 12/16/92). However, mainstream institutions will have to be helped along this path by Black organizational action and pressure.

Pension Funds, Corporate America and Black Banks

Afrikan American members and leaders of pension funds and labor/professional unions, political administrators such as mayors, comptrollers and treasurers can do more to move their organizations to deposit funds in Black-owned banks, to do business with Black merchants and, perhaps, to invest in Black-owned financial institutions in ways helpful to their growth. The alliance forged between the Teachers Insurance and Annuity Association–College Retirement Equities Fund (TIAA-CREF, the world's largest pension fund and third largest insurance company) and a group of minority banks provides an example of the type of mutually beneficial relationship that can occur between such organizations and Black financial institutions.

TIAA-CREF with its 1.6 million participants, was headed by Afrikan-American Clifton B. Wharton, Jr. as chairman and CEO until he joined the Clinton administration as an Undersecretary of State. This mammoth organization which provides comprehensive retirement, insurance and investment programs for over 5,000 colleges, universities, independent schools and non-profit organizations, administers over $112 billion in assets. It is heavily invested in virtually every Fortune 500 Corporation. It also invests in large entrepreneurial undertakings. For example, it is reported to have invested $650 million in the largest mall in the United States — Minnesota's, Mall of America (*Black Enterprise*, 6/93).

In July 1992 the New York State-based TIAA-CREF, then under the leadership of Clifton Wharton, Jr., entered into an accord with

Chicago's Black-owned Drexel National Bank (with deposits of $118 million and assets of $128 million) to create a program for urban economic development (*Black Enterprise*, 6/93). According to *Black Enterprise*, "The pension fund deposited $125 million in a Drexel account that distributed the funds to several minority banks. Ten percent of the deposit's earnings go toward the National Bankers Association [the Black professional bankers organization] Scholarship Fund. Additionally, TIAA-CREF purchased $100,000 worth of certificates of deposit from 14 minority banks."

Any number of beneficial relations are possible between Black-owned financial institutions and major corporations. As stated previously, such relations need not necessarily impinge on these institutions' community-based autonomy and ability to manage themselves. For instance, when ARCO invested $1 million in Los Angeles' Founders National Bank ($93 million in assets, $78 million in deposits) it did so in the form of purchasing nonvoting preferred stock. It also offered to match dollar for dollar any new capital investment made by other corporations during 1993. Founders also received a $1 million infusion from the Bank of America, which also sold it two of its South Central L.A. branch offices. Moreover, ARCO may exercise an option to reinvest the dividends from its share in Founders into the bank thereby providing up to an additional $2 million in capital if its investment challenge is met. Thus, a total of possibly $4 million dollars could be realized from ARCO's original investment (*Black Enterprise*, 6/93).

General Motors, the largest private sector employer of Blacks in the world with 21 percent of its employees minorities, has purchased over $1 billion in supplies and services from 400 minority-owned companies for the past five years. Its Minority Enterprises Inc., a small business investment company created in 1970, provides a model for corporate relations with the Afrikan American community. So does its Minority Dealer Development Programs which service over 180 minority-owned dealerships and dealership start-ups. In the current context, GM "maintains the equivalent of $6 million in average daily balances with 94 minority-owned banks" (*New York Amsterdam News*, 8/21/93). While not as sufficiently supportive of Afrikan American economic development as it should and could be relative to the consumer support it receives from the Afrikan American community, its general economic relationship to the community provides a working model for other corporations. The community, through systematic consumer actions, could advance and require of other corporations that they develop the type of relationship to Black banks modeled after that of GM and those institutions.

Overall, the Afrikan American community is poorly served by its banks and financial institutions, both Black-owned and non-Black-owned. The under-service to the community by Black-owned banks and financial institutions is primarily due to certain structural weaknesses which characterize the economic nature of the community, as discussed by Light above; and more importantly, due to the inadequate capital levels, capital reserves and deposit accounts which endemically characterize those institutions. Despite their difficulties, many Black-owned banks are heroically committed to the Afrikan American community and contribute mightily to its well-being. A prime example of this was cited by *Black Enterprise* magazine (6/93) with reference to Broadway Federal Savings and Loan Association of Los Angeles:

> No thrift had as tough a year as Broadway Federal Savings and Loan Association. Its Los Angeles-based banking headquarters was burned to the ground during last May's riots. Yet almost immediately, CEO Paul C. Hudson built temporary offices across the street from the original site. Despite the fire, Hudson is committed to the community. Last year he offered up to $15 million in loans so that riot-affected businesses could make their payrolls. New headquarters for the $18 million asset thrift will open this year.

This type of commitment can be multiplied a hundred-fold to the benefit of the Afrikan American community if it were to fully commit itself to the strengthening of its financial institutions. The failure to do so spells its immanent economic and political demise. And such a wound would be self-inflicted in that by not investing and depositing its resources in its own financial institutions, while it continues to invest them in White-owned institutions in the Afrikan American community, it damages its own finance institutional base. That is, while the community increasingly deposits its resources in White-owned financial institutions, these same institutions are not only underservicing it but actually are economically strangling it to death.

Black Financial Self-Help

The Community Reinvestment Act has yet to live up to its potential to revitalize Afrikan American neighborhoods. However, community development organizations that have developed their community lending expertise have worked with lenders to obtain nearly $35 billion in loans to low and moderate-income neighborhoods under the Act (*New York Times*, 8/27/93).

The Afrikan American community must be acutely aware of the very severe damage it has done and is doing to itself by invariably depositing its monies in White-owned banks. It has virtually decimated its own economic sector and fatally wounded its economic body politic by so foolishly placing its monies in institutions which give it little or nothing in return. What is worse than receiving little or nothing in return for the billions of dollars it places in the hands of White financial institutions, is the fact that by doing so not only is its own money made unavailable to it for its own economic, social and residential improvement and growth, but its monies are made easily available to White and immigrant merchants and business groups who exploit it remorselessly. Consequently, its monies are utilized to help finance "White flight" — to help build White suburbs and edge-cities and the superhighways which lead to them. Afrikan American monies deposited in White-owned banks are utilized to help relocate factories and other business facilities out of reach of inner-city residents, thereby increasing their unemployment, criminality and general social degeneration. White-owned financial institutions use Afrikan American aggregate savings to finance the development and economic empowerment of all nations other than those of the Afrikan Diaspora. By depositing its monies with White-owned institutions without demanding and getting abundant returns for so doing, the Afrikan American community is literally choking itself and the Pan-Afrikan community to death by its own hands. It is committing economic suicide.

The Expansion of Black-owned Banks. However, all the responsibility for the poor success and retarded growth of Black-owned financial institutions cannot be exclusively laid on the presumed irresponsibility of Black consumers. Black-owned banks themselves must also share that responsibility with Black consumers. These banks must also take primary responsibility for their own growth and success. Black-owned banks and services must pursue business much more aggressively, both inside and outside the community. We continue to emphasize the fact that the economic development of the Afrikan American community depends on the ability of its businesses and professional organizations to expand both internally and externally. We are pleased to report that a growing number of Black-owned banks and financial services are rising to the challenge.

One of the mavericks is this regard is the Citizens Trust Company Bank, the largest Black-owned bank in Atlanta. This bank, founded prior to Great Depression, in fact in 1921, is now aggressively pursuing White, Korean and Hispanic customers. In seeking to diversify its customer base and gain a competitive edge Citizens put up 13 billboards in English, Korean and Spanish in both minority and predominantly White areas in 1992. This year it plans to open two branches in predominantly White areas.

While Citizens Trust Bank takes advantage of its maturity to expand its business horizons, banking "upstart" United Bank of Philadelphia has taken advantage of its youth. The Black-controlled, full-service commercial bank officially opened on March 23, 1992, after struggling for nearly five recession-filled years to raise $6 million in capital. In doing so, it is the first Black-controlled bank to receive a charter in Philadelphia since 1923. In August 1993, United Bank acquired two Chase Federal Savings and Loan Association branches. Chase Federal had total assets of $17.3 million and liabilities of $19.5 million (BE, 6/94). United Bank, with assets of $40 million, in September, 1993 entered into a cooperative venture with PNC Bank, a major commercial bank, that will allow it to purchase branches of a failed thrift, Home Unity Federal Savings and Loan Association, through the Resolution Trust Corporation (RTC). These two branches had combined deposits of $65 million. United Bank also acquired approximately $35 million in deposits from another Philadelphia bank branch which had been sold to PNC Bank. Moreover, United Bank will operate two new Philadelphia branch locations. As reported by the *New York Amsterdam News*, United Bank "paid a premium of $7,007 to assume approximately $100 million in deposits. As part of the minority assistance package made available by the RTC, United Bank has been given an option to purchase approximately $100 million in residential mortgages or consumer loans from RTC. In addition, the RTC has agreed to provide a loan to United Bank equal to two-thirds of the capital required by its primary regulators to support the acquisition...." United Bank is now the 18th largest Black-owned bank, with $75 million in assets and $67 million in deposits.

United Bank brilliantly illustrates the possibilities an aggressive Black-owned financial institution may realize by broadening its vision and by taking quick advantage of business opportunities whenever they may occur. By a judicious and competent use of previously untried methods, Black-owned banks can discover new opportunities to strengthen and expand their financial portfolios and as a result, better serve the national and international Afrikan communities.

Liberty Bank and Trust Company of New Orleans provides another example of aggressive Black-owned banking, achieving growth and financial clout through enhancing its commitment to the Afrikan American community. Liberty Bank's growth has been such that it moved from Nº 13 to Nº 8 on *Black Enterprise's* Top 25 Financial Companies list in 1994. This phenomenal growth can in good part be attributed to Liberty Bank's acquisition of its third financial institution in the last two years (*Black Enterprise*, 7/1994). Liberty Bank in 1992 bought Corpus Christi Federal Credit Union, the first whole-bank purchase of a credit union by a commercial bank, according to executive vice president Gregory St. Etienne. In March 1994, Liberty acquired the assets of Life Federal Savings Bank of Baton Rouge, Louisiana. Led by Alden J. McDonald, Jr. CEO, Liberty Bank recently acquired the White-owned Carrollton Homestead Bank with assets of $33.16 million. In 1993, Liberty Bank had $96.5 million in assets. At the rate Liberty is growing it seems a solid bet that it will achieve its central goal of building a regional banking empire.

Interstate Banking

Another approach to strengthening the competitiveness and power of Black-owned financial institutions and with them, the Afrikan American community, is through pooling resources, forming consortiums, entering new markets and mergers. For example, Seaway National Bank of Chicago recently became a municipal bond trustee. United Bank of Philadelphia introduced a national credit card in July, 1993. An unusual approach to building a wider base of customers, to providing a broader range of services and products, lowering costs, as well as increasing competitiveness for Black-owned banks, is daringly demonstrated by the Omnibanc Corporation of Detroit.

This corporation, owner of Omnibanc in suburban Detroit, announced in August 1993 its proposed interstate merger with Indecorp. Inc. — the Black-owned, Chicago-based holding company that owns two banks, Independence Bank (with assets of $159 million) and Drexel National Bank (with assets of $135 million). The combined assets of Indecorp, $294 million, and Omnibanc with assets of $26 million, would make Omnibanc America's largest Black-owned holding company and the only multistate Black-owned banking company. In pursuing its goals Omnibanc is riding the crest of a wave in mainstream banking — nation-wide branch banking and bank mergers. Both the House and Senate Banking Committees have approved of a bill that will allow banks to set up branches in other states without the costly process of retaining separate banking companies. In recent years the banking industry has been rapidly consolidating in tandem with the lifting of interstate barriers. The current bill proposes to lift all interstate barriers to interstate banking and is likely to accelerate the pace of bank mergers and change how banks do business. Competition among regional banks is likely to heat up as they penetrate each other's markets. Small and mid-size banks will be placed under heavy competitive pressure, bought out or merged. Superregional banks will also appear. These trends in banking need not be as ominous for Black-owned banks as they may first appear even though they may prove problematic for a number of them. Two small Black-owned banks, New Atlantic Bank of Norfolk, VA. (assets of $15 million) and Emerald City Bank, formerly Liberty Bank of Seattle (assets of $10.5 million), were both also acquired by a majority-owned bank in 1993. Boston Bank of Commerce, with some $68 million in assets, is struggling for its life.

However, as modeled by Omnibanc, Black-owned banks may strengthen their positions by taking advantage of the new interstate legislation and consolidate through acquisitions and mergers. The top 25 Afrikan American commercial banks and savings and loan institutions achieved assets of $2.9 billion in 1993 from $2.8 billion in 1992. They posted $3.06 billion in deposits in 1993 compared to $2.90 billion in 1992. Black-owned banks, S&Ls and Insurance Companies generated total assets of $4.2 billion in 1993 compared to $4.05 billion 1992. If these institutions through acquisitions, mergers and various alliances could reorganize themselves as regional, superregional or nationwide banks, then they possibly could become two or three such banks with assets of $2 billion or $1.5 billion each. Such a consolidation should permit the new banks and financial institutions to diversify geographically, to expand their products and services across a wider customer base and drive down costs. They should achieve rapid growth as they spread and improve their services to poor and minority communities as well as mainstream communities and new areas of business. They possibly could engage in more lucrative forms of international investment and trade. Their increased size and more efficient organization could be translated into great financial and political clout on the local, regional, national and international scene. Louis Prezeau, president of City National Bank of Newark, N.J., corroborates this sentiment. In an interview with *Black Enterprise* magazine (6/94), he expresses his feelings relative to interstate banking in this way:

> When I look at interstate banking today, we minority bankers should consider the benefits of mergers, both as a means to garner financial strength and to tap into technological benefits.

As indicated in our earlier discussion, Prezeau is no idle talker. He is a banking activist. According to *Black Enterprise*, Prezeau's City National has "established a $50 line of credit with AT&T, ...City will act as the leader of a syndicate of more than 50 minority banks located throughout the country."

Increasingly, the number and convenience of Automated Teller Machines (ATMs), the placement of mini-branch offices in supermarkets and other retail outlets, automating as many services as possible in as many banking locations as profitable, forming partnerships and alliances with other financial and service institutions to provide innovative financial and service packages, can propel consolidated Black-owned banks into the mainstream of banking and finance while remaining rooted in and committed to the Afrikan community.

Where the locating of branch banks in low income neighborhoods may prove too costly or not cost-effective, Black-owned banks might by various means establish check-cashing services. Such facilities now offer a wide array of services (albeit at higher prices than comparable bank services) e.g., the cashing of checks, paying of bills, buying lottery tickets, collection of welfare benefits. Lines of credit up to $100,000+ may be opened to underwrite fledgling check cashing facilities. National legislation now under consideration requiring banks to cash government checks for a lower fee; for allowing customers to make bank account deposits at check-cashing stores; permitting community financial institutions like credit unions to cash checks, etc., can be supported by Black-owned banks if it is in their interest to do so. Of course the option for these banks to compete head-on with the check-cashing firms through designing low-cost checking accounts for low income customers and welfare recipients through branch bank expansion and ATMs in poor neighborhoods, remains to be accepted.

The financial clout of the Afrikan American community depends on mutuality of relations with and among its financial institutions. These institutions must strengthen their ties and services to the community. They must reach out to its low-income constituents, its fledgling businesses, its talented youth and social institutions. They must help to increase the credit worthiness of the community's inhabitants as well as enhance and stabilize their employment. The community, in turn, must do all within its power to support and enrich its financial institutions for these are its material resources for economic growth, development, security, and political power.

Ultimately, the community can look only to itself for economic salvation. And it can achieve such salvation only to the degree that it assumes the greatest degree of control possible over its own money and wealth and utilize these to the greatest possible extent in its own economic and political interests.

Chapter 27

Financing Black Economic Development

BEGINNING WITH THIS CHAPTER through chapter 30 we will suggest and describe a number of ways an Afrikan American and Pan–Afrikan economic system may be financed by initiatives set forth and controlled by the Afrikan American and Pan–Afrikan community itself. These suggestions are not exhaustive in breadth and depth. They are not written with the expertise of a professionally trained and experienced economist. Their main purpose is to stimulate and focus discourse in the Afrikan community regarding the means of financing its economic development and enhancing its economic well-being and politicoeconomic power. More than merely catalyzing discourse, we hope the corrections and refinements as well as the creative approaches and our suggestions might move others to generate, serve as platforms for community actions that will lead to tangible positive results.

Development Banks

In the context of the Afrikan American community as a nation-within-a-nation, the placing of large deposits in developmental banks or loan funds by individuals and institutions would be similar in effect to the expansion of the money supply by the Federal Reserve Bank of the United States. This would especially be the case if regional development banks (after having received large deposits from many sources) could make more sizable loans to local community banks, CDCUs and other financial institutions which in turn make loans to consumers and businesses. In fact, if the new deposits in Black-owned banks were cycled through a chain of Black-owned banks in the form of loans (with the checks written by consumers based on those loans drawn on Black-owned banks), the money supply would be greatly expanded since every time any bank in the chain opened an account for a new borrower the total number of people and businesses authorized to write checks would have expanded. The money supply refers to "the sum of currency outside the banking system (i.e., in our own pockets) plus the total of demand deposits [e.g., checking and savings accounts]."[1] Martin Mayer explains expansion of the money supply thusly:

> Each time a bank creates a deposit by making a loan, it sets in motion a chain of money creation. The borrower writes checks on his account, the proceeds of those checks are deposited at other banks, the other banks make loans, the borrowers at other banks write checks on *their* accounts, still other banks enter new deposits on the proceeds of those checks, and so on. A bank cannot safely lend the entire proceeds of a deposit — and cannot legally do so in the United States, where all bank supervisory agencies (except the State of Illinois) set "reserve requirements" — so the quantity of new money created diminishes at each stop, as the images diminish in the mirrors. But unless somebody breaks the chain by taking out currency the banks will keep creating deposits, creating new quantities of M_1. If the retained reserves are 20 percent, a $100 deposit of new money — dug out of South African goldfields, printed by a government, imported from abroad — can produce a chain of $80, $64, $51.20, $40.96, etc., to a total of another $400.[2]

Checks are forms of money. As the Black community increases the volume of its bank and financial institutional reserves, it stimulates credit expansion (i.e., checking accounts). Therefore "an increased amount of loanable funds thus becomes available for business and consumer borrowing. As business activity picks up, firms increase hiring, and the unemployment rate falls."[3]

---

1. R. Heilbroner and L. Thurow, *Economics Explained.* See page 237 for an illustration related to this concept.

2. M. Mayer, *The Bankers.* pp. 35–36.

3. W. Carnes and S. Slider, *The Atlas of Economic Indicators: A Visual Guide to Market Forces and the Federal Reserves* (New York: Harper Collins, 1992).

One of the ways banks may more directly engage in the economic development of their communities without violating the traditional rules and laws of banking is to found and organize or support a network of banks designed specifically for that purpose — community-development banks. Community-development banks are financial institutions which provide capital for the business and infrastructural development of their communities. Community-development banks are one among a number of institutions designed to aid depressed areas, including community credit unions and revolving loan funds.

These institutions which provide loans to small businesses may be publicly and/or privately financed. President Clinton has also proposed the government creation of a network of community development banks. In July 1993, the Clinton administration publicly proposed the establishment of a $382-million pool to be allotted over four years, from which existing development corporations, loan funds and credit unions would be able to draw as they compete for grants. The Clinton administration is also proposing a $850 million fund to help finance community-development institutions. According to the *Wall Street Journal* (January 19, 1993) the money would be used to finance banks, credit unions and revolving loan funds. By such means, "The money would provide technical assistance to community groups in launching lending operations and would help capitalize lenders once they got going. Every dollar of federal capital would have to be matched by $2 of private funds." According to the same *Wall Street Journal* article, "The development bank that won Mr. Clinton over to the idea is the South Shore Bank in Chicago, which helped turn around a declining neighborhood by financing a revitalization plan."

Unlike more conventional banks, South Shore Bank specializes in providing loans to fledgling minority entrepreneurs, to buy and renovate small apartment buildings in poor Chicago communities, an approach shunned by many other banks. According to the *Journal* 6/23/93):

> The bank and its affiliates have financed the rehabilitation of about 30% of the 25,000 apartments in South Shore, helping to rescue a neighborhood that fell on hard times about 25 years ago as middle-income Whites fled and lower-income Blacks moved in.
>
> Yet the bank has been consistently profitable, and its loan-loss figures compare favorably with those of similar-sized banks. Last year's losses were a respectable 0.67% of loans outstanding. It has been stuck with just one piece of real estate in the past three years.

The article goes on to indicate that South Shore Bank has achieved these ends based on its "willingness to make loans as much on character as on collateral." The Bank has seemingly developed its capacity "to discern the good risks and also to keep close tabs on them after they borrow." In fact, Richard Turner, senior vice president for lending at South Shore Bank, is reported to have said that "We spend a hell of a lot more time...working with the borrower one-on-one." In this context it is interesting to note that contrary to common business stereotypes, defaults on loans by minority businesses and organizations are not significantly greater than defaults by White-owned businesses and organizations. According to the *Wall Street Journal* (1/13/93), community development loan funds "have lent $106 million in the last six years and made available $760 million in public and private capital for inner-city housing and businesses by agreeing to handle the riskiest portion of loans.... They also have surprisingly low loan losses — less than 1% of all loans..." [based on information supplied by the National Association of Community Development Loan Funds, a trade group representing 42 of the nonprofit funds]. Apparently, a major reason for the low default rates of start-up businesses in the inner-city is due in large part to the willingness of the funds to work closely with borrowers to develop their business plans and businesses.

It is also important to note that South Shore Bank, according to the *Wall Street Journal* (6/13/92), "is owned by foundations, churches and big corporations, the ultimate in patient capital, but it borrows and lends at a profit just like any other bank." Other private development loan funds, such as the Delaware Valley Community Reinvestment Fund of the Germantown section of Philadelphia, the Cascadia Revolving Fund of Seattle, and Nueva Esperanza, a community development corporation founded by Philadelphia's Hispanic clergy, report low default rates for the loans they make to minority business ventures. Cascadia Revolving Fund reports that all but $1,400 of the $1.4 million it has lent to businesses since 1987 has been paid back (WSJ, 1/13/93). Private, non-profit loan funds can, unlike their counterparts, afford to provide loans to their borrowers at fewer points above prime rate. Additionally, they more readily recruit volunteers, e.g., lawyers and accountants, to work both with them and their borrowers.

From the foregoing discussion we can divine a number of directions for the development of community-development banks and loan funds from within the Afrikan American community itself. As we suggested in the prior section dealing with the institutional Black church, individual churches, church associations, professional organizations and other organized groups, either together or separately, can fund development banks or loan funds designed to make or facilitate loans of various sizes (it is possible for such banks or funds t Business Administration guarantees) to upstarting Black-owned businesses and economic development projects. Development loan funds or banks cannot only be community and city-based but regionally based as well. For example, in May 1992, utilizing the support from the banking community and private foundations across New York City, the Brooklyn Economic Development Assistance Corporation announced the founding of the Regional Economic Developmental Corporation. This organization is essentially a mini-loan program for small businesses, offering $5,000–$25,000 loans to businesses with sales of less than $1 million.

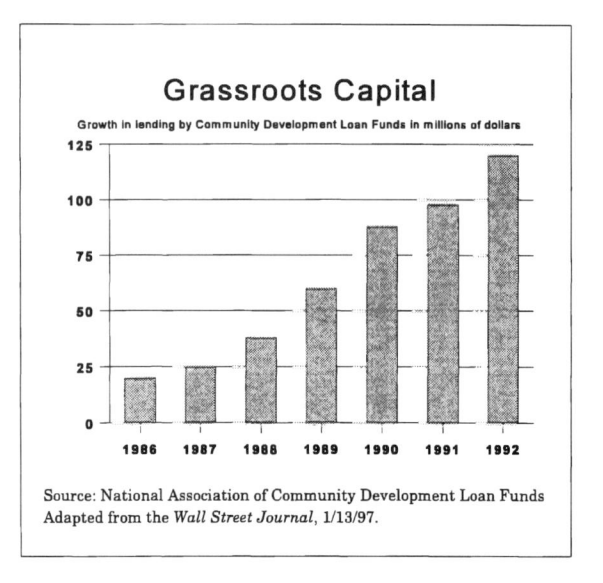

Grassroots Capital

Growth in lending by Community Development Loan Funds in millions of dollars

Source: National Association of Community Development Loan Funds
Adapted from the *Wall Street Journal*, 1/13/97.

Credit Unions

The credit union movement, a prime example of cooperative economics, is growing rapidly by all measures. Total credit union membership has increased by 13.4 million since 1985. Its total membership at the end of 1992 amounted to 64.3 million members. This rapid growth in both membership and assets is occurring at the same time banks and S&Ls are retrenching or shrinking. Compared with 1.9 percent growth for commercial banks and a shrinkage of 9.7 percent for the S&Ls, the assets of the nation's credit unions grew by over 10 percent in 1992. Also in 1992, credit union lending expanded by 1.7 percent compared with a contraction of 1.4 percent for the banks and 11.7 percent for the S&Ls.

Traditionally, consumer-oriented credit unions may lend as little as $50 or $300 for a member to make a purchase of important personal or household items, services, furnishing or appliances. Credit unions like the Germantown Federal Credit Union of Philadelphia, with some 3,000 members and $2.3 million in assets, may provide personal loans of up to $20,000 (*Black Enterprise*, 9/93). Like many churches, Atlanta's Wheat Street Federal Credit Union with some $1.2 million in assets, has made loans over $1.5 million to its members over its 37-year history. While local banks may require anywhere from a $200–$500+ minimum to open a deposit checking account, credit unions may typically open an account for as little as $5. Consequently, credit unions provide excellent means of imbuing youths with thrifty attitudes, savings behavior and financial knowledge.

Youth credit unions such as the D. Edward Wells Federal Credit Union of Springfield, Mass., with its 644 members and $30,000 in assets, can provide teenagers with early experience in how to manage the credit union, how to perform in various positions such as tellers, clerks, officers, members of the board of directors. They may learn how to set policies as well as grant loans (BE, 9/93). The D.E. Wells Youth Credit Union is overseen by an 11-member board. It offers savings accounts and loans, and accepts deposits as small as 5 cents. Seventy-five percent of the graduates of the youth credit union have gone on to college. Contrary to racial stereotypes regarding the irresponsibility of Black youth, "there has not been a single incident of delinquency with any of the 100 loans by the youngsters" (NYT, 2/10/94).

The Northwest Baptist Federal Credit Union of Seattle, Washington, was founded thirty-six years ago. In its 35th year it founded its Youth Credit Union Program (Y-CUP). Y-CUP was formed in March, 1993 to involve and train youth in managing a credit union. By year's end Y-CUP's 44 accounts had accumulated $23,102.92. Membership in the organization is open to youths from six months to 19 years old. The Northwest Baptist Federal Credit Union grew by 17.7% in 1993 to achieve a record high of $3.5 million in assets. It paid $135,748 in dividends to its members. It floated total loans of $1.8 million.

The youth credit union movement is rapidly growing in a number of Afrikan American neighborhoods. In addition to the D.E. Wells Youth Credit Union, the Central Brooklyn Youth Credit Union provides another brilliant example of the viability and promise of using credit unions as means of introducing Afrikan American youths to the world of banking and finance. The Central Brooklyn Youth Credit Union is one of 11 projects designed to teach economic lessons to children as well as help them to develop a sense of fiscal responsibility. The *New York Times* told the story of Central Brooklyn Youth Credit Union and of the youth credit union movement sponsored by the National Federation of Community Credit Unions, in its February 10, 1994 edition. In part, it reported that:

...in central Brooklyn, at the nexus of neighborhoods that include Bedford-Stuyvesant, Crown Heights and Prospect Heights, there is a movement to develop fiscal responsibility. The Central Brooklyn Youth Credit Union, one of 11 such projects awarded grants by the National Federation of Community Development Credit Unions, is coming into being.

The youth credit unions, including ones in Harlem and Hempstead, L.I., received an average of $15,000 in start-up funds early in 1993. The general goals are to infuse low-income minority children with concepts of ownership and to equip them with skills for jobs in the financial services industry. The new credit unions are modeled after the D.E. Wells Youth Credit Union in Springfield, Mass., which was formed in 1988 and has 1,000 members and $30,000 in assets....

The youth credit union in Brooklyn, coordinated by the Central Brooklyn Partnership, a coalition of neighborhood development organizations and churches, will draw its membership from the area's children. Recruited from schools and church groups, the children ages 8 to 18 will run it. They will deposit in it. They will own it.

"It's about a lot more than business," said Angela Riley, an officer with the partnership and an adviser to the youth credit union. "It's about what leadership means. It's about what it means to build an institution."

A number of inner-city neighborhoods presumably abandoned or undeserved by banks or traumatized by social disruptions, such as urban riots, are establishing credit unions to service their populations. For example, Walls Community Credit was formed after 1965. Mount Pleasant, of Washington, D.C., formed its credit union after a riot in that area. In November 1992, the South Central People's Federal Credit Union (SCPFCU) was chartered in riot-torn South Central, Los Angeles (BE, 9/93). The SCPFCU is designed to provide small business loans and other financial services to its 650,000 residents.

After the demise of New York City's largest Black-owned commercial bank, Freedom National Bank, and the closing of its major branch in Central Brooklyn in 1990, a Black community of 750,000 residents, the Central Brooklyn Credit Union was founded in January, 1993. Founded by Errol T. Lewis and Mark Winston Griffith whose research indicated that even though the community had some $629 million on deposit at its local banks (*The City Sun*, 10/27–11/2/93), as of the late 1980s *less than* one penny out of every dollar deposited in local banks was returned by way of home lending to the community. The credit union offers savings accounts, loans and other financial services to neighborhood individuals, churches, and businesses. The Central

Brooklyn Credit Union has more than 600 members and assets of $1.5 million since its inception, and aims to raise $5 million more in the near future. This union which provides technical assistance as well as loans to small businesses, has been remarkably successful in gaining community as well as institutional support. An example of the latter is provided by the fact that Central Brooklyn Credit Union managed to obtain a $100,000 deposit from Chase Manhattan Bank as its way of reinvesting in the Central Brooklyn community. A major money center bank, Chemical Bank of New York, donated a previously closed branch to the fledgling credit union.

Types of Credit Unions

We shall briefly discuss two types of credit unions. The first is a federally or state chartered credit union like those operated by churches, unions and membership organizations of various types for the sole benefit of their depositors, more commonly referred to as shareholders. The second type of credit union, an organization more in line with our interests herein, is called the community development credit union (CDCU).

The following cursory description of federal credit unions is taken from a publication titled *Federal Credit Unions*, published by the National Credit Union Administration (NCUA) (Rev. Sept., 1988). According to NCUA, "a federal credit union is a member-owned cooperation organized to promote thrift among its members and to make loans to its members from these accumulated savings." Credit unions are a more than $200-billion industry that provides a wide array of financial services to a highly diverse array of customers. By 1989 credit union membership reached almost sixty million and total credit union assets almost tripled from $69 billion in 1980 to $196 billion by year-end 1988.[4] The principal purpose of a Federal Credit Union is to encourage and support its members to accumulate savings out of their income as a means of building economic security for themselves and their families. Credit unions provide their members with essentially the same array of services as do commercial and S&L banks. Moreover, share accounts in federal credit unions are insured up to $100,000 per account by NCUA. Furthermore, credit union savings are further protected through a number of federal regulations and standard by-laws which include the requirements that (NCUA. *Federal Credit Unions*. Rev. 9/88):

---

4. The American Bankers Association, *The Credit Union Industry: Trends, Structure, and Competitiveness* (Washington, D.C.: A.B.A., 1990).

(1) All persons handling or having custody of credit union funds must be bonded.
(2) The affairs of the credit union and the records of the treasurer are audited by the supervisory committee.
(3) The [Federal Credit Unions] Act and the bylaws provide for the setting aside of a reserve for uncollectible loans.
(4) The surplus funds of the credit union may be invested only in specified investments.
(5) All federal credit unions are supervised and are periodically examined by the National Credit Union Administration.

According to the Credit Union National Association (CUNA) in its *Credit Union Profile*, December 31, 1987, credit union products and services include the following as outlined in Table 27–1.

Federal credit unions that are members of strong organizations such as the Community Service Credit Union Council, Credit Union Service Organizations, the World Council of Credit Unions, and the Credit Union National Association, permit individual credit unions to offer a broad variety of operational and financial services. These include the following:

Operational services...credit and debt card services; check cashing and wire transfers; internal audits for credit unions; ATM, electronic funds, and accounting services data processing; shared credit union branch operation; sale of repossessed collateral; management, development, sale or lease of fixed assets; sale, lease, or servicing of computer hardware or software; management and personnel training and support; payment item processing; locator, marketing and research services; record retention and storage; microfilm and microfiche services; alarm monitoring and other security services; debt collection; credit analysis, consumer mortgage loan origination (but not commercial real estate development loans); loan processing and servicing; coin and currency services; and provision of forms and supplies.

[F]inancial services...include financial planning and counseling; retirement counseling; investment advice; securities brokerage; estate planning; income tax preparation; acting as administrator for prepaid legal service plans; developing and administering IRA, Keogh and other benefit plans; trust services; real estate brokerage; travel agency services; agent for sale of insurance; personal property leasing; and provision of vehicle warranty programs.[5]

A credit union member of the New York Community Financial Network and National Credit Union Organizations may also engage

---

5. *The Credit Union Industry: Trends, Structure, and Competitiveness* (The American Bankers Association, 1990).

**CREDIT UNION PRODUCTS
AND SERVICES ANALYZED BY CUNA**

Personal Loans: Transaction Services 1:
  Unsecured
  Share Secured
  Cosigner
  Overdraft Protection
  Variable Rate

Vehicle Loans:
  Used Auto
  New Auto
  Balloon Auto Transaction Services 11:
  Auto Leasing
  Plan, Boat R.V.
  Variable Rate

Mortgage Loans:
  First Mortgage
    Balloon
    Fixed Rate
    Adjustable Rate
  Home Equity
  Other 2nd Mortgages

Miscellaneous Loans:
  Home Improvement
  Stock Secured
  GSLs
  Other Student Loans
  Consolidation
  Member Business

Savings:
  Certificates
  Money Market Accounts
  IRAs
  Vacation Clubs
  Christmas Clubs
  Trust Accounts

ATM Cards
Credit Cards
Debit Cards
Share Drafts
Business Checking
In-house Share Draft Processing
CU owned ATMs

Payroll Deduction
Direct Deposit of Net
  Pay
Pre-Authorized Debits
Originate ACH
Receive ACH
Telephone Bill Paying
Home Banking

Insurance Services:
Life Savings Insurance
Loan Protection Ins.
Including Disability
Member-Pay Credit-Life
Member-Pay Credit-Dis.
Life Insurance
Auto Insurance
Homeowner's Insurance

Miscellaneous Services:
Discount Brokerage
Remedial Counseling
Financial Planning
Service Package for
Retirees
Special Programs for
Youth
Safe Deposit Boxes
Group Legal Services

Source: CUNA's *Credit Union Profile*, December 31, 1987.

Table 27–1

in: financing small businesses; providing financial services; job training; management training; as well as sponsor church and youth credit union development projects.

According to NCUA, "membership in a Federal Credit Union is limited to those groups or persons with a common bond of employment, association or residence as specified in its charter." The most pertinent aspect about credit unions relative to the Afrikan American community has to do with control and management. As described by the NCUA, "control of management is in the hands of the members of the credit union. A volunteer board of directors is elected at the annual meeting of the members. Each member has one vote regardless of the number of shares owned." Every depositor is a shareholder in the union. The organization is completely owned by and operated by its members. In other words, a credit union is a democratic bank where members pool their savings and make loans to each other. A major advantage of starting a credit union in contrast to starting a bank is that a credit union may be opened with little or no initial equity. That is, organizers who wish to found a credit union are not required to meet minimum capital requirements.

Thus we see that the credit union provides a very viable instrument for the economic betterment of individuals, families, organizations and the community. It allows the community to be in far greater control of its monetary and economic resources and of its political economic empowerment. Through the credit union the community directly invests in itself. Its monies are available for its exclusive use and advancement. This places it in a superior league relative to banks. More important for economic well-being and development is the fact that through credit unions, "Thousands of poor people are making deposits in savings accounts, opening and using checking accounts, and submitting loan applications that traditional bankers would only throw in the wastebasket."[6]

New Jersey's First Credit Union. First Baptist Church on High Street in Cranford, New Jersey, is a true credit union pioneer. In March, 1994, the church celebrated the 50th anniversary of the founding of its credit union. Established under the patronage of the late Reverend Benjamin W.P. Allen, a staunch believer in community self-help, First Baptist's credit union is the oldest such institution in New Jersey (*The Sunday Star Ledger*, 2/13/94). "During the Great Depression and World War II, Allen helped organize food and coal clubs. With bulk purchasing, members could heat their homes and feed their families at a minimum cost," according to the *Star Ledger*. However, the paper notes that "perhaps his greatest contribution to the church started July 31, 1944, when the first church credit union ever chartered by the state of New Jersey opened.... Allen was instrumental in helping other churches start credit unions. One of them, the St. James AME Church in Newark, has the largest church credit union in the state." First Baptist's own 189-member credit union has assets of more than $396,000. One of only 21 credit unions in New Jersey, First Baptist's credit union and congregation have a clear sense of their economic

---

6. K. Tholin and J. Pogge, *Banking Services for the Poor: Community Development Credit Unions* (Chicago: Woodstock Institute, 1991).

mission in the Black community. Their 50th anniversary theme: *Economic Development: An Essential Mission of the Collective Black Church,* leaves no doubt about that.

Church-based credit unions in various neighborhoods and communities must not only seek to expand those unions but to combine their efforts in ways which would have a greater impact within the Afrikan American community. As a whole, one of the ways this can be done consistent with the tradition of cooperative economics is through the establishment and operation of community development credit unions. We shall now briefly discuss this type of credit union organization.

Community Development Credit Unions

Community development credit unions, in line with regular credit unions, offer credit and financial services that are very often scarcely available to or affordable for a very large number of low-income individuals and families. Just like regular credit unions, they make credit and services available with minimal or no support from government, philanthropic organizations, or other outside sources of assistance. However, community development credit unions play a role quite distinct from that of regular federal credit unions as well as from traditional banks. Citing an analysis of community development credit unions, specialists Tholin and Pogge (1991) indicate that:

Community development credit unions are different from banks, other credit unions, other community development organizations and even other community financial institutions, such as loan funds or development banks in at least two important ways.

(1) the primary members of a community development credit union are precisely those who are not likely to be served by standard banks and credit unions; and the financial services needed by their members may be different from those offered by other financial institutions.

(2) the community development credit union is primarily designed to promote local community development through lending activities, a mission they share with the other development financial institutions, such as loan funds and development banks. However, unlike other development lenders, community development credit unions specialize in small loans made directly to people — home buyers and improvers, students, workers, and small business people.

Tholin and Pogge (1991) further indicate that as of 1990, there were some 300 of these credit unions in 40 states and approximately

70% were located in inner-city communities in large metropolitan areas (National Federation of Community Development Credit Unions (NFCDCU). While most CDCUs serve their local area, *many associational credit unions may serve a particular group in several communities.* Furthermore, as Tholin and Pogge contend, "community development credit unions are committed to the development of community control and leadership-control over the credit union itself, and through the credit union, over the economic resources of the community." Credit unions enhance the development of a sense of social interest, social responsibility and reliability as they encourage savings through regular deposits or payroll deductions. By providing account services to people who may not have had them before; by providing financial management responsibilities to their staffs, volunteers, interested members and trainees; by providing their clients with attractive credit facilities and valuable know-how — credit unions help bring people into and familiarize them with the financial mainstream, thereby enhancing their ability to qualify for loans and other financial services.

While lending far more for housing than other purposes, many CDCUs make small business loans. These loans made to small entrepreneurs or self-employed members are structured along the lines of a bank-based consumer loan. A number of CDCUs make business lending a key part of their lending activities. Moreover, these business-focused unions develop specialized expertise in analyzing and monitoring business loans while often providing other business support services.

Like banks, CDCUs must establish and maintain reserve accounts in order to protect their depositor's funds from uncollectible loans. Reserve account contributions are required to be made before dividends are declared. However, reserve accounts provide additional support benefits for the CDCU. They function in the same ways as capital reserves for a traditional bank. Interest income realized from investing the reserves and earned on loans provide unencumbered funds for further growth in assets, to finance operations, or to distribute to members as dividends. There are three primary sources for credit union deposits: individual members, organizational members and (for CDCUs) non-members. Non-member deposits are usually available only to federally chartered credit unions and some state-chartered credit unions that meet certain specified standards. It's important to note that foundations can place non-member deposits in CDCUs. Such deposits can provide CDCUs with very sizable support for new community development initiatives, with substantial deposits at below market interest rates, and with deposits that can serve as collateral for specific community development loans to other organizations or individuals. Tholin and Pogge (1991) suggest that non-member deposits can "be made to support early operations of a new credit union; to start new programs, such as credit counseling or development lending; to fund needed capital expenditures; or to build reserves.... Grant support could enable additional staffing for a community organizer, a community development officer, or a community financial coordinator."

Traditional banks may also provide support to CDCUs. There are a number of reasons for them to do so: (1) CDCUs help to fill the void left by banks that have abandoned certain communities; (2) CDCUs provide services for very low-income people who are members of communities that cannot provide profitable markets and accounts for banks; (3) financial support of CDCUs by banks is now recognized by federal regulators as one of the important means by which they can satisfy Community Reinvestment Act requirements. Banks may contribute to the support of CDCUs by making low-interest deposits in them, by making direct general loans, grants for funding salaries of staff persons, for general operations, and to support various financial services. Banks may also donate property, equipment or services. Property may include buildings, e.g., abandoned branches, computers and other types of office equipment. Services may include marketing and public relations assistance, training for credit union tellers or loan officers.

Churches can play a crucial role in assisting development credit unions by utilizing their institutional resources, influence with banks and other financial institutions, political influence, organizing community efforts, and by encouraging their members to support CDCUs. Churches can make deposits in CDCUs. Tholin and Pogge (1991) suggest that "credit unions can also be an investment option for individual congregations, providing an alternative to certificate of deposit or money market funds."

State and local governments can contribute to CDCUs in a variety of ways. The interest of these entities in CDCUs flow from the fact these organizations are civic in their orientation and take responsibility for helping improve social and economic conditions in low-income communities. State and local governments may help to increase CDCU reserves by placing some portion of their public deposits generated by taxes and fees with the credit unions. These deposits may be placed with credit unions in ways that they can be used to support additional or increased community reinvestment. Moreover, as suggested by Tholin and Pogge (1991), "States and cities should be encouraged to design public deposit programs targeted to CDCUs as a way of supporting their community development mission." They further suggest that local governments can help to expand and strengthen the activities of CDCUs by permitting them to be agents for packaging loans for city and state finance programs. Since a very sizable number of Blacks head municipal governments and have been elected to state and local legislative bodies, the suggestions made here are increasingly more realistic and feasible.

The Community Development Corporation

The Community Development Corporation (CDC) as the title implies, is an officially incorporated group whose primary aim is to help the members of a particular community advance their economic development and enhance their well-being through the ownership and control of the resources of their community. The CDC strives to expand economic and social opportunity to help establish community stability and self-determination. While the CDC may be funded by federal agencies, the CDC, more truly a community corporation, is financed through stocks and bonds sold in the local community. Thus through the CDC the community invests in itself, may come to own important assets within its boundaries, and can develop a community commonwealth from earnings and dividends as well as any assets it may acquire as the result of the CDC's effectiveness. The CDC operates in many ways as an ordinary stock company, a for-profit company that sells its shares to local residents and earns its income from making equity investments (i.e., by becoming owners and part-owners) in productive entrepreneurial properties and developmental projects. Through the CDC the community may purchase retail and other properties owned by outsiders and aliens and thereby return them to community ownership and control. Consequently, monies and other resources which previously flowed out of the community, draining it of its resources and wealth, would be substantially slowed and reduced. Through community-based corporate planning and developmental projects the CDC may serve to attract new businesses and investments into the community, thus increasing its economic viability. William Tabb summarizes some key functions of CDCs.

> Most schemes for community development corporations (CDC's) propose (1) expanding economic and educational opportunities through the purchase and management of properties and businesses; (2) improving the health, safety and living conditions through CDC-

sponsored health centers, housing projects, and so on; (3) enhancing personal dignity and independence through the expansion of opportunities for meaningful decision-making and self-determination; and (4) at the discretion of the corporation, using its profits to pay a "community dividend" rather than a return to stockholders. The relation between CDC-sponsored businesses and privately owned ones is hard to delineate satisfactorily.[7]

The CDC can become a crucial talent and resource pool for the community through its acting as a source of knowledge, expertise, capital, assistance, and as a generator of new ideas and projects for community ventures.

Caution is advised here as well in regard to the prior reviews. To the extent that the CDC is not self-sustaining, i.e., supported or financed substantially by the community, that is, by both the local and ethnic community as a national or regional whole; to the extent that it is dependent on financing from large corporations, foundations, and government agencies — it may be mortally crippled or destroyed by their withdrawal of support. This was the fate of the vast majority of CDCs established during the 1960s and 70s. Due to relatively weak internal inner-city markets, poor public service, high levels of antisocial behavior; the persistent drain of resources from the inner-city which retards the large accumulation of capital, the CDC may judiciously invest some portions of its capital in other investment instruments outside the immediate community. This may require some ethical investment in major corporations, government bonds, retail/wholesale outlets in downtown areas and shopping malls (where the vast majority of the inner-city and suburban working Blacks spend their working day as well as their earnings). Investments in businesses in Afrikan nations and communities across the diaspora, engaging in export-import services, the selling of services, etc., should also be considered with the intention of accumulating significant amounts of capital to speed and enhance local economic development. However, special care must be taken that outside investment activities not lead to the neglect of local development.

Venture Capital

The economy of the Afrikan American community is essentially a "Third World" economy. This means that it is generally underdeveloped, greatly undercapitalized, and investments in its enterprises considered to be high-risk. That is, its enterprises are generally small,

---

7. W. Tabb, *The Political Economy of the Black Ghetto*, p. 52.

managerially inept and inefficient; are poorly organized, understocked, ill-equipped, low-profit sole proprietorships. Moreover, the enterprises are generally un-associated and uncoordinated, i.e., not systemically organized as collectives or as a whole. There is, therefore, little or no infrastructural means for the enterprises that exist to mutually support each other, mutually expand and strengthen their specific markets and their economy as a whole, and to protect their markets against the incursions of outsiders. There are few Afrikan American business associations and business leagues organized to strategically and tactically expand into and successfully penetrate the marketplaces of other communities or to pioneer and develop new markets. But above all, the central problem faced by Afrikan American entrepreneurialism is *undercapitalization* — i.e., the relative inaccessibility, or more simply, the meagerness or absence of money, capital, and capital resources.

The Afrikan American community can be perceived from an economic perspective as a newly developing nation. Accordingly, investments in its enterprises when measured by "standard" (i.e., Eurocentric) credit or investment grade criteria, are generally considered uncreditworthy or high-risk, i.e., the probability of business failure is high or return on investment highly unlikely or low. Consequently, Black enterprises or would-be enterprises are caught up in a vicious cycle — they are considered high-risk investments because they are generally undercapitalized and they are undercapitalized because they are considered high-risk. These are the economic horns of a dilemma which has ensnared Black enterprise and from which it must escape into freedom and growth. But this type of dilemma is not unique to the Afrikan American economy. It is generally present in all underdeveloped or newly industrializing economies or newly developing market situations. Many nations now considered economically mature, secure and advanced passed through the stage where investing in their enterprises was considered very risky or high-risk investing. Among these nations must be included the United States during its early development in the 17th, 18th, 19th and early 20th centuries. However, the existence of high-risk investment opportunities does not in and of itself negate investment in them. Generally, two approaches to such a situation are used: the organization of investment so as to spread and/or reduce risk (e.g., partnerships, corporate investment, government subsidies and guarantees); and the organization of funds which are willing to invest capital in uncertain business situations in spite of the relatively high risks involved (this does not imply that such investments are reckless or uncalculated). The latter approach pretty much defines the role of venture capital, of venture capitalists, and of venture capital firms.

As we pointed out earlier, it was the venture capital investments by European financiers, cartels, stock companies, merchant banks, firms, and the like in fledgling American enterprises which helped to substantially finance and organize the economic growth and development of U.S. economy in general. Economic enterprise must be supported in spite of risk, if economic growth is to occur. New enterprises, the growth and development of ongoing enterprises, the entry into or development of new markets and industrial innovation, require the long-term and well-funded commitment of resources to organizations that can plan, develop, and coordinate productive capabilities and activities that promote economic prosperity.

Financial commitment by venture capitalists, very wealthy individuals or families, venture capital funds and organizations, is key to building Afrikan American and Pan–Afrikan business organizations to the point where they can gain competitive advantage in a number of business or industrial fields. Some venture capital funds already operate in the Black community in the form of microloan funds, some community development corporation funds, commonwealth and foundation funds. Government backed agencies such as the Small Business Administration (SBA) and Minority Enterprise Small Business Investment Companies (MESBICs), which are functionally designed to supply equity financing and long-term debt financing to small businesses owned by nonwhites, may be, in effect, considered venture capital funds or organizations. Some corporations also provide venture capital resources to Black or minority businesses. For example, the money center bank, Bankers Trust of New York City, through its Bankers Trust Community Development Group's venture capital program finances such projects as a Harlem-based microloan program; a central Brooklyn nonprofit-owned construction company; and a Queens business start-up fund. However, the experience of Black enterprises with these sources of venture capital has been such that there is little reason to recommend their exclusive use by the Black community. Despite their smaller capital bases, we believe that community-based and funded venture capital enterprises, organizations with no strings tied to governments and non-Black financiers, are ultimately the most effective organizations for financing and supporting Black enterprise. Black-owned venture capital funds should be able to exhibit a deeper and more functional understanding of the problems and needs of Black enterprises. They should also exhibit a greater tolerance, creativity and flexibility when it comes to providing the most productive and least risky approach to supporting the growth and development of Black enterprise.

We believe that a large enough variety of wealthy individuals and families, highly profitable corporations and businesses, religious and secular organizations exist in the Afrikan American community which can combine their resources to form venture capital firms. Such firms can be corporations and therefore be publicly traded in the over-the-counter market or owned by its shareholders. A Black-owned venture capital firm may back start-up Black-owned companies that demonstrate promise in their market or some edge in a new technology or market. It may specialize in bringing to market Black-owned firms already established and profitable that have not yet issued stock. The venture capital company may provide consulting, make loans, and invest in the client company as a partner or in its securities. For both a private or public traded venture capital firm, it is the company's close links with, and equity holdings in, any number of other productive firms which makes it a valuable asset or its stocks valuable to shareholders and investment managers. Investing in a well-funded, well-diversified, smart venture capital firm is like owning an investment trust or a type of mutual fund. Buying stock in or owning a top-notch venture capital company is like buying proxy ownership in the companies with which the venture capital company has entered into partnership or a good portion of whose securities are owned by the company. Such ownership by a venture capital firm may give them a value beyond its own assets.

We do not mean to imply that investing in venture capital firms is guaranteed to be profitable or earn high returns on investment. The very fact that it is a "venture" capital firm, i.e., it specializes in relatively high-risk investments, should disabuse us of that idea. However, like any other type of investment, return is predicated on any number of the usual factors and conditions that influence the increasing or declining yields of a particular financial instrument or entity. The venture capital firm plays a very important role in advancing the development of fledgling enterprises and economies and for that reason alone, should be developed by the Afrikan American community as a key instrument for funding its own enterprises and economic development.

The Business Development Company. The venture capital approach we just described is similar to that of a lesser well-known approach to capitalizing small businesses known as the business development company or BDC. The BDC was created by Congress in 1980 to provide growth financing for small-businesses. Unlike MESBICs and other small-business financing vehicles overseen by the Small Business Administration, BDCs are regulated by the Securities Exchange Commission. This is the case because BDCs sell stock to the public. The funds these companies obtain from selling stock are used to invest in start-up businesses and other small companies.

There are approximately 50 BDCs now operating in the country. They own or manage assets of more than $2 billion and have helped to fund hundreds of small businesses. The investment portfolios of BDCs generally consist of stock in private firms or lightly traded public companies. At this time this relatively little-noticed and minimally regulated corner of the venture capital industry remains little understood and somewhat problematic relative to methods for accurately determining the value of a BDC's investment portfolio. However, the functional role of the BDC is worth investigating and perhaps founding as one of a number of possible ways to finance small business development in the Afrikan American community.

Black-owned Venture Capital Funds in the Expansion of the Afrikan American Economy

As we have alluded to elsewhere, if we consider the Afrikan American economy to be essentially a "Third World" economy, its development and achievement of parity with "first world" economies requires the investment of a relatively high level of high-risk or venture capital. This means that large sums of money must be made available to create and expand Black-owned businesses. Venture capital represents one of the major means by which funds are used by existing and new Black-owned companies to underwrite the development, production or marketing of new products, services and technologies by Black-owned companies. Such a new or expanding company may develop, innovate, produce or market regular or new products and services using new or innovative technologies or through creating economies of scale (An *economy of scale* exists when the per unit cost of production falls as the level of production increases).

In a United States with a mature but dynamic economy, Black-owned companies or newly developed Black-owned corporate entities can help to substantially and rapidly expand a Black American economy through becoming involved in joint-ventures, mergers or consolidations, acquisitions and takeovers. A *joint venture* refers to a business partnership between independent companies usually operating under the authority of a specially designated and compensated manager, for the purpose of achieving a particular business objective or completing a business deal. A merger involves the complete absorption of one business by another where the acquiring business retains its name and identity after having acquired all the assets and liabilities of the acquired business. A consolidation is a merger where the acquiring company and the acquired firm both legally terminate their previous existence and become part of a new company, often operating under a new name. An acquisition may involve the purchase of a firm's voting stock by the acquiring firm in exchange for cash, shares of stock, or other securities. An acquisition may also involve the acquiring of another firm by buying most or all of its assets. This is essentially the same as buying the company. Acquisitions may be further classified as horizontal (acquiring a firm in the same industry as the bidding firm); vertical (acquiring a firm which produces goods or services pertinent to the production or marketing process of the acquiring firm); and conglomerate (acquiring a firm in a business not related to that of the bidding firm). A takeover generally refers to the transference of control of a firm from one group of shareholders to another. Control in this instance may be defined as achieving a majority vote on the board of directors.

By engaging in mergers, consolidations, acquisitions, joint ventures, alliances, takeovers and the like, the Black business establishment can (1) acquire ongoing, already established, successful firms, thereby avoiding the more risky and often painful task of starting a business from scratch; (2) gain access to the know-how, technology, organization, talent, assets, contacts, and the like that are already operationally present in the acquired firm; (3) create "virtual" corporations by vertically and/or horizontally integrating itself into an alliance with other companies whose productive output is complementary to their own in order to produce a finished product or service which neither company could have produced alone; (4) gain access to new markets and the means of distributing and marketing products which were not previously available; (5) create employment and training opportunities for Blacks at the various levels of business and trade which were previously restricted; (6) gain access to and knowledge of leading technologies and organizational techniques as well as access to a talented, creative and productive staff; (7) enter into new industries previously closed to Blacks; (8) speed the transfer of technology from the acquired or allied companies to other Black-owned companies, to Afrika and across the Afrikan Diaspora, and (9) increase the wealth, power and influence of Afrikans in the national and international economies of the world.

UNC Ventures: Black Venture Capital in Action. Venture capital firms are often very instrumental in helping companies get started, expand and develop the kinds of relations and achieve some of the goals we just enumerated. If such relations and goals are to be substantially realized by the Afrikan American community, it must greatly increase its supply of venture capital firms as well as greatly enhance their capital resources and prowess. Of course, a number of Black-owned venture firms already exist and have measurably contributed to the growth of Black-owned businesses. Such firms may serve as models and catalysts for the creation of more firms like themselves. One such firm is UNC Ventures Inc. which, since 1971, has leveraged more than $1 billion in financing for minority and Black-owned businesses. *Black Enterprise* (11/94) further describes UNC's achievements as follows:

> Since opening its doors in 1971, UNC has helped create or expand more than 50 businesses owned by minorities, ranging in size from $1 million to $100 million.
> Their two funds, UNC Ventures Inc. and UNC Ventures II L.P., have raised more than $28 million that has been leveraged into more than $1 billion and created about 7,000 new jobs.
> UNC recently announced the formation of a third venture capital fund, UNC Ventures III L.P., which plans to raise $100 million that's earmarked to develop at least 25 companies with annual sales ranging from $25 to $100 million.
> The third fund, UNC managers say, will concentrate on emerging opportunities, but their primary focus remains the same: providing capital to enable minority entrepreneurs to succeed, while creating economic development in areas underserved by traditional financiers. It is a worthy goal that has attracted corporate giants such as Aetna Life & Casualty, American Express and IBM.

Located in Boston, UNC is headed by Edward Dugger III, 45 years old, who is its president. UNC, originally called the Urban National Corp., was founded by two White Harvard graduate students who convinced the mega-investment firms Morgan Stanley and J.P. Morgan to raise funds for their firm. Dugger joined the company in 1974 and became its chief executive after the two White principals left the firm in 1975 and 1976. Dugger's wife, Elizabeth Harris, joined the company in 1990 as vice president. She handles venture investing, portfolio management and strategic planning.

In addition to its original investors including such corporations as Chevron, Cigna, the Ford Foundation, John Hancock, the Massachusetts Institute of Technology, Mobil Oil, the Rockefeller family and

Yale University, Dugger has recruited a sizable number of other corporations, foundations and financial institutions to invest in his efforts to grow and nurture minority businesses. His work with the Boston Bank of Commerce and with Envirotest Systems Corp. clearly illustrates what can be accomplished by a competent and well-backed venture capital firm operating in the Black community. *Black Enterprise* describes UNC's work with these companies thusly:

> One of the businesses that benefitted from UNC Ventures is the Boston Bank of Commerce, New England's only black-owned bank.
>
> During 1990 and 1991, banks throughout the country were struggling to survive. Those that could, raised capital to spur continued growth and protect against future losses. But how does a bank raise capital at a time when many are failing? The answer for BBOC was UNC Ventures.
>
> "UNC stepped up and agreed to make an investment. The fact that they stood up helped us to go to other investors," says Ronald Homer, BBOC's chairman and CEO, who notes that the investment climate during those years made it virtually impossible for banks to attract investors.
>
> UNC Partners Inc., the investment manager for UNC Ventures Funds, assumed the roles of lead investor and financial advisor to BBOC. They were able to convince several other prominent Boston corporations to invest in the bank, including Harvard University, the Bank of Boston, Reebok, State Street Bank, Fleet Bank, Boston Safe, Amelia Peabody Trust, Hyman Trust and Greenwich Capital.
>
> "Their assistance was critical to the bank's survival," Homer says. "We wouldn't be here if they hadn't helped."

Black Enterprise goes on to describe UNC's work with Envirotest:

> Dugger likes to point to UNC's most successful company, Envirotest Systems Corp. in Tucson, Arizona. UNC helped black partners Slivy Edmonds and Chester Davenport put together $57 million in financing to buy Hamilton Test Systems, a division of United Technologies that had $35 million in annual sales.
>
> The partners eventually bought their largest competitor, Systems Control Inc. Envirotest, a publicly traded, $90 million company, is now one of the largest in the auto emissions testing field. It was No. 11 on the 1994 **BE INDUSTRIAL/SERVICE 100**. So far, Envirotest has won the two largest emissions testing contracts — New York and Pennsylvania — and has a $1.5 billion work backlog. Since going public on NASDAQ, their stock has jumped from $16 to $27 a share.
>
> "They [Edmonds and Davenport] didn't have any particular experience in this business," Dugger says. "But they had a lot of

vision, and they have a strategy.... This was very successful for us because it went public at $16 a share. Our cost was $.77 per share." A look at another UNC venture might prove instructive.

Ragan Henry had a good if not unique idea. He wanted to buy several radio stations throughout the country and start a major black-owned broadcasting company.

The problem was that Henry — a Harvard-trained lawyer and a partner at a prestigious Philadelphia law firm — had absolutely no experience in radio.

Few doubted that the Hamilton, Ohio, native, who interrupted law school to serve two years in the military, would succeed at any endeavor he pursued. Still, few were willing to underwrite his dream.

With the help of Boston-based UNC Ventures Inc., Henry bought WAOK-AM in Atlanta and WGIV-AM in Charlotte, N.C., in 1974. His company, Broadcast Enterprises Network Inc., soon owned five stations.

Back in those days, black professionals "couldn't go to a radio station owner and say, "I want to buy you," recalls Edward Dugger III, the 45-year-old president of UNC. Even if they could have, their lack of experience would have kept traditional financing sources from investing.

"We had to make those kinds of leaps of faith all the time," Dugger says. "If you look at almost any industry [back then], you didn't find blacks operating them."

By 1990 Henry — who was inducted into the National Broadcasters Hall of Fame in 1991 — owned more than 60 stations throughout the country.

"The bottom line is: their [UNC] being involved helped me to get the other backers I needed," says Henry, whose latest radio venture is called US Radio Corp. "They gave me the equity that I didn't have. They helped us to get started. They were there at the beginning.

UNC reports that between 1984 and 1993, 61% of its investments have been with Black entrepreneurs. UNC, which invests throughout the United States, reports that it invested 33% of its funds in computer and electronics companies, 23% in communications services, 9% in transportation, 9% in real estate and 16% in a variety of other companies. UNC is developing a fund which will be largely dedicated to completing acquisitions in contrast to start-ups. He explained that "the rationale for that is simply that a company that is acquired has an existing marketplace. It has middle management in place, who know the skeletons and can help in the operation of the company from day one" (BE, ibid). He went on to say that, "Rather than starting at ground zero and going to $10 million over five years, they [minority entrepreneurs] can acquire a company that has $10 million in revenues and over five years can go to $50 million." Dugger is seeking to attract public and private pension funds, endowments, and individual investors to underwrite UNC's special fund concentrating on acquisitions.

UNC and other Black-owned or controlled venture capital funds can contribute very significantly to the expansion and empowerment of an Afrikan American and Pan–Afrikan economic system. However, to ensure that such expansion and Pan-powerment are steady, appropriate and Black controlled, the funding of Black-owned venture capital companies must increasingly draw their underwriting funds from Black-owned and controlled corporations, endowment and pension funds, and Black individual investors. Perhaps venture capital firms like UNC will help to develop the critical mass of Black corporate, institutional and private investors whose combined resources will markedly reduce the dependency of Black-owned venture capital concerns and brokers on White-owned corporations as their chief investment or only underwriting sources.

Chapter 28

ROTATING CREDIT ASSOCIATIONS
The Prime Importance of Saving

ALL THE PREVIOUSLY DISCUSSED METHODS for financing economic development in the Afrikan American community, as well as the methods yet to be discussed, involve at some level increasing the aggregate savings of the community. They all involve some level of capital accumulation, i.e., the accumulation or the centralized collection of relatively large sums of money and other resources which are to be used to fund economic growth and development. The problem with which we are concerned is the economic development of the Black American community as well as the Pan–Afrikan community. We are imminently interested in how these communities can build up a critical mass of capital or money in institutions over which they have control; to fund the founding of new businesses and other financial entities; to fund the expansion of those which already exist; to invest in mainstream corporations and institutions such that the behavior of those corporations and institutions can be significantly influenced by the community, and to fund the development and growth of a Pan–Afrikan economic system. These goals can only be achieved through increased savings on the part of the national Black community. It is from accumulated capital or wealth, from savings and reserves, that a nation covers, or pays for, or can invest in its continuing growth and development. Even though borrowing from other communities, i.e., their institutions, or receiving relatively large-scale transfers of money and other forms of capital from them in the form of government grants, aid, loans, etc., may be used to bring about capital accumulation for economic development, development funded almost exclusively by these means will not continue to advance unless significantly supported by substantial communal savings. Extensive borrowing from outside the community, unsupported by extensive communal savings or other forms of community-based capital accumulation, leads to high levels of community debt, the servicing of which may consume so much of the community's income that little if any of it is left to maintain existing institutions, to fund improvement and to meet increasing needs, let alone to fund new growth and development. Over time, such a situation inevitably leads to economic stagnation, deterioration and collapse. The reduction and withdrawal of grants and other forms of capital transfers generated by the government and non-government organizations from outside the community, uncompensated by increased savings, i.e., wealth accumulation and income from within the community, lead to the same ends. Moreover, onerous indebtedness to and dependency on grants from outside communities inevitably leads to community political-economic weakness, if not powerlessness. Ultimately, inadequacy or withdrawal of outside support may bring about various forms of social disorganization and the community becomes plagued by a host of social problems such as poverty, un- and underemployment, inadequate health care and education, disease and criminality. Such is the state of a large segment of the Afrikan American and Pan–Afrikan communities today.

As stated so succinctly by Geertz, *"Unless the basic savings habits of the people of a country can be altered, the prospects for sustained economic growth are dim indeed."*[1] Specifically, if the Afrikan American community is to advance its economic development and growth and is to enhance its political economic powers vis-à-vis the United States and the world, to paraphrase Geertz, there must be a radical change in the propensity to save on the part of the individual, organizational and institutional members of the community. This not only requires marked reductions in the ruinously high levels of consumer spending and indebtedness the community has incurred relative to other communities, but also the operational development of savings schemes and institutions such as have already been discussed and are to be discussed.

---

1. Clifford Geertz, "The Rotating Credit Association: A 'Middle Rung' In Development," *Economic Development and Cultural Change*, 10 April 1962: 241–63.

The Rotating Credit Association

We have argued that an economic system is first and foremost a social system, a system defined by a dynamic, yet organized and stereotypical set of social customs, relations, attitudes, expectations, values and institutions which characterize the behavior of the members of a specific community relative to each other, to nonmembers and to other communities. We may refer to such patterned social relations between persons, groups and communities as an economic system when they involve the *systematic* production, management, distribution, exchange, and consumption of usable resources. Hence, significant changes in social relations, attitudes, values and institutional organization may be reflected in commensurate changes in a community's economic character, status and wealth. Thus any attempt to change the savings/income ratio of a people requires commensurate changes in their social attitudes and relations, and to some degree, changes in their society or culture. The recommendations made so far for financing Afrikan American economic development and power involve changing the customary social attitudes, values, relations and institutions in the Black community that once such changes occur and are facilitated by appropriate social practice, changes will occur which will greatly enhance the community's fortune, well-being and power.

We contend that the Afrikan American community may in some ways be perceived as a developing nation. Geertz contends that what is needed for the economic advancement and empowerment of a developing nation "...particularly in the early stages, is an institution which can combine local popular appeal with the sort of savings effects a developing economy demands; and institutions which can act as an educational mechanism for a people moving from a static economy to a dynamic one, at the same time as it operates to bring about the restriction of increased consumption such a transformation implies." One such institution to which Geertz is referring is called the *rotating credit association*. We discussed this type of association in Chapter 14 when we discussed how Koreans financed their businesses in America. Though this institution is broadly diffused throughout the developing and under-developed world, "stretching from Japan on the East throughout Southeast Asia and India to Africa on the West..." (Geertz), it has an original and long history in Afrika. It is currently and extensively practiced by Afrikan-Caribbeans both inside and outside the United States to fund various economic ventures and initiatives. Geertz (1962) describes the rotating credit association in the following:

The basic principle upon which the rotating credit association is founded is everywhere the same: a lump sum fund composed of fixed contributions from each member of the association is distributed, at fixed intervals and as a whole to each member of the association in turn. Thus, if there are ten members of the association, if the association meets weekly, and if the weekly contribution from each member is one dollar, then each week over a ten-week period a different member will receive ten dollars (i.e., counting his own contribution). If interest payments are calculated, by one mechanism or another, as part of the system, the numerical simplicity is destroyed, but the essential principle of rotating access to a continually reconstituted capital fund remains intact. Whether the fund is in kind or in cash; whether the order the members receive the fund is fixed by lot, by agreement, or by bidding; whether the time period over which the society runs is many years or a few weeks; whether the sums involved are minute or rather large; whether the members are few or many; and whether the association is composed of urban traders or rural peasants, of men or women, the general structure of institution is constant.

The rotating credit association places the group's or community's monies completely under its control. Basically, all monies raised within the association are made directly available to its members without the interference of middle-men institutions or the taxation and regulative policies of government agencies. The rotating credit association avoids the technical and structural as well as racial difficulties which attend formalized banking and financial institutional approaches to finance. Associations can be used to help create the concrete investment opportunities in a community that are the bases for the growth and development of more formal institutions such as banks. The rotating credit association originates in a community of interested persons, still the major source for financing new business (not loans from banks and other mainstream financial institutions), and therefore "fits into community patterns and yet aims at planned and "goal-directed" savings" (Geertz, 1962). We have demonstrated that the Korean "Kye", a basic rotating credit association, as well as the Japanese "Ko", "Miyin", "Tanamoshi"; the Chinese "hui"; the Nigerian "esusu", "dashi"; the Caribbean "susu", "partners", "the meeting", "boxi money", figure very significantly in the financing of business and personal enterprises. Koreans and Cubans are outstanding current examples of how credit associations can be used to develop very significant and rapid economic development as well as to very significantly help lift a group out of poverty, reduce or eliminate its dependency on government and private largesse.

In its basic form, a member in a rotating credit association receives the total "pot" or money pool. His turn is generally determined by lot or by agreement. Members simply meet and agree among themselves to contribute a sum of money every week or month, or some other cyclical period, each one receiving the entire "pot" once during the chosen time cycle; often the cycle may begin anew with the same or additional members if desired. Members of one association can be concurrent members of one or more other associations. In some instances, one member of an association may take or occupy two or more positions or hold multiple shares in the same association, and contribute as if he were two or more persons, and collect commensurately. In the basic association each recipient of the "pot" or fund takes responsibility for hosting the next meeting of the association and provides refreshments and food for other members. Thus, association meetings, which may include friends, neighbors, kin, and trusted associates, take place in a festive social environment that serves to strengthen social solidarity as much as to reach economic goals. For many members, the creation of communal or social harmony and the provision of mutual assistance is the association's primary attraction, compared with the money they receive. In traditional rural settings the medium which is rotated between members of an association may not be money but cooperative labor. Geertz (1962) describes the exchange of cooperative labor (in rural Java):

> The two major types of cooperative labor are "group work" and "exchange work." In group work, a whole neighborhood applies its labor to certain labor-intensive tasks: clearing a man's fields, erecting his house, etc. In such a pattern all the nearby neighbors are invited and are obligated to come, and the host provides a large feast at the close of the work. In "exchange work," several households work on each other's land in turn. Reciprocality is exact and specific, and usually work is returned within a short period of time.

While the "group work" and "exchange work" concepts discussed by Geertz are not readily applicable in current inner-city climes, modified forms of these approaches may apply. Forms of economic exchange, e.g., professional services, business services, labor, equipment, etc., services for other services, can be utilized by an association to reduce costs of establishing businesses. "Sweat equity" involves the situation where labor, materials, and other services supplied by members in establishing a new enterprise may be converted into the ownership of shares or stock in that establishment.

Typically, urban rotating credit associations may be more specifically economic than social institutions. They may take on more complex forms than the basic traditional associations. For example, Light describes the operation of a Cantonese association or "hui" thusly:

> Instead of a lottery to determine which member of the club would take the pot, each eligible member might submit a sealed bid indicating how much interest he was prepared to pay to have the use of the money. The high bidder received the pot. This system of hui operation placed a clear premium on not needing the money. Those who wanted the money in the early rounds of the hui would have to compete and pay a high interest. On the other hand, wealthier members who were not in need of money could collect the high interest paid by members who needed the use of their surplus. This form of hui created an investment opportunity for the wealthy and tended to enlist the profit motive in the extension of credit. Of course, even in this more capitalistic form of mutual aid, the interest actually paid by members in need of money tended to be less than what they would have paid for equivalent funds obtained from the town moneylender.[2]

In reviewing rotating credit associations of southern China, Japan, and West Afrika which were transferred to and employed in the United States by overseas immigrant communities, Light concludes that these institutions were the principal devices for capitalizing small business. He further intimates that:

> West Indian blacks brought the West African rotating credit association to the United States; they too used this traditional practice to finance small businesses. American-born Negroes apparently did not employ a similar institution. Hence, *the rotating credit association suggests itself as a specific tradition in the field of business which accounts, in some measure, for the differential business success of American-born Negroes, West Indian Negroes, and Orientals.*[3]
> [Emphasis added]

As noted earlier, the rotating credit association has a long and original history in many parts of Afrika, "including West Africa from which the progenitors of American Negroes were abducted as slaves" (Light, ibid). Geertz (1962) describes rotating credit associations as they appear across a number of Afrikan peoples including the Bulu of

---

2. See Light's *Ethnic Enterprises in America*, 1972, for descriptions of various types of rotating credit associations, p. 24.

3. Ibid., p. 23.

the French Cameroon, the Nupe in Central Nigeria, the Yoruba of Nigeria, the Ibo also of Nigeria, and Keta, a town in Ghana. Thus this form of loan funding is very much the heritage of Afrikans born in the United States. An illustrative example of how an Afrikan-based rotating credit association can advance the economic growth and development of an Afrikan people is provided by citations from a *New York Times* article (November 30, 1987) titled "Informal Capitalism Grows in Cameroon."

–Grassroots Credit System, Douala, Cameroon.

When Samuel Nanci needed $35,000 to open his Joie de Vivre Bar here, he did not bother with banks. Instead he turned to the tontine, an informal credit system rooted in African tradition. Without signing a paper or filling out a form, Mr. Nanci emerged from his monthly tontine meeting with $35,000 in cash.

For years development economists saw African's tontines as archaic tribal institutions that would die out with the rise of modern economies based on European-style banking systems. But now many economists see the tontine as a highly efficient method of promoting grassroots efforts in capitalism.

They cite Cameroon. In the first half of the 1980s, this Central African nation had the continent's highest average economic growth rate, 7 percent a year. Cameroonians rate of participation in tontines — 47 percent — was the highest in five French-speaking Afrikan countries surveyed by Marcomer Gallup International. By contrast only 13 percent of the people surveyed in the five nations had savings accounts.

"Bank don't match the mentality of the people," said Theodorvet-Marie Fansi, the director of an economic consulting firm here. "They are colonial structures."

"I have attended tontines where the monthly pot is $1 million," said Antoine L. Ntsimi, a Cameroonian banker with a business degree from the University of Chicago. With a tontine loan, Mr. Ntsimi recently started construction of a four-story, $850,000 building that will hold offices, retail stores and apartments. In Cameroon bankers complain of loan delinquency rates as high as 50 percent. But tontine payments are taken so seriously that borrowers faced with delinquency have been known to commit suicide.

Tontines work, economists say, because their loans are backed by *social pressure*, a system familiar to Africans. Banks perform poorly because their loans are backed by paper guarantees made to strangers, a concept alien to Africans.

Tontines exist in much of sub-Saharan Africa, from Burkina Faso to Ghana to Zaire and Rwanda. But Cameroon's Bamileke tribesmen have popularized interest-bearing tontines to such an extent that bankers complain that tontines contribute to the current crisis in banking liquidity.

In their original form, tontines allowed peasants to pool their labor rather than their money. With the introduction of the money economy in the 20th century, tontines took on a financial character, as informal savings associations. Every month each member would contribute a fixed share into a "pot." In a 12-member group, each member would receive the pot once a year.

The most recent innovation is the interest-bearing tontine. Each month, members bid the amount of interest they will pay for the tontine pot. Interest payments are collected in a separate loan fund and are distributed to members when the tontine is dissolved. Tontines are usually formed for two-year periods and were generally limited to 24 members.

In contrast, banks here pay 7 percent annual interests on savings, and lend money at 13 percent a year. Inflation is about 13 percent. Interest earned on savings is subject to a 10 percent tax, while tontines go unrecorded.

The more advantageous rates offered by tontines can be traced to their lack of overhead, their ability to set rates according to supply and demand and their high payment record.

* * * *

...Tontines, built on trust, are generally made up of homogenous groups — people from the same ethnic background, the same workplace or the same neighborhood.

"When people go in banks, they don't feel the same urgency to reimburse the loan," Mr. Ntsimi said. "If you don't make your payment to the tontine, you are rejected by the community. If you are banned from one group, you are banned from the others."

Thus we see that a traditional Afrikan financial approach can be very profitably adapted to the modern economic system. This approach, which is fundamentally communal and cooperative in nature, befits Afrikan values and the economic circumstances with which they must cope. Similar circumstances are faced by Afrikan Americans and may be resolved by similar means. The re-institution of rotating credit associations in the Afrikan American community will have to develop in tandem with the re-institution of higher levels of trustworthiness, reliability, faithfulness, loyalty, cooperativeness, empathy, Afrikan identity and Afrikan-centered consciousness as primary factors in interpersonal relations between the members of this community, since these are the social underpinnings of a truly functional credit association. Beginning associations should involve the use of contributions which can rather easily be maintained by members since the primary objectives may be to enhance social solidarity, cooperativeness and other positive social traits, as well as familiarize members with the workings of the system. Moreover, as Geertz intimates, "The fact that the money is delivered immediately upon collection to the winner, so that no one has to be trusted to hold cash belonging to anyone else for any length of time, reduces the likelihood of embezzlement." Members of duly constituted bodies such as churches, fraternities, sororities and other such organizations may find it easier to establish associations because of the more legalistic relations which may inhere between them.

As Geertz contends, the rotating credit association is an intermediate institution, mediating two contradictory socioeconomic systems. As such, it can be utilized to facilitate the transformation or adaptation of a more traditional, perhaps in the current economic context, inadequate economic system into or to a more modern and complex economic system. In this regard, Geertz goes on to say:

> The rotating credit association is...a product of a shift from traditionalistic agrarian society to an increasingly fluid commercial one, whether this shift be very slow or very rapid. It, too, mobilizes familiar motivations and applies them to unfamiliar purposes, while serving at the same time to reconstruct those motivations on a more flexible basis. The *arisan, ko, hui, dashi,* or *esusu* is essentially, then, an educational mechanism in terms of which peasants learn to be traders, not merely in the narrow occupational sense, but in the broad cultural sense; an institution which acts to change their whole value framework from one emphasizing particularistic, diffuse, affective, and ascriptive ties between individuals, to one emphasizing — *within economic contexts* — universalistic, affectively neutral, and achieved ties between them. The rotating credit association is thus a socializing mechanism, in that broad sense in which "socialization" refers not simply to the process by which the child learns to be an adult, but the learning of *any* new patterns of behavior which are of functional importance in society, even by adults. The theoretical as well as the practical interest of the association lies in its ability to organize traditional relationships in such a way that they are slowly but steadily transformed into non-traditional ones, as an institution whose functional significance is primarily to facilitate social and cultural change in respect to economic problems and processes....

The rotating credit association can be used in the Afrikan American community to raise large sums of money far beyond those raised by relatively small and intimate groups. We think that organizational associations, associations composed of small, medium or large organizations, e.g., churches, fraternities, sororities, trade and professional associations, business groups, can become the sources of very large sums of money, generating pools of thousands, hundreds of thousands and millions of dollars which can be used by those groups or their constituents to found, develop, maintain and expand business, financial and cultural institutions. Organizational credit associations would permit these organizations to lend each other large sums of money at little or no interest. Ten churches which are members of an association that could raise $1,000 or $5,000 a month each, can make available to each of its members from $10,000 to $50,000 per month in turn, over a 10-month period. Larger churches could raise much larger sums. Secular organizations can do the same. They could be used by groups to make institutional investments in major corporations, to found or buy corporations. By these means they may come to achieve growing influence in the general American economy and may come to participate to a significant extent in the larger, global economic system. They may thereby achieve growing influence on American domestic and foreign policy. The principles of rotating credit associations suggest that the Afrikan American community has the means of lifting itself up by its own bootstraps right in its hands. It only needs the will to do so.

While the recipient member of a credit association may dispose of the "pot" in any way which pleases him/her or it (an organization, which is our focus presently), we dare to suggest that in the case of institutional (e.g., churches, large secular organizations) associations where very large sums are collected, they contribute their "pot" to a local or regional community development credit union, development bank, or loan fund. An association which may raise say $1 million per month may within a year provide such institutions with $12 million. The advantage of making such contributions based on association membership is that the institution and its members' original funds are not actually depleted or diminished by their grant to a financial establishment or loan fund since the money granted, in effect, has been saved especially for that purpose. Thus, the institution is enabled to give without a loss to itself.

The "Susu Account"

It is interesting to note that the legitimacy and value of rotating credit associations are now beginning to be recognized by mainstream financial institutions. Excerpts from the following article published in *New York Newsday* (5/15/93) and titled "Joining the Club" demonstrates how an Afrikan American manager of residential lending at

Chase Community Development Corporation, a unit of Chase Manhattan Bank, one of the largest banks in the United States, helped to establish credit association or "sou-sou" funds as acceptable for down-payment and mortgage payments on real estate.

> Clara Slade of Brooklyn recently became a homeowner, thanks to her sou-sou. Sou-sous are informal, private savings clubs that are common in neighborhoods with large concentrations of immigrants. They have different names in different places — Koreans call them kaes, for instance — but their purpose is always the same. They provide a means of savings for people who often have little experience with banks, or limited access to them.
>
> Every two weeks, Slade and 23 other members of a sou-sou contribute $100 each to a pot, and members take turns collecting the pooled money.
>
> Slade, who has been president of the sou-sou for 11 years, used a $2,400 pot to help obtain a loan from Chase Community Development Corp. for the purchase of a Brooklyn duplex.
>
> A year ago most lenders in the region would have turned down Slade's mortgage application when they learned the down payment hadn't come entirely from her own savings, or was not a verifiable gift from a family member. Now, however, many lenders will accept down payments accumulated through savings clubs.
>
> The more liberal policy on sou-sou money is a reflection of lenders' eagerness to increase business among immigrants and minorities. Under pressure from federal regulators and others who claim they are underserving minority neighborhoods, lenders have begun to recruit immigrant and minority buyers and have established loan programs and counseling services targeted at low- and moderate-income persons. They have also shown increasing willingness to consider cultural differences in applying lending criteria.
>
> There's another reason for the change of heart: The area real estate market has been depressed for several years, and lenders are looking for new business....
>
> Lenders' attitudes toward savings clubs began to change when many banks established units to specifically serve minority and immigrant communities. Mortgage officers working in those neighborhoods lobbied hard to have their supervisors recognize the legitimacy of the savings clubs.
>
> Beryl Riley, manager of residential lending at Chase Community Development Corp., knew nothing about sou-sous when she began her career with Chase three years ago, and neither did most of the senior loan officers at the bank. It quickly became clear to her, as it has to others in the lending industry, that sou-sous are one of the primary ways people save in immigrant communities.

She also knew that if her unit of Chase Manhattan Bank, which lends mortgage money to low- and moderate-rate income buyers, was going to broaden its appeal to minorities and immigrants, she had to find a way for Chase to understand how sou-sous work...

Riley was instrumental in getting the Federal National Mortgage Association [commonly referred to as Fannie Mae], which buys mortgages from lenders and sells them to investors, to recognize sou-sous. Fannie Mae's willingness to accept savings club money as down payment on loans it buys was a critical step in winning over lenders, most of whom follow Fannie Mae's guidelines.

"We kept hearing about how important these [savings clubs] are, and we took up the issue in 1992," said Martin Levine, Fannie Mae's senior vice president for low- and moderate-income lending programs. "Now Fannie Mae allows the use of sou-sous because it is such a common way to save in some cultures."

Three months ago Fannie Mae began a program in which "we not only cite sou-sous as an eligible plan, we also gave lenders specific questions to ask when dealing with sou-sous," Levine said.

Lenders who accept money from savings clubs generally require a letter from the club's administrator saying how many people participate in the club, how much money each member contributes and how long the club has been in operation...

"Sou-sou funds are a reality in the marketplace, and as long as we can verify how the money is saved, we give it our best effort to make the loan," [Michael] Burke [vice president of the affordable mortgage program at Chemical Bank] said.

Thus we see that the rotating credit association is a viable concept and can fully function as an intermediate institution.

Micro-Loan Funds and Underwriters' Loans

An increasingly common mode of helping businesses to grow and expand in local communities is through the support of micro-loan funds. Usually sponsored by state and local government development corporations and by mainstream commercial banks, these funds provide short term financing to small businesses, ranging from $5,000 to $10,000 and more for a maximum of about three years at a modest interest rate. Loans as high as $50,000 or $75,000 may be thought of as macro-loans by lenders with relatively large sums of capital. More specifically, a micro-loan is a *business* loan as opposed to consumer debt or home-equity loans. An increasing number of banks, consequently, are finding that micro-loans of the $20,000-and-up range can be profitable and are now more willing to float such loans than in the past. Non-profit groups are increasingly active in providing smaller loans. Non-profits may receive funding from the Small Business Administration to establish micro-lending programs. The only blanket restriction the SBA and banks have on how micro-fund loans are used, is that they not be used for retiring old debt. Micro-loan funds may be sponsored by religious and other institutions or civic or professional organizations. Loans from the funds may be used to finance business improvements, for the purchase of machinery, equipment, inventory, working capital or leasehold improvements, and for business start-ups. The rates and terms of micro-loans vary widely. According to *Inc.* magazine (4/94), "Some of the smallest macro-lenders charge interest rates roughly comparable with those on Consumer Credit Cards and want to be paid back in six months. On the other hand, banks and nonprofit lenders working with the SBA tend to charge a couple of points fewer and extend credit for longer" (around three years). Generally, collateral requirements tend to be less demanding than regular business loans and the loans may be approved according to a set of criteria quite different from those used for conventional loans.

Micro-loans are offered to sole proprietorships, partnerships, and corporations in a variety of markets. Moreover, micro-loan funds may provide various types of technical assistance such as the development of business plans, the processing of business applications and forms, bookkeeping practice, general oversight and support services. Detailed information regarding the financial background of the business and the entrepreneur is gathered and critically evaluated primarily as means of determining and improving the ability of the applicant to successfully carry a loan and to succeed in business. Micro-loans funds may be geographically restricted in their area of activity, while some others may be geographically extensive. For example, the Harlem Loan Fund, which lends up to $10,000 for all business purposes, restricts its lending to businesses located in East, West, and Central Harlem. According to *Inc.* magazine (4/94) the nonprofit microlender, Accion International of Cambridge, Mass., "which currently has lending programs in Tucson, Ariz., and Brooklyn, N.Y., and expects to add four more, generally makes loans for inventory and other working-capital needs."

The SBA supplies a full list of microlenders (call the SBA district office or its "answer line" at 800-827-5722). *The Directory of Microenterprise Programs*, published by the Aspen Institute, Washington, D.C. (202-736-5851) furnishes information on more than 190 microlending programs in the United States.

Underwriters or "Good Faith" Loans. In situations where an applicant's ability to carry a loan is difficult to verify with reasonable confidence or where his collateral is inadequate or nonexistent, some loan funds or financial institutions may make "good faith" loans based on the applicant's credit record, character and/or reputation. A good faith loan may be underwritten by a number of the applicant's friends and creditors. That is, if an applicant's friends and supporters have faith in his ability to succeed in business and are willing to provide him necessary business support, they may endorse or co-sign his application and place their credit standing behind and "under" his. By their underwriting the applicant's loan application his personal supporters may guarantee the loan against default. Obviously, the more people who endorse the loan, the better; the higher their reputation and credibility, the better. A relatively large number of underwriters compared to the size of the loan, the lesser the risk to each of them in case of default. Generally, the support of highly valued friends and associates as underwriters maximizes the drive of the applicant to succeed in business and to repay the loan.

Small Business Incubators: Creating a Conducive Environment for Black Entrepreneurship

It is a well-known fact that the first two to five years are crucial to the survival of a business and that a relative few make it through their early years. More concisely, the majority of business start-ups in America fail within 2–3 years of opening. It generally takes about five years before a business breaks even and begins to become profitable. The two most frequently cited reasons for small business failure are management problems and undercapitalization. Although small business entrepreneurs may possess considerable business experience in and knowledge of their business, its related products, technologies and markets, and may cater to a market niche or segment not served by other firms, they may still fail due to the lack of a crucial set of business resources or services.[4] It is at this crucial juncture that the small business incubator may play a saving role.

According to Allen and Rahman (1985) of the Institute of Public Administration at the Pennsylvania State University, "A small business incubator is a facility that aids the early-stage growth of companies by providing rental space, shared office services, and business consulting assistance." They go on to intimate that "the universal purpose of an incubator is to increase the chances of a firm

---

4. D. Allen and S. Rahman, "Small Business Incubators: A Positive Environment For Entrepreneurship," in *Journal of Small Business Management*, July 1985.

surviving its formative years." Essential incubators function to provide facilities, fill knowledge gaps, reduce the early costs of doing business such as by the reducing of rent and service fees, and the provision of a local enterprise network. Incubator facilities may be basically financed or sponsored by any number of types of sources. Corporations, investor groups and other private sector formations primarily interested in property development, sales and investment opportunities may found and/or support incubators. Public sector sponsors may include a variety of non-profit agencies, groups and institutions. Non-community development corporations and federal, state, and local agencies or organizations may sponsor incubators as a way of creating jobs, enhancing economic development and diversification as well as community stabilization. Incubators may provide local educational and skills development organizations, universities and vocational-technical schools with the opportunity to train residents and students in various vocations, business and professional skills.

Incubators may occupy facilities of various types — new facilities, renovated and improved buildings. They may buy or lease buildings such as vacant schools, abandoned manufacturing facilities, vacant businesses. A local industrial development authority or other developmental or nonprofit agency(ies) may underwrite leasing costs. Space may be donated by sponsoring organizations. These types of spatial arrangements may allow small business tenants to rent their spaces at less than market rates. Fixed and sliding rates may be charged. That is, rental arrangements between sponsors and tenants may be determined by the tenants' profits, job creation, or length of stay.

The chief service advantage an incubator provides is its on-site provision of shared services and business consulting assistance (Allen and Rahman, ibid). Such services may include: financial consulting assistance, management assistance, general business assistance, professional business assistance and physical services. Allen and Rahman point to the benefits of incubator services and assistance:

> By providing shared services, the fledgling firm can hire fewer support staff, and avoid the purchases or lease of office equipment. With support services located in the facility, tenant's document processing and other service requests can be handled quickly.

Photocopying services, shipping, receiving and mailing, conference room services are most often provided by the incubator. Clerical support and business plan assistance are also generally provided.

Contracting organizations affiliated with the incubator may provide a small business development center, venture and seed capital assistance, health and benefit packages, legal counseling and representation. Other services, e.g., export assistance, may be offered depending on the sponsor.

Incubator tenants may include a variety of businesses — wholesale, retail and leasing services; business services; technology and product manufacturing.

Incubators can provide an economical opportunity for expansion of the local economy, the creation of jobs, community revitalization and stabilization, increased goods and services, and enhanced trade relations. They, in addition to providing affordable rents and services, and placement of entrepreneurs among peers, provide increased and sounder investment opportunities for local institutions, individuals, groups and firms.

One Afrikan American incubator among a growing number of such organizations is the Linwood Square Mall in Kansas City, Missouri. Opened in June 1994, the overwhelming community support and nearly 90 percent occupied at that time, Linwood Square is sponsored by the Donald Maxwell Community Development Corporation.

Small Business Administration Loans

Government Guaranteed Loans. Investing in start-up business involves considerable risks under the best of economic circumstances. The causes of start-up failure are many but the major ones include undercapitalization, i.e., inadequate funds for supporting the business through the first years of profitability, for acquiring adequate stock, equipment, staff, etc., and managerial inadequacy or lack of know-how. Given the problems to which start-ups are prone as well as their high failure rates, regular banks and other investments and loan sources are quite reluctant to extend capital support to these types of businesses. The situation is even more acute if the business is headed or owned by an Afrikan American and is located in an Afrikan American neighborhood given the economic conditions which generally prevail.

Therefore, in the interest of fostering the growth of small business and of reducing the risks involved with start-up and struggling small businesses, the U.S. government makes guaranteed loans available to these entities by means of its Small Business Administration (SBA). The Small Business Administration is designed to allay risks by guaranteeing bank loans to small businesses. In this instance, under the sponsorship of the SBA, should a business fail to complete its loan obligation to the lending bank, the government would make good the defaulted loan by paying the bank in place of the delinquent or failed business. The SBA also provides management assistance and supervision to the borrowing business if need be.

In pursuit of an SBA-sponsored loan the borrowing business seeks a loan from a number of banks. If the banks to which the business applies for credit (usually three) consider it to be too much a credit risk to tender it a loan based on its qualifications alone, then either of the banks may offer the applicant a loan with proviso that the government (through the auspices of the SBA) guarantees its repayment should it fail to do so. The SBA offers full faith and credit guarantees of 90 percent on loans up to $155,000 and 85 percent on larger loans to a maximum guarantee amount of $750,000. It may guarantee as much as 75 percent of small loans. A loan for as little as $25,000 may be obtained. Loan maturity may extend as long as 12 years. Loan rates may range 2–3 percent over prime, i.e., the interest rate banks charge their best and most substantial borrowers — unusually large, stable, reliable corporations or institutions. The successful business borrower is permitted by the SBA to use its proceeds for real estate, business furniture, fixtures, stock, supplies, machinery and equipment, working capital and, to a limited degree, to refinance existing debt and to launch a new business.

The Small Business Administration and Black-owned Businesses. Much has been made of the SBA's ability to foster the growth and development of small minority and female-owned businesses, especially its ability to foster the maturation of "Black capitalism". However, relative to fostering the growth and development of Black-owned small businesses — once its central reason for being — its record has been far less-than-brilliant. In July 1994 the *Wall Street Journal* reported that the SBA acknowledges "that its loan guarantee program has poorly served minorities and women." In fact, Erskine Bowles, administrator of the SBA is quoted as intimating that "We're the largest small-business lender in the country. If we were a bank, we could be accused of redlining" (i.e., of deliberately refusing to float loans in certain locales, usually poor and/or predominantly Black or minority neighborhoods). In 1993, SBA guaranteed 26,812 loans that totaled about $6.4 billion. It expects to guarantee $7 billion of loans in 1994 and $9 billion in 1995.

Research commissioned by SBA itself revealed that Black entrepreneurs received only 3 percent of the agency's guaranteed loans in 1993. This particular rate has held essentially steady since

SBA's inception. It is also interesting to note at this juncture that a significant number of SBA loans to Black-owned businesses only turned out to be apparent because these firms were exposed as fronts for White-owned businesses or that White investors covertly owned over 50 percent of the business. Hispanic business owners were granted 5 percent of SBA funds, and women 14 percent. This trend is followed across each SBA district in the country.

New Approaches to Lending by the SBA. There is some evidence that the low proportion of SBA loans proffered to Black entrepreneurs and businesses is the result of deliberate SBA policy. The *Wall Street Journal* (7/11/94) reports that the California Reinvestment Committee, a non-profit group that advocates loans to minorities and low-income groups, "did a study of SBA lending practices between 1990 and 1992 and found discrimination against African American and Hispanic applicants." In fairness, some of the SBA's apparent discriminatory behavior may be due to the approval process used by banks and other lenders over which the agency has little or no control. Frankly speaking, both SBA and banks and other lenders engage in racial discrimination in making loans to Blacks and other minorities.

In light of the revelations just discussed SBA has pledged to increase its efforts to reach out to the minority and women entrepreneurial segments of the marketplace. The *Wall Street Journal* (7/11/94) reports that "The district directors not only have agreed to improve the percentage of guaranteed loans for these groups but also to aggressively market SBA's loan programs to lenders and to minority and women's business groups." Instead of waiting for banks to approach it with small business loan applications that meet the standards for a government guarantee, the SBA has chosen to actively initiate demands among potential borrowers by directly contacting and visiting lenders monthly and by providing lenders quick service, e.g., deciding whether a loan qualifies for an SBA guarantee within five days. The SBA has instituted new loan programs such as the "new Low Doc programs [which] will allow local offices to use a simple one-page application for loans up to $50,000. Another pilot program aimed at women business owners allows them to be certified as pre-qualifying for an SBA guaranteed loan before they approach a bank" (WSJ, 7/11/94).

The fact that the SBA district office which includes Houston, Texas, made 70 loans to Black-owned businesses in 1993 as the result of aggressive efforts on its part, compared with only 14 made in Richmond, Virginia, which has a slightly higher percentage of Black-owned businesses, seems to indicate that active marketing can make a substantial difference in the number of businesses enabled to start up and grow. Aggressive SBA district offices may be aided in their marketing efforts by banks being required to demonstrate that they are meeting local needs by making equitable loans and services to minority neighborhoods and businesses. This implies that active neighborhood and business groups may help to increase both bank and SBA support for Black-owned business and business start-up by pressuring these institutions under the Community Reinvestment Act and by other means if necessary.

The Afrikan American Development Corporation: National Underwriter of Black Economic Power

We have just discussed underwriting on a grassroots, primary group scale. However, if the Afrikan American community as a whole is to fulfill its economic promise it must fund underwriting on a massive scale. This can be accomplished through the founding and operation of a national development corporation designed primarily to insure risks across a broad spectrum of commercial transactions within the Afrikan American community and between Afrikan American and non-Afrikan American firms.

Bazelon (ibid) speaks directly to the point when he wrote, "underwriting is the greatest credit invention of them all, after alienable paper itself (gold tomorrow).... the endorsement of negotiable paper. That's really all it is, endorsement or guaranty — one man's credit standing behind, "written under," another's. Here, reputation becomes superbly generalized — nothing at all is promised, that is, put on the line, except the promise to pay if the first fellow doesn't." Underwriting allows the putting into operation a first principle of capitalism — use what one has in order to get more. The underwriter in effect collateralizes the borrower who uses the collateral supplied by the underwriter as money-making property on which the borrower can get credit. In this context Bazelon both asks and answer's his own question: "Everybody knows that it is a fact, but have you ever asked yourself *why* it is that the rich get richer? The answer is really very simple: the more you have, the more you can borrow. The underwriter supplies the "have" which can be used to get more."

In a broader context Theodore Cross (ibid) provides us with a general rationale for developing an Afrikan American Development Corporation as the major underwriting institution in the Black community. He refers to this institution as a "national minority development corporation" (NMDC). Furthermore, he envisions it as independently chartered and funded by the federal government. Obviously, we believe such an arrangement would not be independent nor workable if tied to the impetuous political vagaries of the U.S. congress and government. The independence of such an organization could only be assured if it were chartered and funded by the Afrikan American community exclusively.

However, the rationale Cross posits for the functional existence of a national development corporation is a compelling one. He describes the economic context in the U.S. which requires the setting up of an underwriting organization such as a development corporation.

> The idea of a national minority development corporation may best be understood within the context of the vast economic distance between blacks and whites in this country. An advanced economy, which, for the most part, is driven by contractual relationships, actually contributes to this distance. In the United States, as in any free and well-developed economy, virtually all employment and commercial transactions occur under promissory relationships which look to the performance of a future act. People *promise* labor or managerial employment. People and institutions *agree* to borrow, lend, and repay money. People in commerce and institutions *contract* with others to supply goods and machinery. Investment capital is promised, and rewards are reciprocally promised or expected on the part of those who use or rent investment capital. Accordingly, *the instrument of the commercial promise is the principal mechanism for the distribution of income, goods, and capital.*
>
> As a result, one's well-being within the society is highly dependent on whether or not one is, in fact, participating in the vast network of commercial and employment promises that are made every day.
>
> In any given situation, the likelihood of a particular set of commercial promises being made and accepted is largely dependent on whether each party involved in the exchange of promises believes that the other party will perform his promise or keep his "part of the bargain." It follows that whenever significant fear, uncertainty, or ignorance arises about the possible completion of an offered promise, serious obstacles are presented to employment, investment, trade, and other exchanges.
>
> Since the mercantile promise necessarily contemplates completion of a future act, the important question is always the *perceived expectation* about whether the promise will be fulfilled. This counts far more than the reality of the statistical probability that the promise will, in fact, be fulfilled. For instance, on Friday, June 20, 1969, the former Penn Central Company was insolvent. This meant that, objectively viewed, the company definitely could not and would

not keep its promises to repay its debts. Nevertheless, on that same day the company borrowed tens of millions of dollars. This was possible because others still *believed* in the company's ability to keep its promises to repay its debts and to act responsibly in commercial transactions.[5]

Both Bazelon and Cross emphasize the fact that the *appearance* of credibility in the eyes of creditors or parties to a business deal is more productively important than the reality of whether the debtor can pay or the dealer can "hold up his end of the deal." Cross goes on to contend:

> Since appearances and beliefs often count for more than reality in such transactions, a person or group that *appears* credible in fact possesses economic power and bargaining strength. Conversely, a person or group *perceived* as unreliable or incapable of keeping promises has no economic power. Any collective prejudgment holding that a certain group is a poor commercial risk will induce those subscribing to it to refuse to make any economic transactions with the group thus stigmatized. Over a period of time, this perception has the capacity to reduce the group to the powerless and subservient economic status of an outcast class. In virtually all cases, the outcast group will function wholly outside the network of commercial promises that allocates goods and benefits within the economy.*

An Afrikan American National Development Corporation (NDC) would greatly help to overcome the problems generated by "the lack of Black credibility" by placing the economic weight of a large and financially credible organization behind and warranting the undertakings of Afrikan American entrepreneurs and economic and social development agencies. Cross provides an example of the kinds of underwriting activities a national development corporation would undertake. (This, in effect, essentially describes the underwriting role of the SBA and other governmental and private agencies.)

> For example, it would underwrite minority covenants to protect the value of capital, promises to repay loans, and undertakings to manufacture and deliver goods. It would certify and insure a contractor's pledge to construct a building, a merchant's promise to pay rent under a commercial lease, and a mortgage covenant secured by a minority-operated factory. The NMDC would be charged to identify a whole range of organizations in low-income and minority communities — community development corporations, minority banks, credit unions, retail and production cooperatives, contractors, entrepre-

---

5. T. Cross, *Black Power Imperative*, p. 802; and Ibid., p.805*

neurs, and housing cooperatives — and where necessary, to underwrite their commercial undertakings as well as their capital and credit needs.[6]

Cross summarizes the activities of an NDC as follows.

THE RANGE OF RISK-REDUCTION ACTIVITIES OF A NATIONAL MINORITY DEVELOPMENT CORPORATION
Firming up the Bargaining Power of Minority Groups to Enable Them to Negotiate Entry into the Economic Mainstream

- Guarantee credits to assist minority groups to purchase large-scale business enterprises.
- Support minority job creation by providing broad credit guarantees and investment insurance to attract additional investment funds to inner-city and rural neighborhood corporations.
- Indemnify established bonding companies against above-average losses on performance bonds of minority contractors.
- Underwrite credit risks on home mortgage loans developed by minority mortgage bankers for resale to large institutional investors.
- Guarantee inventory borrowings of minority retailers and wholesalers.
- Improve the ability of minority banks and savings institutions to attract deposits by providing a secondary market for their mortgages and other loans.

Source: Theodore Cross, *The Black Power Imperative*, p. 803.

Table 28–1

Cases in Point

A national and regional Black-owned or controlled underwriting organization of the type we are suggesting could step in and positively resolve business problems faced by Black-owned firms such as the ones cited below. In this instance, as reported by the *Wall Street Journal* (5/16/94), Black-owned companies with good track records or business prospects are often rejected when they apply for credit or loans, apparently because of the race of their owners. These companies, though already in business and somewhat profitable but in need of funds for expansion, purchasing supplies and equipment to satisfy firm contracts, are nevertheless often turned down by White-owned banks. A Black-owned underwriting organization could possibly solve these kinds of problems by underwriting the credit applications of such companies.

---

6. Ibid., p. 805.

'Still Tough'

"From where we are sitting — in the trenches — the reception [for Black Americans] at banks isn't any better," says Stanley Tucker, executive director of the Maryland Small Business Development Financing Authority. "There's a perception of easing, but entrepreneurs will tell you that it's still tough," he says.

Warren Thompson, president of **Thomas Hospitality** in Reston, Va., found that out early this year. A number of major banks turned down his bid to refinance some of the debt incurred in his $13.1 million buyout of 31 Bob's Big Boy restaurants. Even though Mr. Thompson's restaurants had combined sales of about $35 million last year and nearly all are profitable, the banks were uncomfortable with his business and growth strategy, he adds.

Bankers haven't been any more hospitable to Wendell Kelly, president of **QualitiCare Medical Services** Inc., a Baltimore distributor of medical supplies. Even though his company expects revenue of nearly $17 million in its first full year of operation and will be profitable, his requests to expand his credit line have received a cool reception at local banks, Mr. Kelly says.

Subcontractor Work

The continued lack of finance also is hampering some initiatives to promote minority-owned businesses. Anna Richards, who recruits minority businesses to act as subcontractors for **McDonnell Douglas** Corp., the huge aerospace concern, says McDonnell awarded more than $100 million in contracts to minority vendors, but some African-American companies couldn't begin the work because they couldn't get any bank to provide the working capital. She says the banks refused the deals, even when the companies had firm orders.

It is encouraging to note that there seems to be an increasing number of private venture capital companies being developed to deal specifically with financing Black-owned and minority-owned businesses. One, the Levmark Corporation, is included in the following report by the *Wall Street Journal* (5/16/94):

Three Capital Pools

In spite of the gloom surrounding bank lending, there is some optimism about the prospects of equity financing. As previously reported, three different capital pools are being organized to funnel money to venture funds focused on minority businesses. And about a dozen new venture capital funds aimed at individual businesses also are in the works, reports the Private Equity Analyst, a newsletter in Wellesley, Mass. The new investment funds include **Levmark** Corp.,

New Rochelle, N.Y., which is attempting to raise $75 million, and **TSG Ventures** Inc., Stamford, Conn., which wants to form a $200 million fund.

To be sure, many black entrepreneurs are obtaining financing, and the sources are often unconventional and the structuring is highly innovative. Pittsburgh's Carnegie Mellon University, for example, designed an unusual bidding procedure for the construction of its $18 million research facility at the Pittsburgh Technology Center. It allowed contractors to bid for the project in smaller parts, thus enabling five small minority-owned companies to participate. And to solve the working-capital problem, it agreed to finance the purchase of supplies by its minority contractors by writing joint checks for the purchases — checks jointly addressed to the contractor and the supplier.

Increasing, too, some corporations are stepping up to provide the financing that minority entrepreneurs need. QualitiCare's $4 million in start-up capital came from a loan provided by a major pharmaceutical supplier. And nearly all of the financing of the 31 restaurants by Warren Thompson was arranged by **Marriot International** Inc. and **Shoney's** Inc.

Besides the straightforward approach to financing Black-owned businesses as represented by the Levmark Corporation, this report demonstrates that other creative methods of finance can be developed once institutions and/or organizations sincerely commit themselves to the task of financing viable Black enterprises.

Financing The National Development Corporation. It goes without saying that an underwriting corporation such as the one we are now discussing will require sufficiently large capital and borrowing power to provide it with the necessary funds to confidently support the high-risk activities in which it must engage, and to provide it with the relative financial independence and strength to complete its economic mission against political and economic opposition. The question is: How is the Afrikan American National Corporation to be financed by the Afrikan American community? The answer is: The Afrikan American community must "tax" itself to do so. That is, the community must pledge, in a way similar to the "10–36" pledges initiated by Reverend Leon Sullivan (described herein), to give a fraction of its monthly income for a limited period of time to funding the National Development Corporation.

What would be the mechanism by which monetary pledges by community members could be reliably forwarded to the national corporation? In answer to this question, we will borrow liberally from a funding idea advocated by Kermit Eady, head of the Black United Fund, a non-profit corporation in New York City, for financing that organization's charitable and developmental activities. He suggested that employed Afrikan Americans instruct their banks to deduct or withdraw from their bank accounts a specified amount of money each month to be sent to his organization. Of course, retired persons and others who receive income from pensions or retirement funds, or who have ample wealth need not be excluded in this matter. Organizational accounts could also apply this technique. The amount of the pledge and the number of the installments made to pay the pledge as well as the period of time over which it will be paid will be left to the discretion of the pledgee. Banks can enter this arrangement willingly because they profit from charging a modest fee for executing the transaction.

The power of the approach to liberally funding a national corporation we just described, can be garnered by a quick review of Afrikan American employment statistics. The Afrikan American civilian labor force was expected to reach 14.4 million employed in 1994. The total was 14.1 million in 1993. Ideally, if all 14.4 million Blacks who were employed pledged 10 dollars per month for 36 months to the national corporation, then after three years that organization would receive a total of $5,204,000,000 or $5.2 billion. The sum could amount to between $5–7 billion if similar pledges by retirees and other non-working Blacks were made. This sum could approach $10 billion if Black churches and secular organizations would pledge substantial resources. This is idealistic, of course, and is unlikely to be realized. A more realistic number of Blacks employees, say, 1–2 million, pledging a more modest amount, say, $5 a month over three years, could still fund a substantial national corporation. This would especially be the case if they were enthusiastically supported by the other sources of pledges we just mentioned. A national corporation capitalized at a minimum of $3 billion could have a visible impact on the Afrikan American and general American economies.

Cross (ibid) gives an example of how a private nonprofit corporation known as the Opportunity Funding Corporation (OFC), which began operations in 1970 capitalized at $7.4 million, in the course of a decade directly generated 1,200 new jobs, and indirectly, perhaps 3,600 new jobs. He further reveals that "with capital of only $7.4 million, OFC produced in excess of $30 million of private investment in low-income communities. In addition, OFC maintained over $5 million of its funds on deposit in some forty-five financial institutions, all situated in poverty communities." One can extrapolate from these figures the impact of a $5–10 billion funding corporation operating on behalf of the Afrikan American community.

It is worthwhile to note that if the Afrikan American National Developmental Corporation is a non-profit fund, contributions to it would be tax deductible. Thus, Black income which is taxed by a federal, state and local systems to help support political-economic regimes often hostile to Black economic and political empowerment, could be legally diverted instead to support the political-economic interests of the community.

If the national corporation is to be a for-profit organization, then the contribution would not be tax deductible, but nevertheless worthwhile. The corporation could consider its contributors as shareholders who own equity in the corporation proportionate to their investment. In this instance, contributors could expect a return on their investment. The corporation would earn its profits by charging fees for its services and funding activities, and by budgeting its income in ways that would permit it to construct reserves to cover possible losses. Either approach — non-profit or for-profit — is feasible and productive. Only the approval and support of the community is required for their enactment. Finally, underwriting institutions like the national one we have proposed may be founded to serve certain industries, local communities, metropolitan areas, states, and regions. A national network of such institutions may allow the syndication of their efforts and resources in underwriting large projects and/or to spread investment risks.

Chapter 29

The Investment Club

Investment Trends in the Black Community

One of our central arguments herein is that the limited political influence and relative poverty of the Afrikan American community is closely related to its limited ownership of wealth, that is, of financial and business assets as well as human capital. Swinton (1994) notes that in 1988, Afrikan Americans had a net worth per capita of $9,359 compared to $44,980 for European Americans. (This compares with $10,651 vs. $51,191 in 1992 dollars.) He goes on to indicate that in 1988 "76.58 percent of White households had earned interest at financial institutions but only 44.48 percent of Black households had this type of wealth...those Blacks who had interest-earning assets at financial institutions had mean holdings worth $5,008 compared to $21,748 for White households." This is related to the fact that Blacks, in 1988, earned an average of $766 interest per capita from assets at financial institutions versus $6,421 for Whites. (This compares with $872 vs. $7,308 in 1992 dollars.) In 1992, the median Black family income was $21,761. The median White family income was $39,320. Thus, the median Black family income was 55.3% of the median White family income. Blacks are far less likely compared to Whites, to invest in equities — stocks and bonds or mutual funds, equity in businesses, IRAs and Keoghs. The Black middle-class is hardly more likely to purchase financial instruments such as stocks than are working-class White ethnics striving to upgrade their social status. The discrepancy in investments between Blacks and Whites may in large part be due to the fact that the Black middle-class is relatively young and has enjoyed affluence for only a relatively short time, and for psycho-historical reasons, has developed different spending patterns. More basic reasons for the discrepancy may be a lack of strong interest in long-range investment and a lack of familiarity with investment instruments and procedures.

There is also a relatively poor grasp by the Black middle and upper classes of the relationship between true political influence, power, and wealth, along with a continuing and unfounded belief on their part that the American economy will, without fail, provide them increasing income from wages and salaries. The rather low interest many Blacks demonstrate in making investments, while probably reflecting their generally low wages and high cost of living, on a deeper level reflects the fact that the economic role of Blacks in the American economy — as determined by dominant Whites — is that of secondary laborers, salaried workers or professionals, and above all, as that of consumers, not producers or owners. In line with the latter role, the spending patterns of many Black middle-classers resemble those of the newly rich or White yuppies — buying cars, imported beer, expensive stereos and other trendy products at significantly above national average rates. There is one major exception to this trend — the Black middle-class invests in mutual funds far below the national average. This orientation has lowered the general aggregate savings of the Afrikan American community and contributes to its prevailing social problems. As implied earlier, Black Americans must radically increase and appropriately increase their aggregate savings if they are to achieve increased economic self-sufficiency and political power. Along with the ways we have already discussed for increasing aggregate savings in the Black community, we shall discuss very briefly their increase through investment in financial instruments, specifically through investment clubs.

Investment Clubs

An investment club typically consists of 10-20 persons, most often comprised of family members, friends, and/or people from all walks of life who meet regularly to learn investment principles, to combine their monies to build an investment portfolio (a combination of stocks, bonds and other investment properties), and exchange information with each other. Most clubs, whether incorporated or partnerships, meet once a month to deposit their monthly investment — usually from 20 to 50 dollars — to review studies of stocks and to select a stock in which to invest. Many investment clubs are formed by experienced investors. While an investment club helps its members to learn more about investing, to build some familiarity and knowledge about corporations and the stock market, to help each member accumulate through small monthly payments and over the years a substantial security account, it may also be founded on a combination of social interests and goals. According to the National Association of Investors Corporation (NAIC), a governing body representing 7,600 investment clubs with a total of over 140,000 members, modern investment clubs operate according to the following principles:

1. Invest a set sum once a month in common stocks, regardless of general market conditions. This helps you obtain lower average costs.
2. Reinvest dividends and capital gains immediately. Your money grows faster if earnings are reinvested. This is compound income at work.
3. Buy growth stocks — companies whose sales are increasing at a rate faster than industry in general. The companies should have good prospects for continued growth. In other words, they should be stronger companies five years from now.
4. Invest in different fields. Diversification helps spread risk and opportunity.

Despite the fact that investment club members may be considered non-professional money managers, the overall performance of the stocks they select for investment is remarkable. As noted by *Black Enterprise* magazine (6/92):

> It's inconceivable that the performance of stocks chosen by investment clubs would stack up to those chosen by mutual fund managers. But in fact the stocks that professional money managers picked haven't performed as well. At least according to a survey by NAIC that shows over a nine-year period, almost 82% of NAIC accounts equaled or exceeded the earnings rate of S&P 500. But only 19% of professional money managers equaled or exceeded the S&P 500 during the same period, says NAIC's O'Hara.

Investment clubs have in common their focus on growth and regular investing. With a history of compounded annual earnings at an average rate of 14.96% (*Black Enterprise*, 6/92), portfolios fully invested in select stocks, bonds or funds, these organizations, by building long-term value, help their members to save for retirement, to fund their or their children's education, or to help finance a business.

THE POWER OF COMPOUNDING

How saving $100 a month at a specific rate adds up over time.

Interest	5 Years	10 Years	15 Years	20 Years	25 Years	30 Years	35 Years
5%	$6,810	$15,502	$26,595	$40,754	$58,823	$81,886	$111,319
6%	$6,984	$16,331	$28,839	$45,577	$67,977	$97,953	$138,068
8%	$7,345	$18,137	$33,994	$57,294*	$91,528	$141,830	$215,740
10%	$7,723	$20,161	$40,192	$72,453	$124,409	$208,084	$342,845
12%	$8,119	$22,427	$47,643	$92,083	$170,401	$308,423	$551,668
14%	$8,534	$24,964	$56,600	$117,513	$234,794	$460,610	$895,339

*Example: By investing $100 per month at an interest rate of 8%, in 20 years you would have a total of $57,294.

Source: *The Black Woman's Guide to Financial Independence: Money Management Strategies for the 1990s*, Hyde Park Publishing, Oakland, 1991.

Table 29-1

Investment Clubs as Financiers of Black-owned Businesses. Investment clubs may also engage in entrepreneurial ventures. Though traditionally conservative, investment clubs, particularly Afrikan American clubs, may cautiously invest in fledgling Black-owned corporations or well-established Black-owned corporations seeking public financing. For example, in December 1991, Black Entertainment Television Holdings Inc. made an initial public offering (IPO) through the selling of shares. The offering raised $72.3 million. As noted by *Black Enterprise* magazine (5/92), "Investors, including many middle-class African Americans, bid the stock up from $17 to $26.37 a share." Increasingly, Black-owned corporations are making initial public offerings or joint stock exchanges as a way of raising funds to enhance growth and expand services. Thus, through investing in Black-owned corporations Afrikan American investors may help to initiate and sustain the growth and development of Afrikan American enterprises as well as earn acceptable returns on their investments.

One of the Afrikan American investment clubs which invested in Black Entertainment Television Holdings Inc. and in the Calvert-Ariel Growth Fund — a small capitalization fund worth some $260 million, founded and headed by 37-year-old Afrikan American John W. Rogers, Jr.[1] — is the Afrikan American Washington Women's Investment Club (WWIC). (See *Black Enterprise*, 4/92, for a full story on equity investment specialist John W. Rogers, Jr.) The WWIC is a group of 21 Black women, formed in 1987 in Washington, D.C. (*Black Enterprise*, 6/92). This club, which was initiated by an investment of $500 by each of its members and sustained by monthly dues of $60, amassed a portfolio valued at more than $100,000. Their portfolio of stocks and mutual funds during the almost five years of its existence, averaged about 20% a year in spite of the volatility of the market. Over the long-term this group may develop a portfolio worth millions to its members and families as well as to the community.

Conceivably, through an investment committee or an asset management organization large Black organizations may form an investment consortium as a way of investing a relatively large sum of money regularly and earning sizable returns to be reinvested or invested in part in economic development projects.

Whether as small intimate clubs of investors or larger more formal clubs, Afrikan Americans as investors are crucial to the economic development and the politicoeconomic empowerment of the Afrikan American community as a whole.

---

1. Also founder and president of Chicago-based Ariel Capital Management Inc. which, as of December 1991, was managing $1.6 billion.

For advice concerning the founding and operation of an investment club the reader is advised to begin with articles in *Black Enterprise*, June 1992 and April 1993. He or she may also contact the National Association of Investment Clubs, 1515 E. Eleven Mills, MI 48061. (For a very readable introduction to the development of investment clubs see Kathryn Shaw's book.[2])

Deep knowledge of how the market works, the development of a keen ability to invest in and use it, are not only important for long-term personal or small group gain but crucial to the expansion of the Black-owned business establishment into the broader national and international marketplace.

Investment Companies

The establishment and rapid increase in the number and size of Black-owned investment companies (or investment trusts) would do much to increase the influence of the Afrikan American community in the nation and its capital markets. Investment companies, currently referred to as mutual funds, "are organizations which have as their sole purpose the ownership of securities (of all types, including government bonds) for investment" (Kristein, 1969). A mutual fund is an investment collective where a group of investors pool their assets under professional management in order to purchase, hold, and/or trade various types of securities. The economic goal of the investment company is to increase the value of its investors' capital. A mutual fund is a corporation. The investor in a mutual fund is therefore an owner, not a lender, who shares in the profits and losses and in the income and expenses derived from the fund's management of a relatively large and diversified portfolio, i.e., securities of various types. In practice, a mutual fund sells securities to investors among the general public. Investors are thereby permitted to purchase a proportionate or small share of the fund's portfolio. When an investor purchases shares in a fund the amount he invests (or a portion thereof, depending on the type of fund in which he invests) is actually invested in securities.

Investing in mutual funds carries a number of advantages for both small and large investors lacking access to investment counsel.[3] These include: professional management; division of risk (because the fund spreads the investment dollars over many different industry and

---

2. Kathryn Shaw, *Investment Clubs: Low Cost Education in the Stock Market* (Williamsburg, Michigan: Lake Shore Press, 1991).

3. Babson - United Investment Advisors, Inc. *Successful Investing*. 4th ed. (New York: Fireside Book).

company stocks and securities); information (re: readily available information regarding the fund's performance); freedom from emotional involvement (and being swayed by strong feelings, hunches, etc., rather than expert knowledge and experience); freedom from housekeeping (i.e., securing stock certificates since they are held by the fund); automatic reinvestment of income dividends and capital gains distributions (i.e., dividends may be converted into additional shares, thereby compounding the investment); instant diversification (by investing in a mutual fund the investor, with a relatively small amount of monies, immediately invests in a number of different industries and their securities); and exchange privileges (in large funds who sponsor a variety of different subsidiary funds with different objectives, services, programs, the investor may switch part or all of his principal from one fund to another in a family of funds).

It must be kept in mind that the performance of mutual funds vary greatly. The investor may be subject to experiencing little or no growth in asset value, growth or decline in the value of his assets depending on the performance of the fund in which he invests.

From a collective point of view, investment companies or mutual funds have become important factors in capital markets including the markets for new securities. Some funds form a prominent and influential segment of large institutional investors whose impact on the market and influence in the corporate sector is enormous. There now exists enough persons and corporations in the Afrikan American community with the means and wealth for founding mutual funds initially worth at least $100–200 million.

Wealth and Knowledge: A Case in Point

The late Afrikan American Reginald Lewis, CEO of The Lewis Company (TLC), Wall Street lawyer and financier, provides an illustrious example of how creative, aggressive market know-how can be utilized by intrepid Afrikan American businesspersons to gain wealth and power in the global marketplace. A graduate of predominantly Black, Virginia State College, Lewis was ranked by *Fortune* magazine as one of the 400 richest Americans, with personal assets valued at $400 million. Lewis, who died of brain cancer at age 50, became a Wall Street legend and business role model in the Afrikan American community after having parlayed a $1 million investment in the McCall Pattern Company into the majority ownership and control of the multinational Beatrice International Holdings Inc., which had sales of some $1.7 billion in 1993. Beatrice International is an international food processor and distributor. This corporation, which is by far the nation's largest Black-owned company, owns food processing and distribution centers scattered around Western Europe.

Lewis' ascension to the top of the global market hierarchy makes for a remarkable story and demonstrates a multitude of possibilities for other Afrikan American businesspersons. Other Afrikan Americans must duplicate his feat if the community is to gain real power in the nation and world. We cannot tell Reginald Lewis' full story here. We will only outline very briefly his rise as a way of demonstrating how a sound knowledge of the market along with other personal and social characteristics can be creatively and boldly combined to penetrate the higher echelons of American/global business and finance.

Reginald Lewis was born in Baltimore, Maryland, and after graduating Virginia State College, graduated the Harvard Law School in 1968. After Harvard he joined the New York law firm of Paul Weiss, Rifkin, Wharton & Garrison as an associate. He soon left that firm to found his own corporate law practice, Lewis & Clarkson (with Charles Clarkson as junior law partner). While his new firm did not fulfill his great expectations of representing a significant number of prominent clients (even though he did land a few, such as Aetna Life & Casualty Co.), he gained valuable experience representing corporations that were acquiring other corporations. He gained an intimate and practiced knowledge of how acquisitions and other large financial transactions were done.

Like many Black professionals seeking to enter into areas where few, if any, other Blacks operate and where access is jealously guarded by old-line White corporate and professional interests, Lewis had no dependable, knowledgeable and deeply sympathetic mentor to guide him through often treacherous terrain. He compensated for this lack by assiduously studying successful companies such as Norton Simon Inc. and Warner Communications Inc. Based on his experience and studies, Lewis sought to enter the field of corporate finance in a "big way" by acquiring a prominent corporate asset. After a number of faltering attempts he managed in 1983 to acquire the McCall Pattern Company, a primary seller of home-sewing patterns, then a subsidiary of the Chicago conglomerate, Esmark Inc. With only $1 million of his own money Lewis arranged a leveraged buy-out of McCall for $22.5 million, meaning that aside from his own $1 million, virtually all the rest of the purchase price was borrowed. Despite his fractional input on the purchase price (half of the layout being financed by a loan from Equitable's venture capital unit for minority-owned businesses), Lewis emerged as a controlling owner of his new acquisition. After cutting costs and raising the profits of McCall's and repaying its debts early, Lewis sold the company to a British firm for $63 million in cash, plus $19 million through a recapitalization plan, and prior distributions. All told, Lewis received $90 million on an investment of $1 million within a three-year period — a 90 to 1 return on investment. These two deals established Lewis' ability to do truly big deals. Joining with Cleve Christoff, a friend at Citicorp, Lewis began analyzing the foreign operations of Beatrice, which was for sale under the aegis of Salomon Brothers, Inc. In June 1987, they notified Salomon Brothers of their tentative bid of $950 million for the company. At the time Beatrice put up its international units for sale they included a conglomeration "of 64 companies operating in 31 countries, ranging from a sausage producer in Spain to an ice cream maker in Germany" (NYT, 1/20/93). As noted by the *Wall Street Journal*:

> Their overture was met with bewilderment. A Salomon executive demanded a meeting with the pair, telling them: "Quite frankly, no one knows who the hell you are." More than a dozen major companies were looking at the Beatrice businesses, too.

With the steady support of Michael Milken, then at the peak of his power as junk bond *major domo* at Drexel Burnham Lambert, Lewis won the Beatrice auction for an offering of $985 million. Unfortunately, some six years after his outstanding coup, Lewis died in January, 1993. However, prior to his untimely death Lewis was able to plan the transfer of the responsibility for running his company to his half-brother, Jean S. Fugett, a 41-year-old Baltimore lawyer. Consequently, the primary ownership and control of the company, which employs 5,000 men and women, has remained within the family and the Afrikan American business community. In its obituary, the *New York Times* (1/20/93) in reviewing Lewis' life and career noted the following contributions he made to the Afrikan American community:

> Mr. Lewis considered his contributions to educational institutions to be his most important legacy. In the 1st few years, he gave vast sums to several schools, including Virginia State and Howard universities. In New York, he gave large contributions to Abyssinian Baptist Church and the scholarship foundation of Kappa Alpha Psi Fraternity, of which he was a member.
>
> Mr. Lewis was a member of the boards of WNET in New York and the NAACP Legal Defense and Education Fund. He was also a member of the Business Roundtable and the Economic Advisory Committee of New York City. Mayor David Dinkins had nominated him to be a member of the city's Municipal Assistance Corporation.

Reginald Lewis demonstrates how a Black man in the face of racist and financial restraints, with a little money and a lot of ingenuity, a facile social intelligence and deep knowledge of his field, lots of heart and self-confidence, and a little luck, can break out of the Black business reservation and range freely across the full terrain of national and international business. Lewis began his trek with $1 million. Today, there are many more Afrikan Americans with hundreds times the personal and financial wealth he began with. There are now Afrikan American athletes who are multimillionaires; Black entertainers worth more than $400 million dollars, who earn upwards of $60 million per year; Black business persons who have amassed fortunes of over $200 million. For example, Bill Cosby, famous comedian and television star who is reportedly worth $400 million and continues to earn millions from residuals, has made serious offers to purchase the National Broadcasting Corporation. Berry Gordy sold Motown for some $300 million. John Johnson of *Ebony* magazine fame has amassed a fortune surpassing $100 million. In fact, Johnson Publishing Company, Inc. achieved sales of $293.8 million in 1993. Entertainers such as Michael Jackson have amassed fortunes in the tens of millions, a number approaching $100 million or more. Black entertainers are among the highest paid in the entertainment industry. For example, *Forbes* magazine's (9/93) list of the nation's highest-paid entertainers for 1992 and 1993 in terms of estimates of total gross earnings include Oprah Winfrey, № 1 at $98 million [increased since]; Bill Cosby, № 3 at $66 million; Prince, № 5 at $49 million; Michael Jackson, № 12 at $42 million; and Eddie Murphy, № 21 at $30 million. The realization that these entertainers have been at the top of their professions for more than several years gives us some idea of their combined earnings and worth at this time. The five entertainers listed here earned roughly $300 million in 1992–1993 alone. The earnings of these stars combined with those of the lesser millionaire Afrikan American entertainers and sports figures indicate the hundreds of millions of dollars, perhaps a billion or more, earned yearly by a relatively small collection of individuals. Corporate relations and investments among such individuals would be quite significant for the economic advancement of the Afrikan American community and Afrikan peoples worldwide. There are millions more dollars held by Black institutions and organizations. These millions, appropriately leveraged, organized into various consortiums, partnerships and other economic formations instrumentally manipulated by a people imbued with an Afrikan-centered consciousness, intentionality, purpose, free-wielding highly flexible creativity and ingenuity — and an iron-willed determination to win liberation by any means necessary — can deeply penetrate the American economy and establish the Afrikan American community as a national and international force to be reckoned with.

Chapter 30

Franchises, Cooperatives, Corporations and Collective Capitalism

Franchises

WHILE NOT A MEANS OF PRODUCING aggregate savings or of financing community development, the franchise industry does provide possible avenues for the rather rapid increase in the business ownership of the Afrikan American community. The current time is somewhat propitious for the wholesale entry of Afrikan Americans into the $75 billion franchise industry since an increasing number of business-format franchisers are more receptive to Afrikan American would-be owners. Moreover, since April 1992, the International Franchise Association through its special subsidiary organization, the Alliance for Minority Opportunities in Franchising, is actively seeking to increase the number of opportunities for women and minorities to own franchises.

The active negotiation to increase Afrikan American employment and ownership in the franchise industry by organizations such as the NAACP (see the *New York Times*, 8/31/93) is also creating a more receptive atmosphere for Afrikan American entry into the industry. However, the increasing entry of Afrikan Americans into the franchise industry is by no means a flood — it is barely a trickle. According to the U.S. Department of Commerce through its Minority Business Development Agency, in 1988 the number of minorities in franchising was projected to amount to 14,000 or merely 2.5% of the nation's 550,000 franchises to be owned in 1990. When the issue becomes what percentage of the nation's franchises are *Black owned* compared to *minority owned*, the picture is starkly clearer. *Black Enterprise* magazine provides an annual review of the *BE Franchise 50*, a listing of the franchisors with the most Black-owned units. In 1992, Afrikan Americans owned only 5% or 2,632 units of the 52,641 franchises represented by the *BE Franchise 50*. In 1993, that figure increased to 5.6% or 4,159 of the 74,273 franchises represented by the *BE Franchise 50*. Obviously, the Afrikan American community has a long way to go if it is to achieve significant ownership in one of America's fastest growing business sectors. According to *Black Enterprise* (9/93), "In 1991, franchises employed 7.0 million people in more than 60 industries. Gross sales for 1992 were $813 billion...an 8% increase over 1991... A new franchise opens every 6.5 minutes of each business day." Moreover, the growing number of franchises *consistently* outperformed the Fortune 500 companies in providing new jobs in America.

The franchise industry, like the rest of American industry, is no bed of roses for Afrikan Americans. However, as the saying goes, "when there are only lemons, make lemonade." Despite its prickly and fickle nature, franchising does provide significant business opportunities for Afrikan Americans and a number of solid mobilization platforms for Afrikan-centered, Afrikan American businesspersons to begin an assault on the American economic and political system. Franchising provides significant business opportunities for Afrikan Americans for the following reasons:

- Franchising often involves less risk than building a business from the ground up.

- Franchisees have a built-in recognition factor, are generally well-defined and operator-ready.

- Franchisees receive on-the-job training on how to expertly operate every facet of their outlets and franchisers may provide advertising, equipment, supplies, business counseling, and a starting customer-base.

Note: This section is primarily based on *Black Enterprise* 9/92, 5/93 and 9/93).

Some franchise companies have established recruitment programs specifically designed to attract minority franchisers and may also provide special financial credits, waivers, reduced liquidity requirements, and loan guarantees. For example, Kentucky Fried Chicken guarantees 15 to 20 loans annually made by local banks to minority franchisers. According to *Black Enterprise*, KFC "has franchised 192 minority-owned restaurants, for a total of $6.9 million, of which $4.3 million has already been repaid."

The failure rate of franchise start-ups tends to be far lower than most small businesses. According to *Black Enterprise*, the U.S. Department of Commerce reported that "less than 5% of franchises failed on an annual basis between 1971 and 1987. In fact, in many industry segments, more than 85% of franchised units opened since 1986 were still owned in 1991 by the person who originally bought the outlet."

Generally speaking, start-up costs for many franchises are relatively low. While an initial investment in a McDonald's unit may cost more than $600,000, a Burger King at least $400,000, and franchises require an average of $150,000, an abundance of franchise opportunities may require start-up costs for as little as $10,000 or less. Home-based franchises generally require low-cost start-up charges and provide many other perks, including flexibility and convenience.

Some Afrikan American Franchisees

Larry Lundy — Pizza Hut. Afrikan American Larry Lundy, who saved for twenty years and planned for two more, launched the largest Afrikan American franchise thus far by purchasing 31 New Orleans-area Pizza Hut restaurants in February 1992 for approximately $15.5 million (*Black Enterprise*, 9/93). Lundy was a nine-year veteran of Pizza Hut Inc. and stepped down as vice president of restaurant development there on assuming ownership of the outlets. In 1992, the total volume of sales was estimated at $20 million (*Black Enterprise*, 5/92). In 1993, Lundy achieved sales of $23.3 million. Lundy, whose restaurants employed approximately 1,000 workers in 1992, anticipates adding additional stores in the immediate future, thereby boosting sales to $50 million. During his 3½ years at Pizza Hut, Lundy led the building and development of 1,100 new stores.

Warren Thompson — Shoney's. In June 1992 Warren M. Thompson, CEO of Thompson Hospitality L.P. (THLP) and former Marriott Restaurant Group executive, purchased 31 Bob's Big Boy restaurants from the Marriott Corporation. He plans to convert at least 26 of the 31 Bob's Big Boys to Shoney's eateries in the near future. Eleven Bob's Big Boys have been converted to Shoney's so far. Thompson recently opened a new catering service and plans to open new fast-food facilities. Reston, Virginia-based THLP had revenues of $34.3 million in 1993 (BE, 6/94) and looks forward to achieving revenues of $45 million by 1995. Each of THLP's Big Boy restaurants generates an average of $1.1 million annually, while each of its Shoney's generates about $1.6 million annually. The fascinating and instructive story of how Warren Thompson and THLP became the fifth largest Shoney's Inc. franchisee, is told by *Black Enterprise* (6/94):

> It's roughly four years since the former Marriott Corp. executive decided to venture out on his own and form THLP, currently the fifth-largest Shoney's Inc. franchisee. Thompson, who has an M.B.A. from the University of Virginia, had served nine years with Marriott Corp., rising through the ranks to become a regional vice president of Host International, a food service subsidiary of the Bethesda, Md.-based company.
>
> In 1990, Marriott decided to exit the family restaurant business, selling its Roy Rogers fast-food chain to Hardee's Food Systems Inc. of North Carolina. When Marriott decided to sell the Big Boy restaurants two years later, Thompson's track record convinced the hotel chain that he was capable of running the restaurants profitably.
>
> A close friend and TLC Beatrice International alumnus, Darryl B. Thompson, 31 (no relation), helped to enlist 15 people to invest $2 million. Using his expertise in mergers and acquisitions, the former special assistant to the late TLC Chairman Reginald Lewis structured the deal with Shoney, THLP and Marriott. With Shoney's as a backer and equity partner and Marriott financing the deal, THLP was able to acquire the suffering Big Boys. Under the deal, THLP would convert 26 of the restaurants to Shoney's in two years.
>
> THLP's acquisition windfall came on the heels of a 1989 class-action suit filed against Shoney's by its African-American employees. They accused the company of discriminatory policies in hiring and promotions, and they won. Shoney's was required to pay $105 million in back pay and damages and to meet certain goals in ending discriminatory practices.
>
> Taylor Henry, chairman and CEO of Shoney's Inc., says that since the suit, Shoney's has worked closely with African-American organizations to improve employment policies and to increase minority franchise ownership. Henry insists, however, that the deal with Thompson just made good business sense.
>
> Thompson agrees: "I presented a good business deal to Shoney's and they recognized it as such. It does have some social implications,

some strategic advantages for Shoney's, but I think the deal was done for economic reasons." Indeed the **BE 100s** company will pay 10% of its royalties to Shoney's over the next 20 years.

C. Alexander West and *Al Carter* – BLOCKBUSTER VIDEO AND DENNY'S. Mention should also be made of Atlanta-based New Day Investments Inc., headed by Afrikan Americans C. Alexander West and Al Carter, who own the nation's largest Black-owned Blockbuster Video franchise. They purchased 23 video outlets in Baltimore, Syracuse and Rochester, N.Y., in April 1992. Concentrating on customers in inner-city neighborhoods and with an experienced management team, NDI raised its revenues 12% within a year of purchasing the franchise. It is important to note that NDI acquired the Blockbuster Video stores from Cox Communications Inc. in a deal financed by private investors and the Levmark Corporation, a New York-based Afrikan American-owned investment firm (*Black Enterprise*, 5/93). New Day Investments currently employs approximately 400 workers. West and Carter are looking and planning to employ 20,000 workers by the year 2000 as NDI Video adds 20 new Blockbuster stores and invests in a number of units of a new footwear franchise. Achieving revenues of $20 million in 1992, West and Carter's goal is to generate $500 million by the turn of the century.

In November 1994, NDI made giant strides toward achieving the long-term earnings goal by acquiring contractual rights to operate as many as 47 Denny's restaurants over the next six years (WSJ, 11/9/94; NYT, 11/9/94). The *Wall Street Journal* described NDI's business deal the following way:

> Under terms of the agreement, NDI Inc. will buy 17 restaurants in New York and New Jersey from Denny's parent, Flagstar Co., this year. In addition, Atlanta-based NDI has the right to buy five more company-owned stores in 1995 and has agreed to build 25 new Denny's under a five-year expansion plan. The price of the transaction wasn't disclosed.
>
> The agreement with NDI, which also operates 23 Blockbuster Video stores, is the most tangible evidence of Flagstar's attempt to boost minority ownership of its stores. Two African-American franchisees began operating individual restaurants earlier this year.

The *Journal* goes on to indicate that "In return for its commitment to Denny's, NDI, which was founded in 1991, appears to be getting a group of healthy restaurants in highly populated territory. Average sales per restaurant at the 17 stores is $1.4 million a year, well above the company-wide average of $1.2 million..." The 47 stores to be acquired by NDI would make it the third largest Denny's franchisee. The company's contract with Denny's exemplifies the trend where large franchisors seek to enter into deals with experienced business operators. Flagstar Company, Denny's parent, also has a program called Fast Track, designed to encourage first-time franchisees through individualized academic and in-restaurant training. Fast Track graduates will be offered, with financial assistance, an opportunity to acquire a franchise.

It is apparent that Denny's contract with NDI is a part of its agreement with the NAACP to add 53 minority-owned restaurants by 1997 as part of a settlement of a lawsuit filed by thousands of Black customer allegations that they had been discriminated against when seeking services in a number of Denny's restaurants across the country (see discussion below). Until very recently, none of Denny's 1500 stores were owned by Afrikan Americans. NDI's initial group of restaurants will be located in upstate New York and in south and central New Jersey.

Blacks and Burger King

The customer base of Burger King is 40 percent minority. The largest percentage of this group is Black. Fourteen percent of Burger King's 6,200 domestic outlets are ethnic-owned restaurants. Three and a half percent or 217 of these outlets are Black-owned. Black-owned V&J Foods Inc., founded and headed by Valerie Daniels-Carter, is by far the largest Black-owned Burger King franchise (*Black Enterprise*, 9/94). Founded 10 years ago, V&J Foods owns 32 Burger King outlets in Wisconsin and Michigan. The Milwaukee-based corporation grossed $23 million in 1993. In May 1993, V&J Foods, which already owned 15 outlets, acquired 17 more. *Black Enterprise* summaries V&J Foods corporate history as follows:

> Perhaps the biggest success story on Burger King's books is Valerie Daniels-Carter, a former financial analyst, and John Daniels, a corporate and real estate lawyer. The brother-sister team started in 1984 with one Burger King unit that was built up from the ground, taking $40,000 in personal savings to pay the franchise fee (the total investment for a site is around $300,000 to $1.2 million). That first year, V&J Foods earned $900,000 in revenues.
>
> Three years later, the duo added two more outlets. Then came a slew of acquisitions between 1990 and 1992 — 15 in all. But the granddaddy of them all was the acquisition of 17 Burger Kings in Detroit last year.

"When we started out, we wanted to get into a business we could expand," says Daniels-Carter, explaining why they chose a Burger King franchise. "We looked at each site as a situational opportunity." V&J has its eyes fixed on nontraditional settings for future Burger King outlets.

In fact, a part of Burger King's overall objective is to build restaurants in these kinds of "nontraditional" settings anchored by other businesses and institutions, such as gas stations, convenience stores and college campuses. The company is specifically targeting historically black colleges. For example, a Burger King franchise will open this month at Xavier University in New Orleans and will be run by Cedric Smith, a black franchisee who owns four other Burger Kings in Indianapolis.

Burger King's Commitment. V&J Foods exemplifies the trend which Burger King has been encouraging, that is, encouraging Black-owned franchise owners "to expand in terms of multiple units and locations," according to Burger King's Chief Financial Officer and Chairperson of Burger King's Diversity Action Council (DAC), Scott Colabuono.

Burger King's $100 million Business Deal. In its September 1994 edition, *Black Enterprise* reported that Burger King has made a $100-million commitment to the Black American community. It revealed that:

Burger King's latest commitment referred to as the Eight-point Plan, sets aside $100 million to develop minority franchises and suppliers over the next five years. Another half million will help underwrite and sponsor minority community events.

Half of the $100 million is earmarked as start-up capital in the procurement area. "We will help minority suppliers in two ways," says Rachelle Hood-Phillips, vice president of diversity affairs. One is through loan guarantees: "Burger King will go to a third-party lender and agree to back the loan if there's a default." A second approach is direct investing: "We will lend companies the money directly," she explains, "but in return, we want a share of their profits."

The other $50 million is targeted to the development funds for new and existing minority franchise owners. "The program is set up so we can do loan guarantees, leasing and capital restructuring," says Hood-Phillips, "whatever it takes to help that individual buy or develop a site."

Burger King has received over 1,200 inquiries. Of that group, 550 are under serious consideration as potential franchisees, another 200 as suppliers.

The program will be driven by Burger King's Diversity Action Council (DAC). The group of four Burger King executives and 10 minority community leaders and business owners, formed in 1991, will meet quarterly.

Denny's Commitment. Flagstar Companies Inc. of Spartanburg, S.C., parent company of Denny's Restaurants, has also made a multimillion commitment to the Black American community. However, unlike Burger King's, Denny's commitment is essentially involuntary. It is the outcome of a $46 million settlement of two class-action discrimination suits filed against the franchise by the Martin Luther King, Jr. All Children's Choir of Raleigh, N.C., and 18 Black young people from San Jose, California. The latter group alleged that a Denny's restaurant made them pay for their meals before they were served. This demand was apparently made because of their race. The All Children's Choir claimed that it was refused service also because of the race of its members. *Black Enterprise* (9/94) outlines the settlement as follows:

> As part of the settlement last May, the $1.5 billion family-restaurant chain signed a Fair Share Agreement with the NAACP. The pact calls for greater minority participation in franchising, management, marketing, purchasing and professional services...
>
> The NAACP...plan[s] to devote special attention to the Denny's deal. "It has a larger dollar impact and more specific goals than other agreements," adds [Fred] Rasheed [the NAACP's director of economic development].
>
> Among Denny's seven-year goals: 53 new minority-owned restaurants.
>
> Flagstar reports that, in the first nine months into the program, 28 African-American applicants are under review, 103 minority managers were hired, over $1.5 million went to minority ad agencies and 3.3% ($20 million) of purchasing contracts went to minority suppliers. Flagstar also appointed an African-American, Vera King Farris, to its 11-member board.
>
> By way of a 12-month FastTrack training program, "We are looking to move up current Denny's employees into the system and to recruit African-Americans who are already in business," says Norman Hill, vice president of field human resources. Plans are in the works to refranchise 135 units by 1995. Prospective black franchisees will be drawn from that employee pool, notes Hill.

Are Franchise Company Commitments 'For Real"? In line with commitments like those made by Burger King and Denny's are those promised by other franchise companies. In fact, a spokesperson for the International Franchise Association (IFA) in Washington D.C. which represents some 800 franchisors and 2,400 franchisees, claims that an increasing number of franchise companies are actively seeking to attract Afrikan American franchisees. *Black Enterprise* (9/94) quotes spokesperson Ferrian Barnes-Bryant, vice president of research/minority and women's affairs with the IFA, as saying that franchise companies are seeking to recruit Afrikan Americans "through formal minority recruitment programs and by showing a sensitivity to the problems and needs of minority franchises." However, *Black Enterprise* goes on to report that "many industry insiders representing the interests of franchisees have their doubts." Spokesperson for an organization representing women franchisees based in Chicago, is reported by the magazine as denigrating the publicized efforts of some franchise companies to actively recruit Black franchisees as "nothing but smoke and mirrors." Though minorities are often the number one customers of a number of franchise companies and a crucially significant segment of the market for many others, where attempts on their part to recruit Black franchisees are not purely deceptive they represent, at best, lackadaisical efforts to recruit female and minority vendors and franchisees, the last and lowest priorities on their lists. *Black Enterprise*, in reference to franchisees such as V&J Foods cited above and to the reported efforts of franchise companies to recruit Afrikan American franchisees, hits the nail on its head when it concludes:

> These megafranchises reflect the significant gains of African-Americans in the industry. But the hard truth is that most franchise companies don't have African-American owners and aren't looking for any. In fact, most don't track how many black-owned units they have.
> The resurgence of programs to help minorities gain entrance into franchising could change all that. But it's going to take more than spoken or written promises to ensure that black potential franchise owners aren't pushed through a revolving door of opportunity.

What Is Required for Increased Franchise Ownership by Blacks. It is up to the Afrikan American community and its relevant community organizations to see to it that the franchise companies they support commercially provide it with a fair share of the ownership of their outlets, of the suppliers, professionals, advertisers, and other vendors who service these outlets and their parent companies, and of the employees at all levels who form the operating staffs of these outlets and their parent firms. Moreover, it is important that the community should own significant equity in the parent corporations and sit on their boards of directors. The community can no longer just accept as its bottom-line demand being courteously treated by franchise outlets in exchange for spending billions of dollars with them while they continue to deny its members equal opportunities at all levels of their organizations. These objectives require that the Black community as a community of consumers be vigilant and intensely monitor the behavior and organization of the franchise companies their consumer dollars enrich. This also requires that Black consumers organize their behavior relative to these companies in ways that can exert maximal pressure against them, if need be, to achieve fair shares of ownership and employment opportunities. One of the ways the Afrikan American community can do this is through vigorously supporting programs like the NAACP's "Operation FairShare," which, relative to franchise companies, focuses on five areas: "employment, upward mobility, minority purchasing, inclusion of Blacks on organizational boards and philanthropic contributions to black organizations" (*Black Enterprise*, 9/94).

Franchise start-ups, like any other business venture, must be entered into with great caution, meticulous study and realistic expectations. Like any other start-up business, a franchise start-up requires long hours, attention to details, commitment and persistence. Franchises vary greatly in quality, honesty, helpfulness and yield. Many are "churns" — i.e., where money is made more by the selling of a particular location over and over again rather than adjusting the business to particular locales, or where the franchisers are more interested in selling units than seeking to assure the franchisee's maximum success.

It is not necessary that all Black-owned franchises be located in Black communities. Overall, the franchising industry does provide an economic "leg-up" for the Afrikan American community. An as yet atypical group of Afrikan American individuals and corporate groups have begun to make their mark in this industry. They demonstrate the investment possibilities open to Black institutional and individual investors in a rapidly growing market.

A Call for Black-owned Franchise Companies. Be that as it may, the real bottom line of the community should be to found and operate its own franchise companies. There is no reason, except for a lack of collective will and organizational lethargy, why the Black community cannot fund the financing of franchise companies and outlets to service its needs and those of other non-Afrikan communities and firms. Many franchise outlets cost as little as $2,500 to start up. A number of business and professional franchises do not require the large capital and real estate investments which are typical of fast food outlets.

The Black American population approaches 40 million persons, a population much or a bit larger or near the same size as many European countries and other prosperous countries and communities world-wide. The number of persons of Afrikan descent in the world approaches 1 billion or more. There is no reason, except for a lack of creative will and self-abnegation, why the Afrikan American and world-wide Afrikan-descended population should not become the primary markets of Afrikan-owned business organizations. The combination of creative financing, cooperative economics and the politics of Afrikan-centered consciousness and identity can make the dream of building an Afrikan-based economic infrastructure that will enhance the economic quality of life for all Afrikan peoples a reality.

Co-operatives

Co-operatives or co-ops are business enterprises owned, controlled, and patronized by a group of people referred to as its members [and often by non-members]. Co-operatives are established by voluntarily pooling together the capital investments of their members, purchasing wholesale lots of products and distributing them proportionately among the members or by selling them and distributing the return on sales among the members. Generally, the primary purposes of cooperatives include providing their members and/or customers and users with needed goods and services at reasonably low net costs in the form and quality they desire; the supplying to their community and membership with needed goods and services at the lowest possible prices. Their primary purpose also involves the provision of services — not profits — and the furnishing of employment and decent living wages to community workers. The Cooperative League of the United States sums up the essence of a cooperative thusly:

> Any business, enterprise, or institution that belongs to the same group of people which it primarily serves with commodities or services and whose purpose of existence is to meet some need of that group, can correctly be called a cooperative.

Cooperative principles include the following:

1. Open membership.
2. Democratic control — one vote for each member-owner, regardless of the number of shares held.

3. Limited return on invested capital.
4. All net savings distributed in proportion to patronage [or shares].

Cooperative practices include the following:

1. Business for cash to extent practical.
2. Sales at going market prices.
3. Constant expansion.
4. Continuous education.[1]

Our definition of a cooperative is very general since the cooperative concept has different meanings for different people and since there are quite a number of different types of co-ops which serve different purposes. The type we are interested in within the context of our discussion may be referred to as a retail cooperative and the cooperative corporation. However, before we define what we mean by these terms we want to stress the fact that cooperatives are financed by their owner/members, or simply, members who join the cooperative by buying a share or shares at a fixed-fee per share. Obviously, the larger number of people who become members through purchasing shares and patronizing the cooperative, the better. And the more it continues to expand its membership and services at a constant and adequate rate, the more likely its success. Continuous education of its members and employees are also essential to its success.

A cooperative corporation is one which has incorporated under its state's statutes or in some instances, under state statutes other than one where the cooperative is located (Honigsberg, et al. 1985). Cooperatives are licensed by state governments and therefore differ in definition, organization, function and other legal parameters, accordingly. Honigsberg and colleagues (1985) indicate that "cooperative corporations are entitled to benefits common to all corporations..." plus additional advantages. These writers also note that "Many coops, by legal definition, do not make a profit — even when they make one. They have a "surplus" or a "net margin" or a "savings". Distribution of the surplus or savings is in some cases referred to as "patronage refunds". How cooperative "profit" or surplus is distributed depends on the form of the corporation, i.e., whether it is a for-profit or non-profit body, and on various IRS, federal and state specifications and regulations. For example, at least in 1985, New York State allowed

---

1. Jerry Voorhis, *American Cooperatives: Where They Come From...What They Do...Where They Are Going....* (New York: Harper & Row, 1951); and Peter Honigsberg, Bernard Kamoroff, & Jim Beatty, *We Own It: Starting & Managing Coops, Collectives & Employee-Owned Ventures* (Laytonville, CA: Bell Springs Publishing, 1982).

co-ops to conduct business for any legal purpose; required that they be organized as non-profit corporations; allowed general reserves, i.e., a certain percentage of surplus (profits), to be retained and not distributed to members for various purposes including expansion, educational expenses, etc.; allowed patronage refunds (i.e., refunds to members based on amount of business they transacted with the co-op) and dividends limited to no more than 12% (Honigsberg, et al. 1985). Some states require that all members of a cooperative be individuals; others allow organizations, e.g., corporations and other co-ops, to be members. Where cash dividends are paid to members, many states limit the maximum amount payable in any given year to one percent of the member's investment.

Co-ops in their many varieties and in their democratic, communal organization, management and control, like revolving credit associations, are very compatible with the current economic status of the Afrikan American community and with the spirit and traditional communal orientation of Afrikan culture. Their organization and management generate a sense of social solidarity and cooperativeness within the community, two very valuable social attitudes necessary for community survival, advancement, and empowerment. Small cooperatives such as food and consumer coops, whether sponsored by collectives of individuals or organizational associations such as churches or secular organizations, may enable communities of Afrikan Americans to establish viable Black-owned businesses and thereby penetrate the monopolization of their community markets by aliens. Through various co-ops the community can reduce prices and increase services to its members and can, through efficient service and relatively lower prices, competitively drive from its midst discourteous, price-gouging, exploitative merchants and vendors who are only interested in the community to the extent to which they may rob it of vital resources and suck its socioeconomic blood.

Co-ops as Large Businesses

While co-ops are valuable small business resources, they can become platforms for entry into larger entrepreneurial activities. We can get some sense of the larger possibilities cooperatives can actualize from the following citation taken from the introduction to the book, *We Own It*, by Honigsberg and colleagues:

> All across the country there are some 50,000 cooperatives serving over 40 million households. Among the most visible serving consumers are food and other retail cooperatives, housing cooperatives and

child care centers. Serving the agricultural community are a wide range of farm supply, production and marketing cooperatives. There are also hundreds of worker owned and operated businesses in the United States employing thousands of employee-owners.

Some of the largest businesses in the country and some of the smallest are coops and employee owned ventures. Sunkist, Ocean Spray and Land O'Lakes are giant farm coops. Yellow Cab Company is a cooperative owned by the cab drivers and dispatchers. Sunset Scavenger, the company which hauls garbage for the city of San Francisco, is employee owned. So is Little Professor Book Centers, a chain of over 100 stores.

Possibly the largest consumer cooperative in the United States, with 300,000 members, is Recreational Equipment Incorporated (REI). It is a forty year old organization based in Seattle with other locations in Anchorage, Portland, Berkeley, Los Angeles and Minneapolis. REI has established an enviable record of producing and retailing quality recreation equipment especially for mountaineering. REI outfitted the first American team to successfully climb Mt. Everest.

Probably the most activist consumer coop in the U.S., and one of the largest, is the Consumers Cooperative of Berkeley known to everybody in the San Francisco Bay Area as "the Coop". The Coop operates supermarkets, pharmacies, hardware and camping stores; it has a membership of more than 100,000. One of the Coop's stores has the largest per capita volume of any supermarket outlet west of the Mississippi....

Cooperatives, collectives and worker owned businesses can provide the framework, the guidelines, the ways and means for people who want to work, shop and live cooperatively....

A cooperative is a social organization as much as it is an economic one. Coops are, first and last, people — people who can work together, who can understand and respect one another, who can agree on common needs and goals and how they're to be accomplished. It is the people who will make or break any business, and it is this "working together" which will require the most work of all.

Honigsberg and his colleagues clearly indicate that a cooperative is not necessarily a small operation. In fact, *Forbes* (8/94) reports that Land O'Lakes, based in Arden Hills, Minn., is a $2.7 billion (1993 revenues) co-operative owned by about 8,200 dairy and livestock farmers and 1,000 local operatives concentrated in Minnesota, Wisconsin, Iowa and North and South Dakota.

By means of co-ops the Afrikan American community could establish a major network of low-price commercial alternatives to the market systems which now exist, especially in the inner-cities across the country. Under the leadership of the National Congress of Black Churches or a similar organization of the major Black Church denominations, a network of large food and other types of co-ops could open simultaneously or in rapid, systematic succession across the nation. Using their combined buying power they could offer the nation's Black and minority communities large varieties of high quality commodities and merchandise at low prices. An excellent example of the possibilities offered by a federation of food cooperatives is provided by citations from the *New York Times* (6/5/94 – "Beyond Supermarkets: A Shopper's Guide"):

The Co-ops: Taking 'Control Over The Food Supply'

Back in 1973, when people talked a lot about acquiring what Joe Holtz calls "control over the food supply," not to mention saving money, Mr. Holtz and a dozen of his neighbors took over a community-center closet and formed the Park Slope Food Co-op. Today, when people talk even more about saving money, the co-op is more than 5,000 members strong and spills across more than 5,000 square feet in its own building at 782 Union Street.

They may sound like relics of the 60's, but food co-ops are thriving, and growing, as alternatives to supermarket shopping in the 90's. The National Cooperative Business Association says requests for informational books and videos it publishes have surged this year, with 1,000 through May, compared with 1,500 for all last year.

"In hard economic times, co-operatives tend to grow," said Leta Mach, the association's spokeswoman, noting that while many co-ops begun in the 60's failed later, the recent incarnations are more businesslike.

At the Park Slope co-op, everything still seems to be done in the collective spirit. Mr. Holtz, though he looks like the person in command, is actually one of six co-managers. Shoppers are the workers are the managers.

The vegetarians predominate, and spanking clean produce, much of it organic, is clearly a priority, but the co-op also carries such supermarket standards as chicken, Kix cereal and a shelf full of Pepperidge Farm cookies. There is no red meat, though, and no diapers. Members can request certain items, but in this super-democratic system, the others have to vote to carry them. (Steak has not come up yet, but Soy Boy Not Dogs won in a landslide.)

Prices on most items are fairly low, though organic produce is almost always more expensive than supermarket produce. The food is labeled with one price — essentially what it costs wholesale — and a 20 percent markup is added to most items at the checkout aisle.

On a recent visit, a bag of Terra Chips, the potato-chip alternative that usually retails for $4 and up, cost $2.81. A five-pound bag of Eastern potatoes was $1.76, compared with an average of $2.09 in Manhattan stores in *The Times's* informal survey, and $1.43 for stores outside Manhattan.

The co-op has paid workers, but by and large it is the members who make the show go. In addition to paying a $100 deposit for inventory and other capital expenses, they must perform about three hours of service every four weeks, from checking identification cards at the entrance (only members are welcome) to mopping floors to watching toddlers in the store's child-care center. The penalty for skipping a shift is two makeup shifts. In the last few years, membership has grown an average of 17 percent annually, Mr. Holtz said, while sales have expanded by 20 percent, to an annual $7.2 million....

One organization, the Hudson Valley Federation of Food Cooperatives, reachable at (914) 473-5400, offers advice on how to set up food co-ops and can refer people to existing ones near them. Bruce Meltzer, the company's marketing director, said about 60 percent of its food is sold to co-ops similar to Ms. Steinberg's, also known as buying clubs; the minimum order is $400. In a bow to technology, the company will send free software to anyone who wants to scan price lists and place orders by computer. Additional information is available from the National Cooperative Business Association in Washington, at (800) 636-6222.

DuBois saw cooperativism among Afrikan Americans as the means by which the "...subtle but real ways the communalism of the African clan can be transferred to the Negro American group...." DuBois also recognized that in order for this to be realized and for other values crucial to Afrikan survival, liberation and high quality of life to be actualized, a unique and courageous, committed and creative, highly intelligent, visionary, yet practical leadership cadre must also be realized and activated on behalf of Afrikan peoples at home and abroad.

The Non-Profit Mode of Economic Development

One of the major reasons economic development is retarded in the Afrikan American community is because it seeks to finance that development using "standard American business practices", that is, by attempting to follow the same general business start-up and operational methods used by the White community. For example, in starting businesses Black entrepreneurs, like their White counterparts, may seek to start and finance their start-up and ongoing businesses by borrowing from banks and other financial institutions — usually White-owned — and by seeking the financial support of family and friends. The difficulties Black entrepreneurs incur in obtaining monies from financial institutions are too well known to be described here. The poverty, values and organization of Black families and friends often make it difficult for Black entrepreneurs to utilize them as financial resources for starting business enterprises. However, as demonstrated in the preceding section, other, more *appropriate* methods for financing economic development exist in the Afrikan American community. If it is to maximize its economic potential, the Afrikan American community must break its ordinary mind-set as to how economic development may be initiated, a mind-set conditioned by observing White American business practices. It must realize that the entrepreneurial practices which characterize the White community are not "standard", i.e., that they are the best or most appropriate means for developing and doing business in all economic contexts or communities without regard for wide differences in economic values, organizations, conditions and circumstances which characterize various national, cultural and ethnic communities. It is arguable that a major reason Black enterprise has had difficulty realizing its potential cannot be attributed, as is usually the case, to the absence of the "spirit of enterprise" in Black Americans, but may be due in part to having their spirits crushed after many failing attempts to develop their enterprises using "standard American (White) business practices" instead of creating and utilizing — *appropriate business practices* — practices based on the values and organization of the Afrikan American community and economy.

The racial discrimination practiced by White-owned financial institutions; the relative absence of large pools of financial capital under the control of Black-owned financial houses; and the relative poverty of Black families, together militate against Black economic development along the lines followed by White Americans. Afrikan American economic development, to be *appropriate development* given the prevailing economic conditions of the Afrikan American community, must be much more collective or cooperative in nature and spirit than is the case in the White community, a community of large, private (and public) financial institutions. The method used by the *Mom & Pop Convenience* Store in South Los Angeles, which was financed by $500,000 solicited directly from the community (discussed below), is one example of what we may refer to as an appropriate business practice in the Afrikan American community. This practice rests on the realization that the community itself is the best and most lucrative source of capital for Black enterprise and economic development. This approach provides an opportunity for all the individual and institutional members of the community to contribute to its economic development and well-being, no matter how small or large or in what form (some may contribute free or discounted labor, goods and services, skills and other helpful activities). Moreover, it provides the opportunity for more enterprises serving the community to be truly community owned.

A review of the early history of Black enterprise in America will demonstrate that much of the financing of community enterprises, e.g., the initial financing of banks, insurance companies, etc., was done through Black collectives such as Black churches and fraternal orders.

A major means for financing current Black enterprise may be achieved by developing enterprises as not-for-profit or non-profit corporations, or by establishing and operating a for-profit enterprise under the ownership of a non-profit corporation. It must be kept in mind that a non-profit corporation is not necessarily a poor or poverty-stricken organization, not necessarily an organization that does not generate a large cash flow or does not pay its officers and employees well. A large, wealthy Black Church, with its ministerial staff and other employees, demonstrates that a non-profit organization can generate large cash flows, maintain a well-paid staff and provide ample services.

> A not-for-profit corporation is defined basically as "a corporation, no part of the income of which is distributable to its members, directors or officers." This does not mean that a not-for-profit corporation cannot make money. In fact, both not-for-profit and business (for-profit) corporations may make money, but in figuring "profits," expenses are subtracted from the gross receipts the corporation takes in. In a not-for-profit corporation, the money that remains as "profits" after the payment of expenses may not be distributed to the corporation's members, directors, or officers, but must be applied to further the corporation's purposes or to expand its facilities. However, "reasonable compensation for services rendered" is a legitimate corporate "expense" to be subtracted from gross receipts in order to arrive at "profits," and salaries are one way in which members, directors, or officers may receive funds from a nonprofit corporation. (Another instance is if the corporation's purposes incidentally benefit members, directors, and officers as well as the other groups it serves (such as a director of a day-care center whose eligible child attends the center), or if the corporation dissolves and its assets are distributed to its members.)

A business corporation is strikingly different. While a nonprofit corporation may not issue stock or pay dividends, a business corporation may issue and sell a variety of instruments which evidence interests in itself, and may reward the holders of these interests with a portion of corporate profits.[2]

Thus, it is possible for not-for-profit corporations (such as churches, civic, social and professional organizations) to sponsor the establishment of retail and other business outlets through the raising of funds for such purposes from community, private, government, corporate sources and foundations who may receive tax deductions for their charitable contributions. This approach to establishing enterprises in the community would (1) allow for the raising of debt-free, interest-free funds for financing a business; (2) the establishment of community-owned businesses which would function as sources of employment and training for community youths and adults in entrepreneuring thereby reducing unemployment, crime and other social problems; (3) enhance community pride and self-esteem; (4) allow for the compensation of business managers and permanent staff commensurate with their counterparts who run the non-profit corporation's businesses, who run or own private businesses which are privately financed. (For example, a private store owner may really earn, say, $30,000 in income per year *after* raising money to start the business and paying his usual costs of doing and maintaining his business. Conversely, the manager of a similar business owned by a non-profit corporation may, earn the same income without having to be himself responsible for start-up and other costs of doing business as is the case with private business ownership); (5) allow the business to offer competitive or lower prices to its customers than its privately owned competitors due to possible lower overhead costs; and may (6) garner broad community consumer support because such support may be perceived by consumers to be a type of positive social action, as a means of contributing to the well-being of the community as a whole.

This approach need not be seen as designed to negate the development and growth of private enterprise in the community. In fact, such an approach may actually facilitate and support the development of private enterprise in the community. There is no reason why the Afrikan American nation should not construct a mixed economy, as is the case with many other nations.

Perhaps Black non-profit organizations can contribute to the development of Black, privately owned enterprises by initially

---

2. M. Diamond & J. Williams, *How To Incorporate: A Handbook for Entrepreneurs and Professionals* (New York: John Wiley & Sons, 1987), pp. 7-8.

financing, establishing and operating businesses, franchises and services themselves. After a period of stabilizing these firms, training and developing their managerial and operational personnel, and locating buyers, these organizations can then sell them to their employees or to qualified Black business persons interested in their purchase. Joint ventures with other organizations or private interests may also be pursued.

Black Church Organization Acquires Private Business. The full acquisition of The Church Insurance Partnership Agency Inc. (CIPA) on July 1, 1993, by the Congress of National Black Churches (CNBC) provides an example of how the acquisition and the operation of a private or semi-private enterprise by a non-profit corporation may occur. The CIPA was an independent, multi-line insurance agency prior to its complete acquisition by the CNBC. Established in 1984, CIPA, then jointly owned by the CNBC and Aetna Life and Casualty, provided insurance services to Black Churches across the nation.[3] While continuing to provide these and other services CIPA, now a wholly-owned subsidiary of The Church Management Services Corporation, a CNBC company, is according to the *New York Amsterdam News*, "the first African American commercial insurance company to be independently operated and jointly owned by the CNBC's eight member denominations." The CIPA, which relocated from Hartford, Connecticut to Washington, D.C. in order to centralize its operations, is engaged in the continuing development of a comprehensive line of products for churches, including property, casualty, life, retirement and disability insurance. In fact, the CNBC introduced a new line of property and casualty national insurance programs on January 1, 1994. CIPA demonstrates that Black non-profit agencies such as the organized, institutional Black Church can acquire and operate businesses which function to serve both its organizational interests and the interests of the Black community as a whole.

A CASE IN POINT
Community Organizations and Institutions:
The Struggle for Economic Democracy in South Afrika

At this point in time, not long after South Afrika's first nationwide, non-racial elections, Afrikan South Afrikans (Blacks) in the new multiethnic society suffer an unemployment rate of 25-50 percent.

---
3. "Black Churches acquire Ownership of Insurance Firm," *Amsterdam News*, 3/12/94.

Afrikan South Afrikans own 2% or less of the $210 billion capitalization on the Johannesburg Stock Exchange. Whites in South Afrika own or hold title to 86% of South Afrika's land while constituting just 13% of its total population, and own 90% of its economic wealth. This leaves the rest of Afrikan and "Colored" South Afrikans who constitute 87% of its total population with title to just 14% of its land and 10% of its wealth. As one leading Afrikan South Afrikan put it — "it's a recipe for revolution".

It is obvious that the gaining of political democracy, e.g., equal access to public accommodations by Afrikans, will not resolve potentially explosive racial and political conflicts which threaten to destabilize the whole South Afrikan nation unless and until economic democracy is also instituted for Afrikans. This simply means that ownership and control of South Afrika's wealth, land, economic resources and production must be equitably and proportionately shared between its White and non-white populations. Moreover, this means that Afrikans must, through individual, corporate, and institutional means not only found, buy and establish or expand new and existing businesses which operate in both the national and international economies, but must acquire high levels of equity in the major corporations and financial institutions now exclusively owned and controlled by Whites. Afrikan South Afrikans must form joint ventures and partnerships with major foreign corporations who wish to do business in the country.

However, given the virtual absence of paucity Black capital, the achievement of economic democracy for Afrikans faces overwhelming social and economic obstacles. New or unusual methods for achieving economic democracy must be found. There are some indications that such approaches are being discovered and utilized. For example, Afrikan South Afrikan, Donald Ncube, a former executive and board member of Anglo-American, South Afrika's largest conglomerate, assembled an unusual group of investors to acquire Black majority ownership of African Life, a formerly White-owned insurance company which caters essentially to the Black market. Ncube acquired 51% of the company by going to *"black organizations that control money and assets but are outside the traditional financial markets. They include trade unions, church groups, trusts and Stokvels or community pools of money that were set up to allow blacks to get around the lack of bank financing"*[4] [Emphasis added]. The purchase of a majority stake in African Life by the consortium of Black institutional investors led by Ncube, "marks a breakthrough in

---

4. "Blacks Enter South African Boardrooms," *Wall Street Journal*, March 3, 1994.

black empowerment because it brings existing black capital into the mainstream economy" (WSJ, 3/3/94). This cooperative venture which places ownership of a major social and economic asset for a buying price of 160 million rand ($50 million U.S.) in the hands of a broad cross-section of the Black working community, sets an exemplary standard for Afrikans across the diaspora, especially Afrikan Americans. Adrian Arnott, African Life's outgoing chairman, speaks to the possibilities of this approach when he was quoted as noting that "This is a new sort of alliance between business and the black community that I'd like to think is a strategic coup" (WSJ, ibid). The work of Ncube and his investors provides a fine example of an investment approach that can be very productively utilized by the pooling of community and institutional capital in the Afrikan American community. These pooled capital resources may be used to purchase and invest in already well-established business firms at home and abroad.

While Ncube's approach is instructive, other indigenous South Afrikan-led investor groups or consortia are also providing examples for achieving economic democracy through acquiring control of previously White-dominated companies. Dr. Nthato Motlana, M.D., Nelson Mandela's personal physician, led a group of investors in acquiring 10% of Metropolitan Life and in acquiring a majority interest in the *Sowetan*, a newspaper from the Argus media group (WSJ, ibid). The *Sowetan* is South Afrika's largest daily newspaper, with a circulation of about 225,000. Ninety-nine percent of its readership is Black, and before its acquisition by Afrikan investors was 100%-owned by the white Argus Group. Dr. Motlana's group, Prosper Africa Group, has also acquired a 20% share of a new cellular telephone venture valued at $29 million. It must be noted that Dr. Motlana's approach to acquiring significant and majority interests in previously White-owned companies is highly controversial in the South Afrikan community, especially because he achieved those ends without putting up his own money and because Argus still retains a major role in the *Sowetan*. The Motlana group's purchase of their 20% share of the cellular phone venture was "financed in part by a soft loan from the Industrial Development Corp. and in part by banks and other partners (WSJ, ibid). In fact, Dr. Motlana's group acquired 52% of the *Sowetan* by swapping part of its cellular stake with Argus.

Another controversial transaction involving deals made by an Afrikan South Afrikan investment group with major White corporations is that made by Thebe Investment Corporation. *Business Week* describes the transactions of Thebe Corporation thusly:

A few local deals are stirring up controversy, however. Thebe Investment Corp., headed by Vusi Khanyile, former head of the African National Congress finance division, was established by a trust fund headed by Nelson Mandela and other ANC leaders. Critics charge that it is unfairly dominating the shift to black entrepreneurship, first with an educational-publishing deal with Macmillan Boleswa, a Swaziland-based Macmillan unit that had a lock on the schoolbook market in much of southern Africa. Thebe received 25% of equity in the company in return, it seemed to critics, for little more than a channel of communication to the ANC's education honchos.

Subsequent Thebe deals haven't quieted fears that its main strategy is to enter spheres where government licensing is required. Already, it plans to take over from South African Airways, the state-owned airline, in partnership with a group led by the former CEO of Canada's Air Ontario. And it's getting a foothold in one of the two lucrative cellular phone networks scheduled to start Mar. 31.

Khanyile says Thebe's goal is to advance black economic empowerment and that opposition to Thebe is orchestrated by political opponents. But Mandela has personally acknowledged the problem, telling businesspeople at an election campaign meeting recently that the ANC was seriously contemplating breaking its links with Thebe soon.[5]

While the business deals of Dr. Motlana's Prosper Africa Group, and Vusi Khanyil's Thebe Investment Corp. stir controversy, it must be kept in mind that their approaches, in very good part, reflect the problem of the lack of sufficient Black capital with which to finance business deals along more conventional lines. These deals and others like them that have led to cries of tokenism and opportunism by their critics, indicate the aggravating presence of a dilemma faced by a Black nation seeking to achieve economic democracy without sufficient capital of its own. The *Wall Street Journal* aptly describes the dilemma which faces Afrikan South Afrikan investors.

Charges of Tokenism

But the trend is controversial. Buyers are accused of tokenism; sellers are viewed as opportunists. "Quite frankly, it's largely a situation in which persons who have a certain amount of political clout are using money they don't have to acquire businesses they probably won't run," says Stephen Friedman, director of the Center for Policy Studies.

The controversy reflects a quandary surrounding these transactions. How can blacks expand their economic muscle when apartheid

---

5. "The Color of Money is Starting to Change," *Business Week*, 3/14/94.

has deprived them of the means to build up capital to do so? And when they manage to leapfrog obstacles — obtaining soft loans that can be repaid with dividends from their investments, for example — they're accused of getting favors because of their race or political connections.

"It's a Catch-22," says Frank Kilbourn, manager of corporate finance at Standard Merchant Bank, which has been active in the black empowerment trend. "If you don't want to be accused of tokenism, you don't do anything that isn't strictly commercial. And since they don't have capital, if you don't want to do something that isn't strictly commercial, you end up doing nothing. You have to find ways to cross the bridge from nonparticipation to capitalism."

The other alternative to capitalistic approaches utilized by Afrikan South Afrikan investment groups to achieve economic democracy in Black-led South Afrika would certainly include heavy government intervention into the economy in the interest of economic justice for Afrikans, e.g., the confiscation and redistribution of previously White-owned assets to the majority Black population, or nationalization of all or large parts of the economy under an Afrikan South Afrikan government. Both these alternatives have thus far been rejected by the Afrikan National Congress, led by Nelson Mandela.

Afrikan Americans face similar problems in their pursuit of economic democracy as those faced by Afrikan South Afrikans, though not near as acute. The fact must be accepted that if social rebellion stemming from the painful absence of economic justice and democracy is to be averted in both situations, some form of "socialization" of the national wealth will have to occur. If the nationalization of wealth is unacceptable to both Blacks and Whites or if reparations are unacceptable by Whites, then a form of less satisfactory, but more expedient, "concessionary capitalism or financing" will have to be undertaken. An instance of concessionary financing or "concessionary-like" financing is that of Dr. Motlana's group having been provided with "soft" loans in order to purchase shares in a very profitable growing concern or a new venture which is expected to be highly lucrative (e.g., the cellular telephone venture) and repaying the loans with earned dividends gained from ownership of or equity in the concern or venture. A general concessionary agreement may give to the grantee the right, or make it possible for the grantee or lender to exploit or purchase certain (potentially) profitable assets placed at his disposal by a business or government for a sum consisting of a minimal payment plus (perhaps) a percentage of the income from returns. Concessionary loans to groups or institutions in the Afrikan

American community would possibly allow them to purchase relatively large or significant shares in large or high growth potential corporations, loans which may be repaid from the group's or institution's own monetary resources, or from earnings or sales of the purchased assets. Outright grants would allow the purchase of shares or equity with minimal or no repayment.

However, it is important to note the most common means by which Afrikans are getting a foothold in the mainstream South Afrikan economy. *Business Week* magazine (3/14/94) describes it this way:

> *BIGGEST PUSH.* While some black-led consortiums have begun to buy up business stakes, the more common route to black ownership so far is through joint-venture deals with foreign, mostly U.S., corporations seeking to reestablish a presence in the country they left in the tumultuous 1980s. Digital Equipment Corp. returned to Johannesburg last year to sell workstations. Apple Computer Inc. is in the process of setting up a sales office with some black partners.
>
> The biggest push is toward deals in consumer goods. First, Nike Inc. announced it was contracting a Soweto-based business group to produce leisurewear and distribute footwear through 400 outlets in South Africa in a deal worth $6 million. Then came the Reebok deal. Although the initial capital injection is just a little more than $1 million, the new partners see scope for rapid expansion and even manufacturing, creating as many as 450 jobs.

What we find of interest here is the apparent willingness of certain American-based multinational corporations to enter into joint-venture deals or partnerships with Black South African groups while they have demonstrated little or no interest in making such deals with Black Americans. We have noted that joint-venture deals have been entered into by a few of the corporations with American Indian nations. This suggests the issue as to whether or not these concessions to Black South Afrikans and to American Indians may be in large part due to the fact that they are citizens of, or are, nations; that they control access to markets and territory; that they are represented by a legitimated governing body or leadership establishment which is supported by a loyal constituency; that their markets are not totally or non-resistantly open for exploitation by outsiders. This further suggests that since Black Americans are not perceived as a cohesive nation, as exercising territorial or market prerogatives under the governance of a recognizable and respected leadership establishment and since the Black American community is not organized along the lines of a quasi-nation, major corporations and businesses owned by aliens feel they have no need to enter into mutually profitable joint ventures with its members, groups and institutions who constitute that community. Therefore, the community is merely exploited by the alien businesses who do business with or in it while contributing little or nothing to its social well-being. If alien businesses, then, were forced to deal with an Afrikan American nation their economic and social outcomes would be markedly different from what they are today and much more beneficial to the Afrikan American community.

A Note on Concessionary Financing

Concessionary financing has a long history in the United States, spanning some four hundred years. In concessionary financing, for example, the government commonly concedes or gives certain grantees the right to exploit natural resources placed at their disposal in return for minimal payments and/or some relatively minimal return on sales or earnings. The government may grant franchises which allows for the exclusive operation of a public utility in a specified area (Kristein, 1969). Recall that the federal government in 1850 began a massive land grant program for private railroads which eventually totaled over 130 million acres containing billions of dollars of petroleum and mineral reserves. The railroads disposed of these lands through the selling and leasing of real estate. They also profited by selling timber and other resources found on the land. The government leases public lands today to private companies for the exploration of oil, gas, and other minerals for absurdly minimal rates, leaving the companies to reap enormous profits at public expense. Currently, government contract awards to private enterprises amount to more than $3 trillion and are major sources of sales, revenues, and profits for those enterprises. A report in the *New York Times* (5/17/94) titled "Forced, U.S. Sells Gold Land for Trifle" substantiates this statement, as the following citation shows.

> WASHINGTON, May 16 — Acting under a mining law it hopes Congress may soon change, the Clinton Administration today reluctantly granted a Canadian-based company the right to mine Nevada gold worth billions of dollars without ever paying royalties.
>
> But it did so only under a direct order from a Federal judge. The company, American Barrick Resources, paid the Federal Government just $9,765 to take title to about 1,949 acres of publicly owned land at its Goldstrike mines in Elko, Nev. The mines hold 30 million ounces of gold.
>
> The company recently won a court order forcing the Administration to sell the land for about $5 an acre, the kind of deal that mining companies have long been entitled to under the Mining Act of 1872.

Congress is considering legislation to charge royalties of up to 8 percent on minerals taken from publicly owned land. But Barrick has now escaped that possibility. Royalties over the years might have cost the company hundreds of millions of dollars....

Aside from the immense potential wealth involved, with gold selling at $380 an ounce, the transaction completed today was not unusual.

Prompted by the fear of changes in the law, hundreds of mining companies have filed applications under the existing law to obtain title to their proven claims for no more than $5 an acre.

The Mining Act of 1872, signed by President Ulysses S. Grant, was meant to provide an incentive for the settlement of the West.

It has not been substantially changed since then. So while the states and private landowners routinely charge royalties for mining on their property, the Federal Government does not charge for hard-rock minerals like gold, silver, copper, platinum and uranium. In contrast, coal, oil and gas companies must pay royalties to mine or drill on Federal land....

Any company, or for that matter any individual prospector, can stake a claim on Federal land and mine metals there virtually free of charge. And if they like, the claimholders can patent the land, buying it outright from the Government for no more than $5 an acre.

The government not only grants concessions of the sort just mentioned, but often aids private ventures in financing some of their business undertakings by underwriting some of their business activities, and in other ways, such as protecting them against certain risks and competition.

Concessions similar to those granted by governments may be granted by private enterprises. For example, a corporation may grant an entrepreneur a franchise to sell or distribute products and/or services it produces in a certain area on very favorable terms. The corporation may not only assume most of the burden of promotion but may use its own credibility to help obtain or underwrite loans given to the entrepreneur in helping him to finance his franchise. This type of arrangement may occur in the outright purchase of a property from a corporation by an entrepreneur.

An example of concessionary financing is provided by the NAACP's fair share agreement. The NAACP helps Black entrepreneurs achieve ownership of franchises and favorable purchasing, marketing, finance, banking and insurance services through its fair-share agreements with various franchisers, corporations and government contractors. The NAACP's fair-share agreement in 1993 with the Flagstar Companies, the parent of Denny's, provided for an increase in Black employees, Black ownership and management of Denny's restaurants as well as the increased use of Black subcontractors. This agreement is said to be worth $1 billion to the Afrikan American community (NYT, 8/31/93 – "The NAACP means Business"). Specifically, Flagstar "agreed with the NAACP to invest $1 billion over seven years to double the number of Denny's franchises owned by minorities, add hundreds of African-American managers and sharply increase purchasing from minority enterprises" (WSJ, 3/11/94 – "Denny Begins Repairing Its Image and Its Attitude").

Box 30-1 Corporations vs Proprietorships

America is a corporate culture. This means it is dominated economically and politically by its corporations and their elite leaders. As Bazelon (1963) intimates, "America was founded by colonizing corporations which subsequently became state governments." Quoting political scientist Earl Latham, he further notes that "the basic form of the public government in America derived from the provenance of a commercial corporation."

The stock corporation is essentially designed to engage in risk-sharing ventures by guaranteeing limited personal liability for its owners or investors; to accumulate and organize and direct relatively large quantities of monetary, material and human capital in more or less circumscribed technological and market areas. The corporate approach allows a group of investors to enter into rather risky but potentially very profitable ventures with a good degree of self-confidence and an increased possibility for success. Observing the ability of corporations to organize and direct large masses of men and productive capital in rather limited areas or markets, Bazelon suggested "that a corporation is a form of industrial or technological or financial government." He goes on to assert that:

> The corporate order is a system of *private* government. This privacy, however, is not to be comprehended in terms of private property or the private discretion of individuals. The corporate order is largely private *from* — from public accountability, whether indirectly through that other national government or directly to any of its various constituencies. The rulers of the corporate system are not elected by anybody, and they are not answerable for the exercise of their more important powers to any elected officials. The privacy of this private government serves mainly to ensure its authoritarian nature — it has nothing to do with the free action of individuals, which is what most of us usually think of when the word "private" is used. Professor Edward S. Mason, one of our leading authorities on the corporate system, has suggested that the corporation was inevitable because of

the enlarged "entrepreneurial discretion" the form allows — meaning the capacity to command large groups of men and materials toward a particular purpose, much the same as in an army. And like an army, the individual corporation is (except in very rare instances) a one-party state. In other areas of government, we have no difficulty in recognizing this as a feature of dictatorship; it is only the studied absence of clear thinking that keeps us from recognizing the political fact in this area. The significance of these authoritarian centers for our otherwise somewhat democratic order is sharpened when we note, for instance, that Peter Drucker has called the few hundred business enterprises dominating the American economy "the only meaningful units of local government."

Further attesting to their essential authoritarianism, the really important activities of private corporate governments are not governed by any constitution.[6]

The corporate culture includes great centers of private power and is the most active and influential political center of political life in America. Major corporations are the centers of power around which and by means of which markets are organized; centers of power around which are gathered and organized thousands of dependent and interdependent affiliated enterprises (Berle, 1963). The relatively limited role played by the government in the corporate system provides the basis for the fact that influential corporations make decisions which affect the socioeconomic and political character of locales, regions and nations in ways which often far exceed the scope of their ownership and economic interests. In light of the development of large trading blocs – e.g., the European Union, the North American Free Trade Association, the trading nations of South-eastern Asia, Japan, and the accords ratified during the most recent General Agreement on Tariffs and Trade – it seems safe to suggest that multinational corporations may at some point exercise power which will exceed the sovereignty of "autonomous" nation-states. For many of these entities this is already the case.

Hence, in view of the power of corporations in both private and public life, in both the economic and political life of America and the world, if Afrikan Americans and Afrikan-descended peoples are to exercise persuasive power and influence in these areas, they must found and develop and gain significant equity in both small and large corporations.

According to current business statistics, approximately 94% of Black-owned enterprises are sole proprietorships. At 3 percent, partnerships are the next most frequent type of business organization. Three percent of Black-owned firms are sole corporations, meaning they are owned by 30 or fewer shareholders. The sole proprietorship is the oldest form of business organization wherein a single individual provides capi-

---

6. Ibid.

tal, management, control and ownership of a business under his or her sole direction. A partnership is created by the mutually written or oral agreement of two or more persons as to the co-ownership of a business for profit. As delineated by Kristein, the general advantages and disadvantages of the ownership, operation, and management of sole proprietorships, partnerships and corporations are as follows:

Operation, Ownership, and Management. In the operation of a business, certain advantages and disadvantages of the sole proprietorship result from one-man control of the firm. Advantages include the fact that the proprietor is spurred on by the impetus of personal incentive; his affairs are secret; and he has great flexibility in making decisions in regard to the location, policies, and activities of the business. Disadvantages generally include the owner's lack of interested advisers and helpers; difficulty in transferring ownership; and the fact that desired permanence of the business depends upon his continued effectiveness. It is easy to dissolve a sole proprietorship, but one may well question whether an amount anywhere near to the going-concern value is likely to be obtained.

The partnership, like the sole proprietorship, benefits from strong motivation of the partners and from the pooling of their abilities to facilitate efficient management. But there is some disadvantage in the loss of secrecy and in diminished flexibility, because of divided authority, although the latter may be avoided in part by a carefully drawn partnership agreement. Like the sole proprietor, each partner is responsible for all debts of the business. The partnership may be dissolved by any of the following circumstances: mutual agreement, withdrawal of a partner, death, insanity, bankruptcy of a partner, bankruptcy of the business, stated termination in the agreement, court order, or war between the nations of the partners. As in the case of the sole proprietorship, dissolution usually involves a considerable loss in the value of the business, a disadvantage offset only in part by partnership insurance and plans for succession.

The advantages of the corporate form in this area center around the permanence of the organization, the ease of transferring and realizing on one's investment by selling the securities representing ownership in established markets (thus allowing for easy transfer of property to heirs without liquidation), and the ability to employ professional management and give it a direct interest in the success of the business. The disadvantages lie in the lack of flexibility, of adaptability, and of personal incentive; and the care with which the charter must be drawn in order to carry on the business effectively and prevent *ultra vires* acts (acts not authorized by provisions of the charter which may lead to suits by stockholders or third parties). The dissolution of large corporations is a complicated legal matter.[7]

Greenberg correctly points out that "the corporation is a form of organization different from other forms of business enterprise." He goes on to point out two of the especially important features of the corporation.

1. The corporation is considered a person with unlimited life span in the eyes of the law, and as a "person" it has the ability to buy and sell, sue and be sued, hire and fire, and so on. This gives it tremendous flexibility and continuity compared to other forms of business enterprise.
2. In the small proprietorship, the owner is liable to an unlimited extent for all small business losses. He may be forced to sell home and possessions to settle business debts. The corporation, on the other hand, has the advantage of *limited liability*. No investor is liable for more than his initial investment, and as a result, the corporation is a more attractive investment than the single proprietorship or partnership. Limited liability allows the corporation to attract backers more easily and to accumulate capital. Limited liability is the basis for almost unlimited capital accumulation, and helps account for the staggering growth in the size of corporations. The growth is of such magnitude, in fact, that in the relatively short span of a century and a half American society has been transformed from an economy of small businesses and widespread proprietorship, to one in which the bulk of economic activity is conducted by a relative handful of firms. Measured in terms of gross receipts, for instance, corporations account for about 80 percent of all business activity, though they comprise but 10 percent of all business firms. The growth of corporations has been so spectacular that there remains no doubt that today they dominate the American economy whether measured in terms of capital, production, investment, new products, consumer impact, or employment.[8]

The Limited Liability Partnership

The major disadvantage of a regular partnership — where each partner is held personally liable if the business partnership is sued or where the negligent action of one partner jeopardizes all the partners — may be legally avoided in many states. The limited liability company or partnership is designed to assure or protect the personal assets of each partner if their business is sued. Only the assets of their busi-

---
7. Marvin Kristein, *Corporation Finance* (New York: Barnes & Noble, 1969).
8. Greenberg, *Serving the Few*, pp. 36-37.

ness can be placed at risk. With limited liability partnership, professionals can be held responsible for their own actions or negligence but not those of partners.

More than 40 states, with the major exception of California, have enacted laws which allow limited liability partnerships. This privilege is often extended to sole proprietorships as well. With the limited liability format, the professional's dread of putting the homes and life savings of all the partners at risk is eased should a partner be wrongfully accused of negligence or malfeasance or loses a suit where he or she must pay the accuser huge awards.

The limited liability format provides the same tax advantages as does the regular partnership. It also carries the same tax benefits as an "S" corporation — with taxes assessed only at the individual level. With both the regular partnership and the limited liability partnership, profits and losses flow directly to partners. Consequently, the double taxation related to corporate earnings are avoided. The advantage of the limited liability format for the sole proprietorship resides in the fact that in the case of lawsuits the person or company suing can only go after the assets of the business, not the personal assets of the owner. The most widespread use of this format will probably occur in real estate businesses where unavoidable accidents can prove financially disastrous for the real estate investor. ■

Investment Banking

New corporations are primarily funded through the selling of stock certificates or stocks. Stock certificates provide legal evidence of the number of shares of corporate stock owned by the stockholder. Through the purchase of capital stock, stockholders provide the corporation with its financial means of production in the expectation that the continuing growth and prosperity of the business will pay them acceptable or high dividends and will enhance the value of their ownership shares. Established and ongoing corporations may obtain funds to finance further growth and expansion, reorganization and other business activities, from profits they have retained and other internal sources; from loans, mortgages and other liabilities as well as the sale from new issues of corporate securities, i.e., of various classes of stocks and bonds. These securities are commonly sold to individual and institutional investors in the capital markets, e.g., the over-the-counter market, the New York, American, and other stock exchanges. They may also be sold through private placement, that is, sold by private negotiation directly to individual investors, corporate investors, insurance companies, commercial banks and pension funds.

The purchaser of a stock certificate issued by a corporation owns a share of that organization proportionate to his ownership of all the common stock outstanding and has the right to vote in the selection of corporate officers. He also shares in any dividends declared by the corporate board of directors.

The bondholder through his purchase of corporate bonds is simply lending money to a corporation. "A bond is a credit instrument whereby the corporation attains money (or property or services) from the investing public in exchange for a promise to pay a stipulated rate of interest at specified intervals in a specific way and to repay the principal at a set time.[9] Unlike stockholders, bondholders have no vote and no influence on the management. Bonds are sold by institutions, governments, agencies, corporations, and the like when they need to raise cash for business or for other economic purposes. In buying bonds, the bondholder becomes a creditor because he, she, or it (institutions and organizations purchase bonds also) has by doing so, loaned money to the company, institution or government. According to the *Wall Street Journal*, "As of 1987, about 80% of all money borrowed by corporations was accomplished through bond issues."[10]

The Role of Investment Banks or Bankers. Our interest here more specifically concerns the role of investment banks or investment bankers in the financing and funding of corporations. Generally, an investment bank intermediates or "goes between" corporations and municipalities (who are looking to sell or issue securities in order to raise money to fund their operations) and their prospective investors. The investment bank advises both the sellers and buyers in the particulars of the issue before and after the sale. For the seller, it provides advice regarding such matters as pricing and/or the setting of interest rates. Moreover, it may act as both a broker and dealer, i.e., buying and selling securities for or to individual and institutional investors. The investment bank underwrites a new issue of securities by assuming the risk of buying the issue from a corporation or municipality thereby guaranteeing that it will receive a stipulated sum on a specified date. The bank seeks to quickly recoup its payments to the corporation or municipality by reselling the new issue to the investing public directly or through other dealers. The bank earns its profits from the difference in the price it pays for the corporate or municipal securities it purchases and the price it receives from selling them to investors.

In sum, the primary functions of investment banks or bankers include the following:

---

9. Kristein, 1969.

10. R. Warman, A. Siegel & K. Morris, *Guide to Understanding Money and Markets* (New York: Access Press, 1990).

His knowledge of corporation finance and the money market enables the investment banker to channel a portion of the savings of the economy into corporate-investment projects which he judges to be worthwhile in terms of their potential profitability. Thus he helps to make the market in which he transacts business a more responsive and efficient allocating mechanism.

From the point of view of corporate management, the competent investment banker (1) guarantees the receipt of long-term investment funds in the amount and at the time needed; (2) provides efficient distribution of new securities to the public by "placing them well" (among investors instead of speculators), thus aiding future financing; (3) gives specialized financial advice and market support for a new issue; and (4) may provide continuing financial advice and assistance.

From the point of view of the investing public, a dependable investment banker (1) investigates carefully the corporations whose securities are being offered; (2) provides sound investment advice (he cannot, of course, guarantee success) appropriate to the financial position and outlook of the investor; (3) gives the investor assurance that the security has been properly and legally issued and contains appropriate protective provisions; and (4) may organize "protective committees" of investors if the issue or the corporation becomes involved in difficulties such as reorganization and bankruptcy.[11]

We have indicated that in addition to underwriting and selling corporate and institutional securities investment banks underwrite and sell government securities as well. Specifically, investment bankers may use their financial expertise to manage and market government bond sales. Federal, state and municipal bonds are issued by the federal, state and local governments to finance past and present government deficits as well as to finance government-sponsored projects. These securities are also sold to wealthy individuals and institutions and to the general public via mutual funds which include government securities in their portfolios.

Black-owned Investment Banks. The managing and marketing of government bonds, as is the case with corporate securities, form a very big and lucrative market. For example, some $278.3 billion of municipal securities were sold in 1992.[12] Blacks, women, and minority-owned investment banks, of which only six are among the top 25 underwriters of long-term and short-term municipal bonds sold

---

11. M. Kristein, *Corporation Finance*, 1969.

12. Note: "States, cities, counties and towns issue bonds to pay for a wide variety of publicly beneficial projects – schools, highways, stadiums, sewage systems, bridges, and many others." *The Wall Street Journal: Guide to Understanding Money and Markets*, 1990.

in 1992, participated in only 7.5 percent of 868 offerings that year. It is interesting and disturbing to note that Black-owned investment bankers who possess the necessary expertise and good track records (though their capitalization is relatively small) have yet to be taken seriously, to have their abilities and the experience of their top people acknowledged. This is particularly puzzling in face of the fact that a number of large cities such as New York City, Washington, D.C., Atlanta, Detroit, Chicago, and others have established special programs and policies ostensibly beneficial to minority firms, and are headed by Afrikan American mayors or include a significant number of Afrikan Americans as top government officials. Since being politically well connected is an important part of garnering contracts from government, it is implicit that the failure of Black-owned investment banks to capture more municipal business speaks to weaknesses in Afrikan American political and economic organization, cohesion, and ethnocentrism.

As implied by Kristein's comments cited above, the major value of investment bankers to the community is their knowledge of corporate finance and of the money market; their functional ability to help direct a portion of the community's savings into worthwhile and potentially profitable projects which benefit both investors and the community at large. It is in this light that the increase in the number, size, and influence of investment banks are to be encouraged in the Afrikan American and the Pan–Afrikan communities. Obviously, Black-owned financial institutions which can facilitate the selling of the securities of Black-owned corporations to well-placed Black individual and institutional investors as well as a wholesome mix of non-Black investors are sorely needed in the community. This is particularly the case for corporations making initial public offerings — the first offer by a company to sell its stock certificates or bonds in order to fund and finance its business activities.

Afrikan American investment bankers are beginning to make deep and impressive inroads in public finance, particularly since 1993. That year two of the top 15 Black investment banks senior-managed, i.e., led in the underwriting, managing and marketing of the issuance of new securities by setting their terms and deciding how they will be distributed for sale, more than $1.6 billion worth of deals (*Black Enterprise*, 1994). For example, the second largest Black-owned investment bank, Grigsby Brandford and Co. Inc., beat out top-ranking Goldman Sachs and Co. to lead-manage a $503 million refinancing of the Los Angeles Convention and Exhibition Center. This was the largest municipal bond deal in Los Angeles history. The fourth largest Black-owned investment bank, WR Lazard & Co., became the first minority firm to lead a sale of New York City securities to the public (BE, 6/94). *Black Enterprise* (6/94) further reported the following regarding the four largest Black-owned investment banks:

> In 1993, the nation's 300 largest investment banks underwrote 13,529, or 99.9%, of all new long-term municipal issues, excluding private placements and nonprofit issues, worth $288.4 billion. Four black firms — Pryor, McClendon, Counts & Co. Inc. (PMC); M.R. Beal & Co.; Grigsby Brandford; and WR Lazard — were among the top 70 banks leading 79 issues worth $4.38 billion.

The largest Black-owned investment bank, Pryor, McClendon, Counts & Co. Inc., led all minority firms in lead-managing 13 deals worth $1.665 billion, thereby ranking 15th "among the nation's long-term municipal new issue underwriters, participating in 270 transactions totaling $36.3 billion" (BE, 6/94). A part of PMC's business in 1993 included making a $6 million deal for facilities at Tougaloo College, a historically Black institution located near Jackson, Miss. PMC led the largest sale ever by a minority firm when in 1993 it sold $823 million worth of tax revenue bonds for Pennsylvania Intergovernmental Cooperation Authority.

Box 30-2   Why Blacks Should Own Government Securities

While impressive strides were made in public finance by Black-owned investment banks, several of these institutions derived most of their income from managing and marketing corporate-related and/or taxable fixed-income business despite resistance from the institutionalized racism of the industry and mainstream investment banks.

Besides encouraging the development of investment banks who can manage and market government securities, the Afrikan American general public and institutional public should be encouraged to invest heavily and as prudently as possible in government securities. This should be the case not only because of the tax benefits which ownership of such securities confer (gains from many such securities are generally not taxed) but also because Afrikan Americans can own and profit from owning the debt that their taxes, and frequent job cuts during municipal debt crises, are utilized to pay. It must be kept in mind that the bulk of municipal debt in the form of municipal bonds is owned by wealthy White American individuals, large White American-owned banks and financial institutions who earn large tax-free incomes from increased taxes paid by urban Black workers, urban businesses and institutions to service the interest on municipal debt. At times when the debt of cities with large or majority Black populations cannot be paid through regular tax collection, it is paid through cutting costs by reducing municipal and state budgets, by the firing of Black municipal workers, and the cutting of services of vital institutions such as hospitals and schools, as well as by increasing the tax burdens of Black and other minority citizens. Consequently, Black Americans are further impoverished, underserved and exploited by wealthy White American individual, corporate, and institutional investors. Further deterioration of the urban Afrikan American community in this fashion can only be relieved by the growth of urban tax bases through the increased ownership of businesses and the increased creation of jobs and wealth by Black Americans themselves, in addition to the increased ability of individual Black American investors, Black-owned banks and financial institutions, pension funds, and other institutions to purchase and own city and government debt — debt that they would then owe more to themselves than to others. ◘

The Struggle to Maintain True Black Ownership of Black-owned Investment Banks. The decree by many Government agencies that some of the bonds they issue be sold by minority-owned brokerage firms has obviously benefitted Black-owned securities businesses. We have already alluded to the benefits these firms could gain from the increased presence of Blacks in mayoral and other high administrative offices across the country. It is estimated that as a partial result of these two situations some 300 minority-owned brokerage firms have been established (*New York Times*, 8/11/94). Together they have garnered a significant share of the $2 billion in fees earned from selling public securities. The phenomenal growth of Black and minority-owned firms in the public securities industry seems now to have stimulated a "white brokers' backlash", that is, a reactionary effort on the part of White-owned brokerage firms to recapture some of their lost business from minority-owned firms by methods which when not nefarious, or illegal, are certainly dangerous to the health of the Black securities industry. The *New York Times* (8/11/94) recently revealed some of the methods utilized by big firms to take business slated for minorities.

> Now, Wall Street firms, among them Merrill Lynch and Bear Stearns and regional brokerages are finding ways to capture some of this business for themselves. They are buying stakes in minority-owned firms, enabling them to profit from these set-aside programs too.
> It is a trend that troubles many independent well-established minority-owned firms. They say that they are losing business to these new competitors, who are perverting the intent of affirmative action.

The Black Enterprise 15 Largest Black-owned Investment Banks

RANK	COMPANY	Senior-Managed Issues* (Millions of dollars)	Co-Managed Issues* (Billions of dollars)
1	Pryor, McClendon, Counts & Co. Inc.	$1,665.0	$42.4
2	Grigsby Brandford & Co. Inc.	$1,651.1	$30.0
3	M.R. Beal & Co.	$575.0	$23.6
4	WR Lazard & Co.	$492.4	$33.6
5	The Chapman Co.	$33.1	$5.0
6	Howard Gary & Co.	$15.5	$3.9
7	Charles A. Bell Securities Corp.	$14.4	$2.8
8	Weldon, Sullivan, Carmichael & Co.	$9.4	$0.7
9	Apex Securities Inc.	**	$7.1
10	Utendahl Capital Partners L.P.	**	$5.6
11	United Daniels Securities Inc.	**	$3.9
12	Sturdivant & Co. Inc.	**	$1.7
13	Ward & Associates Inc.	**	$0.9
14	Doley Securities Inc.	**	$0.8
15	Rideau Lyons & Co. Inc.	**	$0.7

*This is for all issues including municipal, agency, corporate and mortgage-backed securities for the year ending Dec. 31, 1993.
**These investment banks did not participate as senior managers for municipal, agency, corporate and mortgagee-backed securities for the year ending Dec. 31, 1993.
Source: Securities Data Co. Inc., Newark, NJ. 1994. Adapted from *Black Enterprise*, June 1994.

Table 30–1

"Women and minority firms built from scratch on a shoestring are now up against firms that are a quasi-subsidiary or arm of major underwriting firms," said Robert B. Lamb, a professor at the Stern School of Business at New York University, who plans to publish a study on minority-owned firms.

B.E. 15 Largest Black-owned Investment Companies (updated)

Rank	Company	Senior-Managed Issues* (Millions of dollars)	Co-Managed Issues* (Billions of dollars)
1	Utendahl Capital Partners	2,800.000	2.400
2	Rideau Lyons & Co. Inc.	1,118.180	0.058
3	M.R. Beal & Co.	612.133	18.200
4	Apex Securities Inc.	494.735	2.605
5	Jackson Securities Inc.	337.000	2.000
6	Blaylock & Partners, L.P.	320.000	1,956
7	Pryor, McClendon, Counts & Co. Inc.	303.000	12.930
8	Howard Gary & Co.	250.893	1.516
9	SBK-Brooks Investment Corp	201.070	3.304
10	Powell Capital Markets Inc.	168.074	0.105
11	The Williams Capital Group, L.P.	125.000	2.850
12	Charles A. Bell Securities Corp.	121.300	0.215
13	The Chapman Co.	30.100	1,800
14	W.R. Lazard & Co.***	**	0.603
15	Doley Securities	**	0.450

*This is for all issues including municipal, agency, corporate and mortgage-backed securities for the year ending Dec. 31, 1996.
**These investment banks did not participate as senior managers for municipal, agency, corporate and mortgagee-backed securities for the year ending Dec. 31, 1996.
Source: Securities Data Co. Inc., Newark, N.J. 1994.
Adapted from *Black Enterprise*, June 1997.

Table 30–2

Among the most outspoken executives of established black firms is Napoleon Brandford 3d, vice chairman of Grigsby Brandford & Company, a black-owned firm in San Francisco. "African-American firms are an endangered species," he said. "This is an attempt to circumvent inclusion or prevent major African-American firms from getting to the next level. These are not minority firms."

The *Times* goes on to intimate that "about half of the 300 or so minority-owned firms are illegitimate." A large number of these firms are actually so-called "storefront" minority-firms which are small but politically well connected operations which more often than not, "have no employees, no ability to sell bonds and no intention of building a business." These "storefront" firms use their political connections to attain a portion of bonds they then hand over to Wall Street firms for a share of the profits when they are sold by these White-owned establishments. More ominous than this trend is the one which involves the situation where large Wall Street firms help to establish and take interest in Black-owned firms and use the influence they gain over them to win business from Federal agencies. Consequently, these White-owned companies compete unfairly against or undermine truly Black-owned brokerage firms. The *New York Times* (8/11/94) reports on two such cases involving presumably Black-owned firms.

> The most successful has been Merrill Lynch's investment in Utendahl Capital Partners headed by John O. Utendahl, an African-American and former Merrill Lynch trader. Merrill Lynch has invested $3 million and extended a $9.9 million line of credit for a 25 percent stake in Utendahl.
>
> In its first year Utendahl participated in underwriting syndicates that have sold $9.8 billion in Government mortgage-backed securities. Its assets have swollen to $13.9 million from $100,000, and its surplus capital, a rough indication of net worth, has reached $12.2 million.
>
> Merrill declined to discuss its involvement in Utendahl beyond describing it as a "passive, minority-ownership interest." A spokeswoman for Utendahl also declined to comment. But others are not so reticent.
>
> "It cloaks Merrill Lynch in minority status," said Harold E. Doley Jr., who is black and heads Doley Securities Inc., a brokerage firm. "It's as though these big firms are creating their own minority firms."
>
> **Resentment is Stirred**
> "I resent it," said Donald Rice, president and chief executive of GB Derivatives, an affiliate of Grigsby Brandford. "Merrill's relationship in not some uninvolved third party providing capital. This is an ongoing relationship. Merrill people sit on the Utendahl board. The original offices were at Merrill. It was established as a bit of a front."
>
> Bear Stearns invested $10 million for a 25 percent stake on Blaylock & Company, headed by Ronald Blaylock, who is black and

a former Paine Webber trader. "We're really independent of Bear Stearns on a day-to-day basis," Blaylock said. "But if they can help us they will."

The *Times* goes on to report that "Regional [White-owned] brokers are also embracing minority-owned firms to stanch the loss of business to them." It revealed that the Black-owned firm, Ward Associates of Atlanta, joined forces with the White-owned firm, J.C. Bradford and Company, to create Ward, Bradford & Company, "which is 40 percent owned by Bradford and 60 percent owned by Felker Ward, chief executive of Ward & Associates." Jackson Securities of Atlanta, whose chairman is former mayor Maynard Jackson, is 15 percent white-owned by Wheat First Butcher Singer Inc. of Richmond, Virginia. These and other partially white-owned Black firms may reasonably argue that their partnerships or alliances allow them to better weather market risks, increase the availability of capital and marketing clout. However, where such relationships involve mere influence-peddling by Black-owned firms for White firms, or the mere turning over of bonds Black-owned firms receive through set-asides or quota programs to their White cohorts without selling them on their own, they defeat the very purpose of set-aside programs. And more important, these pass-along Black-owned firms endanger the viability and existence of valid Black-owned firms. The *Times* provides an example of two minority-owned firms which are allegedly involved in questionable dealings with White-owned firms.

An S.E.C. Investigation

The S.E.C. is investigating reports of potential abuses involving minority-owned firms in at least three states – Louisiana, Florida and Georgia – as part of a larger investigation into political influence-peddling and questionable campaign contributions in municipal finance.

For instance, in Louisiana, the S.E.C. is investigating an arrangement in which a local minority-owned firm got $240,000 in fees from First Boston and Lazard Frères but sold no bonds. The two Wall Street firms said the payment was suggested by local politicians.

As another example, The S.E.C. is investigating AIBC Investment Services in Miami, partly owned by a Hispanic city commissioner, which received $350,000 last year without selling a single bond.

Robin L. Wiessman, a principal at Artemis Capital Group, speaks directly to the point when she is reported to have said that "The whole point of economic opportunity programs is to create a level field, ..." We are witnessing, an attempt by some White-owned brokerage firms in concert with some nominal Black-owned firms, to tilt the field in their favor and to the disfavor of their Black-owned counterparts.

Why We Are Concerned. We are concerned about the fortunes of Black-owned investment banks as individual firms and about Afrikan American investment bankers as individuals. However, our greatest concern is institutional. It is the investment bank as an institution for raising large sums of money to finance the founding, operation and expansion of socioeconomically productive corporations and socio-cultural institutions which benefit the community both materially and socially which concerns us most. If the Afrikan American and Pan–Afrikan communities are to grow, develop, and prosper economically, if they are to escape economic and political dependency and enter into trade relations with other communities as equals, then investment banks or institutions which function in similar ways, i.e., institutions which facilitate the community's ability to own and finance its own economic and cultural establishments, must be operationally founded in order to achieve these ends. And in order for them to follow the dictates of the community they must be owned by it and by members of the community who are responsive to its needs.

The Evolution of Black-owned Investment Banking. The current evolutionary direction of Black-owned investment banks parallels that of their White counterparts. Those White institutions began as buyers and sellers of Government securities. Economic historian Vincent Carosso informs us that starting after the Revolution, "The principal users of investment banking service were governments, which issued bonds to finance wars, new banks, internal improvements, and railroad companies — the Nation's first big enterprises." He goes on to reveal that "one of the earliest and most important" ancestors of the modern investment banker" was the "loan contractor," who bought securities to resell at a profit. Incorporated commercial banks also performed investment banking functions. The buying and selling of new and old securities to investors, both large and small, institutional and individual, at home and abroad, on the account of their investors or their own, made investment banks one of the most important institutions for fostering the growth of the preponderant American and European social and economic systems.

While before 1873 government and railroad bonds dominated the securities markets and were the primary, if not the only, business of investment bankers, corporate shares increasingly shared the markets thereafter. Carosso (1970) further informs us that "After

1870 innumerable family-owned enterprises organized themselves as corporations... Most of the capital for these large enterprises could not be supplied through reinvestment of earnings. The heads of these new industrial giants, like the railroad leaders before them, turned to investment bankers for the funds they required."

Parallel Road for Black-owned Investment Banks. We envision the evolutionary path of Black-owned investment houses to parallel those of White-owned houses. Beginning with the buying and selling of government securities — hopefully selling a very significant proportion of these to Black individual, institutional and mutual fund investors — we see Black-owned investment banks increasingly moving into the business of helping to finance the development of Black owned or controlled industrial facilities and combinations and providing Black-owned manufacturing companies and other industries with capital derived mainly from selling securities in the Afrikan worldwide community and the progressive communities of other ethnic groups.

We should note that Afrikan American investment banking institutions need not and do not confine their activities to the selling of the securities of federal, state and local governments, of American-owned, i.e., White-owned, businesses and institutions, and of Black-owned corporations. Black-owned investment banks may sell the securities of continental Afrikan and Afrikan-Caribbean governments and agencies, of corporations owned or controlled by the nationals of these locales, of joint-stock companies owned by Afrikan Americans and overseas Afrikans, and the like. Therefore, Black-owned investment institutions may provide the means by which Afrikans all over the world can help to finance the growth and stability of their national, governmental structures, institutions, industrial and service establishments.

Black-owned Investment Banking Syndication. The next major evolutionary milestone in the history of American investment banking and in American economic expansion was the creation and development of the syndicate during the late 1800s up to 1914. It was during these years that the United States was undergoing vast expansion "from an agricultural, rural, loosely organized country into an industrial, urban, and highly organized nation" (Carosso, ibid). In what Carosso refers to as "probably the most important and far-reaching change in their method of operations to be introduced after the Civil War," the investment banker adopted the syndicate in order to finance the vast economic expansion of the American economy. He relates that "Since many enterprises needed more than any single banker could command or dared to risk, investment bankers joined together in syndicates, as these groups came to be called, pooling their resources and talents and sharing the risk as widely as possible. They employed two types of syndicates: those that were used to float specific issues of securities and those that were used to put through a merger, from acquiring the component companies to placing the securities of the new corporations."

The formation of investment banking pools by Black-owned investment bankers will prove necessary to the rapid and expansive growth of Afrikan American and Pan-Afrikan corporations. Syndications of Black-owned investment banks may underwrite Black-owned national and multinational corporations, organize the merger of Black-owned corporations or their conglomeration as well as corporate takeovers and other industrial combinations which will enable Afrikan nations, communities and corporations to move into the front ranks of the world's most industrially and technologically advanced nations and peoples.

Harold E. Doley, Jr.: Black Pioneer In Investment Banking. Investment banker Harold Doley, Jr., CEO of New Orleans-based Doley Securities, Inc., is symbolic of both the pioneering past and future of Black investment banking and of Black entrepreneurialism in general. His current investment activities in Afrika give substance to our discussion of alliances, joint ventures and the like, between continental Afrikans and Afrikan Americans as means of achieving mutual prosperity and of constructing the Pan-Afrikan economic system.

Doley scored a first in Afrikan American history when twenty years ago he became the first Black person to buy a seat on the New York Stock Exchange. Only a broker whose firm is a member of a stock exchange can trade stocks on that exchange. The New York Stock Exchange is an unincorporated association of individuals and corporations and only its members can use its facilities to buy and sell its listed securities. Its member firms are said to hold *seats* on the exchange. Member firms such as Doley's firm, employ registered representatives, or "brokers," who transact business with the general public.

In 1993, Doley securities helped to underwrite more than $800 million in municipal, government and corporate issues (*New York Times*, 9/18/94). Doley successfully penetrated the lily-White "in-crowd" world of securities trading in 1976, by representing a full spectrum of individual, business and institutional accounts. A number of his institutional accounts included Black-owned insurance companies and historically Black universities and colleges. Doley accomplished these goals prior to the existence of minority assistance programs and government set-asides.

Doley Securities, Inc. and the Afrikan American-Continental Afrikan Connection. Doley has restricted his investment banking activities to neither the confines of Wall Street nor to the borders of the continental United States. Doley Securities is an international investment banking house. For the past eight years he has committed himself to raising private capital for Afrikan development. According to the *Times*:

> Since 1986 Doley Securities has co-managed more than $1 billion in foreign bonds sold in the United States for the African Development Bank. His firm is now sole agent of a $100 million medium-term note issue for that bank. And Mr. Doley is financial adviser to an African utility agency that is raising $500 million to bring electricity to the rural areas. He beams that such undertaking brings "true development" to the people of Africa.

According to the *Times*, Doley expects to earn 40 percent of his firm's revenues in 1994 from selling Afrikan securities in the United States. He deservedly expects to reap some benefits from his social and business commitments to Afrikan economic development. Doley is founder of the U.S.–Africa Chamber of Commerce. This organization which functions as a networking medium, meets monthly to promote business and provide information on tax codes relative to Afrika. In 1993, Doley was appointed as the United States ambassador and executive director of the African Development Bank in Abidjan, Ivory Coast. The African Development Bank includes 53-member nations and some $40 billion in assets. It primarily functions to finance Afrikan projects for railroads, schools, farms and hospitals.

Doley's Afrikan-centered activities include more than bilateral relations between the U.S. and Afrika. He has interests in the Caribbean as well. A new member of his staff is former California congressman, Mervyn Dymally, who serves as vice chairman of the corporation. Dymally, while chairman of the Subcommittee on African Affairs, pushed legislation that secured $1 billion in aid to Afrika. He also persuaded the California legislature to permit state agencies to invest in African Development Bank bonds.

Other Black-owned Investment Banks and Afrika. As a prominent Black-owned investment banker who trades in Afrika, Doley Securities is not alone. Bernard Beal, owner of M.R. Beal, a major Black-owned investment bank, remarked that "Doley's in the middle of the pack of black investment banks in Africa. But he's blazed the trail there." The *Times* further revealed that besides Doley's firm:

> ...several other black firms have also established beachheads in Africa.
> According to Michael Sukarsa, the president of the 21st Century Africa Inc., which brings together businesspeople in Africa with investors, the current leader in Africa is actually Pryor, McClendon, Counts & Company. That Philadelphia-based firm owns part of a consolidated acceptance bank in Accra, Ghana, was a founding partner of the African Export-Import Bank in Abidjan, Ivory Coast, and owns part of a venture capital firm in Harare, Zimbabwe. M.R. Beal has an office in Dakar, Senegal, and assists African agencies and clients with debt buybacks and debt-to-equity swaps.

Black-owned Investment Banks: Bridges to Diasporan Afrikan Self-Ownership. The story of Harold Doley and Doley Securities as well as the other Black-owned investment banks who engage in international finance between the U.S. and Afrika, substantiates our theorizing about the benefits of Afrikan American-Afrikan trade and business alliances, partnerships, joint ventures, portfolio and direct investments, and the like. These institutions directly bridge the gap between socially responsible Afrikan American individual and institutional investors and the Afrikan continent in need of funds to finance its economic and social development. They accomplish this by channeling a portion of the aggregate savings of the Black American community into Afrikan governmental, infrastructural, and corporate investment projects which they and their investors judge to be worthwhile in terms of their potential social/economic profitability.

We hope that Black-owned investment banks like Doley Securities, with its $100 million of mid-term notes issued by the Afrikan Development Bank and its $500 million of securities issued by an Afrikan agency, will aggressively pursue Afrikan American individual and institutional investors and persuade them to purchase the bulk of their offerings.

Black investment banks help to provide the opportunity for Afrikan Americans to directly invest in the development of the Motherland and to be part-owners of Her material wealth and among the primary beneficiaries of Her social and economic productivity.

Afrikan American investment and trade relations with Afrika can move us a measurable distance toward the realization of Garvey's famous dream of making "Afrika for the Afrikans, those at home and those abroad."

Syndication as a Method of Finance. Syndication as a method of finance is greatly underutilized by the Afrikan American community. This is one of the major reasons why despite its huge consumer buying power it creates relatively few community-owned businesses and owns relatively little wealth based on investment in the nation's and its own economic resources, corporations and institutions. Webster's dictionary[13] defines a syndicate as "a group of persons or firms authorized jointly to promote some common interest." In the context of our present discussion, Webster's New World Dictionary (1984) defines a syndicate as "an association of individuals or corporations formed for a project requiring much capital." The formation of syndicates to purchase and sell securities (i.e., stocks, bonds, and other credit and investment instruments) issued by corporations, governments and institutions, in their modern form dates back to the last thirty years of the nineteenth century. Its more primary features have been traced back to the latter part of the Middle Ages on through to the 17th and 18th centuries. Carosso (ibid) describes the development of the syndicate in the U.S.:

> To perform more effectively the functions they assumed during the later decades of the nineteenth century, investment bankers adopted the syndicate, probably the most important and far-reaching change in their method of operations to be introduced in the period after the Civil War. Financing the vast economic expansion of these years, which transformed the United States from an agricultural, rural, loosely organized country into an industrial, urban, and highly organized nation, required huge outlays of capital. Since many enterprises needed more than any single banker could command or dared risk, investment bankers joined together in syndicates, as these groups came to be called, pooling their resources and talents and sharing the risk as widely as possible. They employed two general types of syndicates: those that were used to float specific issues of securities and those that were used to put through a merger, from acquiring the component companies to placing the securities of the new corporation.[14]

---

13. *The New Webster's Dictionary of the English Language* International Edition, 1991.
14. Carosso, *Investing Banking in America*, p. 51.

Carosso discusses the various advantages syndication provides banks, two of which include the following:

> Even a strong banking house was "reluctant to put all or a major portion of its resources in any one issue of securities." The risk of failure was too great.
>
> The syndicate provided the machinery through which a banker could participate in the profitable business of floating new securities while limiting his possible losses. One prominent Boston banker likened it to a "temporary" corporation. "It is formed," he said, "to handle something which is perhaps not conveniently handled by individual banking houses or by individuals." By allowing investment bankers to "combine and limit themselves," the syndicate made it possible for them "to compete with the great aggregations of capital, such as the [commercial] banks and insurance companies," a consideration that became especially important during the first two decades of the twentieth century.
>
> Participation in a syndicate afforded the investment banker other advantages as well. It allowed him to diversify his commitments; permitted him to invest in several ventures simultaneously, thus accumulating a variety of securities suitable to the needs of different groups of investors; and provided a convenient way of developing new banking ties and strengthening old ones. Because of the syndicate's flexibility, it could be employed in every kind of flotation.[15]

Since syndicates are "temporary" corporations or groups, they dissolve upon completion of their financial mission or upon completion of the transactions for which they are responsible. The participant in a syndicate may be a member of a number of syndicates at the same time. This is reminiscent of, or is similar to the more ancient Afrikan "susu" or rotating credit association, a form of syndicate where participants also spread risk, raised sizable loans by pooling resources, dissolved upon completion of their mission, and where a participant could be a member of a number of associations simultaneously.

Loan Syndicates. Investment banks may form syndicates not only to buy and sell securities; they may do so to buy and sell loans. In this instance, a lead investment house may put together a corporate loan package by assembling groups of banks to put up the cash. The *New York Times* (8/31/94) explains the objective of this approach to corporate finance:

> ...the aim of the investment bankers is simply to service corporate borrowers that generally have more difficulty raising cash to expand,

---

15. Ibid., pp. 54-55.

make acquisitions or recapitalize, while helping themselves to some of the lush fees that commercial banks have long enjoyed for arranging and syndicating such loans.

The *Times* delineates the more risky nature of these "junk" loans (a junk or *leveraged bond* or loan is one issued or floated for a corporation without an investment rating or with below-investment-grade credit rating which pays high interest yields in compensation for added risk):

> Leveraged loans, like junk bonds, are risky because they are generally made to companies with below-investments-grade credit ratings, meaning that there is a greater chance of default. They are also made at yields above regular market rates.
>
> But unlike bonds, which mostly have fixed rates, the loans have a variable rate that will rise with market interest rates. The loans also give the lender the first claim on the company's assets if it goes bust. So while bond buyers are often spooked by rising rates, banks and other institutions are often more willing to step into the breach with adjustable-rate junk loans.

The *Times* further reveals:

> Junk loans are not really new. During the corporate takeover and leveraged-buyout boom of the late 1980's, loans from commercial banks financed many of the deals. The market peaked in 1989, when more than $186 billion in leveraged loans were written, compared with only $25 billion in junk bonds....
>
> But what makes the market more attractive and less risky for Wall Street now than it was in the 1980's is that the loan business is beginning to look more like the securities business. While commercial banks have traditionally lent money and waited for it to be paid back, a rising number of banks have been trading their loans to other banks, insurance companies, private money managers and mutual funds.

Our interest here is not in creating a junk loan market of the type just described. It is the principle of the phenomenon which interests us — the principle of pooling resources across a broad spectrum of lenders, spreading and reducing risk, and raising sizable amounts of capital thereby. By utilizing this principle, groups of individuals, organizations, business firms or institutions in the Afrikan American community can finance the Black-owned enterprises using resources already in their possession. Their current need to beseech outsiders and the danger of either being rejected or falling under the restrictions and control of them can be avoided by using communal syndication. The participant in loan syndicates can gain satisfaction by contributing to the economic growth and development of the community, expanding employment opportunities, helping to increase Black economic and political power, as well as possibly earning a handsome return on their investments. Individuals, companies and lead organizations who through personal and business contacts can raise cash to service corporate borrowers, may earn very significant fees for their services. However, legal limitations and restrictions, Securities and Exchange Commission regulations if they apply, must be punctiliously observed. Borrowing companies must be thoroughly investigated, their financial conditions, business plan, organization, prospects, etc. disclosed in great detail. Honesty and trust must be maintained at all costs. The wisdom of supporting entrepreneurial undertakings can be fatally damaging and the community suffer irreversible economic failure if questionable or fraudulent schemes are perpetrated by unscrupulous or careless persons, firms and organizations in the name of community economic development.

Syndication of Microloans. Many start-up and successful ongoing businesses may require more money than they can obtain from a single microloan fund. Even though their probability for success are high, or despite the fact they have already established a good business and credit track record, they may still be unable to attain loans from commercial banks. New, expanding, or well-established firms may require a short-term loan in order to set-up, to fulfill a particular order for its products or services, or to meet certain contractual obligations, where increased sales and earnings are anticipated, or payment is to be released to it immediately upon or shortly after completion of the order or fulfillment of the obligation. Moreover, there may exist any number of business opportunities which, but for an absence of appropriate funds, could be profitably exploited by a competent, reputable firm to increase its sales, earnings, size, number of employees, etc., as well as its ability to provide new and better quality services to the community. However, such undertakings may require loans of between $10,000 and $100,000 or more, sums which cannot be tendered by few, if any, single microloan fund. We must remain mindful of the fact that if small businesses are to grow bigger, i.e., to become middle-size or large firms, their growth must be financed beyond what reinvestment of earnings, returns from current sales and savings could afford. Loans must be attained from outside sources. Yet because of racial prejudice on the part of commercial banks and other financial institutions, or because such firms may lack credible investment-grade ratings, or may exhibit other economic characteristics which make them unattractive or appear to be high-risk investments to regular lenders, loans from these sources may be unavailable.

For example, Renaissance Capital of Atlanta, Georgia, makes good use of syndication to fund the growth of fledgling Black companies. Renaissance, whose president is Anita Stephens, is what is referred to as a Specialized Small Business Investment Corporation (SSBIC). SSBICs are typically private companies licensed and funded in part by the Small Business Administration. Like other SSBICs, Renaissance combines the funds it receives from the SBA with funds from private sources, e.g., major banks and corporations, to provide venture capital to minority enterprises. For example, in helping businessman Horace Williams of Greenville, S.C. to buy 17 Pizza Hut franchises in that city and Atlanta, Renaissance syndicated financing among six other SSBICs. It also raised $1.5 million by selling subordinated debt (bonds) and equities (shares) and $5 million through bank financing.

While a microloan fund may, after thorough investigation, deem such a firm as eligible for funds, it may also recognize that the size of loan it can tender would be insufficient to meet the firm's need. Even if the microloan fund could lend the requisite amount to meet the firm's needs, floating such a loan might strain or nearly deplete its resources, reduce its ability to lend funds to other firms, or expose it to considerable difficulty or bankruptcy should the firm default on its payments. This situation need not stymie the growth of fledgling or expanding Black-owned businesses or endanger a particular microloan fund if other arrangements can be made. One such arrangement would involve the organization of a syndicate composed of microlenders, where legally permissible, who would pool or combine a proportionate share of each of their resources to provide a firm with a sizable loan, which each individual lender could not or would not prudently or legally provide. In this instance, each member of the loan pool would expose only a fraction of their resources to possible default by the borrower and earn a proportionate return on investment should the loan prove successful. Such a syndicate would allow its members to spread and share risk, by that reducing negative consequences to a minimum in case of default. It also allows its members to diversify their portfolio of loans thereby strengthening the resources and reserves of their companies against business reversals of one or more of their borrowers as well as increasing overall income of their companies should their portfolios be of good or high quality.

A loan syndicate also enables each member to simultaneously support a larger number of borrowers than each could do single-handedly. This would lead to an accelerated increase in the number of businesses in the community, a more rapid expansion of established businesses and a measurable improvement in their range and quality of merchandise and services, an increase in their profitability and competitiveness, as well as contribute substantially to the economic expansion, power, and well-being of the community.

An Afrikan American Stock Market?

We discussed earlier the primary role investment bankers play, along with brokers or traders in securities (investment bankers may themselves act as brokers or traders), in facilitating the offering and marketing of new securities, e.g., stocks and bonds. The issuance and selling of securities usually take place in the capital market. We shall define the capital market momentarily. However, it is important to keep in mind that the financing of a corporation generally involves the receipt of money from investors in exchange for investors' claims to some of the corporation's assets used for earning profit, and/or claims on the future income of the business. It should also be recalled that new corporations may seek to finance their operations through seeking outside sources of funds, usually through the selling of stock certificates or bonds to investors. An established corporation, although it may be able to retain sufficient profits or may borrow enough from banks in order to expand its operations and to increase profits, may decide it more prudent or necessary to periodically seek outside sources of funds through selling new issues of stock or bonds (Kristein, ibid). It is for such reasons that corporations enter into the capital market where, as described by Kristein:

> ...investors possessing surplus funds exchange them for claims on the future income of the business owners who desire to obtain, and make profitable use of, more funds than they have currently earned. Participants in *the capital market* include, therefore, on the one hand, those lenders or investors (individuals, government departments, banks, and insurance companies) who provide the bulk of the funds needed by business owners, and, on the other hand, those borrowers, (companies and local, state, and federal governments) who seek to obtain funds [Emphasis added].

Hence, as can be surmised from the foregoing citation, the "capital market" is a general term which refers to a system of exchange where specific types of securities or credit instruments are offered for sale in order to raise short-term, intermediate-term, or long-term capital to finance corporate and governmental operations.[16] The capital market includes a number of specialized groups of money markets, each involved with the exchange of a specific type of equity or credit for money, e.g., markets for "commercial paper", government securities, intermediate-term obligations, and for long-term bonds and a variety of types of mortgages.

The whole of several groups of markets are bisected into primary and secondary markets. Primary markets involve the first-time or original selling of securities by governments and corporations. The secondary market is a system where corporate stocks and bonds are offered for resale by the purchasers; where investors can liquidate their holdings quickly and economically (hopefully); where corporate and government securities are bought and sold after the original sale. In sum, "In a primary market transaction, the corporation is the seller and the transaction raises money for the corporation... A secondary market transaction involves the owner or creditor selling to another. It is therefore the secondary markets that provide the means for transferring ownership of corporate securities."[17] Going public is one of two types of primary market transactions. The second is referred to as private placements. A private placement involves the negotiated selling of securities to a specific buyer, usually to large financial institutions such as life insurance companies, mutual pension or endowment funds. Private placements do not have to be registered with the Securities and Exchange Commission and do not require the involvement of underwriters, by that avoiding the variety of regulatory requirements and expense of public offerings.

The New York Exchange, for example, is the most important of a number of securities exchanges where there are secondary markets for the resale of corporate stocks and bonds. Investors who purchase securities already listed and selling on stock exchanges (e.g., the New York, the American and other regional exchanges) through brokers, do not supply new funds to corporations.

---

16. Note: Short-term bonds and debt securities refer to loans to various companies and governmental bodies, which mature in less than one year. Medium-term debt securities mature in one to five years. Long-term debt securities mature after five years or more. Generally, long-term credit instruments are called *bonds*; short-term and medium-term credit instruments are called *bills* and *notes*.

The *capital market* generally involves the selling and buying of long-term securities, like stocks and bonds. The *money market* involves the selling and buying of short-term debt securities. This market is usually referred to as the money market because its instruments can be most quickly turned into spendable cash.

17. S. Ross, R. Westerfield & B. Jordan, *Fundamentals of Corporate Finance* (Boston: Irwin, 1991).

New funds are only obtained by corporations when new securities are issued and sold (usually, through the facilities of investment bankers). Generally, newly issued securities are sold initially in the *over-the-counter* (OTC) market. The OTC market is maintained by dealers in stocks and bonds who bid for an offer to purchase them either as principals for their own account or on behalf of their customers" (Kristein, ibid). When a company issues stocks for the first time, it is said to be going public. This refers to the fact that the owners of the company are selling to the general public part-ownership in their institution. This process is referred to as an initial public offering (IPO). The OTC market also sells a broad variety of bonds, including Federal and Municipal bonds, as well as nearly all the stocks issued by banks and insurance companies, and the stocks of thousands of small- and medium-size, publicly owned corporations. Unlike the organized, registered stock exchanges, e.g., the New York, American, and other exchanges located in the various regions of the country, where only members of these exchanges can buy and sell the securities listed there (most of the members being brokers who are in the business of selling the securities they buy to the public) — anyone can buy and sell unlisted securities in the OTC market. Someone wishing to buy securities on the OTC market need only negotiate their sale with someone owning the stock in question.

The over-the-counter as a secondary market is where the great majority of U.S. stocks are traded. The OTC is an electronic marketplace. It is a highly sophisticated network of brokers who, while studying the activity of the market on their computer screens, trade with other brokers by telephone.

The performance of initial public offerings, i.e., new issues of stock, by various corporations varies widely. That is, the offering price for new shares a company places on the OTC market may rapidly increase or decline on its offering date or some relatively short time thereafter. It is not unusual for a large percentage of the shares of a company which are perceived as being a "hot deal", i.e., as having excellent or good prospects for success or whose shares are expected to rise rapidly in price, may be bought through private placement by major institutional buyers. Generally, institutional investors receive better information during initial public offerings; may be solicited to for orders before offerings occur. Such courtesies are usually not offered to individual investors. Institutional investors are the biggest buyers and holders of blocks of IPOs issued by the "hottest corporations". Small investors therefore tend to get only a relatively smaller portion of the hottest deals and a larger portion of the weaker deals.

The U.S. IPO market is among the most productive in the world. In 1993, underwriters for IPOs raised $57.5 billion for fledgling companies, some $17.5 billion more than they raised in the prior year.

Black-owned Enterprise IPOs. The first Black-owned company to trade on the New York Stock Exchange was the Washington D.C.-based Black Entertainment Television (BET) Holdings Inc., a cable vision and magazine publishing company. It completed its initial public offering (IPO) of stock in 1991. The Parks Sausage Co. and Johnson Products Co. first debuted on the National Association of Securities Dealers Automated Quotation (NASDAQ) and American Stock Exchanges (AMEX) in 1970. Parks Sausage, the first Black-owned company to go public, raised $1.5 million in its IPO of 1969. Johnson Products (later sold to the IVAX Corp. in 1993) was the first Black-owned company to trade in the American Stock Exchange. It also completed a $6.5 million IPO in 1969.

The Need for an Afrikan American Stock Market

Our preceding discussions along with the ones to follow should make it imminently clear that the Afrikan American community needs to develop a stock market — a meeting place for buyers and sellers of securities. This may mean the establishment under the aegis of the Securities and Exchange Commission, of capital marketplaces operating across Black America. There are 14 regional exchanges currently operating in cities other than New York City, where the New York and the American Stock Exchanges are located. More realistically, the founding and operation of a "Black Stock Market" would involve the full participatory entry into the American capital market systems of large numbers of Blacks comprehensively trained in finance and business, of large numbers of well-trained and licensed Black financial brokers, and increasing numbers of Black-owned or Black-led corporations dedicated to assisting the Afrikan community in achieving economic and political self-determination and power.

More Afrikan American brokers and other Afrikan Americans with a deep knowledge of the operation of capital markets, must follow the example of Marvin Terry, CEO, Marvin Terry & Company, Inc., of Harlem, New York City. Like Terry, they must dedicate themselves to the training of corps of individuals and groups in finance, business, and asset management. Training may include the development of brokers, the teaching of developing financial know-how to lay- and business-persons and those directly involved in investing in capital markets, and operating community-wide educational programs. These programs should also be designed to educate Black consumers and leaders of community institutions in the ways of making economic choices that work in their best interests and in the best interests of the community as a whole.

Marvin Terry & Company (MTC) is the only Afrikan American-owned, community-based investment company in the greater Harlem area in New York City. MTC is registered with the Securities and Exchange Commission, a member of the National Association of Securities Dealers, and is licensed regionally. A fully-licensed brokerage firm, MTC offers investment advice and asset management services to the Harlem and regional Black communities. It serves individual investors, retirees, churches, investment clubs, non-profit and for-profit organizations. MTC takes a distinct interest in small as well as large investors. MTC realizes small investors as a whole may have a very measurable social impact in their communities. But more important is MTC's involvement in organizing minority and community-based businesses into cohesive investment units; its provision of community education programs; its training of community-oriented financial and stockbrokers; and its sponsorship of the MTC Scholarship Fund, which provides stipends to help talented individuals to realize their goals in the area of financial services. The Afrikan American community needs the services of many more investment companies like MTC.

The Afrikan American community cannot become a powerful political and economic factor in America unless it establishes a significant presence in national as well as international capital markets. Achievement of this goal must begin with seeing to it that very large numbers of Blacks are employed and operate in these markets so that the whole Pan–Afrikan community can benefit from their knowledge, experience and expertise.

Making "Inroads" on Wall Street. The paucity of Afrikan Americans with an intimate, working knowledge of capital markets can only be remediated by seeing to it that more of them are employed in all areas of the industry. This has not been the case in the past. However, since 1970, when it was founded, Inroads Inc., a nonprofit organization that helps Black, Hispanic, and American Indian college students gain entry into the corporate world, has been instrumental in reversing past trends. According to Inroads president and chief executive officer Charles Story, Inroad's mission "is to develop and place talented minority youth in business and industry and prepare them for corporate and community leadership" (WSJ, 11/25/94). Inroads does this by providing minority students with real-life work experience at more than a dozen top-notch securities firms including Merrill Lynch & Co.; Goldman Sachs & Co.; Dean Witter Discover & Co.'s Dean Witter Reynolds unit; Alex. Brown Inc.'s Alex. Brown & Sons Inc. operations; and Morgan Stanley Group Inc.

When Inroads was formed in 1970 it placed 25 students with 17 participating firms. In 1994 it placed more than 5,400 minority interns with approximately 800 companies. According to the *Wall Street Journal* (11/25/94) "Of the 686 Inroads interns who graduated from college in 1993, 399 of them, or 58%, were offered employment by their sponsors, with 367 students accepting those offers."

Inroads has many corporate sponsors besides those in the securities industry. These sponsors, which include such Fortune 500 companies as Coca-Cola Co., I.B.M., G.E., Johnson & Johnson and Ford Motor Company, agree to provide their student workers with vigorous training at wages up to $15 per hour. Corporate fees that include about $4,000 an intern paid to Inroads, are the primary sources of the organization's funds, which are supplemented by grants and contributions from other sources. Only students with a minimum 3.0 (B) grade-point average are referred to companies.

Inroads' interns are not being accepted for training and offered employment by their corporate sponsors due to some reparative change of heart on their part. Their efforts in this regard have in good part been motivated by their being the subjects in September 1994 of the U.S. Commission on Civil Rights hearings on entrepreneurial and employment opportunities for women and minorities on Wall Street and the availability, or the lack thereof, of training programs designed to increase their employability. A preliminary study of the commission released in October 1994 revealed, unsurprisingly, that "women and minorities are severely under-represented in the securities industry in the New York area, especially compared with other sectors of financial services, such as insurance and banking" (WSJ, ibid). This trend had already been noted by Thomas Powell, managing director of Inroads' branch at 120 Wall Street, NYC. Even today, Powell reports that "the greatest concentration of our interns are in commercial banks," not the brokerage firms, a situation Inroads is struggling to rectify. Women and minorities still find it markedly more difficult to secure employment as managers or in high-paying posts in the upper echelons of investment banking.

The efforts of Inroads must be reinforced by the Afrikan American community and its civil rights organizations. Organizations like

Inroads — dedicated to increasing the know-how and experience of Afrikan Americans in crucially important industries and fields — must be founded and multiplied many-fold if the community is to produce the thousands of trained businesspersons, managers, technicians and other skilled personnel it needs to build and operate an Afrikan American and Pan–Afrikan political-economic system which will deliver Afrikan peoples from subordination and dependency, poverty and powerlessness.

Chapter 31

THE CRISIS OF LEADERSHIP

Leaders and Followers

IN THE UNITED STATES OF AMERICA the primary source of the host of problems which plague the Afrikan American community is powerlessness. Powerlessness is also the source of the host problems which plague Afrikan nations and peoples across the Diaspora. Afrikan communities, both at home and abroad, are corrupted by weaknesses which if not remediated by their acquisition of power will inevitably lead to their absolute corruption and final demise. Rollo May asserted "Power is essential for all living things. If we neglect the factor of power, as is the tendency in our day of reaction against the destructive effects of the misuse of power, we shall lose values that are essential to our existence as humans."

In our beginning chapters we contended, in line with the consensus of many other students of power, that power is created, defined and sustained by organized relationships between persons and between groups. James MacGregor Burns defines the primary basis of social power thusly: "Power is a *relationship* among persons." He goes on to say:

> To define power not as a property or entity or possession but as a ***relationship*** in which two or more persons tap motivational bases in one another and bring varying resources to bear in the process is to

perceive power as drawing a vast range of human behavior into its orbit. The arena of power is no longer the exclusive preserve of a power elite or an establishment or persons clothed with legitimacy. Power is ubiquitous; it permeates human relationships. It exists whether or not it is quested for. It is the glory and the burden of most of humanity.[1]

Thus, according to Burns, social power is, in essence, *collective,* and involves two essentials, intentionality (i.e., purpose, motive) and resources. Power, then, involves dynamic relationships between powerholders and power recipients and the motives and resources they utilize in their efforts to achieve mutual or individual goals. Our concern in this brief chapter is with the intentionalities and resources of a particular class of powerholders, i.e., Afrikan American leaders, and their relationships to the Afrikan American community and whether their interaction with it leads to its empowerment or disempowerment. Time and space does not allow us to critically analyze the individual and organizational leadership in the community in any detail. Therefore, we will confine ourselves to very cursory and preliminary critiques of their predominant ideological tendencies. And these will be reviewed relative only to their ability to enhance or diminish the power of the community.

The relative powerlessness of Afrikan Americans, as we have demonstrated, is not due to an absence of resources but to the misjudgment and misguided intentionalities of their leadership. The vast resources of the Afrikan American community and their potential for conversion into formidable political-economic power have been ruinously wasted or prostituted by leaders whose ineptness borders on treachery.

For our purposes herein we shall follow Burns' description of leadership:

Leadership over human beings is exercised when persons with certain motives and purposes mobilize, in competition or conflict with others, institutional, political, psychological, and other resources so as to arouse, engage, and satisfy the motives of followers. This is done in order to realize goals mutually held by *both* leaders and followers, as in Lenin's calls for peace, bread, and land. In brief, leaders with motive and power bases tap followers' motives in order to realize the purposes of both leaders and followers. Not only must motivation be relevant, as in power generally, but its purposes must be realized and satisfied. Leadership is exercised in a condition of *conflict* or *competi-*

---

1. James MacGregor Burns, *Leadership* (New York: Harper Torchlight, 1978), p. 15.

tion in which leaders contend in appealing to the motive bases of potential followers....

Leaders are a particular kind of power holder. Like power, leadership is relational, collective, and purposeful. Leadership shares with power the central function of achieving purpose....

The crucial variable, again, is *purpose*. Some define leadership as leaders making followers do what *followers* would not otherwise do, or as leaders making followers do what the *leaders* want them to do; I define leadership as leaders inducing followers to act for certain goals that represent the values and the motivations — the wants and needs, the aspirations and expectations — *of both leaders and followers*. And the genius of leadership lies in the manner in which leaders see and act on their own and their followers' values and motivations.

Leadership, unlike naked power-wielding is thus inseparable from followers' needs and goals.[2]

In the political arena, in reference to his discussion of the leadership of Mao Tse-Tung, Burns intimates that "one of the supreme qualities of the gifted political leader is to understand not only the needs of potential followers *but the way in which those needs could be activated and channeled*" [Emphasis added]. Furthermore, Burns implies that "the classical role of the great leader...is to comprehend not only the existing needs of followers but to *mobilize within them newer motivations and aspirations* that in the future [will] furnish a popular foundation for [a new] kind of leadership." [Emphasis added]

We argue here that the crises of the Afrikan American and Pan-Afrikan communities as a whole are one with the crises of leadership of those communities. Moreover, we contend that these crises of leadership flow from its intellectual and ideological bankrupcty, its wrongheaded sense of purpose or intentionality, its inability to recognize and articulate the fundamental needs of its followers and its impaired ability to pragmatically satisfy those needs if they were recognized and articulated. Black leadership as presently constituted, precisely operates against the most basic interests of the Afrikan community. It is therefore unwittingly allied with other inimical forces arrayed against the community. It is imperative that this leadership be razed from its ideological foundation so that a new leadership structure capable of realizing the needs of the Afrikan community can be constructed on its ruins.

Essentially, a crisis of leadership occurs when the intentions and needs of leadership are severely mismatched with those of its

---

2. Ibid., p. 18.

followers. The intentions of leadership are to a significant degree indicated by its ideological orientations or attitudes in addition to its behavioral history. In this final chapter, therefore, we will very broadly review the general needs of the Afrikan American community and see in what ways the ideological intents and political orientations certain Black leadership organizations empower or disempower the community.

The Cry For New Leadership

Forty years after the United States Supreme Court outlawed segregation of the races in America's schools, supposedly in the interest of providing Afrikan Americans with "equal education" through racial integration, the majority of Black students find themselves hypersegregated in urban ghetto schools, entrapped in an education system in severe crisis and in imminent danger of total collapse. Forty years after Blacks in Montgomery, Alabama, won the right to ride in the front of the bus, Blacks in urban America are virtually the only ones, along with other forlorn minorities, riding the buses — buses to nowhere. Thirty years after gaining the right to vote, having benefitted from passage of the great 1964 voting rights act, Blacks in urban and rural America vote for Black politicians who cannot improve their plight. They can vote for the president of the United States, the only problem being that their urban votes are no longer crucially influential in determining who will be elected president. Therefore, the major parties gain political supremacy by running hard against Black images and Black interests. Twenty years after passing fair housing legislation Blacks are hypersegregated in urban ghettos and suburban neighborhoods. Worse still, many Blacks are homeless, sleeping on the sidewalks, under bridges and in abandoned buildings. After twenty-five years of affirmative action Blacks find themselves with the highest unemployment rates, locked out of corporate America, drifting into poverty evermore rapidly, begging for handouts on the streets of America. Twenty-five years after the initiation of Black capitalism Blacks find their community markets dominated by aliens. Black business persons find that they can do little business in America or with America. After forty years of being America's moral conscience, Blacks find their communities being devastated by immorality; after preaching brotherly, race-transcending love, they find themselves the most hated of races. For Blacks in America, thirty years after hearing the ringing words: "Free at last! Free at last! Thank God Almighty, I'm free at last!" America has become even more a prison, sealing their bodies, hopes and aspirations in dungeons of despair.

For Afrikan Americans, all the promises of the Civil Rights Era have been betrayed, everything has been reversed. The more Black officials have been elected the worse the Black electorate has fared; Black homelessness became a national scandal during the tenure of a Black Secretary of Housing; the Black community was overrun with AIDS, drug addiction, tuberculosis, all sorts of diseases and maladies during the tenure of a Black man as Secretary of Health; Black nations were overrun by the imperial armies of the United States while a Black man was Head of the Joint Chiefs of Staff; the more Black judges appointed to the bench, the more Black men become police commissioners and police officers, the more Black men fill America's prisons and the more Black-on-Black violence ravages America's Black ghettos. While some 60 distinguished Black men and women sat on some 165 major corporate boards, Blacks were the only ethnic group who suffered net employment losses in major American corporations. At the time when Afrikan Americans suffered net losses in employment and other minority groups and Whites achieved net increases, Black conservative men presided as the heads of the Equal Economic Opportunity Commission. At the time when the masses of Blacks are ghettoized in America's declining cities and no longer live on, own or work the land, a Black man presided as Secretary of Agriculture. In 1993, at the appointment of a Black woman as Surgeon General, an ardent advocate of sex education and the dispensing of condoms, Black teenage pregnancy and female-headed families threaten the very foundations of Black family culture and Black cultural viability.

There is a pervasive sense of foreboding and impending doom among Afrikans who let themselves look reality dead in the face. In the face of the tremendous deterioration of their quality of life — mounting unemployment, increasing poverty, crime, moral degradation; devastating miseducation and the even more devastating lack of education; overwhelming drug addiction and insensate violence, homicide, terror, prostitution, disease and corruption; in the face of children having children, social incivility, a youth culture whose raucous music speaks of nihilism, rape, robbery and murder, the degradation and venal hatred of Black women, of everything Black; in the face of unfulfilled longings for the satisfaction of basic needs in the midst of the "affluent society" — the need for food, shelter, for physical safety and security, for belonging, love, acceptance, higher self-esteem, knowledge and understanding, freedom and autonomy, achievement, creativity and self-realization; in the face of all these needs unfulfilled, the Afrikan community in ever-rising crescendos emits a heart-rendering cry for new leadership. Even old leaders are calling for new leadership. The persistent call for leadership in the Black community is a call for help, a call for a set of leading persons, organizations and ideas who can provide the community with a sense of unity, definition, direction, power, with a developmental plan and the wherewithal to realize its abundant human potential.

The most persistent complaints the community makes concerning its current leadership are that they have either been co-opted by the ruling White regime; are outdated in terms of values, goals and techniques; are not truly and deeply committed to the welfare of the people; are self-centered, self-serving, egocentric, corrupt; out of touch with current and future realities; timid and cannot recognize the needs of the people or articulate those needs in ways which move the people toward their satisfaction; are intellectually inept and are not effectively educating the masses and inspiring them to realize the enormous power which lies dormant within themselves.

We will not debate or critically evaluate these complaints. We believe that even if the contemporary Black leadership accurately gauged and articulated the needs of the Afrikan American community, it could not necessarily empower it as such. Though a match between leadership intentions and those of the community is necessary to Black empowerment, it in itself is not sufficient. The generation of social power requires appropriate organization, tactics and strategies — and a unifying vision or sense of mission. It requires a guiding set of ideas or an ideology whose attempted realization defines the social attitudes, relations and institutions which together can empower a people. A people are empowered or disempowered by the guiding ideologies of the leaders to whom they pledge allegiance. Though leaders recognize the needs of their followers and are at one with them in terms of their own needs, their choice of inappropriate social-political ideologies and goals may bring both themselves and their followers to despair.

In light of the foregoing discussion we think it more appropriate and productive to critically look at the ideological orientation of certain types of leadership establishments which prevail or are emergent in the Afrikan American community today, than to critically analyze the individual leaders and their politics. While grouping persons into categories is a hazardous undertaking, inevitably some do not fit neatly into a particular category or may "straddle the fence," we do think that if this is done with due precautions, categorization can be a time-saving and productive activity. With this in mind we will immediately launch into brief critiques of three ideological orientations exhibited by Black leadership today— the assimilationist /moralist, the neo-conservative/bourgeois, and the cultural nationalist.

The Assimilationist/Moralistic-oriented Leadership Establishment

The assimilationist/moralistic leadership establishment, hereafter referred to as the assimilationists, is arguably the predominant leadership group in the Afrikan American community today. This leadership establishment is primarily comprised of civil rights organizations such as the National Association for the Advancement of Colored People (NAACP), the National Urban League and the Southern Christian Leadership Conference (SCLC). This establishment is heavily influenced and in many instances led by congeries of Black ministers. Consequently, it is closely allied with the institutional Black Church and its leadership who, forming the most influential leadership group in the Black community, accounts significantly for its moralistic and moralizing orientation.

Besides seeking to attain full and equal civil rights, the groups which make up the assimilationist leadership establishment see the integration or assimilation of Blacks into virtually all social areas with Whites as their ultimate social and political goal. Their penultimate goal appears to be that of total psychosocial, politicoeconomic merging of Blacks with Whites to the point where the Black community will lose its ethnic identity, residential and cultural distinctiveness, self-reference and visibility as an Afrikan people or as a community of persons of Afrikan descent. They seek to not be seen as possessing "color" but to be characterized in deracialized abstract terms.

The moralistic coloring of this leadership establishment follows from its belief that separation by race is morally reprehensible, that ethnic exclusivity is morally unconscionable. More pertinent, however, is its belief that racism, especially in the form of White supremacy and all that it implies, represents a fundamentally moral problem — a problem founded on racial prejudice, stereotypes, deviations from Christian ethics, lack of racial or humanistic enlightenment and moral will. The assimilationist/moralistic establishment essentially overlooks the economic rationale for one race dominating another. Consequently, while pursuing legal and legislative remedies for racial discrimination, while vigorously protesting racial injustice, this group advocates what Cornel West[3] calls "the politics of conversion", or "a love ethic". In other words, dominant Whites must be converted or "born again" to the fundamental beliefs of the Christian religion, Christian charity, brotherhood and love, or some humanistic equivalent thereof. Politically, the belief is that Whites must become true believers in and doers of the Word. If this moral goal is achieved then Blacks would be liberated and empowered the same as Whites. Thus it follows from the logic of this ideological orientation that the freedom and well-being of Blacks are dependent on the conversion of Whites to unconditional humanity through legalistic measures and moralistic appeals to their presumed "better nature", and above all, through the "redemptive love" and self-sacrifice of Blacks.

The tenacious adherence of the assimilationists to the moralistic, non-economic, non-ethnic-based, non-Afrikan-centered approaches to the problems confronting Afrikan peoples is apparently based on their belief that White power over Blacks is essentially a moral problem or a problem involving the inadequate enforcement of constitutional guarantees; their almost absolute faith in the idea that the merging of Blacks and Whites into one represents the only possible route to freedom for Blacks; and their absolute faith that once these two groups are integrated they cannot be dis-integrated.

Neither the NAACP, Urban League, SCLC or the institutional Black Church has proposed or sought to realize ethnically based, sociocultural, politicoeconomic, technologico-military development plans for Afrikan peoples — things essential to their survival and advancement. In fact, these organizations have a history of opposing and seeing the drafting and execution of such plans as racist, nationalistic, separatist and self-segregating. While this opposition may point to a lack of confidence in the idea that such developmental plans are intellectually and organizationally achievable or desirable for Afrikans, it appears to be motivated more by the unfounded belief that the inevitable assimilation of Blacks and Whites will make such efforts on the part of Blacks unnecessary. By becoming indistinguishable from Whites, Blacks would thereby automatically inherit the power, prestige, privilege and material advantages Whites already enjoy. Thus the pursuit of power by Blacks, which would require the full active development of ethnically based organizations and institutions, is perceived as counterproductive, as a hindrance to racial merger — the supreme goal of Black assimilationists.

Consequently, the assimilationist leadership is terrified by the Black Power movement. It readily allies itself with dominant Whites

---

3. Cornel West, *Race Matters* (Boston: Beacon Press, 1993).

to mortally combat such. Evidently, a racial balance of power that can protect the human rights and ensure the exercise of freedom and justice of Blacks presents an undesirable alternative to what is a patently false race-merging fantasy, a delusion having absolutely no substantiating foundation in human history. A racial balance of power apparently has no appeal to the establishment whose inferiority complexes and traumatized egos are such that any other approach besides racial merger is to them unthinkable or unimaginable.

The assimilationist leadership establishment defines liberty and equality, i.e., freedom, in terms of individual liberty, equality of socioeconomic opportunity, equality before the law, equal opportunity to participate fully in the election and processes of government without regard to race, color, or creed. It seeks to gain and involve public agencies in the protection of the private liberties and civil rights of Blacks against governmental and private racial oppression and discrimination. It hopes that the achievement of these ends would enable it to influence government and private agencies to expand the liberties of Blacks and their opportunities to gain education, nutrition, health, employment and housing equal to that of Whites. However, the expectation on the part of the assimilationists that race as a basis for the abridgement of equal rights and opportunity would lose all significance once the formal achievement of egalitarian civil rights and individual liberties as well as the establishment and commissioning of numerous public and private agencies to protect as well as affirm the equal rights and opportunities of Blacks was achieved, has proved to be an abysmal failure. While the Black community has acquired the right to vote, a substantial modicum of individual liberties and civil rights, it has not yet achieved the fundamentally important ability to effectively influence the government or private-corporate interests to live according to their egalitarian credos and to satisfy the economic and social needs of the largest majority of Black people.

Thus, at this juncture that the assimilationist leadership establishment has not achieved racial assimilation, it has achieved the right of Blacks to vote while they suffer homelessness, un- and underemployment, grossly inadequate education, continuing racial discrimination, injustice, and oppression. While this establishment has secured individual liberties (within expanded limits), other abstract rights and liberties for the Afrikan American community, such rights and liberties have not curtailed the amoral liberalism of rampant teenage pregnancy, devastating drug trafficking and addictions, Black-on-Black criminality and violence, cultural vulgarity and incivility, educational underachievement, disruptedness and drop-outism, and the paucity of business ownership and economic impoverishment in the community.

While the bourgeois assimilationists have used their newly acquired liberties to stick their toes into the American mainstream, to take advantage of their accumulated skills, class privileges and access to some mainstream prerogatives; while they have escaped or are seeking to escape from the urban masses into the suburbs and edge cities of America, the "dangerous classes" abandoned in the inner-cities engage in a titanic struggle against their destruction by the economic demands of White supremacy and their own reactionary self-destruction. However, the assimilationists forebodingly sense that the struggles of the urban masses against destruction will inevitably engulf them as well. For their fate, their fervent wishes and self-deceptions to the contrary is inextricably tied to the fate of the masses of Black people. Thus the problems of inner-city Blacks are also the problems of assimilationist Blacks. Therein lies the dilemma of the assimilationists. And this dilemma has paralyzed their leadership and having paralyzed it, made it impotent, ineffective, and spurned by the Black masses.

The Dilemma of Assimilationist Leadership

The central dilemma of the assimilationist leadership involves the fact that the resolution of problems faced by the Black community requires that it empowers itself first through its reclamation of the Afrikan-centered consciousness and identity. The achievement of Black Power involves a revolutionary confrontation with and neutralization of the White Power establishment with which the assimilationists seek total acceptance. The avoidance of this very confrontation motivates the assimilationist to seek refuge in the pursuit of a fantasized raceless society. For assimilationists, true freedom is the freedom of a mythical raceless society.

Apparently, the assimilationists have never stopped to consider the possibility that the raceless society may never come into existence — that racism may be a permanent feature of human nature and sociopolitical relations. They evidently have never considered the possibility that even if a raceless society were to become an actuality in the far distant future the Afrikan race, given its current vulnerabilities, may not be around to enjoy its benefits. If the assimilationist could at least hypothesize the permanence of racism, they may accept the rationality of seeking to ensure the ability of Afrikan peoples to survive by developing their sociocultural, politicoeconomic, military and technological abilities to do so.

The assimilationists obviously have underestimated the tenacity of Whites to maintain the fundamental racial status quo which has proved to be of such obvious and opulent material benefit to them and has also provided them the exhilarating psychic benefits of racial superiority. They did not seriously consider and prepare, apparently, for the possibility that Whites would vigorously play the political and economic game of taking back with one hand what they gave with the other, a game where just as Blacks are permitted to enter the rules are *suddenly* changed and Blacks must protest again to have the rules changed anew.

Sidney Wilhelm describes this new form of "invisible racism" adeptly:

Are Negroes advancing toward equality? No doubt about it, they are indeed. But where is the advancement leading them? As legal retributions seemingly preclude racial segregation and discrimination in education, transportation, military service, housing, and so forth, whites turn to other ways of depriving the Negro people. The new efforts are designed not to subjugate or oppress the black minority, but rather to isolate it. Whites wish to avoid contact with blacks. And this is more readily accomplished by treating any Negro the same as any white. When the Negro dons the military uniform, equality keeps him out of reach of officer ranks and within combat units; as job requirements rise drastically, equality in evaluating applicants regardless of race excludes the Negro just as effectively as discrimination, so massively unqualified is he in terms of what is now required for employment; the denial of employment and promotion on the basis of equality reduces the Negro to economic servitude just as impressively as Southern sharecropping; Negro college admissions remain low for integrated education when judged by educational standards expected of whites; equal economic standards for loans and home mortgages keep the Negro from new housing in the suburbs just as efficiently as restrictive covenants; the equal application of the neighborhood unit within ghettos as the basis of school districting leads to *de facto* educational segregation and results in racial separation just as surely as *de jure* educational segregation.

Such revamping of old prejudices indicates the coming trend in race relations. *Racial discrimination has not been removed entirely; racism is still a fundamental feature of White America.* It would be a mistake to say no discrimination exists in housing, education, employment, or elsewhere; we have seen racism flourishing in such areas. *But as equality becomes more and more a fact of life, we cannot avoid its concomitant of increasing racial separation!* Whites are more anxious than ever to introduce equality where equality fosters racial division within America. This arrangement facilitates Negro removal from the affairs of White America with full compliance to an idealistic democratic precept rather than Negro entrance into mainstream American life. The Negro moves from the plantation to the ghetto as the nation concedes equality on economic terms and upholds racism: "What white Americans have never fully understood — but what the Negroes can never forget — " the *Report of the National Advisory Commission on Civil Disorders* so cogently testifies, "is that white society is deeply implicated in the ghetto. White institutions created it, white institutions maintain it, and white society condones it." *White America intends to forget about its black minority.*[4] [Emphasis added]

In many areas the efforts of the assimilationists have proved very beneficial for Afrikans in America and abroad; however, the range, depth and endurance of these benefits are exceedingly questionable. It is absolutely clear that in regard to the empowerment of the Afrikan American community their failure has been colossal and catastrophic! The very phantasmic central goal of the assimilationists — that of a raceless society, a society where Afrikanicity would be of no significance, would be invisible, obviates against the construction and use of Black Power based on Afrikan-centered consciousness and identity, racial solidarity and unity, and against the construction of a powerful Pan–Afrikan politicoeconomic system. As indicated above, the construction of race-based systems and institutions of any kind requiring relative racial exclusion or separation on the part of Blacks, represents for them intolerable obstacles on the pathway to the achievement of a raceless society — their hearts' desire. This obsession registers the presence in the collective assimilationist psyche of a near-psychotic, mind-numbing ambivalence toward race and power. Ultimately, the assimilationists must destroy the very vehicle they utilize to achieve the goals for which they strive. As is evident throughout the history of the civil rights movement, the assimilationists find it necessary to use Black Power in the form of *organized, Black-based protests,* marches, boycotts, class lawsuits, sit-ins, affirmative action programs, bloc voting, and so forth, to achieve what they perceive as assimilated equality. In other words, the achievement of racial assimilation requires the use of blackness as a basis for organization. Consequently, the assimilationists find themselves in the untenable position of trying to preserve their political cake while

---

4. Sidney Wilhelm, *Who Needs the Negro?* (New York: Anchor Books, 1971), pp. 152-53.

eating it too. Cruse (ibid) speaks to this self-defeating contradiction when he notes the changes in race relations presaged and precipitated by the Supreme Court decision of 1954:

> What would propel the politics of these changes was the enhanced power of the black vote, based in the expanded black urban ghettos. *Here a contradictory fact of life ran counter to civil rights hopes and goals.* One prominent white liberal put it: *'The urban ghetto was at one time and the same time the force that constricted Negro life and aspirations and yet formed the base for black political power and the activities of civil-rights organizations.* Because the black vote was often tied to democratic city machines, it was not as effective a voice of protest as some believed it could have been. Here a case of demographics worked in mysterious ways for civil rights wonders to perform. Only the segregated black urban ghetto could produce such political power. *Yet, the individual benefactors, the appointed and elected public officials and politicians whose status was predicated on the very existence of the urban ghettos would reject the legitimacy of the ghettos' existence. The general logic of this political leadership would be to eschew and disdain all social policy aimed at internal economic, social and cultural improvements of the ghettos on the assumption that such improvements amounted to the perpetuation of segregation. The civil rights influence of white liberalism had, from the outset, played a dominant role in fostering this logic.* By the 1950s, before the persistence of segregated black urban ghettoes (i.e., communities) would render public school desegregation a mockery, a prominent liberal commentator had to admit:
>
>> *Without the urban base, the Negro protest movement would have remained small, and without the political leverage the urban masses provided, it would have remained impotent.* Though no one realized it at the time, and though other factors were also essential in bringing about the events that were to follow, by midcentury the vote of the black ghetto in the North had reached the proportions that made possible the civil rights revolution.[5]
>> [Emphasis added]

And yet the assimilationists have willfully resisted the full and independent political, social and economic organization of their power base, the foundations of their class standing and prestige — the urban Black masses. To put it more prosaically, the assimilationists are prone to kill the Afrikan goose that lays the golden eggs of Black Power. What is worse, it has permitted the masses to sink into economic submarginality and political impotence. As Cruse further contends:

---

5. Harold Cruse, *Plural But Equal*, pp. 216–17.

Because of its unprecedented and unexpected social and economic evolution, this class and its various spokesmen and spokeswomen cannot admit in a political and/or economic fashion that, for all intents, it has written off the contemporary condition of the black underclass as a lost cause. (Apropos of DuBois's critique of 1934, only the state and the uplift forces and agencies of the nation can help save the black underclass.) Flushed with the civil rights optimism of the liberal consensus, the emergent new class both denied and evaded the self evident existence and the growth of a permanent underclass with its ominous signs of black family disintegration as outlined in the controversial Moynihan Report of 1965, *The Negro Family — A Case for National Action.*[6]

The ideological as well as behavioral orientation of the assimilationist leadership establishment have not been merely irrelevant vis-à-vis the Afrikan American community, especially its urban masses, but as Cruse argues, "is *detrimental* to future development in the political, economic, educational, and cultural dimensions of the black cause. More than that, the traditional *civil rights leadership will oppose any attempt on the part of an alternate leadership to organize blacks into an independent political bloc.*" We must conclude that assimilationist ideology has lived far past its usefulness and must immediately undergo political euthanasia if the Afrikan community is to live.

Black Neo-Conservatism

In terms of their ideological or direct organizational influence on the political and economic character and behavior of the Afrikan American community as a whole, a nascent group of Black American ideologues commonly referred to as "Black conservatives," "Black neo-conservatives," does not merit discussion here. This group of theorists and polemicists has no significant organization or constituency in the Afrikan American community to speak of. It nevertheless has managed to worm its way into the consciousness of the community and society in general. Moreover, the Black neoconservative establishment is used by the White conservative establishment as cannon fodder in defense of White racism and domination against both Black and White liberals and Black nationalists. Black neoconservatism has defined itself in opposition to constant call of assimilationists for government intervention and largesse in the uplift of the socially depressed and politically oppressed Black masses. It also opposes the

---

6. Ibid., p. 390.

belief that government and industry should make special efforts on behalf of Blacks in reparation for harm done in the past resulting from White racism. This stance by the Black "neo-con" establishment does not in anyway stand in the way of its members' or advocates' voracious pursuit and acceptance of any high offices offered by both government and industry, whether in the name of affirmative action, quotas, or just plain "help wanted." Black neo-conservatives have been ably assisted in this regard by White neo-conservatives, conservatives and crypto-racists, due to their ideological compatibility with the values and goals of the White supremacist establishment. This has led to their receiving favorable exposure in the mainstream print and electronic media, to their being appointed to influential offices and professional positions such as heads of the EEOC, the Civil Rights Commission, and to the U.S. Supreme Court under conservative administrations, and to departmental chairs at prestigious universities. These well-paid propagandists, themselves "the prime beneficiaries of precisely those maximum social, educational and professional advances resulting from civil rights legislation" (Cruse) paradoxically oppose the very collectivistic civil rights activities which have made their occupational positions possible. Their central thesis is that the current condition of Afrikans at home and abroad is no longer the result of historical or contemporary machinations of White supremacy, racial bigotry and discrimination. Some Black neoconservatives go so far as to argue that the past oppression of Blacks and their continuing racial domination by Whites, whose significance they vigorously downplay, does not provide satisfactory explanations of the current socioeconomic subordination and marginality of Afrikan Americans and of Afrikans across the Diaspora. Martin Kilson, professor of government at Harvard University and an Afrikan American, summarizes the relationship between mainstream, i.e., White, conservatism and Black neo-conservatism thusly:

> At no point in the twentieth century have the claims of black Americans for social and political parity (organized by constitutionalistic and nonviolent pressure groups like the National Association for the Advancement of Colored People) gained serious support from conservative leaders and intellectuals, secular or religious — support, that is, comparable to that which the liberal and moderate sectors among white leadership have sustained on behalf of equality of status and mobility for blacks. From the end of Reconstruction in the 1880s to the late 1960s, American conservatives typically ignored the authoritarian and violent racial-caste practices and values arrayed against black Americans in southern states where the vast majority

of blacks lived. Although American conservatives have, throughout this century, often embraced freedom movements elsewhere in the world — in Europe, Latin America, East Asia — they have always firmly resisted a proactive embrace of the black American civil rights movement as a bona fide movement fully worthy of their support. So it is in the shadow of this dismal record of mainstream American conservatism vis-à-vis black Americans' long and arduous quest for equality of status that new black conservatives have emerged.[7]

Kilson goes on to summarize the main tenets of Black neoconservative discourse relating to Black Americans.

This discourse has centered on several basic arguments concerning the black experience in the post-civil rights era. First, black conservatives assert that federal court decisions and civil rights legislation since the middle 1960s have created a color-blind milieu for black mobility, making it counter-productive for blacks to persist in viewing themselves as victims of racism and so in need of unique public policies. A second argument, linked to the first, claims that the failure of blacks and their leadership to recognize the prevalence of a color-blind American society has hindered the development of self-help or ethnic-uplift strategies for closing the black/white mobility gap. The third argument — basic to black conservative discourse — claims that affirmative action practices go too far in distorting what black conservatives perceive as the high-merit ideals that govern American occupational mobility. Black conservatives are especially concerned that such distortion of merit ideals tends to devalue the real achievement of successful black Americans, because whites will ask: "Did they make it by themselves or by affirmative action?"

The argument by conservatives on behalf of a new color-blind American society asserts that, since the middle 1960s, we can talk only of *an American racist past* — legalized housing segregation, lynchings, segregated public and private schools — and no longer of *an American racist legacy*, in the form of persistent or vestigial attitudes, values, norms, and informal practices that prevail within a variety of institutions (economic, social, political) in our post-civil rights era. In short, conservatives — black and white — claim that through legislation and judicial decisions, America's culture of racism has been vanquished, leaving no meaningful and significant traces and practices.

Generally, Black neoconservatives argue that current liberal Black leadership's obsessive concern with past racial injustice and compensatory affirmative action hinders the development and execution of

---

7. "Anatomy of Black Conservatism," *Transition*, Issue 59, 1993.

"self-help strategies." It is ironic that these advocates of "self-help" among Black Americans are themselves a group of "client-scholars", i.e., mercenary intellectuals, attached to the umbilical cords of the financial and institutional bastions of the conservative White American power establishment like the Heritage, Scaife, Bradley, and Olin foundations. One of the major functions of these institutions is to fund the work of both Black and White critics of Black struggles for civil rights, racial equality and affirmative action, and of the Afrocentric movement. Consequently, Black neo-cons essentially serve to rewrite traditional White conservative and racist ideological canards, trying to win for them legitimacy in the Afrikan American community by making it appear that these warmed-over, self-serving White supremacist contentions originate from their own independent minds. The central function and role of the Black neoconservative is to put a Black face on White Power.

If a central tendency of Black and White neoconservative argument can be discerned, it may best be defined in terms of an extreme White American mythological individualistic, "blaming the victim" ideological orientation. This particular White conservative tendency has been well delineated and refuted by authors William Ryan[8] and Michael Lewis. American individualism relative to its conceptual use by neo-conservatives [and a class of neo-liberals] is best defined by Michael Lewis under the rubric *the individual-as-central sensibility*. He defines it thusly:

> The emergence of this individualistic moral sensibility is of considerable significance, for as we shall see it has become central to the existence of the American *culture of inequality* — an interpretation of unequal outcomes given the assumption of equal chances. It is a sensibility that virtually ignores the impact of social structure upon personal achievement and mobility. According to this sensibility, it is the individual alone who is socially significant, who determines what his or her contribution to the commonweal will be, and who is therefore responsible for the degree of personal success achieved. Society is seen as benign, offering up opportunities and waiting to be enriched by those who have the will and the capacity to make productive use of them. This sensibility therefore removes inequality of personal perquisites from the category of social conditions in need of reform. If such inequality is seen as the product of traditional restrictions on opportunity it becomes a target for social reformers to whom it is the arbitrary and unjust outcome of a reactionary system. If, however, such inequality is simply an indication of differentials in

---

8. William Ryan, *Blaming The Victim* (New York: Vintage Books, 1976).

the productive exertion of individuals, free to exercise their ambitions and talents to the fullest, then the presumption of social arbitrariness cannot be sustained and only the individual can be held accountable for the state of his or her well-being. If inequality exists it is nothing more than a reflection of different personal qualities....

These explanations suggest that, because of inadequate personality structures, some people are self-defeating and therefore incapable of making the most of the opportunities which society (once again benign) proffers. Because they subscribe to poverty or lower-class subcultural world-views, some are inadequately motivated to make their way in a middle-class-dominated urban-industrial world. Because of the absence of a strong paternal model of conventional masculine competence, some boys grow up in families which ill-prepare them to participate fully and successfully in the economic mainstream. Because they lack sufficient cognitive skills to read at expected levels or reason adequately with figures, some people simply do not qualify for vocational opportunities which hold out real promise of personal success. Because of insufficient knowledge of what it takes to get along and work well with others (interpersonal competence), some are unable to make the best use of whatever productive talent they possess.[9]

While more sophisticated versions of this argument, ones preferred by liberal social scientists may attribute individual and group failure to psychodynamic makeup, cultural deprivation or orientation, family background, socialization practices, educational, cognitive and/or interpersonal incompetencies, the neoconservatives are more likely to attribute them to moral deficiencies. For the neoconservative, individuals and groups fail because of a lack of will, of desire to achieve, of drive; of the appropriate moral and social values. Failure is due to laziness, welfare dependency, a love of "low life" pleasures, and the like. The failed individual or group lacks self-respect and is not interested in striving for social respectability as defined by middle-class norms and behavior. Thus, according to this logic, as Lewis further contends, ..."success" (and its attendant perquisites) comes to be understood as being within the grasp of any individual who possesses the will and develops the necessary competence to succeed, ...alternatively "failure" (or visible disadvantage) comes to be understood as the price an individual must pay for personal dissolution and/or incompetence...."

This line of argumentation makes it saliently apparent why Black neoconservatives who utilize it are so immediately and tightly

---

9. Michael Lewis, *The Culture of Inequality* (New York: New American Library, 1978), pp. 8–9.

embraced by White conservatives and are so readily and copiously given White conservative and right-wing ideological, media, institutional and monetary support. Obviously this line absolves Whites and the White supremacist establishment of all historical and contemporary blame and reparative responsibility for the subordination and deprivation of Blacks. Under the rationalizing regime of this argument, White-dominated society is assumed to be fairly egalitarian and benign. Its very structure and functionality are perceived as having little significant formative impact on the personal and group morals, virtues and competencies thought to be crucial for individual and collective success. The Black neoconservative establishment, with its apparent need to rationalize its lack of ethnic connectedness and identity; its refusal to acknowledge and repay its debt to Black community activism; its refusal to take responsibility for helping to liberate the community from White domination; in its desire to enjoy the fruits of the good fortune bequeathed it by the death of numberless Black martyrs to the cause of racial justice and equality; undisturbed by the crying needs of contemporary Afrikan peoples, wants to convince Black Americans that in America opportunity is virtually unlimited and that limitations are not inequitably imposed on them by the functional imperatives of contemporary White American racism and capitalism.

We have neither the space nor time to refute the ahistorical and patently unsubstantiated idealistic arguments of the Black neoconservatives. We agree with Cruse when he contends, and goes on to establish, that "conservative arguments used to explain away racism or racial discrimination as the most important cause of black economic disadvantages...are historically and sociologically of dubious validity."

The neoconservatives seem to readily overlook the fact that even if it were absolutely true that Whites no longer engaged in racial discrimination, due to historical circumstances Blacks would remain disadvantaged relative to Whites. This would be the case simply due to the accumulated material and sociopolitical, sociocultural benefits Whites have inherited from the free labor of Black slaves; from the centuries-long racial domination and exploitation of Blacks. That is, even if they absolutely no longer practiced racial discrimination Whites would continue to enjoy an overwhelming competitive advantage over Blacks based on their near-400 years of accumulated assets alone. Moreover, neoconservatives overlook the fact that after 400 years of White racist social conditioning of Blacks; of White physical and psychic violence against Black bodies, minds and souls; of all types and combinations of physical and social restraints and frustrations visited on Blacks by White supremacy, that the mere removal of those conditioning paradigms and social limitations in the last 20 to 30 years would enable Blacks to take full positive advantage of the alleged new freedoms and opportunities now available to them. For a tree bent by restraints since it was a sapling, in its later maturity does not immediately stand straight because those restraints are rather suddenly removed. The gambler who has played with loaded dice, who has had all the odds in his favor, who owns the "house", who has virtually stripped his marks of all their material and social assets, does them little favor when he, for whatever reason — without justly compensating them for having cheated them before — decides to "play fair" with unloaded dice. This is especially the case when he still controls the "house", sets the rules of the game, and plays with his huge accumulated cache of filthy lucre or blood money. Centuries of White oppression have so conditioned the emotional, social and behavioral orientations of Blacks to be compatible with White domination that even their complete emancipation from it would make it appear that they desire to remain subordinated or are innately incapable of independent existence. In fact, the physical, social, political and economic conditioning of Blacks by Whites continues unabated to this moment — Black neoconservative obtuseness and psychological denial notwithstanding! Blacks are *yet* to be emancipated from White domination and exploitation.

It is important to note that Black neoconservatives generally revel in making insidious comparisons between American Blacks and various immigrant groups, even Black immigrant groups who have achieved economic and professional success while native-born Black Americans presumably have lingered behind. Often this putative situation is explained in terms of the cohesiveness of the other groups, their co-operativeness, willingness to work hard, thrift, family values, morals, and the like, compared to relative impairment or absence of such virtues among Black Americans. The Black neoconservative overlooks the fact that even if this argument could be empirically verified, it is of little primary explanatory value. People are not born innately prepared to be what their culture needs for them to be if it is to sustain and advance itself. They must be socialized, i.e., socially conditioned, taught and trained to be the persons they must be if they are to positively contribute to the well-being of their culture and to their own personal well-being. Members of immigrant groups have been *socialized* to function as they do. In light of this basic sociological fact, it is the role of the student of Black American socioeconomic behavior not to merely describe Black cultural traits by way of explaining the social conditions of Blacks, but to provide a psychohistorical explanation for their evolution and presence among Blacks, of the means by which these traits were and are conditioned and socialized in Blacks by and within the context of the larger White-dominated American society. Furthermore, it is the role of the student to analyze and explain how the traits he attributes to Black Americans, putative traits such as "laziness," apathy, disunity, etc., are not only induced in them by their American experience (apparently since they have nothing to do with their Blackness, since other Black immigrants do not exhibit them), but what politicoeconomic function they serve in maintaining America's White–Black power differential and the American racial status quo. Finally, after such analyses are completed it is incumbent that alternative socialization processes, social and institutional arrangements, reconstructed racial attitudes and relations be prescribed so as to re-socialize Black Americans in ways which will transform their disadvantages into advantages. These tasks the Black neoconservative ideologues have refused to undertake. Consequently, they can only present reactionary arguments in place of promulgating proactive, pragmatic programs for resolving the problems faced by Black Americans and Afrikans across the Diaspora.

Furthermore, as we alluded to in our discussion of the assimilationist leadership establishment, the Black neoconservatives overlook the "indian giving" propensities of dominant Whites. That is, what they give with one hand they take with the other. Consequently, even if Whites decided to be absolutely racially non-discriminatory in hiring Blacks they would still maintain overwhelming competitive advantage due to the existence and practice of racial discrimination in areas pertinent to qualifying for job opportunities. For example, let us say that White-owned companies engage in absolutely no racial discrimination in the hiring of Black computer scientists. Moreover, let us say they may even give these scientists a certain number of extra credits due to the past dominatory practices relative to their White counterparts. We contend that a strong bias in favor of hiring a much larger number of White scientists would still functionally exist not just because of their larger percentage in the population, but more tellingly, because of race and class-based differences in the funding, staffing and organization of courses in computer science which inhere between predominantly Black urban schools and predominantly White suburban schools. This structural dynamic in the education of Blacks and Whites ensures that while the Blacks who "make it" will not be discriminated against or may be even favored to some degree, there will be relatively few of them who will qualify to receive the blessings of racially non-discriminatory employment. Ironically, it will probably be more likely under these circumstances that those Black scientists who are hired and who are either unaware of the operation of the structural differentials in the education of Blacks and Whites or who have forgotten these things as the result of so enjoying the rarified atmosphere of "racial equality", are more likely to become neophyte Black neoconservatives than Black scientists who perceive things differently. They will more likely argue that based on their lack of experience of negative racial discrimination in hiring, the significance of race in accelerating or retarding social mobility has drastically declined or disappeared.

The Black neoconservative, like the Black assimilationist, is a fanatical believer that fairy tales do come true — that the king always offers his daughter, the beautiful princess, and half his kingdom to the triumphant hero who slays the dragon. And they live happily ever after. Harking back to some of the preachments of B.T. Washington, they believe that when the Black man demonstrates his worth and proves himself worthy of the White man's respect he will be accepted as an equal in the White man's domain and live happily ever after! This never-never-land perspective is based on numerous faulty and completely unwarranted assumptions, central among which is the assumption that the White man will always rule a Kingdom he can equally divide with his Black dragonslayers; that he is inclined or compelled by nature to give away or share his daughters and his wealth with his Black underlings, hero or none; that he will not take both daughter and the given half of his Kingdom back should the need arise.

The Black neoconservative argument rests on the very dubious assumption, the one being refuted everyday now that the American economy and social opportunity system will continue to prosper and expand, will offer abundant opportunities continuously, and therefore all Blacks have to do is *qualify* for those opportunities! They need not worry about constructing an ethnically based, Afrikan-centered economy of their own, or worry about creating their own opportunity structure for self-employment; that they can depend on the beneficent White-dominated economic system to meet their needs if only they behave appropriately. In fact, they believe attempts to construct an Afrikan-centered sociocultural, politicoeconomic system would retard Black acceptance in a White or multicultural world — a world, incidentally, where Whites and other groups own and control their own ethnocentric, social and economic systems. Black neocons have infinite faith in the propositions that other non-Afrikan ethnic groups will, in all their *magnanimity*, sacrifice their own ethnic interests, prerogatives and welfare in the interests of democratic ideals and in the interest of economically raising to equality, dependent and militarily weak Afrikans — just as Blacks have sacrificed their own vital interests in the name of *"fraternité et egalité"*. There is absolutely no historical foundation for this genocidally-dangerous guiding fiction so avariciously accepted by Black conservatives and assimilationists alike.

In the face of the ethnically based economic and military power of other ethnic groups; in the face of the fact that individual achievement, success, power, influence, and self-actualization are made possible and take place as a consequence of and within a *social* system, a system of *social* relations, a system of persons and groups and institutions systematically interacting according to societal and cultural commonalities, identities, commitments, obligations, reinforcements, regulations and expectations; in face of the fact, as noted by Parenti, that "while the socialization of owning-class members is designed to foster class loyalties and cohesions, the socialization of the propertyless moves with opposite effect", that White power is the result of White solidarity against non-whites; — in the face of all these obvious facts, the Black neoconservative is the consummate individualist. Self-hating, ethnically irresponsible, and extremely desirous of shedding his Afrikan identity which he misperceives as the source of his suffering in a White racist-dominated world, in a world marked from time immemorial by ethnocentrism, the Black neoconservative longs for an atomized individualism for himself and all other Afrikans where he will no longer be "judged by the color of his skin but by the content of his character".

> Under modern capitalism, society itself becomes little more than an impersonal arena of private interests, of people devoid of strong communal bonds, living for individuated, rather than collective, need. Organic links dissolve before the rationalized, restless demands of the market society. Divested of functional productive tasks and communal relations other than the necessity of having to earn money and consume, the individual often has a difficult time "finding" himself or herself. The need to discover "who am I?", a preoccupation unknown to many earlier societies, is mistakenly treated as an interior personal matter having nothing to do with the way society is organized. Implicit in the quest for one's "individuality" is the dubious notion that the individual exists as something abstracted from a

social matrix, apart from the web of tasks, obligations, affections, and collective relationships which give people their identities, their social meaning, and their experience of humanity and of themselves. Thus people search for "autonomy" and seek to free themselves from emotional dependency upon others without questioning whether such an accomplishment is, in the deepest human sense, desirable or possible. Finding so many of their social relations to be loveless, exploitative, and opportunistic, people mistakenly seek to build an individualized autarky, to find "liberation" in a composed isolation....

Yet the question remains for all groups and persons: liberation toward what?[10]

The naive belief in and the desire for unalloyed, uncommitted, ethnically undefinable individuality by the extreme Black neoconservative (for not all Black neoconservatives reject race consciousness and identity) will to his utter surprise neither liberate him individually nor rescue him from his racial identity — as the phrase *Black Conservative* [note: not merely "*conservative*", but "black conservative"] clearly implies. Nomadic individualism will neither enhance the security of Blacks nor necessarily heighten the quality of their lives. This is made clear by the fact that the rise to material well-being and prominence by a sizable class of Black American professionals who haughtily designate themselves as "Americans" or more abstractly, as "human beings", and the rise to power by an Afrikan ruling elite, has been attended by the rapidly accelerating decline into poverty and powerlessness of the Black American and Afrikan masses.

For the neoconservative Black — like the child who believes that when he closes his eyes, the sun disappears — forgets one crucial and disempowering fact: that not because he refuses to identify himself as Afrikan, the ethnocentric world around him will cease to exist, that other ethnics will no longer see him and treat him as a Black, as an Afrikan. A race of self-chosen, disconnected former Blacks or Afrikans must lose the power that can come only from connectedness, from empathic ethnic identity, from ethnically and culturally based organization.

The neoconservatives pose the problems of Afrikan Americans and their solutions in terms of personal and familial character, ethics, morals and behavioral deportment. Their concern is not with the problems of power but with demonstrating presumed moral and characterological deficiencies of Black people, with moral adjurations, idealistic preachments, and vacuous political diatribes. Moreover, since these minions of the White conservative establishment will not

---

10. Michael Parenti, *Power and the Powerless*, pp. 105-6.

"bite the hands that feed them" — White conservative foundations and think tanks — they dare not challenge White Power with Black Power. They cannot present Black America with proactive proposals for Afrikan liberation and empowerment, only reactionary and accommodative ones. They achieve victory over White racism by simply denying its existence and its threat to the well-being and survival of Afrikan peoples everywhere, a threat only to be overcome by Black empowerment.

Black neoconservative ideology is, therefore, in the main, disempowering for Afrikan peoples. Consequently, Afrikan peoples whose fundamental ailment is powerlessness can only do themselves a vital service by rejecting it in all haste.

Black Nationalist Leadership

Nationalism is an ideology of a thousand faces. While we all may have a similar sense of what it involves, we cannot all agree on any one definition of it. As an ideological and political concept, nationalism is related to the equally unwieldy concept of "nation". Rooted in the prefix "nat" — "to be born", nation implies an entity composed of persons who are born or adopted members of a people who share a common language, territory, economic life, worldview, a set of social experiences, values, thinking and behavioral orientations. The word "nation" is an abstract symbol which is evoked and utilized to elicit certain concrete states of consciousness and "to legitimate numerous social actions and movements often having very diverse aims."[11] Verdery relates nationalism to nation in the following way.

> Nationalism, in this perspective, is the political utilization of the symbol nation through discourse and political activity, as well as the sentiment that draws people into responding to this symbol's use. Nationalism is a quintessentially homogenizing, differentiating, or classifying discourse: one that aims its appeal at people presumed to have certain things in common as against people thought not to have any mutual connections. In modern nationalisms, among the most important things to have in common are certain forms of culture and tradition, and specific history.

Citing the work of anthropologist John Borneman,[12] Verdery distinguishes "between nationalism and nationess, the former referring to conscious sentiments that take the nation as an object of

---

11. Kathrine Verdery, "Whither 'Nation' and 'Nationalism'?: Nation and Nationalism: What are they?" *Daedalus*, Summer, 1993.

12. John Borneman, *Belonging in the Two Berlins: Kin, State, Nation* (Cambridge: Cambridge Univ. Press, 1992).

active devotion, the latter to daily interactions and practices that produce an inherent and often unarticulated feeling of belonging, of being home."

One of the central bases for assuming a sense of nation may be ethnicity. Ethnicity, the sense of common descent, whether real or imputed, especially when validated by generations of common historical experience and when allied with nationalism, has been the most potent force in people's attempts to achieve self-determination, to struggle against domination and exploitation by alien peoples. Nationalism undergirded by the sense of nation, provides the basis for mutual support, solidarity, identity, structure and cohesion to a people who otherwise may feel atomized, insecure, vulnerable, bereft of stabilizing norms, values and affirmative social relations. Through nation-ness and nationalism the individual transcends his existential aloneness and shares in the much broader virtues and powers of the group. His power and that of the group of which he is a member are one.

The power of the group amplifies and extends the power of its individual members. Nationalism has been used by nation-states to facilitate the consolidation of a distinct people(s) and territory as well as to create colonies and empires. Conversely, it has been, and can be utilized to overthrow colonial and imperial domination. Nationalism creates a collective, focused power which enables a people to achieve ends which, as separate individuals pursuing their own unrelated self-interested ends, they could never achieve. The power generated by nationalism is the bane and harbinger of destruction to those who wish to establish or maintain imperial control over other peoples. This is the main reason it is defamed vociferously by imperialistic peoples and nations despite the fact that it is the main instrument of their own domination of other peoples and nations. Nationalism is often catalytically brought into active existence by oppression. As an instrument of power it is often logically chosen as a means of overcoming oppressive and repressive conditions by a people who perceive themselves to be oppressed by another. Such is the case in regard to Black peoples and in regard to Black Nationalism.

Why Black Nationalism?

Nationalism is a double-edged sword. It can be wielded as a tool of oppression by cohesively organized peoples or nation-states such as those of Western Europe, who used it to impose their exploitative rule over many non-European nations and peoples, or by White Americans to enslave and otherwise dominate Black Americans. It can also be used as a tool to organize an oppressed people, nation-states, to best achieve their liberation from oppression and/or to achieve sovereignty or self-determination and to gain control of a national territory.

While the nationalism of some peoples or nation-states may be evoked and utilized to realize some racial sense of superiority or "manifest destiny" or to motivate one group to commandeer and exploit the resources of another, the nationalism of some peoples or nation-states is evoked and utilized to liberate themselves from their oppressive exploitation by imperialistic peoples or nation-states; to increase and realize their inherent socioeconomic potentials without necessarily implying that they are racially superior to, or intend to dominate other peoples or other states. The former nationalism intends to achieve or maintain national self-determination while denying that status to others in so far as it is able to do so. The latter nationalism intends to achieve and sustain national self-determination while not engaging in imperialism by denying autonomy or independent nationhood to others. Thus nationalism by definition and intention is not a monolithic concept and therefore all nationalisms are not the same or are equally racially or politically pernicious or counterproductive as some Eurocentric and liberal intellectuals and government spokespersons would have us believe.

Black or Afrikan nationalism is of the second variety — a nationalism of liberation and self-determination, not of conquest and domination. It is premised on the precept that Blacks as a people should not be the subjects of another people nor should they subject other peoples; that Black peoples and nations should exercise their full rights to develop and utilize their material, human and spiritual resources primarily for their own benefit and well-being and for the benefit and well-being of others as they see fit to do. They view their personhood and humanity, their nationality and ethnicity as equal to that of any and all other persons or peoples, that they are not the inferiors of others and are not destined by god or man to exist in forced servitude to others. And when, and if, and for however long they may be willfully subjected to the domination of others, they are commissioned by their inalienable right to freedom as human beings to resist such domination and overthrow it as soon as humanly possible. This is the bedrock credo of Black nationalism today as it manifests itself in the United States of America, across the Diaspora and in the world.

To paraphrase Jean Jacques Rousseau, the Afrikan is born free but he is everywhere in chains. Throughout this volume and in hundreds of volumes and papers scattered around this globe we have chronicled the material sufferings and political vassalage of Afrikans at home and abroad, the largest proportion of these situations wrought by the hands of alien peoples. However, a crucial and substantial proportion of Afrikan suffering has been and is wrought by their own hands. Black nationalism recognizes that the power of Afrikan peoples to achieve liberation and self-determination lies within their grasp. Afrikan liberation and self-determination will not and cannot be willed or given to Afrikan peoples by non-Afrikan peoples. They must be won through the self-sustained exercise of power generated by Afrikans themselves.

The primary tools used by Black [or Afrikan] nationalists in breaking the mental chains of subordination of Afrikan peoples to other peoples are historical and cultural re-armament. Black nationalism recognizes that European peoples' domination of Black peoples has been primarily achieved and maintained by their stringently clever falsification of the consciousness of Black peoples; by their conditioning of oppressed Blacks to behave in self-defeating, self-destructive ways. This falsification of Afrikan consciousness and the related conditioning of Afrikan misbehavior, combined with the material and social deprivations imposed on Afrikans under the aegis of European economic and military prowess, describes the fundamental context of Afrikan American and Pan–Afrikan socioeconomic, sociocultural subordination and physical peril. These conditions must be hastily and soundly rectified if Afrikans in America and the world-over are to survive and prosper in freedom.

Black Cultural Nationalism. While there have been very notable attempts to address the material or economic deprivation of Blacks and the powerlessness these conditions breed, especially attempts by the Honorable Marcus Mosiah Garvey and the Nation of Islam under the leadership of the Honorable Elijah Muhammad and Malcolm X, the bulk of the attention and energy of Black nationalists have been focused on the rectification of falsifications of Afrikan history and culture. Efforts in this regard on the part of many prominent past and contemporary Black nationalists have been referred to as Black cultural nationalism, in contrast to what we might refer to as Black economic nationalism. (The reader should keep in mind that these "nationalisms" are not by any means mutually exclusive, but are merely a matter of emphasis — having important consequences nevertheless.)

Cultural nationalists seek to restore in Afrikan peoples a knowledge and practice of their true history and culture, mainly through education and the use of various cultural artforms. They generally believe that the cultural revolution must necessarily precede or is a form of political revolution (and presumably economic revolution). Black cultural nationalists believe that Black people must free themselves culturally before they free themselves politically. Black nationalism as ideology is based on the belief that Black people in America constitute a cultural Nation.

The impact of resuscitated Afrikan and Black American history and culture has been remarkably significant in culturally revolutionizing the mind, consciousness and behavior of many in the Black community today. The growing acceptance of the ideology of Afrocentricity, Black or Afrikana Studies, Afrikan-centered and multicultural curricula; the proliferation of Afrikan study groups, Afrikan-centered seminars, forums, conferences and lectures; the establishment of Afrikan cultural institutions; the growing enactment of Afrikan-centered socialization practices and social rituals; the increased consumption of Afrikan-styled items, products, art, artifacts and wearables; the tremendously expanded trade and readership in Black American and Afrikan-centered books and literature, brilliantly attest to the effectiveness of cultural nationalism in reorienting and reconfiguring the consciousness and cultural attitudes of many in the Afrikan national and international communities. Let us hasten to add that Black nationalism has always had a significant constituency in the Afrikan American community. This constituency tends to expand during periods of crisis and to contract under the heavy-handed influences of a combination of state welfarism, concessional White liberalism allied with Black assimilationism per organizations like the NAACP, the National Urban League and other civil rights organizations, and perhaps, better economic times. Cultural nationalism has to a measurable extent even penetrated the consciousness of the traditional civil rights leadership. The tentative embrace of the Honorable Louis Farrakhan by the head of the NAACP, Ben Chavis [since deposed], and by other assimilationist leaders and some leading ministers in the institutional Black Church, seems to indicate that the message of Black nationalism is being listened to, if not put into practice, by Black establishments which not so long ago patently disavowed its preachments.

Contemporary Black Nationalism: Absence of Organization, Creed and Plans

The relatively remarkable success of cultural nationalism in changing the cultural consciousness and tastes of a sizable segment of the Afrikan American community simultaneously highlights its crucial success, failings and vulnerabilities. The cultural success of cultural nationalism has not been paralleled by Black social, economic and political success. While the cultural indoctrination of Black America moved apace, the social disorganization and deterioration of the Black urban community easily out-paced it. The monopolization of the Black community's economic infrastructure by alien groups has been astoundingly rapid and gripping. Unemployment in the Black community has reached Great Depression levels and continues to rise. The political clout of the Afrikan American community has diminished and is increasingly neutralized by the growing political and economic clout of other minority groups. All of these events along with others already discussed have converged to disempower Black America. In the face of this and other indicators we must conclude, therefore, that cultural nationalism and Black nationalism in general, have not yet been able to convert Black and Afrikan cultural sentiment, Black and Afrikan history, culture and pride into tangible Black Power. In this instance it has reached essentially the same impasse as that reached by the assimilationism and the Black neoconservativism. They all have been unable or unwilling to convert their ideological achievements into programmatic, tangible, bankable, politicoeconomic imperatives for Afrikans in the Americas and across the Diaspora. Relative to Black nationalists, there are a number of important reasons for this situation. We shall now list a few of the most important ones.

Reactionary-Compensatory Blackness and Afrikanicity. Black nationalists have rightly responded to Eurocentric, White supremacist assaults on the collective body, mind, soul of Afrikan people. However, their response has too often involved a reactionary obsession with demonstrating the equality of Afrikan humanity, the primal and extraordinary accomplishments and qualities of Afrikan history and culture. While re-educating the Afrikan community about its true history and culture and the true nature of White imperialism and racism, contemporary Black nationalism has demonstrated inadequate concern with organizing effective means of *overthrowing* politicoeconomic oppression of the community by Whites and other ethnic groups. Huey Newton's critique of cultural nationalism still seems apropos, even if a bit overstated — "The cultural nationalists are concerned with returning to the old Afrikan culture and thereby regaining their identity and freedom. In other words, they feel that the Afrikan culture will automatically bring political freedom" (*The*

Movement, August 1968). We believe that this somewhat "magical thinking" while of utmost importance in restoring the critically wounded Afrikan ego to vital health, has retarded the equally important ability of the nationalists to provide the political rationales, theories, developmental plans, working organizations and systems to enable Afrikan peoples to regain their sovereignty and to enhance their well-being and standing in the world.

Militant Retreat. The critique originally leveled against cultural nationalism by Robert Allen still holds true for an important segment of the nationalist community. Allen (ibid) correctly points out that the belief "that black culture and art [and the mere individual and group reclamation of Afrikan culture and identity] alone will somehow bring about a revolution...has allowed a passive retreat into "blackness" on the part of some of those who call themselves revolutionaries." He goes on to say, "These so-called black revolutionaries measure their militancy by how much "black awareness" they have or how "bad" they can talk. Verbal militance thus replaces action, and the net result is passive nonresistance to oppression. Black culture becomes a badge to be worn rather than an experience to be shared." While fully supportive of the need for a deepening awareness of Black culture and history and the absolutely crucial role it must, has, and does play in motivating and shaping Black activism and the politics of Afrikan liberation, we concur with Allen when he cautions that cultural nationalism can become a retreat into reaction "if it is not firmly incorporated into a revolutionary political movement."

A Paucity of Intellectual Vision. Black nationalism is ideally a mass or people's movement. It seeks to encompass the Afrikan masses and involve them intimately in their own liberation from oppression and in the determination of their own political destiny. The chief opponents of Black nationalists have traditionally been bourgeois, assimilationist, liberal, and conservative intellectuals, both Black and White. The people-orientedness and *anti*bourgeois-ism of Black nationalism and its supporters have bred in many of its influential leaders a paralyzing ambivalence towards an often overt contempt for intellectuals and intellection or theorizing in general. This is not to say that Black Nationalists have no positive regard for intellectuals, for there exist highly regarded nationalist intellectuals both past and present. In fact, on the whole the most popular nationalist intellectuals tend to be those who most effectively expose the nature, history and pernicious effects of White racism, who present a history, cultural anthropology and sociopsychological characterization supportive of and flattering to the collective and individual egos of Afrikan people.

While these types of intellectuals are justifiably popular and honored and the work they do vitally necessary to Afrikan liberation, the place and role of intellectuals who cover other concerns vital to Afrikan liberation have not been productively recognized or reinforced by the Black nationalist movement as a whole. The overwhelming popularity of charismatic intellectuals whose acclaim is basically founded on exposés of White racism and racist depravity and on flattering or uplifting portrayals of Afrikan history and culture, has unwittingly operated at the cost of submerging Black nationalist intellectuals whose pursuit of broader visions for Afrikan peoples are future-oriented, pragmatic and concerned with dealing directly with the contemporary reality of Afrikan life in the Americas and across the Diaspora. The critique Cruse made of the role played by intellectuals in the Civil Rights Movement, that this "movement is at an impasse precisely because it lacks a real functional corps of intellectuals able to confront and deal perceptively with American realities on a level that social conditions demand," applies equally to the current nationalist movement. The same can be said with regard to the global realities confronting Afrikan peoples worldwide.

Nationalists must recognize nothing is more practical and powerful than broad, solid intellectual perspectives and theories; perspectives and theories drawn from a broad array of knowledge, experience and thought, even some of which may have been developed by the imperialistic, Eurocentric establishment; perspectives and theories inextricably tied to creating the social practices which will actualize the hopes and visions of the people.

Lack of Definition and Organization. We have written of Black nationalism as if it were a clearly defined creed propagated by an organized group of dedicated advocates and activists. That this is most certainly not the case, is Black nationalism's greatest failing. The actual empowerment of Black people under the banner of Black nationalism cannot occur as long as the two main ingredients necessary for power — definition and organization — are missing or underdeveloped. Obviously, Black nationalists and nationalistic organizations functionally exist. But the absence of a consensually clarified set of goals and a working well-coordinated system of interdependent nationalist organizations, makes impossible the conversion of ambiguously defined nationalist sentiments into a powerful political-economic-cultural movement. Such a movement must become the vehicle for liberation and racial ascendancy of Afrikan peoples in the world of the twenty-first century.

Even if Black nationalist motives and purposes were perfectly defined and matched, Black Power would still prove elusive without organizational appropriateness and a sufficiency of human and material resources. The past and present popularity of Black nationalistic leaders and spokespersons, writers and lecturers, organizations and groups, point to broad support in the Afrikan community for Black nationalist ideological values and goals. Today, the Black nationalist-oriented Nation of Islam leader, the Honorable Louis Farrakhan, has a large national, international and personal following, exerts broad appeal and influence in the Afrikan community as measured by his ability to draw very large crowds and assemblies. He, without doubt, is the one of the most popular platform speakers today. There are a sizable number of lesser known nationalists who are held in high esteem across broad segments of the national and international Afrikan community. However, all this is for naught without broad agreement on purpose and without a unifying/unified nationalist organization.

Despite their declining relevance as a leadership establishment and the disempowering logic of their ideologies, the national scope of their organization has permitted the assimilationists to set the agenda, frame and shape the political/economic/ cultural issues of the Afrikan American community. In sum, while the assimilationists advocate ideological orientations and programs that have proved not only to be patent failures in certain vital areas but concretely injurious to the broader economic needs and interests of Afrikan peoples, they are organized. They also have White liberal organizational monetary support. While the Black neoconservatives are the recipients of White conservative organizational and monetary support, the Black nationalist leadership establishment which advocates a popular and empowering ideology is largely bereft of the organizational infrastructure which would allow it to garner the monetary and political support of its many supporters, sympathizers and would-be followers.

A Black Nationalist Party

To be maximally powerful and effective the nationalist movement must first officially and organizationally establish its existence and reason for being. It must organize a national political party and economic system with a solid, well-trained and informed, well-organized base of grassroots organizations on local, state, regional, national and international levels. On these levels and especially on the national and international levels the nationalists must replace the assimilationist and neoconservative organizations as the primary and legitimate leader on behalf of the Afrikan American community. They must provide the community with a viable, workable plan for economic development, development based on a mixed economy of primarily cooperative, self-help, economic institutions and collective enterprises, corporate and proprietary businesses. A Black nationalist party must provide the training, know-how and personnel with which to organize the Black community nationally. It must organize a Black-based political economy which will assume control of the internal communal markets of the community and which can successfully penetrate and effectively influence the national and international marketplace. The Black nationalist party must become the primary political arm of the Afrikan American community, its chief negotiator with other mainstream and third party organizations, the principal agency for forming coalitions with other groups, all in furthering the vital interests of the community and protecting its physical, socioeconomic and sociopsychological integrity as mandated by the community.

Parallel Institutions. A major problem a nationalistic party must face in becoming actively accepted and supported by the people is its legitimacy — that is, it must exist and act in accord with the consent of the people, according to rules, rituals, traditions and cultural values established by the people. It is only when a nationalistic party is perceived as morally and materially legitimate by the community that it can accomplish the missions it will be assigned to complete by the people.

To a significant degree, the legitimation of a Black nationalist party rests on its ability to arrive at a definition of the vital socioeconomic interests and goals acceptable to the Afrikan community and its demonstration that it is capable of realizing those interests and goals in terms of its organizational know-how.

In tandem with its own legitimation process a nationalist party must, to a significant degree, de-legitimate its rivals as representatives of the people. While we cannot in this space discuss the number of ways this delegitimation process can be approached, let us say that in general it involves the clear pointing out the inability of its political rivals and of the powers-that-be to adequately define and satisfy the needs of the people. Moreover, the nationalists must clearly demonstrate how current government policy and the policy of their rivals are actually injurious to the people's interests and well-being.

If a Black nationalist party is to delegitimate the assimilationists, neoconservatives and the White power structure as well as reduce their capacity to structure the desires, thoughts and behavioral tendencies, dependency relations, and common interests of the Black community in their selfish interests, then it must imaginatively develop and actuate an alternative set of rules and social relations, create exclusive autonomous institutions and spaces — protected from the influence of the powers-that-be — that can counteract the institutions and social power relations of the dominant power structure.

To achieve the necessary credibility and support it must attain in order to be accepted as the community's legitimate representative party, a Black nationalist party must prove itself capable of resolving important community problems. For example, a well-organized, highly regarded and trained nationalist party, by very significantly helping to reduce the ravages of drug abuse and miseducation would undoubtedly gain the gratitude and support of a beleaguered Black community. Black nationalist cultural institutions which through manhood and womanhood education and rites of passage can very significantly help to curb violence, teenage pregnancy, school dropout-ism, adolescent incivility, and the like, would undoubtedly gain legitimacy as the true representative of the people. If a Black nationalist party can protect against police brutality; can institute Afrikan-centered schools and cultural programs which markedly enhance the academic and cultural development of Black children; can demonstrate the capacity to establish and maintain successful commercial enterprises against fierce competition from other ethnic groups, and the like, its legitimacy and community support will be assured and its ability to focus and wield Black Power decisively in the interest of Black people and humanity multiplied many-fold. However, these laudable ends cannot be achieved unless and until Black nationalists are organized through conventions, conferences, strategy and training sessions on the national, state, regional and local levels. This party must be organized under a ratified constitution with a workable system of checks and balances and a clearly defined order of election and succession to office. Above all, if it is to be a major instrument of Black Power, the nationalist party must be fully aware that it is the achievement of genuine Black Power, a power which can effectively and successfully rival the power of Whites and of any other ethnic group as well as work with them in the interest of all humankind, which must be its primary goal and reason for being. For without power the people will perish. Power to the People!

Bibliography

Akoto, Kwame Agyei. 1992. *Nationbuilding: Theory and Practice in Afrikan Centered Education*. Washington, D.C.: Pan Afrikan World Institute.

Allen, D. & Rahman, S. "Small Business Incubators: A Positive Environment for Entrepreneurship," *Journal of Small Business Management,* 1985.

Allen, Gary. "The Bankers: Conspiratorial Origins of the Federal Reserve," *American Opinion,* 1978.

American Bankers Association, 1990. *The Credit Union Industry: Trends, Structure, and Competitiveness*. Washington, D.C.: A.B.A.

Anmbry, Margaret. 1992. *Consumer Power: How Americans Spend*. Chicago: Probus. Publishing Co.

Ardener, Shirley. "The Comparative Study of Rotating Credit Associations," *Journal of the Royal Anthropological Institute 94 Pt. 2,* 1964.

Austin, J.L. 1975. *How To Do Things With Words*, 2nd ed., (Urmsson, J.O. & Sbisa, M., eds.). Washington, D.C.: Howard University Press.

Babson-United Investment Advisors, Inc. *Successful Investing,* 4th ed. New York: Fireside Book.

Baltzell, E. Digby. 1958. *Philadelphia Gentlemen: The Making of a National Upper Class*. Glencoe, New York: The Free Press.

Bazelon, David. 1963. *The Paper Economy*. New York: Vintage Books.

Becker, Howard. 1963. *Outsiders: Studies in the Sociology of Deviance*. Glencoe, New York: The Free Press.

Beetham, David. 1991. *The Legitimation of Power*. New Jersey: Humanities Press.

Berle, Jr., A.A. 1958. *Economic Power and the Free Society*. New York: Fund for the Republic.

_____ , 1959. *Power Without Property*. New York: Harcourt Brace Jovanovich.

Blumberg, Paul. 1980. *Inequality In An Age of Decline*. Cambridge: Oxford Univ. Press.

Borneman, John. 1992. *Belonging in the Two Berlins: Kin, State, Nation*. Cambridge: Cambridge Univ. Press.

Bourdieu, Pierre, 1991. *Language and Symbolic Power* (John B. Thompson, ed.). Cambridge, Mass.: Harvard Univ. Press.

Brown, Michael & Tiffen, Paul. 1992. *Short Changed: Africa and World Trade.* Boulder, Colorado: Pluto Press.

Buchanan, Anne. 1982. *Food, Poverty and Power.* Nottingham, England: Bertrand Russell House.

Burns, James MacGregor. 1978. *Leadership.* New York: Harper Torchlight.

Butler, John Sibley. 1991. *Entrepreneurship and Self-Help Among Black Americans: A Reconsideration of Race and Economics.* Albany, New York: State University of New York Press.

Carnes, W. Stansbury & Slider, Stephen D. 1992. *The Atlas of Economic Indicators: A Visual Guide to Market Forces and the Federal Reserves.* New York: Harper.

Carosso, Vincent P. 1970. *Investment Banking in America: A History.* Cambridge, Mass.: Harvard Univ. Press.

Chu, Chin-Ning. 1991. *The Asian Mind Game.* New York: Rawson Associates.

Clark, Kenneth B. 1965. *Ghetto: Dilemmas of Social Power.* New York: Harper & Row.

Coleman, James. 1969. *Psychology and Effective Behavior.* Glenview, Illinois: Scott, Foresman & Co.

Cookson, Jr., Peter W. and Persell, Caroline H. 1985. *Preparing for Power: America's Elite Boarding Schools.* New York: Basic Books.

Cross, Theodore. 1987. *The Black Power Imperative: Racial Inequality and the Politics of Nonviolence.* New York: Faulkner Books.

Cruse, Harold. 1987. *Plural but Equal: A Critical Study of Blacks and Minorities and America's Plural Society.* New York: William Morrow.

Dager, Albert J. 1990. *Vengeance Is Ours: The Church in Dominion.* Michigan: Sword Publishers.

Dahl, Robert A, "A Critique of the Ruling Elite Model," *American Political Science Review,* June, 1958.

Davidson, Basil. 1966. *A History of West Africa: To The Nineteenth Century.* New York: Doubleday-Anchor Books.

Davis, Mike. "Who Killed L.A.? The War Against the Cities." *Crossroads,* No. 32, 1993.

Diamond, M. & Williams, J. 1987. *How To Incorporate: A Handbook for Entrepreneurs and Professionals.* New York: John Wiley & Sons.

Domhoff, William G. 1967. *Who Rules America?* New Jersey: Prentice Hall Press.

⸻, 1979. *The Powers That Be: Processes of Ruling Class Domination in America.* New York: Vintage Books.

⸻, 1983. *Who Rules America Now? A View for the '80s.* New Jersey: Prentice Hall.

DuBois, W.E.B. 1968. *Dusk of Dawn: An Essay Toward an Autobiography of a Race Concept.* New York: Schocken.

Dye, Thomas R. 1983. *Power and Society: An Introduction to the Social Sciences,* 3rd ed. California: Brooks-Cole.

_____, 1990. *Power and Society: An Introduction to the Social Sciences,* 5th ed. California: Brooks-Cole.
Ellsworth, Scott. 1992. *Death in a Promised Land: The Tulsa Race Riot of 1921.* Baton Rouge, Louisiana: Louisiana State University Press.
Frazier, E. Franklin. 1962. *The Black Bourgeoisie: The Rise of a Middle Class in the United States.* New York: Collier-Macmillan.
Frazier, E. Franklin and Lincoln, C. Eric. 1974. *The Negro Church in America.* New York: Schocken Books.
Fromm, Erich. 1941. *Escape from Freedom.* New York: Holt, Rinehart and Winston.
Fusfeld, Daniel R. & Bates, Timothy. 1984. *The Political Economy of the Urban Ghetto.* Chicago: Southern Illinois Univ. Press.
Galbraith, John Kenneth. 1968. *The New Industrial State.* New York: Houghton Mifflin.
_____, 1983. *The Anatomy of Power.* Boston: Houghton Mifflin.
Garvey, Amy J. 1970. *Garvey and Garveyism.* New York: Macmillan.
Geertz, Clifford. "The Rotating Credit Association: A Middle Rung in Development," *Economic Development and Cultural Change.* 1962.
Gerth, H., & Mills, C.W. 1953. *Character and Social Structure: The Psychology of Social Institutions.* New York: Harcourt Brace Jovanovich.
Greenberg, Edward. 1974. *Serving the Few: Corporate Capitalism and the Bias of Government Policy.* New York: John Wiley.
Greider, William. 1974. *Who Will Tell the People: The Betrayal of American Democracy.* New York: Simon & Schuster.
Harris, Abram L. 1936. *The Negro as Capitalist.* College Park, Md.: McGrath Publishing Company.
Heilbroner, Robert L. 1985. *The Nature and Logic of Capitalism.* New York: W.W. Norton.
_____, 1988. *Behind the Veil of Economics: Essays in the Worldly Philosophy.* New York: W.W. Norton.
Heilbroner, Robert L., and Thurow, L. 1987. *Economics Explained.* New York: Simon & Schuster.
Hofheinz, R. & Calder, K. 1982. *The Eastasia Edge.* New York: Basic Books.
Honigsberg, Pete., Kamofoff, Bernard & Beatty, Jim. 1982. *We Own It: Starting & Managing Coops, Collectives & Employee-Owned Ventures.* Laytonville, CA: Bell Springs Publishing.
Horowitz, David and Kolodney, David. 1974. *The Poverty Establishment* (Pamela Roby, ed.). New Jersey: Prentice-Hall.
Horton, Paul B. & Hunt, Chester L. 1968. *Sociology.* New York: McGraw-Hill.
Humphreys, Jeffrey. *Black Buying Power by Place of Residence: 1990–1995.* Vol. 54, No. 4, Georgia Business and Economic Conditions, 1994.
Kambon, Kobi K. 1992. *The African Personality in America: An African-Centered Framework.* Tallahassee, Florida. Nubian Nation Publications.

Katznelson, Ira and Kesselman, Mark. 1975. *The Politics of Power: A Critical Introduction to American Government.* New York: Harcourt Brace Jovanovich.

Keen, David. 1994. *The Benefits of Famine: A Political Economy of Famine Relief in the South Western Sudan 1983-1989.* New Jersey: Princeton University Press.

Kennedy, Paul. 1988. *The Rise and Fall of the Great Powers.* New York: Random House.

———, 1993. *Preparing for the 21st Century: Winners and Losers.* New York: Random House.

Kotkin, Joel. 1993. *Tribes: How Race, Religion and Identity Determine Success in the New Global Economy.* New York: Random House.

Kristein, Marvin. 1969. *Corporation Finance.* New York: Barnes & Noble.

Krugman, Paul. 1994. *Peddling Prosperity: Economic Sense and Nonsense in the Age of Diminished Expectations.* New York: W.W. Norton.

Laing, R.D. 1971. *Self and Others.* Baltimore, Maryland: Penguin Books.

Lappé, Frances M. & Collins, Joseph. 1977. *Food First: Beyond the Myth of Society.* Boston: Houghton Mifflin.

Lazonick, William. 1991. *Business Organization and the Myth of the Market Economy.* New York: Cambridge Univ. Press.

Lewis, Michael. 1978. *The Culture of Inequality.* New York: New American Library.

Light, Ivan. 1972. *Ethnic Enterprise in America: Business and Welfare among Chinese, Japanese, and Blacks.* California: Univ. of California Press.

Light, Ivan & Bonacich, Edna. 1988. *Immigrant Entrepreneurs: Koreans in Los Angeles 1965-1982.* California: Univ. of California Press.

Lincoln, C. Eric. 1990. *The Black Church in the African American Experience.* Durham, North Carolina: Duke Univ. Press.

Mann, Michael. 1986. *The Sources of Social Power: A History of Power from the Beginning to A.D. 1760*, vol. 1. New York: Cambridge Univ. Press.

Massey, Douglas & Denton, Nancy. 1993. *American Apartheid: Segregation and the Making of the Underclass.* Mass.: Harvard Univ. Press.

May, Rollo. 1977. *Power and Innocence.* New York: W.W. Norton.

Mayer, Martin. 1974. *The Bankers.* New York: Ballantine Books.

McConnell, Campbell R. & Brue, Stanley L. 1990. *Economics.* 11th ed. New York: McGraw-Hill.

Meier, August. 1966. *Negro Thought in America 1880-1915.* Ann Arbor, Michigan: Univ. of Michigan.

Mills, C.W. 1956. *The Power Elite.* New York: Oxford University Press.

Mische, Gerald & Patricia. 1977. *Toward A Human World Order: Beyond the National Security Straitjacket.* New York: Paulist Press.

National Urban League. *The State of Black America 1988-1994.*

Offiong, Daniel A. 1982. *Imperialism and Dependency: Obstacles to African Development.* Washington, D.C.: Howard Univ. Press.

O'Hare, W.P. 1983. *Wealth and Economic Status: A Perspective on Racial Inequality.* Washington, D.C.: Joint Center for Political Studies.

Parenti, Michael. 1977. *Democracy for the Few.* 2nd ed. New York: St. Martin's Press.
_____, 1978. *Power and the Powerless.* New York: St. Martin's Press.
_____, 1986. *Inventing Reality: The Politics of the Mass Media.* New York: St. Martin's Press.
_____, 1988. *Democracy for the Few* 5th ed. New York: St. Martin's Press.
_____, 1993. *Inventing Reality: The Politics of News Media*, 2nd ed. New York: St. Martin's Press.
Parsons, Talcott. 1964. *Social Structure and Personality.* New York: The Free Press.
Piore, Michael J. "Public and Private Responsibility in On-the-Job Training of Disadvantaged Worker," *Department of Economics Working Paper,* No. 23. Cambridge, Mass.: Massachusetts Institute of Technology Press. 1968.
Reiman, J. 1990. *The Rich Get Richer and the Poor Get Prison: Ideology, Class, and Criminal Justice*, 3rd ed. New York: Macmillan.
Reisman, David. 1973. *The Lonely Crowd.* New Haven: Yale University Press.
Rohaytn, Felix."World Capital: The Needs and the Risk," *The New York Review of Books,* 1994.
Ross, Robert & Trachte, Kent. 1990. *Global Capitalism: The Leviathan.* Albany, New York: State University of New York Press.
Ross, S., Westerfield, R. & Jordan, B. 1991. *Fundamentals of Corporate Finance.* Boston: Irwin.
Ryan, William. 1976. *Blaming the Victim.* New York: Vintage Books.
Sallach, David. "Class Domination and Ideological Hegemony," *Sociological Quarterly,* Winter, 1974.
Samuelson, Paul A. & Nordham, William D. 1992. *Economics,* 14th ed. New York: McGraw-Hill.
Schiller, Bradley R. 1991. *The Economy Today,* 5th ed. New York: McGraw-Hill.
Seybold, Peter. 1987. *The Structure of Power in America.* (Michael Schwartz, ed.). New York: Holmes & Meier.
Shaw, Kathryn. 1991. *Investment Clubs: Low Cost Education in the Stock Market.* Williamsburg, Michigan: Lake Shore Press.
Smith, James D. "An Estimate of the Income of the Very Rich," *Papers in Quantative Economics.* Lawrence, Kansas: Univ of Kansas Press, 1968.
Smith. J.C. 1990. *The Neurotic Foundations of Social Order: Psychoanalytic Roots of Patriarchy.* New York: NYU Press.
Smith, James D. and Franklin, Stephen D. "The Concentration of Personal Wealth, 1922–1969," *American Economic Review*, May, 1974.
Sowell, Thomas. 1981. *Ethnic America: A History.* New York: Basic Books.
Stampp, Kenneth M. 1956. *The Peculiar Institution: Slavery in the Ante-Bellum South.* New York: Vintage Books.
Stuart, M.S. 1940. *An Economic Detour: A History of Insurance in the Lives of American Negroes.* Johnson Repr.

Swinton, David. *The State of Black America*. New York: National Urban League 1993.

Tabb, William K. 1970. *The Political Economy of the Black Ghetto*. New York: W.W. Norton.

The American Bankers Association. *The Credit Union Industry: Trends, Structure, and Competitiveness*. Washington, D.C.: American Bankers Association, 1990.

Tholin, K. & Pogge, J. 1991. *Banking Services for the Poor: Community Development Credit Unions*. Chicago: Woodstock Institute.

Thomas, Mark. "Who's Afraid of the Big Bad Trade Deficit," *Second Thoughts: Myths and Morals of U.S. Economic History*. (Donald N. McCloskey, ed.). New York: Oxford University Press.

Tidwell, Billy J. "Afrikan Americans and the 21st Century Labor Market: Improving the Fit," in *The State of Black America*. New York: National Urban League. 1993.

Toffler, Alvin. 1990. *Powershift: Knowledge, Wealth & Violence at the Edge of the 21st Century*. New York: Bantam Books.

U.S. National Advisory Commission on Civil Disorders. 1958. *The Kerner Report*. New York: Pantheon Books.

Verdery, Kathrine. "Whither 'Nation' and 'Nationalism'?: Nation and Nationalism: What are They?" *Daedalus*, Summer, 1993.

Voorhis, Jerry. 1951. *American Cooperatives: Where They Come From ...What They Do...Where They Are Going...* New York: Harper & Row.

Warman, R., Siegel, A. & Morris, K. 1990. *Guide to Understanding Money and Markets*. New York: Access Press.

Wartenberg, Thomas E. 1990. *The Forms of Power: From Domination to Transformation*. Philadelphia: Temple University Press.

Wellman, David T., 1977. *Portraits of White Racism*. New York: Cambridge Univ. Press.

West, Cornel. 1993. *Race Matters*. Boston: Beacon Press.

Wilhelm, Sidney. 1971. *Who Needs the Negro?* New York: Anchor Books.

Wilkins, Mira. 1989. *The History of Foreign Investment in the United States to 1914*. Cambridge, Mass.: Harvard University Press.

Williams, Chancellor. 1974. *The Destruction of Black Civilization*. Chicago: Third World Press.

Wilson, William Julius. 1990. *The Truly Disadvantaged: The Inner City, The Underclass & Public Policy*. Chicago: Univ. of Chicago Press.

Wrong, Dennis. 1988. *Power: Its Forms, Bases and Uses*. Chicago: Univ. of Chicago Press.

Zinn, Howard. 1984. *The Twentieth Century: A People's History*. New York: Harper & Row.

Index

A.M.E. Christian Recorder, 557
A.M.E. Church Review, 557
Abdul-Ghaffar, Faruq, 645
Abernathy, Ralph, 559
Abyssinian Baptist Church, 446, 562, 565, 763
Active Transportation Company, 671
Adams, Charles, 569
Advanced Technology Solutions, 673
Advisory committees, 157, 171, 172
Affirmative action, 142, 201, 203, 214, 236, 243, 278, 282, 285, 293, 460, 484, 486, 596, 601, 802, 827, 835, 838-840
Afghans, 317, 333
AFL-CIO, 262, 268
Africa and America (Crummell), 426
Africa, emerging market, 398
African Development Bank, 373, 810
African Export-Import Bank, 811
African Grove Playhouse, 427
African Life, 786
African Masonic Lodge of Boston, 558
African Methodist Episcopal Zion Church, 427, 560
African Society for Mutual Aid, 427
African
    stock markets, 406; stocks, 399
African Development Public Investment Corporation, 407
Africa's economic crisis, 367
Afrikan
    Americans in Liberia, 425; consciousness, 91, 92, 98, 99, 123, 129, 851; investment fund, 376, 394, 406; liberation, 133, 232, 237, 238, 240, 430, 848, 851, 854, 855; studies, 207, 233
Afrikan American
    community as colony, 248, 249; economic system, 50, 511, 591; entrepreneurial milestones, 417; investment in Afrika, 373, 375, 425; leadership, 49, 352, 375, 430; stock market, 817, 820; trade, 429, 431
Afrikan American National Corporation, 752
Afrikan Americans are not immigrants, 436
The Afrikan Personality in America (Kambon), 134
Afrikan trade, 429, 430, 629, 811
Afrikan-centered
    consciousness, 26, 52, 64, 67, 125, 144, 231, 233, 505, 532, 533, 544, 546, 551, 552, 591, 630, 675, 736, 764, 776, 833, 835; culture, 80, 356; identity, 82, 98, 205, 364, 533
Afrikan-manufactured goods, 510
Afrikan-owned firms, 502
Afrocentric
    consciousness, 135, 632, 638, 840; communalism, 79; curricula, 231, 244; education, 234; goods and services, 639; ideology, 231-233, 244; movement, 182, 231-233, 240, 244, 625, 632, 638, 840; policy-formation, 55; "sneakers", 403; thematic elements, 620; toys, 635; trade, 628; weddings, 638

Afro-Bets, 637
AIDS, 148, 178, 321, 377, 644, 647, 651, 742, 792, 828
Air Commerce Act, 34
Akoto, Kwame Agyei, 129, 130
Alcoholic beverages, 602, 604
Alexander, Herbert, 211
Alexis, Marcus, 362, 363
Ali, Muhammad, 649
Aliaga, David & Carlos, 334
Allen Christian Church, 565, 568, 664
Allen African Methodist Episcopal (A.M.E.) Church, 569, 576
Allen, Benjamin W.P., 714
Allen, D., 742
Allen, Gary, 300
Allen, Richard, 427, 556
Allen Robert, 854
Allen and Rahman, 564, 742, 743
All-Black State in Oklahoma Territory, 428
All-Black towns, 423, 428
"America and the World 1993," 370
America versus Japan, 496
American
  decline, 260; hegemony, 302; higher education, 187; press, 225, 235, 557; standard of living, 258, 269, 291, 371; support, 405, 496
American Apartheid (Massey & Denton), 506
American apartheid, 236, 557
American Bankers Association, 711, 712
American Baptist Home Mission Society, 190
American Colonization Society, 427
American Cooperatives (Voorhis), 777
American Demographics, 527, 536, 542, 545, 602, 604
American Enterprise Institute (AEI), 175, 176, 179, 180
American Express, 159, 298, 376, 404, 725
American Missionary Association, 190
American Opinion, 300
American Petroleum Institute, 158
American Political Science Review, 186

Amsden, Alice, 496
Amsterdam News, see *The New York Amsterdam News*
An Economic Detour, 432, 436
Andean Pact, 529
Anderson, Jack, 158
Anderson, K. Tucker, 177
Anderson John D., 189-192
Anheuser-Busch, 324, 605-607
Anmbry, Margaret, 602
The Annual Guide to Public Policy Experts, 181
Apple Computer, 274, 790
Archer Street, 422
Ardener, Shirley, 576
Ariel Capital Management Inc., 759
Arisan, 737
Articulate tribe, 144
Articulated tribal state, 145
Ashaway Inc., 651
The Asian Mind Game (Chu), 313
Asian-born immigrants, 346
Asia's Next Giant (Amsden), 496
"Asia's Wealth" (*Business Week*), 355
"Assignment workers", 274
Assimilationist leadership establishment, 443, 830, 832, 844
Association of Community Organizations for Reform Now (ACORN), 551, 658, 662
AT&T, 175, 346, 402, 702
Atlantic Monthly, 140, 215, 494
The Atlas of Economic Indicators (Carnes & Slider), 705
Austin, J.L., 87
Autonomy, 64, 65, 95, 106, 108, 119, 122, 123, 305, 316, 392, 696, 828, 850
Avery, B., 340
Ayitley, G., 374
Azor, 428

Bakewell, Danny, 543
Baldwin, Horace, 559
Baldwin, Joseph (a.k.a. Kobi Kambon), 134, 559
Bamileke tribesmen, 735
Banana/tractor ratio, 379
Bank relations, 572

The Bankers: Conspiratorial Origins of the Federal Reserve (Allen), 300
The Bankers (Mayer), 680, 705
Banking, 201, 271, 297, 299, 300, 315, 336, 337, 392, 395, 400, 402, 465-467, 571, 622, 648, 658, 664-666, 669, 670, 678, 680, 682-685, 689-692, 694, 695, 697, 699-702, 705, 706, 708, 709, 713, 714, 732, 735, 736, 792, 797, 807-810, 812, 813, 822
Banking Services for the Poor (Tholin & Pogge), 714
Barbagli and Dei, 115
Barnes-Bryant, F., 774
Bases of power, 27-29, 31, 204, 220, 247
Bates, Timothy, 254, 255, 350, 438, 439, 660
Bazelon, David, 30, 747, 749, 793
BE 100s, 687, 770
Beal, M.R., 801, 803, 804, 811
Beame, A., 296
Bean, R., 347
Beatty, Jim, 777
Becker, Howard, 167
Beckman, 187
Becoat, Bill, 637, 638
Beetham, David, 17, 19-21, 31, 33, 153, 162, 167, 224
Behavioral revolution, 186
Behind the Veil of Economics (Heilbroner), 358
Belgium, 367
Bell, Rosalind A., 636, 803, 804
The Bell Curve (Murray & Herrnstein), 182
Belonging in the Two Berlins (Borneman), 848
The Benefits of Famine (Keen), 377
Benign neglect of Afrika, 370
Benin, 416
Benson, W., 423
Berean Missionary Baptist, 564
Bergman, 261
Berle, A.A., 36, 48, 298, 794
Berry, Simon, 423, 646, 764
Big Red News, 329
Binga State Bank, 682

Biological annihilation, 444
Black
 assimilationist leadership, 74; assimilationists, 73, 443, 831; bourgeois leadership, 442, 443; bourgeoisie, 235, 236, 238-241, 243, 344; business elite, 361; buying power, 589, 590, 592; consumer dollars, 327, 461, 485, 594; consumer market, 520, 591, 621, 627, 632, 689; conventions, 1, 343, 425, 426, 615-617, 619, 681, 858; cultural nationalism, 851; decline, 260; education, 189, 191, 192, 608; face on White power, 456, 840; firms, 473, 485, 554, 587, 599, 801, 804, 806, 811; higher education, 189-193; immigrants, 346, 844; immigration, 426; intelligence agency, 201, 203, 204; Islam, 81, 82; job losses, 282-285; joblessness, 292; main streets, 425; media establishment, 235, 237, 240, 241, 243; militant and liberation politics, 198; Nationalism, 182, 237, 240, 244, 430, 443, 582, 634, 849-855; nationalist movements, 492; nationalist party, 856-858; neo-conservative leadership, 74; political party, 216, 217, 219; powerlessness, 97, 102, 104; radio, 234, 320; self-help, 420, 443, 557; studies, 244, 411; suburbs, 461, 504, 536, 537, 539, 540, 542, 545, 546; underclass, 837; wealth ownership, 472
The Black Bourgeoisie (Frazier), 235
Black Brotherhood Collective, 360, 362, 364, 365
Black Brotherhood United Fund, 542
Black Business Network, 361, 362
Black Church, 68-71, 73-75, 80-83, 189, 488, 490, 530, 535, 549, 555-562, 564, 567, 569-572, 574-576, 578, 579, 581, 609, 614, 689, 707, 715, 780, 783, 785, 830, 831, 852

The Black Church in the African American Experience (Lincoln), 556, 560
Black Cross Navigation and Trading Company, 430
Black Durham, 420
Black Enterprise, 234, 239, 244, 292, 361, 434, 476, 477, 483, 520, 550, 561, 564, 567, 572, 603, 626, 637, 639-643, 681, 687, 692, 695-697, 700-702, 709, 720-722, 725, 726, 757, 759, 760, 767-775, 782, 783, 800, 801, 803, 804
Black Enterprise Board of Economists, 483
Black Entertainment Television (BET), 759
Black main streets
Archer Street, 214, 531, 696
Greenwood Avenue, 421-433
Black national vision, 551
Black power, 16, 22, 28, 34, 35, 49, 53, 54, 79, 92, 93, 96, 98, 99, 108, 115, 120, 123, 145, 198, 199, 202-204, 206, 208, 232, 252, 273, 365, 397, 443, 491, 518, 590, 591, 749, 750, 831, 833, 835, 836, 848, 853, 856, 858
Black power
advocates, 198, 199; conference, 198
The Black Power Imperative (Cross), 34, 35, 202, 252, 749, 750
Black Resource Guide, 550
Black South Afrikans, 790
Black Tulsa, 421, 422, 425
Black-owned
auto dealers, 547; banks, 448, 465, 467, 533, 557, 572, 597, 665, 676, 680, 682, 684-693, 695, 697-702, 705, 802; businesses, 207, 231, 421, 453, 456, 472, 483, 485, 489, 490, 519, 533, 534, 544, 554, 585, 587, 590, 591, 599, 602, 604, 606, 617, 621, 624, 639, 654, 655, 660-662, 665, 671, 673, 686, 692, 708, 723, 725, 745, 746, 752, 759, 778, 816; commercial banks, 546, 688; enterprise, 489, 820; financial establishments, 695; financial institutions, 489, 572, 686, 690, 695, 698, 700, 800; firms, 474, 476, 489, 490, 597, 653, 655, 660, 722, 750, 794, 805-807; insurance companies, 547, 574, 688, 810; investment bank, 799-803, 807-809, 811; manufacturing, 391, 392, 519, 808; publishing, 489; shopping centers, 447-448; supermarkets, 448
Blackbook, 548, 550
Blackwell, Lucien, 322
Blaming the Victim (Ryan), 840
Blumberg, Paul, 256, 258, 262-264, 276
Body Shop, 577, 578, 580
Boleswa, 788
Bonacich, Edna, 46, 330, 337, 350, 351, 533, 534, 576
Bonds, 30, 161, 300, 471, 475, 499, 573, 611, 678, 718, 719, 750, 755-757, 760, 797-802, 805-807, 810, 812, 814, 816-819, 846; and securities, 161; bond market, 573, 574; foreign, 810; junk, 814; long-term, 818; municipal, 611, 799, 801, 819; railroad, 807; short-term, 818; stocks and, 718, 755, 797, 817-819
Borneman, John, 848
Botswana, 373, 393, 394, 399, 401
Bourdieu, Pierre, 86, 87, 552, 553
Bourgeois
class retainers, 75; leadership establishment, 360, 442
Boutte, Alvin, 689
Boycotts, 242, 618, 619, 835
Boyd, 535
Bradshaw, W.A., 692
Bravo supermarkets, 334
Bressant-Kibwe, Dent & Kim, 629
Bretton Woods, 269, 296, 408
Brezinski, Z. 311
Brides Today, 639
Bridge Street African Methodist Episcopal Church, 565
Briggs, Vernon, 435

Brimmer, A.F., 292, 363
British finance, 401
Brookings Institution, 176, 180
Broom Jumping: A Celebration of Love (Green), 639
Broom Lady, 639
Brotherhood Crusade, 542, 543
Brown, Corrine, 322
Brown, Michael, 367, 368, 373, 390
Brown, Ron, 361
Brown and Tiffen, 367, 368, 373, 390
Brue, Stanley L., 30, 679
Buchanan, Anne., 378-381
Bunker, Ellsworth, 298
Bunting, John, 680
Bureau of Applied Social Research, 188
Bureaucratic agencies, 163
Burger King, 478, 479, 565, 597, 768, 771-773
Burkina Faso, 735
Burns, Arthur, 160
Burns, James MacGregor, 824, 825, 826
Burrell Communications Group, 477, 520, 624
Bush, George, 139, 158, 159, 177, 180, 276, 353, 474
Business
  association networks, 338; ownership, 295, 470, 472, 474, 476, 483, 485, 510, 580, 601, 766, 784, 833; tradition, 417, 418
Business Council, 169, 174, 175, 549
Business Development Company (BDC), 722, 723
Business Organization and the Myth of the Market Economy (Lazonick), 493
Business Roundtable, 159, 160, 763
Business Week, 159, 160, 345, 348, 355, 361-363, 369, 634, 787, 788, 790
Burger King, 478, 479, 565, 597, 768, 771-773
Butler, John Sibley, 253, 350, 417, 420 432, 433, 435
Butler, 156
Butts, Calvin, 565

Calder, Kent, 488
Cameroon, 370, 401, 416, 735
Campaign finance, 211
Campaigns, 45, 195, 203, 209, 211, 232, 323, 405, 578, 580, 609, 624, 648
Campbell, Robert, 427
Canada, 256, 257, 264, 267, 268, 271, 312, 346, 352, 396, 413, 427, 436
Candidate-selection process, 154, 209-212
Capital accumulation, 161, 684, 729, 730, 796
Capital Savings Bank, 558
Capitalism, 32, 75, 78, 79, 121, 150, 188, 229, 265, 271, 272, 287, 289, 301-303, 305, 308, 353, 354, 358, 359, 367, 377, 378, 418, 487-489, 496, 512, 543, 581, 648, 735, 747, 766, 789, 827, 842, 846
Caribbean, 10, 218, 229, 327, 340, 341, 346, 347, 390, 412, 414, 423, 426-428, 462, 490, 528, 529, 550, 560, 616, 638, 732, 808, 810
CARICOM, 529
Carnegie, 183-185, 190, 402, 752
Carnegie Commission on Higher Education, 185
Carnegie Endowment for International Peace, 180, 316
Carnegie Foundation, 173, 198
Carnes, W., 705
Carosso, Vincent, 807, 808, 812, 813
Carson, Emmett D., 561
Cartel power, 35
Cartels, 32, 409, 721
Carter, Al., 770-772
Carver Federal Savings, 564, 597, 688
Casarda, 254
Cato Institute, 176, 180, 449
Cato Journal, 180
Center for Advanced Study in the Behavioral Sciences, 188
Central Afrikan Customs and Economic Union, 529
Central and South America, 229, 327, 346, 528
Central Brooklyn Youth Credit Union, 709, 710

Chaliand, Gerard, 380
Chamber of Commerce, 160, 423, 455-457, 810
Character and Social Structure (Gerth & Mills), 114
Charade of Western Aid, 381
Chase Manhattan Bank, 174, 175, 674, 711, 739, 740
Chavis, Ben, 852
Chemical Bank, 314, 315, 658, 659, 666, 711
Chen, Carolyn, 333
Cheney, Dick, 303
Cherokee Nation, 612
Chevy Chase Federal Savings, 669
Chicago Defender, 235
Chief assets of developing countries, 374
China, 271, 275, 297, 312, 313, 331-333, 354, 355, 396, 404, 405, 495, 690, 734
Chinatown, 314, 315, 331, 332
Chinese
 frugality and ethnic chauvinism, 332; social relationships, 314
Choctaws, 610
Choi, 335, 336
Christian churches, 330
Christoff, Cleve, 763
Chu, Chin-Ning, 313
Chumpies, 644, 645
Church
 associations, 572, 575, 707; as growth industry, 555
Church Insurance Partnership Agency (CIPA) Inc., 785
Church, R.R., 419
Citibank, 177, 228
Citibank Special Asian Banking Center, 315
Citizens Trust Company Bank, 698
City News, 559, 571
The City Sun, 239, 285, 321, 349, 434, 521, 598, 627, 663, 666, 710
Civil Rights
 leadership, 601, 837, 852; era, 236, 559, 828, 839; movement, 492, 555, 596, 598, 599, 601, 835, 839, 855

Civil War, 417-419, 425, 427, 428, 555, 557, 614, 808, 812
Clark, Kenneth B., 503, 634
Clarkson, Charles, 762
Class consciousness, 143-147, 150, 169, 223
Clayton, Eva, 322
Clinton, Bill, 194, 275, 664, 686, 691, 695, 706, 791
Clough, Michael, 404, 405
Coca-Cola, 321, 361, 362, 448, 477, 597, 598, 606, 608, 822
Coercion, 12-16, 18, 22, 26, 41, 153
Coercive power, 12-14, 20, 138, 247, 251, 252, 288
Cointelpro, 232
Cold War, 302, 371, 375, 398
Cole, John A., 692
Coleman, James, 89, 102-105, 109, 113
Collective
 capitalism, 487-489, 766; consciousness, 393, 553; internationalism, 304
Collins, Joseph, 382
Colonial
 economic growth, 401; era, 400
Colonialism, 44, 130, 251, 374, 377, 378, 382, 456, 484
 continuing reign of, 382
Colonization, 123, 374, 425-427, 429
 in Africa, 426
Columbia University, 188
Commercial banks, 184, 546, 573, 676, 678, 679, 686-688, 701, 708, 740, 797, 807, 814-816
Committee for Economic Development (CED), 169, 173, 174, 176, 180
Committee on Comparative Politics, 188
Communist Manifesto, 221
Community Association of East Harlem Triangle, 446
Community Development Credit Union (CDCU), 575, 711, 715-717, 738
Community Reinvestment Act of 1977, 663, 695
"Comparative Study of Rotating

Credit Associations" (Ardener), 576
Compensation, 160, 161, 783, 784, 814
Concessionary loans, 669, 789
Concord Baptist Church, 565
Cone Communications, 579, 580
Congo, 373, 426
Congress of National Black Churches (CNBC) 489, 571, 575, 785
Congressional Black Caucus (in Korea), 322
Congressional subcommittees, 163
Conquest of the Skies (Soberg), 34
Conservative
  Black and Hispanic scholars, 182; ideology, 213
Conservatives, 177, 182, 229, 232, 837-840, 842, 846
Consumer Power: How Americans Spend (Anmbry), 602
Consumerism, 149, 150, 513, 651
Consumer cooperatives, 779
Continental Afrikan Nations, 425, 490
Cooke, Jay, 402
Cookson and Persell, 148, 149
Cooperative
  corporation, 777; economics, 77, 489, 502, 542, 715, 776; investment, 162, 263-267, 271, 367, 373, 391, 400, 455; retail, 777
Cooperative League of the United States, 776
Co-ops, 776-781
Coors, 176, 605, 606
Corporate
  oligarchy, 211; philanthropy, 189, 191, 193, 607, 608
Corporation Finance (Kristein), 796, 799
Corpus Christi Federal Credit Union, 700
Cosby, Bill, 361, 362, 764
Cosmetics industry, 603, 651
  hair, 343, 419, 477-479, 603, 627, 628, 634
Council on Foreign Relations, 169, 172-176

Cox, Oliver, 443, 770
Crain's New York Business, 694
Credit
  union loans, 678; accounts, 254; association, 47, 340, 467, 489 576, 730-740, 778; 813; card, 462, 700; consumer, 466, 741; discrimination, 669; economy, 465; rating, 814; rotating, 47, 576, 729-738, 740, 813; tax, 293; union(s), 53, 467, 559, 565, 573, 575, 676, 678, 682, 686, 691, 700, 702, 706, 708-717, 738, 749
Credit Union Industry: Trends, Structure, and Competitiveness, 711, 712
Creditors, 155, 161, 742, 749
Crenshaw High School, 647
Cross, Theodore, 32, 34, 35, 202-204, 251, 252, 350, 747-750, 753
Cross Colours, 637-643
Crossroads, 595
Cromwell, John Wesley, 343
Crowder, Bob, 645-647
Crummell, Alexander, 426, 427
Cruse, Harold, 74, 75, 433, 434, 437, 442, 443, 504, 836-838, 842, 855
Cuban immigrants, 437
Cuffee, Paul, 427, 428
Cultivating cash, 335
Cultural
  analysis, 63; identity, 59-61, 63, 126, 143, 144, 308, 316, 405, 641, 643, 644
The Culture of Inequality (Lewis), 77-79, 840, 841
Currency devaluation, 368
C-Town supermarket, 334

D. Edward Wells Federal Credit Union, 709
Dager, Albert A., 61
Dahl, Robert, 186, 329
Dahomey, 416
The Daily Challenge, 561
Dangerous economic straits of contemporary Afrika, 366
Daniels-Carter, 771, 772
"Dashi", 737 *see also* Rotating credit

Data bank, 410, 411, 413
Davenport, C., 726
Davidson, Basil, 415, 416
Davis, Mike, 595
De Gaulle, Charles, 383
De Tocqueville, Alexis, 504
Death in a Promised Land (Ellsworth), 422, 424
Debt, 161, 254, 257, 269, 273, 314, 367, 373, 375, 376, 391, 401, 408, 439, 507, 508, 574, 667, 671, 672, 712, 721, 730, 740, 741, 745, 751, 784, 801, 802, 811, 816, 818, 842
Defense strategy objectives, 304
Deindustrialization, 255
Delaney, Martin, 427
Democracy for the Few (Parenti), 158, 172, 213, 298
Democratic defectors, 216
Democratic Leadership Council (DLC), 214
Democrats, 193, 194, 212-216, 285
Demopublicans, 212
Denny's, 770, 771, 773, 792, 793
Denton, Nancy, 503, 506
Department of Economics Working Paper, 253
Descartes, Rene, 191
The Destruction of Black Civilization (Williams), 52
Destruction of Black family power, 64
Desynchronization, 328
Diallo, D., 373
Diamond, M., 784
DiBassy, M., 630
Differences in ethnic identity and consciousness, 332
Diffused
  Black American tribe, 162
  tribal identity, 145
Diffusion of technology, 262
Dinkins, David, 320, 323, 324, 649, 763
Diop, Mohamed, 629-631
Direct
  foreign investment, 263, 264, 266, 267, 367, 391; investment, 264-267, 289, 408; private investment in Afrika, 375

Directory of Corporate Philanthropy, 607
The Disuniting of America, 231
Dis-affirmative action, 278
Dixie Industrial Company, 423
Doley, H., 805, 809-811
Doley Securities, 803, 804, 811
Dollars and Sense, 550, 606, 615
Dolls, 634, 635
Domestic
  and foreign policy, 183, 509, 738; demand management, 368, 369
Domhoff, William, 148, 149, 154, 157, 169, 172, 173, 176, 178, 179, 184, 211, 212, 223, 226, 227
Dominicans of New York City, 333
Douglass, Frederick, 236, 681
Douglass National Bank, 682
Dow Chemical, 214
Downsizing, 263, 284, 285
Drake, L., 626
Drexel National Bank, 696, 700
Drucker, Peter, 403, 794
Drug
  abuse, 238, 349, 858; addiction, 120, 239, 270, 350, 508, 515, 644, 828
Du Sable, Jean B., 417
DuBois, W.E.B., 61, 205, 417, 420, 504, 511-515, 556, 588, 589, 781
Dugger III, E., 725-728
Duncan, C., 362
DuPont, 159, 160, 195, 549
Durham, 419-421, 425
The Dusk of Dawn (DuBois), 205, 511, 515, 588
Dye, Thomas, 8, 27, 29, 30, 58, 115, 116, 120, 122, 136-138, 146, 156, 220, 221, 247

Eason, Yla, 634
East Asia, 266, 271, 304, 305, 312, 327, 328, 354-356, 375, 408, 839
The Eastasia Edge (Hofheinz & Calder), 488
Ebony, 234-236, 239, 244, 361, 520, 630, 633, 764
Echoes of decline, 255
Economic

brothels, 439; deprivation, 238, 851; destiny, 286, 287, 311, 323; development, 36, 51, 55, 82, 176, 180, 181, 206, 244, 251, 263, 296, 310, 317, 326, 340, 343, 361, 386, 389, 390, 392, 394, 402, 403, 413, 420, 432, 433, 446, 450, 454, 456, 465, 488, 495, 497, 499, 513, 534, 535, 542, 543, 546, 556, 558, 559, 561-564, 566, 567, 571, 575, 580, 581, 584, 587, 589, 598, 608, 611, 616, 620, 621, 662, 680, 681, 686, 691, 692, 696, 698, 704, 706, 708, 715, 718, 719, 722, 725, 729-732, 743, 759, 781-783, 810, 815, 857; mismanagement, 375; outlook of Black America, 260; power, 30, 32, 45, 46, 74, 138, 218, 246-248, 252, 264, 270, 277, 312, 313, 316, 327, 350, 353, 354, 357, 358, 431-433, 457, 466, 518, 531, 591, 643, 650, 690, 747, 749, 825; powerlessness, 246, 353; segmentation, 253; stagnation of the Black community, 332; underdevelopment, 251; well-being, 20, 57, 192, 235, 254, 256, 260, 329, 338, 345, 455, 458, 469, 470, 494, 508, 545, 689, 704, 714
Economic Community of West Africa States (ECOWAS), 529
Economic Development and Cultural Change (Geertz), 730
Economic Policy Institute, 181
Economics, 77, 178, 179, 207, 244, 249, 253, 282, 287, 289, 307, 308, 339, 347, 358, 368, 374, 395, 403, 420, 489, 492-494, 502, 525, 536, 542, 556, 581, 643, 676, 679, 715, 776
Economics Explained (Heilbroner), 299, 705
Economics of Afrocentrism, 588, 626
Economies of scale, 500, 723
Edmonds, S., 726
Edsall, T.& M., 215
Educational philanthropy, 190
Edwards, Bishop, 568, 569
Eisenbach, J. 197

Eisenhower, Dwight, 160
Electoral politics, 209
Ellsworth, Scott, 421, 422, 424
Ellsworth, 156
EM (Ebony Man), 236, 244
Emerge magazine, 234, 237, 240, 244, 520, 581
Emerging market, 398
Employee ownership, 673, 674
Employment loss, 279
Empowerment, 3, 49, 63, 70, 82, 84, 92, 115, 129, 135, 196, 197, 202, 239, 243, 248, 277, 316, 345, 362, 403, 414, 415, 435, 464, 474, 475, 497, 510, 516, 542, 555, 609, 611, 620, 686, 691, 698, 714, 728, 731, 754, 759, 778, 787-789, 825, 829, 835, 848, 855
Endowment and investment programs, 573
Engels, F.,146
Enterprise groups, 489
Entertainment industry, 764
Entrepreneurial history, 344, 431, 433
Entrepreneurship, 46, 47, 250, 330, 351, 417, 418, 420, 439, 443, 467, 533, 535, 578, 612, 616, 641, 643, 673, 742, 788
Entrepreneurship and Self-Help among Black Americans (Butler), 417, 420
Envirotest, 477, 482, 726
Equal Credit Opportunity Act, 669
Equal Employment Opportunity Commission (EEOC), 279, 281, 282, 284, 285, 287, 838
Ernst and Young, 264
Erosion of American preeminence, 257
Erving, Julius, 361, 362
Escape from Freedom (Fromm), 102
Essence
of domination 657, 658; of class rule, 168; of injustice, 459; of power, 33, 357
Essence Communication, 477, 520, 633
Essence magazine, 234, 236, 239, 244,

874 ✦ Index

362, 520
"Esusu", 732 *see also* Rotating credit
Ethnic
  American enclaves, 527, 528; constituencies, 143; identification, 441; resources, 27, 46, 47, 49, 332, 335, 342, 359, 533, 534, 542
Ethnic America (Sowell), 437
Ethnic Enterprises in America (Light), 684, 734
Ethnicity, 39, 45, 46, 48, 66, 94, 105-108, 137, 138, 310, 311, 316, 317, 325, 335, 355, 356, 359, 360, 362, 364, 406, 441, 528, 613, 635, 849, 850
Ethnic-based values and solidarity, 332
Ethnocentrism, 66, 76, 102, 105-108, 147, 149, 344, 352, 591, 800, 846
European Economic Community, 297
European finance (of American railroads), 402
Exxon, 159, 175

Fair Housing Act, 669
Fair Share Agreement, 773, 792
Fallows, James, 494-496
Family
  disruptions, 508; incomes, 257; instability, 460, 507
Family Savings Bank, 533, 692, 693
Fansi, T., 735
Farrakhan, Louis, 81, 582, 852, 856
Farris, V.K., 773
Faunteroy, Walter, 559
Faustian bargain, 323
Federal
  aid, 160; budget deficit, 257
Federal anti-Afrikan policies, *34*
Federal Communication Commission (FCC), 34
Federal Home Loan Bank, 532
Federal Reserve, 139, 160, 292, 299, 300, 363, 440, 659, 704
Federal Reserve System, 299, 300
Filer, 348
The Final Call, 616, 617, 651
Final payback, 324

Financial-corporate world government, 297
Financing Politics, 211
Firestone Rubber Company, 430
First African Methodist Episcopal (FAME), Church 561
First Fidelity Bancorp, 693, 694
Flagstar, 770, 771, 773, 792, 793
Flake, Floyd, 564, 565
Floating currency, 367
Focus, 182, 202
Food as weapon, 380
Food First (Lappé & Collins), 382
Food from the 'Hood, 647-649
Food stamps, 386, 568
Food, Poverty and Power (Buchanan), 379
Forbes, 342, 351, 352, 630, 631, 764, 779
Ford Foundation, 178, 181, 185-187, 189, 198, 202, 446, 447, 725
Ford II, Henry, 199
Ford Motor Company, 671, 822
Ford, Rockefeller and Carnegie, 173
Foreign
  competition, 260, 261, 263, 275, 289, 388, 498; direct investment (FDI), 264, 265, 267, 289, 408
Foreign Affairs, 173, 267, 322, 370, 403-405, 442
The Forms of Power (Wartenberg), 6, 8-10, 12-15, 23, 24, 72, 312
Fortas, Abe, 298
Fortune, 266-268, 394, 609-611, 761
Fortune 500, 159, 607, 661, 695, 767, 822
Foundation
  Ameliors, 694; Bradley, 840; Carnegie, 173, 180; Enterprise, 565; Ford, 173,178, 181, 185-187, 198, 202, 447; Heritage, 176; Olin, 840; Progressive Freedom, 196, 197; Rockefeller, 173, 447, 694; Russell Sage, 188; Scaife 840; Sloan, 193; Taconic, 193
Foundation(s) 55, 119, 168, 169, 173-176, 178, 179,181-186, 189-191, 193, 194, 198, 202, 228, 287, 297, 445-449, 563, 565, 567, 574,

608, 694, 707, 708, 716, 719, 721, 725, 726, 763, 784, 840, 848; influence, 197-200
Founders National Bank, 533, 696
Founding fathers, 156
Fountain, G., 660
Fractional reserve system, 679
France, 383, 396, 495, 637
Fraternal lodges, 421, 556-558
Frazier, E.F., 235, 238, 241, 420, 555, 556
Free
  market, 33, 35, 79, 300, 301, 368, 492, 493; trade, 35, 251, 268, 300, 301, 328, 496, 497, 501, 528, 529, 794
Free African Society, 427, 556
Freedman's Savings and Trust, 681
Freedom's Journal, 235
Freeing of prices, 368
Freeman, Richard, 276
Frey, William H., 351, 352
Friedman, Milton & Rose, 494, 788
Fromm, Erich, 102, 108
Fugett, Jean S., 763
Full-employment, 267, 277, 440
Fulton Mall, 462, 463
Function of education, 206
Fundamentals of Corporate Finance, 818
Fusfeld and Bates, 254, 255, 350, 438, 439
The Future of Africa (Crummell), 426

Gabon, 373, 383
Galbraith, John K., 36, 45, 301
Gama, Paul, 457, 458
Gambling profits, 611
Games industry, 635
Gardner, John, 198
Garvey, Amy Jacques, 429
Garvey, Hon. Marcus, 82, 344, 420, 425, 428-430, 443, 510, 530, 601, 628, 812, 851
Geertz, Clifford, 730-734, 737
General Agreement on Tariffs and Trade (GATT), 296, 389, 390, 794
General Education Board, 190-193
General Electric (GE), 174,175, 198, 402, 450
General Motors (GM), 161, 174, 175, 266, 696
General System of Preferences (GSP), 390
Georgia Pacific, 214
Germany, 160, 257, 261, 262, 304, 312, 381, 396, 494, 496
Gerth, H. 114
Ghana, 2, 340, 342, 371-373, 393, 394, 399, 401, 416, 630, 735, 811
Ghigis Afrikan Fashion, 341
Giant farm coops, 779
Gift horse, 447
Gilder, George, 182
Gingrich, Newt, 177, 193-197
Giuliani administration, 182
Givens, Kelly, 626
Global
  containment, 143, 371; economy, 256, 269, 287, 301, 302, 311, 312, 316, 317, 345, 514, 515, 528, 529; humanitarianism, 371; network based on mutual trust, 311; policy, 404; tribes, 311, 316
Global Capitalism (Ross & Trachte), 265
Globalization, 268, 273, 327, 328, 406
Goble, Paul, 316
Goizueta, Roberto, 608
Goodwin, Lamond, 376
Gopac, 194-197
Gorée Island, 630
Gospel of Wealth (Carnegie), 183
Government
  bonds and securities, 161; grants, 464, 563, 568, 691, 730
Graves, Earl, 361, 480
Grayson, Jaynell, 648
Great Depression, 420, 425, 440, 684, 698, 714, 853
Greater Christ Temple Church, 568
Greater profits, 351
Green, Danita, 639
Green grocers, 330
Greenberg, Edward, 264, 265, 301
Greenberg, Stanley, 216
Greenberg, Steven, 452
Greenwood (Avenue), 421-423 *see also*

Black main streets
Greider, William, 158, 159, 175, 176, 213-215
Griffey, Dick, 407
Griffith, Mark W., 710
Grigsby Brandford, 800, 801, 803-805
Grogan, Paul, 450, 451
Gross
 domestic product (GDP), 257, 292, 354, 376, 394; national product (GNP), 256, 354, 367, 372, 377, 367, 381, 399, 401
Growth of Asian American Enterprises, 329
Guanxi, 355
Guide to Understanding Money and Markets (Warman & Siegel), 798, 799
Gulf Oil, 158, 305, 563
G-7 nations, 376

Habituation, 308
Hacker, Andrew, 141-143, 438, 504
Hair care, 477-479, 603, 627
Hamilton, Alexander, 400
Hammi Bank, 337
Hancock, Paul, 669
Hankel, Wilhelm, 449, 464, 465, 467
Harlem Loan Fund, 741
Harlem Third World Institute, 410
Harriman, Averell, 298
Harris, Elizabeth, 725
Harris, Abram, 683
Hartford Memorial Baptist Church, 569
Harvard Business Review, 312, 328
Hasbro Inc., 635
Hausa States, 416
Hayes, Bernetta J., 615
Heilbroner, Robert, 287-289, 299, 300, 358, 359, 705
Heilbroner and Thurow, 299, 300
Henderson, Lenneal, 474-476
Heritage Foundation, 176, 181
Hernandez, Aileen, 284
Herndon, Alonzo, 558
Herter, Jr., Christian, 199
Hirsch, Glenn K., 226
Hispanic(s), 182, 278, 279, 281, 282, 284-286, 332, 334, 335, 452, 461, 468, 510, 521, 526-531, 585, 604, 632, 634, 635, 653, 654, 658, 663, 664, 690, 699, 707, 746, 806, 821
"Hispanic merchants thrive", 334
The History of Foreign Investment in the United States to 1914 (Wilkins), 400
A History of West Africa (Davidson), 415, 416
Hofheinz R. & Calder, K., 488
Holtz, Joe, 780, 781
Holyfields, Marilyn, 616
Home and motor vehicle equity, 483
Homeboys, 644-647
Homegirls, 644, 645
Homeland Fashions, 629, 630
Homestead Act, 34
Hong Kong, 271, 312, 354, 390
Honigsberg, Pete, 777-779
"Honorary whites", 142
Hooks, Benjamin, 559
Hoover Institution, 176, 181
Horizontal trade 386, 387
"Horizontal corporations", 502, 724
Horowitz, David, 182, 183, 198, 199
Horowitz and Kolodney, 182, 183, 198
Horton, Paul, 41-43, 59, 100-102, 105-107, 147
Housing loans, 664, 692
Houston, Wade, 671
How To Do Things With Words (Austin), 87
How to Incorporate (Diamond & Williams), 784
Huddle, Donald, 347
Hudson, Paul C., 697
Hudson, Wade & Cheryl, 636, 637
Hudson Valley Federation, 781
"Hui", 734, 737
Human
 capital, 46, 57, 249, 259, 342, 399, 441, 470, 483, 487, 534, 535, 551, 755, 793; rights, 28, 182, 375, 442, 619, 832
Hunt, Chester, 41, 42, 59, 100-102, 105-107, 147
Hurd, Maude, 662, 663
Hussein, Saddam, 302

Hyong, Rev, Henry H., 322
Hypersegregation, 349, 504

Ibo, 340, 735
Identity
  Afrikan, 64, 99, 125, 135, 467, 551, 650, 736, 846; collective, 39, 40, 45, 77, 129, 148, 359; cultural, 59-61, 63, 126, 143, 144, 308, 316, 405, 641, 643, 644; culture and, 59; ethnic, 41, 47, 105, 107, 310, 311, 315, 317, 332, 341-343, 528, 582, 613, 830, 847; group, 48, 81, 309, 310, 316, 365; personal, 60; self-, 63, 103-106, 116, 127, 144; sense of, 47; social, 25, 106
Ideological
  hegemony, 226; propaganda, 20, 224; thrust, 236, 244; warfare, 232, 233, 244
Ideology
  Afrocentric, 231-234, 244; assimilationist, 442, 837; assimilationistic, 352; conservative, 213; discrediting Afrocentric, 232; economic, 49, 193, 491, 492, 494, 496, 501, 510, 556; ethnic, 441; Eurocentric, 25, 120, 232; group, 45, 48; laissez-faire, 496; need for, 222; neoconservative, 848; network, 179, 233; political, 73, 75, 582; process, 154, 223, 225, 227; race, 46
Immigrant Entrepreneurs (Light & Bonacich), 46
Immigration, 331, 342, 345, 346, 348-352, 405, 426, 428, 434, 435, 442
Imports of alcohol and perfumes, 380
Income distribution, 257
Incubators, 742-744
Indian reservations, 611
Indonesia, 354, 355, 396
Indonesia's GNP, 377
Industrial
  decentralization, 254; philanthropy, 189-193
Industrial Revolution, 258, 274, 292, 402

Inequality
  21, 28, 29, 77-79, 113, 137, 148, 201, 226, 252, 257, 276, 289, 290, 353, 460, 470-472, 474, 476, 483, 682, 840, 841; index, 471, 474
Inequality In An Age of Decline (Blumberg), 256, 262
Inequality index, 471, 474
Information revolution, 292
Initial public offering (IPO), 759, 819, 820
Inner-city communities, 258, 262, 349, 350, 439, 447, 450, 452, 461, 542, 662, 716
Institute for Contemporary Studies, 176
Institutional
  Black Church, 68, 488, 490, 560, 561, 570, 574, 581, 609, 689, 707, 785, 830, 831, 852; oligarchs, 210
The Insurgent Socialist, 226
Interest rates, 247, 300, 368, 369, 395, 462, 661, 717, 741, 798, 814
International Business Machines (IBM), 159, 175, 269, 275, 298, 673, 674, 725, 822
International Center for Economic Policy Studies, 182
International Monetary Fund (IMF), 173, 296, 367-369, 395, 407-409
International Trade Center, 409, 413
Inventing Reality: The Politics of the Mass Media (Parenti), 225, 228
Investment
  bank, 798, 800, 801, 807, 811; clubs, 756, 757, 759, 760, 821; policies of the ruling elite, 162; portfolio, 501; rate, 257
Investment Clubs (Shaw), 760

J.C. Penney, 632
Jackson, Michael, 361, 764
Jackson, Jesse L., 214, 442, 559, 597, 649
Jacobs, Johan, 455
Jacobs, John, 361
James, Sharpe, 694
Japan, 257, 261, 262, 264, 271, 291, 297, 302, 304, 312, 328, 354, 371,

373, 396, 403, 494, 496, 497, 508, 509, 528, 731, 734, 794
Japanese 239, 269, 303, 311, 350, 420, 432, 433, 436, 437, 491, 527, 682-684; business 508, 649; economic culture, 488; economy, 328; firms, 262; foreign investment, 265; industry, 262; "Ko", 732; market economy, 509
Jihad, 83
"Jobless recovery", 291
Jobs
    blue-collar, 254, 255, 268, 279, 283, 347, 349, 597; job loss, 279, 285; move abroad, 267; loss of manufacturing, 258; manufacturing, 258, 531
Johnson, 156, 822
Johnson, Anthony 417
Johnson, Charles, 651
Johnson, Charlie, 671
Johnson, Earvin "Magic", 640
Johnson, John, 361, 764
Johnson, Lonnie, 637, 638
Johnson, Lyndon B., 284, 563
Johnson Products, 627, 820
Johnson Publishing, 477, 482, 633
Johnson, Robert, 361
Johnson-Houston, Inc., 671
Joint Center for Political and Economic Studies, 181, 202
Joint Council on Economic Education, 178
Joint ventures, 266, 267, 323, 396, 398, 399, 403, 410, 411, 449, 458, 502, 609, 613, 642, 675, 724, 785, 786, 791, 809, 811
Jones, Absalom, 427, 556
Jones, Carl, 639-643
Jones, Quincy, 361
Jones, Wiley, 419
Jordan, B., 818n
Jordan, Michael, 361
Jordan, Vernon, 363
The Journal see *The Wall Street Journal*
Journal of Small Business Management, 742
Journal of the Royal Anthropological Institute, 576
Juch, Myong Y., 324
Jupiter Transportation System, 671
Justice Department, 659, 669
Just-Us-Books, 637, 638

Kambon, Kobi, 134
Kamofoff, Bernard, 777n
Kani, Karl, 453, 478, 642, 643
Kao, John, 312
Karrow, Russ, 284
Katznelson and Kesselman, 147
Keen, David, 377, 502, 760
Keh, 336
Keller, Edward B., 580
Kelly, Jill, 463
Kelly, Wendell, 751
Kennedy, Paul, 261, 373, 375
Kennedy's Fried Chicken, 333
Kente cloth, 625, 626, 629, 630, 638, 639
Kentucky Fried Chicken, 333, 569, 768
Kenya, 370, 393, 399, 401, 634
Kenya and Baby Kiana, 634
Kerner Commission, 199, 248, 504
Kesselman, Mark, 147
Khanyile, 788
Kiana (doll), 634
Kilson, Martin, 838, 839
Kim, Jae T., 319
Kim Il Sung, 302
Kim Young Sam, 322
King, Martin Luther, 44, 74, 559, 567, 619, 773
King, Rodney, 318, 531, 532
Kinzer and Sagarin, 418
Kluckhon, Clyde, 59
Ko, 737
Koch, Charles, 177
Kohler, Terry, 195
Koh-Taylor, Kwi-Sook, 320
Kolodney, David, 182, 183, 198, 199
Korea United Technologies, 322
Korean(s), 45-47, 143, 144, 247, 266, 315, 317-325, 330, 331, 335-338, 340, 342, 349, 351, 353, 419, 438, 465, 491, 527, 531, 532, 542, 581, 699, 732
Korean Americans, 143, 247, 317,

323, 325, 342, 353, 438
Korean Association of Greater New York (KAGNY), 319, 320
Korean entrepreneurial success, 330
Korean-American Bank, 337
Kotkin, Joel, 311, 312, 528
Kowaliga, 423
Kristein, Martin, 760, 791, 795, 796, 798, 799, 817, 819
Krugman, Paul, 289-292
Ku Klux Klan, 34, 428
Kuba cloth, 628
Kye (Keh), 337
K-Mart, 404, 632

Labor
Black, 253, 386; camps, 84; cheap, 290, 351, 379; contract, 273; cooperative, 733; demands, 272; displaced, 159; displacement, 348; division of, 110, 136, 388; force, 253, 267, 292, 293, 498, 753; foreign, 272; global, 267; globalization of, 273; low-wage, 378, 438, 439; market, 181, 253, 258, 260, 274, 276, 347, 353, 585; movement, 512; organized, 160, 277, 278, 306; power, 272; secondary, 253, 254; segmented, 253; skilled, 261, 290, 435; surplus, 253, 277, 440, 602; uncompensated, 31; unions, 159, 214, 229, 512; unskilled, 249, 290
Lafon, Thomy, 418
Laing, R.D., 127
Laissez-faire (economics), 75, 223, 492, 493, 495-497
Lake, 500
Lamb, Robert B., 803
Land of America (Wolf), 34
Language and Symbolic Power (Bourdieu), 552
Lappé, Frances, 382
Largest creditor nation, 257
Largest debtor nation, 257
Latham, Earl, 793
Latin America, 180, 305, 341, 345, 346, 352, 373, 375, 408, 413, 501, 529, 839

Lawsuits, 797, 835
Lazard, W.R., 801, 803, 804, 806
Lazonick, William, 487, 493-495, 497-500
Leadership
assimilationist black, 82; black bourgeois, 442, 443; black community, 67; black preacher, 69, 73; civil rights, 601, 837, 852; crisis of, 203, 826; democratic, 214; elite, 43; new black, 199; secular, 68, 73; U.S. global, 304
The Leasing of Federal Land for Fossil Fuel Production (McDonald), 34
Lee, Spike, 361, 649
Legislative committees, 158, 163
The Legitimation of Power (Beetham), 20, 162, 224
Legodi, Max, 456, 457
Lenin, V.I., 221
Leverage, 43, 144, 186, 252, 314, 339, 450, 513, 554, 571, 573, 620, 725, 762, 764, *814*, 836
Lewis, Ed., 362
Lewis, Errol T., 710
Lewis, Michael 77, 78, 840, 841
Lewis, Reginald, 761-764, 769
Liberalism, 118, 223, 442, 832, 836, 852
Liberian Exodus and Joint Stock Company, 428
Liberty Bank and Trust Company, 699
Light, Ivan, 46, 47, 330, 337, 350, 351, 533, 534, 576, 681, 684, 686, 697, 734
Light and Bonacich, 46, 330, 337, 350, 351, 533, 534, 576
Limbaugh, Rush, 230
Limited liability company, 796
Lincoln, C. Eric, 556, 558, 560, 573-575, 681
Liquor, 318, 319, 330, 419, 602, 647 malt, 319, 602, 647
Llewellyn, J. Bruce, 362, 448
Loan
housing, 664, 692; syndicates, 813, 815
Lobbyists, 41, 157-159, 162

Local economic networks, 317
Local Initiative Support Corporation (LISC), 445-448, 450, 456
London Stock Exchange, 402
The Lonely Crowd (Reisman), 120
Long-term sublimation, 557
Lopez, Carlos, 647, 648
Losing Ground (Murray), 182, 277
Lowery, Joseph, 559
Lundy Enterprises, 480
Lundy, Larry, 768

Major U.S. investments abroad, 264
Malcolm X, 413, 530, 582, 649, 851
Mali, 416, 631
Mandela, Nelson, 616, 618, 619, 788, 789
Manhattan Institute of Policy Research, 182
Manhattan Spirit, 319, 321
Mankiller, Wilma, 612
Mann, Michael, 37-39, 76
Manufacturing jobs, loss of, 258
Marcuse, Herbert, 185
Marshall, Thurgood, 320
Martin Marietta, 214
Marx, Karl, 146, 221, 224
Mason, Edward S., 793
Massey & Denton, 503, 506
Master Plan, 53, 54, 294, 449
Maughan, Deryck, 408
Mauritius, 393, 394, 399
May, Rollo 5-7, 824
Maybury-Lewis, David, 76
Mayer, Martin, 680, 705
McCloskey, Donald N.
McConnell and Brue, 30, 679
McCraw, Thomas, 496
McDonald, Steven L., 34
McDonald's, 280, 339, 569, 602, 605, 626, 768
McDonald, Jr., Alden J., 700
McDonnell Douglas, 751
McGee, Patricia, 610, 611, 614
McLean, Elys A., 619
Mechanics and Farmers Bank, 420, 684
Media broadcast, 239; conglomerates, 228; electronic, 224, 233, 234, 236, 237, 239, 244, 285, 505, 519, 838; mass, 67, 120, 121, 181, 225, 227-229, 233, 389; power, 204; print, 194, 224, 228, 236, 237, 239
Meese, Edward, 176
Meier, August, 168, 343, 344, 419, 425, 558
Melman, Michael, 261
Mendenhall Ministries, 567
Merrick, 558
Merrill Lynch, 802, 805, 822
Mescalero Apache, 612
Methodist Episcopal Freedman's Aid Society, 190
Metropolitan Applied Research Center, 181, 198, 202
Mexican(s), 334, 347, 348, 405, 432, 436, 437, 527, 528
Michaels, Marguerite, 370, 371
Microlenders, 741
Micro-loans, 740, 741, 815
Milder, David, 463
Miles, Jacob R., 636
Military 11, 32, 33, 37, 38, 75, 84, 152, 161, 173, 180, 193, 212, 244, 270, 286, 305, 310, 325, 345, 351, 357, 360, 361, 375, 510, 727, 831, 834, 851; budget, 212; contractors, 613; dominance, 260; establishment, 81, 83, 141, 183; force, 25, 162, 261, 262; hegemony, 301, 306; might, 25, 303; power, 26, 108, 138, 261, 357, 358, 846; spending, 260; strategy, 244; supremacy, 297; priorities of the U.S., 261; threat, 305; vandalism, 375; warfare, 58, 361
Military-industrial complex, 140, 306
Milken, Michael, 763
Mills, C. Wright, 114, 138, 154, 357
Milosevic, M., 302
Mining Act of 1872, 791, 792
Minority Bank Monitor, 687
Minority firms, 800, 801, 803, 805
Minority-owned restaurants, 768, 771, 773
Minton, 417

Mische, Gerald & Patricia, 270
Missionary philanthropy, 189-191
Metsa Mitchell's, 639
Monopoly, 11, 15, 17, 18, 20, 34, 40, 164, 204, 223, 226, 265, 324, 357, 359, 402, 447, 493, 495, 500, 511, 532, 543
Montague, Ashley, 56
Montgomery Bus Boycott, 190
Montgomery, Isaiah T., 423
Moore, Richard B., 426
Moral-religious-ethical system, 68
Morehouse College, 559
Morgan, 174, 175, 196, 228, 298, 394, 399, 446, 725, 822
Morgan Guaranty, 174, 175, 228
Morland, Miles, 394
Morocco, 393, 394
Morris, K., 798n
Morris, Robert, 400
Motlana, Dr. Nthato, 787
Mound Bayou, 423
Moynihan, Daniel P., 311, 837
Muhammad, Elijah, 81, 510, 530, 581-583, 851
Muhammad, Samir, 644, 645
Murphy, Eddie, 764
Murray, Charles, 182
Music, 59, 112, 121, 332, 416, 421, 424, 479, 544, 625, 640, 649, 651, 828; rap, 234; retrograde, 239
Mutual
  aid societies, 419, 556, 557; funds, 404, 407, 408, 471, 472, 573, 574, 620, 677, 755, 756, 759-761, 799, 814
Myrdal, Gunnar, 504
Myth of individualism, 75, 492

Nader, Ralph, 658, 659
Nation, concept of, 507; sense of, 517, 518, 551, 552, 582, 613, 849
Nation of Islam (NOI), 80-83, 511, 530, 581, 582, 584, 601, 851, 856
National Alliance of Businessmen, 199
National Association of Black Social Workers, 55, 488, 614
National Association of Investors Corporation (NAIC), 757
National Association of Minority Contractors, 433
National Bureau of Economic Research, 178, 348
National Credit Union Administration (NCUA), 711, 712
National debt, 257, 507, 508
National Negro Business League, 419, 420, 423, 558
National Opinion Research Center, 188
National Security Council, 173
National Urban League, 197, 198, 257, 258, 260, 361, 476, 557, 560, 614, 830, 852
Nationalism, 106, 155, 182, 237, 240, 244, 316, 317, 344, 430, 443, 582, 634, 848-855
Nationbuilding: Theory and Practice (Akoto), 130
North Atlantic Treaty Organization (NATO), 177, 302
The Nature and Logic of Capitalism (Heilbroner), 287
Navajos, 612
Ncube, Donald, 786, 787
Ndoye, Makhtar, 342, 343
Need for ideology, 222
Negro as a consumer, 512, 588
The Negro As Capitalist (Harris), 682
Negro Business Directory, 423
The Negro Church in America (Frazier), 555, 556
Negro press, 235, 238, 239
Neo-conservatives, 838, 840
The Neurotic Foundations of Social Order (Smith), 119
New Afrikan self-identity, 63
New Agenda of the Black Church, 567
New Chinatown in Brooklyn, 331
New Community Corporation, 463
New Deal, 160
The Lewis Company, 761 *see also* TLC Beatrice
The New Industrial State (Galbraith), 301
New obsolescence, 277
New York Age, 235

882 ✦ Index

The New York Amsterdam News, 320, 322, 565, 614, 617, 617, 628, 658, 696, 699, 785
The New York Review of Books, 296, 373
The New York Times (NYT), 139, 140, 194, 195, 197, 228, 231, 240, 269, 271, 273, 296, 302, 303, 305, 314, 318-320, 321, 323-325, 330, 331, 333, 334, 337, 338, 347, 367, 369, 372, 377, 382, 383, 398, 399, 401, 413, 433, 440, 445, 446, 450, 454-458, 463, 464. 527, 529, 531-535, 544, 562, 574, 577, 579, 608, 611, 612, 628, 629, 639, 642, 647, 658, 659, 662, 663, 669, 670, 673, 674, 697, 709, 735, 763, 766, 770, 780, 791, 793, 802, 805, 806, 809-811, 813, 814
Newspaper chains, 228
Newsweek, 48, 228, 231, 632
Niang, Sulayman, 341
Nietzsche, Friedrich, 6, 72, 73
Nigeria, 339-341, 370, 377, 393, 399, 401, 427, 735
Nigerians, 339, 634, 732
Nixon, Richard M., 160
Noneconomic liberalism, 442
Nordham, William D., 676
North American Free Trade Agreement (NAFTA), 268, 296, 328, 405, 528, 529, 655
North Star, 235
Northwest Baptist Federal Credit Union, 709
Not-for-profit(s), 464, 620, 783, 784
Ntsimi, Antoine, L., 735, 736

***The Official Report on the Niger Valley Exploring Party* (Delaney), 427**
Offiong, Daniel, 249
Oklahoma, 421, 423, 428, 523, 525, 592, 593, 613
Oklahoma Gold Rush, 34
Oklahoma Sun, 421
Oligopoly, 301
Olmec Corp., 634
Omnibanc, 700, 701

Onye Aghalanwaneya Mbaise, 340
"Open market", 77, 300,301, 387, 388, 432, 500, 509
Operation Breadbasket, 596, 597
Operation PUSH, 362, 596, 597
Opportunities Industrialization Centers of America (OIC), 563
Ordinance of 1785 (federal), 34
Organization for Economic Cooperation and Development (OECD), 256
Origins of power, 56
The Outsiders: Studies in the Sociology of Deviance (Becker), 167
Over-the-counter (OTC) market, 722, 797, 819
Owens, Major, 322
Ownership is sovereignty, 295
O'Hare, W.P., 470

Pacific Rim, 529
Pan–Afrikan, 3, 49, 51, 55, 83, 123, 130, 135, 206, 218, 248, 273, 277, 305,394,395, 403, 404, 430, 466, 510, 511, 514, 546, 554, 560, 591, 596, 601, 641, 650, 652, 675, 691, 698, 704, 721, 728-730, 800, 807, 809, 821, 823, 826, 835, 851
Parenti, Michael, 6, 8, 29, 44, 146, 147, 150, 154, 155, 158, 160, 163, 165, 172, 174, 210, 212, 213, 225, 227, 228, 230, 297, 298, 846, 847
Park Slope Food Co-op, 780
Parsons, Talcott, 113, 122
Parsons and White, 122
Patriarchy, 119
Pax Americana, 303, 305
Paxon, Bill, 195
Payne, Donald, 322
The Peculiar Institution (Stampp), 65
Peddling Prosperity (Krugman), 289
Penny Saver Bank, 558
Pension funds, 465, 573, 677, 692, 695, 728, 797, 802
Pentagon's Defense Planning Guidance for the Fiscal Years 1994–1999, 302-304
People's Advocate, 343
Pepsico, 159, 605, 606, 626

Perez, Danny, 326
Permanent
　economic depression, 255, 440
　war economy, 260, 261
Persell, Caroline H., 148, 149
Personal care products and services, 603
Philadelphia Gentlemen (Baltzell), 149
Philanthropic institutions, 182
Philanthropy, 189-193, 450, 606-608, 648
Philanthropy and Cultural Imperialism (Anderson), 189
Phillipe, Gerald, 198
Pierce, 417
Pilgrimage to My Motherland (Campbell), 427
Piore, Michael J., 253
Pizza Hut, 480, 569, 768, 816
Plural But Equal (Cruse), 74
Pogge, J., 714-718
Pohang Iron and Steel Corporation, 322
Policies of the U.S. government, 183, 263
Policy, 41, 139, 159, 160, 163, 171-185, 197, 198, 202, 206, 211-213, 215-218, 223, 241, 249, 262, 265, 278, 297, 301-303, 325, 328, 348, 367, 369-371, 408, 432, 440, 443, 486, 528, 574, 595, 649, 660, 663, 683, 739, 746, 788, 836, 857; economic, 180-182, 366, 441, 486, 510; foreign, 52, 173, 178, 180, 181, 183, 289, 302, 306, 351, 371, 388, 404, 405, 509, 510, 738; immigration, 350; of deterrence, 303
Politics of Broadcast Regulation (Krasnow & Longley), 34
Policy Review, 181
Policy-formation process, 55, 154, 166, 167, 200, 204, 209
Policy-planning groups, 168, 169, 171, 172, 204
Political
　directorate, 357; powerlessness, 28, 74, 246, 470, 492, 613

The Political Economy of the Black Ghetto (Tabb), 249, 719
The Political Economy of the Urban Ghetto (Fusfeld & Bates), 255, 439
Poriotis, Westley, 284
Portfolio investments, 265, 398, 400, 573
Post-industrial America, 254
Post-riot loan funds, 531
Poverty: 7, 28, 128, 140, 255, 258, 267, 276, 291, 339, 347, 349, 351, 361, 372, 377, 379, 381, 384, 386, 388, 438, 439, 441, 449, 460, 461, 468, 470, 483, 484, 508, 515, 556, 563, 583, 591, 611, 614, 629, 652, 730, 732, 754, 755, 782, 783, 823, 827, 828, 841, 847; culture of, 78-80
The Poverty Establishment (Horowitz & Kolodney), 182, 183, 199
Powell, Adam Clayton, 326, 559, 562, 563, 565
Powell, Colin, 361, 362
Powell, Thomas, 822
Power
　and influence, 20, 144, 145, 155, 165, 200, 246, 247, 325, 329, 354, 380, 459, 513, 515, 528, 584, 652, 724, 794; differentials, 127, 308; elite, 138, 154, 169, 171, 211, 223, 232, 357, 825; of ideas, 220; of investment funds, 407; of the White House, 159
Power and Innocence (May), 6
Power and Society (Dye), 8, 136, 156, 221, 247
Power and the Powerless (Parenti), 44, 147, 150, 210, 847
Power elite, 154, 169, 171, 211, 223
The Power Elite (Mills), 138, 357
Preemption Act (federal), 34
Preferential Trade Area of East and Southern Africa, 529
Preparing for the 21st Century (Kennedy), 261
Presbyterian Board of Missions for the Freedmen, 190
Press
　African American, 32, 259, 348, 361-363, 418, 474-476, 548, 556,

557, 560, 571, 597, 598, 603, 627, 631, 746, 785; black bourgeois press, 236; black nationalist, 245; black, 231, 235, 236, 238, 240, 241; Negro, 235, 238, 239; white, 237, 240 white liberal, 67, 234, 236, 281, 648, 836, 856
Prezeau, Louis, 572, 693, 694, 701, 702
Prince George's County, 543
Prince Hall, 427, 558
Private
 capital, 162, 295, 407, 408, 693, 707, 810; financial capital, 296; financial-corporate complex, 297, 299; government, 297, 299, 300, 793; placements, 801, 818
Privatization, 177, 297, 395
Privileged access, 31, 167, 383, 493, 498-500
Problem of Afrikan debt, 375
Progress and Freedom Foundation, 196, 197
Propaganda agencies, 178
Prosper Africa Group, 787, 788
Protestant Ethic and the Spirit of Capitalism (Weber), 581
Protestantism and the Rise of Capitalism (Tawney), 581
Prudential-Bache, 214
Prussia, 495
Pryor, McClendon, Counts, 801, 803, 804, 811
Psychology and Effective Behavior (Coleman), 103
Public
 land, 34; opinion polls, 213
Publishing, 180, 240, 489, 534, 613, 637
Punjabi Sikhs, 333

Quaker Oats, 605, 606, 632
Quarterly Review of Black Books, 239

Race
 -coded images, 216; solidarity, 344, 475
Race Matters (West), 831
Racial

discrimination, 17, 32, 120, 142, 286, 293, 420, 435, 459, 470, 559, 746, 782, 830, 832, 834, 842, 844, 845; disparities, 470, 483, 670; minorities, 214; preferences, 433; prejudgment, 35, 252; quotas (*100%*) for whites, 32, 34; self-alienation, 375
Racism, 24, 66, 73, 76, 106, 108, 117, 132, 145, 203, 204, 251, 253, 256, 273, 282, 348, 357, 374, 428, 433, 486, 506, 515, 625, 801, 830, 833-835, 837-839, 842, 848, 853-855
Radio Act (federal), 34,
Rahman, S., 742, 743
Railroads, 400, 402, 791, 810
Raising ethnic rivalries, 372
Ralston, 77
RAND Corporation, 178, 302
Rangel, Charles, 409
Rap music, 234
Ratcliff, Wesley, 673-675
Rawls, Lou, 607
Reagan, Ronald, 160, 176, 197, 216, 474, 664
Reagan-Bush, 139, 158, 180, 276, 353
Real gross domestic product, 257
Recession, 275, 277-280, 282-285, 326, 328, 440, 533, 681, 699
Reconstruction, 189, 344, 428, 557, 838
Records and tapes market, 228
Recreational Equipment Incorporated, 779
Regional threats and risk, 305
Regionalization, 327, 328, 405
"A Register of Trades of Colored People in the City of Philadelphia and Districts", 418
Recreational Equipment Inc., 779
Reich, William, 285
Reiman, J., 221, 222
Reisman, David, 120
Relations and Duties of Free Colored Men (Crummell), 426
Religion, 39, 69, 70, 80-82, 120, 124, 213, 310, 311, 329, 361, 442, 528, 556, 574, 582, 831
Religious New Rightists, 229

Renaissance Capital of Atlanta, 816
Reparations, 459, 460, 483, 486, 487, 501, 667, 789
Repression of Afrikan American economic power, 431
Republican party, 193, 194, 213, 215, 216; triumph of, 193
Republicans, 194, 195, 213, 241
Research and Development, 160, 164, 218, 262, 268, 270, 488, 498
Research and higher education, 183
Reserve account, 716
Resolution Trust Corporation, 699
Resources for the Future, 178
Retail Initiative Corporation, 445
Revolution, 181, 186, 188, 221, 228, 231, 239, 258, 274, 292, 401, 402, 496, 532, 807, 836, 852, 854
Reynolds, Paul, 467, 468
Re-engineering, 274, 275
The Rich Get Richer and the Poor Get Prison (Reiman), 222
Ridgley, James, 644, 645
Right wing politics, 194
Riley, Beryl, 739, 740
Riley, Carole, 626
Riley, Angela, 710
The Rise and Fall of the Great Powers (Kennedy), 261
Roberts, Joseph Jenkins, 427
Roberts, Owen, 197
Roby, Pamela, 183n
Rockefeller, David, 198
Rockefeller, 173, 182, 190, 192, 447, 725; *see also* Foundations
Roddick, Anita, 577
Rogers, John W., 759, 769
Rohaytn, Felix, 296, 395
Roper Starch, 579, 580
Ross, S., 818
Ross and Trachte, 265
Rotating credit, 47, 576, 729-738, 740, 813: tontines, 735, 736; "boxi money", 732; "esusu", 732; "hui", 732; "partners", 732; "the meeting", 732
Rotating credit associations, 47, 576, 730-737, 740, 813
Rousseau, Jean Jacques, 118, 850

Rowen, Henry S., 396
Rueben, Luch J., 692
Ruiz-Tagle, E.F., 529
Ruling elite, 23, 33, 79, 117, 120, 145-147, 149, 150, 153, 155, 157, 162, 167, 178, 185, 186, 189, 197, 205, 211, 212, 226, 232, 233, 250, 357, 449, 847
Russell Sage Foundation, 188
Russia, 375, 396, 512
Ryan, William, 129, 840

S.S. General Goethals, 430
Sahara, 367, 372, 398, 415
Saharan Berbers, 416
Saiki, Patricia, 329
Sallach, David, 226
Salomon Brothers, 408, 763
Samuelson, Paul, 676, 677
Sanlam Properties, 454-456
Sarria, Mark, 649
Saul Mortgage, 670
Savings clubs, 340, 739, 740
Savings rate, 250, 257, 354, 365, 584, 585
Schattschneider, Elmer E., 146, 154
Schiller, Bradley, 676-678
Schwab, Klaus, 328
Schwartz, M., 168, 172, 176, 186
Schwarz, Benjamin C., 302, 303
Scott, Arthur B., 661
Scott, Lori, 633
Scully, John, 274
Seagrams, 605, 606
Seaway National Bank of Chicago, 700
Second government, 162, 297
Second Thoughts (McCloskey), 402
Secondary market transaction, 818
Segmented labor market, 253
Segregation, 74, 350, 432, 433, 437, 438, 443, 456, 483, 503, 506, 512- 515, 542, 599, 624, 827, 834, 836, 839
Self and Others (Laing), 127
Self-determination, 82, 382, 443, 455, 460, 466, 484, 498, 718, 719, 820, 849-851; driven recovery, 375; hatred, 12, 78, 126, 375, 621; help, 67, 199, 200, 343, 345, 415,

417, 420, 443, 531, 556, 557, 697, 714, 839, 857
The Selig Center for Economic Growth, 589
Senegalese, 339-343, 630, 631
Senseless civil wars, 375
Serving the Few (Greenberg), 265, 301, 796
Seybold, Peter, 168, 172, 185-187
Shabazz, Malcolm & Betty, 342, 362
Shakespeare, Locke, Descartes, 191
Share accounts, 711
Share of the major occupations, 259
Sharpton, Alfred, 320
Shaw, Kathryn, 760
Sheffield, John Lord, 401
Shell Oil, 177
Shoprite, 454, 455, 457
Short Changed (Brown & Tiffen), 367
Shuttlesworth, Fred, 559
Siegel, A., 798
Sierra Leone, 341, 427
Simi Valley, 533
Simpson, O.J., 362
Singapore, 271, 312, 354, 355
Singh, Pamjit, 333
Skelly, Thomas, 271, 272
Skerritt, John C., 274
Skullduggery of White businessmen, 430
Slade, Clara, 739
Slave
 family, 65; trade, 251, 374; freed, 434; ordinances, *34*
Slaveholdings (of the founding fathers), 156
Slavery, 19, 64-66, 68, 84, 107, 249, 278, 306, 417, 418, 427, 435, 483, 484, 486, 559, 650, 651, 657 *see also* Reparations
Slavery and Christianity, 69-71
Sloan Foundation, 193
Slider, S., 705
Smadja, Claude, 328
Small Business Administration (SBA), 329, 337, 392, 708, 721, 723, 741, 744-747, 749, 816
Small Business Incubators, 742
Smith, J.C., 117, 119n, 356, 357, 360, 365n
Smith, H.T., 616, 617
Smith, Adam, 33, 289, 301, 495
Smith, Cedric, 772
Smith, James D., 179
Smith & Smith, 648
Social
 arrangements, 33, 100; class, 43, 107, 136-138, 141, 146, 243, 620; clubs, 149, 334; conflict, 275; consciousness, 25, 310; engineering, 89, 185, 252, 629; ideology, 221; institutions, 48, 114, 141, 149, 185, 227, 247, 254, 324, 360, 439, 487, 509, 510, 556, 580, 582, 584, 589, 668, 702, 734; kinship, 338; organization, 29, 31, 36-38, 40, 41, 64, 68, 74, 247, 498, 779; power, 16-18, 23, 27, 28, 33, 37-39, 41-43, 45, 46, 51, 56, 63, 66, 76, 91, 93, 95, 96, 101, 102, 105, 106, 109, 111, 114, 148, 166, 167, 227, 229, 308, 310, 312, 329, 335, 431, 494, 618, 652, 684, 685, 824, 825, 829, 858; problems, 128, 129, 258, 262, 273, 339, 343, 350, 396, 439, 441, 460, 467, 505-507, 579, 611, 730, 756, 784
Social Science Research Council, 188
Social Structure and Personality (Parsons), 113, 122
Socialization, 61
Sociological Quarterly, 226
Sociology, 42, 167, 207, 417
Solidarity, 25, 39-41, 51, 96, 149, 240, *329*, 356, 375, 533, 534, 641, 835, 846, 849: ethnic, 45, 46, 332, 338, 341-343, 441; group, 45-48, 106, 107; racial (race), 205, 343-345, 375, 443, 475, 505, 557, 835; social, 41, 443, 733, 737, 778
Songhai, 416
The Sources of Social Power (Mann), 37, 76
South Afrikan Customs Union (SACU), 529
South Afrikan Development Coordination Conference (SADCC), 529
South Central People's Federal Credit

Union, 710
South Korea, 322, 337, 345, 351, 371, 372, 390 *see also* Korea
Southern Education Board, 190
Southern Utes, 612
South-Central Los Angeles, 531, 534, 542, 543, 647, 663
Sou-sou, 739 *see also* Rotating credit
Soviet Union, 264, 303-305, 346, 370, 372, 375, 408
Sowell, Thomas, 182, 436, 437
The Sowetan, 787
Soweto, 454-457, 790
Soweto Chamber of Commerce, 456, 457
Specialized Small Business Investment Corporation (SSBIC), 816
Spelman College, 559, 626
Spices, Eugene, 637
St. Luke's Bank, 558
Stalin, Joseph, 221
Stampp, Kenneth, 64, 65, 70
Standard Oil, 183, 199
Stanford University, 176, 181, 289
The State of Black America, 257-260, 275, 276, 353, 469, 470, 474-476, 550, 560, 561, 571, 603, 604
Stephens, Anita, 816
Stewart, T. McCants, 426
Stock (s), 66, 158, 237, 265, 298, 394, 396, 402, 407, 428, 430, 436, 451, 471, 476, 519, 572, 573, 606, 608, 609, 674, 678, 692, 693, 696, 713, 718, 721-724, 726, 733, 744, 745, 755- 757, 759-761, 784, 786, 793, 798, 808, 809, 812, 817-820; Afrikan stock markets, 406; Afrikan stocks, 399; certificates, 30, 761, 797, 800, 817; fledgling markets, 399
Stock markets, 393, 398, 399, 401, 406
Stocks and mutual funds, 472, 759
Stokes, Carl, 198
Strange, William, 430
Street vendors, 324-326, 631
The Structure of Power in America (Anker et al.), 168, 186
Stuart, M.S., 436
Suburban Blacks, 536, 545

Sub-Saharan Afrika, 267, 296, 305, 368, 371, 372, 373, 376, 391, 398, 401, 407, 735
Successful Investing (Babson), 760
Sullivan, John, 348,
Sullivan, Leon, 448, 562, 563, 752
The Sunday Star Ledger, 714
Super Soaker, 637
"Susu", 465, 500, 732, 813 *see also* Rotating credit
Swanepoel, Jacobus A., 454, 455
Swartz, Bartley, 644, 645
Sweden, 256, 403
Swinton, David, 276, 353, 469, 470, 474, 483, 486, 755
Switzerland, 256, 396
Syndication, 754, 808, 812, 813, 815, 816
Syndication of microloans, 815

Tabb, William, 249, 718, 719
Tafoya, Margaret, 613
Taiwan, 312, 332, 342, 354, 355, 390, 404, 637
Tanner, Tucker, 557
Target Market News, 603, 604
Tariffs, 380, 385, 388-390, 495, 528, 794
Tawney, 581
Tax revenues, 161
Technological changes, 290
Television and radio stations, 228
Terkel, Studs, 504
Terry, Marvin, 820, 821
Texas Playboys, 421
Theology, 68, 69, 71, 73, 75, 81, 581
Think tanks, 149, 169, 175-179, 184, 193, 194, 202, 207, 848
Third World 251, 263, 266, 267, 378, 379, 413, 465; elites, 480
Tholin and Pogge, 715-718
Thomas, Mark, 400, 402
Thomas, Ralph C., 433
Thompson, John B., 86, 87
Thompson, Warren, 751, 752, 768, 769
Thompson Hospitality, L.P., 479, 482, 768
Thornton, Steve, 384

Threads 4 Life Corp., 641
Thrift institutions, 337
Thurow, L., 299, 300, 705
TIAA-CREF, 695, 696
Tidwell, Billy J., 258, 260
Tiffen and Brown, 367, 368, 373, 390
The Times (see *The New York Times*)
TLC Beatrice, 448, 477, 482, 769
Toffler, Alvin, 27, 28
Tontines, 735, 736
Tony Brown's Journal, 244
Tourism, 394, 410, 612-617, 630
Toward A Human World Order (Mische), 270
Toys and games industry, 634-636
Trachte, Kent, 265
Trade
  alliances, 402, 403, 406, 431; associations, 157, 218, 546, 548, 549; barriers, 268, 385, 389; bilateral, 376, 390, 405, 493, 528, 810; deficit(s), 257, 260, 402, 508, 509, 586; horizontal, 205, 387, 724; imbalance, 386, 441; multilateral, 376, 528; vertical, 205, 387, 724
Transactions accounts, 677
Transportation, 335, 400, 407, 411, 462, 478, 480, 517-519, 530, 603, 671, 672, 727, 834
Trans-Atlantic slave trade, 251
Tribes (Kotkin), 311, 528
Trojan Horse, 446, 447
True Reformer's Bank, 558
Tulsa Star, 421
Tulsa, the Black promised land, 421
Tunisia, 393, 394
Turner, Bishop H.M., 428
Turner, Margery, 282
Turner, Richard, 707
Tuskegee Institute, 559
The Twentieth Century (Zinn), 7, 20
Tyco Industries, 634
Tyranny, 299, 300, 306, 361, 375

UNC Ventures, 725-727
Unemployment, 28, 139, 250, 255, 257, 273, 277, 289-293, 326, 395, 406, 440, 441, 476, 531, 611, 698, 705, 784, 785, 827, 828, 853
United Bank of Philadelphia, 699, 700
United Nations Children's Fund, 373
United Nations Development Program (UNDP), 373
United Negro College Fund (UNCF), 192, 363, 549, 607, 647; TV Marathon, 607
United Negro Improvement Association (UNIA), 425, 428-430, 601
United States
  competitiveness, 257; hegemony, 302; interests, 188; post-cold war mission, 303; sells gold land, 791; strategic interest in Africa, 371
University-educated elites, 342
Upper-class
  private prep schools, 148; schooling, 148
Upscale, 234, 244, 576, 650
Urban Coalition, 198
Urban planning, 542
USAID, 371

V&J Foods Inc., 771
Verdery, Kathrine, 848
Village Taxi company, 334
Vivian, C.T., 559
Voorhis, Jerry, 777

Wage growth, 257
Waldron, Milton, 558
Walker, C.J., 419
Walker, Thomas, 639, 640
Walker, Wyatt T., 559
The Wall Street Journal (WSJ), 140, 177, 199, 228, 269, 273, 279, 281, 285, 287, 316-318, 331, 346, 374, 396, 407, 408, 436, 461, 462, 520, 532, 568, 573, 594, 624, 625, 636, 660, 663, 665, 672, 693, 706-708, 745, 746, 750, 751, 763, 770, 786, 788, 798, 799, 822
Walmart, 404
War, 25, 34, 52, 58, 83, 84, 141, 181, 185, 186, 189, 190, 198, 232, 256, 260-262, 269, 278, 291, 302-304, 316, 324, 333, 350, 360, 371, 372, 375, 398, 400, 416-419, 425, 427,

428, 430, 435, 496, 555, 557, 563, 614, 656, 662, 714, 795, 808, 812
War
 against the cities, 595; damages compensation to US companies, 160-161
Warfare, 58, 84, 232, 233, 244, 360, 361
Warman, R., 798
Wartenberg, Thomas, 6, 8-10, 12-15, 23, 24, 72, 312
Washington, Booker T., 200, 344, 420, 421, 430, 432, 434, 443, 510, 530, 558, 845
The Washington Post, 228, 339, 341, 343, 670
The Washington Quarterly, 180
Washington Women's Investment Club (WWIC), 759
Watchdog committees, 666
Watkins, Kevin, 369
We Own It (Kamofoff & Beatty), 777
Wealth and Economic Status (O'Hare), 470
Wealth and Poverty (Gilder), 182
Wealth and power, 30, 32, 79, 80, 157, 221, 222, 239, 353, 361, 460, 486, 583, 585, 629, 684, 685, 694, 761
Weary, Dolphus, 567
Weber, Max, 581
Webster, Frank, 283
Weddings, 638
Welfare and social services, 386
Welfarism of the rich, 161
Wellman, David, 24, 145
Wells Federal Credit Union, 709
West, C. Alexander, 770
West, Cornel, 831
West Indian immigrants, 437
Westerfield, R., 818
Western aid, 381
Weyrich, Paul, 196
Wharton, Clifton, 695, 762
Wheat Street Baptist Church, 566
Wheat Street Charitable Foundation, 567
Whigham, Charles L., 694
White
 American theological mythologies, 75; America's culture, 77; capitalism, 289, 308; corporate elite, 138, 139, 192, 198, 229, 243, 364; mobs, 422; power establishment, 93, 94, 833; supremacists, 453, 456; supremacy, 8, 26, 64, 94, 99, 102, 104, 117, 119, 132, 193, 202, 227, 231- 233, 237-240, 243, 308, 377, 392, 456, 459, 486, 830, 833, 838, 843
Whitlow, Henry, 423
Whitlock, Mark, 561, 566
Who Needs the Negro? (Wilhelm), 835
Who Rules America Now? (Domhoff), 148, 179, 184
Who Will Tell The People (Greider), 154, 159, 215
Who's Who in America, 174
Wilkins, Mira, 198, 400
Williams, Chancellor, 52-55, 182, 511
Williams, Horace, 816
Williams, J., 784
Williams, Walter, 182
Willis, Bob, 421
Wilson, William Julius, 258
Wimes, Angela, 680, 684
Winfrey, Oprah, 764
Wolfe, Alan, 298
Work, John, 282
World Bank, 173, 296, 367-370, 372, 390, 393, 395, 407-409, 449
"Worldwide Web of Chinese Business," 312
Wrong, Dennis, 8-12, 14, 16-18, 21-23, 36, 39, 40, 329
Wyatt, James, 631

Yankelovich Partners, 520, 624
Yavapai Tribe, 610
Young, Andrew, 559
Young, Whitney, 198
Youngblood, Johnny Ray, 564
Younger, Donna, 340, 581

Zambia, 394, 401
Zimbabwe, 393, 394, 399, 401, 811
Zinn, Howard, 7, 20, 154
Zion Baptist Church, 562

Editor's Note

We worked at a feverish pace into many a dawn to meet the demands of our time and our people. We blazed the path to contribute to the development of our people with the full understanding that storm clouds lay on the horizon. We enjoyed a quickened walk in the sun. The walk in the sun was too good to last. The harshest adversity struck. Just weeks from editorial completion of this work the esteemed author and friend passed very suddenly. Our community responded with astonishment and anguish. From near and afar tributes poured in. I recall the despair and trepidation. Folks pondered where do we go from here. Concern for the completion of this mammoth work abounded. The task fell to me to conclude this encyclopedic treatise. Revolutionary psychologist, brother, thinker, master teacher, humanitarian, activist Dr. Amos Wilson joined the pantheon of the ancestors on Saturday, January 14, 1995.

Though near completion, the final phases took an unexpected three years. This attests to the multi-disciplinary scholarship and superhuman workload charged us by Dr. Wilson. The unfurling nature of the material in this work required frequent updating along with meticulous referencing and indexing. Scholastic excellence compelled that signature work be done in honor to the eminence, sagacity, clairvoyance, fortitude, and magnanimity of our Brother. Through thunder and life challenges my commitment culminated in the bringing of this offering to our people. The privilege was mine.

To Amos, this one is for you wherever you are. May you continue to be an advocate for your people in the land of the ancestors. This one is for you my friend, wherever you are, somewhere out there. As so many can attest, a simple stroll with you is a light year of memoirs. We give thanks.

At Afrikan World InfoSystems, be assured that the mission continues apace. Listen out for the unstilled enduring pen of Amos Wilson. Our struggles continue. Stay resolute!

– Sababu N. Plata
Executive Editor
February, 1998

Brief Profiles of Six Other Books by Amos Wilson

Black-on-Black Violence: The Psychodynamics of Black Self-Annihilation in Service of White Domination represents a distinct milestone in criminology and Afrikan studies. The main thesis of this book is that the operational existence of Black-on-Black violence in the United States is psychologically and economically mandated by the White American-dominated status quo. The criminalization of the Black American male is a psychopolitically engineered process geared to maintain dependency and powerlessness of the Afrikan American and Pan-Afrikan communities. Wilson, beyond blaming the victimizer, exposes the psychosocial and intrapsychical dynamics of Black-on-Black criminality.   PB. Pages: 224

Understanding Black Adolescent Male Violence: Its Remediation and Prevention succinctly details how American society creates and sustains Black-on-Black criminality in the inner cities across the U.S. It asserts that Black-on-Black adolescent violence is rooted in historical and contemporary White-on-Black violence. It further points out how the adolescent crises of black males interact with the pervasive false consciousness induced in the collective psyche of the Afrikan American community by White-on-Black violence.

This book provides very practical, remedial and preventative approaches to this problem which threatens the vitality of the whole Afrikan American community.   PB. PAGES: 100

Awakening the Natural Genius of Black Children. Afrikan children are naturally precocious and gifted. They begin life with a "natural head start." Intelligence is not fixed at birth. There is clear evidence that the quality of children's educational experiences during infancy and early childhood are substantially related to their measured intelligence, academic achievement and social behavior. Professor Wilson reveals the daily routines, child-rearing practices, parent-child inter-actions, games and play materials, parent training and pre-school programs which have made demonstrably outstanding and lasting differences in the intellectual, academic and social performance of Afrikan American children.
PB. PAGES: 144

Developmental Psychology of the Black Child
- Are Black and White children the same?
- Is the Black child a White child who happens to be "painted" Black?
- Are there any significant differences in the mental and physical development of Black and White children?
- Do Black parents socialize their children to be inferior to White children?

This pioneering book looks at these and other related questions from an Afrikan perspective. The topics of growth, development and education are scholarly explored.   PB. PAGES: 216

The Falsification of Afrikan Consciousness is a triple feature. The first, *The Role of Eurocentric Historiography in the European Oppression of Afrikan People*, was among the first contemporary analyses which delineated the role Eurocentric history writing plays in rationalizing European oppression of Afrikan peoples and in the falsification of Afrikan consciousness. It explicates why we should study history; how history writing shapes the psychology of peoples and individuals; how Eurocentric history as mythology creates historic amnesia in Afrikans in order to rob them of the material, mental, social and spiritual wherewithal for overcoming poverty and oppression.

Part II, *Eurocentric Political Dogmatism: Its Relationship to Mental Health Misdiagnosis of Afrikan Peoples*, advances that the alleged mental and behavioral maladaptiveness of oppressed Afrikan peoples is a political-economic necessity for the maintenance of White domination and imperialism. It indicts the Eurocentric mental health establishment for entering into collusion with the Eurocentric political establishment to oppress and exploit Afrikan peoples by officially sanctioning egregious practices through its misdiagnosing, mislabeling, and mistreating of Afrikan peoples' behavioral reactions to their oppression and their efforts to win their freedom and independence.   PB. Pages: 152

Afrikan-Centered Consciousness versus the New World Order: *Garveyism in the Age of Globalism* consists of two spellbinding lectures buttressed by a scintillating overview. This text challenges the false perception that the "New World Order" is somehow ordained; that if Afrikan people are to progress, they have no other alternative but to remain colonized by White Western interests. This is patently false. Dr. Wilson debunks this myth with an insightful analysis of the Legacy of Marcus Garvey and the proven validity of Afrikan-centered consciousness as necessary psychological and material tools in the struggle for true liberation.

Wilson puts forth his treatise in ways that grab the reader and simultaneously reduces the much-touted strategic thinking of the proponents of the New World Order to the newspeak it really is.
◆ A NEW RELEASE   PB. Pages: 152

To Order the Works of DR AMOS N. WILSON

BOOKS	ISBN	PRICE
BLUEPRINT FOR BLACK POWER * soft cover	1-879164-06-X	$40.00
BLUEPRINT FOR BLACK POWER* case bound	1-879164-07-8	$60.00
The Developmental Psychology of the Black Child	0-933524-01-3	$12.00
The Falsification of Afrikan Consciousness *also in hard cover*	1-879164-02-7	$13.00
Awakening the Natural Genius of Black Children	1-879164-01-9	$13.00
Understanding Black Adolescent Male Violence	1-879164-03-5	$ 9.00
BLACK-ON-BLACK Violence	1-879164-00-0	$17.00
Afrikan-centered Consciousness vs the New World Order	1-879164-09-4	$13.00

* Shipping & Handling for BLUEPRINT FOR BLACK POWER   1 copy $6.50   2 copies $8.50
Shipping & Handling for all other titles   1-2 Books $5.95   3-5 Books $9.95

AUDIO CASSETTES (Soon on CD and DVD)	CATALOG NUMBER	PRICE
The Third Reconstruction: Moving Beyond Civil and Human Rights into Afrikan Revolution *plus bonus* Who Will Bell the Cat?...	2T911502	$15.00
Who Will Bell the Cat? *De-*constructing the U.S. Violence Initiative Agenda	1T921809	$8.00
Tools of Empire: Construction, Destruction, and Reconstruction of Afrikan Civilizations 3500BCE to 2100AD	2T199102	$15.00
Black-on-Black Violence: White-engineered Self-annihilation in the Black Community	2T912402	$15.00
Culture and Identity: Critical Analyses and Pragmatic Approaches for the Imperiled Afrikan Future	2T932401	$15.00
European Historiography and Oppression Exposed: An Afrikan Analysis and Perspective	2T890205	$15.00
Death at an Early Age: The Failure of the American Education System	2T199906	$15.00
Effectuating an Afrikan Revolutionary Psychotherapy	2T840124	$15.00
Afrikan-centered Consciousness, Personality and Culture as Instruments of Power	2T942109	$15.00
European Psychological Warfare Against Afrikans	2T891502	$15.00
The Psychology of Cooperative Economics in the Afrikan-American Community	2T200006	$15.00

Shipping & Handling   1-2 Cassette Sets $4.95   3-5 Cassette Sets $6.95   ✱ Call about Compact Disk

✦ Note: Prices are subject to change *without* notice

To Order by Telephone call 718 462-1830
E-Mail: AFRIKANWORLD @ AOL.COM

To Order by Mail:
Copy/Fill order information and send remittance to:
 Afrikan World InfoSystems, Order Dept.
 743 Rogers Avenue, Suite 6
 Brooklyn, New York 11226

Name	Tel.
Address	
City	Apt.
State	Zip
Certified Check/Money Order for $_____	
Payable to: **Afrikan World InfoSystems**	

PLEASE FILL ORDER BLANK

Qty	Book ISBN / Cassette Cat #	Price
	Subtotal	$_____
	8.625% Sales Tax (NY residents only)	$_____
	*Shipping & Handling	$_____
	COD Shipments only	$ (6.00)
	Total Order	$_____